Literary and Political Essays

Literary and Political Essays

George Orwell

ALMA CLASSICS

ALMA CLASSICS
an imprint of

ALMA BOOKS LTD
60 High Street
Wimbledon Village
London SW19 5EE
United Kingdom
www.almaclassics.com

Represented by:
Authorised Rep Compliance Ltd
Ground Floor
71 Lower Baggot Street
Dublin, D02 P593
Ireland
www.arccompliance.com

For the publication details of each essay, see the relevant headnote
This edition first published by Alma Classics in 2025

Cover: David Wardle

Edited text, notes and extra material © Alma Books Ltd

Printed in Great Britain by CPI Group (UK) Ltd, Croydon CR0 4YY

ISBN: 978-1-84749-515-0

All rights reserved. No part of this publication may be reproduced, stored in or introduced into a retrieval system, or transmitted, in any form or by any means (electronic, mechanical, photocopying, recording or otherwise), without the prior written permission of the publisher. This book is sold subject to the condition that it shall not be resold, lent, hired out or otherwise circulated without the express prior consent of the publisher.

Contents

Literary and Political Essays	1
A Farthing Newspaper	3
The Spike	6
A Hanging	13
Clink	17
Common Lodging Houses	25
On Kipling's Death	28
Shooting an Elephant	30
In Defence of the Novel	36
Bookshop Memories	41
Spilling the Spanish Beans	45
Why I Joined the Independent Labour Party	51
Marrakech	53
Not Counting Niggers	58
Democracy in the British Army	62
Boys' Weeklies	66
Charles Dickens	87
Inside the Whale	126
Notes on the Way	156
The Limit to Pessimism	159
New Words	162
Prophecies of Fascism	170
Charles Reade	173
My Country Right or Left	176
The Lion and the Unicorn	180
The Proletarian Writer	225
The Frontiers of Art and Propaganda	231
Tolstoy and Shakespeare	234
The Meaning of a Poem	238
Literature and Totalitarianism	241
Wells, Hitler and the World State	244
The Art of Donald McGill	249

No, Not One	258
Rudyard Kipling	263
The Rediscovery of Europe	275
Pacifism and the War	284
Looking Back on the Spanish War	288
Pamphlet Literature	304
W.B. Yeats	307
Literature and the Left	312
Poetry and the Microphone	315
Who Are the War Criminals?	322
Mark Twain – the Licensed Jester	328
A Hundred Up	332
The English People	334
Propaganda and Demotic Speech	365
Benefit of Clergy	371
Raffles and Miss Blandish	379
Arthur Koestler	389
Tobias Smollett	398
Funny, But Not Vulgar	402
Oysters and Brown Stout	407
A New Year Message	410
In Defence of P.G. Wodehouse	414
Anti-Semitism in Britain	426
Notes on Nationalism	434
You and the Atom Bomb	449
What Is Science?	452
Good Bad Books	455
Revenge Is Sour	458
Through a Glass, Rosily	461
Catastrophic Gradualism	464
Introduction to *Love of Life and Other Stories*	468
Freedom of the Park	474
Politics and the English Language	477
The Sporting Spirit	488
In Defence of English Cooking	491
Nonsense Poetry	493
Pleasure Spots	497
A Nice Cup of Tea	501
The Politics of Starvation	503

The Prevention of Literature	507
Books vs. Cigarettes	518
Decline of the English Murder	522
In Front of Your Nose	525
Introduction to *The Position of Peggy Harper*	528
Some Thoughts on the Common Toad	532
A Good Word for the Vicar of Bray	535
Confessions of a Book Reviewer	539
James Burnham and the Managerial Revolution	542
Why I Write	559
Politics vs. Literature	565
Riding Down from Bangor	580
How the Poor Die	585
Lear, Tolstoy and the Fool	593
Towards European Unity	607
In Defence of Comrade Zilliacus	612
George Gissing	617
Writers and Leviathan	624
Such, Such Were the Joys	630
Reflections on Gandhi	663
Conrad's Place and Rank in English Letters	670
The Question of the Pound Award	671
Abbreviations	672
Note on the Texts	673
Notes	673
Extra Material	745

Other books by GEORGE ORWELL
published by Alma Classics

NOVELS

Burmese Days

A Clergyman's Daughter

Keep the Aspidistra Flying

Coming Up for Air

Animal Farm

Nineteen Eighty-Four

NON-FICTION

Down and Out in Paris and London

Homage to Catalonia

The Road to Wigan Pier

Literary and Political Essays

A Farthing Newspaper*

The *Ami du Peuple** is a Paris newspaper. It was established about six months ago, and it has achieved something really strange and remarkable in the world where everything is a "sensation", by being sold at ten centimes, or rather less than a farthing the copy. It is a healthy, full-sized sheet, with news, articles and cartoons quite up to the usual standard, and with a turn for sport, murders, nationalist sentiment and anti-German propaganda. Nothing is abnormal about it except its price.

Nor is there any need to be surprised at this last phenomenon, because the proprietors of the *Ami du Peuple* have just explained all about it, in a huge manifesto which is pasted on the walls of Paris wherever bill-sticking is not *défendu*. On reading this manifesto one learns with pleased surprise that the *Ami du Peuple* is not like other newspapers; it was the purest public spirit, uncontaminated by any base thoughts of gain, which brought it to birth. The proprietors, who hide their blushes in anonymity, are emptying their pockets for the mere pleasure of doing good by stealth. Their objects, we learn, are to make war on the great trusts, to fight for a lower cost of living, and above all to combat the powerful newspapers which are strangling free speech in France. In spite of the sinister attempts of these other newspapers to put the *Ami du Peuple* out of action, it will fight on to the last. In short, it is all that its name implies.

One would cheer this last stand for democracy a great deal louder, of course, if one did not happen to know that the proprietor of the *Ami du Peuple* is M. Coty, a great industrial capitalist, and also proprietor of the *Figaro* and the *Gaulois*.* One would also regard the *Ami du Peuple* with less suspicion if its politics were not anti-radical and anti-socialist, of the goodwill-in-industry, shake-hands-and-make-it-up species. But all that is beside the point at this moment. The important questions, obviously, are these: does the *Ami du Peuple* pay its way? And if so, how?

The second question is the one that really matters. Since the march of progress is going in the direction of always bigger and nastier trusts, any departure is worth noticing which brings us nearer to that day when the newspaper will be simply a sheet of advertisement and propaganda, with a little well-censored news to sugar the pill. It is quite possible that the *Ami du Peuple* exists on its advertisements, but it is equally possible that it makes only an indirect profit, by putting across the sort of propaganda wanted by M. Coty and his associates. In the above-mentioned manifesto, it was declared that the proprietors might rise to an even dizzier height of philanthropy by giving away the *Ami du Peuple* free of charge. This is not so impossible as it may sound. I have seen a daily paper (in India) which was given away free for some time with apparent profit to its backers, a ring of advertisers who found a free newspaper to be a cheap and satisfactory means of blowing their own trumpet. Their paper was rather above the average Indian level, and it supplied, of course, just such news as they themselves approved, and no other. That obscure Indian paper forecast the logical goal of modern journalism – and the *Ami du Peuple* should be noticed as a new step in the same direction.

But whether its profits are direct or indirect, the *Ami du Peuple* is certainly prospering. Its circulation is already very large, and though it started out as a mere morning paper it has now produced an afternoon and late evening edition. Its proprietors speak with perfect truth when they declare that some of the other papers have done their best to crush this new champion of free speech. These others (they, too, of course, acting from the highest altruistic motives) have made a gallant attempt to have it excluded from the newsagents' shops, and have even succeeded as far as the street-corner kiosks are concerned. In some small shops, too, whose owners are socialists, one will even see the sign *"Ici on ne vend pas l'Ami du Peuple"** exhibited in the windows. But the *Ami du Peuple* is not worrying. It is sold in the streets and the cafés with great vigour, and it is sold by barbers and tobacconists and all kinds of people who have never done any news agency before. Sometimes it is simply left out on the boulevard in great piles, together with a tin for the two-sou pieces, and with no attendant whatever. One can see that the proprietors are determined, by hook or by crook, to make it the most widely read paper in Paris.

And supposing they succeed – what then? Obviously the *Ami du Peuple* is going to crowd out of existence one or more of the less prosperous papers – already several are feeling the pinch. In the end, they will presumably either be destroyed or they will survive by imitating the tactics of the *Ami du Peuple*. Hence every paper of this kind, whatever its intentions, is the enemy of free speech. At present France is the home of free speech, in the press if not elsewhere. Paris alone has daily papers by the dozen, nationalist, socialist and communist, clerical and anti-clerical, militarist and anti-militarist, pro-Semitic and anti-Semitic. It has the *Action française*, a royalist paper and still one of the leading dailies, and it has *L'Humanité*, the reddest daily paper outside Soviet Russia. It has *La Libertà*, which is written in Italian and yet may not even be sold in Italy, much less published there.* Papers are printed in Paris in French, English, Italian, Yiddish, German, Russian, Polish and languages whose very alphabets are unrecognizable by a Western European. The kiosks are stuffed with papers, all different. The press combine,* about which French journalists are already grumbling, does not really exist yet in France. But the *Ami du Peuple*, at least, is doing its gallant best to make it a reality.

A FARTHING NEWSPAPER

And supposing that this kind of thing is found to pay in France, why should it not be tried elsewhere? Why should we not have our farthing, or at least our halfpenny newspaper in London? While the journalist exists merely as the publicity agent of big business, a large circulation, got by fair means or foul, is a newspaper's one and only aim. Till recently various of our newspapers achieved the desired level of "net sales" by the simple method of giving away a few thousand pounds now and again in football competition prizes. Now the football competitions have been stopped by law, and doubtless some of the circulations have come down with an ugly bump. Here, then, is a worthy example for our English press magnates. Let them imitate the *Ami du Peuple* and sell their papers at a farthing. Even if it does no other good whatever, at any rate the poor devils of the public will at last feel that they are getting the correct value for their money.

The Spike*

It was late afternoon. Forty-nine of us, forty-eight men and one woman, lay on the green waiting for the spike to open. We were too tired to talk much. We just sprawled about exhaustedly, with home-made cigarettes sticking out of our scrubby faces. Overhead the chestnut branches were covered with blossom, and beyond that great woolly clouds floated almost motionless in a clear sky. Littered on the grass, we seemed dingy, urban riff-raff. We defiled the scene, like sardine tins and paper bags on the seashore.

What talk there was ran on the Tramp Major of this spike. He was a devil, everyone agreed, a tartar, a tyrant, a bawling, blasphemous, uncharitable dog. You couldn't call your soul your own when he was about, and many a tramp had he kicked out in the middle of the night for giving a back answer. When you came to be searched he fair held you upside down and shook you. If you were caught with tobacco there was hell to pay, and if you went in with money (which is against the law) God help you.

I had eightpence on me. "For the love of Christ, mate," the old hands advised me, "don't you take it in. You'd get seven days for going into the spike with eightpence!"

So I buried my money in a hole under the hedge, marking the spot with a lump of flint. Then we set about smuggling our matches and tobacco, for it is forbidden to take these into nearly all spikes, and one is supposed to surrender them at the gate. We hid them in our socks, except for the 20 or so per cent who had no socks, and had to carry the tobacco in their boots, even under their very toes. We stuffed our ankles with contraband until anyone seeing us might have imagined an outbreak of elephantiasis. But it is an unwritten law that even the sternest Tramp Majors do not search below the knee, and in the end only one man was caught. This was Scotty, a little hairy tramp with a bastard accent sired by cockney out of Glasgow. His tin of cigarette ends fell out of his sock at the wrong moment, and was impounded.

At six the gates swung open and we shuffled in. An official at the gate entered our names and other particulars in the register and took our bundles away from us. The woman was sent off to the workhouse, and we others into the spike. It was a gloomy, chilly, lime-washed place, consisting only of a bathroom and dining room and about a hundred narrow stone cells. The terrible Tramp Major met us at the door and herded us into the bathroom to be stripped and searched. He was a gruff, soldierly man of forty, who gave the tramps no more ceremony than sheep at the dipping pond, shoving them this way and that and shouting oaths in their faces. But when he came to myself, he looked hard at me, and said:

"You are a gentleman?"

"I suppose so," I said.

He gave me another long look. "Well, that's bloody bad luck, guv'nor," he said, "that's bloody bad luck, that is." And thereafter he took it into his head to treat me with compassion, even with a kind of respect.

It was a disgusting sight, that bathroom. All the indecent secrets of our underwear were exposed – the grime, the rents and patches, the bits of string doing duty for buttons, the layers upon layers of fragmentary garments, some of them mere collections of holes held together by dirt. The room became a press of steaming nudity, the sweaty odours of the tramps competing with the sickly, sub-faecal stench native to the spike. Some of the men refused the bath, and washed only their "toerags", the horrid, greasy little clouts which tramps bind round their feet. Each of us had three minutes in which to bathe himself. Six greasy, slippery roller towels had to serve for the lot of us.

When we had bathed our own clothes were taken away from us and we were dressed in the workhouse shirts, grey cotton things like nightshirts, reaching to the middle of the thigh. Then we were sent into the dining room, where supper was set out on the deal tables. It was the invariable spike meal, always the same, whether breakfast, dinner or supper – half a pound of bread, a bit of margarine and a pint of so-called tea. It took us five minutes to gulp down the cheap, noxious food. Then the Tramp Major served us with three cotton blankets each, and drove us off to our cells for the night. The doors were locked on the outside a little before seven in the evening, and would stay locked for the next twelve hours.

The cells measured eight feet by five, and had no lighting apparatus except a tiny barred window high up in the wall and a spyhole in the door. There were no bugs, and we had bedsteads and straw palliasses, rare luxuries both. In many spikes one sleeps on a wooden shelf, and in some on the bare floor, with a rolled-up coat for a pillow. With a cell to myself, and a bed, I was hoping for a sound night's rest. But I did not get it, for there is always something wrong in the spike, and the peculiar shortcoming here, as I discovered immediately, was the cold. May had begun, and in honour of the season – a little sacrifice to the gods of spring, perhaps – the authorities had cut off the steam from the hot pipes. The cotton blankets were almost useless. One spent the night in turning from side to side, falling asleep for ten minutes and waking half frozen, and watching for dawn.

As always happens in the spike, I had at last managed to fall comfortably asleep when it was time to get up. The Tramp Major came marching down the passage with his heavy tread, unlocking the doors and yelling to us to show a leg. Promptly the passage was full of squalid shirt-clad figures rushing for the bathroom, for there was only one tub full of water between us all in the morning, and it was first come first served. When I arrived twenty tramps had already washed their faces. I gave one glance at the black scum on top of the water, and decided to go dirty for the day.

We hurried into our clothes, and then went to the dining room to bolt our breakfast. The bread was much worse than usual, because the military-minded idiot of a Tramp Major had cut it into slices overnight, so that it was as hard as ship's biscuit. But we were glad of our tea after the cold, restless night. I do not know what tramps would do without tea, or rather the stuff they miscall tea. It is their food, their medicine, their panacea for all evils. Without the half gallon or so of it that they suck down a day, I truly believe they could not face their existence.

After breakfast we had to undress again for the medical inspection, which is a precaution against smallpox. It was three quarters of an hour before the doctor arrived, and one had time now to look about him and see what manner of men we were. It was an instructive sight. We stood shivering naked to the waist in two long ranks in the passage. The filtered light, bluish and cold, lighted us up with unmerciful clarity. No one can imagine, unless he has seen such a thing, what pot-bellied, degenerate curs we looked. Shock heads, hairy, crumpled faces, hollow chests, flat feet, sagging muscles – every kind of malformation and physical rottenness was there. All were flabby and discoloured, as all tramps are under their deceptive sunburn. Two or three figures seen there stay ineradicably in my mind. Old "Daddy", aged seventy-four, with his truss and his red, watering eyes; a herring-gutted starveling, with sparse beard and sunken cheeks, looking like the corpse of Lazarus in some primitive picture; an imbecile, wandering hither and thither with vague giggles, coyly pleased because his trousers constantly slipped down and left him nude. But few of us were greatly better than these; there were not ten decently built men among us, and half, I believe, should have been in hospital.

This being Sunday, we were to be kept in the spike over the weekend. As soon as the doctor had gone we were herded back to the dining room, and its door shut upon us. It was a lime-washed, stone-floored room, unspeakably dreary with its furniture of deal boards and benches, and its prison smell. The windows were so high up that one could not look outside, and the sole ornament was a set of "Rules" threatening dire penalties to any casual who misconducted himself. We packed the room so tight that one could not move an elbow without jostling somebody. Already, at eight o'clock in the morning, we were bored with our captivity. There was nothing to talk about except the petty gossip of the road, the good and bad spikes, the charitable and uncharitable counties, the iniquities of the police and the Salvation Army. Tramps hardly ever get away from these subjects; they talk, as it were, nothing but shop. They have nothing worthy to be called conversation, because emptiness of belly leaves no speculation in their souls. The world is too much with them. Their next meal is never quite secure, and so they cannot think of anything except the next meal.

Two hours dragged by. Old Daddy, witless with age, sat silent, his back bent like a bow and his inflamed eyes dripping slowly onto the floor. George, a dirty old tramp notorious for the queer habit of sleeping in his hat, grumbled about a parcel of tommy* that he had lost on the road. Bill the moocher, the best-built man of us all, a Herculean sturdy beggar who smelt of beer even after twelve hours in the spike, told tales of mooching, of pints stood him in the boozers and of a parson who had peached to the police and got him seven days. William and Fred, two young ex-fishermen from Norfolk, sang a sad song about Unhappy Bella, who was betrayed and died in the snow. The imbecile drivelled about an imaginary toff who had once given him 257 golden sovereigns. So the time passed, with dull talk and dull obscenities. Everyone was smoking, except Scotty, whose tobacco had been seized, and he was so miserable in his smokeless state that I stood him the makings of a cigarette. We smoked furtively, hiding our cigarettes like schoolboys when we heard the Tramp Major's step, for smoking, though connived at, was officially forbidden.

Most of the tramps spent ten consecutive hours in this dreary room. It is hard to imagine how they put up with it. I have come to think that boredom is the worst of all a tramp's evils, worse than hunger and discomfort, worse even than the constant feeling of being socially disgraced. It is a silly piece of cruelty to confine an ignorant man all day with nothing to do; it is like chaining a dog in a barrel. Only an educated man, who has consolations within himself, can endure confinement. Tramps, unlettered types as nearly all of them are, face their poverty with blank, resourceless minds. Fixed for ten hours on a comfortless bench, they know no way of occupying themselves, and if they think at all it is to whimper about hard luck and pine for work. They have not the stuff in them to endure the horrors of idleness. And so, since so much of their lives is spent in doing nothing, they suffer agonies from boredom.

I was much luckier than the others, because at ten o'clock the Tramp Major picked me out for the most coveted of all jobs in the spike, the job of helping in the workhouse kitchen. There was not really any work to be done there, and I was able to make off and hide in a shed used for storing potatoes, together with some workhouse paupers who were skulking to avoid the Sunday-morning service. There was a stove burning there, and comfortable packing cases to sit on, and back numbers of the *Family Herald*,* and even a copy of *Raffles** from the workhouse library. It was paradise after the spike.

Also, I had my dinner from the workhouse table, and it was one of the biggest meals I have ever eaten. A tramp does not see such a meal twice in the year, in the spike or out of it. The paupers told me that they always gorged to the bursting point on Sundays, and went hungry six days of the week. When the meal was over the cook set me to do the washing-up, and told me to throw away the food that remained. The wastage was astonishing; great dishes of beef, and bucketfuls of bread and vegetables, were pitched away like rubbish, and then defiled with tea leaves. I filled five dustbins to overflowing with good food. And while I did so my fellow tramps were sitting two hundred yards away in the spike, their bellies half filled with the spike dinner of the everlasting bread and tea, and perhaps two cold boiled potatoes each in honour of Sunday. It appeared that the food was thrown away from deliberate policy, rather than that it should be given to the tramps.

At three I left the workhouse kitchen and went back to the spike. The boredom in that crowded, comfortless room was now unbearable. Even smoking had ceased, for a tramp's only tobacco is picked-up cigarette ends and, like a browsing beast, he starves if he is long away from the pavement-pasture. To occupy the time I talked with a rather superior tramp, a young carpenter who wore a collar and tie, and was on the road, he said, for lack of a set of tools. He kept a little aloof from the other tramps, and held himself more like a free man than a casual. He had literary tastes, too, and carried one of Scott's novels* on all his wanderings. He told me he never entered a spike unless driven there by hunger, sleeping under hedges and behind ricks in preference. Along the south coast he had begged by day and slept in bathing machines for weeks at a time.

We talked of life on the road. He criticized the system which makes a tramp spend fourteen hours a day in the spike, and the other ten in walking and dodging the police. He spoke of his own case – six months at the public charge for want of three pounds' worth of tools. It was idiotic, he said.

Then I told him about the wastage of food in the workhouse kitchen, and what I thought of it. And at that he changed his tune immediately. I saw that I had awakened the pew renter* who sleeps in every English workman. Though he had been famished along with the rest, he at once saw reasons why the food should have been thrown away rather than given to the tramps. He admonished me quite severely.

"They have to do it," he said. "If they made these places too pleasant you'd have all the scum of the country flocking into them. It's only the bad food as keeps all that scum away. These tramps are too lazy to work, that's all that's wrong with them. You don't want to go encouraging of them. They're scum."

I produced arguments to prove him wrong, but he would not listen. He kept repeating:

"You don't want to have any pity on these tramps – scum, they are. You don't want to judge them by the same standards as men like you and me. They're scum, just scum."

It was interesting to see how subtly he disassociated himself from his fellow tramps. He has been on the road six months, but in the sight of God, he seemed to imply, he was not a tramp. His body might be in the spike, but his spirit soared far away, in the pure ether of the middle classes.

THE SPIKE

The clock's hands crept round with excruciating slowness. We were too bored even to talk now, the only sound was of oaths and reverberating yawns. One would force his eyes away from the clock for what seemed an age, and then look back again to see that the hands had advanced three minutes. Ennui clogged our souls like cold mutton fat. Our bones ached because of it. The clock's hands stood at four, and supper was not till six, and there was nothing left remarkable beneath the visiting moon.*

At last six o'clock did come, and the Tramp Major and his assistant arrived with supper. The yawning tramps brisked up like lions at feeding time. But the meal was a dismal disappointment. The bread, bad enough in the morning, was now positively uneatable; it was so hard that even the strongest jaws could make little impression on it. The older men went almost supperless, and not a man could finish his portion, hungry though most of us were. When we had finished, the blankets were served out immediately, and we were hustled off once more to the bare, chilly cells.

Thirteen hours went by. At seven we were awakened, and rushed forth to squabble over the water in the bathroom, and bolt our ration of bread and tea. Our time in the spike was up, but we could not go until the doctor had examined us again, for the authorities have a terror of smallpox and its distribution by tramps. The doctor kept us waiting two hours this time, and it was ten o'clock before we finally escaped.

At last it was time to go, and we were let out into the yard. How bright everything looked, and how sweet the winds did blow, after the gloomy, reeking spike! The Tramp Major handed each man his bundle of confiscated possessions, and a hunk of bread and cheese for midday dinner, and then we took the road, hastening to get out of sight of the spike and its discipline. This was our interim of freedom. After a day and two nights of wasted time we had eight hours or so to take our recreation, to scour the roads for cigarette ends, to beg and to look for work. Also, we had to make our ten, fifteen, or it might be twenty miles to the next spike, where the game would begin anew.

I disinterred my eightpence and took the road with Nobby, a respectable, downhearted tramp who carried a spare pair of boots and visited all the Labour Exchanges. Our late companions were scattering north, south, east and west, like bugs into a mattress. Only the imbecile loitered at the spike gates, until the Tramp Major had to chase him away.

Nobby and I set out for Croydon. It was a quiet road, there were no cars passing, the blossom covered the chestnut trees like great wax candles. Everything was so quiet and smelt so clean, it was hard to realize that only a few minutes ago we had been packed with that band of prisoners in a stench of drains and soft soap. The others had all disappeared; we two seemed to be the only tramps on the road.

Then I heard a hurried step behind me, and felt a tap on my arm. It was little Scotty, who had run panting after us. He pulled a rusty tin box from his pocket. He wore a friendly smile, like a man who is repaying an obligation.

"Here y'are, mate," he said cordially. "I owe you some fag ends. You stood me a smoke yesterday. The Tramp Major give me back my box of fag ends when we come out this morning. One good turn deserves another – here y'are."

And he put four sodden, debauched, loathly cigarette ends into my hand.

A Hanging*

It was in Burma,* a sodden morning of the rains. A sickly light, like yellow tinfoil, was slanting over the high walls into the jail yard. We were waiting outside the condemned cells, a row of sheds fronted with double bars, like small animal cages. Each cell measured about ten feet by ten and was quite bare within except for a plank bed and a pot of drinking water. In some of them brown silent men were squatting at the inner bars, with their blankets draped round them. These were the condemned men, due to be hanged within the next week or two.

One prisoner had been brought out of his cell. He was a Hindu, a puny wisp of a man, with a shaven head and vague liquid eyes. He had a thick, sprouting moustache, absurdly too big for his body, rather like the moustache of a comic man on the films. Six tall Indian warders were guarding him and getting him ready for the gallows. Two of them stood by with rifles and fixed bayonets, while the others handcuffed him, passed a chain through his handcuffs and fixed it to their belts, and lashed his arms tight to his sides. They crowded very close about him, with their hands always on him in a careful, caressing grip, as though all the while feeling him to make sure he was there. It was like men handling a fish which is still alive and may jump back into the water. But he stood quite unresisting, yielding his arms limply to the ropes, as though he hardly noticed what was happening.

Eight o'clock struck and a bugle call, desolately thin in the wet air, floated from the distant barracks. The superintendent of the jail, who was standing apart from the rest of us, moodily prodding the gravel with his stick, raised his head at the sound. He was an army doctor, with a grey toothbrush moustache and a gruff voice. "For God's sake hurry up, Francis," he said irritably. "The man ought to have been dead by this time. Aren't you ready yet?"

Francis, the head jailer, a fat Dravidian* in a white drill suit and gold spectacles, waved his black hand. "Yes sir, yes sir," he bubbled. "All iss satisfactorily prepared. The hangman iss waiting. We shall proceed."

"Well, quick march, then. The prisoners can't get their breakfast till this job's over."

We set out for the gallows. Two warders marched on either side of the prisoner, with their rifles at the slope; two others marched close against him, gripping him by arm and shoulder, as though at once pushing and supporting him. The rest of us, magistrates and the like, followed behind. Suddenly, when we had gone ten yards, the procession stopped short without any order or warning. A dreadful thing had happened – a dog, come goodness knows whence, had appeared in the yard. It came bounding among us with a loud volley of barks, and leapt round us wagging its whole body, wild with glee at finding so many human beings together. It was a large woolly dog, half Airedale, half pariah. For a moment it pranced round us, and then, before anyone could stop it, it had made a dash for the prisoner and, jumping up, tried to lick his face. Everyone stood aghast, too taken aback even to grab at the dog.

"Who let that bloody brute in here?" said the superintendent angrily. "Catch it, someone!"

A warder, detached from the escort, charged clumsily after the dog, but it danced and gambolled just out of his reach, taking everything as part of the game. A young Eurasian jailer picked up a handful of gravel and tried to stone the dog away, but it dodged the stones and came after us again. Its yaps echoed from the jail walls. The prisoner, in the grasp of the two warders, looked on incuriously, as though this was another formality of the hanging. It was several minutes before someone managed to catch the dog. Then we put my handkerchief through its collar and moved off once more, with the dog still straining and whimpering.

It was about forty yards to the gallows. I watched the bare brown back of the prisoner marching in front of me. He walked clumsily with his bound arms, but quite steadily, with that bobbing gait of the Indian who never straightens his knees. At each step his muscles slid neatly into place, the lock of hair on his scalp danced up and down, his feet printed themselves on the wet gravel. And once, in spite of the men who gripped him by each shoulder, he stepped slightly aside to avoid a puddle on the path.

It is curious, but till that moment I had never realized what it means to destroy a healthy, conscious man. When I saw the prisoner step aside to avoid the puddle, I saw the mystery, the unspeakable wrongness, of cutting a life short when it is in full tide. This man was not dying, he was alive just as we were alive. All the organs of his body were working – bowels digesting food, skin renewing itself, nails growing, tissues forming – all toiling away in solemn foolery. His nails would still be growing when he stood on the drop, when he was falling through the air with a tenth of a second to live. His eyes saw the yellow gravel and the grey walls, and his brain still remembered, foresaw, reasoned – reasoned even about puddles. He and we were a party of men walking together, seeing, hearing, feeling, understanding the same world, and in two minutes, with a sudden snap, one of us would be gone – one mind less, one world less.

The gallows stood in a small yard, separate from the main grounds of the prison, and overgrown with tall prickly weeds. It was a brick erection like three sides of a shed, with planking on top, and above that two beams and a crossbar with the rope dangling. The hangman, a grey-haired convict in the white uniform of the prison, was waiting beside his machine. He greeted us with a servile crouch as we entered. At a word from Francis the two warders, gripping the prisoner more closely than ever, half led, half pushed him to the gallows and helped him clumsily up the ladder. Then the hangman climbed up and fixed the rope round the prisoner's neck.

We stood waiting, five yards away. The warders had formed in a rough circle round the gallows. And then, when the noose was fixed, the prisoner began crying out on his god. It was a high, reiterated cry of "Ram!* Ram! Ram! Ram!", not urgent and fearful like a prayer or a cry for help, but steady, rhythmical, almost like the tolling of a bell. The dog answered the sound with a whine. The hangman, still standing on the gallows, produced a small cotton bag like a flour bag and drew it down over the prisoner's face. But the sound, muffled by the cloth, still persisted, over and over again: "Ram! Ram! Ram! Ram! Ram!"

The hangman climbed down and stood ready, holding the lever. Minutes seemed to pass. The steady, muffled crying from the prisoner went on and on – "Ram! Ram! Ram!" – never faltering for an instant. The superintendent, his head on his chest, was slowly poking the ground with his stick; perhaps he was counting the cries, allowing the prisoner a fixed number – fifty, perhaps, or a hundred. Everyone had changed colour. The Indians had gone grey like bad coffee, and one or two of the bayonets were wavering. We looked at the lashed, hooded man on the drop, and listened to his cries – each cry another second of life; the same thought was in all our minds: oh, kill him quickly, get it over, stop that abominable noise!

Suddenly the superintendent made up his mind. Throwing up his head he made a swift motion with his stick. "Chalo!"* he shouted almost fiercely.

There was a clanking noise, and then dead silence. The prisoner had vanished, and the rope was twisting on itself. I let go of the dog, and it galloped immediately to the back of the gallows – but when it got there it stopped short, barked, and then retreated into a corner of the yard, where it stood among the weeds, looking timorously out at us. We went round the gallows to inspect the prisoner's body. He was dangling with his toes pointed straight downwards, very slowly revolving, as dead as a stone.

The superintendent reached out with his stick and poked the bare body; it oscillated slightly. "*He's* all right," said the superintendent. He backed out from under the gallows, and blew out a deep breath. The moody look had gone out of his face quite suddenly. He glanced at his wristwatch. "Eight minutes past eight. Well, that's all for this morning, thank God."

The warders unfixed bayonets and marched away. The dog, sobered and conscious of having misbehaved itself, slipped after them. We walked out of the gallows yard, past the condemned cells with their waiting prisoners, into the big central yard of the prison. The convicts, under the command of warders armed with lathis,* were already receiving their breakfast. They squatted in long rows, each man holding a tin pannikin,* while two warders with buckets marched round ladling out rice; it seemed quite a homely, jolly scene, after the hanging. An enormous relief had come upon us now that the job was done. One felt an impulse to sing, to break into a run, to snigger. All at once everyone began chattering gaily.

The Eurasian boy walking beside me nodded towards the way we had come, with a knowing smile: "Do you know, sir, our friend" (he meant the dead man), "when he heard his appeal had been dismissed, he pissed on the floor of his cell. From fright. Kindly take one of my cigarettes, sir. Do you not admire my new silver case, sir? From the boxwallah,* two rupees eight annas.* Classy European style."

Several people laughed – at what, nobody seemed certain.

Francis was walking by the superintendent, talking garrulously: "Well, sir, all hass passed off with the utmost satisfactoriness. It wass all finished – flick! – like that. It iss not always so – oah, no! I have known cases where the doctor wass obliged to go beneath the gallows and pull the prisoner's legs to ensure decease. Most disagreeable!"

"Wriggling about, eh? That's bad," said the superintendent.

"Ach, sir, it iss worse when they become refractory! One man, I recall, clung to the bars of hiss cage when we went to take him out. You will scarcely credit, sir, that it took six warders to dislodge him, three pulling at each leg. We reasoned with him. 'My dear fellow,' we said, 'think of all the pain and trouble you are causing to us!' But no, he would not listen! Ach, he wass very troublesome!"

I found that I was laughing quite loudly. Everyone was laughing. Even the superintendent grinned in a tolerant way. "You'd better all come out and have a drink," he said quite genially. "I've got a bottle of whisky in the car. We could do with it."

We went through the big double gates of the prison, into the road. "Pulling at his legs!" exclaimed a Burmese magistrate suddenly, and burst into a loud chuckling. We all began laughing again. At that moment Francis's anecdote seemed extraordinarily funny. We all had a drink together, native and European alike, quite amicably. The dead man was a hundred yards away.

Clink*

This trip was a failure, as the object of it was to get into prison, and I did not, in fact, get more than forty-eight hours in custody; however, I am recording it, as the procedure in the police court etc. was fairly interesting. I am writing this eight months after it happened, so am not certain of any dates, but it all happened a week or ten days before Christmas 1931.

I started out on Saturday afternoon with four or five shillings, and went out to the Mile End Road, because my plan was to get drunk and incapable, and I thought they would be less lenient towards drunkards in the East End. I bought some tobacco and a "Yank mag"* against my forthcoming imprisonment, and then, as soon as the pubs opened, went and had four or five pints, topping up with a quarter bottle of whisky, which left me with twopence in hand. By the time the whisky was low in the bottle I was tolerably drunk – more drunk than I had intended, for it happened that I had eaten nothing all day, and the alcohol acted quickly on my empty stomach. It was all I could do to stand upright, though my brain was quite clear – with me, when I am drunk, my brain remains clear long after my legs and speech have gone. I began staggering along the pavement in a westward direction, and for a long time did not meet any policemen, though the streets were crowded and all the people pointed and laughed at me. Finally I saw two policemen coming. I pulled the whisky bottle out of my pocket and, in their sight, drank what was left, which nearly knocked me out, so that I clutched a lamp-post and fell down. The two policemen ran towards me, turned me over and took the bottle out of my hand.

THEY: "'Ere, what you bin drinking?" (For a moment they may have thought it was a case of suicide.)

I: "Thass my boll whisky. You lea' me alone."

THEY: "Coo, 'e's fair bin bathing in it! What you bin doing of, eh?"

I: "Bin in boozer, 'avin' bit o' fun. Christmas, ain't it?"

THEY: "No, not by a week it ain't. You got mixed up in the dates, you 'ave. You better come along with us. We'll look after yer."

I: "Why sh'd I come along you?"

THEY: "Jest so's we'll look after you and make you comfortable. You'll get run over, rolling about like that."

I: "Look. Boozer over there. Less go in 'ave drink."

THEY: "You've 'ad enough for one night, ole chap. You best come with us."

I: "Where you takin' me?"

THEY: "Jest somewhere as you'll get a nice quiet kip with a clean sheet and two blankets and all."

I: "Shall I get drink there?"

THEY: "Course you will. Got a boozer on the premises, we 'ave."

All this while they were leading me gently along the pavement. They had my arms in the grip (I forget what it is called) by which you can break a man's arm with one twist, but they were as gentle with me as though I had been a child. I was internally quite sober, and it amused me very much to see the cunning way in which they persuaded me along, never once disclosing the fact that we were making for the police station. This is, I suppose, the usual procedure with drunks.

When we got to the station (it was Bethnal Green, but I did not learn this till Monday) they dumped me in a chair and began emptying my pockets while the sergeant questioned me. I pretended, however, to be too drunk to give sensible answers, and he told them in disgust to take me off to the cells, which they did. The cell was about the same size as a casual-ward* cell (about ten feet by five feet by ten feet high), but much cleaner and better appointed. It was made of white porcelain bricks, and was furnished with a WC, a hot-water pipe, a plank bed, a horsehair pillow and two blankets. There was a tiny barred window high up near the roof, and an electric bulb behind a guard of thick glass was kept burning all night. The door was steel, with the usual spyhole and aperture for serving food through. The constables in searching me had taken away my money, matches, razor, and also my scarf – this, I learnt afterwards, because prisoners have been known to hang themselves on their scarves.

There is very little to say about the next day and night, which were unutterably boring. I was horribly sick, sicker than I have ever been from a bout of drunkenness, no doubt from having an empty stomach. During Sunday I was given two meals of bread and marge and tea (spike quality), and one of meat and potatoes – this, I believe, owing to the kindness of the sergeant's wife, for I think only bread and marge is provided for prisoners in the lock-up. I was not allowed to shave, and there was only a little cold water to wash in. When the charge sheet was filled up I told the story I always tell, viz. my name was Edward Burton, and my parents kept a cake shop in Blythburgh, where I had been employed as a clerk in a draper's shop; that I had had the sack for drunkenness, and my parents, finally getting sick of my drunken habits, had turned me adrift. I added that I had been working as an outside porter at Billingsgate, and having unexpectedly "knocked up" six shillings on Saturday, had gone on the razzle. The police were quite kind, and read me lectures on drunkenness, with the usual stuff about seeing that I still had some good in me, etc. etc. They offered to let me out on bail on my own recognizance, but I had no money and nowhere to go, so I elected to stay in custody. It was very dull, but I had my "Yank mag", and could get a smoke if I asked the constable on duty in the passage for a light – prisoners are not allowed matches, of course.

CLINK

The next morning very early they turned me out of my cell to wash, gave me back my scarf, and took me out into the yard and put me in the Black Maria.* Inside, the Black Maria was just like a French public lavatory, with a row of tiny locked compartments on either side, each just large enough to sit down in. People had scrawled their names, offences and the lengths of their sentences all over the walls of my compartment; also, several times, variants on this couplet:

> Detective Smith knows how to gee;
> Tell him he's a cunt from me.

("Gee" in this context means to act as an *agent provocateur*.) We drove round to various stations, picking up about ten prisoners in all, until the Black Maria was quite full. They were quite a jolly crowd inside. The compartment doors were open at the top, for ventilation, so that you could reach across, and somebody had managed to smuggle matches in, and we all had a smoke. Presently we began singing, and, as it was near Christmas, sang several carols. We drove up to Old Street Police Court singing:

> *Adeste, fideles, læti, triumphantes,*
> *Adeste, adeste ad Bethlehem*, etc.*

which seemed to me rather inappropriate.

At the police court they took me off and put me in a cell identical with the one at Bethnal Green, even to having the same number of bricks in it – I counted in each case. There were three men in the cell besides myself. One was a smartly dressed, florid, well-set-up man of about thirty-five, whom I would have taken for a commercial traveller or perhaps a bookie, and another a middle-aged Jew, also quite decently dressed. The other man was evidently a habitual burglar. He was a short, rough-looking man with grey hair and a worn face, and at this moment in such a state of agitation over his approaching trial that he could not keep still an instant. He kept pacing up and down the cell like a wild beast, brushing against our knees as we sat on the plank bed, and exclaiming that he was innocent – he was charged, apparently, with loitering with intent to commit burglary. He said that he had nine previous convictions against him, and that in these cases, which are mainly of suspicion, old offenders are nearly always convicted. From time to time he would shake his fist towards the door and exclaim "Fucking toerag! Fucking toerag!", meaning the "split" who had arrested him.

Presently two more prisoners were put into the cell, an ugly Belgian youth charged with obstructing traffic with a barrow, and an extraordinary hairy creature who was either deaf and dumb or spoke no English. Except this last all the prisoners talked about their cases with the utmost freedom. The florid, smart man, it appeared, was a public house "guv'nor" (it is a sign of how utterly the London publicans are in the claws of the brewers that they are always referred to as "governors", not "landlords", being, in fact, no better than employees), and had embezzled the Christmas Club money. As usual, he was head over ears in debt to the brewers, and no doubt had taken some of the money in hopes of backing a winner. Two of the subscribers had discovered this a few days before the money was due to be laid out, and laid an information.* The "guv'nor" immediately paid back all save £12, which was also refunded before his case came up for trial. Nevertheless, he was certain to be sentenced, as the magistrates are hard on these cases – he did, in fact, get four months later in the day. He was ruined for life, of course. The brewers would file bankruptcy proceedings and sell up all his stock and furniture, and he would never be given a pub licence again. He was trying to brazen it out in front of the rest of us, and smoking cigarettes incessantly from a stock of Gold Flake packets he had laid in – the last time in his life, I dare say, that he would have quite enough cigarettes. There was a staring, abstracted look in his eyes all the time while he talked. I think the fact that his life was at an end, as far as any decent position in society went, was gradually sinking into him.

The Jew had been a buyer at Smithfield for a kosher butcher. After working seven years for the same employer he suddenly misappropriated £28, went up to Edinburgh – I don't know why Edinburgh – and had a "good time" with tarts, and came back and surrendered himself when the money was gone. £16 of the money had been repaid, and the rest was to be repaid by monthly instalments. He had a wife and a number of children. He told us, what interested me, that his employer would probably get into trouble at the synagogue for prosecuting him. It appears that the Jews have arbitration courts of their own, and a Jew is not supposed to prosecute another Jew, at least in a breach of trust case like this, without first submitting it to the arbitration court.

One remark made by these men struck me – I heard it from almost every prisoner who was up for a serious offence. It was, "It's not the prison I mind, it's losing my job." This is, I believe, symptomatic of the dwindling power of the law compared with that of the capitalist.

They kept us waiting several hours. It was very uncomfortable in the cell, for there was not room for all of us to sit down on the plank bed, and it was beastly cold in spite of the number of us. Several of the men used the WC, which was disgusting in so small a cell, especially as the plug did not work. The publican distributed his cigarettes generously, the constable in the passage supplying lights. From time to time an extraordinary clanking noise came from the cell next door, where a youth who had stabbed his "tart" in the stomach – she was likely to recover, we heard – was locked up alone. Goodness knows what was happening, but it sounded as though he were chained to the wall. At about ten they gave us each a mug of tea – this, it appeared, not provided by the authorities but by the police-court missionaries – and shortly afterwards shepherded us along to a sort of large waiting room where the prisoners awaited trial.

There were perhaps fifty prisoners here, men of every type, but on the whole much more smartly dressed than one would expect. They were strolling up and down with their hats on, shivering with the cold. I saw here a thing which interested me greatly. When I was being taken to my cell I had seen two dirty-looking ruffians, much dirtier than myself and presumably drunks or obstruction cases, being put into another cell in the row. Here, in the waiting room, these two were at work with notebooks in their hands, interrogating prisoners. It appeared that they were "splits", and were put into the cells disguised as prisoners, to pick up any information that was going – for there is complete freemasonry between prisoners, and they talk without reserve in front of one another. It was a dingy trick, I thought.

All the while the prisoners were being taken by ones and twos along a corridor to the court. Presently a sergeant shouted "Come on the drunks!" and four or five of us filed along the corridor and stood waiting at the entrance of the court. A young constable on duty there advised me:

"Take your cap off when you go in, plead guilty and don't give back any answers. Got any previous convictions?"

"No."

"Six bob you'll get. Going to pay it?"

"I can't. I've only twopence."

"Ah well, it don't matter. Lucky for you Mr Brown isn't on the bench this morning. Teetotaller he is. He don't half give it to the drunks. Coo!"

The drunk cases were dealt with so rapidly that I had not even time to notice what the court was like. I only had a vague impression of a raised platform with a coat of arms over it, clerks sitting at tables below, and a railing. We filed past the railing like people passing through a turnstile, and the proceedings in each case sounded like this:

"Edward-Burton-drunk-and-incapable-Drunk?-Yes-Six-shillings-move-on-NEXT!"

All this in the space of about five seconds. At the other side of the court we reached a room where a sergeant was sitting at a desk with a ledger.

"Six shillings?" he said.

"Yes."

"Going to pay it?"

"I can't."

"All right, back you go to your cell."

And they took me back and locked me in the cell from which I had come, about ten minutes after I had left it.

The publican had also been brought back, his case having been postponed, and the Belgian youth, who, like me, could not pay his fine. The Jew was gone, whether released or sentenced we did not know. Throughout the day prisoners were coming and going, some waiting trial, some until the Black Maria was available to take them to prison. It was cold, and the nasty faecal stench in the cell became unbearable. They gave us our dinner at about two o'clock – it consisted of a mug of tea and two slices of bread and marge for each man. Apparently this was the regulation meal. One could, if one had friends outside, get food sent in, but it struck me as damnably unfair that a penniless man must face his trial with only bread and marge in his belly; also unshaven – I, at this time, had had no chance of shaving for over forty-eight hours – which is likely to prejudice the magistrates against him.

Among the prisoners who were put temporarily in the cell were two friends or partners named apparently Snouter and Charlie, who had been arrested for some street offence – obstruction with a barrow, I dare say. Snouter was a thin, red-faced, malignant-looking man, and Charlie a short, powerful, jolly man. Their conversation was rather interesting.

CHARLIE: "Cripes, it ain't 'alf fucking cold in 'ere. Lucky for us ole Brown ain't on today. Give you a month as soon as look at yer."

SNOUTER: (bored, and singing)

> Tap, tap, tapetty tap,
> I'm a perfect devil at that;
> Tapping 'em 'ere, tapping 'em there,
> *I* bin tapping 'em everywhere—

CHARLIE: "Oh, fuck off with yer tapping! Scrumping's what yer want at this time of year. All them rows of turkeys in the winders, like rows of fucking soldiers with no clo'es on – don't it make yer fucking mouth water to look at 'em. Bet yer a tanner I'ave one of 'em afore tonight."

SNOUTER: "What's 'a good? Can't cook the bugger over the kip-'ouse fire, can you?"

CHARLIE: "Oo wants to cook it? I know where I can flog it for a bob or two, though."

SNOUTER: "'S no good. Chanting's the game this time of year. Carols. Fair twist their 'earts round, I can, when I get on the mournful. Old tarts weep their fucking eyes out when they 'ear me. I won't 'alf give them a doing this Christmas. I'll kip indoors if I 'ave to cut it out of their bowels."

CHARLIE: "Ah, *I* can sling you a bit of a carol. 'Ymns, too." (He begins singing in a good bass voice.)

> Jesu, lover of my soul,
> Let me to thy bosom fly—

THE CONSTABLE ON DUTY: (looking through the grille) "Nah then, in 'ere, nah then! What yer think this is? Baptist prayer meeting?"

CHARLIE: (in a low voice as the constable disappears) "Fuck off, pisspot." (He hums.)

> While the gathering waters roll,
> While the tempest still is 'igh!*

"You won't find many in the 'ymnal as I can't sling you. Sung bass in the choir my last two years in Dartmoor, I did."

SNOUTER: "Ah? Wassit like in Dartmoor now? D'you get jam now?"

CHARLIE: "Not jam. Gets cheese, though, twice a week."

SNOUTER: "Ah? 'Ow long was you doing?"

CHARLIE: "Four year."

SNOUTER: "Four years without cunt – cripes! Fellers inside'd go 'alf mad if they saw a pair of legs (a woman), eh?"

CHARLIE: "Ah well, in Dartmoor we used to fuck old women down on the allotments. Take 'em under the 'edge in the mist. Spud-grabbers they was – ole trots seventy years old. Forty of us was caught and went through 'ell for it. Bread and water, chains – everything. I took my Bible oath as I wouldn't get no more stretches after that."

SNOUTER: "Yes, you! 'Ow come you got in the stir lars' time, then?"

CHARLIE: "You wouldn't 'ardly believe it, boy. I was narked – narked by my own sister! Yes, my own fucking sister. My sister's a cow if ever there was one. She got married to a religious maniac, and 'e's so fucking religious that she's got fifteen kids now. Well, it was 'im put 'er up to narking me. But I got it back on 'em, *I* can tell you. What do you think I done first thing, when I come out of the stir? I bought a 'ammer, and I went round to my sister's 'ouse and smashed 'er piano to fucking matchwood. I did. 'There,' I says, 'that's what you get for narking me! You mare!' I says." Etc. etc.

This kind of conversation went on more or less all day between these two, who were only in for some petty offence and were quite pleased with themselves. Those who were going to prison were silent and restless, and the look on some of the men's faces – respectable men under arrest for the first time – was dreadful. They took the publican out at about three in the afternoon, to be sent off to prison. He had cheered up a little on learning from the constable on duty that he was going to the same prison as Lord Kylsant.* He thought that by sucking up to Lord K. in jail he might get a job from him when he came out.

I had no idea how long I was going to be incarcerated, and supposed that it would be several days at least. However, between four and five o'clock they took me out of the cell, gave back the things which had been confiscated and shot me into the street forthwith. Evidently the day in custody served instead of the fine. I had only twopence and had had nothing to eat all day except bread and marge and was damnably hungry; however, as always happens when it is a choice between tobacco and food, I bought tobacco with my twopence. Then I went down to the Church Army shelter in the Waterloo Road, where you get a kip, two meals of bread and corned beef and tea and a prayer meeting, for four hours' work at sawing wood.

The next morning I went home, got some money, and went out to Edmonton. I turned up at the casual ward about nine at night, not downright drunk but more or less under the influence, thinking this would lead to prison – for it is an offence under the Vagrancy Act for a tramp to come drunk to the casual ward. The porter, however, treated me with great consideration, evidently feeling that a tramp with money enough to buy drink ought to be respected. During the next few days I made several more attempts to get into trouble by begging under the noses of the police, but I seemed to bear a charmed life – no one took any notice of me. So, as I did not want to do anything serious which might lead to investigations about my identity, etc., I gave it up. The trip, therefore, was more or less a failure, but I have recorded it as a fairly interesting experience.

Common Lodging Houses*

Common lodging houses, of which there are several hundred in London, are night shelters specially licensed by the LCC.* They are intended for people who cannot afford regular lodgings, and in effect they are extremely cheap hotels. It is hard to estimate the lodging-house population, which varies continually, but it always runs into tens of thousands, and in the winter months probably approaches 50,000. Considering that they house so many people and that most of them are in an extraordinarily bad state, common lodging houses do not get the attention they deserve.

To judge the value of the LCC legislation on this subject, one must realize what life in a common lodging house is like. The average lodging house ("doss house", it used to be called) consists of a number of dormitories and a kitchen, always subterranean, which also serves as a sitting room. The conditions in these places, especially in southern quarters such as Southwark or Bermondsey, are disgusting. The dormitories are horrible fetid dens, packed with anything up to a hundred men, and furnished with beds a good deal inferior to those in a London casual ward. Normally these beds are about five feet six inches long by two feet six inches wide, with a hard convex mattress and a cylindrical pillow like a block of wood; sometimes, in the cheaper houses, not even a pillow. The bedclothes consist of two raw-umber-coloured sheets, supposed to be changed once a week, but actually, in many cases, left on for a month, and a cotton counterpane; in winter there may be blankets, but never enough. As often as not the beds are verminous, and the kitchens invariably swarm with cockroaches or black beetles. There are no baths, of course, and no room where any privacy is attainable. These are the normal and accepted conditions in all ordinary lodging houses. The charges paid for this kind of accommodation vary between 7*d*. and 1/1*d*. a night. It should be added that, low as these charges sound, the average common lodging house brings in something like £40 net profit a week to its owner.

Besides the ordinary dirty lodging houses, there are a few score, such as the Rowton Houses* and the Salvation Army hostels, that are clean and decent. Unfortunately, all of these places set off their advantages by a discipline so rigid and tiresome that to stay in them is rather like being in jail. In London (curiously enough it is better in some other towns) the common lodging house where one gets both liberty and a decent bed does not exist.

The curious thing about the squalor and discomfort of the ordinary lodging house is that these exist in places subject to constant inspection by the LCC.

When one first sees the murky, troglodytic cave of a common-lodging-house kitchen, one takes it for a corner of the early nineteenth century which has somehow been missed by the reformers; it is a surprise to find that common lodging houses are governed by a set of minute and (in intention) exceedingly tyrannical rules. According to the LCC regulations, practically everything is against the law in a common lodging house. Gambling, drunkenness or even the introduction of liquor, swearing, spitting on the floor, keeping tame animals, fighting – in short, the whole social life of these places – are all forbidden. Of course, the law is habitually broken, but some of the rules are enforceable, and they illustrate the dismal uselessness of this kind of legislation. To take an instance: some time ago the LCC became concerned about the closeness together of beds in common lodging houses, and enacted that these must be at least three feet apart. This is the kind of law that is enforceable, and the beds were duly moved. Now, to a lodger in an already overcrowded dormitory it hardly matters whether the beds are three feet apart or one foot – but it does matter to the proprietor, whose income depends upon his floor space. The sole real result of this law, therefore, was a general rise in the price of beds. Please notice that though the space between the beds is strictly regulated, nothing is said about the beds themselves – nothing, for instance, about their being fit to sleep in. The lodging housekeepers can, and do, charge a shilling for a bed less restful than a heap of straw, and there is no law to prevent them.

Another example of LCC regulations. From nearly all common lodging houses women are strictly excluded; there are a few houses specially for women, and a very small number – too small to affect the general question – to which both men and women are admitted. It follows that any homeless man who lives regularly in a lodging house is entirely cut off from female society – indeed, cases even happen of man and wife being separated owing to the impossibility of getting accommodation in the same house. Again, some of the cheaper lodging houses are habitually raided by slumming parties, who march into the kitchen uninvited and hold lengthy religious services. The lodgers dislike these slumming parties intensely, but they have no power to eject them. Can anyone imagine such things being tolerated in a hotel? And yet a common lodging house is only a hotel at which one pays 8*d*. a night instead of 10/6*d*. This kind of petty tyranny can, in fact, only be defended on the theory that a man poor enough to live in a common lodging house thereby forfeits some of his rights as a citizen.

One cannot help feeling that this theory lies behind the LCC rules for common lodging houses. All these rules are in the nature of interference legislation – that is, they interfere, but not for the benefit of the lodgers. Their emphasis is on hygiene and morals, and the question of comfort is left to the lodging-house proprietor, who, of course, either shirks it or solves it in the spirit of organized charity. It is worth pointing out the improvements that could actually be made in common lodging houses by legislation. As to cleanliness, no law will ever enforce that, and in any case it is a minor point. But the sleeping accommodation, which is the important thing, could easily be brought up to a decent standard. Common lodging houses are places in which one pays to sleep, and most of them fail in their essential purpose, for no one can sleep well in a rackety dormitory on a bed as hard as bricks. The LCC would be doing an immense service if they compelled lodging-house keepers to divide their dormitories into cubicles and, above all, to provide comfortable beds: for instance, beds as good as those in the London casual wards. And there seems no sense in the principle of licensing all houses for "men only" or "women only" as though men and women were sodium and water and must be kept apart for fear of an explosion; the houses should be licensed for both sexes alike, as they are in some provincial towns. And the lodgers should be protected by law against various swindles which the proprietors and managers are now able to practise on them. Given these conditions, common lodging houses would serve their purpose, which is an important one, far better than they do now. After all, tens of thousands of unemployed and partially employed men have literally no other place in which they can live. It is absurd that they should be compelled to choose, as they are at present, between an easy-going pigsty and a hygienic prison.

On Kipling's Death*

Rudyard Kipling was the only popular English writer of this century who was not at the same time a thoroughly bad writer. His popularity was, of course, essentially middle-class. In the average middle-class family before the War, especially in Anglo-Indian families, he had a prestige that is not even approached by any writer of today. He was a sort of household god with whom one grew up and whom one took for granted whether one liked him or whether one did not. For my own part I worshipped Kipling at thirteen, loathed him at seventeen, enjoyed him at twenty, despised him at twenty-five, and now again rather admire him. The one thing that was never possible, if one had read him at all, was to forget him. Certain of his stories, for instance 'The Strange Ride', 'Drums of the Fore and Aft' and 'The Mark of the Beast',* are about as good as it is possible for that kind of story to be. They are, moreover, exceedingly well told. For the vulgarity of his prose style is only a surface fault; in the less obvious qualities of construction and economy he is supreme. It is, after all (see the *Times Literary Supplement*), much easier to write inoffensive prose than to tell a good story. And his verse, though it is almost a byword for badness, has the same peculiarly memorable quality.

> I've lost Britain, I've lost Gaul,
> I've lost Rome, and, worst of all,
> I've lost Lalage!*

may be only a jingle, and 'The Road to Mandalay'* may be something worse than a jingle, but they do "stay by one". They remind one that it needs a streak of genius even to become a byword.

What is much more distasteful in Kipling than sentimental plots or vulgar tricks of style is the imperialism to which he chose to lend his genius. The most one can say is that when he made it the choice was more forgivable than it would be now. The imperialism of the eighties and nineties was sentimental, ignorant and dangerous, but it was not entirely despicable. The picture then called up by the word "empire" was a picture of overworked officials and frontier skirmishes, not of Lord Beaverbrook* and Australian butter. It was still possible to be an imperialist and a gentleman, and of Kipling's *personal* decency there can be no doubt. It is worth remembering that he was the most widely popular English writer of our time, and yet that no one, perhaps, so consistently refrained from making a vulgar show of his personality.

ON KIPLING'S DEATH

If he had never come under imperialist influences, and if he had developed, as he might well have done, into a writer of music-hall songs, he would have been a better and more lovable writer. In the role he actually chose, one was bound to think of him, after one had grown up, as a kind of enemy, a man of alien and perverted genius. But now that he is dead, I for one cannot help wishing that I could offer some kind of tribute – a salute of guns, if such a thing were available – to the storyteller who was so important to my childhood.

Shooting an Elephant*

In Moulmein,* in Lower Burma, I was hated by large numbers of people – the only time in my life that I have been important enough for this to happen to me. I was sub-divisional police officer of the town, and in an aimless, petty kind of way anti-European feeling was very bitter. No one had the guts to raise a riot, but if a European woman went through the bazaars alone somebody would probably spit betel juice* over her dress. As a police officer I was an obvious target and was baited whenever it seemed safe to do so. When a nimble Burman tripped me up on the football field and the referee (another Burman) looked the other way, the crowd yelled with hideous laughter. This happened more than once. In the end the sneering yellow faces of young men that met me everywhere, the insults hooted after me when I was at a safe distance, got badly on my nerves. The young Buddhist priests were the worst of all. There were several thousands of them in the town and none of them seemed to have anything to do except stand on street corners and jeer at Europeans.

All this was perplexing and upsetting. For at that time I had already made up my mind that imperialism was an evil thing and the sooner I chucked up my job and got out of it the better. Theoretically – and secretly, of course – I was all for the Burmese and all against their oppressors, the British. As for the job I was doing, I hated it more bitterly than I can perhaps make clear. In a job like that you see the dirty work of Empire at close quarters. The wretched prisoners huddling in the stinking cages of the lock-ups, the grey, cowed faces of the long-term convicts, the scarred buttocks of the men who had been flogged with bamboos – all these oppressed me with an intolerable sense of guilt. But I could get nothing into perspective. I was young and ill-educated and I had had to think out my problems in the utter silence that is imposed on every Englishman in the East. I did not even know that the British Empire is dying, still less did I know that it is a great deal better than the younger empires that are going to supplant it. All I knew was that I was stuck between my hatred of the empire I served and my rage against the evil-spirited little beasts who tried to make my job impossible. With one part of my mind I thought of the British Raj as an unbreakable tyranny, as something clamped down, *in sæcula sæculorum*,* upon the will of prostrate peoples; with another part I thought that the greatest joy in the world would be to drive a bayonet into a Buddhist priest's guts. Feelings like these are the normal by-products of imperialism; ask any Anglo-Indian official, if you can catch him off duty.

One day something happened which in a roundabout way was enlightening. It was a tiny incident in itself, but it gave me a better glimpse than I had had before of the real nature of imperialism – the real motives for which despotic governments act. Early one morning the sub-inspector at a police station the other end of the town rang me up on the phone and said that an elephant was ravaging the bazaar. Would I please come and do something about it? I did not know what I could do, but I wanted to see what was happening, and I got onto a pony and started out. I took my rifle, an old .44 Winchester and much too small to kill an elephant, but I thought the noise might be useful *in terrorem*.* Various Burmans stopped me on the way and told me about the elephant's doings. It was not, of course, a wild elephant, but a tame one which had gone "must". It had been chained up, as tame elephants always are when their attack of "must" is due, but on the previous night it had broken its chain and escaped. Its mahout,* the only person who could manage it when it was in that state, had set out in pursuit, but he had taken the wrong direction and was now twelve hours' journey away, and in the morning the elephant had suddenly reappeared in the town. The Burmese population had no weapons and were quite helpless against it. It had already destroyed somebody's bamboo hut, killed a cow and raided some fruit stalls and devoured the stock; also it had met the municipal rubbish van and, when the driver jumped out and took to his heels, had turned the van over and inflicted violence upon it.

The Burmese sub-inspector and some Indian constables were waiting for me in the quarter where the elephant had been seen. It was a very poor quarter, a labyrinth of squalid bamboo huts, thatched with palm leaf, winding all over a steep hillside. I remember that it was a cloudy, stuffy morning at the beginning of the rains. We began questioning the people as to where the elephant had gone, and as usual failed to get any definite information. That is invariably the case in the East; a story always sounds clear enough at a distance, but the nearer you get to the scene of events the vaguer it becomes. Some of the people said that the elephant had gone in one direction, some said that he had gone in another, some professed not even to have heard of any elephant. I had almost made up my mind that the whole story was a pack of lies, when we heard yells a little distance away. There was a loud, scandalized cry of "Go away, child! Go away this instant!" and an old woman with a switch in her hand came round the corner of a hut, violently shooing away a crowd of naked children. Some more women followed, clicking their tongues and exclaiming; evidently there was something there that the children ought not to have seen. I rounded the hut and saw a man's dead body sprawling in the mud. He was an Indian, a black Dravidian coolie, almost naked, and he could not have been dead many minutes. The people said that the elephant had come suddenly upon him round the corner of the hut, caught him with its trunk, put its foot on his back and ground him into the earth. This was the rainy season and the ground was soft, and his face had scored a trench a foot deep and a couple of yards long. He was lying on his belly with arms crucified and head sharply twisted to one side. His face was coated with mud, the eyes wide open, the teeth bared and grinning with an expression of unendurable agony. (Never tell me, by the way, that the dead look peaceful. Most of the corpses I have seen looked devilish.) The friction of the great beast's foot had stripped the skin from his back as neatly as one skins a rabbit. As soon as I saw the dead man I sent an orderly to a friend's house nearby to borrow an elephant rifle. I had already sent back the pony, not wanting it to go mad with fright and throw me if it smelt the elephant.

The orderly came back in a few minutes with a rifle and five cartridges, and meanwhile some Burmans had arrived and told us that the elephant was in the paddy fields below, only a few hundred yards away. As I started forward practically the whole population of the quarter flocked out of their houses and followed me. They had seen the rifle and were all shouting excitedly that I was going to shoot the elephant. They had not shown much interest in the elephant when he was merely ravaging their homes, but it was different now that he was going to be shot. It was a bit of fun to them, as it would be to an English crowd; besides, they wanted the meat. It made me vaguely uneasy. I had no intention of shooting the elephant – I had merely sent for the rifle to defend myself if necessary – and it is always unnerving to have a crowd following you. I marched down the hill, looking and feeling a fool, with the rifle over my shoulder and an ever-growing army of people jostling at my heels. At the bottom, when you got away from the huts, there was a metalled road and beyond that a miry waste of paddy fields a thousand yards across, not yet ploughed but soggy from the first rains and dotted with coarse grass. The elephant was standing eighty yards from the road, his left side towards us. He took not the slightest notice of the crowd's approach. He was tearing up bunches of grass, beating them against his knees to clean them and stuffing them into his mouth.

I had halted on the road. As soon as I saw the elephant I knew with perfect certainty that I ought not to shoot him. It is a serious matter to shoot a working elephant – it is comparable to destroying a huge and costly piece of machinery – and obviously one ought not to do it if it can possibly be avoided. And at that distance, peacefully eating, the elephant looked no more dangerous than a cow. I thought then and I think now that his attack of "must" was already passing off – in which case he would merely wander harmlessly about until the mahout came back and caught him. Moreover, I did not in the least want to shoot him. I decided that I would watch him for a little while to make sure that he did not turn savage again, and then go home.

But at that moment I glanced round at the crowd that had followed me. It was an immense crowd, 2,000 at the least and growing every minute. It blocked the road for a long distance on either side. I looked at the sea of yellow faces above the garish clothes – faces all happy and excited over this bit of fun, all certain that the elephant was going to be shot. They were watching me as they would watch a conjuror about to perform a trick. They did not like me, but with the magical rifle in my hands I was momentarily worth watching. And suddenly I realized that I should have to shoot the elephant after all. The people expected it of me and I had got to do it; I could feel their 2,000 wills pressing me forward, irresistibly. And it was at this moment, as I stood there with the rifle in my hands, that I first grasped the hollowness, the futility of the white man's dominion in the East. Here was I, the white man with his gun, standing in front of the unarmed native crowd, seemingly the leading actor of the piece – but in reality I was only an absurd puppet pushed to and fro by the will of those yellow faces behind. I perceived in this moment that when the white man turns tyrant it is his own freedom that he destroys. He becomes a sort of hollow, posing dummy, the conventionalized figure of a *sahib*.* For it is the condition of his rule that he shall spend his life in trying to impress the "natives" and so in every crisis he has got to do what the "natives" expect of him. He wears a mask, and his face grows to fit it. I had got to shoot the elephant. I had committed myself to doing it when I sent for the rifle. A *sahib* has got to act like a *sahib*; he has got to appear resolute, to know his own mind and do definite things. To come all that way, rifle in hand, with 2,000 people marching at my heels, and then to trail feebly away, having done nothing – no, that was impossible. The crowd would laugh at me. And my whole life, every white man's life in the East, was one long struggle not to be laughed at.

But I did not want to shoot the elephant. I watched him beating his bunch of grass against his knees, with that preoccupied grandmotherly air that elephants have. It seemed to me that it would be murder to shoot him. At that age I was not squeamish about killing animals, but I had never shot an elephant and never wanted to. (Somehow it always seems worse to kill a *large* animal.) Besides, there was the beast's owner to be considered. Alive, the elephant was worth at least £100; dead, he would only be worth the value of his tusks – five pounds, possibly. But I had got to act quickly. I turned to some experienced-looking Burmans who had been there when we arrived, and asked them how the elephant had been behaving. They all said the same thing: he took no notice of you if you left him alone, but he might charge if you went too close to him.

It was perfectly clear to me what I ought to do. I ought to walk up to within, say, twenty-five yards of the elephant and test his behaviour. If he charged I could shoot, if he took no notice of me it would be safe to leave him until the mahout came back. But also I knew that I was going to do no such thing. I was a poor shot with a rifle and the ground was soft mud into which one would sink at every step. If the elephant charged and I missed him, I should have about as much chance as a toad under a steamroller. But even then I was not thinking particularly of my own skin, only the watchful yellow faces behind. For at that moment, with the crowd watching me, I was not afraid in the ordinary sense, as I would have been if I had been alone. A white man mustn't be frightened in front of "natives" – and so, in general, he isn't frightened. The sole thought in my mind was that if anything went wrong those two thousand Burmans would see me pursued, caught, trampled on and reduced to a grinning corpse like that Indian up the hill. And if that happened it was quite probable that some of them would laugh. That would never do. There was only one alternative. I shoved the cartridges into the magazine and lay down on the road to get a better aim.

The crowd grew very still, and a deep, low, happy sigh, as of people who see the theatre curtain go up at last, breathed from innumerable throats. They were going to have their bit of fun after all. The rifle was a beautiful German thing with cross-hair sights. I did not then know that in shooting an elephant one should shoot to cut an imaginary bar running from earhole to earhole. I ought therefore, as the elephant was sideways on, to have aimed straight at his earhole; actually I aimed several inches in front of this, thinking the brain would be further forward.

When I pulled the trigger I did not hear the bang or feel the kick – one never does when a shot goes home – but I heard the devilish roar of glee that went up from the crowd. In that instant, in too short a time, one would have thought, even for the bullet to get there, a mysterious, terrible change had come over the elephant. He neither stirred nor fell, but every line of his body had altered. He looked suddenly stricken, shrunken, immensely old, as though the frightful impact of the bullet had paralysed him without knocking him down. At last, after what seemed a long time – it might have been five seconds, I dare say – he sagged flabbily to his knees. His mouth slobbered. An enormous senility seemed to have settled upon him. One could have imagined him thousands of years old. I fired again into the same spot. At the second shot he did not collapse but climbed with desperate slowness to his feet and stood weakly upright, with legs sagging and head drooping. I fired a third time. That was the shot that did for him. You could see the agony of it jolt his whole body and knock the last remnant of strength from his legs. But in falling he seemed for a moment to rise, for as his hind legs collapsed beneath him he seemed to tower upwards like a huge rock toppling, his trunk reaching skyward like a tree. He trumpeted, for the first and only time. And then down he came, his belly towards me, with a crash that seemed to shake the ground even where I lay.

I got up. The Burmans were already racing past me across the mud. It was obvious that the elephant would never rise again, but he was not dead. He was breathing very rhythmically with long rattling gasps, his great mound of a side painfully rising and falling. His mouth was wide open – I could see far down into caverns of pale-pink throat. I waited a long time for him to die, but his breathing did not weaken. Finally I fired my two remaining shots into the spot where I thought his heart must be. The thick blood welled out of him like red velvet, but still he did not die. His body did not even jerk when the shots hit him, the tortured breathing continued without a pause. He was dying, very slowly and in great agony, but in some world remote from me where not even a bullet could damage him further. I felt that I had got to put an end to that dreadful noise. It seemed dreadful to see the great beast lying there, powerless to move and yet powerless to die, and not even to be able to finish him. I sent back for my small rifle and poured shot after shot into his heart and down his throat. They seemed to make no impression. The tortured gasps continued as steadily as the ticking of a clock.

In the end I could not stand it any longer and went away. I heard later that it took him half an hour to die. Burmans were arriving with dahs* and baskets even before I left, and I was told they had stripped his body almost to the bones by the afternoon.

Afterwards, of course, there were endless discussions about the shooting of the elephant. The owner was furious, but he was only an Indian and could do nothing. Besides, legally I had done the right thing, for a mad elephant has to be killed, like a mad dog, if its owner fails to control it. Among the Europeans opinion was divided. The older men said I was right; the younger men said it was a damn shame to shoot an elephant for killing a coolie, because an elephant was worth more than any damn Coringhee coolie.* And afterwards I was very glad that the coolie had been killed; it put me legally in the right and it gave me a sufficient pretext for shooting the elephant. I often wondered whether any of the others grasped that I had done it solely to avoid looking a fool.

In Defence of the Novel*

It hardly needs pointing out that at this moment the prestige of the novel is extremely low, so low that the words "I never read novels", which even a dozen years ago were generally uttered with a hint of apology, are now *always* uttered in a tone of conscious pride. It is true that there are still a few contemporary or roughly contemporary novelists whom the intelligentsia consider it permissible to read – but the point is that the ordinary good-bad novel is habitually ignored while the ordinary good-bad book of verse or criticism is still taken seriously. This means that if you write novels you automatically command a less intelligent public than you would command if you had chosen some other form. There are two quite obvious reasons why this must presently make it impossible for good novels to be written. Even now the novel is visibly deteriorating, and it would deteriorate much faster if most novelists had any idea who reads their books. It is, of course, easy to argue (*vide* for instance Belloc's queerly rancorous essay)* that the novel is a contemptible form of art and that its fate does not matter. I doubt whether that opinion is even worth disputing. At any rate, I am taking it for granted that the novel is worth salvaging and that in order to salvage it you have got to persuade intelligent people to take it seriously. It is therefore worthwhile to analyse one of the main causes – in my opinion, *the* main cause – of the novel's lapse in prestige.

The trouble is that the novel is being shouted out of existence. Question any thinking person as to why he "never reads novels", and you will usually find that, at bottom, it is because of the disgusting tripe that is written by the blurb-reviewers. There is no need to multiply examples. Here is just one specimen, from last week's *Sunday Times*: "If you can read this book and not shriek with delight, your soul is dead." That or something like it is now being written about *every* novel published, as you can see by studying the quotes on the blurbs. For anyone who takes the *Sunday Times* seriously, life must be one long struggle to catch up. Novels are being shot at you at the rate of fifteen a day, and every one of them an unforgettable masterpiece which you imperil your soul by missing. It must make it so difficult to choose a book at the library, and you must feel so guilty when you fail to shriek with delight. Actually, however, no one who matters is deceived by this kind of thing, and the contempt into which novel reviewing has fallen is extended to novels themselves. When *all* novels are thrust upon you as works of genius, it is quite natural to assume that all of them are tripe. Within the literary intelligentsia this assumption is now taken for granted. To admit that you like novels is nowadays almost equivalent to admitting that you have a hankering after coconut ice or prefer Rupert Brooke to Gerard Manley Hopkins.*

All this is obvious. What I think is rather less obvious is the way in which the present situation has arisen. On the face of it, the book ramp is a quite simple and cynical swindle. Z writes a book which is published by Y and reviewed by X in the *Weekly W*. If the review is a bad one Y will remove his advertisement, so X has to hand out "unforgettable masterpiece" or get the sack. Essentially that *is* the position, and novel reviewing has sunk to its present depth largely because every reviewer has some publisher or publishers twisting his tail by proxy. But the thing is not so crude as it looks. The various parties to the swindle are not consciously acting together, and they have been forced into their present position partly against their will.

To begin with, one ought not to assume, as is so often done (see for instance Beachcomber's column,* *passim*), that the novelist enjoys and is even in some way responsible for the reviews he gets. Nobody *likes* being told that he has written a palpitating tale of passion which will last as long as the English language – though, of course, it is disappointing not to be told that, because all novelists are being told the same, and to be left out presumably means that your books won't sell. The hack review is in fact a sort of commercial necessity, like the blurb on the dust jacket, of which it is merely an extension. But even the wretched hack reviewer is not to be blamed for the drivel he writes. In his special circumstances he could write nothing else. For even if there were no question of bribery, direct or indirect, there can be no such thing as good novel criticism so long as it is assumed that *every novel is worth reviewing*.

A periodical gets its weekly wad of books and sends off a dozen of them to X, the hack reviewer, who has a wife and family and has got to earn his guinea, not to mention the half-crown per vol. which he gets by selling his review copies. There are two reasons why it is totally impossible for X to tell the truth about the books he gets. To begin with, the chances are that eleven out of the twelve books will fail to rouse in him the faintest spark of interest. They are not more than ordinarily bad, they are merely neutral, lifeless and pointless. If he were not paid to do so he would never read a line of any of them, and in nearly every case the only truthful review he could write would be: "This book inspires in me no thoughts whatever." But will anyone pay you to write that kind of thing? Obviously not. As a start, therefore, X is in the false position of having to manufacture, say, three hundred words about a book which means nothing to him whatever. Usually he does it by giving a brief résumé of the plot (incidentally betraying to the author the fact that he hasn't read the book) and handing out a few compliments which for all their fulsomeness are about as valuable as the smile of a prostitute.

But there is a far worse evil than this. X is expected not only to say what a book is about but to give his opinion as to whether it is good or bad. Since

X can hold a pen he is probably not a fool, at any rate not such a fool as to imagine that *The Constant Nymph** is the most terrific tragedy ever written. Very likely his own favourite novelist, if he cares for novels at all, is Stendhal, or Dickens, or Jane Austen, or D.H. Lawrence, or Dostoevsky – or at any rate, someone immeasurably better than the ordinary run of contemporary novelists. He has got to start, therefore, by immensely lowering his standards. As I have pointed out elsewhere, to apply a decent standard to the ordinary run of novels is like weighing a flea on a spring balance intended for elephants. On such a balance as that a flea would simply fail to register; you would have to start by constructing another balance which revealed the fact that there are big fleas and little fleas. And this approximately is what X does. It is no use monotonously saying, of book after book, "This book is tripe," because, once again, no one will pay you for writing that kind of thing. X has got to discover something which is *not* tripe, and pretty frequently, or get the sack. This means sinking his standards to a depth at which, say, Ethel M. Dell's *Way of an Eagle** is a fairly good book. But on a scale of values which makes *The Way of an Eagle* a good book, *The Constant Nymph* is a superb book, and *The Man of Property** is – what? A palpitating tale of passion, a terrific, soul-shattering masterpiece, an unforgettable epic which will last as long as the English language, and so on and so forth. (As for any *really* good book, it would burst the thermometer.) Having started with the assumption that all novels are good, the reviewer is driven ever upwards on a topless ladder of adjectives. And *sic itur ad Gould.** You can see reviewer after reviewer going the same road. Within two years of starting out with at any rate moderately honest intentions, he is proclaiming with maniacal screams that Miss Barbara Bedworthy's *Crimson Night* is the most terrific, trenchant, poignant, unforgettable, of the earth earthy* and so forth masterpiece which has ever, etc. etc. etc. There is no way out of it when you have once committed the initial sin of pretending that a bad book is a good one. But you cannot review novels for a living without committing that sin. And meanwhile every intelligent reader turns away, disgusted, and to despise novels becomes a kind of snobbish duty. Hence the queer fact that it is possible for a novel of real merit to escape notice, merely because it has been praised in the same terms as tripe.

Various people have suggested that it would be all to the good if no novels were reviewed at all. So it would, but the suggestion is useless, because nothing of the kind is going to happen. No paper which depends on publishers' advertisements can afford to throw them away, and though the more intelligent publishers probably realize that they would be no worse off if the blurb-review were abolished, they cannot put an end to it for the same reason as the nations cannot disarm – because nobody wants to be the first to start. For a long time yet the blurb-reviews are going to continue, and they are going to grow worse and worse; the only remedy is to contrive in some way that they shall be disregarded. But this can only happen if somewhere or other there is decent novel reviewing which will act as a standard of comparison. That is to say, there is need of just *one* periodical (one would be enough for a start) which makes a speciality of novel reviewing but refuses to take any notice of tripe, and in which the reviewers *are* reviewers and not ventriloquists' dummies clapping their jaws when the publisher pulls the string.

It may be answered that there are such periodicals already. There are quite a number of highbrow magazines, for instance, in which the novel reviewing, what there is of it, is intelligent and not suborned. Yes, but the point is that periodicals of that kind do not make a speciality of novel reviewing, and certainly make no attempt to keep abreast of the current output of fiction. They belong to the highbrow world, the world in which it is already assumed that novels, as such, are despicable. But the novel is a popular form of art, and it is no use to approach it with the *Criterion–Scrutiny* assumption* that literature is a game of back-scratching (claws in or claws out according to circumstances) between tiny cliques of highbrows. The novelist is primarily a storyteller, and a man may be a very good storyteller (*vide* for instance Trollope, Charles Reade, Mr Somerset Maugham*) without being in the narrow sense an "intellectual". Five thousand novels are published every year, and Ralph Straus* implores you to read all of them, or would if he had all of them to review. The *Criterion* probably deigns to notice a dozen. But between the dozen and the 5,000 there may be 100 or 200 or even 500 which at different levels have genuine merit, and it is on these that any critic who cares for the novel ought to concentrate.

But the first necessity is some method of *grading*. Great numbers of novels never ought to be mentioned at all (imagine for instance the awful effects on criticism if every serial in *Peg's Paper** had to be solemnly reviewed!), but even the ones that are worth mentioning belong to quite different categories. *Raffles* is a good book, and so is *The Island of Dr Moreau*, and so is *La Chartreuse de Parme*,* and so is *Macbeth* – but they are "good" at very different levels. Similarly, *If Winter Comes* and *The Well-Beloved* and *An Unsocial Socialist* and *Sir Launcelot Greaves** are all bad books, but at different levels of "badness". This is the fact that the hack reviewer has made it his special business to obscure. It ought to be possible to devise a system, perhaps quite a rigid one, of grading novels into classes A, B, C and so forth, so that whether a reviewer praised or damned a book, you would at least know how seriously he meant it to be taken. As for the reviewers, they would have to be people who really cared for the art of the novel (and that means, probably, neither highbrows nor lowbrows nor midbrows, but elastic-brows), people interested in technique and still more interested in discovering what a book is *about*. There are plenty of such people in existence; some of the very worst of the hack reviewers, though now past praying for, started like that, as you can see by glancing at their earlier work. Incidentally, it would be a good thing if more novel reviewing were done by amateurs. A man who is not a practised writer but has just read a book which has deeply impressed him is more likely to tell you what it is *about* than a competent but bored professional. That is why American reviews, for all their stupidity, are better than English ones; they are more amateurish, that is to say, more serious.

I believe that in some such way as I have indicated the prestige of the novel could be restored. The essential need is a paper that would keep abreast of current fiction and yet refuse to sink its standards. It would have to be an obscure paper, for the publishers would not advertise in it; on the other hand, once they had discovered that somewhere there was praise that was real praise, they would be ready enough to quote it on their blurbs. Even if it were a very obscure paper it would probably cause the general level of novel reviewing to rise, for the drivel in the Sunday papers only continues because there is nothing with which to contrast it. But even if the blurb reviewers continued exactly as before, it would not matter so long as there also existed decent reviewing to remind a few people that serious brains can still occupy themselves with the novel. For just as the Lord promised that he would not destroy Sodom if ten righteous men could be found there,* so the novel will not be utterly despised while it is known that somewhere or other there is even a handful of novel reviewers with no straws in their hair.*

At present, if you care about novels and still more if you write them, the outlook is depressing in the extreme. The word "novel" calls up the words "blurb", "genius" and "Ralph Straus" as automatically as "chicken" calls up "bread sauce". Intelligent people avoid novels almost instinctively; as a result, established novelists go to pieces and beginners who "have something to say" turn in preference to almost any other form. The degradation that must follow is obvious. Look for instance at the fourpenny novelettes that you see piled up on any cheap stationer's counter. These things are the decadent offspring of the novel, bearing the same relation to *Manon Lescaut** and *David Copperfield** as the lapdog bears to the wolf. It is quite likely that before long the average novel will be not much different from the fourpenny novelette, though doubtless it will still appear in a seven and sixpenny binding and amid a flourish of publishers' trumpets. Various people have prophesied that the novel is doomed to disappear in the near future. I do not believe that it will disappear, for reasons which would take too long to set forth but which are fairly obvious. It is much likelier, if the best literary brains cannot be induced to return to it, to survive in some perfunctory, despised and hopelessly degenerate form, like modern tombstones, or the Punch and Judy show.

Bookshop Memories*

When I worked in a second-hand bookshop – so easily pictured, if you don't work in one, as a kind of paradise where charming old gentlemen browse eternally among calf-bound folios – the thing that chiefly struck me was the rarity of really bookish people. Our shop had an exceptionally interesting stock, yet I doubt whether 10 per cent of our customers knew a good book from a bad one. First-edition snobs were much commoner than lovers of literature, but oriental students haggling over cheap textbooks were commoner still, and vague-minded women looking for birthday presents for their nephews were commonest of all.

Many of the people who came to us were of the kind who would be a nuisance anywhere but have special opportunities in a bookshop. For example, the dear old lady who "wants a book for an invalid" (a very common demand, that), and the other dear old lady who read such a nice book in 1897 and wonders whether you can find her a copy. Unfortunately she doesn't remember the title or the author's name or what the book was about, but she does remember that it had a red cover. But apart from these there are two well-known types of pest by whom every second-hand bookshop is haunted. One is the decayed person smelling of old breadcrusts who comes every day, sometimes several times a day, and tries to sell you worthless books. The other is the person who orders large quantities of books for which he has not the smallest intention of paying. In our shop we sold nothing on credit, but we would put books aside, or order them if necessary, for people who arranged to fetch them away later. Scarcely half the people who ordered books from us ever came back. It used to puzzle me at first. What made them do it? They would come in and demand some rare and expensive book, would make us promise over and over again to keep it for them, and then would vanish never to return. But many of them, of course, were unmistakable paranoiacs. They used to talk in a grandiose manner about themselves and tell the most ingenious stories to explain how they had happened to come out of doors without any money – stories which, in many cases, I am sure they themselves believed. In a town like London there are always plenty of not quite certifiable lunatics walking the streets, and they tend to gravitate towards bookshops, because a bookshop is one of the few places where you can hang about for a long time without spending any money. In the end one gets to know these people almost at a glance. For all their big talk there is something moth-eaten and aimless about them. Very often, when we were dealing with an obvious paranoiac, we would put aside the books he asked for and then put them back on the shelves the moment he had gone. None of them, I noticed, ever attempted to take books away without paying for them; merely to order them was enough – it gave them, I suppose, the illusion that they were spending real money.

Like most second-hand bookshops we had various sidelines. We sold second-hand typewriters, for instance, and also stamps – used stamps, I mean. Stamp collectors are a strange, silent, fish-like breed, of all ages, but only of the male sex; women, apparently, fail to see the peculiar charm of gumming bits of coloured paper into albums. We also sold sixpenny horoscopes compiled by somebody who claimed to have foretold the Japanese earthquake.* They were in sealed envelopes and I never opened one of them myself, but the people who bought them often came back and told us how "true" their horoscopes had been. (Doubtless any horoscope seems "true" if it tells you that you are highly attractive to the opposite sex and your worst fault is generosity.) We did a good deal of business in children's books, chiefly "remainders".* Modern books for children are rather horrible things, especially when you see them in the mass. Personally I would sooner give a child a copy of Petronius Arbiter* than *Peter Pan*, but even Barrie* seems manly and wholesome compared with some of his later imitators. At Christmas time we spent a feverish ten days struggling with Christmas cards and calendars, which are tiresome things to sell but good business while the season lasts. It used to interest me to see the brutal cynicism with which Christian sentiment is exploited. The touts from the Christmas-card firms used to come round with their catalogues as early as June. A phrase from one of their invoices sticks in my memory. It was: 2 *doz. Infant Jesus with rabbits.*

But our principal sideline was a lending library – the usual "twopenny no-deposit" library of five or six hundred volumes, all fiction. How the book thieves must love those libraries! It is the easiest crime in the world to borrow a book at one shop for twopence, remove the label and sell it at another shop for a shilling. Nevertheless booksellers generally find that it pays them better to have a certain number of books stolen (we used to lose about a dozen a month) than to frighten customers away by demanding a deposit.

Our shop stood exactly on the frontier between Hampstead and Camden Town, and we were frequented by all types from baronets to bus conductors. Probably our library subscribers were a fair cross section of London's reading public. It is therefore worth noting that of all the authors in our library the one who "went out" the best was – Priestley? Hemingway? Walpole? Wodehouse? No, Ethel M. Dell, with Warwick Deeping a good second and Jeffery Farnol, I should say, third.* Dell's novels, of course, are read solely by women, but by women of all kinds and ages and not, as one might expect, merely by wistful spinsters and the fat wives of tobacconists. It is not true that men don't read novels, but it is true that there are whole branches of fiction that they avoid.

Roughly speaking, what one might call the *average* novel – the ordinary, good-bad, Galsworthy-and-water stuff which is the norm of the English novel – seems to exist only for women. Men read either the novels it is possible to respect, or detective stories. But their consumption of detective stories is terrific. One of our subscribers to my knowledge read four or five detective stories every week for over a year, besides others which he got from another library. What chiefly surprised me was that he never read the same book twice. Apparently the whole of that frightful torrent of trash (the pages read every year would, I calculated, cover nearly three quarters of an acre) was stored for ever in his memory. He took no notice of titles or author's names, but he could tell by merely glancing into a book whether he had "had it already".

In a lending library you see people's real tastes, not their pretended ones, and one thing that strikes you is how completely the "classical" English novelists have dropped out of favour. It is simply useless to put Dickens, Thackeray, Jane Austen, Trollope, etc. into the ordinary lending library; nobody takes them out. At the mere sight of a nineteenth-century novel people say "Oh, but that's *old*!" and shy away immediately. Yet it is always fairly easy to *sell* Dickens, just as it is always easy to sell Shakespeare. Dickens is one of those authors whom people are "always meaning to" read, and, like the Bible, he is widely known at second hand. People know by hearsay that Bill Sikes was a burglar and that Mr Micawber had a bald head, just as they know by hearsay that Moses was found in a basket of bulrushes and saw the "back parts" of the Lord.* Another thing that is very noticeable is the growing unpopularity of American books. And another – the publishers get into a stew about this every two or three years – is the unpopularity of short stories. The kind of person who asks the librarian to choose a book for him nearly always starts by saying "I don't want short stories", or "I do not desire little stories", as a German customer of ours used to put it. If you ask them why, they sometimes explain that it is too much fag to get used to a new set of characters with every story; they like to "get into" a novel which demands no further thought after the first chapter. I believe, though, that the writers are more to blame here than the readers. Most modern short stories, English and American, are utterly lifeless and worthless, far more so than most novels. The short stories which *are* stories are popular enough: *vide* D.H. Lawrence, whose short stories are as popular as his novels.

Would I like to be a bookseller *de métier*?* On the whole – in spite of my employer's kindness to me, and some happy days I spent in the shop – no.

Given a good pitch and the right amount of capital, any educated person ought to be able to make a small secure living out of a bookshop. Unless one goes in for "rare" books it is not a difficult trade to learn, and you start at a great advantage if you know anything about the insides of books. (Most booksellers don't. You can get their measure by having a look at the trade papers where they advertise their wants. If you don't see an ad for Boswell's *Decline and Fall* you are pretty sure to see one for *The Mill on the Floss* by T.S. Eliot.*) Also, it is a humane trade which is not capable of being vulgarized beyond a certain point. The combines can never squeeze the small independent bookseller out of existence as they have squeezed the grocer and the milkman. But the hours of work are very long – I was only a part-time employee, but my employer put in a seventy-hour week, apart from constant expeditions out of hours to buy books – and it is an unhealthy life. As a rule, a bookshop is horribly cold in winter, because if it is too warm the windows get misted over, and a bookseller lives on his windows. And books give off more and nastier dust than any other class of objects yet invented, and the top of a book is the place where every bluebottle prefers to die.

But the real reason why I should not like to be in the book trade for life is that while I was in it I lost my love of books. A bookseller has to tell lies about books, and that gives him a distaste for them; still worse is the fact that he is constantly dusting them and hauling them to and fro. There was a time when I really did love books – loved the sight and smell and feel of them, I mean, at least if they were fifty or more years old. Nothing pleased me quite so much as to buy a job lot of them for a shilling at a country auction. There is a peculiar flavour about the battered unexpected books you pick up in that kind of collection: minor eighteenth-century poets, out-of-date gazetteers, odd volumes of forgotten novels, bound numbers of ladies' magazines of the sixties. For casual reading – in your bath, for instance, or late at night when you are too tired to go to bed, or in the odd quarter of an hour before lunch – there is nothing to touch a back number of the *Girl's Own Paper*.* But as soon as I went to work in the bookshop I stopped buying books. Seen in the mass, five or ten thousand at a time, books were boring and even slightly sickening. Nowadays I do buy one occasionally, but only if it is a book that I want to read and can't borrow, and I never buy junk. The sweet smell of decaying paper appeals to me no longer. It is too closely associated in my mind with paranoiac customers and dead bluebottles.

Spilling the Spanish Beans*

The Spanish war has probably produced a richer crop of lies than any event since the Great War of 1914–18, but I honestly doubt, in spite of all those hecatombs of nuns who have been raped and crucified before the eyes of *Daily Mail* reporters, whether it is the pro-fascist newspapers that have done the most harm. It is the left-wing papers, the *News Chronicle** and the *Daily Worker*,* with their far subtler methods of distortion, that have prevented the British public from grasping the real nature of the struggle.

The fact which these papers have so carefully obscured is that the Spanish government (including the semi-autonomous Catalan government) is far more afraid of the revolution than of the fascists. It is now almost certain that the war will end with some kind of compromise, and there is even reason to doubt whether the government, which let Bilbao fall without raising a finger, wishes to be too victorious, but there is no doubt whatever about the thoroughness with which it is crushing its own revolutionaries. For some time past a reign of terror – forcible suppression of political parties, a stifling censorship of the press, ceaseless espionage and mass imprisonment without trial – has been in progress. When I left Barcelona in late June the jails were bulging; indeed, the regular jails had long since overflowed and the prisoners were being huddled into empty shops and any other temporary dump that could be found for them. But the point to notice is that the people who are in prison now are not fascists but revolutionaries; they are there not because their opinions are too much to the right, but because they are too much to the left. And the people responsible for putting them there are those dreadful revolutionaries at whose very name Garvin* quakes in his galoshes – the communists.

Meanwhile the war against Franco continues, but, except for the poor devils in the front-line trenches, nobody in Government Spain thinks of it as the real war. The real struggle is between revolution and counter-revolution: between the workers who are vainly trying to hold on to a little of what they won in 1936 and the liberal–communist bloc who are so successfully taking it away from them.* It is unfortunate that so few people in England have yet caught up with the fact that communism is now a counter-revolutionary force – that communists everywhere are in alliance with bourgeois reformism and using the whole of their powerful machinery to crush or discredit any party that shows signs of revolutionary tendencies. Hence the grotesque spectacle of communists assailed as wicked "Reds" by right-wing intellectuals who are in essential agreement with them. Mr Wyndham Lewis,* for instance, ought to love the communists, at least temporarily. In Spain the communist–liberal alliance has been almost completely victorious. Of all that the Spanish workers won for themselves in 1936 nothing solid remains, except for a few collective farms and a certain amount of land seized by the peasants last year – and presumably even the peasants will be sacrificed later, when there is no longer any need to placate them. To see how the present situation arose, one has got to look back to the origins of the civil war.

Franco's bid for power differed from those of Hitler and Mussolini in that it was a military insurrection, comparable to a foreign invasion, and therefore had not much mass backing, though Franco has since been trying to acquire one. Its chief supporters, apart from certain sections of Big Business, were the landowning aristocracy and the huge, parasitic Church. Obviously a rising of this kind will array against it various forces which are not in agreement on any other point. The peasant and the worker hate feudalism and clericalism – but so does the "liberal" bourgeois, who is not in the least opposed to a more modern version of fascism, at least so long as it isn't called fascism. The "liberal" bourgeois is genuinely liberal up to the point where his own interests stop. He stands for the degree of progress implied in the phrase *"la carrière ouverte aux talents"*.* For clearly he has no chance to develop in a feudal society where the worker and the peasant are too poor to buy goods, where industry is burdened with huge taxes to pay for bishops' vestments, and where every lucrative job is given as a matter of course to the friend of the catamite of the duke's illegitimate son. Hence, in the face of such a blatant reactionary as Franco, you get for a while a situation in which the worker and the bourgeois, in reality deadly enemies, are fighting side by side. This uneasy alliance is known as the Popular Front (or, in the communist press, to give it a spuriously democratic appeal, People's Front). It is a combination with about as much vitality, and about as much right to exist, as a pig with two heads or some other Barnum and Bailey* monstrosity.

In any serious emergency the contradiction implied in the Popular Front is bound to make itself felt. For even when the worker and the bourgeois are both fighting against fascism, they are not fighting for the same things; the bourgeois is fighting for bourgeois democracy, i.e. capitalism, the worker, in so far as he understands the issue, for socialism. And in the early days of the revolution the Spanish workers understood the issue very well. In the areas where fascism was defeated they did not content themselves with driving the rebellious troops out of the towns; they also took the opportunity of seizing land and factories and setting up the rough beginnings of a workers' government by means of local committees, workers' militias, police forces, and so forth. They made the mistake, however (possibly because most of the active revolutionaries were anarchists with a mistrust of all parliaments), of leaving the Republican government in nominal control. And, in spite of various changes in personnel, every subsequent government had been of approximately the same bourgeois-reformist character. At the beginning this seemed not to matter, because the government, especially in Catalonia, was almost powerless and the bourgeoisie had to lie low or even (this was still happening when I reached Spain in December) to disguise themselves as workers. Later, as power slipped from the hands of the anarchists into the hands of the communists and right-wing socialists, the government was able to reassert itself, the bourgeoisie came out of hiding and the old division of society into rich and poor reappeared, not much modified. Henceforward every move, except a few dictated by military emergency, was directed towards undoing the work of the first few months of revolution. Out of the many illustrations I could choose, I will cite only one, the breaking up of the old workers' militias, which were organized on a genuinely democratic system, with officers and men receiving the same pay and mingling on terms of complete equality, and the substitution of the Popular Army (once again, in communist jargon, "People's Army"), modelled as far as possible on an ordinary bourgeois army, with a privileged officer caste, immense differences of pay, etc. etc. Needless to say, this is given out as a military necessity, and almost certainly it does make for military efficiency, at least for a short period. But the undoubted purpose of the change was to strike a blow at equalitarianism. In every department the same policy has been followed, with the result that only a year after the outbreak of war and revolution you get what is in effect an ordinary bourgeois state, with, in addition, a reign of terror to preserve the status quo.

This process would probably have gone less far if the struggle could have taken place without foreign interference. But the military weakness of the government made this impossible. In the face of Franco's foreign mercenaries they were obliged to turn to Russia for help, and though the quantity of arms supplied by Russia has been greatly exaggerated (in my first three months in Spain I saw only one Russian weapon, a solitary machine gun), the mere fact of their arrival brought the communists into power. To begin with, the Russian aeroplanes and guns, and the good military qualities of the International Brigades (not necessarily communist but under communist control), immensely raised the communist prestige. But, more important, since Russia and Mexico were the only countries openly supplying arms, the Russians were able not only to get money for their weapons but to extort terms as well. Put in their crudest form, the terms were: "Crush the revolution or you get no more arms." The reason usually given for the Russian attitude is that if Russia appeared to be abetting the revolution, the Franco-Soviet pact (and the hoped-for alliance with Great Britain) would be imperilled; it may be also that the spectacle of a genuine revolution in Spain would rouse unwanted echoes in Russia. The communists, of course, deny that any direct pressure has been exerted by the Russian government. But this, even if true, is hardly relevant, for the communist parties of all countries can be taken as carrying out Russian policy – and it is certain that the Spanish Communist Party, plus the right-wing socialists whom they control, plus the communist press of the whole world, have used all their immense and ever-increasing influence upon the side of counter-revolution.

In the first half of this article I suggested that the real struggle in Spain, on the government side, has been between revolution and counter-revolution – that the government, though anxious enough to avoid being beaten by Franco, has been even more anxious to undo the revolutionary changes with which the outbreak of war was accompanied.

Any communist would reject this suggestion as mistaken or wilfully dishonest. He would tell you that it is nonsense to talk of the Spanish government crushing the revolution, because the revolution never happened, and that our job at present is to defeat fascism and defend democracy. And in this connection it is most important to see just how the communist anti-revolutionary propaganda works. It is a mistake to think that this has no relevance in England, where the Communist Party is small and comparatively weak. We shall see its relevance quickly enough if England enters into an alliance with the USSR, or perhaps even earlier, for the influence of the Communist Party is bound to increase – visibly is increasing – as more and more of the capitalist class realize that latter-day communism is playing their game.

Broadly speaking, communist propaganda depends upon terrifying people with the (quite real) horrors of fascism. It also involves pretending – not in so many words, but by implication – that fascism has nothing to do with capitalism. Fascism is just a kind of meaningless wickedness, an aberration, "mass sadism", the sort of thing that would happen if you suddenly let loose an asylumful of homicidal maniacs. Present fascism in this form, and you can mobilize public opinion against it, at any rate for a while, without provoking any revolutionary movement. You can oppose fascism by bourgeois "democracy", meaning capitalism. But meanwhile you have got to get rid of the troublesome person who points out that fascism and bourgeois "democracy" are Tweedledum and Tweedledee.* You do it at the beginning by calling him an impracticable visionary. You tell him that he is confusing the issue, that he is splitting the anti-fascist forces, that this is not the moment for revolutionary phrase-mongering, that for the moment we have got to fight against fascism without enquiring too closely what we are fighting *for*. Later, if he still refuses to shut up, you change your tune and call him a traitor. More exactly, you call him a Trotskyist.*

And what is a Trotskyist? This terrible word – in Spain at this moment you can be thrown into jail and kept there indefinitely, without trial, on the mere rumour that you are a Trotskyist – is only beginning to be bandied to and fro in England. We shall be hearing more of it later. The word "Trotskyist" (or "Trotsky-fascist") is generally used to mean a disguised fascist who poses as an ultra-revolutionary in order to split the left-wing forces. But it derives its peculiar power from the fact that it means three separate things. It can mean one who, like Trotsky, wished for world revolution; or a member of the actual organization of which Trotsky is head (the only legitimate use of the word); or the disguised fascist already mentioned. The three meanings can be telescoped one into the other at will. Meaning number one may or may not carry with it meaning number two, and meaning number two almost invariably carries with it meaning number three. Thus: "XY has been heard to speak favourably of world revolution; therefore he is a Trotskyist; therefore he is a fascist." In Spain, to some extent even in England, *anyone* professing revolutionary socialism (i.e. professing the things the Communist Party professed until a few years ago) is under suspicion of being a Trotskyist in the pay of Franco or Hitler.

The accusation is a very subtle one, because in any given case, unless one happened to know the contrary, it might be true. A fascist spy probably *would* disguise himself as a revolutionary. In Spain, everyone whose opinions are to the left of those of the Communist Party is sooner or later discovered to be a Trotskyist, or at least, a traitor. At the beginning of the war the POUM, an opposition communist party roughly corresponding to the English ILP,* was an accepted party and supplied a minister to the Catalan government; later it was expelled from the government; then it was denounced as Trotskyist; then it was suppressed, every member that the police could lay their hands on being flung into jail.

Until a few months ago the anarcho-syndicalists were described as "working loyally" beside the communists. Then the anarcho-syndicalists were levered out of the government; then it appeared that they were not working so loyally; now they are in the process of becoming traitors. After that will come the turn of the left-wing socialists. Caballero,* the left-wing socialist ex-premier, until May 1937 the idol of the communist press, is already in outer darkness, a Trotskyist and "enemy of the people". And so the game continues. The logical end is a regime in which every opposition party and newspaper is suppressed and every dissentient of any importance is in jail. Of course, such a regime will be fascism. It will not be the same as the fascism Franco would impose, it will even be better than Franco's fascism to the extent of being worth fighting for, but it will be fascism. Only, being operated by communists and liberals, it will be called something different.

Meanwhile, can the war be won? The communist influence has been against revolutionary chaos and has therefore, apart from the Russian aid, tended to produce greater military efficiency. If the anarchists saved the government from August to October 1936, the communists have saved it from October onwards. But in organizing the defence they have succeeded in killing enthusiasm (inside Spain, not outside). They made a militarized conscript army possible, but they also made it necessary. It is significant that as early as January of this year voluntary recruiting had practically ceased. A revolutionary army can sometimes win by enthusiasm, but a conscript army has got to win with weapons, and it is unlikely that the government will ever have a large preponderance of arms unless France intervenes or unless Germany and Italy decide to make off with the Spanish colonies and leave Franco in the lurch. On the whole, a deadlock seems the likeliest thing.

And does the government seriously intend to win? It does not intend to lose, that is certain. On the other hand, an outright victory, with Franco in flight and the Germans and Italians driven into the sea, would raise difficult problems, some of them too obvious to need mentioning. There is no real evidence and one can only judge by the event, but I suspect that what the government is playing for is a compromise that would leave the war situation essentially in being. All prophecies are wrong, therefore this one will be wrong, but I will take a chance and say that though the war may end quite soon or may drag on for years, it will end with Spain divided up, either by actual frontiers or into economic zones. Of course, such a compromise might be claimed as a victory by either side, or by both.

All that I have said in this article would seem entirely commonplace in Spain, or even in France. Yet in England, in spite of the intense interest the Spanish war has aroused, there are very few people who have even heard of the enormous struggle that is going on behind the government lines. Of course, this is no accident. There has been a quite deliberate conspiracy (I could give detailed instances) to prevent the Spanish situation from being understood. People who ought to know better have lent themselves to the deception on the ground that if you tell the truth about Spain it will be used as fascist propaganda.

It is easy to see where such cowardice leads. If the British public had been given a truthful account of the Spanish war they would have had an opportunity of learning what fascism is and how it can be combated. As it is, the *News Chronicle* version of fascism as a kind of homicidal mania peculiar to Colonel Blimps* bombinating in the economic void has been established more firmly than ever. And thus we are one step nearer to the great war "against fascism" (cf. 1914, "against militarism") which will allow fascism, British variety, to be slipped over our necks during the first week.

Why I Joined the Independent Labour Party*

Perhaps it will be frankest to approach it first of all from the personal angle.

I am a writer. The impulse of every writer is to "keep out of politics". What he wants is to be left alone so that he can go on writing books in peace. But unfortunately it is becoming obvious that this ideal is no more practicable than that of the petty shopkeeper who hopes to preserve his independence in the teeth of the chain stores.

To begin with, the era of free speech is closing down. The freedom of the press in Britain was always something of a fake, because in the last resort, money controls opinion; still, so long as the legal right to say what you like exists, there are always loopholes for an unorthodox writer. For some years past I have managed to make the capitalist class pay me several pounds a week for writing books against capitalism. But I do not delude myself that this state of affairs is going to last for ever. We have seen what has happened to the freedom of the press in Italy and Germany, and it will happen here sooner or later. The time is coming – not next year, perhaps not for ten or twenty years, but it is coming – when every writer will have the choice of being silenced altogether or of producing the dope that a privileged minority demands.

I have got to struggle against that, just as I have got to struggle against castor oil, rubber truncheons and concentration camps. And the only regime which, in the long run, will dare to permit freedom of speech is a socialist regime. If fascism triumphs I am finished as a writer – that is to say, finished in my only effective capacity. That of itself would be a sufficient reason for joining a socialist party.

I have put the personal aspect first, but obviously it is not the only one.

It is not possible for any thinking person to live in such a society as our own without wanting to change it. For perhaps ten years past I have had some grasp of the real nature of capitalist society. I have seen British imperialism at work in Burma, and I have seen something of the effects of poverty and unemployment in Britain. In so far as I have struggled against the system, it has been mainly by writing books which I hoped would influence the reading public. I shall continue to do that, of course, but at a moment like the present writing books is not enough. The tempo of events is quickening; the dangers which once seemed a generation distant are staring us in the face. One has got to be actively a socialist, not merely sympathetic to socialism, or one plays into the hands of our always-active enemies.

Why the ILP more than another?

Because the ILP is the only British party – at any rate the only one large enough to be worth considering – which aims at anything I should regard as socialism.

I do not mean that I have lost all faith in the Labour Party. My most earnest hope is that the Labour Party will win a clear majority in the next general election. But we know what the history of the Labour Party has been, and we know the terrible temptation of the present moment – the temptation to fling every principle overboard in order to prepare for an imperialist war. It is vitally necessary that there should be in existence some body of people who can be depended on, even in the face of persecution, not to compromise their socialist principles.

I believe that the ILP is the only party which, as a party, is likely to take the right line either against imperialist war or against fascism when this appears in its British form. And meanwhile the ILP is not backed by any moneyed interest, and is systematically libelled from several quarters. Obviously it needs all the help it can get, including any help I can give it myself.

Finally, I was with the ILP contingent in Spain. I never pretended, then or since, to agree in every detail with the policy the POUM* put forward and the ILP supported, but the general course of events has borne it out. The things I saw in Spain brought home to me the fatal danger of mere negative "anti-fascism". Once I had grasped the essentials of the situation in Spain I realized that the ILP was the only British party I felt like joining – and also the only party I could join with at least the certainty that I would never be led up the garden path in the name of capitalist democracy.

Marrakech*

As the corpse went past the flies left the restaurant table in a cloud and rushed after it, but they came back a few minutes later.

The little crowd of mourners – all men and boys, no women – threaded their way across the marketplace between the piles of pomegranates and the taxis and the camels, wailing a short chant over and over again. What really appeals to the flies is that the corpses here are never put into coffins, they are merely wrapped in a piece of rag and carried on a rough wooden bier on the shoulders of four friends. When the friends get to the burying ground they hack an oblong hole a foot or two deep, dump the body in it and fling over it a little of the dried-up, lumpy earth, which is like broken brick. No gravestone, no name, no identifying mark of any kind. The burying ground is merely a huge waste of hummocky earth, like a derelict building lot. After a month or two no one can even be certain where his own relatives are buried.

When you walk through a town like this – 200,000 inhabitants, of whom at least 20,000 own literally nothing except the rags they stand up in – when you see how the people live, and still more how easily they die, it is always difficult to believe that you are walking among human beings. All colonial empires are in reality founded upon that fact. The people have brown faces – besides, there are so many of them! Are they really the same flesh as yourself? Do they even have names? Or are they merely a kind of undifferentiated brown stuff, about as individual as bees or coral insects? They rise out of the earth, they sweat and starve for a few years, and then they sink back into the nameless mounds of the graveyard and nobody notices that they are gone. And even the graves themselves soon fade back into the soil. Sometimes, out for a walk, as you break your way through the prickly pear, you notice that it is rather bumpy underfoot, and only a certain regularity in the bumps tells you that you are walking over skeletons.

I was feeding one of the gazelles in the public gardens.

Gazelles are almost the only animals that look good to eat when they are still alive; in fact, one can hardly look at their hindquarters without thinking of mint sauce. The gazelle I was feeding seemed to know that this thought was in my mind, for though it took the piece of bread I was holding out it obviously did not like me. It nibbled rapidly at the bread, then lowered its head and tried to butt me, then took another nibble and then butted again.

Probably its idea was that if it could drive me away the bread would somehow remain hanging in mid-air.

An Arab navvy working on the path nearby lowered his heavy hoe and sidled towards us. He looked from the gazelle to the bread and from the bread to the gazelle, with a sort of quiet amazement, as though he had never seen anything quite like this before. Finally he said shyly in French:

"*I* could eat some of that bread."

I tore off a piece and he stowed it gratefully in some secret place under his rags. This man is an employee of the municipality.

When you go through the Jewish quarters you gather some idea of what the medieval ghettos were probably like. Under their Moorish rulers the Jews were only allowed to own land in certain restricted areas, and after centuries of this kind of treatment they have ceased to bother about overcrowding. Many of the streets are a good deal less than six feet wide, the houses are completely windowless, and sore-eyed children cluster everywhere in unbelievable numbers, like clouds of flies. Down the centre of the street there is generally running a little river of urine.

In the bazaar huge families of Jews, all dressed in the long black robe and little black skullcap, are working in dark fly-infested booths that look like caves. A carpenter sits cross-legged at a prehistoric lathe, turning chair legs at lightning speed. He works the lathe with a bow in his right hand and guides the chisel with his left foot, and thanks to a lifetime of sitting in this position his left leg is warped out of shape. At his side his grandson, aged six, is already starting on the simpler parts of the job.

I was just passing the coppersmiths' booths when somebody noticed that I was lighting a cigarette. Instantly, from the dark holes all round, there was a frenzied rush of Jews, many of them old grandfathers with flowing grey beards, all clamouring for a cigarette. Even a blind man somewhere at the back of one of the booths heard a rumour of cigarettes and came crawling out, groping in the air with his hand. In about a minute I had used up the whole packet. None of these people, I suppose, works less than twelve hours a day, and every one of them looks on a cigarette as a more or less impossible luxury.

As the Jews live in self-contained communities they follow the same trades as the Arabs, except for agriculture. Fruit sellers, potters, silversmiths, blacksmiths, butchers, leather-workers, tailors, water carriers, beggars, porters – whichever way you look you see nothing but Jews. As a matter of fact there are 13,000 of them, all living in the space of a few acres. A good job Hitler isn't here. Perhaps he is on his way, however. You hear the usual dark rumours about the Jews, not only from the Arabs but from the poorer Europeans.

"Yes, *mon vieux*,* they took my job away from me and gave it to a Jew. The Jews! They're the real rulers of this country, you know. They've got all the money. They control the banks, finance – everything."

"But," I said, "isn't it a fact that the average Jew is a labourer working for about a penny an hour?"

"Ah, that's only for show! They're all moneylenders really. They're cunning, the Jews."

In just the same way, a couple of hundred years ago, poor old women used to be burned for witchcraft when they could not even work enough magic to get themselves a square meal.

All people who work with their hands are partly invisible, and the more important the work they do, the less visible they are. Still, a white skin is always fairly conspicuous. In northern Europe, when you see a labourer ploughing a field, you probably give him a second glance. In a hot country, anywhere south of Gibraltar or east of Suez, the chances are that you don't even see him. I have noticed this again and again. In a tropical landscape one's eye takes in everything except the human beings. It takes in the dried-up soil, the prickly pear, the palm tree and the distant mountain, but it always misses the peasant hoeing at his patch. He is the same colour as the earth, and a great deal less interesting to look at.

It is only because of this that the starved countries of Asia and Africa are accepted as tourist resorts. No one would think of running cheap trips to the distressed areas. But where the human beings have brown skins their poverty is simply not noticed. What does Morocco mean to a Frenchman? An orange grove or a job in government service. Or to an Englishman? Camels, castles, palm trees, Foreign Legionnaires, brass trays and bandits. One could probably live here for years without noticing that for nine tenths of the people the reality of life is an endless, back-breaking struggle to wring a little food out of an eroded soil.

Most of Morocco is so desolate that no wild animal bigger than a hare can live on it. Huge areas which were once covered with forest have turned into a treeless waste where the soil is exactly like broken-up brick. Nevertheless a good deal of it is cultivated, with frightful labour. Everything is done by hand. Long lines of women, bent double like inverted capital Ls, work their way slowly across the fields, tearing up the prickly weeds with their hands, and the peasant gathering lucerne for fodder pulls it up stalk by stalk instead of reaping it, thus saving an inch or two on each stalk. The plough is a wretched wooden thing, so frail that one can easily carry it on one's shoulder, and fitted underneath with a rough iron spike which stirs the soil to a depth of about four inches. This is as much as the strength of the animals is equal to. It is usual to plough with a cow and a donkey yoked together. Two donkeys would not be quite strong enough, but on the other hand two cows would cost a little more to feed. The peasants possess no harrows, they merely plough the soil several times over in different directions, finally leaving it in rough furrows, after which the whole field has to be shaped with hoes into small oblong patches, to conserve water. Except for a day or two after the rare rainstorms there is never enough water. Along the edges of the fields channels are hacked out to a depth of thirty or forty feet to get at the tiny trickles which run through the subsoil.

Every afternoon a file of very old women passes down the road outside my house, each carrying a load of firewood. All of them are mummified with age and the sun, and all of them are tiny. It seems to be generally the case in primitive communities that the women, when they get beyond a certain age, shrink to the size of children. One day a poor old creature who could not have been more than four feet tall crept past me under a vast load of wood. I stopped her and put a five-sou piece (a little more than a farthing) into her hand. She answered with a shrill wail, almost a scream, which was partly gratitude but mainly surprise. I suppose that from her point of view, by taking any notice of her, I seemed almost to be violating a law of nature. She accepted her status as an old woman, that is to say as a beast of burden. When a family is travelling it is quite usual to see a father and a grown-up son riding ahead on donkeys, and an old woman following on foot, carrying the baggage.

But what is strange about these people is their invisibility. For several weeks, always at about the same time of day, the file of old women had hobbled past the house with their firewood, and though they had registered themselves on my eyeballs I cannot truly say that I had seen them. Firewood was passing – that was how I saw it. It was only that one day I happened to be walking behind them, and the curious up-and-down motion of a load of wood drew my attention to the human being underneath it. Then for the first time I noticed the poor old earth-coloured bodies, bodies reduced to bones and leathery skin, bent double under the crushing weight. Yet I suppose I had not been five minutes on Moroccan soil before I noticed the overloading of the donkeys and was infuriated by it. There is no question that the donkeys are damnably treated. The Moroccan donkey is hardly bigger than a St Bernard dog; it carries a load which in the British Army would be considered too much for a fifteen-hands mule, and very often its packsaddle is not taken off its back for weeks together. But what is peculiarly pitiful is that it is the most willing creature on earth – it follows its master like a dog and does not need either bridle or halter. After a dozen years of devoted work it suddenly drops dead, whereupon its master tips it into the ditch and the village dogs have torn its guts out before it is cold.

This kind of thing makes one's blood boil, whereas – on the whole – the plight of the human beings does not. I am not commenting, merely pointing to a fact. People with brown skins are next door to invisible. Anyone can be sorry for the donkey with its galled back, but it is generally owing to some kind of accident if one even notices the old woman under her load of sticks.

MARRAKECH

* * *

As the storks flew northward the Negroes were marching southward – a long, dusty column, infantry, screw-gun batteries and then more infantry, four or five thousand men in all, winding up the road with a clumping of boots and a clatter of iron wheels.

They were Senegalese, the blackest Negroes in Africa, so black that sometimes it is difficult to see whereabouts on their necks the hair begins. Their splendid bodies were hidden in reach-me-down khaki uniforms, their feet squashed into boots that looked like blocks of wood, and every tin hat seemed to be a couple of sizes too small. It was very hot and the men had marched a long way. They slumped under the weight of their packs and the curiously sensitive black faces were glistening with sweat.

As they went past a tall, very young Negro turned and caught my eye. But the look he gave me was not in the least the kind of look you might expect. Not hostile, not contemptuous, not sullen, not even inquisitive. It was the shy, wide-eyed Negro look, which actually is a look of profound respect. I saw how it was. This wretched boy, who is a French citizen and has therefore been dragged from the forest to scrub floors and catch syphilis in garrison towns, actually has feelings of reverence before a white skin. He has been taught that the white race are his masters, and he still believes it.

But there is one thought which every white man (and in this connection it doesn't matter twopence if he calls himself a socialist) thinks when he sees a black army marching past. "How much longer can we go on kidding these people? How long before they turn their guns in the other direction?"

It was curious, really. Every white man there has this thought stowed somewhere or other in his mind. I had it, so had the other onlookers, so had the officers on their sweating chargers and the white NCOs* marching in the ranks. It was a kind of secret which we all knew and were too clever to tell; only the Negroes didn't know it. And really it was almost like watching a flock of cattle to see the long column, a mile or two miles of armed men, flowing peacefully up the road, while the great white birds drifted over them in the opposite direction, glittering like scraps of paper.

Not Counting Niggers*

A dozen years ago anyone who had foretold the political line-up of today would have been looked on as a lunatic. And yet the truth is that the present situation – not in detail, of course, but in its main outlines – ought to have been predictable even in the golden age before Hitler. Something like it was bound to happen as soon as British security was seriously threatened.

In a prosperous country, above all in an imperialist country, left-wing politics are always partly humbug. There can be no real reconstruction that would not lead to at least a temporary drop in the English standard of life, which is another way of saying that the majority of left-wing politicians and publicists are people who earn their living by demanding something that they don't genuinely want. They are red-hot revolutionaries as long as all goes well, but every real emergency reveals instantly that they are shamming. One threat to the Suez Canal, and "anti-fascism" and "defence of British interests" are discovered to be identical.

It would be very shallow as well as unfair to suggest that there is *nothing* in what is now called "anti-fascism" except a concern for British dividends. But it is a fact that the political obscenities of the past two years, the sort of monstrous harlequinade in which everyone is constantly bounding across the stage in a false nose – Quakers shouting for a bigger army, communists waving Union Jacks, Winston Churchill posing as a democrat – would not have been possible without this guilty consciousness that we are all in the same boat. Much against their will the British governing class have been forced into the anti-Hitler position. It is still possible that they will find a way out of it, but they are arming in the obvious expectation of war and they will almost certainly fight when the point is reached at which the alternative would be to give away some of their own property instead of, as hitherto, other people's. And meanwhile the so-called opposition, instead of trying to stop the drift to war, are rushing ahead, preparing the ground and forestalling any possible criticism. So far as one can discover the English people are still extremely hostile to the idea of war, but in so far as they are becoming reconciled to it, it is not the militarists but the "anti-militarists" of five years ago who are responsible. The Labour Party keeps up a pettifogging grizzle against conscription at the same time as its own propaganda makes any real struggle against conscription impossible. The Bren machine guns pour from the factories, books with titles like *Tanks in the Next War*, *Gas in the Next War*, etc. pour from the press, and the warriors of the *New Statesman* gloze over the nature of the process by means of such phrases as "Peace Bloc", "Peace Front", "Democratic Front", and, in general, by pretending that the world is an assemblage of sheep and goats, neatly partitioned off by national frontiers.

In this connection it is well worth having a look at Mr Streit's much-discussed book, *Union Now*. Mr Streit, like the partisans of the "Peace Bloc", wants the democracies to gang up against the dictatorships, but his book is outstanding for two reasons. To begin with he goes further than most of the others and offers a plan which, even if it is startling, is constructive. Secondly, in spite of a rather 1920ish American *naïveté*, he has an essentially decent cast of mind. He genuinely loathes the thought of war, and he does not sink to the hypocrisy of pretending that any country which can be bought or bullied into the British orbit instantly becomes a democracy. His book therefore presents a kind of test case. In it you are seeing the sheep-and-goats theory at its *best*. If you can't accept it in that form you will certainly never accept it in the form handed out by the Left Book Club.*

Briefly, what Mr Streit suggests is that the democratic nations, starting with fifteen which he names, should voluntarily form themselves into a union – not a league or an alliance, but a union similar to the United States, with a common government, common money and complete internal free trade. The initial fifteen states are, of course, the USA, France, Great Britain, the self-governing dominions of the British Empire and the smaller European democracies, not including Czechoslovakia, which still existed when the book was written.* Later, other states could be admitted to the Union when and if they "proved themselves worthy". It is implied all along that the state of peace and prosperity existing within the Union would be so enviable that everyone else would soon be pining to join it.

It is worth noticing that this scheme is not so visionary as it sounds. Of course it is not going to happen, nothing advocated by well-meaning literary men ever happens, and there are certain difficulties which Mr Streit does not discuss – but it is of the order of things which *could* happen. Geographically the USA and the Western European democracies are nearer to being a unit than, for instance, the British Empire. Most of their trade is with one another, they contain within their own territories everything they need, and Mr Streit is probably right in claiming that their combined strength would be so great as to make any attack on them hopeless, even if the USSR joined up with Germany. Why then does one see at a glance that this scheme has something wrong with it? What is there about it that smells – for it *does* smell, of course?

What it smells of, as usual, is hypocrisy and self-righteousness. Mr Streit himself is not a hypocrite, but his vision is limited. Look again at his list of sheep and goats. No need to boggle at the goats (Germany, Italy and Japan); they are goats right enough, and billies at that. But look at the sheep! Perhaps the USA will pass inspection if one does not look too closely. But what about France? What about England? What about even Belgium and Holland? Like everyone of his school of thought, Mr Streit has coolly lumped the huge British and French empires – in essence nothing but mechanisms for exploiting cheap coloured labour – under the heading of democracies!

Here and there in the book, though not often, there are references to the "dependencies" of the democratic states. "Dependencies" means subject races. It is explained that they are to go on being dependencies, that their resources are to be pooled among the states of the Union, and that their coloured inhabitants will lack the right to vote in Union affairs. Except where the tables of statistics bring it out, one would never for a moment guess what *numbers* of human beings are involved. India, for instance, which contains more inhabitants than the whole of the "fifteen democracies" put together, gets just a page and a half in Mr Streit's book, and that merely to explain that as India is not yet fit for self-government the status quo must continue. And here one begins to see what would really be happening if Mr Streit's scheme were put into operation. The British and French empires, with their 600 million disenfranchised human beings, would simply be receiving fresh police forces; the huge strength of the USA would be behind the robbery of India and Africa. Mr Streit is letting cats out of bags, but *all* phrases like "Peace Bloc", "Peace Front", etc. contain some such implication; all imply a tightening-up of the existing structure. The unspoken clause is always "not counting niggers". For how can we make a "firm stand" against Hitler if we are simultaneously weakening ourselves at home? In other words, how can we "fight fascism" except by bolstering up a far vaster injustice?

For of course it *is* vaster. What we always forget is that the overwhelming bulk of the British proletariat does not live in Britain, but in Asia and Africa. It is not in Hitler's power, for instance, to make a penny an hour a normal industrial wage; it is perfectly normal in India, and we are at great pains to keep it so. One gets some idea of the real relationship of England and India when one reflects that the per capita annual income in England is something over eighty pounds, and in India about seven pounds. It is quite common for an Indian coolie's leg to be thinner than the average Englishman's arm. And there is nothing racial in this, for well-fed members of the same races are of normal physique; it is due to simple starvation. This is the system which we all live on and which we denounce when there seems to be no danger of its being altered. Of late, however, it has become the first duty of a "good anti-fascist" to lie about it and help to keep it in being.

What real settlement, of the slightest value, can there be along these lines? What meaning would there be, even if it were successful, in bringing down Hitler's system in order to stabilize something that is far bigger and in its different way just as bad?

But apparently, for lack of any real opposition, this is going to be our objective. Mr Streit's ingenious ideas will not be put into operation, but something resembling the "Peace Bloc" proposals probably will. The British and Russian governments are still haggling, stalling and uttering muffled threats to change sides, but circumstances will probably drive them together. And what then? No doubt the alliance will stave off war for a year or two. Then Hitler's move will be to feel for a weak spot or an unguarded moment; then our move will be more armaments, more militarization, more propaganda, more war-mindedness – and so on, at increasing speed. It is doubtful whether prolonged war preparation is morally any better than war itself; there are even reasons for thinking that it may be slightly worse. Only two or three years of it, and we may sink almost unresisting into some local variant of Austro-fascism. And perhaps a year or two later, in reaction against this, there will appear something we have never had in England yet – a real fascist movement. And because it will have the guts to speak plainly it will gather into its ranks the very people who ought to be opposing it.

Further than that it is difficult to see. The downward slide is happening because nearly all the socialist leaders, when it comes to the pinch, are merely His Majesty's Opposition, and nobody else knows how to mobilize the decency of the English people, which one meets with everywhere when one talks to human beings instead of reading newspapers. Nothing is likely to save us except the emergence within the next two years of a real mass party whose first pledges are to refuse war and to right imperial injustice. But if any such party exists at present, it is only as a possibility, in a few tiny germs lying here and there in unwatered soil.

Democracy in the British Army*

When the Duke of Wellington described the British Army as "the scum of the earth, enlisted for drink",* he was probably speaking no more than the truth. But what is significant is that his opinion would have been echoed by any non-military Englishman for nearly 100 years subsequently.

The French Revolution and the new conception of "national" war changed the character of most Continental armies, but England was in the exceptional position of being immune from invasion and of being governed during most of the nineteenth century by a non-military bourgeoisie. Consequently its army remained, as before, a small professional force more or less cut off from the rest of the nation. The war scare of the sixties produced the Volunteers, later to develop into the Territorials,* but it was not till a few years before the Great War that there was serious talk of universal service. Until the late nineteenth century the total number of white troops, even in wartime, never reached a quarter of a million men, and it is probable that every great British land battle between Blenheim and Loos was fought mainly by foreign soldiers.

In the nineteenth century the British common soldier was usually a farm labourer or slum proletarian who had been driven into the army by brute starvation. He enlisted for a period of at least seven years – sometimes as much as twenty-one years – and he was inured to a barrack life of endless drilling, rigid and stupid discipline, and degrading physical punishments. It was virtually impossible for him to marry, and even after the extension of the franchise he lacked the right to vote. In Indian garrison towns he could kick the "niggers" with impunity, but at home he was hated or looked down upon by the ordinary population, except in wartime, when for brief periods he was discovered to be a hero. Obviously such a man had severed his links with his own class. He was essentially a mercenary, and his self-respect depended on his conception of himself not as a worker or a citizen but simply as a fighting animal.

Since the war the conditions of army life have improved and the conception of discipline has grown more intelligent, but the British Army has retained its special characteristics – small size, voluntary enlistment, long service and emphasis on regimental loyalty. Every regiment has its own name (not merely a number, as in most armies), its history and relics, its special customs, traditions, etc. etc., thanks to which the whole army is honeycombed with snobberies which are almost unbelievable unless one has seen them at close quarters. Between the officers of a "smart" regiment and those of an ordinary infantry regiment, or still more a regiment of the Indian army, there is a degree of jealousy almost amounting to a class difference. And there is no question that the long-term private soldier often identifies with his own regiment almost as closely as the officer does. The effect is to make the narrow "non-political" outlook of the mercenary come more easily to him. In addition, the fact that the British Army is rather heavily officered probably diminishes class friction and thus makes the lower ranks less accessible to "subversive" ideas.

But the thing which above all else forces a reactionary viewpoint on the common soldier is his service in overseas garrisons. An infantry regiment is usually quartered abroad for eighteen years consecutively, moving from place to place every four or five years, so that many soldiers serve their entire term in India, Africa, China, etc. They are only there to hold down a hostile population and the fact is brought home to them in unmistakable ways. Relations with the "natives" are almost invariably bad, and the soldiers – not so much the officers as the men – are the obvious targets for anti-British feeling. Naturally they retaliate, and as a rule they develop an attitude towards the "niggers" which is far more brutal than that of the officials or businessmen. In Burma I was constantly struck by the fact that the common soldiers were the best-hated section of the white community, and, judged simply by their behaviour, they certainly deserved to be. Even as near home as Gibraltar they walk the streets with a swaggering air which is directed at the Spanish "natives". And in practice some such attitude is absolutely necessary; you could not hold down a subject empire with troops infected by notions of class solidarity. Most of the dirty work of the French Empire, for instance, is done not by French conscripts but by illiterate Negroes and by the Foreign Legion, a corps of pure mercenaries.

To sum up: in spite of the technical advances which do not allow the professional officer to be quite such an idiot as he used to be, and in spite of the fact that the common soldier is now treated a little more like a human being, the British Army remains essentially the same machine as it was fifty years ago. A little while back any socialist would have admitted this without argument. But we happen to be at a moment when the rise of Hitler has scared the official leaders of the Left into an attitude not far removed from jingoism. Large numbers of left-wing publicists are almost openly agitating for war. Without discussing this subject at length, it can be pointed out that a left-wing party which, within a capitalist society, becomes a war party, has already thrown up the sponge, because it is demanding a policy which can only be carried out by its opponents. The Labour leaders are intermittently aware of this – witness their shufflings on the subject of conscription. Hence, in among the cries of "Firm front!", "British prestige!", etc., there mingles a quite contradictory line of talk. It is to the effect that "this time" things are going to be "different". Militarization is not going to mean militarization. Colonel Blimp is no longer Colonel Blimp. And in the more soft-boiled left-wing papers a phrase is bandied to and fro – "democratizing the army". It is worth considering what it implies.

"Democratizing" an army, if it means anything, means doing away with the predominance of a single class and introducing a less mechanical form of discipline. In the British Army this would mean an entire reconstruction which would rob the army of efficiency for five to ten years. Such a process is only doubtfully possible while the British Empire exists, and quite unthinkable while the simultaneous aim is to "stop Hitler". What will actually happen during the next couple of years, war or no war, is that the armed forces will be greatly expanded, but the new units will take their colour from the existing professional army. As in the Great War, it will be the same army, only bigger. Poorer sections of the middle class will be drawn on for the supply of officers, but the professional military caste will retain its grip. As for the new militias, it is probably quite a mistake to imagine that they are the nucleus of a "democratic army" in which all classes will start from scratch. It is fairly safe to prophesy that even if there is no class favouritism (as there will be, presumably), militiamen of bourgeois origin will tend to be promoted first. Hore-Belisha* and others have already hinted as much in a number of speeches. A fact not always appreciated by socialists is that in England the whole of the bourgeoisie is to some extent militarized. Nearly every boy who has been to a public school has passed through the OTC* (theoretically voluntary but in practice compulsory), and though this training is done between the ages of thirteen and eighteen, it ought not to be despised. In effect the militiaman with an OTC training behind him will start with several months' advantage of the others. In any case the Military Training Act* is only an experiment, aimed partly at impressing opinion abroad and partly at accustoming the English people to the idea of conscription. Once the novelty has worn off some method will be devised of keeping proletarians out of positions of command.

It is probable that the nature of modern war has made "democratic army" a contradiction in terms. The French army, for instance, based on universal service, is hardly more democratic than the British. It is just as much dominated by the professional officer and the long-service NCO, and the French officer is probably rather more "Prussian" in outlook than his British equivalent. The Spanish government militias during the first six months of war – the first year, in Catalonia – were a genuinely democratic army, but they were also a very primitive type of army, capable only of defensive actions. In that particular case a defensive strategy, coupled with propaganda, would probably have had a better chance of victory than the methods casually adopted. But if you want military efficiency in the ordinary sense, there is no escaping from the professional soldier, and so long as the professional soldier is in control he will see to it that the army is not democratized. And what is true within the armed forces is true of the nation as a whole; every increase in the strength of the military machine means more power for the forces of reaction. It is possible that some of our left-wing jingoes are acting with their eyes open. If they are, they must be aware that the *News Chronicle* version of "defence of democracy" leads directly *away* from democracy, even in the narrow nineteenth-century sense of political liberty, independence of the trade unions and freedom of speech and the press.

Boys' Weeklies*

You never walk far through any poor quarter in any big town without coming upon a small newsagent's shop. The general appearance of these shops is always very much the same: a few posters for the *Daily Mail* and the *News of the World* outside, a poky little window with sweet bottles and packets of Players, and a dark interior smelling of liquorice allsorts and festooned from floor to ceiling with vilely printed twopenny papers, most of them with lurid cover illustrations in three colours.

Except for the daily and evening papers, the stock of these shops hardly overlaps at all with that of the big newsagents. Their main selling line is the twopenny weekly, and the number and variety of these are almost unbelievable. Every hobby and pastime – cage birds, fretwork, carpentering, bees, carrier pigeons, home conjuring, philately, chess – has at least one paper devoted to it, and generally several. Gardening and livestock keeping must have at least a score between them. Then there are the sporting papers, the radio papers, the children's comics, the various snippet papers such as *Tit-Bits*, the large range of papers devoted to the movies and all more or less exploiting women's legs, the various trade papers, the women's story papers (the *Oracle*, *Secrets*, *Peg's Paper*, etc. etc.), the needlework papers – these so numerous that a display of them alone will often fill an entire window – and in addition the long series of "Yank mags" (*Fight Stories*, *Action Stories*, *Western Short Stories*, etc.), which are imported shop-soiled from America and sold at twopence-halfpenny or threepence. And the periodical proper shades off into the fourpenny novelette, the *Aldine Boxing Novels*, the *Boys' Friend Library*, the *Schoolgirls' Own Library* and many others.

Probably the contents of these shops is the best available indication of what the mass of the English people really feels and thinks. Certainly nothing half so revealing exists in documentary form. Bestseller novels, for instance, tell one a great deal, but the novel is aimed almost exclusively at people above the £4-a-week level. The movies are probably a very unsafe guide to popular taste, because the film industry is virtually a monopoly, which means that it is not obliged to study its public at all closely. The same applies to some extent to the daily papers, and most of all to the radio. But it does not apply to the weekly paper with a smallish circulation and specialized subject matter. Papers like the *Exchange and Mart*, for instance, or *Cage-Birds*, or the *Oracle*, or *Prediction*, or the *Matrimonial Times*, only exist because there is a definite demand for them, and they reflect the minds of their readers as a great national daily with a circulation of millions cannot possibly do.

Here I am only dealing with a single series of papers, the boys' twopenny weeklies, often inaccurately described as "penny dreadfuls". Falling strictly within this class there are at present ten papers, the *Gem*, *Magnet*, *Modern Boy*, *Triumph* and *Champion*, all owned by the Amalgamated Press, and the *Wizard*, *Rover*, *Skipper*, *Hotspur* and *Adventure*, all owned by D.C. Thomson & Co. What the circulations of these papers are, I do not know. The editors and proprietors refuse to name any figures, and in any case the circulation of a paper carrying serial stories is bound to fluctuate widely. But there is no question that the combined public of the ten papers is a very large one. They are on sale in every town in England, and nearly every boy who reads at all goes through a phase of reading one or more of them. The *Gem* and *Magnet*, which are much the oldest of these papers, are of rather different type from the rest, and they have evidently lost some of their popularity during the past few years. A good many boys now regard them as old-fashioned and "slow". Nevertheless, I want to discuss them first, because they are more interesting psychologically than the others, and also because the mere survival of such papers into the 1930s is a rather startling phenomenon.

The *Gem* and *Magnet* are sister papers (characters out of one paper frequently appear in the other), and were both started more than thirty years ago. At that time, together with *Chums* and the old *Boy's Own Paper* (*BOP*), they were the leading papers for boys, and they remained dominant till quite recently. Each of them carries every week a 15,000- or 20,000-word school story, complete in itself, but usually more or less connected with the story of the week before. The *Gem* in addition to its school story carries one or more adventure serials. Otherwise the two papers are so much alike that they can be treated as one, though the *Magnet* has always been the better known of the two, probably because it possesses a really first-rate character in the fat boy Billy Bunter.*

The stories are stories of what purports to be public-school life, and the schools (Greyfriars in the *Magnet* and St Jim's in the *Gem*) are represented as ancient and fashionable foundations of the type of Eton or Winchester. All the leading characters are fourth-form boys aged fourteen or fifteen, older or younger boys only appearing in very minor parts. Like Sexton Blake and Nelson Lee,* these boys continue week after week and year after year, never growing any older. Very occasionally a new boy arrives or a minor character drops out, but in at any rate the last twenty-five years the personnel has barely altered. All the principal characters in both papers – Bob Cherry, Tom Merry, Harry Wharton, Johnny Bull, Billy Bunter and the rest of them – were at Greyfriars or St Jim's long before the Great War, exactly the same age as at present, having much the same kind of adventures and talking almost exactly the same dialect. And not only the characters but the whole atmosphere of both the *Gem* and *Magnet* has been preserved unchanged, partly by means of very elaborate stylization. The stories in the *Magnet are* signed "Frank Richards" and those in the *Gem*

"Martin Clifford", but a series lasting thirty years could hardly be the work of the same person every week.* Consequently they have to be written in a style that is easily imitated – an extraordinary, artificial, repetitive style, quite different from anything else now existing in English literature. A couple of extracts will do as illustrations. Here is one from the *Magnet*:

Groan!
"Shut up, Bunter!"
Groan!
Shutting up was not really in Billy Bunter's line. He seldom shut up, though often requested to do so. On the present awful occasion the fat Owl of Greyfriars was less inclined than ever to shut up. And he did not shut up! He groaned, and groaned, and went on groaning.
Even groaning did not fully express Bunter's feeling. His feelings, in fact, were inexpressible.
There were six of them in the soup! Only one of the six uttered sounds of woe and lamentation. But that one, William George Bunter, uttered enough for the whole party and a little over.
Harry Wharton & Co stood in a wrathy and worried group. They were landed and stranded, diddled, dished and done! Etc. etc. etc.

Here is one from the *Gem*:

"Oh cwumbs!"
"Oh gum!"
"Oooogh!"
"Urrggh!"
Arthur Augustus sat up dizzily. He grabbed his handkerchief and pressed it to his damaged nose. Tom Merry sat up, gasping for breath. They looked at one another.
"Bai Jove! This is a go, deah boy!" gurgled Arthur Augustus. "I have been thwown into quite a fluttah! Oogh! The wottahs! The wuffians! The feahful outsidahs! Wow!" Etc. etc. etc.

Both of these extracts are entirely typical; you would find something like them in almost every chapter of every number, today or twenty-five years ago. The first thing that anyone would notice is the extraordinary amount of tautology (the first of these two passages contains a hundred and twenty-five words and could be compressed into about thirty), seemingly designed to spin out the story, but actually playing its part in creating the atmosphere. For the same reason various facetious expressions are repeated over and over again; "wrathy", for instance, is a great favourite, and so is "diddled, dished and done". "Oooogh!", "Grooo!" and "Yaroo!" (stylized cries of pain) recur constantly, and so does "Ha! Ha! Ha!", always given a line to itself, so that sometimes a quarter of a column or thereabouts consists of "Ha! Ha! Ha!" The slang ("Go and eat coke!" "What the thump!", "You frabjous ass!", etc. etc.) has never been altered, so that the boys are now using slang which is at least thirty years out of date. In addition, the various nicknames are rubbed in on every possible occasion. Every few lines we are reminded that Harry Wharton & Co. are "the Famous Five", Bunter is always "the fat Owl" or "the Owl of the Remove", Vernon-Smith is always "the Bounder of Greyfriars", Gussy (the Honourable Arthur Augustus D'Arcy) is always "the swell of St Jim's", and so on and so forth. There is a constant, untiring effort to keep the atmosphere intact and to make sure that every new reader learns immediately who is who. The result has been to make Greyfriars and St Jim's into an extraordinary little world of their own, a world which cannot be taken seriously by anyone over fifteen, but which at any rate is not easily forgotten. By a debasement of the Dickens technique a series of stereotyped "characters" has been built up, in several cases very successfully. Billy Bunter, for instance, must be one of the best-known figures in English fiction; for the mere number of people who know him he ranks with Sexton Blake, Tarzan,* Sherlock Holmes and a handful of characters in Dickens.

Needless to say, these stories are fantastically unlike life at a real public school. They run in cycles of rather differing types, but in general they are the clean-fun, knockabout type of story, with interest centring round horseplay, practical jokes, ragging masters, fights, canings, football, cricket and food. A constantly recurring story is one in which a boy is accused of some misdeed committed by another and is too much of a sportsman to reveal the truth. The "good" boys are "good" in the clean-living Englishman tradition – they keep in hard training, wash behind their ears, never hit below the belt, etc. etc. – and by way of contrast there is a series of "bad" boys, Racke, Crooke, Loder and others, whose badness consists in betting, smoking cigarettes and frequenting public houses. All these boys are constantly on the verge of expulsion, but as it would mean a change of personnel if any boy were actually expelled, no one is ever caught out in any really serious offence. Stealing, for instance, barely enters as a motif. Sex is completely taboo, especially in the form in which it actually arises at public schools. Occasionally girls enter into the stories, and very rarely there is something approaching a mild flirtation, but it is always entirely in the spirit of clean fun. A boy and a girl enjoy going for bicycle rides together – that is all it ever amounts to. Kissing, for instance, would be regarded as "soppy". Even the bad boys are presumed to be completely sexless. When the *Gem* and *Magnet* were started, it is probable that there was a deliberate intention to get away from the guilty sex-ridden atmosphere that pervaded so much of the earlier literature for boys. In the nineties the *Boy's*

Own Paper, for instance, used to have its correspondence columns full of terrifying warnings against masturbation, and books like *St Winifred's* and *Tom Brown's School Days** were heavy with homosexual feeling, though no doubt the authors were not fully aware of it. In the *Gem* and *Magnet* sex simply does not exist as a problem. Religion is also taboo; in the whole thirty years' issue of the two papers the word "God" probably does not occur, except in "God save the King". On the other hand, there has always been a very strong "temperance" strain. Drinking and, by association, smoking are regarded as rather disgraceful even in an adult ("shady" is the usual word), but at the same time as something irresistibly fascinating, a sort of substitute for sex. In their moral atmosphere the *Gem* and *Magnet* have a great deal in common with the Boy Scout movement, which started at about the same time.

All literature of this kind is partly plagiarism. Sexton Blake, for instance, started off quite frankly as an imitation of Sherlock Holmes, and still resembles him fairly strongly; he has hawk-like features, lives in Baker Street, smokes enormously and puts on a dressing gown when he wants to think. The *Gem* and *Magnet* probably owe something to the school-story writers who were flourishing when they began, Gunby Hadath, Desmond Coke* and the rest, but they owe more to nineteenth-century models. In so far as Greyfriars and St Jim's are like real schools at all, they are much more like Tom Brown's Rugby than a modern public school. Neither school has an OTC, for instance; games are not compulsory, and the boys are even allowed to wear what clothes they like. But without doubt the main origin of these papers is *Stalky & Co.** This book has had an immense influence on boys' literature, and it is one of those books which have a sort of traditional reputation among people who have never even seen a copy of it. More than once in boys' weekly papers I have come across a reference to *Stalky & Co.* in which the word was spelt "Storky". Even the name of the chief comic among the Greyfriars masters, Mr Prout, is taken from *Stalky & Co.* and so is much of the slang: "jape", "merry", "giddy", "bizney" (business), "frabjous",* "don't" for "doesn't" – all of them out of date even when *Gem* and *Magnet* started. There are also traces of earlier origins. The name "Greyfriars" is probably taken from Thackeray,* and Gosling, the school porter in the *Magnet*, talks in an imitation of Dickens's dialect.

With all this, the supposed "glamour" of public-school life is played for all it is worth. There is all the usual paraphernalia – lock-up, roll-call, house matches, fagging, prefects, cosy teas round the study fire, etc. etc. – and constant reference to the "old school", the "old grey stones" (both schools were founded in the early sixteenth century), the "team spirit" of the "Greyfriars men". As for the snob appeal, it is completely shameless. Each school has a titled boy or two whose titles are constantly thrust in the reader's face; other boys have the names of well-known aristocratic families – Talbot, Manners, Lowther. We are forever being reminded that Gussy is the Honourable Arthur A. D'Arcy, son of Lord Eastwood, that Jack Blake is heir to "broad acres", that Hurree Jamset Ram Singh (nicknamed Inky) is the Nabob of Bhanipur, that Vernon-Smith's father is a millionaire. Till recently the illustrations in both papers always depicted the boys in clothes imitated from those of Eton; in the last few years Greyfriars has changed over to blazers and flannel trousers, but St Jim's still sticks to the Eton jacket, and Gussy sticks to his top hat. In the school magazine which appears every week as part of the *Magnet*, Harry Wharton writes an article discussing the pocket money received by the "fellows in the Remove", and reveals that some of them get as much as five pounds a week! This kind of thing is a perfectly deliberate incitement to wealth fantasy. And here it is worth noticing a rather curious fact, and that is that the school story is a thing peculiar to England. So far as I know, there are extremely few school stories in foreign languages. The reason, obviously, is that in England education is mainly a matter of status. The most definite dividing line between the petite bourgeoisie and the working class is that the former pay for their education, and within the bourgeoisie there is another unbridgeable gulf between the "public" school and the "private" school. It is quite clear that there are tens and scores of thousands of people to whom every detail of life at a "posh" public school is wildly thrilling and romantic. They happen to be outside that mystic world of quadrangles and house colours, but they yearn after it, daydream about it, live mentally in it for hours at a stretch. The question is, Who are these people? Who reads the *Gem* and *Magnet*?

Obviously one can never be quite certain about this kind of thing. All I can say from my own observation is this. Boys who are likely to go to public schools themselves generally read the *Gem* and *Magnet*, but they nearly always stop reading them when they are about twelve; they may continue for another year from force of habit, but by that time they have ceased to take them seriously. On the other hand, the boys at very cheap private schools, the schools that are designed for people who can't afford a public school but consider the council schools "common", continue reading the *Gem* and *Magnet* for several years longer. A few years ago I was a teacher at two of these schools myself. I found that not only did virtually all the boys read the *Gem* and *Magnet*, but that they were still taking them fairly seriously when they were fifteen or even sixteen. These boys were the sons of shopkeepers, office employees and small business and professional men, and obviously it is this class that the *Gem* and *Magnet* are aimed at. But they are certainly read by working-class boys as well. They are generally on sale in the poorest quarters of big towns, and I have known them to be read by boys whom one might expect to be completely immune from public-school "glamour". I have seen a young coal miner, for instance, a lad who had already worked a year or two underground, eagerly reading the *Gem*. Recently I offered a batch of English papers to some British legionaries of the French Foreign Legion in North Africa; they picked out the *Gem* and

Magnet first. Both papers are much read by girls,* and the Pen Pals' department of the *Gem* shows that it is read in every corner of the British Empire, by Australians, Canadians, Palestine Jews, Malays, Arabs, Straits Chinese, etc. etc. The editors evidently expect their readers to be aged round about fourteen, and the advertisements (milk chocolate, postage stamps, water pistols, blushing cured, home conjuring tricks, itching powder, the Phine Phun Ring which runs a needle into your friend's hand, etc. etc.) indicate roughly the same age; there are also the Admiralty advertisements, however, which call for youths between seventeen and twenty-two. And there is no question that these papers are also read by adults. It is quite common for people to write to the editor and say that they have read every number of the *Gem* or *Magnet* for the past thirty years. Here, for instance, is a letter from a lady in Salisbury:

> I can say of your splendid yarns of Harry Wharton & Co. of Greyfriars, that they never fail to reach a high standard. Without doubt they are the finest stories of their type on the market today, which is saying a good deal. They seem to bring you face to face with Nature. I have taken the *Magnet* from the start, and have followed the adventures of Harry Wharton & Co. with rapt interest. I have no sons, but two daughters, and there's always a rush to be the first to read the grand old paper. My husband, too, was a staunch reader of the *Magnet* until he was suddenly taken away from us.

It is well worth getting hold of some copies of the *Gem* and *Magnet*, especially the *Gem*, simply to have a look at the correspondence columns. What is truly startling is the intense interest with which the pettiest details of life at Greyfriars and St Jim's are followed up. Here, for instance, are a few of the questions sent in by readers:

> "What age is Dick Roylance?" "How old is St Jim's?" "Can you give me a list of the Shell* and their studies?" "How much did D'Arcy's monocle cost?" "How is it fellows like Crooke are in the Shell and decent fellows like yourself are only in the Fourth?" "What are the form captain's three chief duties?" "Who is the chemistry master at St Jim's?" (From a girl:) "Where is St Jim's situated? *Could* you tell me how to get there, as I would love to see the building? Are you boys just 'phoneys', as I think you are?"

It is clear that many of the boys and girls who write these letters are living a complete fantasy life. Sometimes a boy will write, for instance, giving his age, height, weight, chest and biceps measurements and asking which member of the Shell or Fourth Form he most exactly resembles. The demand for a list of the studies on the Shell passage, with an exact account of who lives in each, is a very common one. The editors, of course, do everything in their power to keep up the illusion. In the *Gem* Jack Blake is supposed to write the answers to correspondents, and in the *Magnet* a couple of pages is always given up to the school magazine (the *Greyfriars Herald*, edited by Harry Wharton), and there is another page in which one or other character is written up each week. The stories run in cycles, two or three characters being kept in the foreground for several weeks at a time. First there will be a series of rollicking adventure stories, featuring the Famous Five and Billy Bunter; then a run of stories turning on mistaken identity, with Wibley (the make-up wizard) in the star part; then a run of more serious stories in which Vernon-Smith is trembling on the verge of expulsion. And here one comes upon the real secret of the *Gem* and *Magnet* and the probable reason why they continue to be read in spite of their obvious out-of-dateness.

It is that the characters are so carefully graded as to give almost every type of reader a character he can identify himself with. Most boys' papers aim at doing this, hence the boy assistant (Sexton Blake's Tinker, Nelson Lee's Nipper, etc.) who usually accompanies the explorer, detective or what not on his adventures. But in these cases there is only one boy, and usually it is much the same type of boy. In the *Gem* and *Magnet* there is a model for very nearly everybody. There is the normal, athletic, high-spirited boy (Tom Merry, Jack Blake, Frank Nugent), a slightly rowdier version of this type (Bob Cherry), a more aristocratic version (Talbot, Manners), a quieter, more serious version (Harry Wharton) and a stolid, "bulldog" version (Johnny Bull). Then there is the reckless, daredevil type of boy (Vernon-Smith), the definitely "clever", studious boy (Mark Linley, Dick Penfold) and the eccentric boy who is not good at games but possesses some special talent (Skinner, Wibley). And there is the scholarship boy (Tom Redwing), an important figure in this class of story because he makes it possible for boys from very poor homes to project themselves into the public-school atmosphere. In addition there are Australian, Irish, Welsh, Manx, Yorkshire and Lancashire boys to play upon local patriotism. But the subtlety of characterization goes deeper than this. If one studies the correspondence columns one sees that there is probably *no* character in the *Gem* and *Magnet* whom some or other reader does not identify with, except the out-and-out comics, Coker, Billy Bunter, Fisher T. Fish (the money-grubbing American boy) and, of course, the masters. Bunter, though in his origin he probably owed something to the fat boy in *Pickwick*, is a real creation. His tight trousers against which boots and canes are constantly thudding, his astuteness in search of food, his postal order which never turns up, have made him famous wherever the Union Jack waves. But he is not a subject for daydreams. On the other hand, another seeming figure of fun, Gussy (the Honourable Arthur A. D'Arcy, "the swell of St Jim's"), is evidently much admired. Like everything else in the *Gem* and *Magnet*, Gussy is at least thirty years out of date. He is the "knut"* of the early twentieth century or even the "masher" of the nineties ("Bai Jove, deah boy!" and "Weally, I shall be obliged to give you a feahful thwashin'!"), the monocled idiot who made good on the fields of Mons and Le Cateau. And his evident popularity goes to show how deep the snob appeal of this type is. English people are extremely fond of the titled ass (cf. Lord Peter Wimsey*) who always turns up trumps in the moment of emergency. Here is a letter from one of Gussy's girl admirers:

> I think you're too hard on Gussy. I wonder he's still in existence, the way you treat him. He's my hero. Did you know I write lyrics? How's this – to the tune of 'Goody Goody'?
>
>> Gonna get my gas mask, join the ARP*
>> 'Cos I'm wise to all those bombs you drop on me.
>>> Gonna dig myself a trench
>>> Inside the garden fence;
>> Gonna seal my windows up with tin
>> So that the tear gas can't get in;
>> Gonna park my cannon right outside the kerb
>> With a note to Adolf Hitler: "Don't disturb!"
>>> And if I never fall in Nazi hands
>>> That's soon enough for me
>> Gonna get my gas mask, join the ARP.
>
> P.S. – Do you get on well with girls?

I quote this in full because (dated April 1939) it is interesting as being probably the earliest mention of Hitler in the *Gem*. In the *Gem* there is also a heroic fat boy, Fatty Wynn, as a set-off against Bunter. Vernon-Smith, "the Bounder of the Remove", a Byronic character, always on the verge of the sack, is another great favourite. And even some of the cads probably have their following. Loder, for instance, "the rotter of the Sixth", is a cad, but he is also a highbrow and given to saying sarcastic things about football and the team spirit. The boys of the Remove only think him all the more of a cad for this, but a certain type of boy would probably identify with him. Even Racke, Crooke and Co. are probably admired by small boys who think it diabolically wicked to smoke cigarettes. (A frequent question in the correspondence column: "What brand of cigarettes does Racke smoke?")

Naturally the politics of the *Gem* and *Magnet* are conservative, but in a completely pre-1914 style, with no fascist tinge. In reality their basic political assumptions are two: nothing ever changes, and foreigners are funny. In the *Gem* of 1939 Frenchmen are still Froggies and Italians are still Dagoes. Mossoo, the French master at Greyfriars, is the usual comic-paper Frog, with pointed beard, pegtop trousers, etc. Inky, the Indian boy, though a rajah, and therefore possessing snob appeal, is also the comic babu of the *Punch* tradition. ("'The rowfulness is not the proper caper, my esteemed Bob,' said Inky. 'Let dogs delight in the barkfulness and bitefulness, but the soft answer is the cracked pitcher that goes longest to a bird in the bush, as the English proverb remarks.'") Fisher T. Fish is the old-style stage Yankee ("Waal, I guess," etc.) dating from a period of Anglo-American jealousy. Wun Lung, the Chinese boy (he has rather faded out of late, no doubt because some of the *Magnet*'s readers are Straits Chinese), is the nineteenth-century pantomime Chinaman, with saucer-shaped hat, pigtail and pidgin English. The assumption all along is not only that foreigners are comics who are put there for us to laugh at, but that they can be classified in much the same way as insects. That is why in all boys' papers, not only the *Gem* and *Magnet*, a Chinese is invariably portrayed with a pigtail. It is the thing you recognize him by, like the Frenchman's beard or the Italian's barrel organ. In papers of this kind it occasionally happens that when the setting of a story is in a foreign country some attempt is made to describe the natives as individual human beings, but as a rule it is assumed that foreigners of any one race are all alike and will conform more or less exactly to the following patterns:

> FRENCHMAN: Excitable. Wears beard, gesticulates wildly.
> SPANIARD, MEXICAN, etc.: Sinister, treacherous.
> ARAB, AFGHAN, etc.: Sinister, treacherous.
> CHINESE: Sinister, treacherous. Wears pigtail.
> ITALIAN: Excitable. Grinds barrel organ or carries stiletto.
> SWEDE, *Dane, etc.*: Kind-hearted, stupid.
> NEGRO: Comic, very faithful.

The working classes only enter into the *Gem* and *Magnet* as comics or semi-villains (racecourse touts etc.). As for class friction, trade unionism, strikes, slumps, unemployment, fascism and civil war – not a mention. Somewhere or other in the thirty years' issue of the two papers you might perhaps find the word "socialism", but you would have to look a long time for it. If the Russian Revolution is anywhere referred to, it will be indirectly, in the word "Bolshy" (meaning a person of violent disagreeable habits). Hitler and the Nazis are just beginning to make their appearance, in the sort of reference I quoted above. The war crisis of September 1938 made just enough impression to produce a story in which Mr Vernon-Smith, the Bounder's millionaire father, cashed in on the general panic by buying up country houses in order to sell them to "crisis scuttlers". But that is probably as near to noticing the European situation as the *Gem* and *Magnet* will come, until the war actually starts.* That does not mean that these papers are unpatriotic – quite the contrary! Throughout the Great War the *Gem* and *Magnet* were perhaps the most consistently and cheerfully patriotic papers in England. Almost every week the boys caught a spy or pushed a conchie into the army, and during the rationing period EAT LESS BREAD was printed in large type on every page. But their patriotism has nothing whatever to do with power politics or "ideological" warfare. It is more akin to family loyalty, and actually it gives one a valuable clue to the attitude of ordinary people, especially the huge untouchable block of the middle class and the better-off working class. These people are patriotic to the middle of their bones, but they do not feel that what happens in foreign countries is any of their business. When England is in danger they rally to its defence as a matter of course, but in between times they are not interested. After all, England is always in the right and England always wins, so why worry? It is an attitude that has been shaken during the past twenty years, but not so deeply as is sometimes supposed. Failure to understand it is one of the reasons why left-wing political parties are seldom able to produce an acceptable foreign policy.

The mental world of the *Gem* and *Magnet*, therefore, is something like this:

The year is 1910 – or 1940, but it is all the same. You are at Greyfriars, a rosy-cheeked boy of fourteen in posh, tailor-made clothes, sitting down to tea in your study on the Remove passage after an exciting game of football which was won by an odd goal in the last half-minute. There is a cosy fire in the study, and outside the wind is whistling. The ivy clusters thickly round the old grey stones. The King is on his throne and the pound is worth a pound. Over in Europe the comic foreigners are jabbering and gesticulating, but the grim grey battleships of the British Fleet are steaming up the Channel and at the outposts of Empire the monocled Englishmen are holding the niggers at bay. Lord Mauleverer has just got another fiver and we are all settling down to a tremendous tea of sausages, sardines, crumpets, potted meat, jam and doughnuts. After tea we shall sit round the study fire having a good laugh at Billy Bunter and discussing the team for next week's match against Rookwood. Everything is safe, solid and unquestionable. Everything will be the same for ever and ever. That approximately is the atmosphere.

But now turn from the *Gem* and *Magnet* to the more up-to-date papers which have appeared since the Great War. The truly significant thing is that they have more points of resemblance to the *Gem* and *Magnet* than points of difference. But it is better to consider the differences first.

There are eight of these newer papers, the *Modern Boy*, *Triumph*, *Champion*, *Wizard*, *Rover*, *Skipper*, *Hotspur* and *Adventure*. All of these have appeared since the Great War, but except for the *Modern Boy* none of them is less than five years old. Two papers which ought also to be mentioned briefly here, though they are not strictly in the same class as the rest, are the *Detective Weekly* and the *Thriller*, both owned by the Amalgamated Press. The *Detective Weekly* has taken over Sexton Blake. Both of these papers admit a certain amount of sex interest into their stories, and though certainly read by boys, they are not aimed at them exclusively. All the others are boys' papers pure and simple, and they are sufficiently alike to be considered together. There does not seem to be any notable difference between Thomson's publications and those of the Amalgamated Press.

As soon as one looks at these papers one sees their technical superiority to the *Gem* and *Magnet*. To begin with, they have the great advantage of not being written entirely by one person. Instead of one long complete story, a number of the *Wizard* or *Hotspur* consists of half a dozen or more serials, none of which goes on for ever. Consequently there is far more variety and far less padding, and none of the tiresome stylization and facetiousness of the *Gem* and *Magnet*. Look at these two extracts, for example:

> Billy Bunter groaned.
>
> A quarter of an hour had elapsed out of the two hours that Bunter was booked for extra French.
>
> In a quarter of an hour there were only fifteen minutes! But every one of those minutes seemed inordinately long to Bunter. They seemed to crawl by like tired snails.
>
> Looking at the clock in Classroom No. 10 the fat Owl could hardly believe that only fifteen minutes had passed. It seemed more like fifteen hours, if not fifteen days!
>
> Other fellows were in extra French as well as Bunter. They did not matter. Bunter did! (*Magnet*.)

After a terrible climb, hacking out handholds in the smooth ice every step of the way up, Sergeant Lionheart Logan of the Mounties was now clinging like a human fly to the face of an icy cliff, as smooth and treacherous as a giant pane of glass.

An Arctic blizzard, in all its fury, was buffeting his body, driving the blinding snow into his face, seeking to tear his fingers loose from their handholds and dash him to death on the jagged boulders which lay at the foot of the cliff a hundred feet below.

Crouching among those boulders were eleven villainous trappers who had done their best to shoot down Lionheart and his companion, Constable Jim Rogers – until the blizzard had blotted the two Mounties out of sight from below. (*Wizard*.)

The second extract gets you some distance with the story, the first takes a hundred words to tell you that Bunter is in the detention class. Moreover, by not concentrating on school stories (in point of numbers the school story slightly predominates in all these papers, except the *Thriller* and *Detective Weekly*), the *Wizard*, *Hotspur*, etc. have far greater opportunities for sensationalism. Merely looking at the cover illustrations of the papers which I have on the table in front of me, here are some of the things I see. On one a cowboy is clinging by his toes to the wing of an aeroplane in mid-air and shooting down another aeroplane with his revolver. On another a Chinese is swimming for his life down a sewer with a swarm of ravenous-looking rats swimming after him. On another an engineer is lighting a stick of dynamite while a steel robot feels for him with its claws. On another a man in airman's costume is fighting bare-handed against a rat somewhat larger than a donkey. On another a nearly naked man of terrific muscular development has just seized a lion by the tail and flung it thirty yards over the wall of an arena, with the words, "Take back your blooming lion!" Clearly no school story can compete with this kind of thing. From time to time the school buildings may catch fire or the French master may turn out to be the head of an international anarchist gang, but in a general way the interest must centre round cricket, school rivalries, practical jokes, etc. There is not much room for bombs, death rays, sub-machine guns, aeroplanes, mustangs, octopuses, grizzly bears or gangsters.

Examination of a large number of these papers shows that, putting aside school stories, the favourite subjects are Wild West, Frozen North, Foreign Legion, crime (always from the detective's angle), the Great War (Air Force or Secret Service, not the infantry), the Tarzan motif in varying forms, professional football, tropical exploration, historical romance (Robin Hood, Cavaliers and Roundheads, etc.) and scientific invention. The Wild West still leads, at any rate as a setting, though the Red Indian seems to be fading out. The one theme that is really new is the scientific one. Death rays, Martians, invisible men, robots, helicopters and interplanetary rockets figure largely; here and there there are even far-off rumours of psychotherapy and ductless glands. Whereas the *Gem* and *Magnet* derive from Dickens and Kipling, the *Wizard*, *Champion*, *Modern Boy*, etc. owe a great deal to H.G. Wells, who, rather than Jules Verne, is the father of "scientifiction". Naturally it is the magical, Martian aspect of science that is most exploited, but one or two papers include serious articles on scientific subjects, besides quantities of informative snippets. (Examples: "A Kauri tree in Queensland, Australia, is over 12,000 years old"; "Nearly 50,000 thunderstorms occur every day"; "Helium gas costs £1 per 1,000 cubic feet"; "There are over 500 varieties of spiders in Great Britain"; "London firemen use 14,000,000 gallons of water annually", etc. etc.) There is a marked advance in intellectual curiosity and, on the whole, in the demand made on the reader's attention. In practice the *Gem* and *Magnet* and the post-war papers are read by much the same public, but the mental age aimed at seems to have risen by a year or two years – an improvement probably corresponding to the improvement in elementary education since 1909.

The other thing that has emerged in the post-war boys' papers, though not to anything like the extent one would expect, is bully worship and the cult of violence.

If one compares the *Gem* and *Magnet* with a genuinely modern paper, the thing that immediately strikes one is the absence of the leader principle. There is no central dominating character; instead there are fifteen or twenty characters, all more or less on an equality, with whom readers of different types can identify. In the more modern papers this is not usually the case. Instead of identifying with a schoolboy of more or less his own age, the reader of the *Skipper*, *Hotspur*, etc. is led to identify with a G-man, with a Foreign Legionary, with some variant of Tarzan, with an air ace, a master spy, an explorer, a pugilist – at any rate with some single all-powerful character who dominates everyone about him and whose usual method of solving any problem is a sock on the jaw. This character is intended as a superman, and as physical strength is the form of power that boys can best understand, he is usually a sort of human gorilla; in the Tarzan type of story he is sometimes actually a giant, eight or ten feet high. At the same time the scenes of violence in nearly all these stories are remarkably harmless and unconvincing. There is a great difference in tone between even the most bloodthirsty English paper and the threepenny Yank mags, *Fight Stories*, *Action Stories*, etc. (not strictly boys' papers, but largely read by boys). In the Yank mags you get real bloodlust, really gory descriptions of the all-in, jump-on-his-testicles style of fighting, written in a jargon that has been perfected by people who brood endlessly on violence. A paper like *Fight Stories*, for instance, would have very little appeal except to sadists and masochists. You can see the comparative gentleness of the English civilization by the amateurish way in which prizefighting is always described in the boys' weeklies. There is no specialized vocabulary. Look at these four extracts, two English, two American:

When the gong sounded, both men were breathing heavily, and each had great red marks on his chest, Bill's chin was bleeding, and Ben had a cut over his right eye.

Into their corners they sank, but when the gong clanged again they were up swiftly, and they went like tigers at each other. (*Rover*.)

He walked in stolidly and smashed a clublike right to my face. Blood spattered and I went back on my heels, but surged in and ripped my right under his heart. Another right smashed full on Sven's already battered mouth, and, spitting out the fragments of a tooth, he crashed a flailing left to my body. (*Fight Stories*.)

It was amazing to watch the Black Panther at work. His muscles rippled and slid under his dark skin. There was all the power and grace of a giant cat in his swift and terrible onslaught.

He volleyed blows with a bewildering speed for so huge a fellow. In a moment Ben was simply blocking with his gloves as well as he could. Ben was really a past-master of defence. He had many fine victories behind him. But the Negro's rights and lefts crashed through openings that hardly any other fighter could have found. (*Wizard*.)

Haymakers which packed the bludgeoning weight of forest monarchs crashing down under the axe hurled into the bodies of the two heavies as they swapped punches. (*Fight Stories*.)

Notice how much more knowledgeable the American extracts sound. They are written for devotees of the prize ring; the others are not. Also, it ought to be emphasized that on its level the moral code of the English boys' papers is a decent one. Crime and dishonesty are never held up to admiration, there is none of the cynicism and corruption of the American gangster story. The huge sale of the Yank mags in England shows that there is a demand for that kind of thing, but very few English writers seem able to produce it. When hatred of Hitler became a major emotion in America, it was interesting to see how promptly "anti-fascism" was adapted to pornographic purposes by the editors of the Yank mags. One magazine which I have in front of me is given up to a long, complete story, 'When Hell Came to America', in which the agents of a "blood-maddened European dictator" are trying to conquer the USA with death rays and invisible aeroplanes. There is the frankest appeal to sadism, scenes in which the Nazis tie bombs to women's backs and fling them off heights to watch them blown to pieces in mid-air, others in which they tie naked girls together by their hair and prod them with knives to make them dance, etc. etc. The editor comments solemnly on all this, and uses it as a plea for tightening up restrictions against immigrants. On another page of the same paper: "LIVES OF THE HOTCHA CHORUS GIRLS. Reveals all the intimate secrets and fascinating pastimes of the famous Broadway Hotcha girls, NOTHING IS OMITTED. Price 10c." "HOW TO LOVE. 10c." "FRENCH PHOTO RING, 25c." "NAUGHTY NUDIES TRANSFERS. From the outside of the glass you see a beautiful girl, innocently dressed. Turn it around and look through the glass and oh! what a difference! Set of 3 transfers 25c." etc. etc. etc. There is nothing at all like this in any English paper likely to be read by boys. But the process of Americanization is going on all the same. The American ideal, the "he-man", the "tough guy", the gorilla who puts everything right by socking everybody else on the jaw, now figures in probably a majority of boys' papers. In one serial now running in the *Skipper* he is always portrayed, ominously enough, swinging a rubber truncheon.

The development of the *Wizard*, *Hotspur*, etc., as against the earlier boys' papers, boils down to this: better technique, more scientific interest, more bloodshed, more leader-worship. But, after all, it is the *lack* of development that is the really striking thing.

To begin with, there is no political development whatever. The world of the *Skipper* and the *Champion* is still the pre-1914 world of the *Magnet* and the *Gem*. The Wild West story, for instance, with its cattle-rustlers, lynch law and other paraphernalia belonging to the eighties, is a curiously archaic thing. It is worth noticing that in papers of this type it is always taken for granted that adventures only happen at the ends of the earth, in tropical forests, in Arctic wastes, in African deserts, on Western prairies, in Chinese opium dens – everywhere, in fact, except the places where things really *do* happen. That is a belief dating from thirty or forty years ago, when the new continents were in process of being opened up. Nowadays, of course, if you really want adventure, the place to look for it is in Europe. But apart from the picturesque side of the Great War, contemporary history is carefully excluded. And except that Americans are now admired instead of being laughed at, foreigners are exactly the same figures of fun that they always were. If a Chinese character appears, he is still the sinister pigtailed opium smuggler of Sax Rohmer;* no indication that things have been happening in China since 1912 – no indication that a war is going on there, for instance. If a Spaniard appears, he is still a "Dago" or "greaser" who rolls cigarettes and stabs people in the back; no indication that things have been happening in Spain. Hitler and the Nazis have not yet appeared, or are barely making their appearance. There will be plenty about them in a little while, but it will be from a strictly patriotic angle (Britain versus Germany), with the real meaning of the struggle kept out of sight as much as possible. As for the Russian Revolution, it is extremely difficult to find any reference to it in any of these papers. When Russia is mentioned at all it is usually in an information snippet (example: "There are 29,000 centenarians in the USSR"), and any reference to the Revolution is indirect and twenty years out of date. In one story in the *Rover*, for instance, somebody has a tame bear, and as it is a Russian bear, it is nicknamed Trotsky – obviously an echo of the 1917–23 period and not of recent controversies. The clock has stopped at 1910. Britannia rules the waves, and no one has heard of slumps, booms, unemployment, dictatorships, purges or concentration camps.

And in social outlook there is hardly any advance. The snobbishness is somewhat less open than in the *Gem* and *Magnet* – that is the most one can possibly say. To begin with, the school story, always partly dependent on snob appeal, is by no means eliminated. Every number of a boys' paper includes at least one school story, these stories slightly outnumbering the Wild Westerns. The very elaborate fantasy life of the *Gem* and *Magnet* is not imitated and there is more emphasis on extraneous adventure, but the social atmosphere (old grey stones) is much the same. When a new school is introduced at the beginning of a story we are often told in just about those words that "it was a very posh school". From time to time a story appears which is ostensibly directed *against* snobbery. The scholarship boy (cf. Tom Redwing in the *Magnet*) makes fairly frequent appearances, and what is essentially the same theme is sometimes presented in this form; there is great rivalry between two schools, one of which considers itself more "posh" than the other, and there are fights, practical jokes, football matches, etc., always ending in the discomfiture of the snobs. If one glances very superficially at some of these stories it is possible to imagine that a democratic spirit has crept into the boys' weeklies, but when one looks more closely one sees that they merely reflect the bitter jealousies that exist within the white-collar class. Their real function is to allow the boy who goes to a cheap private school (*not* a council school) to feel that his school is just as "posh" in the sight of God as Winchester or Eton. The sentiment of school loyalty ("We're better than the fellows down the road"), a thing almost unknown to the real working class, is still kept up. As these stories are written by many different hands, they do, of course, vary a good deal in tone. Some are reasonably free from snobbishness; in others money and pedigree are exploited even more shamelessly than in the *Gem* and *Magnet*. In one that I came across an actual *majority* of the boys mentioned were titled.

Where working-class characters appear, it is usually either as comics (jokes about tramps, convicts, etc.) or as prizefighters, acrobats, cowboys, professional footballers and Foreign Legionaries – in other words, as adventurers. There is no facing of the facts about working-class life, or, indeed, about *working* life of any description. Very occasionally one may come across a realistic description of, say, work in a coal mine, but in all probability it will only be there as the background of some lurid adventure. In any case the central character is not likely to be a coal miner. Nearly all the time the boy who reads these papers – in nine cases out of ten a boy who is going to spend his life working in a shop, in a factory or in some subordinate job in an office – is led to identify with people in positions of command, above all with people who are never troubled by shortage of money. The Lord Peter Wimsey figure, the seeming idiot who drawls and wears a monocle but is always to the fore in moments of danger, turns up over and over again. (This character is a great favourite in Secret Service stories.) And, as usual, the heroic characters all have to talk BBC; they may talk Scottish or Irish or American, but no one in a star part is ever permitted to drop an aitch. Here it is worth comparing the social atmosphere of the boys' weeklies with that of the women's weeklies, the *Oracle*, the *Family Star*, *Peg's Paper*, etc.

The women's papers are aimed at an older public and are read for the most part by girls who are working for a living. Consequently they are on the surface much more realistic. It is taken for granted, for example, that nearly everyone has to live in a big town and work at a more or less dull job. Sex, so far from being taboo, is *the* subject. The short, complete stories, the special feature of these papers, are generally of the "came the dawn" type: the heroine narrowly escapes losing her "boy" to a designing rival, or the "boy" loses his job and has to postpone marriage, but presently gets a better job. The changeling fantasy (a girl brought up in a poor home is "really" the child of rich parents) is another favourite. Where sensationalism comes in, usually in the serials, it arises out of the more domestic type of crime, such as bigamy, forgery or sometimes murder; no Martians, death rays or international anarchist gangs. These papers are at any rate aiming at credibility, and they have a link with real life in their correspondence columns, where genuine problems are being discussed. Ruby M. Ayres's column of advice in the *Oracle*,* for instance, is extremely sensible and well written. And yet the world of the *Oracle* and *Peg's Paper* is a pure fantasy world. It is the same fantasy all the time, pretending to be richer than you are. The chief impression that one carries away from almost every story in these papers is of frightful, overwhelming "refinement". Ostensibly the characters are working-class people, but their habits, the interiors of their houses, their clothes, their outlook and, above all, their speech are entirely middle class. They are all living at several pounds a week above their income. And needless to say, that is just the impression that is intended. The idea is to give the bored factory girl or worn-out mother of five a dream life in which she pictures herself – not actually as a duchess (that convention has gone out) but as, say, the wife of a bank manager. Not only is a five-to-six-pound-a-week standard of life set up as the ideal, but it is tacitly assumed that that is how working-class people really *do* live. The major facts are simply not faced. It is admitted, for instance, that people sometimes lose their jobs – but then the dark clouds roll away and they get better jobs instead. No mention of unemployment as something permanent and inevitable, no mention of the dole, no mention of trade unionism. No suggestion anywhere that there can be anything wrong with the system *as a system*; there are only individual misfortunes, which are generally due to somebody's wickedness and can in any case be put right in the last chapter. Always the dark clouds roll away, the kind employer raises Alfred's wages, and there are jobs for everybody except the drunks. It is still the world of the *Wizard* and the *Gem*, except that there are orange blossoms instead of machine guns.

The outlook inculcated by all these papers is that of a rather exceptionally stupid member of the Navy League in the year 1910. Yes, it may be said, but what does it matter? And in any case, what else do you expect?

Of course no one in his senses would want to turn the so-called penny dreadful into a realistic novel or a socialist tract. An adventure story must of its nature be more or less remote from real life. But, as I have tried to make clear, the unreality of the *Wizard* and the *Gem* is not so artless as it looks. These papers exist because of a specialized demand, because boys at certain ages find it necessary to read about Martians, death rays, grizzly bears and gangsters. They get what they are looking for, but they get it wrapped up in the illusions which their future employers think suitable for them. To what extent people draw their ideas from fiction is disputable. Personally I believe that most people are influenced far more than they would care to admit by novels, serial stories, films and so forth, and that from this point of view the worst books are often the most important, because they are usually the ones that are read earliest in life. It is probable that many people who could consider themselves extremely sophisticated and "advanced" are actually carrying through life an imaginative background which they acquired in childhood from (for instance) Sapper* and Ian Hay.* If that is so, the boys' twopenny weeklies are of the deepest importance. Here is the stuff that is read somewhere between the ages of twelve and eighteen by a very large proportion, perhaps an actual majority, of English boys, including many who will never read anything else except newspapers – and along with it they are absorbing a set of beliefs which would be regarded as hopelessly out of date in the Central Office of the Conservative Party. All the better because it is done indirectly, there is being pumped into them the conviction that the major problems of our time do not exist, that there is nothing wrong with laissez-faire capitalism, that foreigners are unimportant comics and that the British Empire is a sort of charity concern which will last for ever. Considering who owns these papers, it is difficult to believe that this is unintentional. Of the twelve papers I have been discussing (i.e. twelve including the *Thriller* and *Detective Weekly*) seven are the property of the Amalgamated Press, which is one of the biggest press combines in the world and controls more than a hundred different papers. The *Gem* and *Magnet*, therefore, are closely linked up with the *Daily Telegraph* and the *Financial Times*. This in itself would be enough to rouse certain suspicions, even if it were not obvious that the stories in the boys' weeklies are politically vetted. So it appears that if you feel the need of a fantasy life in which you travel to Mars and fight lions bare-handed (and what boy doesn't?) you can only have it by delivering yourself over, mentally, to people like Lord Camrose.* For there is no competition. Throughout the whole of this run of papers the differences are negligible, and on this level no others exist. This raises the question, why is there no such thing as a left-wing boys' paper?

At first glance such an idea merely makes one slightly sick. It is so horribly easy to imagine what a left-wing boys' paper would be like, if it existed. I remember in 1920 or 1921 some optimistic person handing round communist tracts among a crowd of public-school boys. The tract I received was of the question-and-answer kind:

> Q. "Can a Boy communist be a Boy Scout, Comrade?"
> A. "No, Comrade."
> Q. "Why, Comrade?"
> A. "Because, Comrade, a Boy Scout must salute the Union Jack, which is the symbol of tyranny and oppression," etc. etc.

Now, suppose that at this moment somebody started a left-wing paper deliberately aimed at boys of twelve or fourteen. I do not suggest that the whole of its contents would be exactly like the tract I have quoted above, but does anyone doubt that they would be *something* like it? Inevitably such a paper would either consist of dreary uplift or it would be under communist influence and given over to adulation of Soviet Russia; in either case no normal boy would ever look at it. Highbrow literature apart, the whole of the existing left-wing press, in so far as it is at all vigorously "left", is one long tract. The one socialist paper in England which could live a week on its merits *as a paper* is the *Daily Herald*, and how much socialism is there in the *Daily Herald*? At this moment, therefore, a paper with a "left" slant and at the same time likely to have an appeal to ordinary boys in their teens is something almost beyond hoping for.

But it does not follow that it is impossible. There is no clear reason why every adventure story should necessarily be mixed up with snobbishness and gutter patriotism. For, after all, the stories in the *Hotspur* and the *Modern Boy* are not conservative tracts; they are merely adventure stories with a conservative bias. It is fairly easy to imagine the process being reversed. It is possible, for instance, to imagine a paper as thrilling and lively as the *Hotspur*, but with subject matter and "ideology" a little more up to date. It is even possible (though this raises other difficulties) to imagine a women's paper at the same literary level as the *Oracle*, dealing in approximately the same kind of story, but taking rather more account of the realities of working-class life. Such things have been done before, though not in England. In the last years of the Spanish monarchy there was a large output in Spain of left-wing novelettes, some of them evidently of anarchist origin. Unfortunately at the time when they were appearing I did not see their social significance, and I lost the collection of them that I had, but no doubt copies would still be procurable. In get-up and style of story they were very similar to the English fourpenny novelette, except that their inspiration was "left". If, for instance, a story described police pursuing anarchists through the mountains, it would be from the point of view of the anarchists and not of the police. An example nearer to hand is the Soviet film *Chapaiev*,* which has been shown a number of times in London. Technically, by the standards of the time when it was made, *Chapaiev* is a first-rate film, but mentally, in spite of the unfamiliar Russian background, it is not so very remote from Hollywood. The one thing that lifts it out of the ordinary is the remarkable performance by the actor who takes the part of the White officer (the fat one) – a performance which looks very like an inspired piece of gagging. Otherwise the atmosphere is familiar. All the usual paraphernalia is there – heroic fight against odds, escape at the last moment, shots of galloping horses, love interest, comic relief. The film is in fact a fairly ordinary one, except that its tendency is "left". In a Hollywood film of the Russian Civil War the Whites would probably be angels and the Reds demons. In the Russian version the Reds are angels and the Whites demons. That also is a lie, but, taking the long view, it is a less pernicious lie than the other.

Here several difficult problems present themselves. Their general nature is obvious enough, and I do not want to discuss them. I am merely pointing to the fact that, in England, popular imaginative literature is a field that left-wing thought has never begun to enter. *All* fiction from the novels in the mushroom libraries* downwards is censored in the interests of the ruling class. And boys' fiction above all, the blood-and-thunder stuff which nearly every boy devours at some time or other, is sodden in the worst illusions of 1910. The fact is only unimportant if one believes that what is read in childhood leaves no impression behind. Lord Camrose and his colleagues evidently believe nothing of the kind, and, after all, Lord Camrose ought to know.

Charles Dickens*

I

Dickens is one of those writers who are well worth stealing. Even the burial of his body in Westminster Abbey was a species of theft, if you come to think of it.

When Chesterton* wrote his introductions to the Everyman edition of Dickens's works, it seemed quite natural to him to credit Dickens with his own highly individual brand of medievalism, and more recently a Marxist writer, Mr T.A. Jackson, has made spirited efforts to turn Dickens into a bloodthirsty revolutionary.* The Marxist claims him as "almost" a Marxist, the Catholic claims him as "almost" a Catholic, and both claim him as a champion of the proletariat (or "the poor", as Chesterton would have put it). On the other hand, Nadezhda Krupskaya, in her little book on Lenin,* relates that towards the end of his life Lenin went to see a dramatized version of *The Cricket on the Hearth*,* and found Dickens's "middle-class sentimentality" so intolerable that he walked out in the middle of a scene.

Taking "middle-class" to mean what Krupskaya might be expected to mean by it, this was probably a truer judgement than those of Chesterton and Jackson. But it is worth noticing that the dislike of Dickens implied in this remark is something unusual. Plenty of people have found him unreadable, but very few seem to have felt any hostility towards the general spirit of his work. Some years ago Mr Bechhofer Roberts published a full-length attack on Dickens in the form of a novel (*This Side Idolatry*),* but it was a merely personal attack, concerned for the most part with Dickens's treatment of his wife. It dealt with incidents which not one in a thousand of Dickens's readers would ever hear about, and which no more invalidate his work than the second-best bed invalidates *Hamlet*.* All that the book really demonstrated was that a writer's literary personality has little or nothing to do with his private character. It is quite possible that in private life Dickens was just the kind of insensitive egoist that Mr Bechhofer Roberts makes him appear. But in his published work there is implied a personality quite different from this, a personality which has won him far more friends than enemies. It might well have been otherwise, for even if Dickens was a bourgeois, he was certainly a subversive writer, a radical, one might truthfully say a rebel. Everyone who has read widely in his work has felt this. Gissing,* for instance, the best of the writers on Dickens, was anything but a radical himself, and he disapproved of this strain in Dickens and wished it were not there, but it never occurred to him to deny it. In *Oliver Twist, Hard Times, Bleak House, Little Dorrit*,* Dickens attacked English institutions with a ferocity that has never since been approached. Yet he managed to do it without making himself hated, and, more than this, the very people he attacked have swallowed him so completely that he has become a national institution himself. In its attitude towards Dickens the English public has always been a little like the elephant which feels a blow with a walking stick as a delightful tickling. Before I was ten years old I was having Dickens ladled down my throat by schoolmasters in whom even at that age I could see a strong resemblance to Mr Creakle, and one knows without needing to be told that lawyers delight in Serjeant Buzfuz* and that *Little Dorrit* is a favourite in the Home Office. Dickens seems to have succeeded in attacking everybody and antagonizing nobody. Naturally this makes one wonder whether after all there was something unreal in his attack upon society. Where exactly does he stand, socially, morally and politically? As usual, one can define his position more easily if one starts by deciding what he was *not*.

In the first place he was *not*, as Messrs Chesterton and Jackson seem to imply, a "proletarian" writer. To begin with, he does not write about the proletariat, in which he merely resembles the overwhelming majority of novelists, past and present. If you look for the working classes in fiction, and especially English fiction, all you find is a hole. This statement needs qualifying, perhaps. For reasons that are easy enough to see, the agricultural labourer (in England a proletarian) gets a fairly good showing in fiction, and a great deal has been written about criminals, derelicts and, more recently, the working-class intelligentsia. But the ordinary town proletariat, the people who make the wheels go round, have always been ignored by novelists. When they do find their way between the covers of a book, it is nearly always as objects of pity or as comic relief. The central action of Dickens's stories almost invariably takes place in middle-class surroundings. If one examines his novels in detail one finds that his real subject matter is the London commercial bourgeoisie and their hangers-on – lawyers, clerks, tradesmen, innkeepers, small craftsmen and servants. He has no portrait of an agricultural worker, and only one (Stephen Blackpool in *Hard Times*) of an industrial worker. The Plornishes in *Little Dorrit* are probably his best picture of a working-class family – the Peggottys,* for instance, hardly belong to the working class – but on the whole he is not successful with this type of character. If you ask any ordinary reader which of Dickens's proletarian characters he can remember, the three he is almost certain to mention are Bill Sikes, Sam Weller and Mrs Gamp.* A burglar, a valet and a drunken midwife – not exactly a representative cross section of the English working class.

Secondly, in the ordinarily accepted sense of the word, Dickens is not a "revolutionary" writer. But his position here needs some defining.

Whatever else Dickens may have been, he was not a hole-and-corner soul-saver, the kind of well-meaning idiot who thinks that the world will be perfect if you amend a few by-laws and abolish a few anomalies. It is worth comparing him with Charles Reade,* for instance. Reade was a much better informed man than Dickens, and in some ways more public-spirited. He really hated the abuses he could understand, he showed them up in a series of novels which for all their absurdity are extremely readable, and he probably helped to alter public opinion on a few minor but important points. But it was quite beyond him to grasp that, given the existing form of society, certain evils *cannot* be remedied. Fasten upon this or that minor abuse, expose it, drag it into the open, bring it before a British jury, and all will be well – that is how he sees it. Dickens at any rate never imagined that you can cure pimples by cutting them off. In every page of his work one can see a consciousness that society is wrong somewhere at the root. It is when one asks "Which root?" that one begins to grasp his position.

The truth is that Dickens's criticism of society is almost exclusively moral. Hence the utter lack of any constructive suggestion anywhere in his work. He attacks the law, parliamentary government, the educational system and so forth, without ever clearly suggesting what he would put in their places. Of course it is not necessarily the business of a novelist, or a satirist, to make constructive suggestions, but the point is that Dickens's attitude is at bottom not even *destructive*. There is no clear sign that he wants the existing order to be overthrown, or that he believes it would make very much difference if it *were* overthrown. For in reality his target is not so much society as "human nature". It would be difficult to point anywhere in his books to a passage suggesting that the economic system is wrong *as a system*. Nowhere, for instance, does he make any attack on private enterprise or private property. Even in a book like *Our Mutual Friend*,* which turns on the power of corpses to interfere with living people by means of idiotic wills, it does not occur to him to suggest that individuals ought not to have this irresponsible power. Of course one can draw this inference for oneself, and one can draw it again from the remarks about Bounderby's will at the end of *Hard Times*, and indeed from the whole of Dickens's work one can infer the evil of laissez-faire capitalism – but Dickens makes no such inference himself. It is said that Macaulay* refused to review *Hard Times* because he disapproved of its "sullen socialism". Obviously Macaulay is here using the word "socialism" in the same sense in which, twenty years ago, a vegetarian meal or a Cubist picture used to be referred to as "Bolshevism". There is not a line in the book that can properly be called socialistic; indeed, its tendency if anything is pro-capitalist, because its whole moral is that capitalists ought to be kind, not that workers ought to be rebellious. Bounderby is a bullying windbag and Gradgrind has been morally blinded, but if they were better men, the system would work well enough – that, all through, is the implication. And so far as social criticism goes, one can never extract much more from Dickens than this, unless one deliberately reads meanings into him. His whole "message" is one that at first glance looks like an enormous platitude: if men would behave decently the world would be decent.

Naturally this calls for a few characters who are in positions of authority and who *do* behave decently. Hence that recurrent Dickens figure, the Good Rich Man. This character belongs especially to Dickens's early optimistic period. He is usually a "merchant" (we are not necessarily told what merchandise he deals in), and he is always a superhumanly kind-hearted old gentleman who "trots" to and fro, raising his employees' wages, patting children on the head, getting debtors out of jail and, in general, acting the fairy godmother. Of course he is a pure dream figure, much further from real life than, say, Squeers or Micawber.* Even Dickens must have reflected occasionally that anyone who was so anxious to give his money away would never have acquired it in the first place. Mr Pickwick,* for instance, had "been in the city", but it is difficult to imagine him making a fortune there. Nevertheless this character runs like a connecting thread through most of the earlier books. Pickwick, the Cheerybles, old Chuzzlewit, Scrooge* – it is the same figure over and over again, the good rich man, handing out guineas. Dickens does however show signs of development here. In the books of the middle period the good rich man fades out to some extent. There is no one who plays this part in *A Tale of Two Cities*, nor in *Great Expectations** – *Great Expectations* is, in fact, definitely an attack on patronage – and in *Hard Times* it is only very doubtfully played by Gradgrind after his reformation. The character reappears in a rather different form as Meagles in *Little Dorrit* and John Jarndyce in *Bleak House* – one might perhaps add Betsy Trotwood in *David Copperfield*. But in these books the good rich man has dwindled from a "merchant" to a rentier. This is significant. A rentier is part of the possessing class; he can and, almost without knowing it, does make other people work for him, but he has very little direct power. Unlike Scrooge or the Cheerybles, he cannot put everything right by raising everybody's wages. The seeming inference from the rather despondent books that Dickens wrote in the fifties is that by that time he had grasped the helplessness of well-meaning individuals in a corrupt society. Nevertheless in the last completed novel, *Our Mutual Friend** (published 1864–65), the good rich man comes back in full glory in the person of Boffin. Boffin is a proletarian by origin and only rich by inheritance, but he is the usual deus ex machina, solving everybody's problems by showering money in all directions. He even "trots" like the Cheerybles. In several ways *Our Mutual Friend* is a return to the earlier manner, and not an unsuccessful return either. Dickens's thoughts seem to have come full circle. Once again, individual kindliness is the remedy for everything.

One crying evil of his time that Dickens says very little about is child labour. There are plenty of pictures of suffering children in his books, but usually they are suffering in schools rather than in factories. The one detailed account of child labour that he gives is the description in *David Copperfield* of little David washing bottles in Murdstone & Grinby's warehouse. This, of course, is autobiography. Dickens himself, at the age of ten, had worked in Warren's blacking factory in the Strand, very much as he describes it here. It was a terribly bitter memory to him, partly because he felt the whole incident to be discreditable to his parents, and he even concealed it from his wife till long after they were married. Looking back on this period, he says in *David Copperfield*:

> It is a matter of some surprise to me, even now, that I can have been so easily thrown away at such an age. A child of excellent abilities and with strong powers of observation, quick, eager, delicate, and soon hurt bodily or mentally, it seems wonderful to me that nobody should have made any sign in my behalf. But none was made; and I became, at ten years old, a little labouring hind in the service of Murdstone & Grinby.

And again, having described the rough boys among whom he worked:

> No words can express the secret agony of my soul as I sunk into this companionship [...] and felt my hopes of growing up to be a learned and distinguished man crushed in my bosom.

Obviously it is not David Copperfield who is speaking; it is Dickens himself. He uses almost the same words in the autobiography that he began and abandoned a few months earlier. Of course Dickens is right in saying that a gifted child ought not to work ten hours a day pasting labels on bottles, but what he does not say is that *no* child ought to be condemned to such a fate, and there is no reason for inferring that he thinks it. David escapes from the warehouse, but Mick Walker and Mealy Potatoes and the others are still there, and there is no sign that this troubles Dickens particularly. As usual, he displays no consciousness that the *structure* of society can be changed. He despises politics, does not believe that any good can come out of Parliament – he had been a parliamentary shorthand writer, which was no doubt a disillusioning experience – and he is slightly hostile to the most hopeful movement of his day, trade unionism. In *Hard Times* trade unionism is represented as something not much better than a racket, something that happens because employers are not sufficiently paternal. Stephen Blackpool's refusal to join the union is rather a virtue in Dickens's eyes. Also, as Mr Jackson has pointed out, the apprentices' association in *Barnaby Rudge*,* to which Sim Tappertit belongs, is probably a hit at the illegal or barely legal unions of Dickens's own day, with their secret assemblies, passwords and so forth. Obviously he wants the workers to be decently treated, but there is no sign that he wants them to take their destiny into their own hands, least of all by open violence.

As it happens, Dickens deals with revolution in the narrower sense in two novels, *Barnaby Rudge* and *A Tale of Two Cities*. In *Barnaby Rudge* it is a case of rioting rather than revolution. The Gordon Riots of 1780,* though they had religious bigotry as a pretext, seem to have been little more than a pointless outburst of looting. Dickens's attitude to this kind of thing is sufficiently indicated by the fact that his first idea was to make the ringleaders of the riots three lunatics escaped from an asylum. He was dissuaded from this, but the principal figure of the book is in fact a village idiot. In the chapters dealing with the riots Dickens shows a most profound horror of mob violence. He delights in describing scenes in which the "dregs" of the population behave with atrocious bestiality. These chapters are of great psychological interest, because they show how deeply he had brooded on this subject. The things he describes can only have come out of his imagination, for no riots on anything like the same scale had happened in his lifetime. Here is one of his descriptions, for instance:

> If Bedlam gates had been flung open wide, there would not have issued forth such maniacs as the frenzy of that night had made. There were men there who danced and trampled on the beds of flowers as though they trod down human enemies, and wrenched them from their stalks, like savages who twisted human necks. There were men who cast their lighted torches in the air, and suffered them to fall upon their heads and faces, blistering the skin with deep unseemly burns. There were men who rushed up to the fire, and paddled in it with their hands as if in water; and others who were restrained by force from plunging in, to gratify their deadly longing. On the skull of one drunken lad – not twenty, by his looks – who lay upon the ground with a bottle to his mouth, the lead from the roof came streaming down in a shower of liquid fire, white hot, melting his head like wax. [...] But of all the howling throng not one learnt mercy from, or sickened at, these sights; nor was the fierce, besotted, senseless rage of one man glutted.

You might almost think you were reading a description of "red" Spain by a partisan of General Franco. One ought, of course, to remember that when Dickens was writing, the London "mob" still existed. (Nowadays there is no mob, only a flock.) Low wages and the growth and shift of population had brought into existence a huge, dangerous slum proletariat, and until the early middle of the nineteenth century there was hardly such a thing as a police force. When the brickbats began to fly there was nothing between shuttering your windows and ordering the troops to open fire. In *A Tale of Two Cities* he is dealing with a revolution which was really *about* something, and Dickens's attitude is different, but not entirely different. As a matter of fact, *A Tale of Two Cities* is a book which tends to leave a false impression behind, especially after a lapse of time.

The one thing that everyone who has read *A Tale of Two Cities* remembers is the Reign of Terror.* The whole book is dominated by the guillotine – tumbrils thundering to and fro, bloody knives, heads bouncing into the basket and sinister old women knitting as they watch. Actually these scenes only occupy a few chapters, but they are written with terrible intensity, and the rest of the book is rather slow going. But *A Tale of Two Cities* is not a companion volume to *The Scarlet Pimpernel*.* Dickens sees clearly enough that the French Revolution was bound to happen and that many of the people who were executed deserved what they got. If, he says, you behave as the French aristocracy had behaved, vengeance will follow. He repeats this over and over again. We are constantly being reminded that while "my lord" is lolling in bed, with four liveried footmen serving his chocolate and the peasants starving outside, somewhere in the forest a tree is growing which will presently be sawn into planks for the platform of the guillotine, etc. etc. etc. The inevitability of the Terror, given its causes, is insisted upon in the clearest terms:

> It was too much the way [...] to talk of this terrible Revolution as if it were the only harvest ever known under the skies that had not been sown – as if nothing had ever been done, or omitted to be done, that had led to it – as if observers of the wretched millions in France, and of the misused and perverted resources that should have made them prosperous, had not seen it inevitably coming, years before, and had not in plain terms recorded what they saw.

And again:

> All the devouring and insatiate monsters imagined since imagination could record itself, are fused in the one realization, Guillotine. And yet there is not in France, with its rich variety of soil and climate, a blade, a leaf, a root, a sprig, a peppercorn, which will grow to maturity under conditions more certain than those that have produced this horror. Crush humanity out of shape once more, under similar hammers, and it will twist itself into the same tortured forms.

In other words, the French aristocracy had dug their own graves. But there is no perception here of what is now called historic necessity. Dickens sees that the results are inevitable, given the causes, but he thinks that the causes might have been avoided. The Revolution is something that happens because centuries of oppression have made the French peasantry subhuman. If the wicked nobleman could somehow have turned over a new leaf, like Scrooge, there would have been no Revolution, no jacquerie, no guillotine – and so much the better. This is the opposite of the "revolutionary" attitude. From the "revolutionary" point of view the class struggle is the main source of progress, and therefore the nobleman who robs the peasant and goads him to revolt is playing a necessary part, just as much as the Jacobin who guillotines the nobleman. Dickens never writes anywhere a line that can be interpreted as meaning this. Revolution as he sees it is merely a monster that is begotten by tyranny and always ends by devouring its own instruments. In Sydney Carton's vision at the foot of the guillotine, he foresees Defarge and the other leading spirits of the Terror all perishing under the same knife – which, in fact, was approximately what happened.

And Dickens is very sure that revolution *is* a monster. That is why everyone remembers the revolutionary scenes in *A Tale of Two Cities*; they have the quality of nightmare, and it is Dickens's own nightmare. Again and again he insists upon the meaningless horrors of revolution – the mass butcheries, the injustice, the ever-present terror of spies, the frightful bloodlust of the mob. The descriptions of the Paris mob – the description, for instance, of the crowd of murderers struggling round the grindstone to sharpen their weapons before butchering the prisoners in the September massacres – outdo anything in *Barnaby Rudge*. The revolutionaries appear to him simply as degraded savages – in fact, as lunatics. He broods over their frenzies with a curious imaginative intensity. He describes them dancing the "Carmagnole", for instance:

> There could not be fewer than five hundred people, and they were dancing like five thousand demons. [...] They danced to the popular Revolution song, keeping a ferocious time that was like a gnashing of teeth in unison. [...] They advanced, retreated, struck at one another's hands, clutched at one another's heads, spun round alone, caught one another, and spun round in pairs, until many of them dropped. [...] Suddenly they stopped again, paused, struck out the time afresh, forming into lines the width of the public way, and, with their heads low down and their hands high up, swooped screaming off. No fight could have been half so terrible as this dance. It was so emphatically a fallen sport – a something, once innocent, delivered over to all devilry.

He even credits some of these wretches with a taste for guillotining children. The passage I have abridged above ought to be read in full. It and others like it show how deep was Dickens's horror of revolutionary hysteria. Notice, for instance, that touch, "with their heads low down and their hands high up" etc., and the evil vision it conveys. Madame Defarge is a truly dreadful figure, certainly Dickens's most successful attempt at a *malignant* character. Defarge and others are simply "the new oppressors who have risen on the destruction of the old", the revolutionary courts are presided over by "the lowest, cruellest and worst populace", and so on and so forth. All the way through Dickens insists upon the nightmare insecurity of a revolutionary period, and in this he shows a great deal of prescience. "A law of the suspected, which struck away all security for liberty or life, and delivered over any good and innocent person to any bad and guilty one; prisons gorged with people who had committed no offence, and could obtain no hearing" – it would apply pretty accurately to several countries today.

The apologists of any revolution generally try to minimize its horrors; Dickens's impulse is to exaggerate them – and from a historical point of view he has certainly exaggerated. Even the Reign of Terror was a much smaller thing than he makes it appear. Though he quotes no figures, he gives the impression of a frenzied massacre lasting for years, whereas in reality the whole of the Terror, so far as the number of deaths goes, was a joke compared with one of Napoleon's battles. But the bloody knives and the tumbrils rolling to and fro create in his mind a special, sinister vision which he has succeeded in passing on to generations of readers. Thanks to Dickens, the very word "tumbril" has a murderous sound; one forgets that a tumbril is only a sort of farm cart. To this day, to the average Englishman, the French Revolution means no more than a pyramid of severed heads. It is a strange thing that Dickens, much more in sympathy with the ideas of the Revolution than most Englishmen of his time, should have played a part in creating this impression.

If you hate violence and don't believe in politics, the only major remedy remaining is education. Perhaps society is past praying for, but there is always hope for the individual human being, if you can catch him young enough. This belief partly accounts for Dickens's preoccupation with childhood.

No one, at any rate no English writer, has written better about childhood than Dickens. In spite of all the knowledge that has accumulated since, in spite of the fact that children are now comparatively sanely treated, no novelist has shown the same power of entering into the child's point of view. I must have been about nine years old when I first read *David Copperfield*. The mental atmosphere of the opening chapters was so immediately intelligible to me that I vaguely imagined they had been written *by a child*. And yet when one rereads the book as an adult and sees the Murdstones, for instance, dwindle from gigantic figures of doom into semi-comic monsters, these passages lose nothing. Dickens has been able to stand both inside and outside the child's mind, in such a way that the same scene can be wild burlesque or sinister reality, according to the age at which one reads it. Look, for instance, at the scene in which David Copperfield is unjustly suspected of eating the mutton chops; or the scene in which Pip, in *Great Expectations*, coming back from Miss Havisham's house and finding himself completely unable to describe what he has seen, takes refuge in a series of outrageous lies – which, of course, are eagerly believed. All the isolation of childhood is there. And how accurately he has recorded the mechanisms of the child's mind, its visualizing tendency, its sensitiveness to certain kinds of impression. Pip relates how in his childhood his ideas about his dead parents were derived from their tombstones:

> The shape of the letters on my father's, gave me an odd idea that he was a square, stout, dark man, with curly black hair. From the character and turn of the inscription, "ALSO GEORGIANA, WIFE OF THE ABOVE", I drew a childish conclusion that my mother was freckled and sickly. To five little stone lozenges, each about a foot and a half long, which were arranged in a neat row beside their grave, and were sacred to the memory of five little brothers of mine [...] I am indebted for a belief I religiously entertained that they had all been born on their backs with their hands in their trouser pockets, and had never taken them out in this state of existence.

There is a similar passage in *David Copperfield*. After biting Mr Murdstone's hand, David is sent away to school and obliged to wear on his back a placard saying *Take care of him. He bites*. He looks at the door in the playground where the boys have carved their names, and from the appearance of each name he seems to know in just what tone of voice the boy will read out the placard:

> There was one boy – a certain J. Steerforth – who cut his name very deep and very often, who, I conceived, would read it in a rather strong voice, and afterwards pull my hair. There was another boy, one Tommy Traddles, who I dreaded would make game of it, and pretend to be dreadfully frightened of me. There was a third, George Demple, who I fancied would sing it.

When I read this passage as a child, it seemed to me that those were exactly the pictures that those particular names would call up. The reason, of course, is the sound associations of the words (Demple – "temple"; Traddles – probably "skedaddle"). But how many people, before Dickens, had ever noticed such things? A sympathetic attitude towards children was a much rarer thing in Dickens's day than it is now. The early nineteenth century was not a good time to be a child. In Dickens's youth children were still being "solemnly tried at a criminal bar, where they were held up to be seen",* and it was not so long since boys of thirteen had been hanged for petty theft. The doctrine of "breaking the child's spirit" was in full vigour, and *The Fairchild Family** was a standard book for children till late into the century. This evil book is now issued in pretty-pretty expurgated editions, but it is well worth reading in the original version. It gives one some idea of the lengths to which child discipline was sometimes carried. Mr Fairchild, for instance, when he catches his children quarrelling, first thrashes them, reciting Doctor Watts's "Let dogs delight to bark and bite"* between blows of the cane, and then takes them to spend the afternoon beneath a gibbet where the rotting corpse of a murderer is hanging. In the earlier part of the century scores of thousands of children, aged sometimes as young as six, were literally worked to death in the mines or cotton mills, and even at the fashionable public schools boys were flogged till they ran with blood for a mistake in their Latin verses. One thing which Dickens seems to have recognized, and which most of his contemporaries did not, is the sadistic sexual element in flogging. I think this can be inferred from *David Copperfield* and *Nicholas Nickleby*. But mental cruelty to a child infuriates him as much as physical, and though there is a fair number of exceptions, his schoolmasters are generally scoundrels.

Except for the universities and the big public schools, every kind of education then existing in England gets a mauling at Dickens's hands. There is Doctor Blimber's Academy, where little boys are blown up with Greek until they burst, and the revolting charity schools of the period, which produced specimens like Noah Claypole and Uriah Heep, and Salem House, and Dotheboys Hall, and the disgraceful little dame school kept by Mr Wopsle's great-aunt.* Some of what Dickens says remains true even today. Salem House is the ancestor of the modern "prep school", which still has a good deal of resemblance to it – and as for Mr Wopsle's great-aunt, some old fraud of much the same stamp is carrying on at this moment in nearly every small town in England. But, as usual, Dickens's criticism is neither creative nor destructive. He sees the idiocy of an educational system founded on the Greek lexicon and the wax-ended cane; on the other hand, he has no use for the new kind of school that is coming up in the fifties and sixties, the "modern" school, with its gritty insistence on "facts". What, then, *does* he want? As always, what he appears to want is a moralized version of the existing thing – the old type of school, but with no caning, no bullying or underfeeding, and not quite so much Greek. Doctor Strong's school, to which David Copperfield goes after he escapes from Murdstone & Grinby's, is simply Salem House with the vices left out and a good deal of "old grey stones" atmosphere thrown in:

> Doctor Strong's was an excellent school, as different from Mr Creakle's as good is from evil. It was very gravely and decorously ordered, and on a sound system; with an appeal, in everything, to the honour and good faith of the boys [...] which worked wonders. We all felt that we had a part in the management of the place, and in sustaining its character and dignity. Hence, we soon became warmly attached to it – I am sure I did for one, and I never knew, in all my time, of any boy being otherwise – and learnt with

a good will, desiring to do it credit. We had noble games out of hours, and plenty of liberty; but even then, as I remember, we were well spoken of in the town, and rarely did any disgrace, by our appearance or manner, to the reputation of Doctor Strong and Doctor Strong's boys.

In the woolly vagueness of this passage one can see Dickens's utter lack of any educational theory. He can imagine the *moral* atmosphere of a good school, but nothing further. The boys "learnt with a good will", but what did they learn? No doubt it was Doctor Blimber's curriculum, a little watered down. Considering the attitude to society that is everywhere implied in Dickens's novels, it comes as rather a shock to learn that he sent his eldest son to Eton and sent all his children through the ordinary educational mill. Gissing seems to think that he may have done this because he was painfully conscious of being undereducated himself. Here perhaps Gissing is influenced by his own love of classical learning. Dickens had had little or no formal education, but he lost nothing by missing it, and on the whole he seems to have been aware of this. If he was unable to imagine a better school than Doctor Strong's, or, in real life, than Eton, it was probably due to an intellectual deficiency rather different from the one Gissing suggests.

It seems that in every attack Dickens makes upon society he is always pointing to a change of spirit rather than a change of structure. It is hopeless to try and pin him down to any definite remedy, still more to any political doctrine. His approach is always along the moral plane, and his attitude is sufficiently summed up in that remark about Strong's school being as different from Creakle's "as good is from evil". Two things can be very much alike and yet abysmally different. Heaven and hell are in the same place. Useless to change institutions without a "change of heart" – that, essentially, is what he is always saying.

If that were all, he might be no more than a cheer-up writer, a reactionary humbug. A "change of heart" is in fact *the* alibi of people who do not wish to endanger the status quo. But Dickens is not a humbug, except in minor matters, and the strongest single impression one carries away from his books is that of a hatred of tyranny. I said earlier that Dickens is not *in the accepted sense* a revolutionary writer. But it is not at all certain that a merely moral criticism of society may not be just as "revolutionary" – and revolution, after all, means turning things upside down – as the politico-economic criticism which is fashionable at this moment. Blake was not a politician, but there is more understanding of the nature of capitalist society in a poem like "I wander through each charter'd street"* than in three quarters of socialist literature. Progress is not an illusion, it happens, but it is slow and invariably disappointing. There is always a new tyrant waiting to take over from the old – generally not quite so bad, but still a tyrant. Consequently two viewpoints are always tenable. The one, how can you improve human nature until you have changed the system? The other, what is the use of changing the system before you have improved human nature? They appeal to different individuals, and they probably show a tendency to alternate in point of time. The moralist and the revolutionary are constantly undermining one another. Marx exploded a hundred tons of dynamite beneath the moralist position, and we are still living in the echo of that tremendous crash. But already, somewhere or other, the sappers are at work and fresh dynamite is being stamped in place to blow Marx at the moon. Then Marx, or somebody like him, will come back with yet more dynamite, and so the process continues, to an end we cannot yet foresee. The central problem – how to prevent power from being abused – remains unsolved. Dickens, who had not the vision to see that private property is an obstructive nuisance, had the vision to see that. "If men would behave decently the world would be decent" is not such a platitude as it sounds.

II

More completely than most writers, perhaps, Dickens can be explained in terms of his social origin, though actually his family history was not quite what one would infer from his novels. His father was a clerk in government service, and through his mother's family he had connections with both the army and the navy. But from the age of nine onwards he was brought up in London in commercial surroundings, and generally in an atmosphere of struggling poverty. Mentally he belongs to the small urban bourgeoisie, and he happens to be an exceptionally fine specimen of this class, with all the "points", as it were, very highly developed. That is partly what makes him so interesting. If one wants a modern equivalent, the nearest would be H.G. Wells, who has had a rather similar history and who obviously owes something to Dickens as a novelist. Arnold Bennett* was essentially of the same type, but, unlike the other two, he was a Midlander, with an industrial and Nonconformist rather than commercial and Anglican background.

The great disadvantage, and advantage, of the small urban bourgeois is his limited outlook. He sees the world as a middle-class world, and everything outside these limits is either laughable or slightly wicked. On the one hand, he has no contact with industry or the soil; on the other no contact with the governing classes. Anyone who has studied Wells's novels in detail will have noticed that though he hates the aristocrat like poison, he has no particular objection to the plutocrat, and no enthusiasm for the proletarian. His most hated types, the people he believes to be responsible for all human ills, are kings, landowners, priests, nationalists, soldiers, scholars and peasants. At first sight a list beginning with kings and ending with peasants looks like a mere omnium gatherum,* but in reality all these people have a common factor. All of them are archaic types, people who are governed by tradition and whose eyes are turned towards the past – the opposite, therefore, of the rising bourgeois who has put his money on the future and sees the past simply as a dead hand.

Actually, although Dickens lived in a period when the bourgeoisie was really a rising class, he displays this characteristic less strongly than Wells. He is almost unconscious of the future and has a rather sloppy love of the picturesque (the "quaint old church" etc.). Nevertheless his list of most hated types is like enough to Wells's for the similarity to be striking. He is vaguely on the side of the working class – has a sort of generalized sympathy with them because they are oppressed – but he does not in reality know much about them; they come into his books chiefly as servants, and comic servants at that. At the other end of the scale he loathes the aristocrat and – going one better than Wells in this – loathes the big bourgeois as well. His real sympathies are bounded by Mr Pickwick on the upper side and Mr Barkis on the lower. But the term "aristocrat", for the type Dickens hates, is vague and needs defining.

Actually Dickens's target is not so much the great aristocracy, who hardly enter into his books, as their petty offshoots, the cadging dowagers who live up mews in Mayfair, and the bureaucrats and professional soldiers. All through his books there are countless hostile sketches of these people, and hardly any that are friendly. There are practically no friendly pictures of the landowning class, for instance. One might make a doubtful exception of Sir Leicester Dedlock; otherwise there is only Mr Wardle (who is a stock figure – the "good old squire") and Haredale in *Barnaby Rudge*, who has Dickens's sympathy because he is a persecuted Catholic. There are no friendly pictures of soldiers (i.e. officers), and none at all of naval men. As for his bureaucrats, judges and magistrates, most of them would feel quite at home in the Circumlocution Office.* The only officials whom Dickens handles with any kind of friendliness are, significantly enough, policemen.

Dickens's attitude is easily intelligible to an Englishman, because it is part of the English puritan tradition, which is not dead even at this day. The class Dickens belonged to, at least by adoption, was growing suddenly rich after a couple of centuries of obscurity. It had grown up mainly in the big towns, out of contact with agriculture, and politically impotent; government, in its experience, was something which either interfered or persecuted. Consequently it was a class with no tradition of public service and not much tradition of usefulness. What now strikes us as remarkable about the new moneyed class of the nineteenth century is their complete irresponsibility; they see everything in terms of individual success, with hardly any consciousness that the community exists. On the other hand, a Tite Barnacle, even when he was neglecting his duties, would have some vague notion of what duties he was neglecting. Dickens's attitude is never irresponsible; still less does he take the money-grubbing Smilesian line* – but at the back of his mind there is usually a half-belief that the whole apparatus of government is unnecessary. Parliament is simply Lord Coodle and Sir Thomas Doodle, the Empire is simply Major Bagstock and his Indian servant, the army is simply Colonel Chowser and Doctor Slammer, the public services are simply Bumble and the Circumlocution Office – and so on and so forth. What he does not see, or only intermittently sees, is that Coodle and Doodle and all the other corpses left over from the eighteenth century *are* performing a function which neither Pickwick nor Boffin would ever bother about.

And of course this narrowness of vision is in one way a great advantage to him, because it is fatal for a caricaturist to see too much. From Dickens's point of view "good" society is simply a collection of village idiots. What a crew! Lady Tippins! Mrs Gowan! Lord Verisopht! The Honourable Bob Stables! Mrs Sparsit (whose husband was a Powler)! The Tite Barnacles! Nupkins! It is practically a casebook in lunacy. But at the same time his remoteness from the landowning-military-bureaucratic class incapacitates him for full-length satire. He only succeeds with this class when he depicts them as mental defectives. The accusation which used to be made against Dickens in his lifetime, that he "could not paint a gentleman", was an absurdity, but it is true in this sense, that what he says against the "gentleman" class is seldom very damaging. Sir Mulberry Hawk, for instance, is a wretched attempt at the wicked baronet type. Harthouse in *Hard Times* is better, but he would be only an ordinary achievement for Trollope or Thackeray. Trollope's thoughts hardly move outside the "gentleman" class, but Thackeray has the great advantage of having a foot in two moral camps. In some ways his outlook is very similar to Dickens's. Like Dickens, he identifies with the puritanical moneyed class against the card-playing, debt-bilking aristocracy. The eighteenth century, as he sees it, is sticking out into the nineteenth in the person of the wicked Lord Steyne. *Vanity Fair** is a full-length version of what Dickens did for a few chapters in *Little Dorrit*. But by origins and upbringing Thackeray happens to be somewhat nearer to the class he is satirizing. Consequently he can produce such comparatively subtle types as, for instance, Major Pendennis and Rawdon Crawley.* Major Pendennis is a shallow old snob, and Rawdon Crawley is a thick-headed ruffian who sees nothing wrong in living for years by swindling tradesmen – but what Thackeray realizes is that according to their tortuous code they are neither of them bad men. Major Pendennis would not sign a dud cheque, for instance. Rawdon certainly would, but on the other hand he would not desert a friend in a tight corner. Both of them would behave well on the field of battle – a thing that would not particularly appeal to Dickens. The result is that at the end one is left with a kind of amused tolerance for Major Pendennis and with something approaching respect for Rawdon – and yet one sees, better than any diatribe could make one, the utter rottenness of that kind of cadging, toadying life on the fringes of smart society. Dickens would be quite incapable of this. In his hands both Rawdon and the major would dwindle to traditional caricatures. And, on the whole, his attacks on "good" society are rather perfunctory. The aristocracy and the big bourgeoisie exist in his books chiefly as a kind of "noises off", a haw-hawing chorus somewhere in the wings, like Podsnap's dinner parties. When he produces a really subtle and damaging portrait, like John Dorrit or Harold Skimpole, it is generally of some rather middling, unimportant person.

One very striking thing about Dickens, especially considering the time he lived in, is his lack of vulgar nationalism. All peoples who have reached the point of becoming nations tend to despise foreigners, but there is not much doubt that the English-speaking races are the worst offenders. One can see this from the fact that as soon as they become fully aware of any foreign race, they invent an insulting nickname for it. Wop, Dago, Froggy, Squarehead, Kike, Sheeny, Nigger, Wog, Chink, Greaser, Yellowbelly – these are merely a selection. Any time before 1870 the list would have been shorter, because the map of the world was different from what it is now, and there were only three or four foreign races that had fully entered into the English consciousness. But towards these, and especially towards France, the nearest and best-hated nation, the English attitude of patronage was so intolerable that English "arrogance" and "xenophobia" are still a legend. And of course they are not a completely untrue legend even now. Till very recently nearly all English children were brought up to despise the southern European races, and history as taught in schools was mainly a list of battles won by England. But one has got to read, say, the *Quarterly Review** of the 1830s to know what boasting really is. Those were the days when the English built up their legend of themselves as "sturdy islanders" and "stubborn hearts of oak" and when it was accepted as a kind of scientific fact that one Englishman was the equal of three foreigners. All through nineteenth-century novels and comic papers there runs the traditional figure of the "Froggy" – a small ridiculous man with a tiny beard and a pointed top hat, always jabbering and gesticulating, vain, frivolous and fond of boasting of his martial exploits, but generally taking to flight when real danger appears. Over against him was John Bull, the "sturdy English yeoman",* or (a more public-school version) the "strong, silent Englishman" of Charles Kingsley,* Tom Hughes* and others.

Thackeray, for instance, has this outlook very strongly, though there are moments when he sees through it and laughs at it. The one historical fact that is firmly fixed in his mind is that the English won the battle of Waterloo. One never reads far in his books without coming upon some reference to it. The English, as he sees it, are invincible because of their tremendous physical strength, due mainly to living on beef. Like most Englishmen of his time, he has the curious illusion that the English are larger than other people (Thackeray, as it happened, *was* larger than most people), and therefore he is capable of writing passages like this:

I say to you that you are better than a Frenchman. I would lay even money that you who are reading this are more than five feet seven in height, and weigh eleven stone; while a Frenchman is five feet four and does not weigh nine. The Frenchman has after his soup a dish of vegetables, where you have one of meat. You are a different and superior animal – a French-beating animal (the history of hundreds of years has shown you to be so)...* etc. etc.

There are similar passages scattered all through Thackeray's works. Dickens would never be guilty of anything of the kind. It would be an exaggeration to say that he nowhere pokes fun at foreigners, and of course, like nearly all nineteenth-century Englishmen, he is untouched by European culture. But never anywhere does he indulge in the typical English boasting, the "island race", "bulldog breed", "right little tight little island" style of talk. In the whole of *A Tale of Two Cities* there is not a line that could be taken as meaning "Look how these wicked Frenchmen behave!" The one place where he seems to display a normal hatred of foreigners is in the American chapters of *Martin Chuzzlewit*. This, however, is simply the reaction of a generous mind against cant. If Dickens were alive today he would make a trip to Soviet Russia and come back with a book rather like Gide's *Retour de l'URSS*.* But he is remarkably free from the idiocy of regarding nations as individuals. He seldom even makes jokes turning on nationality. He does not exploit the comic Irishman and the comic Welshman, for instance, and not because he objects to stock characters and ready-made jokes, which obviously he does not. It is perhaps more significant that he shows no prejudice against Jews. It is true that he takes it for granted (*Oliver Twist* and *Great Expectations*) that a receiver of stolen goods will be a Jew, which at the time was probably justified. But the "Jew joke", endemic in English literature until the rise of Hitler, does not appear in his books, and in *Our Mutual Friend* he makes a pious though not very convincing attempt to stand up for the Jews.

Dickens's lack of vulgar nationalism is in part the mark of a real largeness of mind, and in part results from his negative, rather unhelpful political attitude. He is very much an Englishman, but he is hardly aware of it – certainly the thought of being an Englishman does not thrill him. He has no imperialist feeling, no discernible views on foreign politics, and is untouched by the military tradition. Temperamentally he is much nearer to the small Nonconformist tradesman who looks down on the "redcoats" and thinks that war is wicked – a one-eyed view, but, after all, war *is* wicked. It is noticeable that Dickens hardly writes of war, even to denounce it. With all his marvellous powers of description, and of describing things he had never seen, he never describes a battle, unless one counts the attack on the Bastille in *A Tale of Two Cities*. Probably the subject would not strike him as interesting, and in any case he would not regard a battlefield as a place where anything worth settling could be settled. It is one up to the lower-middle-class, puritan mentality.

III

Dickens had grown up near enough to poverty to be terrified of it, and in spite of his generosity of mind, he is not free from the special prejudices of the shabby-genteel. It is usual to claim him as a "popular" writer, a champion of the "oppressed masses". So he is, so long as he thinks of them as oppressed – but there are two things that condition his attitude. In the first place, he is a south of England man, and a cockney at that, and therefore out of touch with the bulk of the real oppressed masses, the industrial and agricultural labourers. It is interesting to see how Chesterton, another cockney, always presents Dickens as the spokesman of "the poor", without showing much awareness of who "the poor" really are. To Chesterton "the poor" means small shopkeepers and servants. Sam Weller, he says, "is the great symbol in English literature of the populace peculiar to England" – and Sam Weller is a valet! The other point is that Dickens's early experiences have given him a horror of proletarian roughness. He shows this unmistakably whenever he writes of the very poorest of the poor, the slum dwellers. His descriptions of the London slums are always full of undisguised repulsion:

> The ways were foul and narrow; the shops and houses wretched; and people half naked, drunken, slipshod and ugly. Alleys and archways, like so many cesspools, disgorged their offences of smell, and dirt, and life, upon the straggling streets; and the whole quarter reeked with crime, and filth, and misery... etc. etc.*

There are many similar passages in Dickens. From them one gets the impression of whole submerged populations whom he regards as being beyond the pale. In rather the same way the modern doctrinaire socialist contemptuously writes off a large block of the population as "lumpenproletariat". Dickens also shows less understanding of criminals than one would expect of him. Although he is well aware of the social and economic causes of crime, he often seems to feel that when a man has once broken the law he has put himself outside human society. There is a chapter at the end of *David Copperfield* in which David visits the prison where Littimer and Uriah Heep are serving their sentences. Dickens actually seems to regard the horrible "model" prisons, against which Charles Reade delivered his memorable attack in *It Is Never Too Late to Mend*,* as too humane. He complains that the food is too good! As soon as he comes up against crime or the worst depths of poverty, he shows traces of the "I've always kept myself respectable" habit of mind.

The attitude of Pip (obviously the attitude of Dickens himself) towards Magwitch in *Great Expectations* is extremely interesting. Pip is conscious all along of his ingratitude towards Joe, but far less so of his ingratitude towards

Magwitch. When he discovers that the person who has loaded him with benefits for years is actually a transported convict, he falls into frenzies of disgust. "The abhorrence in which I held the man, the dread I had of him, the repugnance with which I shrank from him, could not have been exceeded if he had been some terrible beast," etc. etc. So far as one can discover from the text, this is not because when Pip was a child he had been terrorized by Magwitch in the churchyard; it is because Magwitch is a criminal and a convict. There is an even more "kept-myself-respectable" touch in the fact that Pip feels as a matter of course that he cannot take Magwitch's money. The money is not the product of a crime, it has been honestly acquired – but it is an ex-convict's money and therefore "tainted". There is nothing psychologically false in this, either. Psychologically the latter part of *Great Expectations* is about the best thing Dickens ever did; throughout this part of the book one feels: "Yes, that is just how Pip would have behaved." But the point is that in the matter of Magwitch, Dickens identifies with Pip, and his attitude is at bottom snobbish. The result is that Magwitch belongs to the same queer class of characters as Falstaff and, probably, Don Quixote – characters who are more pathetic than the author intended.

When it is a question of the non-criminal poor, the ordinary, decent, labouring poor, there is of course nothing contemptuous in Dickens's attitude. He has the sincerest admiration for people like the Peggottys and the Plornishes. But it is questionable whether he really regards them as equals. It is of the greatest interest to read Chapter XI of *David Copperfield* and side by side with it the autobiographical fragment (parts of this are given in Forster's *Life*)* in which Dickens expresses his feelings about the blacking factory episode a great deal more strongly than in the novel. For more than twenty years afterwards the memory was so painful to him that he would go out of his way to avoid that part of the Strand. He says that to pass that way "made me cry, after my eldest child could speak". The text makes it quite clear that what hurt him most of all, then and in retrospect, was the enforced contact with "low" associates:

> No words can express the secret agony of my soul as I sunk into this companionship; compared these everyday associates with those of my happier childhood. [...] But I held some station at the blacking warehouse too. [...] I soon became at least as expeditious and as skilful with my hands as either of the other boys. Though perfectly familiar with them, my conduct and manners were different enough from theirs to place a space between us. They, and the men, always spoke of me as "the young gentleman". A certain man [...] used to call me "Charles" sometimes in speaking to me; but I think it was mostly when we were very confidential. [...] Poll Green uprose once, and rebelled against the "young-gentleman" usage; but Bob Fagin settled him speedily.

It was as well that there should be "a space between us", you see. However much Dickens may admire the working classes, he does not wish to resemble them. Given his origins, and the time he lived in, it could hardly be otherwise. In the early nineteenth century class animosities may have been no sharper than they are now, but the surface differences between class and class were enormously greater. The "gentleman" and the "common man" must have seemed like different species of animal. Dickens is quite genuinely on the side of the poor against the rich, but it would be next door to impossible for him not to think of a working-class exterior as a stigma. In one of Tolstoy's fables the peasants of a certain village judge every stranger who arrives from the state of his hands. If his palms are hard from work, they let him in; if his palms are soft, out he goes. This would be hardly intelligible to Dickens; all his heroes have soft hands. His younger heroes – Nicholas Nickleby, Martin Chuzzlewit, Edward Chester, David Copperfield, John Harmon – are usually of the type known as "walking gentlemen". He likes a bourgeois exterior and a bourgeois (not aristocratic) accent. One curious symptom of this is that he will not allow anyone who is to play a heroic part to speak like a working man. A comic hero like Sam Weller, or a merely pathetic figure like Stephen Blackpool, can speak with a broad accent, but the *jeune premier** always speaks the then equivalent of BBC. This is so, even when it involves absurdities. Little Pip, for instance, is brought up by people speaking broad Essex, but talks upper-class English from his earliest childhood; actually he would have talked the same dialect as Joe, or at least as Mrs Gargery. So also with Biddy Wopsle, Lizzie Hexam, Sissie Jupe, Oliver Twist – one ought perhaps to add Little Dorrit. Even Rachel in *Hard Times* has barely a trace of Lancashire accent, an impossibility in her case.

One thing that often gives the clue to a novelist's real feelings on the class question is the attitude he takes up when class collides with sex. This is a thing too painful to be lied about, and consequently it is one of the points at which the "I'm-not-a-snob" pose tends to break down.

One sees that at its most obvious where a class distinction is also a colour distinction. And something resembling the colonial attitude ("native" women are fair game, white women are sacrosanct) exists in a veiled form in all-white communities, causing bitter resentment on both sides. When this issue arises, novelists often revert to crude class feelings which they might disclaim at other times. A good example of "class-conscious" reaction is a rather forgotten novel, *The People of Clopton* by Andrew Barton.* The author's moral code is quite clearly mixed up with class hatred. He feels the seduction of a poor girl by a rich man to be something atrocious, a kind of defilement, something quite different from her seduction by a man in her own walk of life. Trollope deals with this theme twice (*The Three Clerks* and *The Small House at Allington**) and, as one might expect, entirely from the upper-class angle. As he sees it, an affair with a barmaid or a landlady's daughter is simply an "entanglement" to be escaped from. Trollope's moral standards are strict, and he does not allow the seduction actually to happen, but the implication is always that a working-class girl's feelings do not greatly matter. In *The Three Clerks* he even gives the typical class reaction by noting that the girl "smells". Meredith (*Rhoda Fleming*) takes more the "class-conscious" viewpoint. Thackeray, as often, seems to hesitate. In *Pendennis* (Fanny Bolton) his attitude is much the same as Trollope's; in *A Shabby Genteel Story* it is nearer to Meredith's.*

One could divine a good deal about Trollope's social origin, or Meredith's, or Barton's, merely from their handling of the class-sex theme. So one can with Dickens, but what emerges, as usual, is that he is more inclined to identify himself with the middle class than with the proletariat. The one incident that seems to contradict this is the tale of the young peasant girl in Doctor Manette's manuscript in *A Tale of Two Cities*. This, however, is merely a costume piece put in to explain the implacable hatred of Madame Defarge, which Dickens does not pretend to approve of. In *David Copperfield*, where he is dealing with a typical nineteenth-century seduction, the class issue does not seem to strike him as paramount. It is a law of Victorian novels that sexual misdeeds must not go unpunished, and so Steerforth is drowned on Yarmouth sands, but neither Dickens, nor old Peggotty, nor even Ham, seems to feel that Steerforth has added to his offence by being the son of rich parents. The Steerforths are moved by class motives, but the Peggottys are not – not even in the scene between Mrs Steerforth and old Peggotty; if they were, of course, they would probably turn against David as well as against Steerforth.

In *Our Mutual Friend* Dickens treats the episode of Eugene Wrayburn and Lizzie Hexam very realistically and with no appearance of class bias. According to the "unhand me, monster" tradition, Lizzie ought either to "spurn" Eugene or to be ruined by him and throw herself off Waterloo Bridge; Eugene ought to be either a heartless betrayer or a hero resolved upon defying society. Neither behaves in the least like this. Lizzie is frightened by Eugene's advances and actually runs away from them, but hardly pretends to dislike them; Eugene is attracted by her, has too much decency to attempt seducing her and dare not marry her because of his family. Finally they are married and no one is any the worse, except perhaps Mr Twemlow, who will lose a few dinner engagements. It is all very much as it might have happened in real life. But a "class-conscious" novelist would have given her to Bradley Headstone.

But when it is the other way about – when it is a case of a poor man aspiring to some woman who is "above" him – Dickens instantly retreats into the middle-class attitude. He is rather fond of the Victorian notion of a woman (woman with a capital W) being "above" a man. Pip feels that Estella is "above" him, Esther Summerson is "above" Guppy, Little Dorrit is "above" John Chivery, Lucie Manette is "above" Sydney Carton. In some of these the "above"-ness is merely moral, but in others it is social. There is a scarcely mistakable class reaction when David Copperfield discovers that Uriah Heep is plotting to marry Agnes Wickfield. The disgusting Uriah suddenly announces that he is in love with her:

> "Oh, Master Copperfield, with what a pure affection do I love the ground my Agnes walks on."
>
> I believe I had the delirious idea of seizing the red-hot poker out of the fire, and running him through with it. It went from me with a shock, like a ball fired from a rifle: but the image of Agnes, outraged by so much as a thought of this red-headed animal's, remained in my mind (when I looked at him, sitting all awry as if his mean soul griped his body) and made me giddy. [...] "I believe Agnes Wickfield to be as far above *you* [David says later on], and as far removed from all *your* aspirations, as that moon herself."

Considering how Heep's general lowness – his servile manners, dropped aitches and so forth – has been rubbed in throughout the book, there is not much doubt about the nature of Dickens's feelings. Heep, of course, is playing a villainous part, but even villains have sexual lives; it is the thought of the "pure" Agnes in bed with a man who drops his aitches that really revolts Dickens. But his usual tendency is to treat a man in love with a woman who is "above" him as a joke. It is one of the stock jokes of English literature, from Malvolio onwards. Guppy in *Bleak House* is an example, John Chivery is another, and there is a rather ill-natured treatment of this theme in the "swarry" in *Pickwick Papers*. Here Dickens describes the Bath footmen as living a kind of fantasy life, holding dinner parties in imitation of their "betters" and deluding themselves that their young mistresses are in love with them. This evidently strikes him as very comic. So it is, in a way, though one might question whether it is not better for a footman even to have delusions of this kind than simply to accept his status in the spirit of the catechism.

In his attitude towards servants Dickens is not ahead of his age. In the nineteenth century the revolt against domestic service was just beginning, to the great annoyance of everyone with over £500 a year. An enormous number of the jokes in nineteenth-century comic papers deal with the uppishness of servants. For years *Punch* ran a series of jokes called "Servant Gal-isms", all turning on the then astonishing fact that a servant is a human being. Dickens is sometimes guilty of this kind of thing himself. His books abound with the ordinary comic servants; they are dishonest (*Great Expectations*), incompetent (*David Copperfield*), turn up their noses at good food (*Pickwick Papers*), etc. etc. – all rather in the spirit of the suburban housewife with one downtrodden cook-general. But what is curious, in a nineteenth-century radical, is that when he wants to draw a sympathetic picture of a servant, he creates what is recognizably a feudal type. Sam Weller, Mark Tapley, Clara Peggotty are all of them feudal figures. They belong to the genre of the "old family retainer"; they identify themselves with their master's family and are at once doggishly faithful and completely familiar. No doubt Mark Tapley and Sam Weller are derived to some extent from Smollett,* and hence from Cervantes – but it is interesting that Dickens should have been attracted by such a type. Sam Weller's attitude is definitely medieval. He gets himself arrested in order to follow Mr Pickwick into the Fleet, and afterwards refuses to get married because he feels that Mr Pickwick still needs his services. There is a characteristic scene between them:

> "Vages or no vages, board or no board, lodgin' or no lodgin', Sam Veller, as you took from the old inn in the Borough, sticks by you, come what may..."
>
> "My good fellow," said Mr Pickwick, when Mr Weller had sat down again, rather abashed at his own enthusiasm, "you are bound to consider the young woman also."
>
> "I do consider the young 'ooman, sir," said Sam. "I have considered the young 'ooman. I've spoke to her. I've told her how I'm sitivated; she's ready to vait till I'm ready, and I believe she vill. If she don't, she's not the young 'ooman I take her for, and I give her up with readiness."

It is easy to imagine what the young woman would have said to this in real life. But notice the feudal atmosphere. Sam Weller is ready as a matter of course to sacrifice years of life to his master, and he can also sit down in his master's presence. A modern manservant would never think of doing either. Dickens's views on the servant question do not get much beyond wishing that master and servant would love one another. Sloppy in *Our Mutual Friend*, though a wretched failure as a character, represents the same kind of loyalty as Sam Weller. Such loyalty, of course, is natural, human and likeable – but so was feudalism.

What Dickens seems to be doing, as usual, is to reach out for an idealized version of the existing thing. He was writing at a time when domestic service must have seemed a completely inevitable evil. There were no labour-saving devices, and there was huge inequality of wealth. It was an age of enormous families, pretentious meals and inconvenient houses, when the slavey drudging fourteen hours a day in the basement kitchen was something too normal to be noticed. And given the *fact* of servitude, the feudal relationship is the only tolerable one. Sam Weller and Mark Tapley are dream figures, no less than the Cheerybles. If there have got to be masters and servants, how much better that the master should be Mr Pickwick and the servant should be Sam Weller. Better still, of course, if servants did not exist at all – but this Dickens is probably unable to imagine. Without a high level of mechanical development, human equality is not practically possible; Dickens goes to show that it is not imaginable either.

IV

It is not merely a coincidence that Dickens never writes about agriculture and writes endlessly about food. He was a cockney, and London is the centre of the earth in rather the same sense that the belly is the centre of the body. It is a city of consumers, of people who are deeply civilized but not primarily useful. A thing that strikes one when one looks below the surface of Dickens's books is that, as nineteenth-century novelists go, he is rather ignorant. He knows very little about the way things really happen. At first sight this statement looks flatly untrue, and it needs some qualification.

Dickens had had vivid glimpses of "low life" – life in a debtor's prison, for example – and he was also a popular novelist and able to write about ordinary people. So were all the characteristic English novelists of the nineteenth century. They felt at home in the world they lived in, whereas a writer nowadays is so hopelessly isolated that the typical modern novel is a novel about a novelist. Even when Joyce, for instance, spends a decade or so in patient efforts to make contact with the "common man", his "common man" finally turns out to be a Jew, and a bit of a highbrow at that.* Dickens at least does not suffer from this kind of thing. He has no difficulty in introducing the common motives, love, ambition, avarice, vengeance and so forth. What he does not noticeably write about, however, is *work*.

In Dickens's novels anything in the nature of work happens offstage. The only one of his heroes who has a plausible profession is David Copperfield, who is first a shorthand writer and then a novelist, like Dickens himself. With most of the others, the way they earn their living is very much in the background. Pip, for instance, "goes into business" in Egypt; we are not told what business, and Pip's working life occupies about half a page of the book. Clennam has been in some unspecified business in China, and later goes into another barely specified business with Doyce. Martin Chuzzlewit is an architect, but does not seem to get much time for practising. In no case do their adventures spring directly out of their work. Here the contrast between Dickens and, say, Trollope is startling. And one reason for this is undoubtedly that Dickens knows very little about the professions his characters are supposed to follow. What exactly went on in Gradgrind's factories? How did Podsnap make his money? How did Merdle work his swindles? One knows that Dickens could never follow up the details of parliamentary elections and Stock Exchange rackets as Trollope could. As soon as he has to deal with trade, finance, industry or politics he takes refuge in vagueness, or in satire. This is the case even with legal processes, about which actually he must have known a good deal. Compare any lawsuit in Dickens with the lawsuit in *Orley Farm*,* for instance.

And this partly accounts for the needless ramifications of Dickens's novels, the awful Victorian "plot". It is true that not all his novels are alike in this.

A Tale of Two Cities is a very good and fairly simple story, and so in its different way is *Hard Times* – but these are just the two which are always rejected as "not like Dickens" – and incidentally they were not published in monthly numbers.* The two first-person novels are also good stories, apart from their sub-plots. But the typical Dickens novel, *Nicholas Nickleby*, *Oliver Twist*, *Martin Chuzzlewit*, *Our Mutual Friend*, always exists round a framework of melodrama. The last thing anyone ever remembers about these books is their central story. On the other hand, I suppose no one has ever read them without carrying the memory of individual pages to the day of his death. Dickens sees human beings with the most intense vividness, but he sees them always in private life, as "characters", not as functional members of society – that is to say, he sees them statically. Consequently his greatest success is *The Pickwick Papers*, which is not a story at all, merely a series of sketches; there is little attempt at development – the characters simply go on and on, behaving like idiots, in a kind of eternity. As soon as he tries to bring his characters into action, the melodrama begins. He cannot make the action revolve round their ordinary occupations; hence the crossword puzzle of coincidences, intrigues, murders, disguises, buried wills, long-lost brothers, etc. etc. In the end even people like Squeers and Micawber get sucked into the machinery.

Of course it would be absurd to say that Dickens is a vague or merely melodramatic writer. Much that he wrote is extremely factual, and in the power of evoking visual images he has probably never been equalled. When Dickens has once described something you see it for the rest of your life. But in a way the concreteness of his vision is a sign of what he is missing. For, after all, that is what the merely casual onlooker always sees – the outward appearance, the non-functional, the surfaces of things. No one who is really involved in the landscape ever sees the landscape. Wonderfully as he can describe an *appearance*, Dickens does not often describe a *process*. The vivid pictures that he succeeds in leaving in one's memory are nearly always the pictures of things seen in leisure moments, in the coffee rooms of country inns or through the windows of a stagecoach; the kind of things he notices are inn signs, brass door-knockers, painted jugs, the interiors of shops and private houses, clothes, faces and, above all, food. Everything is seen from the consumer angle. When he writes about Coketown he manages to evoke, in just a few paragraphs, the atmosphere of a Lancashire town as a slightly disgusted southern visitor would see it. "It had a black canal in it, and a river that ran purple with evil-smelling dye, and vast piles of buildings full of windows where there was a rattling and a trembling all day long, and where the piston of the steam-engine worked monotonously up and down, like the head of an elephant in a state of melancholy madness." That is as near as Dickens ever gets to the machinery of the mills. An engineer or a cotton-broker would see it differently – but then neither of them would be capable of that impressionistic touch about the heads of the elephants.

In a rather different sense his attitude to life is extremely unphysical. He is a man who lives through his eyes and ears rather than through his hands and muscles. Actually his habits were not so sedentary as this seems to imply. In spite of rather poor health and physique, he was active to the point of restlessness; throughout his life he was a remarkable walker, and he could at any rate carpenter well enough to put up stage scenery. But he was not one of those people who feel a need to use their hands. It is difficult to imagine him digging at a cabbage patch, for instance. He gives no evidence of knowing anything about agriculture, and obviously knows nothing about any kind of game or sport. He has no interest in pugilism, for instance. Considering the age in which he was writing, it is astonishing how little physical brutality there is in Dickens's novels. Martin Chuzzlewit and Mark Tapley, for instance, behave with the most remarkable mildness towards the Americans who are constantly menacing them with revolvers and bowie knives. The average English or American novelist would have had them handing out socks on the jaw and exchanging pistol shots in all directions. Dickens is too decent for that; he sees the stupidity of violence, and also he belongs to a cautious urban class which does not deal in socks on the jaw, even in theory. And his attitude towards sport is mixed up with social feelings. In England, for mainly geographical reasons, sport, especially field sports, and snobbery are inextricably mingled. English socialists are often flatly incredulous when told that Lenin, for instance, was devoted to shooting. In their eyes shooting, hunting, etc. are simply snobbish observances of the landed gentry; they forget that these things might appear differently in a huge virgin country like Russia. From Dickens's point of view almost any kind of sport is at best a subject for satire. Consequently one side of nineteenth-century life – the boxing, racing, cockfighting, badger-digging, poaching, rat-catching side of life, so wonderfully embalmed in Leech's illustrations to Surtees* – is outside his scope.

What is more striking, in a seemingly "progressive" radical, is that he is not mechanically minded. He shows no interest either in the details of machinery or in the things machinery can do. As Gissing remarks, Dickens nowhere describes a railway journey with anything like the enthusiasm he shows in describing journeys by stagecoach. In nearly all of his books one has a curious feeling that one is living in the first quarter of the nineteenth century, and in fact, he does tend to return to this period. *Little Dorrit*, written in the middle fifties, deals with the late twenties; *Great Expectations* (1861) is not dated, but evidently deals with the twenties and thirties. Several of the inventions and discoveries which have made the modern world possible (the electric telegraph, the breech-loading gun, India rubber, coal gas, wood-pulp paper) first appeared in Dickens's lifetime, but he scarcely notes them in his books. Nothing is queerer than the vagueness with which he speaks of Doyce's "invention" in *Little Dorrit*. It is represented as something extremely ingenious and revolutionary, "of great importance to his country and his fellow creatures", and it is also an important minor link in the book – yet we are never told what the "invention" is! On the other hand, Doyce's physical appearance is hit off with the typical Dickens touch; he has a peculiar way of moving his thumb, a way characteristic of engineers. After that, Doyce is firmly anchored in one's memory, but, as usual, Dickens has done it by fastening on something external.

There are people (Tennyson* is an example) who lack the mechanical faculty but can see the social possibilities of machinery. Dickens has not this stamp of mind. He shows very little consciousness of the future. When he speaks of human progress it is usually in terms of *moral* progress – men growing better; probably he would never admit that men are only as good as their technical development allows them to be. At this point the gap between Dickens and his modern analogue, H.G. Wells, is at its widest. Wells wears the future round his neck like a millstone, but Dickens's unscientific cast of mind is just as damaging in a different way. What it does is to make any *positive* attitude more difficult for him. He is hostile to the feudal, agricultural past and not in real touch with the industrial present. Well, then, all that remains is the future (meaning science, "progress" and so forth), which hardly enters into his thoughts. Therefore, while attacking everything in sight, he has no definable standard of comparison. As I have pointed out already, he attacks the current educational system with perfect justice, and yet, after all, he has no remedy to offer except kindlier schoolmasters. Why did he not indicate what a school *might* have been? Why did he not have his own sons educated according to some plan of his own, instead of sending them to public schools to be stuffed with Greek? Because he lacked that kind of imagination. He has an infallible moral sense, but very little intellectual curiosity. And here one comes upon something which really is an enormous deficiency in Dickens, something that really does make the nineteenth century seem remote from us – that he has no ideal of *work*.

With the doubtful exception of David Copperfield (merely Dickens himself), one cannot point to a single one of his central characters who is primarily interested in his job. His heroes work in order to make a living and to marry the heroine, not because they feel a passionate interest in one particular subject. Martin Chuzzlewit, for instance, is not burning with zeal to be an architect; he might just as well be a doctor or a barrister. In any case, in the typical Dickens novel, the deus ex machina enters with a bag of gold in the last chapter and the hero is absolved from further struggle. The feeling, "This is what I came into the world to do. Everything else is uninteresting. I will do this even if it means starvation", which turns men of differing temperaments into scientists, inventors, artists, priests, explorers and revolutionaries – this motif is almost entirely absent from Dickens's books. He himself, as is well known, worked like a slave and believed in his work as few novelists have ever done. But there seems to be no calling except novel-writing (and perhaps acting) towards which he can imagine this kind of devotion. And, after all, it is natural enough, considering his rather negative attitude towards society. In the last resort there is nothing he admires except common decency. Science is uninteresting and machinery is cruel and ugly (the heads of the elephants). Business is only for ruffians like Bounderby. As for politics – leave that to the Tite Barnacles. Really there is no objective except to marry the heroine, settle down, live solvently and be kind. And you can do that much better in private life.

Here, perhaps, one gets a glimpse of Dickens's secret imaginative background. What did he think of as the most desirable way to live? When Martin Chuzzlewit had made it up with his uncle, when Nicholas Nickleby had married money, when John Harmon had been enriched by Boffin – what did they *do*?

The answer evidently is that they did nothing. Nicholas Nickleby invested his wife's money with the Cheerybles and "became a rich and prosperous merchant", but as he immediately retired into Devonshire, we can assume that he did not work very hard. Mr and Mrs Snodgrass "purchased and cultivated a small farm, more for occupation than profit". That is the spirit in which most of Dickens's books end – a sort of radiant idleness. Where he appears to disapprove of young men who do not work (Harthouse, Harry Gowan,* Richard Carstone, Wrayburn before his reformation), it is because they are cynical and immoral or because they are a burden on somebody else; if you are "good", and also self-supporting, there is no reason why you should not spend fifty years in simply drawing your dividends. Home life is always enough. And, after all, it was the general assumption of his age. The "genteel sufficiency", the "competence", the "gentleman of independent means" (or "in easy circumstances") – the very phrases tell one all about the strange, empty dream of the eighteenth- and nineteenth-century middle bourgeoisie. It was a dream of *complete idleness*. Charles Reade conveys its spirit perfectly in the ending of *Hard Cash*.* Alfred Hardie, hero of *Hard Cash*, is the typical nineteenth-century novel hero (public-school style), with gifts which Reade describes as amounting to "genius". He is an old Etonian and a scholar of Oxford, he knows most of the Greek and Latin classics by heart, he can box with prizefighters and win the Diamond Sculls at Henley.* He goes through incredible adventures in which, of course, he behaves with faultless heroism, and then, at the age of twenty-five, he inherits a fortune, marries his Julia Dodd and settles down in the suburbs of Liverpool, in the same house as his parents-in-law:

> They all lived together at Albion Villa, thanks to Alfred. [...] Oh, you happy little villa! You were as like Paradise as any mortal dwelling can be. A day came, however, when your walls could no longer hold all the happy inmates. Julia presented Alfred with a lovely boy; enter two nurses and the villa

showed symptoms of bursting. Two months more, and Alfred and his wife overflowed into the next villa. It was but twenty yards off; and there was a double reason for the migration. As often happens after a long separation, Heaven bestowed on Captain and Mrs Dodd another infant to play about their knees, etc. etc. etc.

This is the type of the Victorian happy ending – a vision of a huge, loving family of three or four generations, all crammed together in the same house and constantly multiplying, like a bed of oysters. What is striking about it is the utterly soft, sheltered, effortless life that it implies. It is not even a violent idleness, like Squire Western's.* That is the significance of Dickens's urban background and his non-interest in the blackguardly-sporting-military side of life. His heroes, once they had come into money and "settled down", would not only do no work; they would not even ride, hunt, shoot, fight duels, elope with actresses or lose money at the races. They would simply live at home in feather-bed respectability, and preferably next door to a blood relation living exactly the same life:

> The first act of Nicholas, when he became a rich and prosperous merchant, was to buy his father's old house. As time crept on, and there came gradually about him a group of lovely children, it was altered and enlarged; but none of the old rooms were ever pulled down, no old tree was ever rooted up, nothing with which there was any association of bygone times was ever removed or changed.
>
> Within a stone's-throw was another retreat enlivened by children's pleasant voices too; and here was Kate [...] the same true, gentle creature, the same fond sister, the same in the love of all about her, as in her girlish days.

It is the same incestuous atmosphere as in the passage quoted from Reade. And evidently this is Dickens's ideal ending. It is perfectly attained in *Nicholas Nickleby*, *Martin Chuzzlewit* and *Pickwick*, and it is approximated to in varying degrees in almost all the others. The exceptions are *Hard Times* and *Great Expectations* – the latter actually has a "happy ending", but it contradicts the general tendency of the book, and it was put in at the request of Bulwer-Lytton.*

The ideal to be striven after, then, appears to be something like this: £100,000, a quaint old house with plenty of ivy on it, a sweetly womanly wife, a horde of children and no work. Everything is safe, soft, peaceful and, above all, domestic. In the moss-grown churchyard down the road are the graves of the loved ones who passed away before the happy ending happened. The servants are comic and feudal, the children prattle round your feet, the old friends sit at your fireside, talking of past days, there is the endless succession of enormous meals, the cold punch and sherry negus, the feather beds and warming pans, the Christmas parties with charades and blind man's buff – but nothing ever happens, except the yearly childbirth. The curious thing is that it is a genuinely happy picture, or so Dickens is able to make it appear. The thought of that kind of existence is satisfying to him. This alone would be enough to tell one that more than a hundred years have passed since Dickens's first book was written. No modern man could combine such purposelessness with so much vitality.

V

By this time anyone who is a lover of Dickens, and who has read as far as this, will probably be angry with me.

I have been discussing Dickens simply in terms of his "message", and almost ignoring his literary qualities. But every writer, especially every novelist, *has* a "message", whether he admits it or not, and the minutest details of his work are influenced by it. All art is propaganda. Neither Dickens himself nor the majority of Victorian novelists would have thought of denying this. On the other hand, not all propaganda is art. As I said earlier, Dickens is one of those writers who are felt to be worth stealing. He has been stolen by Marxists, by Catholics and, above all, by conservatives. The question is, what is there to steal? Why does anyone care about Dickens? Why do *I* care about Dickens?

That kind of question is never easy to answer. As a rule, an aesthetic preference is either something inexplicable or it is so corrupted by non-aesthetic motives as to make one wonder whether the whole of literary criticism is not a huge network of humbug. In Dickens's case the complicating factor is his familiarity. He happens to be one of those "great authors" who are ladled down everyone's throat in childhood. At the time this causes rebellion and vomiting, but it may have different after-effects in later life. For instance, nearly everyone feels a sneaking affection for the patriotic poems that he learnt by heart as a child, 'Ye Mariners of England', 'The Charge of the Light Brigade'* and so forth. What one enjoys is not so much the poems themselves as the memories they call up. And with Dickens the same forces of association are at work. Probably there are copies of one or two of his books lying about in an actual majority of English homes. Many children begin to know his characters by sight before they can even read, for on the whole Dickens was lucky in his illustrators. A thing that is absorbed as early as that does not come up against any critical judgement. And when one thinks of this, one thinks of all that is bad and silly in Dickens – the cast-iron "plots", the characters who don't come off, the *longueurs*, the paragraphs in blank verse, the awful pages of "pathos". And then the thought arises: when I say I like Dickens, do I simply mean that I like thinking about my childhood? Is Dickens merely an institution?

If so, he is an institution that there is no getting away from. How often one really thinks about any writer, even a writer one cares for, is a difficult thing to decide – but I should doubt whether anyone who has actually read Dickens can go a week without remembering him in one context or another. Whether you approve of him or not, he is *there*, like the Nelson Column. At any moment some scene or character, which may come from some book you cannot even remember the name of, is liable to drop into your mind. Micawber's letters! Winkle in the witness box! Mrs Gamp! Mrs Wititterly and Sir Tumley Snuffim! Todgers's! (George Gissing said that when he passed the Monument it was never of the Fire of London that he thought, always of Todgers's.) Mrs Leo Hunter! Squeers! Silas Wegg and the Decline and Fall-Off of the Russian Empire! Miss Mills and the Desert of Sahara! Wopsle acting Hamlet! Mrs Jellyby! Mantalini! Jerry Cruncher! Barkis! Pumblechook! Tracy Tupman! Skimpole! Joe Gargery! Pecksniff! – and so it goes on and on. It is not so much a series of books, it is more like a world. And not a purely comic world either, for part of what one remembers in Dickens is his Victorian morbidness and necrophilia and the blood-and-thunder scenes – the death of Sikes, Krook's spontaneous combustion, Fagin in the condemned cell, the women knitting round the guillotine. To a surprising extent all this has entered even into the minds of people who do not care about it. A music-hall comedian can (or at any rate could quite recently) go on the stage and impersonate Micawber or Mrs Gamp with a fair certainty of being understood, although not one in twenty of the audience had ever read a book of Dickens's right through. Even people who affect to despise him quote him unconsciously.

Dickens is a writer who can be imitated, up to a certain point. In genuinely popular literature – for instance, the Elephant and Castle version of *Sweeney Todd** – he has been plagiarized quite shamelessly. What has been imitated, however, is simply a tradition that Dickens himself took from earlier novelists and developed, the cult of "character", i.e. eccentricity. The thing that cannot be imitated is his fertility of invention, which is invention not so much of characters, still less of "situations", as of turns of phrase and concrete details. The outstanding, unmistakable mark of Dickens's writing is the *unnecessary detail*. Here is an example of what I mean. The story given below is not particularly funny, but there is one phrase in it that is as individual as a fingerprint. Mr Jack Hopkins, at Bob Sawyer's party, is telling the story of the child who swallowed its sister's necklace:

> Next day, child swallowed two beads; the day after that, he treated himself to three, and so on, till in a week's time he had got through the necklace – five-and-twenty beads in all. The sister, who was an industrious girl and seldom treated herself to a bit of finery, cried her eyes out at the loss of the necklace; looked high and low for it; but I needn't say, didn't find it. A few days afterwards, the family were at dinner – baked shoulder of mutton and potatoes

under it – the child, who wasn't hungry, was playing about the room, when suddenly there was heard the devil of a noise, like a small hailstorm. "Don't do that, my boy," says the father. "I ain't a-doin' nothing," said the child. "Well, don't do it again," said the father. There was a short silence, and then the noise began again, worse than ever. "If you don't mind what I say, my boy," said the father, "you'll find yourself in bed, in something less than a pig's whisper." He gave the child a shake to make him obedient, and such a rattling ensued as nobody ever heard before. "Why, dam' me, it's *in* the child," said the father; "he's got the croup in the wrong place!" "No, I haven't, father," said the child, beginning to cry, "it's the necklace; I swallowed it, father." The father caught the child up, and ran with him to the hospital, the beads in the boy's stomach rattling all the way with the jolting; and the people looking up in the air, and down in the cellars, to see where the unusual sound came from. "He's in the hospital now," said Jack Hopkins, "and he makes such a devil of a noise when he walks about, that they're obliged to muffle him in a watchman's coat, for fear he should wake the patients."

As a whole, this story might come out of any nineteenth-century comic paper. But the unmistakable Dickens touch, the thing nobody else would have thought of, is the baked shoulder of mutton and potatoes under it. How does this advance the story? The answer is that it doesn't. It is something totally unnecessary, a florid little squiggle on the edge of the page – only it is by just these squiggles that the special Dickens atmosphere is created. The other thing one would notice here is that Dickens's way of telling a story takes a long time. An interesting example, too long to quote, is Sam Weller's story of the obstinate patient in Chapter XLIV of *The Pickwick Papers*. As it happens, we have a standard of comparison here, because Dickens is plagiarizing, consciously or unconsciously. The story is also told by some ancient Greek writer. I cannot now find the passage, but I read it years ago as a boy at school, and it runs more or less like this:

A certain Thracian, renowned for his obstinacy, was warned by his physician that if he drank a flagon of wine it would kill him. The Thracian thereupon drank the flagon of wine and immediately jumped off the housetop and perished. "For," said he, "in this way I shall prove that the wine did not kill me."

As the Greek tells it, that is the whole story – about six lines. As Sam Weller tells it, it takes round about 1,000 words. Long before getting to the point we have been told all about the patient's clothes, his meals, his manners, even the newspapers he reads, and about the peculiar construction of the doctor's carriage, which conceals the fact that the coachman's trousers do not match his coat. Then there is the dialogue between the doctor and the patient. "'Crumpets is wholesome, sir,' said the patient. 'Crumpets is *not* wholesome, sir,' says the doctor, wery fierce," etc. etc. In the end the original story has been buried under the details. And in all of Dickens's most characteristic passages it is the same. His imagination overwhelms everything, like a kind of weed. Squeers stands up to address his boys, and immediately we are hearing about Bolder's father who was two pounds ten short, and Mobbs's stepmother who took to her bed on hearing that Mobbs wouldn't eat fat and hoped Mr Squeers would flog him into a happier state of mind. Mrs Leo Hunter writes a poem, 'Expiring Frog'; two full stanzas are given. Boffin takes a fancy to pose as a miser, and instantly we are down among the squalid biographies of eighteenth-century misers, with names like Vulture Hopkins and the Revd Blewberry Jones, and chapter headings like "The Story of the Mutton Pies" and "The Treasures of a Dunghill". Mrs Harris, who does not even exist, has more detail piled onto her than any three characters in an ordinary novel. Merely in the middle of a sentence we learn, for instance, that her infant nephew has been seen in a bottle at Greenwich Fair, along with the pink-eyed lady, the Prussian dwarf and the living skeleton. Joe Gargery describes how the robbers broke into the house of Pumblechook, the corn and seed merchant – "and they took his till, and they took his cashbox, and they drinked his wine, and they partook of his wittles, and they slapped his face, and they pulled his nose, and they tied him up to his bedpust, and they give him a dozen, and they stuffed his mouth full of flowering annuals to perwent his crying out." Once again the unmistakable Dickens touch, the flowering annuals – but any other novelist would only have mentioned about half of these outrages. Everything is piled up and up, detail on detail, embroidery on embroidery. It is futile to object that this kind of thing is rococo – one might as well make the same objection to a wedding cake. Either you like it or you do not like it. Other nineteenth-century writers, Surtees, Barham,* Thackeray, even Marryat,* have something of Dickens's profuse, overflowing quality, but none of them on anything like the same scale. The appeal of all these writers now depends partly on period flavour, and though Marryat is still officially a "boys' writer" and Surtees has a sort of legendary fame among hunting men, it is probable that they are read mostly by bookish people.

Significantly, Dickens's most successful books (not his *best* books) are *The Pickwick Papers*, which is not a novel, and *Hard Times* and *A Tale of Two Cities*, which are not funny. As a novelist his natural fertility greatly hampers him, because the burlesque which he is never able to resist is constantly breaking into what ought to be serious situations. There is a good example of this in the opening chapter of *Great Expectations*. The escaped convict, Magwitch, has just captured the six-year-old Pip in the churchyard. The scene starts terrifyingly enough, from Pip's point of view. The convict, smothered in mud and with his chain trailing from his leg, suddenly starts up among the tombs, grabs the child, turns him upside down and robs his pockets. Then he begins terrorizing him into bringing food and a file:

He held me by the arms in an upright position on the top of the stone, and went on in these fearful terms:

"You bring me, tomorrow morning early, that file and them wittles. You bring the lot to me, at that old Battery over yonder. You do it, and you never dare to say a word or dare to make a sign concerning your having seen such a person as me, or any person sumever, and you shall be let to live. You fail, or you go from my words in any partickler, no matter how small it is, and your heart and liver shall be tore out, roasted and ate. Now, I ain't alone, as you may think I am. There's a young man hid with me, in comparison with which young man I am a Angel. That young man hears the words I speak. That young man has a secret way pecooliar to himself, of getting at a boy, and at his heart, and at his liver. It is in wain for a boy to attempt to hide himself from that young man. A boy may lock his door, may be warm in bed, may tuck himself up, may draw the clothes over his head, may think himself comfortable and safe, but that young man will softly creep and creep his way to him and tear him open. I am keeping that young man from harming you at the present moment, but with great difficulty. I find it wery hard to hold that young man off of your inside. Now, what do you say?"

Here Dickens has simply yielded to temptation. To begin with, no starving and hunted man would speak in the least like that. Moreover, although the speech shows a remarkable knowledge of the way in which a child's mind works, its actual words are quite out of tune with what is to follow. It turns Magwitch into a sort of pantomime wicked uncle, or, if one sees him through the child's eyes, into an appalling monster. Later in the book he is to be represented as neither, and his exaggerated gratitude, on which the plot turns, is to be incredible because of just this speech. As usual, Dickens's imagination has overwhelmed him. The picturesque details were too good to be left out. Even with characters who are more of a piece than Magwitch he is liable to be tripped up by some seductive phrase. Mr Murdstone, for instance, is in the habit of ending David Copperfield's lessons every morning with a dreadful sum in arithmetic. "If I go into a cheesemonger's shop, and buy five thousand Double Gloucester cheeses at fourpence halfpenny each, present payment," it always begins. Once again the typical Dickens detail, the Double Gloucester cheeses. But it is far too human a touch for Murdstone; he would have made it five thousand cashboxes. Every time this note is struck, the unity of the novel suffers. Not that it matters very much, because Dickens is obviously a writer whose parts are greater than his wholes. He is all fragments, all details – rotten architecture, but wonderful gargoyles – and never better than when he is building up some character who will later on be forced to act inconsistently.

Of course it is not usual to urge against Dickens that he makes his characters behave inconsistently. Generally he is accused of doing just the opposite. His characters are supposed to be mere "types", each crudely representing some single trait and fitted with a kind of label by which you recognize him. Dickens is "only a caricaturist" – that is the usual accusation, and it does him both more and less than justice. To begin with, he did not think of himself as a caricaturist, and was constantly setting into action characters who ought to have been purely static. Squeers, Micawber, Miss Mowcher,* Wegg, Skimpole, Pecksniff and many others are finally involved in "plots" where they are out of place and where they behave quite incredibly. They start off as magic-lantern slides and they end by getting mixed up in a third-rate movie. Sometimes one can put one's finger on a single sentence in which the original illusion is destroyed. There is such a sentence in *David Copperfield*. After the famous dinner party (the one where the leg of mutton was underdone), David is showing his guests out. He stops Traddles at the top of the stairs:

> "Traddles," said I, "Mr Micawber don't mean any harm, poor fellow: but if I were you I wouldn't lend him anything."
>
> "My dear Copperfield," returned Traddles smiling, "I haven't got anything to lend."
>
> "You have got a name, you know," I said.

At the place where one reads it this remark jars a little, though something of the kind was inevitable sooner or later. The story is a fairly realistic one, and David is growing up; ultimately he is bound to see Mr Micawber for what he is, a cadging scoundrel. Afterwards, of course, Dickens's sentimentality overcomes him and Micawber is made to turn over a new leaf. But from then on the original Micawber is never quite recaptured, in spite of desperate efforts. As a rule, the "plot" in which Dickens's characters get entangled is not particularly credible, but at least it makes some pretence at reality, whereas the world to which they belong is a never-never land, a kind of eternity. But just here one sees that "only a caricaturist" is not really a condemnation. The fact that Dickens is always thought of as a caricaturist, although he was constantly trying to be something else, is perhaps the surest mark of his genius. The monstrosities that he created are still remembered as monstrosities, in spite of getting mixed up in would-be probable melodramas. Their first impact is so vivid that nothing that comes afterwards effaces it. As with the people one knew in childhood, one seems always to remember them in one particular attitude, doing one particular thing. Mrs Squeers is always ladling out brimstone and treacle, Mrs Gummidge is always weeping, Mrs Gargery is always banging her husband's head against the wall, Mrs Jellyby is always scribbling tracts while her children fall into the area – and there they all are, fixed for ever like little twinkling miniatures painted on snuffbox lids, completely fantastic and incredible, and yet somehow more solid and infinitely more memorable than the efforts of serious novelists. Even by the standards of his time Dickens was an exceptionally artificial writer. As Ruskin said, he "chose to work in a circle of stage fire". His characters are even more distorted and simplified than Smollett's. But there are no rules in novel writing, and for any work of art there is only one test worth bothering about – survival. By this test Dickens's characters have succeeded, even if the people who remember them hardly think of them as human beings. They are monsters, but at any rate they *exist*.

But all the same there is a disadvantage in writing about monsters. It amounts to this: that it is only certain moods that Dickens can speak to. There are large areas of the human mind that he never touches. There is no poetic feeling anywhere in his books, and no genuine tragedy, and even sexual love is almost outside his scope. Actually his books are not so sexless as they are sometimes declared to be, and considering the time in which he was writing, he is reasonably frank. But there is not a trace in him of the feeling that one finds in *Manon Lescaut, Salammbô, Carmen, Wuthering Heights*.* According to Aldous Huxley,* D.H. Lawrence once said that Balzac was "a gigantic dwarf", and in a sense the same is true of Dickens. There are whole worlds which he either knows nothing about or does not wish to mention. Except in a rather roundabout way, one cannot *learn* very much from Dickens. And to say this is to think almost immediately of the great Russian novelists of the nineteenth century. Why is it that Tolstoy's grasp seems to be so much larger than Dickens's – why is it that he seems able to tell you so much more *about yourself*? It is not that he is more gifted, or even, in the last analysis, more intelligent. It is because he is writing about people who are growing. His characters are struggling to make their souls, whereas Dickens's are already finished and perfect. In my own mind Dickens's people are present far more often and far more vividly than Tolstoy's, but always in a single unchangeable attitude, like pictures or pieces of furniture. You cannot hold an imaginary conversation with a Dickens character as you can with, say, Pierre Bezukhov.* And this is not merely because of Tolstoy's greater seriousness, for there are also comic characters that you can imagine yourself talking to – Bloom, for instance, or Pécuchet, or even Wells's Mr Polly.* It is because Dickens's characters have no mental life. They say perfectly the thing that they have to say, but they cannot be conceived as talking about anything else. They never learn, never speculate. Perhaps the most meditative of his characters is Paul Dombey, and his thoughts are mush. Does this mean that Tolstoy's novels are "better" than Dickens's? The truth is that it is absurd to make such comparisons in terms of "better" and "worse". If I were forced to compare Tolstoy with Dickens, I should say that Tolstoy's appeal will probably be wider in the long run, because Dickens is scarcely intelligible outside the English-speaking culture;

on the other hand, Dickens is able to reach simple people, which Tolstoy is not. Tolstoy's characters can cross a frontier; Dickens's can be portrayed on a cigarette card.* But one is no more obliged to choose between them than between a sausage and a rose. Their purposes barely intersect.

VI

If Dickens had been *merely* a comic writer, the chances are that no one would now remember his name. Or at best a few of his books would survive in rather the same way as books like *Frank Fairlegh*, *Mr Verdant Green* and *Mrs Caudle's Curtain Lectures*,* as a sort of hangover of the Victorian atmosphere, a pleasant little whiff of oysters and brown stout. Who has not felt sometimes that it was "a pity" that Dickens ever deserted the vein of *Pickwick* for things like *Little Dorrit* and *Hard Times*? What people always demand of a popular novelist is that he shall write the same book over and over again, forgetting that a man who would write the same book twice could not even write it once. Any writer who is not utterly lifeless moves upon a kind of parabola, and the downward curve is implied in the upward one. Joyce has to start with the frigid competence of *Dubliners* and end with the dream language of *Finnegans Wake*, but *Ulysses* and *Portrait of the Artist** are part of the trajectory. The thing that drove Dickens forward into a form of art for which he was not really suited, and at the same time caused us to remember him, was simply the fact that he was a moralist, the consciousness of "having something to say". He is always preaching a sermon, and that is the final secret of his inventiveness. For you can only create if you can *care*. Types like Squeers and Micawber could not have been produced by a hack writer looking for something to be funny about. A joke worth laughing at always has an idea behind it, and usually a subversive idea. Dickens is able to go on being funny because he is in revolt against authority, and authority is always there to be laughed at. There is always room for one more custard pie.

His radicalism is of the vaguest kind, and yet one always knows that it is there. That is the difference between being a moralist and a politician. He has no constructive suggestions, not even a clear grasp of the nature of the society he is attacking, only an emotional perception that something is wrong. All he can finally say is "Behave decently", which, as I suggested earlier, is not necessarily so shallow as it sounds. Most revolutionaries are potential Tories, because they imagine that everything can be put right by altering the *shape* of society; once that change is effected, as it sometimes is, they see no need for any other. Dickens has not this kind of mental coarseness. The vagueness of his discontent is the mark of its permanence. What he is out against is not this or that institution but, as Chesterton put it, "an expression on the human face". Roughly speaking, his morality is the Christian morality, but in spite of his Anglican upbringing he was essentially a Bible Christian, as he took care to make plain when writing his will.* In any case he cannot properly be described as a religious man. He "believed", undoubtedly, but religion in the devotional sense does not seem to have entered much into his thoughts.* Where he is Christian is in his quasi-instinctive siding with the oppressed against the oppressors. As a matter of course he is on the side of the underdog, always and everywhere. To carry this to its logical conclusion one has got to change sides when the underdog becomes an upperdog, and in fact Dickens does tend to do so. He loathes the Catholic Church, for instance, but as soon as the Catholics are persecuted (*Barnaby Rudge*) he is on their side. He loathes the aristocratic class even more, but as soon as they are really overthrown (the revolutionary chapters in *A Tale of Two Cities*) his sympathies swing round. Whenever he departs from this emotional attitude he goes astray. A well-known example is at the ending of *David Copperfield*, in which everyone who reads it feels that something has gone wrong. What is wrong is that the closing chapters are pervaded, faintly but noticeably, by the cult of success. It is the gospel according to Smiles, instead of the gospel according to Dickens. The attractive, out-at-elbow characters are got rid of, Micawber makes a fortune, Heep gets into prison – both of these events are flagrantly impossible – and even Dora is killed off to make way for Agnes. If you like, you can read Dora as Dickens's wife and Agnes as his sister-in-law, but the essential point is that Dickens has "turned respectable" and done violence to his own nature. Perhaps that is why Agnes is the most disagreeable of his heroines, the real legless angel of Victorian romance, almost as bad as Thackeray's Laura.*

No grown-up person can read Dickens without feeling his limitations, and yet there does remain his native generosity of mind, which acts as a kind of anchor and nearly always keeps him where he belongs. It is probably the central secret of his popularity. A good-tempered antinomianism rather of Dickens's type is one of the marks of Western popular culture. One sees it in folk stories and comic songs, in dream figures like Mickey Mouse and Popeye the Sailor (both of them variants of Jack the Giant Killer), in the history of working-class socialism, in the popular protests (always ineffective but not always a sham) against imperialism, in the impulse that makes a jury award excessive damages when a rich man's car runs over a poor man; it is the feeling that one is always on the side of the underdog, on the side of the weak against the strong. In one sense it is a feeling that is fifty years out of date. The common man is still living in the mental world of Dickens, but nearly every modern intellectual has gone over to some or other form of totalitarianism. From the Marxist or fascist point of view, nearly all that Dickens stands for can be written off as "bourgeois morality". But in moral outlook no one could be more "bourgeois" than the English working classes. The ordinary people in the Western countries have never entered, mentally, into the world of "realism" and power politics. They may do so before long, in which case Dickens will be as out of date as the cab horse. But in his own age and ours he has been popular chiefly because he was able to express in a comic, simplified and therefore memorable form the native decency of the common man. And it is important that from this point of view people of very different types can be described as "common". In a country like England, in spite of its class structure there does exist a certain cultural unity. All through the Christian ages, and especially since the French Revolution, the Western world has been haunted by the idea of freedom and equality; it is only an *idea*, but it has penetrated to all ranks of society. The most atrocious injustices, cruelties, lies, snobberies exist everywhere, but there are not many people who can regard these things with the same indifference as, say, a Roman slave owner. Even the millionaire suffers from a vague sense of guilt, like a dog eating a stolen leg of mutton. Nearly everyone, whatever his actual conduct may be, responds emotionally to the idea of human brotherhood. Dickens voiced a code which was and on the whole still is believed in, even by people who violate it. It is difficult otherwise to explain why he could be both read by working people (a thing that has happened to no other novelist of his stature) and buried in Westminster Abbey.

When one reads any strongly individual piece of writing, one has the impression of seeing a face somewhere behind the page. It is not necessarily the actual face of the writer. I feel this very strongly with Swift, with Defoe, with Fielding, Stendhal, Thackeray, Flaubert, though in several cases I do not know what these people looked like and do not want to know. What one sees is the face that the writer *ought* to have. Well, in the case of Dickens I see a face that is not quite the face of Dickens's photographs, though it resembles it. It is the face of a man of about forty, with a small beard and a high colour. He is laughing, with a touch of anger in his laughter, but no triumph, no malignity. It is the face of a man who is always fighting against something, but who fights in the open and is not frightened, the face of a man who is *generously angry* – in other words, of a nineteenth-century liberal, a free intelligence, a type hated with equal hatred by all the smelly little orthodoxies which are now contending for our souls.

Inside the Whale*

I

When Henry Miller's novel *Tropic of Cancer* appeared in 1935, it was greeted with rather cautious praise, obviously conditioned in some cases by a fear of seeming to enjoy pornography. Among the people who praised it were T.S. Eliot, Herbert Read, Aldous Huxley, John dos Passos, Ezra Pound* – on the whole, not the writers who are in fashion at this moment. And in fact the subject matter of the book, and to a certain extent its mental atmosphere, belong to the twenties rather than to the thirties.

Tropic of Cancer is a novel in the first person, or autobiography in the form of a novel, whichever way you like to look at it. Miller himself insists that it is straight autobiography, but the tempo and method of telling the story are those of a novel. It is a story of the American Paris, but not along quite the usual lines, because the Americans who figure in it happen to be people without money. During the boom years, when dollars were plentiful and the exchange value of the franc was low, Paris was invaded by such a swarm of artists, writers, students, dilettanti, sightseers, debauchees and plain idlers as the world has probably never seen. In some quarters of the town the so-called artists must actually have outnumbered the working population – indeed, it has been reckoned that in the late twenties there were as many as 30,000 painters in Paris, most of them impostors. The populace had grown so hardened to artists that gruff-voiced lesbians in corduroy breeches and young men in Grecian or medieval costume could walk the streets without attracting a glance, and along the Seine banks by Notre Dame it was almost impossible to pick one's way between the sketching stools. It was the age of dark horses and neglected genii; the phrase on everybody's lips was "*Quand je serai lancé*".* As it turned out, nobody was "*lancé*", the slump descended like another Ice Age, the cosmopolitan mob of artists vanished, and the huge Montparnasse cafés which only ten years ago were filled till the small hours by hordes of shrieking poseurs have turned into darkened tombs in which there are not even any ghosts. It is this world – described in, among other novels, Wyndham Lewis's *Tarr** – that Miller is writing about, but he is dealing only with the underside of it, the lumpenproletarian fringe which has been able to survive the slump because it is composed partly of genuine artists and partly of genuine scoundrels. The neglected genii, the paranoiacs who are always "going to" write the novel that will knock Proust into a cocked hat, are there, but they are only genii in the rather rare moments when they are not scouting about for the next meal. For the most part it is a story of bug-ridden rooms in working men's hotels, of fights, drinking bouts, cheap brothels, Russian refugees, cadging, swindling and temporary jobs. And the whole atmosphere of the poor quarters of Paris as a foreigner sees them – the cobbled alleys, the sour reek of refuse, the bistros with their greasy zinc counters and worn brick floors, the green waters of the Seine, the blue cloaks of the Republican Guard, the crumbling iron urinals, the peculiar sweetish smell of the Métro stations, the cigarettes that come to pieces, the pigeons in the Luxembourg Gardens – it is all there, or at any rate the feeling of it is there.

On the face of it no material could be less promising. When *Tropic of Cancer* was published the Italians were marching into Abyssinia and Hitler's concentration camps were already bulging. The intellectual focuses of the world were Rome, Moscow and Berlin. It did not seem to be a moment at which a novel of outstanding value was likely to be written about American deadbeats cadging drinks in the Latin Quarter. Of course a novelist is not obliged to write directly about contemporary history, but a novelist who simply disregards the major public events of the moment is generally either a footler or a plain idiot. From a mere account of the subject matter of *Tropic of Cancer* most people would probably assume it to be no more than a bit of naughty-naughty left over from the twenties. Actually, nearly everyone who read it saw at once that it was nothing of the kind, but a very remarkable book. How or why remarkable? That question is never easy to answer. It is better to begin by describing the impression that *Tropic of Cancer* has left on my own mind.

When I first opened *Tropic of Cancer* and saw that it was full of unprintable words, my immediate reaction was a refusal to be impressed. Most people's would be the same, I believe. Nevertheless, after a lapse of time the atmosphere of the book, besides innumerable details, seemed to linger in my memory in a peculiar way. A year later Miller's second book, *Black Spring*,* was published. By this time *Tropic of Cancer* was much more vividly present in my mind than it had been when I first read it. My first feeling about *Black Spring* was that it showed a falling off, and it is a fact that it has not the same unity as the other book. Yet after another year there were many passages in *Black Spring* that had also rooted themselves in my memory. Evidently these books are of the sort to leave a flavour behind them – books that "create a world of their own", as the saying goes. The books that do this are not necessarily good books – they may be good bad books like *Raffles* or the Sherlock Holmes stories, or perverse and morbid books like *Wuthering Heights* or *The House with the Green Shutters*.* But now and again there appears a novel which opens up a new world not by revealing what is strange, but by revealing what is familiar. The truly remarkable thing about *Ulysses*, for instance, is the commonplaceness of its material. Of course there is much more in *Ulysses* than this, because Joyce is a kind of poet and also an elephantine pedant, but his real achievement has been to get the familiar onto paper. He dared – for it is a matter of *daring* just as much as of technique – to expose the imbecilities of the inner mind, and in doing so he discovered an America which was under everybody's nose. Here is a whole world of stuff which you have lived with since childhood, stuff which you supposed to be of its nature incommunicable, and somebody has managed to communicate it. The effect is to break down, at any rate momentarily, the solitude in which the human being lives. When you read certain passages in *Ulysses* you feel that Joyce's mind and your mind are one, that he knows all about you though he has never heard your name, that there exists some world outside time and space in which you and he are together. And though he does not resemble Joyce in other ways, there is a touch of this quality in Henry Miller. Not everywhere, because his work is very uneven, and sometimes, especially in *Black Spring*, tends to slide away into mere verbiage or into the squashy universe of the Surrealists. But read him for five pages, ten pages, and you feel the peculiar relief that comes not so much from understanding as from *being understood*. "He knows all about me," you feel; "he wrote this specially for me." It is as though you could hear a voice speaking to you, a friendly American voice, with no humbug in it, no moral purpose, merely an implicit assumption that we are all alike. For the moment you have got away from the lies and simplifications, the stylized, marionette-like quality of ordinary fiction, even quite good fiction, and are dealing with the recognizable experiences of human beings.

But what kind of experience? What kind of human beings? Miller is writing about the man in the street, and it is incidentally rather a pity that it should be a street full of brothels. That is the penalty of leaving your native land. It means transferring your roots into shallower soil. Exile is probably more damaging to a novelist than to a painter or even a poet, because its effect is to take him out of contact with working life and narrow down his range to the street, the café, the church, the brothel and the studio. On the whole, in Miller's books you are reading about people living the expatriate life, people drinking, talking, meditating and fornicating, not about people working, marrying and bringing up children; a pity, because he would have described the one set of activities as well as the other. In *Black Spring* there is a wonderful flashback of New York, the swarming Irish-infested New York of the O. Henry* period, but the Paris scenes are the best, and, granted their utter worthlessness as social types, the drunks and deadbeats of the cafés are handled with a feeling for character and a mastery of technique that are unapproached in any at all recent novel. All of them are not only credible but completely familiar; you have the feeling that all their adventures have happened to yourself. Not that they are anything very startling in the way of adventures. Henry gets a job with a melancholy Indian student, gets another job at a dreadful French school during a cold snap when the lavatories are frozen solid, goes on drinking bouts in Le Havre with his friend Collins, the sea captain, goes to brothels where there are wonderful Negresses, talks with his friend Van Norden, the novelist, who has got the great novel of the world in his head but can never bring himself to begin writing it. His friend Karl, on the verge of starvation, is picked up by a wealthy widow who wishes to marry him. There are interminable, Hamlet-like conversations in which Karl tries to decide which is worse, being hungry or sleeping with an old woman. In great detail he describes his visits to the widow, how he went to the hotel dressed in his best, how before going in he neglected to urinate, so that the whole evening was one long crescendo of torment, etc. etc. And after all, none of it is true, the widow doesn't even exist – Karl has simply invented her in order to make himself seem important. The whole book is in this vein, more or less. Why is it that these monstrous trivialities are so engrossing? Simply because the whole atmosphere is deeply familiar, because you have all the while the feeling that these things are happening to *you*. And you have this feeling because somebody has chosen to drop the Geneva language* of the ordinary novel and drag the realpolitik of the inner mind into the open. In Miller's case it is not so much a question of exploring the mechanisms of the mind as of owning up to everyday facts and everyday emotions. For the truth is that many ordinary people, perhaps an actual majority, do speak and behave in just the way that is recorded here. The callous coarseness with which the characters in *Tropic of Cancer* talk is very rare in fiction, but it is extremely common in real life; again and again I have heard just such conversations from people who were not even aware that they were talking coarsely. It is worth noticing that *Tropic of Cancer* is not a young man's book. Miller was in his forties when it was published, and though since then he has produced three or four others, it is obvious that this first book had been lived with for years. It is one of those books that are slowly matured in poverty and obscurity, by people who know what they have got to do and therefore are able to wait. The prose is astonishing, and in parts of *Black Spring* it is even better. Unfortunately I cannot quote; unprintable words occur almost everywhere. But get hold of *Tropic of Cancer*, get hold of *Black Spring* and read especially the first hundred pages. They give you an idea of what can still be done, even at this late date, with English prose. In them, English is treated as a spoken language, but spoken *without fear*, i.e. without fear of rhetoric or of the unusual or poetical word. The adjective has come back, after its ten years' exile. It is a flowing, swelling prose, a prose with rhythms in it, something quite different from the flat, cautious statements and snack-bar dialects that are now in fashion.

When a book like *Tropic of Cancer* appears, it is only natural that the first thing people notice should be its obscenity. Given our current notions of literary decency, it is not at all easy to approach an unprintable book with detachment. Either one is shocked and disgusted, or one is morbidly thrilled, or one is determined above all else not to be impressed. The last is probably the commonest reaction, with the result that unprintable books often get less attention than they deserve. It is rather the fashion to say that nothing is easier than to write an obscene book, that people only do it in order to get themselves talked about and make money, etc. etc. What makes it obvious that this is *not* the case is that books which are obscene in the police-court sense are distinctly uncommon. If there were easy money to be made out of dirty words, a lot more people would be making it. But because "obscene" books do not appear very frequently, there is a tendency to lump them together, as a rule quite unjustifiably. *Tropic of Cancer* has been vaguely associated with two other books, *Ulysses* and *Voyage au bout de la nuit*,* but in neither case is there much resemblance. What Miller has in common with Joyce is a willingness to mention the inane squalid facts of everyday life. Putting aside differences of technique, the funeral scene in *Ulysses*, for instance, would fit into *Tropic of Cancer*; the whole chapter is a sort of confession, an *exposé* of the frightful inner callousness of the human being. But there the resemblance ends. As a novel, *Tropic of Cancer* is far inferior to *Ulysses*. Joyce is an artist, in a sense in which Miller is not and probably would not wish to be, and in any case he is attempting much more. He is exploring different states of consciousness, dream, reverie (the "bronze-by-gold" chapter), drunkenness, etc., and dovetailing them all into a huge complex pattern, almost like a Victorian "plot". Miller is simply a hard-boiled person talking about life, an ordinary American businessman with intellectual courage and a gift for words. It is perhaps significant that he *looks* exactly like everyone's idea of an American businessman. As for the comparison with *Voyage au bout de la nuit*, it is even further from the point. Both books use unprintable words, both are in some sense autobiographical, but that is all. *Voyage au bout de la nuit* is a book with a purpose, and its purpose is to protest against the horror and meaninglessness of modern life – actually, indeed, of *life*. It is a cry of unbearable disgust, a voice from the cesspool. *Tropic of Cancer* is almost exactly the opposite. The thing has become so unusual as to seem almost anomalous, but it is the book of a man who is happy. So is *Black Spring*, though slightly less so, because tinged in places with nostalgia. With years of lumpenproletarian life behind him, hunger, vagabondage, dirt, failure, nights in the open, battles with immigration officers, endless struggles for a bit of cash, Miller finds that he is enjoying himself. Exactly the aspects of life that fill Céline with horror are the ones that appeal to him. So far from protesting, he is *accepting*. And the very word "acceptance" calls up his real affinity: another American, Walt Whitman.*

But there is something rather curious in being Whitman in the 1930s. It is not certain that if Whitman himself were alive at this moment he would write anything in the least degree resembling *Leaves of Grass*.* For what he is saying, after all, is "I accept", and there is a radical difference between acceptance now and acceptance then. Whitman was writing in a time of unexampled prosperity, but more than that, he was writing in a country where freedom was something more than a word. The democracy, equality and comradeship that he is always talking about are not remote ideals, but something that existed in front of his eyes. In mid-nineteenth-century America men felt themselves free and equal, *were* free and equal, so far as that is possible outside a society of pure communism. There was poverty and there were even class distinctions, but except for the Negroes there was no permanently submerged class. Everyone had inside him, like a kind of core, the knowledge that he could earn a decent living, and earn it without boot-licking. When you read about Mark Twain's Mississippi raftsmen and pilots, or Bret Harte's* Western gold miners, they seem more remote than the cannibals of the Stone Age. The reason is simply that they are free human beings. But it is the same even with the peaceful domesticated America of the eastern states, the America of *Little Women*, *Helen's Babies* and 'Riding Down from Bangor'.* Life has a buoyant, carefree quality that you can feel as you read, like a physical sensation in your belly. It is this that Whitman is celebrating, though actually he does it very badly, because he is one of those writers who tell you what you ought to feel instead of making you feel it. Luckily for his beliefs, perhaps, he died too early to see the deterioration in American life that came with the rise of large-scale industry and the exploiting of cheap immigrant labour.

Miller's outlook is deeply akin to that of Whitman, and nearly everyone who has read him has remarked on this. *Tropic of Cancer* ends with an especially Whitmanesque passage, in which, after the lecheries, the swindles, the fights, the drinking bouts and the imbecilities, he simply sits down and watches the Seine flowing past, in a sort of mystical acceptance of the thing-as-it-is. Only, what is he accepting? In the first place, not America, but the ancient bone heap of Europe, where every grain of soil has passed through innumerable human bodies. Secondly, not an epoch of expansion and liberty, but an epoch of fear, tyranny and regimentation. To say "I accept" in an age like our own is to say that you accept concentration camps, rubber truncheons, Hitler, Stalin, bombs, aeroplanes, tinned food, machine guns, putsches, purges, slogans, Bedaux belts,* gas masks, submarines, spies, provocateurs, press censorship, secret prisons, aspirins, Hollywood films and political murders. Not *only* those things, of course, but those things among others. And on the whole this is Henry Miller's attitude. Not quite always, because at moments he shows signs of a fairly ordinary kind of literary nostalgia. There is a long passage in the earlier part of *Black Spring* in praise of the Middle Ages, which as prose must be one of the most remarkable pieces of writing in recent years, but which displays an attitude not very different from that of Chesterton. In *Max and the White Phagocytes** there is an attack on modern American civilization (breakfast cereals, cellophane, etc.) from the usual angle of the literary man who hates industrialism. But in general the attitude is "Let's swallow it whole". And hence the seeming preoccupation with indecency and with the dirty-handkerchief side of life. It is only seeming, for the truth is that life, ordinary everyday life, consists far more largely of horrors than writers of fiction usually care to admit. Whitman himself "accepted" a great deal that his contemporaries found unmentionable. For he is not only writing of the prairie, he also wanders through the city and notes the shattered skull of the suicide, the "grey sick faces of onanists", etc. etc. But unquestionably our own age, at any rate in Western Europe, is less healthy and less hopeful than the age in which Whitman was writing. Unlike Whitman, we live in a *shrinking* world. The "democratic vistas" have ended in barbed wire. There is less feeling of creation and growth, less and less emphasis on the cradle, endlessly rocking, more and more emphasis on the teapot, endlessly stewing. To accept civilization *as it is* practically means accepting decay. It has ceased to be a strenuous attitude and become a passive attitude – even "decadent", if that word means anything.

But precisely because, in one sense, he is passive to experience, Miller is able to get nearer to the ordinary man than is possible to more purposive writers. For the ordinary man is also passive. Within a narrow circle (home life, and perhaps the trade union or local politics) he feels himself master of his fate, but against major events he is as helpless as against the elements. So far from endeavouring to influence the future, he simply lies down and lets things happen to him. During the past ten years literature has involved itself more and more deeply in politics, with the result that there is now less room in it for the ordinary man than at any time during the past two centuries. One can see the change in the prevailing literary attitude by comparing the books written about the Spanish Civil War with those written about the war of 1914–18. The immediately striking thing about the Spanish-war books, at any rate those written in English, is their shocking dullness and badness. But what is more significant is that almost all of them, right-wing or left-wing, are written from a political angle, by cocksure partisans telling you what to think, whereas the books about the Great War were written by common soldiers or junior officers who did not even pretend to understand what the whole thing was about. Books like *All Quiet on the Western Front, Le Feu, A Farewell to Arms, Death of a Hero, Goodbye to All That, Memoirs of an Infantry Officer* and *A Subaltern on the Somme** were written not by propagandists but by *victims*. They are saying in effect, "What the hell is all this about? God knows. All we can do is to endure." And though he is not writing about war, nor, on the whole, about unhappiness, this is nearer to Miller's attitude than the omniscience which is now fashionable. The *Booster*, a short-lived periodical of which he was part-editor, used to describe itself in its advertisements as "non-political, non-educational, non-progressive, non-cooperative, non-ethical, non-literary, non-consistent, non-contemporary", and Miller's own work could be described in nearly the same terms. It is a voice from the crowd, from the underling, from the third-class carriage, from the ordinary, non-political, non-moral, passive man.

I have been using the phrase "ordinary man" rather loosely, and I have taken it for granted that the "ordinary man" exists, a thing now denied by some people. I do not mean that the people Miller is writing about constitute a majority, still less that he is writing about proletarians. No English or American novelist has as yet seriously attempted that. And again, the people in *Tropic of Cancer* fall short of being ordinary to the extent that they are idle, disreputable and more or less "artistic". As I have said already, this is a pity, but it is the necessary result of expatriation. Miller's "ordinary man" is neither the manual worker nor the suburban householder, but the derelict, the déclassé, the adventurer, the American intellectual without roots and without money. Still, the experiences even of this type overlap fairly widely with those of more normal people. Miller has been able to get the most out of his rather limited material because he has had the courage to identify with it. The ordinary man, the "average sensual man", has been given the power of speech, like Balaam's ass.*

It will be seen that this is something out of date, or at any rate out of fashion. The average sensual man is out of fashion. The passive, non-political attitude is out of fashion. Preoccupation with sex and truthfulness about the inner life are out of fashion. American Paris is out of fashion. A book like *Tropic of Cancer*, published at such a time, must be either a tedious preciosity or something unusual, and I think a majority of the people who have read it would agree that it is not the first. It is worth trying to discover just what this escape from the current literary fashion means. But to do that one has got to see it against its background – that is, against the general development of English literature in the twenty years since the Great War.

II

When one says that a writer is fashionable one practically always means that he is admired by people under thirty. At the beginning of the period I am speaking of, the years during and immediately after the war, the writer who had the deepest hold upon the thinking young was almost certainly Housman.* Among people who were adolescent in the years 1910–25, Housman had an influence which was enormous and is now not at all easy to understand. In

1920, when I was about seventeen, I probably knew the whole of *A Shropshire Lad* by heart. I wonder how much impression *A Shropshire Lad* makes at this moment on a boy of the same age and more or less the same cast of mind? No doubt he has heard of it and even glanced into it; it might strike him as rather cheaply clever – probably that would be about all. Yet these are the poems that I and my contemporaries used to recite to ourselves, over and over, in a kind of ecstasy, just as earlier generations had recited Meredith's 'Love in a Valley', Swinburne's 'Garden of Proserpine',* etc. etc.

> With rue my heart is laden
>   For golden friends I had,
> For many a rose-lipped maiden
>   And many a light-foot lad.
>
> By brooks too broad for leaping
>   The light-foot boys are laid;
> The rose-lipped girls are sleeping
>   In fields where roses fade.

It just tinkles. But it did not seem to tinkle in 1920. Why does the bubble always burst? To answer that question one has to take account of the *external* conditions that make certain writers popular at certain times. Housman's poems had not attracted much notice when they were first published. What was there in them that appealed so deeply to a single generation, the generation born round about 1900?

In the first place, Housman is a "country" poet. His poems are full of the charm of buried villages, the nostalgia of place names, Clunton and Clunbury, Knighton, Ludlow, "on Wenlock Edge", "in summertime on Bredon", thatched roofs and the jingle of smithies, the wild jonquils in the pastures, the "blue, remembered hills". War poems apart, English verse of the 1910–25 period is mostly "country". The reason no doubt was that the rentier-professional class was ceasing once and for all to have any real relationship with the soil – but at any rate there prevailed then, far more than now, a kind of snobbism of belonging to the country and despising the town. England at that time was hardly more an agricultural country than it is now, but before the light industries began to spread themselves it was easier to think of it as one. Most middle-class boys grew up within sight of a farm, and naturally it was the picturesque side of farm life that appealed to them – the ploughing, harvesting, stack-thrashing and so forth. Unless he has to do it himself a boy is not likely to notice the horrible drudgery of hoeing turnips, milking cows with chapped teats at four o'clock in the morning, etc. etc. Just before, just after and, for that matter, during the war was the great age of the "nature poet", the heyday of Richard Jefferies and W.H. Hudson.* Rupert Brooke's 'Grantchester', the star poem of 1913, is nothing but an enormous gush of "country" sentiment, a sort of accumulated vomit from a stomach stuffed with place names. Considered as a poem 'Grantchester' is something worse than worthless, but as an illustration of what the thinking middle-class young of that period *felt* it is a valuable document.

Housman, however, did not enthuse over the rambler roses in the weekending spirit of Brooke and the others. The "country" motif is there all the time, but mainly as a background. Most of the poems have a quasi-human subject, a kind of idealized rustic, in reality Strephon or Corydon* brought up to date. This in itself had a deep appeal. Experience shows that over-civilized people enjoy reading about rustics (key phrase, "close to the soil") because they imagine them to be more primitive and passionate than themselves. Hence the "dark earth" novels of Sheila Kaye-Smith* etc. And at that time a middle-class boy, with his "country" bias, would identify with an agricultural worker as he would never have thought of doing with a town worker. Most boys had in their minds a vision of an idealized ploughman, gypsy, poacher or gamekeeper, always pictured as a wild, free, roving blade, living a life of rabbit-snaring, cockfighting, horses, beer and women. Masefield's *Everlasting Mercy*,* another valuable period piece, immensely popular with boys round about the war years, gives you this vision in a very crude form. But Housman's Maurices and Terences could be taken seriously where Masefield's Saul Kane could not; on this side of him, Housman was Masefield with a dash of Theocritus.* Moreover all his themes are adolescent – murder, suicide, unhappy love, early death. They deal with the simple, intelligible disasters that give you the feeling of being up against the "bedrock facts" of life:

> The sun burns on the half-mown hill,
>   By now the blood is dried;
> And Maurice amongst the hay lies still
>   And my knife is in his side.

And again:

> They hang us now in Shrewsbury jail:
>   The whistles blow forlorn,
> And trains all night groan on the rail
>   To men that die at morn.

It is all more or less in the same tune. Everything comes unstuck. "Dick lies long in the churchyard, and Ned lies long in jail." And notice also the exquisite self-pity – the "nobody loves me" feeling:

> The diamond tears adorning
> > Thy low mound on the lea,
> Those are the tears of morning,
> > That weeps, but not for thee.

Hard cheese, old chap! Such poems might have been written expressly for adolescents. And the unvarying sexual pessimism (the girl always dies or marries somebody else) seemed like wisdom to boys who were herded together in public schools and were half inclined to think of women as something unattainable. Whether Housman ever had the same appeal for girls I doubt. In his poems the women's point of view is not considered; she is merely the nymph, the siren, the treacherous half-human creature who leads you a little distance and then gives you the slip.

But Housman would not have appealed so deeply to the people who were young in 1920 if it had not been for another strain in him, and that was his blasphemous, antinomian, "cynical" strain. The fight that always occurs between the generations was exceptionally bitter at the end of the Great War; this was partly due to the war itself, and partly it was an indirect result of the Russian Revolution, but an intellectual struggle was in any case due at about that date. Owing probably to the ease and security of life in England, which even the war hardly disturbed, many people whose ideas were formed in the eighties or earlier had carried them quite unmodified into the 1920s. Meanwhile, so far as the younger generation was concerned, the official beliefs were dissolving like sandcastles. The slump in religious belief, for instance, was spectacular. For several years the old–young antagonism took on a quality of real hatred. What was left of the war generation had crept out of the massacre to find their elders still bellowing the slogans of 1914, and a slightly younger generation of boys were writhing under dirty-minded celibate schoolmasters. It was to these that Housman appealed, with his implied sexual revolt and his personal grievance against God. He was patriotic, it was true, but in a harmless old-fashioned way, to the tune of red coats and "God save the Queen" rather than steel helmets and "Hang the Kaiser". And he was satisfyingly anti-Christian – he stood for a kind of bitter, defiant paganism, a conviction that life is short and the gods are against you, which exactly fitted the prevailing mood of the young – and all in charming fragile verse that was composed almost entirely of words of one syllable.

It will be seen that I have discussed Housman as though he were merely a propagandist, an utterer of maxims and quotable "bits". Obviously he was more than that. There is no need to underrate him now because he was overrated a few years ago. Although one gets into trouble nowadays for saying so, there is a number of his poems ('Into My Heart an Air That Kills', for instance, and 'Is My Team Ploughing?') that are not likely to remain long out of favour. But at bottom it is always a writer's tendency, his "purpose", his "message", that makes him liked or disliked. The proof of this is the extreme difficulty of seeing any literary merit in a book that seriously damages your deepest beliefs. And no book is ever truly neutral. Some tendency or other is always discernible, in verse as much as in prose, even if it does no more than determine the form and the choice of imagery. But poets who attain wide popularity, like Housman, are as a rule definitely gnomic writers.

After the war, after Housman and the nature poets, there appears a group of writers of completely different tendency – Joyce, Eliot, Pound, Lawrence, Wyndham Lewis, Aldous Huxley, Lytton Strachey.* So far as the middle and late twenties go, these are "the movement", as surely as the Auden–Spender group* have been "the movement" during the past few years. It is true that not all of the gifted writers of the period can be fitted into the pattern. E.M. Forster,* for instance, though he wrote his best book in 1923 or thereabouts, was essentially pre-war, and Yeats does not seem in either of his phases to belong to the twenties. Others who were still living, Moore, Conrad, Bennett, Wells, Norman Douglas,* had shot their bolt before the war ever happened. On the other hand, a writer who should be added to the group, though in the narrowly literary sense he hardly "belongs", is Somerset Maugham. Of course the dates do not fit exactly; most of these writers had already published books before the war, but they can be classified as post-war in the same sense that the younger men now writing are post-slump. Equally of course, you could read through most of the literary papers of the time without grasping that these people *are* "the movement". Even more then than at most times the big shots of literary journalism were busy pretending that the age before last had not come to an end. Squire ruled the *London Mercury*,* Gibbs and Walpole* were the gods of the lending libraries, there was a cult of cheeriness and manliness, beer and cricket, briar pipes and monogamy, and it was at all times possible to earn a few guineas by writing an article denouncing "highbrows". But all the same it was the despised highbrows who had captured the young. The wind was blowing from Europe, and long before 1930 it had blown the beer-and-cricket school naked, except for their knighthoods.

But the first thing one would notice about the group of writers I have named above is that they do not look like a group. Moreover several of them would strongly object to being coupled with several of the others. Lawrence and Eliot were in reality antipathetic, Huxley worshipped Lawrence but was repelled by Joyce, most of the others would have looked down on Huxley, Strachey and Maugham, and Lewis attacked everyone in turn; indeed, his reputation as a writer rests largely on these attacks. And yet there is a certain temperamental similarity, evident enough now, though it would not have been so a dozen years ago. What it amounts to is *pessimism of outlook*. But it is necessary to make clear what is meant by pessimism.

If the keynote of the Georgian poets was "beauty of Nature", the keynote of the post-war writers would be "tragic sense of life". The spirit behind Housman's poems, for instance, is not tragic, merely querulous; it is hedonism disappointed. The same is true of Hardy, though one ought to make an exception of *The Dynasts*.* But the Joyce–Eliot group come later in time – puritanism is not their main adversary; they are able from the start to "see through" most of the things that their predecessors had fought for. All of them are temperamentally hostile to the notion of "progress"; it is felt that progress not only doesn't happen, but *ought not* to happen. Given this general similarity, there are, of course, differences of approach between the writers I have named as well as very different degrees of talent. Eliot's pessimism is partly the Christian pessimism, which implies a certain indifference to human misery, partly a lament over the decadence of Western civilization ("We are the hollow men, we are the stuffed men"* etc. etc.), a sort of twilight-of-the-gods feeling which finally leads him, in *Sweeney Agonistes** for instance, to achieve the difficult feat of making modern life out to be worse than it is. With Strachey it is merely a polite eighteenth-century scepticism mixed up with a taste for debunking. With Maugham it is a kind of stoical resignation, the stiff upper lip of the *pukka sahib** somewhere east of Suez, carrying on with his job without believing in it, like an Antonine Emperor. Lawrence at first sight does not seem to be a pessimistic writer, because, like Dickens, he is a "change-of-heart" man and constantly insisting that life here and now would be all right if only you looked at it a little differently. But what he is demanding is a movement away from our mechanized civilization, which is not going to happen, and which he knows is not going to happen. Therefore his exasperation with the present turns once more into idealization of the past, this time a safely mythical past, the Bronze Age. When Lawrence prefers the Etruscans* (*his* Etruscans) to ourselves it is difficult not to agree with him, and yet, after all, it is a species of defeatism, because that is not the direction in which the world is moving. The kind of life that he is always pointing to, a life centring round the simple mysteries – sex, earth, fire, water, blood – is merely a lost cause. All he has been able to produce, therefore, is a wish that things would happen in a way in which they are manifestly not going to happen. "A wave of generosity or a wave of death", he says, but it is obvious that there are no waves of generosity this side of the horizon. So he flees to Mexico, and then dies at forty-five, a few years before the wave of death gets going. It will be seen that once again I am speaking of these people as though they were not artists, as though they were merely propagandists putting a "message" across. And once again it is obvious that all of them are more than that. It would be absurd, for instance, to look on *Ulysses* as *merely* a show-up of the horror of modern life, the "dirty *Daily Mail* era", as Pound put it. Joyce actually is more of a "pure artist" than most writers. But *Ulysses* could not have been written by someone who was merely dabbling with word patterns; it is the product of a special vision of life, the vision of a Catholic who has lost his faith. What Joyce is saying is "Here is life without God. Just look at it!" and his technical innovations, important though they are, are there primarily to serve this purpose.

But what is noticeable about all these writers is that what "purpose" they have is very much up in the air. There is no attention to the urgent problems of the moment, above all no politics in the narrower sense. Our eyes are directed to Rome, to Byzantium, to Montparnasse, to Mexico, to the Etruscans, to the subconscious, to the solar plexus – to everywhere except the places where things are actually happening. When one looks back at the twenties, nothing is queerer than the way in which every important event in Europe escaped the notice of the English intelligentsia. The Russian Revolution, for instance, all but vanishes from the English consciousness between the death of Lenin and the Ukraine famine – about ten years. Throughout those years Russia means Tolstoy, Dostoevsky and exiled counts driving taxicabs. Italy means picture galleries, ruins, churches and museums – but not Blackshirts. Germany means films, nudism and psychoanalysis – but not Hitler, of whom hardly anyone had heard till 1931. In "cultured" circles art-for-art's-saking extended practically to a worship of the meaningless. Literature was supposed to consist solely in the manipulation of words. To judge a book by its subject matter was the unforgivable sin, and even to be aware of its subject matter was looked on as a lapse of taste. About 1928, in one of the three genuinely funny jokes that *Punch* has produced since the Great War, an intolerable youth is pictured informing his aunt that he intends to "write". "And what are you going to write about, dear?" asks the aunt. "My dear aunt," says the youth crushingly, "one doesn't write *about* anything, one just *writes*." The best writers of the twenties did not subscribe to this doctrine; their "purpose" is in most cases fairly overt, but it is usually a "purpose" along moral-religious-cultural lines. Also, when translatable into political terms, it is in no case "left". In one way or another the tendency of all the writers in this group is conservative. Lewis, for instance, spent years in frenzied witch-smellings after "Bolshevism", which he was able to detect in very unlikely places. Recently he has changed some of his views, perhaps influenced by Hitler's treatment of artists, but it is safe to bet that he will not go very far leftward. Pound seems to have plumped definitely for fascism, at any rate the Italian variety. Eliot has remained aloof, but if forced at the pistol's point to choose between fascism and some more democratic form of socialism, would probably choose fascism. Huxley starts off with the usual despair-of-life, then, under the influence of Lawrence's "dark abdomen", tries something called Life-Worship, and finally arrives at pacifism – a tenable position, and at this moment an honourable one, but probably in the long run involving rejection of socialism. It is also noticeable that most of the writers in this group have a certain tenderness for the Catholic Church, though not usually of a kind that an orthodox Catholic would accept.

The mental connection between pessimism and a reactionary outlook is no doubt obvious enough. What is perhaps less obvious is just *why* the leading writers of the twenties were predominantly pessimistic. Why always the sense of decadence, the skulls and cactuses, the yearning after lost faith and impossible civilizations? Was it not, after all, *because* these people were writing in an exceptionally comfortable epoch? It is just in such times that "cosmic despair" can flourish. People with empty bellies never despair of the universe, nor even think about the universe, for that matter. The whole period 1910–30 was a prosperous one, and even the war years were physically tolerable if one happened to be a non-combatant in one of the Allied countries. As for the twenties, they were the golden age of the rentier-intellectual, a period of irresponsibility such as the world had never before seen. The war was over, the new totalitarian states had not arisen, moral and religious taboos of all descriptions had vanished, and the cash was rolling in. "Disillusionment" was all the fashion. Everyone with a safe £500 a year turned highbrow and began training himself in *tædium vitæ*.* It was an age of eagles and of crumpets, facile despairs, backyard Hamlets, cheap return tickets to the end of the night. In some of the minor characteristic novels of the period, books like *Told by an Idiot*,* the despair-of-life reaches a Turkish-bath atmosphere of self-pity. And even the best writers of the time can be convicted of a too Olympian attitude, a too great readiness to wash their hands of the immediate practical problem. They see life very comprehensively, much more so than those who come immediately before or after them, but they see it through the wrong end of the telescope. Not that that invalidates their books, as books. The first test of any work of art is survival, and it is a fact that a great deal that was written in the period 1910–30 has survived and looks like continuing to survive. One has only to think of *Ulysses, Of Human Bondage*,* most of Lawrence's early work, especially his short stories, and virtually the whole of Eliot's poems up to about 1930, to wonder what is now being written that will wear so well.

But quite suddenly, in the years 1930–35, something happens. The literary climate changes. A new group of writers, Auden and Spender and the rest of them, has made its appearance, and although technically these writers owe something to their predecessors, their "tendency" is entirely different. Suddenly we have got out of the twilight of the gods into a sort of Boy Scout atmosphere of bare knees and community singing. The typical literary man ceases to be a cultured expatriate with a leaning towards the Church, and becomes an eager-minded schoolboy with a leaning towards communism. If the keynote of the writers of the twenties is "tragic sense of life", the keynote of the new writers is "serious purpose".

The differences between the two schools are discussed at some length in Mr Louis MacNeice's book *Modern Poetry*.* This book is, of course, written entirely from the angle of the younger group and takes the superiority of their standards for granted. According to Mr MacNeice:

> The poets of *New Signatures*,* unlike Yeats and Eliot, are emotionally partisan. Yeats proposed to turn his back on desire and hatred; Eliot sat back and watched other people's emotions with ennui and an ironical self-pity [...]. The whole poetry, on the other hand, of Auden, Spender and Day-Lewis implies that they have desires and hatreds of their own and, further, that they think some things *ought* to be desired and others hated.

And again:

> The poets of *New Signatures* have swung back [...] to the Greek preference for information or statement. The first requirement is to have something to say, and after that you must say it as well as you can.

In other words, "purpose" has come back; the younger writers have "gone into politics". As I have pointed out already, Eliot and Co. are not really so non-partisan as Mr MacNeice seems to suggest. Still, it is broadly true that in the twenties the literary emphasis was more on technique and less on subject matter than it is now.

The leading figures in this group are Auden, Spender, Day-Lewis and MacNeice, and there is a long string of writers of more or less the same tendency – Isherwood, John Lehmann, Arthur Calder-Marshall, Edward Upward, Alec Brown, Philip Henderson,* and many others. As before, I am lumping them together simply according to tendency. Obviously there are very great variations in talent. But when one compares these writers with the Joyce–Eliot generation, the immediately striking thing is how much easier it is to form them into a group. Technically they are closer together, politically they are almost indistinguishable, and their criticisms of one another's work have always been (to put it mildly) good-natured. The outstanding writers of the twenties were of very varied origins; few of them had passed through the ordinary English educational mill (incidentally, the best of them, barring Lawrence, were not Englishmen), and most of them had had at some time to struggle against poverty, neglect and even downright persecution. On the other hand, nearly all the younger writers fit easily into the public-school–university–Bloomsbury pattern. The few who are of proletarian origin are of the kind that is declassed early in life, first by means of scholarships and then by the bleaching tub of London "culture". It is significant that several of the writers in this group have been not only boys but, subsequently, masters at public schools. Some years ago I described Auden as "a sort of gutless Kipling". As criticism this was quite unworthy, indeed it was merely a spiteful remark, but it is a fact that in Auden's work, especially his earlier work, an atmosphere of uplift – something rather like Kipling's 'If' or Newbolt's 'Play Up, Play Up, and Play the Game!'* – never seems to be very far away. Take, for instance, a poem like 'You're leaving now, and it's up to you boys'.* It is pure scoutmaster, the exact note of the ten-minutes-straight talk on the dangers of self-abuse. No doubt there is an element of parody that he intends, but there is also a deeper resemblance that he does not intend. And of course the rather priggish note that is common to most of these writers is a symptom of release. By throwing "pure art" overboard they have freed themselves from the fear of being laughed at and vastly enlarged their scope. The prophetic side of Marxism, for example, is new material for poetry and has great possibilities:

> We are nothing.
> We have fallen
> Into the dark and shall be destroyed.
> Think though, that in this darkness
> We hold the secret hub of an idea
> Whose living sunlit wheel revolves in future years outside.
> (Spender, *Trial of a Judge**)

But at the same time, by being Marxized literature has moved no nearer to the masses. Even allowing for the time lag, Auden and Spender are somewhat farther from being popular writers than Joyce and Eliot, let alone Lawrence. As before, there are many contemporary writers who are outside the current, but there is not much doubt about what *is* the current. For the middle and late thirties, Auden, Spender and Co. *are* "the movement", just as Joyce, Eliot and Co. were for the twenties. And the movement is in the direction of some rather ill-defined thing called communism. As early as 1934 or 1935 it was considered eccentric in literary circles not to be more or less "left", and in another year or two there had grown up a left-wing orthodoxy that made a certain set of opinions absolutely de rigueur on certain subjects. The idea had begun to gain ground (*vide* Edward Upward and others) that a writer must either be actively "left" or write badly. Between 1935 and 1939 the Communist Party had an almost irresistible fascination for any writer under forty. It became as normal to hear that so-and-so had "joined" as it had been a few years earlier, when Roman Catholicism was fashionable, to hear that so-and-so had "been received". For about three years, in fact, the central stream of English literature was more or less directly under communist control. How was it possible for such a thing to happen? And at the same time, what is meant by "communism"? It is better to answer the second question first.

The communist movement in Western Europe began as a movement for the violent overthrow of capitalism, and degenerated within a few years into an instrument of Russian foreign policy. This was probably inevitable when the revolutionary ferment that followed the Great War had died down. So far as I know, the only comprehensive history of this subject in English is Franz Borkenau's book *The Communist International*.* What Borkenau's facts even more than his deductions make clear is that communism could never have developed along its present lines if any real revolutionary feeling had existed in the industrialized countries. In England, for instance, it is obvious that no such feeling has existed for years past. The pathetic membership figures of all extremist parties show this clearly. It is only natural, therefore, that the English communist movement should be controlled by people who are mentally subservient to Russia and have no real aim except to manipulate British foreign policy in the Russian interest. Of course such an aim cannot be openly admitted, and it is this fact that gives the Communist Party its very peculiar character. The more vocal kind of communist is in effect a Russian publicity agent posing as an international socialist. It is a pose that is easily kept up at normal times, but becomes difficult in moments of crisis, because of the fact that the USSR is no more scrupulous in its foreign policy than the rest of the Great Powers. Alliances, changes of front, etc. which only make sense as part of the game of power politics have to be explained and justified in terms of international socialism. Every time Stalin swaps partners, "Marxism" has to be hammered into a new shape. This entails sudden and violent changes of "line", purges, denunciations, systematic destruction of party literature, etc. etc. Every communist is in fact liable at any moment to have to alter his most fundamental convictions, or leave the party. The unquestionable dogma of Monday may become the damnable heresy of Tuesday, and so on. This has happened at least three times during the past ten years. It follows that in any Western country a communist party is always unstable and usually very small. Its long-term membership really consists of an inner ring of intellectuals who have identified with the Russian bureaucracy, and a slightly larger body of working-class people who feel a loyalty towards Soviet Russia without necessarily understanding its policies. Otherwise there is only a shifting membership, one lot coming and another going with each change of "line".

In 1930 the English Communist Party was a tiny, barely legal organization whose main activity was libelling the Labour Party. But by 1935 the face of Europe had changed, and left-wing politics changed with it. Hitler had risen to power and begun to rearm, the Russian Five-Year Plans had succeeded, Russia had reappeared as a great military power. As Hitler's three targets of attack were, to all appearances, Great Britain, France and the USSR, the three countries were forced into a sort of uneasy rapprochement. This meant that the English or French communist was obliged to become a good patriot and imperialist – that is, to defend the very things he had been attacking for the past fifteen years. The Comintern slogans suddenly faded from red to pink. "World revolution" and "Social fascism" gave way to "Defence of democracy" and "Stop Hitler!" The years 1935–39 were the period of anti-fascism and the Popular Front, the heyday of the Left Book Club, when red duchesses and "broad-minded" deans toured the battlefields of the Spanish war and Winston Churchill was the blue-eyed boy of the *Daily Worker*. Since then, of course, there has been yet another change of "line". But what is important for my purpose is that it was during the "anti-fascist" phase that the younger English writers gravitated towards communism.

The fascism–democracy dogfight was no doubt an attraction in itself, but in any case their conversion was due at about that date. It was obvious that laissez-faire capitalism was finished and that there had got to be some kind of reconstruction; in the world of 1935 it was hardly possible to remain politically indifferent. But why did these young men turn towards anything so alien as Russian communism? Why should *writers* be attracted by a form of socialism that makes mental honesty impossible? The explanation really lies in something that had already made itself felt before the slump and before Hitler: middle-class unemployment.

Unemployment is not merely a matter of not having a job. Most people can *get* a job of sorts, even at the worst of times. The trouble was that by 1930 there was no activity, except perhaps scientific research, the arts and left-wing politics, that a thinking person could believe in. The debunking of Western civilization had reached its climax and "disillusionment" was immensely widespread. Who now could take it for granted to go through life in the ordinary middle-class way, as a soldier, a clergyman, a stockbroker, an Indian Civil Servant or what not? And how many of the values by which our grandfathers lived could now be taken seriously? Patriotism, religion, the Empire, the family, the sanctity of marriage, the Old School Tie, birth, breeding, honour, discipline – anyone of ordinary education could turn the whole lot of them inside out in three minutes. But what do you achieve, after all, by getting rid of such primal things as patriotism and religion? You have not necessarily got rid of the need for *something to believe in*. There had been a sort of false dawn a few years earlier when numbers of young intellectuals, including several quite gifted writers (Evelyn Waugh, Christopher Hollis* and others), had fled into the Catholic Church. It is significant that these people went almost invariably to the Roman Church and not, for instance, to the C of E, the Greek Church or the Protestant sects. They went, that is, to the Church with a worldwide organization, the one with a rigid discipline, the one with power and prestige behind it. Perhaps it is even worth noticing that the only latter-day convert of really first-rate gifts, Eliot, has embraced not Romanism but Anglo-Catholicism, the ecclesiastical equivalent of Trotskyism.

But I do not think one need look farther than this for the reason why the young writers of the thirties flocked into or towards the Communist Party. It was simply something to believe in. Here was a church, an army, an orthodoxy, a discipline. Here was a Fatherland and – at any rate since 1935 or thereabouts – a Führer. All the loyalties and superstitions that the intellect had seemingly banished could come rushing back under the thinnest of disguises. Patriotism, religion, empire, military glory – all in one word, Russia. Father, king, leader, hero, saviour – all in one word, Stalin. God – Stalin. The Devil – Hitler. Heaven – Moscow. Hell – Berlin. All the gaps were filled up. So, after all, the "communism" of the English intellectual is something explicable enough. It is the patriotism of the deracinated.

But there is one thing that undoubtedly contributed to the cult of Russia among the English intelligentsia during these years, and that is the softness and security of life in England itself. With all its injustices, England is still the land of habeas corpus, and the overwhelming majority of English people have no experience of violence or illegality. If you have grown up in that sort of atmosphere it is not at all easy to imagine what a despotic regime is like. Nearly all the dominant writers of the thirties belonged to the soft-boiled emancipated middle class and were too young to have effective memories of the Great War. To people of that kind such things as purges, secret police, summary executions, imprisonment without trial, etc. etc. are too remote to be terrifying. They can swallow totalitarianism *because* they have no experience of anything except liberalism. Look, for instance, at this extract from Mr Auden's poem 'Spain'* (incidentally this poem is one of the few decent things that have been written about the Spanish war):

> Tomorrow for the young, the poets exploding like bombs,
> The walks by the lake, the weeks of perfect communion;
> >   Tomorrow the bicycle races
> Through the suburbs on summer evenings. But today the struggle.
>
> Today the deliberate increase in the chances of death,
> The conscious acceptance of guilt in the necessary murder;
> >   Today the expending of powers
> On the flat ephemeral pamphlet and the boring meeting.

The second stanza is intended as a sort of thumbnail sketch of a day in the life of a "good party man". In the morning a couple of political murders, a ten-minutes' interlude to stifle "bourgeois" remorse, and then a hurried luncheon and a busy afternoon and evening chalking walls and distributing leaflets. All very edifying. But notice the phrase "necessary murder". It could only be written by a person to whom murder is at most a *word*. Personally I would not speak so lightly of murder. It so happens that I have seen the bodies of numbers of murdered men – I don't mean killed in battle, I mean murdered. Therefore I have some conception of what murder means – the terror, the hatred, the howling relatives, the post-mortems, the blood, the smells. To me, murder is something to be avoided. So it is to any ordinary person. The Hitlers and Stalins find murder necessary, but they don't advertise their callousness, and they don't speak of it as murder; it is "liquidation", "elimination" or some other soothing phrase. Mr Auden's brand of amoralism is only possible if you are the kind of person who is always somewhere else when the trigger is pulled. So much of left-wing thought is a kind of playing with fire by people who don't even know that fire is hot. The warmongering to which the English intelligentsia gave themselves up in the period 1935–39 was largely based on a sense of personal immunity. The attitude was very different in France, where the military service is hard to dodge and even literary men know the weight of a pack.

Towards the end of Mr Cyril Connolly's recent book *Enemies of Promise** there occurs an interesting and revealing passage. The first part of the book is, more or less, an evaluation of present-day literature. Mr Connolly belongs exactly to the generation of the writers of "the movement", and with not many reservations their values are his values. It is interesting to notice that among prose writers he admires chiefly those specializing in violence – the would-be tough American school, Hemingway, etc. The latter part of the book, however, is autobiographical and consists of an account, fascinatingly accurate, of life at a preparatory school and Eton in the years 1910–20. Mr Connolly ends by remarking:

> Were I to deduce anything from my feelings on leaving Eton, it might be called *The Theory of Permanent Adolescence*. It is the theory that the experiences undergone by boys at the great public schools are so intense as to dominate their lives and to arrest their development.

When you read the second sentence in this passage, your natural impulse is to look for the misprint. Presumably there is a "not" left out, or something. But no, not a bit of it! He means it! And what is more, he is merely speaking the truth, in an inverted fashion. "Cultured" middle-class life has reached a depth of softness at which a public-school education – five years in a lukewarm bath of snobbery – can actually be looked back upon as an eventful period. To nearly all the writers who have counted during the thirties, what more has ever happened than Mr Connolly records in *Enemies of Promise*? It is the same pattern all the time: public school, university, a few trips abroad, then London. Hunger, hardship, solitude, exile, war, prison, persecution, manual labour – hardly even words. No wonder that the huge tribe known as "the right left people" found it so easy to condone the purge-and-OGPU* side of the Russian regime and the horrors of the first Five-Year Plan. They were so gloriously incapable of understanding what it all meant.

By 1937 the whole of the intelligentsia was mentally at war. Left-wing thought had narrowed down to "anti-fascism", i.e. to a negative, and a torrent of hate literature directed against Germany and the politicians supposedly friendly to Germany was pouring from the press. The thing that, to me, was truly frightening about the war in Spain was not such violence as I witnessed, nor even the party feuds behind the lines, but the immediate reappearance in left-wing circles of the mental atmosphere of the Great War. The very people who for twenty years had sniggered over their own superiority to war hysteria were the ones who rushed straight back into the mental slum of 1915. All the familiar wartime idiocies, spy-hunting, orthodoxy-sniffing (Sniff, sniff. Are you a good anti-fascist?), the retailing of incredible atrocity stories, came back into vogue as though the intervening years had never happened. Before the end of the Spanish war, and even before Munich,* some of the better of the left-wing writers were beginning to squirm. Neither Auden nor, on the whole, Spender wrote about the Spanish war in quite the vein that was expected of them. Since then there has been a change of feeling and much dismay and confusion, because the actual course of events has made nonsense of the left-wing orthodoxy of the last few years. But then it did not need very great acuteness to see that much of it was nonsense from the start. There is no certainty, therefore, that the next orthodoxy to emerge will be any better than the last.

On the whole the literary history of the thirties seems to justify the opinion that a writer does well to keep out of politics. For any writer who accepts or partially accepts the discipline of a political party is sooner or later faced with the alternative: toe the line, or shut up. It is, of course, possible to toe the line and go on writing – after a fashion. Any Marxist can demonstrate with the greatest of ease that "bourgeois" liberty of thought is an illusion. But when he has finished his demonstration there remains the psychological *fact* that without this "bourgeois" liberty the creative powers wither away. In the future a totalitarian literature may arise, but it will be quite different from anything we can now imagine. Literature as we know it is an individual thing, demanding mental honesty and a minimum of censorship. And this is even truer of prose than of verse. It is probably not a coincidence that the best writers of the thirties have been poets. The atmosphere of orthodoxy is always damaging to prose, and above all it is completely ruinous to the novel, the most anarchical of all forms of literature. How many Roman Catholics have been good novelists? Even the handful one could name have usually been bad Catholics. The novel is practically a Protestant form of art; it is a product of the free mind, of the autonomous individual. No decade in the past 150 years has been so barren of imaginative prose as the 1930s. There have been good poems, good sociological works, brilliant pamphlets, but practically no fiction of any value at all. From 1933 onwards the mental climate was increasingly against it. Anyone sensitive enough to be touched by the Zeitgeist was also involved in politics. Not everyone, of course, was definitely *in* the political racket, but practically everyone was on its periphery and more or less mixed up in propaganda campaigns and squalid controversies. Communists and near-communists had a disproportionately large influence in the literary reviews. It was a time of labels, slogans and evasions. At the worst moments you were expected to lock yourself up in a constipating little cage of lies; at the best a sort of voluntary censorship ("Ought I to say this? Is it pro-fascist?") was at work in nearly everyone's mind. It is almost inconceivable that good novels should be written in such an atmosphere. Good novels are not written by orthodoxy-sniffers, nor by people who are conscience-stricken about their own unorthodoxy. Good novels are written by people who are *not frightened*. This brings me back to Henry Miller.

III

If this were a likely moment for the launching of "schools" of literature, Henry Miller might be the starting point of a new "school". He does at any rate mark an unexpected swing of the pendulum. In his books one gets right away from the "political animal" and back to a viewpoint not only individualistic but completely passive – the viewpoint of a man who believes the world-process to be outside his control and who in any case hardly wishes to control it.

I first met Miller at the end of 1936, when I was passing through Paris on my way to Spain. What most intrigued me about him was to find that he felt no interest in the Spanish war whatever. He merely told me in forcible terms that to go to Spain at that moment was the act of an idiot. He could understand anyone going there from purely selfish motives, out of curiosity, for instance, but to mix oneself up in such things *from a sense of obligation* was sheer stupidity. In any case my ideas about combating fascism, defending democracy, etc. etc. were all baloney. Our civilization was destined to be swept away and replaced by something so different that we should scarcely regard it as human – a prospect that did not bother him, he said. And some such outlook is implicit throughout his work. Everywhere there is the sense of the approaching cataclysm, and almost everywhere the implied belief that it doesn't matter. The only political declaration which, so far as I know, he has ever made in print is a purely negative one. A year or so ago an American magazine, the *Marxist Quarterly*, sent out a questionnaire to various American writers asking them to define their attitude on the subject of war. Miller replied in terms of extreme pacifism, but a merely personal pacifism, an individual refusal to fight, with no apparent wish to convert others to the same opinion – practically, in fact, a declaration of irresponsibility.

However, there is more than one kind of irresponsibility. As a rule, writers who do not wish to identify themselves with the historical process of the moment either ignore it or fight against it. If they can ignore it, they are probably fools. If they can understand it well enough to want to fight against it, they probably have enough vision to realize that they cannot win. Look, for instance, at a poem like 'The Scholar Gipsy', with its railing against the "strange disease of modern life" and its magnificent defeatist simile in the final stanza.* It expresses one of the normal literary attitudes, perhaps actually the prevailing attitude during the last hundred years. And on the other hand there are the "progressives", the yea-sayers, the Shaw–Wells type, always leaping forward to embrace the ego projections which they mistake for the future. On the whole the writers of the twenties took the first line and the writers of the thirties the second. And at any given moment, of course, there is a huge tribe of Barries and Deepings and Dells* who simply don't notice what is happening. Where Miller's work is symptomatically important is in its avoidance of any of these attitudes. He is neither pushing the world-process forward nor trying to drag it back, but on the other hand he is by no means ignoring it. I should say that he believes in the impending ruin of Western civilization much more firmly than the majority of "revolutionary" writers – only he does not feel called upon to do anything about it. He is fiddling while Rome is burning, and, unlike the enormous majority of people who do this, fiddling with his face towards the flames.

In *Max and the White Phagocytes* there is one of those revealing passages in which a writer tells you a great deal about himself while talking about somebody else. The book includes a long essay on the diaries of Anaïs Nin,* which I have never read, except for a few fragments, and which I believe have not been published. Miller claims that they are the only truly feminine writing that has ever appeared, whatever that may mean. But the interesting passage is one in which he compares Anaïs Nin – evidently a completely subjective, introverted writer – to Jonah in the whale's belly. In passing he refers to an essay that Aldous Huxley wrote some years ago about El Greco's picture *The Dream of Philip the Second*. Huxley remarks that the people in El Greco's pictures always look as though they were in the bellies of whales, and professes to find something peculiarly horrible in the idea of being in a "visceral prison". Miller retorts that, on the contrary, there are many worse things than being swallowed by whales, and the passage makes it clear that he himself finds the idea rather attractive. Here he is touching upon what is probably a very widespread fantasy. It is perhaps worth noticing that everyone, at least every English-speaking person, invariably speaks of Jonah and the *whale*. Of course the creature that swallowed Jonah was a fish, and is so described in the Bible (Jonah 1:17), but children naturally confuse it with a whale, and this fragment of baby talk is habitually carried into later life – a sign, perhaps, of the hold that the Jonah myth has upon our imaginations. For the fact is that being inside a whale is a very comfortable, cosy, homelike thought. The historical Jonah, if he can be so called, was glad enough to escape, but in imagination, in daydream, countless people have envied him. It is, of course, quite obvious why. The whale's belly is simply a womb big enough for an adult. There you are, in the dark, cushioned space that exactly fits you, with yards of blubber between yourself and reality, able to keep up an attitude of the completest indifference, no matter *what* happens. A storm that would sink all the battleships in the world would hardly reach you as an echo. Even the whale's own movements would probably be imperceptible to you. He might be wallowing among the surface waves or shooting down into the blackness of the middle seas (a mile deep, according to Herman Melville), but you would never notice the difference. Short of being dead, it is the final, unsurpassable stage of irresponsibility. And however it may be with Anaïs Nin, there is no question that Miller himself is inside the whale. All his best and most characteristic passages are written from the angle of Jonah, a willing Jonah. Not that he is especially introverted – quite the contrary. In his case the whale happens to be transparent. Only he feels no impulse to alter or control the process that he is undergoing. He has performed the essential Jonah act of allowing himself to be swallowed, remaining passive, *accepting*.

It will be seen what this amounts to. It is a species of quietism, implying either complete unbelief or else a degree of belief amounting to mysticism. The attitude is "*Je m'en fous*"* or "Though He slay me, yet will I trust in Him",* whichever way you like to look at it; for practical purposes both are identical, the moral in either case being "Sit on your bum". But in a time like ours, is this a defensible attitude? Notice that it is almost impossible to refrain from asking this question. At the moment of writing we are still in a period in which it is taken for granted that books ought always to be positive, serious and "constructive". A dozen years ago this idea would have been greeted with titters. ("My dear aunt, one doesn't write *about* anything, one just *writes*.") Then the pendulum swung away from the frivolous notion that art is merely technique, but it swung a very long distance, to the point of asserting that a book can only be "good" if it is founded on a "true" vision of life. Naturally the people who believe this also believe that they are in possession of the truth themselves. Catholic critics, for instance, tend to claim that books are only "good" when they are of Catholic tendency. Marxist critics make the same claim more boldly for Marxist books. For instance, Mr Edward Upward ('A Marxist Interpretation of Literature', in *The Mind in Chains**):

> Literary criticism which aims at being Marxist must [...] proclaim that no book written *at the present time* can be "good" unless it is written from a Marxist or near-Marxist viewpoint.

Various other writers have made similar or comparable statements. Mr Upward italicizes "at the present time" because he realizes that you cannot, for instance, dismiss *Hamlet* on the ground that Shakespeare was not a Marxist. Nevertheless his interesting essay only glances very shortly at this difficulty. Much of the literature that comes to us out of the past is permeated by and in fact founded on beliefs (the belief in the immortality of the soul, for example) which now seem to us false and in some cases contemptibly silly. Yet it is "good" literature, if survival is any test. Mr Upward would no doubt answer that a belief which was appropriate several centuries ago might be inappropriate and therefore stultifying now. But this does not get one much farther, because it assumes that in any age there will be *one* body of belief which is the current approximation to truth, and that the best literature of the time will be more or less in harmony with it. Actually no such uniformity has ever existed. In seventeenth-century England, for instance, there was a religious and political cleavage which distinctly resembled the left–right antagonism of today. Looking back, most modern people would feel that the bourgeois-Puritan viewpoint was a better approximation to truth than the Catholic–feudal one. But it is certainly not the case that all or even a majority of the best writers of the time were Puritans. And more than this, there exist "good" writers whose world view would in *any* age be recognized as false and silly. Edgar Allan Poe is an example. Poe's outlook is at best a wild romanticism and at worst is not far from being insane in the literal clinical sense. Why is it, then, that stories like 'The Black Cat', 'The Tell-Tale Heart', 'The Fall of the House of Usher' and so forth, which might very nearly have been written by a lunatic, do not convey a feeling of falsity? Because they are true within a certain framework, they keep the rules of their own peculiar world, like a Japanese picture. But it appears that to write successfully about such a world you have got to believe in it. One sees the difference immediately if one compares Poe's *Tales* with what is, in my opinion, an insincere attempt to work up a similar atmosphere, Julien Green's *Minuit*.* The thing that immediately strikes one about *Minuit* is that there is no reason why any of the events in it should happen. Everything is completely arbitrary; there is no emotional sequence. But this is exactly what one does *not* feel with Poe's stories. Their maniacal logic, in its own setting, is quite convincing. When, for instance, the drunkard seizes the black cat and cuts its eye out with his penknife, one knows exactly *why* he did it, even to the point of feeling that one would have done the same oneself. It seems therefore that for a creative writer possession of the "truth" is less important than emotional sincerity. Even Mr Upward would not claim that a writer needs nothing beyond a Marxist training. He also needs talent. But talent, apparently, is a matter of being able to *care*, of really *believing* in your beliefs, whether they are true or false. The difference between, for instance, Céline and Evelyn Waugh is a difference of emotional intensity. It is the difference between genuine despair and a despair that is at least partly a pretence. And with this there goes another consideration which is perhaps less obvious: that there are occasions when an "untrue" belief is more likely to be sincerely held than a "true" one.

If one looks at the books of personal reminiscence written about the war of 1914–18, one notices that nearly all that have remained readable after a lapse of time are written from a passive, negative angle. They are the records of something completely meaningless, a nightmare happening in a void. That was not actually the truth about the war, but it was the truth about the individual reaction. The soldier advancing into a machine-gun barrage or standing waist-deep in a flooded trench knew only that here was an appalling experience in which he was all but helpless. He was likelier to make a good book out of his helplessness and his ignorance than out of a pretended power to see the whole thing in perspective. As for the books that were written during the war itself, the best of them were nearly all the work of people who simply turned their backs and tried not to notice that the war was happening. Mr E.M. Forster has described how in 1917 he read 'Prufrock'* and others of Eliot's early poems, and how it heartened him at such a time to get hold of poems that were "innocent of public-spiritedness":

> They sang of private disgust and diffidence, and of people who seemed genuine because they were unattractive or weak. [...] Here was a protest, and a feeble one, and the more congenial for being feeble. [...] He who could turn aside to complain of ladies and drawing rooms preserved a tiny drop of our self-respect, he carried on the human heritage.

That is very well said. Mr MacNeice, in the book I have referred to already, quotes this passage and somewhat smugly adds:

> Ten years later less feeble protests were to be made by poets and the human heritage carried on rather differently. [...] The contemplation of a world of fragments becomes boring and Eliot's successors are more interested in tidying it up.

Similar remarks are scattered throughout Mr MacNeice's book. What he wishes us to believe is that Eliot's "successors" (meaning Mr MacNeice and his friends) have in some way "protested" more effectively than Eliot did by publishing 'Prufrock' at the moment when the Allied armies were assaulting the Hindenburg Line. Just where these "protests" are to be found I do not know. But in the contrast between Mr Forster's comment and Mr MacNeice's lies all the difference between a man who knows what the 1914–18 war was like and a man who barely remembers it. The truth is that in 1917 there was nothing that a thinking and sensitive person could do, except to remain human, if possible. And a gesture of helplessness, even of frivolity, might be the best way of doing that. If I had been a soldier fighting in the Great War, I would sooner have got hold of 'Prufrock' than *The First Hundred Thousand* or Horatio Bottomley's *Letters to the Boys in the Trenches*.* I should have felt, like Mr Forster, that by simply standing aloof and keeping touch with pre-war emotions, Eliot was carrying on the human heritage. What a relief it would have been at such a time, to read about the hesitations of a middle-aged highbrow with a bald spot! So different from bayonet drill! After the bombs and the food queues and the recruiting posters, a human voice! What a relief!

But, after all, the war of 1914–18 was only a heightened moment in an almost continuous crisis. At this date it hardly even needs a war to bring home to us the disintegration of our society and the increasing helplessness of all decent people. It is for this reason that I think that the passive, non-cooperative attitude implied in Henry Miller's work is justified. Whether or not it is an expression of what people *ought* to feel, it probably comes somewhere near to expressing what they *do* feel. Once again it is the human voice among the bomb explosions, a friendly American voice, "innocent of public-spiritedness". No sermons, merely the subjective truth. And along those lines, apparently, it is still possible for a good novel to be written. Not necessarily an edifying novel, but a novel worth reading and likely to be remembered after it is read.

While I have been writing this book* another European war has broken out. It will either last several years and tear Western civilization to pieces, or it will end inconclusively and prepare the way for yet another war which will do the job once and for all. But war is only "peace intensified". What is quite obviously happening, war or no war, is the break-up of laissez-faire capitalism and of the liberal–Christian culture. Until recently the full implications of this were not foreseen, because it was generally imagined that socialism could preserve and even enlarge the atmosphere of liberalism. It is now beginning to be realized how false this idea was. Almost certainly we are moving into an age of totalitarian dictatorships – an age in which freedom of thought will be at first a deadly sin and later on a meaningless abstraction. The autonomous individual is going to be stamped out of existence. But this means that literature, in the form in which we know it, must suffer at least a temporary death. The literature of liberalism is coming to an end and the literature of totalitarianism has not yet appeared and is barely imaginable. As for the writer, he is sitting on a melting iceberg; he is merely an anachronism, a hangover from the bourgeois age, as surely doomed as the hippopotamus. Miller seems to me a man out of the common because he saw and proclaimed this fact a long while before most of his contemporaries – at a time, indeed, when many of them were actually burbling about a renaissance of literature. Wyndham Lewis had said years earlier that the major history of the English language was finished, but he was basing this on different and rather trivial reasons. But from now onwards the all-important fact for the creative writer is going to be that this is not a writer's world. That does not mean that he cannot help to bring the new society into being, but he can take no part in the process *as a writer*. For *as a writer* he is a liberal, and what is happening is the destruction of liberalism. It seems likely, therefore, that in the remaining years of free speech any novel worth reading will follow more or less along the lines that Miller has followed – I do not mean in technique or subject matter, but in implied outlook. The passive attitude will come back, and it will be more consciously passive than before. Progress and reaction have both turned out to be swindles. Seemingly there is nothing left but quietism – robbing reality of its terrors by simply submitting to it. Get inside the whale – or rather, admit that you are inside the whale (for you *are*, of course). Give yourself over to the world-process, stop fighting against it or pretending that you control it; simply accept it, endure it, record it. That seems to be the formula that any sensitive novelist is now likely to adopt. A novel on more positive, "constructive" lines, and not emotionally spurious, is at present very difficult to imagine.

But do I mean by this that Miller is a "great author", a new hope for English prose? Nothing of the kind. Miller himself would be the last to claim or want any such thing. No doubt he will go on writing – anybody who has once started always goes on writing – and associated with him there is a number of writers of approximately the same tendency, Lawrence Durrell, Michael Fraenkel* and others, almost amounting to a "school". But he himself seems to me essentially a man of one book. Sooner or later I should expect him to descend into unintelligibility, or into charlatanism; there are signs of both in his later work. His last book, *Tropic of Capricorn*, I have not even read. This was not because I did not want to read it, but because the police and customs authorities have so far managed to prevent me from getting hold of it. But it would surprise me if it came anywhere near *Tropic of Cancer* or the opening chapters of *Black Spring*. Like certain other autobiographical novelists, he had it in him to do just one thing perfectly, and he did it. Considering what the fiction of the 1930s has been like, that is something.

Miller's books are published by the Obelisk Press in Paris. What will happen to the Obelisk Press, now that war has broken out and Jack Kahane, the publisher, is dead, I do not know, but at any rate the books are still procurable. I earnestly counsel anyone who has not done so to read at least *Tropic of Cancer*. With a little ingenuity, or by paying a little over the published price, you can get hold of it, and even if parts of it disgust you, it will stick in your memory. It is also an "important" book, in a sense different from the sense in which that word is generally used. As a rule novels are spoken of as "important" when they are either a "terrible indictment" of something or other or when they introduce some technical innovation. Neither of these applies to *Tropic of Cancer*. Its importance is merely symptomatic. Here in my opinion is the only imaginative prose writer of the slightest value who has appeared among the English-speaking races for some years past. Even if that is objected to as an overstatement, it will probably be admitted that Miller is a writer out of the ordinary, worth more than a single glance – and, after all, he is a completely negative, unconstructive, amoral writer, a mere Jonah, a passive accepter of evil, a sort of Whitman among the corpses. Symptomatically, that is more significant than the mere fact that 5,000 novels are published in England every year and 4,900 of them are tripe. It is a demonstration of the *impossibility* of any major literature until the world has shaken itself into its new shape.

Notes on the Way*

Reading Mr Malcolm Muggeridge's brilliant and depressing book, *The Thirties*,* I thought of a rather cruel trick I once played on a wasp. He was sucking jam on my plate, and I cut him in half. He paid no attention, merely went on with his meal, while a tiny stream of jam trickled out of his severed oesophagus. Only when he tried to fly away did he grasp the dreadful thing that had happened to him. It is the same with modern man. The thing that has been cut away is his soul, and there was a period – twenty years, perhaps – during which he did not notice it.

It was absolutely necessary that the soul should be cut away. Religious belief, in the form in which we had known it, had to be abandoned. By the nineteenth century it was already in essence a lie, a semi-conscious device for keeping the rich rich and the poor poor. The poor were to be contented with their poverty, because it would all be made up to them in the world beyond the grave, usually pictured as something midway between Kew Gardens and a jeweller's shop. Ten thousand a year for me, two pounds a week for you, but we are all the children of God. And through the whole fabric of capitalist society there ran a similar lie, which it was absolutely necessary to rip out.

Consequently there was a long period during which nearly every thinking man was in some sense a rebel, and usually a quite irresponsible rebel. Literature was largely the literature of revolt or of disintegration. Gibbon,* Voltaire, Rousseau, Shelley, Byron, Dickens, Stendhal, Samuel Butler,* Ibsen, Zola, Flaubert, Shaw, Joyce – in one way or another they are all of them destroyers, wreckers, saboteurs. For 200 years we had sawed and sawed and sawed at the branch we were sitting on. And in the end, much more suddenly than anyone had foreseen, our efforts were rewarded, and down we came. But unfortunately there had been a little mistake. The thing at the bottom was not a bed of roses after all – it was a cesspool full of barbed wire.

It is as though in the space of ten years we had slid back into the Stone Age. Human types supposedly extinct for centuries, the dancing dervish, the robber chieftain, the Grand Inquisitor, have suddenly reappeared, not as inmates of lunatic asylums, but as the masters of the world. Mechanization and a collective economy seemingly aren't enough. By themselves they lead merely to the nightmare we are now enduring: endless war and endless underfeeding for the sake of war, slave populations toiling behind barbed wire, women dragged shrieking to the block, cork-lined cellars where the executioner blows your brains out from behind. So it appears that amputation of the soul *isn't* just a simple surgical job, like having your appendix out. The wound has a tendency to go septic.

The gist of Mr Muggeridge's book is contained in two texts from *Ecclesiastes*: "Vanity of vanities, saith the preacher; all is vanity" and "Fear God, and keep His commandments: for this is the whole duty of man".* It is a viewpoint that has gained a lot of ground lately, among people who would have laughed at it only a few years ago. We are living in a nightmare precisely *because* we have tried to set up an earthly paradise. We have believed in "progress", trusted to human leadership, rendered unto Caesar the things that are God's – that approximately is the line of thought.

Unfortunately Mr Muggeridge shows no sign of believing in God himself. Or at least he seems to take it for granted that this belief is vanishing from the human mind. There is not much doubt that he is right there, and if one assumes that no sanction can ever be effective except the supernatural one, it is clear what follows. There is no wisdom except in the fear of God – but nobody fears God; therefore there is no wisdom. Man's history reduces itself to the rise and fall of material civilizations, one Tower of Babel after another. In that case we can be pretty certain what is ahead of us. Wars and yet more wars, revolutions and counter-revolutions, Hitlers and super-Hitlers – and so downwards into abysses which are horrible to contemplate, though I rather suspect Mr Muggeridge of enjoying the prospect.

It must be about thirty years since Mr Hilaire Belloc, in his book *The Servile State*,* foretold with astonishing accuracy the things that are happening now. But unfortunately he had no remedy to offer. He could conceive nothing between slavery and a return to small-ownership, which is obviously not going to happen and in fact cannot happen. There is little question now of averting a collectivist society. The only question is whether it is to be founded on willing cooperation or on the machine gun. The Kingdom of Heaven, old style, has definitely failed, but on the other hand "Marxist realism" has also failed, whatever it may achieve materially. Seemingly there is no alternative except the thing that Mr Muggeridge and Mr F.A. Voigt,* and the others who think like them, so earnestly warn us against: the much-derided "Kingdom of Earth", the concept of a society in which men know that they are mortal and are nevertheless willing to act as brothers.

Brotherhood implies a common father. Therefore it is often argued that men can never develop the sense of a community unless they believe in God. The answer is that in a half-conscious way most of them have developed it already. Man is not an individual, he is only a cell in an everlasting body, and he is dimly aware of it. There is no other way of explaining why it is that men will die in battle. It is nonsense to say that they only do it because they are driven. If whole armies had to be coerced, no war could ever be fought. Men die in battle – not gladly, of course, but at any rate voluntarily – because of abstractions called "honour", "duty", "patriotism" and so forth.

All that this really means is that they are aware of some organism greater than themselves, stretching into the future and the past, within which they feel themselves to be immortal. "Who dies if England live?"* sounds like a piece of bombast, but if you alter "England" to whatever you prefer, you can see that it expresses one of the main motives of human conduct. People sacrifice themselves for the sake of fragmentary communities – nation, race, creed, class – and only become aware that they are not individuals in the very moment when they are facing bullets. A very slight increase of consciousness, and their sense of loyalty could be transferred to humanity itself, which is not an abstraction.

Mr Aldous Huxley's *Brave New World* was a good caricature of the hedonistic utopia, the kind of thing that seemed possible and even imminent before Hitler appeared, but it had no relation to the actual future. What we are moving towards at this moment is something more like the Spanish Inquisition, and probably far worse, thanks to the radio and the secret police. There is very little chance of escaping it unless we can reinstate the belief in human brotherhood without the need for a "next world" to give it meaning. It is this that leads innocent people like the Dean of Canterbury to imagine that they have discovered true Christianity in Soviet Russia. No doubt they are only the dupes of propaganda, but what makes them so willing to be deceived is their knowledge that the Kingdom of Heaven has somehow got to be brought onto the surface of the earth. We have got to be the children of God, even though the God of the Prayer Book no longer exists.

The very people who have dynamited our civilization have sometimes been aware of this. Marx's famous saying that "religion is the opium of the people"* is habitually wrenched out of its context and given a meaning subtly but appreciably different from the one he gave it. Marx did not say, at any rate in that place, that religion is merely a dope handed out from above; he said that it is something the people create for themselves to supply a need that he recognized to be a real one. "Religion is the sigh of the soul in a soulless world. Religion is the opium of the people." What is he saying except that man does *not* live by bread alone, that hatred is *not* enough, that a world worth living in cannot be founded on "realism" and machine guns? If he had foreseen how great his intellectual influence would be, perhaps he would have said it more often and more loudly.

The Limit to Pessimism*

Mr Malcolm Muggeridge's "message" – for it is a message, though a negative one – has not altered since he wrote *Winter in Moscow*.* It boils down to a simple disbelief in the power of human beings to construct a perfect or even a tolerable society here on earth. In essence, it is the Book of Ecclesiastes with the pious interpolations left out.

No doubt everyone is familiar with this line of thought. Vanity of vanities, all is vanity. The Kingdom of Earth is forever unattainable. Every attempt to establish liberty leads directly to tyranny. One tyrant takes over from another, the captain of industry from the robber baron, the Nazi gauleiter from the captain of industry, the sword gives way to the chequebook and the chequebook to the machine gun, the Tower of Babel perpetually rises and falls. It is the Christian pessimism, but with this important difference, that in the Christian scheme of things the Kingdom of Heaven is there to restore the balance:

> Jerusalem, my happy home,
> Would God I were in thee!
> Would God my woes were at an end,
> Thy joys that I might see!

And after all, even your earthly "woes" don't matter so very greatly, provided that you really "believe". Life is short and even purgatory does not last for ever, so you are bound to be in Jerusalem before long. Mr Muggeridge, needless to say, refuses this consolation. He gives no more evidence of believing in God than of trusting in man. Nothing is open to him, therefore, except an indiscriminate walloping of all human activities whatever. But as a social historian this does not altogether invalidate him, because the age we live in invites something of the kind. It is an age in which every *positive* attitude has turned out a failure. Creeds, parties, programmes of every description have simply flopped, one after another. The only "ism" that has justified itself is pessimism. Therefore at this moment good books can be written from the angle of Thersites,* though probably not very many.

I don't think Mr Muggeridge's history of the thirties is strictly truthful, but I think it is nearer to essential truth than any "constructive" outlook could have made it. He is looking only on the black side, but it is doubtful whether there is any bright side to look on. What a decade! A riot of appalling folly that suddenly becomes a nightmare, a scenic railway ending in a torture chamber.

It starts off in the hangover of the "enlightened" post-war age, with Ramsay MacDonald soft-soaping into the microphone and the League of Nations flapping vague wings in the background, and it ends up with 20,000 bombing planes darkening the sky and Himmler's masked executioner whacking women's heads off on a block borrowed from the Nuremberg museum. In between are the politics of the umbrella and the hand grenade. The National Government* coming in to "save the pound", MacDonald fading out like the Cheshire Cat, Baldwin* winning an election on the disarmament ticket in order to rearm (and then failing to rearm), the June purge, the Russian purges, the glutinous humbug of the abdication, the ideological mix-up of the Spanish war, communists waving Union Jacks, Conservative MPs cheering the news that British ships have been bombed, the Pope blessing Franco, Anglican dignitaries beaming at the wrecked churches of Barcelona, Chamberlain stepping out of his Munich aeroplane with a misquotation from Shakespeare,* Lord Rothermere* acclaiming Hitler as "a great gentleman", the London air-raid sirens blowing a false alarm as the first bombs drop on Warsaw. Mr Muggeridge, who is not loved in "left" circles, is often labelled "reactionary" or even "fascist", but I don't know of any left-wing writer who has flayed MacDonald, Baldwin and Chamberlain with equal ferocity. Mixed up with the buzz of conferences and the crash of guns are the day-to-day imbecilities of the gutter press. Astrology, trunk murders,* the Oxford Groupers* with their "sharing" and their praying batteries, the Rector of Stiffkey* (a great favourite with Mr Muggeridge: he makes several appearances) photographed with naked female acquaintances, starving in a barrel and finally devoured by lions, James Douglas and his dog Bunch,* Godfrey Winn* with his yet more emetic dog and his political reflections ("God and Mr Chamberlain – for I see no blasphemy in coupling these names"), spiritualism, the Modern Girl, nudism, dog racing, Shirley Temple, BO, halitosis, night starvation, should a doctor tell?*

The book ends on a note of extreme defeatism. The peace that is not a peace slumps into a war that is not a war. The epic events that everyone had expected somehow don't happen; the all-pervading lethargy continues just as before. "Shape without form, shade without colour, paralysed force, gesture without motion."* What Mr Muggeridge appears to be saying is that the English are powerless against their new adversaries because there is no longer anything that they believe in with sufficient firmness to make them willing for sacrifice. It is the struggle of people who have no faith against people who have faith in false gods. Is he right, I wonder? The truth is that it is impossible to discover what the English people are really feeling and thinking, about the war or about anything else. It has been impossible all through the critical years. I don't myself believe that he is right. But one cannot be sure until something of a quite unmistakable nature – some great disaster, probably – has brought home to the mass of the people what kind of world they are living in.

THE LIMIT TO PESSIMISM

The final chapters are, to me, deeply moving, all the more because the despair and defeatism that they express is not altogether sincere. Beneath Mr Muggeridge's seeming acceptance of disaster there lies the unconfessed fact that he does after all believe in something – in England. He does not want to see England conquered by Germany, though if one judges merely by the earlier chapters one might well ask what difference it would make. I am told that some months back he left the Ministry of Information to join the army, a thing which none of the ex-warmongers of the Left has done, I believe. And I know very well what underlies these closing chapters. It is the emotion of the middle-class man, brought up in the military tradition, who finds in the moment of crisis that he is a patriot after all. It is all very well to be "advanced" and "enlightened", to snigger at Colonel Blimp and proclaim your emancipation from all traditional loyalties, but a time comes when the sand of the desert is sodden red and what have I done for thee, England, my England?* As I was brought up in this tradition myself I can recognize it under strange disguises, and also sympathize with it, for even at its stupidest and most sentimental it is a comelier thing than the shallow self-righteousness of the left-wing intelligentsia.

New Words*

At present the formation of new words is a slow process (I have read somewhere that English gains about six and loses about four words a year) and no new words are deliberately coined except as names for material objects. Abstract words are never coined at all, though old words (e.g. "condition", "reflex", etc.) are sometimes twisted into new meanings for scientific purposes. What I am going to suggest here is that it would be quite feasible to invent a vocabulary, perhaps amounting to several thousands of words, which would deal with parts of our experience now practically unamenable to language. There are several objections to the idea, and I will deal with these as they arise. The first step is to indicate the kind of purpose for which new words are needed.

Everyone who thinks at all has noticed that our language is practically useless for describing anything that goes on inside the brain. This is so generally recognized that writers of high skill (e.g. Trollope and Mark Twain) will start their autobiographies by saying that they do not intend to describe their inner life, because it is of its nature indescribable. So soon as we are dealing with anything that is not concrete or visible (and even there to a great extent – look at the difficulty of describing anyone's appearance) we find that words are no liker to the reality than chessmen to living beings. To take an obvious case which will not raise side issues, consider a dream. How do you describe a dream? Clearly you *never* describe it, because no words that convey the atmosphere of dreams exist in our language. Of course, you can give a crude approximation of some of the major facts in a dream. You can say "I dreamt that I was walking down Regent Street with a porcupine wearing a bowler hat," etc., but this is no real description of the dream. And even if a psychologist interprets your dream in terms of "symbols", he is still going largely by guesswork; for the *real* quality of the dream, the quality that gave the porcupine its sole significance, is outside the world of words. In fact, describing a dream is like translating a poem into the language of one of Bohn's cribs;* it is a paraphrase which is meaningless unless one knows the original.

I chose dreams as an instance that would not be disputed, but if it were only dreams that were indescribable, the matter might not be worth bothering about. But, as has been pointed out over and over again, the waking mind is not so different from the dreaming mind as it appears – or as we like to pretend that it appears. It is true that most of our waking thoughts are "reasonable" – that is, there exists in our minds a kind of chessboard upon which thoughts move logically and verbally; we use this part of our minds for any straightforward intellectual problem, and we get into the habit of thinking (i.e. thinking in our chessboard moments) that it is the whole of the mind. But obviously it is not the whole. The disordered, unverbal world belonging to dreams is never quite absent from our minds, and if any calculation were possible I dare say it would be found that quite half the volume of our waking thoughts were of this order. Certainly the dream-thoughts take a hand even when we are trying to think verbally; they influence the verbal thoughts, and it is largely they that make our inner life valuable. Examine your thought at any casual moment. The main movement in it will be a stream of nameless things – so nameless that one hardly knows whether to call them thoughts, images or feelings. In the first place there are the objects you see and the sounds you hear, which are in themselves describable in words, but which as soon as they enter your mind become something quite different and totally indescribable.* And besides this there is the dream-life which your mind unceasingly creates for itself – and though most of this is trivial and soon forgotten, it contains things which are beautiful, funny, etc. beyond anything that ever gets into words. In a way this unverbal part of your mind is even the most important part, for it is the source of nearly all *motives*. All likes and dislikes, all aesthetic feeling, all notions of right and wrong (aesthetic and moral considerations are in any case inextricable) spring from feelings which are generally admitted to be subtler than words. When you are asked "Why do you do, or not do, so and so?" you are invariably aware that your *real* reason will not go into words, even when you have no wish to conceal it; consequently you rationalize your conduct, more or less dishonestly. I don't know whether everyone would admit this, and it is a fact that some people seem unaware of being influenced by their inner life, or even of having any inner life. I notice that many people never laugh when they are alone, and I suppose that if a man does not laugh when he is alone his inner life must be relatively barren. Still, every at all individual man has an inner life, and is aware of the practical impossibility of understanding others or being understood – in general, of the star-like isolation in which human beings live. Nearly all literature is an attempt to escape from this isolation by roundabout means, the direct means (words in their primary meanings) being almost useless.

"Imaginative" writing is, as it were, a flank attack upon positions that are impregnable from the front. A writer attempting anything that is not coldly "intellectual" can do very little with words in their primary meanings. He gets his effect, if at all, by using words in a tricky roundabout way, relying on their cadences and so forth, as in speech he would rely upon tone and gesture. In the case of poetry this is too well known to be worth arguing about. No one with the smallest understanding of poetry supposes that

> The mortal moon hath her eclipse endured,
> And the sad augurs mock their own presage*

really *means* what the words "mean" in their dictionary sense. (The couplet is said to refer to Queen Elizabeth having got over her grand climacteric safely.) The dictionary meaning has, as nearly always, *something* to do with the real meaning, but not more than the "anecdote" of a picture has to do with its design. And it is the same with prose, *mutatis mutandis*.* Consider a novel, even a novel which has ostensibly nothing to do with the inner life – what is called a "straight story". Consider *Manon Lescaut*.* Why does the author invent this long rigmarole about an unfaithful girl and a runaway abbé? Because he has a certain feeling, vision, whatever you like to call it, and knows, possibly after experiment, that it is no use trying to convey this vision by describing it as one would describe a crayfish for a book of zoology. But by *not* describing it, by inventing something else (in this case a picaresque novel: in another age he would choose another form) he can convey it, or part of it. The art of writing is in fact largely the perversion of words, and I would even say that the less obvious this perversion is, the more thoroughly it has been done. For a writer who *seems* to twist words out of their meanings (e.g. Gerard Manley Hopkins) is really, if one looks closely, making a desperate attempt to use them straightforwardly. Whereas a writer who seems to have no tricks whatever, for instance the old ballad writers, is making an especially subtle flank attack, though, in the case of the ballad writers, this is no doubt unconscious. Of course one hears a lot of cant to the effect that all good art is "objective" and every true artist keeps his inner life to himself. But the people who say this do not mean it. All they mean is that they want the inner life to be expressed by an exceptionally roundabout method, as in the ballad or the "straight story".

The weakness of the roundabout method, apart from its difficulty, is that it usually fails. For anyone who is not a considerable artist (possibly for them too) the lumpishness of words results in constant falsification. Is there anyone who has ever written so much as a love letter in which he felt that he had said exactly what he intended? A writer falsifies himself both intentionally and unintentionally. Intentionally, because the accidental qualities of words constantly tempt and frighten him away from his true meaning. He gets an idea, begins trying to express it, and then, in the frightful mess of words that generally results, a pattern begins to form itself more or less accidentally. It is not by any means the pattern he wants, but it is at any rate not vulgar or disagreeable; it is "good art". He takes it, because "good art" is a more or less mysterious gift from heaven, and it seems a pity to waste it when it presents itself. Is not anyone with any degree of mental honesty conscious of telling lies all day long, both in talking and writing, simply because lies will fall into artistic shape when truth will not? Yet if words represented meanings as fully and accurately as height multiplied by base represents the area of a parallelogram, at least the *necessity* for lying would never exist. And in the mind of reader or hearer there are further falsifications, because, words not being a direct channel of thought, he constantly sees meanings which are not there. A good illustration of this is our supposed appreciation of foreign poetry. We know from the *Vie Amoureuse du Docteur Watson* stuff of foreign critics that true understanding of foreign literature is almost impossible – yet quite ignorant people profess to get, do get, vast pleasure out of poetry in foreign and even dead languages. Clearly the pleasure they derive may come from something the writer never intended, possibly from something that would make him squirm in his grave if he knew it was attributed to him. I say to myself *Vixi puellis nuper idoneus*,* and I repeat this over and over for five minutes for the beauty of the word "*idoneus*". Yet, considering the gulf of time and culture, and my ignorance of Latin, and the fact that no one even knows how Latin was pronounced, is it possible that the effect I am enjoying is the effect Horace was trying for? It is as though I were in ecstasies over the beauty of a picture, and all because of some splashes of paint which had accidentally got onto the canvas 200 years after it was painted. Notice, I am not saying that *art* would necessarily improve if words conveyed meaning more reliably. For all I know art thrives on the crudeness and vagueness of language. I am only criticizing *words* in their supposed function as vehicles of thought. And it seems to me that from the point of view of exactitude and expressiveness our language has remained in the Stone Age.

The solution I suggest is to invent new words as deliberately as we would invent new parts for a motor-car engine. Suppose that a vocabulary existed which would accurately express the life of the mind, or a great part of it. Suppose that there need be no stultifying feeling that life is inexpressible, no jiggery-pokery with artistic tricks; expressing one's meaning simply being a matter of taking the right words and putting them in place, like working out an equation in algebra. I think the advantages of this would be obvious. It is less obvious, though, that to sit down and deliberately coin words is a common-sense proceeding. Before indicating a way in which satisfactory words might be coined, I had better deal with the objections which are bound to arise.

If you say to any thinking person "Let us form a society for the invention of new and subtler words", he will first of all object that it is the idea of a crank, and then probably say that our present words, properly handled, will meet all difficulties. (This last, of course, is only a theoretical objection. In practice everyone recognizes the inadequacy of language – consider such expressions as "Words fail", "It wasn't what he said, it was the way he said it", etc.) But finally he will give you an answer something like this: "Things cannot be done in that pedantic way. Languages can only grow slowly, like flowers; you can't patch them up like pieces of machinery. Any *made-up* language must be characterless and lifeless – look at Esperanto, etc. The whole meaning of a word is in its slowly acquired associations," etc.

In the first place, this argument, like most of the arguments produced when one suggests changing anything, is a long-winded way of saying that what is must be. Hitherto we have never set ourselves to the deliberate creation of words, and all living languages have grown slowly and haphazard – *therefore* language cannot grow otherwise. At present, when we want to say anything above the level of a geometrical definition, we are obliged to do conjuring tricks with sounds, associations, etc. – *therefore* this necessity is inherent in the nature of words. The non sequitur is obvious. And notice that when I suggest abstract words I am only suggesting an extension of our present practice. For we do now coin concrete words. Aeroplanes and bicycles are invented, and we invent names for them, which is the natural thing to do. It is only a step to coining names for the now unnamed things that exist in the mind. You say to me "Why do you dislike Mr Smith?" and I say "Because he is a liar, coward, etc." and I am almost certainly giving the wrong reason. In my own mind the answer runs "Because he is a — kind of man", — standing for something which I understand, and you would understand if I could tell it you. Why not find a name for —? The only difficulty is to agree about *what* we are naming. But long before this difficulty arises, the reading, thinking type of man will have recoiled from such an idea as the invention of words. He will produce arguments like the one I indicated above, or others of a more or less sneering, question-begging kind. In reality all these arguments are humbug. The recoil comes from a deep unreasoned instinct, superstitious in origin. It is the feeling that any direct rational approach to one's difficulties, any attempt to solve the problems of life as one would solve an equation, can lead nowhere – more, is definitely *unsafe*. One can see this idea expressed everywhere in a roundabout way. All the bosh that is talked about our national genius for "muddling through", and all the squashy godless mysticism that is urged against any hardness and soundness of intellect, mean *au fond** that it is *safer not to think*. This feeling starts, I am certain, in the common belief of children that the air is full of avenging demons waiting to punish presumption.* In adults the belief survives as a fear of too-rational thinking. "I the Lord thy God am a jealous God", "pride comes before a fall", etc. – and the most dangerous pride is the false pride of the intellect. David was punished because he numbered the people – i.e. because he used his intellect scientifically. Thus such an idea as, for instance, ectogenesis, apart from its possible effects upon the health of the race, family life, etc., is felt to be *in itself* blasphemous. Similarly any attack on such a fundamental thing as language, an attack as it were on the very structure of our own minds, is blasphemy and therefore dangerous. To reform language is practically an interference with the work of God – though I don't say that anyone would put it quite in these words. This objection is important, because it would prevent most people from even considering such an idea as the reform of language. And of course the idea is useless unless undertaken by large numbers. For one man, or a clique, to try and make up a language, as I believe James Joyce is now doing, is as absurd as one man trying to play football alone. What is wanted is several thousands of gifted but normal people who would give themselves to word-invention as seriously as people now give themselves to Shakespearean research. Given these, I believe we could work wonders with language.

Now, as to the means. One sees an instance of the successful invention of words, though crude and on a small scale, among the members of large families. All large families have two or three words peculiar to themselves – words which they have made up and which convey subtilized, non-dictionary meanings. They say "Mr Smith is a — kind of man", using some home-made word, and the others understand perfectly; here then, within the limits of the family, exists an adjective filling one of the many gaps left by the dictionary. What makes it possible for the family to invent these words is the basis of their common experience. Without common experience, of course, no word can mean anything. If you say to me "What does bergamot smell like?" I say "Something like verbena", and so long as you know the smell of verbena you are somewhere near understanding me. The method of inventing words, therefore, is the method of analogy based on unmistakable common knowledge; one must have standards that can be referred to without any chance of misunderstanding, as one can refer to a physical thing like the smell of verbena. In effect it must come down to giving words a physical (probably visible) existence. Merely *talking* about definitions is futile; one can see this whenever it is attempted to define one of the words used by literary critics (e.g. "sentimental",* "vulgar", "morbid", etc.). All meaningless – or rather, having a different meaning for everyone who uses them. What is needed is to *show* a meaning in some unmistakable form, and then, when various people have identified it in their own minds and recognized it as worth naming, to give it a name. The question is simply of finding a way in which one can give thought an objective existence.

The thing that suggests itself immediately is the cinematograph. Everyone must have noticed the extraordinary powers that are latent in the film – the powers of distortion, of fantasy, in general of escaping the restrictions of the physical world. I suppose it is only from commercial necessity that the film has been used chiefly for silly imitations of stage plays, instead of concentrating as it ought on things that are beyond the stage. Properly used, the film is the one possible medium for conveying mental processes. A dream, for instance, as I said above, is totally indescribable in words, but it can quite well be represented on the screen. Years ago I saw a film of Douglas Fairbanks's,* part of which was a representation of a dream. Most of it, of course, was silly joking about the dream where you have no clothes on in public, but for a few minutes it really was like a dream, in a manner that would have been impossible in words, or even in a picture, or, I imagine, in music. I have seen the same kind of thing by flashes in other films, for instance in *Dr Caligari** – a film, however, which was for the most part merely silly, the fantastic element being exploited for its own sake and not to convey any definite meaning. If one thinks of it, there is very little in the mind that could not *somehow* be represented by the strange distorting powers of the film. A millionaire with a private cinematograph, all the necessary props and a troupe of intelligent actors could, if he wished, make practically all of his inner life known. He could explain the real reasons of his actions instead of telling rationalized lies, point out the things that seemed to him beautiful, pathetic, funny, etc. – things that an ordinary man has to keep locked up because there are no words to express them. In general, he could make other people understand him. Of course, it is not desirable that any one man, short of a genius, should make a show of his inner life. What is wanted is to discover the now nameless feelings that men have *in common*. All the powerful motives which will not go into words and which are a cause of constant lying and misunderstanding, could be tracked down, given visible form, agreed upon, and named. I am sure that the film, with its almost limitless powers of representation, could accomplish this in the hands of the right investigators, though putting thoughts into visible shape would not always be easy – in fact, at first it might be as difficult as any other art.

A note on the actual form new words ought to take. Suppose that several thousands of people with the necessary time, talents and money undertook to make additions to language; suppose that they managed to agree upon a number of new and necessary words – they would still have to guard against producing a mere Volapük* which would drop out of use as soon as it was invented. It seems to me probable that a word, even a not-yet-existing word, has as it were a natural form – or rather, various natural forms in various languages. If languages were truly expressive there would be no need to play upon the sounds of words as we do now, but I suppose there must always be *some* correlation between the sound of a word and its meaning. An accepted (I believe) and plausible theory of the origin of language is this. Primitive man, before he had words, would naturally rely upon gesture, and like any other animal he would cry out at the moment of gesticulating, in order to attract attention. Now one instinctively makes the gesture that is appropriate to one's meaning, and all parts of the body follow suit including the tongue. Hence, certain tongue movements – i.e. certain sounds – would come to be associated with certain meanings. In poetry one can point to words which, apart from their direct meanings, regularly convey certain ideas by their sound. Thus: "Deeper than did ever *plummet* sound" (Shakespeare – more than once I think); "Past the *plunge of plummet*" (A.E. Housman); "The un*plumbed* salt, estranging sea" (Matthew Arnold), etc.* Clearly, apart from direct meanings, the sound plum- or plun- has something to do with bottomless oceans. Therefore in forming new words one would have to pay attention to appropriateness of sound as well as exactitude of meaning. It would not do, as at present, to clip a new word of any real novelty by making it out of old ones, but it also would not do to make it out of a mere arbitrary collection of letters. One would have to determine the natural form of the word. Like agreeing upon the actual meanings of the words, this would need the cooperation of a large number of people.

I have written all this down hastily, and when I read through it I see that there are weak patches in my argument and much of it is commonplace. To most people in any case the whole idea of reforming language would seem either dilettantish or crankish. Yet it is worth considering what utter incomprehension exists between human beings – at least between those who are not deeply intimate. At present, as Samuel Butler said, the best art (i.e. the most perfect thought transference) must be "lived" from one person to another. It need not be so if our language were more adequate. It is curious that when our knowledge, the complication of our lives and therefore (I think it must follow) our minds develop so fast, language, the chief means of communication, should scarcely stir. For this reason I think that the idea of the deliberate invention of words is at least worth thinking over.

Prophecies of Fascism*

The reprinting of Jack London's *The Iron Heel* brings within general reach a book which has been much sought after during the years of fascist aggression. Like others of Jack London's books it has been widely read in Germany, and it has had the reputation of being an accurate forecast of the coming of Hitler. In reality it is not that. It is merely a tale of capitalist oppression, and it was written at a time when various things that have made fascism possible – for instance, the tremendous revival of nationalism – were not easy to foresee.

Where London did show special insight, however, was in realizing that the transition to socialism was not going to be automatic or even easy. The capitalist class was not going to "perish of its own contradictions" like a flower dying at the end of the season. The capitalist class was quite clever enough to see what was happening, to sink its own differences and counter-attack against the workers – and the resulting struggle would be the most bloody and unscrupulous the world had ever seen.

It is worth comparing *The Iron Heel* with another imaginative novel of the future which was written somewhat earlier and to which it owes something, H.G. Wells's *The Sleeper Wakes*. By doing so one can see both London's limitations and also the advantage to be enjoyed in not being, like Wells, a fully civilized man. As a book, *The Iron Heel* is hugely inferior. It is clumsily written, it shows no grasp of scientific possibilities, and the hero is the kind of human gramophone who is now disappearing even from socialist tracts. But because of his own streak of savagery London could grasp something that Wells apparently could not, and that is that hedonistic societies do not endure.

Everyone who has ever read *The Sleeper Wakes* remembers it. It is a vision of a glittering, sinister world in which society has hardened into a caste system and the workers are permanently enslaved. It is also a world without purpose in which the upper castes for whom the workers toil are completely soft, cynical and faithless. There is no consciousness of any object in life, nothing corresponding to the fervour of the revolutionary or the religious martyr.

In Aldous Huxley's *Brave New World*, a sort of post-war parody of the Wellsian utopia, these tendencies are immensely exaggerated. Here the hedonistic principle is pushed to its utmost; the whole world has turned into a Riviera hotel. But though *Brave New World* was a brilliant caricature of the present (the present of 1930), it probably casts no light on the future. No society of that kind would last more than a couple of generations, because a ruling class which thought principally in terms of a "good time" would soon lose its vitality. A ruling class has got to have a strict morality, a quasi-religious belief in itself, a mystique. London was aware of this, and though he describes the caste of plutocrats who rule the world for seven centuries as inhuman monsters, he does not describe them as idlers or sensualists. They can only maintain their position while they honestly believe that civilization depends on themselves alone, and therefore in a different way they are just as brave, able and devoted as the revolutionaries who oppose them.

In an intellectual way London accepted the conclusions of Marxism, and he imagined that the "contradictions" of capitalism, the unconsumable surplus and so forth, would persist even after the capitalist class had organized themselves into a single corporate body. But temperamentally he was very different from the majority of Marxists. With his love of violence and physical strength, his belief in "natural aristocracy", his animal-worship and exaltation of the primitive, he had in him what one might fairly call a fascist strain. This probably helped him to understand just how the possessing class would behave when once they were seriously menaced.

It is just here that Marxian socialists have usually fallen short. Their interpretation of history has been so mechanistic that they have failed to foresee dangers that were obvious to people who had never heard the name of Marx. It is sometimes urged against Marx that he failed to predict the rise of fascism. I do not know whether he predicted it or not – at that date he could only have done so in very general terms – but it is at any rate certain that his followers failed to see any danger in fascism until they themselves were at the gate of the concentration camp. A year or more *after* Hitler had risen to power official Marxism was still proclaiming that Hitler was of no importance and "Social Fascism" (i.e. democracy) was the real enemy. London would probably not have made this mistake. His instincts would have warned him that Hitler was dangerous. He knew that economic laws do not operate in the same way as the law of gravity, that they can be held up for long periods by people who, like Hitler, believe in their own destiny.

The Iron Heel and *The Sleeper Wakes* are both written from the popular standpoint. *Brave New World*, though primarily an attack on hedonism, is also by implication an attack on totalitarianism and caste rule. It is interesting to compare them with a less well-known utopia which treats the class struggle from the upper or rather the middle-class point of view, Ernest Bramah's *The Secret of the League*.

The Secret of the League was written in 1907, when the growth of the labour movement was beginning to terrify the middle class, who wrongly imagined that they were menaced from below and not from above. As a political forecast it is trivial, but it is of great interest for the light it casts on the mentality of the struggling middle class.

The author imagines a Labour government coming into office with so huge a majority that it is impossible to dislodge them. They do not, however, introduce a full socialist economy. They merely continue to operate capitalism for their own benefit by constantly raising wages, creating a huge army of bureaucrats and taxing the upper classes out of existence. The country is therefore "going to the dogs" in the familiar manner; moreover in their foreign politics the Labour government behave rather like the National Government between 1931 and 1939. Against this there arises a secret conspiracy of the middle and upper classes; the manner of their revolt is very ingenious, provided that one looks upon capitalism as something internal: it is the method of the consumers' strike. Over a period of two years the upper-class conspirators secretly hoard fuel oil and convert coal-burning plants to oil-burning; then they suddenly boycott the principal British industry, the coal industry. The miners are faced with a situation in which they will be able to sell no coal for two years. There is vast unemployment and distress, ending in civil war, in which (thirty years before General Franco!) the upper classes receive foreign aid. After their victory they abolish the trade unions and institute a "strong" non-parliamentary regime – in other words a regime that we should now describe as fascist. The tone of the book is good-natured, as it could afford to be at that date, but the trend of thought is unmistakable.

Why should a decent and kindly writer like Ernest Bramah find the crushing of the proletariat a pleasant vision? It is simply the reaction of a struggling class which felt itself menaced not so much in its economic position as in its code of conduct and way of life. One can see the same purely social antagonism to the working class in an earlier writer of much greater calibre, George Gissing. Time, and Hitler, have taught the middle classes a great deal, and perhaps they will not again side with their oppressors against their natural allies. But whether they do so or not depends partly on how they are handled, and the stupidity of socialist propaganda, with its constant baiting of the "petty bourgeois", has a lot to answer for.

Charles Reade*

Since Charles Reade's books are published in cheap editions one can assume that he still has his following, but it is unusual to meet anyone who has voluntarily read him. In most people his name seems to evoke, at most, a vague memory of "doing" *The Cloister and the Hearth* as a school-holiday task. It is his bad luck to be remembered by this particular book, rather as Mark Twain, thanks to the films, is chiefly remembered by *A Connecticut Yankee in King Arthur's Court*.* Reade wrote several dull books, and *The Cloister and the Hearth* is one of them. But he also wrote three novels which I personally would back to outlive the entire works of Meredith and George Eliot, besides some brilliant long short stories such as 'A Jack of All Trades' and 'The Autobiography of a Thief'.*

What is the attraction of Reade? At bottom it is the same charm as one finds in R. Austin Freeman's detective stories or Lieutenant Commander Gould's collections of curiosities* – the charm of useless knowledge. Reade was a man of what one might call penny-encyclopaedic learning. He possessed vast stocks of disconnected information which a lively narrative gift allowed him to cram into books which would at any rate pass as novels. If you have the sort of mind that takes a pleasure in dates, lists, catalogues, concrete details, descriptions of processes, junk-shop windows and back numbers of the *Exchange and Mart*,* the sort of mind that likes knowing exactly how a medieval catapult worked or just what objects a prison cell of the 1840s contained, then you can hardly help enjoying Reade. He himself, of course, did not see his work in quite this light. He prided himself on his accuracy and compiled his books largely from newspaper cuttings, but the strange facts which he collected were subsidiary to what he would have regarded as his "purpose". For he was a social reformer in a fragmentary way, and made vigorous attacks on such diverse evils as bloodletting, the treadmill, private asylums, clerical celibacy and tight-lacing.

My own favourite has always been *Foul Play*,* which as it happens is not an attack on anything in particular. Like most nineteenth-century novels *Foul Play* is too complicated to be summarized, but its central story is that of a young clergyman, Robert Penfold, who is unjustly convicted of forgery, is transported to Australia, absconds in disguise, and is wrecked on a desert island together with the heroine. Here, of course, Reade is in his element. Of all men who ever lived, he was the best fitted to write a desert-island story. Some desert-island stories, of course, are worse than others, but none is altogether bad when it sticks to the actual concrete details of the struggle to keep alive. A list of the objects in a shipwrecked man's possession is probably the surest winner in fiction, surer even than a trial scene. Nearly thirty years after reading the book I can still remember more or less exactly what things the three heroes of Ballantyne's *Coral Island** possessed between them. (A telescope, six yards of whipcord, a penknife, a brass ring and a piece of hoop iron.) Even a dismal book like *Robinson Crusoe*, so unreadable as a whole that few people even know that the second part exists, becomes interesting when it describes Crusoe's efforts to make a table, glaze earthenware and grow a patch of wheat. Reade, however, was an expert on desert islands, or at any rate he was very well up in the geography textbooks of the time. Moreover he was the kind of man who would have been at home on a desert island himself. He would never, like Crusoe, have been stumped by such an easy problem as that of leavening bread and, unlike Ballantyne, he knew that civilized men cannot make fire by rubbing sticks together.

The hero of *Foul Play*, like most of Reade's heroes, is a kind of superman. He is hero, saint, scholar, gentleman, athlete, pugilist, navigator, physiologist, botanist, blacksmith and carpenter all rolled into one, the sort of compendium of all the talents that Reade honestly imagined to be the normal product of an English university. Needless to say, it is only a month or two before this wonderful clergyman has got the desert island running like a West End hotel. Even before reaching the island, when the last survivors of the wrecked ship are dying of thirst in an open boat, he has shown his ingenuity by constructing a distilling apparatus with a jar, a hot-water bottle and a piece of tubing. But his best stroke of all is the way in which he contrives to leave the island. He himself, with a price on his head, would be glad enough to remain, but the heroine, Helen Rolleston, who has no idea that he is a convict, is naturally anxious to escape. She asks Robert to turn his "great mind" to this problem. The first difficulty, of course, is to discover exactly where the island is. Luckily, however, Helen is still wearing her watch, which is still keeping Sydney time. By fixing a stick in the ground and watching its shadow Robert notes the exact moment of noon, after which it is a simple matter to work out the longitude – for naturally a man of his calibre would know the longitude of Sydney. It is equally natural that he can determine the latitude within a degree or two by the nature of the vegetation. But the next difficulty is to send a message to the outside world. After some thought Robert writes a series of messages on pieces of parchment made from seals' bladders, with ink obtained from cochineal insects. He has noticed that migrant birds often use the island as a stopping place, and he fixes on ducks as the likeliest messengers, because every duck is liable to be shot sooner or later. By a stratagem often used in India he captures a number of ducks, ties a message to each of their legs and lets them go. Finally, of course, one of the ducks takes refuge on a ship, and the couple are rescued, but even then the story is barely half finished. There follow enormous ramifications, plots and counterplots, intrigues, triumphs and disasters, ending with the vindication of Robert, and wedding bells.

In any of Reade's three best books, *Foul Play*, *Hard Cash* and *It Is Never Too Late to Mend*,* it is not fair to say that the sole interest is in the technical detail. His power of descriptive writing, especially of describing violent action, is also very striking, and on a serial-story level he is a wonderful contriver of plots. Simply as a novelist it is impossible to take him seriously, because he has no sense whatever of character or of probability, but he himself had the advantage of believing in even the absurdest details of his own stories. He wrote of life as he saw it, and many Victorians saw it in the same way: that is, as a series of tremendous melodramas, with virtue triumphant every time. Of all the nineteenth-century novelists who have remained readable, he is perhaps the only one who is completely in tune with his own age. For all his unconventionality, his "purpose", his eagerness to expose abuses, he never makes a fundamental criticism. Save for a few surface evils he sees nothing wrong in an acquisitive society, with its equation of money and virtue, its pious millionaires and Erastian clergymen.* Perhaps nothing gives one his measure better than the fact that in introducing Robert Penfold, at the beginning of *Foul Play*, he mentions that he is a scholar and a cricketer and only thirdly and almost casually adds that he is a priest.

That is not to say that Reade's social conscience was not sound so far as it went, and in several minor ways he probably helped to educate public opinion. His attack on the prison system in *It Is Never Too Late to Mend* is relevant to this day, or was so till very recently, and in his medical theories he is said to have been a long way ahead of his time. What he lacked was any notion that the early railway age, with the special scheme of values appropriate to it, was not going to last for ever. This is a little surprising when one remembers that he was the brother of Winwood Reade.* However hasty and unbalanced Winwood Reade's *Martyrdom of Man* may seem now, it is a book that shows an astonishing width of vision, and it is probably the unacknowledged grandparent of the "outlines" so popular today. Charles Reade might have written an "outline" of phrenology, cabinet making or the habits of whales, but not of human history. He was simply a middle-class gentleman with a little more conscience than most, a scholar who happened to prefer popular science to the classics. Just for that reason he is one of the best "escape" novelists we have. *Foul Play* and *Hard Cash* would be good books to send to a soldier enduring the miseries of trench warfare, for instance. There are no problems in them, no genuine "messages", merely the fascination of a gifted mind functioning within very narrow limits, and offering as complete a detachment from real life as a game of chess or a jigsaw puzzle.

My Country Right or Left*

Contrary to popular belief, the past was not more eventful than the present. If it seems so it is because when you look backward things that happened years apart are telescoped together, and because very few of your memories come to you genuinely virgin. It is largely because of the books, films and reminiscences that have come between that the war of 1914–18 is now supposed to have had some tremendous, epic quality that the present one lacks.

But if you were alive during that war, and if you disentangle your real memories from their later accretions, you find that it was not usually the big events that stirred you at the time. I don't believe that the Battle of the Marne, for instance, had for the general public the melodramatic quality that it was afterwards given. I do not even remember hearing the phrase "Battle of the Marne" till years later. It was merely that the Germans were twenty-two miles from Paris – and certainly that was terrifying enough, after the Belgian atrocity stories – and then for some reason they had turned back. I was eleven when the war started. If I honestly sort out my memories and disregard what I have learnt since, I must admit that nothing in the whole war moved me so deeply as the loss of the *Titanic* had done a few years earlier. This comparatively petty disaster shocked the whole world, and the shock has not quite died away even yet. I remember the terrible, detailed accounts read out at the breakfast table (in those days it was a common habit to read the newspaper aloud), and I remember that in all the long list of horrors the one that most impressed me was that at the last the *Titanic* suddenly upended and sank bow foremost, so that the people clinging to the stern were lifted no less than 300 feet into the air before they plunged into the abyss. It gave me a sinking sensation in the belly which I can still all but feel. Nothing in the war ever gave me quite that sensation.

Of the outbreak of war I have three vivid memories which, being petty and irrelevant, are uninfluenced by anything that has come later. One is of the cartoon of the "German Emperor" (I believe the hated name "Kaiser" was not popularized till a little later) that appeared in the last days of July. People were mildly shocked by this guying of royalty ("But he's such a handsome man, really!"), although we were on the edge of war. Another is of the time when the army commandeered all the horses in our little country town, and a cabman burst into tears in the marketplace when his horse, which had worked for him for years, was taken away from him. And another is of a mob of young men at the railway station, scrambling for the evening papers that had just arrived on the London train. And I remember the pile of pea-green papers (some of them were still green in those days), the high collars, the tightish trousers and the bowler hats, far better than I can remember the names of the terrific battles that were already raging on the French frontier.

Of the middle years of the war, I remember chiefly the square shoulders, bulging calves and jingling spurs of the artillerymen, whose uniform I much preferred to that of the infantry. As for the final period, if you ask me to say truthfully what is my chief memory, I must answer simply – margarine. It is an instance of the horrible selfishness of children that by 1917 the war had almost ceased to affect us, except through our stomachs. In the school library a huge map of the Western Front was pinned on an easel, with a red silk thread running across on a zigzag of drawing pins. Occasionally the thread moved half an inch this way or that, each movement meaning a pyramid of corpses. I paid no attention. I was at school among boys who were above the average level of intelligence, and yet I do not remember that a single major event of the time appeared to us in its true significance. The Russian Revolution, for instance, made no impression, except on the few whose parents happened to have money invested in Russia. Among the very young the pacifist reaction had set in long before the war ended. To be as slack as you dared on OTC parades, and to take no interest in the war, was considered a mark of enlightenment. The young officers who had come back, hardened by their terrible experience and disgusted by the attitude of the younger generation to whom this experience meant just nothing, used to lecture us for our softness. Of course they could produce no argument that we were capable of understanding. They could only bark at you that war was "a good thing", it "made you tough", "kept you fit", etc. etc. We merely sniggered at them. Ours was the one-eyed pacifism that is peculiar to sheltered countries with strong navies. For years after the war, to have any knowledge of or interest in military matters, even to know which end of a gun the bullet comes out of, was suspect in "enlightened" circles. 1914–18 was written off as a meaningless slaughter, and even the men who had been slaughtered were held to be in some way to blame. I have often laughed to think of that recruiting poster, "What did you do in the Great War, Daddy?" (a child is asking this question of its shame-stricken father), and of all the men who must have been lured into the army by just that poster and afterwards despised by their children for not being Conscientious Objectors.

But the dead men had their revenge after all. As the war fell back into the past, my particular generation, those who had been "just too young", became conscious of the vastness of the experience they had missed. You felt yourself a little less than a man, because you had missed it. I spent the years 1922–27 mostly among men a little older than myself who had been through the war. They talked about it unceasingly, with horror, of course, but also with a steadily growing nostalgia. You can see this nostalgia perfectly clearly in the English war books. Besides, the pacifist reaction was only a phase, and even the "just too young" had all been trained for war. Most of the English middle class are trained for war from the cradle onwards, not technically but morally. The earliest political slogan I can remember is "We want eight (eight dreadnoughts) and we won't wait". At seven years old I was a member of the Navy League and wore a sailor suit with "HMS *Invincible*" on my cap. Even before my public-school OTC I had been in a private-school cadet corps. On and off, I have been toting a rifle ever since I was ten, in preparation not only for war but for a particular kind of war, a war in which the guns rise to a frantic orgasm of sound, and at the appointed moment you clamber out of the trench, breaking your nails on the sandbags, and stumble across mud and wire into the machine-gun barrage. I am convinced that part of the reason for the fascination that the Spanish Civil War had for people of about my age was that it was so like the Great War. At certain moments Franco was able to scrape together enough aeroplanes to raise the war to a modern level, and these were the turning points. But for the rest it was a bad copy of 1914–18, a positional war of trenches, artillery, raids, snipers, mud, barbed wire, lice and stagnation. In early 1937 the bit of the Aragon front that I was on must have been very like a quiet sector in France in 1915. It was only the artillery that was lacking. Even on the rare occasions when all the guns in Huesca and outside it were firing simultaneously, there were only enough of them to make a fitful unimpressive noise like the ending of a thunderstorm. The shells from Franco's six-inch guns crashed loudly enough, but there were never more than a dozen of them at a time. I know that what I felt when I first heard artillery fired "in anger", as they say, was at least partly disappointment. It was so different from the tremendous, unbroken roar that my senses had been waiting for for twenty years.

I don't quite know in what year I first knew for certain that the present war was coming. After 1936, of course, the thing was obvious to anyone except an idiot. For several years the coming war was a nightmare to me, and at times I even made speeches and wrote pamphlets against it. But the night before the Russo-German Pact* was announced I dreamt that the war had started. It was one of those dreams which, whatever Freudian inner meaning they may have, do sometimes reveal to you the real state of your feelings. It taught me two things: first, that I should be simply relieved when the long-dreaded war started; secondly, that I was patriotic at heart, would not sabotage or act against my own side, would support the war, would fight in it if possible. I came downstairs to find the newspaper announcing Ribbentrop's flight to Moscow. So war was coming, and the government, even the Chamberlain government, was assured of my loyalty. Needless to say this loyalty was and remains merely a gesture. As with almost everyone I know, the government has flatly refused to employ me in any capacity whatever, even as a clerk or a private soldier. But that does not alter one's feelings. Besides, they will be forced to make use of us sooner or later.

If I had to defend my reasons for supporting the war, I believe I could do so. There is no real alternative between resisting Hitler and surrendering to him, and from a socialist point of view I should say that it is better to resist; in any case I can see no argument for surrender that does not make nonsense of the Republican resistance in Spain, the Chinese resistance to Japan, etc. etc. But I don't pretend that that is the emotional basis of my actions. What I knew in my dream that night was that the long drilling in patriotism which the middle classes go through had done its work, and that once England was in a serious jam it would be impossible for me to sabotage. But let no one mistake the meaning of this. Patriotism has nothing to do with conservatism. It is devotion to something that is changing but is felt to be mystically the same, like the devotion of the ex-White Bolshevik to Russia. To be loyal both to Chamberlain's England and to the England of tomorrow might seem an impossibility, if one did not know it to be an everyday phenomenon. Only revolution can save England, that has been obvious for years, but now the revolution has started, and it may proceed quite quickly if only we can keep Hitler out. Within two years, maybe a year, if only we can hang on, we shall see changes that will surprise the idiots who have no foresight. I dare say the London gutters will have to run with blood. All right, let them, if it is necessary. But when the red militias are billeted in the Ritz I shall still feel that the England I was taught to love so long ago and for such different reasons is somehow persisting.

I grew up in an atmosphere tinged with militarism, and afterwards I spent five boring years within the sound of bugles. To this day it gives me a faint feeling of sacrilege not to stand to attention during 'God Save the King'. That is childish, of course, but I would sooner have had that kind of upbringing than be like the left-wing intellectuals who are so "enlightened" that they cannot understand the most ordinary emotions. It is exactly the people whose hearts have *never* leapt at the sight of a Union Jack who will flinch from revolution when the moment comes. Let anyone compare the poem John Cornford wrote not long before he was killed ('Before the Storming of Huesca') with Sir Henry Newbolt's "There's a breathless hush in the close tonight".* Put aside the technical differences, which are merely a matter of period, and it will be seen that the emotional content of the two poems is almost exactly the same. The young communist who died heroically in the International Brigade was public school to the core. He had changed his allegiance but not his emotions. What does that prove? Merely the possibility of building a socialist on the bones of a Blimp, the power of one kind of loyalty to transmute itself into another, the spiritual need for patriotism and the military virtues, for which, however little the boiled rabbits of the Left may like them, no substitute has yet been found.

The Lion and the Unicorn: Socialism and the English Genius*

PART I: ENGLAND YOUR ENGLAND

I

As I write, highly civilized human beings are flying overhead, trying to kill me.

They do not feel any enmity against me as an individual, nor I against them. They are "only doing their duty", as the saying goes. Most of them, I have no doubt, are kind-hearted law-abiding men who would never dream of committing murder in private life. On the other hand, if one of them succeeds in blowing me to pieces with a well-placed bomb, he will never sleep any the worse for it. He is serving his country, which has the power to absolve him from evil.

One cannot see the modern world as it is unless one recognizes the overwhelming strength of patriotism, national loyalty. In certain circumstances it can break down, at certain levels of civilization it does not exist, but as a *positive* force there is nothing to set beside it. Christianity and international socialism are as weak as straw in comparison with it. Hitler and Mussolini rose to power in their own countries very largely because they could grasp this fact and their opponents could not.

Also, one must admit that the divisions between nation and nation are founded on real differences of outlook. Till recently it was thought proper to pretend that all human beings are very much alike, but in fact anyone able to use his eyes knows that the average of human behaviour differs enormously from country to country. Things that could happen in one country could not happen in another. Hitler's June purge, for instance, could not have happened in England. And, as Western peoples go, the English are very highly differentiated. There is a sort of backhanded admission of this in the dislike which nearly all foreigners feel for our national way of life. Few Europeans can endure living in England, and even Americans often feel more at home in Europe.

When you come back to England from any foreign country, you have immediately the sensation of breathing a different air. Even in the first few minutes dozens of small things conspire to give you this feeling. The beer is bitterer, the coins are heavier, the grass is greener, the advertisements are more blatant. The crowds in the big towns, with their mild knobby faces, their bad teeth and gentle manners, are different from a European crowd. Then the vastness of England swallows you up, and you lose for a while your feeling that the whole nation has a single identifiable character. Are there really such things as nations? Are we not forty-six million individuals, all different? And the diversity of it, the chaos! The clatter of clogs in the Lancashire mill towns, the to-and-fro of the lorries on the Great North Road, the queues outside the Labour Exchanges, the rattle of pintables in the Soho pubs, the old maids biking to Holy Communion through the mists of the autumn morning – all these are not only fragments, but *characteristic* fragments, of the English scene. How can one make a pattern out of this muddle?

But talk to foreigners, read foreign books or newspapers, and you are brought back to the same thought. Yes, there *is* something distinctive and recognizable in English civilization. It is a culture as individual as that of Spain. It is somehow bound up with solid breakfasts and gloomy Sundays, smoky towns and winding roads, green fields and red pillar boxes. It has a flavour of its own. Moreover it is continuous, it stretches into the future and the past, there is something in it that persists, as in a living creature. What can the England of 1940 have in common with the England of 1840? But then, what have you in common with the child of five whose photograph your mother keeps on the mantelpiece? Nothing, except that you happen to be the same person.

And above all, it is *your* civilization, it is *you*. However much you hate it or laugh at it, you will never be happy away from it for any length of time. The suet puddings and the red pillar boxes have entered into your soul. Good or evil, it is yours, you belong to it, and this side the grave you will never get away from the marks that it has given you.

Meanwhile England, together with the rest of the world, is changing. And like everything else it can change only in certain directions, which up to a point can be foreseen. That is not to say that the future is fixed, merely that certain alternatives are possible and others not. A seed may grow or not grow, but at any rate a turnip seed never grows into a parsnip. It is therefore of the deepest importance to try and determine what England *is*, before guessing what part England *can play* in the huge events that are happening.

II

National characteristics are not easy to pin down, and when pinned down they often turn out to be trivialities or seem to have no connection with one another. Spaniards are cruel to animals, Italians can do nothing without making a deafening noise, the Chinese are addicted to gambling. Obviously such things don't matter in themselves. Nevertheless, nothing is causeless, and even the fact that Englishmen have bad teeth can tell something about the realities of English life.

Here are a couple of generalizations about England that would be accepted by almost all observers. One is that the English are not gifted artistically. They are not as musical as the Germans or Italians; painting and sculpture have never flourished in England as they have in France. Another is that, as Europeans go, the English are not intellectual. They have a horror of abstract thought; they feel no need for any philosophy or systematic "world view". Nor is this because they are "practical", as they are so fond of claiming for themselves. One has only to look at their methods of town planning and water supply, their obstinate clinging to everything that is out of date and a nuisance, a spelling system that defies analysis, and a system of weights and measures that is intelligible only to the compilers of arithmetic books, to see how little they care about mere efficiency. But they have a certain power of acting without taking thought. Their world-famed hypocrisy – their double-faced attitude towards the Empire, for instance – is bound up with this. Also, in moments of supreme crisis the whole nation can suddenly draw together and act upon a species of instinct, really a code of conduct which is understood by almost everyone, though never formulated. The phrase that Hitler coined for the Germans, "a sleepwalking people", would have been better applied to the English. Not that there is anything to be proud of in being called a sleepwalker.

But here it is worth noting a minor English trait which is extremely well marked though not often commented on, and that is a love of flowers. This is one of the first things that one notices when one reaches England from abroad, especially if one is coming from southern Europe. Does it not contradict the English indifference to the arts? Not really, because it is found in people who have no aesthetic feelings whatever. What it does link up with, however, is another English characteristic which is so much a part of us that we barely notice it, and that is the addiction to hobbies and spare-time occupations, the *privateness* of English life. We are a nation of flower lovers, but also a nation of stamp collectors, pigeon fanciers, amateur carpenters, coupon snippers, darts players, crossword-puzzle fans. All the culture that is most truly native centres round things which even when they are communal are not official – the pub, the football match, the back garden, the fireside and the "nice cup of tea". The liberty of the individual is still believed in, almost as in the nineteenth century. But this has nothing to do with economic liberty, the right to exploit others for profit. It is the liberty to have a home of your own, to do what you like in your spare time, to choose your own amusements instead of having them chosen for you from above. The most hateful of all names in an English ear is Nosy Parker. It is obvious, of course, that even this purely private liberty is a lost cause. Like all other modern people, the English are in process of being numbered, labelled, conscripted, "coordinated". But the pull of their impulses is in the other direction, and the kind of regimentation that can be imposed on them will be modified in consequence. No party rallies, no Youth Movements, no coloured shirts, no Jew-baiting or "spontaneous" demonstrations. No Gestapo either, in all probability.

But in all societies the common people must live to some extent *against* the existing order. The genuinely popular culture of England is something that goes on beneath the surface, unofficially and more or less frowned on by the authorities. One thing one notices if one looks directly at the common people, especially in the big towns, is that they are not puritanical. They are inveterate gamblers, drink as much beer as their wages will permit, are devoted to bawdy jokes, and use probably the foulest language in the world. They have to satisfy these tastes in the face of astonishing, hypocritical laws (licensing laws, lottery acts, etc. etc.) which are designed to interfere with everybody but in practice allow everything to happen. Also, the common people are without definite religious belief, and have been so for centuries. The Anglican Church never had a real hold on them, it was simply a preserve of the landed gentry, and the Nonconformist sects only influenced minorities. And yet they have retained a deep tinge of Christian feeling, while almost forgetting the name of Christ. The power worship which is the new religion of Europe, and which has infected the English intelligentsia, has never touched the common people. They have never caught up with power politics. The "realism" which is preached in Japanese and Italian newspapers would horrify them. One can learn a good deal about the spirit of England from the comic coloured postcards that you see in the windows of cheap stationers' shops. These things are a sort of diary upon which the English people have unconsciously recorded themselves. Their old-fashioned outlook, their graded snobberies, their mixture of bawdiness and hypocrisy, their extreme gentleness, their deeply moral attitude to life, are all mirrored there.

The gentleness of the English civilization is perhaps its most marked characteristic. You notice it the instant you set foot on English soil. It is a land where the bus conductors are good-tempered and the policemen carry no revolvers. In no country inhabited by white men is it easier to shove people off the pavement. And with this goes something that is always written off by European observers as "decadence" or hypocrisy, the English hatred of war and militarism. It is rooted deep in history, and it is strong in the lower middle class as well as the working class. Successive wars have shaken it but not destroyed it. Well within living memory it was common for "the redcoats" to be booed at in the streets and for the landlords of respectable public houses to refuse to allow soldiers on the premises. In peacetime, even when there are two million unemployed, it is difficult to fill the ranks of the tiny standing army, which is officered by the county gentry and a specialized stratum of the middle class, and manned by farm labourers and slum proletarians. The mass of the people are without military knowledge or tradition, and their attitude towards war is invariably defensive. No politician could rise to power by promising them conquests or military "glory", no Hymn of Hate has ever made any appeal to them. In the last war the songs which the soldiers made up and sang of their own accord were not vengeful but humorous and mock-defeatist.* The only enemy they ever named was the sergeant major.

In England all the boasting and flag-wagging, the 'Rule Britannia' stuff, is done by small minorities. The patriotism of the common people is not vocal or even conscious. They do not retain among their historical memories the name of a single military victory. English literature, like other literatures, is full of battle poems, but it is worth noticing that the ones that have won for themselves a kind of popularity are always a tale of disasters and retreats. There is no popular poem about Trafalgar or Waterloo, for instance. Sir John Moore's army at Corunna,* fighting a desperate rearguard action before escaping overseas (just like Dunkirk!) has more appeal than a brilliant victory. The most stirring battle poem in English is about a brigade of cavalry which charged in the wrong direction. And of the last war, the four names which have really engraved themselves on the popular memory are Mons, Ypres, Gallipoli and Passchendaele, every time a disaster. The names of the great battles that finally broke the German armies are simply unknown to the general public.

The reason why the English anti-militarism disgusts foreign observers is that it ignores the existence of the British Empire. It looks like sheer hypocrisy. After all, the English have absorbed a quarter of the earth and held on to it by means of a huge navy. How dare they then turn round and say that war is wicked?

It is quite true that the English are hypocritical about their Empire. In the working class this hypocrisy takes the form of not knowing that the Empire exists. But their dislike of standing armies is a perfectly sound instinct. A navy employs comparatively few people, and it is an external weapon which cannot affect home politics directly. Military dictatorships exist everywhere, but there is no such thing as a naval dictatorship. What English people of nearly all classes loathe from the bottom of their hearts is the swaggering officer type, the jingle of spurs and the crash of boots. Decades before Hitler was ever heard of, the word "Prussian" had much the same significance in England as "Nazi" has today. So deep does this feeling go that for a hundred years past the officers of the British Army, in peacetime, have always worn civilian clothes when off duty.

One rapid but fairly sure guide to the social atmosphere of a country is the parade-step of its army. A military parade is really a kind of ritual dance, something like a ballet, expressing a certain philosophy of life. The goose-step, for instance, is one of the most horrible sights in the world, far more terrifying than a dive-bomber. It is simply an affirmation of naked power; contained in it, quite consciously and intentionally, is the vision of a boot crashing down on a face. Its ugliness is part of its essence, for what it is saying is "Yes, I *am* ugly, and you daren't laugh at me", like the bully who makes faces at his victim. Why is the goose-step not used in England? There are, heaven knows, plenty of army officers who would be only too glad to introduce some such thing. It is not used because the people in the street would laugh. Beyond a certain point, military display is only possible in countries where the common people dare not laugh at the army. The Italians adopted the goose-step at about the time when Italy passed definitely under German control, and, as one would expect, they do it less well than the Germans. The Vichy government, if it survives, is bound to introduce a stiffer parade-ground discipline into what is left of the French army. In the British Army the drill is rigid and complicated, full of memories of the eighteenth century, but without definite swagger; the march is merely a formalized walk. It belongs to a society which is ruled by the sword, no doubt, but a sword which must never be taken out of the scabbard.

And yet the gentleness of English civilization is mixed up with barbarities and anachronisms. Our criminal law is as out of date as the muskets in the Tower. Over against the Nazi Storm Trooper you have got to set that typically English figure, the hanging judge, some gouty old bully with his mind rooted in the nineteenth century, handing out savage sentences. In England people are still hanged by the neck and flogged with the cat-o'-nine-tails. Both of these punishments are obscene as well as cruel, but there has never been any genuinely popular outcry against them. People accept them (and Dartmoor, and Borstal) almost as they accept the weather. They are part of "the law", which is assumed to be unalterable.

Here one comes upon an all-important English trait: the respect for constitutionalism and legality, the belief in "the law" as something above the state and above the individual, something which is cruel and stupid, of course, but at any rate *incorruptible*.

It is not that anyone imagines the law to be just. Everyone knows that there is one law for the rich and another for the poor. But no one accepts the implications of this; everyone takes it for granted that the law, such as it is, will be respected, and feels a sense of outrage when it is not. Remarks like "They can't run me in; I haven't done anything wrong", or "They can't do that; it's against the law", are part of the atmosphere of England. The professed enemies of society have this feeling as strongly as anyone else. One sees it in prison books like Wilfred Macartney's *Walls Have Mouths* or Jim Phelan's *Jail Journey*,* in the solemn idiocies that take place at the trials of conscientious objectors, in letters to the papers from eminent Marxist professors, pointing out that this or that is a "miscarriage of British justice". Everyone believes in his heart that the law can be, ought to be and, on the whole, will be impartially administered. The totalitarian idea that there is no such thing as law, there is only power, has never taken root. Even the intelligentsia have only accepted it in theory.

An illusion can become a half-truth, a mask can alter the expression of a face. The familiar arguments to the effect that democracy is "just the same as" or "just as bad as" totalitarianism never take account of this fact. All such arguments boil down to saying that half a loaf is the same as no bread. In England such concepts as justice, liberty and objective truth are still believed in. They may be illusions, but they are very powerful illusions. The belief in them influences conduct; national life is different because of them. In proof of which – look about you. Where are the rubber truncheons, where is the castor oil? The sword is still in the scabbard, and while it stays there corruption cannot go beyond a certain point. The English electoral system, for instance, is an all but open fraud. In a dozen obvious ways it is gerrymandered in the interest of the moneyed class. But until some deep change has occurred in the public mind, it cannot become *completely* corrupt. You do not arrive at the polling booth to find men with revolvers telling you which way to vote, nor are the votes miscounted, nor is there any direct bribery. Even hypocrisy is a powerful safeguard. The hanging judge, that evil old man in scarlet robe and horsehair wig, whom nothing short of dynamite will ever teach what century he is living in, but who will at any rate interpret the law according to the books and will in no circumstances take a money bribe, is one of the symbolic figures of England. He is a symbol of the strange mixture of reality and illusion, democracy and privilege, humbug and decency, the subtle network of compromises, by which the nation keeps itself in its familiar shape.

III

I have spoken all the while of "the nation", "England", "Britain", as though forty-five million souls could somehow be treated as a unit. But is not England notoriously two nations, the rich and the poor? Dare one pretend that there is anything in common between people with £100,000 a year and people with £1 a week? And even Welsh and Scottish readers are likely to have been offended because I have used the word "England" oftener than "Britain", as though the whole population dwelt in London and the Home Counties and neither north nor west possessed a culture of its own.

One gets a better view of this question if one considers the minor point first. It is quite true that the so-called races of Britain feel themselves to be very different from one another. A Scotsman, for instance, does not thank you if you call him an Englishman. You can see the hesitation we feel on this point by the fact that we call our islands by no less than six different names: England, Britain, Great Britain, the British Isles, the United Kingdom and, in very exalted moments, Albion. Even the differences between north and south England loom large in our own eyes. But somehow these differences fade away the moment that any two Britons are confronted by a European. It is very rare to meet a foreigner, other than an American, who can distinguish between English and Scots or even English and Irish. To a Frenchman, the Breton and the Auvergnat seem very different beings, and the accent of Marseilles is a stock joke in Paris. Yet we speak of "France" and "the French", recognizing France as an entity, a single civilization, which in fact it is. So also with ourselves. Looked at from the outside, even the cockney and the Yorkshireman have a strong family resemblance.

And even the distinction between rich and poor dwindles somewhat when one regards the nation from the outside. There is no question about the inequality of wealth in England. It is grosser than in any European country, and you have only to look down the nearest street to see it. Economically, England is certainly two nations, if not three or four. But at the same time the vast majority of the people *feel* themselves to be a single nation and are conscious of resembling one another more than they resemble foreigners. Patriotism is usually stronger than class hatred, and always stronger than any kind of internationalism. Except for a brief moment in 1920 (the "Hands off Russia" movement) the British working class have never thought or acted internationally. For two and a half years they watched their comrades in Spain slowly strangled, and never aided them by even a single strike.* But when their own country (the country of Lord Nuffield and Mr Montagu Norman*) was in danger, their attitude was very different. At the moment when it seemed likely that England might be invaded, Anthony Eden* appealed over the radio for Local Defence Volunteers. He got a quarter of a million men in the first twenty-four hours, and another million in the subsequent month. One has only to compare these figures with, for instance, the number of conscientious objectors to see how vast is the strength of traditional loyalties compared with new ones.

In England patriotism takes different forms in different classes, but it runs like a connecting thread through nearly all of them. Only the Europeanized intelligentsia are really immune to it. As a positive emotion it is stronger in the middle class than in the upper class – the cheap public schools, for instance, are more given to patriotic demonstrations than the expensive ones – but the number of definitely treacherous rich men, the Laval–Quisling* type, is probably very small. In the working class patriotism is profound, but it is unconscious. The working man's heart does not leap when he sees a Union Jack. But the famous "insularity" and "xenophobia" of the English is far stronger in the working class than in the bourgeoisie. In all countries the poor are more national than the rich, but the English working class are outstanding in their abhorrence of foreign habits. Even when they are obliged to live abroad for years they refuse either to accustom themselves to foreign food or to learn foreign languages. Nearly every Englishman of working-class origin considers it effeminate to pronounce a foreign word correctly. During the war of 1914–18 the English working class were in contact with foreigners to an extent that is rarely possible. The sole result was that they brought back a hatred of all Europeans, except the Germans, whose courage they admired.

In four years on French soil they did not even acquire a liking for wine. The insularity of the English, their refusal to take foreigners seriously, is a folly that has to be paid for very heavily from time to time. But it plays its part in the English mystique, and the intellectuals who have tried to break it down have generally done more harm than good. At bottom it is the same quality in the English character that repels the tourist and keeps out the invader.

Here one comes back to two English characteristics that I pointed out, seemingly at random, at the beginning of the last chapter. One is the lack of artistic ability. This is perhaps another way of saying that the English are outside the European culture. For there is one art in which they have shown plenty of talent, namely literature. But this is also the only art that cannot cross frontiers. Literature, especially poetry, and lyric poetry most of all, is a kind of family joke, with little or no value outside its own language group. Except for Shakespeare, the best English poets are barely known in Europe, even as names. The only poets who are widely read are Byron, who is admired for the wrong reasons, and Oscar Wilde, who is pitied as a victim of English hypocrisy. And linked up with this, though not very obviously, is the lack of philosophical faculty, the absence in nearly all Englishmen of any need for an ordered system of thought or even for the use of logic.

Up to a point, the sense of national unity is a substitute for a "world view". Just because patriotism is all but universal and not even the rich are uninfluenced by it, there can be moments when the whole nation suddenly swings together and does the same thing, like a herd of cattle facing a wolf. There was such a moment, unmistakably, at the time of the disaster in France. After eight months of vaguely wondering what the war was about, the people suddenly knew what they had got to do: first, to get the army away from Dunkirk, and secondly to prevent invasion. It was like the awakening of a giant. Quick! Danger! The Philistines be upon thee, Samson! And then the swift unanimous action – and then, alas, the prompt relapse into sleep. In a divided nation that would have been exactly the moment for a big peace movement to arise. But does this mean that the instinct of the English will always tell them to do the right thing? Not at all – merely that it will tell them to do the same thing. In the 1931 general election, for instance, we all did the wrong thing in perfect unison. We were as single-minded as the Gadarene swine.* But I honestly doubt whether we can say that we were shoved down the slope against our will.

It follows that British democracy is less of a fraud than it sometimes appears. A foreign observer sees only the huge inequality of wealth, the unfair electoral system, the governing-class control over the press, the radio and education, and concludes that democracy is simply a polite name for dictatorship. But this ignores the considerable agreement that does unfortunately exist between the leaders and the led. However much one may hate to admit it, it is almost certain that between 1931 and 1940 the National Government represented the will of the mass of the people. It tolerated slums, unemployment and a cowardly foreign policy. Yes, but so did public opinion. It was a stagnant period, and its natural leaders were mediocrities.

In spite of the campaigns of a few thousand left-wingers, it is fairly certain that the bulk of the English people were behind Chamberlain's foreign policy. More, it is fairly certain that the same struggle was going on in Chamberlain's mind as in the minds of ordinary people. His opponents professed to see in him a dark and wily schemer, plotting to sell England to Hitler, but it is far likelier that he was merely a stupid old man doing his best according to his very dim lights. It is difficult otherwise to explain the contradictions of his policy, his failure to grasp any of the courses that were open to him. Like the mass of the people, he did not want to pay the price either of peace or of war. And public opinion was behind him all the while, in policies that were completely incompatible with one another. It was behind him when he went to Munich, when he tried to come to an understanding with Russia, when he gave the guarantee to Poland, when he honoured it, and when he prosecuted the war half-heartedly. Only when the results of his policy became apparent did it turn against him – which is to say that it turned against its own lethargy of the past seven years. Thereupon the people picked a leader nearer to their mood, Churchill, who was at any rate able to grasp that wars are not won without fighting. Later, perhaps, they will pick another leader who can grasp that only socialist nations can fight effectively.

Do I mean by all this that England is a genuine democracy? No, not even a reader of the *Daily Telegraph* could quite swallow that.

England is the most class-ridden country under the sun. It is a land of snobbery and privilege, ruled largely by the old and silly. But in any calculation about it one has got to take into account its emotional unity, the tendency of nearly all its inhabitants to feel alike and act together in moments of supreme crisis. It is the only great country in Europe that is not obliged to drive hundreds of thousands of its nationals into exile or the concentration camp. At this moment, after a year of war, newspapers and pamphlets abusing the government, praising the enemy and clamouring for surrender are being sold on the streets, almost without interference. And this is less from a respect for freedom of speech than from a simple perception that these things don't matter. It is safe to let a paper like *Peace News** be sold, because it is certain that 95 per cent of the population will never want to read it. The nation is bound together by an invisible chain. At any normal time the ruling class will rob, mismanage, sabotage, lead us into the muck – but let popular opinion really make itself heard, let them get a tug from below that they cannot avoid feeling, and it is difficult for them not to respond. The left-wing writers who denounce the whole of the ruling class as "pro-fascist" are grossly oversimplifying. Even among the inner clique of politicians who brought us to our present pass, it is doubtful whether there were any *conscious* traitors. The corruption that happens in England is seldom of that kind. Nearly always it is more in the nature of self-deception, of the right hand not knowing what the left hand doeth. And being unconscious, it is limited. One sees this at its most obvious in the English press. Is the English press honest or dishonest? At normal times it is deeply dishonest. All the papers that matter live off their advertisements, and the advertisers exercise an indirect censorship over news. Yet I do not suppose there is one paper in England that can be straightforwardly bribed with hard cash. In the France of the Third Republic all but a very few of the newspapers could notoriously be bought over the counter like so many pounds of cheese. Public life in England has never been *openly* scandalous. It has not reached the pitch of disintegration at which humbug can be dropped.

England is not the jewelled isle of Shakespeare's much-quoted message,* nor is it the inferno depicted by Dr Goebbels.* More than either it resembles a family, a rather stuffy Victorian family, with not many black sheep in it but with all its cupboards bursting with skeletons. It has rich relations who have to be kowtowed to and poor relations who are horribly sat upon, and there is a deep conspiracy of silence about the source of the family income. It is a family in which the young are generally thwarted and most of the power is in the hands of irresponsible uncles and bedridden aunts. Still, it is a family. It has its private language and its common memories, and at the approach of an enemy it closes its ranks. A family with the wrong members in control – that, perhaps, is as near as one can come to describing England in a phrase.

IV

Probably the battle of Waterloo *was* won on the playing fields of Eton, but the opening battles of all subsequent wars have been lost there. One of the dominant facts in English life during the past three quarters of a century has been the decay of ability in the ruling class.

In the years between 1920 and 1940 it was happening with the speed of a chemical reaction. Yet at the moment of writing it is still possible to speak of a ruling class. Like the knife which has had two new blades and three new handles, the upper fringe of English society is still almost what it was in the mid nineteenth century. After 1832 the old landowning aristocracy steadily lost power, but instead of disappearing or becoming a fossil they simply intermarried with the merchants, manufacturers and financiers who had replaced them, and soon turned them into accurate copies of themselves. The wealthy shipowner or cotton miller set up for himself an alibi as a country gentleman, while his sons learnt the right mannerisms at public schools which had been designed for just that purpose. England was ruled by an aristocracy constantly recruited from parvenus. And considering what energy the self-made men possessed, and considering that they were buying their way into a class which at any rate had a tradition of public service, one might have expected that able rulers could be produced in some such way.

And yet somehow the ruling class decayed, lost its ability, its daring, finally even its ruthlessness, until a time came when stuffed shirts like Eden or Halifax* could stand out as men of exceptional talent. As for Baldwin, one could not even dignify him with the name of stuffed shirt. He was simply a hole in the air. The mishandling of England's domestic problems during the 1920s had been bad enough, but British foreign policy between 1931 and 1939 is one of the wonders of the world. Why? What had happened? What was it that at every decisive moment made every British statesman do the wrong thing with so unerring an instinct?

The underlying fact was that the whole position of the moneyed class had long ceased to be justifiable. There they sat, at the centre of a vast empire and a worldwide financial network, drawing interest and profits and spending them – on what? It was fair to say that life within the British Empire was in many ways better than life outside it. Still, the Empire was underdeveloped, India slept in the Middle Ages, the Dominions lay empty, with foreigners jealously barred out, and even England was full of slums and unemployment. Only half a million people, the people in the country houses, definitely benefited from the existing system. Moreover, the tendency of small businesses to merge together into large ones robbed more and more of the moneyed class of their function and turned them into mere *owners*, their work being done for them by salaried managers and technicians. For long past there had been in England an entirely functionless class, living on money that was invested they hardly knew where, the "idle rich", the people whose photographs you can look at in the *Tatler* and the *Bystander*,* always supposing that you want to. The existence of these people was by any standard unjustifiable. They were simply parasites, less useful to society than his fleas are to a dog.

By 1920 there were many people who were aware of all this. By 1930 millions were aware of it. But the British ruling class obviously could not admit to themselves that their usefulness was at an end. Had they done that they would have had to abdicate. For it was not possible for them to turn themselves into mere bandits, like the American millionaires, consciously clinging to unjust privileges and beating down opposition by bribery and tear-gas bombs. After all, they belonged to a class with a certain tradition; they had been to public schools where the duty of dying for your country, if necessary, is laid down as the first and greatest of the Commandments. They had to *feel* themselves true patriots, even while they plundered their countrymen. Clearly there was only one escape for them – into stupidity. They could keep society in its existing shape only by being *unable* to grasp that any improvement was possible. Difficult though this was, they achieved it, largely by fixing their eyes on the past and refusing to notice the changes that were going on round them.

There is much in England that this explains. It explains the decay of country life, due to the keeping up of a sham feudalism which drives the more spirited workers off the land. It explains the immobility of the public schools, which have barely altered since the eighties of the last century. It explains the military incompetence which has again and again startled the world. Since the fifties every war in which England has engaged has started off with a series of disasters, after which the situation has been saved by people comparatively low in the social scale. The higher commanders, drawn from the aristocracy, could never prepare for modern war, because in order to do so they would have had to admit to themselves that the world was changing. They have always clung to obsolete methods and weapons, because they inevitably saw each war as a repetition of the last. Before the Boer War they prepared for the Zulu War, before the 1914 for the Boer War, and before the present war for 1914. Even at this moment hundreds of thousands of men in England are being trained with the bayonet, a weapon entirely useless except for opening tins. It is worth noticing that the navy and, latterly, the air force have always been more efficient than the regular army. But the navy is only partially, and the air force hardly at all, within the ruling-class orbit.

It must be admitted that so long as things were peaceful the methods of the British ruling class served them well enough. Their own people manifestly tolerated them. However unjustly England might be organized, it was at any rate not torn by class warfare or haunted by secret police. The Empire was peaceful as no area of comparable size has ever been. Throughout its vast extent, nearly a quarter of the earth, there were fewer armed men than would be found necessary by a minor Balkan state. As people to live under, and looking at them merely from a liberal, *negative* standpoint, the British ruling class had their points. They were preferable to the truly modern men, the Nazis and fascists. But it had long been obvious that they would be helpless against any serious attack from the outside.

They could not struggle against Nazism or fascism, because they could not understand them. Neither could they have struggled against communism, if communism had been a serious force in Western Europe. To understand fascism they would have had to study the theory of socialism, which would have forced them to realize that the economic system by which they lived was unjust, inefficient and out of date. But it was exactly this fact that they had trained themselves never to face. They dealt with fascism as the cavalry generals of 1914 dealt with the machine guns – by ignoring it. After years of aggression and massacres, they had grasped only one fact: that Hitler and Mussolini were hostile to communism. Therefore, it was argued, they *must* be friendly to the British dividend drawer. Hence the truly frightening spectacle of Conservative MPs wildly cheering the news that British ships, bringing food to the Spanish Republican government, had been bombed by

Italian aeroplanes. Even when they had begun to grasp that fascism was dangerous, its essentially revolutionary nature, the huge military effort it was capable of making, the sort of tactics it would use, were quite beyond their comprehension. At the time of the Spanish Civil War, anyone with as much political knowledge as can be acquired from a sixpenny pamphlet on socialism knew that, if Franco won, the result would be strategically disastrous for England – and yet generals and admirals who had given their lives to the study of war were unable to grasp this fact. This vein of political ignorance runs right through English official life, through Cabinet ministers, ambassadors, consuls, judges, magistrates, policemen. The policeman who arrests the "red" does not understand the theories the "red" is preaching; if he did his own position as bodyguard of the moneyed class might seem less pleasant to him. There is reason to think that even military espionage is hopelessly hampered by ignorance of the new economic doctrines and the ramifications of the underground parties.

The British ruling class were not altogether wrong in thinking that fascism was on their side. It is a fact that any rich man, unless he is a Jew, has less to fear from fascism than from either communism or democratic socialism. One ought never to forget this, for nearly the whole of German and Italian propaganda is designed to cover it up. The natural instinct of men like Simon, Hoare,* Chamberlain etc. was to come to an agreement with Hitler. But – and here the peculiar feature of English life that I have spoken of, the deep sense of national solidarity, comes in – they could only do so by breaking up the Empire and selling their own people into semi-slavery. A truly corrupt class would have done this without hesitation, as in France. But things had not gone that distance in England. Politicians who would make cringing speeches about "the duty of loyalty to our conquerors" are hardly to be found in English public life. Tossed to and fro between their incomes and their principles, it was impossible that men like Chamberlain should do anything but make the worst of both worlds.

One thing that has always shown that the English ruling class are *morally* fairly sound is that in times of war they are ready enough to get themselves killed. Several dukes, earls and what nots were killed in the recent campaign in Flanders. That could not happen if these people were the cynical scoundrels that they are sometimes declared to be. It is important not to misunderstand their motives, or one cannot predict their actions. What is to be expected of them is not treachery, or physical cowardice, but stupidity, unconscious sabotage, an infallible instinct for doing the wrong thing. They are not wicked, or not altogether wicked; they are merely unteachable. Only when their money and power are gone will the younger among them begin to grasp what century they are living in.

V

The stagnation of the Empire in the between-war years affected everyone in England, but it had an especially direct effect upon two important subsections of the middle class. One was the military and imperialist middle class, generally nicknamed the Blimps, and the other the left-wing intelligentsia. These two seemingly hostile types, symbolic opposites – the half-pay colonel with his bull neck and diminutive brain, like a dinosaur, the highbrow with his domed forehead and stalk-like neck – are mentally linked together and constantly interact upon one another; in any case they are born to a considerable extent into the same families.

Thirty years ago the Blimp class was already losing its vitality. The middle-class families celebrated by Kipling, the prolific lowbrow families whose sons officered the army and navy and swarmed over all the waste places of the earth from the Yukon to the Irrawaddy, were dwindling before 1914. The thing that had killed them was the telegraph. In a narrowing world, more and more governed from Whitehall, there was every year less room for individual initiative. Men like Clive, Nelson, Nicholson, Gordon* would find no place for themselves in the modern British Empire. By 1920 nearly every inch of the colonial empire was in the grip of Whitehall. Well-meaning, over-civilized men in dark suits and black felt hats, with neatly rolled umbrellas crooked over the left forearm, were imposing their constipated view of life on Malaya and Nigeria, Mombasa and Mandalay. The one-time empire builders were reduced to the status of clerks, buried deeper and deeper under mounds of paper and red tape. In the early twenties one could see, all over the Empire, the older officials, who had known more spacious days, writhing impotently under the changes that were happening. From that time onwards it has been next door to impossible to induce young men of spirit to take any part in imperial administration. And what was true of the official world was true also of the commercial. The great monopoly companies swallowed up hosts of petty traders. Instead of going out to trade adventurously in the Indies one went to an office stool in Bombay or Singapore. And life in Bombay or Singapore was actually duller and safer than life in London. Imperialist sentiment remained strong in the middle class, chiefly owing to family tradition, but the job of administering the Empire had ceased to appeal. Few able men went east of Suez if there was any way of avoiding it.

But the general weakening of imperialism, and to some extent of the whole British morale, that took place during the 1930s, was partly the work of the left-wing intelligentsia, itself a kind of growth that had sprouted from the stagnation of the Empire.

It should be noted that there is now no intelligentsia that is not in some sense "left". Perhaps the last right-wing intellectual was T.E. Lawrence.* Since about 1930 everyone describable as an "intellectual" has lived in a state of chronic discontent with the existing order. Necessarily so, because society as it was constituted had no room for him. In an Empire that was simply stagnant, neither being developed nor falling to pieces, and in an England ruled by people whose chief asset was their stupidity, to be "clever" was to be suspect. If you had the kind of brain that could understand the poems of T.S. Eliot or the theories of Karl Marx, the higher-ups would see to it that you were kept out of any important job. The intellectuals could find a function for themselves only in the literary reviews and the left-wing political parties.

The mentality of the English left-wing intelligentsia can be studied in half a dozen weekly and monthly papers. The immediately striking thing about all these papers is their generally negative, querulous attitude, their complete lack at all times of any constructive suggestion. There is little in them except the irresponsible carping of people who have never been and never expect to be in a position of power. Another marked characteristic is the emotional shallowness of people who live in a world of ideas and have little contact with physical reality. Many intellectuals of the Left were flabbily pacifist up to 1935, shrieked for war against Germany in the years 1935–39, and then promptly cooled off when the war started. It is broadly though not precisely true that the people who were most "anti-fascist" during the Spanish Civil War are most defeatist now. And underlying this is the really important fact about so many of the English intelligentsia – their severance from the common culture of the country.

In intention, at any rate, the English intelligentsia are Europeanized. They take their cookery from Paris and their opinions from Moscow. In the general patriotism of the country they form a sort of island of dissident thought. England is perhaps the only great country whose intellectuals are ashamed of their own nationality. In left-wing circles it is always felt that there is something slightly disgraceful in being an Englishman and that it is a duty to snigger at every English institution, from horse racing to suet puddings. It is a strange fact, but it is unquestionably true that almost any English intellectual would feel more ashamed of standing to attention during 'God Save the King' than of stealing from a poor box. All through the critical years many left-wingers were chipping away at English morale, trying to spread an outlook that was sometimes squashily pacifist, sometimes violently pro-Russian, but always anti-British. It is questionable how much effect this had, but it certainly had some. If the English people suffered for several years a real weakening of morale, so that the fascist nations judged that they were "decadent" and that it was safe to plunge into war, the intellectual sabotage from the Left was partly responsible. Both the *New Statesman* and the *News Chronicle* cried out against the Munich settlement, but even they had done something to make it possible. Ten years of systematic Blimp-baiting affected even the Blimps themselves and made it harder than it had been before to get intelligent young men to enter the armed forces. Given the stagnation of the Empire the military middle class must have decayed in any case, but the spread of a shallow Leftism hastened the process.

It is clear that the special position of the English intellectuals during the past ten years, as purely *negative* creatures, mere anti-Blimps, was a by-product of ruling-class stupidity. Society could not use them, and they had not got it in them to see that devotion to one's country implies "for better, for worse". Both Blimps and highbrows took for granted, as though it were a law of nature, the divorce between patriotism and intelligence. If you were a patriot you read *Blackwood's Magazine** and publicly thanked God that you were "not brainy". If you were an intellectual you sniggered at the Union Jack and regarded physical courage as barbarous. It is obvious that this preposterous convention cannot continue. The Bloomsbury highbrow, with his mechanical snigger, is as out of date as the cavalry colonel. A modern nation cannot afford either of them. Patriotism and intelligence will have to come together again. It is the fact that we are fighting a war, and a very peculiar kind of war, that may make this possible.

VI

One of the most important developments in England during the past twenty years has been the upward and downward extension of the middle class. It has happened on such a scale as to make the old classification of society into capitalists, proletarians and petit bourgeois (small property owners) almost obsolete.

England is a country in which property and financial power are concentrated in very few hands. Few people in modern England *own* anything at all, except clothes, furniture and possibly a house. The peasantry have long since disappeared, the independent shopkeeper is being destroyed, the small businessman is diminishing in numbers. But at the same time modern industry is so complicated that it cannot get along without great numbers of managers, salesmen, engineers, chemists and technicians of all kinds, drawing fairly large salaries. And these in turn call into being a professional class of doctors, lawyers, teachers, artists, etc. etc. The tendency of advanced capitalism has therefore been to enlarge the middle class and not to wipe it out as it once seemed likely to do.

But much more important than this is the spread of middle-class ideas and habits among the working class. The British working class are now better off in almost all ways than they were thirty years ago. This is partly due to the efforts of the trade unions, but partly to the mere advance of physical science. It is not always realized that within rather narrow limits the standard of life of a country can rise without a corresponding rise in real wages. Up to a point, civilization can lift itself up by its boot-tags. However unjustly society is organized, certain technical advances are bound to benefit the whole community, because certain kinds of goods are necessarily held in common. A millionaire cannot, for example, light the streets for himself while darkening them for other people. Nearly all citizens of civilized countries now enjoy the use of good roads, germ-free water, police protection, free libraries and probably free education of a kind. Public education in England has been meanly starved of money, but it has nevertheless improved, largely owing to the devoted efforts of the teachers, and the habit of reading has become enormously more widespread. To an increasing extent the rich and the poor read the same books, and they also see the same films and listen to the same radio programmes. And the differences in their way of life have been diminished by the mass production of cheap clothes and improvements in housing. So far as outward appearance goes, the clothes of rich and poor, especially in the case of women, differ far less than they did thirty or even fifteen years ago. As to housing, England still has slums which are a blot on civilization, but much building has been done during the past ten years, largely by the local authorities. The modern council house, with its bathroom and electric light, is smaller than the stockbroker's villa, but it is recognizably the same kind of house, which the farm labourer's cottage is not. A person who has grown up in a council housing estate is likely to be – indeed, visibly *is* – more middle class in outlook than a person who has grown up in a slum.

The effect of all this is a general softening of manners. It is enhanced by the fact that modern industrial methods tend always to demand less muscular effort and therefore to leave people with more energy when their day's work is done. Many workers in the light industries are less truly manual labourers than is a doctor or a grocer. In tastes, habits, manners and outlook the working class and the middle class are drawing together. The unjust distinctions remain, but the real differences diminish. The old-style "proletarian" – collarless, unshaven and with muscles warped by heavy labour – still exists, but he is constantly decreasing in numbers; he only predominates in the heavy-industry areas of the north of England.

After 1918 there began to appear something that had never existed in England before: people of indeterminate social class. In 1910 every human being in these islands could be "placed" in an instant by his clothes, manners and accent. That is no longer the case. Above all, it is not the case in the new townships that have developed as a result of cheap motor cars and the southward shift of industry. The place to look for the germs of the future England is in light-industry areas and along the arterial roads. In Slough, Dagenham, Barnet, Letchworth, Hayes – everywhere, indeed, on the outskirts of great towns – the old pattern is gradually changing into something new. In those vast new wildernesses of glass and brick the sharp distinctions of the older kind of town, with its slums and mansions, or of the country, with its manor houses and squalid cottages, no longer exist. There are wide gradations of income, but it is the same kind of life that is being lived at different levels, in labour-saving flats or council houses, along the concrete roads and in the naked democracy of the swimming pools. It is a rather restless, cultureless life, centring round tinned food, *Picture Post*,* the radio and the internal-combustion engine. It is a civilization in which children grow up with an intimate knowledge of magnetos and in complete ignorance of the Bible. To that civilization belong the people who are most at home in and most definitely *of* the modern world, the technicians and the higher-paid skilled workers, the airmen and their mechanics, the radio experts, film producers, popular journalists and industrial chemists. They are the indeterminate stratum at which the older class distinctions are beginning to break down.

This war, unless we are defeated, will wipe out most of the existing class privileges. There are every day fewer people who wish them to continue. Nor need we fear that as the pattern changes life in England will lose its peculiar flavour. The new red cities of Greater London are crude enough, but these things are only the rash that accompanies a change. In whatever shape England emerges from the war it will be deeply tinged with the characteristics that I have spoken of earlier. The intellectuals who hope to see it Russianized or Germanized will be disappointed. The gentleness, the hypocrisy, the thoughtlessness, the reverence for law and the hatred of uniforms will remain, along with the suet puddings and the misty skies. It needs some very great disaster, such as prolonged subjugation by a foreign enemy, to destroy a national culture. The Stock Exchange will be pulled down, the horse plough will give way to the tractor, the country houses will be turned into children's holiday camps, the Eton and Harrow match will be forgotten, but England will still be England, an everlasting animal stretching into the future and the past, and, like all living things, having the power to change out of recognition and yet remain the same.

PART II: SHOPKEEPERS AT WAR

I

I began this book to the tune of German bombs, and I begin this second chapter in the added racket of the barrage. The yellow gun flashes are lighting the sky, the splinters are rattling on the housetops, and London Bridge is falling down, falling down, falling down. Anyone able to read a map knows that we are in deadly danger. I do not mean that we are beaten or need be beaten. Almost certainly the outcome depends on our own will. But at this moment we are in the soup, full fathom five, and we have been brought there by follies which we are still committing and which will drown us altogether if we do not mend our ways quickly.

What this war has demonstrated is that private capitalism – that is, an economic system in which land, factories, mines and transport are owned privately and operated solely for profit – *does not work*. It cannot deliver the goods. This fact had been known to millions of people for years past, but nothing ever came of it, because there was no real urge from below to alter the system, and those at the top had trained themselves to be impenetrably stupid on just this point. Argument and propaganda got one nowhere. The lords of property simply sat on their bottoms and proclaimed that all was for the best. Hitler's conquest of Europe, however, was a *physical* debunking of capitalism. War, for all its evil, is at any rate an unanswerable test of strength, like a try-your-grip machine. Great strength returns the penny, and there is no way of faking the result.

When the nautical screw was first invented, there was a controversy that lasted for years as to whether screw steamers or paddle steamers were better. The paddle steamers, like all obsolete things, had their champions, who supported them by ingenious arguments. Finally, however, a distinguished admiral tied a screw steamer and a paddle steamer of equal horsepower stern to stern and set their engines running. That settled the question once and for all. And it was something similar that happened on the fields of Norway and of Flanders. Once and for all it was proved that a planned economy is stronger than a planless one. But it is necessary here to give some kind of definition to those much-abused words, socialism and fascism.

Socialism is usually defined as "common ownership of the means of production". Crudely: the state, representing the whole nation, owns everything, and everyone is a state employee. This does *not* mean that people are stripped of private possessions such as clothes and furniture, but it *does* mean that all productive goods, such as land, mines, ships and machinery, are the property of the state. The state is the sole large-scale producer. It is not certain that socialism is in all ways superior to capitalism, but it is certain that, unlike capitalism, it can solve the problems of production and consumption. At normal times a capitalist economy can never consume all that it produces, so that there is always a wasted surplus (wheat burned in furnaces, herrings dumped back into the sea, etc. etc.) and always unemployment. In time of war, on the other hand, it has difficulty in producing all that it needs, because nothing is produced unless someone sees his way to making a profit out of it.

In a socialist economy these problems do not exist. The state simply calculates what goods will be needed and does its best to produce them. Production is only limited by the amount of labour and raw materials. Money, for internal purposes, ceases to be a mysterious all-powerful thing and becomes a sort of coupon or ration ticket, issued in sufficient quantities to buy up such consumption goods as may be available at the moment.

However, it has become clear in the last few years that "common ownership of the means of production" is not in itself a sufficient definition of socialism. One must also add the following: approximate equality of incomes (it need be no more than approximate), political democracy and abolition of all hereditary privilege, especially in education. These are simply the necessary safeguards against the reappearance of a class system. Centralized ownership has very little meaning unless the mass of the people are living roughly upon an equal level, and have some kind of control over the government. "The state" may come to mean no more than a self-elected political party, and oligarchy and privilege can return, based on power rather than on money.

But what then is fascism?

Fascism, at any rate the German version, is a form of capitalism that borrows from socialism just such features as will make it efficient for war purposes. Internally, Germany has a good deal in common with a socialist state. Ownership has never been abolished, there are still capitalists and workers, and – this is the important point, and the real reason why rich men all over the world tend to sympathize with fascism – generally speaking the same people are capitalists and the same people workers as before the Nazi revolution. But at the same time the state, which is simply the Nazi Party, is in control of everything. It controls investment, raw materials, rates of interest, working hours, wages. The factory owner still owns his factory, but he is for practical purposes reduced to the status of a manager. Everyone is in effect a state employee, though the salaries vary very greatly. The mere *efficiency* of such a system, the elimination of waste and obstruction, is obvious. In seven years it has built up the most powerful war machine the world has ever seen.

But the idea underlying fascism is irreconcilably different from that which underlies socialism. Socialism aims, ultimately, at a world-state of free and equal human beings. It takes the equality of human rights for granted. Nazism assumes just the opposite. The driving force behind the Nazi movement is the belief in human *inequality*. The superiority of Germans to all other races, the right of Germany to rule the world. Outside the German Reich it does not recognize any obligations. Eminent Nazi professors have "proved" over and over again that only Nordic man is fully human, have even mooted the idea that non-Nordic peoples (such as ourselves) can interbreed with gorillas! Therefore, while a species of war-socialism exists within the German state, its attitude towards conquered nations is frankly that of an exploiter. The function of the Czechs, Poles, French, etc. is simply to produce such goods as Germany may need, and get in return just as little as will keep them from open rebellion. If we are conquered, our job will probably be to manufacture weapons for Hitler's forthcoming wars with Russia and America. The Nazis aim, in effect, at setting up a kind of caste system, with four main castes corresponding rather closely to those of the Hindu religion. At the top comes the Nazi Party, second come the mass of the German people, third come the conquered European populations. Fourth and last are to come the coloured peoples, the "semi-apes" as Hitler calls them, who are to be reduced quite openly to slavery.

However horrible this system may seem to us, *it works*. It works because it is a planned system geared to a definite purpose, world conquest, and not allowing any private interest, either of capitalist or worker, to stand in its way. British capitalism does not work, because it is a competitive system in which private profit is and must be the main objective. It is a system in which all the forces are pulling in opposite directions and the interests of the individual are as often as not totally opposed to those of the state.

All through the critical years British capitalism, with its immense industrial plant and its unrivalled supply of skilled labour, was unequal to the strain of preparing for war. To prepare for war on the modern scale you have got to divert the greater part of your national income to armaments, which means cutting down on consumption goods. A bombing plane, for instance, is equivalent in price to fifty small motor cars, or 8,000 pairs of silk stockings, or a million loaves of bread. Clearly you can't have *many* bombing planes without lowering the national standard of life. It is guns or butter, as Marshal Goering* remarked. But in Chamberlain's England the transition could not be made. The rich would not face the necessary taxation, and while the rich are still visibly rich it is not possible to tax the poor very heavily either. Moreover, so long as *profit* was the main object the manufacturer had no incentive to change over from consumption goods to armaments. A businessman's first duty is to his shareholders. Perhaps England needs tanks, but perhaps it pays better to manufacture motor cars. To prevent war material from reaching the enemy is common sense, but to sell in the highest market is a business duty. Right at the end of August 1939 the British dealers were tumbling over one another in their eagerness to sell Germany tin, rubber, copper and shellac – and this in the clear, certain knowledge that war was going to break out in a week or two. It was about as sensible as selling somebody a razor to cut your throat with. But it was "good business".

And now look at the results. After 1934 it was known that Germany was rearming. After 1936 everyone with eyes in his head knew that war was coming. After Munich it was merely a question of how soon the war would begin. In September 1939 war broke out. *Eight months later* it was discovered that, so far as equipment went, the British Army was barely beyond the standard of 1918. We saw our soldiers fighting their way desperately to the coast, with one aeroplane against three, with rifles against tanks, with bayonets against tommy guns. There were not even enough revolvers to supply all the officers. After a year of war the regular army was still short of 300,000 tin hats. There had even, previously, been a shortage of uniforms – this in one of the greatest woollen-goods-producing countries in the world!

What had happened was that the whole moneyed class, unwilling to face a change in their way of life, had shut their eyes to the nature of fascism and modern war. And false optimism was fed to the general public by the gutter press, which lives on its advertisements and is therefore interested in keeping trade conditions normal. Year after year the Beaverbrook press* assured us in huge headlines that *THERE WILL BE NO WAR*, and as late as the beginning of 1939 Lord Rothermere* was describing Hitler as "a great gentleman". And while England in the moment of disaster proved to be short of every war material except ships, it is not recorded that there was any shortage of motor cars, fur coats, gramophones, lipstick, chocolates or silk stockings. And dare anyone pretend that the same tug-of-war between private profit and public necessity is not still continuing? England fights for her life, but business must fight for profits. You can hardly open a newspaper without seeing the two contradictory processes happening side by side. On the very same page you will find the government urging you to save and the seller of some useless luxury urging you to spend. Lend to Defend, but Guinness is Good for You. Buy a Spitfire, but also buy Haig and Haig, Pond's Face Cream and Black Magic Chocolates.

But one thing gives hope – the visible swing in public opinion. If we can survive this war, the defeat in Flanders will turn out to have been one of the great turning points in English history. In that spectacular disaster the working class, the middle class and even a section of the business community could see the utter rottenness of private capitalism. Before that the case against capitalism had never been *proved*. Russia, the only definitely socialist country, was backward and far away. All criticism broke itself against the rat-trap faces of bankers and the brassy laughter of stockbrokers. Socialism? Ha! Ha! Ha! Where's the money to come from? Ha! Ha! Ha! The lords of property were firm in their seats, and they knew it. But after the French collapse there came something that could not be laughed away, something that neither chequebooks nor policemen were any use against – the bombing. Zweee – BOOM! What's that? Oh, only a bomb on the Stock Exchange. Zweee – BOOM! Another acre of somebody's valuable slum-property gone west. Hitler will at any rate go down in history as the man who made the City of London laugh on the wrong side of its face. For the first time in their lives the comfortable were uncomfortable, the professional optimists had to admit that there was something wrong. It was a great step forward. From that time onwards the ghastly job of trying to convince artificially stupefied people that a planned economy might be better than a free-for-all in which the worst man wins – that job will never be quite so ghastly again.

II

The difference between socialism and capitalism is not primarily a difference of technique. One cannot simply change from one system to the other as one might install a new piece of machinery in a factory, and then carry on as before, with the same people in positions of control. Obviously there is also needed a complete shift of power. New blood, new men, new ideas – in the true sense of the word, a revolution.

I have spoken earlier of the soundness and homogeneity of England, the patriotism that runs like a connecting thread through almost all classes. After Dunkirk anyone who had eyes in his head could see this. But it is absurd to pretend that the promise of that moment has been fulfilled. Almost certainly the mass of the people are now ready for the vast changes that are necessary – but those changes have not even begun to happen.

England is a family with the wrong members in control. Almost entirely we are governed by the rich, and by people who step into positions of command by right of birth. Few if any of these people are consciously treacherous, some of them are not even fools, but as a class they are quite incapable of leading us to victory. They could not do it, even if their material interests did not constantly trip them up. As I pointed out earlier, they have been artificially stupefied. Quite apart from anything else, the rule of money sees to it that we shall be governed largely by the old – that is, by people utterly unable to grasp what age they are living in or what enemy they are fighting. Nothing was more desolating at the beginning of this war than the way in which the whole of the older generation conspired to pretend that it was the war of 1914–18 over again. All the old duds were back on the job, twenty years older, with the skull plainer in their faces. Ian Hay was cheering up the troops, Belloc was writing articles on strategy, Maurois doing broadcasts, Bairnsfather drawing cartoons.* It was like a tea party of ghosts. And that state of affairs has barely altered. The shock of disaster brought a few able men like Bevin* to the front, but in general we are still commanded by people who managed to live through the years 1931–39 without even discovering that Hitler was dangerous. A generation of the unteachable is hanging upon us like a necklace of corpses.

As soon as one considers any problem of this war – and it does not matter whether it is the widest aspect of strategy or the tiniest detail of home organization – one sees that the necessary moves cannot be made while the social structure of England remains what it is. Inevitably, because of their position and upbringing, the ruling class are fighting for their own privileges, which cannot possibly be reconciled with the public interest. It is a mistake to imagine that war aims, strategy, propaganda and industrial organization exist in watertight compartments. All are interconnected. Every strategic plan, every tactical method, even every weapon will bear the stamp of the social system that produced it. The British ruling class are fighting against Hitler, whom they have always regarded and whom some of them still regard as their protector against Bolshevism. That does not mean that they will deliberately sell out – but it does mean that at every decisive moment they are likely to falter, pull their punches, do the wrong thing.

Until the Churchill government called some sort of halt to the process, they have done the wrong thing with an unerring instinct ever since 1931. They helped Franco to overthrow the Spanish government, although anyone not an imbecile could have told them that a fascist Spain would be hostile to England. They fed Italy with war materials all through the winter of 1939–40, although it was obvious to the whole world that the Italians were going to attack us in the spring. For the sake of a few hundred thousand dividend drawers they are turning India from an ally into an enemy. Moreover, so long as the moneyed classes remain in control, we cannot develop any but a *defensive* strategy. Every victory means a change in the status quo. How can we drive the Italians out of Abyssinia without rousing echoes among the coloured peoples of our own Empire? How can we even smash Hitler without the risk of bringing the German socialists and communists into power? The left-wingers who wail that "this is a capitalist war" and that "British Imperialism" is fighting for loot have got their heads screwed on backwards. The last thing the British moneyed class wish for is to acquire fresh territory. It would simply be an embarrassment. Their war aim (both unattainable and unmentionable) is simply to hang on to what they have got.

Internally, England is still the rich man's paradise. All talk of "equality of sacrifice" is nonsense. At the same time as factory workers are asked to put up with longer hours, advertisements for "Butler. One in family, eight in staff" are appearing in the press. The bombed-out populations of the East End go hungry and homeless while wealthier victims simply step into their cars and flee to comfortable country houses. The Home Guard swells to a million men in a few weeks, and is deliberately organized from above in such a way that only people with private incomes can hold positions of command. Even the rationing system is so arranged that it hits the poor all the time, while people with over £2,000 a year are practically unaffected by it. Everywhere privilege is squandering goodwill. In such circumstances even propaganda becomes almost impossible. As attempts to stir up patriotic feeling, the red posters issued by the Chamberlain government at the beginning of the war broke all depth records. Yet they could not have been much other than they were, for how could Chamberlain and his followers take the risk of rousing strong popular feeling *against fascism*? Anyone who was genuinely hostile to fascism must also be opposed to Chamberlain himself and to all the others who had helped Hitler into power. So also with external propaganda. In all Lord Halifax's speeches there is not one concrete proposal for which a single inhabitant of Europe would risk the top joint of his little finger. For what war aim can Halifax, or anyone like him, conceivably have, except to put the clock back to 1933?

It is only by revolution that the native genius of the English people can be set free. Revolution does not mean red flags and street fighting – it means a fundamental shift of power. Whether it happens with or without bloodshed is largely an accident of time and place. Nor does it mean the dictatorship of a single class. The people in England who grasp what changes are needed and are capable of carrying them through are not confined to any one class, though it is true that very few people with over £2,000 a year are among them. What is wanted is a conscious open revolt by ordinary people against inefficiency, class privilege and the rule of the old. It is not primarily a question of change of government. British governments do, broadly speaking, represent the will of the people, and if we alter our structure from below we shall get the government we need. Ambassadors, generals, officials and colonial administrators who are senile or pro-fascist are more dangerous than Cabinet ministers whose follies have to be committed in public. Right through our national life we have got to fight against privilege, against the notion that a half-witted public schoolboy is better for command than an intelligent mechanic. Although there are gifted and honest *individuals* among them, we have got to break the grip of the moneyed class as a whole. England has got to assume its real shape. The England that is only just beneath the surface, in the factories and the newspaper offices, in the aeroplanes and the submarines, has got to take charge of its own destiny.

In the short run, equality of sacrifice, "war communism", is even more important than radical economic changes. It is very necessary that industry should be nationalized, but it is more urgently necessary that such monstrosities as butlers and "private incomes" should disappear forthwith. Almost certainly the main reason why the Spanish Republic could keep up the fight for two and a half years against impossible odds was that there were no gross contrasts of wealth. The people suffered horribly, but they all suffered alike. When the private soldier had not a cigarette, the general had not one either. Given equality of sacrifice, the morale of a country like England would probably be unbreakable. But at present we have nothing to appeal to except traditional patriotism, which is deeper here than elsewhere, but is not necessarily bottomless. At some point or another you have got to deal with the man who says "I should be no worse off under Hitler". But what answer can you give him – that is, what answer that you can expect him to listen to – while common soldiers risk their lives for two and sixpence a day, and fat women ride about in Rolls-Royce cars, nursing Pekineses?

It is quite likely that this war will last three years. It will mean cruel overwork, cold dull winters, uninteresting food, lack of amusements, prolonged bombing. It cannot but lower the general standard of living, because the essential act of war is to manufacture armaments instead of consumable goods. The working class will have to suffer terrible things. And they *will* suffer them, almost indefinitely, provided that they know what they are fighting for. They are not cowards, and they are not even internationally minded. They can stand all that the Spanish workers stood, and more. But they will want some kind of proof that a better life is ahead for themselves and their children. The one sure earnest of that is that when they are taxed and overworked they shall see that the rich are being hit even harder. And if the rich squeal audibly, so much the better.

We can bring these things about, if we really want to. It is not true that public opinion has no power in England. It never makes itself heard without achieving something; it has been responsible for most of the changes for the better during the past six months. But we have moved with glacier-like slowness, and we have learnt only from disasters. It took the fall of Paris to get rid of Chamberlain and the unnecessary suffering of scores of thousands of people in the East End to get rid or partially rid of Sir John Anderson.* It is not worth losing a battle in order to bury a corpse. For we are fighting against swift evil intelligences, and time presses, and

> History to the defeated
> May say Alas! But cannot alter or pardon.*

III

During the last six months there has been much talk of "the Fifth Column". From time to time obscure lunatics have been jailed for making speeches in favour of Hitler, and large numbers of German refugees have been interned, a thing which has almost certainly done us great harm in Europe. It is of course obvious that the idea of a large, organized army of Fifth Columnists suddenly appearing on the streets with weapons in their hands, as in Holland and Belgium, is ridiculous. Nevertheless a Fifth Column danger does exist. One can only consider it if one also considers in what way England might be defeated.

It does not seem probable that air bombing can settle a major war. England might well be invaded and conquered, but the invasion would be a dangerous gamble, and if it happened and failed it would probably leave us more united and less Blimp-ridden than before. Moreover, if England were overrun by foreign troops the English people would know that they had been beaten and would continue the struggle. It is doubtful whether they could be held down permanently, or whether Hitler wishes to keep an army of a million men stationed in these islands. A government of —, — and — (you can fill in the names) would suit him better. The English can probably not be bullied into surrender, but they might quite easily be bored, cajoled or cheated into it, provided that, as at Munich, they did not know that they were surrendering. It could happen most easily when the war seemed to be going well rather than badly. The threatening tone of so much of the German and Italian propaganda is a psychological mistake. It only gets home on intellectuals. With the general public the proper approach would be "Let's call it a draw". It is when a peace offer along *those* lines is made that the pro-fascists will raise their voices.

But who are the pro-fascists? The idea of a Hitler victory appeals to the very rich, to the communists, to Mosley's* followers, to the pacifists and to certain sections among the Catholics. Also, if things went badly enough on the Home Front, the whole of the poorer section of the working class might swing round to a position that was defeatist though not actively pro-Hitler.

In this motley list one can see the daring of German propaganda, its willingness to offer everything to everybody. But the various pro-fascist forces are not consciously acting together, and they operate in different ways.

The communists must certainly be regarded as pro-Hitler, and are bound to remain so unless Russian policy changes, but they have not very much influence. Mosley's Blackshirts, though now lying very low, are a more serious danger, because of the footing they probably possess in the armed forces. Still, even in its palmiest days Mosley's following can hardly have numbered 50,000. Pacifism is a psychological curiosity rather than a political movement. Some of the extremer pacifists, starting out with a complete renunciation of violence, have ended by warmly championing Hitler and even toying with anti-Semitism. This is interesting, but it is not important. "Pure" pacifism, which is a by-product of naval power, can only appeal to people in very sheltered positions. Moreover, being negative and irresponsible, it does not inspire much devotion. Of the membership of the Peace Pledge Union,* less than 15 per cent even pay their annual subscriptions. None of these bodies of people, pacifists, communists or Blackshirts, could bring a large-scale stop-the-war movement into being by their own efforts. But they might help to make things very much easier for a treacherous government negotiating surrender. Like the French communists, they might become the half-conscious agents of millionaires.

The real danger is from above. One ought not to pay any attention to Hitler's recent line of talk about being the friend of the poor man, the enemy of plutocracy, etc. etc. Hitler's real self is in *Mein Kampf*, and in his actions. He has never persecuted the rich, except when they were Jews or when they tried actively to oppose him. He stands for a centralized economy which robs the capitalist of most of his power but leaves the structure of society much as before. The state controls industry, but there are still rich and poor, masters and men. Therefore, as against genuine socialism, the moneyed class have always been on his side. This was crystal clear at the time of the Spanish Civil War, and clear again at the time when France surrendered. Hitler's puppet government are not working men but a gang of bankers, gaga generals and corrupt right-wing politicians.

That kind of spectacular, *conscious* treachery is less likely to succeed in England, indeed is far less likely even to be tried. Nevertheless, to many payers of supertax this war is simply an insane family squabble which ought to be stopped at all costs. One need not doubt that a "peace" movement is on foot somewhere in high places; probably a shadow cabinet has already been formed. These people will get their chance not in the moment of defeat but in some stagnant period when boredom is reinforced by discontent. They will not talk about surrender, only about peace, and doubtless they will persuade themselves, and perhaps other people, that they are acting for the best. An army of unemployed led by millionaires quoting the Sermon on the Mount – that is our danger. But it cannot arise when we have once introduced a reasonable degree of social justice. The lady in the Rolls-Royce car is more damaging to morale than a fleet of Goering's bombing planes.

PART III: THE ENGLISH REVOLUTION

I

The English revolution started several years ago, and it began to gather momentum when the troops came back from Dunkirk. Like all else in England, it happens in a sleepy, unwilling way, but it is happening. The war has speeded it up, but it has also increased, and desperately, the necessity for speed.

Progress and reaction are ceasing to have anything to do with party labels. If one wishes to name a particular moment, one can say that the old distinction between Right and Left broke down when *Picture Post* was first published. What are the politics of *Picture Post*? Or of *Cavalcade*, or Priestley's broadcasts,* or the leading articles in the *Evening Standard*? None of the old classifications will fit them. They merely point to the existence of multitudes of unlabelled people who have grasped within the last year or two that something is wrong. But since a classless, ownerless society is generally spoken of as "socialism", we can give that name to the society towards which we are now moving. The war and the revolution are inseparable. We cannot establish anything that a Western nation would regard as socialism without defeating Hitler; on the other hand we cannot defeat Hitler while we remain economically and socially in the nineteenth century. The past is fighting the future and we have two years, a year, possibly only a few months, to see to it that the future wins.

We cannot look to this or to any similar government to put through the necessary changes of its own accord. The initiative will have to come from below. That means that there will have to arise something that has never existed in

England, a socialist movement that actually has the mass of the people behind it. But one must start by recognizing why it is that English socialism has failed.

In England there is only one socialist party that has ever seriously mattered, the Labour Party. It has never been able to achieve any major change, because except in purely domestic matters it has never possessed a genuinely independent policy. It was and is primarily a party of the trade unions, devoted to raising wages and improving working conditions. This meant that all through the critical years it was directly interested in the prosperity of British capitalism. In particular it was interested in the maintenance of the British Empire, for the wealth of England was drawn largely from Asia and Africa. The standard of living of the trade-union workers, whom the Labour Party represented, depended indirectly on the sweating of Indian coolies. At the same time the Labour Party was a socialist party, using socialist phraseology, thinking in terms of an old-fashioned anti-imperialism, and more or less pledged to make restitution to the coloured races. It had to stand for the "independence" of India, just as it had to stand for disarmament and "progress" generally. Nevertheless everyone was aware that this was nonsense. In the age of the tank and the bombing plane, backward agricultural countries like India and the African colonies can no more be independent than can a cat or a dog. Had any Labour government come into office with a clear majority and then proceeded to grant India anything that could truly be called independence, India would simply have been absorbed by Japan, or divided between Japan and Russia.

To a Labour government in power, three imperial policies would have been open. One was to continue administering the Empire exactly as before, which meant dropping all pretensions to socialism. Another was to set the subject peoples "free", which meant in practice handing them over to Japan, Italy and other predatory powers, and incidentally causing a catastrophic drop in the British standard of living. The third was to develop a *positive* imperial policy, and aim at transforming the Empire into a federation of socialist states, like a looser and freer version of the Union of Soviet Republics. But the Labour Party's history and background made this impossible. It was a party of the trade unions, hopelessly parochial in outlook, with little interest in imperial affairs and no contacts among the men who actually held the Empire together. It would have had to hand the administration of India and Africa and the whole job of imperial defence to men drawn from a different class and traditionally hostile to socialism. Overshadowing everything was the doubt whether a Labour government which meant business could make itself obeyed. For all the size of its following, the Labour Party had no footing in the navy, little or none in the army or air force, none whatever in the Colonial Services, and not even a sure footing in the Home Civil Service. In England its position was strong but not unchallengeable, and outside England all the points were in the hands of its enemies. Once in power, the same dilemma would always have faced it: carry out your promises, and risk revolt, or continue with the same policy as the Conservatives, and stop talking about socialism. The Labour leaders never found a solution, and from 1935 onwards it was very doubtful whether they had any wish to take office. They had degenerated into a Permanent Opposition.

Outside the Labour Party there existed several extremist parties, of whom the communists were the strongest. The communists had considerable influence in the Labour Party in the years 1920–26 and 1935–39. Their chief importance, and that of the whole left wing of the Labour movement, was the part they played in alienating the middle classes from socialism.

The history of the past seven years has made it perfectly clear that communism has no chance in Western Europe. The appeal of fascism is enormously greater. In one country after another the communists have been rooted out by their more up-to-date enemies, the Nazis. In the English-speaking countries they never had a serious footing. The creed they were spreading could appeal only to a rather rare type of person, found chiefly in the middle-class intelligentsia, the type who has ceased to love his own country but still feels the need of patriotism, and therefore develops patriotic sentiments towards Russia. By 1940, after working for twenty years and spending a great deal of money, the British communists had barely 20,000 members, actually a smaller number than they had started out with in 1920. The other Marxist parties were of even less importance. They had not the Russian money and prestige behind them, and even more than the communists they were tied to the nineteenth-century doctrine of the class war. They continued year after year to preach this out-of-date gospel, and never drew any inference from the fact that it got them no followers.

Nor did any strong native fascist movement grow up. Material conditions were not bad enough, and no leader who could be taken seriously was forthcoming. One would have had to look a long time to find a man more barren of ideas than Sir Oswald Mosley. He was as hollow as a jug. Even the elementary fact that fascism must not offend national sentiment had escaped him. His entire movement was imitated slavishly from abroad, the uniform and the party programme from Italy and the salute from Germany, with the Jew-baiting tacked on as an afterthought, Mosley having actually started his movement with Jews among his most prominent followers. A man of the stamp of Bottomley or Lloyd George* could perhaps have brought a real British fascist movement into existence. But such leaders only appear when the psychological need for them exists.

After twenty years of stagnation and unemployment, the entire English socialist movement was unable to produce a version of socialism which the mass of the people could even find desirable. The Labour Party stood for a timid reformism, the Marxists were looking at the modern world through nineteenth-century spectacles. Both ignored agriculture and imperial problems, and both antagonized the middle classes. The suffocating stupidity of left-wing propaganda had frightened away whole classes of necessary people, factory managers, airmen, naval officers, farmers, white-collar workers, shopkeepers, policemen. All of these people had been taught to think of socialism as something which menaced their livelihood, or as something seditious, alien, "anti-British" as they would have called it. Only the intellectuals, the least useful section of the middle class, gravitated towards the movement.

A socialist party which genuinely wished to achieve anything would have started by facing several facts which to this day are considered unmentionable in left-wing circles. It would have recognized that England is more united than most countries, that the British workers have a great deal to lose besides their chains, and that the differences in outlook and habits between class and class are rapidly diminishing. In general, it would have recognized that the old-fashioned "proletarian revolution" is an impossibility. But all through the between-war years no socialist programme that was both revolutionary and workable ever appeared – basically, no doubt, because no one genuinely wanted any major change to happen. The Labour leaders wanted to go on and on, drawing their salaries and periodically swapping jobs with the Conservatives. The communists wanted to go on and on, suffering a comfortable martyrdom, meeting with endless defeats and afterwards putting the blame on other people. The left-wing intelligentsia wanted to go on and on, sniggering at the Blimps, sapping away at middle-class morale, but still keeping their favoured position as hangers-on of the dividend drawers. Labour Party politics had become a variant of conservatism; "revolutionary" politics had become a game of make-believe.

Now, however, the circumstances have changed; the drowsy years have ended. Being a socialist no longer means kicking theoretically against a system which in practice you are fairly well satisfied with. This time our predicament is real. It is "the Philistines be upon thee, Samson".* We have got to make our words take physical shape, or perish. We know very well that with its present social structure England cannot survive, and we have got to make other people see that fact and act upon it. We cannot win the war without introducing socialism, nor establish socialism without winning the war. At such a time it is possible, as it was not in the peaceful years, to be both revolutionary and realistic. A socialist movement which can swing the mass of the people behind it, drive the pro-fascists out of positions of control, wipe out the grosser injustices and let the working class see that they have something to fight for, win over the middle classes instead of antagonizing them, produce a workable imperial policy instead of a mixture of humbug and utopianism, bring patriotism and intelligence into partnership – for the first time, a movement of such a kind becomes possible.

II

The fact that we are at war has turned socialism from a textbook word into a realizable policy.

The inefficiency of private capitalism has been proved all over Europe. Its injustice has been proved in the East End of London. Patriotism, against which the socialists fought so long, has become a tremendous lever in their hands. People who at any other time would cling like glue to their miserable scraps of privilege, will surrender them fast enough when their country is in danger. War is the greatest of all agents of change. It speeds up all processes, wipes out minor distinctions, brings realities to the surface. Above all, war brings it home to the individual that he is *not* altogether an individual. It is only because they are aware of this that men will die on the field of battle. At this moment it is not so much a question of surrendering life as of surrendering leisure, comfort, economic liberty, social prestige. There are very few people in England who really want to see their country conquered by Germany. If it can be made clear that defeating Hitler means wiping out class privilege, the great mass of middling people, the £6 a week to £2,000 a year class, will probably be on our side. These people are quite indispensable, because they include most of the technical experts. Obviously the snobbishness and political ignorance of people like airmen and naval officers will be a very great difficulty. But without those airmen, destroyer commanders, etc. etc., we could not survive for a week. The only approach to them is through their patriotism. An intelligent socialist movement will *use* their patriotism, instead of merely insulting it, as hitherto.

But do I mean that there will no opposition? Of course not. It would be childish to expect anything of the kind.

There will be a bitter political struggle, and there will be unconscious and half-conscious sabotage everywhere. At some point or other it may be necessary to use violence. It is easy to imagine a pro-fascist rebellion breaking out in, for instance, India. We shall have to fight against bribery, ignorance and snobbery. The bankers and the larger businessmen, the landowners and dividend drawers, the officials with their prehensile bottoms, will obstruct for all they are worth. Even the middle classes will writhe when their accustomed way of life is menaced. But just because the English sense of national unity has never disintegrated, because patriotism is finally stronger than class hatred, the chances are that the will of the majority will prevail. It is no use imagining that one can make fundamental changes without causing a split in the nation – but the treacherous minority will be far smaller in time of war than it would be at any other time.

The swing of opinion is visibly happening, but it cannot be counted on to happen fast enough of its own accord. This war is a race between the consolidation of Hitler's empire and the growth of democratic consciousness. Everywhere in England you can see a ding-dong battle ranging to and fro – in Parliament and in the government, in the factories and the armed forces, in the pubs and the air-raid shelters, in the newspapers and on the radio. Every day there are tiny defeats, tiny victories. Morrison* for home secretary – a few yards forward. Priestley shoved off the air – a few yards back. It is a struggle between the groping and the unteachable, between the young and the old, between the living and the dead. But it is very necessary that the discontent which undoubtedly exists should take a purposeful and not merely obstructive form. It is time for *the people* to define their war aims. What is wanted is a simple, concrete programme of action, which can be given all possible publicity, and round which public opinion can group itself.

I suggest that the following six-point programme is the kind of thing we need. The first three points deal with England's internal policy, the other three with the Empire and the world:

1. Nationalization of land, mines, railways, banks and major industries.
2. Limitation of incomes, on such a scale that the highest tax-free income in Britain does not exceed the lowest by more than ten to one.
3. Reform of the educational system along democratic lines.
4. Immediate Dominion status for India, with power to secede when the war is over.
5. Formation of an Imperial General Council, in which the coloured peoples are to be represented.
6. Declaration of formal alliance with China, Abyssinia and all other victims of the fascist powers.

The general tendency of this programme is unmistakable. It aims quite frankly at turning this war into a revolutionary war and England into a socialist democracy. I have deliberately included in it nothing that the simplest person could not understand and see the reason for. In the form in which I have put it, it could be printed on the front page of the *Daily Mirror*. But for the purposes of this book a certain amount of amplification is needed.

1. *Nationalization.* One can "nationalize" industry by the stroke of a pen, but the actual process is slow and complicated. What is needed is that the ownership of all major industry shall be formally vested in the state, representing the common people. Once that is done it becomes possible to eliminate the class of mere *owners* who live not by virtue of anything they produce but by the possession of title deeds and share certificates. State ownership implies, therefore, that nobody shall live without working. How sudden a change in the conduct of industry it implies is less certain. In a country like England we cannot rip down the whole structure and build again from the bottom, least of all in time of war. Inevitably the majority of industrial concerns will continue with much the same personnel as before, the one-time owners or managing

directors carrying on with their jobs as state employees. There is reason to think that many of the smaller capitalists would actually welcome some such arrangement. The resistance will come from the big capitalists, the bankers, the landlords and the idle rich, roughly speaking the class with over £2,000 a year – and even if one counts in all their dependants there are not more than half a million of these people in England. Nationalization of agricultural land implies cutting out the landlord and the tithe drawer, but not necessarily interfering with the farmer. It is difficult to imagine any reorganization of English agriculture that would not retain most of the existing farms as units, at any rate at the beginning. The farmer, when he is competent, will continue as a salaried manager. He is virtually that already, with the added disadvantage of having to make a profit and being permanently in debt to the bank. With certain kinds of petty trading, and even the small-scale ownership of land, the state will probably not interfere at all. It would be a great mistake to start by victimizing the smallholder class, for instance. These people are necessary, on the whole they are competent, and the amount of work they do depends on the feeling that they are "their own masters". But the state will certainly impose an upward limit to the ownership of land (probably fifteen acres at the very most), and will never permit any ownership of land in town areas.

From the moment that all productive goods have been declared the property of the state, the common people will feel, as they cannot feel now, that the state *is themselves*. They will be ready then to endure the sacrifices that are ahead of us, war or no war. And even if the face of England hardly seems to change, on the day that our main industries are formally nationalized the dominance of a single class will have been broken. From then onwards the emphasis will be shifted from ownership to management, from privilege to competence. It is quite possible that state ownership will in itself bring about less social change than will be forced upon us by the common hardships of war. But it is the necessary first step without which any *real* reconstruction is impossible.

2. *Incomes*. Limitation of incomes implies the fixing of a minimum wage, which implies a managed internal currency based simply on the amount of consumption goods available. And this again implies a stricter rationing scheme than is now in operation. It is no use at this stage of the world's history to suggest that all human beings should have *exactly* equal incomes. It has been shown over and over again that without some kind of money reward there is no incentive to undertake certain jobs. On the other hand the money reward need not be very large. In practice it is impossible that earnings should be limited quite as rigidly as I have suggested. There will always be anomalies and evasions. But there is no reason why ten to one should not be the maximum normal variation. And within those limits some sense of equality is possible. A man with £3 a week and a man with £1,500 a year can feel themselves fellow creatures, which the Duke of Westminster and the sleepers on the Embankment benches cannot.

3. *Education*. In wartime, educational reform must necessarily be promise rather than performance. At the moment we are not in a position to raise the school leaving age or increase the teaching staffs of the elementary schools. But there are certain immediate steps that we could take towards a democratic educational system. We could start by abolishing the autonomy of the public schools and the older universities and flooding them with state-aided pupils chosen simply on grounds of ability. At present, public-school education is partly a training in class prejudice and partly a sort of tax that the middle classes pay to the upper class in return for the right to enter certain professions. It is true that that state of affairs is altering. The middle classes have begun to rebel against the expensiveness of education, and the war will bankrupt the majority of the public schools if it continues for another year or two. The evacuation is also producing certain minor changes. But there is a danger that some of the older schools, which will be able to weather the financial storm longest, will survive in some form or another as festering centres of snobbery. As for the 10,000 "private" schools that England possesses, the vast majority of them deserve nothing except suppression. They are simply commercial undertakings, and in many cases their educational level is actually lower than that of the elementary schools. They merely exist because of a widespread idea that there is something disgraceful in being educated by the public authorities. The state could quell this idea by declaring itself responsible for *all* education, even if at the start this were no more than a gesture. We need gestures as well as actions. It is all too obvious that our talk of "defending democracy" is nonsense while it is a mere accident of birth that decides whether a gifted child shall or shall not get the education it deserves.

4. *India*. What we must offer India is not "freedom", which, as I have said earlier, is impossible, but alliance, partnership – in a word, equality. But we must also tell the Indians that they are free to secede, if they want to. Without that there can be no equality of partnership, and our claim to be defending the coloured peoples against fascism will never be believed. But it is a mistake to imagine that if the Indians were free to cut themselves adrift they would immediately do so. When a British government *offers* them unconditional independence, they will refuse it. For as soon as they have the power to secede the chief reasons for doing so will have disappeared.

A complete severance of the two countries would be a disaster for India no less than for England. Intelligent Indians know this. As things are at present, India not only cannot defend itself, it is hardly even capable of feeding itself. The whole administration of the country depends on a framework of experts (engineers, forest officers, railwaymen, soldiers, doctors) who are predominantly English and could not be replaced within five or ten years. Moreover, English is the chief lingua franca and nearly the whole of the Indian intelligentsia is deeply anglicized. Any transference to foreign rule – for if the British marched out of India the Japanese and other powers would immediately march in – would mean an immense dislocation. Neither the Japanese, the Russians, the Germans nor the Italians would be capable of administering India even at the low level of efficiency that is attained by the British. They do not possess the necessary supplies of technical experts or the knowledge of languages and local conditions, and they probably could not win the confidence of indispensable go-betweens such as the Eurasians. If India were simply "liberated", i.e. deprived of British military protection, the first result would be a fresh foreign conquest, and the second a series of enormous famines which would kill millions of people within a few years.

What India needs is the power to work out its own constitution without British interference, but in some kind of partnership that ensures its military protection and technical advice. This is unthinkable until there is a socialist government in England. For at least eighty years England has artificially prevented the development of India, partly from fear of trade competition if Indian industries were too highly developed, partly because backward peoples are more easily governed than civilized ones. It is a commonplace that the average Indian suffers far more from his own countrymen than from the British. The petty Indian capitalist exploits the town worker with the utmost ruthlessness, the peasant lives from birth to death in the grip of the moneylender. But all this is an indirect result of the British rule, which aims half-consciously at keeping India as backward as possible. The classes most loyal to Britain are the princes, the landowners and the business community – in general, the reactionary classes who are doing fairly well out of the status quo. The moment that England ceased to stand towards India in the relation of an exploiter, the balance of forces would be altered. No need then for the British to flatter the ridiculous Indian princes, with their gilded elephants and cardboard armies, to prevent the growth of the Indian trade unions, to play off Muslim against Hindu, to protect the worthless life of the moneylender, to receive the salaams of toadying minor officials, to prefer the half-barbarous Gurkha to the educated Bengali. Once check that stream of dividends that flows from the bodies of Indian coolies to the banking accounts of old ladies in Cheltenham, and the whole *sahib*–native nexus, with its haughty ignorance on one side and envy and servility on the other, can come to an end. Englishmen and Indians can work side by side for the development of India, and for the training of Indians in all the arts which, so far, they have been systematically prevented from learning. How many of the existing British personnel in India, commercial or official, would fall in with such an arrangement – which would mean ceasing once and for all to be "*sahibs*" – is a different question. But, broadly speaking, more is to be hoped from the younger men and from those officials (civil engineers, forestry and agriculture experts, doctors, educationists) who have been scientifically educated. The higher officials, the provincial governors, commissioners, judges, etc. are hopeless – but they are also the most easily replaceable.

That, roughly, is what would be meant by Dominion status if it were offered to India by a socialist government. It is an offer of partnership on equal terms until such time as the world has ceased to be ruled by bombing planes. But we must add to it the unconditional right to secede. It is the only way of proving that we mean what we say. And what applies to India applies, *mutatis mutandis*, to Burma, Malaya and most of our African possessions.

5 and 6 explain themselves. They are the necessary preliminary to any claim that we are fighting this for the protection of peaceful peoples against fascist aggression.

Is it impossibly hopeful to think that such a policy as this could get a following in England? A year ago, even six months ago, it would have been, but not now. Moreover – and this is the peculiar opportunity of this moment – it could be given the necessary publicity. There is now a considerable weekly press, with a circulation of millions, which would be ready to popularize – if not *exactly* the programme I have sketched above, at any rate *some* policy along those lines. There are even three or four daily papers which would be prepared to give it a sympathetic hearing. That is the distance we have travelled in the last six months.

But is such a policy realizable? That depends entirely on ourselves.

Some of the points I have suggested are of the kind that could be carried out immediately; others would take years or decades and even then would not be perfectly achieved. No political programme is ever carried out in its entirety. But what matters is that that or something like it should be our declared policy. It is always the *direction* that counts. It is of course quite hopeless to expect the present government to pledge itself to any policy that implies turning this war into a revolutionary war. It is at best a government of compromise, with Churchill riding two horses like a circus acrobat. Before such measures as limitation of incomes become even thinkable, there will have to be a complete shift of power away from the old ruling class. If during this winter the war settles into another stagnant period, we ought in my opinion to agitate for a general election, a thing which the Tory Party machine will make frantic efforts to prevent. But even without an election we can get the government we want, provided that we want it urgently enough. A real shove from below will accomplish it. As to who will be in that government when it comes, I make no guess. I only know that the right men will be there when the people really want them, for it is movements that make leaders and not leaders movements.

Within a year, perhaps even within six months, if we are still unconquered, we shall see the rise of something that has never existed before – a specifically *English* socialist movement. Hitherto there has been only the Labour Party, which was the creation of the working class but did not aim at any fundamental change, and Marxism, which was a German theory interpreted by Russians and unsuccessfully transplanted to England. There was nothing that really touched the heart of the English people. Throughout its entire history the English socialist movement has never produced a song with a catchy tune – nothing like 'La Marseillaise' or 'La Cucaracha', for instance. When a socialist movement native to England appears, the Marxists, like all others with a vested interest in the past, will be its bitter enemies. Inevitably they will denounce it as "fascism". Already it is customary among the more soft-boiled intellectuals of the Left to declare that if we fight against the Nazis we shall "go Nazi" ourselves. They might almost equally well say that if we fight Negroes we shall turn black. To "go Nazi" we should have to have the history of Germany behind us. Nations do not escape from their past merely by making a revolution. An English socialist government will transform the nation from top to bottom, but it will still bear all over it the unmistakable marks of our own civilization, the peculiar civilization which I discussed earlier in this book.

It will not be doctrinaire, nor even logical. It will abolish the House of Lords, but quite probably will not abolish the monarchy. It will leave anachronisms and loose ends everywhere, the judge in his ridiculous horsehair wig and the lion and the unicorn on the soldier's cap buttons. It will not set up any explicit class dictatorship. It will group itself round the old Labour Party and its mass following will be in the trade unions, but it will draw into it most of the middle class and many of the younger sons of the bourgeoisie. Most of its directing brains will come from the new indeterminate class of skilled workers, technical experts, airmen, scientists, architects and journalists, the people who feel at home in the radio and ferro-concrete age. But it will never lose touch with the tradition of compromise and the belief in a law that is above the state. It will shoot traitors, but it will give them a solemn trial beforehand and occasionally it will acquit them. It will crush any open revolt promptly and cruelly, but it will interfere very little with the spoken and written word. Political parties with different names will still exist; revolutionary sects will still be publishing their newspapers and making as little impression as ever. It will disestablish the Church, but will not persecute religion. It will retain a vague reverence for the Christian moral code, and from time to time will refer to England as "a Christian country". The Catholic Church will war against it, but the Nonconformist sects and the bulk of the Anglican Church will be able to come to terms with it. It will show a power of assimilating the past which will shock foreign observers and sometimes make them doubt whether any revolution has happened.

But all the same it will have done the essential thing. It will have nationalized industry, scaled down incomes, set up a classless educational system. Its real nature will be apparent from the hatred which the surviving rich men of the world will feel for it. It will aim not at disintegrating the Empire but at turning it into a federation of socialist states, freed not so much from the British flag as from the moneylender, the dividend drawer and the wooden-headed British official. Its war strategy will be totally different from that of any property-ruled state, because it will not be afraid of the revolutionary after-effects when any existing regime is brought down. It will not have the smallest scruple about attacking hostile neutrals or stirring up native rebellion in enemy colonies. It will fight in such a way that even if it is beaten its memory will be dangerous to the victor, as the memory of the French Revolution was dangerous to Metternich's Europe.* The dictators will fear it as they could not fear the existing British regime, even if its military strength were ten times what it is.

But at this moment, when the drowsy life of England has barely altered, and the offensive contrast of wealth and poverty still exists everywhere, even amid the bombs, why do I dare to say that all these things "will" happen?

Because the time has come when one can predict the future in terms of an "either – or". Either we turn this war into a revolutionary war (I do not say that our policy will be *exactly* what I have indicated above – merely that it will be along those general lines) or we lose it, and much more besides. Quite soon it will be possible to say definitely that our feet are set upon one path or the other. But at any rate it is certain that with our present social structure we cannot win. Our real forces, physical, moral or intellectual, cannot be mobilized.

III

Patriotism has nothing to do with conservatism. It is actually the opposite of conservatism, since it is a devotion to something that is always changing and yet is felt to be mystically the same. It is the bridge between the future and the past. No real revolutionary has ever been an internationalist.

During the past twenty years the negative, fainéant outlook which has been fashionable among English left-wingers, the sniggering of the intellectuals at patriotism and physical courage, the persistent effort to chip away English morale and spread a hedonistic, what-do-I-get-out-of-it attitude to life has done nothing but harm. It would have been harmful even if we had been living in the squashy League of Nations universe that these people imagined. In an age of führers and bombing planes it was a disaster. However little we may like it, toughness is the price of survival. A nation trained to think hedonistically cannot survive amid peoples who work like slaves and breed like rabbits, and whose chief national industry is war. English socialists of nearly all colours have wanted to make a stand against fascism, but at the same time they have aimed at making their own countrymen unwarlike. They have failed, because in England traditional loyalties are stronger than new ones. But in spite of all the "anti-fascist" heroics of the left-wing press, what chance should we have stood when the real struggle with fascism came, if the average Englishman had been the kind of creature that the *New Statesman*, the *Daily Worker* or even the *News Chronicle* wished to make him?

Up to 1935 virtually all English left-wingers were vaguely pacifist. After 1935 the more vocal of them flung themselves eagerly into the Popular Front movement, which was simply an evasion of the whole problem posed by fascism. It set out to be "anti-fascist" in a purely negative way – "against" fascism without being "for" any discoverable policy – and underneath it lay the flabby idea that when the time came the Russians would do our fighting for us. It is astonishing how this illusion fails to die. Every week sees its spate of letters to the press, pointing out that if we had a government with no Tories in it the Russians could hardly avoid coming round to our side. Or we are to publish high-sounding war aims (*vide* books like *Unser Kampf, A Hundred Million Allies: If We Choose*,* etc.), whereupon the European populations will infallibly rise on our behalf. It is the same idea all the time – look abroad for your inspiration; get someone else to do your fighting for you. Underneath it lies the frightful inferiority complex of the English intellectual, the belief that the English are no longer a martial race, no longer capable of enduring.

In truth there is no reason to think that anyone will do our fighting for us yet awhile, except the Chinese, who have been doing it for three years already.* The Russians may be driven to fight on our side by the fact of a direct attack, but they have made it clear enough that they will not stand up to the German army if there is any way of avoiding it. In any case they are not likely to be attracted by the spectacle of a left-wing government in England. The present Russian regime must almost certainly be hostile to any revolution in the West. The subject peoples of Europe will rebel when Hitler begins to totter, but not earlier. Our potential allies are not the Europeans but on the one hand the Americans, who will need a year to mobilize their resources even if Big Business can be brought to heel, and on the other hand the coloured peoples, who cannot be even sentimentally on our side till our own revolution has started. For a long time, a year, two years, possibly three years, England has got to be the shock absorber of the world. We have got to face bombing, hunger, overwork, influenza, boredom and treacherous peace offers. Manifestly it is a time to stiffen morale, not to weaken it. Instead of taking the mechanically anti-British attitude which is usual on the Left, it is better to consider what the world would really be like if the English-speaking culture perished. For it is childish to suppose that the other English-speaking countries, even the USA, will be unaffected if Britain is conquered.

Lord Halifax and all his tribe believe that when the war is over things will be exactly as they were before. Back to the crazy pavement of Versailles, back to "democracy", i.e. capitalism, back to dole queues and the Rolls-Royce cars, back to the grey top hats and the sponge-bag trousers, *in sæcula sæculorum*.

It is of course obvious that nothing of the kind is going to happen. A feeble imitation of it might just possibly happen in the case of a negotiated peace, but only for a short while. Laissez-faire capitalism is dead.* The choice lies between the kind of collective society that Hitler will set up and the kind that can arise if he is defeated.

If Hitler wins this war he will consolidate his rule over Europe, Africa and the Middle East, and if his armies have not been too greatly exhausted beforehand, he will wrench vast territories from Soviet Russia. He will set up a graded caste society in which the German *Herrenvolk* ("master race" or "aristocratic race") will rule over Slavs and other lesser peoples whose job it will be to produce low-priced agricultural products. He will reduce the coloured peoples once and for all to outright slavery. The real quarrel of the fascist powers with British imperialism is that they know that it is disintegrating. Another twenty years along the present line of development, and India will be a peasant republic linked with England only by voluntary alliance. The "semi-apes" of whom Hitler speaks with such loathing will be flying aeroplanes and manufacturing machine guns. The fascist dream of a slave empire will be at an end. On the other hand, if we are defeated we simply hand over our own victims to new masters who come fresh to the job and have not developed any scruples.

But more is involved than the fate of the coloured peoples. Two incompatible visions of life are fighting one another. "Between democracy and totalitarianism," says Mussolini, "there can be no compromise." The two creeds cannot even, for any length of time, live side by side. So long as democracy exists, even in its very imperfect English form, totalitarianism is in deadly danger. The whole English-speaking world is haunted by the idea of human equality, and though it would be simply a lie to say that either we or the Americans have ever acted up to our professions, still, the *idea* is there, and it is capable of one day becoming a reality. From the English-speaking culture, if it does not perish, a society of free and equal human beings will ultimately arise. But it is precisely the idea of human equality – the "Jewish" or "Judaeo-Christian" idea of equality – that Hitler came into the world to destroy. He has, heaven knows, said so often enough. The thought of a world in which black men would be as good as white men and Jews treated as human beings brings him the same horror and despair as the thought of endless slavery brings to us.

It is important to keep in mind how irreconcilable these two viewpoints are. Sometime within the next year a pro-Hitler reaction within the left-wing intelligentsia is likely enough. There are premonitory signs of it already. Hitler's positive achievement appeals to the emptiness of these people and, in the case of those with pacifist leanings, to their masochism. One knows in advance more or less what they will say. They will start by refusing to admit that British capitalism is evolving into something different, or that the defeat of Hitler can mean any more than a victory for the British and American millionaires.

And from that they will proceed to argue that, after all, democracy is "just the same as" or "just as bad as" totalitarianism. There is *not much* freedom of speech in England; therefore there is *no more* than exists in Germany. To be on the dole is a horrible experience; therefore it is *no worse* to be in the torture chambers of the Gestapo. In general, two blacks make a white, half a loaf is the same as no bread.

But in reality, whatever may be true about democracy and totalitarianism, it is not true that they are the same. It would not be true, even if British democracy were incapable of evolving beyond its present stage. The whole conception of the militarized Continental state, with its secret police, its censored literature and its conscript labour, is utterly different from that of the loose maritime democracy, with its slums and unemployment, its strikes and party politics. It is the difference between land power and sea power, between cruelty and inefficiency, between lying and self-deception, between the SS man and the rent collector. And in choosing between them one chooses not so much on the strength of what they now are as of what they are capable of becoming. But in a sense it is irrelevant whether democracy, at its highest or at its lowest, is "better" than totalitarianism. To decide that one would have to have access to absolute standards. The only question that matters is where one's real sympathies will lie when the pinch comes. The intellectuals who are so fond of balancing democracy against totalitarianism and "proving" that one is as bad as the other are simply frivolous people who have never been shoved up against realities. They show the same shallow misunderstanding of fascism now, when they are beginning to flirt with it, as a year or two ago, when they were squealing against it. The question is not, "Can you make out a debating society 'case' in favour of Hitler?" The question is, "Do you genuinely accept that case? Are you willing to submit to Hitler's rule? Do you want to see England conquered, or don't you?" It would be better to be sure on that point before frivolously siding with the enemy. For there is no such thing as neutrality in war; in practice one must help one side or the other.

When the pinch comes, no one bred in the Western tradition can accept the fascist vision of life. It is important to realize that *now*, and to grasp what it entails. With all its sloth, hypocrisy and injustice, the English-speaking civilization is the only large obstacle in Hitler's path. It is a living contradiction of all the "infallible" dogmas of fascism. That is why all fascist writers for years past have agreed that England's power must be destroyed. England must be "exterminated", must be "annihilated", must "cease to exist". Strategically it would be possible for this war to end with Hitler in secure possession of Europe, and with the British Empire intact and British sea power barely affected. But ideologically it is not possible; were Hitler to make an offer along those lines, it could only be treacherously, with a view to conquering England indirectly or renewing the attack at some more favourable moment. England cannot possibly be allowed to remain as a sort of funnel through which deadly ideas from beyond the Atlantic flow into the police states of Europe. And turning it round to our point of view, we see the vastness of the issue before us, the all-importance of preserving our democracy more or less as we have known it. But to *preserve* is always to *extend*. The choice before us is not so much between victory and defeat as between revolution and apathy. If the thing we are fighting for is altogether destroyed, it will have been destroyed partly by our own act.

It could happen that England could introduce the beginnings of socialism, turn this war into a revolutionary war, and still be defeated. That is at any rate thinkable. But, terrible as it would be for anyone who is now adult, it would be far less deadly than the "compromise peace" which a few rich men and their hired liars are hoping for. The final ruin of England could only be accomplished by an English government acting under orders from Berlin. But that cannot happen if England has awakened beforehand. For in that case the defeat would be unmistakable, the struggle would continue, the *idea* would survive. The difference between going down fighting and surrendering without a fight is by no means a question of "honour" and schoolboy heroics. Hitler said once that to *accept* defeat destroys the soul of a nation. This sounds like a piece of claptrap, but it is strictly true. The defeat of 1870 did not lessen the world-influence of France. The Third Republic had more influence, intellectually, than the France of Napoleon III. But the sort of peace that Pétain, Laval* and Co. have accepted can only be purchased by deliberately wiping out the national culture. The Vichy government will enjoy a spurious independence only on condition that it destroys the distinctive marks of French culture: republicanism, secularism, respect for the intellect, absence of colour prejudice. We cannot be *utterly* defeated if we have made our revolution beforehand. We may see German troops marching down Whitehall, but another process, ultimately deadly to the German power-dream, will have been started. The Spanish people were defeated, but the things they learnt during those two and a half memorable years will one day come back upon the Spanish fascists like a boomerang.

A piece of Shakespearean bombast was much quoted at the beginning of the war. Even Mr Chamberlain quoted it once, if my memory does not deceive me:

> Come the four corners of the world in arms
> And we shall shock them: naught shall make us rue
> If England to herself do rest but true.*

It is right enough, if you interpret it rightly. But England has got to be true to herself. She is not being true to herself while the refugees who have sought our shores are penned up in concentration camps, and company directors work out subtle schemes to dodge their Excess Profits Tax. It is goodbye to the *Tatler* and the *Bystander*, and farewell to the lady in the Rolls-Royce car. The heirs of Nelson and of Cromwell are not in the House of Lords. They are in the fields and the streets, in the factories and the armed forces, in the four-ale bar and the suburban back garden – and at present they are still kept under by a generation of ghosts. Compared with the task of bringing the real England to the surface, even the winning of the war, necessary though it is, is secondary. By revolution we become more ourselves, not less. There is no question of stopping short, striking a compromise, salvaging "democracy", standing still. Nothing ever stands still. We must add to our heritage or lose it, we must grow greater or grow less, we must go forward or backward. I believe in England, and I believe that we shall go forward.

The Proletarian Writer*

DISCUSSION BETWEEN GEORGE ORWELL AND DESMOND HAWKINS*

Hawkins: I have always doubted if there is such a thing as proletarian literature – or ever could be. The first question is what people mean by it. What do *you* mean by it? You would expect it to mean literature written specifically for the proletariat, and read by them, but does it?

Orwell: No, obviously not. In that case the most definitely proletarian literature would be some of our morning papers. But you can see by the existence of publications like *New Writing*, or the Unity Theatre,* for instance, that the term has a sort of meaning, though unfortunately there are several different ideas mixed up in it. What people mean by it, roughly speaking, is a literature in which the viewpoint of the working class, which is supposed to be completely different from that of the richer classes, gets a hearing. And that, of course, has got mixed up with socialist propaganda. I don't think the people who throw this expression about mean literature written *by* proletarians. W.H. Davies* was a proletarian, but he would not be called a proletarian writer; Paul Potts* would be called a proletarian writer, but he is not a proletarian. The reason why I am doubtful of the whole conception is that I don't believe the proletariat can create an independent literature while they are not the dominant class. I believe that their literature is and must be bourgeois literature with a slightly different slant. After all, so much that is supposed to be new is simply the old standing on its head. The poems that were written about the Spanish Civil War, for instance, were simply a deflated version of the stuff that Rupert Brooke and Co. were writing in 1914.

Hawkins: Still, I think one must admit that the cult of proletarian literature – whether the theory is right or not – has had some effect. Look at writers like James Hanley, for instance, or Jack Hilton, or Jack Common.* They have something new to say – something at any rate that could not quite be said by anyone who had the ordinary middle-class upbringing. Of course there was a tremendous amount of cant about proletarian literature in the years after the slump,* when Bloomsbury went all Marxist, and communism became fashionable. But the thing had really started earlier. I should say it started just before the last war, when Ford Madox Ford, the editor of the *English Review*, met D.H. Lawrence and saw in him the portent of a new class finding expression in literature. Lawrence's *Sons and Lovers* really did break new ground.

It recorded a kind of experience that simply had not got into print before. And yet it was an experience that had been shared by millions of people. The question is why it had never been recorded earlier. Why would you say there had been no books like *Sons and Lovers* before that time?

Orwell: I think it is simply a matter of education. After all, though Lawrence was the son of a coal miner he had had an education that was not very different from that of the middle class. He was a university graduate, remember. Before a certain date – roughly speaking, before the nineties, when the Education Act began to take effect – very few genuine proletarians could write: that is, write with enough facility to produce a book or a story. On the other hand the professional writers knew nothing about proletarian life. One feels this even with a really radical writer like Dickens. Dickens does not write about the working class; he does not know enough about them. He is for the working class, but he feels himself completely different from them – far more different than the average middle-class person would feel nowadays.

Hawkins: Then, after all, the appearance of the proletariat as a class capable of producing books means a fresh development of literature – completely new subject matter, and a new slant on life?

Orwell: Yes, except in so far as the experience of all classes in society tends to become more and more alike. I maintain that the class distinctions in a country like England are now so unreal that they cannot last much longer. Fifty years ago or even twenty years ago a factory worker and a small professional man, for instance, were very different kinds of creature. Nowadays they are very much alike, though they may not realize it. They see the same films and listen to the same radio programmes, and they wear very similar clothes and live in very similar houses. What used to be called a proletarian – what Marx would have meant by a proletarian – only exists now in the heavy industries and on the land. All the same, there's no doubt that it was a big step forward when the *facts* of working-class life were first got onto paper. I think it has done something to push fiction back towards realities and away from the over-civilized stuff that Galsworthy and so forth used to write. I think possibly the first book that did this was *The Ragged-Trousered Philanthropists*,* which has always seemed to me a wonderful book, although it is very clumsily written. It recorded things that were everyday experience but which simply had not been noticed before – just as, so it is said, no one before 1800 AD ever noticed that the sea was blue. And Jack London was another pioneer in the same line.

Hawkins: And how about language and technique? Cyril Connolly, you may remember, said last week that the great innovations in literature have been made in technique rather than in content. As an example, he said that there is nothing new in Joyce except his technique. But surely these revolutionary proletarians have not shown much interest in technique? Some of them seem to be little different in manner from the pious moralizing lady novelists of the last century. Their revolt is entirely in content, in theme – is that so?

Orwell: I think in the main that's true. It's a fact that written English is much more colloquial now than it was twenty years ago, and that's all to the good. But we've borrowed much more from America than from the speech of the English working class. As for technique, one of the things that strikes one about the proletarian writers, or the people who are called proletarian writers, is how conservative they are. We might make an exception of Lionel Britton's *Hunger and Love*.* But if you look through a volume of *New Writing* or the *Left Review** you won't find many experiments.

Hawkins: Then we come back to this: that what is called proletarian literature stands or falls by its subject matter. The mystique behind these writers, I suppose, is the class war, the hope of a better future, the struggle of the working class against miserable living conditions.

Orwell: Yes, proletarian literature is mainly a literature of revolt. It can't help being so.

Hawkins: And my quarrel with it has always been that it is too much dominated by political considerations. I believe politicians and artists do not go well together. The goal of a politician is always limited, partial, short-term, oversimplified. It has to be, to have any hope of realization. As a principle of action, it cannot afford to consider its own imperfections and the possible virtues of its opponents. It cannot afford to dwell on the pathos and the tragedy of all human endeavour. In short, it must exclude the very things that are valuable in art. Would you agree therefore that when proletarian literature becomes literature it ceases to be proletarian – in the political sense? Or that when it becomes propaganda it ceases to be literature?

Orwell: I think that's putting it too crudely. I have always maintained that every artist is a propagandist. I don't mean a political propagandist. If he has any honesty or talent at all he cannot be that. Most political propaganda is a matter of telling lies, not only about the facts but about your own feelings. But every artist is a propagandist in the sense that he is trying, directly or indirectly, to impose a vision of life that seems to him desirable. I think we are broadly agreed about the vision of life that proletarian literature is trying to impose. As you said just now, the mystique behind it is the class war. That is something real; at any rate, it is something that is believed in. People will die for it as well as write about it. Quite a lot of people died for it in Spain. My point about proletarian literature is that though it has been important and useful so far as it went, it isn't likely to be permanent or to be the beginning of a new age in literature. It is founded on the revolt against capitalism, and capitalism is disappearing. In a socialist state, a lot of our left-wing writers – people like Edward Upward, Christopher Caudwell, Alec Brown, Arthur Calder-Marshall* and all the rest of them – who have specialized in attacking the society they live in would have nothing to attack. Just to revert for a moment to a book I mentioned above, Lionel Britton's *Hunger and Love*. This was an outstanding book and I think in a way it is representative of proletarian literature. Well, what is it about? It is about a young proletarian who wishes he wasn't a proletarian. It simply goes on and on about the intolerable conditions of working-class life, the fact that the roof leaks and the sink smells and all the rest of it. Now, you couldn't found a literature on the fact that the sink smells. As a convention it isn't likely to last so long as the siege of Troy. And behind this book, and lots of others like it, you can see what is really the history of a proletarian writer nowadays. Through some accident – very often it is simply due to having a long period on the dole – a young man of the working class gets a chance to educate himself. Then he starts writing books, and naturally he makes use of his early experiences, his sufferings under poverty, his revolt against the existing system, and so forth. But he isn't really creating an independent literature. He writes in the bourgeois manner, in the middle-class dialect. He is simply the black sheep of the bourgeois family, using the old methods for slightly different purposes. Don't mistake me. I'm not saying that he can't be as good a writer as anyone else – but if he is, it won't be because he is a working man but because he is a talented person who has learnt to write well. So long as the bourgeoisie are the dominant class, literature must be bourgeois. But I don't believe that they will be dominant much longer, or any other class either. I believe we are passing into a classless period, and what we call proletarian literature is one of the signs of the change. But I don't deny for an instant the good that it has done – the vitalizing effect of getting working-class experience and working-class values onto paper.

Hawkins: And, of course, as a positive gain, it has left behind quite a lot of good books.

Orwell: Oh yes, lots. Jack London's book *The Road*, Jack Hilton's *Caliban Shrieks*, Jim Phelan's prison books, George Garrett's sea stories, Private Richards's *Old Soldier Sahib*, James Hanley's *Grey Children*[*] – to name just a few.

Hawkins: All this time we have said nothing about the literature that the proletariat does read – not so much the daily papers, but the weeklies, the twopennies.

Orwell: Yes, I should say that the small weekly press is much more representative. Papers like *Home Chat* or the *Exchange and Mart*, and *Cage Birds*,[*] for instance.

Hawkins: And the literature that really comes out of the people themselves – we have said nothing about that. Take, for instance, the campfire ballads of the men who built the Canadian Pacific Railway; the sea shanties; Negro poems like 'Stagolee';[*] and the old street broadsheets – especially the ones about executions, the sort of thing that must have inspired Kipling's 'Danny Deever'.* And epitaphs, limericks, advertisement jingles – sticking simply to poetry, those are the special literature of the proletariat, aren't they?

Orwell: Yes, and don't forget the jokes on the comic coloured postcards, especially Donald McGill's.* I'm particularly attached to those. And above all the songs that the soldiers made up and sang for themselves in the last war. And the army songs for bugle calls and military marches – those are the real popular poetry of our time, like the ballads in the Middle Ages. It's a pity they are always unprintable.

Hawkins: Yes, but I'm afraid now we are drifting into folk literature, and it seems to me that we must keep the two things distinct. From what you say I imagine that this word "proletarian" is going to be quite meaningless if you detach it from revolutionary politics.

Orwell: Yes, the term "proletariat" is a political term belonging solely to the industrial age.

Hawkins: Well, I think we are completely in agreement that the theory of a separate proletarian literature just doesn't work. For all its apparent difference it comes within the framework of what you call bourgeois writing.

Orwell: By "bourgeois" and "bourgeoisie" I don't mean merely the people who buy and sell things. I mean the whole dominant culture of our time.

Hawkins: If we agree about that, we have still got to assess the contribution that these so-called proletarian writers have made. Because it *is* a contribution and it would be absurd to pass that over in disposing of the theory.

Orwell: I think they have made two kinds of contribution. One is that they have to some extent provided new subject matter, which has also led other writers who are not of the working class to look at things which were under their noses, but not noticed, before. The other is that they have introduced a note of what you might call crudeness and vitality. They have been a sort of voice in the gallery, preventing people from becoming too toney and too civilized.

Hawkins: And then there's another contribution, which you yourself mentioned earlier, and that is language. T.S. Eliot stressed the importance of constantly drawing newly minted words into the language, and in recent years it is pre-eminently from the working class that new words and phrases have come. It may be from the film or the street or through any channel, but the proletarian writer deserves credit for giving modern English much of its raciness and colour.

Orwell: Well, of course, the question is whether it has got much colour! But the thing you can say for the typical prose of the last ten years is that it has not got many frills or unnecessary adjectives. It's plain. It is rather questionable whether the sort of prose that has developed in this way is suitable for expressing very subtle thoughts, but it is excellent for describing action, and it is a good antidote to the over-refined type of prose which used to be fashionable – very good in its way, of course, but tending to emasculate the language altogether.

Hawkins: Well, to conclude – it looks as if the slogan of proletarian literature has made a nice rallying point for some work that was well worth having and it has been a focus for working-class writers, whether they were revolutionary or not, either in technique or in politics or in subject. But the phrase itself as a critical term is virtually useless.

Orwell: It has had a certain use as a label for a rather heterogeneous literature belonging to a transition period, but I do agree with you that for there to be what could really be called a proletarian literature the proletariat would have to be the dominant class.

Hawkins: Yes, and in assuming that it would certainly have to change its character. And that still leaves open the question we have only just touched on – how far can politics be introduced into art without spoiling the art?

The Frontiers of Art and Propaganda*

I am speaking on literary criticism, and in the world in which we are actually living that is almost as unpromising as speaking about peace. This is not a peaceful age, and it is not a critical age. In the Europe of the last ten years literary criticism of the older kind – criticism that is really judicious, scrupulous, fair-minded, treating a work of art as a thing of value in itself – has been next door to impossible.

If we look back at the English literature of the last ten years, not so much at the literature as at the prevailing literary attitude, the thing that strikes us is that it has almost ceased to be aesthetic. Literature has been swamped by propaganda. I do not mean that all the books written during that period have been bad. But the characteristic writers of the time, people like Auden and Spender and MacNeice, have been didactic, political writers, aesthetically conscious, of course, but more interested in subject matter than in technique. And the most lively criticism has nearly all of it been the work of Marxist writers, people like Christopher Caudwell and Philip Henderson and Edward Upward, who look on every book virtually as a political pamphlet and are far more interested in digging out its political and social implications than in its literary qualities in the narrow sense.

This is all the more striking because it makes a very sharp and sudden contrast with the period immediately before it. The characteristic writers of the 1920s – T.S. Eliot, for instance, Ezra Pound, Virginia Woolf – were writers who put the main emphasis on technique. They had their beliefs and prejudices, of course, but they were far more interested in technical innovations than in any moral or meaning or political implication that their work might contain. The best of them all, James Joyce, was a technician and very little else, about as near to being a "pure" artist as a writer can be. Even D.H. Lawrence, though he was more of a "writer with a purpose" than most of the others of his time, had not much of what we should now call social consciousness. And though I have narrowed this down to the 1920s, it had really been the same from about 1890 onwards. Throughout the whole of that period, the notion that form is more important than subject matter, the notion of "art for art's sake", had been taken for granted. There were writers who disagreed, of course – Bernard Shaw was one – but that was the prevailing outlook. The most important critic of the period, George Saintsbury,* was a very old man in the 1920s, but he had a powerful influence up to about 1930, and Saintsbury had always firmly upheld the technical attitude to art. He claimed that he himself could and did judge any book solely on its execution, its *manner*, and was very nearly indifferent to the author's opinions.

Now, how is one to account for this very sudden change of outlook? About the end of the 1920s you get a book like Edith Sitwell's book on Pope,* with a completely frivolous emphasis on technique, treating literature as a sort of embroidery, almost as though words did not have meanings – and only a few years later you get a Marxist critic like Edward Upward asserting that books can be "good" only when they are Marxist in tendency. In a sense both Edith Sitwell and Edward Upward were representative of their period. The question is, why should their outlook be so different?

I think one has got to look for the reason in external circumstances. Both the aesthetic and the political attitude to literature were produced, or at any rate conditioned, by the social atmosphere of a certain period. And now that another period has ended – for Hitler's attack on Poland in 1939 ended one epoch as surely as the great slump of 1931 ended another – one can look back and see more clearly than was possible a few years ago the way in which literary attitudes are affected by external events. A thing that strikes anyone who looks back over the last hundred years is that literary criticism worth bothering about, and the critical attitude towards literature, barely existed in England between roughly 1830 and 1890. It is not that good books were not produced in that period. Several of the writers of that time, Dickens, Thackeray, Trollope and others, will probably be remembered longer than any that have come after them. But there are no literary figures in Victorian England corresponding to Flaubert, Baudelaire, Gautier and a host of others. What now appears to us as aesthetic scrupulousness hardly existed. To a mid-Victorian English writer, a book was partly something that brought him money and partly a vehicle for preaching sermons. England was changing very rapidly, a new moneyed class had come up on the ruins of the old aristocracy, contact with Europe had been severed and a long artistic tradition had been broken. The mid-nineteenth-century English writers were barbarians, even when they happened to be gifted artists, like Dickens.

But in the later part of the century contact with Europe was re-established through Matthew Arnold, Pater, Oscar Wilde* and various others, and the respect for form and technique in literature came back. It is from then that the notion of "art for art's sake" – a phrase very much out of fashion, but still, I think, the best available – really dates. And the reason why it could flourish so long, and be so much taken for granted, was that the whole period between 1890 and 1930 was one of exceptional comfort and security. It was what we might call the golden afternoon of the capitalist age. Even the Great War did not really disturb it. The Great War killed ten million men, but it did not shake the world as this war will shake it and has shaken it already. Almost every European between 1890 and 1930 lived in the tacit belief that civilization would last for ever. You might be individually fortunate or unfortunate, but you had inside you the feeling that nothing would ever fundamentally change. And in that kind of atmosphere intellectual detachment, and also dilettantism, are possible. It is that feeling of continuity, of security, that could make it possible for a critic like Saintsbury, a real old crusted Tory and High Churchman, to be scrupulously fair to books written by men whose political and moral outlook he detested.

But since 1930 that sense of security has never existed. Hitler and the slump shattered it as the Great War and even the Russian Revolution had failed to shatter it. The writers who have come up since 1930 have been living in a world in which not only one's life but one's whole scheme of values is constantly menaced. In such circumstances detachment is not possible. You cannot take a purely aesthetic interest in a disease you are dying from; you cannot feel dispassionately about a man who is about to cut your throat. In a world in which fascism and socialism were fighting one another, any thinking person had to take sides, and his feelings had to find their way not only into his writing but into his judgements on literature. Literature had to become political, because anything else would have entailed mental dishonesty. One's attachments and hatreds were too near the surface of consciousness to be ignored. What books were *about* seemed so urgently important that the way they were written seemed almost insignificant.

And this period of ten years or so in which literature, even poetry, was mixed up with pamphleteering, did a great service to literary criticism, because it destroyed the illusion of pure aestheticism. It reminded us that propaganda in some form or other lurks in every book, that every work of art has a meaning and a purpose – a political, social and religious purpose – that our aesthetic judgements are always coloured by our prejudices and beliefs. It debunked art for art's sake. But it also led for the time being into a blind alley, because it caused countless young writers to try to tie their minds to a political discipline which, if they had stuck to it, would have made mental honesty impossible. The only system of thought open to them at that time was official Marxism, which demanded a nationalistic loyalty towards Russia and forced the writer who called himself a Marxist to be mixed up in the dishonesties of power politics. And even if that was desirable, the assumptions that these writers built upon were suddenly shattered by the Russo-German Pact. Just as many writers about 1930 had discovered that you cannot really be detached from contemporary events, so many writers about 1939 were discovering that you cannot really sacrifice your intellectual integrity for the sake of a political creed – or at least you cannot do so and remain a writer. Aesthetic scrupulousness is not enough, but political rectitude is not enough either. The events of the last ten years have left us rather in the air – they have left England for the time being without any discoverable literary trend – but they have helped us to define, better than was possible before, the frontiers of art and propaganda.

Tolstoy and Shakespeare*

Last week I pointed out that art and propaganda are never quite separable, and that what are supposed to be purely aesthetic judgements are always corrupted to some extent by moral or political or religious loyalties. And I added that in times of trouble, like the last ten years, in which no thinking person can ignore what is happening round him or avoid taking sides, these underlying loyalties are pushed nearer to the surface of consciousness. Criticism becomes more and more openly partisan, and even the pretence of detachment becomes very difficult. But one cannot infer from that that there is no such thing as an aesthetic judgement, that every work of art is simply and solely a political pamphlet and can be judged only as such. If we reason like that we lead our minds into a blind alley in which certain large and obvious facts become inexplicable. And in illustration of this I want to examine one of the greatest pieces of moral, non-aesthetic criticism – *anti*-aesthetic criticism, one might say – that have ever been written: Tolstoy's essay on Shakespeare.*

Towards the end of his life Tolstoy wrote a terrific attack on Shakespeare, purporting to show not only that Shakespeare was not the great man he was claimed to be, but that he was a writer entirely without merit, one of the worst and most contemptible writers the world has ever seen. This essay caused tremendous indignation at the time, but I doubt whether it was ever satisfactorily answered. What is more, I shall point out that in the main it was unanswerable. Part of what Tolstoy says is strictly true, and parts of it are too much a matter of personal opinion to be worth arguing about. I do not mean, of course, that there is no detail in the essay which could not be answered. Tolstoy contradicts himself several times; the fact that he is dealing with a foreign language makes him misunderstand a great deal, and I think there is little doubt that his hatred and jealousy of Shakespeare make him resort to a certain amount of falsification, or at least wilful blindness. But all that is beside the point. In the main what Tolstoy says is justified after its fashion, and at the time it probably acted as a useful corrective to the silly adulation of Shakespeare that was then fashionable. The answer to it is less in anything I can say than in certain things that Tolstoy is forced to say himself.

Tolstoy's main contention is that Shakespeare is a trivial, shallow writer, with no coherent philosophy, no thoughts or ideas worth bothering about, no interest in social or religious problems, no grasp of character or probability, and, in so far as he could be said to have a definable attitude at all, with a cynical, immoral, worldly outlook on life. He accuses him of patching his plays together without caring twopence for credibility, of dealing in fantastic fables and impossible situations, of making all his characters talk in an artificial flowery language completely unlike that of real life. He also accuses him of thrusting anything and everything into his plays – soliloquies, scraps of ballads, discussions, vulgar jokes and so forth – without stopping to think whether they had anything to do with the plot, and also of taking for granted the immoral power politics and unjust social distinctions of the times he lived in. Briefly, he accuses him of being a hasty, slovenly writer, a man of doubtful morals, and, above all, of not being a *thinker*.

Now, a good deal of this could be contradicted. It is not true, in the sense implied by Tolstoy, that Shakespeare is an immoral writer. His moral code might be different from Tolstoy's, but he very definitely *has* a moral code, which is apparent all through his work. He is much more of a moralist than, for instance, Chaucer or Boccaccio. He also is not such a fool as Tolstoy tries to make out. At moments, incidentally, one might say, he shows a vision which goes far beyond his time. In this connection I would like to draw attention to the piece of criticism which Karl Marx – who, unlike Tolstoy, admired Shakespeare – wrote on *Timon of Athens*.* But once again, what Tolstoy says is true on the whole. Shakespeare is not a thinker, and the critics who claimed that he was one of the great philosophers of the world were talking nonsense. His thoughts are simply a jumble, a ragbag. He was like most Englishmen in having a code of conduct but no world view, no philosophical faculty. Again, it is quite true that Shakespeare cares very little about probability and seldom bothers to make his characters coherent. As we know, he usually stole his plots from other people and hastily made them up into plays, often introducing absurdities and inconsistencies that were not present in the original. Now and again, when he happens to have got hold of a foolproof plot – *Macbeth*, for instance – his characters are reasonably consistent, but in many cases they are forced into actions which are completely incredible by any ordinary standard. Many of his plays have not even the sort of credibility that belongs to a fairy story. In any case we have no evidence that he himself took them seriously, except as a means of livelihood. In his sonnets he never even refers to his plays as part of his literary achievement, and only once mentions in a rather shamefaced way that he has been an actor. So far Tolstoy is justified. The claim that Shakespeare was a profound thinker, setting forth a coherent philosophy in plays that were technically perfect and full of subtle psychological observation, is ridiculous.

Only, what has Tolstoy achieved? By this furious attack he ought to have demolished Shakespeare altogether, and he evidently believes that he has done so. From the time when Tolstoy's essay was written, or at any rate from the time when it began to be widely read, Shakespeare's reputation ought to have withered away. The lovers of Shakespeare ought to have seen that their idol had been debunked, that in fact he had no merits, and they ought to have ceased forthwith to take any pleasure in him. But that did not happen. Shakespeare is demolished, and yet somehow he remains standing. So far from his being forgotten as the result of Tolstoy's attack, it is the attack itself that has been almost forgotten. Although Tolstoy is a popular writer in England, both the translations of this essay are out of print, and I had to search all over London before running one to earth in a museum.

It appears, therefore, that though Tolstoy can explain away nearly everything about Shakespeare, there is one thing that he cannot explain away, and that is his popularity. He himself is aware of this, and greatly puzzled by it. I said earlier that the answer to Tolstoy really lies in something he himself is obliged to say. He asks himself how it is that this bad, stupid and immoral writer Shakespeare is everywhere admired, and finally he can only explain it as a sort of worldwide conspiracy to pervert the truth. Or it is a sort of collective hallucination – a hypnosis, he calls it – by which everyone except Tolstoy himself is taken in. As to how this conspiracy or delusion began, he is obliged to set it down to the machinations of certain German critics at the beginning of the nineteenth century. They started telling the wicked lie that Shakespeare is a good writer, and no one since has had the courage to contradict them. Now, one need not spend very long over a theory of this kind. It is nonsense. The enormous majority of the people who have enjoyed watching Shakespeare's plays have never been influenced by any German critics, directly or indirectly. For Shakespeare's popularity is real enough, and it is a popularity that extends to ordinary, by no means bookish people. From his lifetime onwards he has been a stage favourite in England, and he is popular not only in the English-speaking countries but in most of Europe and parts of Asia. Almost as I speak the Soviet government are celebrating the 325th anniversary of his death, and in Ceylon I once saw a play of his being performed in some language of which I did not know a single word. One must conclude that there is something good – something durable – in Shakespeare which millions of ordinary people can appreciate, though Tolstoy happened to be unable to do so. He can survive exposure of the fact that he is a confused thinker whose plays are full of improbabilities. He can no more be debunked by such methods than you can destroy a flower by preaching a sermon at it.

And that, I think, tells one a little more about something I referred to last week: the frontiers of art and propaganda. It shows one the limitation of any criticism that is solely a criticism of subject and of meaning. Tolstoy criticizes Shakespeare not as a poet, but as a thinker and a teacher, and along those lines he has no difficulty in demolishing him. And yet all that he says is irrelevant; Shakespeare is completely unaffected. Not only his reputation but the pleasure we take in him remain just the same as before. Evidently a poet is more than a thinker and a teacher, though he has to be that as well. Every piece of writing has its propaganda aspect, and yet in any book or play or poem or what not that is to endure there has to be a residuum of something that simply is not affected by its moral or meaning – a residuum of something we can only call art. Within certain limits, bad thought and bad morals can be good literature. If so great a man as Tolstoy could not demonstrate the contrary, I doubt whether anyone else can either.

The Meaning of a Poem*

I shall start by quoting the poem called 'Felix Randal',* by Gerard Manley Hopkins, the well-known English poet – he was a Roman Catholic priest – who died in 1893:

> Felix Randal the farrier, O is he dead then? my duty all ended,
> Who have watched his mould of man, big-boned and hardy-handsome
> Pining, pining, till time when reason rambled in it and some
> Fatal four disorders, fleshed there, all contended?
>
> Sickness broke him. Impatient he cursed at first, but mended
> Being anointed and all; though a heavenlier heart began some
> Months earlier, since I had our sweet reprieve and ransom
> Tendered to him. Ah well, God rest him all road ever he offended!
>
> This seeing the sick endears them to us, us too it endears.
> My tongue had taught thee comfort, touch had quenched thy tears,
> Thy tears that touched my heart, child, Felix, poor Felix Randal;
>
> How far from then forethought of, all thy more boisterous years,
> When thou at the random grim forge, powerful amidst peers,
> Didst fettle for the great grey drayhorse his bright and battering sandal!

It is what people call a "difficult" poem – I have a reason for choosing a difficult poem, which I will come back to in a moment – but no doubt the general drift of its meaning is clear enough. Felix Randal is a blacksmith – a farrier. The poet, who is also his priest, has known him in the prime of life as a big powerful man, and then he has seen him dying, worn out by disease and weeping on his bed like a child. That is all there is to it, so far as the "story" of the poem goes.

But now to come back to the reason why I deliberately chose such an obscure and one might say mannered poem. Hopkins is what people call a writer's writer. He writes in a very strange, twisted style – perhaps it is a bad style, really: at any rate, it would be a bad one to imitate – which is not at all easy to understand but which appeals to people who are professionally interested in points of technique. In criticisms of Hopkins, therefore, you will usually find all the emphasis laid on his use of language and his subject matter very lightly touched on. And in any criticism of poetry, of course, it seems natural to judge primarily by the ear. For in verse the words – the sounds of words, their associations, and the harmonies of sound and association that two or three words together can set up – obviously matter more than they do in prose. Otherwise there would be no reason for writing in metrical form. And with Hopkins, in particular, the strangeness of his language and the astonishing beauty of some of the sound effects he manages to bring off seem to overshadow everything else.

The best touch, one might say the especial touch, in this poem is due to a verbal coincidence. For the word that pins the whole poem together and gives it finally an air of majesty, a feeling of being tragic instead of merely pathetic, is that final word "sandal" which no doubt only came into Hopkins's mind because it happened to rhyme with Randal. I ought to perhaps add that the word "sandal" is more impressive to an English reader than it would be to an Oriental, who sees sandals every day and perhaps wears them himself. To us a sandal is an exotic thing, chiefly associated with the ancient Greeks and Romans. When Hopkins describes the carthorse's shoe as a sandal, he suddenly converts the carthorse into a magnificent mythical beast, something like a heraldic animal. And he reinforces that effect by the splendid rhythm of the last line – "Didst fettle for the great grey drayhorse his bright and battering sandal" – which is actually a hexameter, the same metre in which Homer and Virgil wrote. By combination of sound and association he manages to lift an ordinary village death onto the plane of tragedy.

But that tragic effect cannot simply exist in the void, on the strength of a certain combination of syllables. One cannot regard a poem as simply a pattern of words on paper, like a sort of mosaic. This poem is moving because of its sound, its musical qualities, but it is also moving because of an emotional content which could not be there if Hopkins's philosophy and beliefs were different from what they were. It is the poem, first of all, of a Catholic, and secondly of a man living at a particular moment of time, the latter part of the nineteenth century, when the old English agricultural way of life – the old Saxon village community – was finally passing away. The whole feeling of the poem is Christian. It is about death, and the attitude towards death varies in the great religions of the world. The Christian attitude towards death is not that it is something to be welcomed, or that it is something to be met with stoical indifference, or that it is something to be avoided as long as possible, but that it is something profoundly tragic which has to be gone through with. A Christian, I suppose, if he were offered the chance of everlasting life on this earth would refuse it, but he would still feel that death is profoundly sad. Now this feeling conditions Hopkins's use of words. If it were not for his special relationship as priest it would not, probably, occur to him to address the dead blacksmith as "child". And he could not, probably, have evolved that phrase I have quoted, "all thy boisterous years", if he had not the special Christian vision of the necessity and the sadness of death. But, as I have said, the poem is also conditioned by the fact that Hopkins lived at the latter end of the nineteenth century. He had lived in rural communities when they were still distinctly similar to what they had been in Saxon times, but when they were just beginning to break up under the impact of the railway. Therefore he can see a type like Felix Randal, the small independent village craftsman, in perspective, as one can only see something when it is passing away. He can admire him, for instance, as an earlier writer probably could not have done. And that is why in speaking of his work he can evolve phrases like "the random grim forge" and "powerful amidst peers".

But one comes back to the technical consideration that a subject of this kind is very much helped by Hopkins's own peculiar style. English is a mixture of several languages, but mainly Saxon and Norman French, and to this day, in the country districts, there is a class distinction between the two. Many agricultural labourers speak almost pure Saxon. Now, Hopkins's own language is very Saxon; he tends to string several English words together instead of using a single long Latin one, as most people do when they want to express a complicated thought, and he deliberately derived from the early English poets, the ones who come before Chaucer. In this poem, he even uses several dialect words, "road" for way, and "fettle" for fix. The special power he has of recreating the atmosphere of an English village would not belong to him if it were not for the purely technical studies he had made, earlier in his life, of the old Saxon poets. It will be seen that the poem is a synthesis – but more than a synthesis, a sort of growing together – of a special vocabulary and a special religious and social outlook. The two fuse together, inseparably, and the whole is greater than the parts.

I have tried to analyse this poem as well as I can in a short period, but nothing I have said can explain, or explain away, the pleasure I take in it. That is finally inexplicable, and it is just because it *is* inexplicable that detailed criticism is worthwhile. Men of science can study the life process of a flower, or they can split it up into its component elements, but any scientist will tell you that a flower does not become less wonderful, it becomes more wonderful, if you know all about it.

Literature and Totalitarianism*

I said at the beginning of my first talk that this is not a critical age. It is an age of partisanship and not of detachment, an age in which it is especially difficult to see literary merit in a book with whose conclusions you disagree. Politics – politics in the most general sense – have invaded literature, to an extent that does not normally happen, and this has brought to the surface of our consciousness the struggle that always goes on between the individual and the community. It is when one considers the difficulty of writing honest unbiased criticism in a time like ours that one begins to grasp the nature of the threat that hangs over the whole of literature in the coming age.

We live in an age in which the autonomous individual is ceasing to exist – or perhaps one ought to say, in which the individual is ceasing to have the illusion of being autonomous. Now, in all that we say about literature, and (above all) in all that we say about criticism, we instinctively take the autonomous individual for granted. The whole of modern European literature – I am speaking of the literature of the past four hundred years – is built on the concept of intellectual honesty, or, if you like to put it that way, on Shakespeare's maxim, "To thine own self be true". The first thing that we ask of a writer is that he shall not tell lies, that he shall say what he really thinks, what he really feels. The worst thing we can say about a work of art is that it is insincere. And this is even truer of criticism than of creative literature, in which a certain amount of posing and mannerism, and even a certain amount of downright humbug, doesn't matter so long as the writer is fundamentally sincere. Modern literature is essentially an individual thing. It is either the truthful expression of what one man thinks and feels, or it is nothing.

As I say, we take this notion for granted, and yet as soon as one puts it into words one realizes how literature is menaced. For this is the age of the totalitarian state, which does not and probably cannot allow the individual any freedom whatever. When one mentions totalitarianism one thinks immediately of Germany, Russia, Italy, but I think one must face the risk that this phenomenon is going to be worldwide. It is obvious that the period of free capitalism is coming to an end and that one country after another is adopting a centralized economy that one can call socialism or state capitalism according as one prefers. With that the economic liberty of the individual, and to a great extent his liberty to do what he likes, to choose his own work, to move to and fro across the surface of the earth, comes to an end. Now, till recently the implications of this were not foreseen. It was never fully realized that the disappearance of economic liberty would have any effect on intellectual liberty. Socialism was usually thought of as a sort of moralized liberalism. The state would take charge of your economic life and set you free from the fear of poverty, unemployment and so forth, but it would have no need to interfere with your private intellectual life. Art could flourish just as it had done in the liberal-capitalist age, only a little more so, because the artist would not any longer be under economic compulsions.

Now, on the existing evidence, one must admit that these ideas have been falsified. Totalitarianism has abolished freedom of thought to an extent unheard of in any previous age. And it is important to realize that its control of thought is not only negative, but positive. It not only forbids you to express – even to think – certain thoughts, but it dictates what you *shall* think, it creates an ideology for you, it tries to govern your emotional life as well as setting up a code of conduct. And as far as possible it isolates you from the outside world; it shuts you up in an artificial universe in which you have no standards of comparison. The totalitarian state tries, at any rate, to control the thoughts and emotions of its subjects at least as completely as it controls their actions.

The question that is important for us is: can literature survive in such an atmosphere? I think one must answer shortly that it cannot. If totalitarianism becomes worldwide and permanent, what we have known as literature must come to an end. And it will not do – as may appear plausible at first – to say that what will come to an end is merely the literature of post-Renaissance Europe.

There are several vital differences between totalitarianism and all the orthodoxies of the past, either in Europe or in the East. The most important is that the orthodoxies of the past did not change, or at least did not change rapidly. In medieval Europe the Church dictated what you should believe, but at least it allowed you to retain the same beliefs from birth to death. It did not tell you to believe one thing on Monday and another on Tuesday. And the same is more or less true of any orthodox Christian, Hindu, Buddhist or Muslim today. In a sense his thoughts are circumscribed, but he passes his whole life within the same framework of thought. His emotions are not tampered with.

Now, with totalitarianism, exactly the opposite is true. The peculiarity of the totalitarian state is that though it controls thought, it does not fix it. It sets up unquestionable dogmas, and it alters them from day to day. It needs the dogmas, because it needs absolute obedience from its subjects, but it cannot avoid the changes, which are dictated by the needs of power politics. It declares itself infallible, and at the same time it attacks the very concept of objective truth. To take a crude, obvious example, every German up to September 1939 had to regard Russian Bolshevism with horror and aversion, and since September 1939 he has had to regard it with admiration and affection. If Russia and Germany go to war, as they may well do within the next few years, another equally violent change will have to take place. The German's emotional life, his loves and hatreds, are expected, when necessary, to reverse themselves overnight. I hardly need to point out the effect of this kind of thing upon literature. For writing is largely a matter of feeling, which cannot always be controlled from outside. It is easy to pay lip-service to the orthodoxy of the moment, but writing of any consequence can only be produced when a man *feels* the truth of what he is saying; without that, the creative impulse is lacking. All the evidence we have suggests that the sudden emotional changes which totalitarianism demands of its followers are psychologically impossible. And that is the chief reason why I suggest that if totalitarianism triumphs throughout the world, literature, as we have known it, is at an end. And, in fact, totalitarianism does seem to have had that effect so far. In Italy literature has been crippled, and in Germany it seems almost to have ceased. The most characteristic activity of the Nazis is burning books. And even in Russia the literary renaissance we once expected has not happened, and the most promising Russian writers show a marked tendency to commit suicide or disappear into prison.

I said earlier that liberal capitalism is obviously coming to an end, and therefore I may have seemed to suggest that freedom of thought is also inevitably doomed. But I do not believe this to be so, and I will simply say in conclusion that I believe the hope of literature's survival lies in those countries in which liberalism has struck its deepest roots, the non-military countries, Western Europe and the Americas, India and China. I believe – it may be no more than a pious hope – that though a collectivized economy is bound to come, those countries will know how to evolve a form of socialism which is not totalitarian, in which freedom of thought can survive the disappearance of economic individualism. That, at any rate, is the only hope to which anyone who cares for literature can cling. Whoever feels the value of literature, whoever sees the central part it plays in the development of human history, must also see the life-and-death necessity of resisting totalitarianism, whether it is imposed on us from without or from within.

Wells, Hitler and the World State*

In March or April, say the wiseacres, there is to be a stupendous knockout blow at Britain... What Hitler has to do it with, I cannot imagine. His ebbing and dispersed military resources are now probably not so very much greater than the Italians' before they were put to the test in Greece and Africa.

The German air power has been largely spent. It is behind the times and its first-rate men are mostly dead or disheartened or worn out.

In 1914 the Hohenzollern army was the best in the world. Behind that screaming little defective in Berlin there is nothing of the sort. [...] Yet our military "experts" discuss the waiting phantom. In their imaginations it is perfect in its equipment and invincible in discipline. Sometimes it is to strike a decisive "blow" through Spain and North Africa and on, or march through the Balkans, march from the Danube to Ankara, to Persia, to India, or "crush Russia", or "pour" over the Brenner into Italy. The weeks pass and the phantom does none of these things – for one excellent reason. It does not exist to that extent. Most of such inadequate guns and munitions as it possessed must have been taken away from it and fooled away in Hitler's silly feints to invade Britain. And its raw jerry-built discipline is wilting under the creeping realization that the Blitzkrieg is spent, and the war is coming home to roost.

These quotations are not taken from the *Cavalry Quarterly*, but from a series of newspaper articles by Mr H.G. Wells, written at the beginning of this year and now reprinted in a book entitled *Guide to the New World*.* Since they were written, the German army has overrun the Balkans and reconquered Cyrenaica; it can march through Turkey or Spain at such time as may suit it, and it has undertaken the invasion of Russia. How that campaign will turn out I do not know, but it is worth noticing that the German general staff, whose opinion is probably worth something, would not have begun it if they had not felt fairly certain of finishing it within three months. So much for the idea that the German army is a bogey, its equipment inadequate, its morale breaking down, etc. etc.

What has Wells to set against the "screaming little defective in Berlin"? The usual rigmarole about a World State, plus the Sankey Declaration,* which is an attempted definition of fundamental human rights, of anti-totalitarian tendency. Except that he is now especially concerned with federal world control of air power, it is the same gospel as he has been preaching almost without interruption for the past forty years, always with an air of angry surprise at the human beings who can fail to grasp anything so obvious.

What is the use of saying that we need federal world control of the air? The whole question is how we are to get it. What is the use of pointing out that a World State is desirable? What matters is that not one of the five great military powers would think of submitting to such a thing. All sensible men for decades past have been substantially in agreement with what Mr Wells says – but the sensible men have no power and, in too many cases, no disposition to sacrifice themselves. Hitler is a criminal lunatic, and Hitler has an army of millions of men, aeroplanes in thousands, tanks in tens of thousands. For his sake a great nation has been willing to overwork itself for six years and then to fight for two years more, whereas for the common-sense, essentially hedonistic world view which Mr Wells puts forward, hardly a human creature is willing to shed a pint of blood. Before you can even talk of world reconstruction, or even of peace, you have got to eliminate Hitler, which means bringing into being a dynamic not necessarily the same as that of the Nazis but probably quite as unacceptable to "enlightened" and hedonistic people. What has kept England on its feet during the past year? In part, no doubt, some vague idea about a better future, but chiefly the atavistic emotion of patriotism, the ingrained feeling of the English-speaking peoples that they are superior to foreigners. For the last twenty years the main object of English left-wing intellectuals has been to break this feeling down, and if they had succeeded, we might be watching the SS men patrolling the London streets at this moment. Similarly, why are the Russians fighting like tigers against the German invasion? In part, perhaps, for some half-remembered ideal of utopian socialism, but chiefly in defence of Holy Russia (the "sacred soil of the Fatherland", etc. etc.), which Stalin has revived in an only slightly altered form. The energy that actually shapes the world springs from emotions – racial pride, leader-worship, religious belief, love of war – which liberal intellectuals mechanically write off as anachronisms, and which they have usually destroyed so completely in themselves as to have lost all power of action.

The people who say that Hitler is Antichrist, or alternatively, the Holy Ghost, are nearer an understanding of the truth than the intellectuals who for ten dreadful years have kept it up that he is merely a figure out of comic opera, not worth taking seriously. All that this idea really reflects is the sheltered conditions of English life. The Left Book Club was at bottom a product of Scotland Yard, just as the Peace Pledge Union is a product of the navy. One development of the last ten years has been the appearance of the "political book", a sort of enlarged pamphlet combining history with political criticism, as an important literary form. But the best writers in this line – Trotsky, Rauschning, Rosenberg, Silone, Borkenau, Koestler* and others – have none of them been Englishmen, and nearly all of them have been renegades from one or other extremist party, who have seen totalitarianism at close quarters and known the meaning of exile and persecution. Only in the English-speaking countries was it fashionable to believe, right up to the outbreak of war, that Hitler was an unimportant lunatic and the German tanks made of cardboard. Mr Wells, it will be seen from the quotations I have given above, believes something of the kind still. I do not suppose that either the bombs or the German campaign in Greece have altered his opinion. A lifelong habit of thought stands between him and an understanding of Hitler's power.

Mr Wells, like Dickens, belongs to the non-military middle class. The thunder of guns, the jingle of spurs, the catch in the throat when the old flag goes by, leave him manifestly cold. He has an invincible hatred of the fighting, hunting, swashbuckling side of life, symbolized in all his early books by a violent propaganda against horses. The principal villain of his *Outline of History** is the military adventurer, Napoleon. If one looks through nearly any book that he has written in the last forty years one finds the same idea constantly recurring: the supposed antithesis between the man of science who is working towards a planned World State and the reactionary who is trying to restore a disorderly past. In novels, utopias, essays, films, pamphlets, the antithesis crops up, always more or less the same. On the one side science, order, progress, internationalism, aeroplanes, steel, concrete, hygiene: on the other side war, nationalism, religion, monarchy, peasants, Greek professors, poets, horses. History as he sees it is a series of victories won by the scientific man over the romantic man. Now, he is probably right in assuming that a "reasonable", planned form of society, with scientists rather than witch doctors in control, will prevail sooner or later, but that is a different matter from assuming that it is just round the corner. There survives somewhere or other an interesting controversy which took place between Wells and Churchill at the time of the Russian Revolution. Wells accuses Churchill of not really believing his own propaganda about the Bolsheviks being monsters dripping with blood etc. but of merely fearing that they were going to introduce an era of common sense and scientific control, in which flag wavers like Churchill himself would have no place. Churchill's estimate of the Bolsheviks, however, was nearer the mark than Wells's. The early Bolsheviks may have been angels or demons, according as one chooses to regard them, but at any rate they were not sensible men. They were not introducing a Wellsian utopia, but a Rule of the Saints, which, like the English Rule of the Saints,* was a military despotism enlivened by witchcraft trials. The same misconception reappears in an inverted form in Well's attitude to the Nazis. Hitler is all the warlords and witch doctors in history rolled into one. Therefore, argues Wells, he is an absurdity, a ghost from the past, a creature doomed to disappear almost immediately. But unfortunately the equation of science with common sense does not really hold good. The aeroplane, which was looked forward to as a civilizing influence but in practice has hardly been used except for dropping bombs, is the symbol of that fact. Modern Germany is far more scientific than England, and far more barbarous. Much of what Wells has imagined and worked for is physically there in Nazi Germany. The order, the planning, the state encouragement of science, the steel, the concrete, the aeroplanes, are all there, but all in the service of ideas appropriate to the Stone Age. Science is fighting on the side of superstition. But obviously it is impossible for Wells to accept this. It would contradict the world view on which his own works are based. The warlords and the witch doctors *must* fail, the common-sense World State, as seen by a nineteenth-century liberal whose heart does not leap at the sound of bugles, *must* triumph. Treachery and defeatism apart, Hitler *cannot* be a danger. That he should finally win would be an impossible reversal of history, like a Jacobite restoration.

But is it not a sort of parricide for a person of my age (thirty-eight) to find fault with H.G. Wells? Thinking people who were born about the beginning of this century are in some sense Wells's own creation. How much influence any mere writer has, and especially a "popular" writer whose work takes effect quickly, is questionable, but I doubt whether anyone who was writing books between 1900 and 1920, at any rate in the English language, influenced the young so much. The minds of all of us, and therefore the physical world, would be perceptibly different if Wells had never existed. Only, just the singleness of mind, the one-sided imagination that made him seem like an inspired prophet in the Edwardian age, make him a shallow, inadequate thinker now. When Wells was young, the antithesis between science and reaction was not false. Society was ruled by narrow-minded, profoundly incurious people, predatory businessmen, dull squires, bishops, politicians who could quote Horace but had never heard of algebra. Science was faintly disreputable and religious belief obligatory. Traditionalism, stupidity, snobbishness, patriotism, superstition and love of war seemed to be all on the same side; there was need of someone who could state the opposite point of view. Back in the 1900s it was a wonderful experience for a boy to discover H.G. Wells. There you were, in a world of pedants, clergymen and golfers, with your future employers exhorting you to "get on or get out", your parents systematically warping your sexual life, and your dull-witted schoolmasters sniggering over their Latin tags – and here was this wonderful man who could tell you about the inhabitants of the planets and the bottom of the sea, and who *knew* that the future was not going to be what respectable people imagined. A decade or so before aeroplanes were technically feasible Wells knew that within a little while men would be able to fly. He knew that because he himself *wanted* to be able to fly, and therefore felt sure that research in that direction would continue. On the other hand, even when I was a little boy, at a time when the Wright brothers had actually lifted their machine off the ground for fifty-nine seconds, the generally accepted opinion was that if God had meant us to fly He would have given us wings. Up to 1914 Wells was in the main a true prophet. In physical details his vision of the new world has been fulfilled to a surprising extent.

But because he belonged to the nineteenth century and to a non-military nation and class, he could not grasp the tremendous strength of the old world which was symbolized in his mind by fox-hunting Tories. He was, and still is, quite incapable of understanding that nationalism, religious bigotry and feudal loyalty are far more powerful forces than what he himself would describe as sanity. Creatures out of the Dark Ages have come marching into the present, and if they are ghosts they are at any rate ghosts which need a strong magic to lay them. The people who have shown the best understanding of fascism are either those who have suffered under it or those who have a fascist streak in themselves. A crude book like *The Iron Heel*, written nearly thirty years ago, is a truer prophecy of the future than either *Brave New World* or *The Shape of Things to Come*.* If one had to choose among Wells's own contemporaries a writer who could stand towards him as a corrective, one might choose Kipling, who was not deaf to the evil voices of power and military "glory". Kipling would have understood the appeal of Hitler, or for that matter of Stalin, whatever his attitude towards them might be. Wells is too sane to understand the modern world. The succession of lower-middle-class novels which are his greatest achievement stopped short at the other war and never really began again, and since 1920 he has squandered his talents in slaying paper dragons. But how much it is, after all, to have any talents to squander.

The Art of Donald McGill*

Who does not know the "comics" of the cheap stationer's windows, the penny or twopenny coloured postcards with their endless succession of fat women in tight bathing dresses and their crude drawing and unbearable colours, chiefly hedge sparrow's egg tint and Post Office red?

This question ought to be rhetorical, but it is a curious fact that many people seem to be unaware of the existence of these things, or else to have a vague notion that they are something to be found only at the seaside, like nigger minstrels or peppermint rock. Actually they are on sale everywhere – they can be bought at nearly any Woolworth's, for example – and they are evidently produced in enormous numbers, new series constantly appearing. They are not to be confused with the various other types of comic illustrated postcard, such as the sentimental ones dealing with puppies and kittens or the Wendyish,* sub-pornographic ones which exploit the love affairs of children. They are a genre of their own, specializing in very low humour, the mother-in-law, baby's nappy, policemen's boots type of joke, and distinguishable from all the other kinds by having no artistic pretensions. Some half-dozen publishing houses issue them, though the people who draw them seem not to be numerous at any one time.

I have associated them especially with the name of Donald McGill because he is not only the most prolific and by far the best of contemporary postcard artists, but also the most representative, the most perfect in the tradition. Who Donald McGill is, I do not know. He is apparently a trade name, for at least one series of postcards is issued simply as "The Donald McGill Comics", but he is also unquestionably a real person with a style of drawing which is recognizable at a glance. Anyone who examines his postcards in bulk will notice that many of them are not despicable even as drawings, but it would be mere dilettantism to pretend that they have any direct aesthetic value. A comic postcard is simply an illustration to a joke, invariably a "low" joke, and it stands or falls by its ability to raise a laugh. Beyond that it has only "ideological" interest. McGill is a clever draughtsman with a real caricaturist's touch in the drawing of faces, but the special value of his postcards is that they are so completely typical. They represent, as it were, the norm of the comic postcard. Without being in the least imitative, they are exactly what comic postcards have been any time these last forty years, and from them the meaning and purpose of the whole genre can be inferred.

Get hold of a dozen of these things, preferably McGill's – if you pick out from a pile the ones that seem to you funniest, you will probably find that most of them are McGill's – and spread them out on a table. What do you see?

Your first impression is of overwhelming vulgarity. This is quite apart from the ever-present obscenity, and apart also from the hideousness of the colours. They have an utter lowness of mental atmosphere which comes out not only in the nature of the jokes but, even more, in the grotesque, staring, blatant quality of the drawings. The designs, like those of a child, are full of heavy lines and empty spaces, and all the figures in them, every gesture and attitude, are deliberately ugly, the faces grinning and vacuous, the women monstrously parodied, with bottoms like Hottentots. Your second impression, however, is of indefinable familiarity. What do these things remind you of? What are they so like? In the first place, of course, they remind you of the barely different postcards which you probably gazed at in your childhood. But more than this, what you are really looking at is something as traditional as Greek tragedy, a sort of sub-world of smacked bottoms and scrawny mothers-in-law which is a part of Western European consciousness. Not that the jokes, taken one by one, are necessarily stale. Not being debarred from smuttiness, comic postcards repeat themselves less often than the joke columns in reputable magazines, but their basic subject matter, the *kind* of joke they are aiming at, never varies. A few are genuinely witty, in a Max Millerish* style. Examples:

"I like seeing experienced girls home."
  "But I'm not experienced!"
  "You're not home yet!"

"I've been struggling for years to get a fur coat. How did you get yours?"
  "I left off struggling."

Judge: "You are prevaricating, sir. Did you or did you not sleep with this woman?"
  Co-respondent: "Not a wink, my lord!"

In general, however, they are not witty but humorous, and it must be said for McGill's postcards, in particular, that the drawing is often a good deal funnier than the joke beneath it. Obviously the outstanding characteristic of comic postcards is their obscenity, and I must discuss that more fully later. But I give here a rough analysis of their habitual subject matter, with such explanatory remarks as seem to be needed:

Sex. More than half, perhaps three quarters, of the jokes are sex jokes, ranging from the harmless to the all but unprintable. First favourite is probably the illegitimate baby. Typical captions: "Could you exchange this lucky charm for a baby's feeding bottle?" "She didn't ask me to the christening, so I'm not going to the wedding." Also newlyweds, old maids, nude statues and women in bathing dresses. All of these are *ipso facto* funny, mere mention of them being enough to raise a laugh. The cuckoldry joke is very seldom exploited, and there are no references to homosexuality.

Conventions of the sex joke:

a. Marriage only benefits the woman. Every man is plotting seduction and every women is plotting marriage. No woman ever remains unmarried voluntarily.
b. Sex appeal vanishes at about the age of twenty-five. Well-preserved and good-looking people beyond their first youth are never represented. The amorous honeymooning couple reappear as the grim-visaged wife and hapless, moustachioed, red-nosed husband, no intermediate stage being allowed for.

Home life. Next to sex, the henpecked husband is the favourite joke. Typical caption: "Did they get an X-ray of your wife's jaw at the hospital?" – "No, they got a moving picture instead."

Conventions:

a. There is no such thing as a happy marriage.
b. No man ever gets the better of a woman in argument.

Drunkenness. Both drunkenness and teetotalism are *ipso facto* funny.

Conventions:

a. All drunken men have optical illusions.
b. Drunkenness is something peculiar to middle-aged men. Drunken youths or women are never represented.

W.C. jokes. There is not a large number of these. Chamber pots are *ipso facto* funny, and so are public lavatories. A typical postcard, captioned "A Friend in Need", shows a man's hat blown off his head and disappearing down the steps of a ladies' lavatory.

Inter-working-class snobbery. Much in these postcards suggests that they are aimed at the better-off working class and poorer middle class. There are many jokes turning on malapropisms, illiteracy, dropped aitches and the rough manners of slum dwellers. Countless postcards show draggled hags of the stage-charwoman type exchanging "unladylike" abuse. Typical repartee: "I wish you were a statue and I was a pigeon!" A certain number produced since the war treat evacuation from the anti-evacuee angle. There are the usual jokes about tramps, beggars and criminals, and the comic maidservant appears fairly frequently. Also the comic navvy, bargee, etc. – but there are no anti-trade-union jokes. Broadly speaking, everyone with much over or much under £5 a week is regarded as laughable. The "swell" is almost as automatically a figure of fun as the slum dweller.

Stock figures. Foreigners seldom or never appear. The chief locality joke is the Scotsman, who is almost inexhaustible. The lawyer is always a swindler, the clergyman always a nervous idiot who says the wrong thing. The "knut" or "masher" still appears, almost as in Edwardian days, in out-of-date-looking evening clothes and an opera hat, or even with spats and a knobby cane. Another survival is the suffragette, one of the big jokes of the pre-1914 period and too valuable to be relinquished. She has reappeared, unchanged in physical appearance, as the feminist lecturer or temperance fanatic. A feature of the last few years is the complete absence of anti-Jew postcards. The "Jew joke", always somewhat more ill-natured than the "Scotch joke", disappeared abruptly soon after the rise of Hitler.

Politics. Any contemporary event, cult or activity which has comic possibilities (for example, "free love", feminism, ARP,* nudism) rapidly finds its way into the picture postcards, but their general atmosphere is extremely old-fashioned. The implied political outlook is a radicalism appropriate to about the year 1900. At normal times they are not only not patriotic, but go in for a mild guying of patriotism, with jokes about 'God Save the King', the Union Jack, etc. The European situation only began to reflect itself in them at some time in 1939, and first did so through the comic aspects of ARP. Even at this date few postcards mention the war except in ARP jokes (fat woman stuck in the mouth of Anderson shelter; wardens neglecting their duty while young woman undresses at window she had forgotten to black out, etc. etc.). A few express anti-Hitler sentiments of a not very vindictive kind. One, not McGill's, shows Hitler, with the usual hypertrophied backside, bending down to pick a flower. Caption: "What would *you* do, chums?" This is about as high a flight of patriotism as any postcard is likely to attain. Unlike the twopenny weekly papers, comic postcards are not the product of any great monopoly company, and evidently they are not regarded as having any importance in forming public opinion. There is no sign in them of any attempt to induce an outlook acceptable to the ruling class.

Here one comes back to the outstanding, all-important feature of comic postcards – their obscenity. It is by this that everyone remembers them, and it is also central to their purpose, though not in a way that is immediately obvious.

A recurrent, almost dominant motif in comic postcards is the woman with the stuck-out behind. In perhaps half of them, or more than half, even when the point of the joke has nothing to do with sex, the same female figure appears, a plump "voluptuous" figure with the dress clinging to it as tightly as another skin and with breasts or buttocks grossly overemphasized, according to which way it is turned. There can be no doubt that these pictures lift the lid off a very widespread repression, natural enough in a country whose women when young tend to be slim to the point of skimpiness. But at the same time the McGill postcard – and this applies to all other postcards in this genre – is not intended as pornography but, a subtler thing, as a skit on pornography. The Hottentot figures of the women are caricatures of the Englishman's secret ideal, not portraits of it. When one examines McGill's postcards more closely, one notices that his brand of humour only has meaning in relation to a fairly strict moral code. Whereas in papers like *Esquire*, for instance, or *La Vie Parisienne*,* the imaginary background of the jokes is always promiscuity, the utter breakdown of all standards, the background of the McGill postcard is marriage. The four leading jokes are nakedness, illegitimate babies, old maids and newly married couples, none of which would seem funny in a really dissolute or even "sophisticated" society. The postcards dealing with honeymoon couples always have the enthusiastic indecency of those village weddings where it is still considered screamingly funny to sew bells to the bridal bed. In one, for example, a young bridegroom is shown getting out of bed the morning after his wedding night. "The first morning in our own little home, darling!" he is saying. "I'll go and get the milk and paper and bring you a cup of tea." Inset is a picture of the front doorstep; on it are four newspapers and four bottles of milk. This is obscene, if you like, but it is not immoral. Its implication – and this is just the implication that *Esquire* or the *New Yorker* would avoid at all costs – is that marriage is something profoundly exciting and important, the biggest event in the average human being's life. So also with jokes about nagging wives and tyrannous mothers-in-law. They do at least imply a stable society in which marriage is indissoluble and family loyalty taken for granted. And bound up with this is something I noted earlier, the fact that there are no pictures, or hardly any, of good-looking people beyond their first youth. There is the "spooning" couple and the middle-aged, cat-and-dog couple, but nothing in between. The liaison, the illicit but more or less decorous love affair which used to be the stock joke of French comic papers, is not a postcard subject. And this reflects, on a comic level, the working-class outlook which takes it as a matter of course that youth and adventure – almost, indeed, individual life – end with marriage. One of the few authentic class differences, as opposed to class distinctions, still existing in England is that the working classes age very much earlier. They do not live less long, provided that they survive their childhood, nor do they lose their physical activity earlier, but they do lose very early their youthful appearance. This fact is observable everywhere, but can be most easily verified by watching one of the higher age groups registering for military service; the middle- and upper-class members look, on average, ten years younger than the others. It is usual to attribute this to the harder lives that the working classes have to live, but it is doubtful whether any such difference now exists as would account for it. More probably the truth is that the working classes reach middle age earlier because they accept it earlier. For to look young after, say, thirty is largely a matter of wanting to do so. This generalization is less true of the better-paid workers, especially those who live in council houses and labour-saving flats, but it is true enough even of them to point to a difference of outlook. And in this, as usual, they are more traditional, more in accord with the Christian past than the well-to-do women who try to stay young at forty by means of physical jerks, cosmetics and avoidance of childbearing. The impulse to cling to youth at all costs, to attempt to preserve your sexual attraction, to see even in middle age a future for yourself and not merely for your children, is a thing of recent growth and has only precariously established itself. It will probably disappear again when our standard of living drops and our birth rate rises. "Youth's a stuff will not endure"* expresses the normal, traditional attitude. It is this ancient wisdom that McGill and his colleagues are reflecting, no doubt unconsciously, when they allow for no transition stage between the honeymoon couple and those glamourless figures, Mum and Dad.

I have said that at least half McGill's postcards are sex jokes, and a proportion, perhaps 10 per cent, are far more obscene than anything else that is now printed in England. Newsagents are occasionally prosecuted for selling them, and there would be many more prosecutions if the broadest jokes were not invariably protected by double meanings. A single example will be enough to show how this is done. In one postcard, captioned "They didn't believe her", a young woman is demonstrating, with her hands held apart, something about two feet long to a couple of open-mouthed acquaintances. Behind her on the wall is a stuffed fish in a glass case, and beside that is a photograph of a nearly naked athlete. Obviously it is not the fish that she is referring to, but this could never be proved. Now, it is doubtful whether there is any paper in England that would print a joke of this kind, and certainly there is no paper that does so habitually. There is an immense amount of pornography of a mild sort, countless illustrated papers cashing in on women's legs, but there is no popular literature specializing in the "vulgar", farcical aspect of sex. On the other hand, jokes exactly like McGill's are the ordinary small change of the revue and music-hall stage, and are also to be heard on the radio, at moments when the censor happens to be nodding. In England the gap between what can be said and what can be printed is rather exceptionally wide. Remarks and gestures which hardly anyone objects to on the stage would raise a public outcry if any attempt were made to reproduce them on paper. (Compare Max Miller's stage patter with his weekly column in the *Sunday Dispatch*.) The comic postcards are the only existing exception to this rule, the only medium in which really "low" humour is considered to be printable. Only in postcards and on the variety stage can the stuck-out behind, dog and lamp-post, baby's nappy type of joke be freely exploited. Remembering that, one sees what function these postcards, in their humble way, are performing.

What they are doing is to give expression to the Sancho Panza* view of life, the attitude to life that Miss Rebecca West* once summed up as "extracting as much fun as possible from smacking behinds in basement kitchens". The Don Quixote–Sancho Panza combination, which of course is simply the ancient dualism of body and soul in fiction form, recurs more frequently in the literature of the last 400 years than can be explained by mere imitation. It comes up again and again, in endless variations, Bouvard and Pécuchet, Jeeves and Wooster, Bloom and Dedalus,* Holmes and Watson (the Holmes–Watson variant is an exceptionally subtle one, because the usual physical characteristics of two partners have been transposed). Evidently it corresponds to something enduring in our civilization, not in the sense that either character is to be found in a "pure" state in real life, but in the sense that the two principles, noble folly and base wisdom, exist side by side in nearly every human being. If you look into your own mind, which are you, Don Quixote or Sancho Panza? Almost certainly you are both. There is one part of you that wishes to be a hero or a saint, but another part of you is a little fat man who sees very clearly the advantages of staying alive with a whole skin. He is your unofficial self, the voice of the belly protesting against the soul. His tastes lie towards safety, soft beds, no work, pots of beer and women with "voluptuous" figures. He it is who punctures your fine attitudes and urges you to look after Number One, to be unfaithful to your wife, to bilk your debts, and so on and so forth. Whether you allow yourself to be influenced by him is a different question. But it is simply a lie to say that he is not part of you, just as it is a lie to say that Don Quixote is not part of you either, though most of what is said and written consists of one lie or the other, usually the first.

But though in varying forms he is one of the stock figures of literature, in real life, especially in the way society is ordered, his point of view never gets a fair hearing. There is a constant worldwide conspiracy to pretend that he is not there, or at least that he doesn't matter. Codes of law and morals, or religious systems, never have much room in them for a humorous view of life. Whatever is funny is subversive, every joke is ultimately a custard pie, and the reason why so large a proportion of jokes centre round obscenity is simply that all societies, as the price of survival, have to insist on a fairly high standard of sexual morality. A dirty joke is not, of course, a serious attack upon morality, but it is a sort of mental rebellion, a momentary wish that things were otherwise. So also with all other jokes, which always centre round cowardice, laziness, dishonesty or some other quality which society cannot afford to encourage. Society has always to demand a little more from human beings than it will get in practice. It has to demand faultless discipline and self-sacrifice, it must expect its subjects to work hard, pay their taxes and be faithful to their wives, it must assume that men think it glorious to die on the battlefield and women want to wear themselves out with childbearing. The whole of what one may call official literature is founded on such assumptions. I never read the proclamations of generals before battle, the speeches of führers and prime ministers, the solidarity songs of public schools and left-wing political parties, national anthems, temperance tracts, papal encyclicals and sermons against gambling and contraception, without seeming to hear in the background a chorus of raspberries from all the millions of common men to whom these high sentiments make no appeal. Nevertheless, the high sentiments always win in the end, leaders who offer blood, toil, tears and sweat always get more out of their followers than those who offer safety and a good time. When it comes to the pinch, human beings are heroic. Women face childbed and the scrubbing brush, revolutionaries keep their mouths shut in the torture chamber, battleships go down with their guns still firing when their decks are awash. It is only that the other element in man, the lazy, cowardly, debt-bilking adulterer who is inside all of us, can never be suppressed altogether and needs a hearing occasionally.

The comic postcards are one expression of his point of view, a humble one, less important than the music halls, but still worthy of attention. In a society which is still basically Christian, they naturally concentrate on sex jokes; in a totalitarian society, if they had any freedom of expression at all, they would probably concentrate on laziness or cowardice, but at any rate on the unheroic in one form or another. It will not do to condemn them on the ground that they are vulgar and ugly. That is exactly what they are meant to be. Their whole meaning and virtue is in their unredeemed lowness, not only in the sense of obscenity, but lowness of outlook in every direction whatever. The slightest hint of "higher" influences would ruin them utterly. They stand for the worm's-eye view of life, for the music-hall world where marriage is a dirty joke or a comic disaster, where the rent is always behind and the clothes are always up the spout, where the lawyer is always a crook and the Scotsman always a miser, where the newlyweds make fools of themselves on the hideous beds of seaside lodging houses and the drunken, red-nosed husbands roll home at four in the morning to meet the linen-nightgowned wives who wait for them behind the front door, poker in hand. Their existence, the fact that people want them, is symptomatically important. Like the music halls, they are a sort of Saturnalia, a harmless rebellion against virtue. They express only one tendency in the human mind, but a tendency which is always there and will find its own outlet, like water. On the whole, human beings want to be good, but not too good, and not quite all the time. For:

there is a just man that perisheth in his righteousness, and there is a wicked man that prolongeth his life in his wickedness. Be not righteous overmuch; neither make thyself over-wise; why shouldest thou destroy thyself? Be not overmuch wicked, neither be thou foolish: why shouldest thou die before thy time?*

In the past the mood of the comic postcard could enter into the central stream of literature, and jokes barely different from McGill's could casually be uttered between the murders in Shakespeare's tragedies. That is no longer possible, and a whole category of humour, integral to our literature till 1800 or thereabouts, has dwindled down to these ill-drawn postcards, leading a barely legal existence in cheap stationers' windows. The corner of the human heart that they speak for might easily manifest itself in worse forms, and I for one should be sorry to see them vanish.

No, Not One*

Mr Murry* said years ago that the works of the best modern writers, Joyce, Eliot and the like, simply demonstrated the *impossibility* of great art in a time like the present, and since then we have moved onwards into a period in which any sort of *joy* in writing, any such notion as telling a story for the purpose of pure entertainment, has also become impossible. All writing nowadays is propaganda. If, therefore, I treat Mr Comfort's novel as a tract, I am only doing what he himself has done already. It is a good novel as novels go at this moment, but the motive for writing it was not what Trollope or Balzac, or even Tolstoy, would have recognized as a novelist's impulse. It was written in order to put forward the "message" of pacifism, and it was to fit that "message" that the main incidents in it were devised. I think I am also justified in assuming that it is autobiographical, not in the sense that the events described in it have actually happened, but in the sense that the author identifies himself with the hero, thinks him worthy of sympathy and agrees with the sentiments that he expresses.

Here is the outline of the story. A young German doctor who has been convalescent for two years in Switzerland returns to Cologne a little before Munich to find that his wife has been helping war resisters to escape from the country and is in imminent danger of arrest. He and she flee to Holland just in time to escape the massacre which followed on Vom Rath's assassination.* Partly by accident they reach England, he having been seriously wounded on the way. After his recovery he manages to get a hospital appointment, but at the outbreak of war he is brought before a tribunal and put in the B class of aliens. The reason for this is that he has declared that he will not fight against the Nazis, thinking it better to "overcome Hitler by love". Asked why he did not stay in Germany and overcome Hitler by love there, he admits that there is no answer. In the panic following on the invasion of the Low Countries he is arrested a few minutes after his wife has given birth to a baby and kept for a long time in a concentration camp where he cannot communicate with her and where the conditions of dirt, overcrowding, etc. are as bad as anything in Germany. Finally he is packed onto the *Arandora Star** (it is given another name, of course), sunk at sea, rescued, and put in another, somewhat better camp. When he is at last released and makes contact with his wife, it is to find that she has been confined in another camp in which the baby has died of neglect and underfeeding. The book ends with the couple looking forward to sailing for America and hoping that the war fever will not by this time have spread there as well.

NO, NOT ONE

Now, before considering the implications of this story, just consider one or two facts which underlie the structure of modern society and which it is necessary to ignore if the pacifist "message" is to be accepted uncritically.

1. Civilization rests ultimately on coercion. What holds society together is not the policeman but the goodwill of common men, and yet that goodwill is powerless unless the policeman is there to back it up. Any government which refused to use violence in its own defence would cease almost immediately to exist, because it could be overthrown by any body of men, or even any individual, that was less scrupulous. Objectively, whoever is not on the side of the policeman is on the side of the criminal, and vice versa. In so far as it hampers the British war effort, British pacifism is on the side of the Nazis, and German pacifism, if it exists, is on the side of Britain and the USSR. Since pacifists have more freedom of action in countries where traces of democracy survive, pacifism can act more effectively against democracy than for it. Objectively the pacifist is pro-Nazi.

2. Since coercion can never be altogether dispensed with, the only difference is between degrees of violence. During the last twenty years there has been less violence and less militarism inside the English-speaking world than outside it, because there has been more money and more security. The hatred of war which undoubtedly characterizes the English-speaking peoples is a reflection of their favoured position. Pacifism is only a considerable force in places where people feel themselves very safe, chiefly maritime states. Even in such places, turn-the-other-cheek pacifism only flourishes among the more prosperous classes, or among workers who have in some way escaped from their own class. The real working class, though they hate war and are immune to jingoism, are never really pacifist, because their life teaches them something different. To abjure violence it is necessary to have no experience of it.

If one keeps the above facts in mind one can, I think, see the events in Mr Comfort's novel in truer perspective. It is a question of putting aside subjective feelings and trying to see whither one's actions will lead in practice and where one's motives ultimately spring from. The hero is a research worker – a pathologist. He has not been especially fortunate, he has a defective lung, thanks to the carrying-on of the British blockade into 1919, but in so far as he is a member of the middle class, doing work which he has chosen for himself, he is one of a few million favoured human beings who live ultimately on the degradation of the rest. He wants to get on with his work, wants to be out of reach of Nazi tyranny and regimentation, but he will not *act* against the Nazis in any other way than by running away from them. Arrived in England, he is in terror of being sent back to Germany, but refuses to take part in any physical effort to keep the Nazis out of England. His greatest hope is to get to America, with another 3,000 miles of water between himself and the Nazis. He will only get there, you note, if British ships and planes protect him on the way, and having got there he will simply be living under the protection of American ships and planes instead of British ones. If he is lucky he will be able to continue with his work as a pathologist, at the same time keeping up his attitude of moral superiority towards the men who make his work possible. And underlying everything there will still be his position as a research worker, a favoured person living ultimately on dividends which would cease forthwith if not extorted by the threat of violence.

I do not think this is an unfair summary of Mr Comfort's book. And I think the relevant fact is that this story of a German doctor is written by an Englishman. The argument which is implied all the way through, and sometimes explicitly stated, that there is next to no difference between Britain and Germany, political persecution is as bad in one as in the other, those who fight against the Nazis always go Nazi themselves, would be more convincing if it came from a German. There are probably 60,000 German refugees in this country, and there would be hundreds of thousands more if we had not meanly kept them out. Why did they come here if there is virtually no difference between the social atmosphere of the two countries? And how many of them have asked to go back? They have "voted with their feet", as Lenin put it. As I pointed out above, the comparative gentleness of the English-speaking civilization is due to money and security, but that is not to say that no difference exists. Once let it be admitted, however, that there *is* a certain difference, that it matters quite a lot who wins, and the usual short-term case for pacifism falls to the ground. You can be explicitly pro-Nazi without claiming to be a pacifist – and there is a very strong case for the Nazis, though not many people in this country have the courage to utter it – but you can only pretend that Nazism and capitalist democracy are Tweedledum and Tweedledee if you also pretend that every horror from the June purge onwards has been cancelled by an exactly similar horror in England. In practice this has to be done by means of selection and exaggeration. Mr Comfort is in effect claiming that a "hard case" is typical. The sufferings of this German doctor in a so-called democratic country are so terrible, he implies, as to wipe out every shred of moral justification for the struggle against fascism. One must, however, keep a sense of proportion. Before raising a squeal because 2,000 internees have only eighteen latrine buckets between them, one might as well remember what has happened these last few years in Poland, in Spain, in Czechoslovakia, etc. etc. If one clings too closely to the "those who fight against fascism become fascist themselves" formula, one is simply led into falsification. It is not true, for instance, as Mr Comfort implies, that there is widespread spy-mania and that the prejudice against foreigners increases as the war gathers in momentum. The feeling against foreigners, which was one of the factors that made the internment of the refugees possible, has greatly died away, and Germans and Italians are now allowed into jobs that they would have been debarred from in peacetime. It is not true, as he explicitly says, that the only difference between political persecution in England and in Germany is that in England nobody hears about it. Nor is it true that all the evil in our life is traceable to war or war preparation. "I knew," he says, "that the English people, like the Germans, had never been happy since they put their trust in rearmament." Were they so conspicuously happy before? Is it not the truth, on the contrary, that rearmament, by reducing unemployment, made the English people somewhat happier, if anything? From my own observation I should say that, by and large, the war itself has made England happier – and this is not an argument in favour of war, but simply tells one something about the nature of so-called peace.

The fact is that the ordinary short-term case for pacifism, the claim that you can best frustrate the Nazis by not resisting them, cannot be sustained. If you don't resist the Nazis you are helping them, and ought to admit it. For then the long-term case for pacifism can be made out. You can say: "Yes, I know I am helping Hitler, and I want to help him. Let him conquer Britain, the USSR and America. Let the Nazis rule the world; in the end they will grow into something different." That is at any rate a tenable position. It looks forward into human history, beyond the term of our own lives. What is not tenable is the idea that everything in the garden would be lovely *now* if only we stopped the wicked fighting, and that to fight back is exactly what the Nazis want us to do. Which does Hitler fear more, the PPU* or the RAF? Which has he made greater efforts to sabotage? Is he trying to bring America into the war, or to keep America out of it? Would he be deeply distressed if the Russians stopped fighting tomorrow? And after all, the history of the last ten years suggests that Hitler has a pretty shrewd idea of his own interests.

The notion that you can somehow defeat violence by submitting to it is simply a flight from fact. As I have said, it is only possible to people who have money and guns between themselves and reality. But why should they want to make this flight, in any case? Because, rightly hating violence, they do not wish to recognize that it is integral to modern society and that their own fine feelings and noble attitudes are all the fruit of injustice backed up by force. They do not want to learn where their incomes come from. Underneath this lies the hard fact, so difficult for many people to face, that individual salvation is not possible, that the choice before human beings is not, as a rule, between good and evil but between two evils. You can let the Nazis rule the world; that is evil – or you can overthrow them by war, which is also evil. There is no other choice before you, and whichever you choose you will not come out with clean hands. It seems to me that the text for our times is not "Woe to him through whom the evil cometh" but the one from which I took the title of this article, "There is not one that is righteous, no, not one."* We have all touched pitch; we are all perishing by the sword. We do not have the chance, in a time like this, to say "Tomorrow we can all start being good". That is moonshine. We only have the chance of choosing the lesser evil and of working for the establishment of a new kind of society in which common decency will again be possible. There is no such thing as neutrality in this war. The whole population of the world is involved in it, from the Eskimos to the Andamese, and since one must inevitably help one side or the other, it is better to know what one is doing and count the cost. Men like Darlan and Laval* have at any rate had the courage to make their choice and proclaim it openly. The New Order, they say, must be established at all costs, and "*il faut écrabouiller l'Angleterre*".* Mr Murry appears, at any rate at moments, to think likewise. The Nazis, he says, are "doing the dirty work of the Lord" (they certainly did an exceptionally dirty job when they attacked Russia), and we must be careful "lest in fighting against Hitler we are fighting against God". Those are not pacifist sentiments, since if carried to their logical conclusion they involve not only surrendering to Hitler but helping him in his various forthcoming wars, but they are at least straightforward and courageous. I do not myself see Hitler as the saviour, even the unconscious saviour, of humanity, but there is a strong case for thinking him so, far stronger than most people in England imagine. What there is no case for is to denounce Hitler and at the same time look down your nose at the people who actually keep you out of his clutches. That is simply a highbrow variant of British hypocrisy, a product of capitalism in decay, and the sort of thing for which Europeans, who at any rate understand the nature of a policeman and a dividend, justifiably despise us.

Rudyard Kipling*

It was a pity that Mr Eliot should be so much on the defensive in the long essay with which he prefaces this selection of Kipling's poetry, but it was not to be avoided, because before one can even speak about Kipling one has to clear away a legend that has been created by two sets of people who have not read his works. Kipling is in the peculiar position of having been a byword for fifty years. During five literary generations every enlightened person has despised him, and at the end of that time nine tenths of those enlightened persons are forgotten and Kipling is in some sense still there. Mr Eliot never satisfactorily explains this fact, because in answering the shallow and familiar charge that Kipling is a "fascist", he falls into the opposite error of defending him where he is not defensible. It is no use pretending that Kipling's view of life, as a whole, can be accepted or even forgiven by any civilized person. It is no use claiming, for instance, that when Kipling describes a British soldier beating a "nigger" with a cleaning rod in order to get money out of him, he is acting merely as a reporter and does not necessarily approve what he describes. There is not the slightest sign anywhere in Kipling's work that he disapproves of that kind of conduct – on the contrary, there is a definite strain of sadism in him, over and above the brutality which a writer of that type has to have. Kipling *is* a jingo imperialist; he *is* morally insensitive and aesthetically disgusting. It is better to start by admitting that, and then to try to find out why it is that he survives while the refined people who have sniggered at him seem to wear so badly.

And yet the "fascist" charge has to be answered, because the first clue to any understanding of Kipling, morally or politically, is the fact that he was *not* a fascist. He was further from being one than the most humane or the most "progressive" person is able to be nowadays. An interesting instance of the way in which quotations are parroted to and fro without any attempt to look up their context or discover their meaning is the line from 'Recessional',* "Lesser breeds without the Law". This line is always good for a snigger in pansy-left circles. It is assumed as a matter of course that the "lesser breeds" are "natives", and a mental picture is called up of some *pukka sahib* in a pith helmet kicking a coolie. In its context the sense of the line is almost the exact opposite of this. The phrase "lesser breeds" refers almost certainly to the Germans, and especially the pan-German writers, who are "without the Law" in the sense of being lawless, not in the sense of being powerless. The whole poem, conventionally thought of as an orgy of boasting, is a denunciation of power politics, British as well as German. Two stanzas are worth quoting (I am quoting this as politics, not as poetry):

> If, drunk with sight of power, we loose
> Wild tongues that have not Thee in awe,
> Such boastings as the Gentiles use,
> Or lesser breeds without the Law –
> Lord God of hosts, be with us yet,
> Lest we forget – lest we forget!
>
> For heathen heart that puts her trust
> In reeking tube and iron shard,
> All valiant dust that builds on dust,
> And guarding, calls not Thee to guard,
> For frantic boast and foolish word –
> Thy mercy on Thy People, Lord!

Much of Kipling's phraseology is taken from the Bible, and no doubt in the second stanza he had in mind the text from Psalm 127: "Except the Lord build the house, they labour in vain that build it; except the Lord keep the city, the watchman waketh but in vain." It is not a text that makes much impression on the post-Hitler mind. No one, in our time, believes in any sanction greater than military power; no one believes that it is possible to overcome force except by greater force. There is no "Law", there is only power. I am not saying that that is a true belief, merely that it is the belief which all modern men do actually hold. Those who pretend otherwise are either intellectual cowards, or power worshippers under a thin disguise, or have simply not caught up with the age they are living in. Kipling's outlook is pre-fascist. He still believes that pride comes before a fall and that the gods punish hubris. He does not foresee the tank, the bombing plane, the radio and the secret police, or their psychological results.

But in saying this, does not one unsay what I said about Kipling's jingoism and brutality? No, one is merely saying that the nineteenth-century imperialist outlook and the modern gangster outlook are two different things. Kipling belongs very definitely to the period 1885–1902. The Great War and its aftermath embittered him, but he shows little sign of having learnt anything from any event later than the Boer War. He was the prophet of British imperialism in its expansionist phase (even more than his poems, his solitary novel, *The Light That Failed*,* gives you the atmosphere of that time) and also the unofficial historian of the British Army, the old mercenary army which began to change its shape in 1914. All his confidence, his bouncing vulgar vitality, sprang out of limitations which no fascist or near-fascist shares.

Kipling spent the later part of his life in sulking, and no doubt it was political disappointment rather than literary vanity that accounted for this. Somehow history had not gone according to plan. After the greatest victory she had ever known, Britain was a lesser world power than before, and Kipling was quite acute enough to see this. The virtue had gone out of the classes he idealized; the young were hedonistic or disaffected; the desire to paint the map red had evaporated. He could not understand what was happening, because he had never had any grasp of the economic forces underlying imperial expansion. It is notable that Kipling does not seem to realize, any more than the average soldier or colonial administrator, that an empire is primarily a money-making concern. Imperialism as he sees it is a sort of forcible evangelizing. You turn a Gatling gun on a mob of unarmed "natives", and then you establish "the Law", which includes roads, railways and a courthouse. He could not foresee, therefore, that the same motives which brought the Empire into existence would end by destroying it. It was the same motive, for example, that caused the Malayan jungles to be cleared for rubber estates, and which now causes those estates to be handed over intact to the Japanese. The modern totalitarians know what they are doing, and the nineteenth-century English did not know what they were doing. Both attitudes have their advantages, but Kipling was never able to move forward from one into the other. His outlook, allowing for the fact that after all he was an artist, was that of the salaried bureaucrat who despises the "boxwallah"* and often lives a lifetime without realizing that the "boxwallah" calls the tune.

But because he identifies himself with the official class, he does possess one thing which "enlightened" people seldom or never possess, and that is a sense of responsibility. The middle-class Left hate him for this quite as much as for his cruelty and vulgarity. All left-wing parties in the highly industrialized countries are at bottom a sham, because they make it their business to fight against something which they do not really wish to destroy. They have international aims, and at the same time they struggle to keep up a standard of life with which those aims are incompatible. We all live by robbing Asiatic coolies, and those of us who are "enlightened" all maintain that those coolies ought to be set free – but our standard of living, and hence our "enlightenment", demands that the robbery shall continue. A humanitarian is always a hypocrite, and Kipling's understanding of this is perhaps the central secret of his power to create telling phrases. It would be difficult to hit off the one-eyed pacifism of the English in fewer words than in the phrase "making mock of uniforms that guard you while you sleep".* It is true that Kipling does not understand the economic aspect of the relationship between the highbrow and the Blimp. He does not see that the map is painted red chiefly in order that the coolie may be exploited. Instead of the coolie he sees the Indian Civil Servant; but even on that plane his grasp of function, of who protects whom, is very sound. He sees clearly that men can only be highly civilized while other men, inevitably less civilized, are there to guard and feed them.

How far does Kipling really identify himself with the administrators, soldiers and engineers whose praises he sings? Not so completely as is sometimes assumed. He had travelled very widely while he was still a young man, he had grown up with a brilliant mind in mainly philistine surroundings, and some streak in him that may have been partly neurotic led him to prefer the active man to the sensitive man. The nineteenth-century Anglo-Indians, to name the least sympathetic of his idols, were at any rate people who did things. It may be that all that they did was evil, but they changed the face of the earth (it is instructive to look at a map of Asia and compare the railway system of India with that of the surrounding countries), whereas they could have achieved nothing, could not have maintained themselves in power for a single week, if the normal Anglo-Indian outlook had been that of, say, E.M. Forster. Tawdry and shallow though it is, Kipling's is the only literary picture that we possess of nineteenth-century Anglo-India, and he could only make it because he was just coarse enough to be able to exist and keep his mouth shut in clubs and regimental messes. But he did not greatly resemble the people he admired. I know from several private sources that many of the Anglo-Indians who were Kipling's contemporaries did not like or approve of him. They said, no doubt truly, that he knew nothing about India, and on the other hand, he was from their point of view too much of a highbrow. While in India he tended to mix with "the wrong" people, and because of his dark complexion he was wrongly suspected of having a streak of Asiatic blood. Much in his development is traceable to his having been born in India and having left school early. With a slightly different background he might have been a good novelist or a superlative writer of music-hall songs. But how true is it that he was a vulgar flag waver, a sort of publicity agent for Cecil Rhodes?* It is true, but it is not true that he was a yes-man or a time server. After his early days, if then, he never courted public opinion. Mr Eliot says that what is held against him is that he expressed unpopular views in a popular style. This narrows the issue by assuming that "unpopular" means unpopular with the intelligentsia, but it is a fact that Kipling's "message" was one that the big public did not want, and, indeed, has never accepted. The mass of the people, in the nineties as now, were anti-militarist, bored by the Empire and only unconsciously patriotic. Kipling's official admirers are and were the "service" middle class, the people who read *Blackwood's*. In the stupid early years of this century, the Blimps, having at last discovered someone who could be called a poet and who was on their side, set Kipling on a pedestal, and some of his more sententious poems, such as 'If—',* were given almost biblical status. But it is doubtful whether the Blimps have ever read him with attention, any more than they have read the Bible. Much of what he says they could not possibly approve. Few people who have criticized England from the inside have said bitterer things about her than this gutter patriot. As a rule it is the British working class that he is attacking, but not always. That phrase about "the flannelled fools at the wicket and the muddied oafs at the goal"* sticks like an arrow to this day, and it is aimed at the Eton and Harrow match as well as the Cup-Tie Final. Some of the verses he wrote about the Boer War have a curiously modern ring, so far as their subject matter goes. 'Stellenbosch', which must have been written about 1902, sums up what every intelligent infantry officer was saying in 1918, or is saying now, for that matter.

Kipling's romantic ideas about England and the Empire might not have mattered if he could have held them without having the class prejudices which at that time went with them. If one examines his best and most representative work, his soldier's poems, especially *Barrack-Room Ballads*, one notices that what more than anything else spoils them is an underlying air of patronage. Kipling idealizes the army officer, especially the junior officer, and that to an idiotic extent, but the private soldier, though lovable and romantic, has to be a comic. He is always made to speak in a sort of stylized cockney, not very broad but with all the aitches and final gs carefully omitted. Very often the result is as embarrassing as the humorous recitation at a church social. And this accounts for the curious fact that one can often improve Kipling's poems, make them less facetious and less blatant, by simply going through them and transplanting them from cockney into standard speech. This is especially true of his refrains, which often have a truly lyrical quality. Two examples will do (one is about a funeral and the other about a wedding):

> So it's knock out your pipes and follow me!
> And it's finish up your swipes and follow me!
>   Oh, hark to the big drum calling.
>   Follow me – follow me home!*

And again:

> Cheer for the Sergeant's wedding –
>   Give them one cheer more!
> Grey gun-horses in the lando,
>   And a rogue is married to a whore!*

Here I have restored the aitches etc. Kipling ought to have known better. He ought to have seen that the two closing lines of the first of these stanzas are very beautiful lines, and that ought to have overridden his impulse to make fun of a working man's accent. In the ancient ballads the lord and the peasant speak the same language. This is impossible to Kipling, who is looking down a distorting class perspective, and by a piece of poetic justice one of his best lines is spoilt – for "follow me 'ome" is much uglier than "follow me home".

But even where it makes no difference musically the facetiousness of his stage cockney dialect is irritating. However, he is more often quoted aloud than read on the printed page, and most people instinctively make the necessary alterations when they quote him.

Can one imagine any private soldier, in the nineties or now, reading *Barrack-Room Ballads* and feeling that here was a writer who spoke for him? It is very hard to do so. Any soldier capable of reading a book of verse would notice at once that Kipling is almost unconscious of the class war that goes on in an army as much as elsewhere. It is not only that he thinks the soldier comic, but that he thinks him patriotic, feudal, a ready admirer of his officers and proud to be a soldier of the Queen. Of course that is partly true, or battles could not be fought, but "What have I done for thee, England, my England?"* is essentially a middle-class query. Almost any working man would follow it up immediately with "What has England done for me?" In so far as Kipling grasps this, he simply sets it down to "the intense selfishness of the lower classes"* (his own phrase). When he is writing not of British but of "loyal" Indians he carries the "*Salaam, sahib*" motif to sometimes disgusting lengths. Yet it remains true that he has far more interest in the common soldier, far more anxiety that he shall get a fair deal, than most of the "liberals" of his day or our own. He sees that the soldier is neglected, meanly underpaid and hypocritically despised by the people whose incomes he safeguards. "I came to realize," he says in his posthumous memoirs, "the bare horrors of the private's life, and the unnecessary torments he endured."* He is accused of glorifying war, and perhaps he does so, but not in the usual manner, by pretending that war is a sort of football match. Like most people capable of writing battle poetry, Kipling had never been in battle, but his vision of war is realistic. He knows that bullets hurt, that under fire everyone is terrified, that the ordinary soldier never knows what the war is about or what is happening except in his own corner of the battlefield, and that British troops, like other troops, frequently run away:

> I 'eard the knives be'ind me, but I dursn't face my man.
> Nor I don't know where I went to, 'cause I didn't stop to see,
> Till I 'eard a beggar squealin' out for quarter as 'e ran,
> An' I thought I knew the voice an' – it was me!*

Modernize the style of this, and it might have come out of one of the debunking war books of the 1920s. Or again:

> An' now the hugly bullets come peckin' through the dust,
> An' no one wants to face 'em, but every beggar must;
> So, like a man in irons, which isn't glad to go,
> They moves 'em off by companies uncommon stiff an' slow.*

Compare this with:

> "Forward the Light Brigade!"
> Was there a man dismayed?
> No! though the soldier knew
> Someone had blundered.*

If anything, Kipling overdoes the horrors, for the wars of his youth were hardly wars at all by our standards. Perhaps that is due to the neurotic strain in him, the hunger for cruelty. But at least he knows that men ordered to attack impossible objectives *are* dismayed, and also that fourpence a day is not a generous pension.

How complete or truthful a picture has Kipling left us of the long-service, mercenary army of the late nineteenth century? One must say of this, as of what Kipling wrote about nineteenth-century Anglo-India, that it is not only the best but almost the only literary picture we have. He has put on record an immense amount of stuff that one could otherwise only gather from verbal tradition or from unreadable regimental histories. Perhaps his picture of army life seems fuller and more accurate than it is because any middle-class English person is likely to know enough to fill up the gaps. At any rate, reading the essay on Kipling that Mr Edmund Wilson has just published or is just about to publish,* I was struck by the number of things that are boringly familiar to us and seem to be barely intelligible to an American. But from the body of Kipling's early work there does seem to emerge a vivid and not seriously misleading picture of the old pre-machine-gun army – the sweltering barracks in Gibraltar or Lucknow, the red coats, the pipeclayed belts and the pillbox hats, the beer, the fights, the floggings, hangings and crucifixions, the bugle calls, the smell of oats and horse piss, the bellowing sergeants with foot-long moustaches, the bloody skirmishes, invariably mismanaged, the crowded troopships, the cholera-stricken camps, the "native" concubines, the ultimate death in the workhouse. It is a crude, vulgar picture, in which a patriotic music-hall turn seems to have got mixed up with one of Zola's gorier passages, but from it future generations will be able to gather some idea of what a long-term volunteer army was like. On about the same level they will be able to learn something of British India in the days when motor cars and refrigerators were unheard of. It is an error to imagine that we might have had better books on these subjects if, for example, George Moore, or Gissing, or Thomas Hardy, had had Kipling's opportunities. That is the kind of accident that cannot happen. It was not possible that nineteenth-century England should produce a book like *War and Peace*, or like Tolstoy's minor stories of army life, such as 'Sebastopol' or 'The Cossacks', not because the talent was necessarily lacking but because no one with sufficient sensitiveness to write such books would ever have made the appropriate contacts. Tolstoy lived in a great military empire in which it seemed natural for almost any young man of family to spend a few years in the army, whereas the British Empire was and still is demilitarized to a degree which Continental observers find almost incredible. Civilized men do not readily move away from the centres of civilization, and in most languages there is a great dearth of what one might call colonial literature. It took a very improbable combination of circumstances to produce Kipling's gaudy tableau, in which Private Ortheris and Mrs Hauksbee* pose against a background of palm trees to the sound of temple bells, and one necessary circumstance was that Kipling himself was only half civilized.

Kipling is the only English writer of our time who has added phrases to the language. The phrases and neologisms which we take over and use without remembering their origin do not always come from writers we admire. It is strange, for instance, to hear the Nazi broadcasters referring to the Russian soldiers as "robots", thus unconsciously borrowing a word from a Czech democrat whom they would have killed if they could have laid hands on him. Here are half a dozen phrases coined by Kipling which one sees quoted in leaderettes in the gutter press or overhears in saloon bars from people who have barely heard his name. It will be seen that they all have a certain characteristic in common:

East is East, and West is West.

The white man's burden.

What do they know of England who only England know?

The female of the species is more deadly than the male.

Somewhere east of Suez.

Paying the Dane-geld.*

There are various others, including some that have outlived their context by many years. The phrase "killing Kruger with your mouth",* for instance, was current till very recently. It is also possible that it was Kipling who first let loose the use of the word "Huns" for Germans; at any rate he began using it as soon as the guns opened fire in 1914. But what the phrases I have listed above have in common is that they are all of them phrases which one utters semi-derisively (as it might be "For I'm to be Queen o' the May, Mother, I'm to be Queen o' the May"*), but which one is bound to make use of sooner or later. Nothing could exceed the contempt of the *New Statesman*, for instance, for Kipling, but how many times during the Munich period did the *New Statesman* find itself quoting that phrase about paying the Dane-geld?* The fact is that Kipling, apart from his snack-bar wisdom and his gift for packing much cheap picturesqueness into a few words ("palm and pine"* – "east of Suez" – "the road to Mandalay"), is generally talking about things that are of urgent interest. It does not matter, from this point of view, that thinking and decent people generally find themselves on the other side of the fence from him. "White man's burden" instantly conjures up a real problem, even if one feels that it ought to be altered to "black man's burden". One may disagree to the middle of one's bones with the political attitude implied in 'The Islanders', but one cannot say that it is a frivolous attitude. Kipling deals in thoughts which are both vulgar and permanent. This raises the question of his special status as a poet, or verse writer.

Mr Eliot describes Kipling's metrical work as "verse" and not "poetry", but adds that it is "*great* verse", and further qualifies this by saying that a writer can only be described as a "great-verse-writer" if there is some of his work "of which we cannot say whether it is verse or poetry". Apparently Kipling was a versifier who occasionally wrote poems, in which case it was a pity that Mr Eliot did not specify these poems by name. The trouble is that whenever an aesthetic judgement on Kipling's work seems to be called for, Mr Eliot is too much on the defensive to be able to speak plainly. What he does not say, and what I think one ought to start by saying in any discussion of Kipling, is that most of Kipling's verse is so horribly vulgar that it gives one the same sensation as one gets from watching a third-rate music-hall performer recite 'The Pigtail of Wu Fang Fu'* with the purple limelight on his face, *and yet* there is much of it that is capable of giving pleasure to people who know what poetry means. At his worst, and also his most vital, in poems like 'Gunga Din'* or 'Danny Deever', Kipling is almost a shameful pleasure, like the taste for cheap sweets that some people secretly carry into middle life. But even with his best passages one has the same sense of being seduced by something spurious, and yet unquestionably seduced. Unless one is merely a snob and a liar it is impossible to say that no one who cares for poetry could not get any pleasure out of such lines as:

> For the wind is in the palm trees, and the temple bells they say.
> "Come you back, you British soldier, come you back to Mandalay!"*

and yet those lines are not poetry in the same sense as 'Felix Randal' or 'When Icicles Hang by the Wall'* are poetry. One can, perhaps, place Kipling more satisfactorily than by juggling with the words "verse" and "poetry" if one describes him simply as a good bad poet. He is as a poet what Harriet Beecher Stowe* was as a novelist. And the mere existence of work of this kind, which is perceived by generation after generation to be vulgar and yet goes on being read, tells one something about the age we live in.

There is a great deal of good bad poetry in English, all of it, I should say, subsequent to 1790. Examples of good bad poems – I am deliberately choosing diverse ones – are 'The Bridge of Sighs', 'When All the World Is Young, Lad', 'The Charge of the Light Brigade', Bret Harte's 'Dickens in Camp', 'The Burial of Sir John Moore', 'Jenny Kissed Me', 'Keith of Ravelston', 'Casabianca'.* All of these reek of sentimentality, and yet – not these particular poems, perhaps, but poems of this kind, are capable of giving true pleasure to people who can see clearly what is wrong with them. One could fill a fair-sized anthology with good bad poems, if it were not for the significant fact that good bad poetry is usually too well known to be worth reprinting. It is no use pretending that in an age like our own, "good" poetry can have any genuine popularity. It is, and must be, the cult of a very few people, the least tolerated of the arts. Perhaps that statement needs a certain amount of qualification. True poetry can sometimes be acceptable to the mass of the people when it disguises itself as something else. One can see an example of this in the folk poetry that England still possesses, certain nursery rhymes and mnemonic rhymes, for instance, and the songs that soldiers make up, including the words that go to some of the bugle calls. But in general ours is a civilization in which the very word "poetry" evokes a hostile snigger or, at best, the sort of frozen disgust that most people feel when they hear the word "God". If you are good at playing the concertina you could probably go into the nearest public bar and get yourself an appreciative audience within five minutes. But what would be the attitude of that same audience if you suggested reading them Shakespeare's sonnets, for instance? Good bad poetry, however, can get across to the most unpromising audiences if the right atmosphere has been worked up beforehand. Some months back Churchill produced a great effect by quoting Clough's 'Endeavour'* in one of his broadcast speeches. I listened to this speech among people who could certainly not be accused of caring for poetry, and I am convinced that the lapse into verse impressed them and did not embarrass them. But not even Churchill could have got away with it if he had quoted anything much better than this.

In so far as a writer of verse can be popular, Kipling has been and probably still is popular. In his own lifetime some of his poems travelled far beyond the bounds of the reading public, beyond the world of school prize days, Boy Scout singsongs, limp-leather editions, pokerwork and calendars, and out in the yet vaster world of the music halls. Nevertheless, Mr Eliot thinks it worthwhile to edit him, thus confessing to a taste which others share but are not always honest enough to mention. The fact that such a thing as good bad poetry can exist is a sign of the emotional overlap between the intellectual and the ordinary man. The intellectual *is* different from the ordinary man, but only in certain sections of his personality, and even then not all the time. But what is the peculiarity of a good bad poem? A good bad poem is a graceful monument to the obvious. It records in memorable form – for verse is a mnemonic device, among other things – some emotion which very nearly every human being can share. The merit of a poem like 'When All the World Is Young, Lad' is that, however sentimental it may be, its sentiment is "true" sentiment in the sense that you are bound to find yourself thinking the thought it expresses sooner or later – and then, if you happen to know the poem, it will come back into your mind and seem better than it did before. Such poems are a kind of rhyming proverb, and it is a fact that definitely popular poetry is usually gnomic or sententious. One example from Kipling will do:

> White hands cling to the bridle rein,
> Slipping the spur from the booted heel;
> Tenderest voices cry "Turn again!"
> Red lips tarnish the scabbarded steel:
> Down to Gehenna or up to the Throne,
> He travels the fastest who travels alone.*

There is a vulgar thought vigorously expressed. It may not be true, but at any rate it is a thought that everyone thinks. Sooner or later you will have occasion to feel that he travels the fastest who travels alone, and there the thought is, ready made and, as it were, waiting for you. So the chances are that, having once heard this line, you will remember it.

One reason for Kipling's power as a good bad poet I have already suggested – his sense of responsibility, which made it possible for him to have a world view, even though it happened to be a false one. Although he had no direct connection with any political party, Kipling was a conservative, a thing that does not exist nowadays. Those who now call themselves conservatives are either liberals, fascists or the accomplices of fascists. He identified himself with the ruling power and not with the opposition. In a gifted writer this seems to us strange and even disgusting, but it did have the advantage of giving Kipling a certain grip on reality. The ruling power is always faced with the question, "In such and such circumstances, what would you *do*?", whereas the opposition is not obliged to take responsibility or make any real decisions. Where it is a permanent and pensioned opposition, as in England, the quality of its thought deteriorates accordingly. Moreover, anyone who starts out with a pessimistic, reactionary view of life tends to be justified by events, for utopia never arrives and "the gods of the copybook headings",* as Kipling himself put it, always return. Kipling sold out to the British governing class, not financially but emotionally. This warped his political judgement, for the British ruling class were not what he imagined, and it led him into abysses of folly and snobbery, but he gained a corresponding advantage from having at least tried to imagine what action and responsibility are like. It is a great thing in his favour that he is not witty, not "daring", has no wish to *épater les bourgeois*.* He dealt largely in platitudes, and since we live in a world of platitudes, much of what he said sticks. Even his worst follies seem less shallow and less irritating than the "enlightened" utterances of the same period, such as Wilde's epigrams or the collection of cracker mottoes at the end of *Man and Superman*.*

The Rediscovery of Europe*

When I was a small boy and was taught history – very badly, of course, as nearly everyone in England is – I used to think of history as a sort of long scroll with thick black lines ruled across it at intervals. Each of these lines marked the end of what was called a "period", and you were given to understand that what came afterwards was completely different from what had gone before. It was almost like a clock striking. For instance, in 1499 you were still in the Middle Ages, with knights in plate armour riding at one another with long lances, and then suddenly the clock struck 1500, and you were in something called the Renaissance, and everyone wore ruffs and doublets and was busy robbing treasure ships on the Spanish Main. There was another very thick black line drawn at the year 1700. After that it was the eighteenth century, and people suddenly stopped being Cavaliers and Roundheads and became extraordinarily elegant gentlemen in knee breeches and three-cornered hats. They all powdered their hair, took snuff and talked in exactly balanced sentences, which seemed all the more stilted because for some reason I didn't understand they pronounced most of their Ss as Fs. The whole of history was like that in my mind – a series of completely different periods changing abruptly at the end of a century, or at any rate at some sharply defined date.

Now in fact these abrupt transitions don't happen, either in politics, manners or literature. Each age lives on into the next – it must do so, because there are innumerable human lives spanning every gap. And yet there are such things as periods. We feel our own age to be deeply different from, for instance, the early Victorian period, and an eighteenth-century sceptic like Gibbon would have felt himself to be among savages if you had suddenly thrust him into the Middle Ages. Every now and again something happens – no doubt it's ultimately traceable to changes in industrial technique, though the connection isn't always obvious – and the whole spirit and tempo of life changes, and people acquire a new outlook which reflects itself in their political behaviour, their manners, their architecture, their literature and everything else. No one could write a poem like Gray's 'Elegy in a Country Churchyard'* today, for instance, and no one could have written Shakespeare's lyrics in the age of Gray. These things belong in different periods. And though, of course, those black lines across the page of history are an illusion, there are times when the transition is quite rapid, sometimes rapid enough for it to be possible to give it a fairly accurate date. One can say without grossly oversimplifying, "About such and such a year, such and such a style of literature began." If I were asked for the starting point of modern literature – and the fact that we still call it "modern" shows that this particular period isn't finished yet – I should put it at 1917, the year in which T.S. Eliot published his poem 'Prufrock'. At any rate that date isn't more than five years out. It is certain that about the end of the last war the literary climate changed, the typical writer came to be quite a different person, and the best books of the subsequent period seemed to exist in a different world from the best books of only four or five years before.

To illustrate what I mean, I ask you to compare in your mind two poems which haven't any connection with one another, but which will do for purposes of comparison because each is entirely typical of its period. Compare, for instance, one of Eliot's characteristic earlier poems with a poem of Rupert Brooke, who was, I should say, the most admired English poet in the years before 1914. Perhaps the most representative of Brooke's poems are his patriotic ones, written in the early days of the war. A good one is the sonnet beginning

> If I should die, think only this of me:
> That there's some corner of a foreign field
> That is for ever England.*

Now read side by side with this one of Eliot's Sweeney poems; for example, 'Sweeney among the Nightingales' – you know,

> The circles of the stormy moon
> Slide westward toward the River Plate.*

As I say, these poems have no connection in theme or anything else, but it's possible in a way to compare them, because each is representative of its own time and each seemed a good poem when it was written. The second still seems a good poem now.

Not only the technique but the whole spirit, the implied outlook on life, the intellectual paraphernalia of these poems are abysmally different. Between the young Englishman with a public-school and university background, going out enthusiastically to die for his country with his head full of English lanes, wild roses and what not, and the rather jaded cosmopolitan American, getting glimpses of eternity in some slightly squalid restaurant in the Latin Quarter of Paris, there is a huge gulf. That might be only an individual difference, but the point is that you come upon rather the same kind of difference, a difference that raises the same comparisons, if you read side by side almost any two characteristic writers of the two periods. It's the same with the novelists as with the poets – Joyce, Lawrence, Huxley and Wyndham Lewis on the one side, and Wells, Bennett and Galsworthy on the other, for instance. The newer writers are immensely less prolific than the older ones, more scrupulous, more interested in technique, less optimistic and, in general, less confident in their attitude to life. But more than that, you have all the time the feeling that their intellectual and aesthetic background is different, rather as you do when you compare a nineteenth-century French writer such as, say, Flaubert with a nineteenth-century English writer like Dickens. The Frenchman seems enormously more sophisticated than the Englishman, though he isn't necessarily a better writer because of that. But let me go back a bit and consider what English literature was like in the days before 1914.

The giants of that time were Thomas Hardy – who, however, had stopped writing novels some time earlier – Shaw, Wells, Kipling, Bennett, Galsworthy and, somewhat different from the others – not an Englishman, remember, but a Pole who chose to write in English – Joseph Conrad. There were A.E. Housman (*A Shropshire Lad*), and the various Georgian poets, Rupert Brooke and the others. There were also the innumerable comic writers. Sir James Barrie, W.W. Jacobs, Barry Pain* and many others. If you read all those writers I've just mentioned, you would get a not misleading picture of the English mind before 1914. There were other literary tendencies at work – there were various Irish writers, for instance, and in a quite different vein, much nearer to our own time, there was the American novelist Henry James – but the mainstream was the one I've indicated. But what is the common denominator between writers who are individually as far apart as Bernard Shaw and A.E. Housman, or Thomas Hardy and H.G. Wells? I think the basic fact about nearly all English writers of that time is their complete unawareness of anything outside the contemporary English scene. Some are better writers than others, some are politically conscious and some aren't, but they are all alike in being untouched by any European influence. This is true even of novelists like Bennett and Galsworthy, who derived in a very superficial sense from French and perhaps Russian models. All of these writers have a background of ordinary, respectable, middle-class English life, and a half-conscious belief that this kind of life will go on for ever, getting more humane and more enlightened all the time. Some of them, like Hardy and Housman, are pessimistic in outlook, but they all at least believe that what is called progress would be desirable if it were possible. Also – a thing that generally goes with lack of aesthetic sensibility – they are all uninterested in the past, at any rate the remote past. It is very rare to find in a writer of that time anything we should now regard as a sense of history. Even Thomas Hardy, when he attempts a huge poetic drama based on the Napoleonic Wars – *The Dynasts*,* it's called – sees it all from the angle of a patriotic school textbook. Still more, they're all aesthetically uninterested in the past. Arnold Bennett, for instance, wrote a great deal of literary criticism, and it's clear that he is almost unable to see any merit in any book earlier than the nineteenth century, and indeed hasn't much interest in any writer other than his contemporaries. To Bernard Shaw most of the past is simply a mess which ought to be swept away in the name of progress, hygiene, efficiency and what not. H.G. Wells, though later on he was to write a history of the world, looks at the past with the same sort of surprised disgust as a civilized man contemplating a tribe of cannibals. All of these people, whether they liked their own age or not, at least thought it was better than what had gone before, and took the literary standards of their own time for granted. The basis of all Bernard Shaw's attacks on Shakespeare is really the charge – quite true, of course – that Shakespeare wasn't an enlightened member of the Fabian Society. If any of these writers had been told that the writers immediately subsequent to them would hark back to the English poets of the sixteenth and seventeenth centuries, to the French poets of the mid-nineteenth century and to the philosophers of the Middle Ages, they would have thought it a kind of dilettantism.

But now look at the writers who begin to attract notice – some of them had begun writing rather earlier, of course – immediately after the last war: Joyce, Eliot, Pound, Huxley, Lawrence, Wyndham Lewis. Your first impression of them, compared with the others – this is true even of Lawrence – is that something has been punctured. To begin with, the notion of progress has gone by the board. They don't any longer believe that men are getting better and better by having lower mortality rates, more effective birth control, better plumbing, more aeroplanes and faster motor cars. Nearly all of them are homesick for the remote past, or some period of the past, from D.H. Lawrence's ancient Etruscans onwards. All of them are politically reactionary, or at best are uninterested in politics. None of them cares twopence about the various hole-and-corner reforms which had seemed important to their predecessors, such as female suffrage, temperance reform, birth control or prevention of cruelty to animals. All of them are more friendly, or at least less hostile, towards the Christian churches than the previous generation had been. And nearly all of them seem to be aesthetically alive in a way that hardly any English writer since the Romantic Revival had been.

Now, one can best illustrate what I have been saying by means of individual examples, that is, by comparing outstanding books of more or less comparable type in the two periods. As a first example, compare H.G. Wells's short stories – there's a large number of them collected together under the title of *The Country of the Blind* – with D.H. Lawrence's short stories, such as those in *England, My England* and *The Prussian Officer*.*

This isn't an unfair comparison, since each of these writers was at his best, or somewhere near his best, in the short story, and each of them was expressing a new vision of life which had a great effect on the young of his generation. The ultimate subject matter of H.G. Wells's stories is, first of all, scientific discovery, and beyond that the petty snobberies and tragicomedies of contemporary English life, especially lower-middle-class life. His basic "message", to use an expression I don't like, is that science can solve all the ills that humanity is heir to, but that man is at present too blind to see the possibility of his own powers. The alternation between ambitious utopian themes and light comedy, almost in the W.W. Jacobs vein, is very marked in Wells's work. He writes about journeys to the moon and to the bottom of the sea, and also he writes about small shopkeepers dodging bankruptcy and fighting to keep their end up in the frightful snobbery of provincial towns. The connecting link is Wells's belief in science. He is saying all the time, if only that small shopkeeper could acquire a scientific outlook, his troubles would be ended. And of course he believes that this is going to happen, probably in the quite near future. A few more million pounds for scientific research, a few more generations scientifically educated, a few more superstitions shovelled into the dustbin, and the job is done. Now, if you turn to Lawrence's stories, you don't find this belief in science – rather a hostility towards it, if anything – and you don't find any marked interest in the future, certainly not in a rationalized hedonistic future of the kind that Wells deals in. You don't even find the notion that the small shopkeeper, or any of the other victims of our society, would be better off if he were better educated. What you do find is a persistent implication that man has thrown away his birthright by becoming civilized. The ultimate subject matter of nearly all Lawrence's books is the failure of contemporary men, especially in the English-speaking countries, to live their lives intensely enough. Naturally he fixes first on their sexual lives, and it is a fact that most of Lawrence's books centre round sex. But he isn't, as is sometimes supposed, demanding more of what people call sexual liberty. He is completely disillusioned about that, and he hates the so-called sophistication of bohemian intellectuals just as much as he hates the puritanism of the middle class. What he is saying is simply that modern men aren't fully alive, whether they fail through having too narrow standards or through not having any. Granted that they can be fully alive, he doesn't much care what social or political or economic system they live under. He takes the structure of existing society, with its class distinctions and so on, almost for granted in his stories, and doesn't show any very urgent wish to change it. All he asks is that men shall live more simply, nearer to the earth, with more sense of the magic of things like vegetation, fire, water, sex, blood, than they can in a world of celluloid and concrete where the gramophones never stop playing. He imagines – quite likely he is wrong – that savages or primitive peoples live more intensely than civilized men, and he builds up a mythical figure who is not far from being the Noble Savage over again. Finally, he projects these virtues onto the Etruscans, an ancient pre-Roman people who lived in northern Italy and about whom we don't, in fact, know anything. From the point of view of H.G. Wells all this abandonment of science and progress, this actual wish to revert to the primitive, is simply heresy and nonsense. And yet one must admit that whether Lawrence's view of life is true or whether it is perverted, it is at least an advance on the science worship of H.G. Wells or the shallow Fabian progressivism of writers like Bernard Shaw. It is an advance in the sense that it results from seeing through the other attitude and not from falling short of it. Partly that was the effect of the war of 1914–18, which succeeded in debunking both science, progress and civilized man. Progress had finally ended in the biggest massacre in history. Science was something that created bombing planes and poison gas; civilized man, as it turned out, was ready to behave worse than any savage when the pinch came. But Lawrence's discontent with modern machine civilization would have been the same, no doubt, if the war of 1914–18 had never happened.

Now I want to make another comparison, between James Joyce's great novel *Ulysses*, and John Galsworthy's at any rate very large novel sequence *The Forsyte Saga*.* This time it isn't a fair comparison; in effect it's a comparison between a good book and a bad one, and it also isn't quite correct chronologically, because the later parts of *The Forsyte Saga* were written in the 1920s. But the parts of it that anyone is likely to remember were written about 1910, and for my purpose the comparison is relevant, because both Joyce and Galsworthy are making efforts to cover an enormous canvas and get the spirit and social history of a whole epoch between the covers of a single book. *The Man of Property** may not seem to us *now* a very profound criticism of society, but it seemed so to its contemporaries, as you can see by what they wrote about it.

Joyce wrote *Ulysses* in the seven years between 1914 and 1921, working away all through the war, to which he probably paid little or no attention, and earning a miserable living as a teacher of languages in Italy and Switzerland. He was quite ready to work seven years in poverty and complete obscurity so as to get his great book onto paper. But what is it that it was so urgently important for him to express? Parts of *Ulysses* aren't very easily intelligible, but from the book as a whole you get two main impressions. The first is that Joyce is interested to the point of obsession with technique. This has been one of the main characteristics of modern literature, though more recently it has been a diminishing one. You get a parallel development in the plastic arts, painters, and even sculptors, being more and more interested in the material they work in, in the brush-marks of a picture, for instance, as against its design, let alone its subject matter. Joyce is interested in mere words, the sounds and associations of words, even the pattern of words on the paper, in a way that wasn't the case with any of the preceding generation of writers, except to some extent the Polish-English writer Joseph Conrad. With Joyce you are back to the conception of style, of fine writing, or poetic writing, perhaps even to purple passages. A writer like Bernard Shaw, on the other hand, would have said as a matter of course that the sole use of words is to express exact meanings as shortly as possible. And apart from this technical obsession, the other main theme of *Ulysses* is the squalor, even the meaninglessness of modern life after the triumph of the machine and the collapse of religious belief. Joyce – an Irishman, remember, and it's worth noting that the best English writers during the 1920s were in many cases not Englishmen – is writing as a Catholic who has lost his faith but has retained the mental framework which he acquired in his Catholic childhood and boyhood. *Ulysses*, which is a very long novel, is a description of the events of a single day, as seen mostly through the eyes of an out-at-elbow Jewish commercial traveller. At the time when the book came out there was a great outcry and Joyce was accused of deliberately exploiting the sordid, but as a matter of fact, considering what everyday human life is like when you contemplate it in detail, it doesn't seem that he overdid either the squalor or the silliness of the day's events. What you do feel all through, however, is the conviction from which Joyce can't escape, that the whole of this modern world which he is describing has no meaning in it now that the teachings of the Church are no longer credible. He is yearning after the religious faith which the two or three generations preceding him had had to fight against in the name of religious liberty. But finally the main interest of the book is technical. Quite a considerable proportion of it consists of pastiche or parody – parodies of everything from the Irish legends of the Bronze Age down to contemporary newspaper reports. And one can see there that, like all the characteristic writers of his time, Joyce doesn't derive from the English nineteenth-century writers but from Europe and from the remoter past. Part of his mind is in the Bronze Age, another part in the England of Elizabeth. The twentieth century, with its hygiene and its motor cars, doesn't particularly appeal to him.

Now look again at Galsworthy's book, *The Forsyte Saga*, and you see how comparatively narrow its range is. I have said already that this isn't a fair comparison, and indeed from a strictly literary point of view it's a ridiculous one, but it will do as an illustration, in the sense that both books are intended to give a comprehensive picture of existing society. Well, the thing that strikes one about Galsworthy is that though he's trying to be iconoclastic, he has been utterly unable to move his mind outside the wealthy bourgeois society he is attacking. With only slight modifications he takes all its values for granted. All he conceives to be wrong is that human beings are a little too inhumane, a little too fond of money, and aesthetically not quite sensitive enough. When he sets out to depict what he conceives as the desirable type of human being, it turns out to be simply a cultivated, humanitarian version of the upper-middle-class rentier, the sort of person who in those days used to haunt picture galleries in Italy and subscribe heavily to the Society for the Prevention of Cruelty to Animals. And this fact – the fact that Galsworthy hasn't any really deep aversion to the social types he thinks he is attacking – gives you the clue to his weakness. It is that he has no contact with anything outside contemporary English society. He may think he doesn't like it, but he is part of it. Its money and security, the ring of battleships that separated it from Europe, have been too much for him. At the bottom of his heart he despises foreigners, just as much as any illiterate businessman in Manchester. The feelings you have with Joyce or Eliot, or even Lawrence, that they have got the whole of human history inside their heads and can look outwards from their own place and time towards Europe and the past, isn't to be found in Galsworthy or in any characteristic English writer in the period before 1914.

Finally, one more brief comparison. Compare almost any of H.G. Wells's utopia books, for instance *A Modern Utopia*, or *The Dream*, or *Men Like Gods*,* with Aldous Huxley's *Brave New World*. Again it's rather the same contrast, the contrast between the overconfident and the deflated, between the man who believes innocently in progress and the man who happens to have been born later and has therefore lived to see that progress, as it was conceived in the early days of the aeroplane, is just as much of a swindle as reaction.

The obvious explanation of this sharp difference between the dominant writers before and after the war of 1914–18 is the war itself. Some such development would have happened in any case as the insufficiency of modern materialistic civilization revealed itself, but the war speeded the process, partly by showing how very shallow the veneer of civilization is, partly by making England less prosperous and therefore less isolated. After 1918 you couldn't live in such a narrow and padded world as you did when Britannia ruled not only the waves but also the markets. One effect of the ghastly history of the last twenty years has been to make a great deal of ancient literature seem much more modern. A lot that has happened in Germany since the rise of Hitler might have come straight out of the later volumes of Gibbon's *Decline and Fall of the Roman Empire*. Recently I saw Shakespeare's *King John* acted – the first time I had seen it, because it is a play which isn't acted very often. When I had read it as a boy it seemed to me archaic, something dug out of a history book and not having anything to do with our own time. Well, when I saw it acted, what with its intrigues and double-crossings, non-aggression pacts, quislings, people changing sides in the middle of a battle and what not, it seemed to me extraordinarily up to date. And it was rather the same thing that happened in the literary development between 1910 and 1920. The prevailing temper of the time gave a new reality to all sorts of themes which had seemed out of date and puerile when Bernard Shaw and his Fabians were – so they thought – turning the world into a sort of super garden city. Themes like revenge, patriotism, exile, persecution, race hatred, religious faith, loyalty, leader worship, suddenly seemed real again. Tamerlane and Genghis Khan seem credible figures now, and Machiavelli seems a serious thinker, as they didn't in 1910. We have got out of a backwater and back into history. I haven't any unqualified admiration for the writers of the early 1920s, the writers among whom Eliot and Joyce are chief names. Those who followed them have had to undo a great deal of what they did. Their revulsion from a shallow conception of progress drove them politically in the wrong direction, and it isn't an accident that Ezra Pound, for instance, is now shouting anti-Semitism on the Rome radio. But one must concede that their writings are more grown-up, and have a wider scope, than what went immediately before them. They broke the cultural circle in which England had existed for something like a century. They re-established contact with Europe, and they brought back the sense of history and the possibility of tragedy. On that basis all subsequent English literature that matters twopence has rested, and the development that Eliot and the others started, back in the closing years of the last war, has not yet run its course.

Pacifism and the War*

Since I don't suppose you want to fill an entire number of *P.R.* with squalid controversies imported from across the Atlantic, I will lump together the various letters you have sent on to me (from Messrs Savage, Woodcock and Comfort), as the central issue in all of them is the same. But I must afterwards deal separately with some points of fact raised in various of the letters.

Pacifism. Pacifism is objectively pro-fascist. This is elementary common sense. If you hamper the war effort of one side you automatically help that of the other. Nor is there any real way of remaining outside such a war as the present one. In practice, "he that is not with me is against me". The idea that you can somehow remain aloof from and superior to the struggle, while living on food which British sailors have to risk their lives to bring you, is a bourgeois illusion bred of money and security. Mr Savage remarks that "according to this type of reasoning, a German or Japanese pacifist would be 'objectively pro-British'." But of course he would be! That is why pacifist activities are not permitted in those countries (in both of them the penalty is, or can be, beheading) while both the Germans and the Japanese do all they can to encourage the spread of pacifism in British and American territories. The Germans even run a spurious "freedom" station which serves out pacifist propaganda indistinguishable from that of the PPU. They would stimulate pacifism in Russia as well if they could, but in that case they have tougher babies to deal with. In so far as it takes effect at all, pacifist propaganda can only be effective *against* those countries where a certain amount of freedom of speech is still permitted; in other words it is helpful to totalitarianism.

I am not interested in pacifism as a "moral phenomenon". If Mr Savage and others imagine that one can somehow "overcome" the German army by lying on one's back, let them go on imagining it, but let them also wonder occasionally whether this is not an illusion due to security, too much money and a simple ignorance of the way in which things actually happen. As an ex-Indian Civil Servant, it always makes me shout with laughter to hear, for instance, Gandhi named as an example of the success of non-violence. As long as twenty years ago it was cynically admitted in Anglo-Indian circles that Gandhi was very useful to the British government. So he will be to the Japanese if they get there. Despotic governments can stand "moral force" till the cows come home; what they fear is physical force. But though not much interested in the "theory" of pacifism, I *am* interested in the psychological processes by which pacifists who have started out with an alleged horror of violence end up with a marked tendency to be fascinated by the success and power of Nazism. Even pacifists who wouldn't own to any such fascination are beginning to claim that a Nazi victory is desirable in itself. In the letter you sent on to me, Mr Comfort considers that an artist in occupied territory ought to "protest against such evils as he sees", but considers that this is best done by "temporarily accepting the status quo" (like Déat or Bergery,* for instance?). A few weeks back he was hoping for a Nazi victory because of the stimulating effect it would have upon the arts:

> As far as I can see, no therapy short of complete military defeat has any chance of re-establishing the common stability of literature and of the man in the street. One can imagine the greater the adversity the greater the sudden realization of a stream of imaginative work, and the greater the sudden catharsis of poetry, from the isolated interpretation of war as calamity to the realization of the imaginative and actual tragedy of Man. When we have access again to the literature of the war years in France, Poland and Czechoslovakia. I am confident that that is what we shall find.
>
> (FROM A LETTER TO *Horizon*)

I pass over the money-sheltered ignorance capable of believing that literary life is still going on in, for instance, Poland, and remark merely that statements like this justify me in saying that our English pacifists are tending towards active pro-fascism. But I don't particularly object to that. What I object to is the intellectual cowardice of people who are objectively and to some extent emotionally pro-fascist, but who don't care to say so and take refuge behind the formula "I am just as anti-fascist as anyone, but..." The result of this is that so-called peace propaganda is just as dishonest and intellectually disgusting as war propaganda. Like war propaganda, it concentrates on putting forward a "case", obscuring the opponent's point of view and avoiding awkward questions. The line normally followed is "Those who fight against fascism go fascist themselves". In order to evade the quite obvious objections that can be raised to this, the following propaganda-tricks are used:

1. The fascizing processes occurring in Britain as a result of war are systematically exaggerated.

2. The actual record of fascism, especially its pre-war history, is ignored or pooh-poohed as "propaganda". Discussion of what the world would actually be like if the Axis dominated it is evaded.

3. Those who want to struggle against fascism are accused of being wholehearted defenders of capitalist "democracy". The fact that the rich everywhere tend to be pro-fascist and the working class are nearly always anti-fascist is hushed up.

4. It is tacitly pretended that the war is only between Britain and Germany. Mention of Russia and China, and their fate if fascism is permitted to win, is avoided. (You won't find one word about Russia or China in the three letters you sent to me.)

Now as to one or two points of fact which I must deal with if your correspondents' letters are to be printed in full.

My past and present. Mr Woodcock tries to discredit me by saying that (a) I once served in the Indian Imperial Police, (b) I have written articles for the *Adelphi* and was mixed up with the Trotskyists in Spain, and (c) that I am at the BBC "conducting British propaganda to fox the Indian masses". With regard to (a), it is quite true that I served five years in the Indian Police. It is also true that I gave up that job, partly because it didn't suit me but mainly because I would not any longer be a servant of imperialism. I am against imperialism because I know something about it from the inside. The whole history of this is to be found in my writings, including a novel which I think I can claim was a kind of prophecy of what happened this year in Burma.* (b) Of course I have written for the *Adelphi*. Why not? I once wrote an article for a vegetarian paper. Does that make me a vegetarian? I was associated with the Trotskyists in Spain. It was chance that I was serving in the POUM militia and not another, and I largely disagreed with the POUM "line" and told its leaders so freely, but when they were afterwards accused of pro-fascist activities I defended them as best I could. How does this contradict my present anti-Hitler attitude? It is news to me that Trotskyists are either pacifists or pro-fascists. (c) Does Mr Woodcock really know what kind of stuff I put out in the Indian broadcasts? He does not – though I would be quite glad to tell him about it. He is careful not to mention what other people are associated with these Indian broadcasts. One for instance is Herbert Read, whom he mentions with approval. Others are T.S. Eliot, E.M. Forster, Reginald Reynolds, Stephen Spender, J.B.S. Haldane, Tom Wintringham.* Most of our broadcasters are Indian left-wing intellectuals, from liberals to Trotskyists, some of them bitterly anti-British. They don't do it to "fox the Indian masses" but because they know what a fascist victory would mean to the chances of India's independence. Why not try to find out what I am doing before accusing my good faith?

"Mr Orwell is intellectual-hunting again" (Mr Comfort). I have never attacked "the intellectuals" or "the intelligentsia" en bloc. I have used a lot of ink and done myself a lot of harm by attacking the successive literary cliques which have infested this country, not because they were intellectuals but precisely because they were *not* what I mean by true intellectuals. The life of a clique is about five years and I have been writing long enough to see three of them come and two go – the Catholic gang, the Stalinist gang and the present pacifist or, as they are sometimes nicknamed, fascifist gang. My case against all of them is that they write mentally dishonest propaganda and degrade literary

criticism to mutual arse-licking. But even with these various schools I would differentiate between individuals. I would never think of coupling Christopher Dawson with Arnold Lunn, or Malraux with Palme Dutt, or Max Plowman with the Duke of Bedford.* And even the work of one individual can exist at very different levels. For instance Mr Comfort himself wrote one poem I value greatly ('The Atoll in the Mind'), and I wish he would write more of them instead of lifeless propaganda tracts dressed up as novels. But this letter he has chosen to send you is a different matter. Instead of answering what I have said he tries to prejudice an audience to whom I am little known by a misrepresentation of my general line and sneers about my "status" in England. (A writer isn't judged by his "status", he is judged by his work.) That is on a par with "peace" propaganda which has to avoid mention of Hitler's invasion of Russia, and it is not what I mean by intellectual honesty. It is just because I do take the function of the intelligentsia seriously that I don't like the sneers, libels, parrot phrases and financially profitable back-scratching which flourish in our English literary world, and perhaps in yours also.

Looking Back on the Spanish War*

I

First of all the physical memories, the sounds, the smells and the surfaces of things.

It is curious that more vividly than anything that came afterwards in the Spanish war I remember the week of so-called training that we received before being sent to the front – the huge cavalry barracks in Barcelona with its draughty stables and cobbled yards, the icy cold of the pump where one washed, the filthy meals made tolerable by pannikins of wine, the trousered militiawomen chopping firewood, and the roll-call in the early mornings where my prosaic English name made a sort of comic interlude among the resounding Spanish ones, Manuel González, Pedro Aguilar, Ramón Fenellosa, Roque Ballaster, Jaime Domenech, Sebastián Viltron, Ramón Nuvo Bosch. I name those particular men because I remember the faces of all of them. Except for two who were mere riff-raff and have doubtless become good Falangists by this time, it is probable that all of them are dead. Two of them I know to be dead. The eldest would have been about twenty-five, the youngest sixteen.

One of the essential experiences of war is never being able to escape from disgusting smells of human origin. Latrines are an overworked subject in war literature, and I would not mention them if it were not that the latrine in our barracks did its necessary bit towards puncturing my own illusions about the Spanish Civil War. The Latin type of latrine, at which you have to squat, is bad enough at its best, but these were made of some kind of polished stone so slippery that it was all you could do to keep on your feet. In addition they were always blocked. Now I have plenty of other disgusting things in my memory, but I believe it was these latrines that first brought home to me the thought, so often to recur: "Here we are, soldiers of a revolutionary army, defending democracy against fascism, fighting a war which is *about* something, and the detail of our lives is just as sordid and degrading as it could be in prison, let alone in a bourgeois army." Many other things reinforced this impression later – for instance, the boredom and animal hunger of trench life, the squalid intrigues over scraps of food, the mean, nagging quarrels which people exhausted by lack of sleep indulge in.

The essential horror of army life (whoever has been a soldier will know what I mean by the essential horror of army life) is barely affected by the nature of the war you happen to be fighting in. Discipline, for instance, is ultimately the same in all armies. Orders have to be obeyed and enforced by punishment if necessary, the relationship of officer and man has to be the relationship of superior and inferior. The picture of war set forth in books like *All Quiet on the Western Front* is substantially true. Bullets hurt, corpses stink, men under fire are often so frightened that they wet their trousers. It is true that the social background from which an army springs will colour its training, tactics and general efficiency, and also that the consciousness of being in the right can bolster up morale, though this affects the civilian population more than the troops. (People forget that a soldier anywhere near the front line is usually too hungry, or frightened, or cold, or, above all, too tired to bother about the political origins of the war.) But the laws of nature are not suspended for a "red" army any more than for a "white" one. A louse is a louse and a bomb is a bomb, even though the cause you are fighting for happens to be just.

Why is it worthwhile to point out anything so obvious? Because the bulk of the British and American intelligentsia were manifestly unaware of it then, and are now. Our memories are short nowadays, but look back a bit, dig out the files of *New Masses** or the *Daily Worker*, and just have a look at the romantic warmongering muck that our left-wingers were spilling at that time. All the stale old phrases! And the unimaginative callousness of it! The sang-froid with which London faced the bombing of Madrid! Here I am not bothering about the counter-propagandists of the Right, the Lunns, Garvins* *et hoc genus;** they go without saying. But here were the very people who for twenty years had hooted and jeered at the "glory" of war, at atrocity stories, at patriotism, even at physical courage, coming out with stuff that with the alteration of a few names would have fitted into the *Daily Mail* of 1918. If there was one thing that the British intelligentsia were committed to, it was the debunking version of war, the theory that war is all corpses and latrines and never leads to any good result. Well, the same people who in 1933 sniggered pityingly if you said that in certain circumstances you would fight for your country, in 1937 were denouncing you as a Trotsky-fascist if you suggested that the stories in *New Masses* about freshly wounded men clamouring to get back into the fighting might be exaggerated. And the Left intelligentsia made their swing over from "War is hell" to "War is glorious" not only with no sense of incongruity but almost without any intervening stage. Later the bulk of them were to make other transitions equally violent. There must be a quite large number of people, a sort of central core of the intelligentsia, who approved the "King and Country" declaration in 1935, shouted for a "firm line" against Germany in 1937, supported the People's Convention in 1940, and are demanding a Second Front now.*

As far as the mass of the people go, the extraordinary swings of opinion which occur nowadays, the emotions which can be turned on and off like a tap, are the result of newspaper and radio hypnosis. In the intelligentsia I should say they result rather from money and mere physical safety. At a given moment they may be "pro-war" or "anti-war", but in either case they have no realistic picture of war in their minds. When they enthused over the Spanish war they knew, of course, that people were being killed and that to be killed is unpleasant, but they did feel that for a soldier in the Spanish Republican army the experience of war was somehow not degrading. Somehow the latrines stank less, discipline was less irksome. You have only to glance at the *New Statesman* to see that they believed that; exactly similar blah is being written about the Red Army at this moment. We have become too civilized to grasp the obvious. For the truth is very simple. To survive you often have to fight, and to fight you have to dirty yourself. War is evil, and it is often the lesser evil. Those who take the sword perish by the sword, and those who don't take the sword perish by smelly diseases. The fact that such a platitude is worth writing down shows what the years of rentier capitalism have done to us.

II

In connection with what I have just said, a footnote on atrocities.

I have little direct evidence about the atrocities in the Spanish Civil War. I know that some were committed by the Republicans, and far more (they are still continuing) by the fascists. But what impressed me then, and has impressed me ever since, is that atrocities are believed in or disbelieved in solely on grounds of political predilection. Everyone believes in the atrocities of the enemy and disbelieves in those of his own side, without ever bothering to examine the evidence. Recently I drew up a table of atrocities during the period between 1918 and the present; there was never a year when atrocities were not occurring somewhere or other, and there was hardly a single case when the Left and the Right believed in the same stories simultaneously. And stranger yet, at any moment the situation can suddenly reverse itself and yesterday's proved-to-the-hilt atrocity story can become a ridiculous lie, merely because the political landscape has changed.

In the present war we are in the curious situation that our "atrocity campaign" was done largely before the war started, and done mostly by the Left, the people who normally pride themselves on their incredulity. In the same period the Right, the atrocity-mongers of 1914–18, were gazing at Nazi Germany and flatly refusing to see any evil in it. Then as soon as war broke out it was the pro-Nazis of yesterday who were repeating horror stories, while the anti-Nazis suddenly found themselves doubting whether the Gestapo really existed. Nor was this solely the result of the Russo-German Pact. It was partly because before the war the Left had wrongly believed that Britain and Germany would never fight and were therefore able to be anti-German and anti-British simultaneously; partly also because official war propaganda, with its disgusting hypocrisy and self-righteousness, always tends to make thinking people sympathize with the enemy. Part of the price we paid for the systematic lying of 1914–18 was the exaggerated pro-German reaction which followed. During the years 1918–33 you were hooted at in left-wing circles if you suggested that Germany bore even a fraction of responsibility for the war. In all the denunciations of Versailles I listened to during those years I don't think I ever once heard the question "What would have happened if Germany had won?" even mentioned, let alone discussed. So also with atrocities. The truth, it is felt, becomes untruth when your enemy utters it. Recently I noticed that the very people who swallowed any and every horror story about the Japanese in Nanking in 1937 refused to believe exactly the same stories about Hong Kong in 1942. There was even a tendency to feel that the Nanking atrocities had become, as it were, retrospectively untrue because the British government now drew attention to them.

But unfortunately the truth about atrocities is far worse than that they are lied about and made into propaganda. The truth is that they happen. The fact often adduced as a reason for scepticism – that the same horror stories come up in war after war – merely makes it rather more likely that these stories are true. Evidently they are widespread fantasies, and war provides an opportunity of putting them into practice. Also, although it has ceased to be fashionable to say so, there is little question that what one may roughly call the "whites" commit far more and worse atrocities than the "reds". There is not the slightest doubt, for instance, about the behaviour of the Japanese in China. Nor is there much doubt about the long tale of fascist outrages during the last ten years in Europe. The volume of testimony is enormous, and a respectable proportion of it comes from the German press and radio. These things really happened, that is the thing to keep one's eye on. They happened even though Lord Halifax said they happened. The raping and butchering in Chinese cities, the tortures in the cellars of the Gestapo, the elderly Jewish professors flung into cesspools, the machine-gunning of refugees along the Spanish roads – they all happened, and they did not happen any the less because the *Daily Telegraph* has suddenly found out about them when it is five years too late.

III

Two memories, the first not proving anything in particular, the second, I think, giving one a certain insight into the atmosphere of a revolutionary period.

Early one morning another man and I had gone out to snipe at the fascists in the trenches outside Huesca. Their line and ours here lay 300 apart, at which range our aged rifles would not shoot accurately, but by sneaking out to a spot about a hundred yards from the fascist trench you might, if you were lucky, get a shot at someone through a gap in the parapet. Unfortunately the ground between was a flat beet field with no cover except a few ditches, and it was necessary to go out while it was still dark and return soon after dawn, before the light became too good. This time no fascists appeared, and we stayed too long and were caught by the dawn. We were in a ditch, but behind us were 200 yards of flat ground with hardly enough cover for a rabbit. We were still trying to nerve ourselves to make a dash for it when there was an uproar and a blowing of whistles in the fascist trench. Some of our aeroplanes were coming over. At this moment a man, presumably carrying a message to an officer, jumped out of the trench and ran along the top of the parapet in full view. He was half dressed and was holding up his trousers with both hands as he ran. I refrained from shooting at him. It is true that I am a poor shot and unlikely to hit a running man at a hundred yards, and also that I was thinking chiefly about getting back to our trench while the fascists had their attention fixed on the aeroplanes. Still, I did not shoot partly because of that detail about the trousers. I had come here to shoot at "fascists" – but a man who is holding up his trousers isn't a "fascist", he is visibly a fellow creature, similar to yourself, and you don't feel like shooting at him.

What does this incident demonstrate? Nothing very much, because it is the kind of thing that happens all the time in all wars. The other is different. I don't suppose that in telling it I can make it moving to you who read it, but I ask you to believe that it is moving to me, as an incident characteristic of the moral atmosphere of a particular moment in time.

One of the recruits who joined us while I was at the barracks was a wild-looking boy from the backstreets of Barcelona. He was ragged and barefooted. He was also extremely dark (Arab blood, I dare say), and made gestures you do not usually see a European make; one in particular – the arm outstretched, the palm vertical – was a gesture characteristic of Indians. One day a bundle of cigars, which you could still buy dirt cheap at that time, was stolen out of my bunk. Rather foolishly I reported this to the officer, and one of the scallywags I have already mentioned promptly came forward and said quite untruly that twenty-five pesetas had been stolen from his bunk. For some reason the officer instantly decided that the brown-faced boy must be the thief. They were very hard on stealing in the militia, and in theory people could be shot for it. The wretched boy allowed himself to be led off to the guardroom to be searched. What most struck me was that he barely attempted to protest his innocence. In the fatalism of his attitude you could see the desperate poverty in which he had been bred. The officer ordered him to take his clothes off. With a humility which was horrible to me he stripped himself naked, and his clothes were searched. Of course neither the cigars nor the money were there; in fact he had not stolen them. What was most painful of all was that he seemed no less ashamed after his innocence had been established. That night I took him to the pictures and gave him brandy and chocolate. But that too was horrible – I mean the attempt to wipe out an injury with money. For a few minutes I had half believed him to be a thief, and that could not be wiped out.

Well, a few weeks later at the front I had trouble with one of the men in my section. By this time I was a "cabo", or corporal, in command of twelve men. It was static warfare, horribly cold, and the chief job was getting sentries to stay awake and at their posts. One day a man suddenly refused to go to a certain post, which he said quite truly was exposed to enemy fire. He was a feeble creature, and I seized hold of him and began to drag him towards his post. This roused the feelings of the others against me, for Spaniards, I think, resent being touched more than we do. Instantly I was surrounded by a ring of shouting men: "Fascist! Fascist! Let that man go! This isn't a bourgeois army. Fascist!" etc. etc. As best I could in my bad Spanish I shouted back that orders had got to be obeyed, and the row developed into one of those enormous arguments by means of which discipline is gradually hammered out in revolutionary armies. Some said I was right; others said I was wrong. But the point is that the one who took my side the most warmly of all was the brown-faced boy. As soon as he saw what was happening he sprang into the ring and began passionately defending me. With his strange, wild, Indian gesture he kept exclaiming, "He's the best corporal we've got!" ("*¡No hay cabo como él!*") Later on he applied for leave to exchange into my section.

Why is this incident touching to me? Because in any normal circumstances it would have been impossible for good feelings ever to be re-established between this boy and myself. The implied accusation of theft would not have been made any better, probably somewhat worse, by my efforts to make amends. One of the effects of safe and civilized life is an immense oversensitiveness which makes all the primary emotions seem somewhat disgusting. Generosity is as painful as meanness, gratitude as hateful as ingratitude. But in Spain in 1936 we were not living in a normal time. It was a time when generous feelings and gestures were easier than they ordinarily are. I could relate a dozen similar incidents, not really communicable but bound up in my own mind with the special atmosphere of the time, the shabby clothes and the gay-coloured revolutionary posters, the universal use of the word "comrade", the anti-fascist ballads printed on flimsy paper and sold for a penny, the phrases like "international proletarian solidarity", pathetically repeated by ignorant men who believed them to mean something. Could you feel friendly towards somebody, and stick up for him in a quarrel, after you had been ignominiously searched in his presence for property you were supposed to have stolen from him? No, you couldn't – but you might if you had both been through some emotionally widening experience. That is one of the by-products of revolution, though in this case it was only the beginnings of a revolution, and obviously foredoomed to failure.

IV

The struggle for power between the Spanish Republican parties is an unhappy, far-off thing which I have no wish to revive at this date. I only mention it in order to say: believe nothing, or next to nothing, of what you read about internal affairs on the government side. It is all, from whatever source, party propaganda – that is to say, lies. The broad truth about the war is simple enough. The Spanish bourgeoisie saw their chance of crushing the labour movement, and took it, aided by the Nazis and by the forces of reaction all over the world. It is doubtful whether more than that will ever be established.

I remember saying once to Arthur Koestler, "History stopped in 1936," at which he nodded in immediate understanding. We were both thinking of totalitarianism in general, but more particularly of the Spanish Civil War. Early in life I had noticed that no event is ever correctly reported in a newspaper, but in Spain, for the first time, I saw newspaper reports which did not bear any relation to the facts, not even the relationship which is implied in an ordinary lie. I saw great battles reported where there had been no fighting, and complete silence where hundreds of men had been killed. I saw troops who had fought bravely denounced as cowards and traitors, and others who had never seen a shot fired hailed as the heroes of imaginary victories, and I saw newspapers in London retailing these lies and eager intellectuals building emotional superstructures over events that had never happened. I saw, in fact, history being written not in terms of what happened but of what ought to have happened according to various "party lines". Yet in a way, horrible as all this was, it was unimportant. It concerned secondary issues – namely, the struggle for power between the Comintern and the Spanish left-wing parties, and the efforts of the Russian government to prevent revolution in Spain. But the broad picture of the war which the Spanish government presented to the world was not untruthful. The main issues were what it said they were. But as for the fascists and their backers, how could they come even as near to the truth as that? How could they possibly mention their real aims? Their version of the war was pure fantasy, and in the circumstances it could not have been otherwise.

The only propaganda line open to the Nazis and fascists was to represent themselves as Christian patriots saving Spain from a Russian dictatorship. This involved pretending that life in Government Spain was just one long massacre (*vide* the *Catholic Herald* or the *Daily Mail* – but these were child's play compared with the Continental fascist press), and it involved immensely exaggerating the scale of Russian intervention. Out of the huge pyramid of lies which the Catholic and reactionary press all over the world built up, let me take just one point – the presence in Spain of a Russian army. Devout Franco partisans all believed in this; estimates of its strength went as high as half a million. Now, there was no Russian army in Spain. There may have been a handful of airmen and other technicians, a few hundred at the most, but an army there was not. Some thousands of foreigners who fought in Spain, not to mention millions of Spaniards, were witnesses of this. Well, their testimony made no impression at all upon the Franco propagandists, not one of whom had set foot in Government Spain. Simultaneously these people refused utterly to admit the fact of German or Italian intervention, at the same time as the German and Italian press were openly boasting about the exploits of their "legionaries". I have chosen to mention only one point, but in fact the whole of fascist propaganda about the war was on this level.

This kind of thing is frightening to me, because it often gives me the feeling that the very concept of objective truth is fading out of the world. After all, the chances are that those lies, or at any rate similar lies, will pass into history. How will the history of the Spanish war be written? If Franco remains in power his nominees will write the history books, and (to stick to my chosen point) that Russian army which never existed will become historical fact, and schoolchildren will learn about it generations hence. But suppose fascism is finally defeated and some kind of democratic government restored in Spain in the fairly near future – even then, how is the history of the war to be written? What kind of records will Franco have left behind him? Suppose even that the records kept on the government side are recoverable – even so, how is a true history of the war to be written? For, as I have pointed out already, the government also dealt extensively in lies. From the anti-fascist angle one could write a broadly truthful history of the war, but it would be a partisan history, unreliable on every minor point. Yet, after all, *some* kind of history will be written, and after those who actually remember the war are dead, it will be universally accepted. So for all practical purposes the lie will have become truth.

I know it is the fashion to say that most of recorded history is lies anyway. I am willing to believe that history is for the most part inaccurate and biased, but what is peculiar to our own age is the abandonment of the idea that history *could* be truthfully written. In the past people deliberately lied, or they unconsciously coloured what they wrote, or they struggled after the truth, well knowing that they must make many mistakes – but in each case they believed that "the facts" existed and were more or less discoverable. And in practice there was always a considerable body of fact which would have been agreed to by almost everyone. If you look up the history of the last war in, for instance, the *Encyclopædia Britannica*, you will find that a respectable amount of the material is drawn from German sources. A British and a German historian would disagree deeply on many things, even on fundamentals, but there would still be that body of, as it were, neutral fact on which neither would seriously challenge the other. It is just this common basis of agreement, with its implication that human beings are all one species of animal, that totalitarianism destroys. Nazi theory indeed specifically denies that such a thing as "the truth" exists. There is, for instance, no such thing as "science". There is only "German science", "Jewish science", etc. The implied objective of this line of thought is a nightmare world in which the Leader, or some ruling clique, controls not only the future but *the past*. If the Leader says of such and such an event, "It never happened" – well, it never happened. If he says that two and two are five – well, two and two are five. This prospect frightens me much more than bombs – and after our experiences of the last few years that is not a frivolous statement.

But is it perhaps childish or morbid to terrify oneself with visions of a totalitarian future? Before writing off the totalitarian world as a nightmare that can't come true, just remember that in 1925 the world of today would have seemed a nightmare that couldn't come true. Against that shifting phantasmagoric world in which black may be white tomorrow and yesterday's weather can be changed by decree, there are in reality only two safeguards. One is that however much you deny the truth, the truth goes on existing, as it were, behind your back, and you consequently can't violate it in ways that impair military efficiency. The other is that so long as some parts of the earth remain unconquered, the liberal tradition can be kept alive. Let fascism, or possibly even a combination of several fascisms, conquer the whole world, and those two conditions no longer exist. We in England underrate the danger of this kind of thing, because our traditions and our past security have given us a sentimental belief that it all comes right in the end and the thing you most fear never really happens. Nourished for hundreds of years on a literature in which Right invariably triumphs in the last chapter, we believe half instinctively that evil always defeats itself in the long run. Pacifism, for instance, is founded largely on this belief. Don't resist evil, and it will somehow destroy itself. But why should it? What evidence is there that it does? And what instance is there of a modern industrialized state collapsing unless conquered from the outside by military force?

Consider for instance the reinstitution of slavery. Who could have imagined twenty years ago that slavery would return to Europe? Well, slavery has been restored under our noses. The forced labour camps all over Europe and North Africa where Poles, Russians, Jews and political prisoners of every race toil at road-making or swamp-draining for their bare rations are simple chattel slavery. The most one can say is that the buying and selling of slaves by individuals is not yet permitted. In other ways – the breaking-up of families, for instance – the conditions are probably worse than they were on the American cotton plantations. There is no reason for thinking that this state of affairs will change while any totalitarian domination endures. We don't grasp its full implications, because in our mystical way we feel that a regime founded on slavery *must* collapse. But it is worth comparing the duration of the slave empires of antiquity with that of any modern state. Civilizations founded on slavery have lasted for such periods as 4,000 years.

When I think of antiquity, the detail that frightens me is that those hundreds of millions of slaves on whose backs civilization rested generation after generation have left behind them no record whatever. We do not even know their names. In the whole of Greek and Roman history, how many slaves' names are known to you? I can think of two, or possibly three. One is Spartacus and the other is Epictetus.* Also, in the Roman room at the British Museum there is a glass jar with the maker's name inscribed on the bottom: *Felix fecit*.* I have a vivid mental picture of poor Felix (a Gaul with red hair and a metal collar round his neck), but in fact he may not have been a slave; so there are only two slaves whose names I definitely know, and probably few people can remember more. The rest have gone down into utter silence.

V

The backbone of the resistance against Franco was the Spanish working class, especially the urban trade-union members. In the long run – it is important to remember that it is only in the long run – the working class remains the most reliable enemy of fascism, simply because the working class stands to gain most by a decent reconstruction of society. Unlike other classes or categories, it can't be permanently bribed.

To say this is not to idealize the working class. In the long struggle that has followed the Russian Revolution it is the manual workers who have been defeated, and it is impossible not to feel that it was their own fault. Time after time, in country after country, the organized working-class movements have been crushed by open, illegal violence, and their comrades abroad, linked to them in theoretical solidarity, have simply looked on and done nothing – and underneath this, secret cause of many betrayals, has lain the fact that between white and coloured workers there is not even lip-service to solidarity. Who can believe in the class-conscious international proletariat after the events of the past ten years? To the British working class the massacre of their comrades in Vienna, Berlin, Madrid or wherever it might be seemed less interesting and less important than yesterday's football match. Yet this does not alter the fact that the working class will go on struggling against fascism after the others have caved in. One feature of the Nazi conquest of France was the astonishing defections among the intelligentsia, including some of the left-wing political intelligentsia. The intelligentsia are the people who squeal loudest against fascism, and yet a respectable proportion of them collapse into defeatism when the pinch comes. They are far-sighted enough to see the odds against them, and moreover they can be bribed – for it is evident that the Nazis think it worthwhile to bribe intellectuals. With the working class it is the other way about. Too ignorant to see through the trick that is being played on them, they easily swallow the promises of fascism, yet sooner or later they always take up the struggle again. They must do so, because in their own bodies they always discover that the promises of fascism cannot be fulfilled. To win over the working class permanently, the fascists would have to raise the general standard of living, which they are unable and probably unwilling to do. The struggle of the working class is like the growth of a plant. The plant is blind and stupid, but it knows enough to keep pushing upwards towards the light, and it will do this in the face of endless discouragements. What are the workers struggling for? Simply for the decent life which they are more and more aware is now technically possible. Their consciousness of this aim ebbs and flows. In Spain, for a while, people were acting consciously, moving towards a goal which they wanted to reach and believed they could reach. It accounted for the curiously buoyant feeling that life in Government Spain had during the early months of the war. The common people knew in their bones that the Republic was their friend and Franco was their enemy. They knew that they were in the right, because they were fighting for something which the world owed them and was able to give them.

One has to remember this to see the Spanish war in its true perspective. When one thinks of the cruelty, squalor and futility of war – and in this particular case of the intrigues, the persecutions, the lies and the misunderstandings – there is always the temptation to say: "One side is as bad as the other. I am neutral." In practice, however, one cannot be neutral, and there is hardly such a thing as a war in which it makes no difference who wins. Nearly always one side stands more or less for progress, the other side more or less for reaction. The hatred which the Spanish Republic excited in millionaires, dukes, cardinals, playboys, Blimps and what not would in itself be enough to show one how the land lay. In essence it was a class war. If it had been won, the cause of the common people everywhere would have been strengthened. It was lost, and the dividend drawers all over the world rubbed their hands. That was the real issue; all else was froth on its surface.

VI

The outcome of the Spanish war was settled in London, Paris, Rome, Berlin – at any rate not in Spain. After the summer of 1937 those with eyes in their heads realized that the government could not win the war unless there was some profound change in the international set-up, and in deciding to fight on Negrín* and the others may have been partly influenced by the expectation that the world war which actually broke out in 1939 was coming in 1938. The much-publicized disunity on the government side was not a main cause of defeat. The government militias were hurriedly raised, ill-armed and unimaginative in their military outlook, but they would have been the same if complete political agreement had existed from the start. At the outbreak of war the average Spanish factory worker did not even know how to fire a rifle (there had never been universal conscription in Spain), and the traditional pacifism of the Left was a great handicap. The thousands of foreigners who served in Spain made good infantry, but there were very few experts of any kind among them. The Trotskyist thesis that the war could have been won if the revolution had not been sabotaged was probably false. To nationalize factories, demolish churches and issue revolutionary manifestos would not have made the armies more efficient. The fascists won because they were the stronger; they had modern arms and the others hadn't. No political strategy could offset that.

The most baffling thing in the Spanish war was the behaviour of the great powers. The war was actually won for Franco by the Germans and Italians, whose motives were obvious enough. The motives of France and Britain are less easy to understand. In 1936 it was clear to everyone that if Britain would only help the Spanish government, even to the extent of a few million pounds' worth of arms, Franco would collapse and German strategy would be severely dislocated. By that time one did not need to be a clairvoyant to foresee that war between Britain and Germany was coming; one could even foretell within a year or two when it would come. Yet in the most mean, cowardly, hypocritical way the British ruling class did all they could to hand Spain over to Franco and the Nazis. Why? Because they were pro-fascist, was the obvious answer. Undoubtedly they were, and yet when it came to the final showdown they chose to stand up to Germany. It is still very uncertain what plan they acted on in backing Franco, and they may have had no clear plan at all. Whether the British ruling class are wicked or merely stupid is one of the most difficult questions of our time, and at certain moments a very important question. As to the Russians, their motives in the Spanish war are completely inscrutable. Did they, as the pinks believed, intervene in Spain in order to defend democracy and thwart the Nazis? Then why did they intervene on such a niggardly scale and finally leave Spain in the lurch? Or did they, as the Catholics maintained, intervene in order to foster revolution in Spain? Then why did they do all in their power to crush the Spanish revolutionary movements, defend private property and hand power to the middle class as against the working class? Or did they, as the Trotskyists suggested, intervene simply in order to *prevent* a Spanish revolution? Then why not have backed Franco? Indeed, their actions are most easily explained if one assumes that they were acting on several contradictory motives. I believe that in the future we shall come to feel that Stalin's foreign policy, instead of being so diabolically clever as it is claimed to be, has been merely opportunistic and stupid. But at any rate, the Spanish Civil War demonstrated that the Nazis knew what they were doing and their opponents did not. The war was fought at a low technical level and its major strategy was very simple. That side which had arms would win. The Nazis and the Italians gave arms to their Spanish fascist friends, and the Western democracies and the Russians didn't give arms to those who should have been their friends. So the Spanish Republic perished, having "gained what no republic missed".

Whether it was right, as all left-wingers in other countries undoubtedly did, to encourage the Spaniards to go on fighting when they could not win is a question hard to answer. I myself think it was right, because I believe that it is better even from the point of view of survival to fight and be conquered than to surrender without fighting. The effects on the grand strategy of the struggle against fascism cannot be assessed yet. The ragged, weaponless armies of the Republic held out for two and a half years, which was undoubtedly longer than their enemies expected. But whether that dislocated the fascist timetable, or whether, on the other hand, it merely postponed the major war and gave the Nazis extra time to get their war machine into trim, is still uncertain.

VII

I never think of the Spanish war without two memories coming into my mind. One is of the hospital ward at Lérida and the rather sad voices of the wounded militiamen singing some song with a refrain that ended:

Una resolución,
Luchar hasta el fin!*

Well, they fought to the end all right. For the last eighteen months of the war the Republican armies must have been fighting almost without cigarettes, and with precious little food. Even when I left Spain in the middle of 1937, meat and bread were scarce, tobacco a rarity, coffee and sugar almost unobtainable.

The other memory is of the Italian militiaman who shook my hand in the guardroom, the day I joined the militia. I wrote about this man at the beginning of my book on the Spanish war,* and do not want to repeat what I said there. When I remember – oh, how vividly! – his shabby uniform and fierce, pathetic, innocent face, the complex side issues of the war seem to fade away and I see clearly that there was at any rate no doubt as to who was in the right. In spite of power politics and journalistic lying, the central issue of the war was the attempt of people like this to win the decent life which they knew to be their birthright. It is difficult to think of this particular man's probable end without several kinds of bitterness. Since I met him in the Lenin Barracks he was probably a Trotskyist or an anarchist, and in the peculiar conditions of our time, when people of that sort are not killed by the Gestapo they are usually killed by the GPU.* But that does not affect the long-term issues. This man's face, which I saw only for a minute or two, remains with me as a sort of visual reminder of what the war was really about. He symbolizes for me the flower of the European working class, harried by the police of all countries, the people who fill the mass graves of the Spanish battlefields and are now, to the tune of several millions, rotting in forced labour camps.

When one thinks of all the people who support or have supported fascism, one stands amazed at their diversity. What a crew! Think of a programme which at any rate for a while could bring Hitler, Pétain, Montagu Norman, Pavelić, William Randolph Hearst, Streicher, Buchman, Ezra Pound, Juan March, Cocteau, Thyssen, Father Coughlin, the Mufti of Jerusalem, Arnold Lunn, Antonescu, Spengler, Beverly Nichols, Lady Houston and Marinetti* all into the same boat! But the clue is really very simple. They are all people with something to lose, or people who long for a hierarchical society and dread the prospect of a world of free and equal human beings. Behind all the ballyhoo that is talked about "godless" Russia and the "materialism" of the working class lies the simple intention of those with money or privileges to cling to them. Ditto, though it contains a partial truth, with all the talk about the worthlessness of social reconstruction not accompanied by a "change of heart". The pious ones, from the Pope to the yogis of California, are great on the "changes of heart", much more reassuring from their point of view than a change in the economic system. Pétain attributes the fall of France to the common people's "love of pleasure". One sees this in its right perspective if one stops to wonder how much pleasure the ordinary French peasant's or working man's life would contain compared with Pétain's own. The damned impertinence of these politicians, priests, literary men, and what not who lecture the working-class socialist for his "materialism"! All that the working man demands is what these others would consider the indispensable minimum without which human life cannot be lived at all. Enough to eat, freedom from the haunting terror of unemployment, the knowledge that your children will get a fair chance, a bath once a day, clean linen reasonably often, a roof that doesn't leak, and short enough working hours to leave you with a little energy when the day is done. Not one of those who preach against "materialism" would consider life liveable without these things. And how easily that minimum could be attained if we chose to set our minds to it for only twenty years! To raise the standard of living of the whole world to that of Britain would not be a greater undertaking than the war we are now fighting. I don't claim, and I don't know who does, that that would solve anything in itself. It is merely that privation and brute labour have to be abolished before the real problems of humanity can be tackled. The major problem of our time is the decay of the belief in personal immortality, and it cannot be dealt with while the average human being is either drudging like an ox or shivering in fear of the secret police. How right the working classes are in their "materialism"! How right they are to realize that the belly comes before the soul, not in the scale of values but in point of time! Understand that, and the long horror that we are enduring becomes at least intelligible. All the considerations that are likely to make one falter – the siren voices of a Pétain or of a Gandhi, the inescapable fact that in order to fight one has to degrade oneself, the equivocal moral position of Britain, with its democratic phrases and its coolie empire, the sinister development of Soviet Russia, the squalid farce of left-wing politics – all this fades away and one sees only the struggle of the gradually awakening common people against the lords of property and their hired liars and bumsuckers. The question is very simple. Shall people like that Italian soldier be allowed to live the decent, fully human life which is now technically achievable, or shan't they? Shall the common man be pushed back into the mud, or shall he not? I myself believe, perhaps on insufficient grounds, that the common man will win his fight sooner or later, but I want it to be sooner and not later – sometime within the next hundred years, say, and not sometime within the next 10,000 years. That was the real issue of the Spanish war, and of the present war, and perhaps of other wars yet to come.

I never saw the Italian militiaman again, nor did I ever learn his name. It can be taken as quite certain that he is dead. Nearly two years later, when the war was visibly lost, I wrote these verses in his memory:

> The Italian soldier shook my hand
> Beside the guardroom table;
> The strong hand and the subtle hand
> Whose palms are only able
>
> To meet within the sounds of guns,
> But oh! what peace I knew then
> In gazing on his battered face
> Purer than any woman's!
>
> For the flyblown words that make me spew
> Still in his ears were holy,
> And he was born knowing what I had learnt
> Out of books and slowly.
>
> The treacherous guns had told their tale
> And we both had bought it,
> But my gold brick was made of gold –
> Oh, who ever would have thought it?

Good luck go with you, Italian soldier!
But luck is not for the brave;
What would the world give back to you?
Always less than you gave.

Between the shadow and the ghost,
Between the white and the red.
Between the bullet and the lie,
Where would hide your head?

For where is Manuel González,
And where is Pedro Aguilar,
And where is Ramón Fenellosa?
The earthworms know where they are.

Your name and your deeds were forgotten
Before your bones were dry.
And the lie that slew you is buried
Under a deeper lie;

But the thing that I saw in your face
No power can disinherit:
No bomb that ever burst
Shatters the crystal spirit.

Pamphlet Literature*

One cannot adequately review fifteen pamphlets in a thousand words, and if I have picked out that number it is because between them they make a representative selection of eight out of the nine main trends in current pamphleteering. (The missing trend is pacifism: I don't happen to have a recent pacifist pamphlet by me.) I list them under their separate headings, with short comments, before trying to explain certain rather curious features in the revival of pamphleteering during recent years.

1. Anti-Left and crypto-fascist: *A Soldier's New World.* 2d. (Subtitled "An anti-crank pamphlet written in camp"; this wallops the highbrow and proves that the common man does not want socialism. Key phrase: "The Clever Ones have never learnt to delight in simple things.") *Gollancz* in the German Wonderland.* 1s. (Vansittartite.)* *World Order or World Ruin.* 6d. (Anti-planning; G.D.H. Cole* demolished.)

2. Conservative: *Bomber Command Continues*, 7d. (Good specimen of an official pamphlet.)

3. Social Democrat: *The Case of Austria.* 6d. (Published by the Free Austrian Movement.)

4. Communist: *Clear Out Hitler's Agents.* 2d. (Subtitled "An exposure of Trotskyist disruption being organized in Britain"; exceptionally mendacious.)

5. Trotskyist and anarchist: *The Kronstadt Revolt.* 2d. (Anarchist pamphlet, largely an attack on Trotsky.)

6. Non-party radical: *What's Wrong with the Army?* 6d. (A Hurricane Book, well-informed and well-written anti-Blimp document.) *I, James Blunt.* 6d. (Good flesh-creeper, founded on the justified assumption that the mass of the English people haven't yet heard of fascism.) *Battle of Giants.* Unpriced, probably 6d. (Interesting specimen of popular non-communist Russophile literature.)

7. Religious: *A Letter to a Country Clergyman.* 2d. (Fabian pamphlet, left-wing Anglican.) *Fighters Ever.* 6d. (Buchman vindicated.)

8. Lunatic: *Britain's Triumphant Destiny, or Righteousness No Longer on the Defensive.* 6d. (British Israel, profusely illustrated.) *When Russia Invades Palestine.* 1s. (British Israel. The author, A.J. Ferris, BA, has written a long series of pamphlets on kindred subjects, some of them enjoying enormous sales. His *When Russia Bombs Germany*, published in 1940, sold over 60,000.) *Hitler's Story and Programme to Conquer England*, by "Civis Britannicus Sum". 1s. (Specimen passage: "It is a grand thing to 'play the game', and to

know that one is doing it. Then, when the day comes that stumps are drawn or the whistle blows for the last time:

> The *Great Scorer* will come to write against your name,
> Not if you have won or lost; but *How you Played the Game*.")*

These few that I have named are only a drop in the ocean of pamphlet literature, and for the sake of giving a good cross section I have included several that the average reader is likely to have heard of. What conclusions can one draw from this small sample? The interesting fact, not easily explicable, is that pamphleteering has revived upon an enormous scale since about 1935, and has done so without producing anything of real value. My own collection, made during the past six years, would run into several hundreds, but probably does not represent anywhere near 10 per cent of the total output. Some of these pamphlets have had huge sales, especially the religio-patriotic ones, such as those of Mr Ferris, BA, and the scurrilous ones, such as *Hitler's Last Will and Testament*, which is said to have sold several millions. Directly political pamphlets sometimes sell in big numbers, but the circulation of any pamphlet which is "party line" (any party) is likely to be spurious. Looking through my collection, I find that it is practically all trash, interesting only to bibliographies. Though I have classified current pamphlets under nine headings they could be finally reduced to two main schools, roughly describable as Party Line and Astrology. There is totalitarian rubbish and paranoiac rubbish, but in each case it *is* rubbish. Even the well-informed Fabian pamphlets are hopelessly dull, considered as reading matter. The liveliest pamphlets are almost always non-party, a good example being *Bless 'Em All*, which should be regarded as a pamphlet, though it costs one and sixpence.

The reason why the badness of contemporary pamphlets is somewhat surprising is that the pamphlet ought to be *the* literary form of an age like our own. We live in a time when political passions run high, channels of free expression are dwindling and organized lying exists on a scale never before known. For plugging the holes in history the pamphlet is the ideal form. Yet lively pamphlets are very few, and the only explanation I can offer – a rather lame one – is that the publishing trade and the literary papers have never gone to the trouble of making the reading public pamphlet-conscious. One difficulty of collecting pamphlets is that they are not issued in any regular manner, cannot always be procured even in the libraries of museums, and are seldom advertised and still more seldom reviewed. A good writer with something he passionately wanted to say – and the essence of pamphleteering is to have something you want to say *now*, to as many people as possible – would hesitate to cast it in pamphlet form, because he would hardly know how to set about getting it published, and would be doubtful whether the people he wanted to reach would ever read it. Probably he would water his idea down into a newspaper article or pad it out into a book. As a result by far the greater number of pamphlets are either written by lonely lunatics who publish at their own expense, or belong to the sub-world of the crank religions, or are issued by political parties. The normal way of publishing a pamphlet is through a political party, and the party will see to it that any "deviation" – and hence any literary value – is kept out. There have been a few good pamphlets in fairly recent years. D.H. Lawrence's *Pornography and Obscenity* was one, Potocki de Montalk's *Snobbery with Violence* was another, and some of Wyndham Lewis's essays in the *Enemy* really come under this heading.* At present the most hopeful symptom is the appearance of the non-party left-wing pamphlet, such as the Hurricane Books. If productions of this type were as sure of being noticed in the press as are novels or books of verse, something would have been done towards bringing the pamphlet back to the attention of its proper public, and the level of the whole genre might rise. When one considers how flexible a form the pamphlet is, and how badly some of the events of our time need documenting, this is a thing to be desired.

W.B. Yeats*

One thing that Marxist criticism has not succeeded in doing is to trace the connection between "tendency" and literary style. The subject matter and imagery of a book can be explained in sociological terms, but its texture seemingly cannot. Yet some such connection there must be. One knows, for instance, that a socialist would not write like Chesterton or a Tory imperialist like Bernard Shaw, though *how* one knows it is not easy to say. In the case of Yeats, there must be some kind of connection between his wayward, even tortured style of writing and his rather sinister vision of life. Mr Menon is chiefly concerned with the esoteric philosophy underlying Yeats's work, but the quotations which are scattered all through his interesting book serve to remind one how artificial Yeats's manner of writing was. As a rule, this artificiality is accepted as Irishism, or Yeats is even credited with simplicity because he uses short words, but in fact one seldom comes on six consecutive lines of his verse in which there is not an archaism or an affected turn of speech. To take the nearest example:

> Grant me an old man's frenzy,
> Myself must I remake
> Till I am Timon and Lear
> Or that William Blake
> Who beat upon the wall
> Till Truth obeyed his call.*

The unnecessary "that" imports a feeling of affectation, and the same tendency is present in all but Yeats's best passages. One is seldom long away from a suspicion of "quaintness", something that links up not only with the nineties, the Ivory Tower and "calf covers of pissed-on green", but also with Rackham's drawings,* Liberty art fabrics and the *Peter Pan* never-never land, of which, after all, 'The Happy Townland'* is merely a more appetizing example. This does not matter, because, on the whole, Yeats gets away with it, and if his straining after effect is often irritating, it can also produce phrases ("the chill, footless years", "the mackerel-crowded seas"*) which suddenly overwhelm one like a girl's face seen across a room. He is an exception to the rule that poets do not use poetical language:

> How many centuries spent
> The sedentary soul
> In toils of measurement
> Beyond eagle or mole.
> Beyond hearing or seeing,
> Or Archimedes' guess,
> To raise into being
> That loveliness?*

Here he does not flinch from a squashy vulgar word like "loveliness", and after all it does not seriously spoil this wonderful passage. But the same tendencies, together with a sort of raggedness which is no doubt intentional, weaken his epigrams and polemical poems. For instance (I am quoting from memory) the epigram against the critics who damned *The Playboy of the Western World*:*

> Once when midnight smote the air
> Eunuchs ran through hell and met
> On every crowded street to stare
> Upon great Juan riding by;
> Even like these to rail and sweat,
> Staring upon his sinewy thigh.*

The power which Yeats has within himself gives him the analogy ready-made and produces the tremendous scorn of the last line, but even in this short poem there are six or seven unnecessary words. It would probably have been deadlier if it had been neater.

Mr Menon's book is incidentally a short biography of Yeats, but he is above all interested in Yeats's philosophical "system", which in his opinion supplies the subject matter of more of Yeats's poems than is generally recognized. This system is set forth fragmentarily in various places, and at full length in *A Vision*,* a privately printed book which I have never read but which Mr Menon quotes from extensively. Yeats gave conflicting accounts of its origin, and Mr Menon hints pretty broadly that the "documents" on which it was ostensibly founded were imaginary. Yeats's philosophical system, says Mr Menon, "was at the back of his intellectual life almost from the beginning. His poetry is full of it. Without it his later poetry becomes almost completely unintelligible." As soon as we begin to read about the so-called system we are in the middle of a hocus-pocus of Great Wheels, gyres, cycles of the moon, reincarnation, disembodied spirits, astrology and what not. Yeats hedges as to the literalness with which he believed in all this, but he certainly dabbled in spiritualism and astrology, and in earlier life had made experiments in alchemy. Although almost buried under explanations, very difficult to understand, about the phases of the moon, the central idea of his philosophical system seems to be our old friend, the cyclical universe, in which everything happens over and over again. One has not, perhaps, the right to laugh at Yeats for his mystical beliefs – for I believe it could be shown that *some* degree of belief in magic is almost universal – but neither ought one to write such things off as mere unimportant eccentricities. It is Mr Menon's perception of this that gives his book its deepest interest. "In the first flush of admiration and enthusiasm," he says, "most people dismissed the fantastical philosophy as the price we have to pay for a great and curious intellect. One did not quite realize where he was heading. And those who did, like Pound and perhaps Eliot, approved the stand that he finally took. The first reaction to this did not come, as one might have expected, from the politically minded young English poets. They were puzzled because a less rigid or artificial system than that of *A Vision* might not have produced the great poetry of Yeats's last days." It might not, and yet Yeats's philosophy has some very sinister implications, as Mr Menon points out.

Translated into political terms, Yeats's tendency is fascist. Throughout most of his life, and long before fascism was ever heard of, he had had the outlook of those who reach fascism by the aristocratic route. He is a great hater of democracy, of the modern world, science, machinery, the concept of progress – above all, of the idea of human equality. Much of the imagery of his work is feudal, and it is clear that he was not altogether free from ordinary snobbishness. Later these tendencies took clearer shape and led him to "the exultant acceptance of authoritarianism as the only solution. Even violence and tyranny are not necessarily evil because the people, knowing not evil and good, would become perfectly acquiescent to tyranny. [...] Everything must come from the top. Nothing can come from the masses." Not much interested in politics, and no doubt disgusted by his brief incursions into public life, Yeats nevertheless makes political pronouncements. He is too big a man to share the illusions of Liberalism, and as early as 1920 he foretells in a justly famous passage ('The Second Coming'*) the kind of world that we have actually moved into. But he appears to welcome the coming age, which is to be "hierarchical, masculine, harsh, surgical", and is influenced both by Ezra Pound and by various Italian Fascist writers. He describes the new civilization which he hopes and believes will arrive: "An aristocratic civilization in its most completed form, every detail of life hierarchical, every great man's door crowded at dawn by petitioners, great wealth everywhere in a few men's hands, all dependent upon a few, up to the Emperor himself, who is a God dependent on a greater God, and everywhere, in Court, in the family, an inequality made law." The innocence of this statement is as interesting as its snobbishness. To begin with, in a single phrase, "great wealth in a few men's hands", Yeats lays bare the central reality of fascism, which the whole of its propaganda is designed to cover up. The merely political fascist claims always to be fighting for justice: Yeats, the poet, sees at a glance that fascism means injustice, and acclaims it for that very reason. But at the same time he fails to see that the new authoritarian civilization, if it arrives, will not be aristocratic, or what he means by aristocratic. It will not be ruled by noblemen with Van Dyck faces, but by anonymous millionaires, shiny-bottomed bureaucrats and murdering gangsters. Others who have made the same mistake have afterwards changed their views, and one ought not to assume that Yeats, if he had lived longer, would necessarily have followed his friend Pound, even in sympathy. But the tendency of the passage I have quoted above is obvious, and its complete throwing overboard of whatever good the past 2,000 years have achieved is a disquieting symptom.

How do Yeats's political ideas link up with his leaning towards occultism? It is not clear at first glance why hatred of democracy and a tendency to believe in crystal-gazing should go together. Mr Menon only discusses this rather shortly, but it is possible to make two guesses. To begin with, the theory that civilization moves in recurring cycles is one way out for people who hate the concept of human equality. If it is true that "all this", or something like it, "has happened before", then science and the modern world are debunked at one stroke and progress becomes for ever impossible. It does not much matter if the lower orders are getting above themselves, for, after all, we shall soon be returning to an age of tyranny. Yeats is by no means alone in this outlook. If the universe is moving round on a wheel, the future must be foreseeable, perhaps even in some detail. It is merely a question of discovering the laws of its motion, as the early astronomers discovered the solar year. Believe that, and it becomes difficult not to believe in astrology or some similar system. A year before the war, examining a copy of *Gringoire*, the French fascist weekly, much read by army officers, I found in it no less than thirty-eight advertisements of clairvoyants. Secondly, the very concept of occultism carries with it the idea that knowledge must be a secret thing, limited to a small circle of initiates. But the same idea is integral to fascism. Those who dread the prospect of universal suffrage, popular education, freedom of thought, emancipation of women, will start off with a predilection towards secret cults. There is another link between fascism and magic in the profound hostility of both to the Christian ethical code.

No doubt Yeats wavered in his beliefs and held at different times many different opinions, some enlightened, some not. Mr Menon repeats for him Eliot's claim that he had the longest period of development of any poet who has ever lived. But there is one thing that seems constant, at least in all of his work that I can remember, and that is his hatred of modern Western civilization and desire to return to the Bronze Age, or perhaps to the Middle Ages. Like all such thinkers, he tends to write in praise of ignorance. The Fool in his remarkable play, *The Hour-Glass*,* is a Chestertonian figure, "God's fool", the "natural born innocent", who is always wiser than the wise man. The philosopher in the play dies on the knowledge that all his lifetime of thought has been wasted (I am quoting from memory again):

> The stream of the world has changed its course,
> And with the stream my thoughts have run
> Into some cloudy, thunderous spring
> That is its mountain-source;
> Ay, to a frenzy of the mind,
> That all that we have done's undone
> Our speculation but as the wind.*

Beautiful words, but by implication profoundly obscurantist and reactionary – for if it is really true that a village idiot, as such, is wiser than a philosopher, then it would be better if the alphabet had never been invented. Of course, all praise of the past is partly sentimental, because we do not live in the past. The poor do not praise poverty. Before you can despise the machine, the machine must set you free from brute labour. But that is not to say that Yeats's yearning for a more primitive and more hierarchical age was not sincere. How much of all this is traceable to mere snobbishness, product of Yeats's own position as an impoverished offshoot of the aristocracy, is a different question. And the connection between his obscurantist opinions and his tendency towards "quaintness" of language remains to be worked out; Mr Menon hardly touches upon it.

This is a very short book, and I would greatly like to see Mr Menon go ahead and write another book on Yeats, starting where this one leaves off. "If the greatest poet of our times is exultantly ringing in an era of fascism, it seems a somewhat disturbing symptom," he says on the last page, and leaves it at that. It is a disturbing symptom, because it is not an isolated one. By and large the best writers of our time have been reactionary in tendency, and though fascism does not offer any real return to the past, those who yearn for the past will accept fascism sooner than its probable alternatives. But there are other lines of approach, as we have seen during the past two or three years. The relationship between fascism and the literary intelligentsia badly needs investigating, and Yeats might well be the starting point. He is best studied by someone like Mr Menon, who can approach a poet primarily as a poet, but who also knows that a writer's political and religious beliefs are not excrescences to be laughed away but something that will leave their mark even on the smallest detail of his work.

Literature and the Left*

"When a man of true Genius appears in the World, you may know him by this infallible Sign, that all the Dunces are in Conspiracy against him." So wrote Jonathan Swift, 200 years before the publication of *Ulysses*.

If you consult any sporting manual or yearbook you will find many pages devoted to the hunting of the fox and the hare, but not a word about the hunting of the highbrow. Yet this, more than any other, is the characteristic British sport, in season all the year round and enjoyed by rich and poor alike, with no complications from either class feeling or political alignment.

For it should be noted that in its attitude towards "highbrows" – that is, towards any writer or artist who makes experiments in technique – the Left is no friendlier than the Right. Not only is "highbrow" almost as much a word of abuse in the *Daily Worker* as in *Punch*, but it is exactly those writers whose work shows both originality and the power to endure that Marxist doctrinaires single out for attack. I could name a long list of examples, but I am thinking especially of Joyce, Yeats, Lawrence and Eliot. Eliot, in particular, is damned in the left-wing press almost as automatically and perfunctorily as Kipling – and that by critics who only a few years back were going into raptures over the already forgotten masterpieces of the Left Book Club.

Is you ask a "good party man" (and this goes for almost any party of the Left) what he objects to in Eliot, you get an answer that ultimately reduces to this. Eliot is a reactionary (he has declared himself a royalist, an Anglo-Catholic, etc.), and he is also a "bourgeois intellectual", out of touch with the common man: therefore he is a bad writer. Contained in this statement is a half-conscious confusion of ideas which vitiates nearly all politico-literary criticism.

To dislike a writer's politics is one thing. To dislike him because he forces you to think is another, not necessarily incompatible with the first. But as soon as you start talking about "good" and "bad" writers you are tacitly appealing to literary tradition and thus dragging in a totally different set of values. For what is a "good" writer? Was Shakespeare "good"? Most people would agree that he was. Yet Shakespeare is, and perhaps was even by the standards of his own time, reactionary in tendency – and he is also a difficult writer, only doubtfully accessible to the common man. What, then, becomes of the notion that Eliot is disqualified, as it were, by being an Anglo-Catholic royalist who is given to quoting Latin?

Left-wing literary criticism has not been wrong in insisting on the importance of subject matter. It may not even have been wrong, considering the age we live in, in demanding that literature shall be first and foremost propaganda. Where it has been wrong is in making what are ostensibly literary judgements for political ends. To take a crude example, what communist would dare to admit in public that Trotsky is a better writer than Stalin – as he is, of course? To say "X is a gifted writer, but he is a political enemy and I shall do my best to silence him" is harmless enough. Even if you end by silencing him with a tommy gun you are not really sinning against the intellect. The deadly sin is to say "X is a political enemy: therefore he is a bad writer." And if anyone says that this kind of thing doesn't happen, I answer merely: look up the literary pages of the left-wing press, from the *News Chronicle* to the *Labour Monthly*, and see what you find.

There is no knowing just how much the socialist movement has lost by alienating the literary intelligentsia. But it has alienated them, partly by confusing tracts with literature, and partly by having no room in it for a humanistic culture. A writer can vote Labour as easily as anyone else, but it is very difficult for him to take part in the socialist movement *as a writer*. Both the book-trained doctrinaire and the practical politician will despise him as a "bourgeois intellectual", and will lose no opportunity of telling him so. They will have much the same attitude towards his work as a golfing stockbroker would have. The illiteracy of politicians is a special feature of our age – as G.M. Trevelyan* put it, "In the seventeenth century Members of Parliament quoted the Bible, in the eighteenth and nineteenth centuries the classics, and in the twentieth century nothing" – and its corollary is the [political] impotence of writers. In the years following the last war the best English writers were reactionary in tendency, though most of them took no direct part in politics. After them, about 1930, there came a generation of writers who tried very hard to be actively useful in the left-wing movement. Numbers of them joined the Communist Party, and got there exactly the same reception as they would have got in the Conservative Party. That is, they were first regarded with patronage and suspicion, and then, when it was found that they would not or could not turn themselves into gramophone records, they were thrown out on their ears. Most of them retreated into individualism. No doubt they still vote Labour, but their talents are lost to the movement, and – a more sinister development – after them there comes a new generation of writers who, without being strictly non-political, are outside the socialist movement from the start. Of the very young writers who are now beginning their careers, the most gifted are pacifists; a few may even have a leaning towards fascism. There is hardly one to whom the mystique of the socialist movement appears to mean anything. The ten-year-long struggle against fascism seems to them meaningless and uninteresting, and they say so frankly. One could explain this in a number of ways, but the contemptuous attitude of the Left towards "bourgeois intellectuals" is likely to be part of the reason.

Gilbert Murray* relates somewhere or other that he once lectured on Shakespeare to a socialist debating society. At the end he called for questions in the usual way, to receive as the sole question asked: "Was Shakespeare a capitalist?" The depressing thing about this story is that it might well be true. Follow up its implications, and you perhaps get a glimpse of the reason why Céline wrote *Mea Culpa** and Auden is watching his navel in America.

Poetry and the Microphone*

About a year ago I and a number of others were engaged in broadcasting literary programmes to India, and among other things we broadcast a good deal of verse by contemporary and near-contemporary English writers – for example, Eliot, Herbert Read, Auden, Spender, Dylan Thomas, Henry Treece, Alex Comfort, Robert Bridges, Edmund Blunden,* D.H. Lawrence. Whenever it was possible we had poems broadcast by the people who wrote them. Just why these particular programmes (a small and remote outflanking movement in the radio war) were instituted there is no need to explain here, but I should add that the fact that we were broadcasting to an Indian audience dictated our technique to some extent. The essential point was that our literary broadcasts were aimed at the Indian university students, a small and hostile audience, unapproachable by anything that could be described as British propaganda. It was known in advance that we could not hope for more than a few thousand listeners at the most, and this gave us an excuse to be more "highbrow" than is generally possible on the air.

If you are broadcasting poetry to people who know your language but don't share your cultural background, a certain amount of comment and explanation is unavoidable, and the formula we usually followed was to broadcast what purported to be a monthly literary magazine. The editorial staff were supposedly sitting in their office, discussing what to put into the next number. Somebody suggested one poem, someone else suggested another, there was a short discussion and then came the poem itself, read in a different voice, preferably the author's own. This poem naturally called up another, and so the programme continued, usually with at least half a minute of discussion between any two items. For a half-hour programme, six voices seemed to be the best number. A programme of this sort was necessarily somewhat shapeless, but it could be given a certain appearance of unity by making it revolve round a single central theme. For example, one number of our imaginary magazine was devoted to the subject of war. It included two poems by Edmund Blunden, Auden's 'September 1941', extracts from a long poem by G.S. Fraser ('A Letter to Anne Ridler'), Byron's 'Isles of Greece' and an extract from T.E. Lawrence's *Revolt in the Desert*.* These half-dozen items, with the arguments that preceded and followed them, covered reasonably well the possible attitudes towards war. The poems and the prose extract took about twenty minutes to broadcast, the arguments about eight minutes.

This formula may seem slightly ridiculous and also rather patronizing, but its advantage is that the element of mere instruction, the textbook motif, which is quite unavoidable if one is going to broadcast serious and sometimes "difficult" verse, becomes a lot less forbidding when it appears as an informal discussion. The various speakers can ostensibly say to one another what they are in reality saying to the audience. Also, by such an approach you at least give a poem a context, which is just what poetry lacks from the average man's point of view. But of course there are other methods. One which we frequently used was to set a poem in music. It is announced that in a few minutes' time such and such a poem will be broadcast; then the music plays for perhaps a minute, then fades out into the poem, which follows without any title or announcement, then the music is faded in again and plays up for another minute or two – the whole thing taking perhaps five minutes. It is necessary to choose appropriate music, but needless to say, the real purpose of the music is to insulate the poem from the rest of the programme. By this method you can have, say, a Shakespeare sonnet within three minutes of a news bulletin without, at any rate to my ear, any gross incongruity.

These programmes that I have been speaking of were of no great value in themselves, but I have mentioned them because of the ideas they aroused in myself and some others about the possibilities of the radio as a means of popularizing poetry. I was early struck by the fact that the broadcasting of a poem by the person who wrote it does not merely produce an effect upon the audience, if any, but also on the poet himself. One must remember that extremely little in the way of broadcasting poetry has been done in England, and that many people who write verse have never even considered the idea of reading it aloud. By being set down at a microphone, especially if this happens at all regularly, the poet is brought into a new relationship with his work, not otherwise attainable in our time and country. It is a commonplace that in modern times – the last two hundred years, say – poetry has come to have less and less connection either with music or with the spoken word. It needs print in order to exist at all, and it is no more expected that a poet, as such, will know how to sing or even to declaim than it is expected that an architect will know how to plaster a ceiling. Lyrical and rhetorical poetry have almost ceased to be written, and a hostility towards poetry on the part of the common man has come to be taken for granted in any country where everyone can read. And where such a breach exists it is always inclined to widen, because the concept of poetry as primarily something printed, and something intelligible only to a minority, encourages obscurity and "cleverness". How many people do not feel quasi-instinctively that there must be something wrong with any poem whose meaning can be taken in at a single glance? It seems unlikely that these tendencies will be checked unless it again becomes normal to read verse aloud, and it is difficult to see how this can be brought about except by using the radio as a medium. But the special advantage of the radio, its power to select the right audience, and to do away with stage fright and embarrassment, ought here to be noticed.

In broadcasting your audience is conjectural, but it is an audience of *one*. Millions may be listening, but each is listening alone, or as a member of a small group, and each has (or ought to have) the feeling that you are speaking to him individually. More than this, it is reasonable to assume that your audience is sympathetic, or at least interested, for anyone who is bored can promptly switch you off by turning a knob. But though presumably sympathetic, the audience *has no power over you*. It is just here that a broadcast differs from a speech or a lecture. On the platform, as anyone used to public speaking knows, it is almost impossible not to take your tone from the audience. It is always obvious within a few minutes what they will respond to and what they will not, and in practice you are almost compelled to speak for the benefit of what you estimate as the stupidest person present, and also to ingratiate yourself by means of the ballyhoo known as "personality". If you don't do so, the result is always an atmosphere of frigid embarrassment. That grisly thing, a "poetry reading", is what it is because there will always be some among the audience who are bored or all but frankly hostile and who can't remove themselves by the simple act of turning a knob. And it is at bottom the same difficulty – the fact that a theatre audience is not a selected one – that makes it impossible to get a decent performance of Shakespeare in England. On the air these conditions do not exist. The poet *feels* that he is addressing people to whom poetry means something, and it is a fact that poets who are used to broadcasting can read into the microphone with a virtuosity they would not equal if they had a visible audience in front of them. The element of make-believe that enters here does not greatly matter. The point is that in the only way now possible the poet has been brought into a situation in which reading verse aloud seems a natural, unembarrassing thing, a normal exchange between man and man: also he has been led to think of his work as *sound* rather than as a pattern on paper. By that much the reconciliation between poetry and the common man is nearer. It already exists at the poet's end of the ether-waves, whatever may be happening at the other end.

However, what is happening at the other end cannot be disregarded. It will be seen that I have been speaking as though the whole subject of poetry were embarrassing, almost indecent, as though popularizing poetry were essentially a strategic manoeuvre, like getting a dose of medicine down a child's throat or establishing tolerance for a persecuted sect. But unfortunately that or something like it is the case. There can be no doubt that in our civilization poetry is by far the most discredited of the arts, the only art, indeed, in which the average man refuses to discern *any* value. Arnold Bennett was hardly exaggerating when he said that in the English-speaking countries the word "poetry" would disperse a crowd quicker than a fire hose. And as I have pointed out, a breach of this kind tends to widen simply because of its existence, the common man becoming more and more anti-poetry, the poet more and more arrogant and unintelligible, until the divorce between poetry and popular culture is accepted as a sort of law of nature, although in fact it belongs only to our own time and to a comparatively small area of the earth. We live in an age in which the average human being in the highly civilized countries is aesthetically inferior to the lowest savage. This state of affairs is generally looked upon as being incurable by any *conscious* act, and on the other hand is expected to right itself of its own accord as soon as society takes a comelier shape. With slight variations the Marxist, the anarchist and the religious believer will all tell you this, and in broad terms it is undoubtedly true. The ugliness amid which we live has spiritual and economic causes and is not to be explained by the mere going astray of tradition at some point or other. But it does not follow that no improvement is possible within our present framework, nor that an aesthetic improvement is not a necessary part of the general redemption of society. It is worth stopping to wonder, therefore, whether it would not be possible even now to rescue poetry from its special position as the most hated of the arts and win for it at least the same degree of toleration as exists for music. But one has to start by asking: in what way and to what extent is poetry unpopular?

On the face of it, the unpopularity of poetry is as complete as it could be. But on second thoughts, this has to be qualified in a rather peculiar way. To begin with, there is still an appreciable amount of folk poetry (nursery rhymes etc.) which is universally known and quoted and forms part of the background of everyone's mind. There is also a handful of ancient songs and ballads which have never gone out of favour. In addition there is the popularity, or at least the toleration, of "good bad" poetry, generally of a patriotic or sentimental kind. This might seem beside the point if it were not that "good bad" poetry has all the characteristics which, ostensibly, make the average man dislike true poetry. It is in verse, it rhymes, it deals in lofty sentiments and unusual language – all this to a very marked degree, for it is almost axiomatic that bad poetry is more "poetical" than good poetry. Yet if not actively liked it is at least tolerated. For example, just before writing this I have been listening to a couple of BBC comedians doing their usual turn before the nine o'clock news. In the last three minutes one of the two comedians suddenly announces that he "wants to be serious for a moment" and proceeds to recite a piece of patriotic balderdash entitled 'A Fine Old English Gentleman', in praise of His Majesty the King. Now, what is the reaction of the audience to this sudden lapse into the worst sort of rhyming heroics? It cannot be very violently negative, or there would be a sufficient volume of indignant letters to stop the BBC doing this kind of thing. One must conclude that though the big public is hostile to *poetry*, it is not strongly hostile to *verse*. After all, if rhyme and metre were disliked for their own sakes, neither songs nor dirty limericks could be popular. Poetry is disliked because it is associated with unintelligibility, intellectual pretentiousness and a general feeling of Sunday-on-a-weekday. Its name creates in advance the same sort of bad impression as the word "God", or a parson's dog collar. To a certain extent, popularizing poetry is a question of breaking down an acquired inhibition. It is a question of getting people to listen instead of uttering a mechanical raspberry. If true poetry could be introduced to the big public in such a way as to make it seem *normal*, as that piece of rubbish I have just listened to presumably seemed normal, then part of the prejudice against it might be overcome.

It is difficult to believe that poetry can ever be popularized again without some deliberate effort at the education of public taste, involving strategy and perhaps even subterfuge. T.S. Eliot once suggested that poetry, particularly dramatic poetry, might be brought back into the consciousness of ordinary people through the medium of the music hall; he might have added the pantomime, whose vast possibilities do not seem ever to have been completely explored. *Sweeney Agonistes** was perhaps written with some such idea in mind, and it would in fact be conceivable as a music-hall turn, or at least as a scene in a revue. I have suggested the radio as a more hopeful medium, and I have pointed out its technical advantages, particularly from the point of view of the poet. The reason why such a suggestion sounds hopeless at first hearing is that few people are able to imagine the radio being used for the dissemination of anything except tripe. People listen to the stuff that does actually dribble from the loudspeakers of the world, and conclude that it is for that and nothing else that the wireless exists. Indeed the very word "wireless" calls up a picture either of roaring dictators or of genteel throaty voices announcing that three of our aircraft have failed to return. Poetry on the air sounds like the Muses in striped trousers. Nevertheless one ought not to confuse the capabilities of an instrument with the use it is actually put to. Broadcasting is what it is not because there is something inherently vulgar, silly and dishonest about the whole apparatus of microphone and transmitter but because all the broadcasting that now happens all over the world is under the control of governments or great monopoly companies which are actively interested in maintaining the status quo and therefore in preventing the common man from becoming too intelligent. Something of the same kind has happened to the cinema, which, like the radio, made its appearance during the monopoly stage of capitalism and is fantastically expensive to operate. In all the arts the tendency is similar. More and more the channels of production are under control of bureaucrats, whose aim is to destroy the artist or at least to castrate him. This would be a bleak outlook if it were not that the totalitarianization which is now going on, and must undoubtedly continue to go on, in every country of the world, is mitigated by another process which it was not easy to foresee even as short a time as five years ago.

This is, that the huge bureaucratic machines of which we are all part are beginning to work creakily because of their mere size and their constant growth. The tendency of the modern state is to wipe out the freedom of the intellect, and yet at the same time every state, especially under the pressure of war, finds itself more and more in need of an intelligentsia to do its publicity for it. The modern state needs, for example, pamphlet writers, poster artists, illustrators, broadcasters, lecturers, film producers, actors, song composers, even painters and sculptors, not to mention psychologists, sociologists, biochemists, mathematicians and what not. The British government started the present war with the more or less openly declared intention of keeping the literary intelligentsia out of it – yet after three years of war almost every writer, however undesirable his political history or opinions, has been sucked into the various ministries or the BBC and even those who enter the armed forces tend to find themselves after a while in public relations or some other essentially literary job. The government has absorbed these people, unwillingly enough, because it found itself unable to get on without them. The ideal, from the official point of view, would have been to put all publicity into the hands of "safe" people like A.P. Herbert* or Ian Hay – but since not enough of these were available, the existing intelligentsia had to be utilized, and the tone and even to some extent the content of official propaganda have been modified accordingly. No one acquainted with the government pamphlets, ABCA* lectures, documentary films and broadcasts to occupied countries which have been issued during the past two years imagines that our rulers would sponsor this kind of thing if they could help it. Only, the bigger the machine of government becomes, the more loose ends and forgotten corners there are in it. This is perhaps a small consolation, but it is not a despicable one. It means that in countries where there is already a strong liberal tradition, bureaucratic tyranny can perhaps never be complete. The striped-trousered ones will rule, but so long as they are forced to maintain an intelligentsia, the intelligentsia will have a certain amount of autonomy. If the government needs, for example, documentary films, it must employ people specially interested in the technique of the film, and it must allow them the necessary minimum of freedom; consequently, films that are all wrong from the bureaucratic point of view will always have a tendency to appear. So also with painting, photography, scriptwriting, reportage, lecturing and all the other arts and half-arts of which a complex modern state has need.

The application of this to the radio is obvious. At present the loudspeaker is the enemy of the creative writer, but this may not necessarily remain true when the volume and scope of broadcasting increase. As things are, although the BBC does keep up a feeble show of interest in contemporary literature, it is harder to capture five minutes on the air in which to broadcast a poem than twelve hours in which to disseminate lying propaganda, tinned music, stale jokes, faked "discussions" or what have you. But that state of affairs may alter in the way I have indicated, and when that time comes serious experiment in the broadcasting of verse, with complete disregard for the various hostile influences which prevent any such thing at present, would become possible. I don't claim it as certain that such an experiment would have very great results. The radio was bureaucratized so early in its career that the relationship between broadcasting and literature has never been thought out. It is not certain that the microphone is the instrument by which poetry could be brought back to the common people and it is not even certain that poetry would gain by being more of a spoken and less of a written thing. But I do urge that these possibilities exist, and that those who care for literature might turn their minds more often to this much-despised medium, whose powers for good have perhaps been obscured by the voices of Professor Joad* and Dr Goebbels.

Who Are the War Criminals?*

On the face of it, Mussolini's collapse was a story straight out of Victorian melodrama. At long last righteousness had triumphed, the wicked man was discomfited, the mills of God were doing their stuff. On second thoughts, however, this moral tale is less simple and less edifying. To begin with, what crime, if any, has Mussolini committed? In power politics there are no crimes, because there are no laws. And, on the other hand, is there any feature in Mussolini's *internal* regime that could be seriously objected to by any body of people likely to sit in judgement on him? For, as the author of this book abundantly shows – and this in fact is the main purpose of the book – there is not one scoundrelism committed by Mussolini between 1922 and 1940 that has not been lauded to the skies by the very people who are now promising to bring him to trial.

For the purposes of his allegory "Cassius" imagines Mussolini indicted before a British court, with the Attorney General as prosecutor. The list of charges is an impressive one, and the main facts – from the murder of Matteotti* to the invasion of Greece, and from the destruction of the peasants' co-operatives to the bombing of Addis Ababa – are not denied. Concentration camps, broken treaties, rubber truncheons, castor oil – everything is admitted. The only troublesome question is: how can something that was praiseworthy at the time when you did it – ten years ago, say – suddenly become reprehensible now? Mussolini is allowed to call witnesses, both living and dead, and to show by their own printed words that from the very first the responsible leaders of British opinion have encouraged him in everything that he did. For instance, here is Lord Rothermere in 1928:

> In his own country [Mussolini] was the antidote to a deadly poison. For the rest of Europe he has been a tonic which has done to all incalculable good. I can claim with sincere satisfaction to have been the first man in a position of public influence to put Mussolini's splendid achievement in its right light. [...] He is the greatest figure of our age.

Here is Winston Churchill in 1927:

> If I had been an Italian I am sure I should have been wholeheartedly with you in your triumphant struggle against the bestial appetites and passions of Leninism. [...] [Italy] has provided the necessary antidote to the Russian

poison. Hereafter no great nation will be unprovided with an ultimate means of protection against the cancerous growth of Bolshevism.

Here is Lord Mottistone* in 1935:

> I did not oppose [the Italian action in Abyssinia]. I wanted to dispel the ridiculous illusion that it was a nice thing to sympathize with the underdog. [...] I said it was a wicked thing to send arms or connive to send arms to these cruel, brutal Abyssinians and still to deny them to others who are playing an honourable part.

Here is Mr Duff Cooper* in 1938:

> Concerning the Abyssinian episode, the less said now the better. When old friends are reconciled after a quarrel, it is always dangerous for them to discuss its original causes.

Here is Mr Ward Price, of the *Daily Mail*, in 1932:

> Ignorant and prejudiced people talk of Italian affairs as if that nation were subject to some tyranny which it would willingly throw off. With that rather morbid commiseration for fanatical minorities which is the rule with certain imperfectly informed sections of British public opinion, this country long shut its eyes to the magnificent work that the Fascist regime was doing. I have several times heard Mussolini himself express his gratitude to the *Daily Mail* as having been the first British newspaper to put his aims fairly before the world.

And so on, and so on, and so on. Hoare, Simon, Halifax, Neville Chamberlain, Austen Chamberlain, Hore-Belisha, Amery, Lord Lloyd* and various others enter the witness box, all of them ready to testify that, whether Mussolini was crushing the Italian trade unions, non-intervening in Spain, pouring mustard gas on the Abyssinians, throwing Arabs out of aeroplanes or building up a navy for use against Britain, the British government and its official spokesmen supported him through thick and thin. We are shown Lady (Austen) Chamberlain* shaking hands with Mussolini in 1924, Chamberlain and Halifax banqueting with him and toasting "the Emperor of Abyssinia" in 1939, Lord Lloyd buttering up the Fascist regime in an official pamphlet as late as 1940. The net impression left by this part of the trial is quite simply that Mussolini is not guilty. Only later, when an Abyssinian, a Spaniard and an Italian anti-Fascist give their evidence, does the real case against him begin to appear.

Now, the book is a fanciful one, but this conclusion is realistic. It is immensely unlikely that the British Tories will ever put Mussolini on trial. There is nothing that they could accuse him of except his declaration of war in 1940. If the "trial of war criminals" that some people enjoy dreaming about ever happens, it can only happen after revolutions in the Allied countries. But the whole notion of finding scapegoats, of blaming individuals, or parties, or nations for the calamities that have happened to us raises other trains of thought, some of them rather disconcerting.

The history of British relations with Mussolini illustrates the structural weakness of a capitalist state. Granting that power politics are not moral, to attempt to buy Italy out of the Axis – and clearly this idea underlay British policy from 1934 onwards – was a natural strategic move. But it was not a move which Baldwin, Chamberlain and the rest of them were capable of carrying out. It could only have been done by being so strong that Mussolini would not dare to side with Hitler. This was impossible, because an economy ruled by the profit motive is simply not equal to rearming on a modern scale. Britain only began to arm when the Germans were in Calais. Before that, fairly large sums had, indeed, been voted for armaments, but they slid peaceably into the pockets of the shareholders and the weapons did not appear. Since they had no real intention of curtailing their own privileges, it was inevitable that the British ruling class should carry out every policy half-heartedly and blind themselves to the coming danger. But the moral collapse which this entailed was something new in British politics. In the nineteenth and early twentieth centuries, British politicians might be hypocritical, but hypocrisy implies a moral code. It was something new when Tory MPs cheered the news that British ships had been bombed by Italian aeroplanes, or when members of the House of Lords lent themselves to organized libel campaigns against the Basque children who had been brought here as refugees.

When one thinks of the lies and betrayals of those years, the cynical abandonment of one ally after another, the imbecile optimism of the Tory press, the flat refusal to believe that the dictators meant war, even when they shouted it from the housetops, the inability of the moneyed class to see anything wrong whatever in concentration camps, ghettos, massacres and undeclared wars, one is driven to feel that moral decadence played its part as well as mere stupidity. By 1937 or thereabouts it was not possible to be in doubt about the nature of the fascist regimes. But the lords of property had decided that fascism was on their side and they were willing to swallow the most stinking evils so long as their property remained secure. In their clumsy way they were playing the game of Machiavelli, of "political realism", of "anything is right which advances the cause of the Party" – the Party in this case, of course, being the Conservative Party.

All this "Cassius" brings out, but he does shirk its corollary. Throughout his book it is implied that only Tories are immoral. "Yet there is still another England," he says. "This other England detested fascism from the day of its birth. [...] This was the England of the Left, the England of Labour." True, but only part of the truth. The actual behaviour of the Left has been more honourable than its theories. It has fought against fascism, but its representative thinkers have entered just as deeply as their opponents into the evil world of "realism" and power politics.

"Realism" (it used to be called dishonesty) is part of the general political atmosphere of our time. It is a sign of the weakness of "Cassius's" position that one could compile a quite similar book entitled *The Trial of Winston Churchill*, or *The Trial of Chiang Kai-shek*,* or even *The Trial of Ramsay MacDonald*. In each case you would find the leaders of the Left contradicting themselves almost as grossly as the Tory leaders quoted by "Cassius". For the Left has also been willing to shut its eyes to a great deal and to accept some very doubtful allies. We laugh now to hear the Tories abusing Mussolini when they were flattering him five years ago, but who would have foretold in 1927 that the Left would one day take Chiang Kai-shek to its bosom? Who would have foretold just after the General Strike that ten years later Winston Churchill would be the darling of the *Daily Worker*? In the years 1935–39, when almost any ally against fascism seemed acceptable, left wingers found themselves praising Mustapha Kemal and then developing a tenderness for Carol of Rumania.*

Although it was in every way more pardonable, the attitude of the Left towards the Russian regime has been distinctly similar to the attitude of the Tories towards fascism. There has been the same tendency to excuse almost anything "because they're on our side". It is all very well to talk about Lady Chamberlain photographed shaking hands with Mussolini; the photograph of Stalin shaking hands with Ribbentrop* is much more recent. On the whole, the intellectuals of the Left defended the Russo-German Pact. It was "realistic", like Chamberlain's appeasement policy, and with similar consequences. If there is a way out of the moral pigsty we are living in, the first step towards it is probably to grasp that "realism" does *not* pay, and that to sell out your friends and sit rubbing your hands while they are destroyed is not the last word in political wisdom.

This fact is demonstrable in any city between Cardiff and Stalingrad, but not many people can see it. Meanwhile it is a pamphleteer's duty to attack the Right, but not to flatter the Left. It is partly because the Left have been too easily satisfied with themselves that they are where they are now.

Mussolini, in "Cassius's" book, after calling his witnesses, enters the box himself. He sticks to his Machiavellian creed: Might is Right, *væ victis!** He is guilty of the only crime that matters, the crime of failure, and he admits that his adversaries have a right to kill him – but not, he insists, a right to blame him. Their conduct has been similar to his own, and their moral condemnations are all hypocrisy. But thereafter come the other three witnesses, the Abyssinian, the Spaniard and the Italian, who are morally upon a different plane, since they have never temporized with fascism nor had a chance to play at power politics – and all three of them demand the death penalty.

Would they demand it in real life? Will any such thing ever happen? It is not very likely, even if the people who have a real right to try Mussolini should somehow get him into their hands. The Tories, of course, though they would shrink from a real inquest into the origins of the war, are not sorry to have the chance of pushing the whole blame onto a few notorious individuals like Mussolini and Hitler. In this way the Darlan–Badoglio* manoeuvre is made easier. Mussolini is a good scapegoat while he is at large, though he would be an awkward one in captivity. But how about the common people? Would they kill their tyrants, in cold blood and with the forms of law, if they had the chance?

It is a fact that there have been very few such executions in history. At the end of the last war an election was won partly on the slogan "Hang the Kaiser", and yet if any such thing had been attempted the conscience of the nation would probably have revolted. When tyrants are put to death, it should be by their own subjects; those who are punished by a foreign authority, like Napoleon, are simply made into martyrs and legends.

What is important is not that these political gangsters should be made to suffer, but that they should be made to discredit themselves. Fortunately they do do so in many cases, for to a surprising extent the warlords in shining armour, the apostles of the martial virtues, tend not to die fighting when the time comes. History is full of ignominious getaways by the great and famous. Napoleon surrendered to the English in order to get protection from the Prussians, the Empress Eugenie fled in a hansom cab with an American dentist, Ludendorff resorted to blue spectacles, one of the more unprintable Roman emperors tried to escape assassination by locking himself in the lavatory, and during the early days of the Spanish Civil War one leading fascist made his escape from Barcelona, with exquisite fitness, through a sewer.*

It is some such exit that one would wish for Mussolini, and if he is left to himself perhaps he will achieve it. Possibly Hitler also. It used to be said of Hitler that when his time came he would never fly or surrender, but would perish in some operatic manner, by suicide at the very least. But that was when Hitler was successful; during the last year, since things began to go wrong, it is difficult to feel that he has behaved with dignity or courage. "Cassius" ends his book with the judge's summing-up, and leaves the verdict open, seeming to invite a decision from his readers. Well, if it were left to me, my verdict on both Hitler and Mussolini would be: not death, unless it is inflicted in some hurried unspectacular way. If the Germans and Italians feel like giving them a summary court martial and then a firing squad, let them do it. Or better still, let the pair of them escape with a suitcaseful of bearer securities and settle down as the accredited bores of some Swiss *pension*. But no martyrizing, no St Helena business. And, above all, no solemn hypocritical "trial of war criminals", with all the slow cruel pageantry of the law, which after a lapse of time has so strange a way of focusing a romantic light on the accused and turning a scoundrel into a hero.

Mark Twain – the Licensed Jester*

Mark Twain has crashed the lofty gates of the Everyman Library, but only with *Tom Sawyer* and *Huckleberry Finn*,* already fairly well known under the guise of "children's books" (which they are not). His best and most characteristic books, *Roughing It*, *The Innocents at Home*, and even *Life on the Mississippi*,* are little remembered in this country, though no doubt in America the patriotism which is everywhere mixed up with literary judgement keeps them alive.

Although Mark Twain produced a surprising variety of books, ranging from a namby-pamby "life" of Joan of Arc* to a pamphlet so obscene that it has never been publicly printed, all that is best in his work centres about the Mississippi River and the wild mining towns of the West. Born in 1835 (he came of a Southern family, a family just rich enough to own one or perhaps two slaves), he had had his youth and early manhood in the golden age of America, the period when the great plains were opened up, when wealth and opportunity seemed limitless, and human beings felt free, indeed *were* free, as they had never been before and may not be again for centuries. *Life on the Mississippi* and the two other books that I have mentioned are a ragbag of anecdotes, scenic descriptions and social history both serious and burlesque, but they have a central theme which could perhaps be put into these words: "This is how human beings behave when they are not frightened of the sack." In writing these books Mark Twain is not consciously writing a hymn to liberty. Primarily he is interested in "character", in the fantastic, almost lunatic variations which human nature is capable of when economic pressure and tradition are both removed from it. The raftsmen, Mississippi pilots, miners and bandits whom he describes are probably not much exaggerated, but they are as different from modern men, and from one another, as the gargoyles of a medieval cathedral. They could develop their strange and sometimes sinister individuality because of the lack of any outside pressure. The state hardly existed, the churches were weak and spoke with many voices, and land was to be had for the taking. If you disliked your job you simply hit the boss in the eye and moved further west – and moreover, money was so plentiful that the smallest coin in circulation was worth a shilling. The American pioneers were not supermen, and they were not especially courageous. Whole towns of hardy gold miners let themselves be terrorized by bandits whom they lacked the public spirit to put down. They were not even free from class distinctions. The desperado who stalked through the streets of the mining settlement, with a derringer pistol in his waistcoat pocket and twenty corpses to his credit, was dressed in a frock coat and shiny top hat, described himself firmly as a "gentleman" and was meticulous about table manners. But at least it was not the case that a man's destiny was settled from his birth. The "log cabin to White House" myth was true while the free land lasted. In a way, it was for this that the Paris mob had stormed the Bastille, and when one reads Mark Twain, Bret Harte and Whitman it is hard to feel that their effort was wasted.

However, Mark Twain aimed at being something more than a chronicler of the Mississippi and the Gold Rush. In his own day he was famous all over the world as a humorist and comic lecturer. In New York, London, Berlin, Vienna, Melbourne and Calcutta vast audiences rocked with laughter over jokes which have now, almost without exception, ceased to be funny. (It is worth noticing that Mark Twain's lectures were only a success with Anglo-Saxon and German audiences. The relatively grown-up Latin races – whose own humour, he complained, always centred round sex and politics – never cared for them.) But in addition, Mark Twain had some pretensions to being a social critic, even a species of philosopher. He had in him an iconoclastic, even revolutionary vein which he obviously wanted to follow up and yet somehow never did follow up. He might have been a destroyer of humbugs and a prophet of democracy more valuable than Whitman, because healthier and more humorous. Instead he became that dubious thing, a "public figure", flattered by passport officials and entertained by royalty, and his career reflects the deterioration in American life that set in after the Civil War.

Mark Twain has sometimes been compared with his contemporary Anatole France.* This comparison is not so pointless as it may sound. Both men were the spiritual children of Voltaire; both had an ironical, sceptical view of life, and a native pessimism overlaid by gaiety; both knew that the existing social order is a swindle and its cherished beliefs mostly delusions. Both were bigoted atheists and convinced (in Mark Twain's case this was Darwin's doing) of the unbearable cruelty of the universe. But there the resemblance ends. Not only is the Frenchman enormously more learned, more civilized, more alive aesthetically, but he is also more courageous. He does attack the things he disbelieves in; he does not, like Mark Twain, always take refuge behind the amiable mask of the "public figure" and the licensed jester. He is ready to risk the anger of the Church and to take the unpopular side in a controversy – in the Dreyfus case,* for example. Mark Twain, except perhaps in one short essay, 'What Is Man?', never attacks established beliefs in a way that is likely to get him into trouble. Nor could he ever wean himself from the notion, which is perhaps especially an American notion, that success and virtue are the same thing.

In *Life on the Mississippi* there is a queer little illustration of the central weakness of Mark Twain's character. In the earlier part of this mainly autobiographical book the dates have been altered. Mark Twain describes his adventures as a Mississippi pilot as though he had been a boy of about seventeen at the time, whereas in fact he was a young man of nearly thirty. There is a reason for this. The same part of the book describes his exploits in the Civil War, which were distinctly inglorious. Moreover, Mark Twain started by fighting, if he can be said to have fought, on the Southern side, and then changed his allegiance before the war was over. This kind of behaviour is more excusable in a boy than in a man, whence the adjustment of the dates. It is also clear enough, however, that he changed sides because he saw that the North was going to win – and this tendency to side with the stronger whenever possible, to believe that might *must* be right, is apparent throughout his career. In *Roughing It* there is an interesting account of a bandit named Slade, who, among countless other outrages, had committed twenty-eight murders. It is perfectly clear that Mark Twain admires this disgusting scoundrel. Slade was successful; therefore he was admirable. This outlook, no less common today, is summed up in the significant American expression "to *make good*".

In the money-grubbing period that followed the Civil War it was hard for anyone of Mark Twain's temperament to refuse to be a success. The old, simple, stump-whittling, tobacco-chewing democracy which Abraham Lincoln typified was perishing: it was now the age of cheap immigrant labour and the growth of Big Business. Mark Twain mildly satirized his contemporaries in *The Gilded Age*,* but he also gave himself up to the prevailing fever, and made and lost vast sums of money. He even for a period of years deserted writing for business – and he squandered his time on buffooneries, not merely lecture tours and public banquets but, for instance, the writing of a book like *A Connecticut Yankee in King Arthur's Court*,* which is a deliberate flattery of all that is worst and most vulgar in American life. The man who might have been a kind of rustic Voltaire became the world's leading after-dinner speaker, charming alike for his anecdotes and his power to make businessmen feel themselves public benefactors.

It is usual to blame Mark Twain's wife for his failure to write the books he ought to have written, and it is evident that she did tyrannize over him pretty thoroughly. Each morning, Mark Twain would show her what he had written the day before, and Mrs Clemens (Mark Twain's real name was Samuel Clemens) would go over it with the blue pencil, cutting out everything that she thought unsuitable. She seems to have been a drastic blue-penciller even by nineteenth-century standards. There is an account in W.D. Howells's book *My Mark Twain** of the fuss that occurred over a terrible expletive that had crept into *Huckleberry Finn*. Mark Twain appealed to Howells, who admitted that it was "just what Huck would have said", but agreed with Mrs Clemens that the word could not possibly be printed. The word was "hell". Nevertheless, no writer is really the intellectual slave of his wife. Mrs Clemens could not have stopped Mark Twain writing any book he really wanted to write. She may have made his surrender to society easier, but the surrender happened because of that flaw in his own nature, his inability to despise success.

Several of Mark Twain's books are bound to survive, because they contain invaluable social history. His life covered the great period of American expansion. When he was a child it was a normal day's outing to go with a picnic lunch and watch the hanging of an abolitionist, and when he died the aeroplane was ceasing to be a novelty. This period in America produced relatively little literature, and but for Mark Twain our picture of a Mississippi paddle steamer, or a stagecoach crossing the plains, would be much dimmer than it is. But most people who have studied his work have come away with a feeling that he might have done something more. He gives all the while a strange impression of being about to say something and then funking it, so that *Life on the Mississippi* and the rest of them seem to be haunted by the ghost of a greater and much more coherent book. Significantly, he starts his autobiography by remarking that a man's inner life is indescribable. We do not know what he would have said – it is just possible that the unprocurable pamphlet, *1601*,* would supply a clue but we may guess that it would have wrecked his reputation and reduced his income to reasonable proportions.

A Hundred Up*

It is now a hundred years since the final numbers of *Martin Chuzzlewit* were published, and though it came thus early in Dickens's career (it was his fourth novel, if one counts *Pickwick* as a novel), it has more the air of being a potboiler than any of his books except the *Sketches*.* There cannot be many people living who could outline its plot from memory. Whereas books like *Oliver Twist*, or *Bleak House*, or *Great Expectations*, have a central theme which can in some cases be reduced to a single word, the various parts of *Martin Chuzzlewit* have not much more relationship to one another than the sounds produced by a cat walking across the piano. The best characters are "supers".

What do people remember when they think of *Martin Chuzzlewit*? The American interlude, Mrs Gamp, and Todgers's (especially Bailey). Martin Chuzzlewit himself is a stick, Mark Tapley a tedious paradox on two legs, Pecksniff a partial failure. It is ironical that Dickens should have tried, more or less unsuccessfully, to make Pecksniff into a monumental figure of a hypocrite, and at the same time, almost incidentally, should have painted such a devastating picture of hypocrisy in the American chapters. Dickens's comic genius is dependent on his moral sense. He is funniest when he is discovering new sins. To denounce Pecksniff did not call into play his special powers, because, after all, no one supposes that hypocrisy is desirable. But to see through the pretensions of American democracy, or even, at that date, to see that Mrs Gamp was a luxury that society might well do without, did need the eye of a Dickens. The book's lack of any real central theme can be seen in its fearful ending. It is as though Dickens were dissolving into lukewarm treacle, and – as so often when he says something that he does not really feel – whole paragraphs of the final chapter will go straight into blank verse:

> Thy life is tranquil, calm and happy, Tom.
> In the soft strain which ever and again
> Comes stealing back upon the ear, the memory
> Of thine old love may find a voice perhaps;
> But it is a pleasant, softened, whispering memory,
> Like that in which we sometimes hold the dead,
> And does not pain or grieve thee, God be thanked!

Yet the man who could write this stuff could also record the conversations of Bailey, and could not only create Mrs Gamp but could throw in, just for good measure, the metaphysical puzzle Mrs Harris.

The American chapters are a good example of Dickens's habit of telling small lies in order to emphasize what he regards as a big truth. No doubt many of the things he reports actually happened (other travellers of the time confirm him on some details) but his picture of American society as a whole cannot possibly be true – not only because no community is wholly bad, but because the chaos of real life has been deliberately left out. Every incident, every character, is simply an illustration of Dickens's thesis. Moreover, the strongest charge that he makes against the Americans, that they boast of being democratic while actually living on slave labour, is obviously unfair. It implies that American opinion as a whole acquiesced in slavery, whereas a bloody civil war was to be fought mainly on this issue only twenty years later. But Dickens says these things in order to hit at what he feels to be the real fault of the Americans, their ignorant contempt for Europe and unjustified belief in their own superiority. Perhaps there *were* a few Americans who did not edit libellous newspapers or emit sentences like "the libation of freedom must sometimes be quaffed in blood" – but to lay too much stress upon them would have been to spoil the picture. After all, the business of a caricaturist is to make his point, and these chapters have worn very much better than *American Notes*.*

The mental atmosphere of the American interlude is one that has since become familiar to us in the books written by British travellers to Soviet Russia. Some of these report that everything is good, others that everything is bad, but nearly all share the same propagandist outlook. A hundred years ago America, "the land of the free", had rather the same place in the European imagination that Soviet Russia has now, and *Martin Chuzzlewit* is the 1844 equivalent of André Gide's *Retour de l'URSS*.* But it is a sign of the changing temper of the world that Dickens's attack, so much more violent and unfair than Gide's, could be so quickly forgiven.

Martin Chuzzlewit stands somewhere near the turning point of Dickens's literary development, when he was becoming less of a picaresque writer and more of a novelist. The times were changing with the rise of the new cautious middle class, and Dickens was too much alive not to be affected by the atmosphere he lived in. *Martin Chuzzlewit* is his last completely disorderly book. In spite of its frequent flashes of genius, it is difficult to feel that by following up this vein in himself Dickens could have given us anything to compensate for the loss of *Hard Times* and *Great Expectations*.

The English People*

ENGLAND AT FIRST GLANCE

In peacetime, it is unusual for foreign visitors to this country to notice the existence of the English people. Even the accent referred to by Americans as "the English accent" is not in fact common to more than a quarter of the population. In cartoons in Continental papers England is personified by an aristocrat with a monocle, a sinister capitalist in a top hat or a spinster in a Burberry. Hostile or friendly, nearly all the generalizations that are made about England base themselves on the property-owning class and ignore the other forty-five million.

But the chances of war brought to England, either as soldiers or as refugees, hundreds of thousands of foreigners who would not normally have come here, and forced them into intimate contact with ordinary people. Czechs, Poles, Germans and Frenchmen to whom "England" meant Piccadilly and the Derby found themselves quartered in sleepy East Anglian villages, in northern mining towns, or in the vast working-class areas of London whose names the world had never heard until they were blitzed. Those of them who had the gift of observation will have seen for themselves that the real England is not the England of the guidebooks. Blackpool is more typical than Ascot; the top hat is a moth-eaten rarity; the language of the BBC is barely intelligible to the masses. Even the prevailing physical type does not agree with the caricatures, for the tall, lanky physique which is traditionally English is almost confined to the upper classes: the working classes, as a rule, are rather small, with short limbs and brisk movements, and with a tendency among the women to grow dumpy in early middle life.

It is worth trying for a moment to put oneself in the position of a foreign observer, new to England, but unprejudiced, and able because of his work to keep in touch with ordinary, useful, unspectacular people. Some of his generalizations would be wrong, because he would not make enough allowance for the temporary dislocations resulting from war. Never having seen England in normal times, he might underrate the power of class distinctions, or think English agriculture healthier than it is, or be too much impressed by the dinginess of the London streets or the prevalence of drunkenness. But with his fresh eyes he would see a great deal that a native observer misses, and his probable impressions are worth tabulating. Almost certainly he would find the salient characteristics of the English common people to be artistic insensibility, gentleness, respect for legality, suspicion of foreigners, sentimentality about animals, hypocrisy, exaggerated class distinctions and an obsession with sport.

As for our artistic insensibility, ever-growing stretches of beautiful countryside are ruined by planless building, the heavy industries are allowed to convert whole counties into blackened deserts, ancient monuments are wantonly pulled down or swamped by seas of yellow brick, attractive vistas are blocked by hideous statues to nonentities – and all this without any *popular* protest whatever. When England's housing problem is discussed, its aesthetic aspect simply does not enter the mind of the average man. Nor is there any widespread interest in any of the arts, except perhaps music. Poetry, the art in which above all others England has excelled, has for more than a century had no appeal whatever for the common people. It is only acceptable when – as in some popular songs and mnemonic rhymes – it is masquerading as something else. Indeed the very word "poetry" arouses either derision or embarrassment in ninety-eight people out of a hundred.

Our imaginary foreign observer would certainly be struck by our gentleness: by the orderly behaviour of English crowds, the lack of pushing and quarrelling, the willingness to form queues, the good temper of harassed, overworked people like bus conductors. The manners of the English working class are not always very graceful, but they are extremely considerate. Great care is taken in showing a stranger the way; blind people can travel across London with the certainty that they will be helped on and off every bus and across every street. In wartime a few of the policemen carry revolvers, but England has nothing corresponding to the gendarmerie, the semi-military police living in barracks and armed with rifles (sometimes even with tanks and aeroplanes), who are the guardians of society all the way from Calais to Tokyo. And except for certain well-defined areas in half a dozen big towns there is very little crime or violence. The average of honesty is lower in the big towns than in the country, but even in London the news vendor can safely leave his pile of pennies on the pavement while he goes for a drink. The prevailing gentleness of manners is a recent thing, however. Well within living memory it was impossible for a smartly dressed person to walk down Ratcliffe Highway* without being assaulted, and an eminent jurist, asked to name a typically English crime, could answer: "Kicking your wife to death."

There is no revolutionary tradition in England, and even in extremist political parties, it is only the middle-class membership that thinks in revolutionary terms. The masses still more or less assume that "against the law" is a synonym for "wrong". It is known that the criminal law is harsh and full of anomalies and that litigation is so expensive as always to favour the rich against the poor – but there is a general feeling that the law, such as it is, will be scrupulously administered, that a judge or magistrate cannot be bribed, that no one will be punished without trial. An Englishman does not believe in his bones, as a Spanish or Italian peasant does, that the law is simply a racket. It is precisely this general confidence in the law that has allowed a good deal of recent tampering with habeas corpus to escape public notice. But it also causes some ugly situations to end peacefully. During the worst of the London Blitz the authorities tried to prevent the public from using the Tube stations as shelters. The people did not reply by storming the gates – they simply bought themselves penny-halfpenny tickets: they thus had legal status as passengers, and there was no thought of turning them out again.

The traditional English xenophobia is stronger among the working class than the middle class. It was partly the resistance of the trade unions that prevented a really large influx of refugees from the fascist countries before the war, and when the German refugees were interned in 1940, it was not the working class that protested. The difference in habits, and especially in food and language, makes it very hard for English working people to get on with foreigners. Their diet differs a great deal from that of any European nation, and they are extremely conservative about it. As a rule they will refuse even to sample a foreign dish; they regard such things as garlic and olive oil with disgust; life is unliveable to them unless they have tea and puddings. And the peculiarities of the English language make it almost impossible for anyone who has left school at fourteen to learn a foreign language after he has grown up. In the French Foreign Legion, for instance, the British and American legionaries seldom rise out of the ranks, because they cannot learn French, whereas a German learns French in a few months. English working people, as a rule, think it effeminate even to pronounce a foreign word correctly. This is bound up with the fact that the upper classes learn foreign languages as a regular part of their education. Travelling abroad, speaking foreign tongues, enjoying foreign food are vaguely felt to be upper-class habits, a species of snobbery, so that xenophobia is reinforced by class jealousy.

Perhaps the most horrible spectacles in England are the Dogs' Cemeteries in Kensington Gardens, at Stoke Poges (it actually adjoins the churchyard where Gray wrote his famous 'Elegy')* and at various other places. But there were also the Animals' ARP Centres, with miniature stretchers for cats, and in the first year of the war there was the spectacle of Animal Day being celebrated with all its usual pomp in the middle of the Dunkirk evacuation. Although its worst follies are committed by the upper-class women, the animal cult runs right through the nation and is probably bound up with the decay of agriculture and the dwindled birth rate. Several years of stringent rationing have failed to reduce the dog and cat population, and even in poor quarters of big towns the bird fanciers' shops display canary seed at prices ranging up to twenty-five shillings a pint.

THE ENGLISH PEOPLE

Hypocrisy is so generally accepted as part of the English character that a foreign observer would be prepared to meet with it at every turn, but he would find especially ripe examples in the laws dealing with gambling, drinking, prostitution and profanity. He would find it difficult to reconcile the anti-imperialistic sentiments which are commonly expressed in England with the size of the British Empire. If he were a Continental European he would notice with ironical amusement that the English think it wicked to have a big army but see nothing wrong in having a big navy. This too he would set down as hypocrisy – not altogether fairly, for it is the fact of being an island, and therefore not needing a big army, that has allowed British democratic institutions to grow up, and the mass of the people are fairly well aware of this.

Exaggerated class distinctions have been diminishing over a period of about thirty years, and the war has probably speeded up the process, but newcomers to England are still astonished and sometimes horrified by the blatant differences between class and class. The great majority of the people can still be "placed" in an instant by their manners, clothes and general appearance. Even the physical type differs considerably, the upper classes being on an average several inches taller than the working class. But the most striking difference of all is in language and accent. The English working class, as Mr Wyndham Lewis has put it, are "branded on the tongue". And though class distinctions do not exactly coincide with economic distinctions, the contrast between wealth and poverty is very much more glaring, and more taken for granted, than in most countries.

The English were the inventors of several of the world's most popular games, and have spread them more widely than any other product of their culture. The word "football" is mispronounced by scores of millions who have never heard of Shakespeare or Magna Carta. The English themselves are not outstandingly good at all games, but they enjoy playing them, and to an extent that strikes foreigners as childish they enjoy reading about them and betting on them. During the between-war years the football pools did more than any other one thing to make life bearable for the unemployed. Professional footballers, boxers, jockeys and even cricketers enjoy a popularity that no scientist or artist could hope to rival. Nevertheless sport worship is not carried to quite such imbecile lengths as one would imagine from reading the popular press. When the brilliant lightweight boxer, Kid Lewis,* stood for Parliament in his native borough, he only scored 125 votes.

These traits that we have enumerated are probably the ones that would strike an intelligent observer first. Out of them he might feel that he could construct a reliable picture of the English character. But then probably a thought would strike him: is there such a thing as "the English character"? Can one talk about nations as though they were individuals? And supposing that one can, is there any genuine continuity between the England of today and the England of the past?

As he wandered through the London streets, he would notice the old prints in the bookshop windows, and it would occur to him that if these things are representative, then England must have changed a great deal. It is not much more than a hundred years since the distinguishing mark of English life was its brutality. The common people, to judge by the prints, spent their time in an almost unending round of fighting, whoring, drunkenness and bull-baiting. Moreover, even the physical type appears to have changed. Where are they gone, the hulking draymen and low-browed prizefighters, the brawny sailors with their buttocks bursting out of their white trousers, and the great overblown beauties with their swelling bosoms, like the figureheads of Nelson's ships? What had these people in common with the gentle-mannered, undemonstrative, law-abiding English of today? Do such things as "national cultures" really exist?

This is one of those questions, like the freedom of the will or the identity of the individual, in which all the arguments are on one side and instinctive knowledge is on the other. It is not easy to discover the connecting thread that runs through English life from the sixteenth century onwards, but all English people who bother about such subjects feel that it exists. They feel that they understand the institutions that have come to them out of the past – Parliament, for instance, or Sabbatarianism, or the subtle grading of the class system – with an inherited knowledge impossible to a foreigner. Individuals, too, are felt to conform to a national pattern. D.H. Lawrence is felt to be "very English", but so is Blake; Dr Johnson and G.K. Chesterton are somehow the same kind of person. The belief that we resemble our ancestors – that Shakespeare, say, is more like a modern Englishman than a modern Frenchman or German – may be unreasonable, but by existing it influences conduct. Myths which are believed in tend to become true, because they set up a type, or "persona", which the average person will do his best to resemble.

During the bad period of 1940 it became clear that in Britain national solidarity is stronger than class antagonism. If it were really true that "the proletarian has no country", 1940 was the time for him to show it. It was exactly then, however, that class feeling slipped into the background, only reappearing when the immediate danger had passed. Moreover, it is probable that the stolid behaviour of the British town populations under the bombing was partly due to the existence of the national "persona" – that is, to their preconceived idea of themselves. Traditionally the Englishman is phlegmatic, unimaginative, not easily rattled – and since that is what he thinks he ought to be, that is what he tends to become. Dislike of hysteria and "fuss", admiration for stubbornness, are all but universal in England, being shared by everyone except the intelligentsia. Millions of English people willingly accept as their national emblem the bulldog, an animal noted for its obstinacy, ugliness and impenetrable stupidity. They have a remarkable readiness to admit that foreigners are more "clever" than themselves, and yet they feel that it would be an outrage against the laws of God and nature for England to be ruled by foreigners. Our imaginary observer would notice, perhaps, that Wordsworth's sonnets during the Napoleonic War might have been written during this one. He would know already that England has produced poets and scientists rather than philosophers, theologians or pure theorists of any description. And he might end by deciding that a profound, almost unconscious patriotism and an inability to think logically are the abiding features of the English character, traceable in English literature from Shakespeare onwards.

THE MORAL OUTLOOK OF THE ENGLISH PEOPLE

For perhaps 150 years organized religion, or conscious religious belief of any kind, have had very little hold on the mass of the English people. Only about 10 per cent of them ever go near a place of worship except to be married and buried. A vague theism and an intermittent belief in life after death are probably fairly widespread, but the main Christian doctrines have been largely forgotten. Asked what he meant by "Christianity", the average man would define it wholly in ethical terms ("unselfishness", or "loving your neighbour", would be the kind of definition he would give). This was probably much the same in the early days of the Industrial Revolution, when the old village life had been suddenly broken up and the Established Church had lost touch with its followers. But in recent times the Nonconformist sects have also lost much of their vigour, and within the last generation the Bible reading which used to be traditional in England has lapsed. It is quite common to meet with young people who do not know the Bible stories even as *stories*.

But there is one sense in which the English common people have remained more Christian than the upper classes, and probably than any other European nation. This is in their non-acceptance of the modern cult of power worship. While almost ignoring the spoken doctrines of the Church, they have held on to the one that the Church never formulated, because taking it for granted: namely that might is not right. It is here that the gulf between the intelligentsia and the common people is widest. From Carlyle* onwards, but especially in the last generation, the British intelligentsia have tended to take their ideas from Europe and have been infected by habits of thought that derive ultimately from Machiavelli. All the cults that have been fashionable in the last dozen years, communism, fascism and pacifism, are in the last analysis forms of power worship. It is significant that in this country, unlike most others, the Marxist version of socialism has found its warmest adherents in the middle class. Its methods, if not its theories, obviously conflict with what is called "bourgeois morality" (i.e. common decency), and in moral matters it is the proletarians who are bourgeois.

One of the basic folk tales of the English-speaking peoples is Jack the Giant-Killer – the little man against the big man. Mickey Mouse, Popeye the Sailor and Charlie Chaplin are all essentially the same figure. (Chaplin's films, it is worth noticing, were banned in Germany as soon as Hitler came to power, and Chaplin has been viciously attacked by English fascist writers.) Not merely a hatred of bullying, but a tendency to support the weaker side merely because it is weaker, are almost general in England. Hence the admiration for a "good loser" and the easy forgiveness of failures, either in sport, politics or war. Even in very serious matters the English people do not feel that an unsuccessful action is necessarily futile. An example in this war was the campaign in Greece. No one expected it to succeed, but nearly everyone thought that it should be undertaken. And the popular attitude to foreign politics is nearly always coloured by the instinct to side with the underdog.

An obvious recent instance was pro-Finnish sentiment in the Russo-Finnish war of 1940. This was genuine enough, as several by-elections fought mainly on this issue showed. Popular feeling towards the USSR had been increasingly friendly for some time past, but Finland was a small country attacked by a big one, and that settled the issue for most people. In the American Civil War the British working classes sided with the North – the side that stood for the abolition of slavery – in spite of the fact that the Northern blockade of the cotton ports was causing great hardship in Britain. In the Franco-Prussian war, such pro-French sentiment as there was in England was among the working class. The small nationalities oppressed by the Turks found their sympathizers in the Liberal Party, at that time the party of the working class and the lower middle class. And in so far as it bothered with such issues at all, British mass sentiment was for the Abyssinians against the Italians, for the Chinese against the Japanese and for the Spanish Republicans against Franco. It was also friendly to Germany during the period when Germany was weak and disarmed, and it would not be surprising to see a similar swing of sentiment after this war.

The feeling that one ought always to side with the weaker party probably derives from the balance-of-power policy which Britain has followed from the eighteenth century onwards. A European critic would add that it is humbug, pointing in proof to the fact that Britain herself holds down subject populations in India and elsewhere. We don't, in fact, know what settlement the English common people would make with India if the decision were theirs. All political parties and all newspapers of whatever colour have conspired to prevent them from seeing the issue clearly. We do know, however, that they have sometimes championed the weak against the strong when it was obviously not to their own advantage. The best example is the Irish civil war.* The real weapon of the Irish rebels was British public opinion, which was substantially on their side and prevented the British government from crushing the rebellion in the only way possible. Even in the Boer War there was a considerable volume of pro-Boer sentiment, though it was not strong enough to influence events. One must conclude that in this matter the English common people have lagged behind their century. They have failed to catch up with power politics, "realism", *sacro egoismo** and the doctrine that the end justifies the means.

The general English hatred of bullying and terrorism means that any kind of violent criminal gets very little sympathy. Gangsterism on American lines could not flourish in England, and it is significant that the American gangsters have never tried to transfer their activities to this country. At need, the whole nation would combine against people who kidnap babies and fire machine guns in the street – but even the efficiency of the English police force really depends on the fact that the police have public opinion behind them. The bad side of this is the almost universal toleration of cruel and out-of-date punishments. It is not a thing to be proud of that England should still tolerate such punishments as flogging. It continues partly because of the widespread psychological ignorance, partly because men are only flogged for crimes that forfeit nearly everyone's sympathy. There would be an outcry if it were applied to non-violent crimes, or reinstituted for military offences. Military punishments are not taken for granted in England as they are in most countries. Public opinion is almost certainly opposed to the death penalty for cowardice and desertion, though there is no strong feeling against hanging murderers. In general the English attitude to crime is ignorant and old-fashioned, and humane treatment even of child offenders is a recent thing. Still, if Al Capone were in an English jail, it would not be for evasion of income tax.

A more complex question than the English attitude to crime and violence is the survival of puritanism and the world-famed English hypocrisy.

The English people proper, the working masses who make up 75 per cent of the population, are not puritanical. The dismal theology of Calvinism never popularized itself in England as it did for a while in Wales and Scotland. But puritanism in the looser sense in which the word is generally used (that is, prudishness, asceticism, the "killjoy" spirit) is something that has been unsuccessfully forced upon the working class by the class of small traders and manufacturers immediately above them. In its origin it had a clear though unconscious economic motive behind it. If you could persuade the working man that every kind of recreation was sinful, you could get more work out of him for less money. In the early nineteenth century there was even a school of thought which maintained that the working man ought not to marry. But it would be unfair to suggest that the puritan moral code was mere humbug. Its exaggerated fear of sexual immorality, which extended to a disapproval of stage plays, dancing and even bright-coloured clothes, was partly a protest against the real corruption of the later Middle Ages; there was also the new factor of syphilis, which appeared in England about the sixteenth century and worked frightful havoc for the next century or two. A little later there was another new factor in the introduction of distilled liquors – gin, brandy, and so forth – which were very much more intoxicating than the beer and mead which the English had been accustomed to. The "temperance" movement was a well-meant reaction against the frightful drunkenness of the nineteenth century, product of slum conditions and cheap gin. But it was necessarily led by fanatics who regarded not merely drunkenness but even the moderate drinking of alcohol as sinful. During the past fifty years or so there has even been a similar drive against tobacco. 100 years ago, or 200 years ago, tobacco smoking was much disapproved of, but only on the ground that it was dirty, vulgar and injurious to health: the idea that it is a wicked self-indulgence is modern.

This line of thought has never really appealed to the English masses. At most they have been sufficiently intimidated by middle-class puritanism to take some of their pleasures rather furtively. It is universally agreed that the working classes are far more moral than the upper classes, but the idea that sexuality is wicked in itself has no popular basis. Music-hall jokes, Blackpool postcards and the songs the soldiers make up are anything but puritanical. On the other hand, almost no one in England approves of prostitution. There are several big towns where prostitution is extremely blatant, but it is completely unattractive and has never been really tolerated. It could not be regulated and humanized as it has been in some countries, because every English person feels in his bones that it is wrong. As for the general weakening of sex morals that has happened during the past twenty or thirty years, it is probably a temporary thing, resulting from the excess of women over men in the population.

In the matter of drink, the only result of a century of "temperance" agitation has been a slight increase in hypocrisy. The practical disappearance of drunkenness as an English vice has not been due to the anti-drink fanatics but to competing amusements, education, the improvement in industrial conditions and the expensiveness of drink itself. The fanatics have been able to see to it that the Englishman drinks his glass of beer under difficulties and with a faint feeling of wrongdoing, but have not actually been able to prevent him from drinking it. The pub, one of the basic institutions of English life, carries on in spite of the harassing tactics of Nonconformist local authorities. So also with gambling. Most forms of gambling are illegal according to the letter of the law, but they all happen on an enormous scale. The motto of the English people might be the chorus of Marie Lloyd's song 'A Little of What You Fancy Does You Good'.* They are not vicious, not even lazy, but they will have their bit of fun, whatever the higher-ups may say. And they seem to be gradually winning their battle against the killjoy minorities. Even the horrors of the English Sunday have been much mitigated during the past dozen years. Some of the laws regulating pubs – designed in every case to discourage the publican and make drinking unattractive – have been relaxed during the war. And it is a very good sign that the stupid rule forbidding children to enter pubs, which tended to dehumanize the pub and turn it into a mere drinking shop, is beginning to be disregarded in some parts of the country.

Traditionally, the Englishman's home is his castle. In an age of conscription and identity cards this cannot really be true. But the hatred of regimentation, the feeling that your spare time is your own and that a man must not be persecuted for his opinions, is deeply ingrained, and the centralizing processes inevitable in wartime have not destroyed it.

It is a fact that the much-boasted freedom of the British press is theoretical rather than actual. To begin with the centralized ownership of the press means in practice that unpopular opinions can only be printed in books or in newspapers with small circulations. Moreover, the English people as a whole are not sufficiently interested in the printed word to be very vigilant about this aspect of their liberties, and during the last twenty years there has been much tampering with the freedom of the press, with no real popular protest. Even the demonstrations against the suppression of the *Daily Worker** were probably stage-managed by a small minority. On the other hand, freedom of speech is a reality, and respect for it is almost general. Extremely few English people are afraid to utter their political opinions in public, and there are not even very many who want to silence the opinions of others. In peacetime, when unemployment can be used as a weapon, there is a certain amount of petty persecution of "reds", but the real totalitarian atmosphere, in which the state endeavours to control people's thoughts as well as their words, is hardly imaginable.

The safeguard against it is partly the respect for integrity of conscience, and the willingness to hear both sides, which can be observed at any public meeting. But it is also partly the prevailing lack of intellectuality. The English are not sufficiently interested in intellectual matters to be intolerant about them. "Deviations" and "dangerous thoughts" do not seem very important to them. An ordinary Englishman, conservative, socialist, Catholic, communist or what not, almost never grasps the full logical implications of the creed he professes: almost always he utters heresies without noticing it. Orthodoxies, whether of the Right or the Left, flourish chiefly among the literary intelligentsia, the people who ought in theory to be the guardians of freedom of thought.

The English people are not good haters – their memory is very short, their patriotism is largely unconscious, they have no love of military glory and not much admiration for great men. They have the virtues and the vices of an old-fashioned people. To twentieth-century political theories they oppose not another theory of their own, but a moral quality which must be vaguely described as decency. On the day in 1936 when the Germans reoccupied the Rhineland I was in a northern mining town. I happened to go into a pub just after this piece of news, which quite obviously meant war, had come over the wireless, and I remarked to the others at the bar, "The German army has crossed the Rhine." With a vague air of capping a quotation someone answered, "Parley-voo." No more response than that! Nothing will ever wake these people up, I thought. But later in the evening, at the same pub, someone sang a song which had recently come out, with the chorus:

> For you can't do that there 'ere,
> No, you can't do that there 'ere;
> Anywhere else you can do that there,
> But you can't do that there 'ere!

And it struck me that perhaps this was the English answer to fascism. At any rate it is true that it has not happened here, in spite of fairly favourable circumstances. The amount of liberty, intellectual or other, that we enjoy in England ought not to be exaggerated, but the fact that it has not markedly diminished in nearly five years of desperate war is a hopeful symptom.

THE POLITICAL OUTLOOK OF THE ENGLISH PEOPLE

The English people are not only indifferent to fine points of doctrine but are remarkably ignorant politically. They are only now beginning to use the political terminology which has been current for years in Continental countries. If you asked a random group of people from any stratum of the population to define capitalism, socialism, communism, anarchism, Trotskyism, fascism, you would get mostly vague answers, and some of them would be surprisingly stupid ones.

But they are also distinctly ignorant about their own political system. During recent years, for various reasons, there has been a revival of political activity, but over a longer period the interest in party politics has been dwindling. Great numbers of adult English people have never in their lives bothered to vote in an election. In big towns it is quite common for people not to know the name of their MP or what constituency they live in. During the war years, owing to the failure to renew the registers, the young have no votes (at one time no one under twenty-nine had a vote), and do not seem much troubled by the fact. Nor does the anomalous electoral system, which usually favours the Conservative Party, arouse much protest. Attention focuses on policies and individuals (Chamberlain, Churchill, Cripps, Beveridge, Bevin*) rather than on parties. The feeling that Parliament really controls events, and that sensational changes are to be expected when a new government comes in, has been gradually fading ever since the first Labour government in 1923.

In spite of many subdivisions, Britain has in effect only two political parties, the Conservative Party and the Labour Party, which between them broadly represent the main interests of the nation. But during the last twenty years the tendency of these two parties has been to resemble one another more and more. Everyone knows in advance that any government, whatever its political principles may be, can be relied upon not to do certain things. Thus, no Conservative government will ever revert to what would have been called conservatism in the nineteenth century. No socialist government will massacre the propertied class, nor even expropriate them without compensation. A good recent example of the changing temper of politics was the reception given to the Beveridge Report. Thirty years ago any Conservative would have denounced this as state charity, while most socialists would have rejected it as a capitalist bribe. In 1944 the only discussion that arises is about whether it will be adopted in whole or in part. This blurring of party distinctions is happening in almost all countries, partly because everywhere, except perhaps in the USA, the drift is towards a planned economy, partly because in an age of power politics national survival is felt to be more important than class warfare. But Britain has certain peculiarities resulting from its being both a small island and the centre of an empire. To begin with, given the present economic system, Britain's prosperity depends partly on the Empire, while all Left parties are theoretically anti-imperialist. Politicians of the Left are therefore aware – or have recently become aware – that once in power they choose between abandoning some of their principles or lowering the English standard of living. Secondly, it is impossible for Britain to go through the kind of revolutionary process that the USSR went through. It is too small, too highly organized, too dependent on imported food. Civil war in England would mean starvation or conquest by some foreign power, or both. Thirdly and most important of all, civil war is not *morally* possible in England. In any circumstances that we can foresee, the proletariat of Hammersmith will not arise and massacre the bourgeoisie of Kensington: they are not different enough. Even the most drastic changes will have to happen peacefully and with a show of legality, and everyone except the "lunatic fringes" of the various political parties is aware of this.

These facts make up the background of the English political outlook. The great mass of the people want profound changes, but they do not want violence. They want to preserve their own standard of living, and at the same time they want to feel that they are not exploiting less fortunate peoples. If you issued a questionnaire to the whole nation, asking, "What do you want from politics?" the answer would be much the same in the overwhelming majority of cases. Substantially it would be: "Economic security, a foreign policy which will ensure peace, more social equality, and a settlement with India." Of these, the first is by far the most important, unemployment being an even greater nightmare than war. But few people would think it necessary to mention either capitalism or socialism. Neither word has much emotional appeal. No one's heart beats faster at the thought of nationalizing the Bank of England: on the other hand, the old line of talk about sturdy individualism and the sacred rights of property is no longer swallowed by the masses. They know it is not true that "there's plenty of room at the top", and in any case most of them don't want to get to the top: they want steady jobs and a fair deal for their children.

During the last few years, owing to the social frictions arising out of the war, discontent with the obvious inefficiency of old-style capitalism and admiration for Soviet Russia, public opinion has moved considerably to the Left, but without growing more doctrinaire or markedly bitterer. None of the political parties which call themselves revolutionary have seriously increased their following. There are about half a dozen of these parties, but their combined membership, even if one counts the remnants of Mosley's Blackshirts,* would probably not amount to 150,000. The most important of them is the Communist Party, but even the Communist Party, after twenty-five years of existence, must be held to have failed. Although it has had considerable influence at moments when circumstances favoured it, it has never shown signs of growing into a mass party of the kind that exists in France or used to exist in pre-Hitler Germany.

Over a long period of years, Communist Party membership has gone up or down in response to the changes in Russian foreign policy. When the USSR is on good terms with Britain, the British communists follow a "moderate" line hardly distinguishable from that of the Labour Party, and their membership swells to some scores of thousands. When British and Russian policy diverge, the communists revert to a "revolutionary" line and membership slumps again. They can, in fact, only get themselves a worthwhile following by abandoning their essential objectives. The various other Marxist parties, all of them claiming to be the true and uncorrupted successors of Lenin, are in an even more hopeless position. The average Englishman is unable to grasp their doctrines and uninterested in their grievances. And in England the lack of the conspiratorial mentality which has been developed in police-ridden European countries is a great handicap. English people in large numbers will not accept any creed whose dominant notes are hatred and illegality. The ruthless ideologies of the Continent – not merely communism and fascism, but anarchism, Trotskyism, and even ultramontane Catholicism – are accepted in their pure form only by the intelligentsia, who constitute a sort of island of bigotry amid the general vagueness. It is significant that English revolutionary writers are obliged to use a bastard vocabulary whose key phrases are mostly translations. There are no native English words for most of the concepts they are dealing with. Even the word "proletarian", for instance, is not English and the great majority of English people do not know what it means. It is generally used, if at all, to mean simply "poor". But even so it is given a social rather than an economic slant and most people would tell you that a blacksmith or a cobbler is a proletarian and that a bank clerk is not. As for the word "bourgeois", it is used almost exclusively by people who are of bourgeois origin themselves. The only genuinely popular use of the word is as a printer's term. It is then, as one might expect, anglicized and pronounced "boorjoyce".

But there is one abstract political term which is fairly widely used and has a loose but well-understood meaning attached to it. This is the word "democracy". In a way, the English people do feel that they live in a democratic country. Not that anyone is so stupid as to take this in a literal sense. If democracy means either popular rule or social equality, it is clear that Britain is not democratic. It is, however, democratic in the secondary sense which has attached itself to that word since the rise of Hitler. To begin with, minorities have some power of making themselves heard. But more than this, public opinion cannot be disregarded when it chooses to express itself. It may have to work in indirect ways, by strikes, demonstrations and letters to the newspapers, but it can and visibly does affect government policy. A British government may be unjust, but it cannot be quite arbitrary. It cannot do the kind of thing that a totalitarian government does as a matter of course. One example out of the thousands that might be chosen is the German attack on the USSR. The significant thing is not that this was made without a declaration of war – that was natural enough – but that it was made without any propaganda build-up beforehand. The German people woke up to find themselves at war with a country that they had been ostensibly on friendly terms with on the previous evening. Our own government would not dare to do such a thing, and the English people are fairly well aware of this. English political thinking is much governed by the word "They". "They" are the higher-ups, the mysterious powers who do things to you against your will. But there is a widespread feeling that "They", though tyrannical, are not omnipotent. "They" will respond to pressure if you take the trouble to apply it: "They" are even removable. And with all their political ignorance the English people will often show surprising sensitiveness when some small incident seems to show that "They" are overstepping the mark. Hence, in the midst of seeming apathy, the sudden fuss every now and then over a rigged by-election or a too-Cromwellian handling of Parliament.

One thing that is extremely difficult to be certain about is the persistence in England of monarchist sentiment. There cannot be much doubt that at any rate in the south of England it was strong and genuine until the death of King George V. The popular response to the Silver Jubilee in 1935 took the authorities by surprise, and the celebrations had to be prolonged for an extra week. At normal times it is only the richer classes who are overtly royalist: in the West End of London, for instance, people stand to attention for 'God Save the King' at the end of a picture show, whereas in the poorer quarters they walk out. But the affection shown for George V at the Silver Jubilee was obviously genuine, and it was even possible to see in it the survival, or recrudescence, of an idea almost as old as history, the idea of the King and the common people being in a sort of alliance against the upper classes; for example, some of the London slum streets bore during the Jubilee the rather servile slogan "Poor but Loyal". Other slogans, however, coupled loyalty to the King with hostility to the landlord, such as "Long Live the King. Down with the Landlord", or more often, "No Landlords Wanted" or "Landlords Keep Away". It is too early to say whether royalist sentiment was killed outright by the abdication, but unquestionably the abdication dealt it a serious blow. Over the past 400 years it has waxed or waned according to circumstances. Queen Victoria, for instance, was decidedly unpopular during part of her reign, and in the first quarter of the nineteenth century public interest in the royal family was not nearly as strong as it was a hundred years later. At this moment the mass of the English people are probably mildly republican. But it may well be that another long reign, similar to that of George V, would revive royalist feeling and make it – as it was between roughly 1880 and 1936 – an appreciable factor in politics.

THE ENGLISH CLASS SYSTEM

In time of war the English class system is the enemy propagandist's best argument. To Dr Goebbels's charge that England is still "two nations", the only truthful answer would have been that she is in fact three nations. But the peculiarity of English class distinctions is not that they are unjust – for after all, wealth and poverty exist side by side in almost all countries – but that they are anachronistic. They do not exactly correspond to economic distinctions, and what is essentially an industrial and capitalist country is haunted by the ghost of a caste system.

It is usual to classify modern society under three headings: the upper class, or bourgeoisie, the middle class, or petty bourgeoisie, and the working class, or proletariat. This roughly fits the facts, but one can draw no useful inference from it unless one takes account of the subdivisions within the various classes and realizes how deeply the whole English outlook is coloured by romanticism and sheer snobbishness.

England is one of the last remaining countries to cling to the outward forms of feudalism. Titles are maintained and new ones are constantly created, and the House of Lords, consisting mainly of hereditary peers, has real powers. At the same time England has no real aristocracy. The race difference on which aristocratic rule is usually founded was disappearing by the end of the Middle Ages, and the famous medieval families have almost completely vanished. The so-called old families are those that grew rich in the sixteenth, seventeenth and eighteenth centuries. Moreover, the notion that nobility exists in its own right, that you can be a nobleman even if you are poor, was already dying out in the age of Elizabeth, a fact commented on by Shakespeare. And yet, curiously enough, the English ruling class has never developed into a bourgeoisie plain and simple. It has never become purely urban or frankly commercial. The ambition to be a country gentleman, to own and administer land and draw at least a part of your income from rent, has survived every change. So it comes that each new wave of parvenus, instead of simply replacing the existing ruling class, has adopted its habits, intermarried with it, and, after a generation or two, become indistinguishable from it.

The basic reason for this may perhaps be that England is very small and has an equable climate and pleasantly varied scenery. It is almost impossible in England, and not easy even in Scotland, to be more than twenty miles from a town. Rural life is less inherently boorish than it is in bigger countries with colder winters. And the comparative integrity of the British ruling class – for when all is said and done they have not behaved so contemptibly as their European opposite numbers – is probably bound up with their idea of themselves as feudal landowners. This outlook is shared by considerable sections of the middle class. Nearly everyone who can afford to do so sets up as a country gentleman, or at least makes some effort in that direction. The manor house with its park and its walled gardens reappears in reduced form in the stockbroker's weekend cottage, in the suburban villa with its lawn and herbaceous border, perhaps even in the potted nasturtiums on the windowsill of the Bayswater flat. This widespread daydream is undoubtedly snobbish; it has tended to stabilize class distinctions and has helped to prevent the modernization of English agriculture – but it is mixed up with a kind of idealism, a feeling that style and tradition are more important than money.

Within the middle class there is a sharp division, cultural and not financial, between those who aim at gentility and those who do not. According to the usual classification, everyone between the capitalist and the weekly wage earner can be lumped together as "petty bourgeoisie". This means that the Harley Street physician, the army officer, the grocer, the farmer, the senior Civil Servant, the solicitor, the clergyman, the schoolmaster, the bank manager, the speculative builder and the fisherman who owns his own boat are all in the same class. But no one in England feels them to belong to the same class, and the distinction between them is not a distinction of income but of accent, manners and, to some extent, outlook. Anyone who pays any attention to class differences at all would regard an army officer with £1,000 a year as socially superior to a shopkeeper with £2,000 a year. Even within the upper class a similar distinction holds good, the titled person being almost always more deferred to than an untitled person of larger income. Middle-class people are really graded according to their degree of resemblance to the aristocracy: professional men, senior officials, officers in the fighting services, university lecturers, clergymen, even the literary and scientific intelligentsia rank higher than businessmen, though on the whole they earn less. It is a peculiarity of this class that their largest item of expenditure is education. Whereas a successful tradesman will send his son to the local grammar school, a clergyman with half his income will underfeed himself for years in order to send his son to a public school, although he knows that he will get no direct return for the money he spends.

There is, however, another noticeable division in the middle class. The old distinction was between the man who is "a gentleman" and the man who is "not a gentleman". In the last thirty years, however, the demands of modern industry, and the technical schools and provincial universities, have brought into being a new kind of man, middle class in income and to some extent in habits, but not much interested in his own social status. People like radio engineers and industrial chemists, whose education has not been of a kind to give them any reverence for the past, and who tend to live in blocks of flats or housing estates where the old social pattern has broken down, are the most nearly classless beings that England possesses. They are an important section of society, because their numbers are constantly growing. The war, for instance, made necessary the formation of an enormous air force, and so you got thousands of young men of working-class origin graduating into the technical middle class by way of the RAF. Any serious reorganization of industry now will have similar effects. And the characteristic outlook of the technicians is already spreading among the older strata of the middle class. One symptom of this is that intermarriage within the middle class is freer than it used to be. Another is the increasing unwillingness of people below the £2,000-a-year level to bankrupt themselves in the name of education.

Another series of changes, probably dating from the Education Act of 1870, is occurring in the working class. One cannot altogether acquit the English working class either of snobbishness or of servility. To begin with there is a fairly sharp distinction between the better-paid working class and the very poor. Even in socialist literature it is common to find contemptuous references to slum dwellers (the German word *Lumpenproletariat* is much used), and imported labourers with low standards of living, such as the Irish, are greatly looked down on. There is also, probably, more disposition to accept class distinctions as permanent, and even to accept the upper classes as natural leaders, than survives in most countries. It is significant that in the moment of disaster the man best able to unite the nation was Churchill, a Conservative of aristocratic origins. The word "sir" is much used in England, and the man of obviously upper-class appearance can usually get more than his fair share of deference from commissionaires, ticket collectors, policemen and the like. It is this aspect of English life that seems most shocking to visitors from America and the Dominions. And the tendency towards servility probably did not decrease in the twenty years between the two wars: it may even have increased, owing chiefly to unemployment.

But snobbishness is never quite separable from idealism. The tendency to give the upper classes more than their due is mixed up with a respect for good manners and something vaguely describable as culture. In the south of England, at any rate, it is unquestionable that most working-class people want to resemble the upper classes in manners and habits. The traditional attitude of looking down on the upper classes as effeminate and "la-di-dah" survives best in the heavy-industry areas. Hostile nicknames like "toff" and "swell" have almost disappeared, and even the *Daily Worker* displays advertisements for "High-Class Gentleman's Tailor". Above all, throughout southern England there is almost general uneasiness about the cockney accent. In Scotland and northern England snobbishness about the local accents does exist, but it is not nearly so strong or widespread. Many a Yorkshireman definitely prides himself on his broad "U"s and narrow "A"s, and will defend them on linguistic grounds. In London there are still people who say "fice" instead of "face", but there is probably no one who regards "fice" as superior. Even a person who claims to despise the bourgeoisie and all its ways will still take care that his children grow up pronouncing their aitches.

But side by side with this there has gone a considerable growth of political consciousness and an increasing impatience with class privilege. Over a period of twenty or thirty years the working class has grown politically more hostile to the upper class, culturally less hostile. There is nothing incongruous in this: both tendencies are symptoms of the levelling of manners which results from machine civilization and which makes the English class system more and more of an anachronism.

The obvious class differences still surviving in England astonish foreign observers, but they are far less marked, and far less real, than they were thirty years ago. People of different social origins, thrown together during the war in the armed forces, or in factories or offices, or as firewatchers and Home Guards, were able to mingle more easily than they did in the 1914–18 war. It is worth listing the various influences which – mechanically, as it were – tend to make Englishmen of all classes less and less different from one another.

First of all, the improvement in industrial technique. Every year less and less people are engaged in heavy manual labour which keeps them constantly tired and, by hypertrophying certain muscles, gives them a distinctive carriage. Secondly, improvements in housing. Between the two wars rehousing was done mostly by the local authorities, who have produced a type of house (the council house, with its bathroom, garden, separate kitchen and indoor WC) which is nearer to the stockbroker's villa than it is to the labourer's cottage. Thirdly, the mass production of furniture which in ordinary times can be bought on the hire-purchase system. The effect of this is that the interior of a working-class house resembles that of a middle-class house very much more than it did a generation ago. Fourthly, and perhaps most important of all, the mass production of cheap clothes. Thirty years ago the social status of nearly everyone in England could be determined from his appearance, even at 200 yards' distance. The working classes all wore ready-made clothes, and the ready-made clothes were not only ill-fitting but usually followed the upper-class fashions of ten or fifteen years earlier. The cloth cap was practically a badge of status. It was universal among the working class, while the upper classes only wore it for golf and shooting. This state of affairs is rapidly changing. Ready-made clothes now follow the fashions closely, they are made in many different fittings to suit every kind of figure, and even when they are of very cheap cloth they are superficially not very different from expensive clothes. The result is that it grows harder every year, especially in the case of women, to determine social status at a glance.

Mass-produced literature and amusements have the same effect. Radio programmes, for instance, are necessarily the same for everybody. Films, though often extremely reactionary in their implied outlook, have to appeal to a public of millions and therefore have to avoid stirring up class antagonisms. So also with some of the big-circulation newspapers. The *Daily Express*, for instance, draws its readers from all strata of the population. So also with some of the periodicals that have appeared in the past dozen years. *Punch* is obviously a middle- and upper-class paper, but *Picture Post* is not aimed at any particular class. And lending libraries and very cheap books, such as the Penguins, popularize the habit of reading and probably have a levelling effect on literary taste. Even taste in food tends to grow more uniform owing to the multiplication of cheap but fairly smart restaurants such as those of Messrs Lyons.*

We are not justified in assuming that class distinctions are actually disappearing. The essential structure of England is still almost what it was in the nineteenth century. But real differences between man and man are obviously diminishing, and this fact is grasped and even welcomed by people who only a few years ago were clinging desperately to their social prestige.

Whatever may be the ultimate fate of the very rich, the tendency of the working class and the middle class is evidently to merge. It may happen quickly or slowly, according to circumstances. It has been accelerated by the war, and another ten years of all-round rationing, utility clothes, high income tax and compulsory national service may finish the process once and for all. The final effects of this we cannot foresee. There are observers, both native and foreign, who believe that the fairly large amount of individual freedom that is enjoyed in England depends on having a well-defined class system. Liberty, according to some, is incompatible with equality. But at least it is certain that the present drift *is* towards greater social equality, and that this is what the great mass of the English people desire.

THE ENGLISH LANGUAGE

The English language has two outstanding characteristics to which most of its minor oddities can be finally traced. These characteristics are a very large vocabulary and simplicity of grammar.

If it is not the largest in the world, the English vocabulary is certainly among the largest. English is really two languages, Anglo-Saxon and Norman French, and during the last three centuries it has been reinforced on an enormous scale by new words deliberately created from Latin and Greek roots. But in addition the vocabulary is made much larger than it appears by the practice of turning one part of speech into another. For example, almost any noun can be used as a verb: this in effect gives an extra range of verbs, so that you have *knife* as well as *stab*, *school* as well as *teach*, *fire* as well as *burn*, and so on. Then again, certain verbs can be given as many as twenty different meanings simply by adding prepositions to them. (Examples are *get out of*, *get up*, *give out*, *take over*.) Verbs can also change into nouns with considerable freedom, and by the use of affixes such as *-y*, *-ful*, *-like*, any noun can be turned into an adjective. More freely than in most languages, verbs and adjectives can be turned into their opposites by means of the prefix *un-*. And adjectives can be made more emphatic or given a new twist by tying a noun to them; for example, *lily-white*, *sky-blue*, *coal-black*, *iron-hard*, etc.

But English is also, and to an unnecessary extent, a borrowing language. It readily takes over any foreign word that seems to fill a need, often altering the meaning in doing so. A recent example is the word *blitz*. As a verb this word did not appear in print till late in 1940, but it has already become part of the language. Other examples from the vast armoury of borrowed words are *garage, charabanc, alias, alibi, steppe, thug, role, menu, lasso, rendezvous, chemise*. It will be noticed that in most cases an English equivalent exists already, so that borrowing adds to the already large stock of synonyms.

English grammar is simple. The language is almost completely uninflected, a peculiarity which marks it off from almost all languages west of China. Any regular English verb has only three inflections: the third person singular, the present participle and the past participle. Thus, for instance, the verb *to kill* consists of *kill, kills, killing, killed*, and that is all. There is, of course, a great wealth of tenses, very much subtilized in meaning, but these are made by the use of auxiliaries which themselves barely inflect. *May, might, shall, will, should, would* do not inflect at all, except in the obsolete second-person singular. The upshot is that every person in every tense of such a verb as *to kill* can be expressed in only about thirty words including the pronouns, or about forty if one includes the second-person singular. The corresponding number in, for instance, French would be somewhere near 200. And in English there is the added advantage that the auxiliaries which are used to make the tenses are the same in every case.

There is no such thing in English as declension of nouns, and there is no gender. Nor are there many irregular plurals or comparatives. Moreover, the tendency is always towards greater simplicity, both in grammar and syntax. Long sentences with dependent clauses grow more and more unpopular, irregular but time-saving formations such as the "American subjunctive" (*it is necessary that you go* instead of *it is necessary that you should go*) gain ground, and difficult rules, such as the difference between *shall* and *will*, or *that* and *which*, are more and more ignored. If it continues to develop along its present lines English will ultimately have more in common with the uninflected languages of East Asia than with the languages of Europe.

The greatest quality of English is its enormous range not only of meaning but of *tone*. It is capable of endless subtleties, and of everything from the most high-flown rhetoric to the most brutal coarseness. On the other hand, its lack of grammar makes it easily compressible. It is the language of lyric poetry, and also of headlines. On its lower levels it is very easy to learn, in spite of its irrational spelling. It can also for international purposes be reduced to very simple pidgin dialects, ranging from Basic to the "bêche-de-mer"* English used in the South Pacific. It is therefore well suited to be a world lingua franca, and it has in fact spread more widely than any other language.

But there are also great disadvantages, or at least great dangers, in speaking English as one's native tongue. To begin with, as was pointed out earlier in this essay, the English are very poor linguists. Their own language is grammatically so simple that unless they have gone through the discipline of learning a foreign language in childhood, they are often quite unable to grasp what is meant by gender, person and case. A completely illiterate Indian will pick up English far faster than a British soldier will pick up Hindustani. Nearly five million Indians are literate in English and millions more speak it in a debased form. There are some tens of thousands of Indians who speak English as nearly as possible perfectly – yet the number of Englishmen speaking any Indian language perfectly would not amount to more than a few scores. But the great weakness of English is its capacity for debasement. Just because it is so easy to use, it is easy to use *badly*.

To write or even to speak English is not a science but an art. There are no reliable rules: there is only the general principle that concrete words are better than abstract ones, and that the shortest way of saying anything is always the best. Mere correctness is no guarantee whatever of good writing. A sentence like "an enjoyable time was had by all present" is perfectly correct English, and so is the unintelligible mess of words on an income-tax return. Whoever writes English is involved in a struggle that never lets up even for a sentence. He is struggling against vagueness, against obscurity, against the lure of the decorative adjective, against the encroachment of Latin and Greek, and, above all, against the worn-out phrases and dead metaphors with which the language is cluttered up. In speaking, these dangers are more easily avoided, but spoken English differs from written English more sharply than is the case in most languages. In the spoken tongue every word that can be omitted is omitted, every possible abbreviation is used. Meaning is conveyed quite largely by emphasis, though curiously enough the English do not gesticulate, as one might reasonably expect them to do. A sentence like *No, I don't mean that one, I mean that one* is perfectly intelligible when spoken aloud, even without a gesture. But spoken English, when it tries to be dignified and logical, usually takes on the vices of written English, as you can see by spending half an hour either in the House of Commons or at the Marble Arch.

English is peculiarly subject to jargons. Doctors, scientists, businessmen, officials, sportsmen, economists and political theorists all have their characteristic perversion of the language, which can be studied in the appropriate magazines from the *Lancet* to the *Labour Monthly*. But probably the deadliest enemy of good English is what is called "standard English". This dreary dialect, the language of leading articles, White Papers, political speeches and BBC news bulletins, is undoubtedly spreading: it is spreading downwards in the social scale, and outwards into the spoken language. Its characteristic is its reliance on ready-made phrases – *in due course, take the earliest opportunity, warm appreciation, deepest regret, explore every avenue, ring the changes, take up the cudgels, legitimate assumption, the answer is in the affirmative*, etc. etc. – which may once have been fresh and vivid, but have now become mere thought-saving devices, having the same relation to living English as a crutch has to a leg. Anyone preparing a broadcast or writing to *The Times* adopts this kind of language almost instinctively, and it infects the spoken tongue as well. So much has our language been weakened that the imbecile chatter in Swift's essay on polite conversation* (a satire on the upper-class talk of Swift's own day) would actually be rather a good conversation by modern standards.

The temporary decadence of the English language is due, like so much else, to our anachronistic class system. "Educated" English has grown anaemic because for long past it has not been reinvigorated from below. The people likeliest to use simple concrete language, and to think of metaphors that really call up a visual image, are those who are in contact with physical reality. A useful word like *bottleneck*, for instance, would be most likely to occur to someone used to dealing with conveyor belts – or again, the expressive military phrase *to winkle out* implies acquaintance both with winkles and with machine-gun nests. And the vitality of English depends on a steady supply of images of this kind. It follows that language, at any rate the English language, suffers when the educated classes lose touch with the manual workers. As things are at present, nearly every Englishman, whatever his origins, feels the working-class manner of speech, and even working-class idioms, to be inferior. Cockney, the most widespread dialect, is the most despised of all. Any word or usage that is supposedly cockney is looked on as vulgar, even when, as is sometimes the case, it is merely an archaism. An example is *ain't*, which is now abandoned in favour of the much weaker form *aren't*. But *ain't* was good enough English eighty years ago, and Queen Victoria would have said *ain't*.

During the past forty years, and especially the past dozen years, English has borrowed largely from American, while American has shown no tendency to borrow from English. The reason for this is partly political. Anti-British feeling in the United States is far stronger than anti-American feeling in England, and most Americans dislike using a word or phrase which they know to be British. But American has gained a footing in England partly because of the vivid, almost poetic quality of its slang, partly because certain American usages (for instance, the formation of verbs by adding *-ize* to a noun) save time, and most of all because one can adopt an American word without crossing a class barrier. From the English point of view American words have no class label. This applies even to thieves' slang. Words like *stooge* and *stool-pigeon* are considered much less vulgar than words like *nark* and *split*. Even a very snobbish English person would probably not mind calling a policeman a *cop*, which is American, but he would object to calling him a *copper*, which is working-class English. To the working classes, on the other hand, the use of Americanisms is a way of escaping from cockney without adopting the BBC dialect, which they instinctively dislike and cannot easily master. Hence, especially in the big towns, working-class children now use American slang from the moment that they learn to talk. And there is a noticeable tendency to use American words even when they are not slang and when an English equivalent already exists: for instance, *car* for *tram*, *escalator* for *moving staircase*, *automobile* for *motor car*.

This process will probably continue for some time. One cannot check it simply by protesting against it, and in any case many American words and expressions are well worth adopting. Some are necessary neologisms; others (for instance, *fall* for *autumn*) are old words which we ought never to have dropped. But it ought to be realized that on the whole American is a bad influence and has already had a debasing effect.

To begin with, American has some of the vices of English in an exaggerated form. The interchangeability of different parts of speech has been carried further, the distinction between transitive and intransitive verbs tends to break down, and many words are used which have no meaning whatever. For example, whereas English alters the meaning of a verb by tacking a preposition onto it, the American tendency is to burden every verb with a preposition that adds nothing to its meaning (*win out*, *lose out*, *face up to*, etc.). On the other hand, American has broken more completely than English with the past and with literary traditions. It not only produces words like *beautician*, *moronic* and *sexualize*, but often replaces strong primary words by feeble euphemisms. For instance, many Americans seem to regard the word *death* and various words that go with it (*corpse, coffin, shroud*) as almost unmentionable. But above all, to adopt the American language wholeheartedly would probably mean a huge loss of vocabulary. For though American produces vivid and witty turns of speech, it is terribly poor in names for natural objects and localities. Even the streets in American cities are usually known by numbers instead of names. If we really intended to model our language upon American we should have, for instance, to lump the ladybird, the daddy-long-legs, the sawfly, the water boatman, the cockchafer, the cricket, the death-watch beetle and scores of other insects all together under the inexpressive name of *bug*. We should lose the poetic names of our wild flowers, and also, probably, our habit of giving individual names to every street, pub, field, lane and hillock. In so far as American is adopted, that is the tendency. Those who take their language from the films, or from papers such as *Life* and *Time*, always prefer the slick time-saving word to the one with a history behind it. As to accent, it is doubtful whether the American accent has the superiority which it is now fashionable to claim for it. The "educated" English accent, a product of the last thirty years, is undoubtedly very bad and is likely to be abandoned, but the average English person probably speaks as clearly as the average American. Most English people blur their vowel sounds, but most Americans swallow their consonants. Many Americans pronounce, for instance, *water* as though it had no T in it, or even as though it had no consonant in it at all, except the W. On the whole we are justified in regarding the American language with suspicion. We ought to be ready to borrow its best words, but we ought not to let it modify the actual structure of our language.

However, there is no chance of resisting the American influence unless we can put new life into English itself. And it is difficult to do this while words and idioms are prevented from circulating freely among all sections of the population. English people of all classes now find it natural to express incredulity by the American slang phrase "sez you". Many would even tell you in good faith that "sez you" has no English equivalent. Actually it has a whole string of them – for instance, "not half", "I don't think", "come off it", "less of it", "and then you wake up", or simply "gam". But most of these would be considered vulgar: you would never find an expression like "not half" in a *Times* leader, for instance. And on the other hand many necessary abstract words, especially words of Latin origin, are rejected by the working class because they sound public-schoolish, "tony" and effeminate. Language ought to be the joint creation of poets and manual workers, and in modern England it is difficult for these two classes to meet. When they can do so again – as, in a different way, they could in the feudal past – English may show more clearly than at present its kinship with the language of Shakespeare and Defoe.

THE FUTURE OF THE ENGLISH PEOPLE

This is not a book about foreign politics, but if one is to speak of the future of the English people, one must start by considering what kind of world they will probably be living in and what special part they can play in it.

Nations do not often die out, and the English people will still be in existence a hundred years hence, whatever has happened in the meantime. But if Britain is to survive as what is called a "great" nation, playing an important and useful part in the world's affairs, one must taken certain things as assured. One must assume that Britain will remain on good terms with Russia and Europe, will keep its special links with America and the Dominions, and will solve the problem of India in some amicable way. That is perhaps a great deal to assume, but without it there is not much hope for civilization as a whole, and still less for Britain itself. If the savage international struggle of the last twenty years continues, there will only be room in the world for two or three great powers, and in the long run Britain will not be one of them. It has not either the population or the resources. In a world of power politics the English would ultimately dwindle to a satellite people, and the special thing that it is in their power to contribute might be lost.

But what is the special thing that they could contribute? The outstanding and – by contemporary standards – highly original quality of the English is their habit of *not killing one another*. Putting aside the "model" small states, which are in an exceptional position, England is the only European country where internal politics are conducted in a more or less humane and decent manner. It is – and this was true long before the rise of fascism – the only country where armed men do not prowl the streets and no one is frightened of the secret police. And the whole British Empire, with all its crying abuses, its stagnation in one place and exploitation in another, at least has the merit of being internally peaceful. It has always been able to get along with a very small number of armed men, although it contains a quarter of the population of the earth. Between the wars its total armed forces amounted to about 600,000 men, of whom a third were Indians. At the outbreak of war the entire Empire was able to mobilize about a million trained men. Almost as many could have been mobilized by, say, Rumania. The English are probably more capable than most peoples of making revolutionary changes without bloodshed. In England, if anywhere, it would be possible to abolish poverty without destroying liberty. If the English took the trouble to make their own democracy work, they would become the political leaders of Western Europe, and probably of some other parts of the world as well. They would provide the much-needed alternative to Russian authoritarianism on the one hand and American materialism on the other.

But to play a leading part the English have got to know what they are doing, and they have got to retain their vitality. For this, certain developments are needed within the next decade. These are a rising birth rate, more social equality, less centralization and more respect for the intellect.

There has been a small rise in the birth rate during the war years, but that is probably of no significance, and the general curve is downwards. The position is not quite so desperate as it is sometimes said to be, but it can only be put right if the curve not only rises sharply, but does so within ten or at most twenty years. Otherwise the population will not only fall, but, what is worse, will consist predominantly of middle-aged people. If that point is reached, the decline may never be retrievable.

At bottom, the causes of the dwindled birth rate are economic. It is nonsense to say that it has happened because English people do not care for children. In the early nineteenth century they had an extremely high birth rate, and they also had an attitude towards children which now seems to us unbelievably callous. With very little public disapproval, children as young as six were sold into the mines and factories, and the death of a child, the most shocking event that modern people are able to imagine, was looked on as a very minor tragedy. In a sense it is true that modern English people have small families because they are too fond of children. They feel that it is wrong to bring a child into the world unless you are completely certain of being able to provide for him, and at a level not lower than your own. For the last fifty years, to have a big family has meant that your children must wear poorer clothes than others in the same group, must have less food and less attention, and probably must go to work earlier. This held good for all classes except the very rich and the unemployed. No doubt the dearth of babies is partly due to the competing attraction of cars and radios, but its main cause is a typically English mixture of snobbishness and altruism.

The philoprogenitive instinct will probably return when fairly large families are already the rule, but the first steps towards this must be economic ones. Half-hearted family allowances will not do the trick, especially when there is a severe housing shortage, as there is now. People should be better off for having children, just as they are in a peasant community, instead of being financially crippled, as they are in ours. Any government, by a few strokes of the pen, could make childlessness as unbearable an economic burden as a big family is now – but no government has chosen to do so, because of the ignorant idea that a bigger population means more unemployed. Far more drastically than anyone has proposed hitherto, taxation will have to be graded so as to encourage childbearing and to save women with young children from being obliged to work outside the home. And this involves readjustment of rents, better public service in the matter of nursery schools and playing grounds, and the building of bigger and more convenient houses. It also probably involves the extension and improvement of free education, so that the middle-class family shall not, as at present, be crushed out of existence by impossibly high school fees.

The economic adjustments must come first, but a change of outlook is also needed. In the England of the last thirty years it has seemed all too natural that blocks of flats should refuse tenants with children, that parks and squares should be railed off to keep the children out of them, that abortion, theoretically illegal, should be looked on as a peccadillo, and that the main aim of commercial advertising should be to popularize the idea of "having a good time" and staying young as long as possible. Even the cult of animals, fostered by the newspapers, has probably done its bit towards reducing the birth rate. Nor have the public authorities seriously interested themselves in this question till very recently. Britain today has a million and a half less children than in 1914, and a million and a half more dogs. Yet even now, when the government designs a prefabricated house, it produces a house with only two bedrooms – with room, that is to say, for two children at the most. When one considers the history of the years between the wars, it is perhaps surprising that the birth rate has not dropped more catastrophically than it has. But it is not likely to rise to the replacement level until those in power, as well as the ordinary people in the street, come to feel that children matter more than money.

The English are probably less irked by class distinctions, more tolerant of privilege and of absurdities like titles, than most peoples. There is nevertheless, as I have pointed out earlier, a growing wish for greater equality and a tendency, below the £2,000 a year level, for surface differences between class and class to disappear. At present this is happening only mechanically and quite largely as a result of the war. The question is how it can be speeded up. For even the changeover to a centralized economy, which, except, possibly, in the United States, is happening in all countries under one name or another, does of itself guarantee greater equality between man and man. Once civilization has reached a fairly high technical level, class distinctions are an obvious evil. They not only lead great numbers of people to waste their lives in the pursuit of social prestige, but they also cause an immense wastage of talent. In England it is not merely the ownership of property that is concentrated in a few hands. It is also the case that all power, administrative as well as financial, belongs to a single class. Except for a handful of "self-made men" and Labour politicians, those who control our destinies are the product of about a dozen public schools and two universities. A nation is using its capacities to the full when any man can get any job that he is fit for. One has only to think of some of the people who have held vitally important jobs during the past twenty years, and to wonder what would have happened to them if they had been born into the working class, to see that this is not the case in England.

Moreover, class distinctions are a constant drain on morale, in peace as well as in war. And the more conscious, the better educated the mass of the people become, the more this is so. The word "They", the universal feeling that "They" hold all the power and make all the decisions, and that "They" can only be influenced in indirect and uncertain ways, is a great handicap in England. In 1940 "They" showed a marked tendency to give place to "We", and it is time that it did so permanently. Three measures are obviously necessary, and they would begin to produce their effect within a few years.

The first is a scaling-up and scaling-down of incomes. The glaring inequality of wealth that existed in England before the war must not be allowed to recur. Above a certain point – which should bear a fixed relation to the lowest current wage – all income should be taxed out of existence. In theory, at any rate, this has happened already, with beneficial results. The second necessary measure is greater democracy in education. A completely unified system of education is probably not desirable. Some adolescents benefit by higher education, others do not; there is need to differentiate between literary and technical education, and it is better that a few independent experimental schools should remain in existence. But it should be the rule, as it is in some countries already, for all children to attend the same schools up to the age of twelve or at least ten. After that age it becomes necessary to separate the more gifted children from the less gifted, but a uniform educational system for the early years would cut away one of the deepest roots of snobbery.

The third thing that is needed is to remove the class labels from the English language. It is not desirable that all the local accents should disappear, but there should be a manner of speaking that is definitely national and is not merely (like the accent of the BBC announcers) a copy of the mannerisms of the upper classes. This national accent – a modification of cockney, perhaps, or of one of the northern accents – should be taught as a matter of course to all children alike. After that they could, and in some parts of the country they probably would, revert to the local accent, but they should be able to speak standard English if they wished to. No one should be "branded on the tongue". It should be impossible, as it is in the United States and some European countries, to determine anyone's status from his accent.

We need, too, to be less centralized. English agriculture has revived during the war, and the revival may continue, but the English people are still excessively urban in outlook. Culturally, moreover, the country is very much over-centralized. Not only is the whole of Britain in effect governed from London, but the sense of locality – of being, say, an East Anglian or a West Countryman as well as an Englishman – has been much weakened during the past century. The ambition of the farm labourer is usually to get to a town; the provincial intellectual always wants to get to London. In both Scotland and Wales there are nationalist movements, but they are founded on an economic grievance against England rather than on genuine local pride. Nor is there any important literary or artistic movement that is truly independent of London and the university towns.

It is uncertain whether this centralizing tendency is completely reversible, but a good deal could be done to check it. Both Scotland and Wales could and should be a great deal more autonomous than they are at present. The provincial universities should be more generously equipped and the provincial press subsidized. (At present nearly the whole of England is "covered" by eight London newspapers. No newspaper with a large circulation, and no first-class magazine, is published outside London.) The problem of getting people, and especially young, spirited people, to stay on the land would be partly solved if farm labourers had better cottages and if country towns were more civilized and cross-country bus services more efficient. Above all, local pride should be stimulated by teaching in the elementary schools. Every child ought as a matter of course to learn something of the history and topography of its own county. People ought to be proud of their own locality – they ought to feel that its scenery, its architecture and even its cookery are the best in the world. And such feelings, which do exist in some areas of the north but have lapsed throughout the greater part of England, would strengthen national unity rather than weaken it.

It has been suggested earlier that the survival of free speech in England is partly the result of stupidity. The people are not intellectual enough to be heresy-hunters. One does not wish them to grow less tolerant, nor, having seen the results, would one want them to develop the political sophistication that prevailed in pre-Hitler Germany or pre-Pétain France. But the instincts and traditions on which the English rely served them best when they were an exceptionally fortunate people, protected by geography from major disaster. In the twentieth century the narrow interests of the average man, the rather low level of English education, the contempt for "highbrows" and the almost general deadness to aesthetic issues, are serious liabilities.

What the upper classes think about "highbrows" can be judged from the Honours Lists. The upper classes feel titles to be important – yet almost never is any major honour bestowed on anyone describable as an intellectual. With very few exceptions, scientists do not get beyond baronetcies, or literary men beyond knighthoods. But the attitude of the man in the street is no better. He is not troubled by the reflection that England spends hundreds of millions every year on beer and the football pools while scientific research languishes for lack of funds, or that we can afford greyhound tracks innumerable but not even one National Theatre. Between the wars England tolerated newspapers, films and radio programmes of unheard-of silliness, and these produced further stupefaction in the public, blinding their eyes to vitally important problems. This silliness of the English press is partly artificial, since it arises from the fact that newspapers live off advertisements for consumption goods. During the war the papers have grown very much more intelligent without losing their public, and millions of people read papers which they would have rejected as impossibly "highbrow" some years ago. There is, however, not only a low general level of taste but a widespread unawareness that aesthetic considerations can possibly have any importance. Rehousing and town planning, for instance, are normally discussed without even a mention of beauty or ugliness. The English are great lovers of flowers, gardening and "nature", but this is merely a part of their vague aspiration towards an agricultural life. In the main they see no objection to "ribbon development" or to the filth and chaos of the industrial towns. They see nothing wrong in scattering the woods with paper bags and filling every pool and stream with tin cans and bicycle frames. And they are all too ready to listen to any journalist who tells them to trust their instincts and despise the "highbrow".

One result of this has been to increase the isolation of the British intelligentsia. English intellectuals, especially the younger ones, are markedly hostile to their own country. Exceptions can, of course, be found, but it is broadly true that anyone who would prefer T.S. Eliot to Alfred Noyes* despises England, or thinks that he ought to do so. In "enlightened" circles, to express pro-British sentiments needs considerable moral courage. On the other hand, during the past dozen years there has been a strong tendency to develop a violent nationalistic loyalty to some foreign country, usually Soviet Russia. This must probably have happened in any case, because capitalism in its later phases pushes the literary and even the scientific intellectual into a position where he has security without much responsibility. But the philistinism of the English public alienates the intelligentsia still further. The loss to society is very great. It means that the people whose vision is acutest – the people, for instance, who grasped that Hitler was dangerous ten years before this was discovered by our public men – are hardly able to make contact with the masses and grow less and less interested in English problems.

The English will never develop into a nation of philosophers. They will always prefer instinct to logic, and character to intelligence. But they must get rid of their downright contempt for "cleverness". They cannot afford it any longer. They must grow less tolerant of ugliness, and mentally more adventurous. And they must stop despising foreigners. They are Europeans and ought to be aware of it. On the other hand they have special links with the other English speakers overseas, and special imperial responsibilities, in which they ought to take more interest than they have done during these past twenty years. The intellectual atmosphere of England is already very much livelier than it was. The war scotched if it did not kill certain kinds of folly. But there is still need for a conscious effort at national re-education. The first step towards this is an improvement in elementary education, which involves not only raising the school leaving age but spending enough money to ensure that elementary schools are adequately staffed and equipped. And there are immense educational possibilities in the radio, the film and – if it could be freed once and for all from commercial interests – the press.

These, then, appear to be the immediate necessities of the English people. They must breed faster, work harder, and probably live more simply, think more deeply, get rid of their snobbishness and their anachronistic class distinctions, and pay more attention to the world and less to their own backyards. Nearly all of them already love their country, but they must learn to love it intelligently. They must have a clear notion of their own destiny and not listen either to those who tell them that England is finished or to those who tell them that the England of the past can return.

If they can do that they can keep their feet in the post-war world, and if they can keep their feet they can give the example that millions of human beings are waiting for. The world is sick of chaos and it is sick of dictatorship. Of all peoples the English are likeliest to find a way of avoiding both. Except for a small minority they are fully ready for the drastic economic changes that are needed, and at the same time they have no desire either for violent revolution or for foreign conquests. They have known for forty years, perhaps, something that the Germans and the Japanese have only recently learnt, and that the Russians and the Americans have yet to learn: they know that it is not possible for any one nation to rule the earth. They want above all things to live at peace, internally and externally. And the great mass of them are probably prepared for the sacrifices that peace entails.

But they will have to take their destiny into their own hands. England can only fulfil its special mission if the ordinary English in the street can somehow get their hands on power. We have been told very frequently during this war that this time, when the danger is over, there should be no lost opportunities, no recurrence of the past. No more stagnation punctuated by wars, no more Rolls-Royces gliding past dole queues, no return to the England of the Distressed Areas, the endlessly stewing teapot, the empty pram and the Giant Panda.* We cannot be sure that this promise will be kept. Only we ourselves can make certain that it will come true, and if we do not, no further chance may be given us. The past thirty years have been a long series of cheques drawn upon the accumulated goodwill of the English people. That reserve may not be inexhaustible. By the end of another decade it will be finally clear whether England is to survive as a great nation or not. And if the answer is to be "Yes", it is the common people who must make it so.

Propaganda and Demotic Speech*

[...] When you examine government leaflets and White Papers, or leading articles in the newspapers, or the speeches and broadcasts of politicians, or the pamphlets and manifestos of any political party whatever, the thing that nearly always strikes you is their remoteness from the average man. It is not merely that they assume non-existent knowledge: often it is right and necessary to do that. It is also that clear, popular, everyday language seems to be instinctively avoided. The bloodless dialect of government spokesmen (characteristic phrases are: in due course, no stone unturned, take the earliest opportunity, the answer is in the affirmative) is too well known to be worth dwelling on. Newspaper leaders are written either in this same dialect or in an inflated bombastic style with a tendency to fall back on archaic words (peril, valour, might, foe, succour, vengeance, dastardly, rampart, bulwark, bastion) which no normal person would ever think of using. Left-wing political parties specialize in a bastard vocabulary made up of Russian and German phrases translated with the maximum of clumsiness. And even posters, leaflets and broadcasts which are intended to give instructions, to tell people what to do in certain circumstances, often fail in their effect. For example, during the first air raids on London, it was found that innumerable people did not know which siren meant the Alert and which the All Clear. This was after months or years of gazing at ARP posters. These posters had described the Alert as a "warbling note": a phrase which made no impression, since air-raid sirens don't warble, and few people attach any definite meaning to the word.

When Sir Richard Acland,* in the early months of the war, was drawing up a manifesto to be presented to the government, he engaged a squad of Mass Observers* to find out what meaning, if any, the ordinary man attaches to the high-sounding abstract words which are flung to and fro in politics. The most fantastic misunderstandings came to light. It was found, for instance, that most people don't know that "immorality" means anything besides sexual immorality.* One man thought that "movement" had something to do with constipation. And it is a nightly experience in any pub to see broadcast speeches and news bulletins make no impression on the average listener, because they are uttered in stilted bookish language and, incidentally, in an upper-class accent. At the time of Dunkirk I watched a gang of navvies eating their bread and cheese in a pub while the one o'clock news came over. Nothing registered: they just went on stolidly eating. Then, just for an instant, reporting the words of some soldier who had been hauled aboard a boat, the announcer dropped into spoken English, with the phrase, "Well, I've learnt to swim this trip, anyway!" Promptly you could see ears being pricked up: it was ordinary language, and so it got across. A few weeks later, the day after Italy entered the war, Duff Cooper announced that Mussolini's rash act would "add to the ruins for which Italy has been famous". It was neat enough, and a true prophecy, but how much impression does that kind of language make on nine people out of ten? The colloquial version of it would have been: "Italy has always been famous for ruins. Well, there are going to be a damn sight more of them now." But that is not how Cabinet ministers speak, at any rate in public.

Examples of futile slogans, obviously incapable of stirring strong feelings or being circulated by word of mouth, are: "Deserve Victory", "Freedom Is in Peril. Defend It with All Your Might", "Socialism the Only Solution", "Expropriate the Expropriators", "Austerity", "Evolution not Revolution", "Peace Is Indivisible". Examples of slogans phrased in spoken English are: "Hands off Russia", "Make Germany Pay", "Stop Hitler", "No Stomach Taxes", "Buy a Spitfire", "Votes for Women". Examples about midway between these two classes are: "Go to It", "Dig for Victory", "It All Depends on ME", and some of Churchill's phrases, such as "the end of the beginning", "soft underbelly", "blood, toil, tears and sweat" and "never was so much owed by so many to so few". (Significantly, in so far as this last saying has been repeated by word of mouth, the bookish phrase *in the field of human conflict* has dropped out of it.) One has to take into account the fact that nearly all English people dislike anything that sounds high-flown and boastful. Slogans like "They shall not pass", or "Better to die on your feet than live on your knees", which have thrilled Continental nations, seem slightly embarrassing to an Englishman, especially a working man. But the main weakness of propagandists and popularizers is their failure to notice that spoken and written English are two different things.

When recently I protested in print against the Marxist dialect which makes use of phrases like "objectively counter-revolutionary left-deviationism" or "drastic liquidation of petty-bourgeois elements", I received indignant letters from lifelong socialists who told me that I was "insulting the language of the proletariat". In rather the same spirit, Professor Harold Laski devotes a long passage in his last book, *Faith, Reason and Civilization*,* to an attack on Mr T.S. Eliot, whom he accuses of "writing only for the few". Now Eliot, as it happens, is one of the few writers of our time who have tried seriously to write English as it is spoken. Lines like:

And nobody came, and nobody went,
But he took in the milk and he paid the rent*

are about as near to spoken English as print can come. On the other hand, here is an entirely typical sentence from Laski's own writing:

> As a whole, our system was a compromise between democracy in the political realm – itself a very recent development in our history – and an economic power oligarchically organized which was in its turn related to a certain aristocratic vestigia still able to influence profoundly the habits of our society.

This sentence, incidentally, comes from a reprinted lecture – so one must assume that Professor Laski actually stood up on a platform and spouted it forth, parenthesis and all. It is clear that people capable of speaking or writing in such a way have simply forgotten what everyday language is like. But this is nothing to some of the other passages I could dig out of Professor Laski's writings, or better still, from communist literature, or best of all, from Trotskyist pamphlets. Indeed, from reading the left-wing press you get the impression that the louder people yap about the proletariat, the more they despise its language.

I have said already that spoken English and written English are two different things. This variation exists in all languages, but is probably greater in English than in most. Spoken English is full of slang, it is abbreviated wherever possible, and people of all social classes treat its grammar and syntax in a slovenly way. Extremely few English people ever button up a sentence if they are speaking extempore. Above all, the vast English vocabulary contains thousands of words which everyone uses when writing, but which have no real currency in speech – and it also contains thousands more which are really obsolete but which are dragged forth by anyone who wants to sound clever or uplifting. If one keeps this in mind, one can think of ways of ensuring that propaganda, spoken or written, shall reach the audience it is aimed at.

So far as writing goes, all one can attempt is a process of simplification. The first step – and any social survey organization could do this for a few hundreds or thousands of pounds – is to find out which of the abstract words habitually used by politicians are really understood by large numbers of people. If phrases like "unprincipled violation of declared pledges" or "insidious threat to the basic principles of democracy" don't mean anything to the average man, then it is stupid to use them. Secondly, in writing one can keep the spoken word constantly in mind. To get genuine spoken English onto paper is a complicated matter, as I shall show in a moment. But if you habitually say to yourself, "Could I simplify this? Could I make it more like speech?" you are not likely to produce sentences like the one quoted from Professor Laski above; nor are you likely to say "eliminate" when you mean kill, or "static water" when you mean fire tank.

Spoken propaganda, however, offers greater possibilities of improvement. It is here that the problem of writing in spoken English really arises.

Speeches, broadcasts, lectures and even sermons are normally written down beforehand. The most effective orators, like Hitler or Lloyd George, usually speak extempore, but they are very great rarities. As a rule – you can test this by listening at Hyde Park Corner – the so-called extempore speaker only keeps going by endlessly tacking one cliché onto another. In any case, he is probably delivering a speech which he has delivered dozens of times before. Only a few exceptionally gifted speakers can achieve the simplicity and intelligibility which even the most tongue-tied person achieves in ordinary conversation. On the air extempore speaking is seldom even attempted. Except for a few programmes, like *The Brains Trust*,* which in any case are carefully rehearsed beforehand, every word that comes from the BBC has been written down, and is delivered exactly as written. This is not only for censorship reasons: it is also because many speakers are liable to dry up at the microphone if they have no script to follow. The result is the heavy, dull, bookish lingo which causes most radio users to switch off as soon as a talk is announced. It might be thought that one could get nearer to colloquial speech by dictating than by writing – but actually, it is the other way about. Dictating, at any rate to a human being, is always slightly embarrassing. One's impulse is to avoid long pauses, and one necessarily does so by clutching at the ready-made phrases and the dead and stinking metaphors (ring the changes on, ride roughshod over, cross swords with, take up the cudgels for) with which the English language is littered. A dictated script is usually less lifelike than a written one. What is wanted, evidently, is some way of getting ordinary, slipshod, colloquial English onto paper.

But is this possible? I think it is, and by a quite simple method which so far as I know has never been tried. It is this: Set a fairly ready speaker down at the microphone and let him just talk, either continuously or intermittently, on any subject he chooses. Do this with a dozen different speakers, recording it every time. Vary it with a few dialogues or conversations between three or four people. Then play your recordings back and let a stenographer reduce them to writing – not in the shortened, rationalized version that stenographers usually produce, but word for word, with such punctuation as seems appropriate. You would then – for the first time, I believe – have on paper some authentic specimens of spoken English. Probably they would not be readable as a book or a newspaper article is readable, but then spoken English is not meant to be read, it is meant to be listened to. From these specimens you could, I believe, formulate the rules of spoken English and find out how it differs from the written language. And when writing in spoken English had become practicable, the average speaker or lecturer who has to write his material down beforehand could bring it far closer to his natural diction, make it more essentially speakable, than he can at present.

Of course, demotic speech is not solely a matter of being colloquial and avoiding ill-understood words. There is also the question of accent. It seems certain that in modern England the "educated", upper-class accent is deadly to any speaker who is aiming at a large audience. All effective speakers in recent times have had either cockney or provincial accents. The success of Priestley's broadcasts in 1940 was largely due to his Yorkshire accent, which he probably broadened a little for the occasion. Churchill is only a seeming exception to this rule. Too old to have acquired the modern "educated" accent, he speaks with the Edwardian upper-class twang which to the average man's ear sounds like cockney. The "educated" accent, of which the accent of the BBC announcers is a sort of parody, has no asset except its intelligibility to English-speaking foreigners. In England the minority to whom it is natural don't particularly like it, while in the other three quarters of the population it arouses an immediate class antagonism. It is also noticeable that where there is doubt about the pronunciation of a name, successful speakers will stick to the working-class pronunciation even if they know it to be wrong. Churchill, for instance, mispronounced "Nazi" and "Gestapo" as long as the common people continued to do so. Lloyd George during the last war rendered "Kaiser" as "Kayser", which was the popular version of the word.

In the early days of the war the government had the greatest difficulty in inducing people to bother to collect their ration books. At parliamentary elections, even when there is an up-to-date register, it often happens that less than half of the electorate use their votes. Things like these are symptoms of the intellectual gulf between the rulers and the ruled. But the same gulf lies always between the intelligentsia and the common man. Journalists, as we can see by their election forecasts, never know what the public is thinking. Revolutionary propaganda is incredibly ineffective. Churches are empty all over the country. The whole idea of trying to find out what the average man thinks, instead of assuming that he thinks what he ought to think, is novel and unwelcome. Social surveys are viciously attacked from Left and Right alike. Yet some mechanism for testing public opinion is an obvious necessity of modern government, and more so in a democratic country than in a totalitarian one. Its complement is the ability to speak to the ordinary man in words that he will understand and respond to.

At present propaganda only seems to succeed when it coincides with what people are inclined to do in any case. During the present war, for instance, the government has done extraordinarily little to preserve morale: it has merely drawn on the existing reserves of goodwill. And all political parties alike have failed to interest the public in vitally important questions – in the problem of India, to name only one. But some day we may have a genuinely democratic government, a government which will want to tell people what is happening, and what must be done next, and what sacrifices are necessary, and why. It will need the mechanisms for doing so, of which the first are the right words, the right tone of voice. The fact that when you suggest finding out what the common man is like, and approaching him accordingly, you are either accused of being an intellectual snob who wants to "talk down to" the masses, or else suspected of plotting to establish an English Gestapo, shows how sluggishly nineteenth-century our notion of democracy has remained.

Benefit of Clergy: Some Notes on Salvador Dalí*

Autobiography is only to be trusted when it reveals something disgraceful. A man who gives a good account of himself is probably lying, since any life when viewed from the inside is simply a series of defeats. However, even the most flagrantly dishonest book (Frank Harris's autobiographical writings* are an example) can without intending it give a true picture of its author. Dalí's recently published *Life** comes under this heading. Some of the incidents in it are flatly incredible, others have been rearranged and romanticized, and not merely the humiliation but the persistent *ordinariness* of everyday life has been cut out. Dalí is even by his own diagnosis narcissistic, and his autobiography is simply a striptease act conducted in pink limelight. But as a record of fantasy, of the perversion of instinct that has been made possible by the machine age, it has great value.

Here, then, are some of the episodes in Dalí's life, from his earliest years onward. Which of them are true and which are imaginary hardly matters: the point is that this is the kind of thing that Dalí would have *liked* to do.

When he is six years old there is some excitement over the appearance of Halley's comet:

> Suddenly one of my father's office clerks appeared in the drawing-room doorway and announced that the comet could be seen from the terrace. [...] While crossing the hall I caught sight of my little three-year-old sister crawling unobtrusively through a doorway. I stopped, hesitated a second, then gave her a terrible kick in the head as though it had been a ball, and continued running, carried away with a "delirious joy" induced by this savage act. But my father, who was behind me, caught me and led me down into his office, where I remained as a punishment till dinner-time.

A year earlier than this Dalí had "suddenly, as most of my ideas occur" flung another little boy off a suspension bridge. Several other incidents of the same kind are recorded, including (*this was when he was twenty-nine years old*) knocking down and trampling on a girl "until they had to tear her, bleeding, out of my reach".

When he is about five he gets hold of a wounded bat which he puts into a tin pail. Next morning he finds that the bat is almost dead and is covered with ants which are devouring it. He puts it in his mouth, ants and all, and bites it almost in half.

When he is adolescent a girl falls desperately in love with him. He kisses and caresses her so as to excite her as much as possible, but refuses to go further. He resolves to keep this up for five years (he calls it his "five-year plan"), enjoying her humiliation and the sense of power it gives him. He frequently tells her that at the end of five years he will desert her, and when the time comes he does so.

Till well into adult life he keeps up the practice of masturbation, and likes to do this, apparently, in front of a looking glass. For ordinary purposes he is impotent, it appears, till the age of thirty or so. When he first meets his future wife, Gala, he is greatly tempted to push her off a precipice. He is aware that there is something that she wants him to do to her, and after their first kiss the confession is made:

> I threw back Gala's head, pulling it by the hair, and trembling with complete hysteria, I commanded:
> "Now tell me what you want me to do with you! But tell me slowly, looking me in the eye, with the crudest, the most ferociously erotic words that can make both of us feel the greatest shame!"
> [...] Then Gala, transforming the last glimmer of her expression of pleasure into the hard light of her own tyranny, answered:
> "I want you to kill me!"

He is somewhat disappointed by this demand, since it is merely what he wanted to do already. He contemplates throwing her off the bell tower of the cathedral of Toledo, but refrains from doing so.

During the Spanish Civil War he astutely avoids taking sides, and makes a trip to Italy. He feels himself more and more drawn towards the aristocracy, frequents smart salons, finds himself wealthy patrons and is photographed with the plump Vicomte de Noailles, whom he describes as his "Maecenas".* When the European war approaches he has one preoccupation only: how to find a place which has good cookery and from which he can make a quick bolt if danger comes too near. He fixes on Bordeaux, and duly flees to Spain during the Battle of France. He stays in Spain long enough to pick up a few anti-red atrocity stories, then makes for America. The story ends in a blaze of respectability. Dalí, at thirty-seven, has become a devoted husband, is cured of his aberrations, or some of them, and is completely reconciled to the Catholic Church. He is also, one gathers, making a good deal of money.

However, he has by no means ceased to take pride in the pictures of his Surrealist period, with titles like *The Great Masturbator*, *Sodomy of a Skull with a Grand Piano*, etc. There are reproductions of these all the way through the book. Many of Dalí's drawings are simply representational and have a characteristic to be noted later. But from his Surrealist paintings and photographs the two things that stand out are sexual perversity and necrophilia. Sexual objects and symbols – some of them well known, like our old friend the high-heeled slipper, others, like the crutch and the cup of warm milk, patented by Dalí himself – recur over and over again, and there is a fairly well-marked excretory motif as well. Of his painting *Le Jeu Lugubre*, he says, "the drawers bespattered with excrement were painted with such minute and realistic complacency that the whole little Surrealist group was anguished by the question: Is he coprophagic or not?" Dalí adds firmly that he is *not*, and that he regards this aberration as "repulsive", but it seems to be only at that point that his interest in excrement stops. Even when he recounts the experience of watching a woman urinate standing up, he has to add the detail that she misses her aim and dirties her shoes. It is not given to any one person to have all the vices, and Dalí also boasts that he is not homosexual, but otherwise he seems to have as good an outfit of perversions as anyone could wish for.

However, his most notable characteristic is his necrophilia. He himself freely admits to this, and claims to have been cured of it. Dead faces, skulls, corpses of animals occur fairly frequently in his pictures, and the ants which devoured the dying bat make countless reappearances. One photograph shows an exhumed corpse, far gone in decomposition. Another shows the dead donkeys putrefying on top of grand pianos which formed part of the Surrealist film *Le Chien andalou*.* Dalí still looks back on these donkeys with great enthusiasm.

> I "made up" the putrefaction of the donkeys with great pots of sticky glue which I poured over them. Also I emptied their eye sockets and made them larger by hacking them out with scissors. In the same way I furiously cut their mouths open to make the rows of their teeth show to better advantage, and I added several jaws to each mouth, so that it would appear that although the donkeys were already rotting they were vomiting up a little more of their own death, above those other rows of teeth formed by the keys of the black pianos.

And finally there is the picture – apparently some kind of faked photograph – of *Mannequin Rotting in a Taxi-Cab*. Over the already somewhat bloated face and breast of an apparently dead girl, huge snails are crawling. In the caption below the picture Dalí notes that these are Burgundy snails – that is, the edible kind.

Of course, in this long book of 400 quarto pages there is more than I have indicated, but I do not think that I have given an unfair account of its moral atmosphere and mental scenery. It is a book that stinks. If it were possible for a book to give a physical stink off its pages, this one would – a thought that might please Dalí, who before wooing his future wife for the first time rubbed himself all over with an ointment made of goat's dung boiled up in fish glue. But against this has to be set the fact that Dalí is a draughtsman of very exceptional gifts. He is also, to judge by the minuteness and the sureness of his drawings, a very hard worker. He is an exhibitionist and a careerist, but he is not a fraud. He has fifty times more talent than most of the people who would denounce his morals and jeer at his paintings. And these two sets of facts, taken together, raise a question which for lack of any basis of agreement seldom gets a real discussion.

The point is that you have here a direct, unmistakable assault on sanity and decency – and even – since some of Dalí's pictures would tend to poison the imagination like a pornographic postcard – on life itself. What Dalí has done and what he has imagined is debatable, but in his outlook, his character, the bedrock decency of a human being does not exist. He is as antisocial as a flea. Clearly, such people are undesirable, and a society in which they can flourish has something wrong with it.

Now, if you showed this book, with its illustrations, to Lord Elton,* to Mr Alfred Noyes, to *The Times* leader writers who exult over the "eclipse of the highbrow" – in fact, to any "sensible" art-hating English person – it is easy to imagine what kind of response you would get. They would flatly refuse to see any merit in Dalí whatever. Such people are not only unable to admit that what is morally degraded can be aesthetically right, but their real demand of every artist is that he shall pat them on the back and tell them that thought is unnecessary. And they can be especially dangerous at a time like the present, when the Ministry of Information and the British Council put power into their hands. For their impulse is not only to crush every new talent as it appears but to castrate the past as well. Witness the renewed highbrow-baiting that is now going on in this country and America, with its outcry not only against Joyce, Proust and Lawrence, but even against T.S. Eliot.

But if you talk to the kind of person who *can* see Dalí's merits, the response that you get is not as a rule very much better. If you say that Dalí, though a brilliant draughtsman, is a dirty little scoundrel, you are looked upon as a savage. If you say that you don't like rotting corpses, and that people who do like rotting corpses are mentally diseased, it is assumed that you lack the aesthetic sense. Since *Mannequin Rotting in a Taxi-Cab* is a good composition (as it undoubtedly is), it cannot be a disgusting, degrading picture – whereas Noyes, Elton, etc. would tell you that because it is disgusting it cannot be a good composition. And between these two fallacies there is no middle position – or, rather, there is a middle position, but we seldom hear much about it. On the one side *Kulturbolschewismus*;* on the other (though the phrase itself is out of fashion) "Art for Art's sake". Obscenity is a very difficult question to discuss honestly. People are too frightened either of seeming to be shocked or of seeming not to be shocked to be able to define the relationship between art and morals.

It will be seen that what the defenders of Dalí are claiming is a kind of *benefit of clergy*. The artist is to be exempt from the moral laws that are binding on ordinary people. Just pronounce the magic word "art", and everything is OK. Rotting corpses with snails crawling over them are OK; kicking little girls on the head is OK; even a film like *L'Âge d'or** is OK. It is also OK that Dalí should batten on France for years and then scuttle off like a rat as soon as France is in danger. So long as you can paint well enough to pass the test, all shall be forgiven you.

One can see how false this is if one extends it to cover ordinary crime. In an age like our own, when the artist is an altogether exceptional person, he must be allowed a certain amount of irresponsibility, just as a pregnant woman is. Still, no one would say that a pregnant woman should be allowed to commit murder, nor would anyone make such a claim for the artist, however gifted. If Shakespeare returned to the earth tomorrow, and if it were found that his favourite recreation was raping little girls in railway carriages, we should not tell him to go ahead with it on the ground that he might write another *King Lear*. And, after all, the worst crimes are not always the punishable ones. By encouraging necrophilic reveries one probably does quite as much harm as by, say, picking pockets at the races. One ought to be able to hold in one's head simultaneously the two facts that Dalí is a good draughtsman and a disgusting human being. The one does not invalidate or, in a sense, affect the other. The first thing that we demand of a wall is that it shall stand up. If it stands up, it is a good wall, and the question of what purpose it serves is separable from that. And yet even the best wall in the world deserves to be pulled down if it surrounds a concentration camp. In the same way it should be possible to say, "This is a good book or a good picture, and it ought to be burned by the public hangman." Unless one can say that, at least in imagination, one is shirking the implications of the fact that an artist is also a citizen and a human being.

Not, of course, that Dalí's autobiography, or his pictures, ought to be suppressed. Short of the dirty postcards that used to be sold in Mediterranean seaport towns, it is doubtful policy to suppress anything, and Dalí's fantasies probably cast useful light on the decay of capitalist civilization. But what he clearly needs is diagnosis. The question is not so much *what* he is as *why* he is like that. It ought not to be in doubt that he is a diseased intelligence, probably not much altered by his alleged conversion, since genuine penitents, or people who have returned to sanity, do not flaunt their past vices in that complacent way. He is a symptom of the world's illness. The important thing is not to denounce him as a cad who ought to be horsewhipped or to defend him as a genius who ought not to be questioned but to find out *why* he exhibits that particular set of aberrations.

The answer is probably discoverable in his pictures, and those I myself am not competent to examine. But I can point to one clue which perhaps takes one part of the distance. This is the old-fashioned, over-ornate, Edwardian style of drawing to which Dalí tends to revert when he is not being Surrealist. Some of Dalí's drawings are reminiscent of Dürer;* one (p. 113) seems to show the influence of Beardsley;* another (p. 269) seems to borrow something from Blake. But the most persistent strain is the Edwardian one. When I opened the book for the first time and looked at its innumerable marginal illustrations, I was haunted by a resemblance which I could not immediately pin down. I fetched up at the ornamental candlestick at the beginning of Part I (p. 7). What did this remind me of? Finally I tracked it down. It reminded me of a large, vulgar, expensively got-up edition of Anatole France (in translation) which must have been published about 1914. That had ornamental chapter headings and tailpieces after this style. Dalí's candlestick displays at one end a curly fish-like creature that looks curiously familiar (it seems to be based on the conventional dolphin), and at the other is the burning candle. This candle, which recurs in one picture after another, is a very old friend. You will find it, with the same picturesque gouts of wax arranged on its sides, in those phoney electric lights done up as candlesticks which are popular in sham-Tudor country hotels. This candle, and the design beneath it, convey at once an intense feeling of sentimentality. As though to counteract this, Dalí has spattered a quillful of ink all over the page, but without avail. The same impression keeps popping up on page after page. The design at the bottom of p. 62, for instance, would nearly go into *Peter Pan*. The figure on p. 224, in spite of having her cranium elongated into an immense sausage-like shape, is the witch of the fairy-tale books. The horse on p. 234 and the unicorn on p. 218 might be illustrations to James Branch Cabell.* The rather pansified drawings of youths on pp. 97, 100 and elsewhere convey the same impression. Picturesqueness keeps breaking in. Take away the skulls, ants, lobsters, telephones and other paraphernalia, and every now and again you are back in the world of Barrie, Rackham, Dunsany and *Where the Rainbow Ends*.*

Curiously enough, some of the naughty-naughty touches in Dalí's autobiography tie up with the same period. When I read the passage I quoted at the beginning, about the kicking of the little sister's head, I was aware of another phantom resemblance. What was it? Of course! *Ruthless Rhymes for Heartless Homes* by Harry Graham.* Such rhymes were very popular round about 1912, and one that ran:

> Poor little Willy is crying so sore,
> A sad little boy is he,
> For he's broken his little sister's neck
> And he'll have no jam for tea.

might almost have been founded on Dalí's anecdote. Dalí, of course, is aware of his Edwardian leanings, and makes capital out of them, more or less in a spirit of pastiche. He professes an especial affection for the year 1900, and claims that every ornamental object of 1900 is full of mystery, poetry, eroticism, madness, perversity, etc. Pastiche, however, usually implies a real affection for the thing parodied. It seems to be, if not the rule, at any rate distinctly common for an intellectual bent to be accompanied by a non-rational, even childish urge in the same direction. A sculptor, for instance, is interested in planes and curves, but he is also a person who enjoys the physical act of mucking about with clay or stone. An engineer is a person who enjoys the feel of tools, the noise of dynamos and the smell of oil. A psychiatrist usually has a leaning towards some sexual aberration himself. Darwin became a biologist partly because he was a country gentleman and fond of animals. It may be, therefore, that Dalí's seemingly perverse cult of Edwardian things (for example, his "discovery" of the 1900 subway entrances) is merely the symptom of a much deeper, less conscious affection. The innumerable, beautifully executed copies of textbook illustrations, solemnly labelled "*le rossignol*", "*une montre*"* and so on, which he scatters all over his margins, may be meant partly as a joke. The little boy in knickerbockers playing with a diabolo on p. 103 is a perfect period piece. But perhaps these things are also there because Dalí can't help drawing that kind of thing, because it is to that period and that style of drawing that he really belongs.

If so, his aberrations are partly explicable. Perhaps they are a way of assuring himself that he is not commonplace. The two qualities that Dalí unquestionably possesses are a gift for drawing and an atrocious egoism. "At seven," he says in the first paragraph of his book, "I wanted to be Napoleon. And my ambition has been growing steadily ever since." This is worded in a deliberately startling way, but no doubt it is substantially true. Such feelings are common enough. "I knew I was a genius," somebody once said to me, "long before I knew what I was going to be a genius *about*." And suppose that you have nothing in you except your egoism and a dexterity that goes no higher than the elbow; suppose that your real gift is for a detailed, academic, representational style of drawing, your real *métier* to be an illustrator of scientific textbooks. How then do you become Napoleon?

There is always one escape: *into wickedness*. Always do the thing that will shock and wound people. At five, throw a little boy off a bridge, strike an old doctor across the face with a whip and break his spectacles – or, at any rate, dream about doing such things. Twenty years later, gouge the eyes out of dead donkeys with a pair of scissors. Along those lines you can always feel yourself original. And after all, it pays! It is much less dangerous than crime. Making all allowance for the probable suppressions in Dalí's autobiography, it is clear that he has not had to suffer for his eccentricities as he would have done in an earlier age. He grew up in the corrupt world of the 1920s, when sophistication was immensely widespread and every European capital swarmed with aristocrats and rentiers who had given up sport and politics and taken to patronizing the arts. If you threw dead donkeys at people, they threw money back. A phobia for grasshoppers – which a few decades back would merely have provoked a snigger – was now an interesting "complex" which could be profitably exploited. And when that particular world collapsed before the German army, America was waiting. You could even top it all up with religious conversion, moving at one hop and without a shadow of repentance from the fashionable salons of Paris to Abraham's bosom.

That, perhaps, is the essential outline of Dalí's history. But why his aberrations should be the particular ones they were, and why it should be so easy to "sell" such horrors as rotting corpses to a sophisticated public – those are questions for the psychologist and the sociological critic. Marxist criticism has a short way with such phenomena as Surrealism. They are "bourgeois decadence" (much play is made with the phrases "corpse poisons" and "decaying rentier class"), and that is that. But though this probably states a fact, it does not establish a connection. One would still like to know *why* Dalí's leaning was towards necrophilia (and not, say, homosexuality), and *why* the rentiers and the aristocrats should buy his pictures instead of hunting and making love like their grandfathers. Mere moral disapproval does not get one any further. But neither ought one to pretend, in the name of "detachment", that such pictures as *Mannequin Rotting in a Taxi-Cab* are morally neutral. They are diseased and disgusting, and any investigation ought to start out from that fact.

Raffles and Miss Blandish*

Nearly half a century after his first appearance, Raffles, "the amateur cracksman", is still one of the best-known characters in English fiction. Very few people would need telling that he played cricket for England, had bachelor chambers in Albany and burgled the Mayfair houses which he also entered as a guest. Just for that reason he and his exploits make a suitable background against which to examine a more modern crime story such as *No Orchids for Miss Blandish*. Any such choice is necessarily arbitrary – I might equally well have chosen *Arsène Lupin*,* for instance – but at any rate *No Orchids* and the Raffles books* have the common quality of being crime stories which play the limelight on the criminal rather than the policeman. For sociological purposes they can be compared. *No Orchids* is the 1939 version of glamorized crime, *Raffles* the 1900 version. What I am concerned with here is the immense difference in moral atmosphere between the two books, and the change in the popular attitude that this probably implies.

At this date, the charm of *Raffles* is partly in the period atmosphere and partly in the technical excellence of the stories. Hornung was a very conscientious and on his level a very able writer. Anyone who cares for sheer efficiency must admire his work. However, the truly dramatic thing about Raffles, the thing that makes him a sort of byword even to this day (only a few weeks ago, in a burglary case, a magistrate referred to the prisoner as "a Raffles in real life"), is the fact that he is a *gentleman*. Raffles is presented to us – and this is rubbed home in countless scraps of dialogue and casual remarks – not as an honest man who has gone astray but as a public-school man who has gone astray. His remorse, when he feels any, is almost purely social; he has disgraced "the old school", he has lost his right to enter "decent society", he has forfeited his amateur status and become a cad. Neither Raffles nor Bunny appears to feel at all strongly that stealing is wrong in itself, though Raffles does once justify himself by the casual remark that "the distribution of property is all wrong anyway". They think of themselves not as sinners but as renegades, or simply as outcasts. And the moral code of most of us is still so close to Raffles's own that we do feel his situation to be an especially ironical one. A West End club man who is really a burglar! That is almost a story in itself, is it not? But how if it were a plumber or a greengrocer who was really a burglar? Would there be anything inherently dramatic in that? No – although the theme of the "double life", of respectability covering crime, is still there. Even Charles

Peace* in his clergyman's dog collar seems somewhat less of a hypocrite than Raffles in his I Zingari* blazer.

Raffles, of course, is good at all games, but it is peculiarly fitting that his chosen game should be cricket. This allows not only of endless analogies between his cunning as a slow bowler and his cunning as a burglar, but also helps to define the exact nature of his crime. Cricket is not in reality a very popular game in England – it is nowhere near so popular as football, for instance – but it gives expression to a well-marked trait in the English character, the tendency to value "form" or "style" more highly than success. In the eyes of any true cricket lover it is possible for an innings of ten runs to be "better" (i.e. more elegant) than an innings of a hundred runs; cricket is also one of the very few games in which the amateur can excel the professional. It is a game full of forlorn hopes and sudden dramatic changes of fortune, and its rules are so ill-defined that their interpretation is partly an ethical business. When Larwood, for instance, practised bodyline* bowling in Australia he was not actually breaking any rule: he was merely doing something that was "not cricket". Since cricket takes up a lot of time and is rather an expensive game to play, it is predominantly an upper-class game, but for the whole nation it is bound up with such concepts as "good form", "playing the game", etc., and it has declined in popularity just as the tradition of "don't hit a man when he's down" has declined. It is not a twentieth-century game, and nearly all modern-minded people dislike it. The Nazis, for instance, were at pains to discourage cricket, which had gained a certain footing in Germany before and after the last war. In making Raffles a cricketer as well as a burglar, Hornung was not merely providing him with a plausible disguise; he was also drawing the sharpest moral contrast that he was able to imagine.

Raffles, no less than *Great Expectations* or *Le Rouge et le Noir*,* is a story of snobbery, and it gains a great deal from the precariousness of Raffles's social position. A cruder writer would have made the "gentleman burglar" a member of the peerage, or at least a baronet. Raffles, however, is of upper-middle-class origin and is only accepted by the aristocracy because of his personal charm. "We were in Society but not of it," he says to Bunny towards the end of the book, and, "I was asked about for my cricket." Both he and Bunny accept the values of "society" unquestioningly, and would settle down in it for good if only they could get away with a big enough haul. The ruin that constantly threatens them is all the blacker because they only doubtfully "belong". A duke who has served a prison sentence is still a duke, whereas a mere man about town, if once disgraced, ceases to be "about town" for evermore. The closing chapters of the book, when Raffles has been exposed and is living under an assumed name, have a "twilight of the gods" feeling, a mental atmosphere rather similar to that of Kipling's poem 'Gentlemen-Rankers':

Yes, a trooper of the forces –
Who has run his own six horses!*
Etc.

Raffles now belongs irrevocably to the "cohorts of the damned". He can still commit successful burglaries, but there is no way back into Paradise, which means Piccadilly and the MCC.* According to the public-school code there is only one means of rehabilitation: death in battle. Raffles dies fighting against the Boers (a practised reader would foresee this from the start), and in the eyes of both Bunny and his creator this cancels his crimes.

Both Raffles and Bunny, of course, are devoid of religious belief, and they have no real ethical code, merely certain rules of behaviour which they observe semi-instinctively. But it is just here that the deep moral difference between *Raffles* and *No Orchids* becomes apparent. Raffles and Bunny, after all, are gentlemen, and such standards as they do have are not to be violated. Certain things are "not done", and the idea of doing them hardly arises. Raffles will not, for example, abuse hospitality. He will commit a burglary in a house where he is staying as a guest, but the victim must be a fellow guest and not the host. He will not commit murder,* and he avoids violence wherever possible and prefers to carry out his robberies unarmed. He regards friendship as sacred, and is chivalrous though not moral in his relations with women. He will take extra risks in the name of "sportsmanship", and sometimes even for aesthetic reasons. And above all, he is intensely patriotic. He celebrates the Diamond Jubilee ("For sixty years, Bunny, we've been ruled over by absolutely the finest sovereign the world has ever seen") by despatching to the Queen through the post an antique gold cup which he has stolen from the British Museum. He steals, from partly political motives, a pearl which the German Emperor is sending to one of the enemies of Britain, and when the Boer War begins to go badly his one thought is to find his way into the fighting line. At the front he unmasks a spy at the cost of revealing his own identity, and then dies gloriously by a Boer bullet. In this combination of crime and patriotism he resembles his near-contemporary Arsène Lupin, who also scores off the German Emperor and wipes out his very dirty past by enlisting in the Foreign Legion.

It is important to note that by modern standards Raffles's crimes are very petty ones. £400 worth of jewellery seems to him an excellent haul. And though the stories are convincing in their physical detail, they contain very little sensationalism – very few corpses, hardly any blood, no sex crimes, no sadism, no perversions of any kind. It seems to be the case that the crime story, at any rate on its higher levels, has greatly increased in bloodthirstiness during the past twenty years. Some of the early detective stories do not even contain a murder. The Sherlock Holmes stories, for instance, are not all murders, and some of them do not even deal with an indictable crime. So also with the John

Thorndyke stories, while of the Max Carrados stories only a minority are murders.* Since 1918, however, a detective story not containing a murder has been a great rarity, and the most disgusting details of dismemberment and exhumation are commonly exploited. Some of the Peter Wimsey stories,* for instance, display an extremely morbid interest in corpses. The Raffles stories, written from the angle of the criminal, are much less antisocial than many modern stories written from the angle of the detective. The main impression that they leave behind is of boyishness. They belong to a time when people had standards, though they happened to be foolish standards. Their key phrase is "not done". The line that they draw between good and evil is as senseless as a Polynesian taboo, but at least, like the taboo, it has the advantage that everyone accepts it.

So much for *Raffles*. Now for a header into the cesspool. *No Orchids for Miss Blandish*, by James Hadley Chase, was published in 1939, but seems to have enjoyed its greatest popularity in 1940, during the Battle of Britain and the Blitz. In its main outlines its story is this:

Miss Blandish, the daughter of a millionaire, is kidnapped by some gangsters who are almost immediately surprised and killed off by a larger and better organized gang. They hold her to ransom and extract half a million dollars from her father. Their original plan had been to kill her as soon as the ransom money was received, but a chance keeps her alive. One of the gang is a young man named Slim, whose sole pleasure in life consists in driving knives into other people's bellies. In childhood he had graduated by cutting up living animals with a pair of rusty scissors. Slim is sexually impotent, but takes a kind of fancy to Miss Blandish. Slim's mother, who is the real brains of the gang, sees in this the chance of curing Slim's impotence, and decides to keep Miss Blandish in custody till Slim shall have succeeded in raping her. After many efforts and much persuasion, including the flogging of Miss Blandish with a length of rubber hosepipe, the rape is achieved. Meanwhile Miss Blandish's father has hired a private detective, and by means of bribery and torture the detective and the police manage to round up and exterminate the whole gang. Slim escapes with Miss Blandish and is killed after a final rape, and the detective prepares to restore Miss Blandish to her family. By this time, however, she has developed such a taste for Slim's caresses* that she feels unable to live without him, and she jumps out of the window of a skyscraper.

Several other points need noticing before one can grasp the full implications of this book. To begin with, its central story bears a very marked resemblance to William Faulkner's novel *Sanctuary*.* Secondly, it is not, as one might expect, the product of an illiterate hack, but a brilliant piece of writing, with hardly a wasted word or a jarring note anywhere. Thirdly, the whole book, *récit** as well as dialogue, is written in the American language; the author, an Englishman who has (I believe) never been in the United States, seems to have made a complete mental transference to the American underworld. Fourthly, the book sold, according to its publishers, no less than half a million copies.

I have already outlined the plot, but the subject matter is much more sordid and brutal than this suggests. The book contains eight full-dress murders, an unassessable number of casual killings and woundings, an exhumation (with a careful reminder of the stench), the flogging of Miss Blandish, the torture of another woman with red-hot cigarette ends, a striptease act, a third-degree scene of unheard-of cruelty and much else of the same kind. It assumes great sexual sophistication in its readers (there is a scene, for instance, in which a gangster, presumably of masochistic tendency, has an orgasm in the moment of being knifed), and it takes for granted the most complete corruption and self-seeking as the norm of human behaviour. The detective, for instance, is almost as great a rogue as the gangsters, and actuated by nearly the same motives. Like them, he is in pursuit of "five hundred grand". It is necessary to the machinery of the story that Mr Blandish should be anxious to get his daughter back, but apart from this, such things as affection, friendship, good nature or even ordinary politeness simply do not enter. Nor, to any great extent, does normal sexuality. Ultimately only one motive is at work throughout the whole story: the pursuit of power.

It should be noticed that the book is not in the ordinary sense pornography. Unlike most books that deal in sexual sadism, it lays the emphasis on the cruelty and not on the pleasure. Slim, the ravisher of Miss Blandish, has "wet, slobbering lips": this is disgusting, and it is meant to be disgusting. But the scenes describing cruelty to women are comparatively perfunctory. The real high spots of the book are cruelties committed by men upon other men: above all, the third-degreeing of the gangster, Eddie Schultz, who is lashed into a chair and flogged on the windpipe with truncheons, his arms broken by fresh blows as he breaks loose. In another of Mr Chase's books, *He Won't Need It Now*,* the hero, who is intended to be a sympathetic and perhaps even noble character, is described as stamping on somebody's face, and then, having crushed the man's mouth in, grinding his heel round and round in it. Even when physical incidents of this kind are not occurring, the mental atmosphere of these books is always the same. Their whole theme is the struggle for power and the triumph of the strong over the weak. The big gangsters wipe out the little ones as mercilessly as a pike gobbling up the little fish in a pond; the police kill off the criminals as cruelly as the angler kills the pike. If ultimately one sides with the police against the gangsters, it is merely because they are better organized and more powerful, because, in fact, the law is a bigger racket than crime. Might is right: *væ victis*.

As I have mentioned already, *No Orchids* enjoyed its greatest vogue in 1940, though it was successfully running as a play till some time later. It was, in fact, one of the things that helped to console people for the boredom of being bombed. Early in the war the *New Yorker* had a picture of a little man approaching a news stall littered with papers with such headlines as "Great Tank Battles in Northern France", "Big Naval Battle in the North Sea", "Huge Air Battles over the Channel", etc. etc. The little man is saying "*Action Stories*,* please". That little man stood for all the drugged millions to whom the world of the gangsters and the prize ring is more "real", more "tough", than such things as wars, revolutions, earthquakes, famines and pestilences. From the point of view of a reader of *Action Stories*, a description of the London Blitz, or of the struggles of the European underground parties, would be "sissy stuff". On the other hand, some puny gun battle in Chicago, resulting in perhaps half a dozen deaths, would seem genuinely "tough". This habit of mind is now extremely widespread. A soldier sprawls in a muddy trench, with the machine-gun bullets crackling a foot or two overhead, and whiles away his intolerable boredom by reading an American gangster story. And what is it that makes that story so exciting? Precisely the fact that people are shooting at each other with machine guns! Neither the soldier nor anyone else sees anything curious in this. It is taken for granted that an imaginary bullet is more thrilling than a real one.

The obvious explanation is that in real life one is usually a passive victim, whereas in the adventure story one can think of oneself as being at the centre of events. But there is more to it than that. Here it is necessary to refer again to the curious fact of *No Orchids* being written – with technical errors, perhaps, but certainly with considerable skill – in the American language.

There exists in America an enormous literature of more or less the same stamp as *No Orchids*. Quite apart from books, there is the huge array of "pulp magazines", graded so as to cater for different kinds of fantasy, but nearly all having much the same mental atmosphere. A few of them go in for straight pornography, but the great majority are quite plainly aimed at sadists and masochists. Sold at threepence a copy under the title of Yank mags, these things used to enjoy considerable popularity in England, but when the supply dried up owing to the war, no satisfactory substitute was forthcoming. English imitations of the "pulp magazine" do now exist, but they are poor things compared with the original. English crook films, again, never approach the American crook film in brutality. And yet the career of Mr Chase shows how deep the American influence has already gone. Not only is he himself living a continuous fantasy life in the Chicago underworld, but he can count on hundreds of thousands of readers who know what is meant by a "clipshop" or the "hotsquat",* do not have to do mental arithmetic when confronted by "fifty grand" and understand at sight a sentence like "Johnnie was a rummy and only two jumps ahead of the nut-factory". Evidently there are great numbers of English people who are partly Americanized in language and, one ought to add, in moral outlook. For there was no popular protest against

No Orchids. In the end it was withdrawn, but only retrospectively, when a later work, *Miss Callaghan Comes to Grief*,* brought Mr Chase's books to the attention of the authorities. Judging by casual conversations at the time, ordinary readers got a mild thrill out of the obscenities of *No Orchids*, but saw nothing undesirable in the book as a whole. Many people, incidentally, were under the impression that it was an American book reissued in England.

The thing that the ordinary reader *ought* to have objected to – almost certainly would have objected to, a few decades earlier – was the equivocal attitude towards crime. It is implied throughout *No Orchids* that being a criminal is only reprehensible in the sense that it does not pay. Being a policeman pays better, but there is no moral difference, since the police use essentially criminal methods. In a book like *He Won't Need It Now* the distinction between crime and crime prevention practically disappears. This is a new departure for English sensational fiction, in which till recently there has always been a sharp distinction between right and wrong and a general agreement that virtue must triumph in the last chapter. English books glorifying crime (modern crime, that is – pirates and highwaymen are different) are very rare. Even a book like *Raffles*, as I have pointed out, is governed by powerful taboos, and it is clearly understood that Raffles's crimes must be expiated sooner or later. In America, both in life and fiction, the tendency to tolerate crime, even to admire the criminal so long as he is successful, is very much more marked. It is, indeed, ultimately this attitude that has made it possible for crime to flourish upon so huge a scale. Books have been written about Al Capone that are hardly different in tone from the books written about Henry Ford,* Stalin, Lord Northcliffe* and all the rest of the "log cabin to White House" brigade. And switching back eighty years, one finds Mark Twain adopting much the same attitude towards the disgusting bandit Slade,* hero of twenty-eight murders, and towards the Western desperadoes generally. They were successful, they "made good", therefore he admired them.

In a book like *No Orchids* one is not, as in the old-style crime story, simply escaping from dull reality into an imaginary world of action. One's escape is essentially into cruelty and sexual perversion. *No Orchids* is aimed at the power instinct, which *Raffles* or the Sherlock Holmes stories are not. At the same time the English attitude towards crime is not so superior to the American as I may have seemed to imply. It too is mixed up with power worship, and has become more noticeably so in the last twenty years. A writer who is worth examining is Edgar Wallace, especially in such typical books as *The Orator* and the Mr J.G. Reeder stories.* Wallace was one of the first crime-story writers to break away from the old tradition of the private detective and make his central figure a Scotland Yard official. Sherlock Holmes is an amateur, solving his problems without the help and even, in the earlier stories, against the opposition of the police. Moreover, like Lupin, he is essentially an intellectual, even a scientist.

He reasons logically from observed fact, and his intellectuality is constantly contrasted with the routine methods of the police. Wallace objected strongly to this slur, as he considered it, on Scotland Yard, and in several newspaper articles he went out of his way to denounce Holmes by name. His own ideal was the detective inspector who catches criminals not because he is intellectually brilliant but because he is part of an all-powerful organization. Hence the curious fact that in Wallace's most characteristic stories the "clue" and the "deduction" play no part. The criminal is always defeated either by an incredible coincidence, or because in some unexplained manner the police know all about the crime beforehand. The tone of the stories makes it quite clear that Wallace's admiration for the police is pure bully-worship. A Scotland Yard detective is the most powerful kind of being that he can imagine, while the criminal figures in his mind as an outlaw against whom anything is permissible, like the condemned slaves in the Roman arena. His policemen behave much more brutally than British policemen do in real life – they hit people without provocation, fire revolvers past their ears to terrify them and so on – and some of the stories exhibit a fearful intellectual sadism. (For instance, Wallace likes to arrange things so that the villain is hanged on the same day as the heroine is married.) But it is sadism after the English fashion: that is to say, it is unconscious, there is not overtly any sex in it, and it keeps within the bounds of the law. The British public tolerates a harsh criminal law and gets a kick out of monstrously unfair murder trials – but still that is better, on any count, than tolerating or admiring crime. If one must worship a bully, it is better that he should be a policeman than a gangster. Wallace is still governed to some extent by the concept of "not done". In *No Orchids* anything is "done" so long as it leads on to power. All the barriers are down, all the motives are out in the open. Chase is a worse symptom than Wallace, to the extent that all-in wrestling is worse than boxing, or fascism is worse than capitalist democracy.

In borrowing from William Faulkner's *Sanctuary*, Chase only took the plot; the mental atmosphere of the two books is not similar. Chase really derives from other sources, and this particular bit of borrowing is only symbolic. What it symbolizes is the vulgarization of ideas which is constantly happening, and which probably happens faster in an age of print. Chase has been described as "Faulkner for the masses", but it would be more accurate to describe him as Carlyle for the masses. He is a popular writer – there are many such in America, but they are still rarities in England – who has caught up with what it is now fashionable to call "realism", meaning the doctrine that might is right. The growth of "realism" has been the great feature of the intellectual history of our own age. Why this should be so is a complicated question. The interconnection between sadism, masochism, success worship, power worship, nationalism and totalitarianism is a huge subject whose edges have barely been scratched, and even to mention it is considered somewhat indelicate. To take merely the first example that comes to mind, I believe no one has ever pointed out the sadistic element in Bernard Shaw's work, still less suggested that this probably has some connection with Shaw's admiration for dictators. Fascism is often loosely equated with sadism, but nearly always by people who see nothing wrong in the most slavish worship of Stalin. The truth is, of course, that the countless English intellectuals who kiss the arse of Stalin are not different from the minority who give their allegiance to Hitler or Mussolini, nor from the efficiency experts who preached "punch", "drive", "personality" and "learn to be a Tiger man" in the 1920s, nor from the older generation of intellectuals, Carlyle, Creasey* and the rest of them, who bowed down before German militarism. All of them are worshipping power and successful cruelty. It is important to notice that the cult of power tends to be mixed up with a love of cruelty and wickedness *for their own sakes*. A tyrant is all the more admired if he happens to be a bloodstained crook as well, and "the end justifies the means" often becomes, in effect, "the means justify themselves provided they are dirty enough". This idea colours the outlook of all sympathizers with totalitarianism, and accounts, for instance, for the positive delight with which many English intellectuals greeted the Nazi–Soviet Pact. It was a step only doubtfully useful to the USSR, but it was entirely unmoral, and for that reason to be admired; the explanations of it, which were numerous and self-contradictory, could come afterwards.

Until recently the characteristic adventure stories of the English-speaking peoples have been stories in which the hero fights *against odds*. This is true all the way from Robin Hood to Popeye the Sailor. Perhaps the basic myth of the Western world is Jack the Giant-Killer, but to be brought up to date this should be renamed Jack the Dwarf-Killer, and there already exists a considerable literature which teaches, either overtly or implicitly, that one should side with the big man against the little man. Most of what is now written about foreign policy is simply an embroidery on this theme, and for several decades such phrases as "Play the game", "Don't hit a man when he's down" and "It's not cricket" have never failed to draw a snigger from anyone of intellectual pretensions. What is comparatively new is to find the accepted pattern according to which (a) right is right and wrong is wrong, whoever wins, and (b) weakness must be respected disappearing from popular literature as well. When I first read D.H. Lawrence's novels, at the age of about twenty, I was puzzled by the fact that there did not seem to be any classification of the characters into "good" and "bad". Lawrence seemed to sympathize with all of them about equally, and this was so unusual as to give me the feeling of having lost my bearings. Today no one would think of looking for heroes and villains in a serious novel, but in lowbrow fiction one still expects to find a sharp distinction between right and wrong and between legality and illegality. The common people, on the whole, are still living in the world of absolute good and evil from which the intellectuals have long since escaped. But the popularity of *No Orchids* and the American books and magazines to which it is akin shows how rapidly the doctrine of "realism" is gaining ground.

Several people, after reading *No Orchids*, have remarked to me, "It's pure fascism." This is a correct description, although the book has not the smallest connection with politics and very little with social or economic problems. It has merely the same relation to fascism as, say, Trollope's novels have to nineteenth-century capitalism. It is a daydream appropriate to a totalitarian age. In his imagined world of gangsters Chase is presenting, as it were, a distilled version of the modern political scene, in which such things as mass bombing of civilians, the use of hostages, torture to obtain confessions, secret prisons, execution without trial, floggings with rubber truncheons, drownings in cesspools, systematic falsification of records and statistics, treachery, bribery and quislingism are normal and morally neutral, even admirable when they are done in a large and bold way. The average man is not directly interested in politics and, when he reads, he wants the current struggles of the world to be translated into a simple story about individuals. He can take an interest in Slim and Fenner as he could not in the GPU* and the Gestapo. People worship power in the form in which they are able to understand it. A twelve-year-old boy worships Jack Dempsey. An adolescent in a Glasgow slum worships Al Capone. An aspiring pupil at a business college worships Lord Nuffield. A *New Statesman* reader worships Stalin. There is a difference in intellectual maturity, but none in moral outlook. Thirty years ago the heroes of popular fiction had nothing in common with Mr Chase's gangsters and detectives, and the idols of the English liberal intelligentsia were also comparatively sympathetic figures. Between Holmes and Fenner on the one hand, and between Abraham Lincoln and Stalin on the other, there is a similar gulf.

One ought not to infer too much from the success of Mr Chase's books. It is possible that it is an isolated phenomenon, brought about by the mingled boredom and brutality of war. But if such books should definitely acclimatize themselves in England, instead of being merely a half-understood import from America, there would be good grounds for dismay. In choosing *Raffles* as a background for *No Orchids* I deliberately chose a book which by the standards of its time was morally equivocal. Raffles, as I have pointed out, has no real moral code, no religion, certainly no social consciousness. All he has is a set of reflexes – the nervous system, as it were, of a gentleman. Give him a sharp tap on this reflex or that (they are called "sport", "pal", "woman", "king and country" and so forth), and you get a predictable reaction. In Mr Chase's books there are no gentlemen and no taboos. Emancipation is complete; Freud and Machiavelli have reached the outer suburbs. Comparing the schoolboy atmosphere of the one book with the cruelty and corruption of the other, one is driven to feel that snobbishness, like hypocrisy, is a check upon behaviour whose value from a social point of view has been underrated.

Arthur Koestler*

One striking fact about English literature during the present century is the extent to which it has been dominated by foreigners – for example, Conrad, Henry James, Shaw, Joyce, Yeats, Pound and Eliot. Still, if you chose to make this a matter of national prestige and examine our achievement in the various branches of literature, you would find that England made a fairly good showing until you came to what may be roughly described as political writing, or pamphleteering. I mean by this the special class of literature that has arisen out of the European political struggle since the rise of fascism. Under this heading novels, autobiographies, books of "reportage", sociological treatises and plain pamphlets can all be lumped together, all of them having a common origin and to a great extent the same emotional atmosphere.

Some out of the outstanding figures in this school of writers are Silone, Malraux, Salvemini, Borkenau, Victor Serge* and Koestler himself. Some of these are imaginative writers, some not, but they are all alike in that they are trying to write contemporary history, but *unofficial* history, the kind that is ignored in the textbooks and lied about in the newspapers. Also they are all alike in being Continental Europeans. It may be an exaggeration, but it cannot be a very great one, to say that whenever a book dealing with totalitarianism appears in this country, and still seems worth reading six months after publication, it is a book translated from some foreign language. English writers, over the past dozen years, have poured forth an enormous spate of political literature, but they have produced almost nothing of aesthetic value, and very little of historical value either. The Left Book Club, for instance, has been running ever since 1936. How many of its chosen volumes can you even remember the names of? Nazi Germany, Soviet Russia, Spain, Abyssinia, Austria, Czechoslovakia – all that these and kindred subjects have produced, in England, are slick books of reportage, dishonest pamphlets in which propaganda is swallowed whole and then spewed up again, half digested, and a very few reliable guidebooks and textbooks. There has been nothing resembling, for instance, *Fontamara* or *Darkness at Noon*,* because there is almost no English writer to whom it has happened to see totalitarianism from the inside. In Europe, during the past decade and more, things have been happening to middle-class people which in England do not even happen to the working class. Most of the European writers I mentioned above, and scores of others like them, have been obliged to break the law in order to engage in politics at all; some of them have thrown bombs and fought in street battles; many have been in prison or the concentration camp, or fled across frontiers with false names and forged passports. One cannot imagine, say, Professor Laski indulging in activities of that kind. England is lacking, therefore, in what one might call concentration-camp literature. The special world created by secret police forces, censorship of opinion, torture and frame-up trials is, of course, known about and to some extent disapproved of, but it has made very little emotional impact. One result of this is that there exists in England almost no literature of disillusionment about the Soviet Union. There is the attitude of ignorant disapproval, and there is the attitude of uncritical admiration, but very little in between. Opinion on the Moscow sabotage trials, for instance, was divided, but divided chiefly on the question of whether the accused were guilty. Few people were able to see that, whether justified or not, the trials were an unspeakable horror. And English disapproval of the Nazi outrages has also been an unreal thing, turned on and off like a tap according to political expediency. To understand such things one has to be able to imagine oneself as the victim, and for an Englishman to write *Darkness at Noon* would be as unlikely an accident as for a slave trader to write *Uncle Tom's Cabin*.

Koestler's published work really centres about the Moscow trials. His main theme is the decadence of revolutions owing to the corrupting effects of power, but the special nature of the Stalin dictatorship has driven him back into a position not far removed from pessimistic conservatism. I do not know how many books he has written in all. He is a Hungarian whose earlier books were written in German, and five books have been published in England: *Spanish Testament*, *The Gladiators*, *Darkness at Noon*, *Scum of the Earth* and *Arrival and Departure*.* The subject matter of all of them is similar, and none of them ever escapes for more than a few pages from the atmosphere of nightmare. Of the five books, the action of three takes place entirely or almost entirely in prison.

In the opening months of the Spanish Civil War Koestler was the *News Chronicle*'s correspondent in Spain, and early in 1937 he was taken prisoner when the fascists captured Malaga. He was nearly shot out of hand, then spent some months imprisoned in a fortress, listening every night to the roar of rifle fire as batch after batch of Republicans was executed, and being most of the time in acute danger of execution himself. This was not a chance adventure which "might have happened to anybody", but was in accordance with Koestler's lifestyle. A politically indifferent person would not have been in Spain at that date, a more cautious observer would have got out of Malaga before the fascists arrived and a British or American newspaper man would have been treated with more consideration. The book that Koestler wrote about this, *Spanish Testament*, has remarkable passages, but apart from the scrappiness that is usual in a book of reportage, it is definitely false in places. In the prison scenes Koestler successfully establishes the nightmare atmosphere which is, so to speak, his patent, but the rest of the book is too much coloured by the Popular Front orthodoxy of the time. One or two passages even look as though they had been doctored for the purposes of the Left Book Club. At that time Koestler still was, or recently had been, a member of the Communist Party, and the complex politics of the civil war made it impossible for any communist to write honestly about the internal struggle on the government side. The sin of nearly all left-wingers from 1933 onwards is that they have wanted to be anti-fascist without being anti-totalitarian. In 1937 Koestler already knew this, but did not feel free to say so. He came much nearer to saying it – indeed, he did say it, though he put on a mask to do so – in his next book, *The Gladiators*, which was published about a year before the war and for some reason attracted very little attention.

The Gladiators is in some ways an unsatisfactory book. It is about Spartacus, the Thracian gladiator who raised a slaves' rebellion in Italy round about 65 BC, and any book on such a subject is handicapped by challenging comparison with *Salammbô*.* In our own age it would not be possible to write a book like *Salammbô* even if one had the talent. The great thing about *Salammbô*, even more important than its physical detail, is its utter mercilessness. Flaubert could think himself into the stony cruelty of antiquity, because in the midnineteenth century one still had peace of mind. One had time to travel in the past. Nowadays the present and the future are too terrifying to be escaped from, and if one bothers with history it is in order to find modern meanings there. Koestler makes Spartacus into an allegorical figure, a primitive version of the proletarian dictator. Whereas Flaubert has been able, by a prolonged effort of the imagination, to make his mercenaries truly pre-Christian, Spartacus is a modern man dressed up. But this might not matter if Koestler were fully aware of what his allegory means. Revolutions always go wrong – that is the main theme. It is on the question of *why* they go wrong that he falters, and his uncertainty enters into the story and makes the central figures enigmatic and unreal.

For several years the rebellious slaves are uniformly successful. Their numbers swell to 100,000; they overrun great areas of southern Italy; they defeat one punitive expedition after another; they ally themselves with the pirates who at that time were the masters of the Mediterranean; and finally they set to work to build a city of their own, to be named the City of the Sun. In this city human beings are to be free and equal, and above all, they are to be happy: no slavery, no hunger, no injustice, no floggings, no executions. It is the dream of a just society which seems to haunt the human imagination ineradicably and in all ages, whether it is called the Kingdom of Heaven or the classless society, or whether it is thought of as a Golden Age which once existed in the past and from which we have degenerated. Needless to say, the slaves fail to achieve it. No sooner have they formed themselves into a community than their way of life turns out to be as unjust, laborious and fear-ridden as any other. Even the cross, symbol of slavery, has to be revived for the punishment of malefactors. The turning point comes when Spartacus finds himself obliged to crucify twenty of his oldest and most faithful followers. After that the City of the Sun is doomed, the slaves split up and are defeated in detail, the last 15,000 of them being captured and crucified in one batch.

The serious weakness of this story is that the motives of Spartacus himself are never made clear. The Roman lawyer Fulvius, who joins the rebellion and acts as its chronicler, sets forth the familiar dilemma of ends and means. You can achieve nothing unless you are willing to use force and cunning, but in using them you pervert your original aims. Spartacus, however, is not represented as power hungry, nor, on the other hand, as a visionary. He is driven onwards by some obscure force which he does not understand, and he is frequently in two minds as to whether it would not be better to throw up the whole adventure and flee to Alexandria while the going is good. The slaves' republic is in any case wrecked rather by hedonism than by the struggle for power. The slaves are discontented with their liberty because they still have to work, and the final break-up happens because the more turbulent and less civilized slaves, chiefly Gauls and Germans, continue to behave like bandits after the republic has been established. This may be a true account of events – naturally we know very little about the slave rebellions of antiquity – but by allowing the Sun City to be destroyed because Crixus the Gaul cannot be prevented from looting and raping, Koestler has faltered between allegory and history. If Spartacus is the prototype of the modern revolutionary – and obviously he is intended as that – he should have gone astray because of the impossibility of combining power with righteousness. As it is, he is an almost passive figure, acted upon rather than acting, and at times not convincing. The story partly fails because the central problem of revolution has been avoided or, at least, has not been solved.

It is again avoided in a subtler way in the next book, Koestler's masterpiece, *Darkness at Noon*. Here, however, the story is not spoilt, because it deals with individuals and its interest is psychological. It is an episode picked out from a background that does not have to be questioned. *Darkness at Noon* describes the imprisonment and death of an Old Bolshevik,* Rubashov, who first denies and ultimately confesses to crimes which he is well aware he has not committed. The grown-upness, the lack of surprise or denunciation, the pity and irony with which the story is told, show the advantage, when one is handling a theme of this kind, of being a European. The book reaches the stature of tragedy, whereas an English or American writer could at most have made it into a polemical tract. Koestler has digested his material and can treat it on the aesthetic level. At the same time his handling of it has a political implication, not important in this case but likely to be damaging in later books.

Naturally the whole book centres round one question: why did Rubashov confess? He is not guilty – that is, not guilty of anything except the essential crime of disliking the Stalin regime. The concrete acts of treason in which he is supposed to have engaged are all imaginary. He has not even been tortured, or not very severely. He is worn down by solitude, toothache, lack of tobacco, bright lights glaring in his eyes, and continuous questioning, but these in themselves would not be enough to overcome a hardened revolutionary. The Nazis have previously done worse to him without breaking his spirit. The confessions obtained in the Russian state trials are capable of three explanations:

1. That the accused were guilty.
2. That they were tortured, and perhaps blackmailed by threats to relatives and friends.
3. That they were actuated by despair, mental bankruptcy and the habit of loyalty to the Party.

For Koestler's purpose in *Darkness at Noon* 1 is ruled out, and though this is not the place to discuss the Russian purges, I must add that what little verifiable evidence there is suggests that the trials of the Bolsheviks were frame-ups. If one assumes that the accused were not guilty – at any rate, not guilty of the particular things they confessed to – then 2 is the common-sense explanation. Koestler, however, plumps for 3, which is also accepted by the Trotskyist Boris Souvarine, in his pamphlet *Cauchemar en URSS*.* Rubashov ultimately confesses because he cannot find in his own mind any reason for not doing so. Justice and objective truth have long ceased to have any meaning for him. For decades he has been simply the creature of the Party, and what the Party now demands is that he shall confess to non-existent crimes. In the end, though he had to be bullied and weakened first, he is somewhat proud of his decision to confess. He feels superior to the poor Tsarist officer who inhabits the next cell and who talks to Rubashov by tapping on the wall. The Tsarist officer is shocked when he learns that Rubashov intends to capitulate. As he sees it from his "bourgeois" angle, everyone ought to stick to his guns, even a Bolshevik. Honour, he says, consists in doing what you think right. "Honour is to be useful without fuss," Rubashov taps back – and he reflects with a certain satisfaction that he is tapping with his pince-nez while the other, the relic of the past, is tapping with a monocle. Like Bukharin,* Rubashov is "looking out upon black darkness". What is there, what code, what loyalty, what notion of good and evil, for the sake of which he can defy the Party and endure further torment? He is not only alone, he is also hollow. He has himself committed worse crimes than the one that is now being perpetrated against him. For example, as a secret envoy of the Party in Nazi Germany, he has got rid of disobedient followers by betraying them to the Gestapo. Curiously enough, if he has any inner strength to draw upon, it is the memories of his boyhood when he was the son of a landowner. The last thing he remembers, when he is shot from behind, is the leaves of poplar trees on his father's estate. Rubashov belongs to the older generation of Bolsheviks that was largely wiped out in the purges. He is aware of art and literature, and of the world outside Russia. He contrasts sharply with Gletkin, the young GPU man who conducts his interrogation, and who is the typical "good party man", completely without scruples or curiosity, a thinking gramophone. Rubashov, unlike Gletkin, does not have the Revolution as his starting point. His mind was not a blank sheet when the Party got hold of it. His superiority to the other is finally traceable to his bourgeois origin.

One cannot, I think, argue that *Darkness at Noon* is simply a story dealing with the adventures of an imaginary individual. Clearly it is a political book, founded on history and offering an interpretation of disputed events. Rubashov might be called Trotsky, Bukharin, Rakovsky, or some other relatively civilized figure among the Old Bolsheviks. If one writes about the Moscow trials one must answer the question "Why did the accused confess?" and which answer one makes is a political decision. Koestler answers, in effect, "Because these people had been rotted by the Revolution which they served" – and in doing so he comes near to claiming that revolutions are of their nature bad. If one assumes that the accused in the Moscow trials were made to confess by means of some kind of terrorism, one is only saying that one particular set of revolutionary leaders has gone astray. Individuals, and not the situation, are to blame. The implication of Koestler's book, however, is that Rubashov in power would be no better than Gletkin – or rather, only better in that his outlook is still partly pre-revolutionary. Revolution, Koestler seems to say, is a corrupting process. Really enter into the Revolution and you must end up as either Rubashov or Gletkin. It is not merely than "power corrupts": so also do the ways of attaining power. Therefore, all efforts to regenerate society *by violent means* lead to the cellars of the OGPU,* Lenin leads to Stalin, and would have come to resemble Stalin if he had happened to survive.

Of course, Koestler does not say this quite explicitly, and perhaps is not altogether conscious of it. He is writing about darkness, but it is darkness at what ought to be noon. Part of the time he feels that things might have turned out differently. The notion that so-and-so has "betrayed", that things have only gone wrong because of individual wickedness, is ever present in left-wing thought. Later, in *Arrival and Departure*, Koestler swings over much further towards the anti-revolutionary position, but in between these two books there is another, *Scum of the Earth*, which is straight autobiography and has only an indirect bearing upon the problems raised by *Darkness at Noon*. True to his lifestyle, Koestler was caught in France by the outbreak of war and, as a foreigner and a known anti-fascist, was promptly arrested and interned by the Daladier government.* He spent the first nine months of war mostly in a prison camp, then, during the collapse of France, escaped and travelled by devious routes to England, where he was once again thrown into prison as an enemy alien. This time he was soon released, however. The book is a valuable piece of reportage, and together with a few other scraps of honest writing that happened to be produced at the time of the debacle, it is a reminder of the depths that bourgeois democracy can descend to. At this moment, with France newly liberated and the witch-hunt after collaborators in full swing, we are apt to forget that in 1940 various observers on the spot considered that about 40 per cent of the French population was either actively pro-German or completely apathetic. Truthful war books are never acceptable to non-combatants, and Koestler's book did not have a very good reception. Nobody came well out of it – neither the bourgeois politicians, whose idea of conducting an anti-fascist war was to jail every left-winger they could lay their hands on, nor the French communists, who were effectively pro-Nazi and did their best to sabotage the French war effort, nor the common people, who were just as likely to follow mountebanks like Doriot* as responsible leaders. Koestler records some fantastic conversations with fellow victims in the concentration camp, and adds that till then, like most middle-class socialists and communists, he had never made contact with real proletarians, only with the educated minority. He draws the pessimistic conclusion: "Without education of the masses, no social progress; without social progress, no education of the masses." In *Scum of the Earth* Koestler ceases to idealize the common people. He has abandoned Stalinism, but he is not a Trotskyist either. This is the book's real link with *Arrival and Departure*, in which what is normally called a revolutionary outlook is dropped, perhaps for good.

Arrival and Departure is not a satisfactory book. The pretence that it is a novel is very thin; in effect it is a tract purporting to show that revolutionary creeds are rationalizations of neurotic impulses. With all too neat a symmetry, the book begins and ends with the same action – a leap into a foreign country. A young ex-communist who has made his escape from Hungary jumps ashore in Portugal, where he hopes to enter the service of Britain, at that time the only power fighting against Germany. His enthusiasm is somewhat cooled by the fact that the British consulate is uninterested in him and almost ignores him for a period of several months, during which his money runs out and other astuter refugees escape to America. He is successively tempted by the world in the form of a Nazi propagandist, the flesh in the form of a French girl, and – after a nervous breakdown – the Devil in the form of a psychoanalyst. The psychoanalyst drags out of him the fact that his revolutionary enthusiasm is not founded on any real belief in historical necessity, but on a morbid guilt complex arising from an attempt in early childhood to blind his baby brother. By the time that he gets an opportunity of serving the Allies he has lost all reason for wanting to do so, and he is on the point of leaving for America when his irrational impulses seize hold of him again. In practice he cannot abandon the struggle. When the book ends, he is floating down in a parachute over the dark landscape of his native country, where he will be employed as a secret agent of Britain.

As a political statement (and the book is not much more), this is insufficient. Of course it is true in many cases, and it may be true in all cases, that revolutionary activity is the result of personal maladjustment. Those who struggle against society are, on the whole, those who have reason to dislike it, and normal healthy people are no more attracted by violence and illegality than they are by war. The young Nazi in *Arrival and Departure* makes the penetrating remark that one can see what is wrong with the left-wing movement by the ugliness of its women. But after all, this does not invalidate the socialist case. Actions have results, irrespective of their motives. Marx's ultimate motives may well have been envy and spite, but this does not prove that his conclusions were false. In making the hero of *Arrival and Departure* take his final decision from a mere instinct not to shirk action and danger, Koestler is making him suffer a sudden loss of intelligence. With such a history as he has behind him, he would be able to see that certain things have to be done, whether our reasons for doing them are "good" or "bad". History has to move in a certain direction, even if it has to be pushed that way by neurotics. In *Arrival and Departure* Peter's idols are overthrown one after the other. The Russian Revolution has degenerated; Britain, symbolized by the aged consul with gouty fingers, is no better; the international class-conscious proletariat is a myth. But the conclusion (since, after all, Koestler and his hero "support" the war) ought to be that getting rid of Hitler is still a worthwhile objective, a necessary bit of scavenging in which motives are almost irrelevant.

To take a rational political decision one must have a picture of the future. At present Koestler seems to have none, or rather to have two which cancel out. As an ultimate objective he believes in the Earthly Paradise, the Sun State which the gladiators set out to establish, and which has haunted the imagination of socialists, anarchists and religious heretics for hundreds of years. But his intelligence tells him that the Earthly Paradise is receding into the far distance and that what is actually ahead of us is bloodshed, tyranny and privation. Recently he described himself as a "short-term pessimist". Every kind of horror is blowing up over the horizon, but somehow it will all come right in the end. This outlook is probably gaining ground among thinking people: it results from the very great difficulty, once one has abandoned orthodox religious belief, of accepting life on earth as inherently miserable, and on the other hand, from the realization that to make life liveable is a much bigger problem than it recently seemed. Since about 1930 the world has given no reason for optimism whatever. Nothing is in sight except a welter of lies, hatred, cruelty and ignorance, and beyond our present troubles loom vaster ones which are only now entering into the European consciousness. It is quite possible that man's major problems will *never* be solved. But it is also unthinkable! Who is there who dares to look at the world of today and say to himself, "It will always be like this: even in a million years it cannot get appreciably better?" So you get the quasi-mystical belief that for the present there is no remedy, all political action is useless, but that somewhere in space and time human life will cease to be the miserable brutish thing it now is.

The only easy way out is that of the religious believer, who regards this life merely as a preparation for the next. But few thinking people now believe in life after death, and the number of those who do is probably diminishing. The Christian churches would probably not survive on their own merits if their economic basis were destroyed. The real problem is how to restore the religious attitude while accepting death as final. Men can only be happy when they do not assume that the object of life is happiness. It is most unlikely, however, that Koestler would accept this. There is a well-marked hedonistic strain in his writings, and his failure to find a political position after breaking with Stalinism is a result of this.

The Russian Revolution, the central event in Koestler's life, started out with high hopes. We forget these things now, but a quarter of a century ago it was confidently expected that the Russian Revolution would lead to utopia. Obviously this has not happened. Koestler is too acute not to see this, and too sensitive not to remember the original objective. Moreover, from his European angle he can see such things as purges and mass deportations for what they are; he is not, like Shaw or Laski, looking at them through the wrong end of the telescope. Therefore he draws the conclusion: this is what revolutions lead to. There is nothing for it except to be a "short-term pessimist", i.e. to keep out of politics, make a sort of oasis within which you and your friends can remain sane, and hope that somehow things will be better in a hundred years. At the basis of this lies his hedonism, which leads him to think of the Earthly Paradise as desirable. Perhaps, however, whether desirable or not, it isn't possible. Perhaps some degree of suffering is ineradicable from human life; perhaps the choice before man is always a choice of evils; perhaps even the aim of socialism is not to make the world perfect but to make it better. All revolutions are failures, but they are not all the same failure. It is his unwillingness to admit this that has led Koestler's mind temporarily into a blind alley and that makes *Arrival and Departure* seem shallow compared with the earlier books.

Tobias Smollett: Scotland's Best Novelist*

"Realism", a much-abused word, has at least four current meanings, but when applied to novels it normally means a photographic imitation of everyday life. A "realistic" novel is one in which the dialogue is colloquial and physical objects are described in such a way that you can visualize them. In this sense almost all modern novels are more "realistic" than those of the past, because the describing of everyday scenes and the construction of natural-sounding dialogue are largely a matter of technical tricks which are passed on from one generation to another, gradually improving in the process. But there is another sense in which the stilted, artificial novelists of the eighteenth century are more "realistic" than almost any of their successors, and that is in their attitude towards human motives. They may be weak at describing scenery, but they are extraordinarily good at describing scoundrelism. This is true even of Fielding, who in *Tom Jones* and *Amelia** already shows the moralizing tendency which was to mark English novels for 150 years. But it is much truer of Smollett, whose outstanding intellectual honesty may have been connected with the fact that he was not an Englishman.

Smollett is a picaresque novelist, a writer of long, formless tales full of farcical and improbable adventures. He derives to some extent from Cervantes, whom he translated into English and whom he also plagiarized in *Sir Launcelot Greaves*.* Inevitably a great deal that he wrote is no longer worth reading, even including, perhaps, his most praised book, *Humphry Clinker*,* which is written in the form of letters and was considered comparatively respectable in the nineteenth century, because most of its obscenities are hidden under puns. But Smollett's real masterpieces are *Roderick Random* and *Peregrine Pickle*,* which are frankly pornographic in a harmless way and which contain some of the best passages of sheer farce in the English language.

Dickens, in *David Copperfield*, names these two books among his childhood favourites, but the resemblance sometimes claimed as existing between Smollett and Dickens is very superficial. In *Pickwick Papers*, and in several others of Dickens's early books, you have the picaresque form, the endless travelling to and fro, the fantastic adventures, the willingness to sacrifice no matter what amount of probability for the sake of a joke – but the moral atmosphere has greatly altered. Between Smollett's day and Dickens's there had happened not only the French Revolution, but the rise of a new industrial middle class, Low Church in its theology and puritanical in its outlook. Smollett writes of the middle class, but the mercantile and professional middle class, the kind of people who are cousins to a landowner and take their manners from the aristocracy.

Duelling, gambling and fornication seem almost morally neutral to him. It so happens that in private life he was a better man than the majority of writers. He was a faithful husband who shortened his life by overworking for the sake of his family, a sturdy republican who hated France as the country of the Grand Monarchy and a patriotic Scotsman at a time when – the 1745 rebellion being a fairly recent memory – it was far from fashionable to be a Scotsman. But he has very little sense of sin. His heroes do things, and do them on almost every page, which in any nineteenth-century English novel would instantly call forth vengeance from the skies. He accepts as a law of nature the viciousness, the nepotism and the disorder of eighteenth-century society, and therein lies his charm. Many of his best passages would be ruined by any intrusion of the moral sense.

Both *Peregrine Pickle* and *Roderick Random* follow roughly the same course. Both heroes go through great vicissitudes of fortune, travel widely, seduce numerous women, suffer imprisonment for debt, and end up prosperous and happily married. Of the two, Peregrine is somewhat the greater blackguard, because he has no profession – Roderick is a naval surgeon, as Smollett himself had been for a while – and can consequently devote more time to seductions and practical jokes. But neither is ever shown acting from an unselfish motive, nor is it admitted that such things as religious belief, political conviction or even ordinary honesty are serious factors in human affairs.

In the world of Smollett's novels there are only three virtues. One is feudal loyalty (Roderick and Peregrine each have a retainer who is faithful through thick and thin); another is masculine "honour", i.e. willingness to fight on any provocation; and another is female "chastity", which is inextricably mixed up with the idea of capturing a husband. Otherwise anything goes. It is nothing out of the way to cheat at cards, for instance. It seems quite natural to Roderick, when he has got hold of £1,000 from somewhere, to buy himself a smart outfit of clothes and go to Bath posing as a rich man in hopes of entrapping an heiress. When he is in France and out of a job, he decides to join the army, and as the French army happens to be the nearest one, he joins that and fights against the British at the Battle of Dettingen: he is nevertheless ready soon afterwards to fight a duel with a Frenchman who has insulted Britain.

Peregrine devotes himself for months at a time to the elaborate and horribly cruel practical jokes in which the eighteenth century delighted. When, for instance, an unfortunate English painter is thrown into the Bastille for some trifling offence and is about to be released, Peregrine and his friends, playing on his ignorance of the language, let him think that he has been sentenced to be broken on a wheel. A little later they tell him that this punishment has been commuted to castration, and then extract a last bit of fun out of his terrors by letting him think that he is escaping in disguise when he is merely being released from the prison in the normal way.

Why are these petty rogueries worth reading about? In the first place because they are funny. In the Continental writers from whom Smollett derived there may be better things than the description of Peregrine Pickle's adventures on the Grand Tour, but there is nothing better of that particular kind in English. Secondly, by simply ruling out "good" motives and showing no respect whatever for human dignity, Smollett often attains a truthfulness that more serious novelists have missed. He is willing to mention things which do happen in real life but are almost invariably kept out of fiction. Roderick Random, for instance, at one stage of his career, catches a venereal disease – the only English novel hero, I believe, to whom this has happened. And the fact that Smollett, in spite of his fairly enlightened views, takes patronage, official jobbery and general corruption for granted gives great historical interest to certain passages in his books.

Smollett had been for a while in the navy, and in *Roderick Random* we are given not only an unvarnished account of the Cartagena expedition, but an extraordinarily vivid and disgusting description of the inside of a warship, in those days a sort of floating compendium of disease, discomfort, tyranny and incompetence. The command of Roderick's ship is for a while given to a young man of family, a scented homosexual fop who has hardly seen a ship in his life, and who spends the whole voyage in his cabin to avoid contact with the vulgar sailor men, almost fainting when he smells tobacco. The scenes in the debtors' prison are even better. In the prisons of those days, a debtor who had no resources might actually starve to death unless he could keep alive by begging from more fortunate prisoners. One of Roderick's fellow prisoners is so reduced that he has no clothes at all and preserves decency as best he can by wearing a very long beard. Some of the prisoners, needless to say, are poets, and the book includes a self-contained story, 'Mr Melopoyn's Tragedy', which should make anyone who thinks aristocratic patronage a good basis for literature think twice.

Smollett's influence on subsequent English writers has not been as great as that of his contemporary, Fielding. Fielding deals in the same kind of boisterous adventure, but his sense of sin never quite leaves him. It is interesting, in *Joseph Andrews*,* to watch Fielding start out with the intention of writing a pure farce, and then, in spite of himself as it were, begin punishing vice and rewarding virtue in the way that was to be customary in English novels until almost yesterday. Tom Jones would fit into a novel by Meredith, or for that matter by Ian Hay,* whereas Peregrine Pickle seems to belong to a more European background. The writers nearest to Smollett are perhaps Surtees and Marryat, but when sexual frankness ceased to be possible, picaresque literature was robbed of perhaps half of its subject matter. The eighteenth-century inn where it was almost abnormal to go into the right bedroom was a lost dominion.

In our own day various English writers – Evelyn Waugh, for instance, and Aldous Huxley in his early novels – drawing on other sources, have tried to revive the picaresque tradition. One has only to watch their eager efforts to be shocking, and their readiness to be shocked themselves – whereas Smollett was merely trying to be funny in what seemed to him the natural way – to see what an accumulation of pity, decency and public spirit lies between that age and ours.

Funny, But Not Vulgar*

The great age of English humorous writing – not witty and not satirical, but simply humorous – was the first three quarters of the nineteenth century.

Within that period lie Dickens's enormous output of comic writings, Thackeray's brilliant burlesques and short stories, such as 'The Fatal Boots' and 'A Little Dinner at Timmins's', Surtees's *Handley Cross*, Lewis Carroll's *Alice in Wonderland*, Douglas Jerrold's *Mrs Caudle's Curtain Lectures*, and a considerable body of humorous verse by R.H. Barham, Thomas Hood, Edward Lear, Arthur Hugh Clough, Charles Stuart Calverley and others.* Two other comic masterpieces, F. Anstey's *Vice Versa* and the two Grossmiths' *Diary of a Nobody*,* lie only just outside the period I have named. And, at any rate until 1860 or thereabouts, there was still such a thing as comic draughtsmanship: witness Cruikshank's illustrations to Dickens,* Leech's illustrations to Surtees* and even Thackeray's illustrations of his own work.

I do not want to exaggerate by suggesting that, within our own century, England has produced no humorous writing of any value. There have been, for instance, Barry Pain, W.W. Jacobs, Stephen Leacock,* P.G. Wodehouse, H.G. Wells in his lighter moments, Evelyn Waugh, and – a satirist rather than a humorist – Hilaire Belloc. Still, we have not only produced no laugh-getter of anything like the stature of *Pickwick Papers* but, what is probably more significant, there is not and has not been for decades past, any such thing as a first-rate humorous periodical. The usual charge against *Punch*, that it "isn't what it was", is perhaps unjustified at this moment, since *Punch* is somewhat funnier than it was ten years ago – but it is also very much *less* funny than it was ninety years ago.

And comic verse has lost all its vitality – there has been no English light verse of any value within this century, except Mr Belloc's, and a poem or two by Chesterton – while a drawing that is funny in its own right, and not merely because of the joke it illustrates, is a great rarity.

All this is generally admitted. If you want a laugh you are likelier to go to a music hall or a Disney film, or switch on Tommy Handley, or buy a few of Donald McGill's postcards* than to resort to a book or a periodical. It is generally recognized, too, that American comic writers and illustrators are superior to our own. At present we have nobody to set against either James Thurber or Damon Runyon.*

We do not know with certainty how laughter originated or what biological purpose it serves, but we do know, in broad terms, what causes laughter.

A thing is funny when – in some way that is not actually offensive or frightening – it upsets the established order. Every joke is a tiny revolution. If you had to define humour in a single phrase, you might define it as dignity sitting on a tin tack. Whatever destroys dignity and brings down the mighty from their seats, preferably with a bump, is funny. And the bigger the fall, the bigger the joke. It would be better fun to throw a custard pie at a bishop than at a curate. With this general principle in mind, one can, I think, begin to see what has been wrong with English comic writing during the present century.

Nearly all English humorists today are too genteel, too kind-hearted and too consciously lowbrow. P.G. Wodehouse's novels, or A.P. Herbert's verses, seem always to be aimed at prosperous stockbrokers whiling away an odd half-hour in the lounge of some suburban golf course. They and all their kind are dominated by an anxiety not to stir up mud, either moral, religious, political or intellectual. It is no accident that most of the best comic writers of our time – Belloc, Chesterton, "Timothy Shy" and the recent "Beachcomber"* – have been Catholic apologists; that is, people with a serious purpose and a noticeable willingness to hit below the belt. The silly-ass tradition in modern English humour, the avoidance of brutality and horror of intelligence, is summed up in the phrase *funny without being vulgar*. "Vulgar" in this context usually means "obscene," and it can be admitted at once that the best jokes are not necessarily dirty ones. Edward Lear and Lewis Carroll, for instance, never made jokes of that description, and Dickens and Thackeray very rarely.

On the whole, the early Victorian writers avoided sex jokes, though a few, for instance Surtees, Marryat and Barham, retained traces of eighteenth-century coarseness. But the point is that the modern emphasis on what is called "clean fun" is really the symptom of a general unwillingness to touch upon any serious or controversial subject. Obscenity is, after all, a kind of subversiveness. Chaucer's 'Miller's Tale' is a rebellion in the moral sphere, as *Gulliver's Travels* is a rebellion in the political sphere. The truth is that you cannot be memorably funny without *at some point* raising topics which the rich, the powerful and the complacent would prefer to see left alone.

I named above some of the best comic writers of the nineteenth century, but the case becomes much stronger if one draws in the English humorists of earlier ages – for instance, Chaucer, Shakespeare, Swift and the picaresque novelists, Smollett, Fielding and Sterne.* It becomes stronger again if one considers foreign writers, both ancient and modern – for example, Aristophanes, Voltaire, Rabelais, Boccaccio and Cervantes. All of these writers are remarkable for their brutality and coarseness. People are tossed in blankets; they fall through cucumber frames; they are hidden in washing baskets; they rob, lie, swindle and are caught out in every conceivable humiliating situation. And all great humorous writers show a willingness to attack the beliefs and the virtues on which society necessarily rests. Boccaccio treats hell and purgatory as a ridiculous fable; Swift jeers at the very conception of human dignity; Shakespeare makes Falstaff deliver a speech in favour of cowardice in the middle of a battle. As for the sanctity of marriage, it was the principal subject of humour in Christian society for the better part of a thousand years.

All this is not to say that humour is, of its nature, immoral or antisocial. A joke is at most a temporary rebellion against virtue, and its aim is not to degrade the human being but to remind him that he is already degraded. A willingness to make extremely obscene jokes can coexist with very strict moral standards, as in Shakespeare. Some comic writers, like Dickens, have a direct political purpose; others, like Chaucer or Rabelais, accept the corruption of society as something inevitable – but no comic writer of any stature has ever suggested that society is *good*.

Humour is the debunking of humanity, and nothing is funny except in relation to human beings. Animals, for instance, are only funny because they are caricatures of ourselves. A lump of stone could not of itself be funny – but it can become funny if it hits a human being in the eye, or if it is carved into human likeness.

However, there are subtler methods of debunking than throwing custard pies. There is also the humour of pure fantasy, which assaults man's notion of himself as not only a dignified but a rational being. Lewis Carroll's humour consists essentially in making fun of logic, and Edward Lear's in a sort of poltergeist interference with common sense. When the Red Queen remarks, "*I've* seen hills compared with which you'd call that one a valley," she is in her way attacking the bases of society as violently as Swift or Voltaire. Comic verse, as in Lear's poem 'The Courtship of the Yonghy-Bonghy-Bò',* often depends on building up a fantastic universe which is just similar enough to the real universe to rob it of its dignity. But more often it depends on anticlimax – that is, on starting out with a high-flown language and then suddenly coming down with a bump. For instance, Calverley's lines:

> Once, a happy child, I carolled
> On green lawns the whole day through,
> Not unpleasingly apparelled
> In a tightish suit of blue,*

in which the first two lines would give the impression that this is going to be a sentimental poem about the beauties of childhood. Or Mr Belloc's various invocations to Africa in *The Modern Traveller*:

> O Africa, mysterious land,
> Surrounded by a lot of sand,
> And full of grass and trees [...]
> Far land of Ophir, mined for gold
> By lordly Solomon of old,
> Who, sailing northward to Perim,
> Took all the gold away with him
> And left a lot of holes,*
> Etc.

Bret Harte's sequel to 'Maud Muller', with such couplets as:

> But the very day that they were mated
> Maud's brother Bob was intoxicated*

plays essentially the same trick, and so in a different way do Voltaire's mock epic, *La Pucelle*,* and many passages in Byron.

English light verse in the present century – witness the work of Owen Seaman, Harry Graham, A.P. Herbert, A.A. Milne* and others – has mostly been poor stuff, lacking not only in fancifulness but in intellectuality. Its authors are too anxious not to be highbrows – even, though they are writing in verse, not to be poets. Early Victorian light verse is generally haunted by the ghost of poetry; it is often extremely skilful as verse, and it is sometimes allusive and "difficult". When Barham wrote:

> The Callipyge's injured behind,
> Bloudie Jack!
> The de Medici's injured before;
> And the Anadyomene's injured in so many
> Places, I think there's a score,
> If not more,
> Of her fingers and toes on the floor.*

he was performing a feat of sheer virtuosity which the most serious poet would respect. Or, to quote Calverley again, in his 'Ode to Tobacco':

> Thou, who when fears attack,
> Bidst them avaunt, and Black
> Care, at the horseman's back
> Perching, unseatest;
> Sweet when the morn is grey,
> Sweet when they've cleared away

> Lunch, and at close of day
> Possibly sweetest!*

Calverley is not afraid, it will be seen, to put a tax on his reader's attention and to drag in a recondite Latin allusion. He is not writing for lowbrows, and – particularly in his 'Ode to Beer' – he can achieve magnificent anticlimaxes because he is willing to sail close to true poetry and to assume considerable knowledge in his readers.

It would seem that you *cannot* be funny without being vulgar – that is, vulgar by the standards of the people at whom English humorous writing in our own day seems mostly to be aimed. For it is not only sex that is "vulgar". So are death, childbirth and poverty, the other three subjects upon which the best music-hall humour turns. And respect for the intellect and strong political feeling, if not actually vulgar, are looked upon as being in doubtful taste. You cannot be really funny if your main aim is to flatter the comfortable classes: it means leaving out too much. To be funny, indeed, you have got to be serious. *Punch*, for at least forty years past, has given the impression of trying not so much to amuse as to reassure. Its implied message is that all is for the best and nothing will ever really change.

It was by no means with that creed that it started out.

Oysters and Brown Stout*

G.K. Chesterton said once that every novelist writes one book whose title seems to be a summing up of his attitude to life. He instanced, for Dickens, *Great Expectations*, and for Scott, *Tales of a Grandfather*.*

What title would one choose as especially representative of Thackeray? The obvious one is *Vanity Fair*, but I believe that if one looked more closely one would choose either *Christmas Books*, *Burlesques* or *A Book of Snobs** – at any rate, one would choose the title of one of the collections of scraps which Thackeray had previously contributed to *Punch* and other magazines. Not only was he by nature a burlesque writer but he was primarily a journalist, a writer of fragments, and his most characteristic work is not fully separable from the illustrations. Some of the best of these are by Cruikshank, but Thackeray was also a brilliant comic draughtsman himself, and in some of his very short sketches the picture and the letterpress belong organically together. All that is best in his full-length novels seems to have grown out of his contributions to *Punch*, and even *Vanity Fair* has a fragmentary quality that makes it possible to begin reading in it at almost any place, without looking back to see what has happened earlier.

At this date some of his major works – for instance, *Esmond* or *The Virginians** – are barely readable, and only once, in a rather short book, *A Shabby Genteel Story*,* did he write what we should now regard as a serious novel. Thackeray's two main themes are snobbishness and extravagance, but he is at his best when he handles them in the comic vein, because – unlike Dickens, for instance – he has very little social insight and not even a very clear moral code. *Vanity Fair*, it is true, is a valuable social document as well as being an extremely readable and amusing book. It records, with remarkable fidelity so far as physical detail goes, the ghastly social competition of the early nineteenth century, when an aristocracy which could no longer pay its way was still the arbiter of fashion and of behaviour. In *Vanity Fair*, and indeed throughout Thackeray's writings, it is almost exceptional to find anyone living inside his income.

To live in a house which is too big for you, to engage servants whom you cannot pay, to ruin yourself by giving pretentious dinner parties with hired footmen, to bilk your tradesmen, to overdraw your banking account, to live permanently in the clutches of moneylenders – this is almost the norm of human behaviour. It is taken for granted that anyone who is not halfway to being a saint will ape the aristocracy if possible. The desire for expensive clothes, gilded carriages and hordes of liveried servants is assumed to be a natural instinct, like the desire for food and drink. And the people Thackeray is best able to describe are those who are living the fashionable life upon no income whatever – people like Becky Sharp and Rawdon Crawley in *Vanity Fair*, or the innumerable seedy adventurers, Major Loder, Captain Rook, Captain Costigan, Mr Deuceace, whose life is an endless to-and-fro between the card table and the sponging house.

So far as it goes, Thackeray's picture of society is probably true. The types he depicts, the mortgage-ridden aristocrats, the brandy-drinking army officers, the elderly bucks with their stays and their dyed whiskers, the matchmaking mothers, the vulgar City magnates, did exist. But he is observing chiefly externals. In spite of endless musings on the French Revolution, a subject that fascinated him, he does not see that the structure of society is altering: he sees the nationwide phenomenon of snobbery and extravagance without seeing its deeper causes. Moreover, unlike Dickens, he does not see that the social struggle is three-sided: his sympathies hardly extend to the working class, whom he is conscious of chiefly as servants. Nor is he ever certain where he himself stands. He cannot make up his mind whether the raffish upper class or the money-grubbing middle class is more objectionable. Not having any definite social, political or, probably, religious convictions, he can hardly imagine any virtues except simplicity, courage and, in the case of women, "purity". (Thackeray's "good" women, incidentally, are completely intolerable.) The implied moral of both *Vanity Fair* and *Pendennis* is the rather empty one: "Don't be selfish, don't be worldly, don't live outside your income." And *A Shabby Genteel Story* says the same thing in a more delicate way.

But Thackeray's narrow intellectual range is actually an advantage to him when he abandons the attempt to portray real human beings. A thing that is very striking is the vitality of his *minor* writings, even of things that he himself must have thought of as purely ephemeral. If you dip almost anywhere in his collected works – even in his book reviews, for instance – you come upon the characteristic flavour. Partly it is the atmosphere of surfeit which belongs to the early nineteenth century, an atmosphere compounded of oysters, brown stout, brandy and water, turtle soup, roast sirloin, haunch of venison, Madeira and cigar smoke, which Thackeray is well able to convey because he has a good grip on physical detail and is extremely interested in food.

He writes about food perhaps more often even than Dickens, and more accurately. His account of his dinners in Paris – not expensive dinners, either – in 'Memorials of Gormandizing'* is fascinating reading. 'The Ballad of the Bouillabaisse'* is one of the best poems of that kind in English. But the characteristic flavour of Thackeray is the flavour of burlesque, of a world where no one is good and nothing is serious. It pervades all the best passages in his novels, and it reaches its perfection in short sketches and stories like *Doctor*

Birch and His Young Friends, *The Rose and the Ring*, 'The Fatal Boots' and 'A Little Dinner at Timmins's'.*

The Rose and the Ring is a sort of charade, similar in spirit to *The Ingoldsby Legends*,* 'A Little Dinner at Timmins's' is a relatively naturalistic story, and 'The Fatal Boots' is about midway between the two. But in all these and similar pieces Thackeray has got away from the difficulty that besets most novelists and has never been solved by any characteristically English novelist – the difficulty of combining characters who are meant to be real and exist "in the round" with mere figures of fun.

English writers from Chaucer onwards have found it very difficult to resist burlesque, but as soon as burlesque enters the reality of the story suffers. Fielding, Dickens, Trollope, Wells, even Joyce, have all stumbled over this problem. Thackeray, in the best of his short pieces, solves it by making *all* his characters into caricatures. There is no question of the hero of 'The Fatal Boots' existing "in the round". He is as flat as an icon. In 'A Little Dinner at Timmins's' – one of the best comic short stories ever written, though it is seldom reprinted – Thackeray is really doing the same thing as he did in *Vanity Fair*, but without the complicating factor of having to simulate real life and introduce disinterested motives. It is a simple little story, exquisitely told and rising gradually to a sort of crescendo which stops at exactly the right moment. A lawyer who has received an unusually large fee decides to celebrate it by giving a dinner party. He is at once led into much greater expense than he can afford, and there follows a series of disasters which leave him heavily in debt, with his friends alienated and his mother-in-law permanently installed in his home. From start to finish no one has had anything from the dinner party except misery. And when, at the end, Thackeray remarks, "Why, in fact, did the Timminses give that party at all?" one feels the folly of social ambition has been more conclusively demonstrated than it is by *Vanity Fair*. This is the kind of thing that Thackeray could do perfectly, and it is the recurrence of farcical incidents like this, rather than their central story, that makes the longer novels worth reading.

A New Year Message*

For some months past we have intended to make some kind of explanatory statement about *Tribune*'s literary policy, present and future, and the first week of the new year seems a suitable time to do it.

Regular readers of *Tribune* will have noted that during recent months we have printed short stories only intermittently, we have printed less verse than we used to do, and we have altered our system of reviewing, giving a full-length review each week to only one book, and 200-word "shorts" to all the others. The new system of reviewing seems to be giving general satisfaction. By means of it we can cover – including the books in Daniel George's column* – anything up to fifteen books a week, and thus can keep more or less abreast of the current output, which was quite impossible before. We can also in this way make some mention of cheap reprints and even a certain number of pamphlets and periodicals. From time to time we are charged by our readers with concentrating on books which the average person cannot afford to buy, but anyone who chooses to look back through our columns will see that Penguins and other very cheap publications have had their fair share of notice.

The gradual dropping of short stories is deliberate. In future we shall probably abandon short stories almost completely, though we shall not refuse a *good* short story when we happen to get one. We shall also from time to time, as we have done once or twice already, print detachable excerpts from old books. This seems to us a useful thing to do at a time like the present, when so many standard books are unobtainable.

It was only unwillingly that we decided on the dropping of short stories, but the quality of the stories sent in to me makes them, in much more than nine cases out of ten, simply not worth ink and paper. For long past there had been a volume of justified complaints from readers that *Tribune*'s stories were "always so gloomy". The trouble, as anyone who had my job would quickly appreciate, is that one almost never nowadays sees a story with any serious literary pretensions that is *not* gloomy. The reasons for this are many and complex, but I think literary fashion is one of them. A "happy ending", or indeed any admission that anything is right with the world anywhere, seems to be as out of date as Dundreary whiskers, and it hardly seems worth diffusing gloom from the final pages of the paper unless exceptional literary distinction goes with it. Many readers have told me, in writing and by word of mouth, how tired they are of the kind of story that begins "Marjorie's husband was to be hanged on Tuesday, and the children were starving", or "For seven years no ray of sunlight had penetrated the dusty room where William Grocock, a retired insurance agent, lay dying of cancer" – but I don't fancy they are more tired of them than I am myself, who have to work my way through round about twenty such stories every week.

By printing less stories we shall have more room for essays and articles on literary or general (i.e. not directly political) subjects. But upon all those readers who complain that we do not have enough articles on music, or painting, or the drama, or radio, or modern educational methods, or psychoanalysis, or what not, I urge one important consideration: that we have very little space. In most weeks we have well under five pages at our disposal, and we have already been driven into smaller print for the short reviews. It is principally lack of space that has prevented us from undertaking any notes on radio, gramophone records and music generally. We could not do it regularly, and therefore should not be able to keep sufficiently up to date. Nor can we notice concerts, exhibitions, etc., because these occur only in one place, usually London, and *Tribune*'s readers are spread all over the country.

So far I have been dealing with details. But a more general defence, or at least explanation, of our literary policy is needed, because there are certain criticisms of an adverse kind that come up in varying forms over and over again. Our critics are divisible into two main schools. It would be manifestly impossible to satisfy both, and in practice, I should say, impossible to satisfy either.

The first school accuses us of being lowbrow, vulgar, ignorant, obsessed with politics, hostile to the arts, dominated by back-scratching cliques and anxious to prevent talented young writers from getting a hearing. The other school accuses us of being highbrow, arty, bourgeois, indifferent to politics and constantly wasting space on material that can be of no interest to a working man and of no direct use to the socialist movement. Both points need meeting, because between them they express a difficulty that is inherent in running any paper that is not a pure propaganda sheet.

Against the first school, we point out that *Tribune* reaches a large, heterogeneous left-wing audience and cannot be turned into a sort of trade paper for young poets, or a tilting ground on which rival gangs of Surrealists, apocalyptics and what not can fight out their battles. We can assume that our public is intelligent, but not that its primary interests are literary or artistic, and still less that all of our readers have been educated in the same way and will know the same jokes and recognize the same allusions. The smaller literary magazines tend to develop a sort of family atmosphere – almost, indeed, a private language unintelligible to outsiders – and, at the risk of offending a contributor now and then, we have made efforts to prevent that kind of thing from being imported into *Tribune*. We never, for instance, review books written in foreign languages, and we try to cut out avoidable foreign quotations and obscure literary allusions. Nor will we print anything that is verbally unintelligible. I have had several angry letters because of this, but I refuse to be responsible for printing anything that I do not understand. If I can't understand it, the chances are that many of our readers will not be able to either. As to the charge that we are dominated by cliques (contributions sometimes arrive with a sarcastic enquiry as to whether "someone outside the clique" may put a word in), a quick glance through our back numbers would easily disprove it. The number of our contributors is much larger than is usual in a paper of these dimensions, and many of them are people whose work has hardly appeared elsewhere.

The other school of critics presents a more serious difficulty. Any socialist paper which has a literary section is attacked from time to time by the person who says: "What is the use of all this literary stuff? Does it bring socialism any nearer? If not, drop it. Surely our task should be to work for socialism and not waste our time on bourgeois literature?" There are various quick answers to this person (he is easily quelled, for instance, by pointing out that Marx wrote some excellent criticism of Shakespeare), but nevertheless he has a case. Here it is, put in an extreme form by a correspondent in last week's issue:

> May I ask if the book reviews in your paper contribute largely (if at all) to its upkeep? If not, why is so much precious space taken up each week with descriptions of books which (I guess) few of your readers buy?
>
> As a socialist, my aim in life is to destroy Toryism.
>
> For this purpose I require all the ammunition I can get, and I look to *Tribune* as the main source of supply.
>
> You may reply that some of the books would be useful for that purpose, but I think it would be a very small percentage, and in any case I have neither the money to buy nor the time to read them.

This correspondent, by the way, like many others who write in the same vein, is under the misconception that in order to read books you have to buy them. Actually you could read most of the books mentioned in *Tribune* without ever buying a book from one year's end to the other. What else are libraries for – not merely Boots, Smith's, etc., but the public libraries at which anyone who numbers a householder among his acquaintances can get three tickets without any charge whatever? But our correspondent also assumes (a) that a socialist needs no recreations, and (b) that books are of no use to the socialist movement unless they consist of direct propaganda. It is this viewpoint that we tacitly challenge when, for instance, we use up a whole column on a poem, or print a popularization of some little-known dead writer, or give a good review to a book written by a Conservative.

Even the most unpolitical book, even an outright reactionary book, can be of use to the socialist movement if it provides reliable information or forces people to think. But we also assume that books are not to be regarded simply as propaganda, that literature exists in its own right – as a form of recreation, to put it no higher – and that a large number of our readers are interested in it. This involves, unavoidably, a slight divergence between the political and the literary sections of the paper. Obviously we cannot print contributions that grossly violate *Tribune*'s policy. Even in the name of free speech a socialist paper cannot, for instance, throw open its columns to anti-Semitic propaganda. But it is only in this negative sense that any pressure is put upon contributors to the literary end of the paper. Looking through the list of our contributors, I find among them Catholics, communists, Trotskyists, anarchists, pacifists, left-wing Conservatives and Labour Party supporters of all colours. All of them knew, of course, what kind of paper they were writing for and what topics were best left alone, but I think it is true to say that none of them has ever been asked to modify what he had written on the ground that it was "not policy".

This is particularly important in the case of book reviews, in which it is often difficult for the reviewer to avoid indicating his own opinions. To my knowledge, some periodicals coerce their reviewers into following the political line of the paper, even when they have to falsify their own opinions to do so. *Tribune* has never done this. We hold that the reviewer's job is to say what he thinks of the book he is dealing with, and not what we think our readers ought to think. And if, as a result, unorthodox opinions are expressed from time to time – even, on occasion, opinions that contradict some editorial statement at the other end of the paper – we believe that our readers are tough enough to stand a certain amount of diversity. We hold that the most perverse human being is more interesting than the most orthodox gramophone record. And though, in this section of the paper, our main aim is to talk about books as books, we believe that anyone who upholds the freedom of the intellect, in this age of lies and regimentation, is not serving the cause of socialism so badly either.

In Defence of P.G. Wodehouse*

When the Germans made their rapid advance through Belgium in the early summer of 1940, they captured, among other things, Mr P.G. Wodehouse, who had been living throughout the early part of the war in his villa at Le Touquet, and seems not to have realized until the last moment that he was in any danger. As he was led away into captivity, he is said to have remarked, "Perhaps after this I shall write a serious book." He was placed for the time being under house arrest, and from his subsequent statements it appears that he was treated in a fairly friendly way, German officers in the neighbourhood frequently "dropping in for a bath or a party".

Over a year later, on 25th June 1941, the news came that Wodehouse had been released from internment and was living at the Adlon Hotel in Berlin. On the following day the public was astonished to learn that he had agreed to do some broadcasts of a "non-political" nature over the German radio. The full texts of these broadcasts are not easy to obtain at this date, but Wodehouse seems to have done five of them between 26th June and 2nd July, when the Germans took him off the air again. The first broadcast, on 26th June, was not made on the Nazi radio but took the form of an interview with Harry Flannery,* the representative of the Columbia Broadcasting System, which still had its correspondents in Berlin. Wodehouse also published in the *Saturday Evening Post* an article which he had written while still in the internment camp.

The article and the broadcasts dealt mainly with Wodehouse's experiences in internment, but they did include a very few comments on the war. The following are fair samples:

> I never was interested in politics. I'm quite unable to work up any kind of belligerent feeling. Just as I'm about to feel belligerent about some country I meet a decent sort of chap. We go out together and lose any fighting thoughts or feelings.

> A short time ago they had a look at us on parade and got the right idea; at least they sent us to the local lunatic asylum. And I have been there forty-two weeks. There is a good deal to be said for internment. It keeps you out of the saloon and helps you to keep up with your reading. The chief trouble is that it means you are away from home for a long time. When I join my wife I had better take along a letter of introduction to be on the safe side.

* * *

In the days before the war I had always been modestly proud of being an Englishman, but now that I have been some months resident in this bin or repository of Englishmen I am not so sure. [...] The only concession I want from Germany is that she gives me a loaf of bread, tells the gentlemen with muskets at the main gate to look the other way, and leaves the rest to me. In return I am prepared to hand over India, an autographed set of my books, and to reveal the secret process of cooking sliced potatoes on a radiator. This offer holds good till Wednesday week.

The first extract quoted above caused great offence. Wodehouse was also censured for using (in the interview with Flannery) the phrase "whether Britain wins the war or not", and he did not make things better by describing in another broadcast the filthy habits of some Belgian prisoners among whom he was interned. The Germans recorded this broadcast and repeated it a number of times. They seem to have supervised his talks very lightly, and they allowed him not only to be funny about the discomforts of internment but to remark that "the internees at Trost camp all fervently believe that Britain will eventually win". The general upshot of the talks, however, was that he had not been ill-treated and bore no malice.

These broadcasts caused an immediate uproar in England. There were questions in Parliament, angry editorial comments in the press, and a stream of letters from fellow authors, nearly all of them disapproving, though one or two suggested that it would be better to suspend judgement, and several pleaded that Wodehouse probably did not realize what he was doing. On 15th July, the Home Service of the BBC carried an extremely violent postscript by "Cassandra" of the *Daily Mirror*,* accusing Wodehouse of "selling his country". This postscript made free use of such expressions as "quisling" and "worshipping the Führer". The main charge was that Wodehouse had agreed to do German propaganda as a way of buying himself out of the internment camp.

"Cassandra's" postscript caused a certain amount of protest, but on the whole it seems to have intensified popular feeling against Wodehouse. One result of it was that numerous lending libraries withdrew Wodehouse's books from circulation. Here is a typical news item:

Within twenty-four hours of listening to the broadcast of Cassandra, the *Daily Mirror* columnist, Portadown (North Ireland) Urban District Council banned P.G. Wodehouse's books from their public library. Mr Edward McCann said that Cassandra's broadcast had clinched the matter. Wodehouse was funny no longer. (*Daily Mirror*)

In addition the BBC banned Wodehouse's lyrics from the air and was still doing so a couple of years later. As late as December 1944 there were demands in Parliament that Wodehouse should be put on trial as a traitor.

There is an old saying that if you throw enough mud some of it will stick, and the mud has stuck to Wodehouse in a rather peculiar way. An impression has been left behind that Wodehouse's talks (not that anyone remembers what he said in them) showed him up not merely as a traitor but as an ideological sympathizer with fascism. Even at the time several letters to the press claimed that "fascist tendencies" could be detected in his books, and the charge has been repeated since. I shall try to analyse the mental atmosphere of those books in a moment, but it is important to realize that the events of 1941 do not convict Wodehouse of anything worse than stupidity. The really interesting question is how and why he could be so stupid. When Flannery met Wodehouse (released, but still under guard) at the Adlon Hotel in June 1941, he saw at once that he was dealing with a political innocent, and when preparing him for their broadcast interview he had to warn him against making some exceedingly unfortunate remarks, one of which was by implication slightly anti-Russian. As it was, the phrase "whether England wins or not" did get through. Soon after the interview Wodehouse told him that he was also going to broadcast on the Nazi radio, apparently not realizing that this action had any special significance. Flannery comments:

> By this time the Wodehouse plot was evident. It was one of the best Nazi publicity stunts of the war, the first with a human angle. [...] Plack (Goebbels's assistant) had gone to the camp near Gleiwitz to see Wodehouse, found that the author was completely without political sense, and had an idea. He suggested to Wodehouse that in return for being released from the prison camp he write a series of broadcasts about his experiences; there would be no censorship and he would put them on the air himself. In making that proposal Plack showed that he knew his man. He knew that Wodehouse made fun of the English in all his stories and that he seldom wrote in any other way, that he was still living in the period about which he wrote and had no conception of Nazism and all it meant. Wodehouse was his own Bertie Wooster.*

The striking of an actual bargain between Wodehouse and Plack seems to be merely Flannery's own interpretation. The arrangement may have been of a much less definite kind, and to judge from the broadcasts themselves, Wodehouse's main idea in making them was to keep in touch with his public and – the comedian's ruling passion – to get a laugh. Obviously they are not the utterances of a quisling of the type of Ezra Pound or John Amery,* nor, probably, of a person capable of understanding the nature of quislingism. Flannery seems to have warned Wodehouse that it would be unwise to broadcast, but not very forcibly. He adds that Wodehouse (though in one broadcast he refers to himself as an Englishman) seemed to regard himself as an American citizen. He had contemplated naturalization, but had never filled in the necessary papers. He even used, to Flannery, the phrase, "We're not at war with Germany."

I have before me a bibliography of P.G. Wodehouse's works. It names round about fifty books, but is certainly incomplete. It is as well to be honest, and I ought to start by admitting that there are many books by Wodehouse – perhaps a quarter or a third of the total – which I have not read. It is not, indeed, easy to read the whole output of a popular writer who is normally published in cheap editions. But I have followed his work fairly closely since 1911, when I was eight years old, and am well acquainted with its peculiar mental atmosphere – an atmosphere which has not, of course, remained completely unchanged, but shows little alteration since about 1925. In the passage from Flannery's book which I quoted above there are two remarks which would immediately strike any attentive reader of Wodehouse. One is to the effect that Wodehouse "was still living in the period about which he wrote", and the other that the Nazi Propaganda Ministry made use of him because he "made fun of the English". The second statement is based on a misconception to which I will return presently. But Flannery's other comment is quite true and contains in it part of the clue to Wodehouse's behaviour.

A thing that people often forget about P.G. Wodehouse's novels is how long ago the better known of them were written. We think of him as in some sense typifying the silliness of the 1920s and 1930s, but in fact the scenes and characters by which he is best remembered had all made their appearance before 1925. Psmith first appeared in 1909, having been foreshadowed by other characters in early school stories. Blandings Castle, with Baxter and the Earl of Emsworth both in residence, was introduced in 1915. The Jeeves–Wooster cycle began in 1919, both Jeeves and Wooster having made brief appearances earlier. Ukridge appeared in 1924.* When one looks through the list of Wodehouse's books from 1902 onwards, one can observe three fairly well-marked periods. The first is the school-story period. It includes such books as *The Gold Bat*, *The Pothunters*, etc., and has its high spot in *Mike* (1909).* *Psmith in the City*,* published in the following year, belongs in this category, though it is not directly concerned with school life. The next is the American period. Wodehouse seems to have lived in the United States from about 1913 to 1920, and for a while showed signs of becoming Americanized in idiom and outlook. Some of the stories in *The Man with Two Left Feet** (1917) appear to have been influenced by O. Henry, and other books written about this time contain Americanisms (e.g. "highball" for "whisky and soda") which an Englishman would not normally use *in propria persona.** Nevertheless, almost all the books of this period – *Psmith, Journalist*; *The Little Nugget*;

The Indiscretions of Archie; *Piccadilly Jim** and various others – depend for their effect on the *contrast* between English and American manners. English characters appear in an American setting, or vice versa: there is a certain number of purely English stories, but hardly any purely American ones. The third period might fitly be called the country-house period. By the early 1920s Wodehouse must have been making a very large income, and the social status of his characters moved upwards accordingly, though the Ukridge stories form a partial exception. The typical setting is now a country mansion, a luxurious bachelor flat or an expensive golf club. The schoolboy athleticism of the earlier books fades out, cricket and football giving way to golf, and the element of farce and burlesque becomes more marked. No doubt many of the later books, such as *Summer Lightning*,* are light comedy rather than pure farce, but the occasional attempts at moral earnestness which can be found in *Psmith, Journalist*; *The Little Nugget*; *The Coming of Bill*;* *The Man with Two Left Feet* and some of the school stories no longer appear. Mike Jackson has turned into Bertie Wooster. That, however, is not a very startling metamorphosis, and one of the most noticeable things about Wodehouse is his *lack* of development. Books like *The Gold Bat* and *Tales of St Austin's*,* written in the opening years of this century, already have the familiar atmosphere. How much of a formula the writing of his later books had become one can see from the fact that he continued to write stories of English life although throughout the sixteen years before his internment he was living at Hollywood and Le Touquet.

Mike, which is now a difficult book to obtain in an unabridged form, must be one of the best "light" school stories in English. But though its incidents are largely farcical, it is by no means a satire on the public-school system, and *The Gold Bat*, *The Pothunters*, etc. are even less so. Wodehouse was educated at Dulwich, and then worked in a bank and graduated into novel writing by way of very cheap journalism. It is clear that for many years he remained "fixated" on his old school and loathed the unromantic job and the lower-middle-class surroundings in which he found himself. In the early stories the "glamour" of public-school life (house matches, fagging, teas round the study fire, etc.) is laid on fairly thick, and the "play the game" code of morals is accepted with not many reservations. Wrykyn, Wodehouse's imaginary public school, is a school of a more fashionable type than Dulwich, and one gets the impression that between *The Gold Bat* (1904) and *Mike* (1908) Wrykyn itself has become more expensive and moved farther from London. Psychologically the most revealing book of Wodehouse's early period is *Psmith in the City*. Mike Jackson's father has suddenly lost his money, and Mike, like Wodehouse himself, is thrust at the age of about eighteen into an ill-paid subordinate job in a bank. Psmith is similarly employed, though not from financial necessity. Both this book and *Psmith, Journalist* (1915) are unusual in that they display a certain amount of political consciousness. Psmith at this stage chooses to call himself a socialist – in his mind, and no doubt in Wodehouse's, this means no more than ignoring class distinctions – and on one occasion the two boys attend an open-air meeting on Clapham Common and go home to tea with an elderly socialist orator, whose shabby-genteel home is described with some accuracy. But the most striking feature of the book is Mike's inability to wean himself from the atmosphere of school. He enters upon his job without any pretence of enthusiasm, and his main desire is not, as one might expect, to find a more interesting and useful job, but simply to be playing cricket. When he has to find himself lodgings he chooses to settle at Dulwich, because there he will be near a school and will be able to hear the agreeable sound of the ball striking against the bat. The climax of the book comes when Mike gets the chance to play in a county match and simply walks out of his job in order to do so. The point is that Wodehouse here sympathizes with Mike: indeed he identified himself with him, for it is clear enough that Mike bears the same relation to Wodehouse as Julien Sorel* to Stendhal. But he created many other heroes essentially similar. Through the books of this and the next period there passes a whole series of young men to whom playing games and "keeping fit" are a sufficient life-work. Wodehouse is almost incapable of imagining a desirable job. The great thing is to have money of your own, or, failing that, to find a sinecure. The hero of *Something Fresh** (1915) escapes from low-class journalism by becoming physical-training instructor to a dyspeptic millionaire: this is regarded as a step up, morally as well as financially.

In the books of the third period there is no narcissism and no serious interludes, but the implied moral and social background has changed much less than might appear at first sight. If one compares Bertie Wooster with Mike, or even with the rugger-playing prefects of the earliest school stories, one sees that the only real difference between them is that Bertie is richer and lazier. His ideals would be almost the same as theirs, but he fails to live up to them. Archie Moffam, in *The Indiscretions of Archie* (1921), is a type intermediate between Bertie and the earlier heroes: he is an ass, but he is also honest, kind-hearted, athletic and courageous. From first to last Wodehouse takes the public-school code of behaviour for granted, with the difference that in his later, more sophisticated period he prefers to show his characters violating it or living up to it against their will:

"Bertie! You wouldn't let down a pal?"
"Yes, I would."
"But we were at school together, Bertie."
"I don't care."
"The old school, Bertie, the old school!"
"Oh, well – dash it!"

Bertie, a sluggish Don Quixote, has no wish to tilt at windmills, but he would hardly think of refusing to do so when honour calls. Most of the people whom Wodehouse intends as sympathetic characters are parasites, and some of them are plain imbeciles, but very few of them could be described as immoral. Even Ukridge is a visionary rather than a plain crook. The most immoral, or rather unmoral, of Wodehouse's characters is Jeeves, who acts as a foil to Bertie Wooster's comparative high-mindedness and perhaps symbolizes the widespread English belief that intelligence and unscrupulousness are much the same thing. How closely Wodehouse sticks to conventional morality can be seen from the fact that nowhere in his books is there anything in the nature of a sex joke. This is an enormous sacrifice for a farcical writer to make. Not only are there no dirty jokes, but there are hardly any compromising situations: the horns-on-the-forehead motif is almost completely avoided. Most of the full-length books, of course, contain a "love interest", but it is always at the light-comedy level: the love affair, with its complications and its idyllic scenes, goes on and on, but, as the saying goes, "nothing happens". It is significant that Wodehouse, by nature a writer of farces, was able to collaborate more than once with Ian Hay, a serio-comic writer and an exponent (*vide Pip*,* etc.) of the "clean-living Englishman" tradition at its silliest.

In *Something Fresh* Wodehouse had discovered the comic possibilities of the English aristocracy, and a succession of ridiculous but, save in a very few instances, not actually contemptible barons, earls and what not followed accordingly. This had the rather curious effect of causing Wodehouse to be regarded, outside England, as a penetrating satirist of English society. Hence Flannery's statement that Wodehouse "made fun of the English", which is the impression he would probably make on a German or even an American reader. Sometime after the broadcasts from Berlin I was discussing them with a young Indian nationalist who defended Wodehouse warmly. He took it for granted that Wodehouse *had* gone over to the enemy, which from his own point of view was the right thing to do. But what interested me was to find that he regarded Wodehouse as an anti-British writer who had done useful work by showing up the British aristocracy in their true colours. This is a mistake that it would be very difficult for an English person to make, and is a good instance of the way in which books, especially humorous books, lose their finer nuances when they reach a foreign audience. For it is clear enough that Wodehouse is not anti-British, and not anti-upper-class either. On the contrary, a harmless old-fashioned snobbishness is perceptible all through his work. Just as an intelligent Catholic is able to see that the blasphemies of Baudelaire or James Joyce are not seriously damaging to the Catholic faith, so an English reader can see that in creating such characters as Hildebrand Spencer Poyns de Burgh John Hanneyside Coombe-Crombie, 12th Earl of Dreever,* Wodehouse is not really attacking the social hierarchy.

Indeed, no one who genuinely despised titles would write of them so much. Wodehouse's attitude towards the English social system is the same as his attitude towards the public-school moral code – a mild facetiousness covering an unthinking acceptance. The Earl of Emsworth* is funny because an earl ought to have more dignity, and Bertie Wooster's helpless dependence on Jeeves is funny partly because the servant ought not to be superior to the master. An American reader can mistake these two, and others like them, for hostile caricatures because he is inclined to be Anglophobe already and they correspond to his preconceived ideas about a decadent aristocracy. Bertie Wooster, with his spats and his cane, is the traditional stage Englishman. But, as any English reader would see, Wodehouse intends him as a sympathetic figure, and Wodehouse's real sin has been to present the English upper classes as much nicer people than they are. All through his books certain problems are consistently avoided. Almost without exception his moneyed young men are unassuming, good mixers, not avaricious: their tone is set for them by Psmith, who retains his own upper-class exterior but bridges the social gap by addressing everyone as "Comrade".

But there is another important point about Bertie Wooster: his out-of-dateness. Conceived in 1917 or thereabouts, Bertie really belongs to an epoch earlier than that. He is the "knut" of the pre-1914 period, celebrated in such songs as 'Gilbert the Filbert' or 'Reckless Reggie of the Regent's Palace'.* The kind of life that Wodehouse writes about by preference, the life of the "clubman" or "man about town", the elegant young man who lounges all the morning in Piccadilly with a cane under his arm and a carnation in his buttonhole, barely survived into the 1920s. It is significant that Wodehouse could publish in 1936 a book entitled *Young Men in Spats.** For who was wearing spats at that date? They had gone out of fashion quite ten years earlier. But the traditional "knut", the "Piccadilly Johnny", *ought* to wear spats, just as the pantomime Chinese ought to wear a pigtail. A humorous writer is not obliged to keep up to date, and having struck one or two good veins, Wodehouse continued to exploit them with a regularity that was no doubt all the easier because he did not set foot in England during the sixteen years that preceded his internment. His picture of English society had been formed before 1914, and it was a naive, traditional and, at bottom, admiring picture. Nor did he ever become genuinely Americanized. As I have pointed out, spontaneous Americanisms do occur in the books of the middle period, but Wodehouse remained English enough to find American slang an amusing and slightly shocking novelty. He loves to thrust a slang phrase or a crude fact in among Wardour Street English ("With a hollow groan Ukridge borrowed five shillings from me and went out into the night"), and expressions like "a piece of cheese" or "bust him on the noggin" lend themselves to this purpose. But the trick had been developed before he made any American contacts, and his use of garbled quotations is a common device of English writers running back to Fielding. As Mr John Hayward has pointed out, Wodehouse owes a good deal to his knowledge of English literature and especially of Shakespeare.* His books are aimed not, obviously, at a highbrow audience, but at an audience educated along traditional lines. When, for instance, he describes somebody as heaving "the kind of sigh that Prometheus might have heaved when the vulture dropped in for its lunch", he is assuming that his readers will know something of Greek mythology. In his early days the writers he admired were probably Barry Pain, Jerome K. Jerome, W.W. Jacobs, Kipling and F. Anstey, and he has remained closer to them than to the quick-moving American comic writers such as Ring Lardner or Damon Runyon.* In his radio interview with Flannery, Wodehouse wondered whether "the kind of people and the kind of England I write about will live after the war", not realizing that they were ghosts already. "He was still living in the period about which he wrote," says Flannery, meaning, probably, the 1920s. But the period was really the Edwardian age, and Bertie Wooster, if he ever existed, was killed round about 1915.

If my analysis of Wodehouse's mentality is accepted, the idea that in 1941 he consciously aided the Nazi propaganda machine becomes untenable and even ridiculous. He *may* have been induced to broadcast by the promise of an earlier release (he was due for release a few months later, on reaching his sixtieth birthday), but he cannot have realized that what he did would be damaging to British interests. As I have tried to show, his moral outlook has remained that of a public-school boy, and according to the public-school code, treachery in time of war is the most unforgivable of all the sins. But how could he fail to grasp that what he did would be a big propaganda score for the Germans and would bring down a torrent of disapproval on his own head? To answer this one must take two things into consideration. First, Wodehouse's complete lack – so far as one can judge from his printed works – of political awareness. It is nonsense to talk of "fascist tendencies" in his books. There are no post-1918 tendencies at all. Throughout his work there is a certain uneasy awareness of the problem of class distinctions, and scattered through it at various dates there are ignorant though not unfriendly references to socialism. In *The Heart of a Goof** (1926) there is a rather silly story about a Russian novelist, which seems to have been inspired by the factional struggle then raging in the USSR. But the references in it to the Soviet system are entirely frivolous and, considering the date, not markedly hostile. That is about the extent of Wodehouse's political consciousness, so far as it is discoverable from his writings. Nowhere, so far as I know, does he so much as use the word "fascism" or "Nazism". In left-wing circles, indeed in "enlightened" circles of any kind, to broadcast on the Nazi radio, to have any truck with Nazis whatever, would have seemed just as shocking an action before the war as during it. But that is a habit of mind that had been developed during nearly a decade of ideological struggle against fascism. The bulk of the British people, one ought to remember, remained anaesthetic to that struggle until late into 1940. Abyssinia, Spain, China, Austria, Czechoslovakia – the long series of crimes and aggressions had simply slid past their consciousness or were dimly noted as quarrels occurring among foreigners and "not our business". One can gauge the general ignorance from the fact that the ordinary Englishman thought of "fascism" as an exclusively Italian thing and was bewildered when the same word was applied to Germany. And there is nothing in Wodehouse's writings to suggest that he was better informed, or more interested in politics, than the general run of his readers.

The other thing one must remember is that Wodehouse happened to be taken prisoner at just the moment when the war reached its desperate phase. We forget these things now, but until that time feelings about the war had been noticeably tepid. There was hardly any fighting, the Chamberlain government was unpopular, eminent publicists were hinting that we should make a compromise peace as quickly as possible, trade-union and Labour Party branches all over the country were passing anti-war resolutions. Afterwards, of course, things changed. The army was with difficulty extricated from Dunkirk, France collapsed, Britain was alone, the bombs rained on London, Goebbels announced that Britain was to be "reduced to degradation and poverty". By the middle of 1941 the British people knew what they were up against and feelings against the enemy were far fiercer than before. But Wodehouse had spent the intervening year in internment, and his captors seem to have treated him reasonably well. He had missed the turning point of the war, and in 1941 he was still reacting in terms of 1939. He was not alone in this. On several occasions about this time the Germans brought captured British soldiers to the microphone, and some of them made remarks at least as tactless as Wodehouse's. They attracted no attention, however. And even an outright quisling like John Amery was afterwards to arouse much less indignation than Wodehouse had done.

But why? Why should a few rather silly but harmless remarks by an elderly novelist have provoked such an outcry? One has to look for the probable answer amid the dirty requirements of propaganda warfare.

There is one point about the Wodehouse broadcasts that is almost certainly significant – the date. Wodehouse was released two or three days before the invasion of the USSR, and at a time when the higher ranks of the Nazi Party must have known that the invasion was imminent. It was vitally necessary to keep America out of the war as long as possible, and in fact, about this time, the German attitude towards the USA did become more conciliatory than it had been before. The Germans could hardly hope to defeat Russia, Britain and the USA in combination, but if they could polish off Russia quickly – and presumably they expected to do so – the Americans might never intervene.

The release of Wodehouse was only a minor move, but it was not a bad sop to throw to the American isolationists. He was well known in the United States, and he was – or so the Germans calculated – popular with the Anglophobe public as a caricaturist who made fun of the silly-ass Englishman with his spats and his monocle. At the microphone he could be trusted to damage British prestige in one way or another, while his release would demonstrate that the Germans were good fellows and knew how to treat their enemies chivalrously. That presumably was the calculation, though the fact that Wodehouse was only broadcasting for about a week suggests that he did not come up to expectations.

But on the British side similar though opposite calculations were at work. For the two years following Dunkirk, British morale depended largely upon the feeling that this was not only a war for democracy but a war which the common people had to win by their own efforts. The upper classes were discredited by their appeasement policy and by the disasters of 1940, and a social-levelling process appeared to be taking place. Patriotism and left-wing sentiments were associated in the popular mind, and numerous able journalists were at work to tie the association tighter. Priestley's 1940 broadcasts and "Cassandra's" articles in the *Daily Mirror* were good examples of the demagogic propaganda flourishing at that time. In this atmosphere, Wodehouse made an ideal whipping boy. For it was generally felt that the rich were treacherous, and Wodehouse – as "Cassandra" vigorously pointed out in his broadcast – was a rich man. But he was the kind of rich man who could be attacked with impunity and without risking any damage to the structure of society. To denounce Wodehouse was not like denouncing, say, Beaverbrook.* A mere novelist, however large his earnings may happen to be, is not *of* the possessing class. Even if his income touches £50,000 a year he has only the outward semblance of a millionaire. He is a lucky outsider who has fluked into a fortune – usually a very temporary fortune – like the winner of the Calcutta Derby Sweep.* Consequently, Wodehouse's indiscretion gave a good propaganda opening. It was a chance to "expose" a wealthy parasite without drawing attention to any of the parasites who really mattered.

In the desperate circumstances of the time, it was excusable to be angry at what Wodehouse did, but to go on denouncing him three or four years later – and more, to let an impression remain that he acted with conscious treachery – is not excusable. Few things in this war have been more morally disgusting than the present hunt after traitors and quislings. At best it is largely the punishment of the guilty by the guilty. In France, all kinds of petty rats – police officials, penny-a-lining journalists, women who have slept with German soldiers – are hunted down while almost without exception the big rats escape. In England the fiercest tirades against quislings are uttered by Conservatives who were practising appeasement in 1938 and communists who were advocating it in 1940. I have striven to show how the wretched

Wodehouse – just because success and expatriation had allowed him to remain mentally in the Edwardian age – became the *corpus vile** in a propaganda experiment, and I suggest that it is now time to regard the incident as closed. If Ezra Pound is caught and shot by the American authorities, it will have the effect of establishing his reputation as a poet for hundreds of years – and even in the case of Wodehouse, if we drive him to retire to the United States and renounce his British citizenship, we shall end by being horribly ashamed of ourselves. Meanwhile, if we really want to punish the people who weakened national morale at critical moments, there are other culprits who are nearer home and better worth chasing.

Anti-Semitism in Britain*

There are about 400,000 known Jews in Britain, and in addition some thousands or, at most, scores of thousands of Jewish refugees who have entered the country from 1934 onwards. The Jewish population is almost entirely concentrated in half a dozen big towns and is mostly employed in the food, clothing and furniture trades. A few of the big monopolies, such as the ICI,* one or two leading newspapers and at least one big chain of department stores are Jewish-owned or partly Jewish-owned, but it would be very far from the truth to say that British business life is dominated by Jews. The Jews seem, on the contrary, to have failed to keep up with the modern tendency towards big amalgamations and to have remained fixed in those trades which are necessarily carried out on a small scale and by old-fashioned methods.

I start off with these background facts, which are already known to any well-informed person, in order to emphasize that there is no real Jewish "problem" in England. The Jews are not numerous or powerful enough, and it is only in what are loosely called "intellectual circles" that they have any noticeable influence. Yet it is generally admitted that anti-Semitism is on the increase, that it has been greatly exacerbated by the war, and that humane and enlightened people are not immune to it. It does not take violent forms (English people are almost invariably gentle and law-abiding), but it is ill-natured enough, and in favourable circumstances it could have political results. Here are some samples of anti-Semitic remarks that have been made to me during the past year or two:

> Middle-aged office employee: "I generally come to work by bus. It takes longer, but I don't care about using the Underground from Golders Green nowadays. There's too many of the Chosen Race travelling on that line."

> Tobacconist (woman): "No, I've got no matches for you. I should try the lady down the street. *She's* always got matches. One of the Chosen Race, you see."

> Young intellectual, communist or near-communist: "No, I do *not* like Jews. I've never made any secret of that. I can't stick them. Mind you, I'm not anti-Semitic, of course."

> Middle-class woman: "Well, no one could call me anti-Semitic, but I do think the way these Jews behave is too absolutely stinking. The way they push

their way to the head of queues, and so on. They're so abominably selfish. I think they're responsible for a lot of what happens to them."

Milk roundsman: "A Jew don't do no work, not the same as what an Englishman does. 'E's too clever. We work with this 'ere..." (flexes his biceps). "They work with that there..." (taps his forehead).

Chartered accountant, intelligent, left-wing in an undirected way: "These bloody Yids are all pro-German. They'd change sides tomorrow if the Nazis got here. I see a lot of them in my business. They admire Hitler at the bottom of their hearts. They'll always suck up to anyone who kicks them."

Intelligent woman, on being offered a book dealing with anti-Semitism and German atrocities: "Don't show it me, *please* don't show it to me. It'll only make me hate the Jews more than ever."

I could fill pages with similar remarks, but these will do to go on with. Two facts emerge from them. One – which is very important and which I must return to in a moment – is that above a certain intellectual level people are ashamed of being anti-Semitic and are careful to draw a distinction between "anti-Semitism" and "disliking Jews". The other is that anti-Semitism is an irrational thing. The Jews are accused of specific offences (for instance, bad behaviour in food queues) which the person speaking feels strongly about, but it is obvious that these accusations merely rationalize some deep-rooted prejudice. To attempt to counter them with facts and statistics is useless, and may sometimes be worse than useless. As the last of the above-quoted remarks shows, people can remain anti-Semitic, or at least anti-Jewish, while being fully aware that their outlook is indefensible. If you dislike somebody, you dislike him and there is an end of it: your feelings are not made any better by a recital of his virtues.

It so happens that the war has encouraged the growth of antisemitism and even, in the eyes of many ordinary people, given some justification for it. To begin with, the Jews are one people of whom it can be said with complete certainty that they will benefit by an Allied victory. Consequently the theory that "this is a Jewish war" has a certain plausibility, all the more so because the Jewish war effort seldom gets its fair share of recognition. The British Empire is a huge heterogeneous organization held together largely by mutual consent, and it is often necessary to flatter the less reliable elements at the expense of the more loyal ones. To publicize the exploits of Jewish soldiers, or even to admit the existence of a considerable Jewish army in the Middle East, rouses hostility in South Africa, the Arab countries and elsewhere: it is easier to ignore the whole subject and allow the man in the street to go on thinking that Jews are exceptionally clever at dodging military service. Then again, Jews are to be found in exactly those trades which are bound to incur unpopularity with the civilian public in wartime. Jews are mostly concerned with selling food, clothes, furniture and tobacco – exactly the commodities of which there is a chronic shortage, with consequent overcharging, black-marketing and favouritism. And again, the common charge that Jews behave in an exceptionally cowardly way during air raids was given a certain amount of colour by the big raids of 1940. As it happened, the Jewish quarter of Whitechapel was one of the first areas to be heavily blitzed, with the natural result that swarms of Jewish refugees distributed themselves all over London. If one judged merely from these wartime phenomena, it would be easy to imagine that anti-Semitism is a quasi-rational thing, founded on mistaken premises. And naturally the anti-Semite thinks of himself as a reasonable being. Whenever I have touched on this subject in a newspaper article, I have always had a considerable "comeback", and invariably some of the letters are from well-balanced, middling people – doctors, for example – with no apparent economic grievance. These people always say (as Hitler says in *Mein Kampf*) that they started out with no anti-Jewish prejudice but were driven into their present position by mere observation of the facts. Yet one of the marks of anti-Semitism is an ability to believe stories that could not possibly be true. One could see a good example of this in the strange accident that occurred in London in 1942, when a crowd, frightened by a bomb-burst nearby, fled into the mouth of an Underground station, with the result that something over a hundred people were crushed to death. The very same day it was repeated all over London that "the Jews were responsible". Clearly, if people will believe this kind of thing, one will not get much further by arguing with them. The only useful approach is to discover *why* they can swallow absurdities on one particular subject while remaining sane on others.

But now let me come back to that point I mentioned earlier – that there is widespread awareness of the prevalence of anti-Semitic feeling, and unwillingness to admit sharing it. Among educated people, anti-Semitism is held to be an unforgivable sin and in a quite different category from other kinds of racial prejudice. People will go to remarkable lengths to demonstrate that they are *not* anti-Semitic. Thus, in 1943 an intercession service on behalf of the Polish Jews was held in a synagogue in St John's Wood. The local authorities declared themselves anxious to participate in it, and the service was attended by the mayor of the borough in his robes and chain, by representatives of all the churches, and by detachments of RAF, Home Guards, nurses, Boy Scouts and what not. On the surface it was a touching demonstration of solidarity with the suffering Jews. But it was essentially a *conscious* effort to behave decently by people whose subjective feelings must in many cases have been very different. That quarter of London is partly Jewish; anti-Semitism is rife there and, as

I well knew, some of the men sitting round me in the synagogue were tinged by it. Indeed, the commander of my own platoon of Home Guards, who had been especially keen beforehand that we should "make a good show" at the intercession service, was an ex-member of Mosley's Blackshirts. While this division of feeling exists, tolerance of mass violence against Jews, or, what is more important, anti-Semitic legislation, are not possible in England. It is not at present possible, indeed, that anti-Semitism should *become respectable*. But this is less of an advantage than it might appear.

One effect of the persecutions in Germany has been to prevent anti-Semitism from being seriously studied. In England a brief inadequate survey was made by Mass Observation a year or two ago, but if there has been any other investigation of the subject, then its findings have been kept strictly secret. At the same time there has been conscious suppression, by all thoughtful people, of anything likely to wound Jewish susceptibilities. After 1934 the "Jew joke" disappeared as though by magic from postcards, periodicals and the music-hall stage, and to put an unsympathetic Jewish character into a novel or short story came to be regarded as anti-Semitism. On the Palestine issue, too, it was de rigueur among enlightened people to accept the Jewish case as proved and avoid examining the claims of the Arabs – a decision which might be correct on its own merits, but which was adopted primarily because the Jews were in trouble and it was felt that one must not criticize them. Thanks to Hitler, therefore, you had a situation in which the press was in effect censored in favour of the Jews while in private anti-Semitism was on the upgrade, even, to some extent, among sensitive and intelligent people. This was particularly noticeable in 1940 at the time of the internment of the refugees. Naturally, every thinking person felt that it was his duty to protest against the wholesale locking up of unfortunate foreigners who for the most part were only in England because they were opponents of Hitler. Privately, however, one heard very different sentiments expressed. A minority of the refugees behaved in an exceedingly tactless way, and the feeling against them necessarily had an anti-Semitic undercurrent, since they were largely Jews. A very eminent figure in the Labour Party – I won't name him, but he is one of the most respected people in England – said to me quite violently: "We never asked these people to come to this country. If they choose to come here, let them take the consequences." Yet this man would as a matter of course have associated himself with any kind of petition or manifesto against the internment of aliens. This feeling that anti-Semitism is something sinful and disgraceful, something that a civilized person does not suffer from, is unfavourable to a scientific approach, and indeed many people will admit that they are frightened of probing too deeply into the subject. They are frightened, that is to say, of discovering not only that anti-Semitism is spreading but that they themselves are infected by it.

To see this in perspective one must look back a few decades, to the days when Hitler was an out-of-work house painter whom nobody had heard of. One would then find that though anti-Semitism is sufficiently in evidence now, it is probably *less* prevalent in England than it was thirty years ago. It is true that anti-Semitism as a fully thought-out racial or religious doctrine has never flourished in England. There has never been much feeling against intermarriage, or against Jews taking a prominent part in public life. Nevertheless, thirty years ago it was accepted more or less as a law of nature that a Jew was a figure of fun and – though superior in intelligence – slightly deficient in "character". In theory a Jew suffered from no legal disabilities, but in effect he was debarred from certain professions. He would probably not have been accepted as an officer in the navy, for instance, nor in what is called a "smart" regiment in the army. A Jewish boy at a public school almost invariably had a bad time. He could, of course, live down his Jewishness if he was exceptionally charming or athletic, but it was an initial disability comparable to a stammer or a birthmark. Wealthy Jews tended to disguise themselves under aristocratic English or Scottish names, and to the average person it seemed quite natural that they should do this, just as it seems natural for a criminal to change his identity if possible. About twenty years ago, in Rangoon, I was getting into a taxi with a friend when a small ragged boy of fair complexion rushed up to us and began a complicated story about having arrived from Colombo on a ship and wanting money to get back. His manner and appearance were difficult to "place", and I said to him:

"You speak very good English. What nationality are you?"

He answered eagerly in his chi-chi accent: "I am a *Joo*, sir!"

And I remember turning to my companion and saying, only partly in joke, "He admits it openly." All the Jews I had known till then were people who were ashamed of being Jews, or at any rate preferred not to talk about their ancestry, and if forced to do so tended to use the word "Hebrew".

The working-class attitude was no better. The Jew who grew up in Whitechapel took it for granted that he would be assaulted, or at least hooted at, if he ventured into one of the Christian slums nearby, and the "Jew joke" of the music halls and the comic papers was almost consistently ill-natured.* There was also literary Jew-baiting, which in the hands of Belloc, Chesterton and their followers reached an almost Continental level of scurrility. Non-Catholic writers were sometimes guilty of the same thing in a milder form. There has been a perceptible anti-Semitic strain in English literature from Chaucer onwards, and without even getting up from this table to consult a book I can think of passages which *if written now* would be stigmatized as anti-Semitism, in the works of Shakespeare, Smollett, Thackeray, Bernard Shaw, H.G. Wells, T.S. Eliot, Aldous Huxley and various others. Offhand, the only English writers I can think of who, before the days of Hitler, made a definite effort to stick up for Jews are Dickens and Charles Reade. And however little the average intellectual may have agreed with the opinions of Belloc and Chesterton, he did not acutely disapprove of them. Chesterton's endless tirades against Jews, which he thrust into stories and essays upon the flimsiest pretexts, never got him into trouble – indeed Chesterton was one of the most generally respected figures in English literary life. Anyone who wrote in that strain *now* would bring down a storm of abuse upon himself, or more probably would find it impossible to get his writings published.

If, as I suggest, prejudice against Jews has always been pretty widespread in England, there is no reason to think that Hitler has genuinely diminished it. He has merely caused a sharp division between the politically conscious person who realizes that this is not a time to throw stones at the Jews and the unconscious person whose native anti-Semitism is increased by the nervous strain of the war. One can assume, therefore, that many people who would perish rather than admit to anti-Semitic feelings are secretly prone to them. I have already indicated that I believe anti-Semitism to be essentially a neurosis, but of course it has its rationalizations, which are sincerely believed in and are partly true. The rationalization put forward by the common man is that the Jew is an exploiter. The partial justification for this is that the Jew, in England, is generally a small businessman – that is to say a person whose depredations are more obvious and intelligible than those of, say, a bank or an insurance company. Higher up the intellectual scale, anti-Semitism is rationalized by saying that the Jew is a person who spreads disaffection and weakens national morale. Again there is some superficial justification for this. During the past twenty-five years the activities of what are called "intellectuals" have been largely mischievous. I do not think it an exaggeration to say that if the "intellectuals" had done their work a little more thoroughly, Britain would have surrendered in 1940. But the disaffected intelligentsia inevitably included a large number of Jews. With some plausibility it can be said that the Jews are the enemies of our native culture and our national morale. Carefully examined, the claim is seen to be nonsense, but there are always a few prominent individuals who can be cited in support of it. During the past few years there has been what amounts to a counter-attack against the rather shallow Leftism which was fashionable in the previous decade and which was exemplified by such organizations as the Left Book Club. This counter-attack (see for instance such books as Arnold Lunn's *The Good Gorilla* or Evelyn Waugh's *Put Out More Flags**) has an anti-Semitic strain, and it would probably be more marked if the subject were not so obviously dangerous. It so happens that for some decades past Britain has had no nationalist intelligentsia worth bothering about. But British nationalism, i.e. nationalism of an intellectual kind, may revive, and probably will revive if Britain comes out of the present war greatly weakened. The young intellectuals of 1950 may be as naively patriotic as those of 1914. In that case the kind of anti-Semitism which flourished among the anti-Dreyfusards* in France, and which Chesterton and Belloc tried to import into this country, might get a foothold.

I have no hard-and-fast theory about the origins of anti-Semitism. The two current explanations, that it is due to economic causes, or on the other hand, that it is a legacy from the Middle Ages, seem to me unsatisfactory, though I admit that if one combines them they can be made to cover the facts. All I would say with confidence is that anti-Semitism is part of the larger problem of nationalism, which has not yet been seriously examined, and that the Jew is evidently a scapegoat, though *for what* he is a scapegoat we do not yet know. In this essay I have relied almost entirely on my own limited experience, and perhaps every one of my conclusions would be negatived by other observers. The fact is that there are almost no data on this subject. But for what they are worth I will summarize my opinions. Boiled down, they amount to this:

There is more anti-Semitism in England than we care to admit, and the war has accentuated it, but it is not certain that it is on the increase if one thinks in terms of decades rather than years.

It does not at present lead to open persecution, but it has the effect of making people callous to the sufferings of Jews in other countries.

It is at bottom quite irrational and will not yield to argument.

The persecutions in Germany have caused much concealment of anti-Semitic feeling and thus obscured the whole picture.

The subject needs serious investigation.

Only the last point is worth expanding. To study any subject scientifically one needs a detached attitude, which is obviously harder when one's own interests or emotions are involved. Plenty of people who are quite capable of being objective about sea urchins, say, or the square root of 2, become schizophrenic if they have to think about the sources of their own income. What vitiates nearly all that is written about anti-Semitism is the assumption in the writer's mind that *he himself* is immune to it. "Since I know that anti-Semitism is irrational," he argues, "it follows that I do not share it." He thus fails to start his investigation in the one place where he could get hold of some reliable evidence – that is, in his own mind.

It seems to me a safe assumption that the disease loosely called nationalism is now almost universal. Anti-Semitism is only one manifestation of nationalism, and not everyone will have the disease in that particular form. A Jew, for example, would not be anti-Semitic – but then many Zionist Jews seem to me to be merely anti-Semites turned upside down, just as many Indians and Negroes display the normal colour prejudices in an inverted form. The point is that something, some psychological vitamin, is lacking in modern civilization, and as a result we are all more or less subject to this lunacy of believing that whole races or nations are mysteriously good or mysteriously evil. I defy any modern intellectual to look closely and honestly into his own mind without coming upon nationalistic loyalties and hatreds of one kind or another. It is the fact that he can feel the emotional tug of such things, and yet see them dispassionately for what they are, that gives him his status as an intellectual. It will be seen, therefore, that the starting point for any investigation of anti-Semitism should not be "Why does this obviously irrational belief appeal to other people?" but "Why does anti-Semitism appeal to *me*? What is there about it that I feel to be true?" If one asks this question one at least discovers one's own rationalizations, and it may be possible to find out what lies beneath them. Anti-Semitism should be investigated – and I will not say by anti-Semites, but at any rate by people who know that they are not immune to that kind of emotion. When Hitler has disappeared a real enquiry into this subject will be possible, and it would probably be best to start not by debunking anti-Semitism but by marshalling all the justifications for it that can be found, in one's own mind or anybody else's. In that way one might get some clues that would lead to its psychological roots. But that anti-Semitism will be definitively *cured*, without curing the larger disease of nationalism, I do not believe.

Notes on Nationalism*

Somewhere or other Byron makes use of the French word *longueur*, and remarks in passing that though in England we happen not to have the *word*, we have the *thing* in considerable profusion.* In the same way, there is a habit of mind which is now so widespread that it affects our thinking on nearly every subject, but which has not yet been given a name. As the nearest existing equivalent I have chosen the word "nationalism", but it will be seen in a moment that I am not using it in quite the ordinary sense, if only because the emotion I am speaking about does not always attach itself to what is called a nation – that is, a single race or a geographical area. It can attach itself to a church or a class, or it may work in a merely negative sense, *against* something or other and without the need for any positive object of loyalty.

By "nationalism" I mean first of all the habit of assuming that human beings can be classified like insects and that whole blocks of millions or tens of millions of people can be confidently labelled "good" or "bad".* But secondly – and this is much more important – I mean the habit of identifying oneself with a single nation or other unit, placing it beyond good and evil and recognizing no other duty than that of advancing its interests. Nationalism is not to be confused with patriotism. Both words are normally used in so vague a way that any definition is liable to be challenged, but one must draw a distinction between them, since two different and even opposing ideas are involved. By "patriotism" I mean devotion to a particular place and a particular way of life, which one believes to be the best in the world but has no wish to force upon other people. Patriotism is of its nature defensive, both militarily and culturally. Nationalism, on the other hand, is inseparable from the desire for power. The abiding purpose of every nationalist is to secure more power and more prestige, *not* for himself but for the nation or other unit in which he has chosen to sink his own individuality.

So long as it is applied merely to the more notorious and identifiable nationalist movements in Germany, Japan and other countries, all this is obvious enough. Confronted with a phenomenon like Nazism, which we can observe from the outside, nearly all of us would say much the same things about it. But here I must repeat what I said above, that I am only using the word "nationalism" for lack of a better. Nationalism, in the extended sense in which I am using the word, includes such movements and tendencies as communism, political Catholicism, Zionism, anti-Semitism, Trotskyism and pacifism. It does not necessarily mean loyalty to a government or a country, still less to *one's own* country, and it is not even strictly necessary that the units in which it deals should actually exist. To name a few obvious examples, Jewry, Islam, Christendom, the proletariat and the white race are all of them the objects of passionate nationalistic feeling – but their existence can be seriously questioned, and there is no definition of any one of them that would be universally accepted.

It is also worth emphasizing once again that nationalist feeling can be purely negative. There are, for example, Trotskyists who have become simply the enemies of the USSR without developing a corresponding loyalty to any other unit. When one grasps the implications of this, the nature of what I mean by nationalism becomes a good deal clearer. A nationalist is one who thinks solely, or mainly, in terms of competitive prestige. He may be a positive or a negative nationalist – that is, he may use his mental energy either in boosting or in denigrating – but at any rate his thoughts always turn on victories, defeats, triumphs and humiliations. He sees history, especially contemporary history, as the endless rise and decline of great power units, and every event that happens seems to him a demonstration that his own side is on the upgrade and some hated rival on the downgrade. But finally, it is important not to confuse nationalism with mere worship of success. The nationalist does not go on the principle of simply ganging up with the strongest side. On the contrary, having picked his side, he persuades himself that it *is* the strongest, and is able to stick to his belief even when the facts are overwhelmingly against him. Nationalism is power hunger tempered by self-deception. Every nationalist is capable of the most flagrant dishonesty, but he is also – since he is conscious of serving something bigger than himself – unshakeably certain of being in the right.

Now that I have given this lengthy definition, I think it will be admitted that the habit of mind I am talking about is widespread among the English intelligentsia, and more widespread there than among the mass of the people. For those who feel deeply about contemporary politics, certain topics have become so infected by considerations of prestige that a genuinely rational approach to them is almost impossible. Out of the hundreds of examples that one might choose, take this question: which of the three great allies, the USSR, Britain and the USA, has contributed most to the defeat of Germany? In theory it should be possible to give a reasoned and perhaps even a conclusive answer to this question. In practice, however, the necessary calculations cannot be made, because anyone likely to bother his head about such a question would inevitably see it in terms of competitive prestige. He would therefore *start* by deciding in favour of Russia, Britain or America as the case might be, and only *after* this would begin searching for arguments that seemed to support his case. And there are whole strings of kindred questions to which you can only get an honest answer from someone who is indifferent to the whole subject involved, and whose opinion on it is probably worthless in any case. Hence, partly, the remarkable failure in our time of political and military prediction. It is curious to reflect that out of all the "experts" of all the schools, there was not a single one who was able to foresee so likely an event as the Russo-German Pact of 1939.* And when the news of the Pact broke, the most wildly divergent explanations of it were given, and predictions were made which were falsified almost immediately, being based in nearly every case not on a study of probabilities but on a desire to make the USSR seem good or bad, strong or weak. Political or military commentators, like astrologers, can survive almost any mistake, because their more devoted followers do not look to them for an appraisal of the facts but for the stimulation of nationalistic loyalties.* And aesthetic judgements, especially literary judgements, are often corrupted in the same way as political ones. It would be difficult for an Indian nationalist to enjoy reading Kipling or for a conservative to see merit in Mayakovsky,* and there is always a temptation to claim that any book whose tendency one disagrees with must be a bad book from a *literary* point of view. People of strongly nationalistic outlook often perform this sleight of hand without being conscious of dishonesty.

In England, if one simply considers the number of people involved, it is probable that the dominant form of nationalism is old-fashioned British jingoism. It is certain that this is still widespread, and much more so than most observers would have believed a dozen years ago. However, in this essay I am concerned chiefly with the reactions of the intelligentsia, among whom jingoism and even patriotism of the old kind are almost dead, though they now seem to be reviving among a minority. Among the intelligentsia, it hardly needs saying that the dominant form of nationalism is communism – using this word in a very loose sense, to include not merely Communist Party members but "fellow travellers" and Russophiles generally. A communist, for my purpose here, is one who looks upon the USSR as his Fatherland and feels it his duty to justify Russian policy and advance Russian interests at all costs. Obviously such people abound in England today, and their direct and indirect influence is very great. But many other forms of nationalism also flourish, and it is by noticing the points of resemblance between different and even seemingly opposed currents of thought that one can best get the matter into perspective.

Ten or twenty years ago, the form of nationalism most closely corresponding to communism today was political Catholicism. Its most outstanding exponent – though he was perhaps an extreme case rather than a typical one – was G.K. Chesterton. Chesterton was a writer of considerable talent who chose to suppress both his sensibilities and his intellectual honesty in the cause of Roman Catholic propaganda. During the last twenty years or so of his life, his entire output was in reality an endless repetition of the same thing, under its laboured cleverness as simple and boring as "Great is Diana of the Ephesians".* Every book that he wrote, every paragraph, every sentence, every incident in every story, every scrap of dialogue, had to demonstrate beyond possibility of mistake the superiority of the Catholic over the Protestant or the pagan. But Chesterton was not content to think of this superiority as merely intellectual or spiritual: it had to be translated into terms of national prestige and military power, which entailed an ignorant idealization of the Latin countries, especially France. Chesterton had not lived long in France, and his picture of it – as a land of Catholic peasants incessantly singing the 'Marseillaise' over glasses of red wine – had about as much relation to reality as *Chu Chin Chow** has to everyday life in Baghdad. And with this went not only an enormous overestimation of French military power (both before and after 1914–18 he maintained that France, by itself, was stronger than Germany), but a silly and vulgar glorification of the actual process of war. Chesterton's battle poems, such as 'Lepanto' or 'The Ballad of St Barbara', make 'The Charge of the Light Brigade' read like a pacifist tract:* they are perhaps the most tawdry bits of bombast to be found in our language. The interesting thing is that had the romantic rubbish which he habitually wrote about France and the French army been written by somebody else about Britain and the British Army, he would have been the first to jeer. In home politics he was a Little Englander, a true hater of jingoism and imperialism, and according to his lights a true friend of democracy. Yet when he looked outwards into the international field, he could forsake his principles without even noticing that he was doing so. Thus, his almost mystical belief in the virtues of democracy did not prevent him from admiring Mussolini. Mussolini had destroyed the representative government and the freedom of the press for which Chesterton had struggled so hard at home, but Mussolini was an Italian and had made Italy strong, and that settled the matter. Nor did Chesterton ever find a word to say against imperialism and the conquest of coloured races when they were practised by Italians or Frenchmen. His hold on reality, his literary taste and even to some extent his moral sense were dislocated as soon as his nationalistic loyalties were involved.

Obviously there are considerable resemblances between political Catholicism, as exemplified by Chesterton, and communism. So there are between either of these and, for instance, Scottish nationalism, Zionism, anti-Semitism or Trotskyism. It would be an oversimplification to say that all forms of nationalism are the same, even in their mental atmosphere, but there are certain rules that hold good in all cases. The following are the principal characteristics of nationalist thought:

OBSESSION. As nearly as possible, no nationalist ever thinks, talks or writes about anything except the superiority of his own power unit. It is difficult, if not impossible, for any nationalist to conceal his allegiance. The smallest slur upon his own unit, or any implied praise of a rival organization, fills him with uneasiness which he can only relieve by making some sharp retort. If the chosen unit is an actual country, such as Ireland or India, he will generally claim superiority for it not only in military power and political virtue but in art, literature, sport, the structure of the language, the physical beauty of the inhabitants, and perhaps even in climate, scenery and cooking. He will show great sensitiveness about such things as the correct display of flags, relative size of headlines and the order in which different countries are named.* Nomenclature plays a very important part in nationalist thought. Countries which have won their independence or gone through a nationalist revolution usually change their names, and any country or other unit round which strong feelings revolve is likely to have several names, each of them carrying a different implication. The two sides in the Spanish Civil War had between them nine or ten names expressing different degrees of love and hatred. Some of these names (e.g. "Patriots" for Franco supporters or "Loyalists" for government supporters) were frankly question-begging, and there was no single one of them which the two rival factions could have agreed to use. All nationalists consider it a duty to spread their own language to the detriment of rival languages, and among English speakers this struggle reappears in subtler form as a struggle between dialects. Anglophobe Americans will refuse to use a slang phrase if they know it to be of British origin, and the conflict between Latinizers and Germanizers often has nationalist motives behind it. Scottish nationalists insist on the superiority of Lowland Scots, and socialists whose nationalism takes the form of class hatred tirade against the BBC accent and even the broad A. One could multiply instances. Nationalist thought often gives the impression of being tinged by belief in sympathetic magic – a belief which probably comes out in the widespread custom of burning political enemies in effigy, or using pictures of them as targets in shooting galleries.

INSTABILITY. The intensity with which they are held does not prevent nationalist loyalties from being transferable. To begin with, as I have pointed out already, they can be and often are fastened upon some foreign country. One quite commonly finds that great national leaders, or the founders of nationalist movements, do not even belong to the country they have glorified. Sometimes they are outright foreigners, or more often they come from peripheral areas where nationality is doubtful. Examples are Stalin, Hitler, Napoleon, de Valera, Disraeli, Poincaré, Beaverbrook.* The Pan-German movement was in part the creation of an Englishman, Houston Chamberlain.* For the past fifty or a hundred years, transferred nationalism has been a common phenomenon among literary intellectuals. With Lafcadio Hearn* the transference was to Japan, with Carlyle and many others of his time to Germany, and in our own age it is usually to Russia. But the peculiarly interesting fact is that retransference is also possible. A country or other unit which has been worshipped for years may suddenly become detestable, and some other object of affection may take its place with almost no interval. In the first version of H.G. Wells's *Outline of History*,* and others of his writings about that time, one finds the United States praised almost as extravagantly as Russia is praised by communists today: yet within a few years this uncritical admiration had turned into hostility. The bigoted communist who changes in a space of weeks, or even of days, into an equally bigoted Trotskyist is a common spectacle. In Continental Europe fascist movements were largely recruited from among communists, and the opposite process may well happen within the next few years. What remains constant in the nationalist is his own state of mind: the object of his feelings is changeable, and may be imaginary.

But for an intellectual, transference has an important function which I have already mentioned shortly in connection with Chesterton. It makes it possible for him to be much *more* nationalistic – more vulgar, more silly, more malignant, more dishonest – than he could ever be on behalf of his native country, or any unit of which he had real knowledge. When one sees the slavish or boastful rubbish that is written about Stalin, the Red Army, etc. by fairly intelligent and sensitive people, one realizes that this is only possible because some kind of dislocation has taken place. In societies such as ours, it is unusual for anyone describable as an intellectual to feel a very deep attachment to his own country. Public opinion – that is, the section of public opinion of which he as an intellectual is aware – will not allow him to do so. Most of the people surrounding him are sceptical and disaffected, and he may adopt the same attitude from imitativeness or sheer cowardice: in that case he will have abandoned the form of nationalism that lies nearest to hand without getting any closer to a genuinely internationalist outlook. He still feels the need for a Fatherland, and it is natural to look for one somewhere abroad. Having found it, he can wallow unrestrainedly in exactly those emotions from which he believes that he has emancipated himself. God, the King, the Empire, the Union Jack – all the overthrown idols can reappear under different names, and because they are not recognized for what they are they can be worshipped with a good conscience. Transferred nationalism, like the use of scapegoats, is a way of attaining salvation without altering one's conduct.

INDIFFERENCE TO REALITY. All nationalists have the power of not seeing resemblances between similar sets of facts. A British Tory will defend self-determination in Europe and oppose it in India with no feeling of inconsistency. Actions are held to be good or bad not on their own merits but according to who does them, and there is almost no kind of outrage – torture, the use of hostages, forced labour, mass deportations, imprisonment without trial, forgery, assassination, the bombing of civilians – which does not change its moral colour when it is committed by "our" side. The Liberal *News Chronicle* published, as an example of shocking barbarity, photographs of Russians hanged by the

Germans, and then a year or two later published with warm approval almost exactly similar photographs of Germans hanged by the Russians.* It is the same with historical events. History is thought of largely in nationalist terms, and such things as the Inquisition, the tortures of the Star Chamber,* the exploits of the English buccaneers (Sir Francis Drake,* for instance, who was given to sinking Spanish prisoners alive), the Reign of Terror, the heroes of the Mutiny blowing hundreds of Indians from the guns, or Cromwell's soldiers slashing Irishwomen's faces with razors, become morally neutral or even meritorious when it is felt that they were done in the "right" cause. If one looks back over the past quarter of a century, one finds that there was hardly a single year when atrocity stories were not being reported from some part of the world: and yet in not one single case were these atrocities – in Spain, Russia, China, Hungary, Mexico, Amritsar, Smyrna – believed in and disapproved of by the English intelligentsia as a whole. Whether such deeds were reprehensible, or even whether they happened, was always decided according to political predilection.

The nationalist not only does not disapprove of atrocities committed by his own side but he has a remarkable capacity for not even hearing about them. For quite six years the English admirers of Hitler contrived not to learn of the existence of Dachau and Buchenwald. And those who are loudest in denouncing the German concentration camps are often quite unaware, or only very dimly aware, that there are also concentration camps in Russia. Huge events like the Ukraine famine of 1933, involving the deaths of millions of people, have actually escaped the attention of the majority of English Russophiles. Many English people have heard almost nothing about the extermination of German and Polish Jews during the present war. Their own anti-Semitism has caused this vast crime to bounce off their consciousness. In nationalist thought there are facts which are both true and untrue, known and unknown. A known fact may be so unbearable that it is habitually pushed aside and not allowed to enter into logical processes, or on the other hand it may enter into every calculation and yet never be admitted as a fact, even in one's own mind.

Every nationalist is haunted by the belief that the past can be altered. He spends part of his time in a fantasy world in which things happen as they should – in which, for example, the Spanish Armada was a success or the Russian Revolution was crushed in 1918 – and he will transfer fragments of this world to the history books whenever possible. Much of the propagandist writing of our time amounts to plain forgery. Material facts are suppressed, dates altered, quotations removed from their context and doctored so as to change their meaning. Events which, it is felt, ought not to have happened are left unmentioned and ultimately denied.* In 1927 Chiang Kai-shek* boiled hundreds of communists alive, and yet within ten years he had become one of the heroes of the Left. The realignment of world politics had brought him into the anti-fascist camp, and so it was felt that the boiling of the communists "didn't count", or perhaps had not happened. The primary aim of propaganda is, of course, to influence contemporary opinion, but those who rewrite history do probably believe with part of their minds that they are actually thrusting facts into the past. When one considers the elaborate forgeries that have been committed in order to show that Trotsky did not play a valuable part in the Russian Civil War, it is difficult to feel that the people responsible are merely lying. More probably they feel that their own version *was* what happened in the sight of God, and that one is justified in rearranging the records accordingly.

Indifference to objective truth is encouraged by the sealing off of one part of the world from another, which makes it harder and harder to discover what is actually happening. There can often be a genuine doubt about the most enormous events. For example, it is impossible to calculate within millions, perhaps even tens of millions, the number of deaths caused by the present war. The calamities that are constantly being reported – battles, massacres, famines, revolutions – tend to inspire in the average person a feeling of unreality. One has no way of verifying the facts, one is not even fully certain that they have happened, and one is always presented with totally different interpretations from different sources. What were the rights and wrongs of the Warsaw rising of August 1944? Is it true about the German gas ovens in Poland? Who was really to blame for the Bengal famine? Probably the truth is discoverable, but the facts will be so dishonestly set forth in almost any newspaper that the ordinary reader can be forgiven either for swallowing lies or for failing to form an opinion. The general uncertainty as to what is really happening makes it easier to cling to lunatic beliefs. Since nothing is ever quite proved or disproved, the most unmistakable fact can be impudently denied. Moreover, although endlessly brooding on power, victory, defeat, revenge, the nationalist is often somewhat uninterested in what happens in the real world. What he wants is to *feel* that his own unit is getting the better of some other unit, and he can more easily do this by scoring off an adversary than by examining the facts to see whether they support him. All nationalist controversy is at the debating-society level. It is always entirely inconclusive, since each contestant invariably believes himself to have won the victory. Some nationalists are not far from schizophrenia, living quite happily amid dreams of power and conquest which have no connection with the physical world.

I have examined as best I can the mental habits which are common to all forms of nationalism. The next thing is to classify those forms, but obviously this cannot be done comprehensively. Nationalism is an enormous subject. The world is tormented by innumerable delusions and hatreds which cut across one another in an extremely complex way, and some of the most sinister of them have not yet even impinged on the European consciousness. In this essay I am concerned with nationalism as it occurs among the English intelligentsia. In them, much more often than in ordinary English people, it is unmixed with patriotism and can therefore be studied pure. Below are listed the varieties of nationalism now flourishing among English intellectuals, with such comments as seem to be needed. It is convenient to use three headings, Positive, Transferred and Negative, though some varieties will fit into more than one category:

POSITIVE NATIONALISM

1. NEO-TORYISM. Exemplified by such people as Lord Elton, A.P. Herbert, G.M. Young, Professor Pickthorn, by the literature of the Tory Reform Committee and by such magazines as the *New English Review* and the *Nineteenth Century and After*.* The real motive force of neo-Toryism, giving it its nationalistic character and differentiating it from ordinary conservatism, is the desire not to recognize that British power and influence have declined. Even those who are realistic enough to see that Britain's military position is not what it was tend to claim that "English ideas" (usually left undefined) must dominate the world. All neo-Tories are anti-Russian, but sometimes the main emphasis is anti-American. The significant thing is that this school of thought seems to be gaining ground among youngish intellectuals, sometimes ex-communists, who have passed through the usual process of disillusionment and become disillusioned with that. The Anglophobe who suddenly becomes violently pro-British is a fairly common figure. Writers who illustrate this tendency are F.A. Voigt, Malcolm Muggeridge, Evelyn Waugh, Hugh Kingsmill,* and a psychologically similar development can be observed in T.S. Eliot, Wyndham Lewis and various of their followers.

2. CELTIC NATIONALISM. Welsh, Irish and Scottish nationalism have points of difference but are alike in their anti-English orientation. Members of all three movements have opposed the war while continuing to describe themselves as pro-Russian, and the lunatic fringe has even contrived to be simultaneously pro-Russian and pro-Nazi. But Celtic nationalism is not the same thing as Anglophobia. Its motive force is a belief in the past and future greatness of the Celtic peoples, and it has a strong tinge of racialism. The Celt is supposed to be spiritually superior to the Saxon – simpler, more creative, less vulgar, less snobbish, etc. – but the usual power hunger is there under the surface. One symptom of it is the delusion that Eire, Scotland or even Wales could preserve its independence unaided and owes nothing to British protection. Among writers, good examples of this school of thought are Hugh MacDiarmid and Sean O'Casey.* No modern Irish writer, even of the stature of Yeats or Joyce, is completely free from traces of nationalism.

3. ZIONISM. This has the usual characteristics of a nationalist movement, but the American variant of it seems to be more violent and malignant than the British. I classify it under Direct and not Transferred nationalism because it flourishes almost exclusively among the Jews themselves. In England, for several rather incongruous reasons, the intelligentsia are mostly pro-Jew on the Palestine issue, but they do not feel strongly about it. All English people of goodwill are also pro-Jew in the sense of disapproving of Nazi persecution. But any actual nationalistic loyalty, or belief in the innate superiority of Jews, is hardly to be found among Gentiles.

TRANSFERRED NATIONALISM

1. COMMUNISM.

2. POLITICAL CATHOLICISM.

3. COLOUR FEELING. The old-style contemptuous attitude towards "natives" has been much weakened in England, and various pseudoscientific theories emphasizing the superiority of the white race have been abandoned.* Among the intelligentsia, colour feeling only occurs in the transposed form, that is, as a belief in the innate superiority of the coloured races. This is now increasingly common among English intellectuals, probably resulting more often from masochism and sexual frustration than from contact with the oriental and Negro nationalist movements. Even among those who do not feel strongly on the colour question, snobbery and imitation have a powerful influence. Almost any English intellectual would be scandalized by the claim that the white races are superior to the coloured, whereas the opposite claim would seem to him unexceptionable even if he disagreed with it. Nationalistic attachment to the coloured races is usually mixed up with the belief that their sex lives are superior, and there is a large underground mythology about the sexual prowess of Negroes.

4. CLASS FEELING. Among upper-class and middle-class intellectuals, only in the transposed form – i.e. as a belief in the superiority of the proletariat. Here again, inside the intelligentsia, the pressure of public opinion is overwhelming. Nationalistic loyalty towards the proletariat, and most vicious theoretical hatred of the bourgeoisie, can and often do coexist with ordinary snobbishness in everyday life.

5. PACIFISM. The majority of pacifists either belong to obscure religious sects or are simply humanitarians who object to taking life and prefer not to follow their thoughts beyond that point. But there is a minority of intellectual

pacifists whose real though unadmitted motive appears to be hatred of Western democracy and admiration or totalitarianism. Pacifist propaganda usually boils down to saying that one side is as bad as the other, but if one looks closely at the writings of the younger intellectual pacifists, one finds that they do not by any means express impartial disapproval but are directed almost entirely against Britain and the United States. Moreover they do not as a rule condemn violence as such, but only violence used in defence of the Western countries. The Russians, unlike the British, are not blamed for defending themselves by warlike means, and indeed all pacifist propaganda of this type avoids mention of Russia or China. It is not claimed, again, that the Indians should abjure violence in their struggle against the British. Pacifist literature abounds with equivocal remarks which, if they mean anything, appear to mean that statesmen of the type of Hitler are preferable to those of the type of Churchill, and that violence is perhaps excusable if it is violent enough. After the fall of France, the French pacifists, faced by a real choice which their English colleagues have not had to make, mostly went over to the Nazis, and in England there appears to have been some small overlap of membership between the Peace Pledge Union and the Blackshirts. Pacifist writers have written in praise of Carlyle, one of the intellectual fathers of fascism. All in all it is difficult not to feel that pacifism, as it appears among a section of the intelligentsia, is secretly inspired by an admiration for power and successful cruelty. The mistake was made of pinning this emotion to Hitler, but it could easily be retransferred.

NEGATIVE NATIONALISM

1. ANGLOPHOBIA. Within the intelligentsia, a derisive and mildly hostile attitude towards Britain is more or less compulsory, but it is an unfaked emotion in many cases. During the war it was manifested in the defeatism of the intelligentsia, which persisted long after it had become clear that the Axis powers could not win. Many people were undisguisedly pleased when Singapore fell or when the British were driven out of Greece, and there was a remarkable unwillingness to believe in good news, e.g. El Alamein,* or the number of German planes shot down in the Battle of Britain. English left-wing intellectuals did not, of course, actually want the Germans or Japanese to win the war, but many of them could not help getting a certain kick out of seeing their own country humiliated, and wanted to feel that the final victory would be due to Russia, or perhaps America, and not to Britain. In foreign politics many intellectuals follow the principle that any faction backed by Britain must be in the wrong. As a result, "enlightened" opinion is quite largely a mirror image of Conservative policy. Anglophobia is always liable to reversal, hence that fairly common spectacle, the pacifist of one war who is a bellicist in the next.

2. ANTI-SEMITISM. There is little evidence about this at present, because the Nazi persecutions have made it necessary for any thinking person to side with the Jews against their oppressors. Anyone educated enough to have heard the word "anti-Semitism" claims as a matter of course to be free of it, and anti-Jewish remarks are carefully eliminated from all classes of literature. Actually antisemitism appears to be widespread, even among intellectuals, and the general conspiracy of silence probably helps to exacerbate it. People of Left opinions are not immune to it, and their attitude is sometimes affected by the fact that Trotskyists and anarchists tend to be Jews. But anti-Semitism comes more naturally to people of Conservative tendency, who suspect the Jews of weakening national morale and diluting the national culture. Neo-Tories and political Catholics are always liable to succumb to anti-Semitism, at least intermittently.

3. TROTSKYISM. This word is used so loosely as to include anarchists, democratic socialists and even liberals. I use it here to mean a doctrinaire Marxist whose main motive is hostility to the Stalin regime. Trotskyism can be better studied in obscure pamphlets or in papers like the *Socialist Appeal** than in the works of Trotsky himself, who was by no means a man of one idea. Although in some places, for instance in the United States, Trotskyism is able to attract a fairly large number of adherents and develop into an organized movement with a petty führer of its own, its inspiration is essentially negative. The Trotskyist is *against* Stalin just as the communist is *for* him, and, like the majority of communists, he wants not so much to alter the external world as to feel that the battle for prestige is going in his own favour. In each case there is the same obsessive fixation on a single subject, the same inability to form a genuinely rational opinion based on probabilities. The fact that Trotskyists are everywhere a persecuted minority, and that the accusation usually made against them, i.e. of collaborating with the fascists, is obviously false, creates an impression that Trotskyism is intellectually and morally superior to communism – but it is doubtful whether there is much difference. The most typical Trotskyists, in any case, are ex-communists, and no one arrives at Trotskyism except via one of the left-wing movements. No communist, unless tethered to his party by years of habit, is secure against a sudden lapse into Trotskyism. The opposite process does not seem to happen equally often, though there is no clear reason why it should not.

In the classification I have attempted above, it will seem that I have often exaggerated, oversimplified, made unwarranted assumptions and have left out of account the existence of ordinarily decent motives. This was inevitable, because in this essay I am trying to isolate and identify tendencies which exist in all our minds and pervert our thinking, without necessarily occurring in a pure state or operating continuously. It is important at this point to correct the oversimplified picture which I have been obliged to make. To begin with, one has no right to assume that *everyone*, or even every intellectual, is infected by nationalism. Secondly, nationalism can be intermittent and limited. An intelligent man may half succumb to a belief which attracts him but which he knows to be absurd, and he may keep it out of his mind for long periods, only reverting to it in moments of anger or sentimentality, or when he is certain that no important issue is involved. Thirdly, a nationalistic creed may be adopted in good faith from non-nationalist motives. Fourthly, several kinds of nationalism, even kinds that cancel out, can coexist in the same person.

All the way through I have said "the nationalist does this" or "the nationalist does that", using for purposes of illustration the extreme, barely sane type of nationalist who has no neutral areas in his mind and no interest in anything except the struggle for power. Actually such people are fairly common, but they are not worth powder and shot. In real life Lord Elton, D.N. Pritt, Lady Houston, Ezra Pound, Lord Vansittart, Father Coughlin* and all the rest of their dreary tribe have to be fought against, but their intellectual deficiencies hardly need pointing out. Monomania is not interesting, and the fact that no nationalist of the more bigoted kind can write a book which still seems worth reading after a lapse of years has a certain deodorizing effect. But when one has admitted that nationalism has not triumphed everywhere, that there are still people whose judgements are not at the mercy of their desires, the fact does remain that the pressing problems – India, Poland, Palestine, the Spanish Civil War, the Moscow trials, the American Negroes, the Russo-German Pact or what have you – cannot be, or at least never are, discussed upon a reasonable level. The Eltons and Pritts and Coughlins, each of them simply an enormous mouth bellowing the same lie over and over again, are obviously extreme cases, but we deceive ourselves if we do not realize that we can all resemble them in unguarded moments. Let a certain note be struck, let this or that corn be trodden on – and it may be a corn whose very existence has been unsuspected hitherto – and the most fair-minded and sweet-tempered person may suddenly be transformed into a vicious partisan, anxious only to "score" over his adversary and indifferent as to how many lies he tells or how many logical errors he commits in doing so. When Lloyd George, who was an opponent of the Boer War, announced in the House of Commons that the British communiqués, if one added them together, claimed the killing of more Boers than the whole Boer nation contained, it is recorded that Arthur Balfour rose to his feet and shouted "Cad!"* Very few people are proof against lapses of this type. The Negro snubbed by a white woman, the Englishman who hears England ignorantly criticized by an American, the Catholic apologist reminded of the Spanish Armada will all react in much the same way. One prod to the nerve of nationalism, and the intellectual decencies can vanish, the past can be altered, and the plainest facts can be denied.

NOTES ON NATIONALISM

If one harbours anywhere in one's mind a nationalistic loyalty or hatred, certain facts, although in a sense known to be true, are inadmissible. Here are just a few examples. I list below five types of nationalist, and against each I append a fact which it is impossible for that type of nationalist to accept, even in his secret thoughts:

BRITISH TORY: Britain will come out of this war with reduced power and prestige.
COMMUNIST: If she had not been aided by Britain and America, Russia would have been defeated by Germany.
IRISH NATIONALIST: Eire can only remain independent because of British protection.
TROTSKYIST: The Stalin regime is accepted by the Russian masses.
PACIFIST: Those who "abjure" violence can only do so because others are committing violence on their behalf.

All of these facts are grossly obvious if one's emotions do not happen to be involved – but to the kind of person named in each case they are also *intolerable*, and so they have to be denied, and false theories constructed upon their denial. I come back to the astonishing failure of military prediction in the present war. It is, I think, true to say that the intelligentsia have been more wrong about the progress of the war than the common people, and that they were more swayed by partisan feelings. The average intellectual of the Left believed, for instance, that the war was lost in 1940, that the Germans were bound to overrun Egypt in 1942, that the Japanese would never be driven out of the lands they had conquered and that the Anglo-American bombing offensive was making no impression on Germany. He could believe these things because his hatred of the British ruling class forbade him to admit that British plans could succeed. There is no limit to the follies that can be swallowed if one is under the influence of feelings of this kind. I have heard it confidently stated, for instance, that the American troops had been brought to Europe not to fight the Germans but to crush an English revolution. One has to belong to the intelligentsia to believe things like that: no ordinary man could be such a fool. When Hitler invaded Russia, the officials of the MOI* issued "as background" a warning that Russia might be expected to collapse in six weeks. On the other hand the communists regarded every phase of the war as a Russian victory, even when the Russians were driven back almost to the Caspian Sea and had lost several million prisoners. There is no need to multiply instances. The point is that as soon as fear, hatred, jealousy and power worship are involved, the sense of reality becomes unhinged. And, as I have pointed out already, the sense of right and wrong becomes unhinged also. There is no crime, absolutely none, that cannot be condoned when "our" side commits it. Even if one does not deny that the crime has happened, even if one knows that it is exactly the same crime as one has condemned in some other case, even if one admits in an intellectual sense that it is unjustified – still one cannot *feel* that it is wrong. Loyalty is involved, and so pity ceases to function.

The reason for the rise and spread of nationalism is far too big a question to be raised here. It is enough to say that, in the forms in which it appears among English intellectuals, it is a distorted reflection of the frightful battles actually happening in the external world, and that its worst follies have been made possible by the breakdown of patriotism and religious belief. If one follows up this train of thought, one is in danger of being led into a species of conservatism, or into political quietism. It can be plausibly argued, for instance – it is even probably true – that patriotism is an inoculation against nationalism, that monarchy is a guard against dictatorship and that organized religion is a guard against superstition. Or again it can be argued that *no* unbiased outlook is possible, that *all* creeds and causes involve the same lies, follies and barbarities – and this is often advanced as a reason for keeping out of politics altogether. I do not accept this argument, if only because in the modern world no one describable as an intellectual *can* keep out of politics in the sense of not caring about them. I think one must engage in politics – using the word in a wide sense – and that one must have preferences: that is, one must recognize that some causes are objectively better than others, even if they are advanced by equally bad means. As for the nationalistic loves and hatreds that I have spoken of, they are part of the make-up of most of us, whether we like it or not. Whether it is possible to get rid of them I do not know, but I do believe that it is possible to struggle against them, and that this is essentially a *moral* effort. It is a question first of all of discovering what one really is, what one's own feelings really are, and then of making allowance for the inevitable bias. If you hate and fear Russia, if you are jealous of the wealth and power of America, if you despise Jews, if you have a sentiment of inferiority towards the British ruling class, you cannot get rid of those feelings simply by taking thought. But you can at least recognize that you have them, and prevent them from contaminating your mental processes. The emotional urges which are inescapable, and are perhaps even necessary to political action, should be able to exist side by side with an acceptance of reality. But this, I repeat, needs a *moral* effort, and contemporary English literature, so far as it is alive at all to the major issues of our time, shows how few of us are prepared to make it.

You and the Atom Bomb*

Considering how likely we all are to be blown to pieces by it within the next five years, the atomic bomb has not roused so much discussion as might have been expected. The newspapers have published numerous diagrams, not very helpful to the average man, of protons and neutrons doing their stuff, and there has been much reiteration of the useless statement that the bomb "ought to be put under international control". But curiously little has been said, at any rate in print, about the question that is of most urgent interest to all of us, namely: "How difficult are these things to manufacture?"

Such information as we – that is, the big public – possess on this subject has come to us in a rather indirect way, apropos of President Truman's decision not to hand over certain secrets to the USSR. Some months ago, when the bomb was still only a rumour, there was a widespread belief that splitting the atom was merely a problem for the physicists, and that when they had solved it a new and devastating weapon would be within reach of almost everybody. (At any moment, so the rumour went, some lonely lunatic in a laboratory might blow civilization to smithereens, as easily as touching off a firework.)

Had that been true, the whole trend of history would have been abruptly altered. The distinction between great states and small states would have been wiped out, and the power of the state over the individual would have been greatly weakened. However, it appears from President Truman's remarks, and various comments that have been made on them, that the bomb is fantastically expensive and that its manufacture demands an enormous industrial effort, such as only three or four countries in the world are capable of making. This point is of cardinal importance, because it may mean that the discovery of the atomic bomb, so far from reversing history, will simply intensify the trends which have been apparent for a dozen years past.

It is a commonplace that the history of civilization is largely the history of weapons. In particular, the connection between the discovery of gunpowder and the overthrow of feudalism by the bourgeoisie has been pointed out over and over again. And though I have no doubt exceptions can be brought forward, I think the following rule would be found generally true: that ages in which the dominant weapon is expensive or difficult to make will tend to be ages of despotism, whereas when the dominant weapon is cheap and simple, the common people have a chance. Thus, for example, tanks, battleships and bombing planes are inherently tyrannical weapons, while rifles, muskets, longbows and hand grenades are inherently democratic weapons. A complex weapon makes the strong stronger, while a simple weapon – so long as there is no answer to it – gives claws to the weak.

The great age of democracy and of national self-determination was the age of the musket and the rifle. After the invention of the flintlock, and before the invention of the percussion cap, the musket was a fairly efficient weapon, and at the same time so simple that it could be produced almost anywhere. Its combination of qualities made possible the success of the American and French revolutions, and made a popular insurrection a more serious business than it could be in our own day. After the musket came the breech-loading rifle. This was a comparatively complex thing, but it could still be produced in scores of countries, and it was cheap, easily smuggled and economical of ammunition. Even the most backward nation could always get hold of rifles from one source or another, so that Boers, Bulgars, Abyssinians, Moroccans – even Tibetans – could put up a fight for their independence, sometimes with success. But thereafter every development in military technique has favoured the state as against the individual, and the industrialized country as against the backward one. There are fewer and fewer focuses of power. Already, in 1939, there were only five states capable of waging war on the grand scale, and now there are only three – ultimately, perhaps, only two. This trend has been obvious for years, and was pointed out by a few observers even before 1914. The one thing that might reverse it is the discovery of a weapon – or, to put it more broadly, of a method of fighting – not dependent on huge concentrations of industrial plant.

From various symptoms one can infer that the Russians do not yet possess the secret of making the atomic bomb; on the other hand, the consensus of opinion seems to be that they will possess it within a few years. So we have before us the prospect of two or three monstrous superstates, each possessed of a weapon by which millions of people can be wiped out in a few seconds, dividing the world between them. It has been rather hastily assumed that this means bigger and bloodier wars, and perhaps an actual end to the machine civilization. But suppose – and really this is the likeliest development – that the surviving great nations make a tacit agreement never to use the atomic bomb against one another? Suppose they only use it, or the threat of it, against people who are unable to retaliate? In that case we are back where we were before, the only difference being that power is concentrated in still fewer hands and that the outlook for subject peoples and oppressed classes is still more hopeless.

When James Burnham wrote *The Managerial Revolution** it seemed probable to many Americans that the Germans would win the European end of the war, and it was therefore natural to assume that Germany and not Russia would dominate the Eurasian land mass, while Japan would remain master of East Asia. This was a miscalculation, but it does not affect the main argument. For Burnham's geographical picture of the new world has turned out to be correct. More and more obviously the surface of the earth is being parcelled off into three great empires, each self-contained and cut off from contact with the outer world, and each ruled, under one disguise or another, by a self-elected oligarchy. The haggling as to where the frontiers are to be drawn is still going on, and will continue for some years, and the third of the three superstates – East Asia, dominated by China – is still potential rather than actual. But the general drift is unmistakable, and every scientific discovery of recent years has accelerated it.

We were once told that the aeroplane had "abolished frontiers"; actually it is only since the aeroplane became a serious weapon that frontiers have become definitely impassable. The radio was once expected to promote international understanding and cooperation; it has turned out to be a means of insulating one nation from another. The atomic bomb may complete the process by robbing the exploited classes and peoples of all power to revolt, and at the same time putting the possessors of the bomb on a basis of military equality. Unable to conquer one another, they are likely to continue ruling the world between them, and it is difficult to see how the balance can be upset except by slow and unpredictable demographic changes.

For forty or fifty years past, Mr H.G. Wells and others have been warning us that man is in danger of destroying himself with his own weapons, leaving the ants or some other gregarious species to take over. Anyone who has seen the ruined cities of Germany will find this notion at least thinkable. Nevertheless, looking at the world as a whole, the drift for many decades has been not towards anarchy but towards the reimposition of slavery. We may be heading not for general breakdown but for an epoch as horribly stable as the slave empires of antiquity. James Burnham's theory has been much discussed, but few people have yet considered its ideological implications – that is, the kind of world view, the kind of beliefs and the social structure that would probably prevail in a state which was at once *unconquerable* and in a permanent state of "cold war" with its neighbours.

Had the atomic bomb turned out to be something as cheap and easily manufactured as a bicycle or an alarm clock, it might well have plunged us back into barbarism, but it might, on the other hand, have meant the end of national sovereignty and of the highly centralized police state. If, as seems to be the case, it is a rare and costly object as difficult to produce as a battleship, it is likelier to put an end to large-scale wars at the cost of prolonging indefinitely a "peace that is no peace".

What Is Science?*

In last week's *Tribune*, there was an interesting letter from Mr J. Stewart Cook, in which he suggested that the best way of avoiding the danger of a "scientific hierarchy" would be to see to it that every member of the general public was, as far as possible, scientifically educated. At the same time, scientists should be brought out of their isolation and encouraged to take a greater part in politics and administration.

As a general statement, I think most of us would agree with this, but I notice that, as usual, Mr Cook does not define science, and merely implies in passing that it means certain exact sciences whose experiments can be made under laboratory conditions. Thus, adult education tends "to neglect scientific studies in favour of literary, economic and social subjects", economics and sociology not being regarded as branches of science, apparently. This point is of great importance. For the word science is at present used in at least two meanings, and the whole question of scientific education is obscured by the current tendency to dodge from one meaning to the other.

Science is generally taken as meaning either (a) the exact sciences, such as chemistry, physics, etc., or (b) a method of thought which obtains verifiable results by reasoning logically from observed fact.

If you ask any scientist, or indeed almost any educated person, "What is science?" you are likely to get an answer approximating to (b). In everyday life, however, both in speaking and in writing, when people say "science" they mean (a). Science means something that happens in a laboratory: the very word calls up a picture of graphs, test tubes, balances, Bunsen burners, microscopes. A biologist, an astronomer, perhaps a psychologist or a mathematician, is described as a "man of science"; no one would think of applying this term to a statesman, a poet, a journalist or even a philosopher. And those who tell us that the young must be scientifically educated mean, almost invariably, that they should be taught more about radioactivity, or the stars, or the physiology of their own bodies, rather than that they should be taught to think more exactly.

This confusion of meaning, which is partly deliberate, has in it a great danger. Implied in the demand for more scientific education is the claim that if one has been scientifically trained one's approach to *all* subjects will be more intelligent than if one had had no such training. A scientist's political opinions, it is assumed, his opinions on sociological questions, on morals, on philosophy, perhaps even on the arts, will be more valuable than those of a

WHAT IS SCIENCE?

layman. The world, in other words, would be a better place if the scientists were in control of it. But a "scientist", as we have just seen, means in practice a specialist in one of the exact sciences. It follows that a chemist or a physicist, as such, is politically more intelligent than a poet or a lawyer, as such. And, in fact, there are already millions of people who do believe this.

But is it really true that a "scientist", in this narrower sense, is any likelier than other people to approach non-scientific problems in an objective way? There is not much reason for thinking so. Take one simple test – the ability to withstand nationalism. It is often loosely said that "Science is international", but in practice the scientific workers of all countries line up behind their own governments with fewer scruples than are felt by the writers and the artists. The German scientific community, as a whole, made no resistance to Hitler. Hitler may have ruined the long-term prospects of German science, but there were still plenty of gifted men to do the necessary research on such things as synthetic oil, jet planes, rocket projectiles and the atomic bomb. Without them the German war machine could never have been built up.

On the other hand, what happened to German literature when the Nazis came to power? I believe no exhaustive lists have been published, but I imagine that the number of German scientists – Jews apart – who voluntarily exiled themselves or were persecuted by the regime was much smaller than the number of writers and journalists. More sinister than this, a number of German scientists swallowed the monstrosity of "racial science". You can find some of the statements to which they set their names in Professor Brady's *The Spirit and Structure of German Fascism*.*

But, in slightly different forms, it is the same picture everywhere. In England, a large proportion of our leading scientists accept the structure of capitalist society, as can be seen from the comparative freedom with which they are given knighthoods, baronetcies and even peerages. Since Tennyson, no English writer worth reading – one might, perhaps, make an exception of Sir Max Beerbohm* – has been given a title. And those English scientists who do not simply accept the status quo are frequently communists, which means that, however intellectually scrupulous they may be in their own line of work, they are ready to be uncritical and even dishonest on certain subjects. The fact is that a mere training in one or more of the exact sciences, even combined with very high gifts, is no guarantee of a humane or sceptical outlook. The physicists of half a dozen great nations, all feverishly and secretly working away at the atomic bomb, are a demonstration of this.

But does all this mean that the general public should *not* be more scientifically educated? On the contrary! All it means is that scientific education for the masses will do little good, and probably a lot of harm, if it simply boils down to more physics, more chemistry, more biology, etc. to the detriment of literature and history. Its probable effect on the average human being would be to narrow the range of his thoughts and make him more than ever contemptuous of such knowledge as he did not possess – and his political reactions would probably be somewhat less intelligent than those of an illiterate peasant who retained a few historical memories and a fairly sound aesthetic sense.

Clearly, scientific education ought to mean the implanting of a rational, sceptical, experimental habit of mind. It ought to mean acquiring a *method* – a method that can be used on any problem that one meets – and not simply piling up a lot of facts. Put it in those words, and the apologist of scientific education will usually agree. Press him further, ask him to particularize, and somehow it always turns out that scientific education means more attention to the exact sciences, in other words – more *facts*. The idea that science means a way of looking at the world, and not simply a body of knowledge, is in practice strongly resisted. I think sheer professional jealousy is part of the reason for this. For if science is simply a method or an attitude, so that anyone whose thought processes are sufficiently rational can in some sense be described as a scientist – what then becomes of the enormous prestige now enjoyed by the chemist, the physicist, etc. and his claim to be somehow wiser than the rest of us?

A hundred years ago, Charles Kingsley described science as "making nasty smells in a laboratory".* A year or two ago a young industrial chemist informed me, smugly, that he "could not see what was the use of poetry". So the pendulum swings to and fro, but it does not seem to me that one attitude is any better than the other. At the moment, science is on the upgrade, and so we hear, quite rightly, the claim that the masses should be scientifically educated; we do not hear, as we ought, the counter-claim that the scientists themselves would benefit by a little education. Just before writing this, I saw in an American magazine the statement that a number of British and American physicists refused from the start to do research on the atomic bomb, well knowing what use would be made of it. Here you have a group of sane men in the middle of a world of lunatics. And though no names were published, I think it would be a safe guess that all of them were people with some kind of general cultural background, some acquaintance with history or literature or the arts – in short, people whose interests were not, in the current sense of the word, purely scientific.

Good Bad Books*

Not long ago a publisher commissioned me to write an introduction for a reprint of a novel by Leonard Merrick.* This publishing house, it appears, is going to reissue a long series of minor and partly forgotten novels of the twentieth century. It is a valuable service in these bookless days, and I rather envy the person whose job it will be to scout round the threepenny boxes, hunting down copies of his boyhood favourites.

A type of book which we hardly seem to produce in these days, but which flowered with great richness in the late nineteenth and early twentieth centuries, is what Chesterton called the "good bad book":* that is, the kind of book that has no literary pretensions but which remains readable when more serious productions have perished. Obviously outstanding books in this line are *Raffles* and the Sherlock Holmes stories, which have kept their place when innumerable "problem novels", "human documents" and "terrible indictments" of this or that have fallen into deserved oblivion. (Who has worn better, Conan Doyle or Meredith?) Almost in the same class as these I put R. Austin Freeman's earlier stories – 'The Singing Bone', 'The Eye of Osiris' and others – Ernest Bramah's *Max Carrados* and, dropping the standard a bit, Guy Boothby's Tibetan thriller *Doctor Nikola*, a sort of schoolboy version of Huc's *Travels in Tartary*,* which would probably make a real visit to Central Asia seem a dismal anticlimax.

But apart from thrillers, there were the minor humorous writers of the period. For example, Pett Ridge – but I admit his full-length books no longer seem readable – E. Nesbit (*The Treasure Seekers*), George Birmingham, who was good so long as he kept off politics, the pornographic Binstead ("Pitcher" of the *Pink 'Un*), and, if American books can be included, Booth Tarkington's Penrod stories.* A cut above most of these was Barry Pain. Some of Pain's humorous writings are, I suppose, still in print, but to anyone who comes across it I recommend what must now be a very rare book – *The Octave of Claudius*,* a brilliant exercise in the macabre. Somewhat later in time there was Peter Blundell,* who wrote in the W.W. Jacobs vein about Far Eastern seaport towns, and who seems to be rather unaccountably forgotten, in spite of having been praised in print by H.G. Wells.

However, all the books I have been speaking of are frankly "escape" literature. They form pleasant patches in one's memory, quiet corners where the mind can browse at odd moments, but they hardly pretend to have anything to do with real life. There is another kind of good bad book which is more seriously intended, and which tells us, I think, something about the nature of the novel and the reasons for its present decadence. During the last fifty years there has been a whole series of writers – some of them are still writing – whom it is quite impossible to call "good" by any strictly literary standard, but who are natural novelists and who seem to attain sincerity partly because they are not inhibited by good taste. In this class I put Leonard Merrick himself, W.L. George, J.D. Beresford, Ernest Raymond, May Sinclair, and – at a lower level than the others but still essentially similar – A.S.M. Hutchinson.*

Most of these have been prolific writers, and their output has naturally varied in quality. I am thinking in each case of one or two outstanding books: for example, Merrick's *Cynthia*, J.D. Beresford's *A Candidate for Truth*, W.L. George's *Caliban*, May Sinclair's *The Combined Maze* and Ernest Raymond's *We, the Accused*.* In each of these books the author has been able to identify himself with his imagined characters, to feel with them and invite sympathy on their behalf, with a kind of abandonment that cleverer people would find it difficult to achieve. They bring out the fact that intellectual refinement can be a disadvantage to a storyteller, as it would be to a music-hall comedian.

Take, for example, Ernest Raymond's *We, the Accused* – a peculiarly sordid and convincing murder story, probably based on the Crippen case.* I think it gains a great deal from the fact that the author only partly grasps the pathetic vulgarity of the people he is writing about, and therefore does not despise them. Perhaps it even – like Theodore Dreiser's *An American Tragedy** – gains something from the clumsy, long-winded manner in which it is written; detail is piled on detail, with almost no attempt at selection, and in the process an effect of terrible, grinding cruelty is slowly built up. So also with *A Candidate for Truth*. Here there is not the same clumsiness, but there is the same ability to take seriously the problems of commonplace people. So also with *Cynthia* and at any rate the earlier part of *Caliban*. The greater part of what W.L. George wrote was shoddy rubbish, but in this particular book, based on the career of Northcliffe, he achieved some memorable and truthful pictures of lower-middle-class London life. Parts of this book are probably autobiographical, and one of the advantages of good bad writers is their lack of shame in writing autobiography. Exhibitionism and self-pity are the bane of the novelist, and yet if he is too frightened of them his creative gift may suffer.

The existence of good bad literature – the fact that one can be amused or excited or even moved by a book that one's intellect simply refuses to take seriously – is a reminder that art is not the same thing as cerebration. I imagine that by any test that could be devised, Carlyle would be found to be a more intelligent man than Trollope. Yet Trollope has remained readable and Carlyle has not: with all his cleverness he had not even the wit to write in plain straightforward English. In novelists, almost as much as in poets, the connection between intelligence and creative power is hard to establish. A good novelist may be a prodigy of self-discipline like Flaubert, or he may be an intellectual sprawl like Dickens. Enough talent to set up dozens of ordinary writers has been poured into Wyndham Lewis's so-called novels, such as *Tarr* or *Snooty Baronet*.* Yet it would be a very heavy labour to read one of these books right through. Some indefinable quality, a sort of literary vitamin, which exists even in a book like *If Winter Comes*,* is absent from them.

Perhaps the supreme example of the "good bad" book is *Uncle Tom's Cabin*. It is an unintentionally ludicrous book, full of preposterous melodramatic incidents; it is also deeply moving and essentially true; it is hard to say which quality outweighs the other. But *Uncle Tom's Cabin*, after all, is trying to be serious and to deal with the real world. How about the frankly escapist writers, the purveyors of thrills and "light" humour? How about *Sherlock Holmes*, *Vice Versa*, *Dracula*, *Helen's Babies* or *King Solomon's Mines*?* All of these are definitely absurd books, books which one is more inclined to laugh *at* than *with*, and which were hardly taken seriously even by their authors – yet they have survived, and will probably continue to do so. All one can say is that, while civilization remains such that one needs distraction from time to time, "light" literature has its appointed place; also that there is such a thing as sheer skill, or native grace, which may have more survival value than erudition or intellectual power. There are music-hall songs which are better poems than three quarters of the stuff that gets into the anthologies:

> Come where the booze is cheaper,
> Come where the pots hold more,
> Come where the boss is a bit of a sport,
> Come to the pub next door!

Or again:

> Two lovely black eyes –
> Oh, what a surprise!
> Only for calling another man wrong,
> Two lovely black eyes!

I would far rather have written either of those than, say, 'The Blessed Damozel' or 'Love in the Valley'.* And by the same token I would back *Uncle Tom's Cabin* to outlive the complete works of Virginia Woolf or George Moore, though I know of no strictly literary test which would show where the superiority lies.

Revenge Is Sour*

Whenever I read phrases like "war-guilt trials", "punishment of war criminals", and so forth, there comes back into my mind the memory of something I saw in a prisoner-of-war camp in South Germany, earlier this year.

Another correspondent and myself were being shown round the camp by a little Viennese Jew who had been enlisted in the branch of the American army which deals with the interrogation of prisoners. He was an alert, fair-haired, rather good-looking youth of about twenty-five, and politically so much more knowledgeable than the average American officer that it was a pleasure to be with him. The camp was on an airfield, and, after we had been round the cages, our guide led us to a hangar where various prisoners who were in a different category from the others were being "screened".

Up at one end of the hangar about a dozen men were lying in a row on the concrete floor. These, it was explained, were SS officers who had been segregated from the other prisoners. Among them was a man in dingy civilian clothes who was lying with his arm across his face and apparently asleep. He had strangely and horribly deformed feet. The two of them were quite symmetrical, but they were clubbed out into an extraordinary globular shape which made them more like a horse's hoof than anything human. As we approached the group the little Jew seemed to be working himself up into a state of excitement.

"That's the real swine!" he said, and suddenly he lashed out with his heavy army boot and caught the prostrate man a fearful kick right on the bulge of one of his deformed feet.

"Get up, you swine!" he shouted as the man started out of sleep, and then repeated something of the kind in German. The prisoner scrambled to his feet and stood clumsily to attention. With the same air of working himself up into a fury – indeed he was almost dancing up and down as he spoke – the Jew told us the prisoner's history. He was a "real" Nazi: his party number indicated that he had been a member since the very early days, and he had held a post corresponding to a general in the political branch of the SS. It could be taken as quite certain that he had had charge of concentration camps and had presided over tortures and hangings. In short, he represented everything that we had been fighting against during the past five years.

Meanwhile, I was studying his appearance. Quite apart from the scrubby, unfed, unshaven look that a newly captured man generally has, he was a disgusting specimen. But he did not look brutal or in any way frightening: merely neurotic and, in a low way, intellectual. His pale, shifty eyes were deformed by powerful spectacles. He could have been an unfrocked clergyman, an actor ruined by drink, or a spiritualist medium. I have seen very similar people in London common lodging houses, and also in the Reading Room of the British Museum. Quite obviously he was mentally unbalanced – indeed, only doubtfully sane, though at this moment sufficiently in his right mind to be frightened of getting another kick. And yet everything that the Jew was telling me of his history could have been true, and probably was true! So the Nazi torturer of one's imagination, the monstrous figure against whom one had struggled for so many years, dwindled to this pitiful wretch, whose obvious need was not for punishment, but for some kind of psychological treatment.

Later, there were further humiliations. Another SS officer, a large, brawny man, was ordered to strip to the waist and show the blood-group number tattooed on his underarm; another was forced to explain to us how he had lied about being a member of the SS and attempted to pass himself off as an ordinary soldier of the *Wehrmacht*. I wondered whether the Jew was getting any real kick out of this newfound power that he was exercising. I concluded that he wasn't really enjoying it, and that he was merely – like a man in a brothel, or a boy smoking his first cigar, or a tourist traipsing round a picture gallery – *telling* himself that he was enjoying it, and behaving as he had planned to behave in the days when he was helpless.

It is absurd to blame any German or Austrian Jew for getting his own back on the Nazis. Heaven knows what scores this particular man may have had to wipe out; very likely his whole family had been murdered – and, after all, even a wanton kick to a prisoner is a very tiny thing compared with the outrages committed by the Hitler regime. But what this scene, and much else that I saw in Germany, brought home to me was that the whole idea of revenge and punishment is a childish daydream. Properly speaking, there is no such thing as revenge. Revenge is an act which you want to commit when you are powerless and because you are powerless: as soon as the sense of impotence is removed, the desire evaporates also.

Who would not have jumped for joy, in 1940, at the thought of seeing SS officers kicked and humiliated? But when the thing becomes possible, it is merely pathetic and disgusting. It is said that when Mussolini's corpse was exhibited in public, an old woman drew a revolver and fired five shots into it, exclaiming, "Those are for my five sons!" It is the kind of story that the newspapers make up, but it might be true. I wonder how much satisfaction she got out of those five shots, which, doubtless, she had dreamt years earlier of firing. The condition of her being able to get near enough to Mussolini to shoot at him was that he should be a corpse.

In so far as the big public in this country is responsible for the monstrous peace settlement now being forced on Germany, it is because of a failure to see in advance that punishing an enemy brings no satisfaction. We acquiesced in crimes like the expulsion of all Germans from East Prussia – crimes which in some cases we could not prevent but might at least have protested against – because the Germans had angered and frightened us, and therefore we were certain that when they were down we should feel no pity for them. We persist in these policies, or let others persist in them on our behalf, because of a vague feeling that, having set out to punish Germany, we ought to go ahead and do it. Actually there is little acute hatred of Germany left in this country, and even less, I should expect to find, in the army of occupation. Only the minority of sadists, who must have their "atrocities" from one source or another, take a keen interest in the hunting down of war criminals and quislings. If you ask the average man what crime Goering, Ribbentrop* and the rest are to be charged with at their trial, he cannot tell you. Somehow the punishment of these monsters ceases to seem attractive when it becomes possible: indeed, once under lock and key, they almost cease to be monsters.

Unfortunately, there is often need of some concrete incident before one can discover the real state of one's feelings. Here is another memory from Germany. A few hours after Stuttgart was captured by the French army, a Belgian journalist and myself entered the town, which was still in some disorder. The Belgian had been broadcasting throughout the war for the European Service of the BBC, and, like nearly all Frenchmen or Belgians, he had a very much tougher attitude towards "the Boche" than an Englishman or an American would have. All the main bridges into the town had been blown up, and we had to enter by a small footbridge which the Germans had evidently made efforts to defend. A dead German soldier was lying supine at the foot of the steps. His face was a waxy yellow. On his breast someone had laid a bunch of the lilac which was blossoming everywhere.

The Belgian averted his face as we went past. When we were well over the bridge he confided to me that this was the first time he had seen a dead man. I suppose he was thirty-five years old, and for four years he had been doing war propaganda over the radio. For several days after this, his attitude was quite different from what it had been earlier. He looked with disgust at the bomb-wrecked town and the humiliations the Germans were undergoing, and even on one occasion intervened to prevent a particularly bad bit of looting. When he left, he gave the residue of the coffee we had brought with us to the Germans on whom we were billeted. A week earlier he would probably have been scandalized at the idea of giving coffee to a "Boche". But his feelings, he told me, had undergone a change at the sight of *"ce pauvre mort"** beside the bridge: it had suddenly brought home to him the meaning of war. And yet, if we had happened to enter the town by another route, he might have been spared the experience of seeing even one corpse out of the – perhaps – twenty million that the war has produced.

Through a Glass, Rosily*

The recent article by *Tribune*'s Vienna correspondent* provoked a spate of angry letters which, besides calling him a fool and a liar and making other charges of what one might call a routine nature, also carried the very serious implication that he ought to have kept silent even if he knew that he was speaking the truth. He himself made a brief answer in *Tribune*, but the question involved is so important that it is worth discussing it at greater length.

Whenever A and B are in opposition to one another, anyone who attacks or criticizes A is accused of aiding and abetting B. And it is often true, objectively and on a short-term analysis, that he *is* making things easier for B. Therefore, say the supporters of A, shut up and don't criticize: or at least criticize "constructively", which in practice always means favourably. And from this it is only a short step to arguing that the suppression and distortion of known facts is the highest duty of a journalist.

Now, if one divides the world into A and B and assumes that A represents progress and B reaction, it is just arguable that no fact detrimental to A ought ever to be revealed. But before making this claim one ought to realize where it leads. What do we mean by reaction? I suppose it would be agreed that Nazi Germany represented reaction in its worst form or one of its worst. Well, the people in this country who gave most ammunition to the Nazi propagandists during the war are exactly the ones who tell us that it is "objectively" pro-fascist to criticize the USSR. I am not referring to the communists during their anti-war phase: I am referring to the Left as a whole. By and large, the Nazi radio got more material from the British left-wing press than from that of the Right. And it could hardly be otherwise, for it is chiefly in the left-wing press that serious criticism of British institutions is to be found. Every revelation about slums or social inequality, every attack on the leaders of the Tory Party, every denunciation of British imperialism was a gift for Goebbels. And not necessarily a worthless gift, for German propaganda about "British plutocracy" had considerable effect in neutral countries, especially in the earlier part of the war.

Here are two examples of the kind of source from which the Axis propagandists were liable to take their material. The Japanese, in one of their English-speaking magazines in China, serialized Briffault's *Decline and Fall of the British Empire*.* Briffault, if not actually a communist, was vehemently pro-Soviet, and the book incidentally contained some cracks at the Japanese themselves – but from the Japanese point of view this didn't matter, since the main tendency of the book was anti-British. About the same time the German radio broadcast shortened versions of books which they considered damaging to British prestige. Among others they broadcast E.M. Forster's *A Passage to India*.* And so far as I know they didn't even have to resort to dishonest quotation. Just because the book was essentially truthful, it could be made to serve the purposes of fascist propaganda. According to Blake,

> A truth that's told with bad intent
> Beats all the lies you can invent,*

and anyone who has seen his own statements coming back at him on the Axis radio will feel the force of this. Indeed, anyone who has ever written in defence of unpopular causes or been the witness of events which are likely to cause controversy knows the fearful temptation to distort or suppress the facts, simply because any honest statement will contain revelations which can be made use of by unscrupulous opponents. But what one has to consider are the long-term effects. In the long run, can the cause of progress be served by lies, or can it not? The readers who attacked *Tribune*'s Vienna correspondent so violently accused him of untruthfulness, but they also seemed to imply that the facts he brought forward ought not to be published even if true. 100,000 rape cases in Vienna are not a good advertisement for the Soviet regime – therefore, even if they have happened, don't mention them. Anglo-Russian relations are more likely to prosper if inconvenient facts are kept dark.

The trouble is that if you lie to people, their reaction is all the more violent when the truth leaks out, as it is apt to do in the end. Here is an example of untruthful propaganda coming home to roost. Many English people of goodwill draw from the left-wing press an unduly favourable picture of the Indian Congress Party. They not only believe it to be in the right (as it is), but are also apt to imagine that it is a sort of left-wing organization with democratic and internationalist aims. Such people, if they are suddenly confronted with an actual, flesh-and-blood Indian nationalist, are liable to recoil into the attitudes of a Blimp. I have seen this happen a number of times. And it is the same with pro-Soviet propaganda. Those who have swallowed it whole are always in danger of a sudden revulsion in which they may reject the whole idea of socialism. In this and other ways I should say that the net effect of communist and near-communist propaganda has been simply to retard the cause of socialism, though it may have temporarily aided Russian foreign policy.

There are always the most excellent, high-minded reasons for concealing the truth, and these reasons are brought forward in almost the same words by supporters of the most diverse causes. I have had writings of my own kept out of print because it was feared that the Russians would not like them, and I have had others kept out of print because they attacked British imperialism and might be quoted by anti-British Americans. We are told *now* that any frank criticism of the Stalin regime will "increase Russian suspicions", but it is only seven years since we were being told (in some cases by the same newspapers) that frank criticism of the Nazi regime would increase Hitler's suspicions. As late as 1941, some of the Catholic papers declared that the presence of Labour ministers in the British government increased Franco's suspicions and made him incline more towards the Axis. Looking back, it is possible to see that if only the British and American peoples had grasped in 1933 or thereabouts what Hitler stood for, war might have been averted. Similarly, the first step towards decent Anglo-Russian relations is the dropping of illusions. In principle most people would agree to this – but the dropping of illusions means the publication of facts, and facts are apt to be unpleasant.

The whole argument that one mustn't speak plainly because it "plays into the hands of" this or that sinister influence is dishonest, in the sense that people only use it when it suits them. As I have pointed out, those who are most concerned about playing into the hands of the Tories were least concerned about playing into the hands of the Nazis. The Catholics who said "Don't offend Franco because it helps Hitler" had been more or less consciously helping Hitler for years beforehand. Beneath this argument there always lies the intention to do propaganda for some single sectional interest, and to browbeat critics into silence by telling them that they are "objectively" reactionary. It is a tempting manoeuvre, and I have used it myself more than once, but it is dishonest. I think one is less likely to use it if one remembers that the advantages of a lie are always short-lived. So often it seems a positive duty to suppress or colour the facts! And yet genuine progress can only happen through increasing enlightenment, which means the continuous destruction of myths.

Meanwhile there is a curious backhanded tribute to the values of liberalism in the fact that the opponents of free speech write letters to *Tribune* at all. "Don't criticize," such people are in effect saying. "Don't reveal inconvenient facts. Don't play into the hands of the enemy!" Yet they themselves are attacking *Tribune*'s policy with all the violence at their command. Does it not occur to them that if the principles they advocate were put into practice, their letters would never get printed?

Catastrophic Gradualism*

There is a theory which has not yet been accurately formulated or given a name, but which is very widely accepted and is brought forward whenever it is necessary to justify some action which conflicts with the sense of decency of the average human being. It might be called, until some better name is found, the Theory of Catastrophic Gradualism. According to this theory, nothing is ever achieved without bloodshed, lies, tyranny and injustice, but on the other hand no considerable change for the better is to be expected as the result of even the greatest upheaval. History necessarily proceeds by calamities, but each succeeding age will be as bad, or nearly as bad, as the last. One must not protest against purges, deportations, secret police forces and so forth, because these are the price that has to be paid for progress – but on the other hand "human nature" will always see to it that progress is slow or even imperceptible. If you object to dictatorship you are a reactionary, but if you expect dictatorship to produce good results you are a sentimentalist.

At present this theory is most often used to justify the Stalin regime in the USSR, but it obviously could be – and, given appropriate circumstances, would be – used to justify other forms of totalitarianism. It has gained ground as a result of the failure of the Russian Revolution – failure, that is, in the sense that the Revolution has not fulfilled the hopes that it aroused twenty-five years ago. In the name of socialism the Russian regime has committed almost every crime that can be imagined, but at the same time its evolution is *away* from socialism, unless one redefines that word in terms that no socialist of 1917 would have accepted. To those who admit these facts, only two courses are open. One is simply to repudiate the whole theory of totalitarianism, which few English intellectuals have the courage to do: the other is to fall back on Catastrophic Gradualism. The formula usually employed is: "You can't make an omelette without breaking eggs." And if one replies, "Yes, but where is the omelette?", the answer is likely to be: "Oh well, you can't expect everything to happen all in a moment."

Naturally this argument is pushed backward into history, the design being to show that every advance was achieved at the cost of atrocious crimes, and could not have been achieved otherwise. The instance generally used is the overthrow of feudalism by the bourgeoisie, which is supposed to foreshadow the overthrow of capitalism by socialism in our own age. Capitalism, it is argued, was once a progressive force, and therefore its crimes were justified, or at least were unimportant. Thus, in a recent number of the *New Statesman*,

Mr Kingsley Martin,* reproaching Arthur Koestler for not possessing a true "historical perspective", compared Stalin with Henry VIII. Stalin, he admitted, had done terrible things, but on balance he had served the cause of "progress", and a few million "liquidations" must not be allowed to obscure this fact. Similarly, Henry VIII's character left much to be desired, but after all he had made possible the rise of capitalism, and therefore on balance could be regarded as a friend of humanity.

Now, Henry VIII has not a very close resemblance to Stalin – Cromwell would provide a better analogy – but, granting Henry VIII the importance given to him by Mr Martin, where does this argument lead? Henry VIII made possible the rise of capitalism, which led to the horrors of the Industrial Revolution and thence to a cycle of enormous wars, the next of which may well destroy civilization altogether. So, telescoping the process, we can put it like this: "Everything is to be forgiven Henry VIII, because it was ultimately he who enabled us to blow ourselves to pieces with atomic bombs." You are led into similar absurdities if you make Stalin responsible for our present condition and the future which appears to lie before us, and at the same time insist that his policies must be supported. The motives of those English intellectuals who support the Russian dictatorship are, I think, different from what they publicly admit, but it is logical to condone tyranny and massacre if one assumes that progress is inevitable. If each epoch is as a matter of course better than the last, then any crime or any folly that pushes the historical process forward can be justified. Between, roughly, 1750 and 1930 one could be forgiven for imagining that progress of a solid, measurable kind was taking place. Latterly, this has become more and more difficult, whence the theory of Catastrophic Gradualism. Crime follows crime, one ruling class replaces another, the Tower of Babel rises and falls, but one mustn't resist the process – indeed, one must be ready to applaud any piece of scoundrelism that comes off – because in some mystical way, in the sight of God, or perhaps in the sight of Marx, this is "progress". The alternative would be to stop and consider (a) to what extent is history predetermined? and (b) what is meant by progress? At this point one has to call in the Yogi to correct the Commissar.

In his much-discussed essay, Koestler is generally assumed to have come down heavily on the side of the Yogi. Actually, if one assumes the Yogi and the Commissar to be at opposite points of the scale, Koestler is somewhat nearer to the Commissar's end. He believes in action, in violence where necessary, in government, and consequently in the shifts and compromises that are inseparable from government. He supported the war, and the Popular Front before it. Since the appearance of fascism he has struggled against it to the best of his ability, and for many years he was a member of the Communist Party. The long chapter in his book in which he criticizes the USSR is even vitiated by a lingering loyalty to his old Party and by a resulting tendency to make all bad developments date from the rise of Stalin – whereas one ought, I believe, to admit that all the seeds of evil were there from the start and that things would not have been substantially different if Lenin or Trotsky had remained in control. No one is less likely than Koestler to claim that we can put everything right by watching our navels in California. Nor is he claiming, as religious thinkers usually do, that a "change of heart" must come *before* any genuine political improvement. To quote his own words:

> Neither the saint nor the revolutionary can save us; only the synthesis of the two. Whether we are capable of achieving it I do not know. But if the answer is in the negative, there seems to be no reasonable hope of preventing the destruction of European civilization, either by total war's successor Absolute War, or by Byzantine conquest – within the next few decades.

That is to say, the "change of heart" must happen, but it is not really happening unless at each step it issues in action. On the other hand, no change in the structure of society can by itself effect a real improvement. Socialism used to be defined as "common ownership of the means of production", but it is now seen that if common ownership means no more than centralized control, it merely paves the way for a new form of oligarchy. Centralized control is a necessary precondition of socialism, but it no more produces socialism than my typewriter would of itself produce this article I am writing. Throughout history, one revolution after another – although usually producing a temporary relief, such as a sick man gets by turning over in bed – has simply led to a change of masters, because no serious effort has been made to eliminate the power instinct – or if such an effort has been made, it has been made only by the saint, the Yogi, the man who saves his own soul at the expense of ignoring the community. In the minds of active revolutionaries, at any rate the ones who "got there", the longing for a just society has always been fatally mixed up with the intention to secure power for themselves.

Koestler says that we must learn once again the technique of contemplation, which "remains the only source of guidance in ethical dilemmas where the rule-of-thumb criteria of social utility fail". By "contemplation" he means "the will not to will", the conquest of the desire for power. The practical men have led us to the edge of the abyss, and the intellectuals in whom acceptance of power politics has killed first the moral sense, and then the sense of reality, are urging us to march rapidly forward without changing direction. Koestler maintains that history is not at all moments predetermined, but that there are turning points at which humanity is free to choose the better or the worse road. One such turning point (which had not appeared when he wrote the book) is the atomic bomb. Either we renounce it or it destroys us. But renouncing it is both a moral effort and a political effort. Koestler calls for "a new fraternity in a new spiritual climate, whose leaders are tied by a vow of poverty to share the life of the masses, and debarred by the laws of the fraternity from attaining unchecked power". He adds: "If this seems Utopian, then socialism is a Utopia." It may not even be a Utopia – its very name may in a couple of generations have ceased to be a memory – unless we can escape from the folly of "realism". But that will not happen without a change in the individual heart. To that extent, though no further, the Yogi is right as against the Commissar.

Introduction to *Love of Life and Other Stories* by Jack London*

In her little book *Memories of Lenin*,* Nadezhda Krupskaya relates that when Lenin was in his last illness she used to read aloud to him in the evenings:

> Two days before his death I read to him in the evening a tale by Jack London, 'Love of Life' – it is still lying on the table in his room. It was a very fine story. In a wilderness of ice, where no human being had set foot, a sick man, dying of hunger, is making for the harbour of a big river. His strength is giving out, he cannot walk but keeps slipping, and beside him there slides a wolf – also dying of hunger. There is a fight between them: the man wins. Half dead, half demented, he reaches his goal. That tale greatly pleased Ilyich (Lenin). Next day he asked me to read him more Jack London.

However, Krupskaya goes on, the next tale turned out to be "saturated with bourgeois morals", and "Ilyich smiled and dismissed it with a wave of his hand". These two pieces by Jack London were the last things that she read to him.

The story 'Love of Life' is even grimmer than Krupskaya suggests in her short summary of it, for it actually ends with the man eating the wolf, or at any rate biting into its throat hard enough to draw blood. That is the sort of theme towards which Jack London was irresistibly drawn, and this episode of Lenin's deathbed readings is of itself not a bad criticism of London's work. He was a writer who excelled in describing cruelty, whose main theme, indeed, was the cruelty of Nature, or at any rate of contemporary life; he was also an extremely variable writer, much of whose work was produced hurriedly and at low pressure, and he had in him a strain of feeling which Krupskaya is probably right in calling "bourgeois" – at any rate, a strain which did not accord with his democratic and socialist convictions.

During the last twenty years Jack London's short stories have been rather unaccountably forgotten – how thoroughly forgotten, one could gauge by the completeness with which they were out of print. So far as the big public went, he was remembered by various animal books, particularly *White Fang* and *The Call of the Wild* – books which appealed to the Anglo-Saxon sentimentality about animals – and after 1933 his reputation took an upward bound because of *The Iron Heel*, which had been written in 1907, and is in some sense a prophecy of fascism. *The Iron Heel* is not a good book, and on the whole its predictions have not been borne out. Its dates and its geography are ridiculous, and London makes the mistake, which was usual at that time, of assuming that revolution would break out first in the highly industrialized countries. But on several points London was right where nearly all other prophets were wrong, and he was right because of just that strain in his nature that made him a good short-story writer and a doubtfully reliable socialist.

London imagines a proletarian revolution breaking out in the United States and being crushed, or partially crushed, by a counteroffensive of the capitalist class, and, following on this, a long period during which society is ruled over by a small group of tyrants known as the Oligarchs, who are served by a kind of SS known as the Mercenaries. An underground struggle against dictatorship was the kind of thing that London could imagine, and he foresaw certain of the details with surprising accuracy; he foresaw, for instance, that peculiar horror of totalitarian society, the way in which suspected enemies of the regime *simply disappear*. But the book is chiefly notable for maintaining that capitalist society would not perish of its "contradictions", but that the possessing class would be able to form itself into a vast corporation and even evolve a sort of perverted socialism, sacrificing many of its privileges in order to preserve its superior status. The passages in which London analyses the mentality of the Oligarchs are of great interest:

> They, as a class (writes the imaginary author of the book), believed that they alone maintained civilization. It was their belief that, if they ever weakened, the great beast would engulf them and everything of beauty and joy and wonder and good in its cavernous and slime-dripping maw. Without them, anarchy would reign and humanity would drop backward into the primitive night out of which it had so painfully emerged. [...] In short, they alone, by their unremitting toil and self-sacrifice, stood between weak humanity and the all-devouring beast: and they believed it, firmly believed it.
>
> I cannot lay too great stress upon this high ethical righteousness of the whole Oligarch class. This has been the strength of the Iron Heel, and too many of the comrades have been slow or loath to realize it. Many of them have ascribed the strength of the Iron Heel to its system of reward and punishment. This is a mistake. Heaven and hell may be the prime factors of zeal in the religion of a fanatic; but for the great majority of the religious, heaven and hell are incidental to right and wrong. Love of the right, desire for the right, unhappiness with anything less than the right – in short, right conduct, is the prime factor of religion. And so with the Oligarchy. [...] The great driving force of the Oligarchs is the belief that they are doing right.

From these and similar passages it can be seen that London's understanding of the nature of a ruling class – that is, the characteristics which a ruling class must have if it is to survive – went very deep. According to the conventional left-wing view, the "capitalist" is simply a cynical scoundrel, without honour or courage, and intent only on filling his own pockets. London knew that that view is false. But why, one might justly ask, should this hurried, sensational, in some ways childish writer have understood that particular thing so much better than the majority of his fellow socialists?

The answer is surely that London could foresee fascism because he had a fascist streak in himself – or at any rate a marked strain of brutality and an almost unconquerable preference for the strong man as against the weak man. He knew instinctively that the American businessmen would fight when their possessions were menaced, because in their place he would have fought himself. He was an adventurer and a man of action as few writers have ever been. Born into dire poverty, he had already escaped from it at sixteen, thanks to his commanding character and powerful physique; his early years were spent among oyster pirates, gold prospectors, tramps and prizefighters, and he was ready to admire toughness wherever he found it. On the other hand he never forgot the sordid miseries of his childhood, and he never faltered in his loyalty to the exploited classes. Much of his time was spent in working and lecturing for the socialist movement, and when he was already a successful and famous man he could explore the worst depths of poverty in the London slums, passing himself off as an American sailor, and compile a book (*The People of the Abyss**) which still has sociological value. His outlook was democratic in the sense that he hated exploitation and hereditary privilege, and that he felt most at home in the company of people who worked with their hands – but his instinct lay towards acceptance of a "natural aristocracy" of strength, beauty and talent. Intellectually he knew, as one can see from various remarks in *The Iron Heel*, that socialism ought to mean the meek inheriting the earth, but that was not what his temperament demanded. In much of his work one strain in his character simply kills the other off; he is at his best where they interact, as they do in certain of his short stories.

Jack London's great theme is the cruelty of nature. Life is a savage struggle, and victory has nothing to do with justice. In the best of his short stories there is a startling lack of comment, a suspension of judgement, arising out of the fact that he both delights in the struggle and perceives its cruelty. Perhaps the best thing he ever wrote is 'Just Meat'.* Two burglars have got away with a big haul of jewellery; each is intent on swindling the other out of his share, and they poison one another simultaneously with strychnine, the story ending with the two men dead on the floor. There is almost no comment, and certainly no "moral". As Jack London sees it, it is simply a fragment of life, the kind of thing that happens in the present-day world; nevertheless it is doubtful whether such a plot would occur to any writer who was not fascinated by cruelty. Or take a story like 'The *Francis Spaight*'.* The starving crew of a waterlogged ship have decided to resort to cannibalism, and have just nerved themselves to begin when another ship heaves in sight. It is characteristic of Jack London that the second ship should appear after and not before the cabin boy's throat has been cut. A still more typical story is 'A Piece of Steak'.* London's love of boxing and admiration for sheer physical strength, his perception of the meanness and cruelty of a competitive society, and at the same time his instinctive tendency to accept *væ victis* as a law of nature, are all expressed here. An old prizefighter is fighting his last battle; his opponent is a beginner, young and full of vigour, but without experience. The old man nearly wins, but in the end his ring craft is no match for the youthful resilience of the other. Even when he has him at his mercy he is unable to strike the blow that would finish him, because he has been underfed for weeks before the fight and his muscles cannot make the necessary effort. He is left bitterly reflecting that if only he had had a good piece of steak on the day of the fight he would have won.

The old man's thoughts all run upon the theme: "Youth will be served." First you are young and strong, and you knock out older men and make money which you squander; then your strength wanes and in turn you are knocked out by younger men, and then you sink into poverty. This does in fact tell the story of the average boxer's life, and it would be a gross exaggeration to say that Jack London *approves* of the way in which men are used up like gladiators by a society which cannot even bother to feed them. The detail of the piece of steak – not strictly necessary, since the main point of the story is that the younger man is bound to win by virtue of his youth – rubs in the economic implication. And yet there is something in London that takes a kind of pleasure in the whole cruel process. It is not so much an approval of the harshness of Nature as a mystical belief that Nature *is* like that. Nature is "red in tooth and claw". Perhaps fierceness is bad, but fierceness is the price of survival. The young slay the old, the strong slay the weak, by an inexorable law. Man fights against the elements or against his fellow man, and there is nothing except his own toughness to help him through. London would have said that he was merely describing life as it is actually lived, and in his best stories he does so; still, the constant recurrence of the same theme – struggle, toughness, survival – shows which way his inclinations pointed.

London had been deeply influenced by the theory of the survival of the fittest. His book *Before Adam** – an inaccurate but very readable story of prehistory, in which ape-man and early and late Palaeolithic men are all shown as existing simultaneously – is an attempt to popularize Darwin. Although Darwin's main thesis has not been shaken, there has been, during the past twenty or thirty years, a change in the interpretation put upon it by the average thinking man. In the late nineteenth century Darwinism was used as a justification for laissez-faire capitalism, for power politics and for the exploiting of subject peoples. Life was a free-for-all in which the fact of survival was proof of fitness to survive; this was a comforting thought for successful businessmen, and it also led naturally, though not very logically, to the notion of "superior" and "inferior" races. In our day we are less willing to apply biology to politics, partly because we have watched the Nazis do just that thing, with great thoroughness and with horrible results. But when London was writing, a crude version of Darwinism was widespread and must have been difficult to escape. He himself was even capable at times of succumbing to racial mysticism. He toyed for a while with a race theory similar to that of the Nazis, and throughout his work the cult of the "Nordic" is fairly well marked. It ties up on the one hand with his admiration for prizefighters and on the other with his anthropomorphic view of animals – for there seems to be good reason for thinking that an exaggerated love of animals generally goes with a rather brutal attitude towards human beings. London was a socialist with the instincts of a buccaneer and the education of a nineteenth-century materialist. In general the background of his stories is not industrial, nor even civilized. Most of them take place – and much of his own life was lived – on ranches or South Sea islands, in ships, in prison or in the wastes of the Arctic: places where a man is either alone and dependent on his own strength and cunning, or where life is naturally patriarchal.

Nevertheless, London did write from time to time about contemporary industrial society, and on the whole he was at his best when he did so. Apart from his short stories, there are *The People of the Abyss*, *The Road** (a brilliant little book describing London's youthful experiences as a tramp) and certain passages in *The Valley of the Moon** which have the tumultuous history of American trade unionism as their background. Although the tug of his impulses was away from civilization, London had read deeply in the literature of the socialist movement, and his early life had taught him all he needed to know about urban poverty. He himself was working in a factory at the age of eleven, and without that experience behind him he could hardly have written such a story as 'The Apostate'.* In this story, as in all his best work, London does not comment, but he does unquestionably aim at rousing pity and indignation. It is generally when he writes of more primitive scenes that his moral attitude becomes equivocal. Take, for instance, a story like 'Make Westing'.* With whom do London's sympathies lie – with Captain Cullen or with George Dorety? One has the impression that if he were forced to make a choice he would side with the Captain, who commits two murders but does succeed in getting his ship round Cape Horn. On the other hand, in a story like 'The Chinago',* although it is told in the usual pitiless style, the "moral" is plain enough for anyone who wants to find it. London's better angel is his socialist convictions, which come into play when he deals with such subjects as coloured exploitation, child labour or the treatment of criminals, but are hardly involved when he is writing about explorers or animals. It is probably for this reason that a high proportion of his better writings deal with urban life. In stories like 'The Apostate', 'Just Meat', 'A Piece of Steak' and 'Semper Idem',* however cruel and sordid they may seem, something is keeping him on the rails and checking his natural urge towards the glorification of brutality. That "something" is his knowledge, theoretical as well as practical, of what industrial capitalism means in terms of human suffering.

Jack London is a very uneven writer. In his short and restless life he poured forth an immense quantity of work, setting himself to produce 1,000 words every day and generally achieving it. Even his best stories have the curious quality of being well told and yet not well written: they are told with admirable economy, with just the right incidents in just the right place, but the texture of the writing is poor, the phrases are worn and obvious, and the dialogue is erratic. His reputation has had its ups and downs, and for a long period he seems to have been much more admired in France and Germany than in the English-speaking countries. Even before the triumph of Hitler, which brought *The Iron Heel* out of its obscurity, he had a certain renown as a left-wing and "proletarian" writer – rather the same kind of renown as attaches to Robert Tressell, W.B. Traven or Upton Sinclair.* He has also been attacked by Marxist writers for his "fascist tendencies". These tendencies unquestionably existed in him, so much so that if one imagines him as living on into our own day, instead of dying in 1915, it is very hard to be sure where his political allegiance would have lain. One can imagine him in the Communist Party, one can imagine him falling a victim to Nazi racial theory and one can imagine him the quixotic champion of some Trotskyist or anarchist sect. But, as I have tried to make clear, if he had been a politically reliable person he would probably have left behind nothing of interest. Meanwhile his reputation rests mainly on *The Iron Heel*, and the excellence of his short stories has been almost forgotten. A dozen of the best of them are collected in this volume, and a few more are worth rescuing from the museum shelves and the second-hand boxes. It is to be hoped, too, that new editions of *The Road*, *The Jacket*,* *Before Adam* and *The Valley of the Moon* will appear when paper becomes more plentiful. Much of Jack London's work is scamped and unconvincing, but he produced at least six volumes which deserve to stay in print, and that is not a bad achievement from a life of only forty-one years.

Freedom of the Park*

A few weeks ago, five people who were selling papers outside Hyde Park were arrested by the police for obstruction. When taken before the magistrates they were all found guilty, four of them being bound over for six months and the other sentenced to forty shillings' fine or a month's imprisonment. He preferred to serve his term, so I suppose he is still in jail at this moment.

The papers these people were selling were *Peace News*, *Forward* and *Freedom*, besides other kindred literature. *Peace News* is the organ of the Peace Pledge Union; *Freedom* (till recently called *War Commentary*) is that of the anarchists; as for *Forward*, its politics defy definition, but at any rate it is violently Left. The magistrate, in passing sentence, stated that he was not influenced by the nature of the literature that was being sold – he was concerned merely with the fact of obstruction, and that this offence had technically been committed.

This raises several important points. To begin with, how does the law stand on the subject? As far as I can discover, selling newspapers in the street *is* technically obstruction, at any rate if you fail to move on when the police tell you to. So it would be legally possible for any policeman who felt like it to arrest any newsboy for selling the *Evening News*. Obviously this doesn't happen, so that the enforcement of the law depends on the discretion of the police.

And what makes the police decide to arrest one man rather than another? However it may have been with the magistrate, I find it hard to believe that in this case the police were not influenced by political considerations. It is a bit too much of a coincidence that they should have picked on people selling just those papers. If they had also arrested someone who was selling *Truth*, or the *Tablet*, or the *Spectator*, or even the *Church Times*, their impartiality would be easier to believe in.

The British police are not like a Continental gendarmerie or Gestapo, but I do not think one maligns them in saying that, in the past, they have been unfriendly to left-wing activities. They have generally shown a tendency to side with those whom they regarded as the defenders of private property. There were some scandalous cases at the time of the Mosley disturbances. At the only big Mosley meeting I ever attended, the police collaborated with the Blackshirts in "keeping order", in a way in which they certainly would not have collaborated with socialists or communists. Till quite recently "red" and "illegal" were almost synonymous, and it was always the seller of, say, the *Daily Worker*, never the seller of, say, the *Daily Telegraph*, who was moved on and generally harassed. Apparently it can be the same, at any rate at moments, under a Labour government.

A thing I would like to know – it is a thing we hear very little about – is what changes are made in the administrative personnel when there has been a change of government. Does the police officer who has a vague notion that "socialism" means something against the law carry on just the same when the government itself is socialist? It is a sound principle that the official should have no party affiliations, should serve successive governments faithfully and should not be victimized for his political opinions. Still, no government can afford to leave its enemies in key positions, and when Labour is in undisputed power for the first time – and therefore when it is taking over an administration formed by Conservatives – it clearly must make sufficient changes to prevent sabotage. The official, even when friendly to the government in power, is all too conscious that he is a permanency and can frustrate the short-lived ministers whom he is supposed to serve.

When a Labour government takes over, I wonder what happens to Scotland Yard Special Branch? To Military Intelligence? To the Consular Service? To the various colonial administrations – and so on and so forth? We are not told, but such symptoms as there are do not suggest that any very extensive reshuffling is going on. We are still represented abroad by the same ambassadors, and BBC censorship seems to have the same subtly reactionary colour that it always had. The BBC claims, of course, to be both independent and non-political. I was told once that its "line", if any, was to represent the left wing of the government in power. But that was in the days of the Churchill government. If it represents the left wing of the present government, I have not noticed the fact.

However, the main point of this episode is that the sellers of newspapers and pamphlets should be interfered with at all. Which particular minority is singled out – whether pacifists, communists, anarchists, Jehovah's Witnesses or the Legion of Christian Reformers, who recently declared Hitler to be Jesus Christ – is a secondary matter. It is of symptomatic importance that these people should have been arrested at that particular spot. You are not allowed to sell literature inside Hyde Park, but for many years past it has been usual for the paper sellers to station themselves just outside the gates and distribute literature connected with the open-air meetings a hundred yards away. Every kind of publication has been sold there without interference.

As for the meetings inside the park, they are one of the minor wonders of the world. At different times I have listened there to Indian nationalists, temperance reformers, communists, Trotskyists, the SPGB,* the Catholic Evidence Society, freethinkers, vegetarians, Mormons, the Salvation Army, the Church Army and a large variety of plain lunatics, all taking their turn at the rostrum in an orderly way and receiving a fairly good-humoured hearing from the crowd. Granted that Hyde Park is a special area, a sort of Alsatia where outlawed opinions are permitted to walk* – still, there are very few countries in the world where you can see a similar spectacle. I have known Continental Europeans, long before Hitler seized power, come away from Hyde Park astonished and even perturbed by the things they had heard Indian or Irish nationalists saying about the British Empire.

The degree of freedom of the press existing in this country is often overrated. Technically there is great freedom, but the fact that most of the press is owned by a few people operates in much the same way as a state censorship. On the other hand, freedom of speech is real. On the platform, or in certain recognized open-air spaces like Hyde Park, you can say almost anything – and, what is perhaps more significant, no one is frightened to utter his true opinions in pubs, on the tops of buses and so forth.

The point is that the relative freedom which we enjoy depends on public opinion. The law is no protection. Governments make laws, but whether they are carried out and how the police behave depends on the general temper of the country. If large numbers of people are interested in freedom of speech, there will be freedom of speech, even if the law forbids it; if public opinion is sluggish, inconvenient minorities will be persecuted, even if laws exist to protect them. The decline in the desire for intellectual liberty has not been so sharp as I would have predicted six years ago, when the war was starting, but still there has been a decline. The notion that certain opinions cannot safely be allowed a hearing is growing. It is given currency by intellectuals who confuse the issue by not distinguishing between democratic opposition and open rebellion, and it is reflected in our growing indifference to tyranny and injustice abroad. And even those who declare themselves to be in favour of freedom of opinion generally drop their claim when it is their own adversaries who are being persecuted.

I am not suggesting that the arrest of five people for selling harmless newspapers is a major calamity. When you see what is happening in the world today, it hardly seems worth squealing about such a tiny incident. All the same, it is not a good symptom that such things should happen when the war is well over, and I should feel happier if this, and the long series of similar episodes that have preceded it, were capable of raising a genuine popular clamour, and not merely a mild flutter in sections of the minority press.

Politics and the English Language*

Most people who bother with the matter at all would admit that the English language is in a bad way, but it is generally assumed that we cannot by conscious action do anything about it. Our civilization is decadent, and our language – so the argument runs – must inevitably share in the general collapse. It follows that any struggle against the abuse of language is a sentimental archaism, like preferring candles to electric light or hansom cabs to aeroplanes. Underneath this lies the half-conscious belief that language is a natural growth and not an instrument which we shape for our own purposes.

Now, it is clear that the decline of a language must ultimately have political and economic causes: it is not due simply to the bad influence of this or that individual writer. But an effect can become a cause, reinforcing the original cause and producing the same effect in an intensified form, and so on indefinitely. A man may take to drink because he feels himself to be a failure, and then fail all the more completely because he drinks. It is rather the same thing that is happening to the English language. It becomes ugly and inaccurate because our thoughts are foolish, but the slovenliness of our language makes it easier for us to have foolish thoughts. The point is that the process is reversible. Modern English, especially written English, is full of bad habits which spread by imitation and which can be avoided if one is willing to take the necessary trouble. If one gets rid of these habits one can think more clearly, and to think clearly is a necessary first step towards political regeneration: so that the fight against bad English is not frivolous and is not the exclusive concern of professional writers. I will come back to this presently, and I hope that by that time the meaning of what I have said here will have become clearer. Meanwhile, here are five specimens of the English language as it is now habitually written.

These five passages have not been picked out because they are especially bad – I could have quoted far worse if I had chosen – but because they illustrate various of the mental vices from which we now suffer. They are a little below the average, but are fairly representative samples. I number them so that I can refer back to them when necessary:

> 1. I am not, indeed, sure whether it is not true to say that the Milton who once seemed not unlike a seventeenth-century Shelley had not become, out of an experience ever more bitter in each year, more alien [sic] to the founder of that Jesuit sect which nothing could induce him to tolerate.
>
> **PROFESSOR HAROLD LASKI** (ESSAY IN *Freedom of Expression*)*

2. Above all, we cannot play ducks and drakes with a native battery of idioms which prescribes such egregious collocations of vocables as the Basic *put up with* for *tolerate* or *put at a loss* for *bewilder*.

PROFESSOR LANCELOT HOGBEN (*Interglossa*)*

3. On the one side we have the free personality: by definition it is not neurotic, for it has neither conflict nor dream. Its desires, such as they are, are transparent, for they are just what institutional approval keeps in the forefront of consciousness; another institutional pattern would alter their number and intensity; there is little in them that is natural, irreducible or culturally dangerous. But on the other side, the social bond itself is nothing but the mutual reflection of these self-secure integrities. Recall the definition of love. Is not this the very picture of a small academic? Where is there a place in this hall of mirrors for either personality or fraternity?

ESSAY ON PSYCHOLOGY IN *Politics* (NEW YORK)

4. All the "best people" from the gentlemen's clubs, and all the frantic fascist captains, united in common hatred of socialism and bestial horror of the rising tide of the mass revolutionary movement, have turned to acts of provocation, to foul incendiarism, to medieval legends of poisoned wells, to legalize their own destruction to proletarian organizations, and rouse the agitated petty bourgeoisie to chauvinistic fervour on behalf of the fight against the revolutionary way out of the crisis.

COMMUNIST PAMPHLET

5. If a new spirit *is* to be infused into this old country, there is one thorny and contentious reform which must be tackled, and that is the humanization and galvanization of the BBC. Timidity here will bespeak canker and atrophy of the soul. The heart of Britain may be sound and of strong beat, for instance, but the British lion's roar at present is like that of Bottom in Shakespeare's *Midsummer Night's Dream* – as gentle as any sucking dove. A virile new Britain cannot continue indefinitely to be traduced in the eyes, or rather ears, of the world by the effete languours of Langham Place, brazenly masquerading as "standard English". When the Voice of Britain is heard at nine o'clock, better far and infinitely less ludicrous to hear aitches honestly dropped than the present priggish, inflated, inhibited, school-ma'amish arch braying of blameless bashful mewing maidens!

LETTER IN *Tribune*

Each of these passages has faults of its own, but, quite apart from avoidable ugliness, two qualities are common to all of them. The first is staleness of imagery; the other is lack of precision. The writer either has a meaning and cannot express it, or he inadvertently says something else, or he is almost indifferent as to whether his words mean anything or not. This mixture of vagueness and sheer incompetence is the most marked characteristic of modern English prose, and especially of any kind of political writing. As soon as certain topics are raised, the concrete melts into the abstract and no one seems able to think of turns of speech that are not hackneyed: prose consists less and less of *words* chosen for the sake of their meaning and more of *phrases* tacked together like the sections of a prefabricated henhouse. I list below, with notes and examples, various of the tricks by means of which the work of prose construction is habitually dodged:

Dying metaphors. A newly invented metaphor assists thought by evoking a visual image, while on the other hand a metaphor which is technically "dead" (e.g. *iron resolution*) has in effect reverted to being an ordinary word and can generally be used without loss of vividness. But in between these two classes there is a huge dump of worn-out metaphors which have lost all evocative power and are merely used because they save people the trouble of inventing phrases for themselves. Examples are: "ring the changes on", "take up the cudgels for", "toe the line", "ride roughshod over", "stand shoulder to shoulder with", "play into the hands of", "no axe to grind", "grist to the mill", "fishing in troubled waters", "rift within the lute", "on the order of the day", "Achilles heel", "swansong", "hotbed". Many of these are used without knowledge of their meaning (what is a "rift", for instance?), and incompatible metaphors are frequently mixed, a sure sign that the writer is not interested in what he is saying. Some metaphors now current have been twisted out of their original meaning without those who use them even being aware of the fact. For example, "toe the line" is sometimes written "tow the line". Another example is "the hammer and the anvil", now always used with the implication that the anvil gets the worst of it. In real life it is always the anvil that breaks the hammer, never the other way about; a writer who stopped to think what he was saying would be aware of this, and would avoid perverting the original phrase.

Operators, or *verbal false limbs*. These save the trouble of picking out appropriate verbs and nouns, and at the same time pad each sentence with extra syllables which give it an appearance of symmetry. Characteristic phrases are: "render inoperative", "militate against", "prove unacceptable", "make contact with", "be subjected to", "give rise to", "give grounds for", "have the effect of", "play a leading part (role) in", "make itself felt", "take effect", "exhibit a tendency to", "serve the purpose of", etc. etc. The keynote is the elimination of simple verbs. Instead of being a single word, such as "break", "stop", "spoil", "mend", "kill", a verb becomes a *phrase*, made up of a noun or adjective tacked onto some general-purpose verb such as "prove", "serve", "form", "play", "render". In addition, the passive voice is wherever possible used in preference to the active, and noun constructions are used instead of gerunds ("by examination of" instead of "by examining"). The range of verbs is further cut down by means of the -*ize* and *de-* formations, and banal statements are given an appearance of profundity by means of the *not un-* formation. Simple conjunctions and prepositions are replaced by such phrases as "with respect to", "having regard to", "the fact that", "by dint of", "in view of", "in the interests of", "on the hypothesis that" – and the ends of sentences are saved from anticlimax by such resounding commonplaces as "greatly to be desired", "cannot be left out of account", "a development to be expected in the near future", "deserving of serious consideration", "brought to a satisfactory conclusion", and so on and so forth.

Pretentious diction. Words like "phenomenon", "element", "individual" (as noun), "objective", "categorical", "effective", "virtual", "basic", "primary", "promote", "constitute", "exhibit", "exploit", "utilize", "eliminate", "liquidate", are used to dress up simple statements and give an air of scientific impartiality to biased judgements. Adjectives like "epoch-making", "epic", "historic", "unforgettable", "triumphant", "age-old", "inevitable", "inexorable", "veritable", are used to dignify the sordid processes of international politics, while writing that aims at glorifying war usually takes on an archaic colour, its characteristic words being: "realm", "throne", "chariot", "mailed fist", "trident", "sword", "shield", "buckler", "banner", "jackboot", "clarion". Foreign words and expressions such as "cul de sac", "*ancien régime*", "deus ex machina", "*mutatis mutandis*", "status quo", "*Gleichschaltung*", "*Weltanschauung*", are used to give an air of culture and elegance. Except for the useful abbreviations "i.e.", "e.g." and "etc.", there is no real need for any of the hundreds of foreign phrases now current in English. Bad writers, and especially scientific, political and sociological writers, are nearly always haunted by the notion that Latin or Greek words are grander than Saxon ones, and unnecessary words like "expedite", "ameliorate", "predict", "extraneous", "deracinated", "clandestine", "subaqueous" and hundreds of others constantly gain ground from their Anglo-Saxon opposite numbers.* The jargon peculiar to Marxist writing ("hyena", "hangman", "cannibal", "petty bourgeois", "these gentry", "lackey", "flunkey", "mad dog", "White Guard", etc.) consists largely of words and phrases translated from Russian, German or French – but the normal way of coining a new word is to use a Latin or Greek root with the appropriate affix and, where necessary, the -*ize* formation. It is often easier to make up words of this kind ("deregionalize", "impermissible", "extramarital", "non-fragmentatory" and so forth) than to think up the English words that will cover one's meaning. The result, in general, is an increase in slovenliness and vagueness.

Meaningless words. In certain kinds of writing, particularly in art criticism and literary criticism, it is normal to come across long passages which are almost completely lacking in meaning.* Words like "romantic", "plastic", "values", "human", "dead", "sentimental", "natural", "vitality", as used in art criticism, are strictly meaningless, in the sense that they not only do not point to any discoverable object, but are hardly even expected to do so by the reader. When one critic writes, "The outstanding feature of Mr X's work is its living quality," while another writes, "The immediately striking thing about Mr X's work is its peculiar deadness," the reader accepts this as a simple difference of opinion. If words like "black" and "white" were involved, instead of the jargon words "dead" and "living", he would see at once that language in so far as it signifies "something not desirable". The words "democracy", "socialism", "freedom", "patriotic", "realistic", "justice", have each of them several different meanings which cannot be reconciled with one another. In the case of a word like "democracy", not only is there no agreed definition but the attempt to make one is resisted from all sides. It is almost universally felt that when we call a country democratic we are praising it: consequently the defenders of every kind of regime claim that it is a democracy, and fear that they might have to stop using the word if it were tied down to any one meaning. Words of this kind are often used in a consciously dishonest way. That is, the person who uses them has his own private definition, but allows his hearer to think he means something quite different. Statements like "Marshal Pétain was a true patriot", "The Soviet press is the freest in the world", "The Catholic Church is opposed to persecution", are almost always made with intent to deceive. Other words used in variable meanings, in most cases more or less dishonestly, are: "class", "totalitarian", "science", "progressive", "reactionary", "bourgeois", "equality".

Now that I have made this catalogue of swindles and perversions, let me give another example of the kind of writing that they lead to. This time it must of its nature be an imaginary one. I am going to translate a passage of good English into modern English of the worst sort. Here is a well-known verse from Ecclesiastes:

> I returned, and saw under the sun, that the race is not to the swift, nor the battle to the strong, neither yet bread to the wise, nor yet riches to men of understanding, nor yet favour to men of skill; but time and chance happeneth to them all.*

Here it is in modern English:

> Objective consideration of contemporary phenomena compels the conclusion that success or failure in competitive activities exhibits no tendency to be commensurate with innate capacity, but that a considerable element of the unpredictable must invariably be taken into account.

This is a parody, but not a very gross one. Exhibit 3, above, for instance, contains several patches of the same kind of English. It will be seen that I have not made a full translation. The beginning and ending of the sentence follow the original meaning fairly closely, but in the middle the concrete illustrations – race, battle, bread – dissolve into the vague phrase "success or failure in competitive activities". This had to be so, because no modern writer of the kind I am discussing – no one capable of using phrases like "objective consideration of contemporary phenomena" – would ever tabulate his thoughts in that precise and detailed way. The whole tendency of modern prose is away from concreteness. Now analyse these two sentences a little more closely. The first contains forty-nine words but only sixty syllables, and all its words are those of everyday life. The second contains thirty-eight words of ninety syllables: eighteen of its words are from Latin roots, and one from Greek. The first sentence contains six vivid images, and only one phrase ("time and chance") that could be called vague. The second contains not a single fresh, arresting phrase, and in spite of its ninety syllables it gives only a shortened version of the meaning contained in the first. Yet without a doubt it is the second kind of sentence that is gaining ground in modern English. I do not want to exaggerate. This kind of writing is not yet universal, and outcrops of simplicity will occur here and there in the worst-written page. Still, if you or I were told to write a few lines on the uncertainty of human fortunes, we should probably come much nearer to my imaginary sentence than to the one from Ecclesiastes.

As I have tried to show, modern writing at its worst does not consist in picking out words for the sake of their meaning and inventing images in order to make the meaning clearer. It consists in gumming together long strips of words which have already been set in order by someone else, and making the results presentable by sheer humbug. The attraction of this way of writing is that it is easy. It is easier – even quicker, once you have the habit – to say "In my opinion it is a not unjustifiable assumption that" than to say "I think". If you use ready-made phrases, you not only don't have to hunt about for words; you also don't have to bother with the rhythms of your sentences, since these phrases are generally so arranged as to be more or less euphonious. When you are composing in a hurry – when you are dictating to a stenographer, for instance, or making a public speech – it is natural to fall into a pretentious, Latinized style. Tags like "a consideration which we should do well to bear in mind" or "a conclusion to which all of us would readily assent" will save many a sentence from coming down with a bump. By using stale metaphors, similes and idioms, you save much mental effort, at the cost of leaving your meaning vague, not only for your reader but for yourself. This is the significance of mixed metaphors. The sole aim of a metaphor is to call up a visual image. When these images clash – as in "The fascist octopus has sung its swansong", "the jackboot is thrown into the melting pot" – it can be taken as certain that the writer is not seeing a mental image of the objects he is naming; in other words he is not really thinking. Look again at the examples I gave at the beginning of this essay. Professor Laski (1) uses five negatives in fifty-three words. One of these is superfluous, making nonsense of the whole passage, and in addition there is the slip "alien" for akin, making further nonsense, and several avoidable pieces of clumsiness which increase the general vagueness. Professor Hogben (2) plays ducks and drakes with a battery which is able to write prescriptions, and, while disapproving of the everyday phrase "put up with", is unwilling to look "egregious" up in the dictionary and see what it means. (3), if one takes an uncharitable attitude towards it, is simply meaningless: probably one could work out its intended meaning by reading the whole of the article in which it occurs. In (4) the writer knows more or less what he wants to say, but an accumulation of stale phrases chokes him like tea leaves blocking a sink. In (5) words and meaning have almost parted company. People who write in this manner usually have a general emotional meaning – they dislike one thing and want to express solidarity with another – but they are not interested in the detail of what they are saying. A scrupulous writer, in every sentence that he writes, will ask himself at least four questions, thus: What am I trying to say? What words will express it? What image or idiom will make it clearer? Is this image fresh enough to have an effect? And he will probably ask himself two more: Could I put it more shortly? Have I said anything that is avoidably ugly? But you are not obliged to go to all this trouble. You can shirk it by simply throwing your mind open and letting the ready-made phrases come crowding in. They will construct your sentences for you – even think your thoughts for you, to a certain extent – and at need they will perform the important service of partially concealing your meaning even from yourself. It is at this point that the special connection between politics and the debasement of language becomes clear.

In our time it is broadly true that political writing is bad writing. Where it is not true, it will generally be found that the writer is some kind of rebel, expressing his private opinions, and not a "party line". Orthodoxy, of whatever colour, seems to demand a lifeless, imitative style. The political dialects to be found in pamphlets, leading articles, manifestos, White Papers and the speeches of under-secretaries do, of course, vary from party to party, but they are all alike in that one almost never finds in them a fresh, vivid, home-made turn of speech. When one watches some tired hack on the platform mechanically repeating the familiar phrases – "bestial atrocities", "iron heel", "bloodstained tyranny", "free peoples of the world", "stand shoulder to shoulder" – one often has a curious feeling that one is not watching a live human being but some kind of dummy: a feeling which suddenly becomes stronger at moments when the light catches the speaker's spectacles and turns them into blank discs which seem to have no eyes behind them. And this is not altogether fanciful. A speaker who uses that kind of phraseology has gone some distance towards turning himself into a machine. The appropriate noises are coming out of his larynx, but his brain is not involved as it would be if he were choosing his words for himself. If the speech he is making is one that he is accustomed to make over and over again, he may be almost unconscious of what he is saying, as one is when one utters the responses in church. And this reduced state of consciousness, if not indispensable, is at any rate favourable to political conformity.

In our time, political speech and writing are largely the defence of the indefensible. Things like the continuance of British rule in India, the Russian purges and deportations, the dropping of the atom bombs on Japan can indeed be defended, but only by arguments which are too brutal for most people to face, and which do not square with the professed aims of political parties. Thus political language has to consist largely of euphemism, question-begging and sheer cloudy vagueness. Defenceless villages are bombarded from the air, the inhabitants driven out into the countryside, the cattle machine-gunned, the huts set on fire with incendiary bullets: this is called "pacification". Millions of peasants are robbed of their farms and sent trudging along the roads with no more than they can carry: this is called "transfer of population" or "rectification of frontiers". People are imprisoned for years without trial, or shot in the back of the neck or sent to die of scurvy in Arctic lumber camps: this is called "elimination of unreliable elements". Such phraseology is needed if one wants to name things without calling up mental pictures of them. Consider for instance some comfortable English professor defending Russian totalitarianism. He cannot say outright, "I believe in killing off your opponents when you can get good results by doing so." Probably, therefore, he will say something like this:

> While freely conceding that the Soviet regime exhibits certain features which the humanitarian may be inclined to deplore, we must, I think, agree that a certain curtailment of the right to political opposition is an unavoidable concomitant of transitional periods, and that the rigours which the Russian people have been called upon to undergo have been amply justified in the sphere of concrete achievement.

The inflated style is itself a kind of euphemism. A mass of Latin words falls upon the facts like soft snow, blurring the outlines and covering up all the details. The great enemy of clear language is insincerity. When there is a gap between one's real and one's declared aims, one turns as it were instinctively to long words and exhausted idioms, like a cuttlefish squirting out ink. In our age there is no such thing as "keeping out of politics". All issues are political issues, and politics itself is a mass of lies, evasions, folly, hatred and schizophrenia. When the general atmosphere is bad, language must suffer. I should expect to find – this is a guess which I have not sufficient knowledge to verify – that the German, Russian and Italian languages have all deteriorated in the last ten or fifteen years, as a result of dictatorship.

But if thought corrupts language, language can also corrupt thought. A bad usage can spread by tradition and imitation, even among people who should and do know better. The debased language that I have been discussing is in some ways very convenient. Phrases like "a not unjustifiable assumption", "leaves much to be desired", "would serve no good purpose", "a consideration which we should do well to bear in mind" are a continuous temptation, a packet of aspirins always at one's elbow. Look back through this essay, and for certain you will find that I have again and again committed the very faults I am protesting against. By this morning's post I have received a pamphlet dealing with conditions in Germany. The author tells me that he "felt impelled" to write it. I open it at random, and here is almost the first sentence that I see: "(The Allies) have an opportunity not only of achieving a radical transformation of Germany's social and political structure in such a way as to avoid a nationalistic reaction in Germany itself, but at the same time of laying the foundations of a cooperative and unified Europe." You see, he "feels impelled" to write – feels, presumably, that he has something new to say – and yet his words, like cavalry horses answering the bugle, group themselves automatically into the familiar dreary pattern. This invasion of one's mind by ready-made phrases ("lay the foundations", "achieve a radical transformation") can only be prevented if one is constantly on guard against them, and every such phrase anaesthetizes a portion of one's brain.

I said earlier that the decadence of our language is probably curable. Those who deny this would argue, if they produced an argument at all, that language merely reflects existing social conditions, and that we cannot influence its development by any direct tinkering with words and constructions. So far as the general tone or spirit of a language goes, this may be true, but it is not true in detail. Silly words and expressions have often disappeared, not through any evolutionary process but owing to the conscious action of a minority. Two recent examples were "explore every avenue" and "leave no stone unturned", which were killed by the jeers of a few journalists. There is a long list of fly-blown metaphors which could similarly be got rid of if enough people would interest themselves in the job – and it should also be possible to laugh the "not un-" formation* out of existence, to reduce the amount of Latin and Greek in the average sentence, to drive out foreign phrases and strayed scientific words, and, in general, to make pretentiousness unfashionable. But all these are minor points. The defence of the English language implies more than this, and perhaps it is best to start by saying what it does *not* imply.

To begin with, it has nothing to do with archaism, with the salvaging of obsolete words and turns of speech, or with the setting-up of a "standard English" which must never be departed from. On the contrary, it is especially concerned with the scrapping of every word or idiom which has outworn its usefulness. It has nothing to do with correct grammar and syntax, which are of no importance so long as one makes one's meaning clear, or with the avoidance of Americanisms, or with having what is called a "good prose style". On the other hand it is not concerned with fake simplicity and the attempt to make written English colloquial. Nor does it even imply in every case preferring the Saxon word to the Latin one, though it does imply using the fewest and shortest words that will cover one's meaning. What is above all needed is to let the meaning choose the word, and not the other way about. In prose, the worst thing one can do with words is to surrender to them. When you think of a concrete object, you think wordlessly, and then, if you want to describe the thing you have been visualizing, you probably hunt about till you find the exact words that seem to fit it. When you think of something abstract you are more inclined to use words from the start, and unless you make a conscious effort to prevent it, the existing dialect will come rushing in and do the job for you, at the expense of blurring or even changing your meaning. Probably it is better to put off using words as long as possible and get one's meaning as clear as one can through pictures or sensations. Afterwards one can choose – not simply *accept* – the phrases that will best cover the meaning, and then switch round and decide what impression one's words are likely to make on another person. This last effort of the mind cuts out all stale or mixed images, all prefabricated phrases, needless repetitions, and humbug and vagueness generally. But one can often be in doubt about the effect of a word or a phrase, and one needs rules that one can rely on when instinct fails. I think the following rules will cover most cases:

i. Never use a metaphor, simile or other figure of speech which you are used to seeing in print.
ii. Never use a long word where a short one will do.
iii. If it is possible to cut a word out, always cut it out.
iv. Never use the passive where you can use the active.
v. Never use a foreign phrase, a scientific word or a jargon word if you can think of an everyday English equivalent.
vi. Break any of these rules sooner than say anything outright barbarous.

These rules sound elementary, and so they are, but they demand a deep change of attitude in anyone who has grown used to writing in the style now fashionable. One could keep all of them and still write bad English, but one could not write the kind of stuff that I quoted in those five specimens at the beginning of this article.

I have not here been considering the literary use of language, but merely language as an instrument for expressing and not for concealing or preventing thought. Stuart Chase* and others have come near to claiming that all abstract words are meaningless, and have used this as a pretext for advocating a kind of political quietism. Since you don't know what fascism is, how can you struggle against fascism? One need not swallow such absurdities as this, but one ought to recognize that the present political chaos is connected with the decay of language, and that one can probably bring about some improvement by starting at the verbal end. If you simplify your English, you are freed from the worst follies of orthodoxy. You cannot speak any of the necessary dialects, and when you make a stupid remark its stupidity will be obvious, even to yourself. Political language – and with variations this is true of all political parties, from Conservatives to anarchists – is designed to make lies sound truthful and murder respectable, and to give an appearance of solidity to pure wind. One cannot change this all in a moment, but one can at least change one's own habits, and from time to time one can even, if one jeers loudly enough, send some worn-out and useless phrase – some "jackboot", "Achilles heel", "hotbed", "melting pot", "acid test", "veritable inferno" or other lump of verbal refuse – into the dustbin where it belongs.

The Sporting Spirit*

Now that the brief visit of the Dynamo football team* has come to an end, it is possible to say publicly what many thinking people were saying privately before the Dynamos ever arrived. That is, that sport is an unfailing cause of ill will, and that if such a visit as this had any effect at all on Anglo-Soviet relations, it could only be to make them slightly worse than before.

Even the newspapers have been unable to conceal the fact that at least two of the four matches played led to much bad feeling. At the Arsenal match, I am told by someone who was there, a British and a Russian player came to blows and the crowd booed the referee. The Glasgow match, someone else informs me, was simply a free-for-all from the start. And then there was the controversy, typical of our nationalistic age, about the composition of the Arsenal team. Was it really an all-England team, as claimed by the Russians, or merely a league team, as claimed by the British? And did the Dynamos end their tour abruptly in order to avoid playing an all-England team? As usual, everyone answers these questions according to his political predilections. Not quite everyone, however. I noted with interest, as an instance of the vicious passions that football provokes, that the sporting correspondent of the Russophile *News Chronicle* took the anti-Russian line and maintained that Arsenal was *not* an all-England team. No doubt the controversy will continue to echo for years in the footnotes of history books. Meanwhile the result of the Dynamos' tour, in so far as it has had any result, will have been to create fresh animosity on both sides.

And how could it be otherwise? I am always amazed when I hear people saying that sport creates goodwill between the nations, and that if only the common peoples of the world could meet one another at football or cricket, they would have no inclination to meet on the battlefield. Even if one didn't know from concrete examples (the 1936 Olympic Games, for instance) that international sporting contests lead to orgies of hatred, one could deduce it from general principles.

Nearly all the sports practised nowadays are competitive. You play to win, and the game has little meaning unless you do your utmost to win. On the village green, where you pick up sides and no feeling of local patriotism is involved, it is possible to play simply for the fun and exercise – but as soon as the question of prestige arises, as soon as you feel that you and some larger unit will be disgraced if you lose, the most savage combative instincts are aroused. Anyone who has played even in a school football match knows this.

THE SPORTING SPIRIT

At the international level sport is frankly mimic warfare. But the significant thing is not the behaviour of the players but the attitude of the spectators, and, behind the spectators, of the nations who work themselves into furies over these absurd contests, and seriously believe – at any rate for short periods – that running, jumping and kicking a ball are tests of national virtue.

Even a leisurely game like cricket, demanding grace rather than strength, can cause much ill will, as we saw in the controversy over bodyline bowling and over the rough tactics of the Australian team that visited England in 1921. Football, a game in which everyone gets hurt and every nation has its own style of play which seems unfair to foreigners, is far worse. Worst of all is boxing. One of the most horrible sights in the world is a fight between white and coloured boxers before a mixed audience. But a boxing audience is always disgusting, and the behaviour of the women, in particular, is such that the army, I believe, does not allow them to attend its contests. At any rate, two or three years ago, when Home Guards and regular troops were holding a boxing tournament, I was placed on guard at the door of the hall, with orders to keep the women out.

In England, the obsession with sport is bad enough, but even fiercer passions are aroused in young countries where games playing and nationalism are both recent developments. In countries like India or Burma, it is necessary at football matches to have strong cordons of police to keep the crowd from invading the field. In Burma, I have seen the supporters of one side break through the police and disable the goalkeeper of the opposing side at a critical moment. The first big football match that was played in Spain about fifteen years ago led to an uncontrollable riot. As soon as strong feelings of rivalry are aroused, the notion of playing the game according to the rules always vanishes. People want to see one side on top and the other side humiliated, and they forget that victory gained through cheating or through the intervention of the crowd is meaningless. Even when the spectators don't intervene physically they try to influence the game by cheering their own side and "rattling" opposing players with boos and insults. Serious sport has nothing to do with fair play. It is bound up with hatred, jealousy, boastfulness, disregard of all rules and sadistic pleasure in witnessing violence: in other words it is war minus the shooting.

Instead of blah-blahing about the clean, healthy rivalry of the football field and the great part played by the Olympic Games in bringing the nations together, it is more useful to enquire how and why this modern cult of sport arose. Most of the games we now play are of ancient origin, but sport does not seem to have been taken very seriously between Roman times and the nineteenth century. Even in the English public schools the games cult did not start till the later part of the last century. Dr Arnold,* generally regarded as the founder of the modern public school, looked on games as simply a waste of time. Then, chiefly in England and the United States, games were built up into a heavily financed activity, capable of attracting vast crowds and rousing savage passions, and the infection spread from country to country. It is the most violently combative sports, football and boxing, that have spread the widest. There cannot be much doubt that the whole thing is bound up with the rise of nationalism – that is, with the lunatic modern habit of identifying oneself with large power units and seeing everything in terms of competitive prestige. Also, organized games are more likely to flourish in urban communities where the average human being lives a sedentary or at least a confined life, and does not get much opportunity for creative labour. In a rustic community a boy or young man works off a good deal of his surplus energy by walking, swimming, snowballing, climbing trees, riding horses, and by various sports involving cruelty to animals, such as fishing, cockfighting and ferreting for rats. In a big town one must indulge in group activities if one wants an outlet for one's physical strength or for one's sadistic impulses. Games are taken seriously in London and New York, and they were taken seriously in Rome and Byzantium: in the Middle Ages they were played, and probably played with much physical brutality, but they were not mixed up with politics nor a cause of group hatreds.

If you wanted to add to the vast fund of ill will existing in the world at this moment, you could hardly do it better than by a series of football matches between Jews and Arabs, Germans and Czechs, Indians and British, Russians and Poles, and Italians and Yugoslavs, each match to be watched by a mixed audience of 100,000 spectators. I do not, of course, suggest that sport is one of the main causes of international rivalry; big-scale sport is itself, I think, merely another effect of the causes that have produced nationalism. Still, you do make things worse by sending forth a team of eleven men, labelled as national champions, to do battle against some rival team, and allowing it to be felt on all sides that whichever nation is defeated will "lose face".

I hope, therefore, that we shan't follow up the visit of the Dynamos by sending a British team to the USSR. If we must do so, then let us send a second-rate team which is sure to be beaten and cannot be claimed to represent Britain as a whole. There are quite enough real causes of trouble already, and we need not add to them by encouraging young men to kick each other on the shins amid the roars of infuriated spectators.

In Defence of English Cooking*

We have heard a good deal of talk in recent years about the desirability of attracting foreign tourists to this country. It is well known that England's two worst faults, from a foreign visitor's point of view, are the gloom of our Sundays and the difficulty of buying a drink.

Both of these are due to fanatical minorities who will need a lot of quelling, including extensive legislation. But there is one point on which public opinion could bring about a rapid change for the better: I mean cooking.

It is commonly said, even by the English themselves, that English cooking is the worst in the world. It is supposed to be not merely incompetent, but also imitative, and I even read quite recently, in a book by a French writer, the remark: "The best English cooking is, of course, simply French cooking."

Now that is simply not true. As anyone who has lived long abroad will know, there is a whole host of delicacies which it is quite impossible to obtain outside the English-speaking countries. No doubt the list could be added to, but here are some of the things that I myself have sought for in foreign countries and failed to find.

First of all, kippers, Yorkshire pudding, Devonshire cream, muffins and crumpets. Then a list of puddings that would be interminable if I gave it in full: I will pick out for special mention Christmas pudding, treacle tart and apple dumplings. Then an almost equally long list of cakes: for instance, dark plum cake (such as you used to get at Buzzard's before the war), shortbread and saffron buns. Also innumerable kinds of biscuit, which exist, of course, elsewhere, but are generally admitted to be better and crisper in England.

Then there are the various ways of cooking potatoes that are peculiar to our own country. Where else do you see potatoes roasted under the joint, which is far and away the best way of cooking them? Or the delicious potato cakes that you get in the north of England? And it is far better to cook new potatoes in the English way – that is, boiled with mint and then served with a little melted butter or margarine – than to fry them as is done in most countries.

Then there are the various sauces peculiar to England. For instance, bread sauce, horseradish sauce, mint sauce and apple sauce – not to mention redcurrant jelly, which is excellent with mutton as well as with hare, and various kinds of sweet pickle, which we seem to have in greater profusion than most countries.

What else? Outside these islands I have never seen a haggis, except one that came out of a tin, nor Dublin prawns, nor Oxford marmalade, nor several other kinds of jam (marrow jam and bramble jelly, for instance), nor sausages of quite the same kind as ours.

Then there are the English cheeses. There are not many of them but I fancy that Stilton is the best cheese of its type in the world, with Wensleydale not far behind. English apples are also outstandingly good, particularly the Cox's Orange Pippin.

And finally, I would like to put in a word for English bread. All the bread is good, from the enormous Jewish loaves flavoured with caraway seeds to the Russian rye bread which is the colour of black treacle. Still, if there is anything quite as good as the soft part of the crust from an English cottage loaf (how soon shall we be seeing cottage loaves again?) I do not know of it.

No doubt some of the things I have named above could be obtained in Continental Europe, just as it is possible in London to obtain vodka or bird's nest soup. But they are all native to our shores, and over huge areas they are literally unheard of.

South of, say, Brussels, I do not imagine that you would succeed in getting hold of a suet pudding. In French there is not even a word that exactly translates "suet". The French, also, never use mint in cookery and do not use blackcurrants except as a basis of a drink.

It will be seen that we have no cause to be ashamed of our cookery, so far as originality goes or so far as the ingredients go. And yet it must be admitted that there is a serious snag from the foreign visitor's point of view. This is that you practically don't find good English cooking outside a private house. If you want, say, a good, rich slice of Yorkshire pudding you are more likely to get it in the poorest English home than in a restaurant, which is where the visitor necessarily eats most of his meals.

It is a fact that restaurants which are distinctively English and which also sell good food are very hard to find. Pubs, as a rule, sell no food at all, other than potato crisps and tasteless sandwiches. The expensive restaurants and hotels almost all imitate French cookery and write their menus in French, while if you want a good cheap meal you gravitate naturally towards a Greek, Italian or Chinese restaurant. We are not likely to succeed in attracting tourists while England is thought of as a country of bad food and unintelligible by-laws. At present one cannot do much about it, but sooner or later rationing will come to an end, and then will be the moment for our national cookery to revive. It is not a law of nature that every restaurant in England should be either foreign or bad, and the first step towards an improvement will be a less long-suffering attitude in the British public itself.

Nonsense Poetry*

In many languages, it is said, there is no nonsense poetry, and there is not a great deal of it even in English. The bulk of it is in nursery rhymes and scraps of folk poetry, some of which may not have been strictly nonsensical at the start, but have become so because their original application has been forgotten. For example, the rhyme about Margery Daw:

> See-saw, Margery Daw,
> Dobbin shall have a new master.
> He shall have but a penny a day
> Because he can't go any faster.

Or the other version that I learnt in Oxfordshire as a little boy:

> See-saw, Margery Daw,
> Sold her bed and lay upon straw.
> Wasn't she a silly slut
> To sell her bed and lie upon dirt?

It may be that there was once a real person called Margery Daw, and perhaps there was even a Dobbin who somehow came into the story. When Shakespeare makes Edgar in *King Lear* quote "Pillicock sat on Pillicock hill", and similar fragments, he is uttering nonsense, but no doubt these fragments come from forgotten ballads in which they once had a meaning. The typical scrap of folk poetry which one quotes almost unconsciously is not exactly nonsense but a sort of musical comment on some recurring event, such as "One a penny, two a penny, hot-cross buns", or "Polly, put the kettle on, we'll all have tea". Some of these seemingly frivolous rhymes actually express a deeply pessimistic view of life, the churchyard wisdom of the peasant. For instance:

> Solomon Grundy,
> Born on Monday,
> Christened on Tuesday,
> Married on Wednesday,
> Took ill on Thursday,
> Worse on Friday,
> Died on Saturday,

> Buried on Sunday,
> And that was the end of Solomon Grundy.

which is a gloomy story, but remarkably similar to yours or mine.

Until Surrealism made a deliberate raid on the unconscious, poetry that aimed at being nonsense, apart from the meaningless refrains of songs, does not seem to have been common. This gives a special position to Edward Lear, whose nonsense rhymes have just been edited by Mr R.L. Mégroz, who was also responsible for the Penguin edition a year or two before the war.* Lear was one of the first writers to deal in pure fantasy, with imaginary countries and made-up words, without any satirical purpose. His poems are not all of them equally nonsensical; some of them get their effect by a perversion of logic, but they are all alike in that their underlying feeling is sad and not bitter. They express a kind of amiable lunacy, a natural sympathy with whatever is weak and absurd. Lear could fairly be called the originator of the limerick, though verses in almost the same metrical form are to be found in earlier writers, and what is sometimes considered a weakness in his limericks – that is, the fact that the rhyme is the same in the first and last lines – is part of their charm. The very slight change increases the impression of ineffectuality, which might be spoilt if there were some striking surprise. For example:

> There was a young lady of Portugal
> Whose ideas were excessively nautical;
> She climbed up a tree
> To examine the sea,
> But declared she would never leave Portugal.

It is significant that almost no limericks since Lear's have been both printable and funny enough to seem worth quoting. But he is really seen at his best in certain longer poems, such as 'The Owl and the Pussy-Cat' or 'The Courtship of the Yonghy-Bonghy-Bò':

> On the Coast of Coromandel,
> Where the early pumpkins blow,
> In the middle of the woods
> Lived the Yonghy-Bonghy-Bò.
> Two old chairs, and half a candle –
> One old jug without a handle –
> These were all his worldly goods:
> In the middle of the woods,
> These were all the worldly goods

Of the Yonghy-Bonghy-Bò,
Of the Yonghy-Bonghy-Bò.

Later there appears a lady with some white Dorking hens, and an inconclusive love affair follows. Mr Mégroz thinks, plausibly enough, that this may refer to some incident in Lear's own life. He never married, and it is easy to guess that there was something seriously wrong in his sex life. A psychiatrist could no doubt find all kinds of significance in his drawings and in the recurrence of certain made-up words such as "runcible". His health was bad, and as he was the youngest of twenty-one children in a poor family, he must have known anxiety and hardship in very early life. It is clear that he was unhappy and by nature solitary, in spite of having good friends.

Aldous Huxley, in praising Lear's fantasies as a sort of assertion of freedom, has pointed out that the "they" of the limericks represent common sense, legality and the duller virtues generally. "They" are the realists, the practical men, the sober citizens in bowler hats who are always anxious to stop you doing anything worth doing. For instance:

There was an Old Man of Whitehaven,
Who danced a quadrille with a raven;
But they said, "It's absurd
To encourage this bird!"
So they smashed that Old Man of Whitehaven.

To smash somebody just for dancing a quadrille with a raven is exactly the kind of thing that "they" would do. Herbert Read has also praised Lear, and is inclined to prefer his verse to that of Lewis Carroll, as being purer fantasy. For myself, I must say that I find Lear funniest when he is least arbitrary and when a touch of burlesque or perverted logic makes its appearance. When he gives his fancy free play, as in his imaginary names, or in things like 'Three Receipts for Domestic Cookery', he can be silly and tiresome. 'The Pobble Who Has No Toes' is haunted by the ghost of logic, and I think it is the element of sense in it that makes it funny. The Pobble, it may be remembered, went fishing in the Bristol Channel:

And all the Sailors and Admirals cried,
When they saw him nearing the further side –
"He has gone to fish, for his Aunt Jobiska's
Runcible Cat with crimson whiskers!"

The thing that is funny here is the burlesque touch, the Admirals. What is arbitrary – the word "runcible", and the cat's crimson whiskers – is merely rather embarrassing. While the Pobble was in the water some unidentified creatures came and ate his toes off, and when he got home his aunt remarked:

> "It's a fact the whole world knows,
> That Pobbles are happier without their toes,"

which once again is funny because it has a meaning, and one might even say a political significance. For the whole theory of authoritarian governments is summed up in the statement that Pobbles were happier without their toes. So also with the well-known limerick:

> There was an Old Person of Basing,
> Whose presence of mind was amazing;
> He purchased a steed,
> Which he rode at full speed,
> And escaped from the people of Basing.

It is not quite arbitrary. The funniness is in the gentle implied criticism of the people of Basing, who once again are "they", the respectable ones, the right-thinking, art-hating majority.

The writer closest to Lear among his contemporaries was Lewis Carroll, who, however, was less essentially fantastic – and, in my opinion, funnier. Since then, as Mr Mégroz points out in his Introduction, Lear's influence has been considerable, but it is hard to believe that it has been altogether good. The silly whimsiness of present-day children's books could perhaps be partly traced back to him. At any rate, the idea of deliberately setting out to write nonsense, though it came off in Lear's case, is a doubtful one. Probably the best nonsense poetry is produced gradually and accidentally, by communities rather than by individuals. As a comic draughtsman, on the other hand, Lear's influence must have been beneficial. James Thurber, for instance, must surely owe something to Lear, directly or indirectly.

Pleasure Spots*

Some months ago I cut out of a shiny magazine some paragraphs written by a female journalist and describing the pleasure resort of the future. She had recently been spending some time at Honolulu, where the rigours of war do not seem to have been very noticeable. However, "a transport pilot... told me that with all the inventiveness packed into this war, it was a pity someone hadn't found out how a tired and life-hungry man could relax, rest, play poker, drink and make love, all at once, and round the clock, and come out of it feeling good and fresh and ready for the job again." This reminded her of an entrepreneur she had met recently who was planning a "pleasure spot which he thinks will catch on tomorrow as dog racing and dance halls did yesterday". The entrepreneur's dream is described in some detail:

> His blueprints pictured a space covering several acres, under a series of sliding roofs – for the British weather is unreliable – and with a central space spread over with an immense dance floor made of translucent plastic which can be illuminated from beneath. Around it are grouped other functional spaces, at different levels. Balcony bars and restaurants commanding high views of the city roofs, and ground-level replicas. A battery of skittle alleys. Two blue lagoons: one, periodically agitated by waves, for strong swimmers, and another, a smooth and summery pool, for playtime bathers. Sunlight lamps over the pools to simulate high summer on days when the roofs don't slide back to disclose a hot sun in a cloudless sky. Rows of bunks on which people wearing sunglasses and slips can lie and start a tan or deepen an existing one under a sunray lamp.
>
> Music seeping through hundreds of grilles connected with a central distributing stage, where dance or symphonic orchestras play or the radio programme can be caught, amplified and disseminated. Outside, two 1,000-car parks. One, free. The other, an open-air cinema drive-in, cars queueing to move through turnstiles, and the film thrown on a giant screen facing a row of assembled cars. Uniformed male attendants check the cars, provide free aid and water, sell petrol and oil. Girls in white satin slacks take orders for buffet dishes and drinks, and bring them on trays.

Whenever one hears such phrases as "pleasure spot", "pleasure resort", "pleasure city", it is difficult not to remember the often-quoted opening of Coleridge's 'Kubla Khan'.*

> In Xanadu did Kubla Khan
> A stately pleasure-dome decree:
> Where Alph, the sacred river, ran
> Through caverns measureless to man
>   Down to a sunless sea.
> So twice five miles of fertile ground
> With walls and towers were girdled round:
> And there were gardens bright with sinuous rills
> Where blossomed many an incense-bearing tree;
> And here were forests ancient as the hills,
> Enfolding sunny spots of greenery.

But it will be seen that Coleridge has got it all wrong. He strikes a false note straight off with that talk about "sacred" rivers and "measureless" caverns. In the hands of the above-mentioned entrepreneur, Kubla Khan's project would have become something quite different. The caverns, air-conditioned, discreetly lighted and with their original rocky interior buried under layers of tastefully coloured plastics, would be turned into a series of tea grottoes in the Moorish, Caucasian or Hawaiian styles. Alph, the sacred river, would be dammed up to make an artificially warmed bathing pool, while the sunless sea would be illuminated from below with pink electric lights, and one would cruise over it in real Venetian gondolas each equipped with its own radio set. The forests and "spots of greenery" referred to by Coleridge would be cleaned up to make way for glass-covered tennis courts, a bandstand, a roller-skating rink and perhaps a nine-hole golf course. In short, there would be everything that a "life-hungry" man could desire.

I have no doubt that, all over the world, hundreds of pleasure resorts similar to the one described above are now being planned, and perhaps are even being built. It is unlikely that they will be finished – world events will see to that – but they represent faithfully enough the modern civilized man's idea of pleasure. Something of the kind is already partially attained in the more magnificent dance halls, movie palaces, hotels, restaurants and luxury liners. On a pleasure cruise or in a Lyons Corner House* one already gets something more than a glimpse of this future paradise. Analysed, its main characteristics are these:

1. One is never alone.
2. One never does anything for oneself.
3. One is never within sight of wild vegetation or natural objects of any kind.
4. Light and temperature are always artificially regulated.
5. One is never out of the sound of music.

The music – and if possible it should be the same music for everybody – is the most important ingredient. Its function is to prevent thought and conversation, and to shut out any natural sound, such as the song of birds or the whistling of the wind, that might otherwise intrude. The radio is already consciously used for this purpose by innumerable people. In very many English homes the radio is literally never turned off, though it is manipulated from time to time so as to make sure that only light music will come out of it. I know people who will keep the radio playing all through a meal and at the same time continue talking just loudly enough for the voices and the music to cancel out. This is done with a definite purpose. The music prevents the conversation from becoming serious or even coherent, while the chatter of voices stops one from listening attentively to the music and thus prevents the onset of that dreaded thing, thought. For

> The lights must never go out.
> The music must always play,
> Lest we should see where we are;
> Lost in a haunted wood,
> Children afraid of the dark
> Who have never been happy or good.*

It is difficult not to feel that the unconscious aim in the most typical modern pleasure resorts is a return to the womb. For there, too, one was never alone, one never saw daylight, the temperature was always regulated, one did not have to worry about work or food, and one's thoughts, if any, were drowned by a continuous rhythmic throbbing.

When one looks at Coleridge's very different conception of a "pleasure dome", one sees that it revolves partly round gardens and partly round caverns, rivers, forests and mountains with "deep romantic chasms" – in short, round what is called nature. But the whole notion of admiring nature, and feeling a sort of religious awe in the presence of glaciers, deserts or waterfalls, is bound up with the sense of man's littleness and weakness against the power of the universe. The moon is beautiful partly because we cannot reach it; the sea is impressive because one can never be sure of crossing it safely. Even the pleasure one takes in a flower – and this is true even of a botanist who knows all there is to be known about the flower – is dependent partly on the sense of mystery. But meanwhile man's power over nature is steadily increasing. With the aid of the atomic bomb we could literally move mountains; we could even, so it is said, alter the climate of the earth by melting the polar ice caps and irrigating the Sahara. Isn't there, therefore, something sentimental and obscurantist in preferring birdsong to swing music and in wanting to leave a few patches of wildness here and there instead of covering the whole surface of the earth with a network of *Autobahnen** flooded by artificial sunlight?

The question only arises because in exploring the physical universe man has made no attempt to explore himself. Much of what goes by the name of pleasure is simply an effort to destroy consciousness. If one started by asking: what is man? What are his needs? How can he best express himself? one would discover that merely having the power to avoid work and live one's life from birth to death in electric light and to the tune of tinned music is not a reason for doing so. Man needs warmth, society, leisure, comfort and security; he also needs solitude, creative work and the sense of wonder. If he recognized this he could use the products of science and industrialism eclectically, applying always the same test: does this make me more human or less human? He would then learn that the highest happiness does not lie in relaxing, resting, playing poker, drinking and making love simultaneously. And the instinctive horror which all sensitive people feel at the progressive mechanization of life would be seen not to be a mere sentimental archaism but to be fully justified. For man only stays human by preserving large patches of simplicity in his life, while the tendency of many modern inventions – in particular the film, the radio and the aeroplane – is to weaken his consciousness, dull his curiosity and, in general, drive him nearer to the animals.

A Nice Cup of Tea*

If you look up "tea" in the first cookery book that comes to hand you will probably find that it is unmentioned; or at most you will find a few lines of sketchy instructions which give no ruling on several of the most important points.

This is curious, not only because tea is one of the mainstays of civilization in this country, as well as in Eire, Australia and New Zealand, but because the best manner of making it is the subject of violent disputes.

When I look through my own recipe for the perfect cup of tea, I find no fewer than eleven outstanding points. On perhaps two of them there would be pretty general agreement, but at least four others are acutely controversial. Here are my own eleven rules, every one of which I regard as golden:

First of all, one should use Indian or Ceylonese tea. China tea has virtues which are not to be despised nowadays – it is economical, and one can drink it without milk – but there is not much stimulation in it. One does not feel wiser, braver or more optimistic after drinking it. Anyone who uses that comforting phrase "a nice cup of tea" invariably means Indian tea. Secondly, tea should be made in small quantities – that is, in a teapot. Tea out of an urn is always tasteless, while army tea, made in a cauldron, tastes of grease and whitewash. The teapot should be made of china or earthenware. Silver or Britannia-ware pots produce inferior tea and enamel pots are worse – though curiously enough a pewter teapot (a rarity nowadays) is not so bad. Thirdly, the pot should be warmed beforehand. This is better done by placing it on the hob than by the usual method of swilling it out with hot water. Fourthly, the tea should be strong. For a pot holding a quart, if you are going to fill it nearly to the brim, six heaped teaspoons would be about right. In a time of rationing this is not an idea that can be realized on every day of the week, but I maintain that one strong cup of tea is better than twenty weak ones. All true tea lovers not only like their tea strong but like it a little stronger with each year that passes – a fact which is recognized in the extra ration issued to old-age pensioners. Fifthly, the tea should be put straight into the pot. No strainers, muslin bags or other devices to imprison the tea. In some countries teapots are fitted with little dangling baskets under the spout to catch the stray leaves, which are supposed to be harmful. Actually one can swallow tea leaves in considerable quantities without ill effect, and if the tea is not loose in the pot it never infuses properly. Sixthly, one should take the teapot to the kettle and not the other way about. The water should be actually boiling at the moment of impact, which means that one should keep it on the flame while one pours. Some people add that one should only use water that has been freshly brought to the boil, but I have never noticed that this makes any difference. Seventhly, after making the tea, one should stir it, or better, give the pot a good shake, afterwards allowing the leaves to settle. Eighthly, one should drink out of a breakfast cup – that is the cylindrical type of cup, not the flat, shallow type. The breakfast cup holds more, and with the other kind one's tea is always half cold before one has well started on it. Ninthly, one should pour the cream off the milk before using it for tea. Milk that is too creamy always gives tea a sickly taste. Tenthly, one should pour tea into the cup first. This is one of the most controversial points of all; indeed, in every family in Britain there are probably two schools of thought on the subject. The milk-first school can bring forward some fairly strong arguments, but I maintain that my own argument is unanswerable. This is that, by putting the tea in first and then stirring as one pours, one can exactly regulate the amount of milk, whereas one is liable to put in too much milk if one does it the other way round.

Lastly, tea – unless one is drinking it in the Russian style – should be drunk *without sugar*. I know very well that I am in a minority here. But still, how can you call yourself a true tea lover if you destroy the flavour of your tea by putting sugar in it? It would be equally reasonable to put pepper or salt. Tea is meant to be bitter, just as beer is meant to be bitter. If you sweeten it, you are no longer tasting the tea, you are merely tasting the sugar; you could make a very similar drink by dissolving sugar in plain hot water.

Some people would answer that they don't like tea in itself, that they only drink it in order to be warmed and stimulated, and they need sugar to take the taste away. To those misguided people I would say: try drinking tea without sugar for, say, a fortnight and it is very unlikely that you will ever want to ruin your tea by sweetening it again.

These are not the only controversial points that arise in connection with tea drinking, but they are sufficient to show how subtilized the whole business has become. There is also the mysterious social etiquette surrounding the teapot (why is it considered vulgar to drink out of your saucer, for instance?) and much might be written about the subsidiary uses of tea leaves, such as telling fortunes, predicting the arrival of visitors, feeding rabbits, healing burns and sweeping the carpet. It is worth paying attention to such details as warming the pot and using water that is really boiling, so as to make quite sure of wringing out of one's ration the twenty good, strong cups that two ounces, properly handled, ought to represent.

The Politics of Starvation*

A few days ago I received a wad of literature from the "Save Europe Now" Committee, which has been attempting – without much encouragement from the government or help from the press – to increase the supply of food from this country to Europe. They quote a series of statements from authoritative sources, which I will come back to in a moment, and which go to show that whereas we are reasonably well off and the United States is enjoying an orgy of overeating, a good part of Europe is lapsing into brute starvation.

In the *Observer* of 13th January, however, I have just read a signed article by Air Chief Marshal Sir Philip Joubert,* expressing the contrary opinion:

> To one returning from overseas in this seventh winter of war (writes Sir Philip), the appearance of the British people is tragic. They seem morose, lacking in spring; and laughter comes with difficulty. The children look pallid and suety – fat but not fit. They compare very ill with the rosy-cheeked youngsters of Denmark, who have all the meat and fat they need, with plenty of fruit in season.

His main thesis is that we need more meat, fats and eggs – i.e. more of the rationed foods – and less starch. The official figures showing that, in fact, we are healthier than we were before the war convey a false impression: first – this is a quite extraordinary argument – because health and nutrition were admittedly in a bad way before the war, so that the present improvement is nothing to write home about; secondly because the drop in the death rate merely means a "greater expectation of existence" and one must not "confuse existence with life". Unless we can attain "liveliness, vitality, vigour", for which meat, fat, fruit and cane sugar are required, we cannot make the effort needed for the task of reconstruction. Sir Philip ends his article:

> As for those who would cut our present rations further so as to give more to the Germans, there must be many who would reply to their demands: "I would sooner that my children, brought up in freedom and goodwill towards men, should enjoy full vigour than the Germans, who may be using their strength to make war on the world again in another generation."

It will be seen that he is assuming (a) that any further export of food means a cut in rations here, and (b) that it is only proposed to send food to Germany.

And in fact that is the form in which the big public has heard of this project, although those responsible have emphasized from the start that they were only proposing a *voluntary* surrender of certain foodstuffs, by those sections of the population to whom it would do no harm, and were *not* proposing it for the sole benefit of Germany.

Now here are a few facts from the latest bulletin of the "Save Europe Now" Committee. In Budapest, in November, the chemists were closing down for lack of supplies, the hospitals had neither windows, fuel nor anaesthetics, and it was calculated that the town contained 30,000 stray children, some of whom had formed themselves into criminal bands. In December, "independent observers" considered that unless fresh food supplies were brought quickly, a million people would die of starvation in Hungary this winter. In Vienna (November) "the food for hospital surgeons consists of unsweetened coffee, a very thin soup and bread. Less than 500 calories in all", while the Austrian Secretary of State, in December, described the thickly populated areas of eastern Austria as being menaced by "boundless misery, epidemics, crime, physical and moral decline". In Czechoslovakia, in November, the Foreign Minister appealed to Britain and the USA to send fats and meat to save 700,000 "very badly fed children, of whom 50 per cent already have tuberculosis". In Germany, the Saar children are "slowly starving". In the British zone, Field Marshal Montgomery said that he was "entirely dependent on imports of wheat if he was to maintain the present ration scales for the German people, ranging from 1,200 to 1,500 calories". This was in November. About the same time General Eisenhower, speaking of the French zone, said that "the normal ration of 1,100 calories a day for the average consumer was consistently not met". And so on. Meanwhile it appears that our own average consumption is about 2,800 or 2,900 calories a day, while the most recent figures of deaths from tuberculosis, and of deaths of mothers in childbirth and of children of all ages up to five, are the lowest ever recorded. As for the USA, consumption of butter has just risen largely and meat rationing has come to an end. The Secretary of Agriculture estimates that "the lifting of rationing will make meat available for civilians at the rate of 165 lb annually – the pre-war supply was in the neighbourhood of 125 lb".

Even if the above figures do not convey much impression, who has not seen the photographs of skeleton-like children in Greece and other places – children to whom no one would think of applying Sir Philip Joubert's term, "suety"? Yet there has undoubtedly been considerable resistance to the idea that we should send more food to Europe. The "Save Europe Now" Committee, though they are now pursuing more limited aims, started off with the suggestion that those who felt inclined should sacrifice their points,* or some of their points, and that the government should forward the food so saved to the famine-stricken areas. The scheme was discouraged officially, but it also had a cold reception from many private persons. People who would have been in a position to give it good publicity were frankly frightened of it, and the general public was allowed to imagine that what was proposed was to take food from British housewives in order to give it to German war criminals. Indeed, the whole manner in which this business has been discussed illustrates the curious dishonesty that infects every political issue nowadays.

There are two things that make what one might call the official Left, Labour or communist, nervous of any scheme which might mean sending extra food to Germany. One is fear of the working-class reaction. The working classes, so it is said, would resent even a voluntary arrangement which meant, in effect, that people in the higher income groups, who buy unrationed foods and eat some of their meals in restaurants, should give up their surplus. The average woman in the fish queue, it is feared, would answer: "If there's really any food to spare, let *us* have it. Or why not give it to the coal miners?" I don't know whether this would really be the reaction, if the issues were fully explained. I suspect that some of the people who argue thus have in mind the sordid consideration that if we are to sacrifice food in sufficient quantities to make any difference, it would mean not merely giving up points but curtailing restaurant feeding. In practice, whatever it may be in intention, our rationing system is thoroughly undemocratic, and an all-round row on the subject of the export of food might draw attention to this fact. That is part of the reason, I think, why this question has not been fully discussed in print.

But another consideration, even less mentionable, also enters. Food is a political weapon, or is thought of as a political weapon. The hungriest areas are either in the Russian zone or in the parts of Europe that are divided between the USSR and the Western Allies. Many people calculate that if we send more food to, say, Hungary, British or American influence in Hungary will increase – whereas if we let the Hungarians starve and the Russians feed them, they are more likely to look towards the USSR. All those who are strongly Russophile are therefore against sending extra food to Europe, while some people are probably in favour of sending food merely because they see it as a way of weakening Russian prestige. No one has been honest enough to avow such motives, but you have only to look through the lists of those who have – and of those who haven't – supported the "Save Europe Now" campaign to see how the land lies.

The folly of all such calculations lies in supposing that you can ever get good results from starvation. Whatever the ultimate political settlement in Europe may be, it can only be worse if it has been preceded by years of hunger, misery, banditry and ignorance. Air Marshal Joubert advises us to feed ourselves rather than feed German children who will be fighting against us a generation hence. This is the "realistic" view. In 1918 the "realistic" ones were also in favour of keeping up the blockade after the Armistice. We did keep up the blockade, and the children we starved then were the young men who were bombing us in 1940. No one, perhaps, could have foreseen just that result, but people of goodwill could and did foresee that the results of wantonly starving Germany, and of making a vindictive peace, would be evil. So also with raising our own rations, as we shall perhaps be doing before long, while famine descends on Europe. But if we do decide to do this, at least let the issues be plainly discussed, and let the photographs of starving children be well publicized in the press, so that the people of this country may realize just what they are doing.

The Prevention of Literature*

About a year ago I attended a meeting of the PEN Club, the occasion being the tercentenary of Milton's *Areopagitica** – a pamphlet, it may be remembered, in defence of freedom of the press. Milton's famous phrase about the sin of "killing" a book was printed on the leaflets, advertising the meeting, which had been circulated beforehand.

There were four speakers on the platform. One of them delivered a speech which did deal with the freedom of the press, but only in relation to India; another said, hesitantly, and in very general terms, that liberty was a good thing; a third delivered an attack on the laws relating to obscenity in literature. The fourth devoted most of his speech to a defence of the Russian purges. Of the speeches from the body of the hall, some reverted to the question of obscenity and the laws that deal with it; others were simply eulogies of Soviet Russia. Moral liberty – the liberty to discuss sex questions frankly in print – seemed to be generally approved, but political liberty was not mentioned. Out of this concourse of several hundred people, perhaps half of whom were directly connected with the writing trade, there was not a single one who could point out that freedom of the press, if it means anything at all, means the freedom to criticize and oppose. Significantly, no speaker quoted from the pamphlet which was ostensibly being commemorated. Nor was there any mention of the various books that have been "killed" in this country and the United States during the war. In its net effect the meeting was a demonstration in favour of censorship.*

There was nothing particularly surprising in this. In our age, the idea of intellectual liberty is under attack from two directions. On the one side are its theoretical enemies, the apologists of totalitarianism, and on the other its immediate, practical enemies, monopoly and bureaucracy. Any writer or journalist who wants to retain his integrity finds himself thwarted by the general drift of society rather than by active persecution. The sort of things that are working against him are the concentration of the press in the hands of a few rich men, the grip of monopoly on radio and the films, the unwillingness of the public to spend money on books, making it necessary for nearly every writer to earn part of his living by hack work, the encroachment of official bodies like the MOI and the British Council, which help the writer to keep alive but also waste his time and dictate his opinions, and the continuous war atmosphere of the past ten years, whose distorting effects no one has been able to escape. Everything in our age conspires to turn the writer, and every other kind of artist as well, into a minor official, working on themes handed to him from above and never telling what seems to him the whole of the truth. But in struggling against this fate he gets no help from his own side: that is, there is no large body of opinion which will assure him that he is in the right. In the past, at any rate throughout the Protestant centuries, the idea of rebellion and the idea of intellectual integrity were mixed up. A heretic – political, moral, religious or aesthetic – was one who refused to outrage his own conscience. His outlook was summed up in the words of the Revivalist hymn:

> Dare to be a Daniel,
> Dare to stand alone;
> Dare to have a purpose firm,
> Dare to make it known.

To bring this hymn up to date one would have to add a "Don't" at the beginning of each line. For it is the peculiarity of our age that the rebels against the existing order, at any rate the most numerous and characteristic of them, are also rebelling against the idea of individual integrity. "Daring to stand alone" is ideologically criminal as well as practically dangerous. The independence of the writer and the artist is eaten away by vague economic forces, and at the same time it is undermined by those who should be its defenders. It is with the second process that I am concerned here.

Freedom of thought and of the press are usually attacked by arguments which are not worth bothering about. Anyone who has experience of lecturing and debating knows them off backwards. Here I am not trying to deal with the familiar claim that freedom is an illusion, or with the claim that there is more freedom in totalitarian countries than in democratic ones, but with the much more tenable and dangerous proposition that freedom is undesirable and that intellectual honesty is a form of antisocial selfishness. Although other aspects of the question are usually in the foreground, the controversy over freedom of speech and of the press is at the bottom a controversy over the desirability, or otherwise, of telling lies. What is really at issue is the right to report contemporary events truthfully, or as truthfully as is consistent with the ignorance, bias and self-deception from which every observer necessarily suffers. In saying this I may seem to be saying that straightforward "reportage" is the only branch of literature that matters – but I will try to show later that at every literary level, and probably in every one of the arts, the same issue arises in more or less subtilized forms. Meanwhile, it is necessary to strip away the irrelevancies in which this controversy is usually wrapped up.

The enemies of intellectual liberty always try to present their case as a plea for discipline versus individualism. The issue of truth versus untruth is as far as possible kept in the background. Although the point of emphasis may vary, the writer who refuses to sell his opinions is always branded as a mere egoist. He is accused, that is, either of wanting to shut himself up in an ivory tower, or of making an exhibitionist display of his own personality, or of resisting the inevitable current of history in an attempt to cling to unjustified privileges. The Catholic and the communist are alike in assuming that an opponent cannot be both honest and intelligent. Each of them tacitly claims that "the truth" has already been revealed, and that the heretic, if he is not simply a fool, is secretly aware of "the truth" and merely resists it out of selfish motives. In communist literature the attack on intellectual liberty is usually masked by oratory about "petty-bourgeois individualism", "the illusions of nineteenth-century liberalism", etc., and backed up by words of abuse such as "romantic" and "sentimental", which, since they do not have any agreed meaning, are difficult to answer. In this way the controversy is manoeuvred away from its real issue. One can accept, and most enlightened people would accept, the communist thesis that pure freedom will only exist in a classless society, and that one is most nearly free when one is working to bring such a society about. But slipped in with this is the quite unfounded claim that the Communist Party is itself aiming at the establishment of the classless society, and that in the USSR this aim is actually on the way to being realized. If the first claim is allowed to entail the second, there is almost no assault on common sense and common decency that cannot be justified. But meanwhile, the real point has been dodged. Freedom of the intellect means the freedom to report what one has seen, heard and felt, and not to be obliged to fabricate imaginary facts and feelings. The familiar tirades against "escapism", "individualism", "romanticism" and so forth are merely a forensic device, the aim of which is to make the perversion of history seem respectable.

Fifteen years ago, when one defended the freedom of the intellect, one had to defend it against conservatives, against Catholics and to some extent – for they were not of great importance in England – against fascists. Today one has to defend it against communists and "fellow travellers". One ought not to exaggerate the direct influence of the small English Communist Party, but there can be no question about the poisonous effect of the Russian mythos on English intellectual life. Because of it, known facts are suppressed and distorted to such an extent as to make it doubtful whether a true history of our times can ever be written. Let me give just one instance out of the hundreds that could be cited. When Germany collapsed, it was found that very large numbers of Soviet Russians – mostly, no doubt, from non-political motives – had changed sides and were fighting for the Germans. Also, a small but not negligible proportion of the Russian prisoners and Displaced Persons refused to go back to the USSR, and some of them, at least, were repatriated against their will. These facts, known to many journalists on the spot, went almost unmentioned in the British press, while at the same time Russophile publicists in England continued to justify the purges and deportations of 1936–38 by claiming that the USSR "had no quislings". The fog of lies and misinformation that surrounds such subjects as the Ukraine famine, the Spanish Civil War, Russian policy in Poland and so forth is not due entirely to conscious dishonesty, but any writer or journalist who is fully sympathetic to the USSR – sympathetic, that is, in the way the Russians themselves would want him to be – does have to acquiesce in deliberate falsification on important issues. I have before me what must be a very rare pamphlet, written by Maxim Litvinov* in 1918 and outlining the recent events in the Russian Revolution. It makes no mention of Stalin, but gives high praise to Trotsky, and also to Zinoviev, Kamenev* and others. What could be the attitude of even the most intellectually scrupulous communist towards such a pamphlet? At best, the obscurantist attitude of saying that it is an undesirable document and better suppressed. And if for some reason it were decided to issue a garbled version of the pamphlet, denigrating Trotsky and inserting references to Stalin, no communist who remained faithful to his Party could protest. Forgeries almost as gross as this have been committed in recent years. But the significant thing is not that they happen, but that even when they are known about they provoke no reaction from the left-wing intelligentsia as a whole. The argument that to tell the truth would be "inopportune" or would "play into the hands of" somebody or other is felt to be unanswerable, and few people are bothered by the prospect of the lies which they condone getting out of the newspapers and into the history books.

The organized lying practised by totalitarian states is not, as is sometimes claimed, a temporary expedient of the same nature as military deception. It is something integral to totalitarianism, something that would still continue even if concentration camps and secret police forces had ceased to be necessary. Among intelligent communists there is an underground legend to the effect that although the Russian government is obliged now to deal in lying propaganda, frame-up trials and so forth, it is secretly recording the true facts and will publish them at some future time. We can, I believe, be quite certain that this is not the case, because the mentality implied by such an action is that of a liberal historian who believes that the past cannot be altered and that a correct knowledge of history is valuable as a matter of course. From the totalitarian point of view history is something to be created rather than learnt. A totalitarian state is in effect a theocracy, and its ruling caste, in order to keep its position, has to be thought of as infallible. But since, in practice, no one is infallible, it is frequently necessary to rearrange past events in order to show that this or that mistake was not made, or that this or that imaginary triumph actually happened. Then, again, every major change in policy demands a corresponding change of doctrine and a revaluation of prominent historical figures. This kind of thing happens everywhere, but is clearly likelier to lead to outright falsification in societies where only one opinion is permissible at any given moment. Totalitarianism demands, in fact, the continuous alteration of the past, and in the long run probably demands a disbelief in the very existence of objective truth. The friends of totalitarianism in this country usually tend to argue that since absolute truth is not attainable, a big lie is no worse than a little lie. It is pointed out that all historical records are biased and inaccurate, or, on the other hand, that modern physics has proved that what seems to us the real world is an illusion, so that to believe in the evidence of one's senses is simply vulgar philistinism. A totalitarian society which succeeded in perpetuating itself would probably set up a schizophrenic system of thought, in which the laws of common sense held good in everyday life and in certain exact sciences, but could be disregarded by the politician, the historian and the sociologist. Already there are countless people who would think it scandalous to falsify a scientific textbook, but would see nothing wrong in falsifying an historical fact. It is at the point where literature and politics cross that totalitarianism exerts its greatest pressure on the intellectual. The exact sciences are not, at this date, menaced to anything like the same extent. This partly accounts for the fact that in all countries it is easier for the scientists than for the writers to line up behind their respective governments.

To keep the matter in perspective, let me repeat what I said at the beginning of this essay: that in England the immediate enemies of truthfulness, and hence of freedom of thought, are the press lords, the film magnates and the bureaucrats, but that on a long view the weakening of the desire for liberty among the intellectuals themselves is the most serious symptom of all. It may seem that all this time I have been talking about the effects of censorship not on literature as a whole but merely on one department of political journalism. Granted that Soviet Russia constitutes a sort of forbidden area in the British press, granted that issues like Poland, the Spanish Civil War, the Russo-German Pact and so forth are debarred from serious discussion, and that if you possess information that conflicts with the prevailing orthodoxy you are expected to distort it or to keep quiet about it – granted all this, why should literature in the wider sense be affected? Is every writer a politician, and is every book necessarily a work of straightforward "reportage"? Even under the tightest dictatorship, cannot the individual writer remain free inside his own mind and distil or disguise his unorthodox ideas in such a way that the authorities will be too stupid to recognize them? And in any case, if the writer himself is in agreement with the prevailing orthodoxy, why should it have a cramping effect on him? Is not literature, or any of the arts, likeliest to flourish in societies in which there are no major conflicts of opinion and no sharp distinction between the artist and his audience? Does one have to assume that every writer is a rebel, or even that a writer as such is an exceptional person?

Whenever one attempts to defend intellectual liberty against the claims of totalitarianism, one meets with these arguments in one form or another. They are based on a complete misunderstanding of what literature is, and how – one should perhaps rather say why – it comes into being. They assume that a writer is either a mere entertainer or else a venal hack who can switch from one line of propaganda to another as easily as an organ grinder changing tunes. But after all, how is it that books ever come to be written? Above a quite low level, literature is an attempt to influence the viewpoint of one's contemporaries by recording experience. And so far as freedom of expression is concerned, there is not much difference between a mere journalist and the most "unpolitical" imaginative writer. The journalist is unfree, and is conscious of unfreedom, when he is forced to write lies or suppress what seems to him important news; the imaginative writer is unfree when he has to falsify his subjective feelings, which from his point of view are facts. He may distort and caricature reality in order to make his meaning clearer, but he cannot misrepresent the scenery of his own mind: he cannot say with any conviction that he likes what he dislikes, or believes what he disbelieves. If he is forced to do so, the only result is that his creative faculties dry up. Nor can he solve the problem by keeping away from controversial topics. There is no such thing as genuinely non-political literature, and least of all in an age like our own, when fears, hatreds and loyalties of a directly political kind are near to the surface of everyone's consciousness. Even a single taboo can have an all-round crippling effect upon the mind, because there is always the danger that any thought which is freely followed up may lead to the forbidden thought. It follows that the atmosphere of totalitarianism is deadly to any kind of prose writer, though a poet, at any rate a lyric poet, might possibly find it breathable. And in any totalitarian society that survives for more than a couple of generations, it is probable that prose literature, of the kind that has existed during the past 400 years, must actually come to an end.

Literature has sometimes flourished under despotic regimes, but, as has often been pointed out, the despotisms of the past were not totalitarian. Their repressive apparatus was always inefficient, their ruling classes were usually either corrupt or apathetic or half-liberal in outlook, and the prevailing religious doctrines usually worked against perfectionism and the notion of human infallibility. Even so it is broadly true that prose literature has reached its highest levels in periods of democracy and free speculation. What is new in totalitarianism is that its doctrines are not only unchallengeable but also unstable. They have to be accepted on pain of damnation, but on the other hand they are always liable to be altered at a moment's notice. Consider, for example, the various attitudes, completely incompatible with one another, which an English communist or "fellow traveller" has had to adopt towards the war between Britain and Germany. For years before September 1939 he was expected to be in a continuous stew about "the horrors of Nazism" and to twist everything he wrote into a denunciation of Hitler; after September 1939, for twenty months, he had to believe that Germany was more sinned against that sinning, and the word "Nazi", at least so far as print went, had to drop right out of his vocabulary. Immediately after hearing the eight o'clock news bulletin on the morning of 22nd June 1941, he had to start believing once again that Nazism was the most hideous evil the world had ever seen. Now, it is easy for a politician to make such changes; for a writer the case is somewhat different. If he is to switch his allegiance at exactly the right moment, he must either tell lies about his subjective feelings or else suppress them altogether. In either case he has destroyed his dynamo. Not only will ideas refuse to come to him but the very words he uses will seem to stiffen under his touch. Political writing in our time consists almost entirely of prefabricated phrases bolted together like the pieces of a child's Meccano set. It is the unavoidable result of self-censorship. To write in plain, vigorous language one has to think fearlessly, and if one thinks fearlessly one cannot be politically orthodox. It might be otherwise in an "age of faith", when the prevailing orthodoxy has been long established and is not taken too seriously. In that case it would be possible, or might be possible, for large areas of one's mind to remain unaffected by what one officially believed. Even so, it is worth noticing that prose literature almost disappeared during the only age of faith that Europe has ever enjoyed. Throughout the whole of the Middle Ages there was almost no imaginative prose literature and very little in the way of historical writing – and the intellectual leaders of society expressed their most serious thoughts in a dead language which barely altered during a thousand years.

Totalitarianism, however, does not so much promise an age of faith as an age of schizophrenia. A society becomes totalitarian when its structure becomes flagrantly artificial: that is, when its ruling class has lost its function but succeeds in clinging to power by force or fraud. Such a society, no matter how long it persists, can never afford to become either tolerant or intellectually stable. It can never permit either the truthful recording of facts or the emotional sincerity that literary creation demands. But to be corrupted by totalitarianism one does not have to live in a totalitarian country. The mere prevalence of certain ideas can spread a kind of poison that makes one subject after another impossible for literary purposes. Wherever there is an enforced orthodoxy – or even two orthodoxies, as often happens – good writing stops. This was well illustrated by the Spanish Civil War. To many English intellectuals the war was a deeply moving experience, but not an experience about which they could write sincerely. There were only two things that you were allowed to say, and both of them were palpable lies; as a result, the war produced acres of print but almost nothing worth reading.

It is not certain whether the effects of totalitarianism upon verse need be so deadly as its effects on prose. There is a whole series of converging reasons why it is somewhat easier for a poet than for a prose writer to feel at home in an authoritarian society. To begin with, bureaucrats and other "practical" men usually despise the poet too deeply to be much interested in what he is saying. Secondly, what the poet is saying – that is, what his poem "means" if translated into prose – is relatively unimportant even to himself. The thought contained in a poem is always simple, and is no more the primary purpose of the poem than the anecdote is the primary purpose of a picture. A poem is an arrangement of sounds and associations, as a painting is an arrangement of brush-marks. For short snatches, indeed, as in the refrain of a song, poetry can even dispense with meaning altogether. It is therefore fairly easy for a poet to keep away from dangerous subjects and avoid uttering heresies – and even when he does utter them, they may escape notice. But above all, good verse, unlike good prose, is not necessarily an individual product. Certain kinds of poems, such as ballads, or, on the other hand, very artificial verse forms, can be composed cooperatively by groups of people. Whether the ancient English and Scottish ballads were originally produced by individuals, or by the people at large, is disputed – but at any rate they are non-individual in the sense that they constantly change in passing from mouth to mouth. Even in print no two versions of a ballad are ever quite the same. Many primitive peoples compose verse communally. Someone begins to improvise, probably accompanying himself on a musical instrument, somebody else chips in with a line or a rhyme when the first singer breaks down, and so the process continues until there exists a whole song or ballad which has no identifiable author.

In prose, this kind of intimate collaboration is quite impossible. Serious prose, in any case, has to be composed in solitude, whereas the excitement of being part of a group is actually an aid to certain kinds of versification. Verse – and perhaps good verse of its kind, though it would not be the highest kind – might survive under even the most inquisitorial regime. Even in a society where liberty and individuality had been extinguished, there would still be need either for patriotic songs and heroic ballads celebrating victories, or for elaborate exercises in flattery – and these are the kinds of poem that can be written to order, or composed communally, without necessarily lacking artistic value. Prose is a different matter, since the prose writer cannot narrow the range of his thoughts without killing his inventiveness. But the history of totalitarian societies, or of groups of people who have adopted the totalitarian outlook, suggests that loss of liberty is inimical to all forms of literature. German literature almost disappeared during the Hitler regime, and the case was not much better in Italy. Russian literature, so far as one can judge by translations, has deteriorated markedly since the early days of the

Revolution, though some of the verse appears to be better than the prose. Few if any Russian novels that it is possible to take seriously have been translated for about fifteen years. In Western Europe and America large sections of the literary intelligentsia have either passed through the Communist Party or been warmly sympathetic to it, but this whole leftward movement has produced extraordinarily few books worth reading. Orthodox Catholicism, again, seems to have a crushing effect upon certain literary forms, especially the novel. During a period of three hundred years, how many people have been at once good novelists and good Catholics? The fact is that certain themes cannot be celebrated in words, and tyranny is one of them. No one ever wrote a good book in praise of the Inquisition. Poetry might survive, in a totalitarian age, and certain arts or half-arts, such as architecture, might even find tyranny beneficial, but the prose writer would have no choice between silence and death. Prose literature as we know it is the product of rationalism, of the Protestant centuries, of the autonomous individual. And the destruction of intellectual liberty cripples the journalist, the sociological writer, the historian, the novelist, the critic and the poet, in that order. In the future it is possible that a new kind of literature, not involving individual feeling or truthful observation, may arise, but no such thing is at present imaginable. It seems much likelier that if the liberal culture that we have lived in since the Renaissance actually comes to an end, the literary art will perish with it.

Of course, print will continue to be used, and it is interesting to speculate what kinds of reading matter would survive in a rigidly totalitarian society. Newspapers will presumably continue until television technique reaches a higher level, but apart from newspapers it is doubtful even now whether the great mass of people in the industrialized countries feel the need for any kind of literature. They are unwilling, at any rate, to spend anywhere near as much on reading matter as they spend on several other recreations. Probably novels and stories will be completely superseded by film and radio productions. Or perhaps some kind of low-grade sensational fiction will survive, produced by a sort of conveyor-belt process that reduces human initiative to the minimum.

It would probably not be beyond human ingenuity to write books by machinery. But a sort of mechanizing process can already be seen at work in the film and radio, in publicity and propaganda, and in the lower reaches of journalism. The Disney films, for instance, are produced by what is essentially a factory process, the work being done partly mechanically and partly by teams of artists who have to subordinate their individual style. Radio features are commonly written by tired hacks to whom the subject and the manner of treatment are dictated beforehand – even so, what they write is merely a kind of raw material to be chopped into shape by producers and censors. So also with the innumerable books and pamphlets commissioned by government departments. Even more machine-like is the production of short stories, serials and poems for the very cheap magazines. Papers such as *The Writer** abound with advertisements of Literary Schools, all of them offering you ready-made plots at a few shillings a time. Some, together with the plot, supply the opening and closing sentences of each chapter. Others furnish you with a sort of algebraical formula by the use of which you can construct your plots for yourself. Others offer packs of cards marked with characters and situations, which have only to be shuffled and dealt in order to produce ingenious stories automatically. It is probably in some such way that the literature of a totalitarian society would be produced, if literature were still felt to be necessary. Imagination – even consciousness, so far as possible – would be eliminated from the process of writing. Books would be planned in their broad lines by bureaucrats, and would pass through so many hands that when finished they would be no more an individual product than a Ford car at the end of the assembly line. It goes without saying that anything so produced would be rubbish – but anything that was not rubbish would endanger the structure of the state. As for the surviving literature of the past, it would have to be suppressed or at least elaborately rewritten.

Meanwhile totalitarianism has not fully triumphed everywhere. Our own society is still, broadly speaking, liberal. To exercise your right of free speech you have to fight against economic pressure and against strong sections of public opinion, but not, as yet, against a secret police force. You can say or print almost anything so long as you are willing to do it in a hole-and-corner way. But what is sinister, as I said at the beginning of this essay, is that the conscious enemies of liberty are those to whom liberty ought to mean most. The big public do not care about the matter one way or the other. They are not in favour of persecuting the heretic, and they will not exert themselves to defend him. They are at once too sane and too stupid to acquire the totalitarian outlook. The direct, conscious attack on intellectual decency comes from the intellectuals themselves.

It is possible that the Russophile intelligentsia, if they had not succumbed to that particular myth, would have succumbed to another of much the same kind. But at any rate the Russian myth is there, and the corruption it causes stinks. When one sees highly educated men looking on indifferently at oppression and persecution, one wonders which to despise more, their cynicism or their short-sightedness. Many scientists, for example, are the uncritical admirers of the USSR. They appear to think that the destruction of liberty is of no importance so long as their own line of work is for the moment unaffected. The USSR is a large, rapidly developing country which has acute need of scientific workers and, consequently, treats them generously. Provided that they steer clear of dangerous subjects such as psychology, scientists are privileged persons. Writers, on the other hand, are viciously persecuted. It is true that literary prostitutes like Ilya Ehrenburg or Alexei Tolstoy* are paid huge sums of money, but the only thing which is of any value to the writer as such – his freedom of expression – is taken away from him. Some, at least, of the English scientists who speak so enthusiastically of the opportunities enjoyed by scientists in Russia are capable of understanding this. But their reflection appears to be: "Writers are persecuted in Russia. So what? I am not a writer." They do not see that any attack on intellectual liberty, and on the concept of objective truth, threatens in the long run every department of thought.

For the moment the totalitarian state tolerates the scientist because it needs him. Even in Nazi Germany, scientists, other than Jews, were relatively well treated, and the German scientific community, as a whole, offered no resistance to Hitler. At this stage of history, even the most autocratic ruler is forced to take account of physical reality, partly because of the lingering on of liberal habits of thought, partly because of the need to prepare for war. So long as physical reality cannot be altogether ignored, so long as two and two have to make four when you are, for example, drawing the blueprint of an aeroplane, the scientist has his function, and can even be allowed a measure of liberty. His awakening will come later, when the totalitarian state is firmly established. Meanwhile, if he wants to safeguard the integrity of science, it is his job to develop some kind of solidarity with his literary colleagues and not regard it as a matter of indifference when writers are silenced or driven to suicide, and newspapers systematically falsified.

But however it may be with the physical sciences, or with music, painting and architecture, it is – as I have tried to show – certain that literature is doomed if liberty of thought perishes. Not only is it doomed in any country which retains a totalitarian structure, but any writer who adopts the totalitarian outlook, who finds excuses for persecution and the falsification of reality, thereby destroys himself as a writer. There is no way out of this. No tirades against "individualism" and "the ivory tower", no pious platitudes to the effect that "true individuality is only attained through identification with the community", can get over the fact that a bought mind is a spoilt mind. Unless spontaneity enters at some point or another, literary creation is impossible, and language itself becomes ossified. At some time in the future, if the human mind becomes something totally different from what it now is, we may learn to separate literary creation from intellectual honesty. At present we know only that the imagination, like certain wild animals, will not breed in captivity. Any writer or journalist who denies that fact – and nearly all the current praise of the Soviet Union contains or implies such a denial – is, in effect, demanding his own destruction.

Books vs. Cigarettes*

A couple of years ago a friend of mine, a newspaper editor, was firewatching with some factory workers. They fell to talking about his newspaper, which most of them read and approved of, but when he asked them what they thought of the literary section, the answer he got was: "You don't suppose we read that stuff, do you? Why, half the time you're talking about books that cost twelve and sixpence! Chaps like us couldn't spend twelve and sixpence on a book." These, he said, were men who thought nothing of spending several pounds on a day trip to Blackpool.

This idea that the buying, or even the reading, of books is an expensive hobby and beyond the reach of the average person is so widespread that it deserves some detailed examination. Exactly what reading costs, reckoned in terms of pence per hour, is difficult to estimate, but I have made a start by inventorying my own books and adding up their total price. After allowing for various other expenses, I can make a fairly good guess at my expenditure over the last fifteen years.

The books that I have counted and priced are the ones I have here, in my flat. I have about an equal number stored in another place, so that I shall double the final figure in order to arrive at the complete amount. I have not counted oddments such as proof copies, defaced volumes, cheap paper-covered editions, pamphlets, or magazines, unless bound up into book form. Nor have I counted the kind of junky books – old school textbooks and so forth – that accumulate in the bottoms of cupboards. I have counted only those books which I have acquired voluntarily, or else would have acquired voluntarily, and which I intend to keep. In this category I find that I have 442 books, acquired in the following ways:

Bought (mostly second-hand)	251
Given to me or bought with book tokens	33
Review copies and complimentary copies	143
Borrowed and not returned	10
Temporarily on loan	5
Total	442

Now as to the method of pricing. Those books that I have bought I have listed at their full price, as closely as I can determine it. I have also listed at their full price the books that have been given to me, and those that I have temporarily borrowed, or borrowed and kept. This is because book giving, book borrowing and book stealing more or less even out. I possess books that do not strictly speaking belong to me, but many other people also have books of mine, so that the books I have not paid for can be taken as balancing others which I have paid for but no longer possess. On the other hand I have listed the review and complimentary copies at half price. That is about what I would have paid for them second-hand, and they are mostly books that I would only have bought second-hand, if at all. For the prices I have sometimes had to rely on guesswork, but my figures will not be far out. The costs were as follows:

	£	s.	d.
Bought	36	9	0
Gifts	10	10	0
Review copies, etc.	25	11	9
Borrowed and not returned	4	16	9
On loan	3	10	0
Shelves	2	0	0
Total	82	17	6

Adding the other batch of books that I have elsewhere, it seems that I possess altogether nearly 900 books, at a cost of £165 15s. This is the accumulation of about fifteen years – actually more, since some of these books date from my childhood, but call it fifteen years. This works out at £11 1s. a year, but there are other charges that must be added in order to estimate my full reading expenses. The biggest will be for newspapers and periodicals, and for this I think £8 a year would be a reasonable figure. £8 a year covers the cost of two daily papers, one evening paper, two Sunday papers, one weekly review and one or two monthly magazines. This brings the figure up to £19 1s., but to arrive at the grand total one has to make a guess. Obviously one often spends money on books without afterwards having anything to show for it. There are library subscriptions, and there are also the books, chiefly Penguins and other cheap editions, which one buys and then loses or throws away. However, on the basis of my other figures, it looks as though £6 a year would be quite enough to add for expenditure of this kind. So my total reading expenses over the past fifteen years have been in the neighbourhood of £25 a year.

Twenty-five pounds a year sounds quite a lot until you begin to measure it against other kinds of expenditure. It is nearly 9s. 9d. a week, and at present 9s. 9d. is the equivalent of about 83 cigarettes (Players): even before the war it would have bought you less than 200 cigarettes. With prices as they now are, I am spending far more on tobacco than I do on books. I smoke six ounces a week, at half a crown an ounce, making nearly £40 a year. Even before the war when the same tobacco cost 8*d*. an ounce, I was spending over £10 a year on it – and if I also averaged a pint of beer a day, at sixpence, these two items together will have cost me close on £20 a year. This was probably not much above the national average. In 1938 the people of this country spent nearly £10 per head per annum on alcohol and tobacco – however, 20 per cent of the population were children under fifteen and another 40 per cent were women, so that the average smoker and drinker must have been spending much more than £10. In 1944, the annual expenditure per head on these items was no less than £23. Allow for the women and children as before, and £40 is a reasonable individual figure. £40 a year would just about pay for a packet of Woodbines every day and half a pint of mild six days a week – not a magnificent allowance. Of course, all prices are now inflated, including the price of books; still, it looks as though the cost of reading, even if you buy books instead of borrowing them and take in a fairly large number of periodicals, does not amount to more than the combined cost of smoking and drinking.

It is difficult to establish any relationship between the price of books and the value one gets out of them. "Books" includes novels, poetry, textbooks, works of reference, sociological treatises and much else, and length and price do not correspond to one another, especially if one habitually buys books second-hand. You may spend ten shillings on a poem of 500 lines, and you may spend sixpence on a dictionary which you consult at odd moments over a period of twenty years. There are books that one reads over and over again, books that become part of the furniture of one's mind and alter one's whole attitude to life, books that one dips into but never reads through, books that one reads at a single sitting and forgets a week later – and the cost, in terms of money, may be the same in each case. But if one regards reading simply as a recreation, like going to the pictures, then it is possible to make a rough estimate of what it costs. If you read nothing but novels and "light" literature, and bought every book that you read, you would be spending – allowing eight shillings as the price of a book, and four hours as the time spent in reading it – two shillings an hour. This is about what it costs to sit in one of the more expensive seats in the cinema. If you concentrated on more serious books, and still bought everything that you read, your expenses would be about the same. The books would cost more, but they would take longer to read. In either case you would still possess the books after you had read them, and they would be saleable at about a third of their purchase price. If you bought only second-hand books, your reading expenses would, of course, be much less: perhaps sixpence an hour would be a fair estimate. And on the other hand if you don't buy books but merely borrow them from the lending library, reading costs you round about a halfpenny an hour; if you borrow them from the public library, it costs you next door to nothing.

I have said enough to show that reading is one of the cheaper recreations – after listening to the radio probably *the* cheapest. Meanwhile, what is the actual amount that the British public spends on books? I cannot discover any figures, though no doubt they exist. But I do know that before the war this country was publishing annually about 15,000 books, which included reprints and schoolbooks. If as many as 10,000 copies of each book were sold – and even allowing for the schoolbooks, this is probably a high estimate – the average person was only buying, directly or indirectly, about three books a year. These three books taken together might cost £1, or probably less.

These figures are guesswork, and I should be interested if someone would correct them for me. But if my estimate is anywhere near right, it is not a proud record for a country which is nearly 100 per cent literate and where the ordinary man spends more on cigarettes than an Indian peasant has for his whole livelihood. And if our book consumption remains as low as it has been, at least let us admit that it is because reading is a less exciting pastime than going to the dogs, the pictures or the pub, and not because books, whether bought or borrowed, are too expensive.

Decline of the English Murder*

It is Sunday afternoon, preferably before the war. The wife is already asleep in the armchair, and the children have been sent out for a nice long walk. You put your feet up on the sofa, settle your spectacles on your nose, and open the *News of the World*. Roast beef and Yorkshire, or roast pork and apple sauce, followed up by suet pudding and driven home, as it were, by a cup of mahogany-brown tea, have put you in just the right mood. Your pipe is drawing sweetly, the sofa cushions are soft underneath you, the fire is well alight, the air is warm and stagnant. In these blissful circumstances, what is it that you want to read about?

Naturally, about a murder. But what kind of murder? If one examines the murders which have given the greatest amount of pleasure to the British public, the murders whose story is known in its general outline to almost everyone and which have been made into novels and rehashed over and over again by the Sunday papers, one finds a fairly strong family resemblance running through the greater number of them. Our great period in murder, our Elizabethan period, so to speak, seems to have been between roughly 1850 and 1925, and the murderers whose reputation has stood the test of time are the following: Doctor Palmer of Rugeley, Jack the Ripper, Neill Cream, Mrs Maybrick, Doctor Crippen, Seddon, Joseph Smith, Armstrong, and Bywaters and Thompson.* In addition, in 1919 or thereabouts, there was another very celebrated case which fits into the general pattern but which I had better not mention by name, because the accused man was acquitted.*

Of the above-mentioned nine cases, at least four have had successful novels based on them, one has been made into a popular melodrama, and the amount of literature surrounding them, in the form of newspaper write-ups, criminological treatises and reminiscences by lawyers and police officers, would make a considerable library. It is difficult to believe that any recent English crime will be remembered so long and so intimately, and not only because the violence of external events has made murder seem unimportant, but because the prevalent type of crime seems to be changing. The principal cause célèbre of the war years was the so-called Cleft Chin Murder, which has now been written up in a popular booklet; the verbatim account of the trial was published sometime last year by Messrs Jarrolds with an introduction by Mr Bechhofer Roberts.* Before returning to this pitiful and sordid case, which is only interesting from a sociological and perhaps a legal point of view, let me try to define what it is that the readers of Sunday papers mean when they say fretfully that "you never seem to get a good murder nowadays".

In considering the nine murders I named above, one can start by excluding the Jack the Ripper case, which is in a class by itself. Of the other eight, six were poisoning cases, and eight of the ten criminals belonged to the middle class. In one way or another, sex was a powerful motive in all but two cases, and in at least four cases respectability – the desire to gain a secure position in life, or not to forfeit one's social position by some scandal such as a divorce – was one of the main reasons for committing murder. In more than half the cases, the object was to get hold of a certain known sum of money such as a legacy or an insurance policy, but the amount involved was nearly always small. In most of the cases the crime only came to light slowly, as the result of careful investigation which started off with the suspicions of neighbours or relatives – and in nearly every case there was some dramatic coincidence, in which the finger of providence could be clearly seen, or one of those episodes that no novelist would dare to make up, such as Crippen's flight across the Atlantic with his mistress dressed as a boy, or Joseph Smith playing "Nearer, My God, to Thee" on the harmonium while one of his wives was drowning in the next room. The background of all these crimes, except Neill Cream's, was essentially domestic; of twelve victims, seven were either wife or husband of the murderer.

With all this in mind one can construct what would be, from a *News of the World* reader's point of view, the "perfect" murder. The murderer should be a little man of the professional class – a dentist or a solicitor, say – living an intensely respectable life somewhere in the suburbs, and preferably in a semi-detached house, which will allow the neighbours to hear suspicious sounds through the wall. He should be either chairman of the local Conservative Party branch, or a leading Nonconformist and strong temperance advocate. He should go astray through cherishing a guilty passion for his secretary or the wife of a rival professional man, and should only bring himself to the point of murder after long and terrible wrestles with his conscience. Having decided on murder, he should plan it all with the utmost cunning, and only slip up over some tiny, unforeseeable detail. The means chosen should, of course, be poison. In the last analysis he should commit murder because this seems to him less disgraceful, and less damaging to his career, than being detected in adultery. With this kind of background, a crime can have dramatic and even tragic qualities which make it memorable and excite pity for both victim and murderer. Most of the crimes mentioned above have a touch of this atmosphere, and in three cases, including the one I referred to but did not name, the story approximates to the one I have outlined.

Now compare the Cleft Chin Murder. There is no depth of feeling in it. It was almost chance that the two people concerned committed that particular murder, and it was only by good luck that they did not commit several others. The background was not domesticity but the anonymous life of the dance halls and the false values of the American film. The two culprits were an eighteen-year-old ex-waitress named Elizabeth Jones and an American army deserter, posing as an officer, named Karl Hultén. They were only together for six days, and it seems doubtful whether, until they were arrested, they even learnt one another's true names. They met casually in a tea shop, and that night went out for a ride in a stolen army truck. Jones described herself as a striptease artist, which was not strictly true (she had given one unsuccessful performance in this line), and declared that she wanted to do something dangerous, "like being a gun-moll". Hultén described himself as a big-time Chicago gangster, which was also untrue. They met a girl bicycling along the road, and to show how tough he was Hultén ran over her with his truck, after which the pair robbed her of the few shillings that were on her. On another occasion they knocked out a girl to whom they had offered a lift, took her coat and handbag and threw her into a river. Finally, in the most wanton way, they murdered a taxi driver who happened to have £8 in his pocket. Soon afterwards they parted. Hultén was caught because he had foolishly kept the dead man's car, and Jones made spontaneous confessions to the police. In court each prisoner incriminated the other. In between crimes, both of them seem to have behaved with the utmost callousness: they spent the dead taxi driver's £8 at the dog races.

Judging from her letters, the girl's case has a certain amount of psychological interest, but this murder probably captured the headlines because it provided distraction amid the doodlebugs and the anxieties of the Battle of France. Jones and Hultén committed their murder to the tune of V1, and were convicted to the tune of V2.* There was also considerable excitement because – as has become usual in England – the man was sentenced to death and the girl to imprisonment. According to Mr Raymond, the reprieving of Jones caused widespread indignation and streams of telegrams to the home secretary; in her native town, "She should hang" was chalked on the walls beside pictures of a figure dangling from a gallows. Considering that only ten women have been hanged in Britain in this century, and that the practice has gone out largely because of popular feeling against it, it is difficult not to feel that this clamour to hang an eighteen-year-old girl was due partly to the brutalizing effects of war. Indeed, the whole meaningless story, with its atmosphere of dance halls, movie palaces, cheap perfume, false names and stolen cars, belongs essentially to a war period.

Perhaps it is significant that the most talked-of English murder of recent years should have been committed by an American and an English girl who had become partly Americanized. But it is difficult to believe that this case will be so long remembered as the old domestic poisoning dramas, product of a stable society where the all-prevailing hypocrisy did at least ensure that crimes as serious as murder should have strong emotions behind them.

In Front of Your Nose*

Many recent statements in the press have declared that it is almost, if not quite, impossible for us to mine as much coal as we need for home and export purposes, because of the impossibility of inducing a sufficient number of miners to remain in the pits. One set of figures which I saw last week estimated the annual "wastage" of mine workers at 60,000 and the annual intake of new workers at 10,000. Simultaneously with this – and sometimes in the same column of the same paper – there have been statements that it would be undesirable to make use of Poles or Germans because this might lead to unemployment in the coal industry. The two utterances do not always come from the same sources, but there must certainly be many people who are capable of holding these totally contradictory ideas in their heads at a single moment.

This is merely one example of a habit of mind which is extremely widespread, and perhaps always has been. Bernard Shaw, in the preface to *Androcles and the Lion*,* cites as another example the first chapter of the Gospel of Matthew, which starts off by establishing the descent of Joseph, father of Jesus, from Abraham. In the first verse, Jesus is described as "the son of David, the son of Abraham", and the genealogy is then followed up through fifteen verses; then, in the next verse but one, it is explained that as a matter of fact Jesus was *not* descended from Abraham, since he was not the son of Joseph. This, says Shaw, presents no difficulty to a religious believer, and he names as a parallel case the rioting in the East End of London by the partisans of the Tichborne Claimant, who declared that a British working man was being done out of his rights.*

Medically, I believe, this manner of thinking is called schizophrenia: at any rate, it is the power of holding simultaneously two beliefs which cancel out. Closely allied to it is the power of ignoring facts which are obvious and unalterable, and which will have to be faced sooner or later. It is especially in our political thinking that these vices flourish. Let me take a few sample subjects out of the hat. They have no organic connection with each other: they are merely cases, taken almost at random, of plain, unmistakable facts being shirked by people who in another part of their mind are aware of those facts.

Hong Kong. For years before the war everyone with knowledge of Far Eastern conditions knew that our position in Hong Kong was untenable and that we should lose it as soon as a major war started. This knowledge, however, was intolerable, and government after government continued to cling to Hong Kong instead of giving it back to the Chinese. Fresh troops were even pushed into it, with the certainty that they would be uselessly taken prisoner, a few weeks before the Japanese attack began. Then war came, and Hong Kong promptly fell – as everyone had known all along that it would do.

Conscription. For years before the war, nearly all enlightened people were in favour of standing up to Germany; the majority of them were also against having enough armaments to make such a stand effective. I know very well the arguments that are put forward in defence of this attitude; some of them are justified, but in the main they are simply forensic excuses. As late as 1939, the Labour Party voted against conscription, a step which probably played its part in bringing about the Russo-German Pact and certainly had a disastrous effect on morale in France. Then came 1940 and we nearly perished for lack of a large, efficient army, which we could only have had if we had introduced conscription at least three years earlier.

The birth rate. Twenty or twenty-five years ago, contraception and enlightenment were held to be almost synonymous. To this day, the majority of people argue – the argument is variously expressed, but always boils down to more or less the same thing – that large families are impossible for economic reasons. At the same time, it is widely known that the birth rate is highest among the low-standard nations, and, in our population, highest among the worst-paid groups. It is also argued that a smaller population would mean less unemployment and more comfort for everybody, while on the other hand it is well established that a dwindling and ageing population is faced with calamitous and perhaps insoluble economic problems. Necessarily the figures are uncertain, but it is quite possible that in only seventy years our population will amount to about eleven million, over half of whom will be Old Age Pensioners. Since, for complex reasons, most people don't want large families, the frightening facts can exist somewhere or other in their consciousness, simultaneously known and not known.

*UNO.** In order to have any efficacy whatever, a world organization must be able to override big states as well as small ones. It must have power to inspect and limit armaments, which means that its officials must have access to every square inch of every country. It must also have at its disposal an armed force bigger than any other armed force and responsible only to the organization itself. The two or three great states that really matter have never even pretended to agree to any of these conditions, and they have so arranged the constitution of UNO that their own actions cannot even be discussed. In other words, UNO's usefulness as an instrument of world peace is nil. This was just as obvious before it began functioning as it is now. Yet only a few months ago millions of well-informed people believed that it was going to be a success.

There is no use in multiplying examples. The point is that we are all capable of believing things which we *know* to be untrue, and then, when we are finally proved wrong, impudently twisting the facts so as to show that we were right. Intellectually, it is possible to carry on this process for an indefinite time: the only check on it is that sooner or later a false belief bumps up against solid reality, usually on a battlefield.

When one looks at the all-prevailing schizophrenia of democratic societies, the lies that have to be told for vote-catching purposes, the silence about major issues, the distortions of the press, it is tempting to believe that in totalitarian countries there is less humbug, more facing of the facts. There, at least, the ruling groups are not dependent on popular favour and can utter the truth crudely and brutally. Goering could say "Guns before butter", while his democratic opposite numbers had to wrap the same sentiment up in hundreds of hypocritical words.

Actually, however, the avoidance of reality is much the same everywhere, and has much the same consequences. The Russian people were taught for years that they were better off than everybody else, and propaganda posters showed Russian families sitting down to abundant meals while the proletariat of other countries starved in the gutter. Meanwhile the workers in the Western countries were so much better off than those of the USSR that non-contact between Soviet citizens and outsiders had to be a guiding principle of policy. Then, as a result of the war, millions of ordinary Russians penetrated far into Europe, and when they return home the original avoidance of reality will inevitably be paid for in frictions of various kinds. The Germans and the Japanese lost the war quite largely because their rulers were unable to see facts which were plain to any dispassionate eye.

To see what is in front of one's nose needs a constant struggle. One thing that helps towards it is to keep a diary, or, at any rate, to keep some kind of record of one's opinions about important events. Otherwise, when some particularly absurd belief is exploded by events, one may simply forget that one ever held it. Political predictions are usually wrong, but even when one makes a correct one, to discover *why* one was right can be very illuminating. In general, one is only right when either wish or fear coincides with reality. If one recognizes this, one cannot, of course, get rid of one's subjective feelings, but one can to some extent insulate them from one's thinking and make predictions cold-bloodedly, by the book of arithmetic. In private life most people are fairly realistic. When one is making out one's weekly budget, two and two invariably make four. Politics, on the other hand, is a sort of sub-atomic or non-Euclidean world where it is quite easy for the part to be greater than the whole or for two objects to be in the same place simultaneously. Hence the contradictions and absurdities I have chronicled above, all finally traceable to a secret belief that one's political opinions, unlike the weekly budget, will not have to be tested against solid reality.

Introduction to *The Position of Peggy Harper* by Leonard Merrick*

Leonard Merrick died in 1939, but during the later part of his life he wrote, or at any rate published, nothing but short stories. Except for one early and now forgotten book, *Violet Moses,** his full-length novels all belong to the period between 1900 and 1914. There are about a dozen of them in all, and their general level is so high that, though it would be fairly easy to pick out six of them as being better worth reprinting than the rest, it is not easy to narrow the choice down to a single volume.

Merrick has the peculiarity that, though he is by no means a "highbrow" writer, the background of his stories is almost invariably one or other of the arts. Among his full-length novels, the only exceptions to this rule are *The Worldlings*, a story of imposture founded on the Tichborne case, and *One Man's View,** which is a partial exception in so much that the central character is a lawyer. Otherwise the people he habitually writes about are novelists, poets, painters and, most characteristically of all, actors. If there is one thing above all others for which he deserves to be remembered, it is his extraordinarily convincing and glamourless picture of stage life – and this, perhaps, justifies the reprinting of *The Position of Peggy Harper* rather than of, say, *Cynthia* or *The Worldlings*, which are equally good in their different way.

Although nearly all of Merrick's books are about writers or artists, they can be divided fairly sharply into two classes. One class, by which unfortunately he is best known, are his Paris books, mostly collections of short stories, such as *A Chair on the Boulevard.** These stories describe a kind of bohemianism which Merrick had not experienced from the inside and which only doubtfully exists; the atmosphere they are trying to reproduce is that of *Trilby* or even, at their worst, that of W.J. Locke's *Aristide Pujol.** Where Merrick describes *his own* adventures in Paris, as he obviously does in certain chapters in *Cynthia*, for instance, it is quite a different story. Picturesqueness disappears, and in its place there enters that dreadful thing which he understood so well, poverty against a background of gentility. Merrick's shabby-genteel novels are the ones that matter: the best of them, apart from those that have been mentioned already, are *The Man Who Was Good*, *The Actor-Manager*, *The House of Lynch* and *The Quaint Companions.** *Conrad in Quest of His Youth,** one of Merrick's most successful books, deals partly with stage life, but differs from the others in that poverty is not a leading theme in it.

INTRODUCTION TO THE POSITION OF PEGGY HARPER

Money is always a fascinating subject, provided that only small sums are involved. Brute starvation is not interesting, and neither are transactions involving thousands of millions of pounds, but an out-of-work actor pawning his watch chain and wondering whether next week the watch will have to follow it – that is interesting. However, Merrick's books are not simply concerned with the difficulty of making a living. His theme is rather the humiliation which a sensitive and honest person feels when he is forced into contact with people whose standards are commercial. Christopher Tatham, the hero of *Peggy Harper*, writes a melodrama which scores a thunderous success while the comedies into which he has put his real work grow dog-eared on their journey from agent to agent. It is an interesting detail – a reminder that, after all, the status of the literary man *has* risen during the past thirty or forty years – that the sum Tatham receives for his five-act melodrama is fifteen pounds! But the fact that he is underpaid is socially less significant than the fact that he is isolated. Until it is almost too late, he simply does not have the opportunity of making contact with people in any way similar to himself. His silly, snobbish mother, and his prosperous uncle who is "associated with hops", are somewhat further from understanding his point of view than the vulgar actor-manager who buys his melodrama. The foolish engagement into which he enters is the direct result of isolation. When he first meets Peggy Harper, at the age of twenty-one or thereabouts, he probably does not know – never having had the chance to find out – that there exist women who are both attractive and intelligent. Until he has made his mark by individual effort, society has no place for him. The dull commercial world of his family and the vulgar, down-at-heel world of the touring companies are equally hostile to him, and it is largely luck that the one or the other does not swallow him up for good.

Merrick is not consciously, or at any rate not overtly, a "writer with a purpose". The commercialism and philistinism of the English-speaking civilization is something that he inveighs against but assumes to be unchangeable, like the English climate. And there are many of the accepted values of his time that he does not even question. In particular, he everywhere takes for granted the superiority of a "gentleman" to a "bounder" and of a "good accent" to cockney – and in most of his books there are passages which if they were written today would be called snobbish. Actually, Merrick is not a snobbish writer – if he were he would probably write about wealthy or titled people instead of concentrating on the shabby-genteel – but he is too honest to disguise his instinctive preferences. He feels strongly that good manners and delicate sensibilities are important, and that one of the worst horrors of poverty is having to take orders from ill-bred, coarse-fibred people. A beautiful little scene in *Peggy Harper* illustrates the kind of servitude that an educated man in a low-class touring company must be ready to put up with. The word "menace" has occurred in the script of the play that is being rehearsed, and the ignoramus of a stage manager insists that it should be pronounced "manace":

> "What's that – what d'ye call it? 'Menace?' Rats! That's extant, that's altogether extant." He evidently relished his discovery of "extant", which he seemed to believe was a scholarly synonym for "out of date". He looked round for Tatham. "Isn't 'menace' extant, eh?" he enquired.
> "Quite," said Tatham.

Peggy Harper, like most of Merrick's books (the outstanding exception is *The Man Who Was Good*), has a "happy ending", but it is implied all the way through that decency and intelligence are very serious handicaps. In *Cynthia*, which is a story about a novelist, the clash between honesty and bread and butter is even more painful. *Cynthia* is a book which it would not be altogether absurd to mention in the same sentence as George Gissing's *New Grub Street*,* but its theme is one that a good many different writers have handled. The special thing that Merrick could do, and which no one else seems to have done, is to reproduce the atmosphere of low-class theatrical life: the smell of greasepaint and fish and chips, the sordid rivalries, the comfortless Sunday journeys, the lugging of suitcases through the backstreets of unfamiliar towns, the "professional" lodgings presided over by "Ma", the poky bedrooms with the rickety wash-hand stand and the grim white chamber pot under the bed (does Merrick ever mention the chamber pot? Probably not: one just seems to imagine it), and the trudging up and down the Strand on worn-out boot soles, the agents' offices where women in dyed frocks sit waiting their turn, the forlorn collection of press cuttings, the manager who bolts in the middle of the tour with all the takings.

Although Merrick was fairly successful, especially towards the end of his life, as a short-story writer, his full-length novels never "sold" in this country. About 1918 Messrs Hodder and Stoughton issued a uniform edition of his works with introductions by H.G. Wells, G.K. Chesterton, W.D. Howells* and other well-known writers who admired him and felt that he was underrated. The introduction to *Peggy Harper* was written by Sir Arthur Pinero.* The uniform edition, however, was no more successful than earlier editions had been – a fact which is all the more puzzling because throughout his life Merrick's books sold relatively well in the United States.* The obvious explanation of his unpopularity is that he chose to write about artists, whereas the big public, as he himself often remarked, would sooner read about politicians or businessmen; also that his books are what people call "grey", or "gloomy", or "too like real life". It is quite true that the majority of Merrick's books are far from being cheer-up stories. They are lightly written, and for the sake of preserving the comedy form they usually have a "happy ending", but their underlying mood is a bitter one. But it is still not clear why Merrick should have been more popular in America. The American public is presumably no more inclined than the British to take sides with the artist against society; nor did Merrick make any special concessions to American readers, for the subject matter and the whole atmosphere of most of his books are intensely English.

Possibly, from the American point of view, the Englishness was an exotic attraction, while the kind of poverty and failure that Merrick was describing were not quite the kind that Americans are afraid of. At any rate, Merrick's steady refusal to see silver linings where none existed must have had something to do with his unpopularity. It is perhaps significant that *Conrad in Quest of His Youth*, the hero of which is wealthy, was about the most successful of his books. Now that the fear of poverty is a less urgent emotion, and the demand for sunshine stories less insistent, he seems overdue for revival.

Some Thoughts on the Common Toad*

Before the swallow, before the daffodil, and not much later than the snowdrop, the common toad salutes the coming of spring after his own fashion, which is to emerge from a hole in the ground, where he has lain buried since the previous autumn, and crawl as rapidly as possible towards the nearest suitable patch of water. Something – some kind of shudder in the earth, or perhaps merely a rise of a few degrees in the temperature – has told him that it is time to wake up, though a few toads appear to sleep the clock round and miss out a year from time to time; at any rate, I have more than once dug them up, alive and apparently well, in the middle of the summer.

At this period, after his long fast, the toad has a very spiritual look, like a strict Anglo-Catholic towards the end of Lent. His movements are languid but purposeful, his body is shrunken, and by contrast his eyes look abnormally large. This allows one to notice what one might not at another time: that a toad has about the most beautiful eye of any living creature. It is like gold, or more exactly it is like the golden-coloured semi-precious stone which one sometimes sees in signet rings, and which I think is called a chrysoberyl.

For a few days after getting into the water the toad concentrates on building up his strength by eating small insects. Presently he has swollen to his normal size again, and then he goes through a phase of intense sexiness. All he knows, at least if he is a male toad, is that he wants to get his arms round something, and if you offer him a stick, or even your finger, he will cling to it with surprising strength and take a long time to discover that it is not a female toad. Frequently one comes upon shapeless masses of ten or twenty toads rolling over and over in the water, one clinging to another without distinction of sex. By degrees, however, they sort themselves out into couples, with the male duly sitting on the female's back. You can now distinguish males from females, because the male is smaller, darker and sits on top, with his arms tightly clasped round the female's neck. After a day or two the spawn is laid in long strings which wind themselves in and out of the reeds and soon become invisible. A few more weeks, and the water is alive with masses of tiny tadpoles which rapidly grow larger, sprout hind legs, then forelegs, then shed their tails – and finally, about the middle of the summer, the new generation of toads, smaller than one's thumbnail but perfect in every particular, crawl out of the water to begin the game anew.

I mention the spawning of the toads because it is one of the phenomena of spring which most deeply appeal to me, and because the toad, unlike the

SOME THOUGHTS ON THE COMMON TOAD

skylark and the primrose, has never had much of a boost from the poets. But I am aware that many people do not like reptiles or amphibians, and I am not suggesting that in order to enjoy the spring you have to take an interest in toads. There are also the crocus, the mistle thrush, the cuckoo, the blackthorn, etc. The point is that the pleasures of spring are available to everybody, and cost nothing. Even in the most sordid street the coming of spring will register itself by some sign or other, if it is only a brighter blue between the chimney pots or the vivid green of an elder sprouting on a blitzed site. Indeed it is remarkable how nature goes on existing unofficially, as it were, in the very heart of London. I have seen a kestrel flying over the Deptford gasworks, and I have heard a first-rate performance by a blackbird in the Euston Road. There must be some hundreds of thousands, it not millions, of birds living inside the four-mile radius, and if is rather a pleasing thought that none of them pays a halfpenny of rent.

As for spring, not even the narrow and gloomy streets round the Bank of England are quite able to exclude it. It comes seeping in everywhere, like one of those new poison gases which pass through all filters. The spring is commonly referred to as "a miracle", and during the past five or six years this worn-out figure of speech has taken on a new lease of life. After the sort of winters we have had to endure recently, the spring does seem miraculous, because it has become gradually harder and harder to believe that it is actually going to happen. Every February since 1940 I have found myself thinking that this time winter is going to be permanent. But Persephone, like the toads, always rises from the dead at about the same moment. Suddenly, towards the end of March, the miracle happens and the decaying slum in which I live is transfigured. Down in the square the sooty privets have turned bright green, the leaves are thickening on the chestnut trees, the daffodils are out, the wallflowers are budding, the policeman's tunic looks positively a pleasant shade of blue, the fishmonger greets his customers with a smile, and even the sparrows are quite a different colour, having felt the balminess of the air and nerved themselves to take a bath, their first since last September.

Is it wicked to take a pleasure in spring and other seasonal changes? To put it more precisely, is it politically reprehensible, while we are all groaning, or at any rate ought to be groaning, under the shackles of the capitalist system, to point out that life is frequently more worth living because of a blackbird's song, a yellow elm tree in October or some other natural phenomenon which does not cost money and does not have what the editors of left-wing newspapers call a class angle? There is no doubt that many people think so. I know by experience that a favourable reference to "nature" in one of my articles is liable to bring me abusive letters, and though the keyword in these letters is usually "sentimental", two ideas seem to be mixed up in them. One is that any pleasure in the actual process of life encourages a sort of political quietism.

People, so the thought runs, ought to be discontented, and it is our job to multiply our wants and not simply to increase our enjoyment of the things we have already. The other idea is that this is the age of machines and that to dislike the machine, or even to want to limit its domination, is backward-looking, reactionary and slightly ridiculous. This is often backed up by the statement that a love of nature is a foible of urbanized people who have no notion what nature is really like. Those who really have to deal with the soil, so it is argued, do not love the soil, and do not take the faintest interest in birds or flowers, except from a strictly utilitarian point of view. To love the country one must live in the town, merely taking an occasional weekend ramble at the warmer times of year.

This last idea is demonstrably false. Medieval literature, for instance, including the popular ballads, is full of an almost Georgian enthusiasm for nature, and the art of agricultural peoples such as the Chinese and Japanese centres always round trees, birds, flowers, rivers, mountains. The other idea seems to me to be wrong in a subtler way. Certainly we ought to be discontented, we ought not simply to find out ways of making the best of a bad job, and yet if we kill all pleasure in the actual process of life, what sort of future are we preparing for ourselves? If a man cannot enjoy the return of spring, why should he be happy in a labour-saving utopia? What will he do with the leisure that the machine will give him? I have always suspected that if our economic and political problems are ever really solved, life will become simpler instead of more complex, and that the sort of pleasure one gets from finding the first primrose will loom larger than the sort of pleasure one gets from eating an ice to the tune of a Wurlitzer. I think that by retaining one's childhood love of such things as trees, fishes, butterflies and – to return to my first instance – toads, one makes a peaceful and decent future a little more probable, and that by preaching the doctrine that nothing is to be admired except steel and concrete, one merely makes it a little surer that human beings will have no outlet for their surplus energy except in hatred and leader worship.

At any rate, spring is here, even in London N1, and they can't stop you enjoying it. This is a satisfying reflection. How many a time have I stood watching the toads mating, or a pair of hares having a boxing match in the young corn, and thought of all the important persons who would stop me enjoying this if they could? But luckily they can't. So long as you are not actually ill, hungry, frightened or immured in a prison or a holiday camp, spring is still spring. The atom bombs are piling up in the factories, the police are prowling through the cities, the lies are streaming from the loudspeakers, but the earth is still going round the sun, and neither the dictators nor the bureaucrats, deeply as they disapprove of the process, are able to prevent it.

A Good Word for the Vicar of Bray*

Some years ago a friend took me to the little Berkshire church of which the celebrated Vicar of Bray was once the incumbent. (Actually it is a few miles from Bray, but perhaps at that time the two livings were one.) In the churchyard there stands a magnificent yew tree which, according to a notice at its foot, was planted by no less a person than the Vicar of Bray himself. And it struck me at the time as curious that such a man should have left such a relic behind him.

The Vicar of Bray, though he was well equipped to be a leader writer on *The Times*, could hardly be described as an admirable character. Yet, after this lapse of time, all that is left of him is a comic song* and a beautiful tree, which has rested the eyes of generation after generation and must surely have outweighed any bad effects which he produced by his political quislingism.

Thibaw, the last King of Burma,* was also far from being a good man. He was a drunkard, he had 500 wives – he seems to have kept them chiefly for show, however – and when he came to the throne his first act was to decapitate seventy or eighty of his brothers. Yet he did posterity a good turn by planting the dusty streets of Mandalay with tamarind trees which cast a pleasant shade until the Japanese incendiary bombs burned them down in 1942.

The poet James Shirley seems to have generalized too freely when he said that "Only the actions of the just / Smell sweet and blossom in their dust".* Sometimes the actions of the unjust make quite a good showing after the appropriate lapse of time. When I saw the Vicar of Bray's yew tree it reminded me of something, and afterwards I got hold of a book of selections from the writings of John Aubrey* and reread a pastoral poem which must have been written sometime in the first half of the seventeenth century, and which was inspired by a certain Mrs Overall.

Mrs Overall was the wife of a dean and was extensively unfaithful to him. According to Aubrey she "could scarcely denie any one", and she had "the loveliest Eies that were ever seen, but wondrous wanton". The poem* (the "shepherd swaine" seems to have been somebody called Sir John Selby) starts off:

> Downe lay the Shepherd Swaine
> So sober and demure
> Wishing for his wench againe
> So bonny and so pure
> With his head on hillock lowe

> And his arms akimboe
> And all was for the losse of his
> Hye nonny nonny noe...
>
> Sweet she was, as kind a love
> As ever fetter'd Swaine;
> Never such a daynty one
> Shall man enjoy again.
> Sett a thousand on a rowe
> I forbid that any showe
> Ever the like of her
> Hye nonny nonny noe.

As the poem proceeds through another six verses, the refrain "Hye nonny nonny noe" takes on an unmistakably obscene meaning, but it ends with the exquisite stanza:

> But gone she is the prettiest lasse
> That ever trod on plaine.
> What ever hath betide of her
> Blame not the Shepherd Swaine.
> For why? She was her owne Foe,
> And gave herself the overthrowe
> By being so franke of her
> Hye nonny nonny noe.

Mrs Overall was no more an exemplary character than the Vicar of Bray, though a more attractive one. Yet in the end all that remains of her is a poem which still gives pleasure to many people, though for some reason it never gets into the anthologies. The suffering which she presumably caused, and the misery and futility in which her own life must have ended, have been transformed into a sort of lingering fragrance like the smell of tobacco plants on a summer evening.

But to come back to trees. The planting of a tree, especially one of the long-living hardwood trees, is a gift which you can make to posterity at almost no cost and with almost no trouble, and if the tree takes root it will far outlive the visible effect of any of your other actions, good or evil. A year or two ago I wrote a few paragraphs in *Tribune* about some sixpenny rambler roses from Woolworth's which I had planted before the war. This brought me an indignant letter from a reader who said that roses are bourgeois, but I still think that my sixpence was better spent than if it had gone on cigarettes or even on one of the excellent Fabian Research Pamphlets.

A GOOD WORD FOR THE VICAR OF BRAY

Recently, I spent a day at the cottage where I used to live, and noted with a pleased surprise – to be exact, it was a feeling of having done good unconsciously – the progress of the things I had planted nearly ten years ago. I think it is worth recording what some of them cost, just to show what you can do with a few shillings if you invest them in something that grows.

First of all there were the two ramblers from Woolworth's, and three polyantha roses, all at sixpence each. Then there were two bush roses which were part of a job lot from a nursery garden. This job lot consisted of six fruit trees, three rose bushes and two gooseberry bushes, all for ten shillings. One of the fruit trees and one of the rose bushes died, but the rest are all flourishing. The sum total is five fruit trees, seven roses and two gooseberry bushes, all for twelve and sixpence. These plants have not entailed much work, and have had nothing spent on them beyond the original amount. They never even received any manure, except what I occasionally collected in a bucket when one of the farm horses happened to have halted outside the gate.

Between them, in nine years, those seven rose bushes will have given what would add up to 100 or 150 months of bloom. The fruit trees, which were mere saplings when I put them in, are now just about getting in their stride. Last week one of them, a plum, was a mass of blossom, and the apples looked as if they were going to do fairly well. What had originally been the weakling of the family, a Cox's Orange Pippin – it would hardly have been included in the job lot if it had been a good plant – had grown into a sturdy tree with plenty of fruit spurs on it. I maintain that it was a public-spirited action to plant that Cox, for these trees do not fruit quickly and I did not expect to stay there long. I never had an apple off it myself, but it looks as if someone else will have quite a lot. By their fruits ye shall know them, and the Cox's Orange Pippin is a good fruit to be known by. Yet I did not plant it with the conscious intention of doing anybody a good turn. I just saw the job lot going cheap and stuck the things into the ground without much preparation.

A thing which I regret, and which I will try to remedy some time, is that I have never in my life planted a walnut. Nobody does plant them nowadays – when you see a walnut it is almost invariably an old tree. If you plant a walnut you are planting it for your grandchildren, and who cares a damn for his grandchildren? Nor does anybody plant a quince, a mulberry or a medlar. But these are garden trees which you can only be expected to plant if you have a patch of ground of your own. On the other hand, in any hedge or in any piece of waste ground you happen to be walking through, you can do something to remedy the appalling massacre of trees, especially oaks, ashes, elms and beeches, which has happened during the war years.

Even an apple tree is liable to live for about 100 years, so that the Cox I planted in 1936 may still be bearing fruit well into the twenty-first century. An oak or a beech may live for hundreds of years and be a pleasure to thousands or tens of thousands of people before it is finally sawn up into timber. I am not suggesting that one can discharge all one's obligations towards society by means of a private reafforestation scheme. Still, it might not be a bad idea, every time you commit an antisocial act, to make a note of it in your diary, and then, at the appropriate season, push an acorn into the ground.

And, if even one in twenty of them came to maturity, you might do quite a lot of harm in your lifetime and still, like the Vicar of Bray, end up as a public benefactor after all.

Confessions of a Book Reviewer*

In a cold but stuffy bed-sittingroom littered with cigarette ends and half-empty cups of tea, a man in a moth-eaten dressing gown sits at a rickety table, trying to find room for his typewriter among the piles of dusty papers that surround it. He cannot throw the papers away because the waste-paper basket is already overflowing, and besides, somewhere among the unanswered letters and unpaid bills it is possible that there is a cheque for two guineas which he is nearly certain he forgot to pay into the bank. There are also letters with addresses which ought to be entered in his address book. He has lost his address book, and the thought of looking for it, or indeed of looking for anything, afflicts him with acute suicidal impulses.

He is a man of thirty-five, but looks fifty. He is bald, has varicose veins and wears spectacles, or would wear them if his only pair were not chronically lost. If things are normal with him he will be suffering from malnutrition, but if he has recently had a lucky streak he will be suffering from a hangover. At present it is half-past eleven in the morning, and according to his schedule he should have started work two hours ago – but even if he had made any serious effort to start he would have been frustrated by the almost continuous ringing of the telephone bell, the yells of the baby, the rattle of an electric drill out in the street and the heavy boots of his creditors clumping up and down the stairs. The most recent interruption was the arrival of the second post, which brought him two circulars and an income-tax demand printed in red.

Needless to say this person is a writer. He might be a poet, a novelist, or a writer of film scripts or radio features, for all literary people are very much alike, but let us say that he is a book reviewer. Half hidden among the pile of papers is a bulky parcel containing five volumes which his editor has sent with a note suggesting that they "ought to go well together". They arrived four days ago, but for forty-eight hours the reviewer was prevented by moral paralysis from opening the parcel. Yesterday in a resolute moment he ripped the string off it and found the five volumes to be *Palestine at the Crossroads*, *Scientific Dairy Farming*, *A Short History of European Democracy* (this one is 680 pages and weighs four pounds), *Tribal Customs in Portuguese East Africa* and a novel, *It's Nicer Lying Down*, probably included by mistake. His review – 800 words, say – has got to be "in" by midday tomorrow.

Three of these books deal with subjects of which he is so ignorant that he will have to read at least fifty pages if he is to avoid making some howler which will betray him not merely to the author (who of course knows all about the habits of book reviewers) but even to the general reader. By four in the afternoon he will have taken the books out of their wrapping paper but will still be suffering from a nervous inability to open them. The prospect of having to read them, and even the smell of the paper, affects him like the prospect of eating cold ground-rice pudding flavoured with castor oil. And yet curiously enough his copy will get to the office in time. Somehow it always does get there in time. At about nine in the evening his mind will grow relatively clear, and until the small hours he will sit in a room which grows colder and colder, while the cigarette smoke grows thicker and thicker, skipping expertly through one book after another and laying each down with the final comment, "God, what tripe!" In the morning, blear-eyed, surly and unshaven, he will gaze for an hour or two at a blank sheet of paper until the menacing finger of the clock frightens him into action. Then suddenly he will snap into it. All the stale old phrases – "a book that no one should miss", "something memorable on every page", "of special value are the chapters dealing with, etc. etc." – will jump into their places like iron filings obeying the magnet, and the review will end up at exactly the right length and with just about three minutes to go. Meanwhile another wad of ill-assorted, unappetizing books will have arrived by post. So it goes on. And yet with what high hopes this downtrodden, nerve-racked creature started his career, only a few years ago.

Do I seem to exaggerate? I ask any regular reviewer – anyone who reviews, say, a minimum of 100 books a year – whether he can deny in honesty that his habits and character are such as I have described. Every writer, in any case, is rather that kind of person, but the prolonged, indiscriminate reviewing of books is a quite exceptionally thankless, irritating and exhausting job. It not only involves praising trash – though it does involve that, as I will show in a moment – but constantly *inventing* reactions towards books about which one has no spontaneous feelings whatever. The reviewer, jaded though he may be, is professionally interested in books, and out of the thousands that appear annually, there are probably fifty or a hundred that he would enjoy writing about. If he is a top-notcher in his profession he may get hold of ten or twenty of them; more probably he gets hold of two or three. The rest of his work, however conscientious he may be in praising or damning, is in essence humbug. He is pouring his immortal spirit down the drain, half a pint at a time.

The great majority of reviews give an inadequate or misleading account of the book that is dealt with. Since the war publishers have been less able than before to twist the tails of literary editors and evoke a paean of praise for every book that they produce, but on the other hand the standard of reviewing has gone down owing to lack of space and other inconveniences. Seeing the results, people sometimes suggest that the solution lies in getting book reviewing out of the hands of hacks. Books on specialized subjects ought to be dealt with by experts, and on the other hand a good deal of reviewing, especially of novels, might well be done by amateurs. Nearly every book is capable of arousing passionate feeling, if it is only a passionate dislike, in some or other reader, whose ideas about it would surely be worth more than those of a bored professional. But, unfortunately, as every editor knows, that kind of thing is very difficult to organize. In practice the editor always finds himself reverting to his team of hacks – his "regulars", as he calls them.

None of this is remediable so long as it is taken for granted that every book deserves to be reviewed. It is almost impossible to mention books in bulk without grossly overpraising the great majority of them. Until one has some kind of professional relationship with books one does not discover how bad the majority of them are. In much more than nine cases out of ten the only objectively truthful criticism would be "This book is worthless", while the truth about the reviewer's own reaction would probably be: "This book does not interest me in any way, and I would not write about it unless I were paid to." But the public will not pay to read that kind of thing. Why should they? They want some kind of guide to the books they are asked to read, and they want some kind of evaluation. But as soon as values are mentioned, standards collapse. For if one says – and nearly every reviewer says this kind of thing at least once a week – that *King Lear* is a good play and *The Four Just Men** is a good thriller, what meaning is there in the word "good"?

The best practice, it has always seemed to me, would be simply to ignore the great majority of books and to give very long reviews – 1,000 words is a bare minimum – to the few that seem to matter. Short notes of a line or two on forthcoming books can be useful, but the usual middle-length review of about 600 words is bound to be worthless even if the reviewer genuinely wants to write it. Normally he doesn't want to write it, and the week-in, week-out production of snippets soon reduces him to the crushed figure in a dressing gown whom I described at the beginning of this article. However, everyone in this world has someone else whom he can look down on, and I must say, from experience of both trades, that the book reviewer is better off than the film critic, who cannot even do his work at home, but has to attend trade shows at eleven in the morning and, with one or two notable exceptions, is expected to sell his honour for a glass of inferior sherry.

James Burnham and the Managerial Revolution*

James Burnham's book *The Managerial Revolution* made a considerable stir both in the United States and in this country at the time when it was published, and its main thesis has been so much discussed that a detailed exposition of it is hardly necessary. As shortly as I can summarize it, the thesis is this:

Capitalism is disappearing, but socialism is not replacing it. What is now arising is a new kind of planned, centralized society which will be neither capitalist nor, in any accepted sense of the word, democratic. The rulers of this new society will be the people who effectively control the means of production: that is, business executives, technicians, bureaucrats and soldiers, lumped together by Burnham under the name of "managers". These people will eliminate the old capitalist class, crush the working class, and so organize society that all power and economic privilege remain in their own hands. Private property rights will be abolished, but common ownership will not be established. The new "managerial" societies will not consist of a patchwork of small, independent states but of great superstates grouped round the main industrial centres in Europe, Asia and America. These superstates will fight among themselves for possession of the remaining uncaptured portions of the earth, but will probably be unable to conquer one another completely. Internally, each society will be hierarchical, with an aristocracy of talent at the top and a mass of semi-slaves at the bottom.

In his next published book, *The Machiavellians*,* Burnham elaborates and also modifies his original statement. The greater part of the book is an exposition of the theories of Machiavelli and of his modern disciples, Mosca, Michels and Pareto;* with doubtful justification, Burnham adds to these the syndicalist writer Georges Sorel.* What Burnham is mainly concerned to show is that a democratic society has never existed and, so far as we can see, never will exist. Society is of its nature oligarchical, and the power of the oligarchy always rests upon force and fraud. Burnham does not deny that "good" motives may operate in private life, but he maintains that politics consists of the struggle for power, and nothing else. All historical changes finally boil down to the replacement of one ruling class by another. All talk about democracy, liberty, equality, fraternity, all revolutionary movements, all visions of utopia, or "the classless society", or "the Kingdom of Heaven on earth", are humbug (not necessarily conscious humbug) covering the ambitions of some new class which is elbowing its way into power. The English Puritans, the Jacobins, the Bolsheviks were in each case simply power seekers using the hopes of the masses in order to win a privileged position for themselves. Power can sometimes be won or maintained without violence, but never without fraud, because it is necessary to make use of the masses, and the masses would not cooperate if they knew that they were simply serving the purposes of a minority. In each great revolutionary struggle the masses are led on by vague dreams of human brotherhood, and then, when the new ruling class is well established in power, they are thrust back into servitude. This is practically the whole of political history, as Burnham sees it.

Where the second book departs from the earlier one is in asserting that the whole process could be somewhat moralized if the facts were faced more honestly. *The Machiavellians* is subtitled *Defenders of Freedom*. Machiavelli and his followers taught that in politics decency simply does not exist, and, by doing so, Burnham claims, made it possible to conduct political affairs more intelligently and less oppressively. A ruling class which recognized that its real aim was to stay in power would also recognize that it would be more likely to succeed if it served the common good, and might avoid stiffening into a hereditary aristocracy. Burnham lays much stress on Pareto's theory of the "circulation of the elites". If it is to stay in power a ruling class must constantly admit suitable recruits from below, so that the ablest men may always be at the top and a new class of power-hungry malcontents cannot come into being. This is likeliest to happen, Burnham considers, in a society which retains democratic habits – that is, where opposition is permitted and certain bodies such as the press and the trade unions can keep their autonomy. Here Burnham undoubtedly contradicts his earlier opinion. In *The Managerial Revolution*, which was written in 1940, it is taken as a matter of course that "managerial" Germany is in all ways more efficient than a capitalist democracy such as France or Britain. In the second book, written in 1942, Burnham admits that the Germans might have avoided some of their more serious strategic errors if they had permitted freedom of speech. However, the main thesis is not abandoned. Capitalism is doomed, and socialism is a dream. If we grasp what is at issue we may guide the course of the managerial revolution to some extent, but that revolution *is happening*, whether we like it or not. In both books, but especially the earlier one, there is a note of unmistakable relish over the cruelty and wickedness of the processes that are being discussed. Although he reiterates that he is merely setting forth the facts and not stating his own preferences, it is clear that Burnham is fascinated by the spectacle of power, and that his sympathies were with Germany so long as Germany appeared to be winning the war. A more recent essay, 'Lenin's Heir', published in the *Partisan Review* about the beginning of 1945, suggests that this sympathy has since been transferred to the USSR. 'Lenin's Heir', which provoked violent controversy in the American left-wing press, has not yet been reprinted in England, and I must return to it later.

It will be seen that Burnham's theory is not, strictly speaking, a new one. Many earlier writers have foreseen the emergence of a new kind of society, neither capitalist nor socialist, and probably based upon slavery – though most of them have differed from Burnham in not assuming this development to be *inevitable*. A good example is Hilaire Belloc's book *The Servile State*,* published in 1911. *The Servile State* is written in a tiresome style, and the remedy it suggests (a return to small-scale peasant ownership) is for many reasons impossible; still, it does foretell with remarkable insight the kind of things that have been happening from about 1930 onwards. Chesterton, in a less methodical way, predicted the disappearance of democracy and private property, and the rise of a slave society which might be called either capitalist or communist. Jack London, in *The Iron Heel* (1909), foretold some of the essential features of fascism, and such books as Wells's *The Sleeper Awakes* (1900), Zamyatin's *We** (1923) and Aldous Huxley's *Brave New World* (1930) all described imaginary worlds in which the special problems of capitalism had been solved without bringing liberty, equality or true happiness any nearer. More recently, writers like Peter Drucker* and F.A. Voigt have argued that fascism and communism are substantially the same thing. And indeed, it has always been obvious that a planned and centralized society is liable to develop into an oligarchy or a dictatorship. Orthodox Conservatives were unable to see this, because it comforted them to assume that socialism "wouldn't work", and that the disappearance of capitalism would mean chaos and anarchy. Orthodox socialists could not see it, because they wished to think that they themselves would soon be in power, and therefore assumed that when capitalism disappears, socialism takes its place. As a result they were unable to foresee the rise of fascism, or to make correct predictions about it after it had appeared. Later, the need to justify the Russian dictatorship and to explain away the obvious resemblances between communism and Nazism clouded the issue still more. But the notion that industrialism must end in monopoly, and that monopoly must imply tyranny, is not a startling one.

Where Burnham differs from most other thinkers is in trying to plot the course of the "managerial revolution" accurately on a world scale, and in assuming that the drift towards totalitarianism is irresistible and must not be fought against, though it may be guided. According to Burnham, writing in 1940, "managerialism" has reached its fullest development in the USSR, but is almost equally well developed in Germany, and has made its appearance in the United States. He describes the New Deal as "primitive managerialism". But the trend is the same everywhere, or almost everywhere. Always laissez-faire capitalism gives way to planning and state interference, the mere *owner* loses power as against the technician and the bureaucrat, but socialism – that is to say, what used to be called socialism – shows no sign of emerging:

Some apologists try to excuse Marxism by saying that it has "never had a chance". This is far from the truth. Marxism and the Marxist parties have had dozens of chances. In Russia, a Marxist party took power. Within a short time it abandoned socialism; if not in words, at any rate in the effect of its actions. In most European nations there were during the last months of the first world war and the years immediately thereafter, social crises which left a wide-open door for the Marxist parties: without exception they proved unable to take and hold power. In a large number of countries – Germany, Denmark, Norway, Sweden, Austria, England, Australia, New Zealand, Spain, France – the reformist Marxist parties have administered the governments, and have uniformly failed to introduce socialism or make any genuine step towards socialism. [...] These parties have, in practice, at every historical test – and there have been many – either failed socialism or abandoned it. This is the fact which neither the bitterest foe nor the most ardent friend of socialism can erase. This fact does not, as some think, prove anything about the moral quality of the socialist ideal. But it does constitute unblinkable evidence that, whatever its moral quality, socialism is not going to come.

Burnham does not, of course, deny that the new "managerial" regimes, like the regimes of Russia and Nazi Germany, may be *called* socialist. He means merely that they will not *be* socialist in any sense of the word which would have been accepted by Marx, or Lenin, or Keir Hardie, or William Morris, or indeed, by any representative socialist prior to about 1930. Socialism, until recently, was supposed to connote political democracy, social equality and internationalism. There is not the smallest sign that any of these things is in a way to being established anywhere, and the one great country in which something described as a proletarian revolution once happened, i.e. the USSR, has moved steadily away from the old concept of a free and equal society aiming at universal human brotherhood. In an almost unbroken progress since the early days of the Revolution, liberty has been chipped away and representative institutions smothered, while inequalities have increased and nationalism and militarism have grown stronger. But at the same time, Burnham insists, there has been no tendency to return to capitalism. What is happening is simply the growth of "managerialism", which, according to Burnham, is in progress everywhere, though the manner in which it comes about may vary from country to country.

Now, as an interpretation of what *is happening*, Burnham's theory is extremely plausible, to put it at the lowest. The events of, at any rate, the last fifteen years in the USSR can be far more easily explained by this theory than by any other. Evidently the USSR is not socialist, and can only be called socialist if one gives the word a meaning different from what it would have in any other context. On the other hand, prophecies that the Russian regime would revert to capitalism have always been falsified, and now seem further than ever from being fulfilled. In claiming that the process had gone almost equally far in Nazi Germany, Burnham probably exaggerates, but it seems certain that the drift was away from old-style capitalism and towards a planned economy with an adoptive oligarchy in control. In Russia the capitalists were destroyed first and the workers were crushed later. In Germany the workers were crushed first – but the elimination of the capitalists had at any rate begun, and calculations based on the assumption that Nazism was "simply capitalism" were always contradicted by events. Where Burnham seems to go most astray is in believing "managerialism" to be on the upgrade in the United States, the one great country where free capitalism is still vigorous. But if one considers the world movement as a whole, his conclusions are difficult to resist – and even in the United States the all-prevailing faith in laissez-faire may not survive the next great economic crisis. It has been urged against Burnham that he assigns far too much importance to the "managers", in the narrow sense of the word – that is, factory bosses, planners and technicians – and seems to assume that even in Soviet Russia it is these people, and not the Communist Party chiefs, who are the real holders of power. However, this is a secondary error, and it is partially corrected in *The Machiavellians*. The real question is not whether the people who wipe their boots on us during the next fifty years are to be called managers, bureaucrats or politicians: the question is whether capitalism, now obviously doomed, is to give way to oligarchy or to true democracy.

But curiously enough, when one examines the predictions which Burnham has based on his general theory, one finds that in so far as they are verifiable, they have been falsified. Numbers of people have pointed this out already. However, it is worth following up Burnham's predictions in detail, because they form a sort of pattern which is related to contemporary events, and which reveals, I believe, a very important weakness in present-day political thought.

To begin with, writing in 1940, Burnham takes a German victory more or less for granted. Britain is described as "dissolving", and as displaying "all the characteristics which have distinguished decadent cultures in past historical transitions", while the conquest and integration of Europe which Germany achieved in 1940 is described as "irreversible". "England," writes Burnham, "no matter with what non-European allies, cannot conceivably hope to conquer the European continent." Even if Germany should somehow manage to lose the war, she could not be dismembered or reduced to the status of the Weimar Republic, but is bound to remain as the nucleus of a unified Europe. The future map of the world, with its three great superstates, is in any case already settled in its main outlines – and "the nuclei of these three superstates are, whatever may be their future names, the previously existing nations, Japan, Germany and the United States."

Burnham also commits himself to the opinion that Germany will not attack the USSR until after Britain has been defeated. In a condensation of his book published in the *Partisan Review* of May–June 1941, and presumably written later than the book itself, he says:

> As in the case of Russia, so with Germany, the third part of the managerial problem – the contest for dominance with other sections of managerial society – remains for the future. First had to come the death-blow that assured the toppling of the capitalist world order, which meant above all the destruction of the foundations of the British Empire (the keystone of the capitalist world order) both directly and through the smashing of the European political structure, which was a necessary prop of the Empire. This is the basic explanation of the Nazi–Soviet Pact, which is not intelligible on other grounds. The future conflict between Germany and Russia will be a managerial conflict proper; prior to the great world-managerial battles, the end of the capitalist order must be assured. The belief that Nazism is "decadent capitalism" […] makes it impossible to explain reasonably the Nazi–Soviet Pact. From this belief followed the always expected war between Germany and Russia, not the actual war to the death between Germany and the British Empire. The war between Germany and Russia is one of the managerial wars of the future, not of the anticapitalist wars of yesterday and today.

However, the attack on Russia will come later, and Russia is certain, or almost certain, to be defeated. "There is every reason to believe […] that Russia will split apart, with the western half gravitating towards the European base and the eastern towards the Asiatic." This quotation comes from *The Managerial Revolution*. In the above-quoted article, written probably about six months later, it is put more forcibly: "the Russian weaknesses indicate that Russia will not be able to endure, that it will crack apart, and fall towards east and west." And in a supplementary note which was added to the English (Pelican) edition, and which appears to have been written at the end of 1941, Burnham speaks as though the "cracking apart" process were already happening. The war, he says, "is part of the means whereby the western half of Russia is being integrated into the European super-state".

Sorting these various statements out, we have the following prophecies:

1. Germany is bound to win the war.
2. Germany and Japan are bound to survive as great states, and to remain the nuclei of power in their respective areas.
3. Germany will not attack the USSR until after the defeat of Britain.
4. The USSR is bound to be defeated.

However, Burnham has made other predictions besides these. In a short article in the *Partisan Review*, in the summer of 1944, he gives his opinion that the USSR will gang up with Japan in order to prevent the total defeat of the latter, while the American communists will be set to work to sabotage the eastern end of the war. And finally, in an article in the same magazine in the winter of 1944–45, he claims that Russia, destined so short a while ago to "crack apart", is within sight of conquering the whole of Eurasia. This article, which was the cause of violent controversies among the American intelligentsia, has not been reprinted in England. I must give some account of it here, because its manner of approach and its emotional tone are of a peculiar kind, and by studying them one can get nearer to the real roots of Burnham's theory.

The article is entitled 'Lenin's Heir', and it sets out to show that Stalin is the true and legitimate guardian of the Russian Revolution, which he has not in any sense "betrayed" but has merely carried forward on lines that were implicit in it from the start. In itself, this is an easier opinion to swallow than the usual Trotskyist claim that Stalin is a mere crook who has perverted the Revolution to his own ends, and that things would somehow have been different if Lenin had lived or Trotsky had remained in power. Actually there is no strong reason for thinking that the main lines of development would have been very different. Well before 1923 the seeds of a totalitarian society were quite plainly there. Lenin, indeed, is one of those politicians who win an undeserved reputation by dying prematurely.* Had he lived, it is probable that he would either have been thrown out, like Trotsky, or would have kept himself in power by methods as barbarous, or nearly as barbarous, as those of Stalin. The *title* of Burnham's essay, therefore, sets forth a reasonable thesis, and one would expect him to support it by an appeal to the facts.

However, the essay barely touches upon its ostensible subject matter. It is obvious that anyone genuinely concerned to show that there has been continuity of policy as between Lenin and Stalin would start by outlining Lenin's policy and then explain in what way Stalin's has resembled it. Burnham does not do this. Except for one or two cursory sentences he says nothing about Lenin's policy, and Lenin's name only occurs five times in an essay of twelve pages – in the first seven pages, apart from the title, it does not occur at all. The real aim of the essay is to present Stalin as a towering, superhuman figure, indeed a species of demigod, and Bolshevism as an irresistible force which is flowing over the earth and cannot be halted until it reaches the outermost borders of Eurasia. In so far as he makes any attempt to prove his case, Burnham does so by repeating over and over again that Stalin is "a great man" – which is probably true, but is almost completely irrelevant. Moreover, though he does advance some solid arguments for believing in Stalin's genius, it is clear that in his mind the idea of "greatness" is inextricably mixed up with the idea of cruelty and dishonesty. There are curious passages in which it seems to be suggested that Stalin is to be admired *because of* the limitless suffering that he has caused:

> Stalin proves himself a "great man", in the grand style. The accounts of the banquets, staged in Moscow for the visiting dignitaries, set the symbolic tone. With their enormous menus of sturgeon, and roasts, and fowl, and sweets; their streams of liquor; the scores of toasts with which they end; the silent, unmoving secret police behind each guest; all against the winter background of the starving multitudes of besieged Leningrad; the dying millions at the front; the jammed concentration camps; the city crowds kept by their minute rations just at the edge of life; there is little trace of dull mediocrity or the hand of Babbitt.* We recognize, rather, the tradition of the most spectacular of the Tsars, of the Great Kings of the Medes and Persians, of the Khanate of the Golden Horde, of the banquet we assign to the gods of the Heroic Ages in tribute to the insight that insolence, and indifference, and brutality on such a scale remove beings from the human level. [...] Stalin's political techniques show a freedom from conventional restrictions that is incompatible with mediocrity: the mediocre man is custom-bound. Often it is the scale of their operations that sets them apart. It is usual, for example, for men active in practical life to engineer an occasional frame-up. But to carry out a frame-up against tens of thousands of persons, important percentages of whole strata of society, including most of one's own comrades, is so far out of the ordinary that the long-run mass conclusion is either that the frame-up must be true – at least "have some truth in it" – or that power so immense must be submitted to – is a "historical necessity", as intellectuals put it. [...] There is nothing unexpected in letting a few individuals starve for reasons of state; but to starve by deliberate decision, several millions, is a type of action attributed ordinarily only to gods.

In these and other similar passages there may be a tinge of irony, but it is difficult not to feel that there is also a sort of fascinated admiration. Towards the end of the essay Burnham compares Stalin with those semi-mythical heroes, like Moses or Asoka, who embody in themselves a whole epoch, and can justly be credited with feats that they did not actually perform. In writing of Soviet foreign policy and its supposed objectives, he touches an even more mystical note:

> Starting from the magnetic core of the Eurasian heartland, the Soviet power, like the reality of the One of Neo-Platonism overflowing in the descending series of the emanative progression, flows outward, west into Europe, south into the Near East, east into China, already lapping the shores of the Atlantic, the Yellow and China Seas, the Mediterranean, and the Persian

Gulf. As the undifferentiated One, in its progression, descends through the stages of Mind, Soul and Matter, and then through its fatal Return back to itself; so does the Soviet power, emanating from the integrally totalitarian centre, proceed outwards by Absorption (the Baltics, Bessarabia, Bukovina, East Poland), Domination (Finland, the Balkans, Mongolia, North China and, tomorrow, Germany), Orienting Influence (Italy, France, Turkey, Iran, Central and south China...), until it is dissipated in *MH ON*, the outer material sphere, beyond the Eurasian boundaries, of momentary Appeasement and Infiltration (England, the United States).

I do not think it is fanciful to suggest that the unnecessary capital letters with which this passage is loaded are intended to have a hypnotic effect on the reader. Burnham is trying to build up a picture of terrifying, irresistible power, and to turn a normal political manoeuvre like infiltration into "Infiltration" adds to the general portentousness. The essay should be read in full. Although it is not the kind of tribute that the average Russophile would consider acceptable, and although Burnham himself would probably claim that he is being strictly objective, he is in effect performing an act of homage, and even of self-abasement. Meanwhile, this essay gives us another prophecy to add to the list: i.e. that the USSR will conquer the whole of Eurasia, and probably a great deal more. And one must remember that Burnham's basic theory contains, in itself, a prediction which still has to be tested – that is, that whatever else happens, the "managerial" form of society is bound to prevail.

Burnham's earlier prophecy, of a Germany victory in the war and the integration of Europe round the German nucleus, was falsified, not only in its main outlines but in some important details. Burnham insists all the way through that "managerialism" is not only more efficient than capitalist democracy or Marxian socialism, but also more acceptable to the masses. The slogans of democracy and national self-determination, he says, no longer have any mass appeal: "managerialism", on the other hand, can rouse enthusiasm, produce intelligible war aims, establish fifth columns everywhere and inspire its soldiers with a fanatical morale. The "fanaticism" of the Germans, as against the "apathy" or "indifference" of the British, French, etc., is much emphasized, and Nazism is represented as a revolutionary force sweeping across Europe and spreading its philosophy "by contagion". The Nazi fifth columns "cannot be wiped out", and the democratic nations are quite incapable of projecting any settlement which the German or other European masses would prefer to the New Order. In any case, the democracies can only defeat Germany if they go "still further along the managerial road than Germany has yet gone".

The germ of truth in all this is that the smaller European states, demoralized by the chaos and stagnation of the pre-war years, collapsed rather more quickly than they need have done, and might conceivably have accepted the

New Order if the Germans had kept some of their promises. But the actual experience of German rule aroused almost at once such a fury of hatred and vindictiveness as the world has seldom seen. After about the beginning of 1941 there was hardly any need of a positive war aim, since getting rid of the Germans was a sufficient objective. The question of morale, and its relation to national solidarity, is a nebulous one, and the evidence can be so manipulated as to prove almost anything. But if one goes by the proportion of prisoners to other casualties, and the amount of quislingism, the totalitarian states come out of the comparison worse than the democracies. Hundreds of thousands of Russians appear to have gone over to the Germans during the course of the war, while comparable numbers of Germans and Italians had gone over to the Allies before the war started; the corresponding number of American or British renegades would have amounted to a few scores. As an example of the inability of "capitalist ideologies" to enlist support, Burnham cites "the complete failure of voluntary military recruiting in England (as well as the entire British Empire) and in the United States". One would gather from this that the armies of the totalitarian states were manned by volunteers. Actually, no totalitarian state has ever so much as considered voluntary recruitment for any purpose, nor, throughout history, has a large army ever been raised by voluntary means.* It is not worth listing the many similar arguments that Burnham puts forward. The point is that he assumes that the Germans must win the propaganda war as well as the military one, and that, at any rate in Europe, this estimate was not borne out by events.

It will be seen that Burnham's predictions have not merely, when they were verifiable, turned out to be wrong, but that they have sometimes contradicted one another in a sensational way. It is this last fact that is significant. Political predictions are usually wrong, because they are usually based on wish-thinking, but they can have symptomatic value, especially when they change abruptly. Often the revealing factor is the date at which they are made. Dating Burnham's various writings as accurately as can be done from internal evidence, and then noting what events they coincided with, we find the following relationships:

In *The Managerial Revolution* Burnham prophesies a German victory, postponement of the Russo-German war until after Britain is defeated, and, subsequently, the defeat of Russia. The book, or much of it, was written in the second half of 1940 – i.e. at a time when the Germans had overrun Western Europe and were bombing Britain, and the Russians were collaborating with them fairly closely, and in what appeared, at any rate, to be a spirit of appeasement.

In the supplementary note added to the English edition of the book, Burnham appears to assume that the USSR is already beaten and the splitting-up process is about to begin. This was published in the spring of 1942 and presumably written at the end of 1941 – i.e. when the Germans were in the suburbs of Moscow.

The prediction that Russia would gang up with Japan against the USA was written early in 1944, soon after the conclusion of a new Russo-Japanese treaty.

The prophecy of Russian world conquest was written in the winter of 1944, when the Russians were advancing rapidly in eastern Europe while the Western Allies were still held up in Italy and northern France.

It will be seen that at each point Burnham is predicting *a continuation of the thing that is happening*. Now the tendency to do this is not simply a bad habit, like inaccuracy or exaggeration, which one can correct by taking thought. It is a major mental disease, and its roots lie partly in cowardice and partly in the worship of power, which is not fully separable from cowardice.

Suppose in 1940 you had taken a Gallup poll,* in England, on the question "Will Germany win the war?" You would have found, curiously enough, that the group answering "Yes" contained a far higher percentage of intelligent people – people with IQ of over 120, shall we say – than the group answering "No". The same would have held good in the middle of 1942. In this case the figures would not have been so striking, but if you had made the question "Will the Germans capture Alexandria?" or "Will the Japanese be able to hold on to the territories they have captured?", then once again there would have been a very marked tendency for intelligence to concentrate in the "Yes" group. In every case the less-gifted person would have been likelier to give a right answer.

If one went simply by these instances, one might assume that high intelligence and bad military judgement always go together. However, it is not so simple as that. The English intelligentsia, on the whole, were more defeatist than the mass of the people – and some of them went on being defeatist at a time when the war was quite plainly won – partly because they were better able to visualize the dreary years of warfare that lay ahead. Their morale was worse because their imaginations were stronger. The quickest way of ending a war is to lose it, and if one finds the prospect of a long war intolerable, it is natural to disbelieve in the possibility of victory. But there was more to it than that. There was also the disaffection of large numbers of intellectuals, which made it difficult for them not to side with any country hostile to Britain. And deepest of all, there was admiration – though only in a very few cases conscious admiration – for the power, energy and cruelty of the Nazi regime. It would be a useful though tedious labour to go through the left-wing press and enumerate all the hostile references to Nazism during the years 1935–45. One would find, I have little doubt, that they reached their high-water mark in 1937–38 and 1944–45, and dropped off noticeably in the years 1939–42 – that is, during the period when Germany seemed to be winning. One would find, also, the same people advocating a compromise peace in 1940 and approving the dismemberment of Germany in 1945. And if one studied the reactions of the English intelligentsia towards the USSR, there, too, one would find genuinely progressive impulses mixed up with admiration for power and cruelty. It would be grossly unfair to suggest that power worship is the only motive for Russophile feeling, but it is one motive, and among intellectuals it is probably the strongest one.

Power worship blurs political judgement because it leads, almost unavoidably, to the belief that present trends will continue. Whoever is winning at the moment will always seem to be invincible. If the Japanese have conquered South Asia, then they will keep South Asia for ever; if the Germans have captured Tobruk, they will infallibly capture Cairo; if the Russians are in Berlin, it will not be long before they are in London – and so on. This habit of mind leads also to the belief that things will happen more quickly, completely and catastrophically than they ever do in practice. The rise and fall of empires, the disappearance of cultures and religions are expected to happen with earthquake suddenness, and processes which have barely started are talked about as though they were already at an end. Burnham's writings are full of apocalyptic visions. Nations, governments, classes and social systems are constantly described as expanding, contracting, decaying, dissolving, toppling, crashing, crumbling, crystallizing and, in general, behaving in an unstable and melodramatic way. The slowness of historical change, the fact that any epoch always contains a great deal of the last epoch, is never sufficiently allowed for. Such a manner of thinking is bound to lead to mistaken prophecies, because even when it gauges the direction of events rightly it will miscalculate their tempo. Within the space of five years Burnham foretold the domination of Russia by Germany and of Germany by Russia. In each case he was obeying the same instinct: the instinct to bow down before the conqueror of the moment, to accept the existing trend as irreversible. With this in mind one can criticize his theory in a broader way.

The mistakes I have pointed out do not disprove Burnham's theory, but they do cast light on his probable reasons for holding it. In this connection one cannot leave out of account the fact that Burnham is an American. Every political theory has a certain regional tinge about it, and every nation, every culture, has its own characteristic prejudices and patches of ignorance. There are certain problems that must almost inevitably be seen in a different perspective according to the geographical situation from which one is looking at them. Now, the attitude that Burnham adopts, of classifying communism and fascism as much the same thing, and at the same time accepting both of them – or, at any rate, not assuming that either must be violently struggled against – is essentially an American attitude, and would be almost impossible for an Englishman or any other Western European. English writers who consider communism and fascism to be *the same thing* invariably hold that both are monstrous evils which must be fought to the death; on the other hand, any Englishman who believes communism and fascism to be opposites will feel that he ought to side with one or the other.* The reason for this difference of outlook is simple enough and, as usual, is bound up with wish-thinking. If totalitarianism triumphs and the dreams of the geopoliticians come true, Britain will disappear as a world power and the whole of Western Europe will be swallowed by some single great state. This is not a prospect that it is easy for an Englishman to contemplate with detachment. Either he does not want Britain to disappear – in which case he will tend to construct theories proving the thing that he wants – or, like a minority of intellectuals, he will decide that his country is finished and transfer his allegiance to some foreign power. An American does not have to make the same choice. Whatever happens, the United States will survive as a great power, and from the American point of view it does not make much difference whether Europe is dominated by Russia or by Germany. Most Americans who think of the matter at all would prefer to see the world divided between two or three monster states which had reached their natural boundaries and could bargain with one another on economic issues without being troubled by ideological differences. Such a world picture fits in with the American tendency to admire size for its own sake and to feel that success constitutes justification, and it fits in with the all-prevailing anti-British sentiment. In practice, Britain and the United States have twice been forced into alliance against Germany, and will probably, before long, be forced into alliance against Russia – but, subjectively, a majority of Americans would prefer either Russia or Germany to Britain, and as between Russia and Germany would prefer whichever seemed stronger at the moment.* It is, therefore, not surprising that Burnham's world view should often be noticeably close to that of the American imperialists on the one side, or to that of the isolationists on the other. It is a "tough" or "realistic" world view which fits in with the American form of wish-thinking. The almost open admiration for Nazi methods which Burnham shows in the earlier of his two books, and which would seem shocking to almost any English reader, depends ultimately on the fact that the Atlantic is wider than the Channel.

As I have said earlier, Burnham has probably been more right than wrong about the present and the immediate past. For quite fifty years past the general drift has almost certainly been towards oligarchy. The ever-increasing concentration of industrial and financial power; the diminishing importance of the individual capitalist or shareholder and the growth of the new "managerial" class of scientists, technicians and bureaucrats; the weakness of the proletariat against the centralized state; the increasing helplessness of small countries against big ones; the decay of representative institutions and the appearance of one-party regimes based on police terrorism, faked plebiscites, etc. – all these things seem to point in the same direction. Burnham sees the trend and assumes that it is irresistible, rather as a rabbit fascinated by a boa constrictor might assume that a boa constrictor is the strongest thing in the world. When one looks a little deeper, one sees that all his ideas rest upon two axioms which are taken for granted in the earlier book and made partly explicit in the second one. They are:

1. Politics is essentially the same in all ages.
2. Political behaviour is different from other kinds of behaviour.

To take the second point first. In *The Machiavellians*, Burnham insists that politics is simply the struggle for power. Every great social movement, every war, every revolution, every political programme, however edifying and utopian, really has behind it the ambitions of some sectional group which is out to grab power for itself. Power can never be restrained by any ethical or religious code, but only by other power. The nearest possible approach to altruistic behaviour is the perception by a ruling group that it will probably stay in power longer if it behaves decently. But curiously enough, these generalizations only apply to political behaviour, not to any other kind of behaviour. In everyday life, as Burnham sees and admits, one cannot explain every human action by applying the principle of *cui bono?** Obviously, human beings have impulses which are not selfish. Man, therefore, is an animal that can act morally when he acts as an individual, but becomes unmoral when he acts collectively. But even this generalization only holds good for the higher groups. The masses, it seems, have vague aspirations towards liberty and human brotherhood, which are easily played upon by power-hungry individuals or minorities. So that history consists of a series of swindles, in which the masses are first lured into revolt by the promise of utopia, and then, when they have done their job, enslaved over again by new masters.

Political activity, therefore, is a special kind of behaviour, characterized by its complete unscrupulousness, and occurring only among small groups of the population, especially among dissatisfied groups whose talents do not get free play under the existing form of society. The great mass of the people – and this is where (2) ties up with (1) – will always be unpolitical. In effect, therefore, humanity is divided into two classes: the self-seeking, hypocritical minority and the brainless mob whose destiny is always to be led or driven, as one gets a pig back to the sty by kicking it on the bottom or by rattling a stick inside a swill bucket, according to the needs of the moment. And this beautiful pattern is to continue for ever. Individuals may pass from one category to another, whole classes may destroy other classes and rise to the dominant position, but the division of humanity into rulers and ruled is unalterable. In their capabilities, as in their desires and needs, men are not equal. There is an "iron law of oligarchy", which would operate even if democracy were not impossible for mechanical reasons.

It is curious that in all his talk about the struggle for power, Burnham never stops to ask *why* people want power. He seems to assume that power hunger, although only dominant in comparatively few people, is a natural instinct that does not have to be explained, like the desire for food. He also assumes that the division of society into classes serves the same purpose in all ages. This is practically to ignore the history of hundreds of years. When Burnham's master, Machiavelli, was writing, class divisions were not only unavoidable, but desirable. So long as methods of production were primitive, the great mass of the people were necessarily tied down to dreary, exhausting manual labour – and a few people had to be set free from such labour, otherwise civilization could not maintain itself, let alone make any progress. But since the arrival of the machine the whole pattern has altered. The justification for class distinctions, if there is a justification, is no longer the same, because there is no mechanical reason why the average human being should continue to be a drudge. True, drudgery persists; class distinctions are probably re-establishing themselves in a new form, and individual liberty is on the downgrade – but as these developments are now technically avoidable, they must have some psychological cause which Burnham makes no attempt to discover. The question that he ought to ask, and never does ask, is: why does the lust for naked power become a major human motive exactly *now*, when the dominion of man over man is ceasing to be necessary? As for the claim that "human nature" or "inexorable laws" of this and that make socialism impossible, it is simply a projection of the past into the future. In effect, Burnham argues that because a society of free and equal human beings has never existed, it never can exist. By the same argument one could have demonstrated the impossibility of aeroplanes in 1900, or of motor cars in 1850.

The notion that the machine has altered human relationships, and that in consequence Machiavelli is out of date, is a very obvious one. If Burnham fails to deal with it, it can, I think, only be because his own power instinct leads him to brush aside any suggestion that the Machiavellian world of force, fraud and tyranny may somehow come to an end. It is important to bear in mind what I said above: that Burnham's theory is only a variant – an American variant, and interesting because of its comprehensiveness – of the power worship now so prevalent among intellectuals. A more normal variant, at any rate in England, is communism. If one examines the people who, having some idea of what the Russian regime is like, are strongly Russophile, one finds that, on the whole, they belong to the "managerial" class of which Burnham writes. That is, they are not managers in the narrow sense but scientists, technicians, teachers, journalists, broadcasters, bureaucrats, professional politicians – in general, middling people who feel themselves cramped by a system that is still partly aristocratic, and are hungry for more power and more prestige. These people look towards the USSR and see in it, or think they see, a system which eliminates the upper class, keeps the working class in its place and hands unlimited power to people very similar to themselves. It was only *after* the Soviet regime became unmistakably totalitarian that English intellectuals, in large numbers, began to show an interest in it. Burnham, although the English Russophile intelligentsia would repudiate him, is really voicing their secret wish: the wish to destroy the old, equalitarian version of socialism and usher in a hierarchical society where the intellectual can at last get his hands on the whip. Burnham at least has the honesty to say that socialism isn't coming; the others merely say that socialism *is* coming, and then give the word "socialism" a new meaning which makes nonsense of the old one. But his theory, for all its appearance of objectivity, is the rationalization of a wish. There is no strong reason for thinking that it tells us anything about the future, except perhaps the immediate future. It merely tells us what kind of world the "managerial" class themselves, or at least the more conscious and ambitious members of the class, would like to live in.

Fortunately the "managers" are not so invincible as Burnham believes. It is curious how persistently, in *The Managerial Revolution*, he ignores the advantages, military as well as social, enjoyed by a democratic country. At every point the evidence is squeezed in order to show the strength, vitality and durability of Hitler's crazy regime. Germany is expanding rapidly, and "rapid territorial expansion has always been a sign, not of decadence [...] but of renewal". Germany makes war successfully, and "the ability to make war well is never a sign of decadence but of its opposite". Germany also "inspires in millions of persons a fanatical loyalty. This, too, never accompanies decadence." Even the cruelty and dishonesty of the Nazi regime are cited in its favour, since "the young, new, rising social order is, as against the old, more likely to resort on a large scale to lies, terror, persecution". Yet, within only five years this young, new, rising social order had smashed itself to pieces and become, in Burnham's usage of the word, decadent. And this had happened quite largely because of the "managerial" (i.e. undemocratic) structure which Burnham admires. The immediate cause of the German defeat was the unheard-of folly of attacking the USSR while Britain was still undefeated and America was manifestly getting ready to fight. Mistakes of this magnitude can only be made, or at any rate they are most likely to be made, in countries where public opinion has no power. So long as the common man can get a hearing, such elementary rules as not fighting all your enemies simultaneously are less likely to be violated.

But, in any case, one should have been able to see from the start that such a movement as Nazism could not produce any good or stable result. Actually, so long as they were winning, Burnham seems to have seen nothing wrong with the methods of the Nazis. Such methods, he says, only appear wicked because they are new:

> There is no historical law that polite manners and "justice" shall conquer. In history there is always the question of *whose* manners and *whose* justice. A rising social class and a new order of society have got to break through

the old moral codes just as they must break through the old economic and political institutions. Naturally, from the point of view of the old, they are monsters. If they win, they take care in due time of manners and morals.

This implies that literally anything can become right or wrong if the dominant class of the moment so wills it. It ignores the fact that certain rules of conduct have to be observed if human society is to hold together at all. Burnham, therefore, was unable to see that the crimes and follies of the Nazi regime *must* lead by one route or another to disaster. So also with his newfound admiration for Stalinism. It is too early to say in just what way the Russian regime will destroy itself. If I had to make a prophecy, I should say that a continuation of the Russian policies of the last fifteen years – and internal and external policy, of course, are merely two facets of the same thing – can only lead to a war conducted with atomic bombs, which will make Hitler's invasion look like a tea party. But at any rate, the Russian regime will either democratize itself or it will perish. The huge, invincible, everlasting slave empire of which Burnham appears to dream will not be established, or if established will not endure, because slavery is no longer a stable basis for human society.

One cannot always make positive prophecies, but there are times when one ought to be able to make negative ones. No one could have been expected to foresee the exact results of the Treaty of Versailles, but millions of thinking people could and did foresee that those results would be bad. Plenty of people, though not so many in this case, can foresee that the results of the settlement now being forced on Europe will also be bad. And to refrain from admiring Hitler or Stalin – that, too, should not require an enormous intellectual effort. But it is partly a moral effort. That a man of Burnham's gifts should have been able for a while to think of Nazism as something rather admirable, something that could and probably would build up a workable and durable social order, shows what damage is done to the sense of reality by the cultivation of what is now called "realism".

Why I Write*

From a very early age, perhaps the age of five or six, I knew that when I grew up I should be a writer. Between the ages of about seventeen and twenty-four I tried to abandon this idea, but I did so with the consciousness that I was outraging my true nature and that sooner or later I should have to settle down and write books.

I was the middle child of three, but there was a gap of five years on either side, and I barely saw my father before I was eight. For this and other reasons I was somewhat lonely, and I soon developed disagreeable mannerisms which made me unpopular throughout my schooldays. I had the lonely child's habit of making up stories and holding conversations with imaginary persons, and I think from the very start my literary ambitions were mixed up with the feeling of being isolated and undervalued. I knew that I had a facility with words and a power of facing unpleasant facts, and I felt that this created a sort of private world in which I could get my own back for my failure in everyday life. Nevertheless the volume of serious – i.e. seriously intended – writing which I produced all through my childhood and boyhood would not amount to half a dozen pages. I wrote my first poem at the age of four or five, my mother taking it down to dictation. I cannot remember anything about it except that it was about a tiger and the tiger had "chair-like teeth" – a good enough phrase, but I fancy the poem was a plagiarism of Blake's 'Tiger, Tiger'.* At eleven, when the war of 1914–18 broke out, I wrote a patriotic poem which was printed in the local newspaper, as was another, two years later, on the death of Kitchener.* From time to time, when I was a bit older, I wrote bad and usually unfinished "nature poems" in the Georgian style. I also, about twice, attempted a short story, which was a ghastly failure. That was the total of the would-be serious work that I actually set down on paper during all those years.

However, throughout this time I did in a sense engage in literary activities. To begin with there was the made-to-order stuff which I produced quickly, easily and without much pleasure to myself. Apart from schoolwork, I wrote *vers d'occasion*,* semi-comic poems which I could turn out at what now seems to me astonishing speed – at fourteen I wrote a whole rhyming play, in imitation of Aristophanes, in about a week – and helped to edit school magazines, both printed and in manuscript. These magazines were the most pitiful burlesque stuff that you could imagine, and I took far less trouble with them than I now would with the cheapest journalism. But side by side with all this, for fifteen years or more, I was carrying out a literary exercise of a quite different kind: this was the making up of a continuous "story" about myself, a sort of diary existing only in the mind. I believe this is a common habit of children and adolescents. As a very small child I used to imagine that I was, say, Robin Hood, and picture myself as the hero of thrilling adventures, but quite soon my "story" ceased to be narcissistic in a crude way and became more and more a mere description of what I was doing and the things I saw. For minutes at a time this kind of thing would be running through my head: "He pushed the door open and entered the room. A yellow beam of sunlight, filtering through the muslin curtains, slanted onto the table, where a matchbox, half open, lay beside the inkpot. With his right hand in his pocket he moved across to the window. Down in the street a tortoiseshell cat was chasing a dead leaf," etc. etc. This habit continued till I was about twenty-five, right through my non-literary years. Although I had to search, and did search, for the right words, I seemed to be making this descriptive effort almost against my will, under a kind of compulsion from outside. The "story" must, I suppose, have reflected the styles of the various writers I admired at different ages, but so far as I remember it always had the same meticulous descriptive quality.

When I was about sixteen I suddenly discovered the joy of mere words, i.e. the sounds and associations of words. The lines from *Paradise Lost*,

> So hee with difficulty and labour hard
> Moved on: with difficulty and labour hee,*

which do not now seem to me so very wonderful, sent shivers down my backbone – and the spelling "hee" for "he" was an added pleasure. As for the need to describe things, I knew all about it already. So it is clear what kind of books I wanted to write, in so far as I could be said to want to write books at that time. I wanted to write enormous naturalistic novels with unhappy endings, full of detailed descriptions and arresting similes, and also full of purple passages in which words were used partly for the sake of their sound. And in fact my first completed novel, *Burmese Days*,* which I wrote when I was thirty but projected much earlier, is rather that kind of book.

I give all this background information because I do not think one can assess a writer's motives without knowing something of his early development. His subject matter will be determined by the age he lives in – at least this is true in tumultuous, revolutionary ages like our own – but before he ever begins to write he will have acquired an emotional attitude from which he will never completely escape. It is his job, no doubt, to discipline his temperament and avoid getting stuck at some immature stage, or in some perverse mood: but if he escapes from his early influences altogether, he will have killed his impulse to write.

WHY I WRITE

Putting aside the need to earn a living, I think there are four great motives for writing, at any rate for writing prose. They exist in different degrees in every writer, and in any one writer the proportions will vary from time to time, according to the atmosphere in which he is living. They are:

1. Sheer egoism. Desire to seem clever, to be talked about, to be remembered after death, to get your own back on grown-ups who snubbed you in childhood, etc. etc. It is humbug to pretend that this is not a motive, and a strong one. Writers share this characteristic with scientists, artists, politicians, lawyers, soldiers, successful businessmen – in short, with the whole top crust of humanity. The great mass of human beings are not acutely selfish. After the age of about thirty they abandon individual ambition – in many cases, indeed, they almost abandon the sense of being individuals at all – and live chiefly for others, or are simply smothered under drudgery. But there is also the minority of gifted, wilful people who are determined to live their own lives to the end, and writers belong in this class. Serious writers, I should say, are on the whole more vain and self-centred than journalists, though less interested in money.

2. Aesthetic enthusiasm. Perception of beauty in the external world, or, on the other hand, in words and their right arrangement. Pleasure in the impact of one sound on another, in the firmness of good prose or the rhythm of a good story. Desire to share an experience which one feels is valuable and ought not to be missed. The aesthetic motive is very feeble in a lot of writers, but even a pamphleteer or a writer of textbooks will have pet words and phrases which appeal to him for non-utilitarian reasons, or he may feel strongly about typography, width of margins, etc. Above the level of a railway guide, no book is quite free from aesthetic considerations.

3. Historical impulse. Desire to see things as they are, to find out true facts and store them up for the use of posterity.

4. Political purpose – using the word "political" in the widest possible sense. Desire to push the world in a certain direction, to alter other people's idea of the kind of society that they should strive after. Once again, no book is genuinely free from political bias. The opinion that art should have nothing to do with politics is itself a political attitude.

It can be seen how these various impulses must war against one another, and how they must fluctuate from person to person and from time to time. By nature – taking your "nature" to be the state you have attained when you are first adult – I am a person in whom the first three motives would outweigh the fourth. In a peaceful age I might have written ornate or merely descriptive books, and might have remained almost unaware of my political loyalties. As it is I have been forced into becoming a sort of pamphleteer. First I spent five years in an unsuitable profession (the Indian Imperial Police, in Burma), and then I underwent poverty and the sense of failure. This increased my natural hatred of authority and made me for the first time fully aware of the existence of the working classes, and the job in Burma had given me some understanding of the nature of imperialism: but these experiences were not enough to give me an accurate political orientation. Then came Hitler, the Spanish Civil War, etc. By the end of 1935 I had still failed to reach a firm decision. I remember a little poem* that I wrote at that date, expressing my dilemma:

> A happy vicar I might have been
> Two hundred years ago,
> To preach upon eternal doom
> And watch my walnuts grow;
>
> But born, alas, in an evil time,
> I missed that pleasant haven,
> For the hair has grown on my upper lip
> And the clergy are all clean-shaven.
>
> And later still the times were good,
> We were so easy to please,
> We rocked our troubled thoughts to sleep
> On the bosoms of the trees.
>
> All ignorant we dared to own
> The joys we now dissemble;
> The greenfinch on the apple bough
> Could make my enemies tremble.
>
> But girls' bellies and apricots,
> Roach in a shaded stream,
> Horses, ducks in flight at dawn,
> All these are a dream.
>
> It is forbidden to dream again;
> We maim our joys or hide them;
> Horses are made of chromium steel
> And little fat men shall ride them.
>
> I am the worm who never turned,
> The eunuch without a harem;
> Between the priest and the commissar
> I walk like Eugene Aram;*

And the commissar is telling my fortune
While the radio plays,
But the priest has promised an Austin Seven,*
For Duggie always pays.*

I dreamt I dwelt in marble halls,
And woke to find it true;
I wasn't born for an age like this;
Was Smith? Was Jones? Were you?

The Spanish war and other events in 1936–37 turned the scale and thereafter I knew where I stood. Every line of serious work that I have written since 1936 has been written, directly or indirectly, *against* totalitarianism and *for* democratic socialism, as I understand it. It seems to me nonsense, in a period like our own, to think that one can avoid writing of such subjects. Everyone writes of them in one guise or another. It is simply a question of which side one takes and what approach one follows. And the more one is conscious of one's political bias, the more chance one has of acting politically without sacrificing one's aesthetic and intellectual integrity.

What I have most wanted to do throughout the past ten years is to make political writing into an art. My starting point is always a feeling of partisanship, a sense of injustice. When I sit down to write a book, I do not say to myself, "I am going to produce a work of art." I write it because there is some lie that I want to expose, some fact to which I want to draw attention, and my initial concern is to get a hearing. But I could not do the work of writing a book, or even a long magazine article, if it were not also an aesthetic experience. Anyone who cares to examine my work will see that even when it is downright propaganda it contains much that a full-time politician would consider irrelevant. I am not able, and I do not want, completely to abandon the world view that I acquired in childhood. So long as I remain alive and well I shall continue to feel strongly about prose style, to love the surface of the earth and to take pleasure in solid objects and scraps of useless information. It is no use trying to suppress that side of myself. The job is to reconcile my ingrained likes and dislikes with the essentially public, non-individual activities that this age forces on all of us.

It is not easy. It raises problems of construction and of language, and it raises in a new way the problem of truthfulness. Let me give just one example of the cruder kind of difficulty that arises. My book about the Spanish Civil War, *Homage to Catalonia*,* is, of course, a frankly political book, but in the main it is written with a certain detachment and regard for form. I did try very hard in it to tell the whole truth without violating my literary instincts. But among other things it contains a long chapter, full of newspaper quotations and the like, defending the Trotskyists who were accused of plotting with Franco. Clearly such a chapter, which after a year or two would lose its interest for any ordinary reader, must ruin the book. A critic whom I respect read me a lecture about it. "Why did you put in all that stuff?" he said. "You've turned what might have been a good book into journalism." What he said was true, but I could not have done otherwise. I happened to know what very few people in England had been allowed to know: that innocent men were being falsely accused. If I had not been angry about that I should never have written the book.

In one form or another this problem comes up again. The problem of language is subtler and would take too long to discuss. I will only say that of late years I have tried to write less picturesquely and more exactly. In any case I find that by the time you have perfected any style of writing, you have always outgrown it. *Animal Farm** was the first book in which I tried, with full consciousness of what I was doing, to fuse political purpose and artistic purpose into one whole. I have not written a novel for seven years, but I hope to write another fairly soon. It is bound to be a failure, every book is a failure, but I know with some clarity what kind of book I want to write.

Looking back through the last page or two, I see that I have made it appear as though my motives in writing were wholly public-spirited. I don't want to leave that as the final impression. All writers are vain, selfish and lazy, and at the very bottom of their motives there lies a mystery. Writing a book is a horrible, exhausting struggle, like a long bout of some painful illness. One would never undertake such a thing if one were not driven on by some demon whom one can neither resist nor understand. For all one knows that demon is simply the same instinct that makes a baby squall for attention. And yet it is also true that one can write nothing readable unless one constantly struggles to efface one's own personality. Good prose is like a window pane. I cannot say with certainty which of my motives are the strongest, but I know which of them deserve to be followed. And looking back through my work, I see that it is invariably where I lacked a *political* purpose that I wrote lifeless books and was betrayed into purple passages, sentences without meaning, decorative adjectives and humbug generally.

Politics vs. Literature:
An Examination of *Gulliver's Travels**

In *Gulliver's Travels* humanity is attacked, or criticized, from at least three different angles, and the implied character of Gulliver himself necessarily changes somewhat in the process. In Part I he is the typical eighteenth-century voyager, bold, practical and unromantic, his homely outlook skilfully impressed on the reader by the biographical details at the beginning, by his age (he is a man of forty, with two children, when his adventures start), and by the inventory of the things in his pockets, especially his spectacles, which make several appearances. In Part II he has in general the same character, but at moments when the story demands it he has a tendency to develop into an imbecile who is capable of boasting of "our noble Country, the Mistress of Arts and Arms, the Scourge of France" etc. etc., and at the same time of betraying every available scandalous fact about the country which he professes to love. In Part III he is much as he was in Part I, though, as he is consorting chiefly with courtiers and men of learning, one has the impression that he has risen in the social scale. In Part IV he conceives a horror of the human race which is not apparent, or only intermittently apparent, in the earlier books, and changes into a sort of unreligious anchorite whose one desire is to live in some desolate spot where he can devote himself to meditating on the goodness of the Houyhnhnms. However, these inconsistencies are forced upon Swift by the fact that Gulliver is there chiefly to provide a contrast. It is necessary, for instance, that he should appear sensible in Part I and at least intermittently silly in Part II, because in both books the essential manoeuvre is the same, i.e. to make the human being look ridiculous by imagining him as a creature six inches high. Whenever Gulliver is not acting as a stooge there is a sort of continuity in his character, which comes out especially in his resourcefulness and his observation of physical detail. He is much the same kind of person, with the same prose style, when he bears off the warships of Blefuscu, when he rips open the belly of the monstrous rat and when he sails away upon the ocean in his frail coracle made from the skins of Yahoos. Moreover, it is difficult not to feel that in his shrewder moments Gulliver is simply Swift himself, and there is at least one incident in which Swift seems to be venting his private grievance against contemporary society. It will be remembered that when the Emperor of Lilliput's palace catches fire, Gulliver puts it out by urinating on it. Instead of being congratulated on his presence of mind, he finds that he has committed a capital offence by making water in the precincts of the palace, and

> I was privately assured, that the Empress, conceiving the greatest Abhorrence of what I had done, removed to the most distant Side of the Court, firmly resolved that those buildings should never be repaired for her Use; and, in the Presence of her chief Confidents, could not forbear vowing Revenge.

According to Professor G.M. Trevelyan (*England under Queen Anne**), part of the reason for Swift's failure to get preferment was that the Queen was scandalized by *A Tale of a Tub** – a pamphlet in which Swift probably felt that he had done a great service to the English Crown, since it scarifies the Dissenters and still more the Catholics while leaving the Established Church alone. In any case no one would deny that *Gulliver's Travels* is a rancorous as well as a pessimistic book, and that especially in Parts I and III it often descends into political partisanship of a narrow kind. Pettiness and magnanimity, republicanism and authoritarianism, love of reason and lack of curiosity are all mixed up in it. The hatred of the human body with which Swift is especially associated is only dominant in Part IV, but somehow this new preoccupation does not come as a surprise. One feels that all these adventures, and all these changes of mood, could have happened to the same person, and the interconnection between Swift's political loyalties and his ultimate despair is one of the most interesting features of the book.

Politically, Swift was one of those people who are driven into a sort of perverse Toryism by the follies of the progressive party of the moment. Part I of *Gulliver's Travels*, ostensibly a satire on human greatness, can be seen, if one looks a little deeper, to be simply an attack on England, on the dominant Whig Party, and on the war with France, which – however bad the motives of the Allies may have been – did save Europe from being tyrannized over by a single reactionary power. Swift was not a Jacobite nor strictly speaking a Tory, and his declared aim in the war was merely a moderate peace treaty and not the outright defeat of England. Nevertheless there is a tinge of quislingism in his attitude, which comes out in the ending of Part I and slightly interferes with the allegory. When Gulliver flees from Lilliput (England) to Blefuscu (France) the assumption that a human being six inches high is inherently contemptible seems to be dropped. Whereas the people of Lilliput have behaved towards Gulliver with the utmost treachery and meanness, those of Blefuscu behave generously and straightforwardly, and indeed this section of the book ends on a different note from the all-round disillusionment of the earlier chapters. Evidently Swift's animus is, in the first place, against *England*. It is "your Natives" (i.e. Gulliver's fellow countrymen) whom the King of Brobdingnag considers to be "the most pernicious Race of little odious Vermin that Nature ever suffered to crawl upon the surface of the Earth", and the long passage at the end, denouncing colonization and foreign conquest, is plainly aimed at England, although the contrary is elaborately stated. The Dutch, England's allies and target of one of Swift's most famous pamphlets,* are also more or less wantonly attacked in Part III. There is even what sounds like a personal note in the passage in which Gulliver records his satisfaction that the various countries he has discovered cannot be made colonies of the British Crown:

> The *Houyhnhnms*, indeed, appear not to be so well prepared for War, a Science to which they are perfect Strangers, and especially against missive Weapons. However, supposing myself to be a Minister of State, I could never give my advice for invading them. [...] Imagine twenty thousand of them breaking into the midst of an *European* army, confounding the Ranks, overturning the Carriages, battering the Warriors' Faces into Mummy, by terrible Yerks from their hinder Hoofs [...]

Considering that Swift does not waste words, that phrase, "battering the warriors' faces into mummy", probably indicates a secret wish to see the invincible armies of the Duke of Marlborough treated in a like manner. There are similar touches elsewhere. Even the country mentioned in Part III, where "the Bulk of the People consist, in a Manner, wholly of Discoverers, Witnesses, Informers, Accusers, Prosecutors, Evidences, Swearers, together with their several subservient and subaltern Instruments, all under the Colours, the Conduct, and Pay of Ministers of State", is called Langdon, which is within one letter of being an anagram of England. (As the early editions of the book contain misprints, it may perhaps have been intended as a complete anagram.) Swift's *physical* repulsion from humanity is certainly real enough, but one has the feeling that his debunking of human grandeur, his diatribes against lords, politicians, court favourites, etc. have mainly a local application and spring from the fact that he belonged to the unsuccessful party. He denounces injustice and oppression, but he gives no evidence of liking democracy. In spite of his enormously greater powers, his implied position is very similar to that of the innumerable silly-clever Conservatives of our own day – people like Sir Alan Herbert, Professor G.M. Young, Lord Elton, the Tory Reform Committee or the long line of Catholic apologists from W.H. Mallock onwards:* people who specialize in cracking neat jokes at the expense of whatever is "modern" and "progressive", and whose opinions are often all the more extreme because they know that they cannot influence the actual drift of events. After all, such a pamphlet as *An Argument to Prove That the Abolishing of Christianity*, etc. is very like "Timothy Shy" having a bit of clean fun with *The Brains Trust*, or Father Ronald Knox exposing the errors of Bertrand Russell.* And the ease with which Swift has been forgiven – and forgiven, sometimes, by devout believers – for the blasphemies of *A Tale* *of a Tub* demonstrates clearly enough the feebleness of religious sentiments as compared with political ones.

However, the reactionary cast of Swift's mind does not show itself chiefly in his political affiliations. The important thing is his attitude towards science, and, more broadly, towards intellectual curiosity. The famous Academy of Lagado, described in Part III of *Gulliver's Travels*, is no doubt a justified satire on most of the so-called scientists of Swift's own day. Significantly, the people at work in it are described as "Projectors", that is, people not engaged in disinterested research but merely on the lookout for gadgets which will save labour and bring in money. But there is no sign – indeed, all through the book there are many signs to the contrary – that "pure" science would have struck Swift as a worthwhile activity. The more serious kind of scientist has already had a kick in the pants in Part II, when the "Scholars" patronized by the King of Brobdingnag try to account for Gulliver's small stature:

> After much Debate; they concluded unanimously that I was only *Relplum Scalcath*, which is interpreted literally, *Lusus Naturae*; a Determination exactly agreeable to the modern philosophy of *Europe*, whose Professors, disdaining the old Evasion of *occult Causes*, whereby the followers of *Aristotle* endeavoured in vain to disguise their Ignorance, have invented this wonderful Solution of all Difficulties, to the unspeakable Advancement of human Knowledge.

If this stood by itself one might assume that Swift is merely the enemy of *sham* science. In a number of places, however, he goes out of his way to proclaim the uselessness of all learning or speculation not directed towards some practical end:

> The Learning of (the Brobdingnagians) is very defective, consisting only in Morality, History, Poetry and Mathematics, wherein they must be allowed to excel. But, the last of these is wholly applied to what may be useful in Life, to the Improvement of Agriculture, and all mechanical Arts; so that among us it would be little esteemed. And as to Ideas, Entities, Abstractions and Transcendentals, I could never drive the least Conception into their Heads.

The Houyhnhnms, Swift's ideal beings, are backward even in a mechanical sense. They are unacquainted with metals, have never heard of boats, do not, properly speaking, practise agriculture (we are told that the oats which they live upon "grow naturally") and appear not to have invented wheels.* They have no alphabet, and evidently have not much curiosity about the physical world. They do not believe that any inhabited country exists beside their own, and though they understand the motions of the sun and moon, and the nature of eclipses, "this is the utmost Progress of their *Astronomy*". By contrast, the philosophers of the flying island of Laputa are so continuously absorbed in mathematical speculations that before speaking to them one has to attract their attention by flapping them on the ear with a bladder. They have catalogued 10,000 fixed stars, have settled the periods of ninety-three comets and have discovered, in advance of the astronomers of Europe, that Mars has two moons – all of which information Swift evidently regards as ridiculous, useless and uninteresting. As one might expect, he believes that the scientist's place, if he has a place, is in the laboratory, and that scientific knowledge has no bearing on political matters:

> What I [...] thought altogether unaccountable, was the strong Disposition I observed in them towards News and Politics, perpetually enquiring into Public Affairs, giving their judgements in Matters of State, and passionately disputing every Inch of a Party Opinion. I have, indeed, observed the same Disposition among most of the Mathematicians I have known in *Europe*, though I could never discover the least Analogy between the two Sciences; unless those People suppose, that, because the smallest Circle hath as many Degrees as the largest, therefore the Regulation and Management of the World require no more Abilities, than the Handling and Turning of a Globe.

Is there not something familiar in that phrase "I could never discover the least analogy between the two sciences"? It has precisely the note of the popular Catholic apologists who profess to be astonished when a scientist utters an opinion on such questions as the existence of God or the immortality of the soul. The scientist, we are told, is an expert only in one restricted field: why should his opinions be of value in any other? The implication is that theology is just as much an exact science as, for instance, chemistry, and that the priest is also an expert whose conclusions on certain subjects must be accepted. Swift in effect makes the same claim for the politician, but he goes one better in that he will not allow the scientist – either the "pure" scientist or the ad hoc investigator – to be a useful person in his own line. Even if he had not written Part III of *Gulliver's Travels*, one could infer from the rest of the book that, like Tolstoy and like Blake, he hates the very idea of studying the processes of nature. The "reason" which he so admires in the Houyhnhnms does not primarily mean the power of drawing logical inferences from observed facts. Although he never defines it, it appears in most contexts to mean either common sense – i.e. acceptance of the obvious and contempt for quibbles and abstractions – or absence of passion and superstition. In general he assumes that we know all that we need to know already, and merely use our knowledge incorrectly. Medicine, for instance, is a useless science, because if we lived in a more natural way, there would be no diseases. Swift, however, is not a simple-lifer or an admirer of the Noble Savage. He is in favour of civilization and the arts of civilization. Not only does he see the value of good manners, good conversation, and even learning of a literary and historical kind, he also sees that agriculture, navigation and architecture need to be studied and could with advantage be improved. But his implied aim is a static, incurious civilization – the world of his own day, a little cleaner, a little saner, with no radical change and no poking into the unknowable. More than one would expect in anyone so free from accepted fallacies, he reveres the past, especially classical antiquity, and believes that modern man has degenerated sharply during the past hundred years.* In the island of sorcerers, where the spirits of the dead can be called up at will:

> I desired that the Senate of *Rome* might appear before me in one large Chamber, and a modern Representative in Counterview, in another. The first seemed to be an Assembly of Heroes and Demy-Gods, the other a Knot of Pedlars, Pick-pockets, Highwaymen, and Bullies.

Although Swift uses this section of Part III to attack the truthfulness of recorded history, his critical spirit deserts him as soon as he is dealing with Greeks and Romans. He remarks, of course, upon the corruption of imperial Rome, but he has an almost unreasoning admiration for some of the leading figures of the ancient world:

> I was struck with profound Veneration at the Sight of *Brutus*, and could easily discover the most consummate Virtue, the greatest Intrepidity and Firmness of Mind, the truest Love of his Country, and general Benevolence for mankind, in every Lineament of his Countenance. [...] I had the Honour to have much Conversation with *Brutus*, and was told, that his Ancestor *Junius*, *Socrates*, *Epaminondas*, *Cato* the younger, *Sir Thomas More*, and himself, were perpetually together: a *Sextumvirate*, to which all the Ages of the World cannot add a seventh.

It will be noticed that of these six people only one is a Christian. This is an important point. If one adds together Swift's pessimism, his reverence for the past, his incuriosity and his horror of the human body, one arrives at an attitude common among religious reactionaries – that is, people who defend an unjust order of society by claiming that this world cannot be substantially improved and only the "next world" matters. However, Swift shows no sign of having any religious beliefs, at least in any ordinary sense of the words. He does not appear to believe seriously in life after death, and his idea of goodness is bound up with republicanism, love of liberty, courage, "benevolence" (meaning in effect public spirit), "reason" and other pagan qualities. This reminds one that there is another strain in Swift, not quite congruous with his disbelief in progress and his general hatred of humanity.

To begin with, he has moments when he is "constructive" and even "advanced". To be occasionally inconsistent is almost a mark of vitality in utopia books, and Swift sometimes inserts a word of praise into a passage that ought to be purely satirical. Thus, his ideas about the education of the young are fathered onto the Lilliputians, who have much the same views on this subject as the Houyhnhnms. The Lilliputians also have various social and legal institutions (for instance, there are old-age pensions, and people are rewarded for keeping the law as well as punished for breaking it) which Swift would have liked to see prevailing in his own country. In the middle of this passage Swift remembers his satirical intention and adds, "In relating these and the following Laws, I would only be understood to mean the original Institutions, and not the most scandalous Corruptions into which these people are fallen by the degenerate Nature of Man" – but as Lilliput is supposed to represent England, and the laws he is speaking of have never had their parallel in England, it is clear that the impulse to make constructive suggestion has been too much for him. But Swift's greatest contribution to political thought, in the narrower sense of the words, is his attacks, especially in Part III, on what would now be called totalitarianism. He has an extraordinarily clear prevision of the spy-haunted "police state", with its endless heresy hunts and treason trials, all really designed to neutralize popular discontent by changing it into war hysteria. And one must remember that Swift is here inferring the whole from a quite small part, for the feeble governments of his own day did not give him illustrations ready-made. For example, there is the professor at the School of Political Projectors who "shewed me a large Paper of Instructions for discovering Plots and Conspiracies", and who claimed that one can find people's secret thoughts by examining their excrement:

> Because Men are never so serious, thoughtful, and intent, as when they are at Stool, which he found by frequent Experiment: for in such Conjunctures, when he used merely as a Trial to consider what was the best Way of murdering the King, his Ordure would have a Tincture of Green; but quite different when he thought only of raising an Insurrection, or burning the Metropolis.

The professor and his theory are said to have been suggested to Swift by the – from our point of view – not particularly astonishing or disgusting fact that in a recent State Trial some letters found in somebody's privy had been put in evidence. Later in the same chapter we seem to be positively in the middle of the Russian purges:

In the Kingdom of Tribnia, by the Natives called Langdon [...] the Bulk of the People consist, in a Manner, wholly of Discoverers, Witnesses, Informers, Accusers, Prosecutors, Evidences, Swearers. [...] It is first agreed, and settled among them, what suspected Persons shall be accused of a Plot: Then, effectual Care is taken to secure all their Letters and Papers, and put the Owners in Chains. These papers are delivered to a Sett of Artists, very dexterous in finding out the mysterious Meanings of Words, Syllables, and Letters. [...] Where this Method fails, they have two others more effectual, which the Learned among them call *Acrostics* and *Anagrams*. *First*, they can decipher all initial Letters into political Meanings: Thus, N shall signify a Plot, B a Regiment of Horse, L a Fleet at Sea: Or, *Secondly*, by transposing the Letters of the Alphabet in any suspected Paper, they can lay open the deepest Designs of a discontented Party. So, for Example, if I should say in a Letter to a Friend, *Our Brother Tom has just got the Piles*, a skilful Decipherer would discover that the same Letters, which compose that Sentence, may be analysed in the following Words: *Resist – a Plot is brought Home – The Tour*.* And this is the anagrammatic Method.

Other professors at the same school invent simplified languages, write books by machinery, educate their pupils by inscribing the lessons on a wafer and causing them to swallow it, or propose to abolish individuality altogether by cutting off part of the brain of one man and grafting it on to the head of another. There is something queerly familiar in the atmosphere of these chapters, because, mixed up with much fooling, there is a perception that one of the aims of totalitarianism is not merely to make sure that people will think the right thoughts, but actually to make them *less conscious*. Then, again, Swift's account of the Leader who is usually to be found ruling over a tribe of Yahoos, and of the "favourite" who acts first as a dirty-worker and later as a scapegoat, fits remarkably well into the pattern of our own times. But are we to infer from all this that Swift was first and foremost an enemy of tyranny and a champion of the free intelligence? No: his own views, so far as one can discern them, are not markedly liberal. No doubt he hates lords, kings, bishops, generals, ladies of fashion, orders, titles and flummery generally, but he does not seem to think better of the common people than of their rulers, or to be in favour of increased social equality, or to be enthusiastic about representative institutions. The Houyhnhnms are organized upon a sort of caste system which is racial in character, the horses which do the menial work being of different colours from their masters and not interbreeding with them. The educational system which Swift admires in the Lilliputians takes hereditary class distinctions for granted, and the children of the poorest class do not go to school, because "their Business being only to till and cultivate the Earth [...] therefore their Education is of little Consequence to the Public". Nor does he seem to have been strongly in favour of freedom of speech and the press, in spite of the toleration which his own writings enjoyed. The King of Brobdingnag is astonished at the multiplicity of religious and political sects in England, and considers that those who hold "opinions prejudicial to the public" (in the context this seems to mean simply heretical opinions), though they need not be obliged to change them, ought to be obliged to conceal them: for "as it was Tyranny in any government to require the first, so it was Weakness not to enforce the second". There is a subtler indication of Swift's own attitude in the manner in which Gulliver leaves the land of the Houyhnhnms. Intermittently, at least, Swift was a kind of anarchist, and Part IV of *Gulliver's Travels* is a picture of an anarchistic society, not governed by law in the ordinary sense, but by the dictates of "reason", which are voluntarily accepted by everyone. The General Assembly of the Houyhnhnms "exhorts" Gulliver's master to get rid of him, and his neighbours put pressure on him to make him comply. Two reasons are given. One is that the presence of this unusual Yahoo may unsettle the rest of the tribe, and the other is that a friendly relationship between a Houyhnhnm and a Yahoo is "not agreeable to Reason or Nature, or a Thing ever heard of before among them". Gulliver's master is somewhat unwilling to obey, but the "exhortation" (a Houyhnhnm, we are told, is never *compelled* to do anything, he is merely "exhorted" or "advised") cannot be disregarded. This illustrates very well the totalitarian tendency which is implicit in the anarchist or pacifist vision of society. In a society in which there is no law, and in theory no compulsion, the only arbiter of behaviour is public opinion. But public opinion, because of the tremendous urge to conformity in gregarious animals, is less tolerant than any system of law. When human beings are governed by "thou shalt not", the individual can practise a certain amount of eccentricity: when they are supposedly governed by "love" or "reason", he is under continuous pressure to make him behave and think in exactly the same way as everyone else. The Houyhnhnms, we are told, were unanimous on almost all subjects. The only question they ever *discussed* was how to deal with the Yahoos. Otherwise there was no room for disagreement among them, because the truth is always either self-evident, or else it is undiscoverable and unimportant. They had apparently no word for "opinion" in their language, and in their conversations there was no "difference of sentiments". They had reached, in fact, the highest stage of totalitarian organization, the stage when conformity has become so general that there is no need for a police force. Swift approves of this kind of thing because among his many gifts neither curiosity nor good nature was included. Disagreement would always seem to him sheer perversity. "Reason", among the Houyhnhnms, he says, "is not a Point Problematical, as with us, where men can argue with Plausibility on both Sides of a Question; but strikes you with immediate Conviction; as it must needs do, where it is not mingled, obscured or discoloured by Passion and Interest." In other words, we know everything already, so why should dissident opinions be tolerated? The totalitarian society of the Houyhnhnms, where there can be no freedom and no development, follows naturally from this.

We are right to think of Swift as a rebel and iconoclast, but except in certain secondary matters, such as his insistence that women should receive the same education as men, he cannot be labelled "left". He is a Tory anarchist, despising authority while disbelieving in liberty, and preserving the aristocratic outlook while seeing clearly that the existing aristocracy is degenerate and contemptible. When Swift utters one of his characteristic diatribes against the rich and powerful, one must probably, as I said earlier, write off something for the fact that he himself belonged to the less successful party, and was personally disappointed. The "outs", for obvious reasons, are always more radical than the "ins".* But the most essential thing in Swift is his inability to believe that life – ordinary life on the solid earth, and not some rationalized, deodorized version of it – could be made worth living. Of course, no honest person claims that happiness is *now* a normal condition among adult human beings – but perhaps it *could* be made normal, and it is upon this question that all serious political controversy really turns. Swift has much in common – more, I believe, than has been noticed – with Tolstoy, another disbeliever in the possibility of happiness. In both men you have the same anarchistic outlook covering an authoritarian cast of mind; in both a similar hostility to science, the same impatience with opponents, the same inability to see the importance of any question not interesting to themselves; and in both cases a sort of horror of the actual process of life, though in Tolstoy's case it was arrived at later and in a different way. The sexual unhappiness of the two men was not of the same kind, but there was this in common: that in both of them a sincere loathing was mixed up with a morbid fascination. Tolstoy was a reformed rake who ended by preaching complete celibacy, while continuing to practise the opposite into extreme old age. Swift was presumably impotent, and had an exaggerated horror of human dung; he also thought about it incessantly, as is evident throughout this works. Such people are not likely to enjoy even the small amount of happiness that falls to most human beings, and, from obvious motives, are not likely to admit that earthly life is capable of much improvement. Their incuriosity and hence their intolerance spring from the same root.

Swift's disgust, rancour and pessimism would make sense against the background of a "next world" to which this one is the prelude. As he does not appear to believe seriously in any such thing, it becomes necessary to construct a paradise supposedly existing on the surface of the earth, but something quite different from anything we know, with all that he disapproves of – lies, folly, change, enthusiasm, pleasure, love and dirt – eliminated from it. As his ideal being he chooses the horse, an animal whose excrement is not offensive. The

Houyhnhnms are dreary beasts – this is so generally admitted that the point is not worth labouring. Swift's genius can make them credible, but there can have been very few readers in whom they have excited any feeling beyond dislike. And this is not from wounded vanity at seeing animals preferred to men – for, of the two, the Houyhnhnms are much liker to human beings than are the Yahoos, and Gulliver's horror of the Yahoos, together with his recognition that they are the same kind of creature as himself, contains a logical absurdity. This horror comes upon him at his very first sight of them. "I never beheld," he says, "in all my Travels, so disagreeable an Animal, nor one against which I naturally conceived so strong an Antipathy." But in comparison with what are the Yahoos disgusting? Not with the Houyhnhnms, because at this time Gulliver has not seen a Houyhnhnm. It can only be in comparison with himself, i.e. with a human being. Later, however, we are to be told that the Yahoos *are* human beings, and human society becomes insupportable to Gulliver because all men are Yahoos. In that case why did he not conceive his disgust of humanity earlier? In effect we are told that the Yahoos are fantastically different from men, and yet are the same. Swift has overreached himself in his fury, and is shouting at his fellow creatures: "You are filthier than you are!" However, it is impossible to feel much sympathy with the Yahoos, and it is not because they oppress the Yahoos that the Houyhnhnms are unattractive. They are unattractive because the "Reason" by which they are governed is really a desire for death. They are exempt from love, friendship, curiosity, fear, sorrow and – except in their feelings towards the Yahoos, who occupy rather the same place in their community as the Jews in Nazi Germany – anger and hatred. "They have no Fondness for their Colts or Foles, but the Care they take, in educating them, proceeds entirely from the Dictates of *Reason*." They lay store by "Friendship" and "Benevolence", but "these are not confined to particular Objects, but universal to the whole Race". They also value conversation, but in their conversations there are no differences of opinion, and "nothing passed but what was useful, expressed in the fewest and most significant Words". They practise strict birth control, each couple producing two offspring and thereafter abstaining from sexual intercourse. Their marriages are arranged for them by their elders, on eugenic principles, and their language contains no word for "love", in the sexual sense. When somebody dies they carry on exactly as before, without feeling any grief. It will be seen that their aim is to be as like a corpse as is possible while retaining physical life. One or two of their characteristics, it is true, do not seem to be strictly "reasonable" in their own usage of the word. Thus, they place a great value not only on physical hardihood but on athleticism, and they are devoted to poetry. But these exceptions may be less arbitrary than they seem. Swift probably emphasizes the physical strength of the Houyhnhnms in order to make clear that they could never be conquered by the hated human race, while a taste for poetry may figure among their qualities because poetry appeared to Swift as the antithesis of science, from his point of view the most useless of all pursuits. In Part III he names "Imagination, Fancy and Invention" as desirable faculties in which the Laputan mathematicians (in spite of their love of music) were wholly lacking. One must remember that although Swift was an admirable writer of comic verse, the kind of poetry he thought valuable would probably be didactic poetry. The poetry of the Houyhnhnms, he says:

> must be allowed to excel (that of) all other Mortals; wherein the Justness of their Similes, and the Minuteness, as well as exactness, of their Descriptions, are, indeed, inimitable. Their Verses abound very much in both of these; and usually contain either some exalted Notions of Friendship and Benevolence, or the Praises of those who were Victors in Races, and other bodily Exercises.

Alas, not even the genius of Swift was equal to producing a specimen by which we could judge the poetry of the Houyhnhnms. But it sounds as though it were chilly stuff (in heroic couplets, presumably), and not seriously in conflict with the principles of "Reason".

Happiness is notoriously difficult to describe, and pictures of a just and well-ordered society are seldom either attractive or convincing. Most creators of "favourable" utopias, however, are concerned to show what life could be like if it were lived more fully. Swift advocates a simple refusal of life, justifying this by the claim that "Reason" consists in thwarting your instincts. The Houyhnhnms, creatures without a history, continue for generation after generation to live prudently, maintaining their population at exactly the same level, avoiding all passion, suffering from no diseases, meeting death indifferently, training up their young in the same principles – and all for what? In order that the same process may continue indefinitely. The notions that life here and now is worth living, or that it could be made worth living, or that it must be sacrificed for some future good are all absent. The dreary world of the Houyhnhnms was about as good a utopia as Swift could construct, granting that he neither believed in a "next world" nor could get any pleasure out of certain normal activities. But it is not really set up as something desirable in itself, but as the justification for another attack on humanity. The aim, as usual, is to humiliate Man by reminding him that he is weak and ridiculous, and above all that he stinks: and the ultimate motive, probably, is a kind of envy, the envy of the ghost for the living, of the man who knows he cannot be happy for the others who – so he fears – may be a little happier than himself. The political expression of such an outlook must be either reactionary or nihilistic, because the person who holds it will want to prevent society from developing in some direction in which his pessimism may be cheated. One can do this either by blowing everything to pieces, or by averting social change.

Swift ultimately blew everything to pieces in the only way that was feasible before the atomic bomb – that is, he went mad – but, as I have tried to show, his political aims were on the whole reactionary ones.

From what I have written it may have seemed that I am *against* Swift, and that my object is to refute him and even to belittle him. In a political and moral sense I am against him, so far as I understand him. Yet curiously enough he is one of the writers I admire with least reserve, and *Gulliver's Travels*, in particular, is a book which it seems impossible for me to grow tired of. I read it first when I was eight – one day short of eight, to be exact, for I stole and furtively read the copy which was to be given me next day on my eighth birthday – and I have certainly not read it less than half a dozen times since. Its fascination seems inexhaustible. If I had to make a list of six books which were to be preserved when all others were destroyed, I would certainly put *Gulliver's Travels* among them. This raises the question: what is the relationship between agreement with a writer's opinions and enjoyment of his work?

If one is capable of intellectual detachment, one can *perceive* merit in a writer whom one deeply disagrees with, but *enjoyment* is a different matter. Supposing that there is such a thing as good or bad art, then the goodness or badness must reside in the work of art itself – not independently of the observer, indeed, but independently of the mood of the observer. In one sense, therefore, it cannot be true that a poem is good on Monday and bad on Tuesday. But if one judges the poem by the appreciation it arouses, then it can certainly be true, because appreciation, or enjoyment, is a subjective condition which cannot be commanded. For a great deal of his waking life, even the most cultivated person has no aesthetic feelings whatever, and the power to have aesthetic feelings is very easily destroyed. When you are frightened, or hungry, or are suffering from toothache or seasickness, *King Lear* is no better from your point of view than *Peter Pan*. You may know in an intellectual sense that it is better, but that is simply a fact which you remember: you will not *feel* the merit of *King Lear* until you are normal again. And aesthetic judgement can be upset just as disastrously – more disastrously, because the cause is less readily recognized – by political or moral disagreement. If a book angers, wounds or alarms you, then you will not enjoy it, whatever its merits may be. If it seems to you a really pernicious book, likely to influence other people in some undesirable way, then you will probably construct an aesthetic theory to show that it *has* no merits. Current literary criticism consists quite largely of this kind of dodging to and fro between two sets of standards. And yet the opposite process can also happen: enjoyment can overwhelm disapproval, even though one clearly recognizes that one is enjoying something inimical. Swift, whose world view is so peculiarly unacceptable, but who is nevertheless an extremely popular writer, is a good instance of this. Why is it that we don't mind being called Yahoos, although firmly convinced that we are *not* Yahoos?

It is not enough to make the usual answer that of course Swift was wrong, in fact he was insane, but he was "a good writer". It is true that the literary quality of a book is to some small extent separable from its subject matter. Some people have a native gift for using words, as some people have a naturally "good eye" at games. It is largely a question of timing and of instinctively knowing how much emphasis to use. As an example near at hand, look back at the passage I quoted earlier, starting "In the Kingdom of Tribnia, by the Natives called Langdon". It derives much of its force from the final sentence: "And this is the anagrammatic Method." Strictly speaking this sentence is unnecessary, for we have already seen the anagram deciphered, but the mock-solemn repetition, in which one seems to hear Swift's own voice uttering the words, drives home the idiocy of the activities described, like the final tap to a nail. But not all the power and simplicity of Swift's prose, nor the imaginative effort that has been able to make not one but a whole series of impossible worlds more credible than the majority of history books – none of this would enable us to enjoy Swift if his world view were truly wounding or shocking. Millions of people, in many countries, must have enjoyed *Gulliver's Travels* while more or less seeing its antihuman implications – and even the child who accepts Parts I and II as a simple story gets a sense of absurdity from thinking of human beings six inches high. The explanation must be that Swift's world view is felt to be *not* altogether false – or it would probably be more accurate to say, not false all the time. Swift is a diseased writer. He remains permanently in a depressed mood which in most people is only intermittent, rather as though someone suffering from jaundice or the after-effects of influenza should have the energy to write books. But we all know that mood, and something in us responds to the expression of it. Take, for instance, one of his most characteristic works, 'The Lady's Dressing Room'; one might add the kindred poem 'Upon a Beautiful Young Nymph Going to Bed'.* Which is truer, the viewpoint expressed in these poems, or the viewpoint implied in Blake's phrase "the naked female human form divine"?* No doubt Blake is nearer the truth, and yet who can fail to feel a sort of pleasure in seeing that fraud, feminine delicacy, exploded for once? Swift falsifies his picture of the whole world by refusing to see anything in human life except dirt, folly and wickedness, but the part which he abstracts from the whole does exist, and it is something which we all know about while shrinking from mentioning it. Part of our minds – in any normal person it is the dominant part – believes that man is a noble animal and life is worth living, but there is also a sort of inner self which at least intermittently stands aghast at the horror of existence. In the queerest way, pleasure and disgust are linked together. The human body is beautiful; it is also repulsive and ridiculous, a fact which can be verified at any swimming pool. The sexual organs are objects of desire and also of loathing, so much so that in many languages, if not in all languages, their names are used as words of abuse. Meat is delicious, but a butcher's shop makes one feel sick – and indeed all our food springs ultimately from dung and dead bodies, the two things which of all others seem to us the most horrible. A child, when it is past the infantile stage but still looking at the world with fresh eyes, is moved by horror almost as often as by wonder – horror of snot and spittle, of the dogs' excrement on the pavement, the dying toad full of maggots, the sweaty smell of grown-ups, the hideousness of old men, with their bald heads and bulbous noses. In his endless harping on disease, dirt and deformity, Swift is not actually inventing anything – he is merely leaving something out. Human behaviour, too, especially in politics, is as he describes it, although it contains other more important factors which he refuses to admit. So far as we can see, both horror and pain are necessary to the continuance of life on this planet, and it is therefore open to pessimists like Swift to say: "If horror and pain must always be with us, how can life be significantly improved?" His attitude is in effect the Christian attitude, minus the bribe of a "next world" – which, however, probably has less hold upon the minds of believers than the conviction that this world is a vale of tears and the grave is a place of rest. It is, I am certain, a wrong attitude, and one which could have harmful effects upon behaviour, but something in us responds to it, as it responds to the gloomy words of the burial service and the sweetish smell of corpses in a country church.

It is often argued, at least by people who admit the importance of subject matter, that a book cannot be "good" if it expresses a palpably false view of life. We are told that in our own age, for instance, any book that has genuine literary merit will also be more or less "progressive" in tendency. This ignores the fact that throughout history a similar struggle between progress and reaction has been raging, and that the best books of any one age have always been written from several different viewpoints, some of them palpably more false than others. In so far as a writer is a propagandist, the most one can ask of him is that he shall genuinely believe in what he is saying, and that it shall not be something blazingly silly. Today, for example, one can imagine a good book being written by a Catholic, a communist, a fascist, a pacifist, an anarchist, perhaps by an old-style Liberal or an ordinary Conservative; one cannot imagine a good book being written by a spiritualist, a Buchmanite* or a member of the Ku Klux Klan. The views that a writer holds must be compatible with sanity, in the medical sense, and with the power of continuous thought: beyond that what we ask of him is talent, which is probably another name for conviction. Swift did not possess ordinary wisdom, but he did possess a terrible intensity of vision, capable of picking out a single hidden truth and then magnifying it and distorting it. The durability of *Gulliver's Travels* goes to show that, if the force of belief is behind it, a world view which only just passes the test of sanity is sufficient to produce a great work of art.

Riding Down from Bangor*

The reappearance of *Helen's Babies*,* in its day one of the most popular books in the world – within the British Empire alone it was pirated by twenty different publishing firms, the author receiving a total profit of £40 from a sale of some hundreds of thousands or millions of copies – will ring a bell in any literate person over thirty-five. Not that the present edition is an altogether satisfactory one. It is a cheap little book with rather unsuitable illustrations, various American dialect words appear to have been cut out of it, and the sequel, *Other People's Children*, which was often bound up with it in earlier editions, is missing. Still, it is pleasant to see *Helen's Babies* in print again. It had become almost a rarity in recent years, and it is one of the best of the little library of American books on which people born at about the turn of the century were brought up.

The books one reads in childhood, and perhaps most of all the bad and good bad books, create in one's mind a sort of false map of the world, a series of fabulous countries into which one can retreat at odd moments throughout the rest of life, and which in some cases can even survive a visit to the real countries which they are supposed to represent. The pampas, the Amazon, the coral islands of the Pacific, Russia, land of birch tree and samovar, Transylvania with its boyars and vampires, the China of Guy Boothby, the Paris of du Maurier* – one could continue the list for a long time. But one other imaginary country that I acquired early in life was called America. If I pause on the word "America" and, deliberately putting aside the existing reality, call up my childhood vision of it, I see two pictures – composite pictures, of course, from which I am omitting a good deal of the detail.

One is of a boy sitting in a whitewashed stone schoolroom. He wears braces and has patches on his shirt, and if it is summer he is barefooted. In the corner of the school room there is a bucket of drinking water with a dipper. The boy lives in a farmhouse, also of stone and also whitewashed, which has a mortgage on it. He aspires to be President, and is expected to keep the woodpile full. Somewhere in the background of the picture, but completely dominating it, is a huge black Bible. The other picture is of a tall, angular man, with a shapeless hat pulled down over his eyes, leaning against a wooden paling and whittling at a stick. His lower jaw moves slowly but ceaselessly. At very long intervals he emits some piece of wisdom such as "A woman is the orneriest critter there is, 'ceptin' a mule", or "When you don't know a thing to do, don't do a thing" – but more often it is a jet of tobacco juice that issues from the gap in his front teeth. Between them those two pictures summed up my earliest impression of America. And of the two, the first – which, I suppose, represented New England, the other representing the South – had the stronger hold upon me.

The books from which these pictures were derived included, of course, books which it is still possible to take seriously, such as *Tom Sawyer* and *Uncle Tom's Cabin*, but the most richly American flavour was to be found in minor works which are now almost forgotten. I wonder, for instance, if anyone still reads *Rebecca of Sunnybrook Farm*, which remained a popular favourite long enough to be filmed with Mary Pickford in the leading part.* Or how about the "Katy" books by Susan Coolidge (*What Katy Did at School*, etc.),* which, although girls' books and therefore "soppy", had the fascination of foreignness? Louisa M. Alcott's *Little Women* and *Good Wives** are, I suppose, still flickeringly in print, and certainly they still have their devotees. As a child I loved both of them, though I was less pleased by the third of the trilogy, *Little Men*.* That model school where the worst punishment was to have to whack the schoolmaster, on "this hurts me more than it hurts you" principles, was rather difficult to swallow.

Helen's Babies belonged in much the same world as *Little Women*, and must have been published round about the same date. Then there were Artemus Ward, Bret Harte, and various songs, hymns and ballads, besides poems dealing with the civil war, such as 'Barbara Fritchie' ("'Shoot if you must this old grey head, But spare your country's flag,' she said") and 'Little Gifford of Tennessee'.* There were other books so obscure that it hardly seems worth mentioning them, and magazine stories of which I remember nothing except that the old homestead always seemed to have a mortgage on it. There was also *Beautiful Joe*, the American reply to *Black Beauty*,* of which you might just possibly pick up a copy in a sixpenny box. All the books I have mentioned were written well before 1900, but something of the special American flavour lingered on into this century in, for instance, the Buster Brown coloured supplements, and even in Booth Tarkington's "Penrod" stories,* which will have been written round about 1910. Perhaps there was even a tinge of it in Ernest Thompson Seton's animal books (*Wild Animals I Have Known*, etc.),* which have now fallen from favour but which drew tears from the pre-1914 child as surely as *Misunderstood** had done from the children of a generation earlier.

Somewhat later my picture of nineteenth-century America was given greater precision by a song which is still fairly well known and which can be found (I think) in *The Scottish Students' Song Book*.* As usual in these bookless days I cannot get hold of a copy, and I must quote fragments from memory. It begins:

> Riding down from Bangor
> On an Eastern train,
> Bronzed with weeks of hunting
> In the woods of Maine –
> Quite extensive whiskers,
> Beard, moustache as well –
> Sat a student fellow,
> Tall and slim and swell.*

Presently an aged couple and a "village maiden", described as "beautiful, petite", get into the carriage. Quantities of cinders are flying about, and before long the student fellow gets one in his eye: the village maiden extracts it for him, to the scandal of the aged couple. Soon after this the train shoots into a long tunnel, "black as Egypt's night". When it emerges into the daylight again the maiden is covered with blushes, and the cause of her confusion is revealed when

> There suddenly appeared
> A tiny little earring
> In that horrid student's beard!*

I do not know the date of the song, but the primitiveness of the train (no lights in the carriage, and a cinder in one's eye a normal accident) suggests that it belongs well back in the nineteenth century.

What connects this song with books like *Helen's Babies* is first of all a sort of sweet innocence – the climax, the thing you are supposed to be slightly shocked at, is an episode with which any modern piece of naughty-naughty would *start* – and, secondly, a faint vulgarity of language mixed up with a certain cultural pretentiousness. *Helen's Babies* is intended as a humorous, even a farcical book, but it is haunted all the way through by words like "tasteful" and "ladylike", and it is funny chiefly because its tiny disasters happen against a background of conscious gentility. "Handsome, intelligent, composed, tastefully dressed, without a suspicion of the flirt or the languid woman of fashion about her, she awakened to the utmost my every admiring sentiment" – thus is the heroine described, figuring elsewhere as "erect, fresh, neat, composed, bright-eyed, fair-faced, smiling and observant". One gets beautiful glimpses of a now-vanished world in such remarks as: "I believe you arranged the floral decorations at St Zephaniah's Fair last winter, Mr Burton? 'Twas the most tasteful display of the season." But in spite of the occasional use of "'twas" and other archaisms – "parlour" for sitting room, "chamber" for bedroom, "real" as an adverb, and so forth – the book does not "date" very markedly, and many of its admirers imagine it to have been written round about 1900.

Actually it was written in 1875, a fact which one might infer from internal evidence, since the hero, aged twenty-eight, is a veteran of the civil war.

The book is very short and the story is a simple one. A young bachelor is prevailed on by his sister to look after her house and her two sons, aged five and three, while she and her husband go on a fortnight's holiday. The children drive him almost mad by an endless succession of such acts as falling into ponds, swallowing poison, throwing keys down wells, cutting themselves with razors and the like, but also facilitate his engagement to "a charming girl, whom, for about a year, I had been adoring from afar". These events take place in an outer suburb of New York, in a society which now seems astonishingly sedate, formal, domesticated and, according to current conceptions, un-American. Every action is governed by etiquette. To pass a carriage full of ladies when your hat is crooked is an ordeal; to recognize an acquaintance in church is ill-bred; to become engaged after a ten days' courtship is a severe social lapse. We are accustomed to thinking of American society as more crude, adventurous and, in a cultural sense, democratic than our own, and from writers like Mark Twain, Whitman and Bret Harte, not to mention the cowboy and Red Indian stories of the weekly papers, one draws a picture of a wild anarchic world peopled by eccentrics and desperadoes who have no traditions and no attachment to one place. That aspect of nineteenth-century America did of course exist, but in the more populous eastern states a society similar to Jane Austen's seems to have survived longer than it did in England. And it is hard not to feel that it was a better kind of society than that which arose from the sudden industrialization of the later part of the century. The people in *Helen's Babies* or *Little Women* may be mildly ridiculous, but they are uncorrupted. They have something that is perhaps best described as integrity, or good morale, founded partly on an unthinking piety. It is a matter of course that everyone attends church on Sunday morning and says grace before meals and prayers at bedtime; to amuse the children one tells them Bible stories, and if they ask for a song it is probably 'Glory, Glory Hallelujah'. Perhaps it is also a sign of spiritual health in the light literature of this period that death is mentioned freely. "Baby Phil", the brother of Budge and Toddie, has died shortly before *Helen's Babies* opens, and there are various tear-jerking references to his "tiny coffin". A modern writer attempting a story of this kind would have kept coffins out of it.

English children are still Americanized by way of the films, but it would no longer be generally claimed that American books are the best ones for children. Who, without misgivings, would bring up a child on the coloured "comics" in which sinister professors manufacture atomic bombs in underground laboratories while Superman whizzes through the clouds, the machine-gun bullets bouncing off his chest like peas, and platinum blondes are raped, or very nearly, by steel robots and fifty-foot dinosaurs? It is a far cry from Superman to the

Bible and the woodpile. The earlier children's books, or books readable by children, had not only innocence but a sort of native gaiety, a buoyant, carefree feeling, which was the product, presumably, of the unheard-of freedom and security which nineteenth-century America enjoyed. That is the connecting link between books so seemingly far apart as *Little Women* and *Life on the Mississippi*.* The society described in the one is subdued, bookish and home-loving, while the other tells of a crazy world of bandits, gold mines, duels, drunkenness and gambling hells – but in both one can detect an underlying confidence in the future, a sense of freedom and opportunity.

Nineteenth-century America was a rich, empty country which lay outside the mainstream of world events, and in which the twin nightmares that beset nearly every modern man, the nightmare of unemployment and the nightmare of state interference, had hardly come into being. There were social distinctions, more marked than those of today, and there was poverty (in *Little Women*, it will be remembered, the family is at one time so hard up that one of the girls sells her hair to the barber), but there was not, as there is now, an all-prevailing sense of helplessness. There was room for everybody, and if you worked hard you could be certain of a living – could even be certain of growing rich; this was generally believed, and for the greater part of the population it was even broadly true. In other words, the civilization of nineteenth-century America was capitalist civilization at its best. Soon after the civil war the inevitable deterioration started. But for some decades, at least, life in America was much better fun than life in Europe – there was more happening, more colour, more variety, more opportunity – and the books and songs of that period had a sort of bloom, a childlike quality. Hence, I think, the popularity of *Helen's Babies* and other "light" literature, which made it normal for the English child of thirty or forty years ago to grow up with a theoretical knowledge of raccoons, woodchucks, chipmunks, gophers, hickory trees, watermelons and other unfamiliar fragments of the American scene.

How the Poor Die*

In the year 1929 I spent several weeks in the Hôpital X,* in the fifteenth *arrondissement* of Paris. The clerks put me through the usual third degree at the reception desk, and indeed I was kept answering questions for some twenty minutes before they would let me in. If you have ever had to fill up forms in a Latin country you will know the kind of questions I mean. For some days past I had been unequal to translating Réaumur into Fahrenheit, but I know that my temperature was round about 103, and by the end of the interview I had some difficulty in standing on my feet. At my back a resigned little knot of patients, carrying bundles done up in coloured handkerchiefs, waited their turn to be questioned.

After the questioning came the bath – a compulsory routine for all newcomers, apparently, just as in prison or the workhouse. My clothes were taken away from me, and after I had sat shivering for some minutes in five inches of warm water I was given a linen nightshirt and a short blue flannel dressing gown – no slippers, they had none big enough for me, they said – and led out into the open air. This was a night in February and I was suffering from pneumonia. The ward we were going to was 200 yards away and it seemed that to get to it you had to cross the hospital grounds. Someone stumbled in front of me with a lantern. The gravel path was frosty underfoot, and the wind whipped the nightshirt round my bare calves. When we got into the ward I was aware of a strange feeling of familiarity whose origin I did not succeed in pinning down till later in the night. It was a long, rather low, ill-lit room, full of murmuring voices and with three rows of beds surprisingly close together. There was a foul smell, faecal and yet sweetish. As I lay down I saw on a bed nearly opposite me a small, round-shouldered, sandy-haired man sitting half naked while a doctor and a student performed some strange operation on him. First the doctor produced from his black bag a dozen small glasses like wine glasses, then the student burned a match inside each glass to exhaust the air, then the glass was popped onto the man's back or chest and the vacuum drew up a huge yellow blister. Only after some moments did I realize what they were doing to him. It was something called cupping, a treatment which you can read about in old medical textbooks but which till then I had vaguely thought of as one of those things they do to horses.

The cold air outside had probably lowered my temperature, and I watched this barbarous remedy with detachment and even a certain amount of amusement. The next moment, however, the doctor and the student came across to my bed, hoisted me upright and without a word began applying the same set of glasses, which had not been sterilized in any way. A few feeble protests that I uttered got no more response than if I had been an animal. I was very much impressed by the impersonal way in which the two men started on me. I had never been in the public ward of a hospital before, and it was my first experience of doctors who handle you without speaking to you or, in a human sense, taking any notice of you. They only put on six glasses in my case, but after doing so they scarified the blisters and applied the glasses again. Each glass now drew out about a dessertspoonful of dark-coloured blood. As I lay down again, humiliated, disgusted and frightened by the thing that had been done to me, I reflected that now at least they would leave me alone. But no, not a bit of it. There was another treatment coming, the mustard poultice, seemingly a matter of routine like the hot bath. Two slatternly nurses had already got the poultice ready, and they lashed it round my chest as tight as a straitjacket while some men who were wandering about the ward in shirt and trousers began to collect round my bed with half-sympathetic grins. I learnt later that watching a patient have a mustard poultice was a favourite pastime in the ward. These things are normally applied for a quarter of an hour and certainly they are funny enough if you don't happen to be the person inside. For the first five minutes the pain is severe, but you believe you can bear it. During the second five minutes this belief evaporates, but the poultice is buckled at the back and you can't get it off. This is the period the onlookers most enjoy. During the last five minutes, I noted a sort of numbness supervenes. After the poultice had been removed a waterproof pillow packed with ice was thrust beneath my head and I was left alone. I did not sleep and to the best of my knowledge this was the only night of my life – I mean the only night spent in bed – in which I have not slept at all, not even a minute.

During my first hour in the Hôpital X, I had had a whole series of different and contradictory treatments, but this was misleading, for in general you got very little treatment at all, either good or bad, unless you were ill in some interesting and instructive way. At five in the morning the nurses came round, woke the patients and took their temperatures, but did not wash them. If you were well enough you washed yourself; otherwise you depended on the kindness of some walking patient. It was generally patients, too, who carried the bed bottles and the grim bedpan, nicknamed *la casserole*. At eight breakfast arrived, called army-fashion *la soupe*. It was soup, too, a thin vegetable soup with slimy hunks of bread floating about in it. Later in the day the tall, solemn, black-bearded doctor made his rounds, with an *interne* and a troop of students following at his heels, but there were about sixty of us in the ward and it was evident that he had other wards to attend to as well. There were many beds past which he walked day after day, sometimes followed by imploring cries. On the other hand if you had some disease with which the students wanted to familiarize themselves you got plenty of attention of a kind. I myself, with an exceptionally fine specimen of a bronchial rattle, sometimes had as many as a dozen students queueing up to listen to my chest. It was a very queer feeling – queer, I mean, because of their intense interest in learning their job, together with a seeming lack of any perception that the patients were human beings. It is strange to relate, but sometimes as some young student stepped forward to take his turn at manipulating you he would be actually tremulous with excitement, like a boy who has at last got his hands on some expensive piece of machinery. And then ear after ear – ears of young men, of girls, of Negroes – pressed against your back, relays of fingers solemnly but clumsily tapping, and not from any one of them did you get a word of conversation or a look direct in your face. As a non-paying patient, in the uniform nightshirt, you were primarily *a specimen*, a thing I did not resent but could never quite get used to.

After some days I grew well enough to sit up and study the surrounding patients. The stuffy room, with its narrow beds so close together that you could easily touch your neighbour's hand, had every sort of disease in it except, I suppose, acutely infectious cases. My right-hand neighbour was a little red-haired cobbler with one leg shorter than the other, who used to announce the death of any other patient (this happened a number of times, and my neighbour was always the first to hear of it) by whistling to me, exclaiming "*Numéro 43!*" (or whatever it was) and flinging his arms above his head. This man had not much wrong with him, but in most of the other beds within my angle of vision some squalid tragedy or some plain horror was being enacted. In the bed that was foot to foot with mine there lay, until he died (I didn't see him die – they moved him to another bed), a little wizened man who was suffering from I do not know what disease, but something that made his whole body so intensely sensitive that any movement from side to side, sometimes even the weight of the bedclothes, would make him shout out with pain. His worst suffering was when he urinated, which he did with the greatest difficulty. A nurse would bring him the bed bottle and then for a long time stand beside his bed, whistling, as grooms are said to do with horses, until at last with an agonized shriek of "*Je pisse!*" he would get started. In the bed next to him the sandy-haired man whom I had seen being cupped used to cough up blood-streaked mucus at all hours. My left-hand neighbour was a tall, flaccid-looking young man who used periodically to have a tube inserted into his back and astonishing quantities of frothy liquid drawn off from some part of his body. In the bed beyond that a veteran of the war of 1870 was dying, a handsome old man with a white imperial, round whose bed, at all hours when visiting was allowed, four elderly female relatives dressed all in black sat exactly like crows, obviously scheming for some pitiful legacy. In the bed opposite me in the further row was an old bald-headed man with drooping moustaches and greatly swollen face and body, who was suffering from some disease that made him urinate almost incessantly. A huge glass receptacle stood always beside his bed. One day his wife and daughter came to visit him. At the sight of them the old man's bloated face lit up with a smile of surprising sweetness, and as his daughter, a pretty girl of about twenty, approached the bed I saw that his hand was slowly working its way from under the bedclothes. I seemed to see in advance the gesture that was coming – the girl kneeling beside the bed, the old man's hand laid on her head in his dying blessing. But no, he merely handed her the bed bottle, which she promptly took from him and emptied into the receptacle.

About a dozen beds away from me was *numéro 57* – I think that was his number – a cirrhosis of the liver case. Everyone in the ward knew him by sight because he was sometimes the subject of a medical lecture. On two afternoons a week the tall, grave doctor would lecture in the ward to a party of students, and on more than one occasion old *numéro 57* was wheeled on a sort of trolley into the middle of the ward, where the doctor would roll back his nightshirt, dilate with his fingers a huge flabby protuberance on the man's belly – the diseased liver, I suppose – and explain solemnly that this was a disease attributable to alcoholism, commoner in the wine-drinking countries. As usual he neither spoke to his patient nor gave him a smile, a nod or any kind of recognition. While he talked, very grave and upright, he would hold the wasted body beneath his two hands, sometimes giving it a gentle roll to and fro, in just the attitude of a woman handling a rolling pin. Not that *numéro 57* minded this kind of thing. Obviously he was an old hospital inmate, a regular exhibit at lectures, his liver long since marked down for a bottle in some pathological museum. Utterly uninterested in what was said about him, he would lie with his colourless eyes gazing at nothing, while the doctor showed him off like a piece of antique china. He was a man of about sixty, astonishingly shrunken. His face, pale as vellum, had shrunken away till it seemed no bigger than a doll's.

One morning my cobbler neighbour woke me by plucking at my pillow before the nurses arrived. "*Numéro 57!*" He flung his arms above his head. There was a light in the ward, enough to see by. I could see old *numéro 57* lying crumpled up on his side, his face sticking out over the side of the bed, and towards me. He had died sometime during the night; nobody knew when. When the nurses came they received the news of his death indifferently and went about their work. After a long time, an hour or more, two other nurses marched in abreast like soldiers, with a great clumping of sabots, and knotted the corpse up in the sheets, but it was not removed till sometime later. Meanwhile, in the better light, I had had time for a good look at *numéro 57*. Indeed I lay on my side to look at him. Curiously enough he was the first dead European I had seen. I had seen dead men before, but always Asiatics and usually people who had died violent deaths. *Numéro 57*'s eyes were still open, his mouth also open, his small face contorted into an expression of agony. What most impressed me, however, was the whiteness of his face. It had been pale before, but now it was little darker than the sheets. As I gazed at the tiny, screwed-up face it struck me that this disgusting piece of refuse, waiting to be carted away and dumped on a slab in the dissecting room, was an example of "natural" death, one of the things you pray for in the Litany. There you are, then, I thought, that's what is waiting for you, twenty, thirty, forty years hence: that is how the lucky ones die, the ones who live to be old. One wants to live, of course, indeed one only stays alive by virtue of the fear of death, but I think now, as I thought then, that it's better to die violently and not too old. People talk about the horrors of war, but what weapon has man invented that even approaches in cruelty some of the commoner diseases? "Natural" death, almost by definition, means something slow, smelly and painful. Even at that, it makes a difference if you can achieve it in your own home and not in a public institution. This poor old wretch who had just flickered out like a candle end was not even important enough to have anyone watching by his deathbed. He was merely a number, then a "subject" for the students' scalpels. And the sordid publicity of dying in such a place! In the Hôpital X the beds were very close together and there were no screens. Fancy, for instance, dying like the little man whose bed was for a while foot to foot with mine, the one who cried out when the bedclothes touched him! I dare say "*Je pisse!*" were his last recorded words. Perhaps the dying don't bother about such things – that at least would be the standard answer: nevertheless dying people are often more or less normal in their minds till within a day or so of the end.

In the public wards of a hospital you see horrors that you don't seem to meet with among people who manage to die in their own homes, as though certain diseases only attacked people at the lower income levels. But it is a fact that you would not in any English hospitals see some of the things I saw in the Hôpital X. This business of people just dying like animals, for instance, with nobody standing by, nobody interested, the death not even noticed till the morning – this happened more than once. You certainly would not see that in England, and still less would you see a corpse left exposed to the view of the other patients. I remember that once in a cottage hospital in England a man died while we were at tea, and though there were only six of us in the ward the nurses managed things so adroitly that the man was dead and his body removed without our even hearing about it till tea was over. A thing we perhaps underrate in England is the advantage we enjoy in having large numbers of well-trained and rigidly disciplined nurses. No doubt English nurses are dumb enough; they may tell fortunes with tea leaves, wear Union Jack badges and keep photographs of the Queen on their mantelpieces, but at least they don't let you lie unwashed and constipated on an unmade bed, out of sheer laziness. The nurses at the Hôpital X still had a tinge of Mrs Gamp about them, and later, in the military hospitals of Republican Spain, I was to see nurses almost too ignorant to take a temperature. You wouldn't, either, see in England such dirt as existed in the Hôpital X. Later on, when I was well enough to wash myself in the bathroom, I found that there was kept there a huge packing case into which the scraps of food and dirty dressings from the ward were flung, and the wainscotings were infested by crickets.

When I had got back my clothes and grown strong on my legs I fled from the Hôpital X, before my time was up and without waiting for a medical discharge. It was not the only hospital I have fled from, but its gloom and bareness, its sickly smell and, above all, something in its mental atmosphere stand out in my memory as exceptional. I had been taken there because it was the hospital belonging to my *arrondissement*, and I did not learn till after I was in it that it bore a bad reputation. A year or two later the celebrated swindler, Madame Hanaud,* who was ill while on remand, was taken to the Hôpital X, and after a few days of it she managed to elude her guards, took a taxi and drove back to the prison, explaining that she was more comfortable there. I have no doubt that the Hôpital X was quite untypical of French hospitals even at that date. But the patients, nearly all of them working men, were surprisingly resigned. Some of them seemed to find the conditions almost comfortable, for at least two were destitute malingerers who found this a good way of getting through the winter. The nurses connived because the malingerers made themselves useful by doing odd jobs. But the attitude of the majority was: of course this is a lousy place, but what else do you expect? It did not seem strange to them that you should be woken at five and then wait three hours before starting the day on watery soup, or that people should die with no one at their bedside, or even that your chance of getting medical attention should depend on catching the doctor's eye as he went past. According to their traditions that was what hospitals were like. If you are seriously ill, and if you are too poor to be treated in your own home, then you must go into hospital, and once there you must put up with harshness and discomfort, just as you would in the army. But on top of this I was interested to find a lingering belief in the old stories that have now almost faded from memory in England – stories, for instance, about doctors cutting you open out of sheer curiosity or thinking it funny to start operating before you were properly "under". There were dark tales about a little operating room said to be situated just beyond the bathroom. Dreadful screams were said to issue from this room. I saw nothing to confirm these stories and no doubt they were all nonsense, though I did see two students kill a sixteen-year-old boy, or nearly kill him (he appeared to be dying when I left the hospital, but he may have recovered later) by a mischievous experiment which they probably could not have tried on a paying patient. Well within living memory it used to be believed in London that in some of the big hospitals patients were killed off to get dissection subjects. I didn't hear this tale repeated at the Hôpital X, but I should think some of the men there would have found it credible. For it was a hospital in which not the methods, perhaps, but something of the atmosphere of the nineteenth century had managed to survive, and therein lay its peculiar interest.

During the past fifty years or so there has been a great change in the relationship between doctor and patient. If you look at almost any literature before the later part of the nineteenth century, you find that a hospital is popularly regarded as much the same thing as a prison, and an old-fashioned, dungeon-like prison at that. A hospital is a place of filth, torture and death, a sort of antechamber to the tomb. No one who was not more or less destitute would have thought of going into such a place for treatment. And especially in the early part of the last century, when medical science had grown bolder than before without being any more successful, the whole business of doctoring was looked on with horror and dread by ordinary people. Surgery, in particular, was believed to be no more than a peculiarly gruesome form of sadism, and dissection, possible only with the aid of body snatchers, was even confused with necromancy. From the nineteenth century you could collect a large horror literature connected with doctors and hospitals. Think of poor old George III, in his dotage, shrieking for mercy as he sees his surgeons approaching to "bleed him till he faints"! Think of the conversations of Bob Sawyer and Benjamin Allen, which no doubt are hardly parodies, or the field hospitals in *La Débâcle* and *War and Peace*, or that shocking description of an amputation in Melville's *White-Jacket*!* Even the names given to doctors in nineteenth-century English fiction, Slasher, Carver, Sawyer, Fillgrave and so on, and the generic nickname "sawbones", are about as grim as they are comic. The anti-surgery tradition is perhaps best expressed in Tennyson's poem 'The Children's Hospital',* which is essentially a pre-chloroform document though it seems to have been written as late as 1880. Moreover, the outlook which Tennyson records in this poem had a lot to be said for it. When you consider what an operation without anaesthetics must have been like, what it notoriously *was* like, it is difficult not to suspect the motives of people who would undertake such things. For these bloody horrors which the students so eagerly looked forward to ("A magnificent sight if Slasher does it!") were admittedly more or less useless: the patient who did not die of shock usually died of gangrene, a result which was taken for granted. Even now doctors can be found whose motives are questionable. Anyone who has had much illness, or who has listened to medical students talking, will know what I mean. But anaesthetics were a turning point, and disinfectants were another. Nowhere in the world, probably, would you now see the kind of scene described by Axel Munthe in *The Story of San Michele*,* when the sinister surgeon in top hat and frock coat, his starched shirtfront spattered with blood and pus, carves up patient after patient with the same knife and flings the severed limbs into a pile beside the table. Moreover, national health insurance has partly done away with the idea that a working-class patient is a pauper who deserves little consideration. Well into this century it was usual for "free" patients at the big hospitals to have their teeth extracted with no anaesthetic. They didn't pay, so why should they have an anaesthetic – that was the attitude. That too has changed.

And yet every institution will always bear upon it some lingering memory of its past. A barrack room is still haunted by the ghost of Kipling, and it is difficult to enter a workhouse without being reminded of *Oliver Twist*. Hospitals began as a kind of casual ward for lepers and the like to die in, and they continued as places where medical students learnt their art on the bodies of the poor. You can still catch a faint suggestion of their history in their characteristically gloomy architecture. I would be far from complaining about the treatment I have received in any English hospital, but I do know that it is a sound instinct that warns people to keep out of hospitals if possible, and especially out of the public wards. Whatever the legal position may be, it is unquestionable that you have far less control over your own treatment, far less certainty that frivolous experiments will not be tried on you, when it is a case of "accept the discipline or get out". And it is a great thing to die in your own bed, though it is better still to die in your boots. However great the kindness and the efficiency, in every hospital death there will be some cruel, squalid detail, something perhaps too small to be told but leaving terribly painful memories behind, arising out of the haste, the crowding, the impersonality of a place where every day people are dying among strangers.

The dread of hospitals probably still survives among the very poor and in all of us it has only recently disappeared. It is a dark patch not far beneath the surface of our minds. I have said earlier that, when I entered the ward at the Hôpital X, I was conscious of a strange feeling of familiarity. What the scene reminded me of, of course, was the reeking, pain-filled hospitals of the nineteenth century, which I had never seen but of which I had a traditional knowledge. And something, perhaps the black-clad doctor with his frowsy black bag, or perhaps only the sickly smell, played the queer trick of unearthing from my memory that poem of Tennyson's, 'The Children's Hospital', which I had not thought of for twenty years. It happened that as a child I had had it read aloud to me by a sick-nurse whose own working life might have stretched back to the time when Tennyson wrote the poem. The horrors and sufferings of the old-style hospitals were a vivid memory to her. We had shuddered over the poem together, and then seemingly I had forgotten it. Even its name would probably have recalled nothing to me. But the first glimpse of the ill-lit, murmurous room, with the beds so close together, suddenly roused the train of thought to which it belonged, and in the night that followed I found myself remembering the whole story and atmosphere of the poem, with many of its lines complete.

Lear, Tolstoy and the Fool*

Tolstoy's pamphlets are the least known part of his work, and his attack on Shakespeare* is not even an easy document to get hold of, at any rate in an English translation. Perhaps, therefore, it will be useful if I give a summary of the pamphlet before trying to discuss it.

Tolstoy begins by saying that throughout life Shakespeare has aroused in him "an irresistible repulsion and tedium". Conscious that the opinion of the civilized world is against him, he has made one attempt after another on Shakespeare's works, reading and rereading them in Russian, English and German, but "I invariably underwent the same feelings: repulsion, weariness and bewilderment". Now, at the age of seventy-five, he has once again reread the entire works of Shakespeare, including the historical plays, and

> I have felt with even greater force, the same feelings – this time, however, not of bewilderment, but of firm, indubitable conviction that the unquestionable glory of a great genius which Shakespeare enjoys, and which compels writers of our time to imitate him and readers and spectators to discover in him non-existent merits – thereby distorting their aesthetic and ethical understanding – is a great evil, as is every untruth.

Shakespeare, Tolstoy adds, is not merely no genius, but is not even "an average author", and in order to demonstrate this fact he will examine *King Lear* – which, as he is able to show by quotations from Hazlitt, Brandes* and others, has been extravagantly praised and can be taken as an example of Shakespeare's best work.

Tolstoy then makes a sort of exposition of the plot of *King Lear*, finding it at every step to be stupid, verbose, unnatural, unintelligible, bombastic, vulgar, tedious and full of incredible events, "wild ravings", "mirthless jokes", anachronisms, irrelevancies, obscenities, worn-out stage conventions and other faults both moral and aesthetic. *Lear* is, in any case, a plagiarism of an earlier and much better play, *King Leir*, by an unknown author, which Shakespeare stole and then ruined. It is worth quoting a specimen paragraph to illustrate the manner in which Tolstoy goes to work. Act III, Sc. 2 (in which Lear, Kent and the Fool are together in the storm) is summarized thus:

> Lear walks about the heath and says words which are meant to express his despair: he desires that the winds should blow so hard that they (the winds)

should crack their cheeks and that the rain should flood everything, that lightning should singe his white head, and the thunder flatten the world and destroy all germs "that make ungrateful man"! The fool keeps uttering still more senseless words. Enter Kent: Lear says that for some reason during this storm all criminals shall be found out and convicted. Kent, still unrecognized by Lear, endeavours to persuade him to take refuge in a hovel. At this point the fool utters a prophecy in no wise related to the situation and they all depart.

Tolstoy's final verdict on *Lear* is that no unhypnotized observer, if such an observer existed, could read it to the end with any feeling except "aversion and weariness". And exactly the same is true of "all the other extolled dramas of Shakespeare, not to mention the senseless dramatized tales, *Pericles*, *Twelfth Night*, *The Tempest*, *Cymbeline*, *Troilus and Cressida*".

Having dealt with *Lear* Tolstoy draws up a more general indictment against Shakespeare. He finds that Shakespeare has a certain technical skill which is partly traceable to his having been an actor, but otherwise no merits whatever. He has no power of delineating character or of making words and actions spring naturally out of situations; his language is uniformly exaggerated and ridiculous; he constantly thrusts his own random thoughts into the mouth of any character who happens to be handy; he displays a "complete absence of aesthetic feeling"; and his words "have nothing whatever in common with art and poetry". "Shakespeare might have been whatever you like," Tolstoy concludes, "but he was not an artist." Moreover, his opinions are not original or interesting, and his tendency is "of the lowest and most immoral". Curiously enough, Tolstoy does not base this last judgement on Shakespeare's own utterances, but on the statements of two critics, Gervinus* and Brandes. According to Gervinus (or at any rate Tolstoy's reading of Gervinus), "Shakespeare taught [...] that one *may be too good*," while according to Brandes, "Shakespeare's fundamental principle [...] is that *the end justifies the means*." Tolstoy adds on his own account that Shakespeare was a jingo patriot of the worst type, but apart from this he considers that Gervinus and Brandes have given a true and adequate description of Shakespeare's view of life.

Tolstoy then recapitulates in a few paragraphs the theory of art which he had expressed at greater length elsewhere. Put still more shortly, it amounts to a demand for dignity of subject matter, sincerity and good craftsmanship. A great work of art must deal with some subject which is "important to the life of mankind", it must express something which the author genuinely feels and it must use such technical methods as will produce the desired effect. As Shakespeare is debased in outlook, slipshod in execution and incapable of being sincere even for a moment, he obviously stands condemned.

But here there arises a difficult question. If Shakespeare is all that Tolstoy has shown him to be, how did he ever come to be so generally admired? Evidently the answer can only lie in a sort of mass hypnosis, or "epidemic suggestion". The whole civilized world has somehow been deluded into thinking Shakespeare a good writer, and even the plainest demonstration to the contrary makes no impression, because one is not dealing with a reasoned opinion but with something akin to religious faith. Throughout history, says Tolstoy, there has been an endless series of these "epidemic suggestions" – for example, the Crusades, the search for the Philosopher's Stone, the craze for tulip growing which once swept over Holland, and so on and so forth. As a contemporary instance he cites, rather significantly, the Dreyfus case,* over which the whole world grew violently excited for no sufficient reason. There are also sudden short-lived crazes for new political and philosophical theories, or for this or that writer, artist or scientist – for example, Darwin, who (in 1903) is "beginning to be forgotten". And in some cases a quite worthless popular idol may remain in favour for centuries, for "it also happens that such crazes, having arisen in consequence of special reasons accidentally favouring their establishment, correspond in such a degree to the views of life spread in society, and especially in literary circles, that they are maintained for a long time". Shakespeare's plays have continued to be admired over a long period because "they corresponded to the irreligious and immoral frame of mind of the upper classes of his time and ours".

As to the manner in which Shakespeare's fame *started*, Tolstoy explains it as having been "got up" by German professors towards the end of the eighteenth century. His reputation "originated in Germany, and thence was transferred to England". The Germans chose to elevate Shakespeare because, at a time when there was no German drama worth speaking about and French classical literature was beginning to seem frigid and artificial, they were captivated by Shakespeare's "clever development of scenes" and also found in him a good expression of their own attitude towards life. Goethe pronounced Shakespeare a great poet, whereupon all the other critics flocked after him like a troop of parrots, and the general infatuation has lasted ever since. The result has been a further debasement of the drama – Tolstoy is careful to include his own plays when condemning the contemporary stage – and a further corruption of the prevailing moral outlook. It follows that "the false glorification of Shakespeare" is an important evil which Tolstoy feels it his duty to combat.

This, then, is the substance of Tolstoy's pamphlet. One's first feeling is that in describing Shakespeare as a bad writer he is saying something demonstrably untrue. But this is not the case. In reality there is no kind of evidence or argument by which one can show that Shakespeare, or any other writer, is "good". Nor is there any way of definitely proving that – for instance – Warwick Deeping* is "bad". Ultimately there is no test of literary merit except survival, which is itself merely an index to majority opinion. Artistic theories such as Tolstoy's are quite worthless, because they not only start out with arbitrary assumptions but depend on vague terms ("sincere", "important" and so forth) which can be interpreted in any way one chooses. Properly speaking one cannot *answer* Tolstoy's attack. The interesting question is: why did he make it? But it should be noticed in passing that he uses many weak or dishonest arguments. Some of these are worth pointing out, not because they invalidate his main charge but because they are, so to speak, evidence of malice.

To begin with, his examination of *King Lear* is not "impartial", as he twice claims. On the contrary, it is a prolonged exercise in misrepresentation. It is obvious that when you are summarizing *King Lear* for the benefit of someone who has not read it, you are not really being impartial if you introduce an important speech (Lear's speech when Cordelia is dead in his arms) in this manner: "Again begin Lear's awful ravings, at which one feels ashamed, as at unsuccessful jokes." And in a long series of instances Tolstoy slightly alters or colours the passages he is criticizing, always in such a way as to make the plot appear a little more complicated and improbable, or the language a little more exaggerated. For example, we are told that Lear "has no necessity or motive for his abdication", although his reason for abdicating (that he is old and wishes to retire from the cares of state) has been clearly indicated in the first scene. It will be seen that even in the passage which I quoted earlier, Tolstoy has wilfully misunderstood one phrase and slightly changed the meaning of another, making nonsense of a remark which is reasonable enough in its context. None of these misreadings is very gross in itself, but their cumulative effect is to exaggerate the psychological incoherence of the play. Again, Tolstoy is not able to explain why Shakespeare's plays were still in print, and still on the stage, two hundred years after his death (*before* the "epidemic suggestion" started, that is) – and his whole account of Shakespeare's rise to fame is guesswork punctuated by outright misstatements. And again, various of his accusations contradict one another: for example, Shakespeare is a mere entertainer and "not in earnest", but on the other hand he is constantly putting his own thoughts into the mouths of his characters. On the whole it is difficult to feel that Tolstoy's criticisms are uttered in good faith. In any case it is impossible that he should fully have believed in his main thesis – believed, that is to say, that for a century or more the entire civilized world had been taken in by a huge and palpable lie which he alone was able to see through. Certainly his dislike of Shakespeare is real enough, but the reasons for it may be different, or partly different, from what he avows – and therein lies the interest of his pamphlet.

At this point one is obliged to start guessing. However, there is one possible clue, or at least there is a question which may point the way to a clue. It is: why did Tolstoy, with thirty or more plays to choose from, pick out *King Lear* as his especial target? True, *Lear* is so well known and has been so much praised that it could justly be taken as representative of Shakespeare's best work; still, for the purpose of a hostile analysis Tolstoy would probably choose the play he disliked most. Is it not possible that he bore an especial enmity towards this particular play because he was aware, consciously or unconsciously, of the resemblance between Lear's story and his own? But it is better to approach this clue from the opposite direction – that is, by examining *Lear* itself, and the qualities in it that Tolstoy fails to mention.

One of the first things an English reader would notice in Tolstoy's pamphlet is that it hardly deals with Shakespeare as a poet. Shakespeare is treated as a dramatist, and in so far as his popularity is not spurious, it is held to be due to tricks of stagecraft which give good opportunities to clever actors. Now, so far as the English-speaking countries go, this is not true. Several of the plays which are most valued by lovers of Shakespeare (for instance, *Timon of Athens*) are seldom or never acted, while some of the most actable, such as *A Midsummer Night's Dream*, are the least admired. Those who care most for Shakespeare value him in the first place for his use of language, the "verbal music" which even Bernard Shaw, another hostile critic, admits to be "irresistible". Tolstoy ignores this, and does not seem to realize that a poem may have a special value for those who speak the language in which it was written. However, even if one puts oneself in Tolstoy's place and tries to think of Shakespeare as a foreign poet it is still clear that there is something that Tolstoy has left out. Poetry, it seems, is *not* solely a matter of sound and association, and valueless outside its own language group: otherwise, how is it that some poems, including poems written in dead languages, succeed in crossing frontiers? Clearly a lyric like "Tomorrow is Saint Valentine's Day" could not be satisfactorily translated, but in Shakespeare's major work there is something describable as poetry that can be separated from the words. Tolstoy is right in saying that *Lear* is not a very good play, as a play. It is too drawn out and has too many characters and sub-plots. One wicked daughter would have been quite enough, and Edgar is a superfluous character; indeed it would probably be a better play if Gloucester and both his sons were eliminated. Nevertheless, something, a kind of pattern, or perhaps only an atmosphere, survives the complications and the *longueurs*. *Lear* can be imagined as a puppet show, a mime, a ballet, a series of pictures. Part of its poetry, perhaps the most essential part, is inherent in the story and is dependent neither on any particular set of words nor on flesh-and-blood presentation.

Shut your eyes and think of *King Lear*, if possible without calling to mind any of the dialogue. What do you see? Here at any rate is what I see: a majestic old man in a long black robe, with flowing white hair and beard, a figure out of Blake's drawings (but also, curiously enough, rather like Tolstoy), wandering through a storm and cursing the heavens, in company with a Fool and a lunatic.

Presently the scene shifts, and the old man, still cursing, still understanding nothing, is holding a dead girl in his arms while the Fool dangles on a gallows somewhere in the background. This is the bare skeleton of the play, and even here Tolstoy wants to cut out most of what is essential. He objects to the storm as being unnecessary, to the Fool, who in his eyes is simply a tedious nuisance and an excuse for making bad jokes, and to the death of Cordelia, which, as he sees it, robs the play of its moral. According to Tolstoy, the earlier play, *King Leir*, which Shakespeare adapted,

> terminates more naturally and more in accordance with the moral demands of the spectator than does Shakespeare's: namely, by the King of the Gauls conquering the husbands of the elder sisters, and by Cordelia, instead of being killed, restoring Leir to his former position.

In other words the tragedy ought to have been a comedy, or perhaps a melodrama. It is doubtful whether the sense of tragedy is compatible with belief in God; at any rate, it is not compatible with disbelief in human dignity and with the kind of "moral demand" which feels cheated when virtue fails to triumph. A tragic situation exists precisely when virtue does *not* triumph but when it is still felt that man is nobler than the forces which destroy him. It is perhaps more significant that Tolstoy sees no justification for the presence of the Fool. The Fool is integral to the play. He acts not only as a sort of chorus, making the central situation clearer by commenting on it more intelligently than the other characters, but as a foil to Lear's frenzies. His jokes, riddles and scraps of rhyme, and his endless digs at Lear's high-minded folly, ranging from mere derision to a sort of melancholy poetry ("All thy other titles thou hast given away; that thou wast born with"), are like a trickle of sanity running through the play, a reminder that somewhere or other, in spite of the injustices, cruelties, intrigues, deceptions and misunderstandings that are being enacted here, life is going on much as usual. In Tolstoy's impatience with the Fool one gets a glimpse of his deeper quarrel with Shakespeare. He objects, with some justification, to the raggedness of Shakespeare's plays, the irrelevancies, the incredible plots, the exaggerated language: but what at bottom he probably most dislikes is a sort of exuberance, a tendency to take – not so much a pleasure as simply an interest in the actual process of life. It is a mistake to write Tolstoy off as a moralist attacking an artist. He never said that art, as such, is wicked or meaningless, nor did he even say that technical virtuosity is unimportant. But his main aim, in his later years, was to narrow the range of human consciousness. One's interests, one's points of attachment to the physical world and the day-to-day struggle, must be as few and not as many as possible. Literature must consist of parables, stripped of detail and almost independent of language. The parables – this is where

Tolstoy differs from the average vulgar puritan — must themselves be works of art, but pleasure and curiosity must be excluded from them. Science, also, must be divorced from curiosity. The business of science, he says, is not to discover what happens but to teach men how they ought to live. So also with history and politics. Many problems (for example, the Dreyfus case) are simply not worth solving, and he is willing to leave them as loose ends. Indeed his whole theory of "crazes" or "epidemic suggestions", in which he lumps together such things as the Crusades and the Dutch passion of tulip growing, shows a willingness to regard many human activities as mere ant-like rushings to and fro, inexplicable and uninteresting. Clearly he could have no patience with a chaotic, detailed, discursive writer like Shakespeare. His reaction is that of an irritable old man who is being pestered by a noisy child. "Why do you keep jumping up and down like that? Why can't you sit still like I do?" In a way the old man is in the right, but the trouble is that the child has a feeling in its limbs which the old man has lost. And if the old man knows of the existence of this feeling, the effect is merely to increase his irritation: he would make children senile if he could. Tolstoy does not know, perhaps, just *what* he misses in Shakespeare, but he is aware that he misses something, and he is determined that others shall be deprived of it as well. By nature he was imperious as well as egotistical. Well after he was grown up he would still occasionally strike his servant in moments of anger, and somewhat later, according to his English biographer, Derrick Leon,* he felt "a frequent desire upon the slenderest provocation to slap the faces of those with whom he disagreed". One does not necessarily get rid of that kind of temperament by undergoing religious conversion, and indeed it is obvious that the illusion of having been reborn may allow one's native vices to flourish more freely than ever, though perhaps in subtler forms. Tolstoy was capable of abjuring physical violence and of seeing what this implies, but he was not capable of tolerance or humility, and even if one knew nothing of his other writings, one could deduce his tendency towards spiritual bullying from this single pamphlet.

However, Tolstoy is not simply trying to rob others of a pleasure he does not share. He is doing that, but his quarrel with Shakespeare goes further. It is the quarrel between the religious and the humanist attitudes towards life. Here one comes back to the central theme of *King Lear*, which Tolstoy does not mention, although he sets forth the plot in some detail.

Lear is one of the minority of Shakespeare's plays that are unmistakably *about* something. As Tolstoy justly complains, much rubbish has been written about Shakespeare as a philosopher, as a psychologist, as a "great moral teacher" and what not. Shakespeare was not a systematic thinker; his most serious thoughts are uttered irrelevantly or indirectly, and we do not know to what extent he wrote with a "purpose" or even how much of the work attributed to him was actually written by him. In the Sonnets he never even refers to the plays as part of his achievement, though he does make what seems to be a half-ashamed allusion to his career as an actor. It is perfectly possible that he looked on at least half of his plays as mere potboilers and hardly bothered about purpose or probability so long as he could patch up something, usually from stolen material, which would more or less hang together on the stage. However, that is not the whole story. To begin with, as Tolstoy himself points out, Shakespeare has a habit of thrusting uncalled-for general reflections into the mouths of his characters. This is a serious fault in a dramatist, but it does not fit in with Tolstoy's picture of Shakespeare as a vulgar hack who has no opinions of his own and merely wishes to produce the greatest effect with the least trouble. And more than this, about a dozen of his plays, written for the most part later than 1600, do unquestionably have a meaning and even a moral. They revolve round a central subject which in some cases can be reduced to a single word. For example, *Macbeth* is about ambition, *Othello* is about jealousy and *Timon of Athens* is about money. The subject of *Lear* is renunciation, and it is only by being wilfully blind that one can fail to understand what Shakespeare is saying.

Lear renounces his throne but expects everyone to continue treating him as a king. He does not see that if he surrenders power, other people will take advantage of his weakness – also that those who flatter him the most grossly, i.e. Regan and Goneril, are exactly the ones who will turn against him. The moment he finds that he can no longer make people obey him as he did before, he falls into a rage which Tolstoy describes as "strange and unnatural", but which in fact is perfectly in character. In his madness and despair, he passes through two moods which again are natural enough in his circumstances, though in one of them it is probable that he is being used partly as a mouthpiece for Shakespeare's own opinions. One is the mood of disgust in which Lear repents, as it were, for having been a king, and grasps for the first time the rottenness of formal justice and vulgar morality. The other is a mood of impotent fury in which he wreaks imaginary revenges upon those who have wronged him. "To have a thousand with red burning spits / Come hissing in upon 'em!", and:

> It were a delicate stratagem to shoe
> A troop of horse with felt: I'll put't in proof;
> And when I have stol'n upon these sons-in-law,
> Then kill, kill, kill, kill, kill!

Only at the end does he realize, as a sane man, that power, revenge and victory are not worthwhile:

> No, no, no, no! Come, let's away to prison [...]
> and we'll wear out,
> In a wall'd prison, packs and sects of great ones
> That ebb and flow by the moon.

But by the time he makes this discovery it is too late, for his death and Cordelia's are already decided on. That is the story, and, allowing for some clumsiness in the telling, it is a very good story.

But is it not also curiously similar to the history of Tolstoy himself? There is a general resemblance which one can hardly avoid seeing, because the most impressive event in Tolstoy's life, as in Lear's, was a huge and gratuitous act of renunciation. In his old age he renounced his estate, his title and his copyrights, and made an attempt – a sincere attempt, though it was not successful – to escape from his privileged position and live the life of a peasant. But the deeper resemblance lies in the fact that Tolstoy, like Lear, acted on mistaken motives and failed to get the results he had hoped for. According to Tolstoy, the aim of every human being is happiness, and happiness can only be attained by doing the will of God. But doing the will of God means casting off all earthly pleasures and ambitions, and living only for others. Ultimately, therefore, Tolstoy renounced the world under the expectation that this would make him happier. But if there is one thing certain about his later years, it is that he was *not* happy. On the contrary, he was driven almost to the edge of madness by the behaviour of the people about him, who persecuted him precisely *because* of his renunciation. Like Lear, Tolstoy was not humble and not a good judge of character. He was inclined at moments to revert to the attitudes of an aristocrat, in spite of his peasant's blouse, and he even had two children whom he had believed in and who ultimately turned against him – though, of course, in a less sensational manner than Regan and Goneril. His exaggerated revulsion from sexuality was also distinctly similar to Lear's. Tolstoy's remark that marriage is "slavery, satiety, repulsion" and means putting up with the proximity of "ugliness, dirtiness, smell, sores", is matched by Lear's well-known outburst:

> But to the girdle do the gods inherit,
> Beneath is all the fiends;
> There's hell, there's darkness, there's the sulphurous pit,
> Burning, scalding, stench, consumption, etc. etc.

And though Tolstoy could not foresee it when he wrote his essay on Shakespeare, even the ending of his life – the sudden unplanned flight across country, accompanied only by a faithful daughter, the death in a cottage in a strange village – seems to have in it a sort of phantom reminiscence of *Lear*.

Of course, one cannot assume that Tolstoy was aware of this resemblance, or would have admitted it if it had been pointed out to him. But his attitude towards the play must have been influenced by its theme. Renouncing power, giving away your lands, was a subject on which he had reason to feel deeply. Probably, therefore, he would be more angered and disturbed by the moral that Shakespeare draws than he would be in the case of some other play – *Macbeth*, for example – which did not touch so closely on his own life. But what exactly *is* the moral of *Lear*? Evidently there are two morals, one explicit, the other implied in the story.

Shakespeare starts by assuming that to make yourself powerless is to invite an attack. This does not mean that *everyone* will turn against you (Kent and the Fool stand by Lear from first to last), but in all probability *someone* will. If you throw away your weapons, some less scrupulous person will pick them up. If you turn the other cheek, you will get a harder blow on it than you got on the first one. This does not always happen, but it is to be expected, and you ought not to complain if it does happen. The second blow is, so to speak, part of the act of turning the other cheek. First of all, therefore, there is the vulgar, common-sense moral drawn by the Fool: "Don't relinquish power, don't give away your lands." But there is also another moral. Shakespeare never utters it in so many words, and it does not very much matter whether he was fully aware of it. It is contained in the story, which, after all, he made up, or altered to suit his purposes. It is: "Give away your lands if you want to, but don't expect to gain happiness by doing so. Probably you won't gain happiness. If you live for others, you must live *for others*, and not as a roundabout way of getting an advantage for yourself."

Obviously neither of these conclusions could have been pleasing to Tolstoy. The first of them expresses the ordinary, belly-to-earth selfishness from which he was genuinely trying to escape. The other conflicts with his desire to eat his cake and have it – that is, to destroy his own egoism and by so doing to gain eternal life. Of course, *Lear* is not a sermon in favour of altruism. It merely points out the results of practising self-denial for selfish reasons. Shakespeare had a considerable streak of worldliness in him, and if he had been forced to take sides in his own play, his sympathies would probably have lain with the Fool. But at least he could see the whole issue and treat it at the level of tragedy. Vice is punished, but virtue is not rewarded. The morality of Shakespeare's later tragedies is not religious in the ordinary sense, and certainly is not Christian. Only two of them, *Hamlet* and *Othello*, are supposedly occurring inside the Christian era, and even in those, apart from the antics of the ghost in *Hamlet*, there is no indication of a "next world" where everything is to be put right. All of these tragedies start out with the humanist assumption that life, although full of sorrow, is worth living, and that Man is a noble animal – a belief which Tolstoy in his old age did not share.

Tolstoy was not a saint, but he tried very hard to make himself into a saint, and the standards he applied to literature were other-worldly ones. It is important to realize that the difference between a saint and an ordinary human being is a difference of kind and not of degree. That is, the one is not to be regarded as an imperfect form of the other. The saint, at any rate Tolstoy's kind of saint, is not trying to work an improvement in earthly life: he is trying to bring it to an end and put something different in its place. One obvious expression of this is the claim that celibacy is "higher" than marriage. If only, Tolstoy says in effect, we would stop breeding, fighting, struggling and enjoying, if we could get rid not only of our sins but of everything else that binds us to the surface of the earth – including love, in the ordinary sense of caring more for one human being than another – then the whole painful process would be over and the Kingdom of Heaven would arrive. But a normal human being does not want the Kingdom of Heaven: he wants life on earth to continue. This is not solely because he is "weak", "sinful" and anxious for a "good time". Most people get a fair amount of fun out of their lives, but on balance life is suffering, and only the very young or the very foolish imagine otherwise. Ultimately it is the Christian attitude which is self-interested and hedonistic, since the aim is always to get away from the painful struggle of earthly life and find eternal peace in some kind of heaven or Nirvana. The humanist attitude is that the struggle must continue and that death is the price of life. "Men must endure / Their going hence, even as their coming hither: / Ripeness is all" – which is an unchristian sentiment. Often there is a seeming truce between the humanist and the religious believer, but in fact their attitudes cannot be reconciled: one must choose between this world and the next. And the enormous majority of human beings, if they understood the issue, would choose this world. They do make that choice when they continue working, breeding and dying instead of crippling their faculties in the hope of obtaining a new lease of existence elsewhere.

We do not know a great deal about Shakespeare's religious beliefs, and from the evidence of his writings it would be difficult to prove that he had any. But at any rate he was not a saint or a would-be saint: he was a human being, and in some ways not a very good one. It is clear, for instance, that he liked to stand well with the rich and powerful, and was capable of flattering them in the most servile way. He is also noticeably cautious, not to say cowardly, in his manner of uttering unpopular opinions. Almost never does he put a subversive or sceptical remark into the mouth of a character likely to be identified with himself. Throughout his plays the acute social critics, the people who are not taken in by accepted fallacies, are buffoons, villains, lunatics or persons who are shamming insanity or are in a state of violent hysteria. *Lear* is a play in which this tendency is particularly well marked. It contains a great deal of veiled social criticism – a point Tolstoy misses – but it is all uttered either by the Fool, by Edgar when he is pretending to be mad or by Lear during his bouts of madness. In his sane moments Lear hardly ever makes an intelligent remark. And yet the very fact that Shakespeare had to use these subterfuges shows how widely his thoughts ranged. He could not restrain himself from commenting on almost everything, although he put on a series of masks in order to do so. If one has once read Shakespeare with attention, it is not easy to go a day without quoting him, because there are not many subjects of major importance that he does not discuss or at least mention somewhere or other, in his unsystematic but illuminating way. Even the irrelevancies that litter every one of his plays – the puns and riddles, the lists of names, the scraps of reportage like the conversation of the carriers in *Henry IV*, the bawdy jokes, the rescued fragments of forgotten ballads – are merely the products of excessive vitality. Shakespeare was not a philosopher or a scientist, but he did have curiosity: he loved the surface of the earth and the process of life – which, it should be repeated, is *not* the same thing as wanting to have a good time and stay alive as long as possible. Of course, it is not because of the quality of his thought that Shakespeare has survived, and he might not even be remembered as a dramatist if he had not also been a poet. His main hold on us is through language. How deeply Shakespeare himself was fascinated by the music of words can probably be inferred from the speeches of Pistol. What Pistol says is largely meaningless, but if one considers his lines singly they are magnificent rhetorical verse. Evidently, pieces of resounding nonsense ("Let floods o'erswell, and fiends for food howl on," etc.) were constantly appearing in Shakespeare's mind of their own accord, and a half-lunatic character had to be invented to use them up. Tolstoy's native tongue was not English, and one cannot blame him for being unmoved by Shakespeare's verse, nor even, perhaps, for refusing to believe that Shakespeare's skill with words was something out of the ordinary. But he would also have rejected the whole notion of valuing poetry for its texture – valuing it, that is to say, as a kind of music. If it could somehow have been proved to him that his whole explanation of Shakespeare's rise to fame is mistaken, that inside the English-speaking world, at any rate, Shakespeare's popularity is genuine, that his mere skill in placing one syllable beside another has given acute pleasure to generation after generation of English-speaking people – all this would not have been counted as a merit to Shakespeare, but rather the contrary. It would simply have been one more proof of the irreligious, earthbound nature of Shakespeare and his admirers. Tolstoy would have said that poetry is to be judged by its meaning, and that seductive sounds merely cause false meanings to go unnoticed. At every level it is the same issue: this world against the next – and certainly the music of words is something that belongs to this world.

A sort of doubt has always hung round the character of Tolstoy, as round the character of Gandhi. He was not a vulgar hypocrite, as some people declared him to be, and he would probably have imposed even greater sacrifices on himself than he did if he had not been interfered with at every step by the people surrounding him, especially his wife. But on the other hand it is dangerous to take such men as Tolstoy at their disciples' valuation. There is always the possibility – the probability, indeed – that they have done no more than exchange one form of egoism for another. Tolstoy renounced wealth, fame and privilege; he abjured violence in all its forms and was ready to suffer for doing so – but it is not so easy to believe that he abjured the principle of coercion, or at least the *desire* to coerce others. There are families in which the father will say to his child, "You'll get a thick ear if you do that again," while the mother, her eyes brimming over with tears, will take the child in her arms and murmur lovingly, "Now, darling, *is* it kind to Mummy to do that?" And who would maintain that the second method is less tyrannous than the first? The distinction that really matters is not between violence and non-violence, but between having and not having the appetite for power. There are people who are convinced of the wickedness both of armies and of police forces, but who are nevertheless much more intolerant and inquisitorial in outlook than the normal person who believes that it is necessary to use violence in certain circumstances. They will not say to somebody else, "Do this, that and the other or you will go to prison," but they will, if they can, get inside his brain and dictate his thoughts for him in the minutest particulars. Creeds like pacifism and anarchism, which seem on the surface to imply a complete renunciation of power, rather encourage this habit of mind. For if you have embraced a creed which appears to be free from the ordinary dirtiness of politics – a creed from which you yourself cannot expect to draw any material advantage – surely that proves that you are in the right? And the more you are in the right, the more natural that everyone else should be bullied into thinking likewise.

If we are to believe what he says in his pamphlet, Tolstoy had never been able to see any merit in Shakespeare, and was always astonished to find that his fellow writers, Turgenev, Fet* and others, thought differently. We may be sure that in his unregenerate days Tolstoy's conclusion would have been: "You like Shakespeare – I don't. Let's leave it at that." Later, when his perception that it takes all sorts to make a world had deserted him, he came to think of Shakespeare's writings as something dangerous to himself. The more pleasure people took in Shakespeare, the less they would listen to Tolstoy. Therefore nobody must be *allowed* to enjoy Shakespeare, just as nobody must be allowed to drink alcohol or smoke tobacco. True, Tolstoy would not prevent them by force. He is not demanding that the police shall impound every copy of Shakespeare's works. But he will do dirt on Shakespeare, if he can. He will try to get inside the mind of every lover of Shakespeare and kill his enjoyment by every trick he can think of, including – as I have shown in my summary of his pamphlet – arguments which are self-contradictory or even doubtfully honest.

But finally the most striking thing is how little difference it all makes. As I said earlier, one cannot *answer* Tolstoy's pamphlet, at least on its main counts. There is no argument by which one can defend a poem. It defends itself by surviving, or it is indefensible. And if this test is valid, I think the verdict in Shakespeare's case must be "not guilty". Like every other writer, Shakespeare will be forgotten sooner or later, but it is unlikely that a heavier indictment will ever be brought against him. Tolstoy was perhaps the most admired literary man of his age, and he was certainly not its least able pamphleteer. He turned all his powers of denunciation against Shakespeare, like all the guns of a battleship roaring simultaneously. And with what result? Forty years later, Shakespeare is still there, completely unaffected, and of the attempt to demolish him nothing remains except the yellowing pages of a pamphlet which hardly anyone has read, and which would be forgotten altogether if Tolstoy had not also been the author of *War and Peace* and *Anna Karenina*.

Towards European Unity*

A socialist today is in the position of a doctor treating an all but hopeless case. As a doctor, it is his duty to keep the patient alive, and therefore to assume that the patient has at least a chance of recovery. As a scientist, it is his duty to face the facts, and therefore to admit that the patient will probably die. Our activities as socialists only have meaning if we assume that socialism *can* be established, but if we stop to consider what probably *will* happen, then we must admit, I think, that the chances are against us. If I were a bookmaker, simply calculating the probabilities and leaving my own wishes out of account, I would give odds against the survival of civilization within the next few hundred years. As far as I can see, there are three possibilities ahead of us:

1. That the Americans will decide to use the atomic bomb while they have it and the Russians haven't. This would solve nothing. It would do away with the particular danger that is now presented by the USSR, but would lead to the rise of new empires, fresh rivalries, more wars, more atomic bombs, etc. In any case this is, I think, the least likely outcome of the three, because a preventive war is a crime not easily committed by a country that retains any traces of democracy.

2. That the present "cold war" will continue until the USSR, and several other countries, have atomic bombs as well. Then there will only be a short breathing space before *whizz!* go the rockets, *wallop!* go the bombs, and the industrial centres of the world are wiped out, probably beyond repair. Even if any one state, or group of states, emerges from such a war as technical victor, it will probably be unable to build up the machine civilization anew. The world, therefore, will once again be inhabited by a few million, or a few hundred million human beings living by subsistence agriculture, and probably, after a couple of generations, retaining no more of the culture of the past than a knowledge of how to smelt metals. Conceivably this is a desirable outcome, but obviously it has nothing to do with socialism.

3. That the fear inspired by the atomic bomb and other weapons yet to come will be so great that everyone will refrain from using them. This seems to me the worst possibility of all. It would mean the division of the world among two or three vast superstates, unable to conquer one another and unable to be overthrown by any internal rebellion. In all probability their structure would be hierarchic, with a semi-divine caste at the top and outright slavery at the bottom, and the crushing out of liberty would exceed anything that the world has yet seen. Within each state the necessary psychological atmosphere would

be kept up by complete severance from the outer world, and by a continuous phoney war against rival states. Civilizations of this type might remain static for thousands of years.

Most of the dangers that I have outlined existed and were foreseeable long before the atomic bomb was invented. The only way of avoiding them that I can imagine is to present somewhere or other, on a large scale, the spectacle of a community where people are relatively free and happy and where the main motive in life is not the pursuit of money or power. In other words, democratic socialism must be made to work throughout some large area. But the only area in which it could conceivably be made to work, in any near future, is Western Europe. Apart from Australia and New Zealand, the tradition of democratic socialism can only be said to exist – and even there it only exists precariously – in Scandinavia, Germany, Austria, Czechoslovakia, Switzerland, the Low Countries, France, Britain, Spain and Italy. Only in those countries are there still large numbers of people to whom the word "socialism" has some appeal and for whom it is bound up with liberty, equality and internationalism. Elsewhere it either has no foothold or it means something different. In North America the masses are contented with capitalism, and one cannot tell what turn they will take when capitalism begins to collapse. In the USSR there prevails a sort of oligarchical collectivism which could only develop into democratic socialism against the will of the ruling minority. Into Asia even the word "socialism" has barely penetrated. The Asiatic nationalist movements are either fascist in character, or look towards Moscow, or manage to combine both attitudes – and at present all movements among the coloured peoples are tinged by racial mysticism. In most of South America the position is essentially similar; so is it in Africa and the Middle East. Socialism does not exist anywhere, but even as an idea it is at present valid only in Europe. Of course, socialism cannot properly be said to be established until it is worldwide, but the process must begin somewhere, and I cannot imagine it beginning except through the federation of the Western European states, transformed into socialist republics without colonial dependencies. Therefore a socialist United States of Europe seems to me the only worthwhile political objective today. Such a federation would contain about 250 million people, including perhaps half the skilled industrial workers of the world. I do not need to be told that the difficulties of bringing any such thing into being are enormous and terrifying, and I will list some of them in a moment. But we ought not to feel that it is of its nature impossible, or that countries so different from one another would not voluntarily unite. A Western European union is in itself a less improbable concatenation than the Soviet Union or the British Empire.

Now as to the difficulties. The greatest difficulty of all is the apathy and conservatism of people everywhere, their unawareness of danger, their inability to imagine anything new – in general, as Bertrand Russell put it recently, the unwillingness of the human race to acquiesce in its own survival. But there are also active malignant forces working against European unity, and there are existing economic relationships on which the European peoples depend for their standard of life and which are not compatible with true socialism. I list what seem to me to be the four main obstacles, explaining each of them as shortly as I can manage:

1. *Russian hostility*. The Russians cannot but be hostile to any European union not under their own control. The reasons, both the pretended and the real ones, are obvious. One has to count, therefore, with the danger of a preventive war, with the systematic terrorizing of the smaller nations, and with the sabotage of the communist parties everywhere. Above all there is the danger that the European masses will continue to believe in the Russian myth. As long as they believe it, the idea of a socialist Europe will not be sufficiently magnetic to call forth the necessary effort.

2. *American hostility*. If the United States remains capitalist, and especially if it needs markets for exports, it cannot regard a socialist Europe with a friendly eye. No doubt it is less likely than the USSR to intervene with brute force, but American pressure is an important factor because it can be exerted most easily on Britain, the one country in Europe which is outside the Russian orbit. Since 1940 Britain has kept its feet against the European dictators at the expense of becoming almost a dependency of the USA. Indeed, Britain can only get free of America by dropping the attempt to be an extra-European power. The English-speaking Dominions, the colonial dependencies, except perhaps in Africa, and even Britain's supplies of oil, are all hostages in American hands. Therefore there is always the danger that the United States will break up any European coalition by drawing Britain out of it.

3. *Imperialism*. The European peoples, and especially the British, have long owed their high standard of life to direct or indirect exploitation of the coloured peoples. This relationship has never been made clear by official socialist propaganda, and the British worker, instead of being told that, by world standards, he is living above his income, has been taught to think of himself as an overworked, downtrodden slave. To the masses everywhere "socialism" means, or at least is associated with, higher wages, shorter hours, better houses, all-round social insurance, etc. etc. But it is by no means certain that we can afford these things if we throw away the advantages we derive from colonial exploitation. However evenly the national income is divided up, if the income as a whole falls, the working-class standard of living must fall with it. At best there is liable to be a long and uncomfortable reconstruction period for which public opinion has nowhere been prepared. But at the same time the European nations *must* stop being exploiters abroad if they are to build true socialism at home. The first step towards a European socialist federation is for the British to get out of India. But this entails something else.

If the United States of Europe is to be self-sufficient and able to hold its own against Russia and America, it must include Africa and the Middle East. But that means that the position of the indigenous peoples in those countries must be changed out of recognition – that Morocco or Nigeria or Abyssinia must cease to be colonies or semi-colonies and become autonomous republics on a complete equality with the European peoples. This entails a vast change of outlook and a bitter, complex struggle which is not likely to be settled without bloodshed. When the pinch comes the forces of imperialism will turn out to be extremely strong, and the British worker, if he has been taught to think of socialism in materialistic terms, may ultimately decide that it is better to remain an imperial power at the expense of playing second fiddle to America. In varying degrees all the European peoples, at any rate those who are to form part of the proposed union, will be faced with the same choice.

4. *The Catholic Church*. As the struggle between East and West becomes more naked, there is danger that democratic socialists and mere reactionaries will be driven into combining in a sort of Popular Front. The Church is the likeliest bridge between them. In any case the Church will make every effort to capture and sterilize any movement aiming at European unity. The dangerous thing about the Church is that it is *not* reactionary in the ordinary sense. It is not tied to laissez-faire capitalism or to the existing class system, and will not necessarily perish with them. It is perfectly capable of coming to terms with socialism, or appearing to do so, provided that its own position is safeguarded. But if it is allowed to survive as a powerful organization, it will make the establishment of true socialism impossible, because its influence is and always must be against freedom of thought and speech, against human equality and against any form of society tending to promote earthly happiness.

When I think of these and other difficulties, when I think of the enormous mental readjustment that would have to be made, the appearance of a socialist United States of Europe seems to me a very unlikely event. I don't mean that the bulk of the people are not prepared for it, in a passive way. I mean that I see no person or group of persons with the slightest chance of attaining power and at the same time with the imaginative grasp to see what is needed and to demand the necessary sacrifices from their followers. But I also can't at present see any other hopeful objective. At one time I believed that it might be possible to form the British Empire into a federation of socialist republics, but if that chance ever existed, we lost it by failing to liberate India, and by our attitude towards the coloured peoples generally. It may be that Europe is finished and that in the long run some better form of society will arise in India or China. But I believe that it is only in Europe, if anywhere, that democratic socialism could be made a reality in short enough time to prevent the dropping of the atom bombs.

Of course, there are reasons, if not for optimism, at least for suspending judgement on certain points. One thing in our favour is that a major war is not likely to happen immediately. We could, I suppose, have the kind of war that consists in shooting rockets, but not a war involving the mobilization of tens of millions of men. At present any large army would simply melt away, and that may remain true for ten or even twenty years. Within that time some unexpected things might happen. For example, a powerful socialist movement might for the first time arise in the United States. In England it is now the fashion to talk of the United States as "capitalistic", with the implication that this is something unalterable, a sort of racial characteristic like the colour of eyes or hair. But in fact it cannot be unalterable, since capitalism itself has manifestly no future, and we cannot be sure in advance that the next change in the United States will not be a change for the better.

Then, again, we do not know what changes will take place in the USSR if war can be staved off for the next generation or so. In a society of that type, a radical change of outlook always seems unlikely, not only because there can be no open opposition but because the regime, with its complete hold over education, news, etc. deliberately aims at preventing the pendulum swing between generations which seems to occur naturally in liberal societies. But for all we know the tendency of one generation to reject the ideas of the last is an abiding human characteristic which even the NKVD* will be unable to eradicate. In that case there may by 1960 be millions of young Russians who are bored by dictatorship and loyalty parades, eager for more freedom, and friendly in their attitude towards the West.

Or again, it is even possible that if the world falls apart into three unconquerable superstates, the liberal tradition will be strong enough within the Anglo-American section of the world to make life tolerable and even offer some hope of progress. But all this is speculation. The actual outlook, so far as I can calculate the probabilities, is very dark, and any serious thought should start out from that fact.

In Defence of Comrade Zilliacus*

Some weeks ago Mr K. Zilliacus addressed a long and, as usual, abusive letter to *Tribune*, in which he accused it of having no definite and viable foreign policy, but of being in effect an anti-Russian paper while keeping up a show of hostility to Ernest Bevin.* Bevin, he said, was far more realistic than *Tribune*, since he grasped that to oppose Russia it was necessary to rely on America and "bolster up fascism", while *Tribune* was merely sitting on the fence, uttering contradictory slogans and getting nowhere.

I am not often in agreement with Mr Zilliacus, and it is therefore all the more of a pleasure to record my agreement with him on this occasion. Granting him his own special terminology, I think his accusation is fully justified. One must remember, of course, that in the mouths of Mr Zilliacus and his associates, words like democracy, fascism or totalitarianism do not bear quite their normal meanings. In general they tend to turn into their opposites, fascism meaning unfaked elections, democracy meaning minority rule, and so on. But this does not alter the fact that he is dwelling on real issues – issues on which *Tribune* has consistently, over a period of years, failed to make its position clear. He knows that the only big political questions in the world today are: for Russia – against Russia; for America – against America; for democracy – against democracy. And though he may describe his own activities in different words from what most of us would use, at least we can see at a glance where he stands.

But where does *Tribune* stand? I know, or think I know, what foreign policy *Tribune* favours, but I know it by inference and from private contacts. Casual readers can, and to my knowledge do, draw very different impressions. If one had to sum up *Tribune*'s *apparent* policy in a single word, the name one would have to coin for it would be anti-Bevinism. The first rule of this "ism" is that when Bevin says or does something, a way must be found of showing that it is wrong, even if it happens to be what *Tribune* was advocating in the previous week. The second rule is that though Russian policy may be criticized, extenuating circumstances must always be found. The third rule is that when the United States can be insulted, it must be insulted. The effect of framing a policy on these principles is that one cannot even find out what solution *Tribune* offers for the specific problems it most discusses. To take some examples. Is *Tribune* in favour of clearing out of Greece unconditionally? Does *Tribune* think the USSR should have the Dardanelles? Is *Tribune* in favour of unrestricted Jewish immigration into Palestine? Does *Tribune* think Egypt should be allowed to annex the Sudan? In some cases I know the answers, but I think it would be very difficult to discover them simply by reading the paper.

Part of the trouble, I believe, is that after building Bevin up into Public Enemy Number One, *Tribune* has found out that it is not genuinely in disagreement with him. Certainly there are real differences over Palestine, Spain and perhaps Greece, but broadly, I think, he and *Tribune* stand for the same kind of policy. There are, it is generally agreed, only three possible foreign policies for Great Britain. One is to do as Mr Zilliacus would have us do, i.e. to become part of the Russian system, with a government perhaps less servile than that of Poland or Czechoslovakia, but essentially similar. Another is to move definitely into the orbit of the United States. And another is to become part of a federation of Western European socialist republics, including if possible Africa, and again if possible (though this is less likely) the British Dominions. *Tribune*, I infer – for it has never been clearly stated – favours the third policy, and so I believe does Bevin, that is to say, the government. But *Tribune* is not only involved in its personal feud with Bevin; it is also unwilling to face two facts – very unpopular facts at the moment – which must be faced if one is to discuss a Western union seriously. One is that such a union could hardly succeed without a friendly America behind it, and the other is that however peaceful its intentions might be it would be bound to incur Russian hostility. It is exactly here that *Tribune* has failed as an organ of opinion. All its other equivocations, I believe, spring from a dread of flouting fashionable opinion on the subject of Russia and America.

One very noticeable thing in *Tribune* is the pretence that Bevin's policy is exclusively his own. Apparently he is a sort of runaway horse dragging an unwilling Cabinet behind him, and our policy would have been quite different – above all, our relations with the USSR would have been better – if only we had had a more enlightened Foreign Secretary. Now it is obvious that this cannot be so. A minister who is really thwarting the will of the rest of the government does not stay in office for two years. Why then the attempt to put all the blame on one person? Was it not because otherwise it would have been necessary to say a very unpopular thing: namely that a Labour government, as such, is almost bound to be on bad terms with the government of the USSR? With a government headed by Pritt* and Zilliacus we could no doubt have excellent relations, of a kind, with Russia, and with a government headed by Churchill and Beaverbrook we could probably patch up some kind of arrangement – but any government genuinely representative of the Labour movement *must* be regarded with hostility. From the point of view of the Russians and the communists, social democracy is a deadly enemy, and to do them justice they have frequently admitted it. Even such controversial questions as the formation of a Western union are irrelevant here. Even if we had no influence in Europe and made no attempt to interfere there, it would still be to the interest of the Russian government to bring about the failure of the British Labour government, if possible. The reason is clear enough. Social democracy, unlike capitalism, offers an alternative to communism, and if somewhere or other it can be made to work on a big scale – if it turns out that after all it *is* possible to introduce socialism without secret police forces, mass deportations and so forth – then the excuse for dictatorship vanishes. With a Labour government in office, relations with Russia, bad already, were bound to deteriorate. Various observers pointed this out at the time of the general election, but I do not remember *Tribune* doing so, then or since. Was it not because it was easier, more popular, to encourage the widespread delusion that "a government of the Left can get on better with Russia" and that communism is much the same thing as socialism, only more so – and then, when things didn't turn out that way, to register pained surprise and look round for a scapegoat?

And what, I wonder, is behind *Tribune*'s persistent anti-Americanism? In *Tribune* over the past year I can recall three polite references to America (one of those was a reference to Henry Wallace*) and a whole string of petty insults. I have just received a letter from some students at an American university. They ask me if I can explain why *Tribune* thinks it necessary to boo at America. What am I to say to these people? I shall tell them what I believe to be the truth – namely that *Tribune*'s anti-Americanism is not sincere but is an attempt to keep in with fashionable opinion. To be anti-American nowadays is to shout with the mob. Of course it is only a minor mob, but it is a vocal one. Although there was probably some growth of ill feeling as a result of the presence of the American troops, I do not believe the mass of the people in this country are anti-American politically, and certainly they are not so culturally. But politico-literary intellectuals are not usually frightened of mass opinion. What they are frightened of is the prevailing opinion within their own group. At any given moment there is always an orthodoxy, a parrot cry which must be repeated, and in the more active section of the Left the orthodoxy of the moment is anti-Americanism. I believe part of the reason (I am thinking of some remarks in Mr G.D.H. Cole's last 1,143-page compilation*) is the idea that if we can cut our links with the United States we might succeed in staying neutral in the case of Russia and America going to war. How anyone can believe this, after looking at the map and remembering what happened to neutrals in the late war, I do not know. There is also the rather mean consideration that the Americans are *not* really our enemies, that they are unlikely to start dropping atomic bombs on us or even to let us starve to death, and therefore that we can safely take liberties with them if it pays to do so. But at any rate the orthodoxy is there. To speak favourably of America, to recall that the Americans helped us in 1940 when the Russians were supplying the Germans with oil and setting on their Communist Parties to sabotage the war effort, is to be branded as a "reactionary". And I suspect that when *Tribune* joins in the chorus it is more from fear of this label than from genuine conviction.

Surely, if one is going to write about foreign policy at all, there is one question that should be answered plainly. It is: "If you *had* to choose between Russia and America, which would you choose?" It will not do to give the usual quibbling answer, "I refuse to choose." In the end the choice may be forced upon us. We are no longer strong enough to stand alone, and if we fail to bring a Western European union into being, we shall be obliged, in the long run, to subordinate our policy to that of one great power or the other. And in spite of all the fashionable chatter of the moment, everyone knows in his heart that we should choose America. The great mass of people in this country would, I believe, make this choice almost instinctively. Certainly there is a small minority that would choose the other way. Mr Zilliacus, for instance, is one of them. I think he is wrong, but at least he makes his position clear. I also know perfectly well what *Tribune*'s position is. But has *Tribune* ever made it clear?

How subject we are in this country to the intellectual tyranny of minorities can be seen from the composition of the press. A foreign observer who judged Britain solely by its press would assume that the Conservative Party was out and away the strongest party, with the Liberals second, the Communists third and the Labour Party nowhere. The one genuine mass party has no daily paper that is undisputedly its own, and among the political weeklies it has no reliable supporter. Suppose *Tribune* came out with a plain statement of the principles that are implicit in some of its individual decisions – in its support of conscription, for instance. Would it be going against the main body of Labour Party opinion? I doubt it. But it would be going against the fashionable minority who can make things unpleasant for a political journalist. These people have a regular technique of smears and ridicule – a whole specialized vocabulary designed to show that anyone who will not repeat the accepted catchwords is a rather laughable kind of lunatic. Mr Zilliacus, for instance, accuses *Tribune* of being "rabidly anti-Russian" (or "rabidly anti-communist" – it was one or the other). The keyword here is rabid. Other words used in this context are insensate, demented, "sick with hatred" (the *New Republic*'s phrase) and maniacal. The upshot is that if from time to time you express a mild distaste for slave-labour camps or one-candidate elections, you are either insane or actuated by the worst motives. In the same way, when Henry Wallace is asked by a newspaper interviewer why he issues falsified versions of his speeches to the press, he replies: "So you are one of these people who are clamouring for war with Russia?" It doesn't answer the question, but it would frighten most people into silence. Or there is the milder kind of ridicule that consists in pretending that a reasoned opinion is indistinguishable from an absurd out-of-date prejudice. If you do not like communism you are a Red-baiter, a believer in Bolshevik atrocities, the nationalization of women, Moscow Gold, and so on. Similarly, when Catholicism was almost as fashionable among the English intelligentsia as communism is now, anyone who said that the Catholic Church was a sinister organization and no friend to democracy was promptly accused of swallowing the worst follies of the No-Popery organizations, of looking under his bed lest Jesuits should be concealed there, of believing stories about babies' skeletons dug up from the floors of nunneries, and all the rest of it. But a few people stuck to their opinion, and I think it is safe to say that the Catholic Church is less fashionable now than it was then.

After all, what does it matter to be laughed at? The big public, in any case, usually doesn't see the joke, and if you state your principles clearly and stick to them, it is wonderful how people come round to you in the end. There is no doubt about whom *Tribune* is frightened of. It is frightened of the communists, the fellow travellers and the fellow travellers of fellow travellers. Hence its endless equivocations: a paragraph of protest when this one of our friends is shot – silence when that one is shot, denunciation of this faked election – qualified approval of that one, and so on. The result is that in American papers I have more than once seen the phrase "the Foot–Zilliacus group"* (or words to that effect). Of course Foot and Zilliacus are not allies, but they can appear so from the outside. Meanwhile, does this kind of thing even conciliate the people it is aimed at? Does it conciliate Mr Zilliacus, for instance? He has been treated with remarkable tenderness by *Tribune*. He has been allowed to infest its correspondence columns like a perennial weed, and when a little while ago *Tribune* reviewed a book of his,* I looked in vain in that review for any plain statement of what he is or whose interests he is serving. Instead there was only a mild disagreement, a suggestion that he was perhaps a little over-zealous, a little given to special pleading – all this balanced by praise wherever possible, and headed by the friendly title 'The Fighting Propagandist'. But is Mr Zilliacus grateful? On the contrary, only a few weeks later he turns round and without any provocation delivers a good hard boot on the shins.

It is hard to blame him, since he knows very well that *Tribune* is not on his side and does not really like him. But whereas he is willing to make this clear, *Tribune*, in spite of occasional side thrusts, is not. I do not claim for Mr Zilliacus that he is honest, but at least he is sincere. We know where he stands, and he prefers to hit his enemies rather than his friends. Of course it is true that he is saying what is safe and fashionable at this moment, but I imagine he would stick to his opinions if the tide turned.

George Gissing*

In the shadow of the atomic bomb it is not easy to talk confidently about progress. However, if it can be assumed that we are *not* going to be blown to pieces in about ten years' time, there are many reasons, and George Gissing's novels are among them, for thinking that the present age is a good deal better than the last one. If Gissing were still alive he would be younger than Bernard Shaw, and yet already the London of which he wrote seems almost as distant as that of Dickens. It is the fog-bound, gaslit London of the eighties, a city of drunken puritans, where clothes, architecture and furniture had reached their rock bottom of ugliness, and where it was almost normal for a working-class family of ten persons to inhabit a single room. On the whole Gissing does not write of the worst depths of poverty, but one can hardly read his descriptions of lower-middle-class life, so obviously truthful in their dreariness, without feeling that we have improved perceptibly on that black-coated, money-ruled world of only sixty years ago.

Everything of Gissing's – except perhaps one or two books written towards the end of his life – contains memorable passages, and anyone who is making his acquaintance for the first time might do worse than start with *In the Year of the Jubilee*.* It was rather a pity, however, to use up paper in reprinting two of his minor works* when the books by which he ought to be remembered are and have been for years completely unprocurable. *The Odd Women*,* for instance, is about as thoroughly out of print as a book can be. I possess a copy myself, in one of those nasty little red-covered cheap editions that flourished before the 1914 war, but that is the only copy I have ever seen or heard of. *New Grub Street*, Gissing's masterpiece, I have never succeeded in buying. When I have read it, it has been in soup-stained copies borrowed from public lending libraries; so also with *Demos*, *The Nether World** and one or two others. So far as I know only *The Private Papers of Henry Ryecroft*, the book on Dickens and *A Life's Morning** have been in print at all recently. However, the two now reprinted are well worth reading, especially *In the Year of the Jubilee*, which is the more sordid and therefore the more characteristic.

In his introduction Mr William Plomer remarks that "generally speaking, Gissing's novels are about money and women", and Miss Myfanwy Evans says something very similar in introducing *The Whirlpool*. One might, I think, widen the definition and say that Gissing's novels are a protest against the form of self-torture that goes by the name of respectability. Gissing was a bookish, perhaps over-civilized man, in love with classical antiquity, who found himself trapped in a cold, smoky, Protestant country where it was impossible to be comfortable without a thick padding of money between yourself and the outer world. Behind his rage and querulousness there lay a perception that the horrors of life in late-Victorian England were largely unnecessary. The grime, the stupidity, the ugliness, the sex starvation, the furtive debauchery, the vulgarity, the bad manners, the censoriousness – these things were unnecessary, since the puritanism of which they were a relic no longer upheld the structure of society. People who might, without becoming less efficient, have been reasonably happy chose instead to be miserable, inventing senseless taboos with which to terrify themselves. Money was a nuisance not merely because without it you starved; what was more important was that unless you had quite a lot of it – £300 a year, say – society would not allow you to live gracefully or even peacefully. Women were a nuisance because even more than men they were the believers in taboos, still enslaved to respectability even when they had offended against it. Money and women were therefore the two instruments through which society avenged itself on the courageous and the intelligent. Gissing would have liked a little more money for himself and some others, but he was not much interested in what we should now call social justice. He did not admire the working class as such, and he did not believe in democracy. He wanted to speak not for the multitude, but for the exceptional man, the sensitive man, isolated among barbarians.

In *The Odd Women* there is not a single major character whose life is not ruined either by having too little money or by getting it too late in life, or by the pressure of social conventions which are obviously absurd but which cannot be questioned. An elderly spinster crowns a useless life by taking to drink; a pretty young girl marries a man old enough to be her father; a struggling schoolmaster puts off marrying his sweetheart until both of them are middle-aged and withered; a good-natured man is nagged to death by his wife; an exceptionally intelligent, spirited man misses his chance to make an adventurous marriage and relapses into futility – in each case the ultimate reason for the disaster lies in obeying the accepted social code, or in not having enough money to circumvent it. In *A Life's Morning* an honest and gifted man meets with ruin and death because it is impossible to walk about a big town with no hat on. His hat is blown out of the window when he is travelling in the train, and as he has not enough money to buy another, he misappropriates some money belonging to his employer, which sets going a series of disasters. This is an interesting example of the changes in outlook that can suddenly make an all-powerful taboo seem ridiculous. Today, if you had somehow contrived to lose your trousers, you would probably embezzle money rather than walk about in your underpants. In the eighties the necessity would have seemed equally strong in the case of a hat. Even thirty or forty years ago, indeed, bare-headed men were booed at in the street. Then, for no very clear reason, hatlessness became respectable, and today the particular tragedy described by Gissing – entirely plausible in its context – would be quite impossible.

The most impressive of Gissing's books is *New Grub Street*. To a professional writer it is also an upsetting and demoralizing book, because it deals among other things with that much-dreaded occupational disease, sterility. No doubt the number of writers who suddenly lose the power to write is not large, but it is a calamity that *might* happen to anybody at any moment, like sexual impotence. Gissing, of course, links it up with his habitual themes – money, the pressure of the social code and the stupidity of women.

Edwin Reardon, a young novelist – he has just deserted a clerkship after having a fluky success with a single novel – marries a charming and apparently intelligent young woman, with a small income of her own. Here, and in one or two other places, Gissing makes what now seems the curious remark that it is difficult for an educated man who is not rich to get married. Reardon brings it off, but his less successful friend, who lives in an attic and supports himself by ill-paid tutoring jobs, has to accept celibacy as a matter of course. If he did succeed in finding himself a wife, we are told, it could only be an uneducated girl from the slums. Women of refinement and sensibility will not face poverty. And here one notices again the deep difference between that day and our own. Doubtless Gissing is right in implying all through his books that intelligent women are very rare animals, and if one wants to marry a women who is intelligent *and* pretty, then the choice is still further restricted, according to a well-known arithmetical rule. It is like being allowed to choose only among albinos, and left-handed albinos at that. But what comes out in Gissing's treatment of his odious heroine, and of certain others among his women, is that at that date the idea of delicacy, refinement, even intelligence, in the case of a woman, was hardly separable from the idea of superior social status and expensive physical surroundings. The sort of woman whom a writer would want to marry was also the sort of woman who would shrink from living in an attic. When Gissing wrote *New Grub Street* that was probably true, and it could, I think, be justly claimed that it is not true today.

Almost as soon as Reardon is married it becomes apparent that his wife is merely a silly snob, the kind of woman in whom "artistic tastes" are no more than a cover for social competitiveness. In marrying a novelist she has thought to marry someone who will rapidly become famous and shed reflected glory upon herself. Reardon is a studious, retiring, ineffectual man, a typical Gissing hero. He has been caught up in an expensive, pretentious world in which he knows he will never be able to maintain himself, and his nerve fails almost immediately. His wife, of course, has not the faintest understanding of what is meant by literary creation. There is a terrible passage – terrible, at least, to anyone who earns his living by writing – in which she calculates the number of pages that it would be possible to write in a day, and hence the number of novels that her husband may be expected to produce in a year – with the reflection that really it is not a very laborious profession. Meanwhile Reardon has been stricken dumb. Day after day he sits at his desk; nothing happens, nothing comes. Finally, in panic, he manufactures a piece of rubbish; his publisher, because Reardon's previous book had been successful, dubiously accepts it. Thereafter he is unable to produce anything that even looks as if it might be printable. He is finished.

The desolating thing is that if only he could get back to his clerkship and his bachelorhood, he would be all right. The hard-boiled journalist who finally marries Reardon's widow sums him up accurately by saying that he is the kind of man who, if left to himself, would write a fairly good book every two years. But, of course, he is not left to himself. He cannot revert to his old profession, and he cannot simply settle down to live on his wife's money; public opinion, operating through his wife, harries him into impotence and finally into the grave. Most of the other literary characters in the book are not much more fortunate, and the troubles that beset them are still very much the same today. But at least it is unlikely that the book's central disaster would now happen in quite that way or for quite those reasons. The chances are that Reardon's wife would be less of a fool, and that he would have fewer scruples about walking out on her if she made life intolerable for him. A woman of rather similar type turns up in *The Whirlpool* in the person of Alma Frothingham. By contrast there are the three Miss Frenches in *The Year of the Jubilee*, who represent the emerging lower middle class – a class which, according to Gissing, was getting hold of money and power which it was not fitted to use – and who are quite surprisingly coarse, rowdy, shrewish and unmoral. At first sight Gissing's "ladylike" and "unladylike" women seem to be different and even opposite kinds of animal, and this seems to invalidate his implied condemnation of the female sex in general. The connecting link between them, however, is that all of them are miserably limited in outlook. Even the clever and spirited ones, like Rhoda in *The Odd Women* (an interesting early specimen of the New Woman), cannot think in terms of generalities, and cannot get away from ready-made standards. In his heart Gissing seems to feel that women are natural inferiors. He wants them to be better educated, but on the other hand he does not want them to have freedom, which they are certain to misuse. On the whole the best women in his books are the self-effacing, home-keeping ones.

There are several of Gissing's books that I have never read, because I have never been able to get hold of them, and these unfortunately include *Born in Exile*,* which is said by some people to be his best book. But merely on the strength of *New Grub Street*, *Demos* and *The Odd Women* I am ready to maintain that England has produced very few better novelists. This perhaps sounds like a rash statement until one stops to consider what is meant by a novel. The word "novel" is commonly used to cover almost any kind of story – *The Golden Ass,** Anna Karenina, Don Quixote, The Improvisatore,** Madame Bovary, King Solomon's Mines* or anything else you like – but it also has a narrower sense in which it means something hardly existing before the nineteenth century and flourishing chiefly in Russia and France. A novel, in this sense, is a story which attempts to describe credible human beings, and – without necessarily using the technique of naturalism – to show them acting on everyday motives and not merely undergoing strings of improbable adventures. A true novel, sticking to this definition, will also contain at least two characters, probably more, who are described from the inside and on the same level of probability – which, in effect, rules out the novels written in the first person. If one accepts this definition, it becomes apparent that the novel is not an art form in which England has excelled. The writers commonly paraded as "great English novelists" have a way of turning out either not to be true novelists or not to be Englishmen. Gissing was not a writer of picaresque tales, or burlesques, or comedies, or political tracts – he was interested in individual human beings, and the fact that he can deal sympathetically with several different sets of motives, and makes a credible story out of the collision between them, makes him exceptional among English writers.

Certainly there is not much of what is usually called beauty, not much lyricism, in the situations and characters that he chooses to imagine, and still less in the texture of his writing. His prose, indeed, is often disgusting. Here are a couple of samples:

> Not with impunity could her thought accustom itself to stray in regions forbidden, how firm soever her resolve to hold bodily aloof. (*The Whirlpool*)

> The ineptitude of uneducated English women in all that relates to their attire is a fact that it boots not to enlarge upon. (*In the Year of the Jubilee*)

However, he does not commit the faults that really matter. It is always clear what he means; he never "writes for effect"; he knows how to keep the balance between *récit* and dialogue and how to make dialogue sound probable while not contrasting too sharply with the prose that surrounds it. A much more serious fault than his inelegant manner of writing is the smallness of his range of experience. He is only acquainted with a few strata of society, and, in spite of his vivid understanding of the pressure of circumstance on character, does not seem to have much grasp of political or economic forces. In a mild way his outlook is reactionary, from lack of foresight rather than from ill will. Having been obliged to live among them, he regarded the working class as savages, and in saying so he was merely being intellectually honest; he did not see that they were capable of becoming civilized if given slightly better opportunities. But, after all, what one demands from a novelist is not prophecy, and part of the charm of Gissing is that he belongs so unmistakably to his own time, although his time treated him badly.

The English writer nearest to Gissing always seems to be his contemporary, or near-contemporary, Mark Rutherford.* If one simply tabulates their outstanding qualities, the two men appear to be very different. Mark Rutherford was a less prolific writer than Gissing, he was less definitely a novelist, he wrote much better prose, his books belong less recognizably to any particular time, and he was in outlook a social reformer and, above all, a puritan. Yet there is a sort of haunting resemblance, probably explained by the fact that both men lack that curse of English writers, a "sense of humour". A certain low-spiritedness and air of loneliness is common to both of them. There are, of course, funny passages in Gissing's books, but he is not chiefly concerned with getting a laugh – above all, he has no impulse towards burlesque. He treats all his major characters more or less seriously, and with at least an attempt at sympathy. Any novel will inevitably contain minor characters who are mere grotesques or who are observed in a purely hostile spirit, but there is such a thing as impartiality, and Gissing is more capable of it than the great majority of English writers. It is a point in his favour that he had no very strong moral purpose. He had, of course, a deep loathing of the ugliness, emptiness and cruelty of the society he lived in, but he was concerned to describe it rather than to change it. There is usually no one in his books who can be pointed to as the villain, and even when there is a villain he is not punished. In his treatment of sexual matters Gissing is surprisingly frank, considering the time at which he was writing. It is not that he writes pornography or expresses approval of sexual promiscuity, but simply that he is willing to face the facts. The unwritten law of English fiction, the law that the hero as well as the heroine of a novel should be virgin when married, is disregarded in his books, almost for the first time since Fielding.

Like most English writers subsequent to the mid-nineteenth century, Gissing could not imagine any desirable destiny other than being a writer or a gentleman of leisure. The dichotomy between the intellectual and the lowbrow already existed, and a person capable of writing a serious novel could no longer picture himself as fully satisfied with the life of a businessman, or a soldier, or a politician, or what not. Gissing did not, at least consciously, even want to be the kind of writer that he was. His ideal, a rather melancholy one, was to have a moderate private income and live in a small comfortable house in the country, preferably unmarried, where he could wallow in books, especially the Greek and Latin classics. He might perhaps have realized this ideal if he had not managed to get himself into prison immediately after winning an Oxford scholarship; as it was he spent his life in what appeared to him to be hack work, and when he had at last reached the point where he could stop writing against the clock, he died almost immediately, aged only about forty-five. His death, described by H.G. Wells in his *Experiment in Autobiography*,* was of a piece with his life. The twenty novels, or thereabouts, that he produced between 1880 and 1900 were, so to speak, sweated out of him during his struggle towards a leisure which he never enjoyed and which he might not have used to good advantage if he had had it: for it is difficult to believe that his temperament really fitted him for a life of scholarly research. Perhaps the natural pull of his gifts would in any case have drawn him towards novel writing sooner or later. If not, we must be thankful for the piece of youthful folly which turned him aside from a comfortable middle-class career and forced him to become the chronicler of vulgarity, squalor and failure.

Writers and Leviathan*

The position of the writer in an age of state control is a subject that has already been fairly largely discussed, although most of the evidence that might be relevant is not yet available. In this place I do not want to express an opinion either for or against state patronage of the arts, but merely to point out that *what kind* of state rules over us must depend partly on the prevailing intellectual atmosphere: meaning, in this context, partly on the attitude of writers and artists themselves, and on their willingness or otherwise to keep the spirit of liberalism alive. If we find ourselves in ten years' time cringing before somebody like Zhdanov,* it will probably be because that is what we have deserved. Obviously there are strong tendencies towards totalitarianism at work within the English literary intelligentsia already. But here I am not concerned with any organized and conscious movement such as communism, but merely with the effect, on people of goodwill, of political thinking and the need to take sides politically.

This is a political age. War, fascism, concentration camps, rubber truncheons, atomic bombs, etc. are what we daily think about, and therefore to a great extent what we write about, even when we do not name them openly. We cannot help this. When you are on a sinking ship, your thoughts will be about sinking ships. But not only is our subject matter narrowed but our whole attitude towards literature is coloured by loyalties which we at least intermittently realize to be non-literary. I often have the feeling that even at the best of times literary criticism is fraudulent, since in the absence of any accepted standards whatever – any *external* reference which can give meaning to the statement that such and such a book is "good" or "bad" – every literary judgement consists in trumping up a set of rules to justify an instinctive preference. One's real reaction to a book, when one has a reaction at all, is usually "I like this book" or "I don't like it", and what follows is a rationalization. But "I like this book" is not, I think, a non-literary reaction; the non-literary reaction is "This book is on my side, and therefore I must discover merits in it". Of course, when one praises a book for political reasons one may be emotionally sincere, in the sense that one does feel strong approval of it, but also it often happens that party solidarity demands a plain lie. Anyone used to reviewing books for political periodicals is well aware of this. In general, if you are writing for a paper that you are in agreement with, you sin by commission, and if for a paper of the opposite stamp, by omission. At any rate, innumerable controversial books – books for or against Soviet Russia, for or against Zionism, for or against the Catholic Church, etc. – are judged before they are read, and in effect before they are written. One knows in advance what reception they will get in what papers. And yet, with a dishonesty that sometimes is not even quarter-conscious, the pretence is kept up that genuinely literary standards are being applied.

Of course, the invasion of literature by politics was bound to happen. It must have happened, even if the special problem of totalitarianism had never arisen, because we have developed a sort of compunction which our grandparents did not have, an awareness of the enormous injustice and misery of the world, and a guilt-stricken feeling that one ought to be doing something about it, which makes a purely aesthetic attitude towards life impossible. No one, now, could devote himself to literature as single-mindedly as Joyce or Henry James. But unfortunately, to accept political responsibility now means yielding oneself over to orthodoxies and "party lines", with all the timidity and dishonesty that that implies. As against the Victorian writers, we have the disadvantage of living among clear-cut political ideologies and of usually knowing at a glance what thoughts are heretical. A modern literary intellectual lives and writes in constant dread – not, indeed, of public opinion in the wider sense but of public opinion within his own group. As a rule, luckily, there is more than one group, but also at any given moment there is a dominant orthodoxy, to offend against which needs a thick skin and sometimes means cutting one's income in half for years on end. Obviously, for about fifteen years past, the dominant orthodoxy, especially among the young, has been "left". The keywords are "progressive", "democratic" and "revolutionary", while the labels which you must at all costs avoid having gummed upon you are "bourgeois", "reactionary" and "fascist". Almost everyone nowadays, even the majority of Catholics and Conservatives, is "progressive", or at least wishes to be thought so. No one, so far as I know, ever describes himself as a "bourgeois", just as no one literate enough to have heard the word ever admits to being guilty of anti-Semitism. We are all of us good democrats, anti-fascist, anti-imperialist, contemptuous of class distinctions, impervious to colour prejudice, and so on and so forth. Nor is there much doubt that the present-day "left" orthodoxy is better than the rather snobbish, pietistic Conservative orthodoxy which prevailed twenty years ago, when the *Criterion* and (on a lower level) the *London Mercury* were the dominant literary magazines. For at the least its implied objective is a viable form of society which large numbers of people actually want. But it also has its own falsities which, because they cannot be admitted, make it impossible for certain questions to be seriously discussed.

The whole left-wing ideology, scientific and utopian, was evolved by people who had no immediate prospect of attaining power. It was, therefore, an extremist ideology, utterly contemptuous of kings, governments, laws, prisons, police forces, armies, flags, frontiers, patriotism, religion, conventional morality and, in fact, the whole existing scheme of things. Until well within living memory the forces of the Left in all countries were fighting against a tyranny which appeared to be invincible, and it was easy to assume that if only *that* particular tyranny – capitalism – could be overthrown, socialism would follow. Moreover, the Left had inherited from Liberalism certain distinctly questionable beliefs, such as the belief that the truth will prevail and persecution defeats itself, or that man is naturally good and is only corrupted by his environment. This perfectionist ideology has persisted in nearly all of us, and it is in the name of it that we protest when (for instance) a Labour government votes huge incomes to the King's daughters or shows hesitation about nationalizing steel. But we have also accumulated in our minds a whole series of unadmitted contradictions, as a result of successive bumps against reality.

The first big bump was the Russian Revolution. For somewhat complex reasons, nearly the whole of the English Left has been driven to accept the Russian regime as "socialist", while silently recognizing that its spirit and practice are quite alien to anything that is meant by "socialism" in this country. Hence there has arisen a sort of schizophrenic manner of thinking, in which words like "democracy" can bear two irreconcilable meanings, and such things as concentration camps and mass deportations can be right and wrong simultaneously. The next blow to the left-wing ideology was the rise of fascism, which shook the pacifism and internationalism of the Left without bringing about a definite restatement of doctrine. The experience of German occupation taught the European peoples something that the colonial peoples knew already, namely that class antagonisms are not all-important and that there is such a thing as national interest. After Hitler it was difficult to maintain seriously that "the enemy is in your own country" and that national independence is of no value. But though we all know this and act upon it when necessary, we still feel that to say it aloud would be a kind of treachery. And finally, the greatest difficulty of all, there is the fact that the Left is now in power and is obliged to take responsibility and make genuine decisions.

Left governments almost invariably disappoint their supporters because, even when the prosperity which they have promised is achievable, there is always need of an uncomfortable transition period about which little has been said beforehand. At this moment we see our own government, in its desperate economic straits, fighting in effect against its own past propaganda. The crisis that we are now in is not a sudden unexpected calamity, like an earthquake, and it was not caused by the war, but merely hastened by it. Decades ago it could be foreseen that something of this kind was going to happen. Ever since the nineteenth century our national income, dependent partly on interest from foreign investments, and on assured markets and cheap raw materials in colonial countries, had been extremely precarious. It was certain that, sooner or later, something would go wrong and we should be forced to make our exports balance our imports – and when that happened the British standard of living, including the working-class standard, was bound to fall, at least temporarily. Yet the left-wing parties, even when they were vociferously anti-imperialist, never made these facts clear. On occasion they were ready to admit that the British workers had benefited, to some extent, by the looting of Asia and Africa, but they always allowed it to appear that we could give up our loot and yet in some way contrive to remain prosperous. Quite largely, indeed, the workers were won over to socialism by being told that they were exploited, whereas the brute truth was that, in world terms, they were exploiters. Now, to all appearances, the point has been reached when the working-class living standard *cannot* be maintained, let alone raised. Even if we squeeze the rich out of existence, the mass of the people must either consume less or produce more. Or am I exaggerating the mess we are in? I may be, and I should be glad to find myself mistaken. But the point I wish to make is that this question, among people who are faithful to the Left ideology, cannot be genuinely discussed. The lowering of wages and raising of working hours are felt to be inherently anti-socialist measures, and must therefore be dismissed in advance, whatever the economic situation may be. To suggest that they may be unavoidable is merely to risk being plastered with those labels that we are all terrified of. It is far safer to evade the issue and pretend that we can put everything right by redistributing the existing national income.

To accept an orthodoxy is always to inherit unresolved contradictions. Take for instance the fact that all sensitive people are revolted by industrialism and its products, and yet are aware that the conquest of poverty and the emancipation of the working class demand not less industrialization but more and more. Or take the fact that certain jobs are absolutely necessary and yet are never done except under some kind of coercion. Or take the fact that it is impossible to have a positive foreign policy without having powerful armed forces. One could multiply examples. In every such case there is a conclusion which is perfectly plain but which can only be drawn if one is privately disloyal to the official ideology. The normal response is to push the question, unanswered, into a corner of one's mind, and then continue repeating contradictory catchwords. One does not have to search far through the reviews and magazines to discover the effects of this kind of thinking.

I am not, of course, suggesting that mental dishonesty is peculiar to socialists and left-wingers generally, or is commonest among them. It is merely that acceptance of *any* political discipline seems to be incompatible with literary integrity. This applies equally to movements like pacifism and personalism, which claim to be outside the ordinary political struggle. Indeed, the mere sound of words ending in -ism seems to bring with it the smell of propaganda. Group loyalties are necessary, and yet they are poisonous to literature, so long as literature is the product of individuals. As soon as they are allowed to have any influence, even a negative one, on creative writing, the result is not only falsification but often the actual drying up of the inventive faculties.

Well, then what? Do we have to conclude that it is the duty of every writer to "keep out of politics"? Certainly not! In any case, as I have said already, no thinking person can or does genuinely keep out of politics, in an age like the present one. I only suggest that we should draw a sharper distinction than we do at present between our political and our literary loyalties, and should recognize that a willingness to *do* certain distasteful but necessary things does not carry with it any obligation to swallow the beliefs that usually go with them. When a writer engages in politics he should do so as a citizen, as a human being, but not *as a writer*. I do not think that he has the right, merely on the score of his sensibilities, to shirk the ordinary dirty work of politics. Just as much as anyone else, he should be prepared to deliver lectures in draughty halls, to chalk pavements, to canvass voters, to distribute leaflets, even to fight in civil wars if it seems necessary. But whatever else he does in the service of his party, he should never write for it. He should make it clear that his writing is a thing apart. And he should be able to act cooperatively while, if he chooses, completely rejecting the official ideology. He should never turn back from a train of thought because it may lead to a heresy, and he should not mind very much if his unorthodoxy is smelt out, as it probably will be. Perhaps it is even a bad sign in a writer if he is not suspected of reactionary tendencies today, just as it was a bad sign if he was not suspected of communist sympathies twenty years ago.

But does all this mean that a writer should not only refuse to be dictated to by political bosses, but also that he should refrain from writing *about* politics? Once again, certainly not! There is no reason why he should not write in the most crudely political way, if he wishes to. Only he should do so as an individual, an outsider, at the most an unwelcome guerrilla on the flank of a regular army. This attitude is quite compatible with ordinary political usefulness. It is reasonable, for example, to be willing to fight in a war because one thinks the war ought to be won, and at the same time to refuse to write war propaganda. Sometimes, if a writer is honest, his writings and his political activities may actually contradict one another. There are occasions when that is plainly undesirable – but then the remedy is not to falsify one's impulses but to remain silent.

To suggest that a creative writer, in a time of conflict, must split his life into two compartments may seem defeatist or frivolous – yet in practice I do not see what else he can do. To lock yourself up in an ivory tower is impossible and undesirable. To yield subjectively, not merely to a party machine but even to a group ideology, is to destroy yourself as a writer. We feel this dilemma to be a painful one, because we see the need of engaging in politics while also seeing what a dirty, degrading business it is. And most of us still have a lingering belief that every choice, even every political choice, is between good and evil, and that if a thing is necessary it is also right. We should, I think, get rid of this belief, which belongs to the nursery. In politics one can never do more than decide which of two evils is the lesser, and there are some situations from which one can only escape by acting like a devil or a lunatic. War, for example, may be necessary, but it is certainly not right or sane. Even a general election is not exactly a pleasant or edifying spectacle. If you have to take part in such things – and I think you do have to, unless you are armoured by old age or stupidity or hypocrisy – then you also have to keep part of yourself inviolate. For most people the problem does not arise in the same form, because their lives are split already. They are truly alive only in their leisure hours, and there is no emotional connection between their work and their political activities. Nor are they generally asked, in the name of political loyalty, to debase themselves as workers. The artist, and especially the writer, is asked just that – in fact, it is the only thing that politicians ever ask of him. If he refuses, that does not mean that he is condemned to inactivity. One half of him, which in a sense is the whole of him, can act as resolutely, even as violently if need be, as anyone else. But his writings, in so far as they have any value, will always be the product of the saner self that stands aside, records the things that are done and admits their necessity, but refuses to be deceived as to their true nature.

Such, Such Were the Joys*

I

Soon after I arrived at St Cyprian's (not immediately, but after a week or two, just when I seemed to be settling into the routine of school life) I began wetting my bed. I was now aged eight, so that this was a reversion to a habit which I must have grown out of at least four years earlier.

Nowadays, I believe, bed-wetting in such circumstances is taken for granted. It is a normal reaction in children who have been removed from their homes to a strange place. In those days, however, it was looked on as a disgusting crime which the child committed on purpose and for which the proper cure was a beating. For my part I did not need to be told it was a crime. Night after night I prayed, with a fervour never previously attained in my prayers, "Please God, do not let me wet my bed! Oh, please God, do not let me wet my bed!", but it made remarkably little difference. Some nights the thing happened, others not. There was no volition about it, no consciousness. You did not properly speaking *do* the deed: you merely woke up in the morning and found that the sheets were wringing wet.

After the second or third offence I was warned that I should be beaten next time, but I received the warning in a curiously roundabout way. One afternoon, as we were filing out from tea, Mrs W——, the Headmaster's wife, was sitting at the head of one of the tables, chatting with a lady of whom I knew nothing, except that she was on an afternoon's visit to the school. She was an intimidating, masculine-looking person wearing a riding habit, or something that I took to be a riding habit. I was just leaving the room when Mrs W—— called me back, as though to introduce me to the visitor.

Mrs W—— was nicknamed Flip, and I shall call her by that name, for I seldom think of her by any other. (Officially, however, she was addressed as Mum, probably a corruption of the "Ma'am" used by public schoolboys to their housemasters' wives.) She was a stocky square-built woman with hard red cheeks, a flat top to her head, prominent brows and deep-set, suspicious eyes. Although a great deal of the time she was full of false heartiness, jollying one along with mannish slang ("*Buck* up, old chap!" and so forth), and even using one's Christian name, her eyes never lost their anxious, accusing look. It was very difficult to look her in the face without feeling guilty, even at moments when one was not guilty of anything in particular.

"Here is a little boy," said Flip, indicating me to the strange lady, "who wets his bed every night. Do you know what I am going to do if you wet your bed again?" she added, turning to me. "I am going to get the Sixth Form to beat you."

The strange lady put on an air of being inexpressibly shocked, and exclaimed "I-should-think-so!" And here there occurred one of those wild, almost lunatic misunderstandings which are part of the daily experience of childhood. The Sixth Form was a group of older boys who were selected as having "character" and were empowered to beat smaller boys. I had not yet learnt of their existence, and I misheard the phrase "the Sixth Form" as "Mrs Form". I took it as referring to the strange lady – I thought, that is, that her name was Mrs Form. It was an improbable name, but a child has no judgement in such matters. I imagined, therefore, that it was *she* who was to be deputed to beat me. It did not strike me as strange that this job should be turned over to a casual visitor in no way connected with the school. I merely assumed that "Mrs Form" was a stern disciplinarian who enjoyed beating people (somehow her appearance seemed to bear this out) and I had an immediate terrifying vision of her arriving for the occasion in full riding kit and armed with a hunting whip. To this day I can feel myself almost swooning with shame as I stood, a very small, round-faced boy in short corduroy knickers, before the two women. I could not speak. I felt that I should die if "Mrs Form" were to beat me. But my dominant feeling was not fear or even resentment: it was simply shame because one more person, and that a woman, had been told of my disgusting offence.

A little later, I forget how, I learnt that it was not after all "Mrs Form" who would do the beating. I cannot remember whether it was that very night that I wetted my bed again, but at any rate I did wet it again quite soon. Oh, the despair, the feeling of cruel injustice, after all my prayers and resolutions, at once again waking between the clammy sheets! There was no chance of hiding what I had done. The grim statuesque matron, Margaret by name, arrived in the dormitory specially to inspect my bed. She pulled back the clothes, then drew herself up, and the dreaded words seemed to come rolling out of her like a peal of thunder:

"REPORT YOURSELF to the Headmaster after breakfast!"

I put REPORT YOURSELF in capitals because that was how it appeared in my mind. I do not know how many times I heard that phrase during my early years at St Cyprian's. It was only very rarely that it did not mean a beating. The words always had a portentous sound in my ears, like muffled drums or the words of the death sentence.

When I arrived to report myself, Flip was doing something or other at the long shiny table in the anteroom to the study. Her uneasy eyes searched me as I went past. In the study the Headmaster, nicknamed Sambo, was waiting.

Sambo was a round-shouldered, curiously oafish-looking man, not large but shambling in gait, with a chubby face which was like that of an overgrown baby, and which was capable of good humour. He knew, of course, why I had been sent to him, and had already taken a bone-handled riding crop out of the cupboard, but it was part of the punishment of reporting yourself that you had to proclaim your offence with your own lips. When I had said my say, he read me a short but pompous lecture, then seized me by the scruff of the neck, twisted me over and began beating me with the riding crop. He had a habit of continuing his lecture while he flogged you, and I remember the words "you dir-ty lit-tle boy" keeping time with the blows. The beating did not hurt (perhaps, as it was the first time, he was not hitting me very hard), and I walked out feeling very much better. The fact that the beating had not hurt was a sort of victory and partially wiped out the shame of the bed-wetting. I was even incautious enough to wear a grin on my face. Some small boys were hanging about in the passage outside the door of the anteroom.

"D'you get the cane?"

"It didn't hurt," I said proudly.

Flip had heard everything. Instantly her voice came screaming after me: "Come here! Come here this instant! What was that you said?"

"I said it didn't hurt," I faltered out.

"How dare you say a thing like that? Do you think that is a proper thing to say? Go in and REPORT YOURSELF AGAIN!"

This time Sambo laid on in real earnest. He continued for a length of time that frightened and astonished me – about five minutes, it seemed – ending up by breaking the riding crop. The bone handle went flying across the room.

"Look what you've made me do!" he said furiously, holding up the broken crop.

I had fallen into a chair, weakly snivelling. I remember that this was the only time throughout my boyhood when a beating actually reduced me to tears, and curiously enough I was not even now crying because of the pain. The second beating had not hurt very much either. Fright and shame seemed to have anaesthetized me. I was crying partly because I felt that this was expected of me, partly from genuine repentance, but partly also because of a deeper grief which is peculiar to childhood and not easy to convey: a sense of desolate loneliness and helplessness, of being locked up not only in a hostile world but in a world of good and evil where the rules were such that it was actually not possible for me to keep them.

I knew that the bed-wetting was (a) wicked and (b) outside my control. The second fact I was personally aware of, and the first I did not question. It was possible, therefore, to commit a sin without knowing that you committed it, without wanting to commit it and without being able to avoid it. Sin was not necessarily something that you did – it might be something that happened to you. I do not want to claim that this idea flashed into my mind as a complete novelty at this very moment, under the blows of Sambo's cane; I must have had glimpses of it even before I left home, for my early childhood had not been altogether happy. But at any rate this was the great, abiding lesson of my boyhood: that I was in a world where it was *not possible* for me to be good. And the double beating was a turning point, for it brought home to me for the first time the harshness of the environment into which I had been flung. Life was more terrible, and I was more wicked, than I had imagined. At any rate, as I sat snivelling on the edge of a chair in Sambo's study, with not even the self-possession to stand up while he stormed at me, I had a conviction of sin and folly and weakness such as I do not remember to have felt before.

In general, one's memories of any period must necessarily weaken as one moves away from it. One is constantly learning new facts, and old ones have to drop out to make way for them. At twenty I could have written the history of my schooldays with an accuracy which would be quite impossible now. But it can also happen that one's memories grow sharper after a long lapse of time, because one is looking at the past with fresh eyes and can isolate and, as it were, notice facts which previously existed undifferentiated among a mass of others. Here are two things which in a sense I remembered, but which did not strike me as strange or interesting until quite recently. One is that the second beating seemed to me a just and reasonable punishment. To get one beating, and then to get another and far fiercer one on top of it, for being so unwise as to show that the first had not hurt – that was quite natural. The gods are jealous, and when you have good fortune you should conceal it. The other is that I accepted the broken riding crop as my own crime. I can still recall my feeling as I saw the handle lying on the carpet – the feeling of having done an ill-bred clumsy thing, and ruined an expensive object. *I* had broken it: so Sambo told me, and so I believed. This acceptance of guilt lay unnoticed in my memory for twenty or thirty years.

So much for the episode of the bed-wetting. But there is one more thing to be remarked. This is that I did not wet my bed again – at least, I did wet it once again, and received another beating, after which the trouble stopped. So perhaps this barbarous remedy does work, though at a heavy price, I have no doubt.

II

St Cyprian's was an expensive and snobbish school which was in process of becoming more snobbish, and, I imagine, more expensive. The public school with which it had special connections was Harrow, but during my time an increasing proportion of the boys went on to Eton. Most of them were the children of rich parents, but on the whole they were the unaristocratic rich, the sort of people who live in huge shrubberied houses in Bournemouth or Richmond, and who have cars and butlers but not country estates. There were a few exotics among them – some South American boys, sons of Argentine beef barons, one or two Russians, and even a Siamese prince, or someone who was described as a prince.

Sambo had two great ambitions. One was to attract titled boys to the school, and the other was to train up pupils to win scholarships at public schools, above all at Eton. He did, towards the end of my time, succeed in getting hold of two boys with real English titles. One of them, I remember, was a wretched drivelling little creature, almost an albino, peering upwards out of weak eyes, with a long nose at the end of which a dewdrop always seemed to be trembling. Sambo always gave these boys their titles when mentioning them to a third person, and for their first few days he actually addressed them to their faces as "Lord So-and-So". Needless to say he found ways of drawing attention to them when any visitor was being shown round the school. Once, I remember, the little fair-haired boy had a choking fit at dinner, and a stream of snot ran out of his nose onto his plate in a way horrible to see. Any lesser person would have been called a dirty little beast and ordered out of the room instantly – but Sambo and Flip laughed it off in a "boys will be boys" spirit.

All the very rich boys were more or less undisguisedly favoured. The school still had a faint suggestion of the Victorian "private academy" with its "parlour boarders", and when I later read about that kind of school in Thackeray I immediately saw the resemblance. The rich boys had milk and biscuits in the middle of the morning, they were given riding lessons once or twice a week, Flip mothered them and called them by their Christian names, and above all they were never caned. Apart from the South Americans, whose parents were safely distant, I doubt whether Sambo ever caned any boy whose father's income was much above £2,000 a year. But he was sometimes willing to sacrifice financial profit to scholastic prestige. Occasionally, by special arrangement, he would take at greatly reduced fees some boy who seemed likely to win scholarships and thus bring credit on the school. It was on these terms that I was at St Cyprian's myself: otherwise my parents could not have afforded to send me to so expensive a school.

I did not at first understand that I was being taken at reduced fees; it was only when I was about eleven that Flip and Sambo began throwing the fact in my teeth. For my first two or three years I went through the ordinary educational mill; then, soon after I had started Greek (one started Latin at eight, Greek at ten), I moved into the scholarship class, which was taught, so far as classics went, largely by Sambo himself. Over a period of two or three years the scholarship boys were crammed with learning as cynically as a goose is crammed for Christmas. And with what learning! This business of making a gifted boy's career depend on a competitive examination, taken when he is only twelve or thirteen, is an evil thing at best, but there do appear to be preparatory schools which send scholars to Eton, Winchester, etc. without teaching them to see everything in terms of marks. At St Cyprian's the whole process was frankly a preparation for a sort of confidence trick. Your job was to learn exactly those things that would give an examiner the impression that you knew more than you did know, and as far as possible to avoid burdening your brain with anything else. Subjects which lacked examination value, such as geography, were almost completely neglected, mathematics was also neglected if you were a "classical", science was not taught in any form – indeed it was so despised that even an interest in natural history was discouraged – and even the books you were encouraged to read in your spare time were chosen with one eye on the "English paper". Latin and Greek, the main scholarship subjects, were what counted, but even these were deliberately taught in a flashy, unsound way. We never, for example, read right through even a single book of a Greek or Latin author: we merely read short passages which were picked out because they were the kind of thing likely to be set as an "unseen translation". During the last year or so before we went up for our scholarships, most of our time was spent in simply working our way through the scholarship papers of previous years. Sambo had sheaves of these in his possession, from every one of the major public schools. But the greatest outrage of all was the teaching of history.

There was in those days a piece of nonsense called the Harrow History Prize, an annual competition for which many preparatory schools entered. It was a tradition for St Cyprian's to win it every year, as well we might, for we had mugged up every paper that had been set since the competition started, and the supply of possible questions was not inexhaustible. They were the kind of stupid question that is answered by rapping out a name or a quotation. Who plundered the Begams? Who was beheaded in an open boat? Who caught the Whigs bathing and ran away with their clothes?* Almost all our historical teaching was on this level. History was a series of unrelated, unintelligible but – in some way that was never explained to us – important facts with resounding phrases tied to them. Disraeli brought peace with honour. Clive was astonished at his moderation. Pitt called in the New World to redress the balance of the Old.* And the dates, and the mnemonic devices! (Did you know, for example, that the initial letters of "A black Negress was my aunt: there's her house behind the barn" are also the initial letters of the battles in the Wars of the Roses?)* Flip, who "took" the higher forms in history, revelled in this kind of thing. I recall positive orgies of dates, with the keener boys leaping up and down in their places in their eagerness to shout out the right answers, and at the same time not feeling the faintest interest in the meaning of the mysterious events they were naming.

"1587?"
"Massacre of St Bartholomew!"
"1707?"
"Death of Aurangzeb!"
"1713?"
"Treaty of Utrecht!"
"1773?"
"Boston Tea Party!"
"1520?"
"Oo, Mum, please, Mum—"
"Please, Mum, please, Mum! Let me tell him, Mum!"
"Well! 1520?"
"Field of the Cloth of Gold!"*
And so on.

But history and such secondary subjects were not bad fun. It was in "classics" that the real strain came. Looking back, I realize that I then worked harder than I have ever done since, and yet at the time it never seemed possible to make quite the effort that was demanded of one. We would sit round the long shiny table, made of some very pale-coloured hard wood, with Sambo goading, threatening, exhorting, sometimes joking, very occasionally praising, but always prodding, prodding away at one's mind to keep it up to the right pitch of concentration, as one might keep a sleepy person awake by sticking pins into him.

"Go on, you little slacker! Go on, you idle, worthless little boy! The whole trouble with you is that you're bone and horn idle. You eat too much, that's why. You wolf down enormous meals, and then when you come here you're half asleep. Go on, now, put your back into it. You're not *thinking*. Your brain doesn't sweat."

He would tap away at one's skull with his silver pencil, which, in my memory, seems to have been about the size of a banana, and which certainly was heavy enough to raise a bump – or he would pull the short hairs round one's ears, or, occasionally, reach out under the table and kick one's shin. On some days nothing seemed to go right, and then it would be: "All right, then, I know what you want. You've been asking for it the whole morning. Come along, you useless little slacker. Come into the study." And then whack, whack, whack, whack, and back one would come, red-wealed and smarting – in later years Sambo had abandoned his riding crop in favour of a thin rattan cane which hurt very much more – to settle down to work again. This did not happen very often, but I do remember, more than once, being led out of the room in the middle of a Latin sentence, receiving a beating and then going straight ahead with the same sentence, just like that. It is a mistake to think such methods do not work. They work very well for their special purpose. Indeed, I doubt whether classical education ever has been or can be successfully carried on without corporal punishment. The boys themselves believed in its efficacy. There was a boy named Beacham, with no brains to speak of, but evidently in acute need of a scholarship. Sambo was flogging him towards the goal as one might do with a foundered horse. He went up for a scholarship at Uppingham, came back with a consciousness of having done badly, and a day or two later received a severe beating for idleness. "I wish I'd had that caning before I went up for the exam," he said sadly – a remark which I felt to be contemptible, but which I perfectly well understood.

The boys of the scholarship class were not all treated alike. If a boy were the son of rich parents to whom the saving of fees was not all-important, Sambo would goad him along in a comparatively fatherly way, with jokes and digs in the ribs and perhaps an occasional tap with the pencil, but no hair-pulling and no caning. It was the poor but "clever" boys who suffered. Our brains were a gold mine in which he had sunk money, and the dividends must be squeezed out of us. Long before I had grasped the nature of my financial relationship with Sambo, I had been made to understand that I was not on the same footing as most of the other boys. In effect there were three castes in the school. There was the minority with an aristocratic or millionaire background, there were the children of the ordinary suburban rich, who made up the bulk of the school, and there were a few underlings like myself, the sons of clergyman, Indian Civil Servants, struggling widows and the like. These poorer ones were discouraged from going in for "extras" such as shooting and carpentry, and were humiliated over clothes and petty possessions. I never, for instance, succeeded in getting a cricket bat of my own, because "Your parents wouldn't be able to afford it." This phrase pursued me throughout my schooldays. At St Cyprian's we were not allowed to keep the money we brought back with us, but had to "give it in" on the first day of term, and then from time to time were allowed to spend it under supervision. I and similarly placed boys were always choked off from buying expensive toys like model aeroplanes, even if the necessary money stood to our credit. Flip, in particular, seemed to aim consciously at inculcating a humble outlook in the poorer boys. "Do you think that's the sort of thing a boy like you should buy?" I remember her saying to somebody – and she said this in front of the whole school: "You know you're not going to grow up with money, don't you? Your people aren't rich. You must learn to be sensible. Don't get above yourself!" There was also the weekly pocket money, which we took out in sweets, dispensed by Flip from a large table. The millionaires had sixpence a week, but the normal sum was threepence. I and one or two others were only allowed twopence. My parents had not given instructions to this effect, and the saving of a penny a week could not conceivably have made any difference to them: it was a mark of status. Worse yet was the detail of the birthday cakes. It was usual for each boy, on his birthday, to have a large iced cake with candles, which was shared out at tea between the whole school. It was provided as a matter of routine and went on his parents' bill. I never had such a cake, though my parents would have paid for it readily enough. Year after year, never daring to ask, I would miserably hope that this year a cake would appear. Once or twice I even rashly pretended to my companions that this time I *was* going to have a cake. Then came teatime, and no cake, which did not make me more popular.

Very early it was impressed upon me that I had no chance of a decent future unless I won a scholarship at a public school. Either I won my scholarship, or I must leave school at fourteen and become, in Sambo's favourite phrase, "a little office boy at forty pounds a year". In my circumstances it was natural that I should believe this. Indeed, it was universally taken for granted at St Cyprian's that unless you went to a "good" public school (and only about fifteen schools came under this heading) you were ruined for life. It is not easy to convey to a grown-up person the sense of strain, of nerving oneself for some terrible, all-deciding combat, as the date of the examination crept nearer – eleven years old, twelve years old, then thirteen, the fatal year itself! Over a period of about two years, I do not think there was ever a day when "the exam", as I called it, was quite out of my waking thoughts. In my prayers it figured invariably: and whenever I got the bigger portion of a wishbone, or picked up a horseshoe, or bowed seven times to the new moon, or succeeded in passing through a wishing gate without touching the sides, then the wish I earned by doing so went on "the exam" as a matter of course. And yet curiously enough I was also tormented by an almost irresistible impulse *not* to work. There were days when my heart sickened at the labours ahead of me, and I stood stupid as an animal before the most elementary difficulties. In the holidays, also, I could not work. Some of the scholarship boys received extra tuition from a certain Mr Batchelor, a likeable, very hairy man who wore shaggy suits and lived in a typical bachelor's "den" – book-lined walls, overwhelming stench of tobacco – somewhere in the town. During the holidays Mr Batchelor used to send us extracts from Latin authors to translate, and we were supposed to send back a wad of work once a week. Somehow I could not do it. The empty paper and the black Latin dictionary lying on the table, the consciousness of a plain duty shirked, poisoned my leisure, but somehow I could not start, and by the end of the holidays I would only have sent Mr Batchelor fifty or a hundred lines. Undoubtedly part of the reason was that Sambo and his cane were far away. But in term time, also, I would go through periods of idleness and stupidity when I would sink deeper and deeper into disgrace and even achieve a sort of feeble, snivelling defiance, fully conscious of my guilt and yet unable or unwilling – I could not be sure which – to do any better. Then Sambo or Flip would send for me, and this time it would not even be a caning.

Flip would search me with her baleful eyes. (What colour were those eyes, I wonder? I remember them as green, but actually no human being has green eyes. Perhaps they were hazel.) She would start off in her peculiar, wheedling, bullying style, which never failed to get right through one's guard and score a hit on one's better nature.

"I don't think it's awfully decent of you to behave like this, is it? Do you think it's quite playing the game by your mother and father to go on idling your time away, week after week, month after month? Do you *want* to throw all your chances away? You know your people aren't rich, don't you? You know they can't afford the same things as other boys' parents. How are they to send you to a public school if you don't win a scholarship? I know how proud your mother is of you. Do you *want* to let her down?"

"I don't think he wants to go to a public school any longer," Sambo would say, addressing himself to Flip with a pretence that I was not there. "I think he's given up that idea. He wants to be a little office boy at forty pounds a year."

The horrible sensation of tears – a swelling in the breast, a tickling behind the nose – would already have assailed me. Flip would bring out her ace of trumps:

"And do you think it's quite fair to *us*, the way you're behaving? After all we've done for you? You *do* know what we've done for you, don't you?" Her eyes would pierce deep into me, and though she never said it straight out, I did know. "We've had you here all these years – we even had you here for a week in the holidays so that Mr Batchelor could coach you. We don't *want* to have to send you away, you know, but we can't keep a boy here just to eat up our food, term after term. *I* don't think it's very straight, the way you're behaving. Do you?"

I never had any answer except a miserable "No, Mum", or "Yes, Mum", as the case might be. Evidently it was *not* straight, the way I was behaving. And at some point or other the unwanted tear would always force its way out of the corner of my eye, roll down my nose, and splash.

Flip never said in plain words that I was a non-paying pupil, no doubt because vague phrases like "all we've done for you" had a deeper emotional appeal. Sambo, who did not aspire to be loved by his pupils, put it more brutally, though, as was usual with him, in pompous language. "You are living on my bounty" was his favourite phrase in this context. At least once I listened to these words between blows of the cane. I must say that these scenes were not frequent, and except on one occasion they did not take place in the presence of other boys. In public I was reminded that I was poor and that my parents "wouldn't be able to afford" this or that, but I was not actually reminded of my dependent position. It was a final unanswerable argument, to be brought forth like an instrument of torture when my work became exceptionally bad.

To grasp the effect of this kind of thing on a child of ten or twelve, one has to remember that the child has little sense of proportion or probability. A child may be a mass of egoism and rebelliousness, but it has no accumulated experience to give it confidence in its own judgements. On the whole it will accept what it is told, and it will believe in the most fantastic way in the knowledge and powers of the adults surrounding it. Here is an example.

I have said that at St Cyprian's we were not allowed to keep our own money. However, it was possible to hold back a shilling or two, and sometimes I used furtively to buy sweets which I kept hidden in the loose ivy on the playing-field wall. One day when I had been sent on an errand I went into a sweetshop a mile or more from the school and bought some chocolates. As I came out of the shop I saw on the opposite pavement a small sharp-faced man who seemed to be staring very hard at my school cap. Instantly a horrible fear went through me. There could be no doubt as to who the man was. He was a spy placed there by Sambo! I turned away unconcernedly, and then, as though my legs were doing it of their own accord, broke into a clumsy run. But when I got round the next corner I forced myself to walk again, for to run was a sign of guilt, and obviously there would be other spies posted here and there about the town. All that day and the next I waited for the summons to the study, and was surprised when it did not come. It did not seem to me strange that the headmaster of a private school should dispose of an army of informers, and I did not even imagine that he would have to pay them. I assumed that any adult, inside the school or outside, would collaborate voluntarily in preventing us from breaking the rules. Sambo was all-powerful; it was natural that his agents should be everywhere. When this episode happened I do not think I can have been less than twelve years old.

I hated Sambo and Flip, with a sort of shamefaced, remorseful hatred, but it did not occur to me to doubt their judgement. When they told me that I must either win a public-school scholarship or become an office boy at fourteen, I believed that those were the unavoidable alternatives before me. And above all, I believed Sambo and Flip when they told me they were my benefactors. I see now, of course, that from Sambo's point of view I was a good speculation. He sank money in me, and he looked to get it back in the form of prestige. If I had "gone off", as promising boys sometimes do, I imagine that he would have got rid of me swiftly. As it was I won him two scholarships when the time came, and no doubt he made full use of them in his prospectuses. But it is difficult for a child to realize that a school is primarily a commercial venture. A child believes that the school exists to educate and that the schoolmaster disciplines him either for his own good or from a love of bullying. Flip and Sambo had chosen to befriend me, and their friendship included canings, reproaches and humiliations, which were good for me and saved me from an office stool. That was their version, and I believed in it. It was therefore clear that I owed them a vast debt of gratitude. But I was *not* grateful, as I very well knew. On the contrary, I hated both of them. I could not control my subjective feelings, and

I could not conceal them from myself. But it is wicked, is it not, to hate your benefactors? So I was taught, and so I believed. A child accepts the codes of behaviour that are presented to it, even when it breaks them. From the age of eight, or even earlier, the consciousness of sin was never far away from me. If I contrived to seem callous and defiant, it was only a thin cover over a mass of shame and dismay. All through my boyhood I had a profound conviction that I was no good, that I was wasting my time, wrecking my talents, behaving with monstrous folly and wickedness and ingratitude – and all this, it seemed, was inescapable, because I lived among laws which were absolute, like the law of gravity, but which it was not possible for me to keep.

III

No one can look back on his schooldays and say with truth that they were altogether unhappy.

I have good memories of St Cyprian's, among a horde of bad ones. Sometimes on summer afternoons there were wonderful expeditions across the Downs to a village called Birling Gap, or to Beachy Head, where one bathed dangerously among the chalk boulders and came home covered with cuts. And there were still more wonderful midsummer evenings when, as a special treat, we were not driven off to bed as usual but allowed to wander about the grounds in the long twilight, ending up with a plunge into the swimming bath at about nine o'clock. There was the joy of waking early on summer mornings and getting in an hour's undisturbed reading (Ian Hay, Thackeray, Kipling and H.G. Wells were the favourite authors of my boyhood) in the sunlit, sleeping dormitory. There was also cricket, which I was no good at but with which I conducted a sort of hopeless love affair up to the age of about eighteen. And there was the pleasure of keeping caterpillars – the silky green and purple puss moth, the ghostly green poplar hawk, the privet hawk, large as one's third finger, specimens of which could be illicitly purchased for sixpence at a shop in the town – and, when one could escape long enough from the master who was "taking the walk", there was the excitement of dredging the dew ponds on the Downs for enormous newts with orange-coloured bellies. This business of being out for a walk, coming across something of fascinating interest and then being dragged away from it by a yell from the master, like a dog jerked onwards by the leash, is an important feature of school life, and helps to build up the conviction, so strong in many children, that the things you most want to do are always unattainable.

Very occasionally, perhaps once during each summer, it was possible to escape altogether from the barrack-like atmosphere of school, when Brown, the second master, was permitted to take one or two boys for an afternoon of butterfly hunting on a common a few miles away. Brown was a man with white hair and a red face like a strawberry, who was good at natural history, making models and plaster casts, operating magic lanterns, and things of that kind. He and Mr Batchelor were the only adults in any way connected with the school whom I did not either dislike or fear. Once he took me into his room and showed me in confidence a plated, pearl-handled revolver – his "six-shooter", he called it – which he kept in a box under his bed. And oh, the joy of those occasional expeditions! The ride of two or three miles on a lonely little branch line, the afternoon of charging to and fro with large green nets, the beauty of the enormous dragonflies which hovered over the tops of the grasses, the sinister killing bottle with its sickly smell, and then tea in the parlour of a pub with large slices of pale-coloured cake! The essence of it was in the railway journey, which seemed to put magic distances between yourself and school.

Flip, characteristically, disapproved of these expeditions, though not actually forbidding them. "And have you been catching *little butterflies*?" she would say with a vicious sneer when one got back, making her voice as babyish as possible. From her point of view, natural history ("bug hunting" she would probably have called it) was a babyish pursuit which a boy should be laughed out of as early as possible. Moreover it was somehow faintly plebeian, it was traditionally associated with boys who wore spectacles and were no good at games, it did not help you to pass exams, and above all it smelt of science and therefore seemed to menace classical education. It needed a considerable moral effort to accept Brown's invitation. How I dreaded that sneer of *little butterflies*! Brown, however, who had been at the school since its early days, had built up a certain independence for himself: he seemed able to handle Sambo, and ignored Flip a good deal. If it ever happened that both of them were away, Brown acted as deputy headmaster, and on those occasions instead of reading the appointed lesson for the day at morning chapel, he would read us stories from the Apocrypha.*

Most of the good memories of my childhood, and up to the age of about twenty, are in some way connected with animals. So far as St Cyprian's goes, it also seems, when I look back, that all my good memories are of summer. In winter your nose ran continually, your fingers were too numb to button your shirt (this was an especial misery on Sundays, when we wore Eton collars), and there was the daily nightmare of football – the cold, the mud, the hideous greasy ball that came whizzing at one's face, the gouging knees and trampling boots of the bigger boys. Part of the trouble was that in winter, after the age of about ten, I was seldom in good health, at any rate during term time. I had defective bronchial tubes and a lesion in one lung which was not discovered till many years later. Hence I not only had a chronic cough, but running was a torment to me. In those days however, "wheeziness", or "chestiness", as it was called, was either diagnosed as imagination or was looked on as essentially a moral disorder, caused by overeating. "You wheeze like a concertina," Sambo would say disapprovingly as he stood behind my chair. "You're perpetually stuffing yourself with food, that's why." My cough was referred to as a "stomach cough", which made it sound both disgusting and reprehensible. The cure for it was hard running, which, if you kept it up long enough, ultimately "cleared your chest".

It is curious, the degree – I will not say of actual hardship, but of squalor and neglect that was taken for granted in upper-class schools of that period. Almost as in the days of Thackeray, it seemed natural that a little boy of eight or ten should be a miserable, snotty-nosed creature, his face almost permanently dirty, his hands chapped, his nails bitten, his handkerchief a sodden horror, his bottom frequently blue with bruises. It was partly the prospect of actual physical discomfort that made the thought of going back to school lie in one's breast like a lump of lead during the last few days of the holidays. A characteristic memory of St Cyprian's is the astonishing hardness of one's bed on the first night of term. Since this was an expensive school, I took a social step upwards by attending it, and yet the standard of comfort was in every way far lower than in my own home, or, indeed, than it would have been in a prosperous working-class home. One only had a hot bath once a week, for instance. The food was not only bad, it was also insufficient. Never before or since have I seen butter or jam scraped on bread so thinly. I do not think I can be imagining the fact that we were underfed, when I remember the lengths we would go in order to steal food. On a number of occasions I remember creeping down at two or three o'clock in the morning through what seemed like miles of pitch-dark stairways and passages – barefooted, stopping to listen after each step, paralysed with about equal fear of Sambo, ghosts and burglars – to steal stale bread from the pantry. The assistant masters had their meals with us, but they had somewhat better food, and if one got half a chance it was usual to steal leftover scraps of bacon rind or fried potato when their plates were removed.

As usual, I did not see the sound commercial reason for this underfeeding. On the whole I accepted Sambo's view that a boy's appetite is a sort of morbid growth which should be kept in check as much as possible. A maxim often repeated to us at St Cyprian's was that it is healthy to get up from a meal feeling as hungry as when you sat down. Only a generation earlier than this it had been common for school dinners to start off with a slab of unsweetened suet pudding, which, it was frankly said, "broke the boys' appetites". But the underfeeding was probably less flagrant at preparatory schools, where a boy was wholly dependent on the official diet, than at public schools, where he was allowed – indeed, expected – to buy extra food for himself. At some schools, he would literally not have had enough to eat unless he had bought regular supplies of eggs, sausages, sardines, etc. – and his parents had to allow him money for this purpose. At Eton, for instance, at any rate in College, a boy was given no solid meal after midday dinner. For his afternoon tea he was given only tea and bread and butter, and at eight o'clock he was given a miserable supper of soup or fried fish, or more often bread and cheese, with water to drink. Sambo went down to see his eldest son at Eton and came back in snobbish ecstasies over the luxury in which the boys lived. "They give them fried fish for supper!" he exclaimed, beaming all over his chubby face. "There's no school like it in the world." Fried fish! The habitual supper of the poorest of the working class! At very cheap boarding schools it was no doubt worse. A very early memory of mine is of seeing the boarders at a grammar school – the sons, probably, of farmers and shopkeepers – being fed on boiled lights.*

Whoever writes about his childhood must beware of exaggeration and self-pity. I do not want to claim that I was a martyr or that St Cyprian's was a sort of Dotheboys Hall. But I should be falsifying my own memories if I did not record that they are largely memories of disgust. The overcrowded, underfed, underwashed life that we led *was* disgusting, as I recall it. If I shut my eyes and say "school", it is of course the physical surroundings that first come back to me: the flat playing field with its cricket pavilion and the little shed by the rifle range, the draughty dormitories, the dusty splintery passages, the square of asphalt in front of the gymnasium, the raw-looking pinewood chapel at the back. And at almost every point some filthy detail obtrudes itself. For example, there were the pewter bowls out of which we had our porridge. They had overhanging rims, and under the rims there were accumulations of sour porridge, which could be flaked off in long strips. The porridge itself, too, contained more lumps, hairs and unexplained black things than one would have thought possible, unless someone were putting them there on purpose. It was never safe to start on that porridge without investigating it first. And there was the slimy water of the plunge bath – it was twelve or fifteen feet long, the whole school was supposed to go into it every morning, and I doubt whether the water was changed at all frequently – and the always-damp towels with their cheesy smell, and, on occasional visits in the winter, the murky seawater of the local baths, which came straight in from the beach and on which I once saw floating a human turd. And the sweaty smell of the changing room with its greasy basins, and, giving on this, the row of filthy, dilapidated lavatories, which had no fastenings of any kind on the doors, so that whenever you were sitting there someone was sure to come crashing in. It is not easy for me to think of my schooldays without seeming to breathe in a whiff of something cold and evil-smelling – a sort of compound of sweaty stockings, dirty towels, faecal smells blowing along corridors, forks with old food between the prongs, neck-of-mutton stew, and the banging doors of the lavatories and the echoing chamber pots in the dormitories.

It is true that I am by nature not gregarious, and the WC and dirty-handkerchief side of life is necessarily more obtrusive when great numbers of human beings are crushed together in a small space. It is just as bad in an army, and worse, no doubt, in a prison. Besides, boyhood is the age of disgust. After one has learnt to differentiate, and before one has become hardened – between seven and eighteen, say – one seems always to be walking the tightrope over a cesspool. Yet I do not think I exaggerate the squalor of school life, when I remember how health and cleanliness were neglected, in spite of the hoo-ha about fresh air and cold water and keeping in hard training. It was common to remain constipated for days together. Indeed, one was hardly encouraged to keep one's bowels open, since the only aperients tolerated were castor oil or another almost equally horrible drink called liquorice powder. One was supposed to go into the plunge bath every morning, but some boys shirked it for days on end, simply making themselves scarce when the bell sounded, or else slipping along the edge of the bath among the crowd, and then wetting their hair with a little dirty water off the floor. A little boy of eight or nine will not necessarily keep himself clean unless there is someone to see that he does it. There was a new boy named Hazel, a pretty, mother's darling of a boy, who came a little while before I left. The first thing I noticed about him was the beautiful pearly whiteness of his teeth. By the end of that term his teeth were an extraordinary shade of green. During all that time, apparently, no one had taken sufficient interest in him to see that he brushed them.

But of course the differences between home and school were more than physical. That bump on the hard mattress, on the first night of term, used to give me a feeling of abrupt awakening, a feeling of: "This is reality; this is what you are up against." Your home might be far from perfect, but at least it was a place ruled by love rather than by fear, where you did not have to be perpetually on your guard against the people surrounding you. At eight years old you were suddenly taken out of this warm nest and flung into a world of force and fraud and secrecy, like a goldfish into a tank full of pike. Against no matter what degree of bullying you had no redress. You could only have defended yourself by sneaking, which, except in a few rigidly defined circumstances, was the unforgivable sin. To write home and ask your parents to take you away would have been even less thinkable, since to do so would have been to admit yourself unhappy and unpopular, which a boy will never do. Boys are Erewhonians: they think that misfortune is disgraceful and must be concealed at all costs.* It might perhaps have been considered permissible to complain to your parents about bad food, or an unjustified caning, or some other ill-treatment inflicted by masters and not by boys. The fact that Sambo never beat the richer boys suggests that such complaints were made occasionally. But in my own peculiar circumstances I could never have asked my parents to intervene on my behalf. Even before I understood about the reduced fees, I grasped that they were in some way under an obligation to Sambo, and therefore could not protect me against him. I have mentioned already that throughout my time at St Cyprian's I never had a cricket bat of my own. I had been told this was because "your parents couldn't afford it". One day in the holidays, by some casual remark, it came out that they had provided ten shillings to buy me one: yet no cricket bat appeared. I did not protest to my parents, let alone raise the subject with Sambo. How could I? I was dependent on him, and the ten shillings was merely a fragment of what I owed him. I realize now, of course, that it is immensely unlikely that Sambo had simply stuck to the money. No doubt the matter had slipped his memory. But the point is that I assumed that he had stuck to it, and that he had a right to do so if he chose.

How difficult it is for a child to have any real independence of attitude could be seen in our behaviour towards Flip. I think it would be true to say that every boy in the school hated and feared her. Yet we all fawned on her in the most abject way, and the top layer of our feelings towards her was a sort of guilt-stricken loyalty. Flip, although the discipline of the school depended more on her than on Sambo, hardly pretended to dispense strict justice. She was frankly capricious. An act which might get you a caning one day might next day be laughed off as a boyish prank, or even commended because it "showed you had guts". There were days when everyone cowered before those deep-set, accusing eyes, and there were days when she was like a flirtatious queen surrounded by courtier-lovers, laughing and joking, scattering largesse, or the promise of largesse ("And if you win the Harrow History Prize I'll give you a new case for your camera!"), and occasionally even packing three or four favoured boys into her Ford car and carrying them off to a tea shop in town, where they were allowed to buy coffee and cakes. Flip was inextricably mixed up in my mind with Queen Elizabeth, whose relations with Leicester and Essex and Raleigh* were intelligible to me from a very early age. A word we all constantly used in speaking of Flip was "favour". "I'm in good favour," we would say, or "I'm in bad favour." Except for the handful of wealthy or titled boys, no one was permanently in good favour, but on the other hand even the outcasts had patches of it from time to time. Thus, although my memories of Flip are mostly hostile, I also remember considerable periods when I basked under her smiles, when she called me "old chap" and used my Christian name, and allowed me to frequent her private library, where I first made acquaintance with *Vanity Fair*. The high-water mark of good favour was to be invited to serve at table on Sunday nights when Flip and Sambo had guests to dinner. In clearing away, of course, one had a chance to finish off the scraps, but one also got a servile pleasure from standing behind the seated guests and darting deferentially forward when something was wanted. Whenever one had the chance to suck up, one did suck up, and at the first smile one's hatred turned into a sort of cringing love. I was always tremendously proud when I succeeded in making Flip laugh. I have even, at her command, written *vers d'occasion*, comic verses to celebrate memorable events in the life of the school.

I am anxious to make it clear that I was not a rebel, except by force of circumstances. I accepted the codes that I found in being. Once, towards the end of my time, I even sneaked to Brown about a suspected case of homosexuality. I did not know very well what homosexuality was, but I knew that it happened and was bad, and that this was one of the contexts in which it was proper to sneak. Brown told me I was "a good fellow", which made me feel horribly ashamed. Before Flip one seemed as helpless as a snake before the snake-charmer. She had a hardly varying vocabulary of praise and abuse, a whole series of set phrases, each of which promptly called forth the appropriate response. There was "*Buck* up, old chap!", which inspired one to paroxysms of energy; there was "Don't *be* such a fool!" (or, "It's path*e*tic, isn't it?"), which made one feel a born idiot; and there was "It isn't very straight of you, is it?", which always brought one to the brink of tears. And yet all the while, at the middle of one's heart, there seemed to stand an incorruptible inner self who knew that whatever one did – whether one laughed or snivelled or went into frenzies of gratitude for small favours – one's only true feeling was hatred.

IV

I had learnt early in my career that one can do wrong against one's will, and before long I also learnt that one can do wrong without ever discovering what one has done or why it was wrong. There were sins that were too subtle to be explained, and there were others that were too terrible to be clearly mentioned. For example, there was sex, which was always smouldering just under the surface and which suddenly blew up into a tremendous row when I was about twelve.

At some preparatory schools homosexuality is not a problem, but I think that St Cyprian's may have acquired a "bad tone" thanks to the presence of the South American boys, who would perhaps mature a year or two earlier than an English boy. At that age I was not interested, so I do not actually know what went on, but I imagine it was group masturbation. At any rate, one day the storm suddenly burst over our heads. There were summonses, interrogations, confessions, floggings, repentances, solemn lectures of which one understood nothing except that some irredeemable sin known as "swinishness" or "beastliness" had been committed. One of the ringleaders, a boy named Horne, was flogged, according to eyewitnesses, for a quarter of an hour continuously before being expelled. His yells rang through the house. But we were all implicated, more or less, or felt ourselves to be implicated. Guilt seemed to hang in the air like a pall of smoke. A solemn, black-haired imbecile of an assistant master, who was later to be a Member of Parliament, took the older boys to a secluded room and delivered a talk on the Temple of the Body.

"Don't you realize what a wonderful thing your body is?" he said gravely. "You talk of your motor-car engines, your Rolls-Royces and Daimlers and so on. Don't you understand that no engine ever made is fit to be compared with your body? And then you go and wreck it, ruin it – for life!"

He turned his cavernous black eyes on me and added sadly:

"And you, whom I'd always believed to be quite a decent person after your fashion – you, I hear, are one of the very worst."

A feeling of doom descended upon me. So I was guilty too. I too had done the dreadful thing, whatever it was, that wrecked you for life, body and soul, and ended in suicide or the lunatic asylum. Till then I had hoped that I was innocent, and the conviction of sin which now took possession of me was perhaps all the stronger because I did not know what I had done. I was not among those who were interrogated and flogged, and it was not until the row was well over that I even learnt about the trivial accident that had connected my name with it. Even then I understood nothing. It was not till about two years later that I fully grasped what that lecture on the Temple of the Body had referred to.

At this time I was in an almost sexless state, which is normal, or at any rate common, in boys of that age; I was therefore in the position of simultaneously knowing and not knowing what used to be called the Facts of Life. At five or six, like many children, I had passed through a phase of sexuality. My friends were the plumber's children up the road, and we used sometimes to play games of a vaguely erotic kind. One was called "playing at doctors", and I remember getting a faint but definitely pleasant thrill from holding a toy trumpet, which was supposed to be a stethoscope, against a little girl's belly. About the same time I fell deeply in love, a far more worshipping kind of love than I have ever felt for anyone since, with a girl named Elsie at the convent school which I attended. She seemed to me grown up, so I suppose she must have been fifteen. After that, as so often happens, all sexual feelings seemed to go out of me for many years. At twelve I knew more than I had known as a young child, but I understood less, because I no longer knew the essential fact that there is something pleasant in sexual activity. Between roughly seven and fourteen, the whole subject seemed to me uninteresting and, when for some reason I was forced to think of it, disgusting. My knowledge of the so-called Facts of Life was derived from animals, and was therefore distorted, and in any case was only intermittent. I knew that animals copulated and that human beings had bodies resembling those of animals – but that human beings also copulated I only knew, as it were, reluctantly, when something, a phrase in the Bible, perhaps, compelled me to remember it. Not having desire, I had no curiosity, and was willing to leave many questions unanswered. Thus,

I knew in principle how the baby gets into the woman, but I did not know how it gets out again, because I had never followed the subject up. I knew all the dirty words, and in my bad moments I would repeat them to myself, but I did not know what the worst of them meant, nor want to know. They were abstractly wicked, a sort of verbal charm. While I remained in this state, it was easy for me to remain ignorant of any sexual misdeeds that went on about me, and to be hardly wiser even when the row broke. At most, through the veiled and terrible warnings of Flip, Sambo and all the rest of them, I grasped that the crime of which we were all guilty was somehow connected with the sexual organs. I had noticed, without feeling much interest, that one's penis sometimes stands up of its own accord (this starts happening to a boy long before he has any conscious sexual desires), and I was inclined to believe, or half-believe, that *that* must be the crime. At any rate, it was something to do with the penis – so much I understood. Many other boys, I have no doubt, were equally in the dark.

After the talk on the Temple of the Body (days later, it seems in retrospect; the row seemed to continue for days), a dozen of us were seated at the long shiny table which Sambo used for the scholarship class, under Flip's lowering eye. A long, desolate wail rang out from a room somewhere above. A very small boy named Ronalds, aged no more than about ten, who was implicated in some way, was being flogged, or was recovering from a flogging. At the sound, Flip's eyes searched our faces, and settled upon me.

"*You see*," she said.

I will not swear that she said, "You see what you have done," but that was the sense of it. We were all bowed down with shame. It was *our* fault. Somehow or other we had led poor Ronalds astray: *we* were responsible for his agony and his ruin. Then Flip turned upon another boy named Heath. It is thirty years ago, and I cannot remember for certain whether she merely quoted a verse from the Bible, or whether she actually brought out a Bible and made Heath read it; but at any rate the text indicated was: "Whoso shall offend one of these little ones that believe in me, it were better for him that a millstone were hanged about his neck, and that he were drowned in the depth of the sea."*

That, too, was terrible. Ronalds was one of these little ones, we had offended him; it were better that a millstone were hanged about our necks and that we were drowned in the depth of the sea.

"Have you thought about that, Heath – have you thought what it means?" Flip said. And Heath broke down into snivelling tears.

Another boy, Beacham, whom I have mentioned already, was similarly overwhelmed with shame by the accusation that he "had black rings round his eyes".

"Have you looked in the glass lately, Beacham?" said Flip. "Aren't you ashamed to go about with a face like that? Do you think everyone doesn't know what it means when a boy has black rings round his eyes?"

Once again the load of guilt and fear seemed to settle down upon me. Had *I* got black rings round my eyes? A couple of years later I realized that these were supposed to be a symptom by which masturbators could be detected. But already, without knowing this, I accepted the black rings as a sure sign of depravity, *some* kind of depravity. And many times, even before I grasped the supposed meaning, I have gazed anxiously into the glass, looking for the first hint of that dreaded stigma, the confession which the secret sinner writes upon his own face.

These terrors wore off, or became merely intermittent, without affecting what one might call my official beliefs. It was still true about the madhouse and the suicide's grave, but it was no longer acutely frightening. Some months later it happened that I once again saw Horne, the ringleader who had been flogged and expelled. Horne was one of the outcasts, the son of poor middle-class parents, which was no doubt part of the reason why Sambo had handled him so roughly. The term after his expulsion he went on to Eastbourne College, the small local public school, which was hideously despised at St Cyprian's and looked on as "not really" a public school at all. Only a very few boys from St Cyprian's went there, and Sambo always spoke of them with a sort of contemptuous pity. You had no chance if you went to a school like that: at the best your destiny would be a clerkship. I thought of Horne as a person who at thirteen had already forfeited all hope of any decent future. Physically, morally and socially he was finished. Moreover I assumed that his parents had only sent him to Eastbourne College because after his disgrace no "good" school would have him.

During the following term, when we were out for a walk, we passed Horne in the street. He looked completely normal. He was a strongly built, rather good-looking boy with black hair. I immediately noticed that he looked better than when I had last seen him – his complexion, previously rather pale, was pinker and that he did not seem embarrassed at meeting us. Apparently he was not ashamed either of having been expelled, or of being at Eastbourne College. If one could gather anything from the way he looked at us as we filed past, it was that he was glad to have escaped from St Cyprian's. But the encounter made very little impression on me. I drew no inference from the fact that Horne, ruined in body and soul, appeared to be happy and in good health. I still believed in the sexual mythology that had been taught me by Sambo and Flip. The mysterious, terrible dangers were still there. Any morning the black rings might appear round your eyes and you would know that you too were among the lost ones. Only it no longer seemed to matter very much. These contradictions can exist easily in the mind of a child, because of its own vitality. It accepts – how can it do otherwise? – the nonsense that its elders tell it, but its youthful body, and the sweetness of the physical world, tell it another story. It was the same with hell, which up to the age of about fourteen I officially believed in. Almost certainly hell existed, and there were occasions when a vivid sermon could scare you into fits. But somehow it never lasted. The fire that waited for you was real fire, it would hurt in the same way as when you burnt your finger, and *for ever*, but most of the time you could contemplate it without bothering.

V

The various codes which were presented to you at St Cyprian's – religious, moral, social and intellectual – contradicted one another if you worked out their implications. The essential conflict was between the tradition of nineteenth-century asceticism and the actually existing luxury and snobbery of the pre-1914 age. On the one side were Low-Church Bible Christianity, sex puritanism, insistence on hard work, respect for academic distinction, disapproval of self-indulgence; on the other, contempt for "braininess", and worship of games, contempt for foreigners and the working class, an almost neurotic dread of poverty, and, above all, the assumption not only that money and privilege are the things that matter but that it is better to inherit them than to have to work for them. Broadly, you were bidden to be at once a Christian and a social success, which is impossible. At the time I did not perceive that the various ideals which were set before us cancelled out. I merely saw that they were all, or nearly all, unattainable, so far as I was concerned, since they all depended not only on what you did but on what you *were*.

Very early, at the age of only ten or eleven, I reached the conclusion – no one told me this, but on the other hand I did not simply make it up out of my own head; somehow it was in the air I breathed – that you were no good unless you had £100,000. I had perhaps fixed on this particular sum as a result of reading Thackeray. The interest on £100,000 would be £4,000 a year (I was in favour of a safe 4 per cent), and this seemed to me the minimum income that you must possess if you were to belong to the real top crust, the people in the country houses. But it was clear that I could never find my way into that paradise, to which you did not really belong unless you were born into it. You could only *make* money, if at all, by a mysterious operation called "going into the City", and when you came out of the City, having won your £100,000, you were fat and old. But the truly enviable thing about the top-notchers was that they were rich while young. For people like me, the ambitious middle class, the examination passers, only a bleak, laborious kind of success was possible. You clambered upwards on a ladder of scholarships into the Civil Service or the Indian Civil Service, or possibly you became a barrister. And if at any point you "slacked" or "went off" and missed one of the rungs in the ladder, you became "a little office boy at forty pounds a year". But even if you climbed to the highest niche that was open to you, you could still only be an underling, a hanger-on of the people who really counted.

Even if I had not learnt this from Sambo and Flip, I would have learnt it from the other boys. Looking back, it is astonishing how intimately, intelligently snobbish we all were, how knowledgeable about names and addresses, how swift to detect small differences in accents and manners and the cut of clothes. There were some boys who seemed to drip money from their pores even in the bleak misery of the middle of a winter term. At the beginning and end of the term, especially, there was naively snobbish chatter about Switzerland, and Scotland with its gillies and grouse moors, and "my uncle's yacht", and "our place in the country", and "my pony" and "my pater's touring car". There never was, I suppose, in the history of the world a time when the sheer vulgar fatness of wealth, without any kind of aristocratic elegance to redeem it, was so obtrusive as in those years before 1914. It was the age when crazy millionaires in curly top hats and lavender waistcoats gave champagne parties in rococo houseboats on the Thames, the age of diabolo and hobble skirts, the age of the "knut" in his grey bowler and cutaway coat, the age of *The Merry Widow*, Saki's novels, *Peter Pan* and *Where the Rainbow Ends*,* the age when people talked about chocs and cigs and ripping and topping and heavenly, when they went for divvy weekends at Brighton and had scrumptious teas at the Troc.* From the whole decade before 1914 there seems to breathe forth a smell of the more vulgar, un-grown-up kinds of luxury, a smell of brilliantine and crème de menthe and soft-centred chocolates – an atmosphere, as it were, of eating everlasting strawberry ices on green lawns to the tune of the Eton Boating Song. The extraordinary thing was the way in which everyone took it for granted that this oozing, bulging wealth of the English upper and upper middle classes would last for ever, and was part of the order of things. After 1918 it was never quite the same again. Snobbishness and expensive habits came back, certainly, but they were self-conscious and on the defensive. Before the war the worship of money was entirely unreflecting and untroubled by any pang of conscience. The goodness of money was as unmistakable as the goodness of health or beauty, and a glittering car, a title or a horde of servants was mixed up in people's minds with the idea of actual moral virtue.

At St Cyprian's, in term time, the general bareness of life enforced a certain democracy, but any mention of the holidays and the consequent competitive swanking about cars and butlers and country houses promptly called class distinctions into being. The school was pervaded by a curious cult of Scotland, which brought out the fundamental contradiction in our standard of values. Flip claimed Scottish ancestry, and she favoured the Scottish boys, encouraging them to wear kilts in their ancestral tartan instead of the school uniform, and even christened her youngest child by a Gaelic name. Ostensibly we were supposed to admire the Scots because they were "grim" and "dour" ("stern" was perhaps the key word), and irresistible on the field of battle. In the big schoolroom there was a steel engraving of the charge of the Scots

Greys at Waterloo, all looking as though they enjoyed every moment of it. Our picture of Scotland was made up of burns, braes, kilts, sporrans, claymores, bagpipes and the like, all somehow mixed up with the invigorating effects of porridge, Protestantism and a cold climate. But underlying this was something quite different. The real reason for the cult of Scotland was that only very rich people could spend their summers there. And the pretended belief in Scottish superiority was a cover for the bad conscience of the occupying English, who had pushed the Highland peasantry off their farms to make way for the deer forests, and then compensated them by turning them into servants. Flip's face always beamed with innocent snobbishness when she spoke of Scotland. Occasionally she even attempted a trace of Scottish accent. Scotland was a private paradise which a few initiates could talk about and make outsiders feel small.

"You going to Scotland this hols?"

"Rather! We go every year."

"My pater's got three miles of river."

"My pater's giving me a new gun for the twelfth. There's jolly good black game where we go. Get out, Smith! What are you listening for? You've never been in Scotland. I bet you don't know what a blackcock looks like."

Following on this, imitations of the cry of a blackcock, of the roaring of a stag, of the accent of "our gillies", etc. etc.

And the questionings that new boys of doubtful social origin were sometimes put through – questionings quite surprising in their mean-minded particularity, when one reflects that the inquisitors were only twelve or thirteen!

"How much a year has your pater got? What part of London do you live in? Is that Knightsbridge or Kensington? How many bathrooms has your house got? How many servants do your people keep? Have you got a butler? Well, then, have you got a cook? Where do you get your clothes made? How many shows did you go to in the hols? How much money did you bring back with you?" etc. etc.

I have seen a little new boy, hardly older than eight, desperately lying his way through such a catechism:

"Have your people got a car?"

"Yes."

"What sort of car?"

"Daimler."

"How many horsepower?"

(Pause, and leap in the dark.) "Fifteen."

"What kind of lights?"

The little boy is bewildered.

"What kind of lights? Electric or acetylene?"

(A longer pause, and another leap in the dark.) "Acetylene."

"Coo! He says his pater's car's got acetylene lamps. They went out years ago. It must be as old as the hills."

"Rot! He's making it up. He hasn't got a car. He's just a navvy. Your pater's a navvy."

And so on.

By the social standards that prevailed about me, I was no good, and could not be any good. But all the different kinds of virtue seemed to be mysteriously interconnected and to belong to much the same people. It was not only money that mattered: there were also strength, beauty, charm, athleticism and something called "guts" or "character", which in reality meant the power to impose your will on others. I did not possess any of these qualities. At games, for instance, I was hopeless. I was a fairly good swimmer and not altogether contemptible at cricket, but these had no prestige value, because boys only attach importance to a game if it requires strength and courage. What counted was football, at which I was a funk. I loathed the game, and since I could see no pleasure or usefulness in it, it was very difficult for me to show courage at it. Football, it seemed to me, is not really played for the pleasure of kicking a ball about, but is a species of fighting. The lovers of football are large, boisterous, nobbly boys who are good at knocking down and trampling on slightly smaller boys. That was the pattern of school life – a continuous triumph of the strong over the weak. Virtue consisted in winning: it consisted in being bigger, stronger, handsomer, richer, more popular, more elegant, more unscrupulous than other people – in dominating them, bullying them, making them suffer pain, making them look foolish, getting the better of them in every way. Life was hierarchical and whatever happened was right. There were the strong, who deserved to win and always did win, and there were the weak, who deserved to lose and always did lose, everlastingly.

I did not question the prevailing standards, because so far as I could see there were no others. How could the rich, the strong, the elegant, the fashionable, the powerful be in the wrong? It was their world, and the rules they made for it must be the right ones. And yet from a very early age I was aware of the impossibility of any *subjective* conformity. Always at the centre of my heart the inner self seemed to be awake, pointing out the difference between the moral obligation and the psychological *fact*. It was the same in all matters, worldly or other-worldly. Take religion, for instance. You were supposed to love God, and I did not question this. Till the age of about fourteen I believed in God, and believed that the accounts given of him were true. But I was well aware that I did not love him. On the contrary, I hated him, just as I hated Jesus and the Hebrew patriarchs. If I had sympathetic feelings towards any character in the Old Testament, it was towards such people as Cain, Jezebel, Haman, Agag, Sisera; in the New Testament my friends, if any, were Ananias, Caiaphas, Judas and Pontius Pilate. But the whole business of religion seemed to be strewn with psychological impossibilities. The Prayer Book told you, for example, to love God and fear him – but how could you love someone whom you feared? With your private affections it was the same. What you *ought* to feel was usually clear enough, but the appropriate emotion could not be commanded. Obviously it was my duty to feel grateful towards Flip and Sambo – but I was not grateful. It was equally clear that one ought to love one's father, but I knew very well that I merely disliked my own father, whom I had barely seen before I was eight and who appeared to me simply as a gruff-voiced elderly man forever saying "Don't". It was not that one did not want to possess the right qualities or feel the correct emotions, but that one could not. The good and the possible never seemed to coincide.

There was a line of verse that I came across not actually while I was at St Cyprian's but a year or two later, and which seemed to strike a sort of leaden echo in my heart. It was: "The armies of unalterable law."* I understood to perfection what it meant to be Lucifer, defeated and justly defeated, with no possibility of revenge. The schoolmasters with their canes, the millionaires with their Scottish castles, the athletes with their curly hair – these were the armies of unalterable law. It was not easy, at that date, to realize that in fact it *was* alterable. And according to that law I was damned. I had no money, I was weak, I was ugly, I was unpopular, I had a chronic cough, I was cowardly, I smelt. This picture, I should add, was not altogether fanciful. I was an unattractive boy. St Cyprian's soon made me so, even if I had not been so before. But a child's belief in its own shortcomings is not much influenced by facts. I believed, for example, that I "smelt", but this was based simply on general probability. It was notorious that disagreeable people smelt, and therefore presumably I did so too. Again, until after I had left school for good I continued to believe that I was preternaturally ugly. It was what my schoolfellows had told me, and I had no other authority to refer to. The conviction that it was *not possible* for me to be a success went deep enough to influence my actions till far into adult life. Until I was about thirty I always planned my life on the assumption not only that any major undertaking was bound to fail, but that I could only expect to live a few years longer.

But this sense of guilt and inevitable failure was balanced by something else: that is, the instinct to survive. Even a creature that is weak, ugly, cowardly, smelly and in no way justifiable still wants to stay alive and be happy after its own fashion. I could not invert the existing scale of values, or turn myself into a success, but I could accept my failure and make the best of it. I could resign myself to being what I was, and then endeavour to survive on those terms.

To survive, or at least to preserve any kind of independence, was essentially criminal, since it meant breaking rules which you yourself recognized. There was a boy named Johnny Hale who for some months oppressed me horribly. He was a big, powerful, coarsely handsome boy with a very red face and curly black hair, who was forever twisting somebody's arm, wringing somebody's ear, flogging somebody with a riding crop (he was a member of the Sixth Form) or performing prodigies of activity on the football field. Flip loved him (hence the fact that he was habitually called by his Christian name) and Sambo commended him as a boy who "had character" and "could keep order". He was followed about by a group of toadies who nicknamed him Strong Man.

One day, when we were taking off our overcoats in the changing room, Hale picked on me for some reason. I "answered him back", whereupon he gripped my wrist, twisted it round and bent my forearm back upon itself in a hideously painful way. I remember his handsome, jeering red face bearing down upon mine. He was, I think, older than I, besides being enormously stronger. As he let go of me a terrible, wicked resolve formed itself in my heart. I would get back on him by hitting him when he did not expect it. It was a strategic moment, for the master who had been "taking" the walk would be coming back almost immediately, and then there could be no fight. I let perhaps a minute go by, walked up to Hale with the most harmless air I could assume, and then, getting the weight of my body behind it, smashed my fist into his face. He was flung backwards by the blow, and some blood ran out of his mouth. His always sanguine face turned almost black with rage. Then he turned away to rinse his mouth at the washing basins.

"*All right!*" he said to me between his teeth as the master led us away.

For days after this he followed me about, challenging me to fight. Although terrified out of my wits, I steadily refused to fight. I said that the blow in the face had served him right, and there was an end of it. Curiously enough he did not simply fall upon me there and then, which public opinion would probably have supported him in doing. So gradually the matter tailed off, and there was no fight.

Now, I had behaved wrongly, by my own code no less than his. To hit him unawares was wrong. But to refuse afterwards to fight knowing that if we fought he would beat me – that was far worse: it was cowardly. If I had refused because I disapproved of fighting, or because I genuinely felt the matter to be closed, it would have been all right – but I had refused merely because I was afraid. Even my revenge was made empty by that fact. I had struck the blow in a moment of mindless violence, deliberately not looking far ahead and merely determined to get my own back for once and damn the consequences. I had had time to realize that what I did was wrong, but it was the kind of crime from which you could get some satisfaction. Now all was nullified. There had been a sort of courage in the first act, but my subsequent cowardice had wiped it out.

The fact I hardly noticed was that though Hale formally challenged me to fight, he did not actually attack me. Indeed, after receiving that one blow he never oppressed me again. It was perhaps twenty years before I saw the significance of this. At the time I could not see beyond the moral dilemma that is presented to the weak in a world governed by the strong: break the rules or perish. I did not see that in that case the weak have the right to make a different set of rules for themselves – because, even if such an idea had occurred to me, there was no one in my environment who could have confirmed me in it. I lived in a world of boys, gregarious animals, questioning nothing, accepting the law of the stronger and avenging their own humiliations by passing them down to someone smaller. My situation was that of countless other boys, and if potentially I was more of a rebel than most, it was only because, by boyish standards, I was a poorer specimen. But I never did rebel intellectually, only emotionally. I had nothing to help me except my dumb selfishness, my inability – not, indeed, to despise myself, but to *dislike* myself; my instinct to survive.

It was about a year after I hit Johnny Hale in the face that I left St Cyprian's for ever. It was the end of a winter term. With a sense of coming out from darkness into sunlight I put on my Old Boy's tie as we dressed for the journey. I well remember the feeling of that brand-new silk tie round my neck, a feeling of emancipation, as though the tie had been at once a badge of manhood and an amulet against Flip's voice and Sambo's cane. I was escaping from bondage. It was not that I expected, or even intended, to be any more successful at a public school than I had been at St Cyprian's. But still, I was escaping. I knew that at a public school there would be more privacy, more neglect, more chance to be idle and self-indulgent and degenerate. For years past I had been resolved – unconsciously at first, but consciously later on – that when once my scholarship was won I would "slack off" and cram no longer. This resolve, by the way, was so fully carried out that between the ages of thirteen and twenty-two or -three I hardly ever did a stroke of avoidable work.

Flip shook hands to say goodbye. She even gave me my Christian name for the occasion. But there was a sort of patronage, almost a sneer, in her face and in her voice. The tone in which she said goodbye was nearly the tone in which she had been used to say *little butterflies*. I had won two scholarships, but I was a failure, because success was measured not by what you did but by what you *were*. I was "not a good type of boy" and could bring no credit on the school. I did not possess character or courage or health or strength or money, or even good manners, the power to look like a gentleman.

"Goodbye," Flip's parting smile seemed to say. "It's not worth quarrelling now. You haven't made much of a success of your time at St Cyprian's, have you? And I don't suppose you'll get on awfully well at a public school either. We made a mistake, really, in wasting our time and money on you. This kind of education hasn't much to offer to a boy with your background and your outlook. Oh, don't think we don't understand you! We know all about those ideas you have at the back of your head, we know you disbelieve in everything we've taught you, and we know you aren't in the least grateful for all we've done for you. But there's no use in bringing it all up now. We aren't responsible for you any longer, and we shan't be seeing you again. Let's just admit that you're one of our failures and part without ill feeling. And so, goodbye."

That at least was what I read into her face. And yet how happy I was, that winter morning, as the train bore me away with the gleaming new silk tie (dark green, pale blue and black, if I remember rightly) round my neck! The world was opening before me, just a little, like a grey sky which exhibits a narrow crack of blue. A public school would be better fun than St Cyprian's, but at bottom equally alien. In a world where the prime necessities were money, titled relatives, athleticism, tailor-made clothes, neatly brushed hair, a charming smile, I was no good. All I had gained was a breathing space. A little quietude, a little self-indulgence, a little respite from cramming – and then, ruin. What kind of ruin I did not know: perhaps the colonies or an office stool, perhaps prison or an early death. But first a year or two in which one could "slack off" and get the benefit of one's sins, like Doctor Faustus. I believed firmly in my evil destiny, and yet I was acutely happy. It is the advantage of being thirteen that you can not only live in the moment but do so with full consciousness, foreseeing the future and yet not caring about it. Next term I was going to Wellington. I had also won a scholarship at Eton, but it was uncertain whether there would be a vacancy, and I was going to Wellington first. At Eton you had a room to yourself – a room which might even have a fire in it. At Wellington you had your own cubicle, and could make yourself cocoa in the evenings. The privacy of it, the grown-upness! And there would be libraries to hang about in, and summer afternoons when you could shirk games and mooch about the countryside alone, with no master driving you along. Meanwhile there were the holidays. There was the .22 rifle that I had bought the previous holidays (the Crackshot, it was called, costing twenty-two and sixpence), and Christmas was coming next week. There were also the pleasures of overeating. I thought of some particularly voluptuous cream buns which could be bought for twopence each at a shop in our town. (This was 1916, and food rationing had not yet started.) Even the detail that my journey money had been slightly miscalculated, leaving about a shilling over – enough for an unforeseen cup of coffee and a cake or two somewhere on the way – was enough to fill me with bliss. There was time for a bit of happiness before the future closed in upon me. But I did know that the future was dark. Failure, failure, failure – failure behind me, failure ahead of me – that was by far the deepest conviction that I carried away.

VI

All this was thirty years ago and more. The question is: does a child at school go through the same kind of experiences nowadays?

The only honest answer, I believe, is that we do not with certainty know. Of course it is obvious that the present-day *attitude* towards education is enormously more humane and sensible than that of the past. The snobbishness that was an integral part of my own education would be almost unthinkable today, because the society that nourished it is dead. I recall a conversation that must have taken place about a year before I left St Cyprian's. A Russian boy, large and fair-haired, a year older than myself, was questioning me.

"How much a year has your father got?"

I told him what I thought it was, adding a few hundreds to make it sound better. The Russian boy, neat in his habits, produced a pencil and a small notebook and made a calculation.

"My father has over two hundred times as much money as yours," he announced with a sort of amused contempt.

That was in 1915. What happened to that money a couple of years later, I wonder? And still more I wonder, do conversations of that kind happen at preparatory schools now?

Clearly there has been a vast change of outlook, a general growth of "enlightenment", even among ordinary, unthinking middle-class people. Religious belief, for instance, has largely vanished, dragging other kinds of nonsense after it. I imagine that very few people nowadays would tell a child that if it masturbates it will end in the lunatic asylum. Beating, too, has become discredited, and has even been abandoned at many schools. Nor is the underfeeding of children looked on as a normal, almost meritorious act. No one now would openly set out to give his pupils as little food as they could do with, or tell them that it is healthy to get up from a meal as hungry as you sat down. The whole status of children has improved, partly because they have grown relatively less numerous. And the diffusion of even a little psychological knowledge has made it harder for parents and schoolteachers to indulge their aberrations in the name of discipline. Here is a case, not known to me personally, but known to someone I can vouch for, and happening within my own lifetime. A small girl, daughter of a clergyman, continued wetting her bed at an age when she should have grown out of it. In order to punish her for this dreadful deed, her father took her to a large garden party and there introduced her to the whole company as a little girl who wetted her bed – and to underline her wickedness he had previously painted her face black. I do not suggest that Flip and Sambo would actually have done a thing like this, but I doubt whether it would have much surprised them. After all, things do change. And yet!...

The question is not whether boys are still buckled into Eton collars on Sunday, or told that babies are dug up under gooseberry bushes. That kind of thing is at an end, admittedly. The real question is whether it is still normal for a schoolchild to live for years amid irrational terrors and lunatic misunderstandings. And here one is up against the very great difficulty of knowing what a child really feels and thinks. A child which appears reasonably happy may actually be suffering horrors which it cannot or will not reveal. It lives in a sort of alien underwater world which we can only penetrate by memory or divination. Our chief clue is the fact that we were once children ourselves, and many people appear to forget the atmosphere of their own childhood almost entirely. Think for instance of the unnecessary torments that people will inflict by sending a child back to school with clothes of the wrong pattern, and refusing to see that this matters! Over things of this kind a child will sometimes utter a protest, but a great deal of the time its attitude is one of simple concealment. Not to expose your true feelings to an adult seems to be instinctive from the age of seven or eight onwards. Even the affection that one feels for a child, the desire to protect and cherish it, is a cause of misunderstanding. One can love a child, perhaps, more deeply than one can love another adult, but it is rash to assume that the child feels any love in return. Looking back on my own childhood, after the infant years were over, I do not believe that I ever felt love for any mature person, except my mother, and even her I did not trust, in the sense that shyness made me conceal most of my real feelings from her. Love, the spontaneous, unqualified emotion of love, was something I could only feel for people who were young. Towards people who were old – and remember that "old" to a child means over thirty, or even over twenty-five – I could feel reverence, respect, admiration or compunction, but I seemed cut off from them by a veil of fear and shyness mixed up with physical distaste. People are too ready to forget the child's *physical* shrinking from the adult. The enormous size of grown-ups, their ungainly, rigid bodies, their coarse, wrinkled skins, their great relaxed eyelids, their yellow teeth, and the whiffs of musty clothes and beer and sweat and tobacco that disengage from them at every movement! Part of the reason for the ugliness of adults, in a child's eyes, is that the child is usually looking upwards, and few faces are at their best when seen from below. Besides, being fresh and unmarked itself, the child has impossibly high standards in the matter of skin and teeth and complexion. But the greatest barrier of all is the child's misconception about age. A child can hardly envisage life beyond thirty, and in judging people's ages it will make fantastic mistakes. It will think that a person of twenty-five is forty, that a person of forty is sixty-five, and so on. Thus, when I fell in love with Elsie I took her to be grown-up. I met her again, when I was thirteen and she, I think, must have been twenty-three; she now seemed to me a middle-aged woman, somewhat past her best. And the child thinks of growing old as an almost obscene calamity, which for some mysterious reason will never happen to itself. All who have passed the age of thirty are joyless grotesques, endlessly fussing about things of no importance and staying alive without, so far as the child can see, having anything to live for. Only child life is real life. The schoolmaster who imagines that he is loved and trusted by his boys is in fact mimicked and laughed at behind his back. An adult who does not seem dangerous nearly always seems ridiculous.

I base these generalizations on what I can recall of my own childhood outlook. Treacherous though memory is, it seems to me the chief means we have of discovering how a child's mind works. Only by resurrecting our own memories can we realize how incredibly distorted is the child's vision of the world. Consider this, for example. How would St Cyprian's appear to me now, if I could go back, at my present age, and see it as it was in 1915? What should I think of Sambo and Flip, those terrible, all-powerful monsters? I should see them as a couple of silly, shallow, ineffectual people, eagerly clambering up a social ladder which any thinking person could see to be on the point of collapse. I would no more be frightened of them than I would be frightened of a dormouse. Moreover, in those days they seemed to me fantastically old, whereas – though of this I am not certain – I imagine they must have been somewhat younger than I am now. And how would Johnny Hale appear, with his blacksmith's arms and his red, jeering face? Merely a scruffy little boy, barely distinguishable from hundreds of other scruffy little boys. The two sets of facts can lie side by side in my mind, because those happen to be my own memories. But it would be very difficult for me to see with the eyes of any other child, except by an effort of the imagination which might lead me completely astray. The child and the adult live in different worlds. If that is so, we cannot be certain that school, at any rate boarding school, is not still for many children as dreadful an experience as it used to be. Take away God, Latin, the cane, class distinctions and sexual taboos, and the fear, the hatred, the snobbery and the misunderstanding might still all be there. It will have been seen that my own main trouble was an utter lack of any sense of proportion or probability. This led me to accept outrages and believe absurdities, and to suffer torments over things which were in fact of no importance. It is not enough to say that I was "silly" and "ought to have known better". Look back into your own childhood and think of the nonsense you used to believe and the trivialities which could make you suffer. Of course my own case had its individual variations, but essentially it was that of countless other boys. The weakness of the child is that it starts with a blank sheet. It neither understands nor questions the society in which it lives, and because of its credulity other people can work upon it, infecting it with the sense of inferiority and the dread of offending against mysterious, terrible laws. It may be that everything that happened to me at St Cyprian's could happen in the most "enlightened" school, though perhaps in subtler forms. Of one thing, however, I do feel fairly sure, and that is that boarding schools are worse than day schools. A child has a better chance with the sanctuary of its home near at hand. And I think the characteristic faults of the English upper and middle classes may be partly due to the practice, general until recently, of sending children away from home as young as nine, eight or even seven.

I have never been back to St Cyprian's. Reunions, old boys' dinners and suchlike leave me something more than cold, even when my memories are friendly. I have never even been down to Eton, where I was relatively happy, though I did once pass through it in 1933 and noted with interest that nothing seemed to have changed, except that the shops now sold radios. As for St Cyprian's, for years I loathed its very name so deeply that I could not view it with enough detachment to see the significance of the things that happened to me there. In a way, it is only within the last decade that I have really thought over my schooldays, vividly though their memory has always haunted me. Nowadays, I believe, it would make very little impression on me to see the place again, if it still exists. (I remember hearing a rumour some years ago that it had been burnt down.) If I had to pass through Eastbourne I would not make a detour to avoid the school – and if I happened to pass the school itself I might even stop for a moment by the low brick wall, with the steep bank running down from it, and look across the flat playing field at the ugly building with the square of asphalt in front of it. And if I went inside and smelt again the inky, dusty smell of the big schoolroom, the rosiny smell of the chapel, the stagnant smell of the swimming bath and the cold reek of the lavatories, I think I should only feel what one invariably feels in revisiting any scene of childhood: how small everything has grown, and how terrible is the deterioration in myself! But it is a fact that for many years I could hardly have borne to look at it again. Except upon dire necessity I would not have set foot in Eastbourne. I even conceived a prejudice against Sussex, as the county that contained St Cyprian's, and as an adult I have only once been in Sussex, on a short visit. Now, however, the place is out of my system for good. Its magic works no longer, and I have not even enough animosity left to make me hope that Flip and Sambo are dead or that the story of the school being burnt down was true.

Reflections on Gandhi*

Saints should always be judged guilty until they are proved innocent, but the tests that have to be applied to them are not, of course, the same in all cases. In Gandhi's case the questions one feels inclined to ask are: to what extent was Gandhi moved by vanity – by the consciousness of himself as a humble, naked old man, sitting on a praying mat and shaking empires by sheer spiritual power – and to what extent did he compromise his own principles by entering into politics, which of their nature are inseparable from coercion and fraud? To give a definite answer one would have to study Gandhi's acts and writings in immense detail, for his whole life was a sort of pilgrimage in which every act was significant. But this partial autobiography,* which ends in the 1920s, is strong evidence in his favour, all the more because it covers what he would have called the unregenerate part of his life and reminds one that inside the saint, or near-saint, there was a very shrewd, able person who could, if he had chosen, have been a brilliant success as a lawyer, an administrator or perhaps even a businessman.

At about the time when the autobiography first appeared I remember reading its opening chapters in the ill-printed pages of some Indian newspaper. They made a good impression on me, which Gandhi himself, at that time, did not. The things that one associated with him – homespun cloth, "soul forces" and vegetarianism – were unappealing, and his medievalist programme was obviously not viable in a backward, starving, overpopulated country. It was also apparent that the British were making use of him, or thought they were making use of him. Strictly speaking, as a nationalist, he was an enemy, but since in every crisis he would exert himself to prevent violence – which, from the British point of view, meant preventing any effective action whatever – he could be regarded as "our man". In private this was sometimes cynically admitted. The attitude of the Indian millionaires was similar. Gandhi called upon them to repent, and naturally they preferred him to the socialists and communists who, given the chance, would actually have taken their money away. How reliable such calculations are in the long run is doubtful; as Gandhi himself says, "in the end deceivers deceive only themselves" – but at any rate the gentleness with which he was nearly always handled was due partly to the feeling that he was useful. The British Conservatives only became really angry with him when, as in 1942, he was in effect turning his non-violence against a different conqueror.

But I could see even then that the British officials who spoke of him with a mixture of amusement and disapproval also genuinely liked and admired him, after a fashion. Nobody ever suggested that he was corrupt, or ambitious in any vulgar way, or that anything he did was actuated by fear or malice. In judging a man like Gandhi one seems instinctively to apply high standards, so that some of his virtues have passed almost unnoticed. For instance, it is clear even from the autobiography that his natural physical courage was quite outstanding: the manner of his death was a later illustration of this, for a public man who attached any value to his own skin would have been more adequately guarded. Again, he seems to have been quite free from that maniacal suspiciousness which, as E.M. Forster rightly says in *A Passage to India*, is the besetting Indian vice, as hypocrisy is the British vice. Although no doubt he was shrewd enough in detecting dishonesty, he seems wherever possible to have believed that other people were acting in good faith and had a better nature through which they could be approached. And though he came of a poor middle-class family, started life rather unfavourably and was probably of unimpressive physical appearance, he was not afflicted by envy or by the feeling of inferiority. Colour feeling, when he first met it in its worst form in South Africa, seems rather to have astonished him. Even when he was fighting what was in effect a colour war he did not think of people in terms of race or status. The governor of a province, a cotton millionaire, a half-starved Dravidian coolie, a British private soldier were all equally human beings, to be approached in much the same way. It is noticeable that even in the worst possible circumstances, as in South Africa, when he was making himself unpopular as the champion of the Indian community, he did not lack European friends.

Written in short lengths for newspaper serialization, the autobiography is not a literary masterpiece, but it is the more impressive because of the commonplaceness of much of its material. It is well to be reminded that Gandhi started out with the normal ambitions of a young Indian student and only adopted his extremist opinions by degrees and, in some cases, rather unwillingly. There was a time, it is interesting to learn, when he wore a top hat, took dancing lessons, studied French and Latin, went up the Eiffel Tower, and even tried to learn the violin – all this with the idea of assimilating European civilization as thoroughly as possible. He was not one of those saints who are marked out by their phenomenal piety from childhood onwards, nor one of the other kind who forsake the world after sensational debaucheries. He makes full confession of the misdeeds of his youth, but in fact there is not much to confess. As a frontispiece to the book there is a photograph of Gandhi's possessions at the time of his death. The whole outfit could be purchased for about £5, and Gandhi's sins, at least his fleshly sins, would make the same sort of appearance if placed all in one heap. A few cigarettes, a few mouthfuls of meat, a few annas* pilfered in childhood from the maidservant, two visits to a brothel (on each occasion he got away without "doing anything"), one narrowly escaped lapse with his landlady in Plymouth, one outburst of temper – that is about the whole collection. Almost from childhood onwards he had a deep earnestness, an attitude ethical rather than religious, but, until he was about thirty, no very definite sense of direction. His first entry into anything describable as public life was made by way of vegetarianism. Underneath his less ordinary qualities one feels all the time the solid middle-class businessmen who were his ancestors. One feels that even after he had abandoned personal ambition he must have been a resourceful, energetic lawyer and a hard-headed political organizer, careful in keeping down expenses, an adroit handler of committees and an indefatigable chaser of subscriptions. His character was an extraordinarily mixed one, but there was almost nothing in it that you can put your finger on and call bad, and I believe that even Gandhi's worst enemies would admit that he was an interesting and unusual man who enriched the world simply by being alive. Whether he was also a lovable man, and whether his teachings can have much value for those who do not accept the religious beliefs on which they are founded, I have never felt fully certain.

Of late years it has been the fashion to talk about Gandhi as though he were not only sympathetic to the Western left-wing movement but were even integrally part of it. Anarchists and pacifists, in particular, have claimed him for their own, noticing only that he was opposed to centralism and state violence and ignoring the other-worldly, anti-humanist tendency of his doctrines. But one should, I think, realize that Gandhi's teachings cannot be squared with the belief that man is the measure of all things, and that our job is to make life worth living on this earth, which is the only earth we have. They make sense only on the assumption that God exists and that the world of solid objects is an illusion to be escaped from. It is worth considering the disciplines which Gandhi imposed on himself and which – though he might not insist on every one of his followers observing every detail – he considered indispensable if one wanted to serve either God or humanity. First of all, no meat eating, and if possible no animal food in any form. (Gandhi himself, for the sake of his health, had to compromise on milk, but seems to have felt this to be a backsliding.) No alcohol or tobacco, and no spices or condiments, even of a vegetable kind, since food should be taken not for its own sake, but solely in order to preserve one's strength. Secondly, if possible, no sexual intercourse. If sexual intercourse must happen, then it should be for the sole purpose of begetting children and presumably at long intervals. Gandhi himself, in his middle thirties, took the vow of *brahmacharya*, which means not only complete chastity but the elimination of sexual desire. This condition, it seems, is difficult to attain without a special diet and frequent fasting. One of the dangers of milk drinking is that it is apt to arouse sexual desire. And finally

– this is the cardinal point – for the seeker after goodness there must be no close friendships and no exclusive loves whatever.

Close friendships, Gandhi says, are dangerous, because "friends react on one another" and through loyalty to a friend one can be led into wrongdoing. This is unquestionably true. Moreover, if one is to love God, or to love humanity as a whole, one cannot give one's preference to any individual person. This again is true, and it marks the point at which the humanistic and the religious attitudes cease to be reconcilable. To an ordinary human being, love means nothing if it does not mean loving some people more than others. The autobiography leaves it uncertain whether Gandhi behaved in an inconsiderate way to his wife and children, but at any rate it makes clear that on three occasions he was willing to let his wife or a child die rather than administer the animal food prescribed by the doctor. It is true that the threatened death never actually occurred, and also that Gandhi – with, one gathers, a good deal of moral pressure in the opposite direction – always gave the patient the choice of staying alive at the price of committing a sin; still, if the decision had been solely his own, he would have forbidden the animal food, whatever the risks might be. There must, he says, be some limit to what we will do in order to remain alive, and the limit is well on this side of chicken broth. This attitude is perhaps a noble one, but, in the sense which – I think – most people would give to the word, it is inhuman. The essence of being human is that one does not seek perfection, that one *is* sometimes willing to commit sins for the sake of loyalty, that one does not push asceticism to the point where it makes friendly intercourse impossible, and that one is prepared in the end to be defeated and broken up by life, which is the inevitable price of fastening one's love upon other human individuals. No doubt alcohol, tobacco and so forth are things that a saint must avoid, but sainthood is also a thing that human beings must avoid. There is an obvious retort to this, but one should be wary about making it. In this yogi-ridden age, it is too readily assumed that "non-attachment" is not only better than a full acceptance of earthly life, but that the ordinary man only rejects it because it is too difficult: in other words, that the average human being is a failed saint. It is doubtful whether this is true. Many people genuinely do not wish to be saints, and it is probable that some who achieve or aspire to sainthood have never felt much temptation to be human beings. If one could follow it to its psychological roots, one would, I believe, find that the main motive for "non-attachment" is a desire to escape from the pain of living, and above all from love, which, sexual or non-sexual, is hard work. But it is not necessary here to argue whether the other-worldly or the humanistic ideal is "higher". The point is that they are incompatible. One must choose between God and man, and all "radicals" and "progressives", from the mildest liberal to the most extreme anarchist, have in effect chosen man.

However, Gandhi's pacifism can be separated to some extent from his other teachings. Its motive was religious, but he claimed also for it that it was a definite technique, a method, capable of producing desired political results. Gandhi's attitude was not that of most Western pacifists. *Satyagraha*, first evolved in South Africa, was a sort of non-violent warfare, a way of defeating the enemy without hurting him and without feeling or arousing hatred. It entailed such things as civil disobedience, strikes, lying down in front of railway trains, enduring police charges without running away and without hitting back, and the like. Gandhi objected to "passive resistance" as a translation of *Satyagraha*: in Gujarati, it seems, the word means "firmness in the truth". In his early days Gandhi served as a stretcher bearer on the British side in the Boer War, and he was prepared to do the same again in the war of 1914–18. Even after he had completely abjured violence he was honest enough to see that in war it is usually necessary to take sides. He did not – indeed, since his whole political life centred round a struggle for national independence, he could not – take the sterile and dishonest line of pretending that in every war both sides are exactly the same and it makes no difference who wins. Nor did he, like most Western pacifists, specialize in avoiding awkward questions. In relation to the late war, one question that every pacifist had a clear obligation to answer was: "What about the Jews? Are you prepared to see them exterminated? If not, how do you propose to save them without resorting to war?" I must say that I have never heard, from any Western pacifist, an honest answer to this question, though I have heard plenty of evasions, usually of the "you're another" type. But it so happens that Gandhi was asked a somewhat similar question in 1938 and that his answer is on record in Mr Louis Fischer's *Gandhi and Stalin*.* According to Mr Fischer, Gandhi's view was that the German Jews ought to commit collective suicide, which "would have aroused the world and the people of Germany to Hitler's violence". After the war he justified himself: the Jews had been killed anyway, and might as well have died significantly. One has the impression that this attitude staggered even so warm an admirer as Mr Fischer, but Gandhi was merely being honest. If you are not prepared to take life, you must often be prepared for lives to be lost in some other way. When, in 1942, he urged non-violent resistance against a Japanese invasion, he was ready to admit that it might cost several million deaths.

At the same time there is reason to think that Gandhi, who after all was born in 1869, did not understand the nature of totalitarianism and saw everything in terms of his own struggle against the British government. The important point here is not so much that the British treated him forbearingly as that he was always able to command publicity. As can be seen from the phrase quoted above, he believed in "arousing the world", which is only possible if the world gets a chance to hear what you are doing. It is difficult to see how Gandhi's methods could be applied in a country where opponents of the regime disappear in the middle of the night and are never heard of again. Without a free press and the right of assembly, it is impossible not merely to appeal to outside opinion but to bring a mass movement into being, or even to make your intentions known to your adversary. Is there a Gandhi in Russia at this moment? And if there is, what is he accomplishing? The Russian masses could only practise civil disobedience if the same idea happened to occur to all of them simultaneously, and even then, to judge by the history of the Ukraine famine, it would make no difference. But let it be granted that non-violent resistance can be effective against one's own government, or against an occupying power: even so, how does one put it into practice internationally? Gandhi's various conflicting statements on the late war seems to show that he felt the difficulty of this. Applied to foreign politics, pacifism either stops being pacifist or becomes appeasement. Moreover the assumption, which served Gandhi so well in dealing with individuals, that all human beings are more or less approachable and will respond to a generous gesture, needs to be seriously questioned. It is not necessarily true, for example, when you are dealing with lunatics. Then the question becomes: who is sane? Was Hitler sane? And is it not possible for one whole culture to be insane by the standards of another? And, so far as one can gauge the feelings of whole nations, is there any apparent connection between a generous deed and a friendly response? Is gratitude a factor in international politics?

These and kindred questions need discussion, and need it urgently, in the few years left to us before somebody presses the button and the rockets begin to fly. It seems doubtful whether civilization can stand another major war, and it is at least thinkable that the way out lies through non-violence. It is Gandhi's virtue that he would have been ready to give honest consideration to the kind of question that I have raised above – and, indeed, he probably did discuss most of these questions somewhere or other in his innumerable newspaper articles. One feels of him that there was much that he did not understand, but not that there was anything that he was frightened of saying or thinking. I have never been able to feel much liking for Gandhi, but I do not feel sure that as a political thinker he was wrong in the main, nor do I believe that his life was a failure. It is curious that when he was assassinated, many of his warmest admirers exclaimed sorrowfully that he had lived just long enough to see his life work in ruins, because India was engaged in a civil war which had always been foreseen as one of the by-products of the transfer of power. But it was not in trying to smooth down Hindu–Muslim rivalry that Gandhi had spent his life. His main political objective, the peaceful ending of British rule, had after all been attained. As usual, the relevant facts cut across one another. On the one hand, the British did get out of India without fighting, an event which very few observers indeed would have predicted until about a year before it happened. On the other hand, this was done by a Labour government, and it is certain that a Conservative government, especially a government headed by Churchill, would have acted differently. But if, by 1945, there had grown up in Britain a large body of opinion sympathetic to Indian independence, how far was this due to Gandhi's personal influence? And if, as may happen, India and Britain finally settle down into a decent and friendly relationship, will this be partly because Gandhi, by keeping up his struggle obstinately and without hatred, disinfected the political air? That one even thinks of asking such questions indicates his stature. One may feel, as I do, a sort of aesthetic distaste for Gandhi, one may reject the claims of sainthood made on his behalf (he never made any such claim himself, by the way), one may also reject sainthood as an ideal and therefore feel that Gandhi's basic aims were anti-human and reactionary – but regarded simply as a politician, and compared with the other leading political figures of our time, how clean a smell he has managed to leave behind!

Conrad's Place and Rank in English Letters*

I cannot answer at great length, as I am ill in bed, but I am happy to give you my opinions for what they are worth.

1. I regard Conrad as one of the best writers of this century, and – supposing that one can count him as an English writer – one of the very few true novelists that England possesses. His reputation, which was somewhat eclipsed after his death, has risen again during the past ten years, and I have no doubt that the bulk of his work will survive. During his lifetime he suffered by being stamped as a writer of "sea stories", and books like *The Secret Agent* and *Under Western Eyes** went almost unnoticed. Actually Conrad only spent about a third of his life at sea and he had only a sketchy knowledge of the Asiatic countries of which he wrote in *Lord Jim*, *Almayer's Folly*,* etc. What he did have, however, was a sort of grown-upness and political understanding which would have been almost impossible to a native English writer at that time. I consider that his best work belongs to what might be called his middle period, roughly between 1900 and 1914. This period includes *Nostromo*, *Chance*, *Victory*,* the two mentioned above, and several outstanding short stories.

2. Yes, Conrad has definitely a slight exotic flavour to me. That is part of his attraction. In the earlier books, such as *Almayer's Folly*, his English is sometimes definitely incorrect, though not in a way that matters. He used I believe to think in Polish and then translate his thoughts into French and finally into English, and one can sometimes follow the process back at least as far as French, for instance in his tendency to put the adjective after the noun. Conrad was one of those writers who in the present century civilized English literature and brought it back into contact with Europe, from which it had been almost severed for a hundred years. Most of the writers who did this were foreigners, or at any rate not quite English – Eliot and James (Americans), Joyce and Yeats (Irish), and Conrad himself, a transplanted Pole.

The Question of the Pound Award*

I think the Bollingen Foundation were quite right to award Pound the prize, if they believed his poems to be the best of the year, but I think also that one ought to keep Pound's career in memory and not feel that his ideas are made respectable by the mere fact of winning a literary prize.

Because of the general revulsion against Allied war propaganda, there has been – indeed, there was, even before the war was over – a tendency to claim that Pound was "not really" a fascist and an anti-Semite, that he opposed the war on pacifist grounds, and that in any case his political activities only belonged to the war years. Some time ago I saw it stated in an American periodical that Pound only broadcast on the Rome radio when "the balance of his mind was upset", and later (I think in the same periodical) that the Italian government had blackmailed him into broadcasting by threats to relatives. All this is plain falsehood. Pound was an ardent follower of Mussolini as far back as the 1920s, and never concealed it. He was a contributor to Mosley's review the *British Union Quarterly*, and accepted a professorship from the Rome government before the war started. I should say that his enthusiasm was essentially for the Italian form of fascism. He did not seem to be very strongly pro-Nazi or anti-Russian, his real underlying motive being hatred of Britain, America and "the Jews". His broadcasts were disgusting. I remember at least one in which he approved the massacre of the East European Jews and "warned" the American Jews that their turn was coming presently. These broadcasts – I did not hear them, but only read them in the BBC monitoring report – did not give me the impression of being the work of a lunatic. Incidentally I am told that in delivering them Pound used to put on a pronounced American accent which he did not normally have, no doubt with the idea of appealing to the isolationists and playing on anti-British sentiment.

None of this is a reason against giving Pound the Bollingen Prize. There are times when such a thing might be undesirable – it would have been undesirable when the Jews were actually being killed in the gas vans, for instance – but I do not think this is one of them. But since the judges have taken what amounts to the "art for art's sake" position, that is, the position that aesthetic integrity and common decency are two separate things, then at least let us keep them separate and not excuse Pound's political career on the ground that he is a good writer. He *may* be a good writer (I must admit that I personally have always regarded him as an entirely spurious writer), but the opinions that he has tried to disseminate by means of his works are evil ones, and I think that the judges should have said so more firmly when awarding him the prize.

Abbreviations

CE: *Critical Essays* (London: Secker & Warburg, [February] 1946)

CEJL1: *The Collected Essays, Journalism and Letters of George Orwell, Vol. 1: An Age Like This, 1920–1940*, ed. Sonia Orwell and Ian Angus (London: Secker & Warburg, 1968)

CEJL2: *The Collected Essays, Journalism and Letters of George Orwell, Vol. 2: My Country Right or Left, 1940–1943*, ed. Sonia Orwell and Ian Angus (London: Secker & Warburg, 1968)

CEJL3: *The Collected Essays, Journalism and Letters of George Orwell, Vol. 3: As I Please, 1943–1945*, ed. Sonia Orwell and Ian Angus (London: Secker & Warburg, 1968)

CEJL4: *The Collected Essays, Journalism and Letters of George Orwell, Vol. 4: In Front of Your Nose, 1945–1950*, ed. Sonia Orwell and Ian Angus (London: Secker & Warburg, 1968)

CNF: *The Collected Non-Fiction: Essays, Articles, Diaries and Letters, 1903–1950*, ed. Peter Davison (London: Penguin, 2017)

IW: *Inside the Whale and Other Essays* (London: Victor Gollancz, [11th March] 1940)

Note on the Texts

The texts in this edition are taken from CEJL1–4. They are ordered chronologically by date of composition where the information is available, and by date of first publication (or broadcast, if applicable) where it is not. Information regarding date of composition is taken from the editorial apparatus of CNF. (CEJL1–4 also occasionally notes the date of composition separately from that of first publication, but because the underlying methodology is not always transparent, and because the information sometimes clashes with that provided in CNF, the latter has been privileged for dating purposes.) For convenience's sake, the titles of the texts are as given in CEJL1–4. Where a title is not the one that appears in the first published version of a text, an explanation is provided in the headnote.

Notes

p. 3, *A Farthing Newspaper*: First published in *G.K.'s Weekly* (29th December 1928); collected in CEJL1.

p. 3, *Ami du Peuple*: *L'Ami du Peuple* was a right-wing newspaper founded by the perfumier François Coty (1874–1934) in 1928. It ceased publication in 1937.

p. 3, *the Figaro and the Gaulois*: Both French daily newspapers; *Le Gaulois* was taken over by *Le Figaro* in 1929.

p. 4, *"Ici on ne vend pas l'Ami du Peuple"*: "Here the *Ami du Peuple* is not on sale" (French).

p. 4, *Action française... published there*: *L'Action française* was a reactionary newspaper that espoused the restoration of the monarchy in the form of the House of Orléans. *L'Humanité* was in the 1920s the official newspaper of the French Communist Party (Parti Communiste Français; PCF). The weekly newspaper *La Libertà* was the official journal of the Paris-based Italian Anti-Fascist Concentration (Concentrazione Antifascista Italiana; CAI).

p. 4, *the press combine*: The ownership of newspapers by large for-profit companies.

p. 6, *The Spike*: First published in the *Adelphi* (April 1931); later shortened and reworked to form Chapters 27 and 35 of *Down and Out in Paris and London* (Victor Gollancz, 1933); collected in CEJL1. "Spike" was an informal term for a "casual ward", part of a workhouse providing short-term relief for the temporarily destitute, as well as for vagrants.

p. 9, *tommy*: A slang term for food, especially bread.

p. 9, *the Family Herald*: A weekly story paper published from 1843 to 1940, with the subtitle "A Domestic Magazine of Useful Information & Amusement".

p. 9, *Raffles*: A popular series of short stories by the English author E.W. Hornung (1866–1921) published between 1898 and 1909, featuring the character A.J. Raffles, a cricketer and "gentleman thief". Orwell writes about this series in 'Raffles and Miss Blandish' (see pp. 379–88).

p. 10, *one of Scott's novels*: The Scottish writer Sir Walter Scott (1771–1832) was the author of a series of historical tales known as the *Waverley* novels.

p. 10, *pew renter*: One who rents a church pew for exclusive use. Orwell here uses the term figuratively and pejoratively, to refer to a person who, despite being of relatively low status, looks down on those perceived to be socially inferior.

p. 11, *and there was... visiting moon*: Cleopatra's words on the death of Antony in Shakespeare's play (Act IV, Sc. 15, ll. 77–78).

p. 13, *A Hanging*: First published in the *Adelphi* (August 1931); collected in CEJL1.

p. 13, *It was in Burma*: For Orwell's time with the Indian Imperial Police in Burma (known today as Myanmar), see his novel *Burmese Days*, published in New York by Harper & Brothers, 1934.

p. 13, *Dravidian*: A member of one of a number of population groups from southern India and Sri Lanka who speak any of the Dravidian family of languages, once spoken throughout the subcontinent but now restricted to its south.

p. 15, *Ram*: A major Hindu deity, also known as Rama.

p. 15, *Chalo*: "Let's go" (Hindi).

p. 16, *lathis*: Long metal-bound bamboo sticks used as weapons in parts of South Asia, especially by the police.

p. 16, *pannikin*: A small metal drinking cup.

p. 16, *boxwallah*: A term used in British India to mean a street pedlar.

p. 16, *annas*: An anna was one sixteenth of a rupee.

p. 17, *Clink*: Written in August 1932; first published in CEJL1. "Clink" is a slang term for prison, originally the name of a notorious prison in Southwark, south London, destroyed by fire in 1780.

p. 17, *"Yank mag"*: An American pulp magazine.

p. 18, *casual-ward*: See note to p. 6.

p. 19, *Black Maria*: A police vehicle for the transportation of prisoners.

p. 19, *Adeste, fideles... ad Bethlehem, etc.*: The opening lines of the original Latin lyrics to the carol 'O Come, All Ye Faithful', as written by the English hymnist John Francis Wade (1711–86), corresponding to the English lines "O come, all ye faithful, joyful and triumphant! / O come ye, O come ye to Bethlehem."

NOTES

p. 20, *laid an information*: Made a statement to a magistrate.

p. 23, *While the gathering... still is 'igh!*: From the hymn 'Jesus, Lover of My Soul' (1740) by Charles Wesley (1707–88).

p. 23, *Lord Kylsant*: Owen Cosby Philipps, 1st Baron Kylsant (1863–1937), was an MP, initially for the Liberal Party and later for the Conservatives, and a businessman in the shipping industry. In 1931 he was sentenced to twelve months' imprisonment for circulating a false prospectus while chairman of the Royal Mail Steam Packet Company.

p. 25, *Common Lodging Houses*: First published in the *New Statesman and Nation* (3rd September 1932); collected in CEJL1.

p. 25, *the LCC*: The London County Council.

p. 25, *such as the Rowton Houses*: A chain of London hostels founded by the philanthropist Montagu Corry, 1st Baron Rowton (1838–1903). The first was opened in Vauxhall in 1892.

p. 28, *On Kipling's Death*: First published in the *New English Weekly* under the title 'Rudyard Kipling' (23rd January 1936); collected in CEJL1 under the present title. The English poet and novelist Rudyard Kipling (b. 1865) died on 18th January 1836.

p. 28, *'The Strange Ride'... 'The Mark of the Beast'*: Three of Kipling's British India-set tales. 'The Strange Ride of Morrowbie Jukes' was first published in *Quartette*, the Christmas annual of the *Civil and Military Gazette*, in 1885, and later appeared in the collection *The Phantom 'Rickshaw and other Eerie Tales* (1888). 'The Drums of the Fore and Aft' was first published in Kipling's *Wee Willie Winkie and Other Child Stories* (1889). 'The Mark of the Beast' was first published in the *Pioneer* in July 1890 and collected in *Life's Handicap* in 1891.

p. 28, *I've lost... Lalage!*: From Kipling's 'Rimini' (1906), subtitled "Marching Song of a Roman Legion of the Later Empire" (ll. 10–12). Rimini is a port on the eastern Adriatic coast of Italy.

p. 28, *'The Road to Mandalay'*: Kipling's poem 'Mandalay' (1890), written from the perspective of a working-class cockney soldier who reminisces about his time in colonial Burma. Mandalay was the capital of Burma until 1885.

p. 28, *Lord Beaverbrook*: Max Aitken, 1st Baron Beaverbrook (1879–1964), was a Canadian-British newspaper publisher and a highly influential figure in British media and politics during the first half of the twentieth century, owning several newspapers, including the *Daily Express*.

p. 30, *Shooting an Elephant*: First published in *New Writing* (Autumn 1936); reprinted in *Penguin New Writing* (November 1940); broadcast on the BBC Home Service on 12th October 1948; collected in CEJL1.

p. 30, *Moulmein*: The fourth-largest city in Burma, now known as Mawlamyine.

p. 30, *betel juice*: A red fluid produced by chewing a preparation of betel (areca) nuts and leaves.

p. 30, *in sæcula sæculorum*: "For ever and ever" (Latin) – a liturgical formula, often used at the end of a prayer.

p. 31, *in terrorem*: "As a warning" (Latin).

p. 31, *mahout*: An elephant keeper or rider.

p. 33, *sahib*: A polite form of address for a gentleman (Urdu).

p. 35, *dahs*: Short, heavy swords used in Burma.

p. 35, *Coringhee coolie*: An outdated term for a Telugu-speaking labourer from Coastal Andhra in India; "Coringhee" comes from Korangi, a village on the Coromandel coast.

p. 36, *In Defence of the Novel*: First published in the *New English Weekly* (12th and 19th November 1936); collected in CEJL1.

p. 36, *Belloc's queerly rancorous essay*: Hilaire Belloc (1870–1953) was a French-English writer, orator, politician and historian. It is not clear which essay Orwell refers to here, but Belloc often expresses a preference for verse and essays over the novel in his work; for example, in his essay 'On an Unknown Country' he writes: "All that can best be expressed in words should be expressed in verse."

p. 37, *Rupert Brooke... Gerard Manley Hopkins*: The English poets Rupert Brooke (1887–1915) and Gerard Manley Hopkins (1844–89).

p. 37, *Beachcomber's column*: This refers to "By the Way", a long-running humorous column in the *Daily Express* written under the pen name "Beachcomber". J.B. Morton (1893–1979) authored the column from 1924 to 1975, succeeding D.B. Wyndham Lewis (1891–1969).

p. 38, *The Constant Nymph*: A bestselling 1924 novel by Margaret Kennedy (1896–1967).

p. 38, *Ethel M. Dell's Way of an Eagle*: The bestselling romantic novel *The Way of an Eagle* (1911) by Ethel M. Dell (1881–1939), whose work enjoyed a loyal and devoted following among the reading public but was derided by critics. Orwell also mentions Dell in the essay 'Bookshop Memories' (see p. 42), and the protagonist of *Keep the Aspidistra Flying* (1936) makes several disparaging comments about her.

p. 38, *The Man of Property*: Published in 1906, *The Man of Property* is the first volume in the trilogy known as *The Forsyte Saga*, about the fortunes of a large upper-middle-class English family, by the English novelist and playwright John Galsworthy (1867–1933).

p. 38, *sic itur ad Gould*: "Thus one journeys to Gould" (Latin). The usual phrase is *sic itur ad astra* ("thus one journeys to the stars"), a phrase from Virgil's *Aeneid* (IX, l. 641). Gerald Gould (1885–1936) was an influential novel reviewer for the *Observer*, who died around the time this piece was published.

p. 38, *of the earth earthy*: "The first man is of the earth, earthy: the second man is the Lord from heaven" (1 Corinthians 15:47). The boilerplate phrase "of the earth earthy" was a review-writing cliché in Orwell's day.

p. 39, *the Criterion–Scrutiny assumption*: The *Criterion* and *Scrutiny: A Quarterly Review* were both influential literary journals. The *Criterion*, which was founded and edited by the American-born British poet T.S. Eliot (1888–1965) and published from 1922 to 1939, is subject to both criticism and praise elsewhere in Orwell's writing: in a 1935 letter to a friend he wrote "for pure snootiness it beats anything I have ever seen", but in 1944 in his 'As I Please' column in *Tribune* he referred to it as "possibly the best literary paper we have ever had". *Scrutiny* was founded by the English literary critics L.C. Knights (1906–97) and F.R. Leavis (1895–1978) in 1932, with the latter remaining its principal editor until it ceased publication in 1953.

p. 39, *Trollope... Maugham*: The English novelist Anthony Trollope (1815–82); the English novelist and dramatist Charles Reade (1814–84), best known for his 1861 historical novel *The Cloister and the Hearth* – see Orwell's essay 'Charles Reade' (pp. 173–75); and the English novelist, short-story writer and playwright W. Somerset Maugham (1874–1965), known for works including *Of Human Bondage* (1915) and *The Moon and Sixpence* (1919).

p. 39, *Ralph Straus*: The literary critic, novelist and biographer Ralph Straus (1882–1950), who was chief fiction reviewer for the *Sunday Times* from 1928 until his death.

p. 39, *Peg's Paper*: A weekly women's magazine with a focus on romantic fiction, published from 1919 to 1940.

p. 39, *Raffles... La Chartreuse de Parme*: For *Raffles*, see third note to p. 9 and the essay 'Raffles and Miss Blandish', pp. 379–88. *The Island of Dr Moreau* is an 1896 science-fiction novel by the English novelist H.G. Wells (1866–1946). *La Chartreuse de Parme* is an 1839 novel by the French novelist Stendhal, pseudonym of Marie Henri Beyle (1783–1842). It was translated into English as *The Charterhouse of Parma*.

p. 39, *If Winter Comes... Sir Launcelot Greaves*: *If Winter Comes* is a bestselling 1921 novel by the English novelist A.S.M. Hutchinson (1879–1971). *The Well-Beloved* is a work by Thomas Hardy (1840–1928), first serialized in 1892 and published as a book in 1897. It is generally considered a minor work in relation to Hardy's better-known novels. *An Unsocial Socialist* is the first novel by the Irish playwright George Bernard Shaw (1856–1950), serialized in 1884 and published as a book in 1887. *The Life and Adventures of Sir Launcelot Greaves* is a picaresque novel by the Scottish writer and surgeon Tobias Smollett (1721–71), serialized in 1760–61 and published as a book in 1762. For Smollett, see Orwell's essay 'Tobias Smollett: Scotland's Best Novelist' (pp. 398–401).

p. 40, *the Lord promised... there*: See Genesis 18:16–33.

p. 40, *with no straws in their hair*: That is, who are not mentally deranged.

p. 40, *Manon Lescaut*: The novel *Histoire du Chevalier des Grieux, et de Manon Lescaut* (1731) by the French writer the Abbé Prévost (1697–1763), published in English in 1934 as *The Story of the Chevalier des Grieux and Manon Lescaut*.

p. 40, *David Copperfield*: The famous novel by the English novelist Charles Dickens (1812–70), serialized in 1849–50 and published as a book in 1850 (Bradbury & Evans).

p. 41, *Bookshop Memories*: First published in *Fortnightly* (November 1936); collected in CEJL1.

p. 42, *the Japanese earthquake*: The Tokyo-Yokohama earthquake that struck the main Japanese island of Honshu on 1st September 1923, devastating Tokyo and killing an estimated 140,000 people.

p. 42, *"remainders"*: Copies of a book sold off by the publisher at a reduced price after demand has fallen.

p. 42, *Petronius Arbiter*: Gaius Petronius Arbiter (d. 66 AD), the likely author of the *Satyricon*, a bawdy novel set in first-century-AD Rome.

p. 42, *Barrie*: The Scottish novelist and playwright J.M. Barrie (1860–1937), best known as the creator of Peter Pan, who featured in the play *Peter Pan, or The Boy Who Wouldn't Grow Up* (1904) and the children's novel *Peter and Wendy* (1911).

p. 42, *Priestley?... third*: Orwell's four suggested writers are the English novelist, playwright and social commentator J.B. Priestley (1894–1984), the American novelist and short-story writer Ernest Hemingway (1899–1961), the bestselling but largely forgotten English novelist Hugh Walpole (1884–1941) and the English writer of humorous novels and short stories P.G. Wodehouse (1881–1975). For Ethel M. Dell, see second note to p. 38. Warwick Deeping (1877–1950) was an English novelist and short-story writer, best known for the bestselling novel *Sorrell and Son* (1925). The English writer Jeffery Farnol (1878–1952) was the author of more than forty romance novels set mostly in the Georgian and Regency periods.

p. 43, *People know... "back parts" of the Lord*: Bill Sikes and Wilkins Micawber are characters in, respectively, Dickens's *Oliver Twist* (serialized in 1837–39 and published as a book in 1838 by Richard Bentley) and *David Copperfield*. The biblical allusion is to Exodus 33:23: "And I will take away mine hand, and thou shalt see my back parts: but my face shall not be seen."

p. 43, *de métier*: "By profession" (French).

p. 44, *Boswell's Decline and Fall... T.S. Eliot*: The hypothetical bookseller confuses, first, *The Life of Samuel Johnson* (1791) by the Scottish author James Boswell (1740–95) – a biography of the English lexicographer, writer and critic Samuel Johnson (1709–84) – with the monumental *History of the Decline and Fall of the Roman Empire* (1776–88) by the English historian Edward Gibbon (1737–94), and then the English novelist George Eliot (1819–80) – the pen name of Mary Ann Evans – with the poet T.S. Eliot.

p. 44, *the Girl's Own Paper*: A story paper catering to girls and young women, published from 1880 until 1956.

p. 45, *Spilling the Spanish Beans*: First published in the *New English Weekly* (29th July and 2nd September 1937); collected in CEJL1.

p. 45, *the News Chronicle*: A daily paper formed by the merger of the *Daily News* and the *Daily Chronicle* in 1930; it ceased publication in 1960, when it was absorbed into the *Daily Mail*.

p. 45, *the Daily Worker*: Founded in 1930 by the Communist Party of Great Britain, and renamed the *Morning Star* in 1966.

p. 45, *Garvin*: The journalist J.L. Garvin (1868–1947), editor of the *Observer* from 1908 to 1942.

p. 45, *The real struggle... taking it away from them*: A reference to the schisms and divisions within the loose coalition of left-wing factions that had formed in Spain ostensibly to fight the Nationalists led by General Francisco Franco (1892–1975), and in particular of the conflict between anarcho-syndicalist (that is, revolutionary trade-unionist) groups and the Soviet-backed International Brigades.

p. 46, *Wyndham Lewis*: The Vorticist artist and novelist Wyndham Lewis (1882–1957). His 1937 novel *The Revenge for Love*, set in the period leading up to the Spanish Civil War, was strongly critical of communist activity in Spain.

p. 46, *la carrière ouverte aux talents*: A maxim espoused by Napoleon Bonaparte, literally meaning "career open to talents", meaning a meritocratic system in which people are employed and rewarded according to their talents rather than their class or connections.

p. 46, *Barnum and Bailey*: The American showman P.T. Barnum (1810–91) and circus manager James Anthony Bailey (1847–1906) merged their companies to found the Barnum & Bailey Circus in 1881, a travelling circus and freak show billed as "the Greatest Show on Earth".

p. 48, *Tweedledum and Tweedledee*: Characters in an English nursery rhyme who appear as two almost identical-looking fat little men in *Through the Looking Glass* (1871) by Lewis Carroll, pseudonym of Charles Lutwidge Dodgson (1832–98).

p. 48, *a Trotskyist*: An adherent of the political or economic principles associated with Leon Trotsky (1879–1940), one of the architects, along with Lenin, of the Russian Revolution of 1917, and who was expelled from the Communist Party by Stalin in 1927.

p. 49, *the POUM... the English ILP*: The United Workers' Marxist Party (Partido Obrero de Unificación Marxista; POUM) was an anti-Stalinist militia linked to Britain's Independent Labour Party (ILP), a political party founded in 1893. The ILP was further to the left than the Labour Representation Committee, founded in 1900 and later rechristened the Labour Party, although the two parties were affiliated between 1906 and 1932. (In 1975, the ILP rejoined the Labour Party.) See Orwell's article 'Why I Joined the Independent Labour Party' (pp. 51–52).

p. 49, *Caballero*: The Spanish politician and trade unionist Francisco Largo Caballero (1869–1946), who served as prime minister of Spain from September 1936 to May 1937.

p. 50, *Colonel Blimps*: Colonel Blimp – a pompous nationalist with distinctive walrus moustache – was a famous cartoon character created in 1934 by New Zealand artist David Low (1891–1963) for Lord Beaverbrook's *Evening Standard*.

p. 51, *Why I Joined the Independent Labour Party*: First published in the *New Leader* under the title 'Why I Join the ILP' (24th June 1938); collected in CEJL1 under the present title.

p. 52, *the POUM*: See first note to p. 49.

p. 53, *Marrakech*: Written by 12th April 1939; first published in *New Writing* (Christmas 1939); collected in CEJL1.

p. 55, *mon vieux*: "Old chap" (French).

p. 57, *NCOs*: Non-commissioned officers.

p. 58, *Not Counting Niggers*: First published in the *Adelphi* (July 1939); collected in CEJL1. This article is a review of the book *Union Now* by the American *New York Times* journalist Clarence Streit (1896–1986), which called for a federal union of fifteen of the world's major democracies, published in March 1939.

p. 59, *the Left Book Club*: A publishing imprint and subscription book club pioneered by the dedicated socialist Victor Gollancz (1893–1967), publisher of several of Orwell's books. It ran from 1936 to 1948, supplying a book to its members each month.

p. 59, *Czechoslovakia... written*: The country of Czechoslovakia, created in the aftermath of the First World War out of the northern part of the former Austro-Hungarian Empire, disintegrated following the Nazi annexation of the majority-German Sudetenland in September 1938.

p. 62, *Democracy in the British Army*: First published in the *Left Forum* (September 1939); collected in CEJL1.

p. 62, *When the Duke of Wellington... enlisted for drink*: This famous remark attributed to the English soldier and statesman Arthur Wellesley, Duke of Wellington (1769–1852), is said to have been made at a banquet following the British victory against the French at the Battle of Vitoria, fought on 21st June 1813.

p. 62, *The war scare... the Territorials*: Public anxiety in Britain at the prospect of a French invasion in the 1860s led to the creation of the Volunteer Force, a citizen army of part-time rifle, artillery and engineer corps raised across the country for home defence. It was a forerunner of the Territorial Army, founded in 1908.

p. 64, *Hore-Belisha*: Leslie Hore-Belisha (1893–1957) was a politician who belonged initially to the Liberal Party and was then an MP and Cabinet minister for the National Liberal Party. He was Secretary of State for War in 1937–40 in the coalition government led by the Conservative statesman Neville Chamberlain (1869–1940), and later joined the Conservative Party. He was responsible for the reintroduction of conscription via the Military Training Act of May 1939,

NOTES

which, initially intended as a temporary measure, required men of twenty and twenty-one to undertake six months of full-time military training, after which they would be transferred to the Army Reserve.

p. 64, *the OTC*: The Officers' Training Corps, British Army reserve units formally established in 1908 to focus on training and leadership development. The OTC initially comprised a junior division in public schools and a senior division in the universities.

p. 64, *the Military Training Act*: See first note to this page.

p. 66, *Boys' Weeklies*: First published (in abridged form) in *Horizon* (March 1940); republished in a slightly revised version in IW; collected in CEJL1.

p. 67, *Billy Bunter*: A fictional schoolboy, a pupil at Greyfriars School in Kent (also fictional), created by the English writer Charles Hamilton (1876–1961), who wrote under the pseudonym Frank Richards. Bunter originally appeared in the children's story paper the *Magnet* between 1908 and 1940, and would later, from 1947, feature in a series of novels.

p. 67, *Sexton Blake and Nelson Lee*: Both fictional detectives who remained popular for several decades in the early twentieth century. The character of Sexton Blake was created by Hal Meredeth, pseudonym of Harry Blyth (1852–98), in 1893 and subsequently appeared in various story papers, comic strips, novels and films, as well as a 1960s television series. Nelson Lee was created in 1894 by Maxwell Scott, pseudonym of John William Staniforth (1863–1927), and featured in the Amalgamated Press papers for around forty years.

p. 68, *The stories in... week*: This is quite incorrect. These stories have been written throughout the whole period by "Frank Richards" and "Martin Clifford", who are one and the same person! See articles in *Horizon*, May 1940, and *Summer Pie*, summer 1944 [ORWELL'S NOTE, 1945].

p. 69, *Tarzan*: The central character in a series of popular stories and novels by the American author Edgar Rice Burroughs (1875–1950) about the son of an English nobleman who is raised by a tribe of great apes in the African jungle and subsequently becomes a heroic adventurer.

p. 70, *St Winifred's and Tom Brown's School Days*: Two novels of public-school life: *St Winifred's, or The World of School* (1862), by the English cleric and schoolmaster Frederic W. Farrar (1831–1903), and *Tom Brown's School Days* (1857), by the English lawyer, politician and author Thomas Hughes (1822–96), set at Rugby School in Warwickshire.

p. 70, *Gunby Hadath, Desmond Coke*: The authors and schoolmasters John Edward Gunby Hadath (1871–1954) and Desmond Coke (1879–1931), both known for their juvenile fiction set in English public schools.

p. 70, *Stalky & Co.*: An 1899 collection of boarding-school stories by Rudyard Kipling.

p. 70, *"frabjous"*: This word in fact comes from Lewis Carroll, specifically from the nonsense poem 'Jabberwocky' that appears in *Through the Looking Glass* (see first note to p. 48): "And hast thou slain the Jabberwock? / Come to my arms, my beamish boy! / O frabjous day! Callooh! Callay!" (ll. 21–23).

p. 70, *"Greyfriars" is probably taken from Thackeray*: In the novels *The History of Pendennis* (1848–50) and *The Newcomes* (1855) by the English novelist William Makepeace Thackeray (1811–63), "Greyfriars" is a fictionalized version of Charterhouse School in Surrey, which Thackeray himself attended.

p. 72, *Both papers are... girls*: There are several corresponding girls' papers. The *Schoolgirl* is companion paper to the *Magnet* and has stories by "Hilda Richards". The characters are interchangeable to some extent. Bessie Bunter, Billy Bunter's sister, figures in the *Schoolgirl* [ORWELL'S NOTE]. "Hilda Richards" was another pseudonym used by Hamilton (for whom, see first note to p. 67).

p. 72, *the Shell*: Like "the Remove", a term denoting an intermediate form in English public-school jargon.

p. 73, *"knut"*: A fashionable, showy young man.

p. 74, *Lord Peter Wimsey*: The protagonist of a series of detective novels and short stories by Dorothy L. Sayers (1893–1957).

p. 74, *the ARP*: Air Raid Precautions, a programme established in the late 1930s to protect civilians from air raids during the Second World War.

p. 75, *until the war actually starts*: This was written some months before the outbreak of war. Up to the end of September 1939 no mention of the war has appeared in either paper [ORWELL'S NOTE].

p. 81, *Sax Rohmer*: The popular novelist Sax Rohmer, pseudonym of the English novelist Arthur Henry Sarsfield Ward (1883–1959), best known for his mystery novels and short stories featuring the Chinese villain Dr Fu Manchu.

p. 83, *Ruby M. Ayres's column of advice in the Oracle*: The prolific English romance novelist Ruby Mildred Ayres (1881–1955) wrote an advice column in the *Oracle* in the 1930s.

p. 84, *Sapper*: Pseudonym of Herman Cyril McNeile (1888–1937), an English soldier and author known for his war stories and thrillers, notably *Bulldog Drummond* (1920).

p. 84, *Ian Hay*: The English novelist, historian, schoolmaster and soldier Ian Hay, pseudonym of John Hay Beith (1876–1952).

p. 84, *Lord Camrose*: The newspaper magnate William Ewart Berry, 1st Viscount Camrose (1879–1954).

p. 85, *the Soviet film Chapaiev*: A 1934 Soviet war film, directed by the brothers Georgi (1899–1946) and Sergei Vasilyev (1900–59), set during the Russian Civil War (1918–21), fought between the Bolshevik Red Army and the counter-revolutionary White Russians. It was based on the novel of the same name by the Bolshevik Dmitry Furmanov (1891–1926).

p. 86, *mushroom libraries*: That is, the cheap lending libraries that proliferated in Britain between the wars.

p. 87, *Charles Dickens*: First published in IW; collected in CEJL1.

p. 87, *Chesterton*: The English literary critic, Roman Catholic convert and writer of fiction G.K. Chesterton (1874–1936).

p. 87, *a Marxist writer... revolutionary*: The book referred to here is *Charles Dickens: The Progress of a Radical* (1937) by the English communist writer T.A. Jackson (1879–1955).

p. 87, *Nadezhda Krupskaya... Lenin*: Nadezhda Krupskaya (1869–1939) was the wife of Vladimir Lenin. Her memoir of her life with Lenin was published in Russian in 1926 and translated into English in 1930 as *Memories of Lenin*.

p. 87, *The Cricket on the Hearth*: One of Dickens's Christmas books, published in December 1845 (Bradbury & Evans).

p. 87, *Mr Bechhofer Roberts... Idolatry*: *This Side Idolatry* is a 1928 novel based on the life of Charles Dickens by the English author C.E. Bechhofer Roberts (1894–1949).

p. 87, *which no more invalidate... Hamlet*: In his will, signed on 25th March 1616, Shakespeare famously bequeathed to his wife, Anne (née Hathaway), his "second-best bed" and nothing else, something that has traditionally been interpreted as a snub.

p. 87, *Gissing*: The English novelist George Gissing (1857–1903), known for his realist novels about the lower middle classes, notably *New Grub Street* (1891), a novel about life on the destitute margins of London literary life. Gissing published *Charles Dickens: A Critical Study* in 1898, and wrote several journal articles on the author and introductions to editions of the works. He also edited a 1903 revised edition of John Forster's biography (see note to p. 105). See Orwell's essay 'George Gissing' (pp. 617–23).

p. 88, *Oliver Twist... Little Dorrit*: For *Oliver Twist*, see first note to p. 43. *Hard Times* was serialized and published as a book in 1854 (Bradbury & Evans). *Bleak House* was serialized in 1852–53 and published as a book in 1853 (Bradbury & Evans). *Little Dorrit* was serialized in 1855–57 and published as a book in 1857 (Bradbury & Evans).

p. 88, *Mr Creakle... Serjeant Buzfuz*: Characters in, respectively, *David Copperfield* and *The Pickwick Papers*.

p. 88, *the Peggottys*: A family in *David Copperfield*.

p. 88, *Bill Sikes, Sam Weller and Mrs Gamp*: Characters in, respectively: *Oliver Twist*; *The Posthumous Papers of the Pickwick Club* (known as *The Pickwick Papers*), Dickens's first novel, serialized in 1836–37 and published as a book in 1837 (Chapman & Hall); and *Martin Chuzzlewit*, serialized in 1843–44 and published as a book in 1844 (Chapman & Hall).

p. 89, *Charles Reade*: See second note to p. 39 and the essay 'Charles Reade' (pp. 173–75).

p. 89, *Our Mutual Friend*: Serialized in 1864–65 and published as a book in 1865 (Chapman & Hall).

p. 89, *Macaulay*: The English historian, essayist, poet and Whig politician Thomas Babington Macaulay (1800–59).

p. 90, *Squeers or Micawber*: Characters in *Nicholas Nickleby* (serialized in 1838–39 and published as a book in 1839 by Chapman & Hall) and *David Copperfield*, respectively.

p. 90, *Mr Pickwick*: The protagonist of *The Pickwick Papers*.

p. 90, *the Cheerybles... Scrooge*: Respectively, Charles and Ned Cheeryble, two characters in *Nicholas Nickleby*; the eponymous hero of *Martin Chuzzlewit*; and the miserly but ultimately repentant protagonist of *A Christmas Carol*, published in 1843 (Chapman & Hall).

p. 90, *A Tale of Two Cities... Great Expectations*: The first was serialized and published as a book in 1859 (Chapman & Hall), the second serialized in 1860–61 and published as a book in 1861 (Chapman & Hall).

p. 90, *Our Mutual Friend*: Serialized in 1864–65 and published as a book in 1865 (Chapman & Hall).

p. 91, *Barnaby Rudge*: Serialized and published as a book in 1841 (Chapman & Hall).

p. 92, *The Gordon Riots of 1780*: A period of civil disorder and violent rioting in London, lasting from 2nd to 8th June 1780. It was sparked by the presentation by Lord George Gordon (1751–93) of a petition to Parliament against recent concessions to Catholics.

p. 93, *Reign of Terror*: The bloodiest period of the French Revolution, from September 1793 to July 1794, during which the radical Jacobins, led by Maximilien de Robespierre (1758–94), ruthlessly executed anyone considered an enemy.

p. 93, *The Scarlet Pimpernel*: A 1905 historical novel by the Hungarian-born British author Baroness Orczy (1865–1947), set during the Reign of Terror. Orczy went on to write a series of novels featuring the Scarlet Pimpernel, the name assumed by an English nobleman who rescued French aristocrats from the guillotine, always evading capture.

p. 96, *"solemnly tried at... seen"*: From Chapter 51 of *Great Expectations*.

p. 96, *The Fairchild Family*: *The History of the Fairchild Family* by the English writer Mary Martha Sherwood (1775–1851) was a bestselling series of children's books published between 1818 and 1847.

p. 97, *"Let dogs delight... bite"*: The first line of the didactic poem 'Against Quarrelling and Fighting' by the English hymnist and poet Isaac Watts (1674–1748), published in the collection *Divine Songs: Attempted in Easy Language for the Use of Children* in 1777.

p. 97, *Doctor Blimber's Academy... Mr Wopsle's great-aunt*: Doctor Blimber's Academy, Salem House and Dotheboys Hall are boarding schools in *Dombey and Son* – serialized in 1846–48 and published as a book in 1848 – *David Copperfield* and *Nicholas Nickleby*, respectively. Noah Claypole and Uriah

Heep are characters in *Oliver Twist* and *David Copperfield*, respectively. In *Great Expectations*, the great-aunt of the small-town church clerk Mr Wopsle runs a chaotic and ineffective evening school.

p. 98, *"I wander through each charter'd street"*: The first line of the poem 'London' by the English artist and poet William Blake (1757–1827), published in *Songs of Experience* in 1794.

p. 99, *Arnold Bennett*: The English novelist, playwright and author of self-help books Arnold Bennett (1867–1931), best known for his novels set in the Staffordshire Potteries ("the Five Towns"), notably *Anna of the Five Towns* (1902).

p. 99, *omnium gatherum*: A cod-Latin term meaning a confused medley.

p. 100, *Circumlocution Office*: A satirical term coined in Dickens's *Little Dorrit* to refer to a bureaucratic government department run by incompetent officials for their own benefit.

p. 100, *the money-grubbing Smilesian line*: A reference to the Scottish author Samuel Smiles (1812–1904), who famously argued in works such as *Self-Help* (1859) for the importance of thrift and self-reliance, and that material progress is best achieved through individual enterprise.

p. 101, *Vanity Fair*: Thackeray's most famous novel, serialized in 1847–48 and published as a book in 1848 (Bradbury & Evans).

p. 101, *Major Pendennis and Rawdon Crawley*: Characters from Thackeray's *The History of Pendennis* and *Vanity Fair*, respectively.

p. 102, *the Quarterly Review*: A literary and political periodical published by John Murray between 1809 and 1967.

p. 102, *John Bull... yeoman*: A character depicted in literature and political caricature as the personification of England, originating in satirical works of the early eighteenth century.

p. 102, *Charles Kingsley*: The Revd Charles Kingsley (1819–75) was a Church of England priest, academic, historian and novelist. While in his lifetime he was known primarily as an advocate of social reform, he is now remembered chiefly as the author of the classic children's book *The Water-Babies* (1863).

p. 102, *Tom Hughes*: See first note to p. 70.

p. 103, *I say to... so*: From Thackeray's humorous 1841 essay 'Memorials of Gormandizing', published in *Fraser's Magazine* in June 1941.

p. 103, *Gide's Retour de l'URSS*: A 1936 travel memoir and reflection on Soviet society by the French writer André Gide (1869–1951). It was published in English as *Return from the USSR*.

p. 104, *The ways were... etc.*: From *A Christmas Carol* ("Stave Four").

p. 104, *It Is Never Too Late to Mend*: An 1856 novel by Charles Reade – for whom, see second note to p. 39 and the essay 'Charles Reade' (pp. 173–75).

p. 105, *Forster's Life*: *The Life of Charles Dickens* (1872) by the English writer John Forster (1812–76) was the first biography of Dickens, published two years after the writer's death.

p. 106, *jeune premier*: Literally, "young first" (French), that is, the male juvenile lead in a play.

p. 106, *The People of... Barton*: Orwell has mistaken the author's name here: *The People of Clopton*, published in 1897, is by George Bartram, a pseudonym of the English author Henry Atton (1853–1915).

p. 106, *The Three Clerks and The Small House at Allington*: Novels published in 1857 and 1864, respectively.

p. 107, *Meredith... Meredith's*: The English novelist and poet George Meredith (1828–1909) is best known for works including *The Ordeal of Richard Feverel* (1859) and *The Egoist* (1879). *Rhoda Fleming* was published in 1865. *A Shabby Genteel Story* is an unfinished novel by Thackeray written around 1840 and published in the collection *Miscellanies* (1857).

p. 109, *Smollett*: See sixth note to p. 39 and Orwell's essay 'Tobias Smollett: Scotland's Best Novelist' (pp. 398–401).

p. 110, *Even when Joyce... at that*: A reference to Leopold Bloom, the protagonist of the modernist novel *Ulysses* (1922) by the Irish writer James Joyce (1882–1941).

p. 110, *Orley Farm*: A novel by Anthony Trollope, published in 1861–62.

p. 111, *A Tale of... numbers*: *Hard Times* was published as a serial in *Household Words* and *Great Expectations* and *A Tale of Two Cities* in *All the Year Round*. Forster says that the shortness of the weekly instalments made it "much more difficult to get sufficient interest into each". Dickens himself complained of the lack of "elbow room". In other words, he had to stick more closely to the story [ORWELL'S NOTE].

p. 112, *Leech's illustrations to Surtees*: R.S. Surtees (1805–64) was an English sports writer, magazine editor and novelist, best remembered as the creator of the popular comic character Jorrocks, a plain-speaking cockney grocer devoted to fox hunting. Several of Surtees's novels were illustrated by the English caricaturist and illustrator John Leech (1817–64).

p. 113, *Tennyson*: The English poet Alfred, Lord Tennyson (1809–92).

p. 114, *Harry Gowan*: Henry Gowan is a character in Dickens's *Little Dorrit*. He is not referred to as "Harry" in the novel, so this is likely an error on Orwell's part.

p. 114, *Hard Cash*: An 1863 novel by Charles Reade – for whom, see second note to p. 39 and the essay 'Charles Reade' (pp. 173–75).

p. 114, *the Diamond Sculls at Henley*: The Diamond Challenge Sculls is a rowing race at the annual Henley Royal Regatta on the River Thames.

p. 115, *Squire Western*: A character from the picaresque novel *The History of Tom Jones, a Foundling* (1749) by the English novelist and playwright Henry Fielding (1707–54).

p. 115, *Bulwer-Lytton*: The English novelist, dramatist and politician Edward Bulwer-Lytton (1803–73), whose best-known fictional works include *The Last Days of Pompeii* (1834) and *Harold, the Last of the Saxon Kings* (1848).

p. 116, *'Ye Mariners of England', 'The Charge of the Light Brigade'*: Respectively, a war song by the Scottish poet Thomas Campbell (1777–1844) and Tennyson's famous poem describing the bungled cavalry charge at the Battle of Balaclava (1854) in the Crimean War.

p. 117, *Sweeney Todd*: The fictional "Demon Barber of Fleet Street", a barber who murders his customers, who first appeared in the penny-dreadful serial *The String of Pearls* (1846–47), and has since become part of London folklore.

p. 119, *Barham*: The Church of England cleric, novelist and humorous poet Richard Harris Barham (1788–1845), best known as the author of *The Ingoldsby Legends* (1837), a popular collection of stories and poetry that claimed to be by "Thomas Ingoldsby of Tappington Manor".

p. 119, *Marryat*: The novelist and Royal Navy officer Frederick Marryat (1792–1848), known as "Captain Marryat", remembered for his sea stories, including *Mr Midshipman Easy* (1836), and his children's novel *The Children of the New Forest* (1847).

p. 121, *Miss Mowcher*: Dickens turned Miss Mowcher into a sort of heroine because the real woman whom he had caricatured had read the earlier chapters and was bitterly hurt. He had previously meant her to play a villainous part. But *any* action by such a character would seem incongruous [ORWELL'S NOTE].

p. 122, *Manon Lescaut... Wuthering Heights*: For *Manon Lescaut*, see third note to p. 40. *Salammbô* is a novel by the French writer Gustave Flaubert (1821–80), published in French in 1862 and in English in 1886. *Carmen* is a novella by the French writer Prosper Mérimée (1803–70), the source material for the opera of the same name by Georges Bizet (1838–75), first performed in 1875. *Wuthering Heights* is the only novel by the English writer Emily Brontë (1818–48), published in 1847.

p. 122, *Aldous Huxley*: The English novelist Aldous Huxley (1894–1963), known among other things for his dystopian novel *Brave New World* (1932). He taught French at Eton College when Orwell was a pupil there.

p. 122, *Pierre Bezukhov*: The protagonist of the epic novel *War and Peace* (1869) by the Russian writer Leo Tolstoy (1828–1910).

p. 122, *Bloom... Mr Polly*: For Bloom, see first note to p. 110. Juste Romain Cyrille Pécuchet is one of the main characters in Flaubert's unfinished comic novel *Bouvard et Pécuchet* (published posthumously in 1881), about two clerks who make use of a legacy to pursue multiple scientific and intellectual endeavours, with disastrous consequences. Alfred Polly is the protagonist of H.G. Wells's comic novel *The History of Mr Polly* (1910).

p. 123, *Dickens's can be... card*: Two series of cigarette cards (collectable trading cards included in packets of cigarettes) entitled "Characters from Dickens" were issued by the tobacco and cigarette manufacturer John Player & Sons in 1913, and reissued as a single series in 1923.

p. 123, *Frank Fairlegh... Mrs Caudle's Curtain Lectures*: Respectively, an 1850 work by the English novelist Frank E. Smedley (1818–64), an 1853 novel by the English clergyman and writer Edward Bradley (1827–89), published under the pseudonym "Cuthbert Bede", and a satirical collection of domestic monologues by the English dramatist and writer Douglas William Jerrold (1803–57), originally featured in *Punch* and published as a book in 1846.

p. 123, *Dubliners... Portrait of the Artist*: Joyce's mostly conventional short-story collection *Dubliners* (1914) was followed first by the semi-autobiographical novel *A Portrait of the Artist as a Young Man* (1916), and then by the modernist *Ulysses*. *Finnegans Wake*, his final and most experimental work, was published in 1939.

p. 124, *he was essentially... will*: In his last will and testament, written on 12th May 1869, Dickens wrote: "I commit my soul to the mercy of God through our Lord and Saviour Jesus Christ, and I exhort my dear children humbly to try to guide themselves by the teaching of the New Testament in its broad spirit, and to put no faith in any man's narrow construction of its letter here or there."

p. 124, *religion in the... thoughts*: From a letter to his youngest son (in 1868): "You will remember that you have never at home been harassed about religious observances, or mere formalities. I have always been anxious not to weary my children with such things, before they are old enough to form opinions respecting them. You will therefore understand the better that I now most solemnly impress upon you the truth and beauty of the Christian Religion, as it came from Christ Himself, and the impossibility of your going far wrong if you humbly but heartily respect it. [...] Never abandon the wholesome practice of saying your own private prayers, night and morning. I have never abandoned it myself, and I know the comfort of it" [ORWELL'S NOTE].

p. 124, *Thackeray's Laura*: Laura Bell is a character in *The History of Pendennis*.

p. 126, *Inside the Whale*: First published in IW; collected in CEJL1. This essay is principally a review of the novel *Tropic of Cancer* by the American writer Henry Miller (1891–1980).

p. 126, *T.S. Eliot... Ezra Pound*: For T.S. Eliot, see first note to p. 39. Herbert Read (1893–1968) was an English literary critic, poet, art historian and philosopher. For Aldous Huxley, see second note to p. 122. The American novelist John dos Passos (1896–1970) is best known for works such as *Manhattan Transfer* (1925) and *USA* (1938). The American modernist poet and critic Ezra Pound (1885–1972) is remembered for works such as *The Cantos* (1917–70).

p. 126, *"Quand je serai lancé"*: "When I have got going" (French).

p. 126, *Tarr*: A modernist novel by Wyndham Lewis, first serialized in 1916–17 and published as a book in 1918.

p. 127, *Black Spring*: A short-story collection published in 1936.

p. 127, *The House with the Green Shutters*: A novel by the Scottish writer George Douglas Brown (1869–1902), published in 1901.

p. 128, *O. Henry*: The pseudonym of the American author William Sydney Porter (1862–1910), best remembered today for his short stories.

p. 129, *Geneva language*: That is, diplomatic, restrained language. The allusion is to the Geneva Convention, an international agreement of 1864 (later revised) governing the treatment of captured and wounded military personnel in wartime.

p. 130, *Voyage au bout de la nuit*: A semi-autobiographical novel by the controversial French writer Louis-Ferdinand Céline (1894–1961), first published in 1932. It appeared in English as *Journey to the End of the Night* in 1934.

p. 130, *Walt Whitman*: The American poet, journalist and essayist Walt Whitman (1819–92).

p. 131, *Leaves of Grass*: A collection of free-verse poetry by Whitman, the first version of which he self-published in 1855; he later published multiple revised and expanded editions.

p. 131, *Bret Harte's*: Bret Harte (1836–1902) was an American short-story writer and poet, best known for fiction set during the California gold rush of 1848–55.

p. 131, *Little Women, Helen's Babies and 'Riding Down from Bangor'*: Respectively: a semi-autobiographical novel by the American writer Louisa May Alcott (1832–88), about four sisters growing up in genteel poverty in Massachusetts, published in 1868; a humorous novel by the American journalist and author John Habberton (1842–1921), first published in 1876; and a traditional song about a railway journey from Bangor, Maine, dating from around 1871.

p. 131, *Bedaux belts*: Leather belts fitted with stopwatches to record the length of time taken by factory workers to perform tasks. Such devices were part of the "Bedaux System" – a time–motion management method designed to maximize industrial efficiency that was devised in the early twentieth century by the French-American efficiency expert Charles Eugène Bedaux (1886–1944).

p. 132, *Max and the White Phagocytes*: A collection of short prose pieces and essays by Miller, published in 1938.

p. 132, *All Quiet on the Western Front... A Subaltern on the Somme*: *All Quiet on the Western Front* is a semi-autobiographical novel by the German novelist Erich Maria Remarque (1898–1970), published in 1929. *Le Feu: journal d'une escouade* (1916), by the French writer Henri Barbusse (1873–1935), was one of the first published novels about the First World War, drawing on the author's experiences as a French soldier on the Western Front. It appeared in English as *Under Fire: The Story of a Squad* in 1917. Hemingway's novel *A Farewell to Arms* (1929) is set on the Italian front during the First World War. *Death of a Hero* (1929) is a novel by the English writer Richard Aldington (1892–1962) set during the First World War. *Goodbye to All That* (1929) is the autobiography of the English soldier, poet, novelist and critic Robert Graves (1895–1985), focusing partly on the author's experiences as an officer in the First World

War. *Memoirs of an Infantry Officer* (1930) is an autobiographical novel by the English soldier, poet and writer Siegfried Sassoon (1886–1967). *A Subaltern on the Somme* is a memoir by the English writer and pacifist Max Plowman (1883–1941), written under the pseudonym "Mark VII", detailing the author's experiences as a junior officer on the Western Front.

p. 133, *Balaam's ass*: A reference to the Bible story in which God gives the power of speech to a donkey (Numbers 22:21–34).

p. 133, *Housman*: The English poet A.E. Housman (1859–1936), best remembered for the collection *A Shropshire Lad* (1896).

p. 134, *Meredith's... 'Garden of Proserpine'*: References to 'Love in the Valley', an 1851 poem (published in an expanded version in 1883) by George Meredith (for whom, see note to p. 107), and an 1866 poem by the English poet Algernon Charles Swinburne (1837–1909).

p. 135, *Richard Jefferies and W.H. Hudson*: The nature writer John Richard Jefferies (1848–87), known for his depictions of English rural life, and the Anglo-Argentine author, naturalist and ornithologist W.H. Hudson (1841–1922).

p. 135, *Strephon or Corydon*: Stock names for rustic male characters in pastoral literature.

p. 135, *Sheila Kaye-Smith*: The novelist Sheila Kaye-Smith (1887–1956), known for her depictions of life in her native rural Sussex.

p. 135, *Everlasting Mercy*: A long poem by the English poet John Masefield (1878–1967), published in 1911, written from the perspective of a self-confessed sinner, Saul Kane, who turns to Christianity.

p. 135, *Theocritus*: The Sicilian-born Greek poet Theocritus (c.310–c.250 BC), best known for his *Idylls*, pastoral poems that inspired Virgil's *Eclogues*.

p. 137, *Lytton Strachey*: The English biographer Lytton Strachey (1880–1932), a prominent member of the Bloomsbury Group, remembered as the author of the iconoclastic *Eminent Victorians* (1918).

p. 137, *the Auden–Spender group*: A reference to the circle around the English poets W.H. Auden (1907–73) and Stephen Spender (1909–95), which included the English poet Cecil Day-Lewis (1904–72), the Irish poet and playwright Louis MacNeice (1907–63) and the British-born US novelist Christopher Isherwood (1904–86).

p. 137, *E.M. Forster*: The English novelist E.M. Forster (1879–1970).

p. 137, *Moore... Norman Douglas*: The Irish writer George Moore (1852–1933), the Polish-born British novelist and short-story writer Joseph Conrad (1857–1924), Arnold Bennett (see first note to p. 99) and the British novelist and travel writer Norman Douglas (1868–1952), now best known for his 1917 novel *South Wind* (1917).

p. 137, *Squire ruled the London Mercury*: J.C. Squire (1884–1958) was editor of the monthly literary periodical the *London Mercury* from 1919 to 1934.

p. 137, *Gibbs and Walpole*: Philip Gibbs (1877–1962) was a prolific English author and journalist. For Walpole, see fifth note to p. 42.

NOTES

p. 138, *The Dynasts*: An epic in verse and prose by Thomas Hardy about the Napoleonic Wars, published in three parts between 1904 and 1908.

p. 138, *"We are... stuffed men"*: From Eliot's 'The Hollow Men' (1925) (ll. 1–2).

p. 138, *Sweeney Agonistes*: Eliot's unfinished verse drama *Sweeney Agonistes: Fragments of an Aristophanic Melodrama* (1932). For the recurring character of Sweeney in Eliot's work, see second note to p. 276.

p. 138, *pukka sahib*: A term of respectful address used in British India, meaning something like "true gentleman".

p. 138, *Lawrence prefers the Etruscans*: In 1927, the English novelist and poet D.H. Lawrence (1885–1930) toured the countryside of Tuscany, subsequently producing *Sketches of Etruscan Places and other Italian Essays*, published posthumously in 1932, in which he discussed his fascination with the ancient civilization of Etruria, a region in western Italy corresponding roughly to modern Tuscany and parts of Umbria.

p. 140, *tædium vitæ*: "Weariness of life" (Latin).

p. 140, *Told by an Idiot*: A 1923 novel by the English writer Rose Macaulay (1881–1958).

p. 140, *Of Human Bondage*: See second note to p. 39.

p. 141, *Modern Poetry*: A work of literary criticism by Louis MacNeice published in 1938.

p. 141, *New Signatures*: Published in 1932 by Hogarth Press, *New Signatures: Poems by Several Hands* was an anthology of verse by nine young poets, including Auden, Spender and Day-Lewis.

p. 141, *John Lehmann... Philip Henderson*: The English poet, editor and publisher John Lehmann (1907–87), who founded the periodicals *New Writing* and the *London Magazine*; the English novelist, critic, memoirist and biographer Arthur Calder-Marshall (1908–92); the English novelist and short-story writer Edward Upward (1903–2009); the English author and translator Alec Brown (1900–62); and the English novelist and critic Philip Henderson (1906–77).

p. 142, *'Play Up... Game!'*: The refrain of 'Vitaï Lampada', an 1892 poem about sportsmanship and duty by the English poet Sir Henry Newbolt (1862–1938).

p. 142, *'You're leaving now... boys'*: Not, in fact, by Auden, but by Day-Lewis, from the tenth poem in the 1933 collection *The Magnetic Mountain* (l. 1).

p. 142, *Trial of a Judge*: A 1938 drama in verse. The quotation is from Act v.

p. 143, *The Communist International*: A historical analysis of the Communist International, known as the "Comintern", an international organization founded in 1919 by Lenin and the Russian Communist Party to promote world communism, by the Austrian writer and academic Franz Borkenau (1900–57), published in 1938.

p. 144, *Evelyn Waugh, Christopher Hollis*: The English novelist Evelyn Waugh (1903–66), known for works such as *Decline and Fall* (1928) and *Brideshead Revisited* (1945), and his friend Christopher Hollis (1902–77), an English teacher,

Conservative politician and writer, were both Catholic converts, having adopted the religion in 1930 and 1924, respectively.

p. 145, *Mr Auden's poem 'Spain'*: First published as a pamphlet in 1937; a revised version, titled 'Spain 1937', was published in Auden's collection *Another Time* (1940).

p. 146, *Enemies of Promise*: A critical and autobiographical work by the English literary critic Cyril Connolly (1903–74), published in 1938.

p. 146, *OGPU*: The Joint State Political Directorate (known by the Russian acronym OGPU), the Soviet secret police from 1923 to 1934, when it was incorporated into the NKVD.

p. 147, *Munich*: A reference to the Munich Agreement of September 1938, signed by Britain, France, Germany and Italy, which ceded the Sudetenland to Germany (see second note to p. 59), in an effort to secure peace in Europe.

p. 149, *'The Scholar Gipsy'... final stanza*: 'The Scholar Gipsy', by the English poet and essayist Matthew Arnold (1822–88), published in the 1853 collection *Poems*, tells of an Oxford student who joins a band of Gypsies. It ends with an extended simile about a trader from the ancient Phoenician port of Tyre who, descrying "intruders on his ancient home" in the form of Grecian merchants, sets sail for the Iberian peninsula.

p. 149, *Barries and Deepings and Dells*: See fourth note to p. 42, fifth note to p. 42 and second note to p. 38, respectively.

p. 149, *Anaïs Nin*: The French-born American diarist and writer of erotica Anaïs Nin (1903–77), who famously had an affair with Miller.

p. 150, "*Je m'en fous*": "I don't give a damn" (French).

p. 150, "*Though He slay me, yet will I trust in Him*": From Job 13:15.

p. 150, *The Mind in Chains*: An anthology of essays with the full title *The Mind in Chains: Socialism and the Cultural Revolution*, edited by Cecil Day-Lewis and published in 1937.

p. 151, *Julien Green's Minuit*: The 1936 novel *Minuit*, written in French by the American writer Julien Green (1900–98).

p. 152, *'Prufrock'*: 'The Love Song of J. Alfred Prufrock', written in 1910–11 and first published in June 1915.

p. 153, *The First Hundred Thousand... Boys in the Trenches*: *The First Hundred Thousand: Being the Unofficial Chronicle of a Unit of "K(1)"* (1915) is a First World War memoir by Ian Hay (for whom, see second note to p. 84). The journalist, financier, newspaper proprietor and politician Horatio Bottomley (1860–1933) was a prominent orator and propagandist during the First World War; no book of this exact title exists, so Orwell may be referring to an article or column in one of Bottomley's publications.

p. 153, *this book*: IW, in which this essay was first published.

p. 154, *Lawrence Durrell, Michael Fraenkel*: The English novelist, poet, playwright and writer of topographical books Lawrence Durrell (1912–90), now best

NOTES

known for his series of interconnected novels the *Alexandria Quartet* (1957–60), and the Lithuanian-American author, poet, essayist and publisher Michael Fraenkel (1896–1957), whose correspondence with Miller was published as *The Michael Fraenkel–Henry Miller Correspondence, Called Hamlet* (1941–43).

p. 156, *Notes on the Way*: First published in *Time and Tide* (6th April 1940); collected in CEJL2.

p. 156, *The Thirties*: *The Thirties: 1930–1940 in Great Britain*, a work by the English journalist and satirist Malcolm Muggeridge (1903–90), first published in 1940.

p. 156, *Gibbon*: See first note to p. 44.

p. 156, *Samuel Butler*: The English novelist and critic Samuel Butler (1835–1902), remembered for the utopian satire *Erewhon, or Over the Range* (1872), about a fictional country of the same name, and the semi-autobiographical *The Way of All Flesh* (published posthumously in 1903).

p. 157, *"Vanity of vanities... duty of man"*: Respectively, Ecclesiastes 1:2 (repeated at 12:8) and 12:13.

p. 157, *Mr Hilaire Belloc... State*: For Belloc, see second note to p. 36. *The Servile State*, published in 1912, is an economic and political treatise critiquing both capitalism and socialism.

p. 157, *Mr F.A. Voigt*: The English journalist Frederick Augustus Voigt (1892–1957), famous for his opposition to dictatorship and totalitarianism in Europe.

p. 158, *"Who dies if England live?"*: The last line of Kipling's 1914 poem 'For All We Have and Are'.

p. 158, *Marx's famous saying... people*: From Marx's introduction to his *Critique of Hegel's Philosophy of Right*, written in 1843. The introduction was published in *Deutsch–Französische Jahrbücher* in February 1844, though the rest of the book remained unpublished during the author's lifetime.

p. 159, *The Limit to Pessimism*: First published in the *New English Weekly*, untitled (25th April 1940); collected in CEJL1 under the present title. This article is a review of Muggeridge's *The Thirties* (see second note to p. 156).

p. 159, *Winter in Moscow*: A satirical account of Stalin's Moscow, first published in 1934.

p. 159, *Thersites*: A soldier of the Greek army who appears in the *Iliad* as a physically deformed, mocking, disparaging character.

p. 160, *the National Government*: A series of coalition governments formed in 1931–35 during the Great Depression, led by the Labour prime minister Ramsay MacDonald (1866–1937).

p. 160, *Baldwin*: The Conservative politician Stanley Baldwin (1867–1947), who served three times as prime minister between 1923 and 1937.

p. 160, *Chamberlain... Shakespeare*: When Neville Chamberlain returned from the signing of the Munich Agreement in September 1938 (see note to p. 147), he famously proclaimed: "I believe it is peace for our time", in fact a reference to a line from the Book of Common Prayer – "Give peace in our time, O Lord" – not Shakespeare.

p. 160, *Lord Rothermere*: The newspaper proprietor Harold Harmsworth, 1st Viscount Rothermere (1868–1940), owner of Associated Newspapers, was a pioneer of tabloid journalism. He co-founded both the *Daily Mail* and the *Daily Mirror* with his brother Alfred Harmsworth, later Viscount Northcliffe (1865–1922).

p. 160, *trunk murders*: A reference to the separate discoveries, in June–July 1934, of two dismembered female bodies inside trunks, both linked to the resort of Brighton on the south coast of England. The two murders are not believed to be connected. Tony Mancini, the lover of the second victim, Violet Kaye, was tried for the second killing but found not guilty.

p. 160, *the Oxford Groupers*: The "Oxford Group" was a Christian organization founded in 1921 by the American Lutheran minister Frank Buchman (1878–1961).

p. 160, *the Rector of Stiffkey*: Harold Davidson (1875–1937), a Church of England priest who was defrocked in 1932 after being found guilty of immorality by a Church court.

p. 160, *James Douglas and his dog Bunch*: A reference to *The Bunch Book* (1932), a biography of Bunch, a Sealyham Terrier, by his owner, the critic and newspaper editor James Douglas (1867–1940), a vocal supporter of censorship.

p. 160, *Godfrey Winn*: The English journalist and columnist Godfrey Winn (1906–71).

p. 160, *should a doctor tell?*: An allusion to a debate conducted in the British popular press in the 1930s about the ethical question of whether a doctor should reveal the truth to a patient suffering from a terminal or otherwise serious illness.

p. 160, *"Shape without form... motion"*: A quotation from T.S. Eliot's 'The Hollow Men' (ll. 11–12).

p. 161, *the sand of the desert is sodden red... England, my England?*: "The sand of the desert is sodden red" is from Newbolt's 'Vitaï Lampada' (see first note to p. 142) (l. 9). "What have I done for thee, England, my England" is a slight misquotation of the first two lines of 'Pro Rege Nostro', a 1900 poem by the English poet William Ernest Henley (1849–1903): "What have I done for you, / England, my England?"

p. 162, *New Words*: Probably written February–April 1940; first published in CEJL2.

p. 162, *Bohn's cribs*: Bohn's Classical Library, cheap English versions of Greek and Latin texts published in the nineteenth century by Henry George Bohn (1790–1884).

p. 163, *the objects you... indescribable*: "The mind, that ocean where each kind / Doth straight its own resemblance find, / Yet it creates, transcending these, / Far other worlds and other seas," etc. [ORWELL'S NOTE]. The quotation is from 'The Garden' (ll. 43–46), by the English metaphysical poet Andrew Marvell (1621–78).

p. 164, *The mortal moon... presage*: Shakespeare's sonnet CVII (ll. 5–6).

p. 164, *mutatis mutandis*: "With the necessary changes" (Latin).

p. 164, *Manon Lescaut*: See third note to p. 40.

p. 165, *Vixi puellis nuper idoneus*: "I have lived my life until recently in a manner attractive to girls" (Latin) – Horace, *Odes* III, 26, l. 1.

p. 166, *au fond*: "Fundamentally" (French).

p. 166, *the common belief... presumption*: The idea is that the demons will come down on you for being too self-confident. Thus children believe that if you hook a fish and say "Got him" before he is landed, he will escape; that if you put your pads on before it is your turn to bat you will be out first ball, etc. Such beliefs often survive in adults. Adults are only less superstitious than children in proportion as they have more power over their environment. In predicaments where everyone is powerless (e.g. war, gambling) everyone is superstitious [ORWELL'S NOTE].

p. 167, *"sentimental"*: I once began making a list of writers whom the critics called "sentimental". In the end it included nearly every English writer. The word is in fact a meaningless symbol of hatred, like the bronze tripods in Homer which were given to guests as a symbol of friendship [ORWELL'S NOTE].

p. 167, *a film of Douglas Fairbanks's*: The American actor and film-maker Douglas Fairbanks (1883–1939) was a major star of the silent-film era. The film referred to here is possibly *When the Clouds Roll By* (1919).

p. 168, *Dr Caligari*: *The Cabinet of Dr Caligari* (1920), a German silent horror film directed by Robert Wiene (1873–1938).

p. 168, *Volapük*: An artificial language created in 1879–80 by the German Catholic priest Johann Martin Schleyer (1831–1912).

p. 169, *"Deeper than did ever... etc.*: Quotations from, respectively: *The Tempest*, Act V, Sc. 1 (l. 65); Housman's 'There Pass the Careless People' (l. 5), published in *A Shropshire Lad* (see second note to p. 133); and Arnold's 1852 poem 'To Marguerite: Continued' (l. 24).

p. 170, *Prophecies of Fascism*: First published in *Tribune*, untitled (12th July 1940); collected in CEJL2 under the present title. This article is a review of four dystopian novels: *The Iron Heel* (1908) by the American writer Jack London (1876–1916), best remembered today for *The Call of the Wild* (1903) and *White Fang* (1906); Wells's *The Sleeper Wakes* (1910), originally serialized in 1899 as *When the Sleeper Wakes*; Huxley's *Brave New World*; and *What Might Have Been* (1907) by the English author Ernest Bramah (1868–1942), published in the United States as *The Secret of the League* (1909).

p. 173, *Charles Reade*: First published in the *New Statesman and Nation* (17th August 1940); collected in CEJL2. For Reade, see second note to p. 39.

p. 173, *A Connecticut Yankee in King Arthur's Court*: An 1889 novel by Mark Twain about a man from contemporary America who is transported back in time to the reign of King Arthur. A silent-film adaptation appeared in 1921, followed by a second screen version in 1931, directed by David Butler (1894–1979) and starring Will Rogers (1879–1935). Both were box-office successes.

p. 173, 'A Jack of All Trades' and 'The Autobiography of a Thief': Two novellas by Read, published together as *Cream* (1858).

p. 173, *R. Austin Freeman's... curiosities*: The English writer R. Austin Freeman (1862–1943) was the author of detective stories mostly featuring the forensic investigator Doctor Thorndyke. The Royal Navy officer and horologist Rupert Gould (1890–1948) was the author of *Oddities: A Book of Unexplained Facts* (1928) and *Enigmas: Another Book of Unexplained Facts* (1929).

p. 173, *Exchange and Mart*: A weekly magazine founded in 1868 that consisted entirely of advertisements, mostly submitted by individuals or small businesses.

p. 173, *Foul Play*: A sensation novel published in 1869.

p. 174, *Coral Island*: *The Coral Island: A Tale of the Pacific Ocean*, an 1857 novel by Scottish author R.M. Ballantyne (1825–94).

p. 175, *Hard Cash and It Is Never Too Late to Mend*: Published in 1863 and 1856, respectively.

p. 175, *Erastian clergymen*: That is, clergymen who subscribed to the belief – wrongly attributed to the Swiss theologian Erastus (1524–83) – that ecclesiastical power should be subordinate to secular power.

p. 175, *Winwood Reade*: Charles Reade was in fact the uncle of the influential historian, philosopher and explorer William Winwood Reade (1838–75), author of *The Martyrdom of Man* (1872).

p. 176, *My Country Right or Left*: First published in *Folios of New Writing* (Autumn 1940); collected in CEJL1.

p. 178, *the Russo-German pact*: On 23rd August 1939 – only a few days before the beginning of the Second World War – the Nazi minister of foreign affairs, Joachim von Ribbentrop (1893–1946), and the Soviet foreign minister, Vyacheslav Molotov (1890–1986), signed the German–Soviet Non-Aggression Pact (also known as the Molotov–Ribbentrop Pact), in which each side committed neither to aid nor to ally itself with an enemy of the other, and Eastern Europe was divided into German and Soviet spheres of influence.

p. 179, *John Cornford... in the close tonight*: Respectively, the poem 'Full Moon at Tierz: Before the Storming of Huesca' (1936) by the English poet and communist John Cornford (1915–36) and Newbolt's 'Vitaï Lampada' (see first note to p. 142), of which "There's a breathless hush in the close tonight" is the first line.

p. 180, *The Lion and the Unicorn: Socialism and the English Genius*: Written by November 1940; a section of 'England Your England' first published as 'The Ruling Class' in *Horizon* (December 1940); full essay first published as the first volume of the "Searchlight Books" series edited by Orwell and the German-born British journalist and prominent Zionist T.R. Fyvel (1907–85) and published by Secker & Warburg (February 1941); collected in CEJL2.

p. 184, *In the last... mock-defeatist*: For example: "I don't want to join the bloody army, / I don't want to go unto the war; / I want no more to roam, / I'd rather stay at home, / Living on the earnings of a whore." But it was not in that spirit that they fought [ORWELL'S NOTE].

p. 184, *Sir John Moore's army at Corunna*: A reference to the Battle of Corunna (La Coruña) on 16th January 1809, part of the Peninsular War (1808–14), during which the commander of the British Army, Sir John Moore (1761–1809), was mortally wounded. The British troops were able to hold off the French attacks until nightfall and evacuate on transport ships overnight. The death of Moore is commemorated in the poem 'The Burial of Sir John Moore at Corunna' (1816) by the Irish clergyman Charles Wolfe (1791–1823).

p. 185, *Wilfred Macartney's... Jim Phelan's Jail Journey*: Wilfred Macartney (1899–1970) was an English socialist convicted of being a Soviet spy. His memoir *Walls Have Mouths: A Record of Ten Years' Penal Servitude* was published in 1936. The Irish author Jim Phelan (1895–1966) wrote several books on tramping and prison life, including *Jail Journey* (1940).

p. 187, *never aided them... strike*: It is true that they aided them to a certain extent with money. Still, the sums raised for the various aid-Spain funds would not equal 5 per cent of the turnover of the football pools during the same period [ORWELL'S NOTE].

p. 187, *Lord Nuffield and Mr Montagu Norman*: The English motor manufacturer and philanthropist William Morris, 1st Viscount Nuffield (1877–1963), and the banker Montagu Norman, 1st Baron Norman (1871–1950), who served as governor of the Bank of England from 1920 to 1944.

p. 187, *Anthony Eden*: The Conservative politician Anthony Eden (1897–1977), who would serve as prime minister from 1955 until his resignation in 1957.

p. 187, *Laval–Quisling*: The French politician Pierre Laval (1883–1945), who served three times as prime minister of France, including in 1942–44, during Vichy France, and the Norwegian military officer Vidkun Quisling (1887–1945), who headed his country's government during German occupation. Both were later tried as Nazi collaborators and executed for treason.

p. 188, *the Gadarene swine*: A reference to the pigs into which Jesus cast the demons that had possessed a madman, and that as a result ran down a steep cliff into the sea and were killed. See (Matthew 8:28–34; Mark 5:1–20; Luke 8:26–39).

p. 189, *Peace News*: A pacifist magazine published between 1936 and 2024.

p. 190, *England is not... message*: A reference to the famous speech by John of Gaunt in *Richard II* in which England is described as, among other things, "this sceptred isle" and "this precious stone set in the silver sea" (Act II, Sc. 1, ll. 40–50).

p. 190, *Dr Goebbels*: The Nazi minister of propaganda Joseph Goebbels (1897–1945).

p. 191, *Halifax*: The Conservative politician Edward Wood, 1st Earl of Halifax (1881–1959), who held several senior posts in government and was a supporter of the policy of appeasement of Adolf Hitler in 1936–38.

p. 191, *the Bystander*: A tabloid magazine published between 1903 and 1940.

p. 193, *Simon, Hoare*: The Liberal politician John Simon, 1st Viscount Simon (1873–1954), a prominent government figure from the beginning of the First World War to the end of the Second World War, and the Conservative politician Samuel Hoare, 1st Viscount Templewood (1880–1959), who held many senior government posts during the 1920s and 1930s.

p. 194, *Clive... Gordon*: Robert Clive, 1st Baron Clive, known as "Clive of India" (1725–74), the first British governor of Bengal; Horatio Nelson, 1st Viscount Nelson (1758–1805), the hero of the Battle of Trafalgar (1805); the East India Company officer John Nicholson (1822–57), famous for his role during the Indian Mutiny of 1857; and the British general Charles George Gordon (1833–85), who became a national hero for crushing the Taiping rebellion (1863–64) in China, and then for suppressing an uprising in Khartoum in Sudan (1884), where he was killed.

p. 194, *T.E. Lawrence*: The British military officer and archaeologist T.E. Lawrence, known as "Lawrence of Arabia" (1888–1935), remembered for his role in the Arab revolt against the Ottomans during the First World War, the subject of his autobiographical book *Seven Pillars of Wisdom* (1926).

p. 196, *Blackwood's Magazine*: A periodical founded in Edinburgh by the publisher William Blackwood (1776–1834), and published between 1817 and 1980. It was regarded as a bastion of conservatism.

p. 198, *Picture Post*: A photojournalistic magazine published from 1938 to 1957.

p. 201, *Marshal Goering*: The senior Nazi politician and military leader Hermann Goering (1893–1946).

p. 202, *the Beaverbrook press*: See fifth note to p. 28.

p. 202, *Lord Rothermere*: See fourth note to p. 160.

p. 203, *Ian Hay... drawing cartoons*: For Ian Hay and Hilaire Belloc, see second note to p. 84 and second note to p. 36, respectively. "Maurois" is the French author Émile Herzog, known under his assumed name André Maurois (1885–1967), and as the author of numerous biographies and popular histories. Bruce Bairnsfather (1887–1959) was a prominent British humorist and cartoonist, best known as the creator of the character "Old Bill", an elderly, pipe-smoking "Tommy" (a private soldier in the British Army).

p. 203, *Bevin*: The trade-union leader and Labour politician Ernest Bevin (1881–1951).

p. 206, *the unnecessary suffering... Sir John Anderson*: The Scottish politician Sir John Anderson (1882–1958), who served as home secretary and minister of home security in 1939–40 under Neville Chamberlain and then under Churchill, was criticized for failing the civilian population, particularly in London's East End, during the early stages of the Blitz in September 1940, by refusing to open London's Underground stations as air-raid shelters, despite public demand. Only after immense pressure did Anderson's ministry relent.

p. 206, *History to the... pardon*: A slightly imprecise quotation of the last two lines of Auden's poem 'Spain': "History to the defeated / May say Alas but cannot help nor pardon." See also note to p. 145.

p. 207, *Mosley's*: A reference to the right-wing politician Oswald Mosley (1896–1980), a former Conservative and then Labour MP, who founded the British Union of Fascists (BUF), known as the "Blackshirts", in 1932.

p. 207, *the Peace Pledge Union*: A pacifist campaigning organization founded in 1934.

p. 208, *Cavalcade, or Priestley's broadcasts*: *Cavalcade* was a weekly news magazine published between 1936 and 1950. J.B. Priestley broadcast a series of short propaganda radio talks in 1940 to strengthen civilian morale during the Battle of Britain.

p. 210, *Bottomley or Lloyd George*: For Bottomley, see first note to p. 153. The Liberal politician David Lloyd George (1863–1945) served as prime minister from 1916 to 1922.

p. 211, *"the Philistines be... Samson"*: Judges 16:20.

p. 213, *Morrison*: The Labour politician Herbert Morrison (1888–1965), who served as home secretary in the wartime coalition.

p. 219, *Metternich's Europe*: That is, the Europe that emerged following the Congress of Vienna (1814–15), which reorganized the Continent after the Napoleonic Wars, and at which the Austrian statesman and diplomat Klemens von Metternich (1773–1859) was a key figure.

p. 220, *Unser Kampf... If We Choose*: Respectively, a 1940 work by the Liberal politician Sir Richard Acland (1906–90) and a book published anonymously in 1940 under the pseudonym "Scipio".

p. 220, *there is no... already*: Written before the outbreak of the war in Greece [ORWELL'S NOTE].

p. 221, *Laissez-faire capitalism is dead*: It is interesting to notice that Mr Kennedy, USA ambassador in London, remarked on his return to New York in October 1940 that as a result of the war "democracy is finished". By "democracy", of course, he meant private capitalism [ORWELL'S NOTE].

p. 223, *Pétain, Laval*: The French general and statesman Philippe Pétain (1856–1951), head of state 1940–44, signed an armistice with Nazi Germany in 1940 and established the Vichy regime (a puppet regime for the Third Reich). For Laval, see fourth note to p. 187.

p. 223, *Come the four corners... true*: A slightly imprecise quotation from the end of *King John*, Act v, Sc. 7: "Come the three corners of the world in arms

/ And we shall shock them. Naught shall make us rue, / If England to itself do rest but true" (ll. 122–24).

p. 225, *The Proletarian Writer*: Broadcast on the BBC Home Service on 6th December 1940; first published in the *Listener* (19th December 1940); collected in CEJL2.

p. 225, *Desmond Hawkins*: The influential English author, editor and critic Desmond Hawkins (1908–99).

p. 225, *New Writing, or the Unity Theatre*: For *New Writing*, see first note to p. 30. The Unity Theatre operated between 1936 and 1994, and until 1975 was located in London's Somers Town district. Its main aim was to bring contemporary social and political issues to a working-class audience. It had had links to the Left Book Club and the Communist Party of Great Britain.

p. 225, *W.H. Davies*: The Welsh poet W.H. Davies (1871–1940), who spent much of his life as a tramp in Britain and in the Unites States.

p. 225, *Paul Potts*: The English poet and writer Paul Potts (1911–90), best known for the memoir *Dante Called You Beatrice* (1960).

p. 225, *James Hanley... Jack Common*: The English writer of Irish descent James Hanley (1897–1985), the English novelist and essayist Jack Hilton (1900–83) and the English essayist and novelist Jack Common (1903–68).

p. 225, *the slump*: The period of national economic downturn in 1930s Britain, which had its origins in the global Great Depression.

p. 226, *The Ragged-Trousered Philanthropists*: A semi-autobiographical novel by the Irish house painter and sign writer Robert Tressell, pseudonym of Robert Noonan (1870–1911), published in 1914.

p. 227, *Hunger and Love*: The only novel written by the English working-class author Lionel Britton (1887–1971), published in 1931.

p. 227, *the Left Review*: A journal set up by the British section of the International Union of Revolutionary Writers, published between 1934 and 1938.

p. 227, *Edward Upward... Arthur Calder-Marshall*: "Christopher Caudwell" was the pseudonym used by the English Marxist writer Christopher St John Sprigg (1907–37). For the other names on this list, see third note to p. 141.

p. 228, *Jack London's... Grey Children*: *The Road* (1907) is London's memoir of his time travelling the United States as a tramp in the 1890s, during a period of economic depression. *Caliban Shrieks* (1935) is an autobiographical work of working-class life by Jack Hilton (for whom, see sixth note to p. 225). For Jim Phelan, see note to p. 185. George Garrett (1896–1966) was an English radical activist, merchant seaman, playwright and author of several sea stories. *Old Soldier Sahib* (1936) is a memoir of military service in India by the Welsh soldier Frank Richards (1883–1961). *Grey Children: A Study in Humbug and Misery* (1937) is a non-fiction work about unemployment in South Wales by James Hanley (for whom, see sixth note to p. 225).

NOTES

p. 228, *Home Chat... Cage Birds*: *Home Chat* was a weekly women's magazine published between 1895 and 1959. For *Exchange and Mart*, see fifth note to p. 173. *Cage Birds* is probably the periodical *Cage Birds and Bird World*, published between 1902 and 1960 (under a different title from 1935).

p. 228, *'Stagolee'*: 'Stagolee', better known as 'Stagger Lee', is a popular American folk song about the murder of the underworld figure Billy Lyons by the African American pimp "Stag" Lee Shelton (1865–1912) in St Louis, Missouri, on Christmas night, 1895.

p. 229, *'Danny Deever'*: An 1890 poem about the execution of a British soldier for murder in India.

p. 229, *Donald McGill*: The English graphic artist Donald McGill (1875–1962), known for illustrating humorous and often risqué postcards, often associated with the seaside. See Orwell's essay 'The Art of Donald McGill' (pp. 249–57).

p. 231, *The Frontiers of Art and Propaganda*: Broadcast on the BBC Overseas Service on 30th April 1941; first published in the *Listener* (29th May 1941); collected in CEJL2.

p. 231, *George Saintsbury*: The influential English literary historian and critic George Saintsbury (1845–1933), noted for his profoundly conservative views.

p. 232, *Edith Sitwell's book on Pope*: The study *Alexander Pope* (1930) by the English poet and critic Edith Sitwell (1887–1964).

p. 232, *Pater, Oscar Wilde*: The English essayist and critic Walter Pater (1839–94) and the Irish playwright, novelist and poet Oscar Wilde (1854–1900) were closely associated with the Aesthetic Movement, a group of writers and artists in the late nineteenth century who were devoted to "art for art's sake".

p. 234, *Tolstoy and Shakespeare*: Broadcast on the BBC Overseas Service on 7th May 1941; first published in the *Listener* (5th June 1941); collected in CEJL2.

p. 234, *Tolstoy's essay on Shakespeare*: Written in 1897 and published in Moscow in 1903. An English translation appeared in 1906, titled *Tolstoy on Shakespeare: A Critical Essay on Shakespeare*, and published alongside another essay, *Shakespeare's Attitude to the Working Classes*, by the American author Ernest Howard Crosby (1856–1907).

p. 235, *the piece of criticism... Timon of Athens*: 'The Power of Money', included in Marx's *Economic and Philosophic Manuscripts of 1844*, compiled and published posthumously in 1932.

p. 238, *The Meaning of a Poem*: Broadcast on the BBC Overseas Service on 14th May 1941; first published in the *Listener* (12th June 1941); collected in CEJL2.

p. 238, *'Felix Randal'*: An 1880 poem by Hopkins written to commemorate the death of Felix Spencer, a Liverpool farrier who died of pleurisy.

p. 241, *Literature and Totalitarianism*: Broadcast on the BBC Overseas Service on 21st May 1941; first published in the *Listener* (19th June 1941); collected in CEJL2.

p. 244, *Wells, Hitler and the World State*: First published in *Horizon* (August 1941); collected in CEJL2.

p. 244, *Guide to the New World*: Wells's *Guide to the New World: A Handbook of Constructive World Revolution* (1941) is an example of the utopian strand of his writing, in which he advocated the reorganization of human society into an enlightened world state.

p. 244, *the Sankey Declaration*: The 1940 Sankey Declaration of the Rights of Man, named after the chairman of the committee that promoted it, John Sankey, 1st Viscount Sankey (1866–1948). H.G. Wells was the most active member of the committee.

p. 246, *Trotsky... Koestler*: For Leon Trotsky, see second note to p. 48. Hermann Rauschning (1887–1982) was a German politician and essayist who broke with Nazism in 1934. Alfred Rosenberg (1893–1946) was a Nazi theorist and ideologue. Ignazio Silone (1900–78) was an Italian writer, best known for his anti-fascist novels. For Borkenau, see note to p. 143. Arthur Koestler (1905–83) was an Austro-Hungarian-born journalist and novelist, best known for the novel *Darkness at Noon* (1940), which exposed the Stalinist purges of the 1930s. See Orwell's essay 'Arthur Koestler' (pp. 389–97).

p. 246, *Outline of History*: A work by H.G. Wells serialized in 1919–20 and published as a single volume in 1920.

p. 246, *the English Rule of the Saints*: The Puritan regime under Oliver Cromwell and the Commonwealth during the Interregnum: the period from the execution of Charles I in 1649 to the Restoration of Charles II in 1660.

p. 248, *The Shape of Things to Come*: A 1933 science-fiction novel by H.G. Wells.

p. 249, *The Art of Donald McGill*: First published in *Horizon* (September 1941); collected in CEJL2.

p. 249, *Wendyish*: Resembling Wendy Darling, a character from J.M. Barrie's Peter Pan stories.

p. 250, *Max Millerish*: A reference to the English comedian Thomas Sargent (1894–1963), known professionally by his stage name Max Miller and billed as "the Cheeky Chappie".

p. 252, *ARP*: See second note to p. 74.

p. 253, *La Vie Parisienne*: A French magazine published between 1863 and 1970, featuring stories, gossip, fashion and risqué pictures of women.

p. 254, *"Youth's a stuff will not endure"*: The last line of 'O Mistress Mine', an Elizabethan song that appears in *Twelfth Night* (Act II, Sc. 3).

p. 255, *Sancho Panza*: The uneducated but worldly-wise squire of Don Quixote in the novel by the Spanish writer Miguel de Cervantes (1547–1616), published between 1605 and 1615. Sancho Panza is noted for his broad humour and his "*sanchismos*" – pills of earthy proverbial wisdom.

NOTES

p. 255, *Miss Rebecca West*: The English author and literary critic Rebecca West (1892–1983), later famous as the author of *Black Lamb and Grey Falcon* (1941) and for her coverage of the Nuremberg trials.

p. 255, *Bouvard... Dedalus*: For Bouvard and Pécuchet, see fourth note to p. 122. Reginald Jeeves and Bertie Wooster are a famous valet-and-master duo who appear in a series of comedic novels and short stories by P.G. Wodehouse. Leopold Bloom and Stephen Dedalus are two of the main characters in Joyce's *Ulysses*.

p. 257, *there is a... time?*: Ecclesiastes 7:15–17.

p. 258, *No, Not One*: First published in the *Adelphi* (October 1941); collected in CEJL2. This article is a review of the novel *No Such Liberty* (1941) by Alex Comfort (1920–2000), then a student at Cambridge and later to achieve fame as a scientist, physician and writer, notably of *The Joy of Sex* (1972).

p. 258, *Mr Murry*: The writer and critic John Middleton Murry (1889–1957), who founded the *Adelphi* literary magazine in 1923. From July 1940 to April 1946 he was editor of *Peace News* (for which, see note to p. 189).

p. 258, *the massacre... Vom Rath's assassination*: The assassination in Paris of the German diplomat Ernst vom Rath (1909–38) by a Polish Jewish teenager was used as a pretext by the Nazis to launch the Kristallnacht pogrom on 9th–10th November 1938.

p. 258, *Arandora Star*: A British passenger ship that, during the Second World War, was first requisitioned as a troopship and then, at the end of June 1940, assigned the task of deporting interned Anglo-Italian and Anglo-German civilians as well as a small number of prisoners of war to Canada. On 2nd July 1940 she was sunk by a German U-boat off the coast of Ireland, with the loss of 805 lives.

p. 261, *the PPU*: The Peace Pledge Union. See second note to p. 207.

p. 261, *"Woe to him... no, not one"*: Respectively, a paraphrase of Jesus's words in Luke 17:1 ("It is impossible but that offences will come: but woe unto him, through whom they come!") and Romans 3:10.

p. 262, *Darlan and Laval*: The French admiral François Darlan (1881–1942) was a prominent figure in the Vichy regime. For Laval, see fourth note to p. 187.

p. 262, *"il faut écrabouiller l'Angleterre"*: "England must be crushed" (French).

p. 263, *Rudyard Kipling*: First published in *Horizon* (February 1942); collected in CEJL2. This article is a response to the publication of *A Choice of Kipling's Verse* (1941), selected and introduced by T.S. Eliot.

p. 263, *'Recessional'*: A poem composed for Queen Victoria's Diamond Jubilee in 1897.

p. 264, *The Light That Failed*: A semi-autobiographical novel published in 1891.

p. 265, *boxwallah*: See third note to p. 16.

p. 265, *"making mock of... sleep"*: From 'Tommy' (l. 17), included in *Barrack-Room Ballads and Other Verses* (1892).

p. 266, *Cecil Rhodes*: The English mining magnate and politician Cecil Rhodes (1853–1902), a strenuous supporter of British imperialism. He served as prime minister of the Cape Colony from 1890 to 1896. He and his British South Africa Company founded the territory of Rhodesia (now Zimbabwe and Zambia), which the company named after him in 1895.

p. 266, *'If—'*: A poem written around 1895 and first published in *Rewards and Fairies* (1910).

p. 267, *"the flannelled fools... goal"*: From the 1902 poem 'The Islanders' (l. 32).

p. 267, *So it's knock... home!*: From 'Follow Me 'Ome' (ll. 5–8), included in the collection *The Seven Seas* (1896).

p. 267, *Cheer for the... whore!*: The refrain of 'The Sergeant's Weddin'' (ll. 9–13, 54–57), included in *The Seven Seas*, where the words "a whore" are replaced by "etc."

p. 268, *"What have I... England"*: See note to p. 161.

p. 268, *"the intense selfishness... classes"*: From 'The Drums of the Fore and Aft' – see second note to p. 28.

p. 268, *I came to realize... he endured*: From the third chapter of Kipling's posthumously published autobiography *Something of Myself: For My Friends Known and Unknown* (1937).

p. 268, *I 'eard the... me!*: From 'That Day' (ll. 17–20), published in *The Seven Seas*.

p. 268, *An' now the... slow*: From 'The 'Eathen' (ll. 53–56), published in *The Seven Seas*.

p. 269, *Forward the Light... blundered*: A slight misquotation from Tennyson's 'The Charge of the Light Brigade' (ll. 9–12).

p. 269, *the essay on... publish*: Published in a volume of collected essays, *The Wound and the Bow* [ORWELL'S NOTE, 1945]. The essay in question, by the American critic, essayist and short-story writer Edmund Wilson (1895–1972), is titled 'The Kipling That Nobody Read'.

p. 270, *Private Ortheris and Mrs Hauksbee*: Recurring characters in Kipling's fiction set in British India. Private Ortheris, a cockney soldier, first appeared in the story 'The Madness of Private Ortheris', featured in *Plain Tales from the Hills* (1888). The sharp-witted society hostess Mrs Hauksbee first appeared in 'Three and – an Extra', also from *Plain Tales from the Hills*.

p. 270, *East is East... Dane-geld*: Respectively: the first line of 'The Ballad of East and West' (1889); the title of an 1899 poem (each verse of which begins "Take up the white man's burden"); a slight paraphrase of the second line of the 1891 poem 'The English Flag' ("And what should they know of England who only England know?"); the refrain of the first four stanzas of the 1911 poem 'The Female of the Species'; a phrase from the first line of the last stanza of 'Mandalay' ("Ship me somewhere east of Suez, where the best is like the worst"); and a phrase from the 1911 poem 'Dane-geld' (l. 14), whose title refers to a land tax levied in Anglo-Saxon England to raise funds for protection against Danish invaders. For 'Mandalay', see fourth note to p. 28.

p. 270, *killing Kruger with your mouth*: From the 1899 poem 'The Absent-Minded Beggar': "When you've finished killing Kruger with your mouth" (l. 3). The reference is to Paul Kruger (1825–1904), president of the South African Republic (the Transvaal) during the Second Boer War (1899–1902), fought between the British Empire and the independent Boer republics of the Transvaal and the Orange Free State. The Boers were Dutch and Huguenot colonists who settled in southern Africa in the seventeenth century.

p. 270, *"For I'm to... May"*: The refrain of Tennyson's 'The May Queen' (1843).

p. 271, *Nothing could exceed... Dane-geld*: On the first page of his recent book, *Adam and Eve*, Mr Middleton Murry quotes the well-known lines:

There are nine and sixty ways
Of constructing tribal lays,
And every single one of them is right.

He attributes these lines to Thackeray. This is probably what is known as a "Freudian error". A civilized person would prefer not to quote Kipling – i.e. would prefer not to feel that it was Kipling who had expressed his thought for him [ORWELL'S NOTE, 1945]. The quotation is in fact from Kipling's 'In the Neolithic Age' (1892). For John Middleton Murry, see second note to p. 258.

p. 271, *"palm and pine"*: From 'Recessional' (see second note to p. 263): "Dominion over palm and pine" (l. 4).

p. 271, *'The Pigtail of Wu Fang Fu'*: The reference is to 'The Pigtail of Li Fang Fu', a musical monologue by Sax Rohmer (for whom, see note to p. 81).

p. 271, *'Gunga Din'*: Kipling's famous poem of 1890.

p. 271, *For the wind... to Mandalay"*: From 'Mandalay' (ll. 3–4). See fourth note to p. 28.

p. 271, *'Felix Randal' or 'When Icicles Hang by the Wall'*: For 'Felix Randal', see second note to p. 238. 'When Icicles Hang by the Wall' is a song from *Love's Labour's Lost*, Act V, Sc. 2.

p. 271, *Harriet Beecher Stowe*: The American novelist Harriet Beecher Stowe (1811–96), author of *Uncle Tom's Cabin* (1852), a vivid account of the reality of slavery in the United States.

p. 272, *'The Bridge of Sighs'... 'Casabianca'*: 'The Bridge of Sighs' is an 1844 poem by the English poet Thomas Hood (1799–1845). 'When All the World Is Young, Lad' is a song from Kingsley's *The Water-Babies* (see third note to p. 102). For 'The Charge of the Light Brigade', see note to p. 116. 'Dickens in Camp' is an 1870 poem by the American author Bret Harte (for whom, see second note to p. 131), written as a tribute to Dickens on his death. For 'The Burial of Sir John Moore', see second note to p. 184. 'Jenny Kissed

Me' is an 1838 poem by the English critic and poet Leigh Hunt (1784–1859). 'Keith of Ravelston' is a ballad by the English poet Sydney Thompson Dobell (1824–74). 'Casabianca' is an 1826 poem by the English poet Felicia Hemans (1793–1835).

p. 272, *'Endeavour'*: A reference to 'Say Not the Struggle Naught Availeth' (1849) by the English poet Arthur Hugh Clough (1819–61). Winston Churchill quoted the last two stanzas of the poem in his "Report on the War" speech of 27th April 1941.

p. 273, *White hands... travels alone*: From the 1888 poem 'The Winners' (ll. 7–10, 5–6). Orwell replaces, intentionally or by mistake, the last two lines of the second stanza with the closing couplet of the first one.

p. 273, *the gods of... headings*: The title of a 1919 poem.

p. 274, *épater les bourgeois*: "Shock the middle classes" (French).

p. 274, *Man and Superman*: A four-act drama by George Bernard Shaw, first performed in 1905.

p. 275, *The Rediscovery of Europe*: Broadcast on the BBC Overseas Service on 10th March 1942; first published in the *Listener* (19th March 1942); collected in CEJL2.

p. 275, *'Elegy in a Country Churchyard'*: 'Elegy Written in a Country Churchyard', a 1750 poem by the English poet Thomas Gray (1716–71).

p. 276, *If I should die... for ever England*: From the first three lines of Brooke's sonnet 'The Soldier', published posthumously in 1915.

p. 276, *Eliot's Sweeney poems... River Plate*: The character of Sweeney – who represents the vulgar, base side of modern man – appears in four of T.S. Eliot's poems: 'Sweeney Among the Nightingales' (1918), 'Mr Eliot's Sunday Morning Service' (1918), 'Sweeney Erect' (1919) and *The Waste Land* (1922), as well as in the play *Sweeney Agonistes* (see third note to p. 138). The quotation is from 'Sweeney among the Nightingales' (ll. 5–6).

p. 277, *W.W. Jacobs, Barry Pain*: W.W. Jacobs (1863–1943) was an English author of humorous short stories. Barry Pain (1864–1928) was an English journalist and humorist.

p. 277, *The Dynasts*: An epic drama in verse and prose by Thomas Hardy, published in three parts between 1904 and 1908.

p. 278, *The Country of the Blind... The Prussian Officer*: Wells's *The Country of the Blind and Other Stories*, a collection of fantasy and science-fiction stories, was published in 1911. Lawrence's collections *England, My England and Other Stories* and *The Prussian Officer and Other Stories* were published in 1922 and 1914, respectively.

p. 280, *The Forsyte Saga*: See third note to p. 38.

p. 280, *The Man of Property*: See third note to p. 38.

p. 282, *H.G. Wells's... Men Like Gods*: Three novels, published in 1905, 1924 and 1923, respectively, in which Wells expounded his vision of an ideal world state run according to socialist principles. For Wells's utopian writings, see also second note to p. 244.

p. 284, *Pacifism and the War*: Dated 12th July 1942; first published in the *Partisan Review* (September–October 1942); collected in CEJL2. This article is Orwell's contribution to a symposium, subtitled "A Controversy", that also contained pieces by the pacifist poet and Christian anarchist Derek Savage (1917–2007), the anarchist thinker George Woodcock (1912–95) and Alex Comfort (see first note to p. 258) – for which, see CEJL2.

p. 285, *Déat or Bergery*: The French Vichy politicians Marcel Déat (1894–1955) and Gaston Bergery (1892–1974).

p. 286, *a novel which... Burma*: For Orwell's novel *Burmese Days*, see second note to p. 13. The reference here is to the collapse of British rule in Burma during the Japanese invasion of 1942.

p. 286, *Herbert Read... Tom Wintringham*: For Read, Eliot and Forster, see second note to p. 126, first note to p. 39 and note to p. 105, respectively. Reginald Reynolds (1905–58) was a left-wing British writer known for his opposition to British imperialism in India. For Spender, see second note to p. 137. J.B.S. Haldane (1892–1964) was an English scientist and communist. Also a communist, the English soldier, author and historian Tom Wintringham (1898–1949) was a founder of the *Left Review* and a key figure in the creation of the Home Guard in 1940.

p. 287, *Christopher Dawson... the Duke of Bedford*: The Welsh scholar and Catholic historian Christopher Dawson (1889–1970); the Madras-born English mountaineer, authority on skiing and Catholic apologist Arnold Lunn (1888–1974); the French novelist, member of the French Resistance and politician André Malraux (1901–76); the British Marxist theoretician of Indian and Swedish descent R. Palme Dutt (1896–1974); the English writer and pacifist Max Plowman (see second note to p. 132); and Hastings Russell, 12th Duke of Bedford (1888–1953), a far-right politician and the co-founder of the British People's Party.

p. 288, *Looking Back on the Spanish War*: Probably written in 1942; sections I, II, III and VII first published in *New Road* ([June] 1943); full version first published in the posthumous collection *Such, Such Were the Joys* (New York: Harcourt, Brace, 1953); collected in CEJL2.

p. 289, *New Masses*: An American Marxist magazine published between 1926 and 1948.

p. 289, *Lunns, Garvins*: For Arnold Lunn, see note to p. 287. For J.L. Garvin, see fourth note to p. 45.

p. 289, *et hoc genus*: Abbreviation of *et hoc genus omne*, meaning "and all their kind" (Latin). The expression derives from Horace's *Satires* I, 2, l. 2.

p. 289, *There must be... Second Front now*: In February 1933 the Oxford Union famously passed a motion that "this House will in no circumstances fight for its

King and Country"; the ramifications of this declaration were still being felt in the middle of the decade. By 1937, though, many on the left had switched to a position of anti-fascist militancy, urging strong action against Nazi Germany. The signing of the Molotov–Ribbentrop Pact (see note to p. 178), however, led to the People's Convention (1940), a Communist Party of Great Britain-backed movement in opposition to the war effort. Hitler's invasion of the Soviet Union in 1941 then brought about another volte-face, as many on the left began to argue that Britain should open a Second Front in Western Europe in order to relieve pressure on Stalin's forces.

p. 297, *Spartacus... Epictetus*: The Thracian gladiator Spartacus (*c*.103–71 BC), one of the leaders of the Third Servile War (73–71 BC), a major slave uprising against the Roman Republic, and the Greek Stoic philosopher Epictetus (*c*.50–*c*.135 AD), who was born into slavery at Hierapolis, in Phrygia.

p. 297, *Felix fecit*: "Felix made this" (Latin).

p. 298, *Negrín*: Juan Negrín (1892–1956), a leader of the Spanish Socialist Workers' Party (Partido Socialista Obrero Español, PSOE) and of the left-leaning Popular Front government during the Spanish Civil War. He served as prime minister of the Second Spanish Republic (1931–39) between May 1937 and March 1939, when he was deposed in a coup orchestrated by the Republican Army officer Segismundo Casado López (1893–1968), who believed that Negrín was planning a Communist takeover. Casado's subsequent attempts to negotiate a peace with Franco failed, leading, on 1st April 1939, to the unconditional surrender demanded by the latter.

p. 300, *Una resolución... hasta el fin!*: "One resolution – to fight to the end!" (Spanish).

p. 300, *my book on the Spanish war*: *Homage to Catalonia*, published by Secker & Warburg in 1938.

p. 301, *the GPU*: OGPU – see second note to p. 146.

p. 301, *Montagu Norman... Marinetti*: The banker Montagu Norman (see second note to p. 187); the Croatian politician Ante Pavelić (1889–1959), founder of the fascist Ustaše organization and leader of the Independent State of Croatia (NDH), a fascist puppet state, from 1941 to 1945; the American newspaper tycoon and politician William Randolph Hearst (1863–1951); the Nazi politician Julius Streicher (1885–1946); the American minister Frank Buchman (see sixth note to p. 160); the poet Ezra Pound (see second note to p. 126); the Spanish magnate Juan March (1880–1962), associated with the Nationalist side during the Spanish Civil War; the French author Jean Cocteau (1889–1963), who was accused of harbouring pro-Nazi sentiments; the German industrialist Fritz Thyssen (1873–1951), an early supporter and financial backer of the Nazi Party; the Canadian-American Catholic priest Charles Coughlin (1891–1979), a supporter of the Nazi and Italian Fascist regimes, and a virulent anti-Semite; the Muslim leader and Arab nationalist Amin al-Husseini (1897–1974), who played a key role in violent opposition to Zionism and was a close ally of the Nazi regime; the author Arnold Lunn (see note to p. 287); the Romanian military officer and wartime dictator Ion Antonescu (1882–1946), a Holocaust facilitator; the German polymath and nationalist Oswald Spengler (1880–1936); the English author Beverley Nichols (1898–1983), a supporter of Mosley (for whom, see first note to p. 207); the English philanthropist and fascist sympathizer Lucy, Lady Houston (1857–1936); and the Italian poet and literary theorist Filippo Tommaso Marinetti (1876–1944), the founder of the Futurist movement, who was a fascist supporter and a co-author of the 'Fascist Manifesto' of 1919.

p. 304, *Pamphlet Literature*: First published in the *New Statesman and Nation* (9th January 1943); collected in CEJL2.

p. 304, *Gollancz*: See first note to p. 59.

p. 304, *Vansittartite*: A reference to the British diplomat Robert Vansittart, 1st Baron Vansittart (1881–1957), who famously embraced a theory (which became known as "Vansittartism") that Germany was addicted to war and predisposed to follow murderous authoritarians. Vansittart proposed forcing the German people to comply with a programme of re-education. If this plan failed, their extermination as a race would be warranted.

p. 304, *G.D.H. Cole*: The English political theorist, economist, historian and Fabian G.D.H. Cole (1889–1959).

p. 305, *The Great Scorer... Played the Game*: The final couplet of the 1941 version of the poem 'Alumnus Football' (originally published in 1908) by the American sportswriter and poet Grantland Rice (1880–1954).

p. 306, *D.H. Lawrence's... this heading*: Lawrence's *Pornography and Obscenity* was published in 1929. Count Geoffrey Potocki de Montalk (1903–97) was a New Zealand poet and polemicist of Polish heritage. His *Snobbery with Violence: A Poet in Gaol* appeared in 1932. The *Enemy* was a magazine of art and literature that ran from 1927 to 1929, with Wyndham Lewis as its founder, editor and primary contributor.

p. 307, *W.B. Yeats*: First published in *Horizon* as 'Review of *The Development of William Butler Yeats* by V.K. Narayana Menon' (January 1943); republished in CE under the present title; collected in CEJL2. V.K. Narayana Menon (1911–97) was an Indian scholar of music. His book about the Irish poet and playwright W.B. Yeats (1865–1939) appeared in 1942.

p. 307, *Grant me an... call*: The third stanza (ll. 13–18) of Yeats's 'An Acre of Grass' (1936), published in his posthumous collection *Last Poems and Two Plays* (1939).

p. 307, *Rackham's drawings*: A reference to the English book illustrator Arthur Rackham (1867–1939).

p. 307, *'The Happy Townland'*: A 1904 poem by Yeats.

p. 307, *"the chill, footless years", "the mackerel-crowded seas"*: The first quotation does not appear to be from one of Yeats's works, but from 'The Swift Years Slip and Slide Adown the Steep', a poem included in the story 'Ula and Urla', collected in *Spiritual Tales*, an 1897 volume of prose and verse by the Scottish poet, biographer and Celtic Revivalist William Sharp (1855–1905), who wrote under the pseudonym Fiona McLeod: "And the chill footless years go over me who am slain" (l. 10). The second is from Yeats's 1927 poem 'Sailing to Byzantium' (l. 4).

p. 308, *How many centuries... loveliness?*: From the 1919 verse drama *The Only Jealousy of Emer* (ll. 7–14).

p. 308, *The Playboy of the Western World*: A 1907 play by the Irish playwright John Millington Synge (1871–1909).

p. 308, *Once when midnight... thigh*: Orwell's version does not quite match the text of the original epigram, published in 1907 and titled 'The Attack on *The Playboy of the Western World*', which reads: "Once, when midnight smote the air, / Eunuchs ran through hell and met / From thoroughfare to thoroughfare, / While that great Juan galloped by; / And like these to rail and sweat / Staring upon his sinewy thigh."

p. 308, *A Vision*: A 1925 work with the full title *An Explanation of Life Founded upon the Writings of Giraldus and upon Certain Doctrines Attributed to Kusta Ben Luka*.

p. 309, *'The Second Coming'*: One of Yeats's most famous poems, first published in 1920 and included in the collection *Michael Robartes and the Dancer* (1921).

p. 310, *The Hour-Glass*: A one-act play first published in 1903.

p. 311, *The Stream of... wind*: The last three lines actually read: "Aye, to some frenzy of the mind / For all that we have done's undone / Our speculation but as the wind."

p. 312, *Literature and the Left*: First published in *Tribune* (4th June 1943); collected in CEJL2.

p. 313, *G.M. Trevelyan*: The influential English historian G.M. Trevelyan (1876–1962).

p. 314, *Gilbert Murray*: The Australian-born British classical scholar Gilbert Murray (1866–1957).

p. 314, *Mea Culpa*: A 1936 pamphlet by Céline (for whom, see first note to p. 130) attacking communism, written following the author's visit to Soviet Russia.

p. 315, *Poetry and the Microphone*: Probably written in summer 1943; first published in *New Saxon Pamphlet* (March 1945); collected in CEJL2.

p. 315, *Eliot... Edmund Blunden*: For Eliot, see first note to p. 39. For Read, see second note to p. 126. For Auden and Spender, see second note to p. 137. For Comfort, see first note to p. 258. The remainder are: the Welsh poet Dylan Thomas (1914–53); the English poet and writer of historical novels for children Henry Treece (1911–66); the English poet Robert Bridges (1844–1930); and the English poet and critic Edmund Blunden (1896–1974).

p. 315, *Auden's 'September 1941'... Revolt in the Desert*: Auden's 'September 1, 1939' was incorrectly titled 'September 1, 1941' in the anthology *Poetry* in *Wartime* (1942), edited by the Tamil poet Meary James Thurairajah Tambimuttu (1915–83), in which most of the poems quoted in this article are to be found. 'A Letter to Anne Ridler' is a poem by the Scottish poet George Sutherland Fraser (1915–80). 'Isles of Greece' is a song from Canto III (ll. 689–784) of Byron's narrative poem *Don Juan*. *Revolt in the Desert* (1927) is an abridged version of Lawrence's *Seven Pillars of Wisdom* – see second note to p. 194.

p. 319, *Sweeney Agonistes*: See third note to p. 138.

p. 320, *A.P. Herbert*: The English humorist and politician A.P. Herbert (1890–1971).

p. 320, *ABCA*: The Army Bureau of Current Affairs, an organization within the British Army formed in 1941 to provide an educational programme for members of the armed forces, focusing on current affairs, citizenship and post-war reconstruction.

p. 321, *Professor Joad*: The philosopher and author C.E.M. Joad (1891–1953), best known during the war as a broadcasting personality, appearing on *The Brains Trust*, a BBC radio discussion programme.

p. 322, *Who Are the War Criminals?*: First published in *Tribune* (22nd October 1943); collected in CEJL2. This article is a review of the book *The Trial of Mussolini* by "Cassius", pseudonym of the Labour politician Michael Foot (1913–2010), published in 1943.

p. 322, *the murder of Matteotti*: The Italian socialist politician Giacomo Matteotti (1885–1924) was kidnapped and killed by Mussolini's secret political police in June 1924.

p. 323, *Lord Mottistone*: The English general and Conservative politician J.E.B. Seely, 1st Baron Mottistone (1868–1947).

p. 323, *Duff Cooper*: The English Conservative politician and diplomat Alfred Duff Cooper, 1st Viscount Norwich, better known as "Duff Cooper" (1890–1954).

p. 323, *Hoare... Lord Lloyd*: For Hoare and Simon, see note to p. 193. For Halifax, see first note to p. 191. For Neville Chamberlain and Hore-Belisha, see first note to p. 64. The English statesman Austen Chamberlain (1863–1937), who held a number of senior government posts in the early twentieth century, was the older half-brother of Neville Chamberlain. The British India-born Conservative politician Leo Amery, also known as "L.S. Amery" (1873–1955), served in Churchill's wartime Cabinet and was one of the most vigorous advocates for total war against Germany. George Lloyd, 1st Baron Lloyd (1879–1941), was a Conservative politician and colonial administrator.

p. 323, *Lady (Austen) Chamberlain*: Ivy Muriel (née Dundas), Lady Chamberlain (1878–1941), wife of Austen Chamberlain.

p. 325, *Chiang Kai-shek*: The Chinese politician, revolutionary and general Chiang Kai-shek (1887–1975), who led the Republic of China from 1928 until his death in 1975.

p. 325, *Mustapha Kemal... Carol of Rumania*: Despite their authoritarianism, both the Turkish general and statesman Kemal Atatürk (1881–1938) – who became the first president of the Turkish republic in 1923 and went on to remodel the country as a modern secular state – and Carol II of Romania (1893–1953), a dictator, were sometimes regarded as potential allies in the 1930s by some on the British Left due to the fact that they were not aligned with the Axis powers.

p. 325, *Ribbentrop*: See note to p. 178.

p. 325, *væ victis*: "Woe to the vanquished" (Latin).

p. 326, *Darlan–Badoglio*: For Darlan, see first note to p. 262. Pietro Badoglio (1871–1956) was an Italian general during both world wars. With the fall of the Fascist regime in July 1943, he became prime minister of Italy.

p. 326, *the Empress Eugenie... through a sewer*: When the Second Empire came to an end with the deposition of Napoleon III in 1870, his wife, Eugénie de Montijo (1826–1920), fled Paris with the assistance of her American dentist, Thomas W. Evans (1823–97). The German general and politician Erich Ludendorff (1865–1937) fled Germany disguised in blue spectacles and a false beard after his country's defeat in 1918. The Roman emperor is probably Marcus Aurelius Antoninus, known posthumously as Elagabalus or Heliogabalus, who reigned from 218–22 AD. The "leading fascist" is Juan March (for whom, see second note to p. 301), whose escape from Barcelona through the city's sewers to avoid capture was widely reported in the European press.

p. 328, *Mark Twain – the Licensed Jester*: First published in *Tribune* (26th November 1943); collected in CEJL2.

p. 328, *Tom Sawyer and Huckleberry Finn*: Novels published in 1876 and 1884, respectively.

p. 328, *Roughing It... Life on the Mississippi*: *Roughing It* and *The Innocents Abroad, or The New Pilgrim's Progress* are works of travel writing, published in 1872 and 1876, respectively. *Life on the Mississippi* is a memoir of Twain's days as a steamboat pilot before the American Civil War, published in 1883.

p. 328, *a namby-pamby "life" of Joan of Arc*: The reference is to the 1896 novel *Personal Recollections of Joan of Arc*.

p. 329, *Anatole France*: The French poet, novelist and journalist Anatole France, pseudonym of Jacques-Anatole-François Thibault (1844–1924).

p. 329, *the Dreyfus case*: The Jewish French army officer Alfred Dreyfus (1859–1935) was arrested, summarily tried and unjustly convicted of treason in 1894–95. After a public outcry, he was pardoned in 1899, and fully exonerated in 1906. The affair was the focus of France's satirical history *L'Île des pingouins* (1908).

p. 330, *The Gilded Age*: *The Gilded Age: A Tale of Today* (1873, a satirical novel co-written by Mark Twain and the American writer Charles Dudley Warner (1829–1900).

p. 330, *A Connecticut Yankee in King Arthur's Court*: See second note to p. 173.

p. 330, *My Mark Twain*: *My Mark Twain: Reminiscences and Criticisms*, a 1910 work by the American novelist and literary critic William Dean Howells (1837–1920).

p. 331, *1601*: *1601: Conversation, as It Was by the Social Fireside, in the Time of the Tudors*, a short, risqué squib first published anonymously in 1880 and finally acknowledged by the author in 1906.

p. 332, *A Hundred Up*: First published in the *Observer* as 'Review of *Martin Chuzzlewit* by Charles Dickens' (13th February 1944); collected in CEJL3 under the present title.

p. 332, *the Sketches*: *Sketches by Boz, Illustrative of Everyday Life and Everyday People*, a series of short pieces by Charles Dickens published between 1833 and 1836, collected in two volumes in 1836. "Boz" was Dickens's pen name.

p. 333, *American Notes*: *American Notes for General Circulation*, an 1842 travelogue.

p. 333, *André Gide's Retour de l'URSS*: See second note to p. 103.

p. 334, *The English People*: Written by 22nd April 1944; first published (in pamphlet form) by Collins as part of the series "Britain in Pictures" (August 1947); collected in CEJL3.

p. 335, *Ratcliffe Highway*: The Ratcliffe Highway, known today simply as "the Highway", is a road that runs between the City of London and Limehouse in the East End. In the nineteenth century it was synonymous with crime and vice, not least because of a series of vicious killings in 1811 that became known as "the Ratcliffe Highway murders".

p. 336, *Gray wrote his famous 'Elegy'*: See second note to p. 275.

p. 337, *Kid Lewis*: The English boxer Ted "Kid" Lewis (1894–1970), who won the World Welterweight Championship in 1915 and 1917.

p. 339, *Carlyle*: The Scottish essayist and historian Thomas Carlyle (1795–1881).

p. 340, *the Irish civil war*: The reference here is to the Irish insurgency against British rule that began with the Easter Rising of 1916, included the Anglo-Irish War of 1919–21 and ended with the partitioning, in December 1921, of the country between the Irish Free State and Northern Ireland, which remained part of the United Kingdom. (The term "Irish Civil War" is today used specifically to refer to the subsequent conflict, fought in 1922–23, between factions within the Irish Free State over the terms of the Anglo-Irish Treaty, which had legislated for the partitioning.)

p. 341, *sacro egoismo*: "Sacred egoism" (Italian). The expression is used to denote a foreign policy in which the national interest is prioritized.

p. 342, *'A Little of What You Fancy Does You Good'*: A 1916 music-hall song popularized by the singer and comedian Marie Lloyd (1870–1922).

p. 343, *the suppression of the Daily Worker*: The *Daily Worker* (see third note to p. 45) was banned from 21st January 1941 to 26th August 1942.

p. 344, *Cripps... Bevin*: Respectively: the English Labour politician Stafford Cripps (1889–1952); the English Liberal politician and economist William Beveridge (1879–1963), author, in November 1942, of the government report *Social Insurance and Allied Services* (known as the "Beveridge Report"), which was influential in the founding of the welfare state; and the Labour politician Ernest Bevin (see second note to p. 203).

p. 346, *Mosley's Blackshirts*: See first note to p. 207.

p. 352, *Messrs Lyons*: A reference to a chain of tea shops owned by J. Lyons & Co., with around 200 outlets throughout England.

p. 354, *"bêche-de-mer" English*: A form of pidgin English used as the national language of Vanuatu in the south-western Pacific. It was originally associated with labourers in the nineteenth-century trade in sea cucumbers from the Pacific region, hence the name.

p. 355, *Swift's essay on polite conversation*: *A Complete Collection of Genteel and Ingenious Conversation*, or *Polite Conversation* (1738).

p. 363, *Alfred Noyes*: The English poet and short-story writer Alfred Noyes (1880–1958).

p. 364, *the Giant Panda*: A reference to a giant panda named Ming who was brought to London Zoo in 1938 and became an icon in wartime Britain.

p. 365, *Propaganda and Demotic Speech*: Written by 28th April 1944; first published in *Persuasion* (Summer 1944); collected in CEJL3.

p. 365, *Sir Richard Acland*: See first note to p. 220.

p. 365, *Mass Observers*: A reference to Mass Observation, a social-research organization founded in 1937 with the aim of documenting the lives of ordinary people via surveys and diaries kept by volunteers.

p. 365, *most people don't... immorality*: In spite of this, Common Wealth has adopted the astonishingly feeble slogan: "What is morally wrong cannot be politically right" [ORWELL'S NOTE]. Common Wealth was a socialist political party established by Acland (see first note to p. 220) and J.B. Priestley.

p. 366, *Professor Harold Laski... Civilization*: Harold Laski (1893–1950) was an English political theorist, economist and revolutionary socialist. *Faith, Reason and Civilization*, in which Laski argued for Stalinism, was published in 1944.

p. 366, *And nobody... paid the rent*: From *Sweeney Agonistes* (see third note to p. 138).

p. 368, *the Brains Trust*: See note to p. 321.

p. 371, *Benefit of Clergy: Some Notes on Salvador Dali*: Probably written in June 1944; first published in CE; collected in CEJL3. In CE, Orwell supplied the following note: "'Benefit of Clergy' made a sort of phantom appearance in the *Saturday Book* for 1944. The book was in print when its publishers, Messrs Hutchinson, decided that this essay must be suppressed on grounds of obscenity. It was accordingly cut out of each copy, though for technical reasons it was impossible to remove its title from the table of contents." *The Saturday Book* was an annual miscellany published from 1941 to 1975.

p. 371, *Frank Harris's autobiographical writings*: A reference to the sexually explicit and scurrilous *My Life and Loves* (1931), the autobiography of the Irish-American journalist, editor and literary personality Frank Harris (1856–1931), which was banned on both sides of the Atlantic until the early 1960s.

p. 371, *Dalí's recently published Life*: *The Secret Life of Salvador Dalí*, published in English in 1942.

p. 372, *The Vicomte de Noailles, whom he describes as his "Maecenas"*: The French nobleman and patron of the arts Charles de Noailles, Vicomte de Noailles (1891–1981), was Dalí's patron. The Roman statesman Gaius Maecenas (c.70–8 BC) was the patron of poets such as Virgil and Horace.

p. 373, *Le Chien andalou*: A reference to the French silent short *Un Chien andalou* (a title meaning "an Andalusian dog"), directed by the Spanish film-maker Luis Buñuel (1900–83), who co-wrote the screenplay with Dalí.

p. 374, *Lord Elton*: The English historian, academic and Labour politician Godfrey Elton, 1st Baron Elton (1892–1973).

p. 374, *Kulturbolschewismus*: "Cultural Bolshevism" (German).

p. 375, *L'Âge d'or*: Dalí mentions *L'Âge d'or* and adds that its first public showing was broken up by hooligans, but he does not say in detail what it was about. According to Henry Miller's account of it, it showed among other things some fairly detailed shots of a woman defecating [ORWELL'S NOTE]. *L'Âge d'or* (a title meaning "the golden age") is a 1930 French Surrealist film directed by Buñuel (for whom, see note to p. 373), controversial for its graphic and subversive content. As with *Un Chien andalou*, Dalí co-wrote the screenplay with Buñuel.

p. 376, *Dürer*: The German painter and printmaker Albrecht Dürer (1471–1528).

p. 376, *Beardsley*: The English illustrator Aubrey Beardsley (1872–98), famous for his risqué black-ink drawings.

p. 376, *James Branch Cabell*: The American writer of fantasy fiction and belletrist James Branch Cabell (1879–1958).

p. 376, *Barrie... Where the Rainbow Ends*: For Barrie and Rackham, see fourth note to p. 42 and third note to p. 307, respectively. Edward Plunkett, 18th Baron Dunsany (1878–1957), commonly known as "Lord Dunsany", was an Anglo-Irish writer of fantasy fiction. *Where the Rainbow Ends* is a 1911 children's play written by the English author Emlie Clifford (1863–1933) and the English actor Reginald Owen (1887–1972), who wrote under the names "Clifford Mills" and "John Ramsey", respectively.

p. 376, *Ruthless Rhymes... Graham*: The English poet Harry Graham (1874–1936) wrote – under the pseudonym "Col. D. Streamer" – and illustrated *Ruthless Rhymes for Heartless Homes* (1899), a volume of comic verse.

p. 377, *"le rossignol", "une montre"*: Respectively, "the nightingale" and "a watch" (French).

p. 379, *Raffles and Miss Blandish*: Written by 28th August 1944; first published in *Horizon* (October 1944); collected in CEJL3. For Raffles, see third note to p. 9. The name "Miss Blandish" refers to *No Orchids for Miss Blandish*, a 1939 crime novel by the English writer René Raymond (1906–85), published under a pseudonym, James Hadley Chase.

p. 379, *Arsène Lupin*: A series of novels, novellas and short stories featuring the gentleman thief Arsène Lupin by the French author Maurice Leblanc (1864–1941).

p. 379, *The Raffles Books*: *Raffles*, *A Thief in the Night* and *Mr Justice Raffles* by E.W. Hornung. The third of these is definitely a failure, and only the first has the true Raffles atmosphere. Hornung wrote a number of crime stories, usually with a tendency to take the side of the criminal. A successful book in rather the same vein as *Raffles* is *Stingaree* [ORWELL'S NOTE]. *Stingaree* is a novel by Hornung about an Australian bushranger, published in 1905.

p. 380, *Charles Peace*: The notorious English burglar and murderer Charles Peace (1832–79).

p. 380, *I Zingari*: An English cricket club founded in 1845 and notable for having no home ground – hence the name, which means "the gypsies" in dialectal Italian.

p. 380, *Larwood... bodyline*: The English cricketer Harold Larwood (1904–95) was the main exponent of the bowling style known as "bodyline" – that is, one in which the cricket ball is bowled at pace, aimed at the body of the batsman in the expectation that when he defends himself with his bat the resulting deflection can be caught by one of the fielders placed nearby on the leg side. His use of this technique during the Marylebone Cricket Club (MCC) tour of Australia in 1932–33 caused a furore and brought to an end his international career.

p. 380, *Le Rouge et le Noir*: *The Red and the Black*, a novel by Stendhal of 1830.

p. 381, *Kipling's... six horses*: The quotation is of l. 5 of Kipling's 1892 poem: "Yea, a trooper of the forces who has run his own six horses." A "gentleman-ranker" was an enlisted soldier qualified through education or background to be an officer.

p. 381, *the MCC*: The Marylebone Cricket Club.

p. 381, *He will not commit murder*: Actually Raffles does kill one man and is more or less consciously responsible for the death of two others. But all three of them are foreigners and have behaved in a very reprehensible manner. He also, on one occasion, contemplates murdering a blackmailer. It is, however, a fairly well-established convention in crime stories that murdering a blackmailer "doesn't count" [ORWELL'S NOTE, 1945].

p. 382, *the John Thorndyke... minority are murders*: For Thorndyke, see fourth note to p. 173. Max Carrados is a blind detective in a series of mystery stories and books by Ernest Bramah (for whom, see note to p. 170).

p. 382, *the Peter Wimsey stories*: See first note to p. 74.

p. 382, *she has developed... caresses*: Another reading of the final episode is possible; it may mean merely that Miss Blandish is pregnant. But the interpretation I have given above seems more in keeping with the general brutality of the book [ORWELL'S NOTE, 1945].

p. 382, *Sanctuary*: A 1931 novel by the American novelist William Faulkner (1897–1962).

p. 382, *récit*: "Narration" (French).

p. 383, *He Won't Need It Now*: A 1941 novel, published under a different pseudonym, James L. Docherty.

p. 384, *Action Stories*: An American pulp magazine published between 1921 and 1950.

p. 384, *"clipshop" or the "hotsquat"*: American underworld slang for a fraudulent gambling house and the electric chair, respectively.

p. 385, *Miss Callaghan Comes to Grief*: Published in 1941 under the pseudonym James Hadley Chase.

p. 385, *Henry Ford*: The American industrialist and magnate Henry Ford (1863–1947), founder of the Ford Motor Company.

p. 385, *Lord Northcliffe*: See fourth note to p. 160.

p. 385, *one finds Mark Twain... Slade*: Twain devotes a chapter in *Roughing It* (for which, see third note to p. 328) to the notorious real-life gunfighter and murderer Joseph "Jack" Slade (1831–64), a legendary figure of the American West.

p. 385, *Edgar Wallace... Mr J.G. Reeder stories*: The English author Edgar Wallace (1875–1932) was a prolific and hugely popular author of thriller stories and novels. *The Orator* (1928) is a collection of his detective stories. J.G. Reeder is a former police officer working for the Director of Public Prosecutions in a series of novels and short stories.

p. 387, *Creasey*: The English author of crime fiction John Creasey (1908–73).

p. 388, *GPU*: OGPU – see second note to p. 146.

p. 389, *Arthur Koestler*: Written by 11th September 1944; first published in CE; collected in CEJL3. For Koestler, see first note to p. 246.

p. 389, *Silone...Victor Serge*: For Silone, see first note to p. 246. For Borkenau, see note to p. 143. For Malraux, see note to p. 287. Gaetano Salvemini (1873–1957) was an Italian socialist, anti-fascist politician and historian. Victor Serge (1890–1947) was a Belgian-born Russian revolutionary and author.

p. 389, *Fontamara or Darkness at Noon*: *Fontamara* (1933), Silone's most famous novel, concerns the exploitation of peasants in a southern Italian village under Mussolini's Fascist regime. For *Darkness at Noon*, see first note to p. 246.

p. 390, *Spanish Testament... Arrival and Departure*: *Spanish Testament* (1937) is a non-fiction work describing Koestler's experiences during the Spanish Civil War. *The Gladiators* (1939) is a novel about the effects of the Spartacus revolt on the Roman Republic. *Scum of the Earth* (1941) is an account of Koestler's life in France in 1939–40. *Arrival and Departure* (1943) is a novel about a refugee and former revolutionary who undergoes psychoanalysis.

p. 391, *Salammbô*: See first note to p. 122.

p. 392, *Old Bolshevik*: A name for the prominent Bolshevik leaders from before the October Revolution of 1917, many of whom went on to hold leading positions in the Soviet Union. Many Old Bolsheviks were removed from power, imprisoned or executed during the Stalinist "Great Purge" of the late 1930s.

p. 393, *Boris Souvarine... en URSS*: Boris Souvarine (1895–1984) was a French Marxist, anti-Stalinist and essayist. His pamphlet *Cauchemar en URSS* (a title meaning "nightmare in the USSR") was published in 1937.

p. 393, *Bukharin*: Nikolai Bukharin (1888–1938), an Old Bolshevik (see note to p. 392) who along with twenty others was tried at the third and final of the Moscow show trials in March 1938, accused of espionage and treason. He was subsequently executed.

p. 394, *OGPU*: See second note to p. 146.

p. 394, *the Daladier government*: Édouard Daladier (1884–1970) was prime minister of France from April 1938 to March 1940.

p. 395, *Doriot*: The French politician Jacques Doriot (1898–1945), who shifted from a communist stance to fascism and founded, in 1936, the ultra-nationalist Parti Populaire Français (PPF).

p. 398, *Tobias Smollett: Scotland's Best Novelist*: First published in *Tribune* (22nd September 1944); collected in CEJL3. For Smollett, see sixth note to p. 39.

p. 398, *Amelia*: Fielding's last novel, published in 1751.

p. 398, *Sir Lancelot Greaves*: See sixth note to p. 39.

p. 398, *Humphry Clinker*: *The Expedition of Humphry Clinker*, a picaresque novel published in 1771.

p. 398, *Roderick Random and Peregrine Pickle*: *The Adventures of Roderick Random* and *The Adventures of Peregrine Pickle*, picaresque novels published in 1748 and 1751, respectively.

p. 400, *Joseph Andrews*: The first of Fielding's novels, published in 1742.

p. 400, *Ian Hay*: See second note to p. 84.

p. 402, *Funny, but Not Vulgar*: Written by 1st December 1944; first published in the *Leader* (28th July 1945); collected in CEJL3.

p. 402, *Surtees's Handley Cross... and others*: For Surtees, see note to p. 112. His Jorrocks novel *Handley Cross* was published in 1843. For *Mrs Caudle's Curtain Lectures*, see second note to p. 123. For R.H. Barham, see first note to p. 119. For Thomas Hood, see first note to p. 272. Edward Lear (1812–88) was an English poet and illustrator, famous for his books of nonsense poetry. For Arthur Hugh Clough, see second note to p. 272. Charles Stuart Calverley (1831–84) was an English poet, wit and translator.

NOTES

p. 402, *F. Anstey's... Diary of a Nobody*: *Vice Versa: A Lesson to Fathers* (1882) is a comic novel by the English writer Thomas Anstey Guthrie (1856–1934), published under the pseudonym F. Anstey. *The Diary of a Nobody* (1892) is a comic novel by the brothers George (1847–1912) and Weedon Grossmith (1854–1919), originally serialized in *Punch* in 1888–89.

p. 402, *Cruikshank's illustrations to Dickens*: The English caricaturist and illustrator George Cruikshank (1792–1878) provided illustrations for a number of Dickens's early works.

p. 402, *Leech's illustrations to Surtees*: See note to p. 112.

p. 402, *Barry Pain... Stephen Leacock*: For Pain and Jacobs, see first note to p. 277. Stephen Leacock (1869–1944) was a Canadian humorist of international renown, author of comic works such as *Sunshine Sketches of a Little Town* (1912) and *Arcadian Adventures with the Idle Rich* (1914).

p. 402, *Tommy Handley... postcards*: Tommy Handley (1892–1949) was an English comedian, best known for *It's That Man Again*, a BBC radio programme that began in 1939. For McGill, see Orwell's essay 'The Art of Donald McGill' (pp. 249–57).

p. 402, *James Thurber or Damon Runyon*: James Thurber (1894–1961) was an American cartoonist and humorist whose work, including short stories such as 'The Secret Life of Walter Mitty' (1939), appeared regularly in the *New Yorker* in the 1930s and 1940s. Damon Runyon (1880–1946) was an American writer best known for stories about New York City's Broadway, including the collection *Guys and Dolls* (1931).

p. 403, *"Timothy Shy"... "Beachcomber"*: "Timothy Shy" was the name used by D.B. Wyndham Lewis (for whom, see second note to p. 37) to sign a long-running column in the *News Chronicle*. For "Beachcomber", see second note to p. 37.

p. 403, *Sterne*: The Irish writer Laurence Sterne (1713–68), author of the comic novel *The Life and Opinions of Tristram Shandy, Gentleman* (1759–67).

p. 404, *'The Courtship of the Yonghy-Bonghy-Bò'*: A nonsense poem published in the collection *Laughable Lyrics* (1877). For Lear, see second note to p. 402.

p. 404, *Once... of blue*: From the 1862 poem 'Ode: "On a Distant Prospect" of Making a Fortune' (ll. 49–52). For Calverley, see second note to p. 402.

p. 405, *The Modern Traveller... a lot of holes*: For Belloc, see second note to p. 36. The collection *The Modern Traveller* was published in 1898. The quotation is from the poem numbered 'V' (ll. 1–3, 19–23).

p. 405, *Bret Harte's sequel... was intoxicated*: From the poem 'Mrs Judge Jenkins: Being the Only Genuine Sequel to "Maud Muller"' (ll. 15–16) by Bret Harte (for whom, see second note to p. 131). It was written in response to 'Maud Muller', an 1856 poem by the American poet John Greenleaf Whittier (1807–92).

p. 405, *La Pucelle*: *La Pucelle d'Orléans* (*The Maid of Orléans*), a bawdy and satirical poem by the French Enlightenment writer Voltaire (1694–1778), whose real name was François-Marie Arouet.

p. 405, *Owen Seaman... A.A. Milne*: Owen Seaman (1861–1936) was an English journalist and writer, and the editor of *Punch* from 1906 to 1932. For Harry Graham, see fifth note to p. 376. For A.P. Herbert, see first note to p. 320. The English children's author A.A. Milne (1882–1956) is best known as the creator of Winnie-the-Pooh.

p. 405, *The Callipyge's injured... floor*: From the humorous poem 'Bloudie Jacke of Shrewsberrie' (ll. 286–92), one of Barham's *Ingoldsby Legends*. See first note to p. 119.

p. 406, *'Ode to Tobacco'... sweetest*: For Calverley, see second note to p. 402. The quotation is of the first stanza of 'Ode to Tobacco' (1862).

p. 407, *Oysters and Brown Stout*: First published in *Tribune* (22nd December 1944); collected in CEJL3.

p. 407, *Tales of a Grandfather*: A series of books on Scottish history by Sir Walter Scott, originally intended for his grandson, published between 1828 and 1830.

p. 407, *Christmas Books... A Book of Snobs*: Thackeray wrote and illustrated five Christmas books, the first four of which were published under the name of "M.A. Titmarsh" ("Michael Angelo Titmarsh"). They are: *Mrs Perkins's Ball* (1846), *Our Street* (1848), *Doctor Birch and His Young Friends* (1849), *The Kickleburys on the Rhine* (1851) and *The Rose and the Ring* (1854). *Burlesques* is a collection of satirical writings and tales published posthumously in 1869. The satirical essays known collectively as *A Book of Snobs* first appeared in *Punch* between 1846 and 1847, and were published in volume form in 1848.

p. 407, *Esmond or The Virginians*: Historical novels published in 1852 and 1857–59, respectively. The full title of the former is *The History of Henry Esmond*.

p. 407, *A Shabby Genteel Story*: See note to p. 107.

p. 408, *'Memorials of Gormandizing'*: See first note to p. 103.

p. 408, *'The Ballad of the Bouillabaisse'*: A humorous poem by Thackeray first published in *Fraser's Magazine* in November 1844.

p. 409, *Doctor Birch... 'A Little Dinner at Timmins's'*: For *Doctor Birch and His Young Friends* and *The Rose and the Ring*, see third note to p. 407. 'The Fatal Boots' and 'A Little Dinner at Timmins's' are novellas published in 1857 and 1856, respectively.

p. 409, *The Ingoldsby Legends*: See first note to p. 119.

p. 410, *A New Year Message*: First published in *Tribune* (5th January 1945); collected in CEJL3.

p. 410, *Daniel George's column*: Daniel George was the pen name of the journalist Daniel George Bunting (1890–1967), a regular contributor to *Tribune*.

p. 414, *In Defence of P.G. Wodehouse*: Written by 20th February 1945; first published in *Windmill* (July 1945); collected in CEJL3.

p. 414, *Harry Flannery*: The American journalist and author Harry Flannery (1900–75) was the Berlin correspondent for the CBS network during the

NOTES

Second World War, an experience that became the subject of his 1942 bestseller *Assignment to Berlin*.

p. 415, *"Cassandra" of the Daily Mirror*: The English journalist William Neil Connor (1909–67) wrote for the *Daily Mirror* under the pen name of "Cassandra".

p. 416, *Flannery comments... Wooster*: From *Assignment to Berlin* (see second note to p. 414). For Bertie Wooster, see third note to p. 255.

p. 416, *John Amery*: The British fascist and Nazi collaborator John Amery (1912–45), son of politician L.S. Amery (for whom, see third note to p. 323).

p. 417, *Ukridge appeared in 1924*: Stanley Featherstonehaugh Ukridge is an avaricious and scheming idler in several short stories and a novel by Wodehouse, notably an eponymously titled ten-story collection published in 1924.

p. 417, *The Gold Bat... Mike (1909)*: Three novels with a public-school setting. *The Gold Bat* and *The Pothunters* (Wodehouse's first published novel), were published in 1904 and 1902, respectively. *Mike* is notable for introducing the dandyish Rupert Psmith, who would become one of Wodehouse's best-loved characters. Orwell incorrectly gives the publication date of *Mike* as 1908 later in this essay.

p. 417, *Psmith in the City*: A 1910 novel continuing the adventures of Mike Jackson and his friend Psmith, both introduced in *Mike* (see previous note).

p. 417, *The Man with Two Left Feet*: A 1917 collection, with the full title *The Man with Two Left Feet and Other Stories*.

p. 417, *in propria persona*: "In his or her own person" (Latin).

p. 418, *Psmith, Journalist... Piccadilly Jim*: Novels published in 1915, 1913, 1921 and 1918, respectively.

p. 418, *Summer Lightning*: One of Wodehouse's "Blandings Castle" novels, set on the country estate of the eccentric Earl of Emsworth, published in 1929.

p. 418, *The Coming of Bill*: A novel published in 1919.

p. 418, *Tales of St Austin's*: A collection of public-school-themed short stories and essays, published in 1903.

p. 419, *Julien Sorel*: The protagonist of Stendhal's *The Red and the Black* (see fourth note to p. 380).

p. 419, *Something Fresh*: The first of the "Blandings Castle" novels, published in 1915.

p. 420, *Pip*: A 1907 novel by Ian Hay (for whom, see second note to p. 84).

p. 420, *Hildebrand... Dreever*: An impecunious young aristocrat, nicknamed "Spennie", in the 1910 novel *A Gentleman of Leisure*.

p. 421, *The Earl of Emsworth*: See second note to p. 418.

p. 421, *'Gilbert... Regent's Palace'*: 'Gilbert the Filbert' was a popular song sung from the perspective of a fashionable, showy young man, or "knut", that featured in the 1914 iteration of the annual musical revue *The Passing Show*, which opened in London in April 1914. It was performed by the English actor

Basil Hallam (1888–1916). 'Reckless Reggie' was a song from the 1917 revue *Bubbly*, devised by the English impresario John Hastings Turner (1891–1956).

p. 421, *Young Men in Spats*: A collection of short stories published in 1936.

p. 422, *As Mr John Hayward... Shakespeare*: 'P.G. Wodehouse' by John Hayward (*The Saturday Book*, 1942). I believe this is the only full-length critical essay on Wodehouse [ORWELL'S NOTE]. John Davy Hayward (1905–65) was an English literary scholar, critic and editor, remembered as a close friend and collaborator of T.S. Eliot.

p. 422, *Barry Pain... Damon Runyon*: For Pain and Jacobs, see first note to p. 277. Jerome K. Jerome (1859–1927) was an English writer and humorist, remembered as the author of the comic novel *Three Men in a Boat* (1889). For Anstey, see third note to p. 402. Ring Lardner (1885–1933) was an American satirist, sports columnist and short-story writer. For Runyon, see eighth note to p. 402.

p. 422, *The Heart of a Goof*: A collection of golf-related short stories.

p. 424, *Beaverbrook*: See fifth note to p. 28.

p. 424, *the Calcutta Derby Sweep*: A lottery based on the result of the Calcutta Derby, a horse race held annually in British India; tickets were sold worldwide, with prizes awarded according to the success of randomly allotted horses.

p. 425, *corpus vile*: "A living or dead body that is of so little value that it can be used for experiment without regard for the outcome" (*OED*).

p. 426, *Anti-Semitism in Britain*: Written by 26th February 1945; first published in the *Contemporary Jewish Record* (April 1945); collected in CEJL3.

p. 426, *the ICI*: Imperial Chemical Industries, now-defunct. It was, for much of its history, the largest manufacturer in Britain.

p. 430, *the "Jew joke"... ill-natured*: It is interesting to compare the "Jew joke" with that other standby of the music halls, the "Scotch joke", which superficially it resembles. Occasionally a story is told (e.g. the Jew and the Scotsman who went into a pub together and both died of thirst) which puts both races on an equality, but in general the Jew is credited *merely* with cunning and avarice while the Scotsman is credited with physical hardihood as well. This is seen, for example, in the story of the Jew and the Scotsman who go together to a meeting which has been advertised as free. Unexpectedly there is a collection, and to avoid this the Jew faints and the Scotsman carries him out. Here the Scotsman performs the athletic feat of carrying the other. It would seem vaguely wrong if it were the other way about [ORWELL'S NOTE].

p. 431, *Arnold Lunn's... Put Out More Flags*: For Lunn, see note to p. 287. *The Good Gorilla*, a book of essays, was published in 1943. Waugh's *Put Out More Flags*, in which the upper-class characters of his darkly comic earlier novels are forced to adjust to the social changes brought about by the outbreak of war, appeared in 1942.

p. 432, *the anti-Dreyfusards*: For the Dreyfus affair, see second note to p. 329.

p. 434, *Notes on Nationalism*: Written by 15th May 1945; first published in *Polemic* (October 1945); collected in CEJL3.

p. 434, *Byron... profusion*: See *Don Juan* III, 97: "I know that what our neighbours call 'longueurs' / (We've not so good a word, but have the thing / In that complete perfection which ensures / An epic from Bob Southey every spring)" (ll. 1–4).

p. 434, *By "nationalism" I... "bad"*: Nations, and even vaguer entities such as the Catholic Church or the proletariat, are commonly thought of as individuals and often referred to as "she". Patently absurd remarks such as "Germany is naturally treacherous" are to be found in any newspaper one opens, and reckless generalizations about national character ("The Spaniard is a natural aristocrat" or "Every Englishman is a hypocrite") are uttered by almost everyone. Intermittently these generalizations are seen to be unfounded, but the habit of making them persists, and people of professedly international outlook, e.g. Tolstoy or Bernard Shaw, are often guilty of them [ORWELL'S NOTE].

p. 436, *It is curious... 1939*: A few writers of conservative tendency, such as Peter Drucker, foretold an agreement between Germany and Russia, but they expected an actual alliance or amalgamation which would be permanent. No Marxist or other left-wing writer, of whatever colour, came anywhere near foretelling the Pact [ORWELL'S NOTE]. The reference is to the book *The End of Economic Man* (1939) by the Austrian-American author Peter Drucker (1909–2005), later famous as a management theorist. For the Molotov–Ribbentrop Pact of 1939, see note to p. 178.

p. 436, *Political or military... loyalties*: The military commentators of the popular press can mostly be classified as pro-Russian or anti-Russian, pro-Blimp or anti-Blimp. Such errors as believing the Maginot Line impregnable, or predicting that Russia would conquer Germany in three months, have failed to shake their reputation, because they were always saying what their own particular audience wanted to hear. The two military critics most favoured by the intelligentsia are Captain Liddell Hart and Major General Fuller, the first of whom teaches that the defence is stronger than the attack, and the second that the attack is stronger than the defence. This contradiction has not prevented both of them from being accepted as authorities by the same public. The secret reason for their vogue in left-wing circles is that both of them are at odds with the War Office [ORWELL'S NOTE]. The critics referred to here are the British military historians and strategists Sir Basil Liddell Hart (1895–1970) and J.F.C. Fuller (1878–1966).

p. 436, *Mayakovsky*: The Russian Futurist poet and playwright Vladimir Mayakovsky (1893–1930).

p. 436, *"Great is Diana of the Ephesians"*: A reference to a story in Acts of the Apostles (19) in which St Paul's preaching in Ephesus provokes an angry response from a crowd of silversmiths – makers of shrines to the goddess Diana – who feel that their culture and livelihoods are threatened. In the ensuing riot the crowd mechanically repeats the chant "Great is Diana of the Ephesians!" for two hours.

p. 437, *Chu Chin Chow*: A musical comedy written by the Australian actor, director and writer Oscar Asche (1871–1936), with music by the English composer Frederic Norton (1869–1946), based on the story of 'Ali Baba and the Forty Thieves' from the *One Thousand and One Nights*.

p. 437, *Chesterton's battle poems... pacifist tract*: The poems by Chesterton are, respectively, one published in 1915 that celebrates the victory of the Holy League at the Battle of Lepanto of 7th October 1571 and another from 1922 about "the patron saint of artillery and of those in danger of sudden death", as the subtitle explains. For 'The Charge of the Light Brigade', see note to p. 116.

p. 438, *the order in... named*: Certain Americans have expressed dissatisfaction because "Anglo-American" is the normal form of combination of these two words. It has been proposed to substitute "America-British" [ORWELL'S NOTE].

p. 438, *de Valera... Beaverbrook*: Respectively: the Irish politician and activist (and later statesman) Éamon de Valera (1882–1975), who campaigned for the official international recognition of the Irish Republic; the English Conservative statesman Benjamin Disraeli (1804–81), prime minister in 1868 and again between 1874 and 1880; the French statesman Raymond Poincaré (1860–1934), president from 1913 to 1920 and three times prime minister (1912–13, 1922–24, 1926–29); and the newspaper magnate Lord Beaverbrook (for whom, see fifth note to p. 28).

p. 438, *Houston Chamberlain*: The British-born German philosopher Houston Stewart Chamberlain (1855–1927), known for his belief in Aryan supremacy, anti-Semitism and advocacy of German ethnonationalism.

p. 438, *Lafcadio Hearn*: Lafcadio Hearn (1850–1904) was a Greek-born writer and translator of Irish descent, later naturalized in Japan, who introduced the culture and literature of Japan to the Western world.

p. 439, *H.G. Wells's Outline of History*: See second note to p. 246.

p. 440, *The Liberal News Chronicle... Russians*: The *News Chronicle* advised its readers to visit the news film at which the entire execution could be witnessed, with close-ups. The *Star* published with seeming approval photographs of nearly naked female collaborationists being baited by the Paris mob. These photographs had a marked resemblance to the Nazi photographs of Jews being baited by the Berlin mob [ORWELL'S NOTE].

p. 440, *the Star Chamber*: An English court that sat at the Palace of Westminster from the late fifteenth to the mid-seventeenth century. Although it was not authorized to use torture, its judgements were often harsh and arbitrary.

p. 440, *Sir Francis Drake*: The English explorer and privateer Sir Francis Drake (*c.*1540–96).

NOTES

p. 440, *Events which, it... denied*: An example is the Russo-German Pact, which is being effaced as quickly as possible from public memory. A Russian correspondent informs me that mention of the Pact is already being omitted from Russian yearbooks which table recent political events [ORWELL'S NOTE]. For the Molotov–Ribbentrop Pact of 1939, see note to p. 178.

p. 440, *Chiang Kai-shek*: See first note to p. 325.

p. 442, *Lord Elton... and After*: For Lord Elton, see first note to p. 374. For A.P. Herbert, see first note to p. 320. G.M. Young (1882–1959) was an English historian, best known for a study of the Victorian era, *Portrait of an Age* (1936). Kenneth Pickthorn (1892–1975) was an English Conservative politician, historian and academic. The Tory Reform Committee, established in 1943, was a group consisting of forty to fifty backbenchers who advocated a commitment to post-war social reform. The right-wing *New English Review* was launched in 1945 by the British journalist and publisher Douglas Francis Jerrold (1893–1964) as a successor to the *English Review*, which, during Jerrold's editorship (1931–35), had adopted a pro-fascist position. The *Nineteenth Century and After* was a monthly literary magazine established in 1877 that, during the twentieth century, became increasingly right-wing in tone. In 1945 its editor was F.A. Voigt (see third note to p. 157).

p. 442, *F.A. Voigt... Hugh Kingsmill*: For Voigt, see third note to p. 157. For Muggeridge, see second note to p. 156. For Waugh, see note to p. 144. Hugh Kingsmill Lunn (1889–1949), known under his pen name Hugh Kingsmill, was an English journalist and the brother of the writer Arnold Lunn (see note to p. 287). From 1945 until his death in 1949 he was the literary editor of the *New English Review* (see previous note).

p. 442, *Hugh MacDiarmid and Sean O'Casey*: Hugh MacDiarmid was the pen name of Christopher Murray Grieve (1892–1978), a leading Scottish poet, journalist and essayist. Sean O'Casey (1880–1964) was an Irish dramatist.

p. 443, *various pseudoscientific theories... abandoned*: A good example is the sunstroke superstition. Until recently it was believed that the white races were much more liable to sunstroke than the coloured, and that a white man could not safely walk about in tropical sunshine without a pith helmet. There was no evidence whatever for this theory, but it served the purpose of accentuating the difference between "natives" and Europeans. During the present war the theory has been quietly dropped and whole armies manoeuvre in the tropics without pith helmets. So long as the sunstroke superstition survived, English doctors in India appear to have believed in it as firmly as laymen [ORWELL'S NOTE].

p. 444, *El Alamein*: The Second Battle of El Alamein (23rd October–11th November 1942), a decisive defeat of the Axis forces by the British Army.

p. 445, *the Socialist Appeal*: A Marxist newspaper published in London between 1941 and 1946.

p. 446, *Lord Elton... Father Coughlin*: For Lord Elton, see first note to p. 374. Denis Pritt (1887–1972) was an English barrister and Labour politician, remembered as a defender of the Soviet Union. For Lady Houston, see second note to p. 301. Ezra Pound (for whom, see second note to p. 126) had pro-fascist sympathies. For Lord Vansittart, see third note to p. 304. For Coughlin, see second note to p. 301.

p. 446, *When Lloyd George... "Cad!"*: Lloyd George was an outspoken critic of the Second Boer War (for which, see third note to p. 270). The Scottish Conservative politician Arthur Balfour (1848–1930) later served as prime minister (1902–05).

p. 447, *the MOI*: The Ministry of Information, a government department responsible for publicity and propaganda during the Second World War.

p. 449, *You and the Atom Bomb*: First published in *Tribune* (19th October 1945); collected in CEJL4.

p. 450, *The Managerial Revolution*: *The Managerial Revolution: What Is Happening in the World*, a 1941 book by the American philosopher and political theorist James Burnham (1905–87). See Orwell's essay 'James Burnham and the Managerial Revolution' (pp. 542–58).

p. 452, *What Is Science?*: First published in *Tribune* (26th October 1945); collected in CEJL4.

p. 453, *The Spirit and Structure of German Fascism*: A 1937 book by the American economist Robert A. Brady (1901–63).

p. 453, *Sir Max Beerbohm*: The English essayist, humorist and artist Sir Max Beerbohm (1872–1956).

p. 454, *"making nasty smells in a laboratory"*: A paraphrase of a passage in Kingsley's *The Water-Babies*, in which the narrator advocates scepticism regarding the claims of scientists: "It is only children who read Aunt Agitate's *Arguments*, or Cousin Cramchild's *Conversations*; or lads who go to popular lectures, and see a man pointing at a few big ugly pictures on the wall, or making nasty smells with bottles and squirts for an hour or two, and calling that anatomy or chemistry – who talk about 'cannot exist' and 'contrary to nature'" (Chapter 2). For Kingsley and *The Water-Babies*, see third note to p. 102.

p. 455, *Good Bad Books*: First published in *Tribune* (2nd November 1945); collected in CEJL4.

p. 455, *Not long ago... Leonard Merrick*: See Orwell's 'Introduction to *The Position of Peggy Harper* by Leonard Merrick' (pp. 528–31).

p. 455, *what Chesterton called the "good bad book"*: While it is true that Chesterton defended popular fiction in works such as the essay 'A Defence of Penny Dreadfuls' (1901), he nowhere used the exact term "good bad book".

p. 455, *R. Austin Freeman's... Huc's Travels in Tartary*: For Freeman, see fourth note to p. 173. For Bramah and his creation Max Carrados, see note to p. 170 and first note to p. 382, respectively. A collection titled simply *Max Carrados* was published in 1914. *Doctor Nikola* (1896) is the second novel in a series about the titular occultist and criminal mastermind by the Australian author Guy Boothby (1867–1905). *Travels in Tartary, Thibet and China, during the Years 1844–5–6* is a travelogue by the French missionary Evariste Régis Huc (1813–60). An English version was published in 1851, translated by the English essayist and critic William Hazlitt (1811–93).

p. 455, *Pett Ridge... Penrod stories*: William Pett Ridge (1859–1930) was an English writer, notably of novels chronicling working-class life, such as *Mord Em'ly* (1898). Edith Nesbit (1858–1924) was the author of novels for children including *Five Children and It* (1902) and *The Railway Children* (1906). *The Story of the Treasure Seekers* was published in 1899. George A. Birmingham was the pen name of the Irish clergyman and novelist James Owen Hannay (1865–1950). The English journalist and author Arthur Morris Binstead (1861–1914) used the nickname "Pitcher" when writing for the *Sporting Times*, known informally as the *Pink 'Un*, which was printed on pink paper. The bestselling American novelist Booth Tarkington (1869–1946) was the author of a trilogy – consisting of *Penrod* (1914), *Penrod and Sam* (1916) and *Penrod Jashber* (1929) – about the adventures of an eleven-year-old boy growing up in the Midwest.

p. 455, *The Octave of Claudius*: An 1897 novel by Barry Pain (for whom, see first note to p. 277) set in ancient Rome during the reign of the emperor Claudius.

p. 455, *Peter Blundell*: The pen name of the English seaman and novelist Frank Nestle Butterworth (1875–1953).

p. 456, *Leonard Merrick... A.S.M. Hutchinson*: For Merrick, see Orwell's 'Introduction to *The Position of Peggy Harper* by Leonard Merrick' (pp. 528–31), and first note to p. 528. The others are, respectively: the English writer W.L. George (1882–1926); the English writer J.D. Beresford (1873–1947); the French-born English novelist Ernest Raymond (1888–1974); the English novelist Mary Amelia St Clair (1863–1946), who wrote under the name May Sinclair; and the English novelist A.S.M. Hutchinson (for whom, see sixth note to p. 39).

p. 456, *Merrick's Cynthia... We, the Accused*: Merrick's novel *Cynthia* was published in 1896. For Beresford, George, Sinclair and Raymond, see previous note. Beresford's *A Candidate for Truth* was published in 1912. W.L. George's *Caliban*, a fictionalized account of the life of Lord Northcliffe (for whom, see fourth note to p. 160), was published in 1920. Sinclair's *The Combined Maze* was published in 1913. Ernest Raymond's crime novel *We, the Accused* was published in 1935.

p. 456, *the Crippen case*: A reference to a famous poisoner, Hawley Harvey Crippen (1862–1910), known as "Doctor Crippen", who killed his wife and dismembered her body.

p. 456, *Theodore Dreiser's An American Tragedy*: Theodore Dreiser (1871–1945) was an American writer and journalist. His novel *An American Tragedy* (1925) was based on a notorious real-life murder.

p. 457, *Tarr* or *Snooty Baronet*: For *Tarr*, see fourth note to p. 126. *Snooty Baronet* is a satirical novel published in 1932.

p. 457, *If Winter Comes*: See sixth note to p. 39.

p. 457, *Vice Versa... King Solomon's Mines*: For *Vice Versa*, see third note to p. 402. For *Helen's Babies*, see third note to p. 131. *King Solomon's Mines* (1885) is a popular adventure novel by the English writer H. Rider Haggard (1856–1925).

p. 457, *'The Blessed Damozel' or 'Love in the Valley'*: 'The Blessed Damozel' is an 1850 poem by the English poet and artist Dante Gabriel Rossetti (1828–82). For 'Love in the Valley', see note to p. 134.

p. 458, *Revenge Is Sour*: First published in *Tribune* (9th November 1945); collected in CEJL4.

p. 460, *Ribbentrop*: See note to p. 178.

p. 460, *"ce pauvre mort"*: "That poor dead man" (French).

p. 461, *Through a Glass, Rosily*: First published in *Tribune* (23rd November 1945); collected in CEJL4. The title alludes to 1 Corinthians 13:12: "For now we see through a glass, darkly; but then face to face: now I know in part; but then shall I know even as also I am known."

p. 461, *The recent article... correspondent*: The article referred to had described the awful conditions in Vienna in the wake of the war, and detailed the abhorrent behaviour of some of the Russian troops occupying the city. Several readers wrote to the magazine in response, protesting against what they called "this slander" on the Red Army.

p. 461, *Briffault's Decline and Fall of the British Empire*: A 1938 book by the French surgeon, social anthropologist and novelist Robert Briffault (1874–1948).

p. 462, *A Passage to India*: A 1924 novel by E.M. Forster.

p. 462, *A truth that's... invent*: From Blake's 'Auguries of Innocence' (ll. 54–55), written around 1803 and published posthumously in 1863.

p. 464, *Catastrophic Gradualism*: First published in *C.W. Review* (November 1945); collected in CEJL4. This article is a review of 'The Yogi and the Commissar' by Arthur Koestler, the title piece of a collection of essays published in 1945.

p. 465, *Mr Kingsley Martin*: The English journalist Kingsley Martin (1897–1969), who edited the *New Statesman* from 1930 to 1960.

p. 468, *Introduction to Love of Life and Other Stories by Jack London*: Written in October or November 1945; first published as the introduction to Jack London, *Love of Life and Other Stories* (London: Paul Elek, [November] 1946); collected in CEJL4. For Jack London, see note to p. 170.

p. 468, *Memories of Lenin*: See fourth note to p. 87.

p. 470, *The People of the Abyss*: A book denouncing the conditions of the poor in the Whitechapel area of London, published in 1903.

p. 470, *'Just Meat'*: A short story first published in 1907.

NOTES

p. 471, *'The Francis Spaight'*: A short story first published in 1911.

p. 471, *'A Piece of Steak'*: A short story first published in 1909.

p. 471, *Before Adam*: A novel serialized in 1906–07 and published in volume form in 1907.

p. 472, *The Road*: See first note to p. 228.

p. 472, *The Valley of the Moon*: A novel serialized in 1913 and published in volume form in the same year.

p. 472, *'The Apostate'*: A short story first published in 1906.

p. 472, *'Make Westing'*: A short story first published in 1908.

p. 472, *'The Chinago'*: A short story first published in 1909.

p. 473, *'Semper Idem'*: A short story first published in 1900.

p. 473, *Robert Tressell... Upton Sinclair*: For Tressell, see note to p. 226. By "W.B. Traven" Orwell means "B. Traven", the pen name of a reclusive, German-language writer of uncertain identity known for his mostly Mexico-set adventure stories, most famously *The Treasure of the Sierra Madre* (1927), as well as for a series of politically engaged novels about the lives of indigenous Mexicans in the period leading up to the outbreak of the Mexican Revolution in 1910. The American writer and socialist Upton Sinclair (1878–1968) was a so-called "muckraker", that is, he used his work as a means of exposing social injustice and to argue for reform.

p. 473, *The Jacket*: A novel serialized in 1914 and published in volume form in 1915. Its US title is *The Star Rover*.

p. 474, *Freedom of the Park*: First published in *Tribune* (7th December 1945); collected in CEJL4.

p. 475, *the SPGB*: The Socialist Party of Great Britain, a Marxist political party unconnected to the Labour Party.

p. 476, *a sort of Alsatia... permitted to walk*: In the seventeenth century, "Alsatia" was the colloquial name of an area in the Whitefriars area of the ward of Farringdon in the City of London that, due to unclear ownership and jurisdiction following the dissolution of the Carmelite Whitefriars monastery that gave it its name, offered protection against prosecution for debtors and other criminals.

p. 477, *Politics and the English Language*: Written by 11th December 1945; first published in *Horizon* (April 1946); collected in CEJL4.

p. 477, *Professor Harold Laski (essay in Freedom of Expression)*: For Laski, see first note to p. 366. The quotation is from Laski's contribution to the collection *Freedom of Expression: A Symposium Based on the Conference Called by the London Centre of the International PEN to Commemorate the Tercentenary of the Publication of Milton's Areopagitica, 22–26th August 1944* (1945). The polemic *Areopagitica: A Speech of Mr John Milton for the Liberty of Unlicenc'd Printing to the Parlament of England* (1644) is a defence of the right to freedom of speech and expression by the English poet John Milton (1608–74).

p. 478, *Professor Lancelot Hogben (Interglossa)*: Lancelot Hogben (1895–1975) was an English zoologist. The quotation is from his *Interglossa: A Draft of an Auxiliary for a Democratic World Order, Being an Attempt to Apply Semantic Principles to Language Design* (1943). "Interglossa" was a constructed language devised by Hogben.

p. 480, *Latin or Greek... numbers*: An interesting illustration of this is the way in which the English flower names which were in use till very recently are being ousted by Greek ones, "snapdragon" becoming "antirrhinum", "forget-me-not" becoming "myosotis", etc. It is hard to see any practical reason for this change of fashion – it is probably due to an instinctive turning away from the more homely word and a vague feeling that the Greek word is scientific [ORWELL'S NOTE].

p. 481, *long passages which... meaning*: Example: "Comfort's catholicity of perception and image, strangely Whitmanesque in range, almost the exact opposite in aesthetic compulsion, continues to evoke that trembling atmospheric accumulative hinting at a cruel, an inexorably serene timelessness [...] Wrey Gardiner scores by aiming at simple bullseyes with precision. Only they are not so simple, and through this contented sadness runs more than the surface bitter-sweet of resignation" (*Poetry Quarterly*) [ORWELL'S NOTE].

p. 481, *I returned, and... all*: Ecclesiastes 9:11.

p. 486, *the "not un-" formation*: One can cure oneself of the "not un-" formation by memorizing this sentence: "A not unblack dog was chasing a not unsmall rabbit across a not ungreen field" [ORWELL'S NOTE].

p. 487, *Stuart Chase*: The American economist, social theorist and writer Stuart Chase (1888–1985).

p. 488, *The Sporting Spirit*: First published in *Tribune* (14th December 1945); collected in CEJL4.

p. 488, *the brief visit... team*: In autumn 1945, the Russian football team Dynamo Moscow toured Britain, playing against leading British clubs.

p. 489, *Dr Arnold*: The English educator and historian Thomas Arnold (1795–1842), headmaster of Rugby School from 1828 to 1841.

p. 491, *In Defence of English Cooking*: First published in the *Evening Standard* (15th December 1945); collected in CEJL3.

p. 493, *Nonsense Poetry*: First published in *Tribune* (21st December 1945); collected in CEJL4.

p. 494, *Edward Lear, whose... war*: A reference to *The Lear Omnibus*, edited by the English writer, critic and poet R.L. Mégroz (1891–1968), first published in 1938, with a new illustrated edition appearing in 1945.

p. 497, *Pleasure Spots*: First published in *Tribune* (11th January 1946); collected in CEJL4.

p. 497, '*Kubla Khan*': 'Kubla Khan, or A Vision in a Dream' a poem by the English poet, critic and philosopher Samuel Taylor Coleridge (1772–1834), completed in 1797 and first published in 1816.

p. 498, *Lyons Corner House*: See note to p. 352.
p. 499, *The lights must... good*: From Auden's 'September 1, 1939' (ll. 47–48, 52–55).
p. 499, *Autobahnen*: "Motorways" (German).
p. 501, *A Nice Cup of Tea*: First published in the *Evening Standard* (12th January 1946); collected in CEJL3.
p. 503, *The Politics of Starvation*: First published in *Tribune* (18th January 1946); collected in CEJL4.
p. 503, *Air Chief Marshal Sir Philip Joubert*: Sir Philip Joubert de la Ferté (1887–1965), a senior commander in the Royal Air Force during the 1930s and the Second World War.
p. 504, *points*: During rationing luxuries like tinned fruit or tinned meat were allocated according to a system of "points".
p. 507, *The Prevention of Literature*: First published in *Polemic* (January 1946); collected in CEJL4.
p. 507, *About a year ago... Areopagitica*: See second note to p. 477.
p. 507, *the meeting was... censorship*: It is fair to say that the PEN Club celebrations, which lasted a week or more, did not always stick at quite the same level. I happened to strike a bad day. But an examination of the speeches (printed under the title *Freedom of Expression*) shows that almost nobody in our own day is able to speak out as roundly in favour of intellectual liberty as Milton could do 300 years ago – and this in spite of the fact Milton was writing in a period of civil war [ORWELL'S NOTE].
p. 510, *Maxim Litvinov*: The Russian revolutionary Maxim Litvinov (1876–1951).
p. 510, *Zinoviev, Kamenev*: The Soviet statesman Grigory Zinoviev (1883–1936), head of the Comintern between 1919 and 1926, and the Russian revolutionary and Soviet politician Lev Kamenev (1883–1936).
p. 516, *The Writer*: *The Writer: A Monthly Magazine for Literary Workers*, a periodical founded in Boston, Massachusetts, in 1887.
p. 516, *Ilya Ehrenburg or Alexei Tolstoy*: The Russian writers Ilya Ehrenburg (1891–1967) and Alexei Nikolayevich Tolstoy (1883–1945).
p. 518, *Books vs. Cigarettes*: First published in *Tribune* (8th February 1946); collected in CEJL4. We have replaced "v." with "vs." in the title.
p. 522, *Decline of the English Murder*: First published in *Tribune* (15th February 1946); collected in CEJL4.
p. 522, *Doctor Palmer of Rugeley... Bywaters and Thompson*: Infamous poisoners and murderers of the Victorian era and the beginning of the twentieth century. William Palmer (1824–56) of Rugeley, Staffordshire, was a notorious poisoner; Thomas Neill Cream (1850–92) was a Scottish-Canadian medical doctor and serial killer who poisoned his victims with strychnine; Florence Maybrick (1862–1941) was an American woman convicted of killing her husband; Frederick Seddon (1872–1912) was a English murderer hanged for

the poisoning by arsenic of his lodger; George Joseph Smith (1872–1915) was a bigamist and serial killer who was hanged for the murders of three women; Herbert Rowse Armstrong (1869–1922) was an English solicitor who was hanged for the murder of his wife; Frederick Bywaters (1902–23) and Edith Thompson (1893–1923) were English lovers executed for the murder of Thompson's husband. For Crippen, see third note to p. 456.

p. 522, *another very celebrated... acquitted*: A reference to the "Green Bicycle Case", one of the most famous and controversial murder cases in British criminal history, in which the victim, Bella Wright (1897–1919), was shot dead and the prime suspect, Ronald Light (1885–1975), was finally acquitted.

p. 522, *the so-called Cleft Chin Murder... Mr Bechhofer Roberts*: This famous murder case took its name from the fact that the victim, the taxi driver George Edward Heath (1910–44), had a cleft chin. The murderers were Karl Hultén (1922–45), a Swedish-born deserter from the US Army, and the eighteen-year-old waitress Elizabeth Jones (b. 1926). Hultén was hanged for his crime, while Jones received a last-minute reprieve. The "popular booklet" is *An Account of the Trial of Carl Gustav Hulten and Elizabeth Maud Jones at the Old Bailey in 1945* by the Australian journalist R. Alwyn Raymond (1922–2003), published by Claud Morris in 1945. The "verbatim account" is *The Trial of Jones and Hulten*, edited by the English barrister and author C.E. Bechhofer Roberts (1894–1949), published by Jarrolds in 1945.

p. 524, *V1... V2*: The V1, nicknamed a "doodlebug", was an unmanned flying bomb developed by the Germans and used against London and southern England from June 1944. The V2 was the world's first long-range ballistic missile, used by the Germans to bomb London from September 1944.

p. 525, *In Front of Your Nose*: First published in *Tribune* (22nd March 1946); collected in CEJL4.

p. 525, *Androcles and the Lion*: A play by George Bernard Shaw which premiered at St James's Theatre, London, in September 1913, and was first published in the UK the same year.

p. 525, *a parallel case... his rights*: In the late 1860s and 1870s a popular movement developed, particularly among working-class people in London's East End, in support of a man who claimed to be Sir Roger Tichborne, heir to a wealthy Catholic aristocratic family, who was missing and presumed dead. In reality, the claimant was the London-born Arthur Orton (1834–98), who since the 1850s had been living in Wagga Wagga in Australia, where, calling himself Thomas Castro, he worked as a butcher. The movement Orton inspired continued to champion his cause for many years after he was sentenced to fourteen years' imprisonment for perjury in 1874.

p. 526, *UNO*: The United Nations (Organization).

p. 528, *Introduction to The Position of Peggy Harper by Leonard Merrick*: Probably written in late February or March 1946; collected in CEJL4. The introduction was commissioned by publishing house Eyre & Spottiswoode for a proposed but ultimately unpublished new edition of *The Position of Peggy Harper* by the largely forgotten English novelist Leonard Merrick (1864–1939), originally published in 1911.

p. 528, *Violet Moses*: A novel published in 1891.

p. 528, *The Worldlings... One Man's View*: The novel *The Worldlings* was published in 1900. For the "Tichborne Case", see third note to p. 525. The novel *One Man's View* was published in 1897.

p. 528, *A Chair on the Boulevard*: A collection of short stories published in 1919.

p. 528, *Trilby... Aristide Pujol*: Respectively, an 1894 sensation novel by the French-British writer George du Maurier (1834–96) and a 1912 novel by the British Guyana-born author William John Locke (1863–1930).

p. 528, *The Man Who Was Good... The Quaint Companions*: Novels published in 1892, 1892, 1907 and 1903, respectively.

p. 528, *Conrad in Quest of His Youth*: A novel published in 1903.

p. 530, *New Grub Street*: See eighth note to p. 87.

p. 530, *W.D. Howells*: See third note to p. 330.

p. 530, *Sir Arthur Pinero*: The English playwright Arthur Wing Pinero (1855–1934).

p. 530, *Merrick's books sold... States*: The American uniform edition was issued by Messrs E.P. Dutton, who also issued a limited edition [ORWELL'S NOTE]. The edition Orwell refers to is *The Complete Works of Leonard Merrick*, published in 1918–19.

p. 532, *Some Thoughts on the Common Toad*: First published in *Tribune* (12th April 1946); collected in CEJL4.

p. 535, *A Good Word for the Vicar of Bray*: First published in *Tribune* (26th April 1946); collected in CEJL4. The title refers to an English cleric – sometimes identified as Simon Aleyn (d. 1565) – who, according to the English historian Thomas Fuller (1608–61) in *Worthies of England* (1662), succeeded in retaining his ecclesiastical office during much of the second half of the sixteenth century despite the upheaval caused by the English Reformation. Thus a "Vicar of Bray" is proverbially one who readily changes his or her principles to suit the times.

p. 535, *a comic song*: A satirical ballad recounting the career of the Vicar of Bray, but locating him instead in the period from the Restoration of the monarchy in 1660 to the Hanoverian succession of 1714.

p. 535, *Thibaw, the last King of Burma*: Thibaw Min (1859–1916), the last king of the Konbaung Dynasty of Burma.

p. 535, *Only the actions... dust*: From the poem 'The Glories of Our Blood and State' (ll. 23–24) by the English dramatist James Shirley (1596–1666), taken from his play *The Contention of Ajax and Ulysses for the Armour of Achilles* (1659).

p. 535, *John Aubrey*: The English antiquary and writer John Aubrey (1626–97), famous for his posthumously published collection of short biographical pieces, *Brief Lives*.

p. 535, *The poem*: Included in a chapter devoted to the English prelate John Overall (1559–1619), dean of St Paul's Cathedral, and his wife.

p. 539, *Confessions of a Book Reviewer*: First published in *Tribune* (3rd May 1946); collected in CEJL4.

p. 541, *The Four Just Men*: A 1905 detective novel by Edgar Wallace (for whom, see fifth note to p. 385).

p. 542, *James Burnham and the Managerial Revolution*: First published in *Polemic* under the title 'Second Thoughts on James Burnham' (May 1946); republished in pamphlet form with the present title by the Socialist Book Centre in summer 1946; collected in CEJL4. For Burnham and *The Managerial Revolution*, see note to p. 450.

p. 542, *The Machiavellians*: *The Machiavellians: Defenders of Freedom*, published in 1943.

p. 542, *Mosca, Michels and Pareto*: The Italian political scientist and journalist Gaetano Mosca (1858–1941), the German-born Italian sociologist Robert Michels (1876–1936) and the Italian sociologist and economist Vilfredo Pareto (1848–1923).

p. 542, *Georges Sorel*: The French political theorist and historian Georges Sorel (1847–1922).

p. 544, *The Servile State*: See second note to p. 157.

p. 544, *Wells's The Sleeper Awakes (1900), Zamyatin's We*: For *The Sleeper Wakes*, see note to p. 170. *We* is a dystopian novel by the Russian author Yevgeny Zamyatin (1884–1937), written in 1920–21 and first published in an English translation in 1924.

p. 544, *Peter Drucker*: See first note to p. 436.

p. 548, *one of those... prematurely*: It is difficult to think of any politician who has lived to be eighty and still been regarded as a success. What we call a "great" statesman normally means one who dies before his policy has had time to take effect. If Cromwell had lived a few years longer he would probably have fallen from power, in which case we should now regard him as a failure. If Pétain had died in 1930, France would have venerated him as a hero and patriot. Napoleon remarked once that if only a cannonball had happened to hit him when he was riding into Moscow, he would have gone down to history as the greatest man who ever lived [ORWELL'S NOTE]. For Pétain, see first note to p. 223.

p. 549, *there is little... of Babbitt*: Babbitt is the titular character of a satirical novel by the American writer Sinclair Lewis (1885–1951), published in 1922. The name became a pejorative byword for respectable bourgeois conformity and complacency.

p. 551, *nor, throughout history... means*: Great Britain raised a million volunteers in the earlier part of the 1914–18 war. This must be a world's record, but the pressures applied were such that it is doubtful whether the recruitment ought to be described as voluntary. Even the most "ideological" wars have

NOTES

been fought largely by pressed men. In the English Civil War, the Napoleonic Wars, the American Civil War, the Spanish Civil War, etc., both sides resorted to conscription or the press gang [ORWELL'S NOTE].

p. 552, *Gallup poll*: That is, an assessment of public opinion achieved by canvassing a representative cross-section of the population. The method is named after its pioneer, the American statistician George Horace Gallup (1901–84).

p. 553, *English writers who... other*: The only exception I am able to think of is Bernard Shaw, who, for some years at any rate, declared communism and fascism to be much the same thing, and was in favour of both of them. But Shaw, after all, is not an Englishman, and probably does not feel his fate to be bound up with that of Britain [ORWELL'S NOTE].

p. 554, *a majority of... moment*: As late as the autumn of 1945, a Gallup poll taken among the American troops in Germany showed that 51 per cent "thought Hitler did much good before 1939". This was after five years of anti-Hitler propaganda. The verdict, as quoted, is not very strongly favourable to Germany, but it is hard to believe that a verdict equally favourable to Britain would be given by anywhere near 51 per cent of the American army [ORWELL'S NOTE].

p. 555, *cui bono?*: "Who gains by it?" (Latin).

p. 559, *Why I Write*: First published in *Gangrel* (Summer 1946); collected in CEJL1.

p. 559, *Blake's 'Tiger, Tiger'*: Published in 1794 as part of the collection *Songs of Experience*.

p. 559, *the death of Kitchener*: Horatio Kitchener, 1st Earl Kitchener (1850–1916), was a British Army field marshal and colonial administrator who was instrumental in the Second Boer War and the First World War. He died in action in 1916 when the ship HMS *Hampshire* struck a German mine near Orkney, Scotland.

p. 559, *vers d'occasion*: Light verse written for a special occasion.

p. 560, *So hee... labour hee*: *Paradise Lost* II, ll. 1021–22.

p. 560, *Burmese Days*: See second note to p. 13.

p. 562, *a little poem*: This poem, usually titled either 'A Little Poem' or 'A Happy Vicar I Might Have Been', first appeared in the *Adelphi* in December 1936.

p. 562, *Eugene Aram*: The noted English scholar Eugene Aram (1704–59), most famous for committing, and initially successfully concealing, a murder. His crime formed the subject of a ballad by Thomas Hood (for whom, see first note to p. 272) and the novel *Eugene Aram* (1832) by Edward Bulwer-Lytton (for whom, see second note to p. 115).

p. 563, *Austin Seven*: An economy car that was produced by the Birmingham-based Austin Motor Company between 1922 and 1939.

p. 563, *Duggie always pays*: Possibly a reference to the bookmaker Douglas Stuart Ltd, whose motto was "Duggie never owes".

p. 563, *Homage to Catalonia*: See second note to p. 300.

p. 564, *Animal Farm*: First published by Secker & Warburg in 1945.

p. 565, *Politics vs. Literature: An Examination of Gulliver's Travels*: First published in *Polemic* (September–October 1946); collected in CEJL4.

p. 566, *England under Queen Anne*: A 1930 work by G.M. Trevelyan (for whom, see note to p. 313).

p. 566, *A Tale of a Tub*: A parodic work published in 1704.

p. 567, *one of Swift's most famous pamphlets*: *The Conduct of the Allies* (1711), in which Swift criticized what he saw as the ingratitude of the Dutch, allies of the British in the War of the Spanish Succession (1701–14), a Europe-wide conflict in which a "Grand Alliance" consisting of Britain, the Netherlands and the Holy Roman Empire sought to thwart French hegemony on the Continent.

p. 567, *Sir Alan Herbert... W.H. Mallock onwards*: For A.P. Herbert, see first note to p. 320. For G.M. Young and the Tory Reform Committee, see first note to p. 442. For Lord Elton, see first note to p. 374. William Hurrell Mallock (1849–1923) was an English novelist and writer on economics, whose work is noted for its pro-Catholic and anti-socialist stance.

p. 567, *such a pamphlet... Bertrand Russell*: The pamphlet is Swift's *An Argument to Prove That the Abolishing of Christianity in England May, as Things Now Stand, Be Attended with Some Inconveniences, and Perhaps Not Produce Those Many Good Effects Proposed Thereby* (1708). For "Timothy Shy" and *The Brains Trust*, see first note to p. 403 and note to p. 321, respectively. In his 1932 book *Broadcast Minds*, the English Catholic priest, theologian, author and radio broadcaster Ronald Knox (1888–1957) criticized the religious opinions of some of the leading scientific publicists of the time, including the Welsh philosopher and mathematician Bertrand Russell (1872–1970).

p. 568, *appear not to have invented wheels*: Houyhnhnms too old to walk are described as being carried in "sledges" or in "a kind of vehicle, drawn like a sledge". Presumably these had no wheels [ORWELL'S NOTE].

p. 570, *believes that modern... years*: The physical decadence which Swift claims to have observed may have been a reality at that date. He attributes it to syphilis, which was a new disease in Europe and may have been more virulent than it is now. Distilled liquors, also, were a novelty in the seventeenth century and must have led at first to a great increase in drunkenness [ORWELL'S NOTE].

p. 572, *The Tour*: "Tower" [ORWELL'S NOTE].

p. 574, *The "outs", for... "ins"*: At the end of the book, as typical specimens of human folly and viciousness, Swift names "a Lawyer, a Pickpocket, a Colonel, a Fool, a Lord, a Gamester, a Politician, a Whore-master, a Physician, an Evidence, a Suborner, an Attorney, a Traitor, or the like". One sees here the irresponsible violence of the powerless. The list lumps together those who break the conventional code, and those who keep it. For instance, if you automatically condemn a colonel, as such, on what grounds do you condemn a traitor? Or again, if you want to suppress pickpockets, you must have laws, which means that you must

NOTES

have lawyers. But the whole closing passage, in which the hatred is so authentic, and the reason given for it so inadequate, is somehow unconvincing. One has the feeling that personal animosity is at work [ORWELL'S NOTE].

p. 578, *'The Lady's Dressing Room'*... *'Upon a Beautiful Young Nymph Going to Bed'*: Poems first published in 1732 and 1734, respectively.

p. 578, *"the naked female human form divine"*: Blake uses the phrase "the human form divine" in his 1789 poem 'The Divine Image', included in his *Songs of Innocence*: "And Love the human form divine" (l. 11), and in his 1794 poem 'A Divine Image' (l. 3), included in his *Songs of Experience*: "Terror the human form divine". However, he makes no mention in either poem of a "naked female" form.

p. 579, *Buchmanite*: See sixth note to p. 160.

p. 580, *Riding Down from Bangor*: First published in *Tribune* (22nd November 1946); collected in CEJL4. The title alludes to the song 'Riding Down from Bangor' (for which, see third note to p. 131).

p. 580, *Helen's Babies*: See third note to p. 131.

p. 580, *the China of Guy Boothby, the Paris of du Maurier*: Boothby's *Doctor Nikola* (for which, see fourth note to p. 455) is set in China and Tibet. Du Maurier's *Trilby* (for which, see fifth note to p. 528) is set in Paris.

p. 581, *Rebecca of Sunnybrook Farm... leading part*: *Rebecca of Sunnybrook Farm* is a 1903 children's novel by the American author and educator Kate Douglas Wiggin (1856–1923). The Canadian-born American actress Mary Pickford (1892–1979) played the book's heroine, Rebecca Randall, in the first film adaptation (1917).

p. 581, *the "Katy" books... etc.*: A series of novels by the American children's author Sarah Chauncey Woolsey (1835–1905), who wrote under the pen name Susan Coolidge. It includes *What Katy Did* (1872), *What Katy Did at School* (1873), *What Katy Did Next* (1886), *Clover* (1888) and *In the High Valley* (1890).

p. 581, *Little Women and Good Wives*: For *Little Women*, see third note to p. 131. *Good Wives*, a sequel, was published in 1869. They are often published together under the title *Little Women* in modern editions.

p. 581, *Little Men*: Published in 1871.

p. 581, *Artemus Ward... 'Little Gifford of Tennessee'*: The American humorist Charles Farrar Browne (1834–67) wrote under the pseudonym "Artemus Ward". For Bret Harte, see second note to p. 131. 'Barbara Fritchie' is an 1863 poem by the American Quaker poet John Greenleaf Whittier (1807–92). 'Little Gifford of Tennessee' is untraced.

p. 581, *Beautiful Joe... Black Beauty*: *Beautiful Joe: An Autobiography* is an 1893 novel by the Canadian children's author Margaret Marshall Saunders (1861–1947), narrated by the eponymous dog. *Black Beauty: His Grooms and Companions, the Autobiography of a Horse* is an 1877 novel by the English author Anna Sewell (1820–78).

p. 581, *the Buster Brown... "Penrod" stories*: Buster Brown was a comic-strip character created in 1902 by the American cartoonist Richard F. Outcault (1863–1928). For Tarkington and "Penrod", see fifth note to p. 455.

p. 581, *Ernest Thompson Seton's... etc.*: Ernest Thompson Seton (1860–1946) was a British-born Canadian-American naturalist and author. His bestselling collection of short stories *Wild Animals I Have Known* (1898) was one of many books he produced in the same genre.

p. 581, *Misunderstood*: An 1869 novel by the English novelist and children's author Florence Montgomery (1843–1923).

p. 581, *The Scottish Students' Song Book*: An annual anthology published between 1891 and 1941.

p. 582, *Riding down... swell*: The text from *The Scottish Students' Song Book* of 1897 reads: "Riding down from Bangor, / On an eastern train, / After weeks of hunting, / In the woods of Maine; / Quite extensive whiskers, / Beard, moustache as well, / Sat a student fellow, / Tall and slim and swell" (ll. 1–4).

p. 582, *There suddenly appeared... beard*: The last three lines of the song read, in *The Scottish Students' Song Book* version: "When then and there appeared / A tiny little earring / In that horrid student's beard."

p. 584, *Life on the Mississippi*: See third note to p. 328.

p. 585, *How the Poor Die*: First published in *Now* (November 1946); collected in CEJL4.

p. 585, *Hôpital X*: The Hôpital Cochin on the Rue du Faubourg-Saint-Jacques, where Orwell was treated for flu from 7th to 22nd March 1929.

p. 590, *Madame Hanaud*: A reference to the French newspaper proprietor Marthe Hanau (1890–1935), who defrauded French financial markets in the 1920s and the 1930s by feeding fraudulent stock tips to financial speculators.

p. 591, *Bob Sawyer... White-Jacket!*: Bob Sawyer and Benjamin Allen are medical students in Dickens's *The Pickwick Papers*. *La Débâcle* (1892) by the French naturalist writer Émile Zola (1840–1902) is set during the collapse of the Second Empire and the Franco-Prussian War (1870–71). *White-Jacket, or The World in a Man-of-War* (1850) by Herman Melville (1819–91) is an account of life at sea based on the author's experiences as a sailor aboard the USS *United States* in 1843–44.

p. 591, *'The Children's Hospital'*: 'In the Children's Hospital' (1880).

p. 591, *The Story of San Michele*: An autobiographical work by the Swedish physician Axel Munthe (1857–1949), published in 1929.

p. 593, *Lear, Tolstoy and the Fool*: First published in *Polemic* (March 1947); collected in CEJL4.

p. 593, *his attack on Shakespeare*: *Shakespeare and the Drama*. Written about 1903 as an introduction to another pamphlet, *Shakespeare and the Working Classes* by Ernest Crosby [ORWELL'S NOTE]. For Tolstoy's essay on Shakespeare and for Crosby, see second note to p. 234. Orwell's version of the title likely comes from the title of the French version, *Shakespeare et le Drame* (1905).

p. 593, *Hazlitt, Brandes*: The reference is to the English essayist, drama and literary critic William Hazlitt (1778–1830) and the Danish critic and scholar Georg Brandes (1842–1927).

p. 594, *Gervinus*: The German literary and political historian Georg Gottfried Gervinus (1805–71).

p. 595, *the Dreyfus case*: See second note to p. 329.

p. 595, *Warwick Deeping*: See fifth note to p. 42.

p. 599, *his English biographer, Derrick Leon*: *Tolstoy: His Life and Work* by the English author and biographer Derrick Leon (1908–44) was published in 1944.

p. 605, *Turgenev, Fet*: The Russian novelist Ivan Turgenev (1818–83), author of realist novels such as *Fathers and Sons* (1862), and the Russian poet Afanasy Fet (1820–92).

p. 607, *Towards European Unity*: First published as 'Toward European Unity' in the *Partisan Review* (July–August 1947); collected in CEJL4.

p. 611, *the NKVD*: The Soviet secret police. See second note to p. 146.

p. 612, *In Defence of Comrade Zilliacus*: Probably written in August–September 1947; first published in CEJL4. The title refers to the Japanese-born British Labour politician Konni Zilliacus (1894–1967). Having come into conflict with the Labour Party leadership, he was expelled from the party in 1949. The following year he lost his seat in Parliament, but was readmitted by Labour in 1952 and returned to the Commons in 1955.

p. 612, *Ernest Bevin*: See second note to p. 203.

p. 613, *Pritt*: See first note to p. 446.

p. 614, *Henry Wallace*: The American politician Henry A. Wallace (1888–1965), who served as vice president of the United States from 1941 to 1945 under President Franklin D. Roosevelt (1882–1945). He was the nominee of the new Progressive Party in the 1948 presidential election.

p. 614, *Mr G.D.H. Cole's last 1,143-page compilation*: *The Intelligent Man's Guide to the Post-War World*, by G.D.H. Cole (for whom, see fourth note to p. 304), published in 1947.

p. 616, *"the Foot–Zilliacus group"*: For Michael Foot, see first note to p. 322.

p. 616, *a little while ago Tribune reviewed a book of his*: Zilliacus's *Mirror of the Present: The Way the World Is Going* (1947) was reviewed by T.R. Fyvel (for whom, see note to p. 180) in June 1947.

p. 617, *George Gissing*: Written around May–June 1948 for *Politics and Letters*, which ceased publication before this essay made it into print; first published in the *London Magazine* (June 1960); collected in CEJL4. For Gissing, see eighth note to p. 87.

p. 617, *In the Year of the Jubilee*: A novel published in 1894.

p. 617, *two of his minor works*: *In the Year of the Jubilee* and *The Whirlpool* by George Gissing [ORWELL'S NOTE]. In 1947 the two novels – the latter originally published in 1897 – were republished by "Watergate Classics", with introductions by the South African-born British novelist, poet and literary editor William Plomer (1903–73) and the English art critic Myfanwy Piper, née Evans (1911–97), respectively.

p. 617, *The Odd Women*: A novel published in 1893.

p. 617, *Demos, The Nether World*: Novels published in 1886 and 1889.

p. 617, *The Private Papers... A Life's Morning*: *The Private Papers of Henry Ryecroft* is a novel published in 1903. For Gissing's *Charles Dickens: A Critical Study*, see eighth note to p. 87. *The Private Papers of Henry Ryecroft* is a novel published in 1888.

p. 620, *Born in Exile*: A novel published in 1892.

p. 621, *The Golden Ass*: A novel by the Latin writer Apuleius (*c*.124–after 170 AD), also known as *The Metamorphoses*.

p. 621, *The Improvisatore*: An autobiographical novel by the Danish author Hans Christian Andersen (1805–75), best known for his fairy tales, first published in 1835.

p. 622, *Mark Rutherford*: The English journalist, novelist and translator William Hale White (1831–1913), best known under his pen name Mark Rutherford.

p. 623, *Experiment in Autobiography*: Published in 1934.

p. 624, *Writers and Leviathan*: Probably written by 20th June 1948; first published in *Politics and Letters* (Summer 1948); collected in CEJL4.

p. 624, *Zhdanov*: The Russian politician Andrei Zhdanov (1896–1948), the Soviet Union's chief propagandist after the Second World War.

p. 630, *Such, Such Were the Joys*: Written by summer 1948; first published in the *Partisan Review* (September–October 1952); collected in CEJL4. In a version of this piece published in the United States, St Cyprian's was called "Crossgates". The text printed here, reproduced from CEJL4, is from Orwell's original typescript (the names of his fellow schoolboys and of the assistant masters have been changed). The quotation used for the title of the essay is from William Blake's poem 'The Ecchoing Green' (l. 17), published in *Songs of Innocence*.

p. 635, *Who plundered... with their clothes?*: Warren Hastings (1732–1818), the first governor general of India (1774–84), was impeached for corruption in 1786 after being accused of extorting money from two Indian princesses, the Begums of Oudh (Awadh), in order to restore the finances of the East India Company. The British admiral John Byng (1704–57) was executed by firing squad (not beheaded) on board HMS *Monarch* after being court-martialled for failing to do his utmost in battle during the Seven Years War (1756). He is widely regarded as having been made a scapegoat for the failings of the government of the day. In 1846, following the repeal of the protectionist Corn Laws by the Tory government under Sir Robert Peel (1788–1850), the future Conservative prime minister Benjamin Disraeli (1804–81), then a backbench MP, remarked that Peel had "caught the Whigs bathing and run away with their clothes" – that is, adopted their free-trade policies.

NOTES

p. 635, *Disraeli brought... balance of the Old*: Prime Minister Benjamin Disraeli declared "peace with honour" on his return from the Congress of Berlin (1878), which settled the Russo-Turkish War of 1877–78. When he was investigated by Parliament for corruption in 1772, Robert Clive (for whom, see first note to p. 194) said in his defence that he was "astonished at [his] own moderation", given the vast riches he could have taken after securing control of Bengal for the British East India Company. It was in fact the Anglo-Irish Tory foreign secretary George Canning (1770–1827), not either Pitt the Elder or Pitt the Younger, who, in 1826, described himself as having "called the New World into existence to redress the balance of the Old", following the British recognition of the newly independent states of Latin America: Argentina, Colombia, Mexico and Brazil.

p. 635, *Did you know... Wars of the Roses?*: The Wars of the Roses (1455–85) were a thirty-year dynastic dispute between supporters of the house of York and those of the house of Lancaster, rival branches of the Plantagenet dynasty that had ruled England since the twelfth century. The conflict ended with the accession in 1485 of the Lancastrian Henry Tudor (1457–1509), who went on to reign as Henry VII, the first of the Tudor dynasty. The battles covered by the (imprecise) mnemonic are: St Albans (first, 1455), Blore Heath (1459), Northampton (1460), Wakefield (1460), Mortimer's Cross (1461), St Albans (second, 1461), Towton (1461) or Tewkesbury (1471), Barnet (1471), and Bosworth Field (1485).

p. 636, *"1587?"... "Field of the Cloth of Gold!"*: On 23rd August 1572 (the eve of the feast of St Bartholomew) a period of violence directed against French Protestants, known as Huguenots, began in Paris. It lasted for several weeks and many thousands were killed. Alamgir I, known as Aurangzeb (1618–1707), was the sixth Mughal emperor of Hindustan, reigning from 1658 until his death. The Peace of Utrecht was a series of treaties that brought to an end the War of the Spanish Succession – for which, see first note to p. 567. The Boston Tea Party was a protest by American colonists in Boston at the imposition of a tax on tea by the British Parliament. It was a prelude to the War of American Independence (1775–83). The Field of the Cloth of Gold was the location, near Calais, of a meeting between Henry VIII (1491–1547) of England and Francis I (1494–1547) of France in 1520. Lavish temporary palaces and pavilions were erected for the occasion.

p. 642, *the Apocrypha*: Biblical or related writings that are not included in the accepted canon of Scripture.

p. 644, *lights*: Animals' lungs, used as food.

p. 645, *Boys are Erewhonians... must be concealed at all costs*: In the morally inverted world of Butler's *Erewhon* (for which, see fourth note to p. 156), illness and other misfortunes – including suffering, fear or unhappiness – are treated as crimes or as matters of personal disgrace.

p. 646, *Leicester and Essex and Raleigh*: Favourites of Elizabeth I: Robert Dudley, 1st Earl of Leicester (1532–88); Robert Devereux, 2nd Earl of Essex (1565–1601); and Sir Walter Raleigh (*c*.1553–1618).

p. 649, *Whoso shall offend... sea*: Matthew 18:6.

p. 652, *The Merry Widow... Where the Rainbow Ends*: *The Merry Widow* is a 1905 operetta by the Austro-Hungarian composer Franz Lehár (1870–1948), with a libretto by Viktor Léon (1858–1940) and Leo Stein (1861–1921), based on the 1861 comedy *L'Attaché d'ambassade* (a title meaning "the embassy attaché") by Henri Meilhac (1830–97). Saki was the pseudonym of the British writer (born in Burma) Hector Hugh Munro (1870–1916), known for his darkly comic short-stories. He was also the author of two novels: *The Unbearable Bassington* (1912) and *When William Came* (1913). For *Where the Rainbow Ends*, see fourth note to p. 376.

p. 652, *the Troc*: The Trocadero, a fashionable restaurant in London.

p. 655, *"The armies of unalterable law"*: The last line of George Meredith's poem 'Lucifer in Starlight' (1883). For Meredith, see note to p. 107.

p. 663, *Reflections on Gandhi*: First published in the *Partisan Review* (January 1949); collected in CEJL4.

p. 663, *this partial autobiography*: *The Story of my Experiments with Truth* by Mahatma Gandhi (1869–1948), serialized in Gujarati in 1925–29 and translated into English by Mahadev Desai (1892–1942). The English edition was published in two volumes in 1927 and 1929.

p. 665, *annas*: See fourth note to p. 16.

p. 667, *Mr Louis Fischer's Gandhi and Stalin*: Louis Fischer (1896–1970) was an American journalist. *Gandhi and Stalin* was published in 1947.

p. 670, *Conrad's Place and Rank in English Letters*: Written on 25th February 1949; first published in *Wiadomości* (10th April 1949); collected in CEJL4. Orwell's piece was written in response to the following two questions, which had been sent to him by the Polish cultural weekly magazine *Wiadomości*, published in London between 1946 and 1981:

> First, what do you believe to be his permanent place and rank in English letters? When Conrad died, some critics were uncertain of his final position, and Virginia Woolf, in particular, doubted whether any of his later novels would survive. Today, on the occasion of a new edition of his collected writings [*The Collected Edition of the Works of Joseph Conrad*, published by J.M. Dent and Sons in 1949], Mr Richard Curle [the Scottish author, critic and journalist Richard Curle (1883–1968)] wrote in *Time and Tide* that Conrad's works now rank among the great classics of the English novel. Which of these views, in your opinion, is correct?
>
> The other question to which we would like to have your answer, is whether you detect in Conrad's work any oddity, exoticism and strangeness (of course, against the background of the English literary tradition), and if so, do you attribute it to his Polish origin?

NOTES

- p. 670, *The Secret Agent and Under Western Eyes*: Novels published in 1907 and 1911, respectively.
- p. 670, *Lord Jim, Almayer's Folly*: Novels published in 1900 and 1895, respectively.
- p. 670, *Nostromo, Chance, Victory*: Novels published in 1904, 1913 and 1915, respectively.
- p. 671, *The Question of the Pound Award*: First published in the *Partisan Review* (May 1949); collected in CEJL4. In 1948, Ezra Pound's *The Pisan Cantos* was controversially awarded the Bollingen Foundation Prize as the best book of poetry for the year. The following April, the editors of *Partisan Review* asked a number of writers, including Orwell, to express their opinion about the judges' decision.

Extra Material

on

George Orwell's

Literary and Political Essays

George Orwell's Life

George Orwell was born Eric Arthur Blair in Motihari in Bengal, on 25th June 1903. His parents were Richard Walmesley Blair (1857–1939), an opium agent in the imperial civil service, and Ida Mabel Blair (née Limouzin, 1875–1943). Richard Blair was from a wealthy background, but occupied a relatively lowly station in life, thus making the family, in Orwell's famous description, "lower-upper-middle class". In the year following his birth, his mother departed for England with Eric and his elder sister Marjorie (1898–1946), and they took residence in Henley-on-Thames. Apart from a three-month visit in 1907, during which another child, Avril (1908–78), was conceived, Richard Blair was entirely absent from his children's lives until his eventual permanent return to England in 1912. Orwell always sought to convey the impression of himself as an unhappy, introverted child, although this was disputed by his sister Avril. It is true, however, that his younger years were punctuated by a number of chest-related illnesses, a foreshadowing of the bronchial problems that would plague him throughout his life. *Early Life*

From the age of eight Eric attended St Cyprian's, a preparatory school in Eastbourne, where, identified as a potential scholarship winner, he was admitted on half-fees. Despite the animosity he felt towards the school – made plain in the essay 'Such, Such Were the Joys' (published posthumously in 1952) – Eric was an academic high-flyer, securing scholarships to two public schools: Wellington College in Berkshire, where he spent a term in spring 1917, and Eton College, fifteen miles from Wellington, where he moved in May 1917 when a place became available. *St Cyprian's and Eton*

In later life Orwell was careful to emphasize that he felt socially isolated at Eton, and that the school had little formative influence on him. As a King's Scholar (KS), Eric belonged to an intellectual elite – although, as he later admitted, "I did no work there and learnt very little." Indeed, despite his early promise and obvious intelligence, his academic record at the school was poor, and it quickly became apparent that he would not be able to pursue a university career. Instead, at the behest of his father, in 1921, after fourteen terms at Eton, Orwell, now eighteen and six foot three, was entered for the Indian Imperial Police.

Burma After passing the police exam, on 27th October 1922 Orwell set sail from Liverpool for Burma – a place he chose because he had relatives there, and because it was close to the Indian postings where his father had spent his working life. Orwell's first months in the country were spent at the police training school in Mandalay, before he was sent on a series of official postings – for which, at least initially, he lacked the necessary experience. After a number of transfers and a promotion, in late 1926 he was dispatched to the Irrawaddy port town of Katha – later fictionalized as "Kyauktada" in *Burmese Days* (1934) – where he contracted dengue fever and was granted six months' leave. He left Burma in July 1927, never to return. Later he claimed that his decision to leave the Burma Police was political – that he could not in good conscience continue to serve an imperialist system that he considered a "racket".

London and Paris Orwell returned to England and announced to his horrified parents his decision to leave the Burma Police and become a writer. He then moved to London, to a single room on the Portobello Road, from where – calling himself "Burton" and dressing like a down-and-out – he began to go on investigative tramping expeditions to London's East End. Then, in spring 1928, and partly supported by his French aunt Nellie Limouzin, he moved to the Rue du Pot de Fer, a bohemian district in Paris's fifth *arrondissement*. Here he wrote an early draft of *Burmese Days* and began to publish articles in French periodicals, as well as making his British journalistic debut in the publications *G.K.'s Weekly* and the *Adelphi*. In February 1929, he fell seriously ill and was admitted to hospital, and shortly afterwards his money was stolen from his lodgings – an incident that was the starting point for what would be his first full-length work, *Down and Out in Paris and London* (1933), whose first half recounts the period of indigence he experienced following the theft.

Southwold, the Suffolk seaside town where Orwell's parents now lived, and where he returned at Christmas 1929, remained his base until the mid-1930s. During this period he pursued and was rejected by Brenda Salkeld, a clergyman's daughter who taught gym at a nearby girls' school, continued to work on *Down and Out in Paris and London*, at this stage called 'A Scullion's Diary', and became a regular contributor to the *Adelphi*. He also persisted with the tramping expeditions, including, in August 1931, a "hopping" – that is, hop-picking – excursion in Kent (a traditional alternative to a summer holiday for poor East End folk). In April 1932, he began teaching at the Hawthorns High School for Boys in Hayes, West London, a private establishment – an experience that, along with the hop-picking trip, he later mined for *A Clergyman's Daughter* (1935). By now he had an agent, Leonard Moore, who, in June 1932, told Orwell that the left-wing publisher Victor Gollancz was interested in 'A Scullion's Diary', already rejected by Jonathan Cape and Faber. Gollancz was worried about libel, but eventually publication of the retitled *Down and Out in Paris and London* was set for January 1933. Orwell chose not to publish the book under his real name – perhaps simply to protect his family – proposing several pseudonyms to Moore, including "Burton", his tramping alias, but in the end settled on "George Orwell" on the basis that it was a "good round English name".

Southwold and First Books

Despite the fact that he was now a published writer, this was not a happy period for Orwell: his pursuit of another woman, Eleanor Jacques, ended in failure when she married another man; shortly before Christmas 1933 he caught pneumonia and, his life seemingly in danger, was admitted to hospital in Uxbridge, where he was teaching at another school, Fray's College (he was discharged in January); and Gollancz turned down *Burmese Days*, fearing legal action from real-life Indian civil servants. However, the novel was accepted by Harpers, who brought out an American edition in 1934. Orwell expressed dissatisfaction with the work, though, claiming that the proofs made him "spew". By this stage he had begun work on his next novel, *A Clergyman's Daughter*, which was sent to Moore in October 1934.

Bookshop and Marriage At the beginning of 1935, Orwell secured a job in a second-hand bookshop, Booklovers' Corner, in Hampstead. Initially he lodged with the owners, the Westropes – who, as members of the Independent Labour Party (ILP), introduced Orwell to the world of earnest political engagement – then moved to a flat at Parliament Hill. Meanwhile, the first half of the year saw the publication of two novels: *A Clergyman's Daughter*, which appeared in March to mixed reviews, and a British edition of *Burmese Days*, published in June, Gollancz having finally been persuaded that it had been purged of any potentially actionable elements. In the spring Orwell held a party at Parliament Hill, where he met Eileen O'Shaughnessy, originally from South Shields, who was studying Psychology at University College London, and a relationship developed over the following summer, during which Orwell moved again, this time to a flat in Kentish Town, which he shared with the writer Rayner Heppenstall and the Communist poet Michael Sayers, although by mid-autumn only Orwell was left.

Expedition to the North and Move to Wallington With another novel, *Keep the Aspidistra Flying*, completed, on 31st January 1936 Orwell left London, following a proposal from Gollancz that he travel to the north of England and produce a work of reportage describing life among the working-class poor for the publisher's fledgling Left Book Club imprint. Thus, armed with a list of contacts supplied by the *Adelphi*'s editor, Richard Rees, Orwell travelled first to the north-west – to Manchester, Wigan (where he made his first visit to a coal mine) and Liverpool – then to South Yorkshire and finally to Headingley in Leeds to stay with his sister Marjorie Dakin. Returning to the south at the end of March, he took on the tenancy of "the Stores" – so named because it was once a shop – a cottage in the village of Wallington, Hertfordshire, previously occupied by Aunt Nellie, which would remain his base for a decade. Here he began to write what would become *The Road to Wigan Pier*, his account of his northern excursion, and – with the help of Eileen, whom he quietly married on 9th June – set about reopening the village shop.

In autumn of the same year, Orwell, disturbed by developments in Spain, where a military uprising against the leftist Republican Popular Front government had led to the outbreak of civil war, elected to join the many thousands of foreign volunteers who, under the aegis of the Communist International Brigades, were flocking to the country to fight with the Republican militia against General Franco's Nationalists. So, with the manuscript of *The Road to Wigan Pier* dispatched to Gollancz on 15th December, and choosing to remain aloof from the International Brigades until he had seen the situation on the ground for himself, Orwell travelled to the Continent a few days before Christmas, meeting with the ILP's John McNair in Barcelona shortly before New Year. Here, motivated only by a desire to fight fascists and ignorant of the complexity of the political situation and the tensions between the many leftist groups that made up the Republican coalition, Orwell joined the United Workers' Marxist Party (POUM), an anti-Stalinist group with links to the ILP. In January 1937, his unit, under the command of Georges Kopp, was ordered to the Aragon front, where Orwell stayed for four months, although he witnessed little fighting. At the end of April he returned to Barcelona, where Eileen was now working in John McNair's office, and where he was caught up in the factional fighting between Communists and other groups. Dismayed by this experience, and by the smearing of the POUM as fascist collaborators in the Communist press, he decided against joining the International Brigades after all, but instead to return to the Aragon front – where, on 20th May, he was struck in the throat by a bullet.

Orwell was taken to hospital first in Lerida, then in Tarragona, where he learnt that the bullet had narrowly missed his main artery; he was then moved to a POUM sanatorium in the Barcelona suburbs, where, contrary to expectations, his voice recovered somewhat. Meanwhile,

Spain

the POUM, which was declared a Trotskyist organization by the pro-Soviet Communists, was outlawed on 16th June, and its leaders rounded up and imprisoned. Orwell – declared unfit and discharged – and Eileen managed to escape from Spain by train and returned to England in July; had they remained, they would probably have been killed. Shortly before his return, he declared in a letter to the writer Cyril Connolly, "I [...] at last really believe in Socialism" – indeed, there can be no doubt that the Spanish experience was the turning point in Orwell's life. On his return, and in view of the parlous international situation, Orwell was politically engaged in a way he had not been until now, and joined the ILP. He strongly rejected political quietism, believing that one had to be an active socialist in order to defeat fascism – although he was against the coming war.

Orwell's first journalistic response to Spain, an article titled 'Eyewitness in Barcelona', was rejected by the editor of the *New Statesman*, Kingsley Martin, on the basis that its anti-Communist stance might prove controversial with his leftist readership. Orwell also guessed, rightly, that Gollancz – whose publishing house had links with the Communist Party of Great Britain – would be uncomfortable with the full-length account of his Spanish adventure that he intended to write. Fortunately, he was approached by Fred Warburg of the newly formed Secker & Warburg – a more open-minded publisher, but one without the commercial standing of Gollancz – who agreed to publish the work. *Homage to Catalonia* – which Orwell wrote on returning to Wallington, where he had now abandoned the shop and turned to animal husbandry – was finished in December 1937, and published in the following April to poor sales.

Spain also had the effect of destroying Orwell's already fragile health. In March 1938, he was admitted to Preston Hall Sanatorium in Aylesford, Kent, apparently suffering from tuberculosis, although he was diagnosed with bronchiectasis. In September, Orwell set off with Eileen on a winter trip to Morocco – anonymously paid for by the novelist L.H. Myers – in order that he might be spared the English winter. Here he wrote another novel, *Coming Up for Air*. The couple left Morocco on 23rd March 1939, returning to Wallington in April. The new novel was published in June – the same month in which Orwell's father, Richard Blair, died.

With the outbreak of war, Eileen went to work at the Censorship Department of the Ministry of Information in Whitehall. Orwell, meanwhile – who performed a volte-face in his attitude to war following the signing of the Molotov–Ribbentrop Pact between Nazi Germany and Russia in August 1939 – was bitterly frustrated by his unfitness for military service, and remained in Wallington, where he planned a book of articles, which would become *Inside the Whale* (published by Gollancz in March 1940). He also became a contributor to Cyril Connolly's newly founded *Horizon*, which went on to become the most celebrated literary magazine of the 1940s, and in which would appear many of Orwell's most important essays, including 'Politics and the English Language' (April 1946). In early 1940, Orwell was somewhat improbably offered the job of theatre critic for *Time and Tide*, a position that enabled him, in May, to move once again to London, to Dorset Chambers, Chagford Street, Marylebone. Shortly afterwards, Orwell joined the St John's Wood company of the Local Defence Volunteers (LDV), later the Home Guard, whose creation allowed Orwell finally to make a contribution to the war effort. That summer, he joined Warburg and the Zionist author Tosco Fyvel in planning a series called Searchlight Books, of which Orwell would contribute the first, an essay about the future of democratic socialism in Britain. The result, *The Lion and the Unicorn: Socialism and the English Genius*, was published in February 1941.

Second World War

In early 1941, Orwell began writing a regular 'London Letter' for the American *Partisan Review*. Then, in August, he was belatedly given a chance to do war work when he took a job with the BBC's Eastern Service, supervising cultural broadcasts to India, Malaya and Indonesia to counter enemy propaganda. Orwell remained at the corporation for two years; among the routine work, he created a literary programme called *Voice*, attracting contributions from, among others, T.S. Eliot, Dylan Thomas, E.M. Forster and William Empson. Nevertheless, he became disillusioned, famously describing the BBC as

War Work with the BBC and Animal Farm

"halfway between a girls' school and a lunatic asylum" and the work as "useless, or slightly worse than useless".

Feeling that he was wasting his time, Orwell left the BBC in November 1943, becoming instead, for the next two years, literary editor of the left-wing *Tribune* magazine, edited by the Labour MP Aneurin Bevan, one of the future architects of the post-war Labour government. Meanwhile, he was planning a new book in which he would illustrate in the form of an allegory the way in which the Soviet regime had betrayed the revolution and become a tyranny. Aware that neither Gollancz nor Secker & Warburg would be willing to touch something so anti-Stalinist, especially now that the Soviet Union was a key ally in the war, Orwell approached Cape, who accepted but subsequently rejected the book (apparently on the advice of a Ministry of Information official named Peter Smollett, later unmasked as a Soviet spy). Eventually, however, Secker & Warburg relented, although *Animal Farm* did not appear in print until August 1945.

Adoption of Richard and Death of Eileen

In 1944, in a move facilitated by Eileen's sister Gwen O'Shaughnessy, a doctor in the north-east, the Orwells adopted a baby boy, whom they called Richard Horatio Blair, who had been born illegitimately in Newcastle upon Tyne. Richard was delayed in coming to London to join his new family, however, when a V-1 fell on the Orwells' residence at Mortimer Crescent, Kilburn, forcing them to seek temporary accommodation; as a result, it was not until October – by which time a new flat had been found in Canonbury Square, Islington – that Richard was brought from Newcastle. Both Orwell and Eileen proved to be devoted and affectionate parents, but the family's happiness was short-lived: on 29th March 1945, with Orwell in Paris as war correspondent for the *Observer* and the *Manchester Evening News*, Eileen died under anaesthetic while undergoing a hysterectomy due to tumours on her uterus.

Move to Jura, Nineteen Eighty-Four, Illness and Death

With the war over, Orwell began to put into action a plan he had been formulating for some time: to retreat to the island of Jura in the Inner Hebrides, where he would be able to concentrate on his writing free from distraction. He settled on a remote farm named Barnhill, where he moved in May 1946, his departure having been delayed in February when he fell ill with what he claimed was gastritis but was in reality a tubercular haemorrhage. On Jura – where he was joined first by his sister Avril and then, in July, by Richard and his nanny, Susan Watson – Orwell commenced a new novel, a dystopian fantasy whose principal theme, totalitarianism, he had been meditating throughout the 1930s and 1940s. Seriously ill once again, in December 1947 Orwell was moved to Hairmyres Hospital near Glasgow, where the consultant, Bruce Dick, confirmed that the author was suffering from fibrotic tuberculosis. He was treated with streptomycin, a brand-new drug that had to be specially imported from the United States, and in July 1948, partially recovered, was able to return to Jura, where he was keen to finish the novel while there was still time. By December his health had deteriorated again, and he was moved to Cranham, a rather austere sanatorium in the Cotswolds, where he remained for eight months.

Warburg found the manuscript of *Nineteen Eighty-Four* "terrifying", while Orwell's friend Malcolm Muggeridge thought it "repugnant" and far-fetched, but the book trade was confident that it would be a bestseller. It was published in June to excellent reviews. Despite the severity of his illness, Orwell began to court Sonia Brownell, part of Connolly's *Horizon* circle and fifteen years his junior, to whom he had unsuccessfully proposed marriage before his departure for Jura. She visited him several times at Cranham, and this time accepted. In September 1949 Orwell was moved to University College Hospital in London, where the marriage took place on 13th October, conducted by the hospital's chaplain. Afterwards Orwell continued to grow weaker, the doctors acknowledging that nothing could be done with such an advanced case of bilateral pulmonary tuberculosis. Then, in the early hours of 21st January 1950, an artery burst in the writer's lungs, killing him. Dismissed as a gold-digger by some, Sonia nevertheless remained a zealous custodian of Orwell's legacy for the rest of her life.

George Orwell's Works

Down and Out in Paris and London   *Down and Out in Paris and London*, Orwell's first full-length work, was a semi-fictionalized memoir consisting of two parts: the first based on his time living in near-destitution in Paris at the end of the 1920s, and the second describing various tramping expeditions he had made in London. It was published by Victor Gollancz in January 1933, to mostly favourable reviews.

Burmese Days   It was followed by *Burmese Days*, a novel set in Kyauktada, a provincial Burmese town, during the twilight of the British Raj. Its central figure is John Flory, a teak merchant blighted by a facial birthmark, who, after losing and then winning again the affections of Elizabeth Lackersteen, is disgraced when a disgruntled native magnate, U Po Kyin, bribes Flory's native mistress to cause a scene on his wedding day. Distraught, Flory commits suicide. Fearing prosecution for libel, Victor Gollancz initially refused to publish the novel; thus it appeared first in the United States, published by Harpers in 1934, with a British edition following in 1935 only after Gollancz had been convinced that none of the characters could be identified with real people.

A Clergyman's Daughter   As with *Burmese Days*, for his next novel Orwell drew on his own experiences, this time to tell the story of Dorothy Hare, whose life of keeping house for her widowed father and fending off the advances of the disreputable Mr Warburton is interrupted when she suffers an attack of amnesia and is found, eight days later, sitting on a London roadside. Eventually, after a series of adventures – including going on a hop-picking expedition to Kent with a group of down-and-outs, being arrested for vagrancy and teaching at a "fourth-rate" private girls' school – Dorothy returns home. *A Clergyman's Daughter*, which was published by Gollancz in March 1935, is the most formally experimental of Orwell's works, although he himself described it as "bollix" and refused to allow it to be reprinted in his lifetime.

Keep the Aspidistra Flying   *Keep the Aspidistra Flying*, which was published by Victor Gollancz in April 1936, was also in part a romanà-clef, drawing on Orwell's experience working in a Hampstead bookshop. Gordon Comstock, a poet "at war" with the world of bourgeois respectability (symbolized by the aspidistra of the title), gives up his job as a copywriter for an advertising agency and goes to work instead in a bookshop run by Mr McKechnie. When he loses his job after going on a drinking binge, he is forced to work instead at a seedy lending library in Lambeth, where he is paid significantly less than he received at Mr McKechnie's. Comstock is satisfied with his reduced circumstances, believing that only by sinking to the very bottom can he thrive as a poet, but when his girlfriend, Rosemary Waterlow, falls pregnant, he goes back to his advertising job and therefore to the civilized world he had tried to leave behind.

Orwell returned to reportage for *The Road to Wigan Pier*, an account of his 1936 expedition to the industrial north of England. The book's first half is a documentary account of his findings, including vivid descriptions of the appalling living conditions endured by the working-class families he met on his journey. In the second half Orwell attempts to account for the failure of socialism – a system he believed capable of redressing the iniquities identified in the first part – of attracting sufficient support to implement its programme, concluding that the class prejudice and "crankiness" of middle-class socialists are to blame. While Orwell was away in Spain early in 1937, Gollancz, concerned that the second half would prove controversial with the middle-class members of his Left Book Club, initially tried to publish the first part on its own; after resistance from Orwell's wife and agent, however, he relented, although he added a foreword in which he attempted to rebut some of Orwell's criticisms. *The Road to Wigan Pier* was published in March 1937.

The Road to Wigan Pier

After *The Road to Wigan Pier* came another work of reportage, this time a personal account of Orwell's experiences and observations fighting with the POUM militia, part of the Republican coalition during the Spanish Civil War. *Homage to Catalonia* was rejected by Gollancz, Orwell's usual publisher, due to its criticism of the Stalin-backed Communists in the conflict – "Gollancz is of course

Homage to Catalonia

part of the Communism racket," Orwell wrote in a letter of July 1937 – but taken on by Secker & Warburg, who were willing to publish books by dissident socialists. It was not a commercial success, however, selling only seven hundred copies in the first year, and was not reprinted during Orwell's lifetime.

Coming Up for Air   Orwell returned to fiction for his seventh book, *Coming Up for Air*. When George Bowling, an unhappy middle-aged insurance salesman living with his family in the West London suburbs, attempts to escape his life of dull petit-bourgeois conformity and relive his idyllic childhood by returning to Lower Binfield, the Oxfordshire town of his childhood, he finds the place changed beyond recognition due to the depredations of "progress". Published in June 1939 by Victor Gollancz, the novel was, unlike *Homage to Catalonia*, a notable commercial success, selling out its initial print run of two thousand copies, and garnered favourable notices.

Animal Farm   After publishing a book of essays, *Inside the Whale* (Gollancz, March 1940), and a tract, *The Lion and the Unicorn: Socialism and the English Genius* (Secker & Warburg, February 1941), in 1943 Orwell returned to fiction with a fable about a group of farm animals who, led by the pigs, overthrow the farmer, Mr Jones, and attempt to establish a new egalitarian order. Their idealism is betrayed, however, and the animals slowly succumb to a dictatorship led by Napoleon, one of the pigs. The book, a transparent allegory describing events in Russia from the 1917 revolution up to the totalitarian tyranny of Stalinism, reflects the left-wing but anti-Communist stance that Orwell had held since his first-hand experience of the Spanish Civil War. Rejected by Gollancz, Cape and other publishers afraid of being associated with such a controversial work given Britain's wartime alliance with Stalin, *Animal Farm* was published by Secker & Warburg in August 1945, and was a resounding commercial success, selling out its initial run of 4,500 copies in just six weeks.

Nineteen Eighty-Four   Orwell's final book, *Nineteen Eighty-Four*, is an exploration of totalitarianism, uncompromising in its desolate vision of a future in which Britain has been absorbed into Oceania, a superstate governed by "the

Party" under the leadership of the mysterious "Big Brother", a place where any independent thought or action is ruthlessly suppressed. It centres on Winston Smith, a worker in the Ministry of Truth who secretly opposes the Party. He embarks on an illicit affair with Julia, a young colleague, but the couple are caught by the Thought Police and Winston is removed to the Ministry of Love for re-education, where he is tortured and beaten. Ultimately he is taken to Room 101, a place containing each individual's worst fear, where a wire cage holding starving rats is strapped to his head. Terrified, he begs O'Brien, his captor, to inflict the punishment on Julia instead – a betrayal that represents the Party's final victory over Winston as an individual. The novel ends with Winston, newly conditioned, proclaiming his love for Big Brother. *Nineteen Eighty-Four* was published in June 1949 by Secker & Warburg.

Select Bibliography

Biographies:
Crick, Bernard, *George Orwell: A Life* (London: Secker & Warburg, 1980)
Bowker, Gordon, *George Orwell* (London: Little, Brown, 2003)
Taylor, D.J., *Orwell: The Life* (London: Chatto & Windus, 2003)

Additional Recommended Background Material:
Coppard, Audrey, and Bernard Crick, eds., *Orwell Remembered* (London: Ariel, 1984)
Hitchens, Christopher, *Why Orwell Matters* (New York: Basic Books, 2002)
Rees, Richard, *George Orwell: Fugitive from the Camp of Victory* (London: Secker & Warburg, 1961)

Websites:
The Orwell Foundation, available at https://www.orwellfoundation.com/
The Orwell Society, available at https://orwellsociety.com/

ALMA CLASSICS

ALMA CLASSICS aims to publish mainstream and lesser-known European classics in an innovative and striking way, while employing the highest editorial and production standards. By way of a unique approach the range offers much more, both visually and textually, than readers have come to expect from contemporary classics publishing.

LATEST TITLES PUBLISHED BY ALMA CLASSICS

473. Sinclair Lewis, *Babbitt*
474. Edith Wharton, *The House of Mirth*
475. George Orwell, *Burmese Days*
476. Virginia Woolf, *The Voyage Out*
477. Charles Dickens, *Pictures from Italy*
478. Fyodor Dostoevsky, *Crime and Punishment*
479. Anton Chekhov, *Small Fry and Other Stories*
480. George Orwell, *Homage to Catalonia*
481. Carlo Collodi, *The Adventures of Pinocchio*
482. Virginia Woolf, *Between the Acts*
483. Alain Robbe-Grillet, *Last Year at Marienbad*
484. Charles Dickens, *The Pickwick Papers*
485. Wilkie Collins, *The Haunted Hotel*
486. Ivan Turgenev, *Parasha and Other Poems*
487. Arthur Conan Doyle, *His Last Bow*
488. Ivan Goncharov, *The Frigate Pallada*
489. Arthur Conan Doyle, *The Casebook of Sherlock Holmes*
490. Alexander Pushkin, *Lyrics Vol. 4*
491. Arthur Conan Doyle, *The Valley of Fear*
492. Gottfried Keller, *Green Henry*
493. Grimmelshausen, *Simplicius Simplicissimus*
494. Edgar Allan Poe, *The Raven and Other Poems*
495. Sinclair Lewis, *Main Street*
496. Prosper Mérimée, *Carmen*
497. D.H. Lawrence, *Women in Love*
498. Albert Maltz, *A Tale of One January*
499. George Orwell, *Coming Up for Air*
500. Anton Chekhov, *The Looking Glass and Other Stories*
501. Ivan Goncharov, *An Uncommon Story*
502. Paul Éluard, *Selected Poems*
503. Ivan Turgenev, *Memoirs of a Hunter*
504. Albert Maltz, *A Long Day in a Short Life*
505. Edith Wharton, *Ethan Frome*
506. Charles Dickens, *The Old Curiosity Shop*
507. Fyodor Dostoevsky, *The Village of Stepanchikovo*
508. George Orwell, *The Clergyman's Daughter*
509. Virginia Woolf, *The New Dress and Other Stories*
510. Ivan Goncharov, *A Serendipitous Error and Two Incidents at Sea*
511. Beatrix Potter, *Peter Rabbit*

www.almaclassics.com